T0181669

Lecture Notes in Computer Science   12663

More information about this subseries at http://www.springer.com/series/7412

Alberto Del Bimbo · Rita Cucchiara ·
Stan Sclaroff · Giovanni Maria Farinella ·
Tao Mei · Marco Bertini ·
Hugo Jair Escalante · Roberto Vezzani (Eds.)

Pattern Recognition

ICPR International Workshops and Challenges

Virtual Event, January 10–15, 2021
Proceedings, Part III

 Springer

Editors
Alberto Del Bimbo (iD)
Dipartimento di Ingegneria
dell'Informazione
University of Firenze
Firenze, Italy

Stan Sclaroff (iD)
Department of Computer Science
Boston University
Boston, MA, USA

Tao Mei
Cloud & AI, JD.COM
Beijing, China

Hugo Jair Escalante (iD)
Computational Sciences Department
National Institute of Astrophysics,
Optics and Electronics (INAOE)
Tonantzintla, Puebla, Mexico

Rita Cucchiara (iD)
Dipartimento di Ingegneria "Enzo Ferrari"
Università di Modena e Reggio Emilia
Modena, Italy

Giovanni Maria Farinella (iD)
Dipartimento di Matematica e Informatica
University of Catania
Catania, Italy

Marco Bertini (iD)
Dipartimento di Ingegneria
dell'Informazione
University of Firenze
Firenze, Italy

Roberto Vezzani (iD)
Dipartimento di Ingegneria "Enzo Ferrari"
Università di Modena e Reggio Emilia
Modena, Italy

ISSN 0302-9743   ISSN 1611-3349 (electronic)
Lecture Notes in Computer Science
ISBN 978-3-030-68795-3   ISBN 978-3-030-68796-0 (eBook)
https://doi.org/10.1007/978-3-030-68796-0

LNCS Sublibrary: SL6 – Image Processing, Computer Vision, Pattern Recognition, and Graphics

This Springer imprint is published by the registered company Springer Nature Switzerland AG
The registered company address is: Gewerbestrasse 11, 6330 Cham, Switzerland

Foreword by General Chairs

It is with great pleasure that we welcome you to the post-proceedings of the 25th International Conference on Pattern Recognition, ICPR2020 Virtual-Milano. ICPR2020 stands on the shoulders of generations of pioneering pattern recognition researchers. The first ICPR (then called IJCPR) convened in 1973 in Washington, DC, USA, under the leadership of Dr. King-Sun Fu as the General Chair. Since that time, the global community of pattern recognition researchers has continued to expand and thrive, growing evermore vibrant and vital. The motto of this year's conference was *Putting Artificial Intelligence to work on patterns*. Indeed, the deep learning revolution has its origins in the pattern recognition community – and the next generations of revolutionary insights and ideas continue with those presented at this 25th ICPR. Thus, it was our honor to help perpetuate this longstanding ICPR tradition to provide a lively meeting place and open exchange for the latest pathbreaking work in pattern recognition.

For the first time, the ICPR main conference employed a two-round review process similar to journal submissions, with new papers allowed to be submitted in either the first or the second round and papers submitted in the first round and not accepted allowed to be revised and re-submitted for second round review. In the first round, 1554 new submissions were received, out of which 554 (35.6%) were accepted and 579 (37.2%) were encouraged to be revised and resubmitted. In the second round, 1696 submissions were received (496 revised and 1200 new), out of which 305 (61.4%) of the revised submissions and 552 (46%) of the new submissions were accepted. Overall, there were 3250 submissions in total, and 1411 were accepted, out of which 144 (4.4%) were included in the main conference program as orals and 1263 (38.8%) as posters (4 papers were withdrawn after acceptance). We had the largest ICPR conference ever, with the most submitted papers and the most selective acceptance rates ever for ICPR, attesting both the increased interest in presenting research results at ICPR and the high scientific quality of work accepted for presentation at the conference.

We were honored to feature seven exceptional Keynotes in the program of the ICPR2020 main conference: David Doermann (Professor at the University at Buffalo), Pietro Perona (Professor at the California Institute of Technology and Amazon Fellow at Amazon Web Services), Mihaela van der Schaar (Professor at the University of Cambridge and a Turing Fellow at The Alan Turing Institute in London), Max Welling (Professor at the University of Amsterdam and VP of Technologies at Qualcomm), Ching Yee Suen (Professor at Concordia University) who was presented with the IAPR 2020 King-Sun Fu Prize, Maja Pantic (Professor at Imperial College UK and AI Scientific Research Lead at Facebook Research) who was presented with the IAPR 2020 Maria Petrou Prize, and Abhinav Gupta (Professor at Carnegie Mellon University and Research Manager at Facebook AI Research) who was presented with the IAPR 2020 J.K. Aggarwal Prize. Several best paper prizes were also announced and awarded, including the Piero Zamperoni Award for the best paper authored by a student, the BIRPA Best Industry Related Paper Award, and Best Paper Awards for each of the five tracks of the ICPR2020 main conference.

The five tracks of the ICPR2020 main conference were: (1) Artificial Intelligence, Machine Learning for Pattern Analysis, (2) Biometrics, Human Analysis and Behavior Understanding, (3) Computer Vision, Robotics and Intelligent Systems, (4) Document and Media Analysis, and (5) Image and Signal Processing. The best papers presented at the main conference had the opportunity for publication in expanded format in journal special issues of *IET Biometrics* (tracks 2 and 3), *Computer Vision and Image Understanding* (tracks 1 and 2), *Machine Vision and Applications* (tracks 2 and 3), *Multimedia Tools and Applications* (tracks 4 and 5), *Pattern Recognition Letters* (tracks 1, 2, 3 and 4), or *IEEE Trans. on Biometrics, Behavior, and Identity Science* (tracks 2 and 3).

In addition to the main conference, the ICPR2020 program offered workshops and tutorials, along with a broad range of cutting-edge industrial demos, challenge sessions, and panels. The virtual ICPR2020 conference was interactive, with real-time live-streamed sessions, including live talks, poster presentations, exhibitions, demos, Q&A, panels, meetups, and discussions – all hosted on the Underline virtual conference platform.

The ICPR2020 conference was originally scheduled to convene in Milano, which is one of the most beautiful cities of Italy for art, culture, lifestyle – and more. The city has so much to offer! With the need to go virtual, ICPR2020 included interactive **virtual tours** of Milano during the conference coffee breaks, which we hoped would introduce attendees to this wonderful city, and perhaps even entice them to visit Milano once international travel becomes possible again.

The success of such a large conference would not have been possible without the help of many people. We deeply appreciate the vision, commitment, and leadership of the ICPR2020 Program Chairs: Kim Boyer, Brian C. Lovell, Marcello Pelillo, Nicu Sebe, René Vidal, and Jingyi Yu. Our heartfelt gratitude also goes to the rest of the main conference organizing team, including the Track and Area Chairs, who all generously devoted their precious time in conducting the review process and in preparing the program, and the reviewers, who carefully evaluated the submitted papers and provided invaluable feedback to the authors. This time their effort was considerably higher given that many of them reviewed for both reviewing rounds. We also want to acknowledge the efforts of the conference committee, including the Challenge Chairs, Demo and Exhibit Chairs, Local Chairs, Financial Chairs, Publication Chair, Tutorial Chairs, Web Chairs, Women in ICPR Chairs, and Workshop Chairs. Many thanks, also, for the efforts of the dedicated staff who performed the crucially important work behind the scenes, including the members of the ICPR2020 Organizing Secretariat. Finally, we are grateful to the conference sponsors for their generous support of the ICPR2020 conference.

We hope everyone had an enjoyable and productive ICPR2020 conference.

Rita Cucchiara
Alberto Del Bimbo
Stan Sclaroff

Preface

The 25th International Conference on Pattern Recognition Workshops (ICPRW 2020) were held virtually in Milan, Italy and rescheduled to January 10 and January 11 of 2021 due to the Covid-19 pandemic. ICPRW 2020 included timely topics and applications of Computer Vision, Image and Sound Analysis, Pattern Recognition and Artificial Intelligence. We received 49 workshop proposals and 46 of them have been accepted, which is three times more than at ICPRW 2018. The workshop proceedings cover a wide range of areas including Machine Learning (8), Pattern Analysis (5), Healthcare (6), Human Behavior (5), Environment (5), Surveillance, Forensics and Biometrics (6), Robotics and Egovision (4), Cultural Heritage and Document Analysis (4), Retrieval (2), and Women at ICPR 2020 (1). Among them, 33 workshops are new to ICPRW. Specifically, the ICPRW 2020 volumes contain the following workshops (please refer to the corresponding workshop proceeding for details):

- CADL2020 – Workshop on Computational Aspects of Deep Learning.
- DLPR – Deep Learning for Pattern Recognition.
- EDL/AI – Explainable Deep Learning/AI.
- (Merged) IADS – Integrated Artificial Intelligence in Data Science, IWCR – IAPR workshop on Cognitive Robotics.
- ManifLearn – Manifold Learning in Machine Learning, From Euclid to Riemann.
- MOI2QDN – Metrification & Optimization of Input Image Quality in Deep Networks.
- IML – International Workshop on Industrial Machine Learning.
- MMDLCA – Multi-Modal Deep Learning: Challenges and Applications.
- IUC 2020 – Human and Vehicle Analysis for Intelligent Urban Computing.
- PATCAST – International Workshop on Pattern Forecasting.
- RRPR – Reproducible Research in Pattern Recognition.
- VAIB 2020 – Visual Observation and Analysis of Vertebrate and Insect Behavior.
- IMTA VII – Image Mining Theory & Applications.
- AIHA 2020 – Artificial Intelligence for Healthcare Applications.
- AIDP – Artificial Intelligence for Digital Pathology.
- (Merged) GOOD – Designing AI in support of Good Mental Health, CAIHA – Computational and Affective Intelligence in Healthcare Applications for Vulnerable Populations.
- CARE2020 – pattern recognition for positive teChnology And eldeRly wEllbeing.
- MADiMa 2020 – Multimedia Assisted Dietary Management.
- 3DHU 2020 – 3D Human Understanding.
- FBE2020 – Facial and Body Expressions, micro-expressions and behavior recognition.
- HCAU 2020 – Deep Learning for Human-Centric Activity Understanding.
- MPRSS - 6th IAPR Workshop on Multimodal Pattern Recognition for Social Signal Processing in Human Computer Interaction.

- CVAUI 2020 – Computer Vision for Analysis of Underwater Imagery.
- MAES – Machine Learning Advances Environmental Science.
- PRAConBE - Pattern Recognition and Automation in Construction & the Built Environment.
- PRRS 2020 – Pattern Recognition in Remote Sensing.
- WAAMI - Workshop on Analysis of Aerial Motion Imagery.
- DEEPRETAIL 2020 - Workshop on Deep Understanding Shopper Behaviours and Interactions in Intelligent Retail Environments 2020.
- MMForWild2020 – MultiMedia FORensics in the WILD 2020.
- FGVRID – Fine-Grained Visual Recognition and re-Identification.
- IWBDAF – Biometric Data Analysis and Forensics.
- RISS – Research & Innovation for Secure Societies.
- WMWB – TC4 Workshop on Mobile and Wearable Biometrics.
- EgoApp – Applications of Egocentric Vision.
- ETTAC 2020 – Eye Tracking Techniques, Applications and Challenges.
- PaMMO – Perception and Modelling for Manipulation of Objects.
- FAPER – Fine Art Pattern Extraction and Recognition.
- MANPU – coMics ANalysis, Processing and Understanding.
- PATRECH2020 – Pattern Recognition for Cultural Heritage.
- (Merged) CBIR – Content-Based Image Retrieval: where have we been, and where are we going, TAILOR – Texture AnalysIs, cLassificatiOn and Retrieval, VIQA – Video and Image Question Answering: building a bridge between visual content analysis and reasoning on textual data.
- W4PR - Women at ICPR.

We would like to thank all members of the workshops' Organizing Committee, the reviewers, and the authors for making this event successful. We also appreciate the support from all the invited speakers and participants. We wish to offer thanks in particular to the ICPR main conference general chairs: Rita Cucchiara, Alberto Del Bimbo, and Stan Sclaroff, and program chairs: Kim Boyer, Brian C. Lovell, Marcello Pelillo, Nicu Sebe, Rene Vidal, and Jingyi Yu. Finally, we are grateful to the publisher, Springer, for their cooperation in publishing the workshop proceedings in the series of Lecture Notes in Computer Science.

December 2020
Giovanni Maria Farinella
Tao Mei

Challenges

Competitions are effective means for rapidly solving problems and advancing the state of the art. Organizers identify a problem of practical or scientific relevance and release it to the community. In this way the whole community can contribute to the solution of high-impact problems while having fun. This part of the proceedings compiles the best of the competitions track of the *25th International Conference on Pattern Recognition (ICPR)*.

Eight challenges were part of the track, covering a wide variety of fields and applications, all of this within the scope of ICPR. In every challenge organizers released data, and provided a platform for evaluation. The top-ranked participants were invited to submit papers for this volume. Likewise, organizers themselves wrote articles summarizing the design, organization and results of competitions. Submissions were subject to a standard review process carried out by the organizers of each competition. Papers associated with seven out the eight competitions are included in this volume, thus making it a representative compilation of what happened in the ICPR challenges.

We are immensely grateful to the organizers and participants of the ICPR 2020 challenges for their efforts and dedication to make the competition track a success. We hope the readers of this volume enjoy it as much as we have.

November 2020

Marco Bertini
Hugo Jair Escalante

ICPR Organization

General Chairs

Rita Cucchiara   Univ. of Modena and Reggio Emilia, Italy
Alberto Del Bimbo   Univ. of Florence, Italy
Stan Sclaroff   Boston Univ., USA

Program Chairs

Kim Boyer   Univ. at Albany, USA
Brian C. Lovell   Univ. of Queensland, Australia
Marcello Pelillo   Univ. Ca' Foscari Venezia, Italy
Nicu Sebe   Univ. of Trento, Italy
René Vidal   Johns Hopkins Univ., USA
Jingyi Yu   ShanghaiTech Univ., China

Workshop Chairs

Giovanni Maria Farinella   Univ. of Catania, Italy
Tao Mei   JD.COM, China

Challenge Chairs

Marco Bertini   Univ. of Florence, Italy
Hugo Jair Escalante   INAOE and CINVESTAV National Polytechnic Institute of Mexico, Mexico

Publication Chair

Roberto Vezzani   Univ. of Modena and Reggio Emilia, Italy

Tutorial Chairs

Vittorio Murino   Univ. of Verona, Italy
Sudeep Sarkar   Univ. of South Florida, USA

Women in ICPR Chairs

Alexandra Branzan Albu   Univ. of Victoria, Canada
Maria De Marsico   Univ. Roma La Sapienza, Italy

Demo and Exhibit Chairs

Lorenzo Baraldi   Univ. Modena Reggio Emilia, Italy
Bruce A. Maxwell   Colby College, USA
Lorenzo Seidenari   Univ. of Florence, Italy

Special Issue Initiative Chair

Michele Nappi   Univ. of Salerno, Italy

Web Chair

Andrea Ferracani   Univ. of Florence, Italy

Corporate Relations Chairs

Fabio Galasso   Univ. Roma La Sapienza, Italy
Matt Leotta   Kitware, Inc., USA
Zhongchao Shi   Lenovo Group Ltd., China

Local Chairs

Matteo Matteucci   Politecnico di Milano, Italy
Paolo Napoletano   Univ. of Milano-Bicocca, Italy

Financial Chairs

Cristiana Fiandra   The Office srl, Italy
Vittorio Murino   Univ. of Verona, Italy

Towards AI Ethics and Explainability
(ICPR EDL-AI Workshop Plenary Talk)

D. Petkovic

CS Department, San Francisco State University, San Francisco, CA, USA
petkovic@sfsu.edu

Abstract. We are witnessing the emergence of an "AI economy and society" where AI technologies are increasingly impacting many aspects of modern life, in business as well as in everyday life. However, AI systems may produce errors, can exhibit overt or subtle bias, may be sensitive to noise in the data, and often lack technical and judicial transparency and explainability. Recently, upon in depth analysis, many cases where AI systems produced seemingly correct results but all based on "wrong reasons" (e.g. classifying X-ray machine and not actual patients' diseases) have been documented, as well as biases (namely increased error rates) for people of color in many already deployed face recognition systems. These shortcomings raise many ethical and policy concerns that impede wider adoption of this potentially very beneficial technology. These broad concerns about AI are often grouped under the rubric "AI Ethics and Values". The technical community, the media, as well as political, regulatory and legal stakeholders have recognized the problem and have begun to seek solutions. However, developing technical solutions and practices to implement and verify these AI Ethics and Values principles has proven to be a substantial challenge. One of the key components of addressing these challenges is making humans understand how the AI systems make their decision which is called AI explainability or transparency. Challenges are compounded due to the fact that some of the most powerful AI techniques like Deep Learning are not amenable to explanations. In this talk the speaker will motivate the need for better AI Explainability based on several case studies and analysis of regulatory and political pressures to do so, followed by brief outline of main approaches to explainability. Strong recommendation will be made for more focus on the needs of real users and adopters of AI technology who are most often domain but not AI experts.

Contents – Part III

**EgoApp 2020 - 2nd Workshop on Applications of Egocentric
Vision 2020**

FAPER - International Workshop on Fine Art Pattern Extraction and Recognition

FBE2020 - Workshop on Facial and Body Expressions, micro-expressions and behavior recognition

EDL-AI - Explainable Deep Learning/AI

Preface

The recent focus of AI and Pattern Recognition communities on the supervised learning approaches, and particularly to Deep Learning/AI, resulted in considerable increase of performance of Pattern Recognition and AI systems, but also raised the question of the trustfulness and explainability of their predictions for decision-making. AI systems may produce errors, can exhibit overt or subtle bias, may be sensitive to noise in the data, and often lack technical and judicial transparency and explainability. In various Pattern Recognition and AI application domains such as health, ecology, autonomous driving cars, security, culture it is mandatory that humans (*e.g.*, adopters, users) understand how the predictions are correlated with the information perception and decision making by the experts. These shortcomings raise many ethical and policy concerns that impede wider adoption of this potentially very beneficial technology. These broad concerns about AI are often grouped under the rubric "AI Ethics and Values". The technical community, the media, as well as political, regulatory and legal stakeholders have recognized the problem and have begun to seek solutions. However, developing technical solutions and practices to implement and verify these AI Ethics and Values principles has proven to be a substantial challenge. This resulted in emergence of a new field, namely Explainable Deep Learning/AI, which aims to develop and evaluate methods to "understand" and "explain" to humans how AI systems produce their decisions so that adoption, verification and audit of these systems can be improved. The goals of the workshop were to bring together research community working on the question of improving the explainability of AI and Pattern Recognition algorithms and systems.

The following topics were proposed for the workshop program:

- "Sensing" or "salient features" of Neural Networks and AI systems - explanation of which features for a given configuration yield predictions both in spatial (images) and temporal (time-series, video) data;
- Attention mechanisms in Deep Neural Networks and their explanation;
- For temporal data, the explanation of which features and at what time are the most prominent for the prediction and what are the time intervals when the contribution of each data is important;
- How the explanation can help on making Deep learning architectures more sparse (pruning) and light-weight;
- When using multimodal data how the prediction in data streams are correlated and explain each other;
- Automatic generation of explanations/justifications of algorithms and systems' decisions;
- Decision making in uncertainty and its explainability;
- Evaluation of the explanations generated by Deep Learning and other AI systems.

Explainability and trustworthiness of AI tools is a very active research topic and we got a strong interest of community with 47 submissions for this workshop. Amongst them, 31 papers were full length and 16 were short papers.

Merely all topics of the workshop were covered. The explanation methods were proposed for convolutional neural networks both 2D and 3D essentially, but also for such classifiers as Random Forests.

Application domains were wide ranging from medical domain such as for Sclerosis classification explanations to classification of data in Maritime domain or in Astrophysics.

Each paper has undergone a single blind review with two expert reviewers in the domain of AI. From 47 submissions we have retained eight oral papers including 3 invited papers from renown researchers in the field and twelve posters, which made the program of the Workshop rich and diverse.

In addition, we have invited five panelists to close the Workshop with panel discussion focused on AI Explainability, moderated by Prof. D. Petkovic.

November 2020

Jenny Benois-Pineau
Dragutin Petkovic
Georges Quénot

Organization

General Chairs

Jenny Benois-Pineau   University of Bordeaux, France
Georges Quénot   CNRS-LIG, France

Program Committee Chairs

Jenny Benois-Pineau   University of Bordeaux , France
Dragutin Petkovic   San Francisco State University, USA
Georges Quénot   CNRS-LIG, France

Program Committee

Alexandre Benoît   Savoie University, France
Jenny Benois-Pineau   University of Bordeaux, France
Christophe Garcia   Institut National des Sciences Appliquées de Lyon, France
Mark T. Keane   University College Dublin, Ireland
Stefanos Kolias   National Technical University of Athens, Greece
Hervé Le Borgne   CEA LIST, France
Noel O'Connor   Dublin City University, Ireland
Georges Qénot   CNRS-LIG, France
Nicolas Thome   CNAM, France

Publication Chairs

Romain Bourqui   University of Bordeaux, France
Romain Giot   University of Bordeaux, France

Panel Chair

Dragutin Petkovic   San Francisco State University, USA

Additional Reviewers

Romain Bourqui   Rafael Padilha
Romain Giot   Sean Quinn
Vitor Araújo Cautiero Horta   Joris Sansen

A Multi-layered Approach for Tailored Black-Box Explanations

Clément Henin[1,2]([✉]) [iD] and Daniel Le Métayer[1]

[1] Univ Lyon, Inria, INSA Lyon, CITI, Villeurbanne, France
{clement.henin,daniel.le-metayer}@inria.fr
[2] École des Ponts ParisTech, Champs-sur-Marne, France

Abstract. Explanations for algorithmic decision systems can take different forms, they can target different types of users with different goals. One of the main challenges in this area is therefore to devise explanation methods that can accommodate this variety of situations. A first step to address this challenge is to allow explainees to express their needs in the most convenient way, depending on their level of expertise and motivation. In this paper, we present a solution to this problem based on a multi-layered approach allowing users to express their requests for explanations at different levels of abstraction. We illustrate the approach with the application of a proof-of-concept system called IBEX to two case studies.

Keywords: Algorithmic Decision System · Explainability · Transparency · Black-box model · Machine-learning · Artificial intelligence · Interactive

1 Introduction

Explainability has generated increased interest during the last decade because accurate ML techniques often lead to opaque Algorithmic Decision Systems (hereafter "ADS") and opacity is a major source of mistrust. Indeed, even if they should not be seen as a silver bullet, well designed explanations can play a key role, not only to enhance trust in a system, but also to allow its users to better understand its outputs and therefore to make a better use of them. In addition, they are necessary to make it possible to challenge decisions based on the results of an ADS. On the legal side, Recital 71 of the European General Data Protection Regulation, which concerns decisions "based solely on automated processing", states that a data subject has the right "to express his or her point of view, to obtain an explanation of the decision reached after such assessment and to challenge the decision."

Explainability methods produce different types of explanations in different ways, based on different assumptions on the system [1]. In this paper, we focus on a category of methods, called "black-box explanation methods", which do not assume the availability of the code of the ADS or its underlying model.

© Springer Nature Switzerland AG 2021
A. Del Bimbo et al. (Eds.): ICPR 2020 Workshops, LNCS 12663, pp. 5–19, 2021.
https://doi.org/10.1007/978-3-030-68796-0_1

The only assumption is that input data can be provided to the ADS and its outputs can be observed.

In practice, explanations can take different forms, they can target different types of users (hereafter "explainees") with different interests. One of the main challenges in this area is therefore to devise explanation methods that can accommodate this variety of situations. This is especially crucial to avoid the "inmates running the asylum" phenomenon [2] and be able to design a system that can be used by lay persons. A first step to address this challenge is to allow explainees to express their needs in the most convenient way, which is not an easy task especially for users lacking technical expertise. In this paper, we present a solution to this problem based on a multi-layered approach allowing users to formulate their requests for explanations at different levels of abstraction. The three levels of abstraction considered here are called respectively the *context*, the *requirements* and the *technical options*:

1. The *context* provides high-level information about the profile of the explainee and his/her objectives.
2. The *requirements* characterize the desired explanations, including, for example, their format, degree of simplicity and generality.
3. The *technical options* are lower-level choices related to the available explanation techniques.

We provide a mapping between the different levels of abstraction to generate explanations tailored to the needs of each explainee. In addition, we make it possible for explainees to react to an explanation. They can, for example, request more detailed, or simpler explanations, or explanations in a different form.

The idea is that lay users should be able to express their needs at the highest level of abstraction, without any knowledge of the requirements and technical options. On the other hand, expert users, for example the designers of the ADS, may prefer to express their requests directly as requirements or technical options. Regardless of the level of abstraction adopted by the user, ultimately his/her needs have to be translated into technical options. In this paper, we describe a heuristic method to derive requirements from contexts and suggest the derivation of technical options from requirements for different explanation methods.

We first present the two higher levels of abstraction (context and requirements) in Sect. 2. In Sect. 3, we show the derivation of requirements from contexts and suggest how technical options can be derived from requirements. In Sect. 4 we illustrate the approach with the application of our proof-of-concept system IBEX (for "Interactive Black-box Explanations") to two case studies. Section 5 discusses related work and Sect. 6 concludes with prospects for future work.

2   Context and Requirements

In this section, we present successively the higher levels of abstraction of our framework: the context (Sect. 2.1) and the requirements (Sect. 2.2). The mapping between these levels is described in Sect. 3. The methodology followed to devise the framework relies on a detailed analysis of existing explanation methods [3] as well as existing literature to identify the needs and the expectations of the users. The most relevant references are included in the text and further discussed in Sect. 5.

2.1 Context

The context is the highest level of abstraction, which should be accessible to any explainee, including lay users, to express their needs in a simple, non technical, way. Contexts are made of the ADS to be explained[1] and four elements related to the explainee's query: *Profile*, *Objective*, *Focus* and *Point of interest*.

- *Profile* takes a value in the set $\{TE, AU, DE, LU\}$. TE represents technical experts, AU auditors, DE domain experts and LU lay users. Technical experts include designers, developers, testers, i.e. people having some knowledge about the design or the techniques used to implement the ADS. Auditors are also assumed to have a high level of expertise but they are involved in a specific task of auditing or evaluating the ADS. Domain experts are not assumed to have any expertise about the ADS itself or the technology used but they are knowledgeable about the application domain. Examples of domain experts include medical doctors, judges or police officers. The last category, lay users, includes users who are not assumed to possess any specific knowledge. They may be persons affected by decisions relying on the ADS or simple citizens.[2]
- *Objective* takes a value in the set $\{I, T, C, A\}$. I represents the improvement of the ADS, T trust enhancement, C challenging a decision and A taking actions based on a decision. The improvement of the ADS includes its testing, assessment of its accuracy and any action to detect potential weaknesses. Trust enhancement includes a variety of objectives related to the use of the ADS (avoiding wrong decisions [1], enhancing the acceptance of the results [1], increasing the predictability of the output [6] and being comfortable with the strengths and limitations of the ADS [7]) or its purpose (causality, transferability [5,8]). Challenging a decision and taking an action based on a decision are two alternative reactions for the person affected by a decision [9]. Actions that can be taken based on a decision include actions that can have an impact on the person's record and therefore on future decisions. An example of action for the customer of a bank could be to reduce his/her outstanding loan balance to increase his/her chances to have his/her new credit application accepted.
- *Focus* characterizes the scope of the explanation. It takes a value in the set $\{G, L\}$. G stands for global explanation and L for local explanation. An explanation is global if the explainee is interested in the behaviour of the ADS for

---

[1] With the associated learning data set, if available.

[2] Other taxonomies of explainees' profiles have already been proposed, in particular in [4] and [5]. Our contribution is consistent with them, but involves some simplifications, justified by pragmatic needs.

the whole input dataset. Otherwise, it is local, which means that the explainee
is interested in the behaviour of the ADS for (or around) a specific input value.
– *Point of interest* defines the input value x which is the point of interest of the
explainee when the focus of the explanation is local (otherwise, the context
does not involve any point of interest).

We should emphasize that some of these elements can be omitted by
explainees if they are not sure about them. The only mandatory element is the
ADS. Explanations can be generated from partially defined contexts. The drawback is that such explanations may not correspond to the expectations of the
explainee who may then have to refine his/her needs through further interaction
steps.

2.2   Requirements

Requirements provide an intermediate level of abstraction. They characterize the
desired explanations more precisely than the context but still in an abstract way.
They can be useful to certain lay users, depending on their level of proficiency,
and to expert users. The requirements are made of seven elements[3]: *Format*, *Simplicity*, *Generality*, *Point of interest*, *Realism*, *Actionability* and *Nature*. Apart
from *Realism*, which is, to the best of our knowledge, an original contribution,
these elements are motivated by previous work and experimental studies, as
mentioned below.

– *Format* includes the different forms of explanations that can be generated
[1,8]. The impact of the format on the acceptance of explanations is analyzed
in [10,11]. Examples of formats include rule based explanations (RB), feature
importance (FI), counterfactual explanations (CF), decision trees (DT) and
partial dependence plots (PD).
– *Simplicity* is a key requirement as it generally relates to understandability
[1,6,12]. It is usually expressed through a fixed scale of values. The current
version of IBEX considers three increasing levels of simplicity: Simplicity =
$\{1, 2, 3\}$.
– *Generality* characterizes the size of the class of input values that should be
covered by the explanation ([6] p. 44). Some authors use the word "cover"
to denote the same concept [12,13]. It is also expressed through a fixed scale
of values. The current version of IBEX considers three increasing levels of
generality: Generality = $\{1, 2, 3\}$. Level 1 covers a single input (the point
of interest), level 3 a wide class of inputs and level 2 is intermediate. Note
that generality is defined only for local explanations since global explanations
cover, by definition, the whole input dataset.
– *Point of interest* has the same definition as above (for contexts). It also
belongs to the requirements for the sake of comprehensiveness (each level is
assumed to be self-contained). Like generality, the point of interest is defined
only for local explanations.

---

[3] In addition to the ADS, as defined in the context.

- *Realism* characterizes the level of realism required for an explanation. By "realism", we mean the fact that the explanation process takes into account the actual distribution of the input data. Realistic explanations are preferable for explainees interested in the actual usage of the ADS. On the other hand, explainees interested in the internal logic of the ADS, independently of its actual usage, may proceed without the constraint of realism. Let us consider this notion with the example of a credit scoring system. The ADS systematically outputs the maximum risk when the application file mentions a previous credit fraud. Although this feature has a tremendous impact on the score, it is rarely used in practice, as few credit applicants are in this situation. The realistic approach takes into account the low probability of this feature while the non-realistic approach only considers the model itself, and thus assigns great importance to this feature. The current version of IBEX considers three increasing levels of realism: Realism $= \{1, 2, 3\}$.
- *Actionability* expresses the fact that actionable explanations should be preferred. An actionable explanation is an explanation involving only actionable features of the input dataset ([9] p. 42). For example, in the input file of a loan applicant, the age variable is not actionable whereas the number of outstanding loans is actionable. The current version of IBEX considers two options: Actionability $= \{T, F\}$. Value T means that actionability is a requirement. In this case, the explainee has to provide the list of actionable features.
- *Nature* corresponds to the presence or absence of probability in the explanations ([6] p. 44). The current version of IBEX considers two options: Nature $= \{T, F\}$. Value F means that probabilistic explanations are not desired and value T that they are acceptable.

Like contexts, requirements can be partially defined. In addition, they may be expressed in terms of preferences rather than fixed choices. For example, a technical expert may characterize simplicity by $3 > 2 > 1$ to express a preference for simple explanations but can also cope with intermediate or complex explanations. On the other hand, lay-users may prefer to characterize simplicity by selecting only value 3. In the following, the former are called soft requirements and the latter hard requirements. In addition, soft requirements may also be prioritized (ranked by order of importance). For example, a technical expert who wants to debug or improve the ADS may consider that generality is more important than simplicity (*general* > *simple*).

3   From Contexts to Explanations

In order to produce explanations, the needs described in the previous section have to be translated into technical options of the generic explainer. In this section, we present the two phases of this process, the translation of the context into requirements in Sect. 3.1 and the translation of requirements into technical options in Sect. 3.2. The whole process is sketched in Fig. 1.

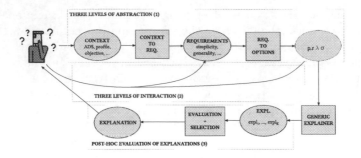

Fig. 1. Overview of the approach.

3.1   From Context to Requirements

The first step of the translation procedure consists in using the *Focus* element of the context to select the subset of formats that can be used. For example, if *Focus = G* (meaning that the explainee is interested in a global explanation), then counterfactual explanations (*CF*) are not appropriate. If *Focus = L* (local explanation), then the *Point of interest* element of the requirements is obtained directly from the same element in the context. The other elements of the requirements are derived from the *Profile* and *Objective* elements of the context as presented in Table 1.

Table 1. Translation of the context into requirements. Hard requirements contain symbol "=" (in black type) and soft requirements contain symbol "<" (in green type). Objectives marked with a star are usedas default settings.

Technical Expert		Domain Expert		
Improve*	*Trust*	*Trust**	*Challenge*	*Action*
format: RB >DT >FI >PD >CF	format: RB >DT >FI >PD >CF	format: RB >DT >FI >PD >CF	format: RB >DT >FI >PD >CF	format = CF
simplicity: 3 >2 >1	simplicity: 3 >2 >1	simplicity: 3 >2 >1	simplicity: 3 >2 >1	simplicity: 3 >2 >1
generality: 3 >2 >1	generality = 3	generality = 3	generality: 1 >2 >3	generality: 1 >2 >3
realism = 1	realism: 3 >2 >1	realism = 3	realism = 1	realism = 2
actionability = F	actionabililty = F	actionability = F	actionability = F	actionability = T
nature = T	nature = T	nature: T >F	nature : F >T	nature = F
general >form >simple	simple >real >form	simple >nat >form	form >nat >simple	simple >gen
Auditor		Lay User		
Trust	*Challenge**	*Trust**	*Challenge*	*Action*
format: RB >DT >FI >PD >CF	format: RB >DT >FI >PD >CF	format: RB >DT >FI >PD >CF	format: RB >DT >FI >PD >CF	format = CF
simplicity: 3 >2 >1	simplicity: 3 >2 >1	simplicity = 3	simplicity = 3	simplicity = 3
generality = 3	generality: 1 >2 >3	generality = 3	generality: 1 >2 >3	generality: 1 >2 >3
realism = 3	realism = 1	realism = 3	realism = 1	realism = 2
actionability = F	actionability = F	actionability = F	actionability = F	actionability = T
nature: T >F	nature: T >F	nature : F >T	nature : F >T	nature = F
simple >nat. >form	form >nat. >simple	nat. >form	form >nat.	

In the following, we provide some intuition about the choices made in Table 1. Usually, simple explanations are preferred over complex explanations ([6] p. 44).

Simplicity is expressed as a soft requirement with a low priority unless the profile is *Lay User*. Lay users generally expect explanations that are as simple as possible, thus a hard requirement is used ($simple = 3$).

The generality of an explanation (which is relevant only for local explanations) enhances the explainee's capabilities to understand the outcomes of the ADS for input values that have similarities with the point of interest. Therefore the values of the generality element should be maximum ($general = 3$) when the objective is to increase the trust in the model ([6] p. 44). On the other hand, when the objective for a lay user is to challenge a specific decision or to take actions to obtain better decisions from the ADS, a lower level of generality is more appropriate.

High levels of realism favour the generation of explanations that are supported by training data [14]. Depending on the context, this choice can be an advantage or a drawback. Explanations that are not supported by training data make it possible to analyze decision boundaries that are part of the model, but are not necessarily reflected in actual field data, as mentioned in the credit scoring example of Sect. 2.2. When the objective of the explainee is trust enhancement, decision boundaries that are actually used must be the primary concern, which justifies the choice of realistic sampling. On the other hand, technical experts may want to investigate these "theoretical" decision boundaries in order to assess the robustness of the model in all conditions.

As shown by previous studies ([6] p. 44), the use of probabilities in explanations is usually not illuminating for explainees ($nature = F$), especially when they are interested in a single point of interest. However some profiles, such as auditors and technical experts, may be interested in an overall view of the situation, which is provided by the use of probabilities ($nature: F > T$).

To conclude this section, we would like to emphasize that Table 1 corresponds to the choices made in IBEX but they are not hard-wired in the implementation. The architecture of the system can accommodate different choices of translation and this flexibility will be used to improve it based on the feedback of the users and field experience.

3.2 From Requirements to Technical Options

The translation of the requirements into technical options depend on the available explanation methods. For instance, simplicity can be translated into an acceptable number of non-zero coefficients for explanations expressed as feature importance or number of nodes for decision trees. Generality has an impact on the range of the sampling of the explanation method, *i.e.* the average distance between the point of interest and the samples. Interested readers can find in [15] the details of the translation for IBEX, which makes it possible to generate different forms of explanations based on a variety of parameters.

In general, the translation procedure may yield several possible solutions (sets of technical options), in particular when soft requirements are involved. In such cases, it is necessary to choose among them the set of technical options that is the most likely to address the needs of the explainee. To address this issue and to ensure that the explanation generated by the explainer will meet the requirements, the translation process of IBEX includes a last *post-hoc evaluation* step: the generation of the explanations corresponding to the different technical options derived in the previous step, followed by an evaluation of their properties.

Generally speaking, the assessment of the qualities of explanations is still an open research question. We consider here their compliance with respect to requirements as defined in Sect. 2.2. More precisely, we focus on the *Simplicity* and *Generality* elements, which are often expressed as soft requirements. The assessment of simplicity is based on the number of items involved in the explanation (*e.g.* the number of rules in a rule-based model, the number of modifications in a counterfactual example, etc.). This use of the size of an explanation as a proxy for simplicity is common [16]. It has some limitations (size does not always reflect simplicity) but it is operational and it can be instantiated to any explanation format. In IBEX, the assessment of generality relies on a test of the explanation on inputs from the population that are close to the point of interest. If the explanation is not valid for a minimum number of inputs (threshold T_1) then the generality is 1; if it is valid for the T_1 closest inputs but not for T_2 inputs ($T_2 > T_1$), then the generality is 2; if it is valid for the T_2 closest inputs then the generality is 3[4].

To conclude this section, it is important to stress that the definition of the needs of the explainee (at one of the three levels of abstractions) is only the first interaction step of the explainee with IBEX. When an explanation has been generated by IBEX based on the set of technical options resulting from the initial step, the explainee can reply to IBEX with a new request. This request can refer to the initial explanation (e.g. asking for a "richer", or "less simple", explanation, or an explanation in a different format) or can be entirely new and expressed again at any level of abstraction. By allowing explainees to interact at a different abstraction levels, IBEX gives them the opportunity to express their needs in a very precise and interactive way.

4   IBEX at Work: Application to Case Studies

In this section, we illustrate our approach with the application of our proof-of-concept system IBEX to two case studies. The implementation of the interaction protocol of IBEX follows directly the approach presented in the previous sections and interested readers can find in [15,17] complementary information about the explanation techniques available in IBEX. The code of IBEX is publicly available[5].

Interactions at any level of abstraction are feasible with IBEX. By default, the interaction is done at the context level which is the most appropriate for lay users. These interactions take place as follows (questions asked by IBEX):

---

[4] In the current version of IBEX, threshold T_1 is set to 10 and T_2 is set to 50.
[5] https://gitlab.inria.fr/chenin/ibex.

1. Choose a data set.
2. Are you interested in global (G) or local (L) explanations?
3. What is your point of interest? (optional question: for local explanations only)
4. How do you want to be considered by IBEX: as a technical expert (TE), a lay user (LU), a domain expert (DE) or an auditor (AU)?
5. What is the objective of the explanation: is it to improve the ADS (I), to enhance your trust in the ADS (T), to challenge the ADS (C), or to take future actions based on results of the ADS (A)?
6. What are your actionable features? (optional question: for objective A only)

The user may skip any of these questions (except the first one) if he/she is not sure about the answer. In any case, IBEX then generates a first explanation based on this (potentially partial) context and asks whether the user has further questions. If so, the user has two options: either ask an entirely new question (simple iteration of the protocol) or ask a question based on the previous explanation. In this case, he/she can express his/her wishes as a tuning of the requirements, for example "simpler explanation", "more general explanation", or "actionable explanation". Alternatively, the user can ask to see the requirements derived from the previous question and modify any of its components by himself/herself. In both cases, IBEX will then generate new technical options and a new explanation based on the new requirements. The user will then have again the options to stop, ask an entirely new question or a question involving the previous answer.

In order to illustrate the benefits of the approach in terms of versatility and interactivity, we consider two possible ways of using IBEX to get explanations about hypothetical ADS based on publicly available datasets.

1. The first situation corresponds to a lay user requesting explanations about the ADS with the objective of enhancing trust (Sect. 4.1).
2. The second situation is a lay user requesting explanations with the objective of taking future actions to improve his/her record (Sect. 4.2).

4.1   Explanations to Enhance Trust

The first case study involves the adult census data set[6]. This data set, which has been extracted from the 1994 US census, contains personal information about American citizens such as their age, education level or marital status. The goal of the ADS is to predict, from these features, if the individual earns more or less than $50,000\$$ per year. A lay user who wants to enhance his/her trust in the ADS would choose the following answers: *data set = adult census, focus = G, profile = LU and objective = T*. From this context, IBEX has generated the explanation presented in Fig. 2. We can see that the explanation is simple, it is composed of a decision tree with only two nodes and three leaves, which is consistent with the choices presented in Table 1.

---

[6] https://archive.ics.uci.edu/ml/datasets/Adult.

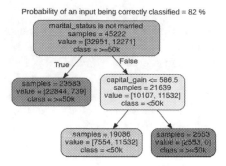

Fig. 2. Explanation generated by IBEX for the adult census data set from the initial context. The explanation is a decision tree applied to the training data set with labels replaced by model's outputs. The following information is associated with each node: number of samples meeting the conditions leading to the subtree (*samples*), numbers of samples belonging respectively to the class $>= 50k$ and to the class $< 50k$ (*value*), and the majority class for this subset of samples (either $< 50k$ or $>= 50k$). To meet the simplicity constraint (only 3 leaves), the tree must be approximate and is therefore only valid for a part of the inputs (*82%*). IBEX has used the following requirements to generate this decision tree: *format* $= DT$, *simplicity* $= 3$, *actionability* $= F$, *nature* $= T$, *realism* $= 3$.

The requirements generated by IBEX for this context are presented in the left part of Fig. 3. We can see that *nature* $= F > T$, meaning that an explanation that does not involve any probability would have been preferred by the user. Nevertheless, the explanation generated by IBEX involves a probability. The reason is that the first explanation formats that were considered by IBEX (*FI* and *PD*, which are non probabilistic, in accordance with the soft requirement *nature* : $F > T$) led to explanations that were considered too complex to satisfy the hard requirement *simplicity* $= 3$. For this reason, the post-hoc evaluation step of IBEX made the choice of a decision tree format.

```
HARD REQUIREMENTS:                    HARD REQUIREMENTS:
      actionability : F                     actionability : F
      simplicity : 3                        simplicity : 2
      generality :                          generality :
      realism : 3                           realism : 3
SOFT REQUIREMENTS:                          format : DT
      nature : F > T                  SOFT REQUIREMENTS:
      format : DT > PD > PC                 nature : F > T
```

Fig. 3. (a) Requirements derived by IBEX from the initial context (G, LU, T) corresponding to the columns Lay User/Trust of Table 1. Because the focus is "Global", formats corresponding to local explanations (RB, FI, CF) are not considered and the generality requirement is empty as it is only applicable to local explanations; (b) Revised requirements based on the user's request "less simple".

Let us assume now that the user is almost satisfied with this first explanation but he/she suspects that the logic of the ADS is much more complex and this explanation is a bit simplistic. Through the IBEX interface, he/she can either request a "less simple" explanation or ask IBEX to show the requirements derived from the previous question and modify by himself/herself the simplicity element. In the first case, IBEX would generate the requirements shown in the right part of Fig. 3 leading to a richer decision tree, as shown in [15].

4.2   Explanations to Take Actions

The second case study concerns the German credit data set[7] which contains information about the credits (amount, duration, purpose, etc.) and the applicants (type of job, number of ongoing credits, etc.). The ADS classifies applications as risky ("bad") or safe ("good"). Let us consider an individual whose credit application has been rejected and who would like to know how to improve it to have it accepted in the future. The profile for this query is lay user (LU) and the objective is to prepare future actions (A) for a specific input (L). From Table 1, we can see that IBEX associates this context with the CF format and the average level *2* of realism. Indeed, level *1* would lead to unlikely modifications of the application that might not be of any practical use. At the other extreme, level a generation method based on a high realism (*3*) would involve only real examples. Restricting the search for counterfactuals to real examples is not necessary in our case and would probably yield counterfactuals that are too far away from the optimal value. Also, possible modifications need to be limited to actionable features (e.g. duration of the credit or number of ongoing credits), which are provided by the explainee. The counterexample generated from this context by IBEX, shown in Table 2, suggests two modifications of the current application: the duration of the credit and telephone ownership.

Table 2. Realistic counterfactual explanations based on actionable features. The first line shows the current attribute values of the Point of Interest while the second line shows the attribute values of a counterfactual (CF) input being classified as "Good" (low credit risk) by the system.

Actionable features	Credit amount	Duration	Ongoing credits	Job	Telephone ownership	Output
Current	10722	47	1	unskilled resident	yes	Bad
CF	10722	36	1	unskilled resident	none	Good

Comparing these two case studies gives insight of the diversity of explanations that can be generated with IBEX. We see that the framework proposed to define the context and the associated requirements offer an understandable way to interact with explanations, event for a lay user. Further examples of the use of IBEX are presented in [17].

---

[7] https://archive.ics.uci.edu/ml/datasets/statlog+(german+credit+data).

5   Related Works

To the best of our knowledge, no existing explanation system provides the diversity of explanations and the interaction capabilities offered by IBEX. Some authors have already proposed taxonomies of explainee's profiles [4,18], explanations' objectives [6,8,19] or combinations of profiles and objectives [5,7,20]. The impact of the type of question on the explanation has been analyzed through a user study in [11]. In the same vein, different forms of explanations are studied in [21]. Some works also aim at identifying appropriate sets of features of explanations [1,6,22]. These contributions are related to this paper in the sense that the categorization of explainees' needs is a key element of our interactive approach. However, the goal of these contributions is to identify and categorize these needs, rather than to design a generic interactive explainer. To the best of our understanding, none of them suggests an operational mapping to actual explanations as presented here.

Some contributions involve a form of interaction with explainees. AIX360 [23] contains eight explainability algorithms and allows users to choose among them based on a taxonomy including criteria such as "understand the data or the model" or "self-explaining model or post-hoc explanations". As it takes into consideration the user's needs, AIX360 provides a first level of interaction with explainees. However, the three levels of abstraction available in IBEX allow for richer interactivity, for instance, by allowing to choose the levels of simplicity, generality and realism of the explanation. Moreover, the generic explainer can be customized to fulfill the requirements of the explainee, which is not possible with the portfolio approach of AIX360. Finally, IBEX offers the possibility to react to an explanation, which is also a distinguishing feature.

Glass-Box [24] allows explainees to interact with an adaptive explainer through a voice-based (or chat-based) interface. The system provides local explanations, under the form of counterfactuals, and allows explainees to react in order to obtain a new explanation. Although Glass-Box has similarities with IBEX, its interactive capabilities are limited to the choice of actionable features for counterfactuals (which is also included in IBEX).

The bLIMEy system (for "build LIME yourself"), is a generic explainer relying on the framework proposed in [3]. However, bLIMEy does not include an analysis of the context of the explainee's query, neither does it include a mapping from this context to technical options, as done in IBEX.

Some authors consider interactive explanation frameworks from a more theoretical point of view. For instance, [25] defines the specifications of a dialogue system for explanations and [26] proposes an interaction protocol for XAI. These works are related to IBEX, and could be useful sources of inspiration to enhance its interaction facilities. However, their goal is not to propose an operational explanation system.

Finally, on the implementation side, many projects have recently emerged to provide implementations of existing methods [27–29]. The goal of these projects is to integrate a variety of existing methods, but they do not include a comprehensive interaction module and a fine-grain decomposition of components as done in IBEX.

6   Conclusion

The main goal of the work described in this paper is to address the variety of needs in terms of explanations of ADS and to design an explanation system that can be used by a wide range of explainees, including lay users. We have shown, through the IBEX prototype, the feasibility of an interactive explanation system based on our multi-layered approach. IBEX is a generic explanation generation system based on a variety of parameters and fine-grained components that can be combined in different ways. The architecture of IBEX and its components are described in [17]. As stated above, IBEX is a proof of concept implementation and it can be improved and extended in several directions. A first improvement concerns the user interface, which is very basic in the current version. In particular, it would be interesting to provide a richer and higher-level language to interact with explainees, for instance a restricted version of natural language that could be used by explainees to express questions such as "Why is it the case that my application has been rejected ?" or "Why has this file been accepted and not this one ?" or to express explanations. In some cases, requirements or technical options for the generation of explanations could be derived directly from such questions. In other cases, the explanation system would in turn ask a question to the explainee in order to allow him/her to refine his/her initial request. Dialogue specifications could rely on models such as [26]. Another extension of the tool would be to include an additional component to deal with input data that are not meaningful for humans, as the pixels of an image for example. An initial task is necessary to extract an interpretable representation from such data, as done in LIME [30], for example.

In order to prove its usability as an explanation system in real life, IBEX should be tested through a randomized user study involving different types of explainees, which we plan to do in the near future with applications in the health care and the judicial sectors. In this perspective, a key aspect of explanations that has not been developed in this paper is their assessment. Different criteria have been proposed to assess the quality of an explanation [31]. Our framework makes it possible to specify quality objectives, either as constraints or as criteria, but it does not provide any help to evaluate the relevance of these objectives (for example through an assessment of the understanding of the explainee). This is a major avenue for further research.

References

1. Guidotti, R., Monreale, A., Ruggieri, S., Turini, F., Giannotti, F., Pedreschi, D.: A survey of methods for explaining black box models. ACM Comput. Surv. (CSUR) 51(5), 1–42 (2018). Article no. 93
2. Miller, T., Howe, P., Sonenberg, L.: Explainable AI: beware of inmates running the asylum. In: IJCAI 2017 Workshop on Explainable AI (XAI), vol. 36 (2017)
3. Henin, C., Le Métayer, D.: Towards a generic framework for black-box explanations of algorithmic decision systems (Extended Version). Inria Research Report 9276. https://hal.inria.fr/hal-02131174

4. Tomsett, R., Braines, D., Harborne, D., Preece, A.D., Chakraborty, S.: Interpretable to whom? A role-based model for analyzing interpretable machine learning systems. CoRR abs/1806.07552 (2018)
5. Arrieta, A.B., et al.: Explainable artificial intelligence (XAI): concepts, taxonomies, opportunities and challenges toward responsible AI. arXiv:1910.10045 [cs]arXiv: 1910.10045
6. Miller, T.: Explanation in artificial intelligence: insights from the social sciences. Artif. Intell. **267**. https://doi.org/10.1016/j.artint.2018.07.007
7. Weller, A.: Challenges for transparency. arXiv:1708.01870 [cs]arXiv: 1708.01870
8. Lipton, Z.C.: The mythos of model interpretability. arXiv:1606.03490 [cs, stat]arXiv: 1606.03490
9. Wachter, S., Mittelstadt, B., Russell, C.: Counterfactual explanations without opening the black box: automated decisions and the GDPR. Harvard J. Law Technol. **31**, 841–887 (2018)
10. Stumpf, S., et al.: Toward harnessing user feedback for machine learning 10 (2007)
11. Lim, B.Y., Dey, A.K., Avrahami, D.: Why and why not explanations improve the intelligibility of context-aware intelligent systems. In: Proceedings of the 27th International Conference on Human Factors in Computing Systems - CHI 2009, p. 2119. ACM Press (2009). https://doi.org/10.1145/1518701.1519023
12. Lakkaraju, H., Kamar, E., Caruana, R., Leskovec, J.: Interpretable & explorable approximations of black box models. arXiv preprint arXiv:1707.01154
13. Ribeiro, M.T., Singh, S., Guestrin, C.: Anchors: high-precision model-agnostic explanations. In: AAAI Conference on Artificial Intelligence (2018)
14. Laugel, T., Lesot, M.-J., Marsala, C., Renard, X., Detyniecki, M.: The dangers of post-hoc interpretability: unjustified counterfactual explanations. arXiv:1907.09294 [cs, stat]arXiv: 1907.09294
15. Henin, C., Le Métayer, D.: A multi-layered approach for interactive black-box explanations. Inria Research Report 9331. https://hal.inria.fr/hal-02498418
16. Doshi-Velez, F., Kim, B.: Towards a rigorous science of interpretable machine learning. arXiv e-prints arXiv:1702.08608 (2017)
17. Henin, C., Le Métayer, D.: A generic framework for black-box explanations. In: Proceedings of the International Workshop on Fair and Interpretable Learning Algorithms (FILA 2020). IEEE (2020)
18. Ras, G., van Gerven, M., Haselager, P. Explanation methods in deep learning: users, values, concerns and challenges. CoRR abs/1803.07517. http://arxiv.org/abs/1803.07517
19. Adadi, A., Berrada, M.: Peeking inside the black-box: a survey on explainable artificial intelligence (XAI). IEEE Access **6**, 52138–52160 (2018). https://doi.org/10.1109/ACCESS.2018.2870052
20. Wolf, C.T.: Explainability scenarios: towards scenario-based XAI design. In: Proceedings of the 24th International Conference on Intelligent User Interfaces - IUI 2019, pp. 252–257. ACM Press (2019). https://doi.org/10.1145/3301275.3302317
21. Poursabzi-Sangdeh, F., Goldstein, D.G., Hofman, J.M., Vaughan, J.W., Wallach, H.: Manipulating and measuring model interpretability. arXiv:1802.07810 [cs]arXiv: 1802.07810
22. Hall, M., et al.: A systematic method to understand requirements for explainable AI (XAI) systems 7 (2019)
23. Arya, V., et al.: One explanation does not fit all: a toolkit and taxonomy of AI explainability techniques. arXiv:1909.03012 [cs, stat]arXiv: 1909.03012

24. Sokol, K., Flach, P.: One explanation does not fit all: the promise of interactive explanations for machine learning transparency. KI - Künstliche Intelligenz. http://dx.doi.org/10.1007/s13218-020-00637-y
25. Walton, D.: A dialogue system specification for explanation. Synthese **182**(3), 349–374 (2011). https://doi.org/10.1007/s11229-010-9745-z
26. Madumal, P., Miller, T., Sonenberg, L., Vetere, F.: A grounded interaction protocol for explainable artificial intelligence. arXiv:1903.02409 [cs]arXiv: 1903.02409
27. Nori, H., Jenkins, S., Koch, P., Caruana, R.: InterpretML: a unified framework for machine learning interpretability. arXiv preprint arXiv:1909.09223
28. Klaise, J., Van Looveren, A., Vacanti, G., Coca, A.: Alibi: Algorithms for monitoring and explaining machine learning models (2020)
29. Biecek, P.: DALEX: explainers for complex predictive models in R. J. Mach. Learn. Res. **19**(84), 1–5 (2018)
30. Ribeiro, M.T., Singh, S., Guestrin, C.: "Why should I trust you?" Explaining the predictions of any classifier. In: Proceedings of the 22nd ACM SIGKDD International Conference on Knowledge Discovery and Data Mining, pp. 1135–1144 (2016)
31. Dhurandhar, A., Iyengar, V., Luss, R., Shanmugam, K.: A formal framework to characterize interpretability of procedures. arXiv:1707.03886 [cs]arXiv: 1707.03886

Post-hoc Explanation Options for XAI in Deep Learning: The *Insight Centre for Data Analytics* Perspective

Eoin M. Kenny[1,2,3], Eoin D. Delaney[1,2,3], Derek Greene[1,2,3], and Mark T. Keane[1,2,3(✉)]

[1] School of Computer Science, University College Dublin, Dublin, Ireland
{eoin.kenny,eoin.delaney}@insight-centre.org, {derek.greene, mark.keane}@ucd.ie
[2] Insight Centre for Data Analytics, University College Dublin, Dublin, Ireland
[3] VistaMilk SFI Research, Cork, Ireland

Abstract. This paper profiles the recent research work on eXplainable AI (XAI), at the Insight Centre for Data Analytics. This work concentrates on post-hoc explanation-by-example solutions to XAI as one approach to explaining black box deep-learning systems. Three different methods of post-hoc explanation are outlined for image and time-series datasets: that is, factual, counterfactual, and semi-factual methods). The future landscape for XAI solutions is discussed.

Keywords: Explainable AI · Interpretable AI · Trust · Artificial Neural Networks · Convolutional neural networks · Case-based reasoning · *k*-nearest neighbors

1 Introduction

In the last five years, the problem of eXplainable AI (XAI) has been highlighted as the public, business and government face AI-based decision-making in people's everyday lives, jobs, and leisure time [11]. In the European Union, the urgency behind this research area has, in part, being driven by GDPR proposals on explaining automated decisions [40]. However, more broadly, it also arises from a deep concern in the academic community that some AI technologies rely on dubious ethical standards and/or unethical design decisions, decisions that may result AI systems coming to be perceived as unfair, unaccountable, and untrustworthy. For instance, consider the issues around bias and consent in prominent datasets [24, 25, 35]; MIT recently apologized for the Tiny Images dataset, when it was revealed to contain verifiably pornographic images shot in non-consensual settings [35].

Facing these challenges, Ireland's national Artificial Intelligence and Data Analytics centre – the *Insight Centre for Data Analytics* (www.insight-centre.org) – has developed an extensive program of engagement with government and business in the field of XAI, as well as advancing research in the area. On the regulatory side, *Insight* has engaged

© Springer Nature Switzerland AG 2021
A. Del Bimbo et al. (Eds.): ICPR 2020 Workshops, LNCS 12663, pp. 20–34, 2021.
https://doi.org/10.1007/978-3-030-68796-0_2

with initiatives at national and international levels in championing a Magna Carta for Data [32], contributing to the European's Commission's High-Level Expert Group in AI [1], and the Joint Strategic Research Innovation and Deployment Agenda for the Artificial Intelligence, Data and Robotics Partnership [12]. On the research side, the *Insight* centre has an extensive program that aims to formulate a coherent solution to the XAI problem (e.g., [7, 20, 26, 30, 41]). In this paper, we present a slice of this work directed at image and time-series data, focussing on how opaque, black-box AI systems can be explained with reference to more interpretable, white-box AI systems; what has been termed the *Twin-Systems* approach to XAI [8, 14, 15, 20] (see Fig. 1).

In the remainder of this introduction we make some of key taxonomic distinctions in XAI for different algorithmic approaches to the problem, before showing a taxonomic matrix for the research area. Then, in later sections, we sketch the algorithmic techniques advanced by *Insight* and initial user tests of these techniques.

A Fundamental Distinction: *Pre-hoc* Versus *Post-hoc*

Many definitional and taxonomic issues arise in XAI, not least because "explanation" has for decades proven to be very hard concept to define across many disciplines, from Philosophy, to the Philosophy of Science, and Psychology [39]. It is, therefore, not surprising that Computer Science and Artificial Intelligence has struggled too [39]. Arguably, we still really do not have precise definitions for the terms "explanation"", "interpretable" and transparent"; though this does not stop us using them on a regular basis. However, notwithstanding these definitional issues, there has been some agreement on a fundamental distinction between "explanation proper" and "explanation as justification". For example, Sørmo *et al.* [39] point out the philosophical distinction between explaining how the system reached some answer (what they call *transparency*) and explaining why the system produced a given answer (*post-hoc justification*). Lipton [27] makes a similar distinction between *transparency* (i.e., *"How does the model work"*) and *post hoc explanation* (i.e., *"What else can the model tell me?"*). The key idea here is that one can causally explain a model directly, in some sense, (e.g., "it optimizes this function using such-and-such a detailed method") or one can explain/justify how it reached some decision with reference to other information (e.g., "the model did this because it used such-and-such data"). The problem XAI faces is that the former may be accurate but can only be comprehended by a handful of people (i.e., how can the general public understand a deep learning algorithm) and the latter may be comprehensible but is too approximate to really explain what happens (e.g., saying certain data was used may also be uninformative or unclear). At present, these two options for explanation have been set somewhat in opposition to one another [37], even though on occasion they shade into one another [11]. Next, we consider these two opposing positions on "model transparency" and "*post-hoc* explanation" in more detail.

Model Transparency. This explanation position has been terminologically cast as "transparency", "simulatability" or "interpretable machine learning". The key idea here is that one can causally explain a model directly, in some sense, (e.g., "it optimizes this function using such-and-such a detailed method"). In this approach, one understands how the whole model works given some representation of it [27] or via some simplified proxy model that "behaves similarly to the original model, but in a way that is easier to explain" [11] (e.g., [10]). Rudin [37] argues that the use of inherently transparent models is the only appropriate solution to XAI in sensitive domains; pointing to her own use of prototypes [5]. There are two major problems with this approach to XAI. First, to date, few pure instances of good proxy models have been proposed to characterize black box systems. Second, when proxy models have been proposed (e.g., decision trees) very little evidence is provided for why they are more interpretable than the original black box; that is, the researchers typically just assert they are more interpretable without supporting user tests. As Lipton [27] points out "neither linear models, rule-based systems, nor decision trees are intrinsically interpretable...Sufficiently high-dimensional models, unwieldy rule lists, and deep decision trees could all be considered less transparent than comparatively compact neural networks". Finally, it should be said, that it is not wholly clear when a proxy model actually becomes an identifiably separate model; for instance, Frosst & Hinton [10] argue that their model is a stand-alone one, not an interpretable proxy to work "alongside" a deep learner. Presumably, at some (as yet undefined) point a proxy model is no longer a facsimile of the original.

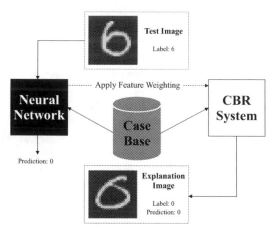

Fig. 1. *The Twin-Systems Explanation Framework*: A deep learning model (Neural Network) produces a miss-classification for an MNIST test image, wrongly labelling a "6" as a "0". This prediction is explained by analysing the feature-weights of the network for that prediction and applying these to a twinned k-NN (Case Based Reasoner/CBR System) to retrieve a nearest neighbor to the test-image in the training set. This explanatory image shows that the model used an image of a "0" that looks very like a "6" to make its prediction of a "0". So, though it miss-classifies the item, it is quite faithful to the data it was given.

***Post-hoc* Explanation.** The other explanation position has been terminologically cast as *justification* or *explainable machine learning*. The key idea here is that one can explain/justify how a model reached some decision with reference to other information (e.g., "the model did this because it used such-and-such data"). Lipton [27] has further divided *post-hoc* explanations into (i) textual explanations of system outputs, (ii) visualizations of learned representations or models (e.g., heat/saliency maps; [42]), and (iii) explanations by example (i.e., the classic case-based reasoning approach). This type of "explanation by justification", is an after-the-prediction explanation step where some evidence is given to elucidate the predictions made by the AI system; though, some techniques, such as visual analytics may operate right across the deep learning pipeline [42]. As we shall see, it has recently become clear that explanation-by-example can be divided into three distinct flavors (i.e., factual, counterfactual, and semi-factual). This paper recounts the systematic work that has been done by researchers at the *Insight Centre for Data Analytics* to explore these *post-hoc* solutions to XAI in image and time-series datasets.

Table 1. The *Insight* taxonomic matrix for explanation-types X datasets

	Explanation type		
Data sets	Factual	Counterfactual	Semi-factual
Tabular	Kenny & Keane [20] Keane & Kenny [14] Keane & Kenny [15] Kenny *et al.* [17] Kenny *et al.* [18]	Keane & Smyth [16]	–
Image	Keane & Kenny [20] Ford *et al.* [8]	Kenny & Keane [19]	Kenny & Keane [19]
Time-series	Nguyen *et al.* [30] Delaney *et al.* [7]	Delaney *et al.* [7]	–

Post-hoc Explanation: Factual, Counterfactual, and Semi-factuals

Traditionally, *post-hoc* explanations were viewed as explanations-by-example where some factual (i.e., nearest neighboring) case was produced to explain some target query [18]. However, there are other explanatory options based on the type of example used in the explanation. Consider a typical scenario where we are trying to explain a black-box classifier giving loan decisions, operating off a traditional tabular dataset with defined features (e.g., gender). Assume you are refused your loan application and, under your GDPR rights, ask for an explanation. The system could give you a *factual example-based explanation* saying "you were refused the loan because your profile is similar to person-x who was also refused the loan". Alternatively, the system could give you a *counterfactual explanation* saying "if you had a higher salary, you would have the profile of person-x who got the loan". Finally, one could also be given a *semi-factual explanation* saying "even if you had a higher salary, you would still *not* have the profile of person-x who got the loan". Of course, computing these alternative explanations is non-trivial and, as such, the lion's share of research has been on factual *post-hoc* explanations (as in CBR), but there is a growing interest in counterfactual [23, 40], and semi-factual explanations

[19, 31]. Finally, almost all of this research has focused on tabular datasets, so here we consider, arguably harder, image and time-series datasets.

A Taxonomic Matrix for *Post-hoc* Explanations
In the previous subsection, we saw how *post-hoc* explanations can be divided into three distinct types – factual, counterfactual, and semi-factual – and noted that while some progress has been made in implementing these strategies for tabular datasets, it is only very recently that researchers have started to consider them for non-tabular datasets. In *Insight*, we have a research program designed to flesh out these *post-hoc* alternatives for explaining different datasets. Accordingly, our research program aims to fill the cells of a matrix created by crossing explanation-types by datasets (see Table 1).

In the remainder of this paper we will sketch some of the solutions we have found when exploring these different explanation-types for image and time-series datasets. So, for image datasets we first consider methods for factual (Sect. 2), counterfactual (Sect. 3), and semi-factual explanations (Sect. 4). Then in the remainder of the paper, we consider counterfactuals explanations for time-series (Sect. 5) before looking to future directions for this work (see Sect. 6).

2   Post-hoc Factual Explanations: Images

A "factual *post-hoc* explanation-by-example" is a long name for the case-based explanations used in CBR[1]. Traditionally, these models deploy a k-NN to solve some classification or regression problem and then use the nearest-neighbors in k to explain the prediction made; where, typically, the prediction is made from some averaging or aggregation of the instances in k [17, 18]. The current use of factual explanations extends this approach to explain black-box deep learning models (Artificial Neural Networks or ANNs) where the nearest neighboring cases from a k-NN twinned with the ANN are selected based on analyzing the feature-weights of the ANN. Recently, Kenny & Keane [20] generalized this explanation option in the *Twin Systems* approach, where the feature-weights for a test-instance in a deep learning model are applied to a k-NN, operating over the same dataset, to find factual explanations (see Fig. 1).

Kenny & Keane [20] also competitively tested several feature-weighting, methods from a literature going back to the 1990s, to determine the most accurate method for capturing ANNs (including, multi-layered perceptrons and convolutional neural networks); these experiments found that a contributions-based method performed best. Recently, Papernot and MacDaniel [33] proposed DkNN as a method for finding factual explanation cases, although they did not consider weighting the k-NN abstraction, which has been found to be crucial [20]. Also, Chen *et al.* [5] replaced the last layer of a CNN with a CBR system to force the black-box to be more transparent. In the present section, we sketch our contributions-based method (see Sect. 2.1) and show how it can be applied to a CNN dealing with the MNIST and CIFAR datasets before considering some of its explanatory results and user-tests.

---

[1] Here, we consider factual *examples* as explanations; but LIME [36] gives factual information about the current test instance via feature importance scores also.

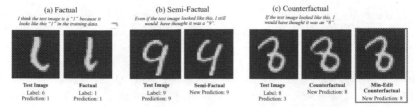

Fig. 2. *Post-hoc* factual, semi-factual, and counterfactual explanations on MNIST showing: (a) a *factual explanation* for a miss-classification of "6" as "1", that uses a nearest-neighbor in latent-space classed as "1", (b) a *semi-factual explanation* for the correct classification of a "9", that shows a synthetic instance with meaningful feature changes that would *not* alter its classification, and (c) a *counterfactual explanation* for the miss-classification of an "8" as a "3", that shows a synthetic test-instance with meaningful feature changes that *would have been* classified as an "8" (n.b., for comparison a counterfactual using a *Min-Edit* method is shown with its human-undetectable feature-changes; from [19]).

2.1 The Method: COLE

A contributions-based feature-weighting method has been found to offer the most accurate analysis of black-box ANNs, with a view to finding factual example-based explanations [20]. This feature-weighting method -- *Contributions Oriented Local Explanations* (COLE) – can be applied to both multi-layered perceptrons (MLPs) and convolutional neural networks (CNNs) to find explanatory cases from the twinned k-NN/CBR model (i.e., a CNN-CBR twin) applied to the same dataset. COLE fits a k-NN model with feature contributions to abstract the ANN function, that are calculated by multiplying a data-instance by weights it used in the final prediction.

To implement this in a CNN there are two possible options. Firstly, the CNN may have several fully connected layers post feature-extraction, in which case we have shown how saliency map techniques can be used to implement COLE [20]. Secondly, there may be a linear classifier post feature-extraction (e.g., the ResNet architectures), in which case contributions can be calculated by taking the Hadamard product of an instance's penultimate activations with the weight vector connected to its final classification (henceforth called C-HP). In both approaches it is possible to highlight the most positively contributing features via a feature activation map (FAM) [20].

2.2 Results: Factual Image-Based Explanations

Figure 2a and 3 shows two examples of factual explanations found using a CNN-CBR twin system approach on the MNIST and CIFAR-10 datasets, for correct and incorrect classifications. In Fig. 2a an incorrect classification is made by the system, where a "6" is miss-classified as a "1" and the explanatory nearest-neighbors tell the user that this occurs because the dataset contains data which looks like the test image and was labelled as "1". Figure 3 shows an example using the CIFAR-10 dataset involving C-HP. It shows the miss-classification of an automobile as a truck. This incorrect prediction is justified by essentially saying to the user *"I think this is a truck because it looks like these trucks I saw before"*. In addition, the FAMs highlight the most important (i.e., the most positively contributing) feature in the classification, which clearly focusses on the vehicle wheels in all images. Since these are a central aspect of both automobiles and trucks, it makes the miss-classification more reasonable.

C-HP has been extensively tested on seventeen classification/regression datasets, which consistently showed C-HP to be the best for both MLPs and CNNs. Furthermore, Ford *et al.* [8] have performed a series of user studies using its explanations for MNIST; they asked people to judge the correctness/reasonableness of the predictions made by the CNN in the presence/absence of explanations. These studies showed that explanations impacted people's perceptions of the correctness of the CNN's predictions. However, these studies also showed that the explanations did *not* improve people's overall trust/satisfaction in the system when it produced miss-classifications (i.e., it did not "explain away" error behaviour). This work also found that people have a low-tolerance for error in such automated systems (i.e., algorithmic aversion).

Fig. 3. A CNN-CBR twin miss-classifies an image of an automobile as a truck. The nearest-neighbours are all trucks, justifying the prediction. Also, a FAM shows the CNN is focused on the wheels in the prediction, features indicative of both automobiles and trucks.

3 Post-hoc Counterfactual Explanations: Images

Although factual explanations have traditionally been the focus for example-based explanations, recently there has been an expanding interest in contrastive-example explanations [19, 23, 40]. Indeed, some have argued that contrastive explanations are much more causally-informative than factual ones, as well as being GDPR-compliant [40]. Most current counterfactual methods only apply to tabular data [16, 28], but some recent work has begun to consider images. To deal with images, generative models have been used to produce counterfactual images with large featural-changes for XAI [38]. Recently however, *Insight* researchers have developed a different approach to generating counterfactuals for image datasets, called PlausIble Exceptionality-Based Contrastive Explanations (PIECE) [19]; it generates counterfactual images by focusing on *exceptional* features (an approach inspired by strategies humans use when generating counterfactuals [4]). The algorithm generates counterfactuals by identifying "exceptional" features in the test image, and then modifying these to be "normal".

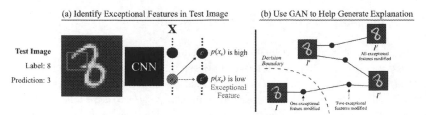

Fig. 4. PIECE explains an incorrect prediction using a counterfactual: the test image labelled as "8" is miss-classified as a "3" by the CNN. To show how the image would have to change for the CNN to classify it as an "8", PIECE generates a counterfactual by (a) identifying the features that have a low probability of occurrence in the counterfactual class c' (i.e., "8" class) before modifying them to be the expected feature values for c', and (b) using a GAN to visualize the image I' (here we show progressive exceptional-feature changes that gradually produce a plausible counterfactual image of an "8").

3.1 The Method: PIECE

PIECE involves two distinct systems, a CNN that is generating predictions to be explained, and a GAN that helps generate explanatory images. This algorithm will work with any trained CNN, provided there is a GAN trained on the same dataset as the CNN. PIECE has three main steps: (i) "exceptional" features are identified in the CNN for a test image from the perspective of the counterfactual class, (ii) these are then modified to be their expected values, and (iii) the resulting latent-feature representation of the explanatory counterfactual is visualized in the pixel-space with help from the GAN.

Figure 4 illustrates how PIECE works in practice to generate a counterfactual image-explanation. Here, the counterfactuals to a test image I, in class c, with latent features x, are denoted as I', c' and x', respectively. Figure 4 shows a test image labelled as class "8" (i.e., c) is miss-classified as class "3" (i.e., c'). Exceptional features are identified using mathematical probability in the extracted feature layer X which have a low chance of occurrence in c'; these are then modified to be their expected feature values for class c' which modify the latent representation x to be x'. This new latent counterfactual representation x' is then visualized in the pixel space as the explanation I' using a GAN.

3.2 Results: Counterfactual Image-Based Explanations

Kenny & Keane [19] have compared PIECE to a simple *Min-Edit* method in a series of experiments (along with several other methods in the literature) to highlight the difference it finds. Figure 2c shows the counterfactual explanations for the miss-classification of an "8" as a "3" for PIECE and *Min-Edit*. PIECE shows a plausible counterfactual which fully removes all irregularities from the perspective of the counterfactual class "8", whilst the Min-Edit counterfactual does not convey meaningful information to help a user understand the difference between the two classes. Furthermore, [19] compared PIECE to a *Min-Edit* approach, generating 193 counterfactual explanations for right and wrong classifications on the MNIST and CIFAR-10 datasets. The evaluation measures assessed the plausibility of the generated instances by virtue of their proximity to the underlying data distribution. On most measures, PIECE was significantly better than the *Min-Edit* approach and other popular methods [19].

4 Post-hoc Semi-factual Explanations: Images

The last missing piece of the puzzle for post-hoc explanations is the largely under researched semi-factual explanations. To understand semi-factuals computationally, it is interesting to contrast them with counterfactuals; whilst counterfactuals are typically described as the minimum distance an instance must travel to cross a decision boundary, a semi-factual can be seen as the *maximal distance* an instance can travel *without* changing its classification (n.b., while still being a plausible instance). An AI loan application system might explain its decision semi-factually by saying "Even if you had asked for a slightly lower amount, you still would have been refused the loan". We have found only one decade-old paper related to semi-factual explanations (see [31] on *a-fortiori* reasoning that was only on tabular data).

4.1 Method and Results: PIECE for Semi-factuals

To implement semi-factual explanations for images, we used the PIECE algorithm, but stop the modification of exceptional features before the decision boundary is crossed. As we shall see, this results in a large, plausible change to the image that does *not* change the classification. For comparison, we compared it again against the *Min-Edit* method; although this time, the method is stopped not after crossing the decision boundary, but one optimization step before, so the classification remains.

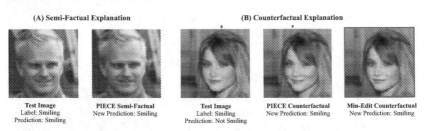

Fig. 5. (A) A semi-factual explanation justifying why the initial classification was definitely correct, in that, even if the image was smiling much less, it still would have classified it as "smiling. (B) A counterfactual explanation conveying to a user why the CNN made a mistake, and how the image would need to look for it to have classified it correctly (as computed by PIECE and Min-Edit)

We measure "good semi-factuals" for images with the L_1 distance between the test image and synthetic explanatory semi-factual in the pixel-space (n.b., the greater the distance the better). Kenny & Keane [19] compared PIECE against the *Min-Edit* method, finding significant differences between the two in terms for how much of the image is modified before reaching the decision boundary. This result shows that that the "blind perturbation" *Min-edit* method is suboptimal for generating semi-factuals close to the decision boundary. Figures 2 and 5 show some examples of semi-factual explanation for the MNIST and CelebA datasets, respectively. Figure 2b shows a semi-factual explanation for the correct classification of a "9" on MNIST. Glossed, the explanation is saying *"Even if the test image looked like this (i.e., closer to a 4), the model would still have thought it was a 9, ergo, the initial classification is definitely correct"*. A similar explanation is conveyed in Fig. 5a for the CelebA dataset.

5 *Post-hoc*, Counterfactual Explanations: Time-Series

We have now demonstrated how nearest neighbor techniques in twin systems can explain the predictions of black-box deep learners (such as CNN's). Next, we focus on explanations in the time-series domain. The current focus in XAI for time series mainly focusses on saliency-based approaches where important sub-sequences or features are highlighted [30]. However, given the immense success of nearest-neighbor classifiers using a variety of distance measures [3, 29], instance-based counterfactual explanations also seem like an exciting avenue to pursue for XAI in time series.

Earlier we highlighted that counterfactual explanations with image-data is a recent development in XAI; however, until very recently, counterfactuals explanations of time-series models have been largely ignored. The best way to understand how counterfactual explanations might be used for explaining time-series data is to explore how they differ from factual explanations. Consider a binary classification system which decides whether a city has Oceanic Climate or a Mediterranean Climate based on weekly temperatures over some historical period. The system explain a prediction factually saying "Amsterdam has an Oceanic Climate because it is most similar to London (a city in the training data) which also has an Oceanic Climate". In contrast, the system might explain its decision counterfactually by saying "If Amsterdam had slightly hotter summers the system would predict the city to have a Mediterranean climate". Tabular methods for counterfactuals [40], quickly become intractable for time-series data because of the number of possible feature dimensions and the domain-specific distance measures (such as DTW). In response to this gap in the literature, some recent proposals have been made to use contrastive methods to explain time-series predictions. Karlsson *et al.* [13] implement explainable time-series tweaking, using an opaque shapelet-based classifier, where they find the minimum number of changes to be performed to the given time series that changes the classification decision. Also, by modifying the original loss function [59] to generate counterfactuals, Ates *et al.* [2] have explored generating counterfactual explanations for multivariate time series classification problems. Also, Labaien *et al.* [21] have progressed contrastive explanations for the predictions of recurrent neural networks in time-series prediction. Recently researchers at *Insight* proposed an instance-based approach, called Native-Guide, for counterfactual generation in time series [7]. This approach has been shown to work with any classifier, using both DTW and Minkowski distance measures.

5.1 The Method: Native-Guide for Time-Series Counterfactuals

The current method – Native Guide – incorporates a strategy where the closest in-sample counterfactual instance to the test-instance is adapted to form a new counterfactual explanation [16, 22, 31]. Here the "Native-Guide" is a counterfactual instance that already exists in the dataset, it is the nearest-neighbor time-series to the query that involves a class change (see Fig. 6). We can retrieve this in-sample counterfactual instance using a

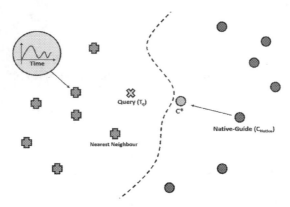

Fig. 6. A time series data set for a binary classification task with two class labels. A query time series T_q (represented as X) and it's Native-Guide C_{Native}. The generated counterfactual C^* is represented by the light circle.

simple 1-NN search. Once this instance is found it is perturbed towards the query until just before the decision boundary. The generated counterfactual instance C^* (the light circle in Fig. 6), should offer better explanations than the original in-sample counterfactual as it is in closer to the query whilst still staying within the distribution of the data. Figure 7 shows a specific example in the climate domain for a counterfactual explanation of a time-series.

When using Euclidean distance perturbation a simple weighted perturbation strategy works well. But, when working with DTW a technique known as weighted Dynamic Barycenter Averaging (DBA) is required to implement the perturbation [9, 34]:

Definition: Weighted average of time series under DTW. *Given a weighted set of time series* $D = (T_1, \beta_1), \ldots, (T_N, \beta_N)D = (T_1, \beta_1), \ldots, (T_N, \beta_N)$, *the average time series under DTW,* $\overline{T}$, *is the time series that minimizes:*

$$argmin\overline{T} = \sum_{i=1}^{N} \beta_i \cdot DTW^2(\overline{T}, T_i)$$

5.2   Results: Native-Guide for Counterfactuals

Native Guide was tested on a climate case-study and over 35 diverse datasets from the UCR archive [6]. In these experiments, a specialized distance-measure (called RCF, see [16]) was used to assess if the generated counterfactuals were in close proximity to the query, along with novelty detection algorithms, to assess if the generated counterfactuals were within the distribution of the data. The generated counterfactual instances that are not within the distribution of the data are referred to as being Out-of-Distribution (OOD). A subset of our results are shown in Table 2 with a full analysis and discussion of results in the original paper [7]. The results highlight that Native-Guide generates proximal and plausible counterfactual explanations for a diverse range of datasets. The generated counterfactual instances are significantly closer to the query when compared to the existing in-sample counterfactual instances.

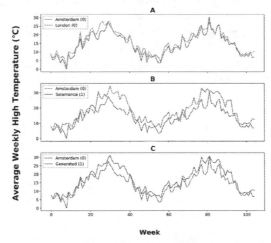

Fig. 7. Different explanations for a queried city (Amsterdam) in the climate prediction task **(A)** Factual Explanation: "Amsterdam has an Oceanic climate because it is most similar to London, which has an Oceanic climate too". **(B)** In-sample Counterfactual Explanation: "If Amsterdam had the same weather profile as Salamanca the system would classify it as having a Mediterranean climate". Salamanca's weather profile is quite different to Amsterdam's (noticeably hotter summers and warmer winters). An explanation that is more similar to the query might be more informative and this motivates the generation of a new counterfactual using Salamanca as a "Native-Guide" **(C)** If Amsterdam had a weather profile like the Generated-Instance then system would classify it as having a Mediterranean climate. This is a better explanation than **B** because the generated time series is much closer to the original query by comparison to Salamanca and is also within the data distribution.

Table 2. Subset of results for UCR Data Experiment (Dynamic Time Warping Implementation). #CF indicates the number of counterfactual instances generated.

Data set	Train size	Test size	#CF	OOD	RCF
ECG200	100	100	23	1	0.304
GunPoint	50	150	14	0	0.151
ItalyPowerDemand	67	1029	51	1	0.323
PhalangesOutlinesCorrect	1800	858	233	6	0.408

6   Future Directions

This paper has briefly summarized the *Insight Centre for Data Analytics'* engagement and contributions to the rapidly evolving and increasingly important field of XAI. The immediate avenue for future work is to fill out the matrix detailed above (in Table 1). This plan underscores the need to explore semi-factual explanations in tabular and time-series datasets. Additionally, we have already considered and published work on natural language counterfactual explanations which focused on the issue of grammatical plausibility [26]; future work in this area will also extend this to factual and semi-factual explanations. Other interesting avenues exist in applying the PIECE algorithm to tabular, text, and time-series datasets, to see if the modification of *exceptional* features to generate contrastive explanations carries over into these other domains. Finally, it is important to reiterate that whatever explanation strategy bears the most fruit computationally will need to be psychologically verified in user tests, such as those in [8].

Acknowledgements. This paper emanated from research funded by (i) Science Foundation Ireland (SFI) to the Insight Centre for Data Analytics (12/RC/2289-P2), (ii) SFI and DAFM on behalf of the Government of Ireland to the VistaMilk SFI Research Centre (16/RC/3835).

References

1. Ala-Pietilä, P.: Landline - 10/10/20: High-Level Expert Group on Artificial Intelligence. https://ec.europa.eu/digital-single-market/en/high-level-expert-group-artificial-intelligence
2. Ates, E., et al.: Counterfactual explanations for machine learning on multivariate time series data. arXiv:2008.10781 (2020)
3. Bagnall, A., et al.: The great time series classification bake off: an experimental evaluation of recently proposed algorithms. Extended Version. arXiv:1602.01711 (2016)
4. Byrne, R.M.J.: Counterfactuals in explainable artificial intelligence (XAI): evidence from human reasoning. In: Proceedings of the 28th International Joint Conference on Artificial Intelligence (IJCAI 2019) (2019)
5. Chen, C., et al.: This looks like that. In: NeurIPS (2020)
6. Dau, H.A., et al.: The UCR time series archive. arXiv:1810.07758 (2019)
7. Delaney, E., et al.: Instance-based counterfactual explanations for time series classification. arXiv:2009.13211 (2020)
8. Ford, C., et al.: Play MNIST for me! User studies on the effects of post-hoc, example-based explanations & error rates on debugging a deep learning, black-box classifier. In: IJCAI 2020 XAI Workshop (2020)
9. Forestier, G., et al.: Generating synthetic time series to augment sparse datasets. In: 2017 IEEE International Conference on Data Mining (2017)
10. Frosst, N., Hinton, G.: Distilling a neural network into a soft decision tree. arXiv:1711.09784 (2017)
11. Gilpin, L.H., et al.: Explaining explanations: an approach to evaluating interpretability of machine learning. arXiv:1806.00069 (2018)
12. Hahn, T.: Landline - 10/10/20: Strategic Research, Innovation and Deployment Agenda. https://ai-data-robotics-partnership.eu/wp-content/uploads/2020/09/AI-Data-Robotics-Partnership-SRIDA-V3.0.pdf
13. Karlsson, I., et al.: Explainable time series tweaking via irreversible and reversible temporal transformations. arXiv:1809.05183 (2018)
14. Keane, M., Kenny, E.: How case-based reasoning explains neural networks: a theoretical analysis of XAI using post-hoc explanation-by-example from a survey of ANN-CBR twin-systems. In: Bach, K., Marling, C. (eds.) ICCBR 2019. LNCS (LNAI), vol. 11680, pp. 155–171. Springer, Cham (2019). https://doi.org/10.1007/978-3-030-29249-2_11
15. Keane, M.T., Kenny, E.M.: The twin-system approach as one generic solution for XAI. In: IJCAI 2019 XAI Workshop (2019)

16. Keane, M.T., Smyth, B.: Good counterfactuals and where to find them: a case-based technique for generating counterfactuals for explainable AI (XAI). In: Watson, I., Weber, R. (eds.) ICCBR 2020. LNCS (LNAI), vol. 12311, pp. 163–178. Springer, Cham (2020). https://doi.org/10.1007/978-3-030-58342-2_11

17. Kenny, E.M., et al.: Bayesian case-exclusion and personalized explanations for sustainable dairy farming. In: Proceedings of the Twenty-Ninth International Joint Conference on Artificial Intelligence (IJCAI 2020) (2020)

18. Kenny, E., et al.: Predicting grass growth for sustainable dairy farming: a CBR system using Bayesian case-exclusion and post-hoc, personalized explanation-by-example (XAI). In: Bach, K., Marling, C. (eds.) ICCBR 2019. LNCS (LNAI), vol. 11680, pp. 172–187. Springer, Cham (2019). https://doi.org/10.1007/978-3-030-29249-2_12

19. Kenny, E.M., Keane, M.T.: On generating plausible counterfactual and semi-factual explanations for deep learning. arXiv:2009.06399 (2020)

20. Kenny, E.M., Keane, M.T.: Twin-systems to explain artificial neural networks using case-based reasoning. In: Proceedings of the 28th International Joint Conference on Artificial Intelligence (IJCAI 2019) (2019)

21. Labaien, J., Zugasti, E., De Carlos, X.: Contrastive explanations for a deep learning model on time-series data. In: Song, M., Song, I.-Y., Kotsis, G., Tjoa, A.M., Khalil, I. (eds.) DaWaK 2020. LNCS, vol. 12393, pp. 235–244. Springer, Cham (2020). https://doi.org/10.1007/978-3-030-59065-9_19

22. Laugel, T., et al.: Defining locality for surrogates in post-hoc interpretablity. arXiv:1806.07498 (2018)

23. Laugel, T., et al.: The dangers of post-hoc interpretability: unjustified counterfactual explanations. In: Proceedings of the Twenty-Eighth International Joint Conference on Artificial Intelligence (IJCAI 2019) (2019)

24. Leavy, S., et al.: Data, power and bias in artificial intelligence. arXiv:2008.0734 (2020)

25. Leavy, S., Meaney, G., Wade, K., Greene, D.: Mitigating gender bias in machine learning data sets. In: Boratto, L., Faralli, S., Marras, M., Stilo, G. (eds.) BIAS 2020. CCIS, vol. 1245, pp. 12–26. Springer, Cham (2020). https://doi.org/10.1007/978-3-030-52485-2_2

26. Linyi, Y., et al.: Generating plausible counterfactual explanations for deep transformers in financial text classification. In: Proceedings of the 28th International Conference on Computational Linguistics (2020)

27. Lipton, Z.C.: The mythos of model interpretability. arXiv:1606.03490 (2017)

28. Mittelstadt, B., et al.: Explaining explanations in AI. In: Proceedings of the Conference on Fairness, Accountability, and Transparency (2019)

29. Mueen, A., Keogh, E.: Extracting optimal performance from dynamic time warping. In: Proceedings of the 22nd ACM SIGKDD International Conference on Knowledge Discovery and Data Mining (2016)

30. Nguyen, T.T., Le Nguyen, T., Ifrim, G.: A model-agnostic approach to quantifying the informativeness of explanation methods for time series classification. In: Lemaire, V., Malinowski, S., Bagnall, A., Guyet, T., Tavenard, R., Ifrim, G. (eds.) AALTD 2020. LNCS (LNAI), vol. 12588, pp. 77–94. Springer, Cham (2020). https://doi.org/10.1007/978-3-030-65742-0_6

31. Nugent, C., et al.: Gaining insight through case-based explanation. J. Intell. Inf. Syst. **32**(3), 267–295 (2009). https://doi.org/10.1007/s10844-008-0069-0

32. O'Sullivan, B.: Landline - 10/10/20: Towards a Magna Carta for Data: Expert Opinion Piece: Engineering and Computer Science Committee. https://www.ria.ie/sites/default/files/ria_magna_carta_data.pdf

33. Papernot, N., McDaniel, P.: Deep k-Nearest neighbors: towards confident, interpretable and robust deep learning. arXiv:1803.04765 (2018)

34. Petitjean, F., et al.: A global averaging method for dynamic time warping, with applications to clustering. Pattern Recogn. **44**, 678–693 (2011)

35. Prabhu, V.U., Birhane, A.: Large image datasets: a pyrrhic win for computer vision? arXiv: 2006.16923 (2020)
36. Ribeiro, M.T., et al.: "Why should I trust you?": explaining the predictions of any classifier. In: Proceedings of the 22nd ACM SIGKDD International Conference on Knowledge Discovery and Data Mining - KDD 2016 (2016)
37. Rudin, C.: Please stop explaining black box models for high stakes decisions. arXiv:1811. 10154 (2018)
38. Seah, J.C.Y., et al.: Chest radiographs in congestive heart failure: visualizing neural network learning. Radiology **290**(2), 514–522 (2019)
39. Sørmo, F., et al.: Explanation in case-based reasoning-perspectives and goals. Artif. Intell. Rev. **24**, 109–143 (2005). https://doi.org/10.1007/s10462-005-4607-7
40. Wachter, S., et al.: Counterfactual explanations without opening the black box: automated decisions and the GDPR. SSRN J. **31** (2017)
41. Horta, V.A.C., Mileo, A.: Towards explaining deep neural networks through graph analysis. In: Anderst-Kotsis, G., et al. (eds.) DEXA 2019. CCIS, vol. 1062, pp. 155–165. Springer, Cham (2019). https://doi.org/10.1007/978-3-030-27684-3_20
42. Hohman, F., Kahng, M., Pienta, R., Chau, D.H.: Visual analytics in deep learning. IEEE Trans. Visual. Comput. Graphics **25**, 2674–2693 (2018)

Expert Level Evaluations for Explainable AI (XAI) Methods in the Medical Domain

Satya M. Muddamsetty$^{(\boxtimes)}$ (iD), Mohammad N. S. Jahromi (iD),
and Thomas B. Moeslund (iD)

Visual Analysis of People Laboratory (VAP), Aalborg University,
Rendsburggade 14, 9000 Aalborg, Denmark
{smmu,mosa,tbm}@create.aau.dk

Abstract. The recently emerged field of explainable artificial intelligence (XAI) attempts to shed lights on 'black box' Machine Learning (ML) models in understandable terms for human. As several explanation methods are developed alongside different applications for a black box model, the need for expert-level evaluation in inspecting their effectiveness becomes inevitable. This is significantly important for sensitive domains such as medical applications where evaluation of experts is essential to better understand how accurate the results of complex ML are and debug the models if necessary. The aim of this study is to experimentally show how the expert-level evaluation of XAI methods in a medical application can be utilized and aligned with the actual explanations generated by the clinician. To this end, we collect annotations from expert subjects equipped with an eye-tracker while they classify medical images and devise an approach for comparing the results with those obtained from XAI methods. We demonstrate the effectiveness of our approach in several experiments.

Keywords: Explainable AI (XAI) · Deep learning · Expert-level explanation · XAI evaluation · Retinal Images · Eye-tracker

1 Introduction

Machine Learning (ML) models are becoming an essential part of the current technology due to their ability to outperform humans in solving particular tasks such as spam detection [8,15], healthcare [5], ophthalmology [24] and autonomous robots [27]. Furthermore, the ML model can be employed to help experts in supporting their decision in domains such as medical or risk analysis where actionable solutions may have serious consequences [13,26]. Recent advances in ML promise to improve retinal diseases screening substantially and to improve diagnosis accuracy. Systems developed using these methods have demonstrated expert-level accuracy in diagnosis for multiple eye diseases including diabetic retinopathy [20], age related macular degeneration (AMD) [11],

A. Del Bimbo et al. (Eds.): ICPR 2020 Workshops, LNCS 12663, pp. 35–46, 2021.
https://doi.org/10.1007/978-3-030-68796-0_3

glaucoma [18] and other anomalies associated with retinal diseases, and to monitor their progression. However, the impact of these models in clinical settings is not completely understood. Previous attempts to use ML algorithms in a computer-assisted diagnosis setting have faced numerous challenges, including both over reliance (repeating errors made by the model) and under reliance (ignoring accurate algorithm predictions) [14,22]. Some of these issues may be avoided if the computer assisted diagnosis system can explain its black box AI predictions [3]. Explainable AI (XAI) aims at decoding the decision of AI (Deep learning/Machine learning) black box to the extent of human-interpretable level. For instance, if we are to use AI algorithms to classify Diabetic Retinopathy (DR) levels from retinal fundus images, can the algorithm generate further interpretable justification for its prediction results? Can that justification be presented visually? Is that visualization aligned closely with expert explanation? Generally, in sensitive domains such as clinical settings, the domain experts (clinicians) are skeptical in supporting interpretations generated by AI diagnosis tools as a result of high involved risk [6,26]. But, if instead of developing various explanation methods for the sensitive domains, the effectiveness of their evaluation method is studied when expert subjects are involved in loop, then AI diagnosis tool gain further trust by the domain experts. Therefore, in addition to improving accuracy of such a tool, the notion of trust, need for transparency and robustness implies how crucial it is to study the effect of expert evaluation in the context of XAI methods.

XAI evaluation methods are broadly classified into three categories [9]: They are, Application-Grounded Evaluation, Human-Grounded Evaluation and Functionally Grounded Evaluation. Application-Grounded Evaluation quantifies how expert-generated explanation can properly help other humans in specific tasks. The quality of this evaluation is tested by employing domain experts to accomplish certain tasks within the context of an application. For example, an ophthalmologist should evaluate a diagnosis system in determining the DR level from retinal fundus images. On the other hand, in the *Human-Grounded Evaluation* evaluations are done using non-expert humans on simplified tasks. For instance non-experts or users will be shown different explanations and the user would choose the best one. The authors in [4,23] evaluated their method using non-experts, asking to identify which XAI method provides good explanation. The Functionally-Grounded Evaluation discussed in [8] is basically independent of human subject. Most of the state-of-art methods falls into this category [1,21]. For example, the authors in [19] proposed casual metrics *insertion* and *deletion* which, are independent of humans to evaluate the faithfulness of the XAI methods. The intuition behind the *deletion* and *insertion* metrics is that the removal or inserting of the 'cause' will make the AI model to change its decision. However, functionally and human grounded evaluations will not be suitable for such sensitive medical domains. In practice, all types of evaluation have equal importance. Choosing a right evaluation method is subject to the explanation context. For instance, if we seek to generate an explanation that is limited to experts or specific application such as a medical diagnosis tool, the Application-grounded evaluation could become more appropriate. This is due to fact that for such a unique application careful expert studies are required. Therefore, to address the specific medical case such as screening the retinal diseases across retinal fundus images, it is necessary to involve domain experts within this field to evaluate the explanations of black box models predictions. One way of performing this task is through an interactive collection of the expert feedback on generating actual explanation using an eye-tracker.

To this end, the main contribution of this paper is to develop a collection of eye-tracking data from 3 expert subjects across 150 retinal fundus images for medical application. Concretely, domain clinicians are equipped with an eye-tracker in an interactive experimental settings to understand how they classify retinal diseases and assess the retinal image quality. The experts evaluate the five DR level (No DR, Mild, Moderate, Severe and Proliferative DR) and the retinal image quality (Good/Bad), respectively. Finally the heatmaps obtained via the eye-tracker can be compared directly by XAI methods. In this work we use heatmaps generated together by two XAI state-of-the-art methods namely SIDU [17], GRAD-CAM [23] using two different evaluation metrics.

The rest of the paper is organized as follows. In Sect. 2 we describe the eye-tracking experiments and data collection. Section 3 describes the XAI methods used for evaluation. Section 4 describes comparison metrics for XAI methods and Sect. 5 shows performance evaluation of XAI methods and comparisons. Finally, Section 6 provides concluding remarks.

2 Eye-Tracking Experiments and Data Collection

In this section, we discuss how we employ expert subjects to collect annotation of medical images with an eye-tracker in an interactive experiment setting. The experts annotation experiments consist of two phases. In the first phase a total of 100 images are randomly drawn from the Retinal Fundus Image Quality Assessment (RFIQA) dataset [16]. Each expert subject (ophthalmologist) is then required to classify each image (stimuli) as a Good/Bad quality. During each session of the experiment an ophthalmologist is equipped with an eye-tracker. In a similar setting, the second phase is conducted to highlight salient regions corresponding to Diabetic Retinopathy (DR) levels (5 grades) in the eye fundus Images. In this setup, in order to utilize different dataset for evaluation, 50 images are selected randomly from the EyePacs dataset [10]. To ensure variance in our experiment, we asked ophthalmologist experts from medical community to participate in the experiments. The data collection protocol as well as hardware setup are discussed in the subsequent section. Note that the collection procedures are identical in both phases.

2.1 Data Collection Protocol

In order to record the eye-fixation (spatial coordinate on the screen) of each expert on the fundus images, we utilized Tobii-X120 eye-tracker [25] as follows:

1. Instructions were given to the expert to sit in front of a screen where the eye-tracker was attached to the base stand of a monitor and facing a subject.
2. In order for the eye-tracker to capture the eye-fixation properly, the subject has to sit within 60 cm distance from the screen. This distance was measured in the IMOTION (Software) [7] where the ultimate data annotation took place.
3. After a careful calibration of the eye-tracker setup done in the IMOTION, a block of stimuli displayed on the screen for the expert to evaluate the good/bad quality of each stimuli (Natural image). Each block of data composed of 25 cells and in each cell, three images were located. The cross-fixation (+) image at in the beginning (1 s duration) in order to refresh the visionary system between each stimuli transition. The second image was the main stimuli presented to the expert and finally a survey with the task question (Good/Bad quality or DR level assessment).
4. Once the eye-fixation were collected for the first block (25 stimuli), a break is given for 10-minutes. This process were repeated for all the stimuli.

Figure 1 illustrates the eye-tracking collection setup with the eye-tracker positioned below the screen and facing to the experts during the experiment. In addition, Fig. 2 shows samples of recorded eye-fixation and their generated heatmaps for an expert subject. Note that the heatmaps generation are done via fitting a Gaussian kernels at each coordinate location of eye-fixation (third column in the figure).

Fig. 1. Eye-tracking data collection from experts for screening the diabetic retinopathy and retinal images quality levels.

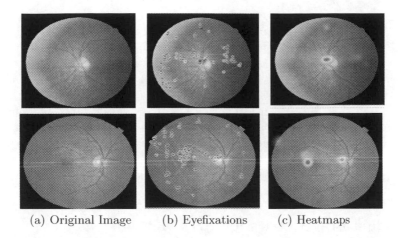

(a) Original Image   (b) Eyefixations   (c) Heatmaps

Fig. 2. Eye-tracking data samples of recorded eye-fixation and their generated heatmaps collected from experts for screening the diabetic retinopathy and retinal images quality levels.

3   Explainable AI Methods

To evaluate the visual explanation on the proposed dataset we considered two most recent visual explanation methods. They are briefly described in Sects. 3.1 and 3.2.'

3.1   SIDU

A new visual explanation method known as SIDU proposed recently in [17] estimates the pixel saliency by extracting the last convolutional layer of the deep CNN model and creating the similarity difference mask which is eventually combined to form a final map for generating the visual explanation of the prediction. This method generates a heatmap based on two steps: Similarity difference and Uniqueness. First, a heatmap of the most salient areas of an image is generated by calculating the similarity difference between sets of feature activation maps. Secondly, it evaluates feature map uniqueness. This step calculates how different a specific feature map is from the others. If a feature map is unique, then it will be labelled as more salient and have a higher weight. The final score that gives the feature importance is given by the dot product between the two values, which is then used to calculate the weighted sum of all feature activation image masks and generate the visual explanation. It was shown via the quantitative and qualitative (human trust) experiments that for both general and critical medical data, the SIDU method outperforms state-of-the-art [17]. The ability of properly localizing the region of interest in the clinical eye fundus images makes SIDU a well-suited method to provide transparent explanation and audit model output that is crucial for sensitive domains such as medical diagnosis.

3.2 GRAD-CAM

Grad-CAM is a method which generates visual explanations via gradient based localization [23]. It extracts the gradients from the last convolution layer of the network. The intuition behind this method is that the layer prior to the classification retains the information of feature relevance while maintaining spatial relations, and therefore it can generate a heatmap (based on a weighted combination of activation maps dependent on gradient score), which highlights the features with a positive influence for the specific class that is chosen as the prediction. Given any CNN model, Grad-CAM is an class-discriminative localization technique which can generate visual explanations without requiring architectural changes or re-training.

4 Comparison Metrics for XAI Methods

To compare heatmaps we choose the two usual metrics used in state-of-the-art methods for evaluation of saliency detection [2]. The main reason for choosing more than one evaluation measure is to ensure that the discussion about the results is as independent as possible from the choice of the metrics. The results of the different evaluation metrics are not necessarily the same, but when two metrics show similarities, then it is easy to interpret the robustness of the methods. These metrics are used do evaluate the performance of the XAI methods are two different kinds of experiments described in Sect. 5.2.

4.1 Area Under ROC Curve (AUC)

The Receiver Operating Characteristics (ROC) measure is one of the most popular and most widely used method in the community for assessing the degree of similarity of two saliency maps and it measures the trade-off between true and false positives at different discrimination threshold values (level sets) [2]. It is a graphical plot which describes the performance of a binary classifier system as its discrimination threshold is varied. It is created by plotting the fraction of true positives out of the total actual positives (TPR = true positive rate) versus the fraction of false positives out of the total actual negatives (FPR = false positive rate), at various threshold values. A good prediction method would give a TPR of 1 at a FPR of 0, yielding a point in the upper left corner of the ROC space that corresponds to a perfect classification. A completely random guess would give a point along a diagonal line from the left bottom to the top right corner. The diagonal divides the ROC space and points above the diagonal represent good classification results (better than random), points below the line poor results (worse than random). Thus, a measure of performance derived from the ROC curve is the AUC (Area Under Curve) which is equal to the probability that a classifier will rank a randomly chosen positive instance higher than a randomly chosen negative one (assuming 'positive' ranks higher than 'negative'). The XAI visual explanation heatmap is treated as a binary classifier of fixations at various threshold values (level sets), and an ROC curve is swept out by measuring the true and false positive rates under each binary classifier (level set).

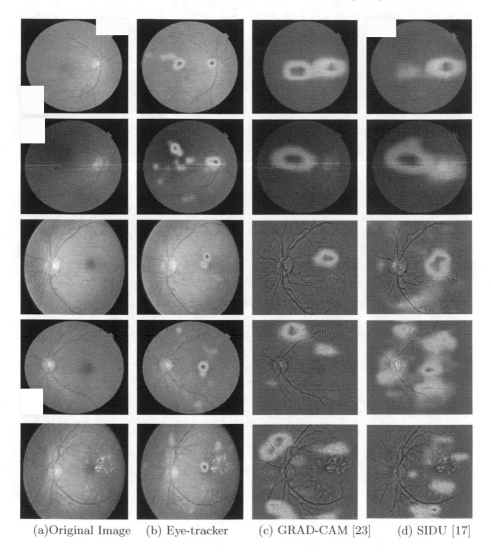

(a)Original Image   (b) Eye-tracker   (c) GRAD-CAM [23]   (d) SIDU [17]

Fig. 3. Comparison of XAI methods visual explanation with human visual explanation (heatmaps). First two rows describes the explanations of good and bad quality of retinal images. Third, fourth and fifth row describes the explanations of mild, moderate and sever DR levels. In a real scenario, the ophthalmologists inspect the image quality or DR levels by looking around exact regions (areas of the heatmaps captured by the eye-tracker in the 2nd column) of the eye fundus images. The generated heatmaps in 3rd and 4th columns by the GRAD-CAM and SIDU demonstrate how the visual explanation methods are closely aligns with human experts. (Color figure online)

4.2   Kullback-Leibler Divergence (KL-DIV)

The Kullback-Leibler Divergence is a metric, which estimates dissimilarity between two probability density functions [2]. To evaluate the XAI methods, the distributions are given by the eye-fixations points and the heatmap (visual explanation maps) produced by the model. Let FM be the probability distribution of the heat map from eye tracking data, and EM be the probability distribution of the visual explanation map. The distributions are normalized and they are given by:

$$EM(x) = \frac{EM(x)}{\sum_{x=1}^{X} FM(x) + \epsilon}, \tag{1}$$

$$FM(x) = \frac{FM(x)}{\sum_{x=1}^{X} FM(x) + \epsilon}, \tag{2}$$

where X is the number of pixels and ϵ is a regularization constant to avoid division by zero. The KL-divergence measure is non-linear and varies in the range of zero to infinity. The lower score indicates that the EM maps have better approximation of the human expert eye-fixation ground truth.

5   Experimental Evaluation and Results

In this section we perform the experimental evaluation of two state-of-the-art XAI methods described in Sect. 3 on proposed dataset. We conducted two experiments, for the given trained CNN models. In first experiment, we evaluated the explanations of retinal fundus image quality predictions and in the second experiment we evaluated the explanations of Diabetic Retinopathy disease level classification.

5.1   Training CNN Models

To evaluate the XAI methods, we trained two CNN models on two different datasets. First, we trained the existing ResNet50 [12] with an additional two FC layers and softmax layer on the Retinal Fundus Image Quality Assessment (RFIQA) dataset from the medical domain. The dataset consists of 9,945 images with two levels of quality, 'Good' and 'Bad'. The retinal images were collected from a large number of patients with retinal diseases [16]. The dataset is split into 80% training, 10% validation and 10% testing. Data augmentation is performed on the training samples. We apply image transformations such as random rotation, width shift, height shift, zooming, horizontal flipping and scaling to the RFIQA training subset to enlarge the dataset. The CNN model is trained over 120 epochs with batch size of 3. We use categorical cross entropy as a loss function and SGD as optimizer with learning rate 10^{-4} and momentum as 0.9. The CNN model is initialized with imagenet weights and trained the whole model on the RFIQA dataset. The CNN model achieves 94% accuracy. The explanation methods uses the trained model for explaining the prediction of the RFIQA test subset with 1028 images whereas the second CNN model is trained for classifying the diabetic retinopathy (DR) disease levels. We used existing ResNet50 [12] model similar to first one. The CNN model is trained on the EyePacs dataset [10].

We initialized with ImageNet pre-trained weights and trained the whole model parameters on EyePacs dataset. The CNN model achieves 85% on test dataset which 10k images of five levels of DR. Both model have 'human like' performance and hence XAI generated heatmaps can be expected to behave similar to those of human expert. The frameworks are implemented on Tensorflow keras with GPU memory of 11 GB, Nvidia, RTX 2080Ti.

5.2 Results and Discussion

In the first experiment, we use the RFIQA images eye-tracking data recordings described in Sect. 2 to generate and evaluate the explanation by the XAI algorithms. To this end, we first generate ground truth heatmaps by applying Gaussian distributions on human expert eye-fixations. These heatmaps are then used to compare with the XAI heatmaps. Table 1 summarizes the results obtained by two different XAI methods on our proposed RFIQA eye-tracking data using AUC and KL-DIV evaluation measures as described in Sect. 4.1 and 4.2 respectively. For the AUC measure, we observe that, GRAD-CAM [23] shows slightly better performances compared to SIDU [17] for both the experts, whereas for the KL-DIV measure both methods performed equally well for expert 1 and for expert 2 GRAD-CAM [23] has shown better performance.

In the second experiment we evaluated XAI methods using DR disease levels eye-tracking data recording described in Sect. 2. We follow a similar procedure for generating the ground truth heatmaps. We collected the eye-fixations from three experts and compared the XAI methods, explanations with the three experts individually. Table 2 summarizes the results obtained by two different XAI methods on our proposed eye-tracking data using two evaluation measures. We observe that SIDU [17] performs better than GRAD-CAM [23] for both AUC and KL-DIV measures for all the experts. Figure 3 shows visual explanations comparisons of XAI methods with human visual explanation of Good, Bad, quality grades and DR disease levels such as No DR, Mild, Moderate, Severe, Proliferative DR levels predictions. From the figure, we can clearly observe that the visual explanations from the XAI methods are closely aligns with human experts. In practice, the doctors verify the visibility of the optical disc and macular regions in a good quality image, corresponding to the highlighted regions in the heatmap 1st row. Similarly, the bad quality image, 2nd row is due to the shadow just above the center of the image, i.e., exactly the region highlighted by the XAI methods. For the DR levels the practitioners look in the lesions such as Microaneurysms (tiny red lesions), Haemorrhages (Bright red lesions), Exudates (Yellow spots) near the optical disk, the macula and the region surrounding to macula and this can be observed in the heatmaps of human experts and XAI methods 3rd, 4th row and 5th row with mild, moderate and Severe DR levels. Therefore from the above two experiments we can conclude that the evaluation of XAI methods in medical domain requires human experts for gaining greater trust and transparency.

Table 1. Evaluation of XAI methods on proposed eye-tracking dataset using AUC and KL-DIV on retinal images quality levels dataset.

XAI methods	AUC measure ↑			KL-DIV measure↓		
	Expert 1	Expert 2	Expert 3	Expert 1	Expert 2	Expert 3
SIDU [17]	0.6545	0.5899	0.6442	11.7712	14.1240	12.231 6
GRAD-CAM [23]	**0.6605**	**0.6125**	**0.6575**	**11.6087**	**13.3929**	**11.7866**

Table 2. Evaluation of XAI methods on proposed eye-tracking using AUC and KL-DIV on DR disease levels dataset.

XAI methods	AUC measure ↑			KL-DIV measure ↓		
	Expert 1	Expert 2	Expert 3	Expert 1	Expert 2	Expert 3
SIDU [17]	**0.6089**	**0.5805**	**0.5834**	**12.9420**	**14.14708**	**13.6627**
GRAD-CAM [23]	0.5734	0.5454	0.5504	14.0974	15.2675	14.6741

6   Concluding Remarks

In this paper we proposed a framework for evaluating explainable AI (XAI) methods using an eye-tracker in the medical domain particularly for the screening of retinal diseases, DR and quality assessment for retinal images. It is designed specifically for evaluating XAI methods in the medical domain. To the best of our knowledge, the proposed eye-tracker dataset is the first of its kind for evaluating the visual explanations in the medical domain by involving human experts (ophthalmologists). Experimental results using two different datasets with different characteristics show the importance of involving human experts in evaluating XAI methods.

References

1. Bach, S., Binder, A., Montavon, G., Klauschen, F., Müller, K., Samek, W.: On pixel-wise explanations for non-linear classifier decisions by layer-wise relevance propagation. PLoS ONE **10**(7) (2015)
2. Bylinskii, Z., Judd, T., Oliva, A., Torralba, A., Durand, F.: What do different evaluation metrics tell us about saliency models? IEEE Trans. Pattern Anal. Mach. Intell. **41**(3), 740–757 (2018)
3. Cabitza, F., Rasoini, R., Gensini, G.F.: Unintended consequences of machine learning in medicine. Jama **318**(6), 517–518 (2017)
4. Chattopadhay, A., Sarkar, A., Howlader, P., Balasubramanian, V.N.: Grad-CAM++: generalized gradient-based visual explanations for deep convolutional networks. In: 2018 IEEE Winter Conference on Applications of Computer Vision (WACV), pp. 839–847. IEEE (2018)
5. Chen, R., Yang, L., Goodison, S., Sun, Y.: Deep-learning approach to identifying cancer subtypes using high-dimensional genomic data. Bioinformatics **36**(5), 1476–1483 (2020)

6. Chromik, M., Schuessler, M.: A taxonomy for human subject evaluation of black-box explanations in XAI. In: ExSS-ATEC@ IUI (2020)
7. De Lemos, J.: Visual attention and emotional response detection and display system, uS Patent App. 11/685,552, 15 November 2007
8. Doshi-Velez, F., Kim, B.: Towards a rigorous science of interpretable machine learning. arXiv preprint arXiv:1702.08608 (2017)
9. Doshi-Velez, F., Kim, B.: Considerations for evaluation and generalization in interpretable machine learning. In: Escalante, H.J., et al. (eds.) Explainable and Interpretable Models in Computer Vision and Machine Learning. TSSCML, pp. 3–17. Springer, Cham (2018). https://doi.org/10.1007/978-3-319-98131-4_1
10. EyePACS: Diabetic retinopathy detection of Kaggle (2015). https://www.kaggle.com/c/diabetic-retinopathy-detection/data
11. Grassmann, F., et al.: A deep learning algorithm for prediction of age-related eye disease study severity scale for age-related macular degeneration from color fundus photography. Ophthalmology **125**(9), 1410–1420 (2018)
12. He, K., Zhang, X., Ren, S., Sun, J.: Deep residual learning for image recognition. In: Proceedings of the IEEE Conference on Computer Vision and Pattern Recognition, pp. 770–778 (2016)
13. Hengstler, M., Enkel, E., Duelli, S.: Applied artificial intelligence and trust–the case of autonomous vehicles and medical assistance devices. Technol. Forecast. Soc. Chang. **105**, 105–120 (2016)
14. Kohli, A., Jha, S.: Why cad failed in mammography. J. Am. Coll. Radiol. **15**(3), 535–537 (2018)
15. Lin, C.F.: Application-grounded evaluation of predictive model explanation methods (2018)
16. Muddamsetty, S.M., Moeslund, T.B.: Multi-level quality assessment of retinal fundus images using deep convolutional neural network. In: VISAPP (2021, submitted to)
17. Muddamsetty, S.M., Mohammad, N.S.J., Moeslund, T.B.: SIDU: similarity difference and uniqueness method for explainable AI. In: 2020 IEEE International Conference on Image Processing (ICIP), pp. 3269–3273 (2020). https://doi.org/10.1109/ICIP40778.2020.9190952
18. Nayak, J., Acharya, R., Bhat, P.S., Shetty, N., Lim, T.C.: Automated diagnosis of glaucoma using digital fundus images. J. Med. Syst. **33**(5), 337 (2009)
19. Petsiuk, V., Das, A., Saenko, K.: RISE: randomized input sampling for explanation of black-box models. In: Proceedings of the British Machine Vision Conference (BMVC) (2018)
20. Raman, R., Srinivasan, S., Virmani, S., Sivaprasad, S., Rao, C., Rajalakshmi, R.: Fundus photograph-based deep learning algorithms in detecting diabetic retinopathy. Eye (2018). https://doi.org/10.1038/s41433-018-0269-y
21. Samek, W., Binder, A., Montavon, G., Lapuschkin, S., Müller, K.R.: Evaluating the visualization of what a deep neural network has learned. IEEE Trans. Neural Netw. Learn. Syst. **28**(11), 2660–2673 (2016)
22. Sayres, R., et al.: Using a deep learning algorithm and integrated gradients explanation to assist grading for diabetic retinopathy. Ophthalmology **126**(4), 552–564 (2019)
23. Selvaraju, R.R., Cogswell, M., Das, A., Vedantam, R., Parikh, D., Batra, D.: Grad-CAM: visual explanations from deep networks via gradient-based localization. In: Proceedings of the IEEE International Conference on Computer Vision, pp. 618–626 (2017)

24. Son, J., Shin, J.Y., Kim, H.D., Jung, K.H., Park, K.H., Park, S.J.: Development and validation of deep learning models for screening multiple abnormal findings in retinal fundus images. Ophthalmology **127**(1), 85–94 (2020)
25. Technology, T.: User manual: Tobii X60 and X120 eye trackers (2008)
26. Weld, D.S., Bansal, G.: The challenge of crafting intelligible intelligence. Commun. ACM **62**(6), 70–79 (2019)
27. You, C., Lu, J., Filev, D., Tsiotras, P.: Advanced planning for autonomous vehicles using reinforcement learning and deep inverse reinforcement learning. Robot. Auton. Syst. **114**, 1–18 (2019)

Samples Classification Analysis Across DNN Layers with Fractal Curves

Adrien Halnaut[✉], Romain Giot[iD], Romain Bourqui[iD], and David Auber[iD]

Univ. Bordeaux, Bordeaux INP, CNRS, LaBRI, UMR5800, 33400 Talence, France
{adrien.halnaut,romain.giot,romain.bourqui,david.auber}@u-bordeaux.fr

Abstract. Deep Neural Networks are becoming the prominent solution when using machine learning models. However, they suffer from a black-box effect that renders complicated their inner workings interpretation and thus the understanding of their successes and failures. Information visualization is one way among others to help in their interpretability and hypothesis deduction. This paper presents a novel way to visualize a trained DNN to depict at the same time its architecture and its way of treating the classes of a test dataset at the layer level. In this way, it is possible to visually detect where the DNN starts to be able to discriminate the classes or where it could decrease its separation ability (and thus detect an oversized network). We have implemented the approach and validated it using several well-known datasets and networks. Results show the approach is promising and deserves further studies.

Keywords: Deep learning · Visualization · Explainable artificial intelligence · Glyph definition

1 Introduction

Deep-learning [19] based approaches are used in various contexts and dominate most historical methods, especially for classification problems. Even when datasets are not large enough to train Deep Neural Networks (DNN), it is possible to use transfer learning with a pre-trained DNN by fine-tuning [10] it, or by extracting features and feeding them to a conventional classifier [34]. Any DNN corresponds to a graph of computational blocks: each block processes the output of one or several previous ones through a simple function parametrized by many weights. Such weights are data-dependent and computed during the training phase.

The black-box feeling is one of the largest issues. Indeed, even if each block is individually well understood mathematically, its behavior depends mainly on the training data (*i.e.*, their impact on the learned weights). As a consequence, one cannot know what treatment these blocks are doing. However, it is well admitted that the first layers extract low-level features, while the latest ones extract high-level features specific to the application problem [8]. Two non-exclusive strategies can help to open this black box. (i) *Explainable deep-learning*

A. Del Bimbo et al. (Eds.): ICPR 2020 Workshops, LNCS 12663, pp. 47–61, 2021.
https://doi.org/10.1007/978-3-030-68796-0_4

where the architecture of the DNN emphasizes its explainability [39], even if it could negatively impact its performance, and (ii) *Interpretable deep-learning* where additional processes extract information by computing a more explainable model [40], computing some saliency information [2,5] or using information visualization techniques [14].

This paper presents a new method for interpretable deep-learning based on information visualization techniques. The task to solve corresponds to the analysis of the data classification over layers. It aims at analyzing how all input samples of a dataset are globally treated by any part of the network. In opposite to most papers of the literature on attribution-based methods, the focus is not for a specific sample. The method *allows focusing on* successive layers that better (or worst) discriminate the samples. It also displays the complete network and the data behavior for each of its computational blocks.

It originality relies on the fact it focuses on both all samples and full architecture and has the advantages of (i) using less screen space than existing methods despite the amount of information to display; (ii) fitting to any network that can be represented as a directed acyclic graph; (iii) using the same encoding for input data, inner blocks and final result.

The remaining of the paper is organized as follows. Section 2 presents related works in visualization for CNN and space filling curves. Section 3 describes the proposed method. Section 4 provides the details of the experimental protocol. Section 5 discusses the results and provide directions for future work. We finally draw conclusions in Sect. 6.

2   Previous Works

Our proposed method aims at visually interpreting how DNN behave using a space-efficient method. For this reason, this section firstly presents previous works on deep neural networks visualization then focus on dense pixel oriented methods.

2.1   Visualization for the Interpretation of Deep Neural Networks

Visualization plays an important role in the tools used to help to explain or interpret how deep models work and to reduce their black-box feeling [14]. Different purposes have been achieved in the literature.

Some works focus on *single views* that can be reused in other works or embedded in more complex applications. GradCam [29] aims at generating a heatmap for a single input to highlight the spatial location that greatly supports the final decision. It is computed thanks to the gradients from the logit of a target class up to the latest convolutional layer and can be straightforwardly visualized and understood with a heatmap when the input feature is an image. Other methods rely on different concepts to achieve the same objective such as LRP [5] on the concept of relevance or other work [2] that only uses information collected during the forward pass. Instead of focusing on a single input sample, it is also possible to focus on the complete dataset. Some use Sankey-diagram analogy [11] to highlight the processing flows. Others project activations obtained at a specific layer in a 2d space to verify how the network sees the data at this specific point [27]. Such an approach is also common in the literature using T-SNE projection [23]; however, an important drawback remains: the representation is not space efficient and there is no guarantee that overlap does not occur. Our proposed method solves these two issues.

Other works create *applications for educational purpose* to visually explain how some specific deep systems perform. For example, Tensorflow playground [32] focuses on simple DNN, CNN 101 [36] focuses on CNN, Ganlab [16] focuses on Gan system and Adversarial Playground [26] illustrates the concept of adversarial examples. Even if they are visually appealing, these systems can hardly be used for industrial scenarios.

In opposite, several complete tools treat *industrial problems*. Some of them are generalist enough to be used in almost any scenario, such as Activis [15] (that focuses on the visualization and comparison of activation of a single selected layer), while some others are restricted to some specific networks or evaluation scenarios. CNNVIS [22] is tailored for CNN and uses a visualization that relies on aggregation of layers (not all layers are depicted), filters (filters that behave similarly are grouped) and data (a subset of the samples are depicted). DQNVIZ [35] has been designed for Deep Q-Network explanation in the specific context of Atari play.

2.2 Hilbert Curve in Information Visualization

Dense pixel-oriented methods aim at improving both the data-ink ratio and the visualization size by displaying a unit of information on a single pixel while avoiding unused pixels. Keim reviewed various pixel-oriented visualizations [17] and asserts that space-filling curves, such as the Hilbert one [13], are among the bests to project ordered elements in a screen space while preserving the distance of the one-dimensional ordering in the two-dimensional arrangement. Blanchard *et al.* [6] have shown that to display images, reduced to a one pixel representation, on an Hilbert curve produces coherent and identifiable clusters. Auber *et al.* [3] have also shown the interest of such visualization, when complemented by tailored interaction techniques, to explore datacubes of several dozen of millions of elements. Since these previous successes, we have selected the Hilbert curve to project our data in a square; a curve of order n contains 4^n elements [3].

3 Proposed Method

Figure 1 describes the proposal with the "Nested blocks and guidelines model" [24] among various description levels: *domain* (who is concerned by which problem), *abstraction* (which data is used or generated to solve which task), *technique* (which methods are used) and *algorithms* (how these methods are implemented).

Additionally, Fig. 2 lists the successive steps involved in the method. The requirements of the proposed method are: to be *space efficient* (R1) while

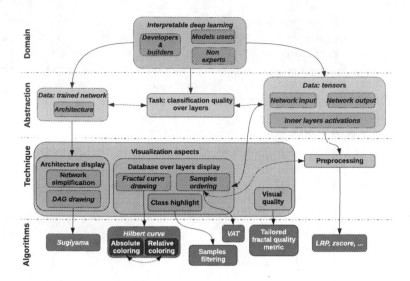

Fig. 1. Nested blocks and guidelines [24] representation of the proposed method. Dotted italic blocks corresponds to existing ones; plain straight blocks are defined in the work.

displaying information from *all samples* (R2) in *all layers* (R3) of the network to solve the *task "classification quality analysis over layers"* (R4).

3.1   Domain Level

The proposed method fits the needs of *networks designers* and *trainers* that want to verify *how* the data is *grouped* by the various *layers* of their *classification network*. From the *analysis* of these groupings, they could infer *hypotheses* that aim at being verified with other techniques. Such hypotheses are related to input sample properties and network errors. *Non experts* would better understand how DNN work by looking at the representation of simple networks and datasets.

3.2   Abstraction Level

The proposed method considers an already trained DNN N with a compatible test dataset D_{test}. N is a network (*i.e.*, graph) of operations (*i.e.*, nodes) $N = (O, E)$. Its sources $s_{\bullet} \in O$ are the identity function on data input (*i.e.*, samples) and its sinks $t_{\bullet} \in O$ are its outputs (*i.e.*, classes probability). N has multiple sources for a multi-modal system, but always a single sink as we are restricted the use case of standard classification. The other nodes $o_{\bullet} \in O \setminus \{s_{\bullet} \cup t_{\bullet}\}$ correspond to any operations (*e.g.*, convolution, pooling, etc.) that compose N; operations related to optimization (*e.g.*, dropout) are not included. The edges $E = O \times O$ model the flow of data over the operations of the network (*i.e.*, they link successive layers).

Each sample $d_i \in D_{test}$ is fed into the network and the output (*i.e.*, activations) of each operation o^j is stored in a_i^j; we assume operations are ordered

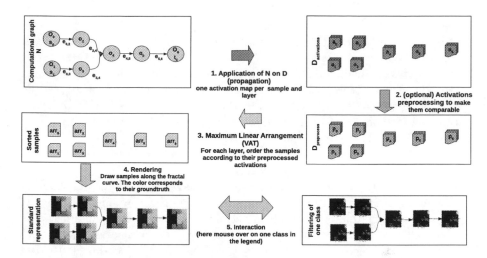

Fig. 2. Summary of the proposed method. Dataset D is fed to the network N. All activations are collected, eventually preprocessed, and finally ordered at each layer. The ordered samples are drawn along a fractal curve at each operation of the network that is placed on the screen using a graph drawing method.

depending on the execution flow. These activations consist of tensors whose order depends on the underlying operation and whose dimensions size depends on the input data of the network. Each operation o^j consumes at least one result $a_i^k | k < j$ computed by a previous operation except for the sources where $a_i^\bullet$ corresponds to the raw data (of the targeted modality in a multimodal scenario). Thus, a sample d_i is represented by a set of activations $A_i = \cup_j \{a_i^j\}$ and the complete dataset D_{test} is represented by an ensemble of sets of activations $D_{activations} = \cup_i \{A_i\}$.

The activations can be optionally preprocessed to fall within compatible domains as their domain is not controlled: $D_{preprocess} = \bigcup_i \bigcup_j \left\{ Preprocessed \left(a_i^j \right) \right\}$. This preprocessing method is a parameter of the workflow.

3.3   Technique Level

As the method aims at displaying (a) the dataset and its *groundtruth* (R2), (b) the *architecture of the network* (R3) and (c) its impact on the *complete dataset* (R4), we propose an encoding relying on both $D_{preprocess}$ and N.

Groundtruth Encoding. The groundtruth of the dataset is depicted with a legend where each class is represented by a colored rectangle followed by a black text. Obviously, the text is the name of the class and the color represents this class in the samples encoding.

Network Encoding. It is straightforward to layout N operations with a graph-drawing algorithm tailored for Directed Acyclic Graphs (networks are always DAG). Such technique is common in the literature [15,37] and aims at computing the coordinates of each node (operation) in a plane while emphasizing the order of operations in the computing flow. Each node is depicted by a glyph that represents the whole dataset as viewed by the network at this specific operation. Thus, a specific encoding is used to map the activations $\bigcup_i \{Preprocessed(a_i^j)\}$ of each node o^j in the screen space.

Like Ganlab [16], a dotted line is drawn between nodes that represents consecutive operations; the flow of data is revealed by the dots moving in flow direction. Some networks can be very deep with successive layers that do not bring additional information because they consist of data reordering. We allow the user to request the visualization of a simplified network where the corresponding nodes are removed (thus, their successors are linked to their predecessors), as such information brings noise to the representation. No special encoding is used to represent this information shrinking.

Samples Encoding. As already explained, we have chosen a pixel-oriented technique that relies on fractal curves (R1). For a given node o^j, a maximal linear arrangement method is used to order the representation a_i^j of each sample d_i in such a way that close samples are positioned closely in the ordering according to a *distance* function. We assume close samples in the output space of o^j corresponds to samples treated similarly by the network (*i.e.*, considered to be similar). Once the samples are ordered, they are projected into a discrete pixel grid using a fractal curve that respects proximity relations. This way, screen space usage can be maximized (1 pixel per sample) and we are assured that close samples are drawn closely on the screen (however close pixels on the screen are not necessarily close in data space). Two visual encodings can represent this curve. The first one, *absolute coloring*, explicitly draws samples of each class with the same color. The second one, *relative coloring*, uses a gray-scale to emphasize label difference between adjacent nodes and identify zones where different labels are present. It can be used *de facto* when the number of classes is higher than the number of discernable colors by a human. When using the *absolute coloring* scheme, the user can choose to only visualize a specific class to analyze the spread of its samples over the layer. The name of the layer is written above its fractal representation, and a quality metric (see later) is written below it.

3.4 Algorithms Level

The model topology is drawn using the well-known Sugiyama [33] algorithm and each node is depicted with a specific fractal-based glyph that represents the ordered samples. The Euclidean distance is used to compare the activations generated for all the samples on the same operation. It reflects the dissimilarity between samples in the Euclidean space; we consider that each neuron activation has the same impact as others in the full network processing. These distances are then compiled into a $n \times n$ sized distance-matrix, n being the number of compared samples. In real use case, some neurons have more impact on the final prediction than others. Some pre- or post-processing methods, such as the LRP [5] methods as done in [11], can be applied to the activation maps in order to reflect that behavior. However, we decided not to apply those methods because of the unsure interpretation on model topologies using branches, such as ResNet [12] or our chimeric *DoubleLeNet5* (Sect. 4.1). Using dissimilarity matrix ordering methods [4], data can be ordered in a queue with similar elements placed next to each other using their dissimilarity matrix. By using the VAT algorithm [30] on the dissimilarity matrices, we found a progressive definition of the clusters (or "black squares" as shown in the original paper) reflecting the progressive recognition by the model over the layers we attempt to show. The order computed by this algorithm can then be applied on a 1d-space to display similar data indexes next to each other. Using a fractal curve, we transformed this 1d-space into a 2d-space which is more suitable for data visualization. The fractal curve chosen to map each sample into a pixel-grid is the Hilbert curve [13] because of its ability to place points in a discrete space (this is not the case of Gosper curve [9]) and the absence of "jumps" in the curve (this is not the case of the Z-order curve [25]) which ensures that two consecutive samples are adjacent. The order in which each sample is positioned is following the same order computed by VAT on the previous step. When the number of test samples is lower than the number of pixels available in the curve, we skip half of the missing positions in the beginning of the curve (and thus half of the missing positions at the end of the curve); which gives a hole in the curve.

In the absolute coloring, each pixel sample is being colored according to its ground-truth class, which is different for each class. In the relative coloring, the colors depend on the number of similar labels for the pixel of interest in its sample ordering. That gives three possible values (0 for an outlier with no neighbors of the same class, 1 for a previous or next label different, and 2 when the three successive samples are of the same class). The absolute colors come from a palette of diverging colors while the relative colors or black (0), gray (1) and white (2). Computing in the ordering space instead of the picture allows to no highlight the visual border inherent to the fractal curve. Placing the cursor on a class in the legend selects this specific class and draws only its samples with the appropriate absolute color.

The machine learning community provides various evaluation metrics (*e.g.*, accuracy or cross-entropy) to evaluate the quality of the network by comparing its output to a ground-truth. By definition, they cannot be applied at each layer, but we still need to provide hints to the user of their efficiency. We have defined a quality metric, based on the quality of the visual representation of a layer, which counts the number of neighbors of a given pixel that are of the same color (*i.e.*, the number of samples that belong to the same class). We normalized it between 0 and 1 to ease its comparison (however, as the normalization does not consider the mandatory borders, 1 is an unreachable value). We assume that to quantify the quality of the visualization is strongly related to the ability of the layer to separate data.

Table 1. Number of layers, parameters and activations per sample for each network.

Network	Layers	Parameters	Activations
LeNet5	10	1 182 006	26 378
DoubleLeNet5	18	1 646 370	54 570
VGG16	18	14 714 688	308 244

4   Experimental Protocol

Several scenarios, that rely on a *test dataset* and a *trained network* (Table 1), illustrate the efficiency of the proposed method.

4.1   Scenarios

Datasets

- *Mnist* [18] is a standard dataset used in handwritten recognition from 28×28 grayscale images. Even simple networks are able to perform almost perfectly on this 10-class dataset. We use it to illustrate what happens with an easy dataset.
- *FashionMnist* [38] shares a similar distribution than *Mnist* and is composed of images of clothes instead of digits. Classification performance is usually lower than with *Mnist*. We use it to illustrate what happens with an average difficulty dataset.

Both datasets are composed of 60 000 samples to train the model and 10 000 samples to evaluate the model.

Networks

- *LeNet5* [20] is a simple and historical CNN that provides good accuracy results on *Mnist*. Its topology is simple enough to get a grasp on how data is being transformed across the model. It is also easy to train with its low parameter count, but that simplicity comes at the cost of lower accuracy results in more complex recognition tasks.
- *DoubleLeNet5* is a chimeric network we have created to illustrate the ability of the system to handle networks with several branches. It consists of two *LeNet5*-like networks that process in parallel two versions of the given input data, one as-is and one with image rotation applied. Those sub-models are concatenated after the reduction to a 128-values long vector by a Dense-type layer from each branch. This model targets the same kinds of data as *LeNet5*, with a minor performance gain.
- *VGG16* [31] is a deep CNN usually used on complex datasets composed of large color images, with a thousand recognizable classes [28]. Its robustness allows it to reach fairly good accuracy results on target tasks, but comes with

a heavy computation cost and cannot be trained in a reasonable amount of time on standard computers. In this paper, the convolutional layers of the *VGG16* model are already pre-trained with the ImageNet dataset, and are not altered when training the prediction layers.

Couples of Network and Dataset. We have selected meaningful combinations of network and dataset.

- *Easy scenario*: *LeNet5* uses *Mnist* which illustrates a well performing system.
- *Generalization scenario*: *LeNet5* uses *FashionMnist* which illustrates a system with more errors.
- *Problematic scenario*: *LeNet5* predicts *FashionMnist* but is trained with *Mnist* which illustrates a system that does not perform well.
- *Simplification scenario*: *VGG16* is processing *Mnist*. It illustrates the use of a complex network to solve a simple task.
- *Realistic scenario*: *DoubleLeNet5* predicts *FashionMnist* which illustrates a network with branches. It illustrates the correct usage of transfer learning for a simpler task.

4.2 Implementation and Execution Infrastructure

The TensorFlow framework is solicited along with Keras to train the studied models with said datasets [1,7]. The intermediate computations between each layer, seen as high-dimensional vectors leading to potentially very large data, are saved into a 52-machines large cluster handling the dissimilarity matrix computation, which makes use of a large pool of memory (around 2 Terabytes in our infrastructure). The resulting matrices are small enough (for our experiments) to fit and be processed on a recent laptop, equipped with a 9th generation Intel i9 CPU, a nVIDIA Quadro T1000 GPU and 16 GB of RAM capacity. The matrix manipulations of the original VAT algorithm are implemented using the ArrayFire library for their efficient matrix computation abilities. This part of the process only produces the data for the visualization tool and thus can be seen as a backend infrastructure. Fractal images are then generated by relying on the Rust *hilbert* library. The visual and interactive part corresponds to an HTML application written in `Typescript` relying on `D3.js` for the visualization, `D3-dag` for the Sugiyama implementation and `webpack` for the build system.

5 Results and Discussion

The complete results are accessible and best viewed online (images are strongly undersized in the paper where 1 pixel represents several samples) at the following address: https://pivert.labri.fr/frac/index.html. Figure 3 depicts still-resized representations of the proposed method for several scenarios, while their confusion matrices are presented in Fig. 4.

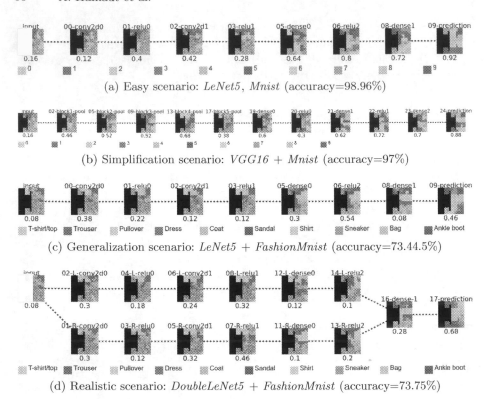

(a) Easy scenario: *LeNet5*, *Mnist* (accuracy=98.96%)

(b) Simplification scenario: *VGG16 + Mnist* (accuracy=97%)

(c) Generalization scenario: *LeNet5 + FashionMnist* (accuracy=73.44.5%)

(d) Realistic scenario: *DoubleLeNet5 + FashionMnist* (accuracy=73.75%)

Fig. 3. Illustration of results on some scenarios. The simplified version of the network is drawn. The confusion matrices are presented in Fig. 4 for comparison with a standard visual evaluation method. Larger images are available here: https://pivert.labri. fr/frac/.

Results. The accuracy for the system of the *easy scenario* is 98.96%. This appears clearly in the latest Hilbert curve where clusters appear neatly. Looking at the successive operations that correspond to activation functions (`01-relu0`, `03-relu1`, `06-relu2`, `09-prediction`), we observe an improvement in the quality of the representation, which means the network improves its discriminability ability over layers. Classes `1` and `0` seem to be highly differentiable since the beginning of the network, as well as a subset of `6, 7, 8`. Discriminability improves greatly at layer `05-dense0`.

The accuracy in the *generalization scenario* reduces to 73.44%. This performance reduction is observed with the latest curve that is saltier as well as the representation of the inner operations. `T-shirt` and `Trouser` classes start to be differentiable at the beginning of the network while `Ankle boots` or `Sandal` are differentiable only at the end of the network.

The *problematic scenario* provides noisy representations associated to the worst quality measures as the network is unable to classify properly. Cluster tendencies may appear because samples of the same class can be somehow

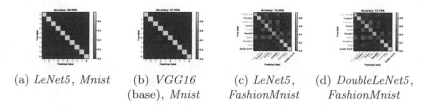

(a) *LeNet5*, *Mnist*   (b) *VGG16*   (c) *LeNet5*,   (d) *DoubleLeNet5*,
                           (base), *Mnist*   *FashionMnist*   *FashionMnist*

Fig. 4. Confusion matrices of the systems presented in Fig. 3.

transformed similarly. The *simplification scenario* has the accuracy of 97% (so lower than *LeNet5*). As a consequence, the cluster frontiers of the latest Hilbert curve is less neat. There is a succession of improvement/decreasing of drawing quality over time. We assume they come from several reasons: they are pretrained and not specialized for the task, and they are too deep and redundant.

The *realistic scenario* illustrates the ability to draw networks with branches. We observe the same tendencies in both branches with an initial increase in the drawing quality then a decrease. They are also confident on the same classes.

Discussion. We observe easily the efficient use of the screen space (remember each sample is drawn once per layer) in comparison to a T-SNE projection [27]. Pixels usage is maximized; but not all points of the curves are used; black pixels correspond to unused pixels because test datasets are smaller than what is technically possible with such display size. It is possible to evaluate larger datasets without using more space on the screen. Another observation is the effectiveness of samples projection over the fractal curve to depict the classification performance over layers. Usually, dataset representation is less and less salty over layers which means the network is better and better at separating classes of samples. *FashionMnist* which is a problem more difficult than *Mnist* is also saltier than the later one: we are able to visually represent this fact.

By construction, the very first node corresponds to the projection of the raw dataset; the noisier it is, the more complex it is to distinguish its samples without extracting additional features. The representation clearly depicts this point and its quality metric is worst for *FashionMnist* than *Mnist*. The very last node corresponds to the projection of the softmax values; the noisier it is, the worst the accuracy is. The final representation is complementary of a confusion matrix (see Fig. 4) as it provides more information.

A labeled dataset is currently needed to color the pixels. It limits the use of the method to a test dataset and not a real world unlabeld dataset. However, it is still possible to use the predicted labels instead of the groundtruth ones to obtain a view of how the network interprets the data.

Figure 5 compares the absolute and relative color schemes for one operation able to differentiate the samples and another one yet not able to differentiate them. Thanks to the color, the absolute one allows to clearly see which classes is subject to more noise than the others, while the relative one allows to better

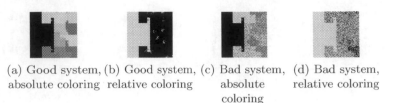

(a) Good system, (b) Good system, (c) Bad system, (d) Bad system,
absolute coloring   relative coloring   absolute   relative coloring
                                          coloring

Fig. 5. Comparison of the absolute and relative color schemes. No data is depicted in black for absolute and light blue for relative color schemes. (Color figure online)

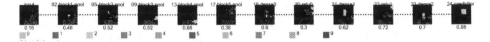

Fig. 6. Analysis of the spread of samples of class 2 over layers. Such representation could indicated an oversizing of the network by looking at the separation effect around layer 17.

see the relative quantity of errors. The relative one is also able by construction to handle many classes.

Focusing on a specific class helps to track the evolution of the treatment of samples for that chosen class over layers. Figure 6 illustrates a possible oversizing of the network by observing that samples of selected class tend to be considered similar around layer 9, whereas it is not the case anymore around layer 17.

Future Work. The method is resource consuming, mainly due to the need of storing dissimilarity matrices in memory. As a future work, it would be interesting to study whether one could use smaller part, or estimation, of the dissimilarities to approach a similar visualization. Additionally, the ordering of the samples highly depend on the Euclidean distance that is known to not be efficient in high dimensional spaces. Other metrics need to be compared.

The approach is satisfactory using interaction, but is not yet self-sufficient. Indeed, it provides a good overview of how the classification is handled but lacks of interactions to track the progression of a single sample or group of samples (in opposite to our previous work that specifically focus on this point [11]) in the network. Such investigations have to be held.

The Hilbert curve is very efficient to place the samples in its reserved space. However, there is a high probability that the number of elements in the dataset to visualize is lower than what is possible with the curve (in our experiment, $4^7 - 10\,000$ pixels are lost, which is roughly 39% of the picture for each layer). It would be interesting to implement additional interactions that use this additional space; or use grid-based projection methods instead of fractal ones. To subsample or sample with replacement the dataset with a number of samples equals to the curve length, and that follows data distribution, could also be interesting. The standard Sugiyama algorithm does not consider the screen space size; a modified method should be used in order to project the graph on the screen in a way that does not necessitate to horizontally scroll the screen to see it [21].

6 Conclusion

Deep learning classifiers are progressively replacing handcrafted and understood standard classifiers for various fields. This performance gain is counterbalanced by a difficulty in understanding how and why they perform well. Information visualization is one solution to this lack of interpretability. We have presented a pipeline consuming a trained network and a dataset and producing an interactive representation depicting both the network's architecture and the behaviors of the test samples at each layer. Such system allows to visually analyze the classification quality over layers of a dataset and could be used to visually detect patterns in the data and propose a hypothesis about the performance of the network. Such hypothesis would need then to be verified by other means.

This approach has been validated on various scenarios and shows its interest and limits that will be overcome in the future. It will be extended with various specific interaction methods to also focus on individual data and, subsampling or dense pixel based method that do not "lost" screen space.

References

1. Abadi, M., et al.: TensorFlow: large-scale machine learning on heterogeneous systems (2015). https://www.tensorflow.org/. Software available from tensorflow.org
2. Fuad, K.A.A., Martin, P.E., Giot, R., Bourqui, R., Benois-Pineau, J., Zemmari, A.: Features understanding in 3D CNNs for actions recognition in video. In: The tenth International Conference on Image Processing Theory, Tools and Applications (IPTA 2020), p. 6 (2020)
3. Auber, D., Novelli, N., Melançon, G.: Visually mining the datacube using a pixel-oriented technique. In: 2007 11th International Conference Information Visualization (IV 2007), pp. 3–10. IEEE (2007)
4. Behrisch, M., Bach, B., Henry Riche, N., Schreck, T., Fekete, J.D.: Matrix reordering methods for table and network visualization. Comput. Graph. Forum **35**(3), 693–716 (2016)
5. Binder, A., Montavon, G., Lapuschkin, S., Müller, K.-R., Samek, W.: Layer-wise relevance propagation for neural networks with local renormalization layers. In: Villa, A.E.P., Masulli, P., Pons Rivero, A.J. (eds.) ICANN 2016. LNCS, vol. 9887, pp. 63–71. Springer, Cham (2016). https://doi.org/10.1007/978-3-319-44781-0_8
6. Blanchard, F., Herbin, M., Lucas, L.: A new pixel-oriented visualization technique through color image. Inf. Vis. **4**(4), 257–265 (2005)
7. Chollet, F., et al.: Keras (2015). https://keras.io
8. Erhan, D., Bengio, Y., Courville, A., Vincent, P.: Visualizing higher-layer features of a deep network. Technical report, University of Montreal (2009)
9. Gardner, M.: Mathematical games-in which "monster" curves force redefinition of the word "curve". Sci. Am. **235**(6), 124–133 (1976)
10. Ghazi, M.M., Yanikoglu, B., Aptoula, E.: Plant identification using deep neural networks via optimization of transfer learning parameters. Neurocomputing **235**, 228–235 (2017)

11. Halnaut, A., Giot, R., Bourqui, R., Auber, D.: Deep dive into deep neural networks with flows. In: 15th International Joint Conference on Computer Vision, Imaging and Computer Graphics Theory and Applications, pp. 231–239 (2020)
12. He, K., Zhang, X., Ren, S., Sun, J.: Deep residual learning for image recognition. In: Proceedings of the IEEE Conference on Computer Vision and Pattern Recognition, pp. 770–778 (2016)
13. Hilbert, D.: Über die stetige abbildung einer linie auf ein flächenstück. In: Dritter Band: Analysis Grundlagen der Mathematik Physik Verschiedenes, pp. 1–2. Springer (1935)
14. Hohman, F., Kahng, M., Pienta, R., Chau, D.H.: Visual analytics in deep learning: an interrogative survey for the next frontiers. IEEE Trans. Visual Comput. Graphics $25(8)$, 2674–2693 (2018)
15. Kahng, M., Andrews, P.Y., Kalro, A., Chau, D.H.: ActiVis: visual exploration of industry-scale deep neural network models. IEEE Trans. Visual Comput. Graphics $24(1)$, 88–97 (2018)
16. Kahng, M., Thorat, N., Chau, D.H.P., Viégas, F.B., Wattenberg, M.: GAN lab: understanding complex deep generative models using interactive visual experimentation. IEEE Trans. Visual Comput. Graphics $25(1)$, 1–11 (2018)
17. Keim, D.A.: Designing pixel-oriented visualization techniques: theory and applications. IEEE Trans. Visual Comput. Graphics $6(1)$, 59–78 (2000)
18. LeCun, Y.: The MNIST database of handwritten digits (1998). http://yann.lecun.com/exdb/mnist/
19. LeCun, Y., Bengio, Y., Hinton, G.: Deep learning. Nature $521(7553)$, 436–444 (2015)
20. LeCun, Y., Bottou, L., Bengio, Y., Haffner, P.: Gradient-based learning applied to document recognition. Proc. IEEE $86(11)$, 2278–2324 (1998)
21. Liu, M., Liu, S., Su, H., Cao, K., Zhu, J.: Analyzing the noise robustness of deep neural networks. In: 2018 IEEE Conference on Visual Analytics Science and Technology (VAST), pp. 60–71. IEEE (2018)
22. Liu, M., Shi, J., Li, Z., Li, C., Zhu, J., Liu, S.: Towards better analysis of deep convolutional neural networks. IEEE Trans. Visual Comput. Graphics $23(1)$, 91–100 (2017)
23. Maaten, L.v.d., Hinton, G.: Visualizing data using t-SNE. J. Mach. Learn. Res. 9, 2579–2605 (2008)
24. Meyer, M., Sedlmair, M., Quinan, P.S., Munzner, T.: The nested blocks and guidelines model. Inf. Vis. $14(3)$, 234–249 (2015)
25. Morton, G.M.: A computer oriented geodetic data base and a new technique in file sequencing. Technical report, International Business Machines Company New York (1966)
26. Norton, A.P., Qi, Y.: Adversarial-playground: a visualization suite showing how adversarial examples fool deep learning. In: 2017 IEEE Symposium on Visualization for Cyber Security (VizSec), pp. 1–4. IEEE (2017)
27. Rauber, P.E., Fadel, S.G., Falcao, A.X., Telea, A.C.: Visualizing the hidden activity of artificial neural networks. IEEE Trans. Visual Comput. Graphics $23(1)$, 101–110 (2017)
28. Russakovsky, O., et al.: ImageNet large scale visual recognition challenge. Int. J. Comput. Vision $115(3)$, 211–252 (2015)
29. Selvaraju, R.R., Cogswell, M., Das, A., Vedantam, R., Parikh, D., Batra, D.: Gradcam: visual explanations from deep networks via gradient-based localization. In: 2017 IEEE International Conference on Computer Vision (ICCV), pp. 618–626 (2017)

30. d. Silva, L.E.B., Wunsch, D.C.: A study on exploiting vat to mitigate ordering effects in fuzzy art. In: 2018 International Joint Conference on Neural Networks (IJCNN), pp. 1–8 (2018)
31. Simonyan, K., Zisserman, A.: Very deep convolutional networks for large-scale image recognition. preprint arXiv:1409.1556 (2014)
32. Smilkov, D., Carter, S., Sculley, D., Viégas, F.B., Wattenberg, M.: Direct-manipulation visualization of deep networks. arXiv preprint arXiv:1708.03788 (2017)
33. Sugiyama, K., Tagawa, S., Toda, M.: Methods for visual understanding of hierarchical system structures. IEEE Trans. Syst. Man Cybern. 11, 109–125 (1981)
34. Tang, Y.: Deep learning using linear support vector machines. In: In ICML (2013)
35. Wang, J., Gou, L., Shen, H.W., Yang, H.: DQNViz: a visual analytics approach to understand deep q-networks. IEEE Trans. Visual Comput. Graphics 25(1), 288–298 (2019)
36. Wang, Z.J., et al.: CNN 101: interactive visual learning for convolutional neural networks. In: Extended Abstracts of the 2020 CHI Conference on Human Factors in Computing Systems, pp. 1–7 (2020)
37. Wongsuphasawat, K., et al.: Visualizing dataflow graphs of deep learning models in TensorFlow. IEEE Trans. Visual Comput. Graphics 24(1), 1–12 (2017)
38. Xiao, H., Rasul, K., Vollgraf, R.: Fashion-MNIST: a novel image dataset for benchmarking machine learning algorithms. arXiv preprint arXiv:1708.07747 (2017)
39. Zhang, Q., Nian Wu, Y., Zhu, S.C.: Interpretable convolutional neural networks. In: Proceedings of the IEEE Conference on Computer Vision and Pattern Recognition, pp. 8827–8836 (2018)
40. Zhang, Q., Yang, Y., Ma, H., Wu, Y.N.: Interpreting CNNs via decision trees. In: Proceedings of the IEEE Conference on Computer Vision and Pattern Recognition, pp. 6261–6270 (2019)

Random Forest Model and Sample Explainer for Non-experts in Machine Learning – Two Case Studies

D. Petkovic$^{(\boxtimes)}$, A. Alavi, D. Cai, and M. Wong

CS Department, San Francisco State University, San Francisco, CA, USA
petkovic@sfsu.edu

Abstract. Machine Learning (ML) is becoming an increasingly critical technology in many areas such as health, business but also in everyday applications of significant societal importance. However, the lack of explainability or ability of ML systems to offer explanation on how they work, which refers to the model (related to the whole data) and sample explainability (related to specific samples) poses significant challenges in their adoption, verification, and in ensuring the trust among users and general public. We present novel integrated Random Forest Model and Sample Explainer – RFEX. RFEX is specifically designed for important class of users who are non-ML experts but are often the domain experts and key decision makers. RFEX provides easy to analyze one-page Model and Sample explainability summaries in tabular format with wealth of explainability information including classification confidence, tradeoff between accuracy and features used, as well as ability to identify potential outlier samples and features. We demonstrate RFEX on two case studies: mortality prediction for COVID-19 patients from the data obtained from Huazhong University of Science and Technology, Wuhan, China, and classification of cell type clusters for human nervous system based on the data from J. Craig Venter Institute. We show that RFEX offers simple yet powerful means of explaining RF classification at model, sample and feature levels, as well as providing guidance for testing and developing explainable and cost-effective operational prediction models.

Keywords: Machine learning · Random Forest · Explainability · COVID-19 · Human nervous system

1 Introduction

Machine Learning (ML) is becoming an increasingly critical technology in many areas ranging from health and business, to everyday applications that directly influence society such as face recognition, self driving cars, policing, credit, rent and loan approvals etc. However, ML systems complexity creates challenges in our ability to audit such systems for true accuracy as well as for ethical, legally transparent and unbiased operation [1, 2, 5, 6, 8–10]. This results in increasing concerns and erosion of trust not only in technical community but importantly among key adopters who are often non-ML experts, as well

© Springer Nature Switzerland AG 2021
A. Del Bimbo et al. (Eds.): ICPR 2020 Workshops, LNCS 12663, pp. 62–75, 2021.
https://doi.org/10.1007/978-3-030-68796-0_5

as in general public and politicians. Indeed, when audited using explainability, many well-known ML systems turned out to be making seemingly correct decisions based on wrong "reasoning" making them useless in real practice (see for example [1, 2]). At a high level, explainability of ML systems should allow human users (including non-ML experts) to gain insights into how ML systems make their decisions. ML explainability can be model based, where it offers insights on how the ML system works on a collection of data as a whole (e.g. the whole training database) and sample based, where it offers insights into how the trained ML system classifies a specific data sample. The latter has been shown to be critical in determining user trust in ML systems [3]. ML explainers can be agnostic to ML methods they try to explain or direct (tied to a specific ML algorithm). ML systems that are explainable achieve many benefits such as: increasing user trust and more likely adoption; improvement in ML quality control and maintenance; reduced production costs (by using only subset of top predictive features); legal transparency; and possibly even new insights into the analyzed domain. The need for explainability does not exclude usefulness of black box models since they are always tried first and may serve among other things to point to ultimate achievable accuracy [4]. Explainable systems can also be used for development, verification and testing of otherwise hard to explain black box systems. Note that some ML methods like Neural Networks and Deep Learning are inherently difficult to explain, while some like tree-based ones (e.g. Random Forest (RF)) are more amenable to explanations. The academic community is addressing this issue with more research, dedicated conferences and workshops e.g. [5–7]. Importantly, many governmental and scientific bodies as well as major companies like Google and Microsoft recently focused on addressing issues in ML, and in all of them explainability or transparency (sometimes called "right to know") figures as a very important factor e.g. [8–10].

Jointly with Stanford University Bioengineering Department we have been working for a number of years in applying ML to biomedical problems [12–14] and in trying to build confidence in our results we got involved in ML explainability, especially of well-known Random Forest (RF) ML method [11]. Our initial attempts to develop very basic RF Explainability focused on model explainer only and were applied to Stanford FEATURE data [12, 14]. In this paper we present several novel contributions: a) New RFEX Sample explainer which provides an easy to interpret explanation of how RF classifies a particular data sample and is designed to directly relate to RFEX Model Explainer. It can also be used to identify potential outliers in training data, an important step in development of ML; b) Significantly updated RFEX Model Explainer from the one in [12]; and c) two case studies demonstrating utility of RFEX, namely: use of RFEX for early prediction of mortality from COVID-19 based on the data from Huazhong University of Science and Technology, Wuhan, China [15]; and case study using the data and findings from J. Craig Venter Institute (JCVI) and Allen Institute for Brain Science [16–18] for classification of human nervous system cell type clusters.

2   Integrated Random Forest Model and Sample Explainer - RFEX

RF is widely used and one of the most powerful ML techniques (as evaluated in [21]), and well supported with open source free tools (e.g. R [22]). It lends itself to explanation being a tree based method. RF is based on a set of ntree decision trees (forest of trees), each trained on a slightly different random partition of training data, voting together to determine sample classification. The parameter voting cutoff is chosen for voting threshold (minimal fraction of ntree trees needed to vote for a particular class to be chosen) and determines RF sensitivity. RF has several built in feature importance (ranking) measures and we use the MDA (Mean Decrease in Accuracy) perturbation measure [11, 22]. For the main classification accuracy measure, to be more precise in case of imbalanced data, we use standard F1 score computed as:

$$F_1 = 2 * (recall * precision)/(recall + precision) \qquad (1)$$

In this paper we focus on the most common case of binary classification with positive (+) class being the class of interest. Multi class problem can be addressed by investigating each class separately with all other classes treated together as - class (like in our second case study). We also leverage very useful RF information (rarely used by others) namely RF voting statistics e.g. number of trees from the set of ntree "forest" voting for + or − class for each tested sample. RFEX approach is unique in that it is user driven, with users defined mainly as adopters with strong domain but low or no ML expertise (a crucial class of users mostly neglected by ML researchers). Following the principles of well proven User Centered Design, an industry best practice for developing usable systems, we started by understanding what users want from ML systems in terms of explainability and in what form. We reviewed published literature, current initiatives and recommendations for ML verification and explainability, spoke to many users, and in [12] ran a formal user trust evaluation for older version of RFEX with 13 users including ML and non-ML experts. This brief study validated viability of RFEX approach and its tabular output. Our findings on explainability requirements are summarized below, in a form of explainability questions and requirements posed by users. These were the key driving factors for the design of RFEX. Questions 1–6 below drove our RFEX Model Explainer design, and questions 7–9 drove our RFEX Sample Explainer design. The ease of use and the format of presenting RFEX were driven by requirement 10.

1. *What is the best accuracy (e.g. using all features) achieved by the chosen ML method?*
2. *How confident should I be in ML classification?*
3. *Which features (preferably small manageable number) are most important for predicting the class of interest?*
4. *What is the tradeoff between using a subset of features and the related accuracy? (I need to reduce the cost of extracting features...)*
5. *What are basic statistics/ranges and separation of feature values between those for + and − class?*
6. *Which (small) groups of features work best together?*
7. *Why was my sample classified incorrectly or correctly? Was it a "reliably" classified/misclassified sample or "marginal"?*
8. *Which features or factors contributed to incorrect classification of the sample?*
9. *Can I identify training samples or features that are "outliers" or "noisy" so I can "clean" my training data?*
10. *Present ML explainability reports in a simple way, not requiring deep ML knowledge; in formats and "components" that I can understand*

2.1 RFEX Model Explainer

RFEX Model Explainer includes: a) basic RF classification accuracy (as it is customarily done today); b) novel classification confidence information related to the tree voting statistics on the whole training data and with the use of all available features (steps 1 and 2 below); and c) much improved one-page RFEX Model Explainer in tabular format with the columns providing explainability data from steps 3–6 below, for each top ranked feature (rows). RFEX Model Summary Table leverages drastic feature (e.g. complexity) reduction by transforming ML problem with (commonly used) hundreds of features to a much more simple to understand representation using only few (e.g. 7–10) top ranked features (using step 4 below) which in all our studies showed to carry almost all predictive power of full classifier [12, 19, 20] - a crucial but nowadays rarely used observation.

1. *RF base accuracy:* We first train the RF classifier on a full training database using all features to establish base (ultimate) RF accuracy (e.g. F1 score) and optimal RF parameters e.g. ntree, mtry and cutoff using standard best practices for RF optimization. RF does not need cross validation since it has a built in one [11] (Explainability requirement 1)

2. *RF Classification Confidence - Voting statistics:* It is defined as the average of fractions of trees in trained RF which voted correctly for all truc + and for all – samples, computed separately as AVVote+ and AVVote– respectively. It is a novel measure reflecting how well the trained trees "agree" in their votes for + and in their votes for – class, with high values (over 90%) indicating very high confidence in RF classification. (Explainability requirement 2)

3. *Feature Rank:* We rank features by their predictive power using RF's standard Mean Decrease in Accuracy (MDA) feature ranking measured from the optimally trained RF classifier in Step 1. In the case of unbalanced training data (e.g. number of + class samples is 10% or less than – class samples), we recommend the use of class specific MDA (separate rankings for + and – class) which, in our experiments, clearly showed different rankings [12, 19]. (Explainability requirement 3)

4. *Cumulative F_1 score*: This measure provides important tradeoffs between using subsets of top ranked features (up to the topK) and RF accuracy by computing "cumulative F_1 score" for each combination of top ranked 2, top ranked 3,…top ranked topK features (in each step a full RF optimization/training is performed, noting that RF has built in cross validation). Users can then choose top ranked feature subset which offers desired F_1 accuracy. (Explainability requirements 3, 4, 6)

5. *Feature Value Statistics:* To present basic feature value statistics (e.g. presence or absence of a "signal" or a high or low range), instead of "feature direction" in [12] we use more common measures of average (AV) and standard deviation (SD) for feature values of + and – class separately. This type of data is familiar to most (including non ML expert) users and offers basic most often needed information and confidence building to domain experts. (Explainability requirement 5)

6. *Feature Class Separation:* To indicate separation of feature value populations for + and – class for each of topK features as a way of confidence measure of individual feature predictive power, we use well established Cohen Distance [23] between feature values of two populations e.g. for + and – class, defined as:

$$\text{Cohen Distance} = \text{ABS}(\text{AV}+ \; - \; \text{AV}-)/\text{SDmax} \qquad (2)$$

where AV+ is the average of feature values for the positive class; AV− is the average of feature values for the negative class; and SDmax is the larger standard deviation of the two feature value populations. ABS is absolute value. We chose Cohen Distance over p-value measure since it provides level of separation vs. only the hypothesis confirmation, and works well for large data sets [23]. As noted in [23], Cohen Distance of less than 0.2 denotes a small separation, from 0.2 to 0.5 indicates a medium, from 0.5 to 0.8 large, and above it a very large separation. Note that feature can have low class separation but still, with other features, may play a significant role in RF prediction. (Explainability requirements 2, 3, 5)

7. To address *ease of use explainability requirement* 10 we set out goals as follows: a) present RFEX Model and Sample Explainers data in one-page tabular format each, rows being topK ranked features (usually 8–10); and b) use explainability measures already understandable or easy to explain to non-experts in ML. The tabular format is a basic format amenable and familiar to "visual inspection" by domain experts. It is possible also to add number of "filters/rules" and visualization options on top of this basic tabular data

2.2 RFEX Sample Explainer

The RFEX Sample Explainer is also designed with our target users in mind for situations when for example: a) they want to understand why and how the trained RF classified a *specific sample* for which they know the ground truth, critical in forming their trust in RF classification [3]; and b) for ML quality control e.g. editing of training data where they want to identify and possibly delete "outlier" training samples or features of marginal "quality". Importantly, RFEX Sample Explainer also has tabular format and directly relates to RFEX Model Explainer (e.g. uses the same set of topK ranked features), with the data as follows:

● *RFEX Sample Explainability Basic Data* such as

  – *CORRECT_CLASS:* Correct (ground truth) class label of tested sample known or assumed by the domain expert used as a reference to determine if the sample was classified correctly by RF;
  – *RF_CLASS_LABEL*: Sample class label as determined by trained RF;
  – SAMPLE_*VOTE_FRACTION:* This novel measure represents the fraction of optimally trained RF trees voting for the CORRECT_CLASS for the given sample. SAMPLE_VOTE_FRACTION, when compared to the *voting cutoff* of the trained RF, helps assess if the sample classification was done "reliably" (i.e. it is much larger than voting cutoff) or was "marginal" or wrong (i.e. it is close to or below voting cutoff), which is important in determining potential sample "outliers". This measure is provided in RF tool R [22]. Rationale for this measure comes from the

observation that outliers participate less frequently in bootstrap data sets used to train each RF tree and they, being far from majority of samples, often do not force node splitting algorithms to create a tree/node to accommodate them, see more discussion in [20] (Explainability requirements 7 and 9).

- *RFEX Sample Summary Table* shows, in a one-page summary, how topK features from RFEX Model Summary (rows) contribute to RF classification of tested sample. The first five columns are the same as in RFEX Model Summary e.g.: *Feature Rank*; Feature *Name; Feature MDA rank; Feature values AV/SD* positive class; *Feature values AV/SD* for negative class. This is then followed by the table columns containing:

  - *Sample Cohen Distance to + class* measured as difference between sample feature value and average of feature values for + class, normalized by standard deviation [23];
  - *Sample Cohen Distance to − class* (analogous to above);
  - *K Nearest Neighbor Ratio or KNN* as a new confidence measure defined for each feature as a fraction of K nearest neighbors of the current feature value that belong to CORRECT_CLASS. KNN complements the *Sample Cohen Distances* in that it is more local and rank based, as well as non-parametric. For K, we recommend 20% of the number of samples of the smaller class which we determined experimentally over several applications.

To investigate further, one can establish simple and intuitive rules to identify *specific features* of tested sample which may cause low SAMPLE_VOTE_FRACTION. One such rule for "flagging" sample i-*th* feature SFi as a potential "outlier" (addressing explainability requirement 8) is suggested as follows, for the case of CORRECT_CLASS being + class:

$$
\begin{aligned}
&\text{IF (\textit{"Sample Cohen Distance of SFi to + class"}) > (\textit{"Sample Cohen Distance of SFi to − class"}) OR} \\
&\text{(\textit{"K Nearest Neighbor Ratio (KNN)" of SFi for + class}) < 0.5\ \textit{THEN Flag SFi s "outlier"}}
\end{aligned} \tag{3}
$$

Threshold of 0.5 for KNN was determined to enforce majority presence of samples of correct class in the neighborhood, and can be changed depending on sensitivity required for determining outliers. To test our hypothesis of usefulness of AVVote+ measure and SAMPLE_VOTE_FRACTION we first conducted a number of experiments using carefully designed synthetic data. These synthetic test data consisted of number of well grouped clusters of + class samples with random− class data, and were compared with the same data but with added + class outliers. Our experiments showed that AVVote+ is higher for well grouped data vs. data with outliers (and correlates with higher F_1 score), and that the outlier data can be identified as the data with low SAMPLE_VOTE_FRACTION (more details are in [20]). As with Model Explainer table, the Sample Summary tabular data is a basic format amenable to visual inspection by domain experts, and it too can be augmented by automated annotation and visualization e.g. in flagging outliers as per rule in Eq. (3). All RFEX steps can easily be automated in the form of a pipeline of processing.

3 RFEX Explanation of Early Mortality Prediction for COVID-19 Patients

In this case study we apply RFEX Model Explainer to the data from the recently published study from Huazhong University of Science and Technology in Wuhan, China [15] on *interpretable* mortality prediction model for COVID-19 patients ("Wuhan data" in this paper). The study used the data from 485 infected patients in the region of Wuhan, China to identify most predicative biomarkers of COVID-19 mortality (including those in early stages of observing the infected patients). Authors of this paper pay great attention to address explainability/interpretability of their ML solution in order to provide easy to understand, verify and adopt "operational predictive model" in practice. The data for the study included patients' basic data, symptom classification by team of physicians, and number of blood tests taken in different times (full details are in [15]). These data comprise feature vectors for ML models with 76 features (mainly blood tests and some basic medical data like age) taken from each patient at different times. The outcomes (which were classes to be predicted by ML) are defined as patient recovery and subsequent discharge from the hospital (negative class) or unfortunately patient mortality (positive class). In their analysis, Wuhan researchers applied two separate categories of experiments: a) prediction of mortality based on the last blood samples taken at "day 0" e.g. the day of the outcome as defined above; and b) analysis of ML prediction of final outcome based on data taken before "day 0" e.g. at days -2; -4; and -7 and earlier. (Note that some patients reached the outcome before 7 days in hospital so this is why the total number of patients in these different times is less than the number of patients at day 0). Wuhan researchers chose XGBoost tree classifiers and achieved impressive results using separate training and validation sets, with F_1 score of 0.978 using only top ranked 3 features out of 76 (LDH + lymphocyte + CRP) taken at day 0. To address the explainability, Wuhan researchers developed a simple decision tree using above 3 top predictive features to serve as guidance for physicians, which they call "clinically operable decision tree" (one more case for simple formats of ML explainability attuned to domain and not ML experts). Notably they used similar approach used in RFEX, namely "cumulative F_1 score", to justify why top 3 features above provide sufficient accuracy. In terms of exploring if ML can be used for *early* predictions (before day 0) they performed a number of separate experiments with data from patients in several preset times before day zero (e.g. days -2, -4, -7) to establish as they call it "prediction horizon". They showed that ML model in some cases can predict outcomes with high accuracy (over 90%) before day 0, and even 10 or more days before the day 0 outcome. Our goals in this case study were several: a) to analyze the data from [15] at day 0 and to compare it with our RFEX Model Summary in Table 1 (accuracy, top predictive features), as well as to compare the explainability presentation formats and their ease of use; b) to further apply RFEX Model Explainer to "historical" data e.g. data taken before day 0 to analyze if early prediction using RF is feasible (Table 2); and c) to explore if the RFEX Model Explainers in Tables 1 and 2 computed at different times differ and how these differences influence explainability and operational application of RF predictors.

Table 1. RFEX Model Summary table for Wuhan data for day 0. Base RF accuracy using all 76 features is F1 = 0.979, for NTREE = 6000, MTRY = 19 and CUTOFF of 0.6. RF Voting statistics: AVVote+ = 0.968

Feature index	Feature name	MDA value	Cumulative F₁ score	AV/SD + class	AV/SD − class	Cohen distance
1	LDH	100.99	0.935	788/439	213/65	1.31
2	hs-CRP	63.14	0.960	129/79	12/26	1.48
3	Lymphocyte %	42.37	0.972	6/6	26/10]	2
4	Neutrophils %	38.20	0.969	90/9	63/12.8]	2.1
5	Lymphocyte count	33.00	0.970	0.58/0.4	1.6/2.4	0.43
6	ASP Aminotransferase	30.72	0.970	92/213	23/16	0.32
7	albumin	28.83	0.974	28/4.9	37/3.9	1.84

Table 2. RFEX Model Summary table for Wuhan data for day -7. Base RF accuracy using all 76 features is F1 = 0.888, for NTREE = 5500, MTRY = 5 and CUTOFF of 0.6. RF Voting statistics: AVVote+ = 0.879

Feature index	Feature name	MDA value	Cumulative F₁ score	AV/SD + class	AV/SD − class	Cohen distance
1	LDH	38.04	0.714	599/286	259/88	1.19
2	Lymphocyte count	30.69	0.806	0.54/0.33	1.2/0.5	1.32
3	Urea	29.82	0.827	10.4/5.8	4.3/1.7	1.05
4	Lymphocyte %	29.76	0.837	7.2/5.2	23.7/11.6	1.42
5	hs-CRP	28.62	0.839	124/77	29/39	1.23
6	Neutrophils %	28.09	0.828	89/6.9	67/13.8	1.59
7	Age	27.42	0.850	70/10	49/14.8	1.42

3.1 RFEX Model Explainer for the Prediction of COVID-19 Mortality from the Data for Day 0

We first applied RFEX Model Explainer to Wuhan data on day 0. These data contained a total of 361 patients, 195 discharged, and 166 mortality cases at day 0, with 76 features/tests done at day 0. We then created RFEX Model Summary data shown in Table 1 showing eight topK ranked features. We now make several observations by visual analysis of Table 1 data which contains all the relevant model explainability information on one page. First, the base accuracy provided by RF using all 76 features yielded very high F₁ score of 0.979 (for NTREE of 6000, MTRY of 19 and CUTOFF of 0.6), confirming very high accuracy classification results in [15]. In addition, high AVVote+ of 0.968 (e.g. on average 96.8% of trees voted for + class data) indicates very high confidence in RF classification. We note that, as in all our experiments where RF produces high F_1 score [19, 20], as well as in second case study in this paper, MDA feature rankings (important step in RFEX) were very stable (practically the same) in experiments with repeated (20) runs of RF using different random seeds. We also suggest that RFEX Model one-page tabular format with the number of explainability measures leads toward better explainability and increasing user trust, as follows. "Cumulative F_1 score" offers more detailed tradeoffs between subsets of features used vs. achievable accuracy, namely for the top 10 ranked features (vs. top 3 in [15]). We for example easily observe that the top 3 ranked features are exactly the same as reported in [15] and that they carry most of the prediction power (e.g., using only these 3 features yields F_1 score of 0.972 vs. base F_1 score of 0.979). Visual analysis of the trend of F_1 scores in "cumulative F_1 score" column shows little gain in using more than 3-4 top ranked features. (Note different situation for data for day -7 below). Feature statistics in columns 5 and 6 allow domain experts to easily observe and check basic statistics/ranges of features for + and − class (analogous to medical test reports), useful in verifying and validating domain relevance of chosen features. Finally, class separation measured by Cohen Distance (column 7) gives yet another measure of feature predictive power. Note that top ranked 4 features have very high separation between + and − class samples (Cohen Distances > 1), yet another confidence building information.

3.2   RFEX Model Explainer for *Early* Prediction of COVID-19 Mortality from the Data for Day -7

We then explored if RF could provide accurate and confident *early prediction* and its explanation, a critical need in this case study. We divided the data into separate data sets for chosen times (in this case -2, -4, -7 days before day 0 outcome) and derived RFEX Model Summary for each data set separately.

In this paper we present results only for day -7 in RFEX Model Summary in Table 2. The data included a total of 196 patients, with 151 discharged and 45 who died, using the same 76 features as for day 0. We show that RF achieved very good base accuracy F_1 score of 0.888 using all 76 features, for NTREE = 5500, MTRY 5, CUTOFF 0.6, with relatively high AVVote+ of 0.879. As expected, RF accuracy in day -7 while high is a bit less than for day 0 and with a bit less confidence (lower AVVote+). Based on this, we conclude, as found in [15], that RF can indeed provide very good and reliable early prediction (7 days before outcome day) with good confidence, albeit with a bit less than for day 0, which is to be expected. MDA feature ranking of top 10 features in repeated runs of RF with different random seeds was again stable, but slightly less stable than in case for the day 0, all consistent relationships with our observations in second case study (with more details in [19]). The question we address next is whether the RF Model Explainers (and thus respective operational RF classifiers) are different in day -7 (Table 2) from the day 0 (Table 1).

We observe that there are indeed some crucial differences of consequence for operational implementation of RF for early prediction (e.g. in day -7) compared to RF prediction model for day 0. We observe that among the top 7 ranked features for day 0 and day -7, 5 of them overlap and have the same "low/high" direction for + and − class samples, with somewhat different feature value (test) statistics, as it is to be expected. We also observe that the top 7 ranked features for day -7 have two features not appearing among the top 7 in day 0, namely "urea" (ranked consistently second or third in multiple RF runs) and "age" (ranked consistently sixth or seventh). This indicates important *early prediction "signal" which may be lost later* given that urea was ranked 10th in day -4, and was not among top 10 in day -2, and that age was ranked seventh to ninth in day -4, and was not among the top 10 in day -2 and day 0. Cohen Distances for urea and age features are above 1 indicating high separation between + and − class, and increasing the confidence in using these measures. By observing statistics of urea and age feature values (columns 5 and 6) one easily sees that + class is indicated by higher urea values (indicating kidney problems) and older patients. Importantly, by comparing the trends of "cumulative F_1 score" column values in Table 1 and Table 2 it is easily seen that there are large differences in concentration of predictive power among the top ranked features. For example, the single top ranked feature in RF Model Explainer for day 0 carries 95% of prediction (e.g. 95% of F_1 score using all features), while this is not the case for day -7 (Table 2), where one needs top 7 ranked features to achieve 95% of the base F_1 score. Besides building confidence in RF classification, this analysis also points to important guidance for operational implementation of early RF prediction (e.g. in day -7) with disclaimer that we are not medical professionals and that our observations are purely based on analysis of explainability information in Tables 1 and 2 and cursory research on meaning of urea test:

- One needs to use *more tests* (e.g. 7 as in Table 2) vs. only top 2–3 tests/features in day 0 (as in Table 1).
- In addition to common measures already deemed important for both day 0 and day -7 RF prediction (LDH, Lymphocyte count, Lymphocyte %, hs-CRP), one has to keep checking for *high urea values in patients of older age.*

4 RFEX Explanation of Classification of Human Nervous System Cell Type Clusters

In this case study we collaborated with the team of Dr. R. Scheuermann from J. Craig Venter Institute (JCVI), and used data ("JCVI data" in this paper) produced in collaboration between JCVI and the Allen Institute for Brain Science as published in [16–18]. The goals of our case study were two-fold: a) to investigate if RFEX Model Summary explains RF classification of cell clusters consistently wrt. independently obtained ground truth in *an easy to use way e.g. only by visual analysis of RFEX data;* and b) to use RFEX Sample Explainer to *easily* identify samples and features that are possibly *"out of range or outliers".* JCVI training data consists of the set of gene expression values from single nuclei samples derived from human middle temporal gyrus (MTG) layer 1 forming 610 features (each measuring expression levels of certain gene) for RF classification. Data contains 871 samples (feature vectors), grouped in 16 different cell type clusters, which constitute the classes for RF classification [16]. We, as in [16], transformed the problem of 16 class classification into a set of 16 binary classifications, where all classes of non interest were grouped into the – class and chosen cell type cluster (class of interest) was considered the + class.

4.1   RFEX Model Explainer Applied to JCVI Data

We analyzed several cell type clusters and we first show the RFEX analysis of cell type cluster *e1*. Cluster for cell type e1 had 299 positive samples and 572 negative (non-e1) samples and thus offered a relatively balanced training data set. Biological (ML independent) analysis from [16] defines and explains cluster e1 as *"A human middle temporal gyrus cortical layer 1 excitatory neuron that selectively expresses TESPA1, LINC00507 and SLC17A7 mRNAs, and lacks expression of KNCP1 mRNA"* which forms our *ground truth explanation* which we aim to verify using only visual analysis of RFEX Model Explainer data. We start by establishing base RF accuracy with all 610 gene features performing a grid search using a range of RF parameters.

We obtained a very high F_1 score of 0.995 with NTREE = 1000, MTRY = 50, CUTOFF of 0.7 for + class (0.3 for – class). High accuracy RF classification for e1 cluster was also confirmed in [17]. *RF Classification Confidence measure - Voting statistics* points to high confidence in RF classification for both + and − samples, indicated by high AVVote+ of 0.97 and AVVote− of 0.99. RFEX Model Summary in Table 3 was then generated showing from "Cumulative F_1 score" column that RF can achieve accuracy of $F_1 = 0.992$ with only 8 topK ranked features (vs. F_1 of 0.995 using all 610 features) thus achieving over 98% dimensionality reduction with practically no loss of accuracy. RFEX Model Explainer in Table 3 indeed provided correct and visually easy to interpret explanations of RF classification verifying ground truth explanation of cluster *e1* from [16] as follows: a) by observing feature ranking in Table 3 one confirms that key four defining genes for e1 cluster are among the top 5 ranked predictors and together achieve cumulative F_1 score of 0.986 – very close to base F_1 score using all features (F_1 of 0.995); and b) one can confirm from Table 3 columns 5 and 6 the correct levels (high or low) of gene expression of these key genes as stated in [16]: top 3 ranked genes show high expressions indicated by high average (AV) for + class feature values, and low AV for − class; KCNIP1 shows low expression indicated by low AV value for the + class vs. high AV for the − class. High Cohen Distance values (column 7) confirm that all highly ranked features show very good separation between + and – classes, and notably this separation is highest for highly ranked features. Interestingly, gene TBR1 also participated strongly in predictions, an information which was *previously unknown* to our JCVI collaborators, thus possibly offering new insights into this problem.

To show usefulness of *RF Voting_Statistics* measure for indicating RF classification confidence, we also computed it for two other cell type clusters form JCVI data, namely *i10* cluster with very low number of + samples (only 16) causing problems in RF classification as expected, and *i1* cluster with a bit more + samples (90). RF classification of *i10* cluster achieved F_1 score of only 0.72 with low AVVote+ of 0.72, and RF classification of *i1* cluster achieved good F_1 score of 0.95 with higher AVVote+ of 0.88 (all AVVote− were in high 0.99 range). This data, together with data for *e1* cluster points to correlation between overall classification accuracy on one hand and confidence measured by AVCVote + (as also found in first case study). Consistent with the first

Table 3. RFEX Model Summary table for JCVI data e1 cluster. Base RF accuracy using all 610 features is $F_1 = 0.995$, for NTREE $= 1000$, MTRY $= 50$ and CUTOFF of 0.7. RF Voting statistics: AVVote+ $= 0.97$

Feature index	Feature name	MDA value	Cumulative F_1 score	AV/SD e1 class	AV/SD non e1 class	Cohen Distance
1	TESPA1	18.8	N/A	363.5/266	3.9/29	1.35
2	LINC00507	16.5	0.980	234/203	1.8/15	1.14
3	SLC17A7	16.3	0.9816	82.8/77	1.1/11	1.06
4	LINC00508	12.8	0.9799	97.4/108	0.6/4.8	0.9
5	KCNIP1	12.7	0.9866	1.0/2.8	310.6/377	0.82
6	NPTX1	12.5	0.9901	142/176	3/21	0.79
7	TBR1	12.3	0.9917	34/57	0.4/4.1	0.59
8	SFTA1P	12.1	0.9917	108/119	1.1/15	0.9

case study, analyzing data for clusters *e1, i1, i10*, we observed that the higher F_1 score is, the more stable is MDA feature ranking [19].

4.2 RFEX Sample Explainer Applied to JCVI Data

In the second part of our case study on the JCVI data, we used our newly developed RFEX Sample Explainer for an important case of quality control similar to work in [17], in order to check if it can help users identify samples and features that are "marginal" or "outliers", and hence possibly not recommended for use for RF training. From the JCVI e1 training data, we chose two correctly classified + class samples with drastically different SAMPLE_VOTE_FRACTION:

- *Sample 1* – correctly and reliably classified (good) e1 cluster + class sample, with high SAMPLE_VOTE_FRACTION of 100% meaning all RF trees voted for it correctly;
- *Sample 2* – correctly classified but possibly "marginal or outlier" e1 cluster + class sample, with the smallest SAMPLE_VOTE_FRACTION, where only 80% of the trees voted correctly for it

RFEX Sample Summary table with top 5 ranked features for sample 2 is shown in Table 4. Simple visual analysis of Table 4 using Eq. (3) clearly points to three possible "outlier" features in sample 2 (ranked 2, 3, 4) among the top 5. Sample 1 did not have any "outlier" features among top 10, details in [19]. To verify our hypothesis that the above "outlier" features (out of 610 features) are responsible for this "marginal" sample 2 receiving low SAMPLE_VOTE_FRACTION we replaced their values with their respective average values for the correct + class and observed considerable increase of the SAMPLE_VOTE_FRACTION from 80% to 93.7% [20].

Table 4. RFEX Sample Summary table for JCVI data, Sample 2 – "marginal or outlier" sample, correctly classified with SAMPLE_VOTE_FRACTION of 80%. Possibly "outlier" features flagged by Eq. (3) are marked ***

Feature Rank	Feature name	Feature MDA rankings	Feature AV/SD for e1 Class	Feature AV/SD for non-e1 Class	Feature Value of tested sample	Sample Cohen Distance To e1 class	Sample Cohen Distance To non e1 class	K Nearest Neighbor ratio
1	TESPA1	18.8	363.5/266	3.9/29	601	0.89	20.6	60/60
2 ***	LINC00507	16.5	234/203	1.8/15	2	1.14	0.01	4/60
3 ***	SLC17A7	16.3	82.8/77	1.1/11	1	1.06	0.009	11/60
4 ***	LINC00508	12.8	97.4/108	0.6/4.8	1	0.89	0.08	31/60
5	KCNIP1	12.7	1.0/2.8	310.6/377	1	0	0.82	51/60

Acknowledgment. We are grateful to researchers from Huazhong University of Science and Technology, Wuhan, China for their prompt response to our inquiry for the COVID-19 data, and Dr. R. Scheuermann and B. Aevermann from JCVI for the data for our case study and their feedback. We are also grateful to Prof. Russ Altman, Stanford University, and Prof. Lester Kobzik (Harvard University) for their feedback and encouragement.

References

1. Szabo, L., Kaiser Health News: Artificial intelligence is rushing into patient care—and could raise risks. Sci. Am. 24 December 2019
2. Kaufman, S., Rosset, S., Perlich, C.: Leakage in data mining: formulation, detection, and avoidance. ACM Trans. Knowl. Discov. Data **6**(4), 1–21 (2012)
3. Dzindolet, M., Peterson, S., Pomranky, R., Pierce, L., Beck, H.: The role of trust in automation reliance. Int. J. Hum.-Comput. Stud. **58**(6), 697–718 (2003)
4. Holm, E.: In defense of black box. Science **364**(6435), 26–27 (2019)
5. Petkovic, D., Kobzik, L., Re, C.: Machine learning and deep analytics for biocomputing: call for better explainability. Pacific Symposium on Biocomputing Hawaii **23**, 623–627 (2018)
6. Petkovic, D., Kobzik, L., Ganaghan, R.: AI ethics and values in biomedicine – technical challenges and solutions. In: Pacific Symposium on Biocomputing, Hawaii, 3–7 January (2020)
7. Vellido, A., Martin-Guerrero, J., Lisboa, P.: Making machine learning models interpretable. European Symposium on Artificial Neural Networks, Computational Intelligence and Machine Learning; 25–27 April, Bruges, Belgium (2012)
8. Future of Life Institute: Asilomar AI Priciples. https://futureoflife.org/ai-principles/?cn-reloaded=1. Accessed 09 2020
9. Asociation of Computing machinery: Statement on Algorithmic Transparency and Accountability, 01 Dec 2017. https://www.acm.org/binaries/content/assets/public-policy/2017_usacm_statement_algorithms.pdf
10. OECD Principles on AI. https://www.oecd.org/going-digital/ai/principles/ Accessed 09 2020
11. Breiman, L.: Random forests. Mach. Learn. **45**(1), 5–32 (2001)

12. Petkovic, D., Altman, R., Wong, M., Vigil, A.: Improving the explainability of Random Forest classifier - user centered approach. Pacific Symposium on Biocomputing. **23**, 204–215 (2018)
13. L. Buturovic, M. Wong, G. Tang, R. Altman, D. Petkovic: "High precision prediction of functional sites in protein structures", PLoS ONE 9(3): e91240. https://doi.org/10.1371/jou rnal.pone.0091240
14. Okada, K., Flores, L., Wong, M., Petkovic, D.: Microenvironment-based protein function analysis by random forest. In: Proceedings of the ICPR (International Conference on Pattern Recognition), Stockholm (2014)
15. Yan, L., et al.: An Interpretable mortality prediction model for COVID-19 patients. Nature Mach. Intell. **2**, pp. 283–288 (2020)
16. Aevermann, B., et al.: Cell type discovery using single cell transcriptomics: implications for ontological representation. Hum. Mol. Gene. **27**(R1), R40–R47 (2018)
17. Aevermann, B., McCorrison, J., Venepally, P., et al.: Production of a preliminary quality control pipeline for single nuclei RNA-seq and its application in the analysis of cell type diversity of post-mortem human brain neocortex. In: Pacific Symposium on Biocomputing Proceedings, vol. 22, pp. 564–575, Hawaii, January 2017
18. Boldog, E., et al.: Transcriptomic and morphophysiological evidence for a specialized human cortical GABAergic cell type. Nat. Neurosci. 2018 **21**(9), 1185–1195. https://doi.org/10.1038/ s41593-018-0205-2. Epub 2018 Aug 27
19. Yang, J., Petkovic, D.: Application of Improved Random Forest Explainability (Rfex 2.0) on Data from JCV Institute LaJolla, California, SFSU CS Department TR 19.01, 16 June 2019. https://cs.sfsu.edu/sites/default/files/technical-reports/RFEX%202%20JCVI_Jizhou% 20Petkovic%20%2006-16-19_0.pdf
20. Alavi, A., Petkovic, D.: Improvements of Explainability of Random Forest Algorithms. SFSU CS Department TR TR 20.01, May 2020. https://cs.sfsu.edu/sites/default/files/technical-rep orts/Ali%20Alavi%20CER%20895%20RFEX%20May%202020.pdf
21. Olson, R.S., Cava, W., Mustahsan, Z., Varik, A., Moore, J.H.: Data-driven advice for applying machine learning to bioinformatics problems. Pac. Symp. Biocomput. **23**, 192–203 (2018)
22. Liaw, A., Wiener, M.: Classification and regression by random forest. R News 2(3), 18–22 (2002). http://CRAN.R-project.org/doc/Rnews/
23. Solla, F., Tran, A., Bertoncelli, D., Musoff, C., Bertoncelli, C.M.: Why a P-value is not enough. Clin Spine Surg. **31**(9), 385–388 (2018)
24. Barlaskar, S., Petkovic, D.: Applying Improved Random Forest Explainability (RFEX 2.0) on synthetic data. SFSU TR 18.01, 11/27/20181; with related toolkit at https://www.youtube. com/watch?v=neSVxbxxiCE

Jointly Optimize Positive and Negative Saliencies for Black Box Classifiers

Hyungsik Jung⬤, Youngrock Oh⬤, Jeonghyung Park⬤,
and Min Soo Kim(✉)⬤

AI Advanced Research Lab., Samsung SDS, Seoul 06765, South Korea
{hs89.jung,y52.oh,jeong.h.park,minsoo07.kim}@samsung.com

Abstract. Neural networks are increasingly applied to high-stakes tasks, such as autonomous driving and medical applications. For these tasks, it is important to explain the contributions of data components to a model prediction. In recent times, mask-based methods have been proposed for visual explanations. They optimize masks that maximally affect the model output. In this work, we propose a novel mask-based saliency method for given black box classifiers. We jointly optimize positive and negative masks to achieve a faithful feature importance map. To optimize them effectively, we define a distance between them in terms of the selected activation maps; the corresponding kernels express the important features of an input image. Then, we impose the distance to the objective function of each mask as a regularizer. By forcing both masks to be dissimilar in terms of the influential features, they can focus on essential parts of an object while alleviating noises.

Keywords: Saliency method · Visual explanation · Explainable AI

1 Introduction

As prediction performances of neural networks have been remarkably improved, they become popular in numerous areas including high-stakes tasks such as autonomous driving [9] and medical applications [3]. Accordingly, the needs for an appropriate explanation of a model prediction have also been increased to use neural network models responsibly. However, due to their black box characteristics and intrinsic complexity, it is difficult to clearly explain why they make a certain prediction.

A lot of *saliency methods* which provide pixel-based feature importance maps, *saliency maps*, have been proposed for visual explanations. They aim to find which pixels of an input image are responsible for a model output. Hence, a reliable saliency method gives a clue of understanding the inner behaviors of the given model, so it helps us to use the model result wisely (e.g. decision making to accept the prediction result or not).

Recently, mask-based methods (MBMs) [5,7,8,22] have been proposed for obtaining a saliency map. They learn a mask (i.e. a saliency map) by optimizing a model prediction with respect to the target class using gradient descent

A. Del Bimbo et al. (Eds.): ICPR 2020 Workshops, LNCS 12663, pp. 76–89, 2021.
https://doi.org/10.1007/978-3-030-68796-0_6

algorithms. There are two basic perspectives to learn a mask: *preservation* and *deletion* [8]. In the preservation, we search for the positive region that maximally activates the target class probability. On the other hand, in the deletion, we try to find the negative region that, when preserved, causes the target class probability to drop significantly. More specifically, the preservation perspective learns a positive saliency by finding out the positive pixels and the deletion perspective learns a negative saliency by detecting the non-negative pixels. These two viewpoints share the idea that the model output is sensitive to the changes of influential pixels.

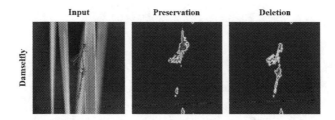

Fig. 1. Saliency maps from the preservation and the deletion. The two masks focus on different parts of the target object.

However, their saliency maps can be quite different for a given image as shown in Fig. 1. Since both perspectives produce meaningful saliency maps, we expect that appropriately combining them amounts to a reliable saliency map. An algorithm called *dual* is proposed from that point of view [5]. It calculates gradients from these perspectives simultaneously and simply adds them to update masks. However, we demonstrate that the gradients calculated from the preservation and deletion conflict with each other, so the compromised gradients in the dual perspective can be obscured in the optimization.

In this work, we propose a new perspective which integrates the preservation and the deletion masks effectively. The proposed saliency method, *joint mask method* (JMM), separately but jointly optimizes the two masks on the basis of MBMs. We separate them to be learned individually to prevent gradients from being ambiguous. Moreover, we encourage the two maps to be similar in the model's aspect; the distance between them is quantified in terms of activation maps, and is decreased by gradient descent algorithms. It helps to figure out essential features clearly. We compare JMM to the other perspectives of MBMs and other state-of-the-art saliency methods, qualitatively and quantitatively. It gives reliable visual explanations and shows better performances on several datasets [6,11,16].

2   Related Works

A saliency map can be calculated from various approaches. The following categories are literature reviews of the notable approaches for visual explanations.

2.1   Class Activation Map

Class activation map (CAM) based methods [4,13,17,23,25] linearly combine activation maps from a designated intermediate convolution layer to visualize a saliency map. Since the activation maps do not change with a fixed pair of a given model and an input image, weight coefficients of the activation maps govern the performance of CAM-based methods. Grad-CAM [17] determines the coefficients of the activation maps using the sum of gradients. Score-CAM [23] overlaps normalized activation maps to an input image and makes predictions to acquire the corresponding coefficients. CAM-based methods are fast and widely applicable to convolutional neural networks, but they are inadequate for generating fine-grained evidence and weak for detecting color dependency.

2.2   Backpropagation-Based Method

Backpropagation-based methods (BBMs) track partial derivatives of a target class output with respect to input pixels for computing a saliency map of a given image [1,18–21,24]. A gradient method [19] simply adopts an unmodified gradient map of an input as a saliency. DeconvNet [24] and Guided-backpropagation [21] are similar to the gradient method but have a difference in way of manipulating nonlinearities at rectified linear units (ReLUs). Since they need a single backward pass to obtain saliency maps, they are computationally efficient. Furthermore, they can provide fine-grained saliency maps unlike CAM-based methods. However, saliency maps generated by BBMs are relatively of low quality and noisy. Additionally, some BBMs [18,21] are fragile to sanity check [2].

2.3   Perturbation-Based Method

Perturbation-based methods (PBMs) focus on how the model prediction of a target class is influenced by distortion of input pixels [12,14,15]. It is based on the idea that if some pixels are responsible for the prediction result, the result will largely fluctuate when we perturb the pixels of interest. RISE [14] produces Bernoulli saliency samples and calculates softmax probabilities of the samples. Next, the probabilities are used to determine the importance of each sample. PBMs are intuitive and can provide fine-grained visualizations but are relatively time-consuming. Moreover, it is difficult to choose the proper regions to be perturbed. If we fail to select the proper regions, the resulting saliencies from PBMs can be noisy with capturing non-essential parts of the input.

2.4   Mask-Based Method

MBMs integrate the concepts of BBMs and PBMs [5,7,8,22]. They first generate a *perturbed image* $\Phi(x, M)$ from a given mask and an original image by:

$$\Phi(x, M) = x \otimes M + x' \otimes (\mathbf{1} - M) \tag{1}$$

where x is the original image and x' is a distorted version of x, respectively. Blurring, average coloring, and black-out are usually employed for distortion. $M : \Lambda \to [0,1]$ is a mask which presents an estimated saliency map where $\Lambda = \{1, \ldots, H\} \times \{1, \ldots, W\}$ is a discrete domain and $\mathbf{1}$ denotes the matrix of the same size with M of which every element is 1.

Each pixel of M, denoted by u, has a value of $M(u)$, which represents the feature importance of the pixel. The pixels with high values maintain the original information of the image. On the other hand, low-valued pixels would lose the information by distortion. Next, an output (i.e. a softmax probability in this work) of a given model f with respect to a target class k, $f_k(\Phi(x, M))$ is calculated using the perturbed image. Lastly, partial derivatives of the model output with respect to M are calculated to update M while freezing the parameters of f. By repeating forward propagation with the perturbed image and backpropagation toward the mask, we can learn meaningful perturbation for the given model and the input image.

MBMs provide reliable visual explanations. Besides, the algorithms automatically determine the pixels to be perturbed. Thus, we do not have to consider the regions of perturbation. However, since MBMs are sensitive to hyperparameters, they should be tuned adequately for a specific pair of a model and a dataset, to attain a faithful saliency map for the pair.

3 Joint Mask Method

In this research, we propose a novel perspective, JMM, for MBMs. It smartly integrates information from the preservation and deletion masks to generate a trustworthy saliency map. In the method, both masks are optimized considering the distance between them. The distance is decided in terms of the selected activation maps of the perturbed images to grasp important features from the model's view.

3.1 Baseline Works

Mask Method. Most of the MBMs are based on [8], which is the first work of suggesting a concept of learning a mask. The authors propose two basic perspectives, preservation and deletion, to learn the mask. The objective functions are given as follows:

$$L_{pre}(f_k, x, M) = \lambda_{l_1} \|M\|_1 + \lambda_{tv} \sum_{u \in \Lambda} \|\nabla M(u)\|_p^p - f_k(\Phi(x, M)) \qquad (2)$$

$$L_{del}(f_k, x, M) = \lambda_{l_1} \|M\|_1 + \lambda_{tv} \sum_{u \in \Lambda} \|\nabla M(u)\|_p^p + f_k(\Phi(x, \mathbf{1} - M)) \qquad (3)$$

where $L_{pre}(\cdot)$ and $L_{del}(\cdot)$ are objective functions of the preservation and deletion, respectively. λ_{l1} and λ_{tv} are weight coefficients of $l1$-norm and total variance regularizers, respectively. We set up $p = 3$ by default.

The preservation tries to find the minimal region which should be retained to increase $f_k(\Phi(x, M))$. On the other hand, the deletion perspective aims to find the smallest region which should be removed to minimize $f_k(\Phi(x, \mathbf{1} - M))$. Total variances of masks are considered in both algorithms to avoid trivial artifacts and reduce noises.

FGVis. Fine-grained visual explanation (FGVis) [22] focuses on preventing a model from artifacts. It kills gradients not to be backpropagated through the model when a perturbed image shows a larger activation value than an original image. In this work, the constraint is applied to all nonlinearities in convolution blocks. The gradient update rule for ReLU is implemented by:

$$\gamma_i^l = \bar{\gamma}_i^l \cdot \mathbf{1}_{[h_i^l(\Phi(x,M)) \leq h_i^l(x)]} \cdot \mathbf{1}_{[h_i^l(\Phi(x,M)) \geq 0]} \qquad (4)$$

where $\bar{\gamma}_i^l$ is the flowing gradient and γ_i^l is the resulting gradient of the i-th neuron in the l-th layer, respectively. $\mathbf{1}_{[\cdot]}$ means the indicator function and $h_i^l(\cdot)$ denotes the activation of the i-th neuron in the l-th layer.

In this work, we combine the above two works as a baseline for all perspectives of MBMs: the preservation, deletion, dual, and JMM. The mask is learned without downsampling for fine-grained explanations. Additionally, total variance and gradient clipping help to avoid learning trivial artifacts.

3.2 Deletion and Negative Saliency

This section describes one of the most important motivations of this work. *Why should we sync positive pixels from the preservation and non-negative pixels from the deletion?* Here is the answer; learning a deletion mask is identical to learning a negative saliency. Assume that we learn a negative mask which suppresses the probability of the target class k. The objective function of the saliency can be formulated by:

$$L_{neg}(f_k, x, M^-) = \lambda_{l_1} \|\mathbf{1} - M^-\|_1 + \lambda_{tv} \sum_{u \in \Lambda} \|\nabla M^-(u)\|_p^p + f_k(\Phi(x, M^-)) \qquad (5)$$

where M^- is the negative mask which gives a clue for the target probability suppression; high-valued pixels of M^- are factors of decreasing the probability. It finds out the maximal region that negatively contributes to the model prediction.

However, it turns out that optimizing (3) and (5) are identical. Since total variances of M^- and $\mathbf{1} - M^-$ are the same, we have:

$$\operatorname*{argmin}_{M^-} L_{neg}(f_k, x, M^-) = \operatorname*{argmin}_{M^-} L_{del}(f_k, x, \mathbf{1} - M^-)$$

$$= \mathbf{1} - \operatorname*{argmin}_{M} L_{del}(f_k, x, M). \qquad (6)$$

Thus, if we minimize the distance between the preservation and deletion masks through optimization, it is equivalent to maximizing the distance between positive and negative saliencies. From this point of view, it is clear that synchronizing the two masks is advantageous for obtaining a more dependable map.

3.3   Integration of Preservation and Deletion Masks

The Problem of Dual. Dual and the proposed JMM utilize the information from the two different perspectives in common. However, there is a difference in the way of using the information. The dual mask can be achieved through the optimization of the following objective function:

$$L_{dual}(f_k, x, M) = \lambda_{l_1} \|M\|_1 + \lambda_{tv} \sum_{u \in \Lambda} \|\nabla M(u)\|_p^p$$
$$- f_k(\Phi(x, M)) + f_k(\Phi(x, 1 - M)). \tag{7}$$

Since the algorithm considers positive and negative saliencies simultaneously to calculate gradients, the gradients can be obscured.

Figure 2a shows a visualized example of gradient maps. For a given input image x (column 1), column 2 and 3 present $\frac{\partial\{-f_k(\Phi(x,M))\}}{\partial M}$ and $\frac{\partial\{f_k(\Phi(x,1-M))\}}{\partial M}$, respectively. They are normalized from -1 to 1 range for visualization, but the signs of the gradients are maintained. The last column shows a gradient-deviation map, which highlights the pixels of opposite gradient signs (i.e. $\frac{\partial\{-f_k(\Phi(x,M))\}}{\partial M}(u) \times \frac{\partial\{f_k(\Phi(x,1-M))\}}{\partial M}(u) < 0$) in white color. If the signs of gradients from the two are different at some pixels, the simply added gradients of the dual probably lose the useful information.

Figure 2b presents a general trend of gradient obscuring. It displays the ratios of gradient-deviation pixels during the optimization process of the dual. We analyze 500 randomly sampled images from ImageNet 2012 validation dataset [16] to quantify the ratios. The ratios are consistently high (close to 0.5) throughout the iterations. Consequently, the dual fails to integrate the information from the preservation and deletion effectively due to gradient obscuration.

Distance Between the Selected Activation Maps. We propose JMM which detaches the learning processes of the preservation and deletion masks. By separating those, JMM helps positive and negative saliencies to be learned in the right direction. For implementation, we separate an optimizer of each mask. Then we add the distance between the two masks to the objective functions of gradient descent algorithms. The objective functions of the preservation and the deletion are revised as follows:

$$L'_{pre}(f_k, x, M_{pre}) = L_{pre}(f_k, x, M_{pre}) + \lambda_d D(M_{pre}, M_{del}), \tag{8}$$

$$L'_{del}(f_k, x, M_{del}) = L_{del}(f_k, x, M_{del}) + \lambda_d D(M_{pre}, M_{del}) \tag{9}$$

where $D(\cdot)$ is the distance measure between the saliencies and λ_d is the weight coefficient of the distance.

Next, we define a distance between the two masks in terms of the selected activation maps from the perturbed images. As a result, the distance is determined in view of the model, not in view of human eyes (i.e. not pixel-based).

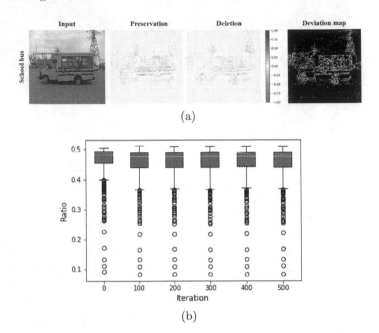

(a)

(b)

Fig. 2. Gradient obscuration in the dual: (a) Example of gradient maps from the preservation and the deletion and the gradient deviation map. (b) The ratios of the pixels where the signs of gradients from the two perspectives are different.

Since kernels of convolutional layers can be indicators for the existence of features, we define a feature-based distance measure as below:

$$D(M_{pre}, M_{del}) = \left\| \frac{A^l_{\tilde{K},pre} - A^l_{\tilde{K},del}}{C} \right\|_p \tag{10}$$

where $\tilde{K}$ is a subset of the whole kernels in l-th layer. Let $A^l_{\kappa}(x)$ represent an activation map of x for a kernel κ and $A^l_{\tilde{K},ori}$ denote the vector obtained by concatenating $\{A^l_{\kappa}(x)\}_{\kappa \in \tilde{K}}$. Correspondingly, $A^l_{\tilde{K},pre}$ and $A^l_{\tilde{K},del}$ indicate $\{A^l_{\kappa}(\Phi(x, M_{pre}))\}_{\kappa \in \tilde{K}}$ and $\{A^l_{\kappa}(\Phi(x, M_{del}))\}_{\kappa \in \tilde{K}}$, respectively. The activation difference is normalized by C, which is an average value of $A^l_{\tilde{K},ori}$.

We select only a few kernels of which activation maps have high standard deviations in the original image. The selection ratio is set to 0.1 by default. By the procedure, the defined distance can only focus on essential features which contribute to the target class probability of the original image. Furthermore, by defining the distance as lp-norm with high p (5 by default), we can enforce regions of activation maps with large differences to have priority of being updated.

Figure 3 demonstrates the effects of defining the distance with respect to the activation maps, not pixels. We can recognize the two superiorities of JMM compared to the dual and pixel-based joint. First, JMM finds out the object more clearly (row 1). Second, it can remove pixel noises (row 2). From the results, we can infer that JMM provides feature-focused saliency maps.

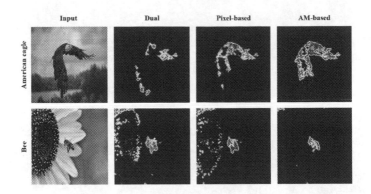

Fig. 3. Saliency maps from the dual, pixel-based joint (jointly optimized with the pixel-level distance), and activation map-based joint (JMM). Note that JMM detects an object of interest precisely (upper figure) and alleviates noises (lower figure).

Implementation Details. At the beginning of the optimization, each mask is learned without considering the distance. This warm-up step helps to extract information from each perspective to some extent. In addition, after optimization, either the preservation or the deletion mask is selected for the final mask based on the softmax score of the mask, $S(M)$, which is defined as follows:

$$S(M) = f_k(\phi(x, M)) + \{1 - f_k(\phi(x, \mathbf{1} - M))\}. \tag{11}$$

Since a faithful saliency map is expected to have high $f_k(\phi(x, M))$ and low $f_k(\phi(x, \mathbf{1}-M))$, this score is reasonable and fair in that the goals of the both perspectives are considered concurrently. The overall procedure of JMM is wrapped up by Algorithm 1. N means the maximum number of iterations and r denotes the ratio for warm-up. N and r are set to 500 and 0.2 by default, respectively.

4   Experiments

Since this work is focused on suggesting a novel perspective of MBMs, we first validate the superiority of JMM over the other perspectives; the preservation, deletion, and dual. Next, we compare JMM with other state-of-the-art saliency methods to verify the competitiveness of JMM. Qualitative and Quantitative analyses are conducted on both experiments.

For all MBMs, we utilize the Adam [10] optimizer with learning rate $\gamma = 0.1$ and median blur perturbation is used for image distortion. For fair comparison among MBMs, we equally set up λ_{l_1} and λ_{tv} for each architecture and dataset pair. λ_d is fixed to 0.05 for all cases.

Algorithm 1. Joint Mask Method

Initialize M_{pre} and M_{del}.
For given f, k, x,
for $i = 0, ..., N - 1$ do
    STEP1. Generate the preservation and deletion perturbed images using (1).
    STEP2. Calculate the preservation and deletion objective functions without considering the distance (i.e. $L(f_k, x, M_{pre})$ and $L(f_k, x, M_{del})$) using (2) and (3), respectively.
    if $i < r \times N$ then
        Goto **STEP5**
    end if
    STEP3. Measure the activation distance, $D(M_{pre}, M_{del})$ with (10).
    STEP4. Recalculate the preservation and deletion objective functions considering the distance (i.e. $L^{'}(f_k, x, M_{pre})$ and $L^{'}(f_k, x, M_{del})$) using (8) and (9), respectively.
    STEP5. Update M_{pre} and M_{del}.
end for
$$M_{JMM} = \underset{M}{\mathrm{argmax}} \left(S(M_{pre}), S(M_{del}) \right)$$

4.1   Comparison with the Other Perspectives

Qualitative Comparison. Figure 4 shows the comparison results among mask-based saliency maps from various perspectives. To identify which perspectives can pinpoint the important features of an object, we select two classes which have distinguishable features from the others; *Pelican* has a large beak and *Siamese cat* has a black face. In both images, JMM shows better results compared to the other perspectives. The preservation provides faint saliencies and cannot recognize the essential parts apparently. The saliency maps from the deletion and dual fail to highlight important features. Contrary to the others, JMM focuses on the prominent features excluding non-essential parts of the objects while alleviating noises.

Reliability Evaluation. We quantify reliability of each perspective using the softmax score $S(M)$ defined by (11) (i.e. the softmax probabilities of perturbed images). By the score, we can verify whether a saliency method can actually figure out the important parts of an image which are responsible for the classification result. Table 1 shows the average scores of the perspectives for COCO[11] and VOC[6]. Randomly sampled images (500 for each dataset) are analyzed to calculate the score. The VGG16 network is used for the experiment with the following parameters: $\lambda_{l_1} = 0.01$ and $\lambda_{tv} = 1.0$.

As shown in Table 1, JMM outperforms all perspectives in both datasets by meaningful margins. It is worthwhile to note that the scores of JMM are beyond those of dual despite direct optimization of the score in dual; the dual maximizes $f_k(\Phi(x, M)) - f_k(\Phi(x, 1 - M))$ as shown in (7). Specifically, contrary to

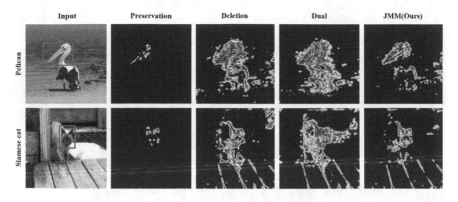

Fig. 4. Comparison with the other MBMs. The VGG16 trained on ImageNet [16] is used for visualization. A bounding box of each image highlights the important features of the target class; a large beak for *Pelican* and a black face for *Siamese cat.*

the negligible drops in $f_k(\phi(x, M))$, JMM provides remarkably enhanced results in terms of $f_k(\phi(x, 1 - M))$ compared to the dual perspective.

Table 1. The average softmax probabilities of the perturbed images and the resulting softmax score. Higher is better for $f_k(\phi(x, M))$ and $S(M)$; Lower is better for $f_k(\phi(x, 1 - M))$.

	COCO				VOC			
	Pre	Del	Dual	JMM	Pre	Del	Dual	JMM
$f_k(\phi(x, M))$	0.913	0.766	0.920	0.918	0.989	0.841	0.992	0.981
$f_k(\phi(x, 1 - M))$	0.474	0.090	0.168	0.114	0.720	0.148	0.249	0.159
$S(M)$	1.439	1.676	1.752	**1.804**	1.269	1.693	1.743	**1.822**

4.2   Comparison with Other Saliency Methods

Qualitative Comparison. Figure 5 presents examples of saliency maps from various saliency methods. The gradient method gives noisy saliency maps in general and fails to highlight the objects in some cases (Zebra and Jeep). Grad-CAM and Score-CAM find out the approximate locations of the objects, but they cannot provide fine-grained saliency maps. Furthermore, they fail to explain a Snorkel example. RISE cannot provide reliable saliency maps since it captures trivial parts of the input images. The vanilla FGVis shows fine-grained but noisy saliencies. Compared to the other methods, JMM provides clear, fine-grained, and stable visual explanations. Sometimes, JMM shows that only a part of objects can be essential features (Mushroom, Zebra, Dragonfly, and Jeep), as already shown in Fig. 4.

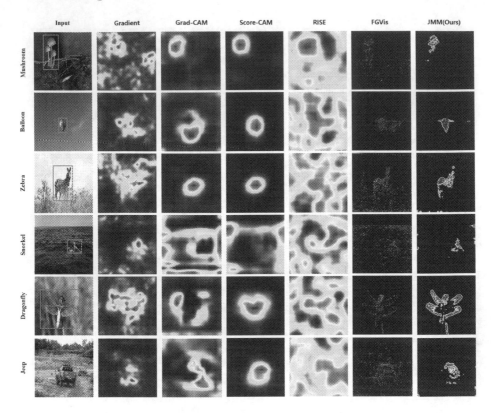

Fig. 5. Comparison with other saliency methods. The VGG16 trained on ImageNet is used for visualization. A bounding box of each input image indicates the whole object of the target class.

Localization Evaluation. It is reasonable to expect that a saliency map overlaps with a target object. However, it is not clear that which part of the object should be covered by the saliency map. For example, if the model classifies an image as *"lion"*, only a part of lion (e.g. a lion's mane) may be essential for the prediction. In other words, a saliency does not necessarily contain the entire object. Therefore, we evaluate localization of saliency methods on VOC segmentation dataset [6] by calculating the area precision P which is defined by:

$$P = \frac{|A_{obj} \cap SL_\tau| + 0.5 \cdot |A_{bd} \cap SL_\tau|}{|SL_\tau|}. \tag{12}$$

Note that each example image in the dataset has pixel-level labels: "background" or "object" or "boundary". In (12), A_{obj} and A_{bd} are the sets of pixels labeled by "object" and "boundary", respectively. $SL_\tau = \{u \in \Lambda : SL(u) > \tau\}$ for the min-max normalized saliency map SL. τ is set to 0.5. We use ResNet50 and set $\lambda_{l_1} = 0.1$ and $\lambda_{tv} = 2.0$ for MBMs.

Table 2 shows that JMM outperforms other saliency methods. From the result, we reason that JMM produces a compact saliency map which focuses on the essential high-level features of the image without noises.

Table 2. Area precision for segmentation of saliency methods.

	Gradient	Grad-CAM	Grad-CAM++	Score-CAM	RISE	FGVis	Dual	Joint
Precision	0.467	0.653	0.552	0.534	0.503	0.563	0.667	**0.722**

4.3 Sanity Check

A reliable saliency method should be dependent on both the model and data; this dependency on a pair of the model and data is defined as *sanity* in [2]. However, some saliency methods do not satisfy the sanity even if they seem to provide visually plausible explanations. To check the sanity of JMM, we refer to the model parameter randomization test which is performed in [2]. In Fig. 6, saliency maps from the trained model and the randomly initialized models are compared. The randomizations are implemented from top to bottom layers.

The trained model before randomization pinpoints the wine-containing part of a glass. However, the models after randomization cannot find the essential part which induces the image to be classified as *red wine*. Since the changes in model parameters cause the changes in classification results, red wine is a misclassified label from the standpoint of the after-randomization models. In other words, by Fig. 6, we prove not only the sanity of JMM, but also the superiority of JMM in terms of preventing trivial artifacts from being captured in a saliency map.

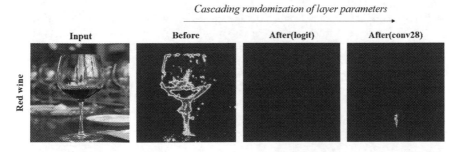

Fig. 6. Sanity check for JMM. The VGG16 trained on ImageNet is analyzed for the test. The following columns are results of JMM with respect to *red wine* class, before and after parameter randomization from top to bottom layers, respectively. Note that after randomization, JMM cannot detect the object.

5   Conclusions

In this work, we propose a novel mask-based saliency method, JMM, which jointly optimizes the preservation and deletion masks with a distance regularizer. The distance between the two masks is defined in terms of activation maps of the perturbed images. It helps the masks to be similar with regard to the essential features.

JMM provides a preferable saliency map compared to various state-of-the-art saliency methods. JMM clearly identifies a region of interest by providing feature-compacted saliency maps. We prove the superiority of JMM quantitatively as well. It gives a higher softmax score than those of the preservation, deletion, and even dual. In addition, JMM presents the highest area precision for the VOC segmentation task.

References

1. Adebayo, J., Gilmer, J., Goodfellow, I., Kim, B.: Local explanation methods for deep neural networks lack sensitivity to parameter values (2018)
2. Adebayo, J., Gilmer, J., Muelly, M., Goodfellow, I., Hardt, M., Kim, B.: Sanity checks for saliency maps. In: Advances in Neural Information Processing Systems, pp. 9505–9515 (2018)
3. Caruana, R., Lou, Y., Gehrke, J., Koch, P., Sturm, M., Elhadad, N.: Intelligible models for healthcare: Predicting pneumonia risk and hospital 30-day readmission. In: Proceedings of the 21th ACM SIGKDD International Conference on Knowledge Discovery and Data Mining, pp. 1721–1730 (2015)
4. Chattopadhay, A., Sarkar, A., Howlader, P., Balasubramanian, V.N.: Grad-cam++: generalized gradient-based visual explanations for deep convolutional networks. In: 2018 IEEE Winter Conference on Applications of Computer Vision (WACV), pp. 839–847 (2018)
5. Dabkowski, P., Gal, Y.: Real time image saliency for black box classifiers. In: Advances in Neural Information Processing Systems, pp. 6967–6976 (2017)
6. Everingham, M., Van Gool, L., Williams, C.K., Winn, J., Zisserman, A.: The pascal visual object classes (VOC) challenge. Int. J. Comput. Vision $88(2)$, 303–338 (2010)
7. Fong, R., Patrick, M., Vedaldi, A.: Understanding deep networks via extremal perturbations and smooth masks. In: Proceedings of the IEEE/CVF International Conference on Computer Vision (ICCV), October 2019
8. Fong, R.C., Vedaldi, A.: Interpretable explanations of black boxes by meaningful perturbation. In: Proceedings of the IEEE International Conference on Computer Vision (ICCV), October 2017
9. Kim, J., Canny, J.: Interpretable learning for self-driving cars by visualizing causal attention. In: Proceedings of the IEEE International Conference on Computer Vision (ICCV), October 2017
10. Kingma, D.P., Ba, J.: Adam: a method for stochastic optimization (2017)
11. Lin, T.-Y., Maire, M., Belongie, S., Hays, J., Perona, P., Ramanan, D., Dollár, P., Zitnick, C.L.: Microsoft COCO: common objects in context. In: Fleet, D., Pajdla, T., Schiele, B., Tuytelaars, T. (eds.) ECCV 2014. LNCS, vol. 8693, pp. 740–755. Springer, Cham (2014). https://doi.org/10.1007/978-3-319-10602-1_48

12. Lundberg, S.M., Lee, S.I.: A unified approach to interpreting model predictions. In: Advances in Neural Information Processing Systems, pp. 4765–4774 (2017)
13. Omeiza, D., Speakman, S., Cintas, C., Weldermariam, K.: Smooth grad-cam++: an enhanced inference level visualization technique for deep convolutional neural network models (2019)
14. Petsiuk, V., Das, A., Saenko, K.: Rise: Randomized input sampling for explanation of black-box models. In: BMVC (2018)
15. Ribeiro, M.T., Singh, S., Guestrin, C.: Why should i trust you?: explaining the predictions of any classifier. In: Proceedings of the 22nd ACM SIGKDD International Conference on Knowledge Discovery and Data Mining, pp. 1135–1144. ACM (2016)
16. Russakovsky, O., Deng, J., Su, H., Krause, J., Satheesh, S., Ma, S., Huang, Z., Karpathy, A., Khosla, A., Bernstein, M., et al.: Imagenet large scale visual recognition challenge. Int. J. Comput. Vision **115**(3), 211–252 (2015)
17. Selvaraju, R.R., Cogswell, M., Das, A., Vedantam, R., Parikh, D., Batra, D.: Grad-cam: visual explanations from deep networks via gradient-based localization. In: Proceedings of the IEEE International Conference on Computer Vision (ICCV), October 2017
18. Shrikumar, A., Greenside, P., Shcherbina, A., Kundaje, A.: Not just a black box: Learning important features through propagating activation differences. arXiv preprint arXiv: 1605.01713 (2016)
19. Simonyan, K., Vedaldi, A., Zisserman, A.: Deep inside convolutional networks: Visualising image classification models and saliency maps (2014)
20. Smilkov, D., Thorat, N., Kim, B., Viégas, F., Wattenberg, M.: Smoothgrad: removing noise by adding noise (2017)
21. Springenberg, J., Dosovitskiy, A., Brox, T., Riedmiller, M.: Striving for simplicity: The all convolutional net. In: ICLR (Workshop Track) (2015)
22. Wagner, J., Kohler, J.M., Gindele, T., Hetzel, L., Wiedemer, J.T., Behnke, S.: Interpretable and fine-grained visual explanations for convolutional neural networks. In: Proceedings of the IEEE/CVF Conference on Computer Vision and Pattern Recognition (CVPR), June 2019
23. Wang, H., et al.: Score-cam: Score-weighted visual explanations for convolutional neural networks. In: Proceedings of the IEEE/CVF Conference on Computer Vision and Pattern Recognition (CVPR) Workshops, June 2020
24. Zeiler, M.D., Fergus, R.: Visualizing and understanding convolutional networks. In: Fleet, D., Pajdla, T., Schiele, B., Tuytelaars, T. (eds.) ECCV 2014. LNCS, vol. 8689, pp. 818–833. Springer, Cham (2014). https://doi.org/10.1007/978-3-319-10590-1_53
25. Zhou, B., Khosla, A., Lapedriza, A., Oliva, A., Torralba, A.: Learning deep features for discriminative localization. In: Proceedings of the IEEE Conference on Computer Vision and Pattern Recognition (CVPR), June 2016

Low Dimensional Visual Attributes: An Interpretable Image Encoding

Pengkai Zhu[✉], Ruizhao Zhu, Samarth Mishra, and Venkatesh Saligrama

Boston University, Boston, MA 02215, USA
{zpk,rzhu,samarthm,srv}@bu.edu

Abstract. Deep convolutional networks (DCNs) as black-boxes make many computer vision models hard to interpret. In this paper, we present an interpretable encoding for images that represents the objects as a composition of parts and the parts themselves as a mixture of learned prototypes. We found that this representation is well suited for low-label image recognition problems such as few-shot learning (FSL), zero-shot learning (ZSL) and domain adaptation (DA). Our image encoding model with simple task predictors performs favorably against state of the art approaches in each of these tasks. Via crowdsourced results, we also show that this image encoding using parts and prototypes is interpretable to humans and agrees with their visual perception.

Keywords: Interpretable deep learning · Zero-shot learning · Few-shot learning · Domain adaptation

1 Introduction

Automated object recognition in images saw a dramatic boost in performance with deep convolutional networks (DCNs). On the large Imagenet [35] image classification dataset, an Alexnet [17] DCN improved top-1 accuracy by about 10% on the prior best method. However, in a range of subsequent research it became apparent that these DCNs require large quantities of data to generalize or to have good predictions on unseen images.

Complex recognition tasks may require a more complex model and hence more data for generalization, going by any theory of learning [20]. However, learning to recognize complex objects as a composition of simpler parts can help learn them without a corresponding combinatorially large training set. This is possibly how humans navigate a range of complex learning problems with sparse data, and a possible approach for dealing with automated recognition problems with a scarcity of labeled training images [30,34].

DCNs with their large parameter sets are also hard to interpret. It is desirable, but hard, to say why a DCN predicted a certain class for a certain image just by looking at the model's outputs at any intermediate layer. An added advantage of a compositional learning model is that its predictions can be probed to find the parts of a complex object it identified.

A. Del Bimbo et al. (Eds.): ICPR 2020 Workshops, LNCS 12663, pp. 90–102, 2021.
https://doi.org/10.1007/978-3-030-68796-0_7

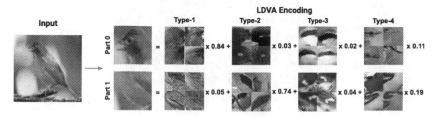

Fig. 1. Our model learns to encode each image using its salient parts and the closeness of each part to certain learned prototypes

In this paper, we present a method, previously introduced in [60], that learns to identify parts in a complex object from its image. It also learns a set of different "prototypes" for these parts, thus encoding an object using its parts and the closeness of these parts to learned prototypes. We refer to this encoding as the Low Dimensional Visual Attributes (LDVA) of an image. Figure 1 illustrates this with a possible encoding our model outputs for an image of a bird.

We evaluate our model that learns to encode images as LDVA in 3 different label-deficient learning problems: Few Shot Learning (FSL) [47], Visual Domain Adaptation (DA) [49] and Zero Shot Learning (ZSL) [1] and found that it performs comparable to state of the art on each of these problems. This indicates that LDVA are closer to semantic attributes (*e.g.* in zero-shot learning datasets) than regular DCN features and are robust to domain shift. They also have a high ratio of inter-class to intra-class variance, making them label-efficient and thus effective in learning with few labeled examples in few shot learning.

Adding to the contributions of [60], we also show that our model's encodings are human interpretable. We do this by crowdsourcing responses to questions regarding the parts and prototypes learned by the model. These responses show that the parts learned by our model are discriminative, the prototypes learned are diverse and the similarity predictions made by the model between parts and prototypes agree with common human perception of visual similarity.

2   Related Work

Label-Limited Image Recognition: Most existing approaches to the label-limited image recognition tasks of few-shot learning, visual domain adaptation or zero-shot learning, can be broadly categorized into three groups: *generative-model based methods*, *feature-space learning methods* and *meta-learning methods*. Generative-model based methods focus on synthesizing new images or features to circumvent the limited availability of labeled data [18,23,57]. Feature-space learning methods attempt to learn a universally generalizable, domain invariant feature space to counteract the limited availability of labels. Deep metric learning [25], visual embedding for zero-shot learning [11,29] and domain alignment [24,50,55] are exemplar works. Finally meta-learning or *learning-to-learn* methods train by learning to adapt to multiple synthetically generated low-label recognition tasks from a label-rich set of images. Meta-learning approaches include learning a "meta-network" that outputs parameters for a network that learns recognition from few labelled images [52] or semantic task descriptions [51] or learning a good initialization for fast-adaptation to a target task [8,26]. Meta-learning has also been used for learning to generalize across multiple visual domains [22].

Interpretable Image Recognition: There are a class of prior work that focus on post-hoc interpretability of deep networks via activation maximization [6,39] and saliency visualization [38,41]. These methods try to discover via visualizations the parts of an input image that a model is most sensitive to and hence that may play a major role in the model's prediction. Another class of methods tries to build in attention based interpretability into DCNs. For instance, Zheng *et al.* [58] proposed a multi-attention convolution network to extract discriminative regions for fine-grained image classification. Chen *et al.* [3] proposed a model that learns prototypical representation for categories, classifying an image according to its similarity to prototypes.

Interpretability in Label-Limited Learning: For label-limited learning, interpretable representations have been explored in prior work, with the motivation that these may distill the salient image features making them domain invariant and generalizable with few labeled examples. For zero-shot learning, Zhu *et al.* [61] proposed to localize attributes by learning semantic-guided attentions, while [16] applied a dense attention module to extract the attention features for all attributes, so as to align the semantic attributes. In order to bridge the gap between the visual and semantic spaces, Zhu *et al.* [59] proposed a multi-part encoder and represented the object as a mixture of visual elements. [43] extensively investigated the benefits of attribute locality and compositionality in the context of zero-shot learning from scratch. For few-shot learning, Tang *et al.* [45] attempted to represent novel objects by the appearance of semantic parts, and Hou *et al.* [13] proposed to use cross-attention networks to discover the most discriminative regions in a transductive setting. Although these approaches address the label-limited tasks in a partially interpretable manner, they fail to provide extensive evidence for the interpretability of the proposed representations. In contrast, we extensively evaluate the interpretability of our model through human interactions via crowdsourcing.

3 Low Dimensional Visual Attributes

The proposed model consists of a cascade of three modules: a part-feature extractor, a part probability encoder and a task specific predictor. The part feature decoder is only used during training and is not a part of the model at inference time. The overall structure of our model is illustrated in Fig. 2. The model is

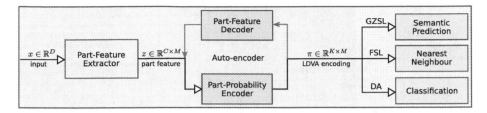

Fig. 2. The proposed network architecture. The part feature extractor decomposes an input image x into M parts and extracts associated features z_m, the part-probability encoder then encodes each part feature as a low-dimensional encoding π_m by projecting the features onto a dictionary of prototypical part types automatically discovered by our model. π_m is then used as inputs to train task-specific predictor models for GZSL, FSL and DA.

end-to-end trainable with a weighted sum of loss functions involving the three different modules.

Part-Feature Extractor. This module is implemented as a multi-attention convolutional neural network (MACNN) [58]. It takes the input of an image x and produces a finite set of part features $z_m(x)$ (where m indexes the different parts) through spatial pooling [60]. The features are encouraged to be diverse and discriminative via respective losses. For full details, refer to Sect. 3.3 of [60].

Part-Probability Encoder. This module uses the high-dimensional part features $z_m(x)$ and for each part, learns K prototypes. These serve as atoms in a dictionary learned for the part features, *i.e.*, the features themselves can be represented as a linear combination of the atoms. The coefficient of each atom represents a probability that the part belongs to the category defined by that particular prototype. The part-feature decoder module (see Fig. 2) only comes into picture for learning this dictionary representation while training. We again refer readers to Section 3.3 of [60] for details.

Task Specific Predictors. For each of the different label-limited recognition tasks, a different task-specific "head" is used, as described in Sect. 4

4   Label-Limited Classification Evaluation

We evaluated the effectiveness of our proposed method on three label-limited classification tasks. For complete details, we refer readers to [60].

Table 1. FSL results on Omniglot and *mini*ImageNet.

Methods	Omniglot		*mini*ImageNet	
	5-way Acc.		5-way Acc.	
	1-shot	5-shot	1-shot	5-shot
Meta Nets [31]	99.0	–	49.2	–
MAML [8]	98.7	**99.9**	48.7	63.1
Proto Nets [40]	98.8	99.7	49.4	68.2
Rel^n Nets [42]	**99.6**	99.8	50.4	65.3
TADAM [33]	–	–	58.5	76.7
LEO [36]	–	–	61.7	77.6
EA-FSL [56]	–	–	**62.6**	78.4
Ours	98.9	99.8	61.7	**78.7**

Table 2. DA classification results.

Methods	M → U	U → M	S → M
CoGAN [28]	91.2	89.1	–
ADDA [46]	89.4	90.1	76.0
DTN [44]	–	–	84.4
UNIT [27]	96.0	93.6	90.5
CyCADA [12]	95.6	96.5	90.4
MSTN [54]	92.9	–	91.7
Self-ensembling [9]	**98.3**	**99.5**	**99.3**
Ours (source π)	94.8	96.1	82.4
Ours (joint π)	**98.8**	96.8	**95.2**

Table 3. GZSL results on CUB, AWA2 and aPY. ts = test classes (unseen classes), tr = train classes (seen classes), H = harmonical mean. The accuracy is class-average Top-1 in %. The highest two accuracies are in **bold face**.

Methods	CUB			AWA2			aPY		
	ts	tr	H	ts	tr	H	ts	tr	H
DEVISE [10]	23.8	53.0	32.8	17.1	74.7	27.8	4.9	76.9	9.2
PSRZSL [2]	24.6	54.3	33.9	20.7	73.8	32.3	13.5	51.4	21.4
SP-AEN [4]	34.7	70.6	46.6	23.3	**90.9**	37.1	13.7	63.4	22.6
GDAN [14]	39.3	66.7	49.5	32.1	67.5	43.5	**30.4**	75.0	**43.4**
CADA-VAE [37]	51.6	53.5	52.4	**55.8**	75.0	**63.9**	–	–	–
SE-GZSL [19]	41.5	53.3	46.7	**58.3**	68.1	62.8	–	–	–
LSD [5]	**53.1**	59.4	**56.1**	–	–	–	22.4	**81.3**	35.1
Ours	33.4	**87.5**	48.4	41.6	**91.3**	57.2	24.5	72.0	36.6
Ours + CS	**59.2**	**74.6**	**66.0**	54.6	87.7	**67.3**	**41.1**	68.0	**51.2**

Few Shot Learning. A learner in this task is required to classify a certain number of test images given K training examples for each of N classes in an "N-way K-shot episode". The task-specific predictor for this task is trained for classification using cross-entropy loss on the base set of classes, and the final classification is done using a nearest-neighbor classifier for a few shot episode. We evaluate on the hand-written character dataset Omniglot [20] and *mini*ImageNet [47].

Unsupervised Visual Domain Adaptation. A learner is required to recognize images in a target domain, while being only given labels for images in a different source domain. We evaluate two variants of our model: (i) The *source-π*

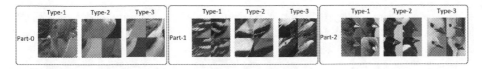

Fig. 3. Example of prototypes in each part on CUB dataset (best viewed in color). (Color figure online)

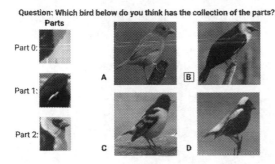

Fig. 4. Exemplar question for discriminability. The workers are asked to select the class they think has the parts provided on the left side. If none of the given classes applies, they should select "None of above". The ground truth class is B in this example which is bounded by a box (Best viewed in color). (Color figure online)

Table 4. Selected classes of CUB for crowd-sourcing. *: the selected unseen classes.

No.	Class
0	Yellow_headed_Blackbird*
1	Bobolink
2	Indigo_Bunting
3	Painted_Bunting*
4	Vermilion_Flycatcher
5	American_Goldfinch
6	Baltimore_Oriole
7	Tree_Swallow
8	Summer_Tanager
9	Prothonotary_Warbler

model trains the task specific head for classification only on the source domain labeled images, while (ii) the *joint-π* model also uses pseudo-labels generated by the source-π model on the target-domain unlabeled images. For evaluation on this task, we use three digit-image datasets: MNIST [21], USPS [15] and SVHN [32].

Generalized Zero Shot Learning. Here, a learner is evaluated for recognizing images from both classes that it sees during training and ones it does not. The learner can leverage certain semantic attributes (typically encoded as a vector) of classes to learn to recognize classes that it has not seen during training. The head for this task, trains to maximize the dot product between the LDVA of images and the semantic attributes of the class to which the image belongs, using a maximum margin loss. Finally classification is done using the LDVA dot products with semantic attributes as scores, and labeling an image as the class with the highest score. The protocol for evaluation follows [53], and we report performance on three datasets: CUB [48], AWA2 [53] and aPY [7].

In Tables 1, 2, and 3, we can see that our model performs favorably compared to state of the art methods on different tasks. Since the model uses very simple task-specific heads, this highlights that the proposed LDVA are discriminative in feature space, are close to semantic attributes and are domain invariant. Their low dimensionality makes them suitable for generalizing with few labelled images.

5   Interpretability

5.1   Learned Part and Prototypes

In Fig. 3, we show examples of parts and prototypes learned by our model on the CUB dataset of bird images. The examples representing a prototype are selected via nearest neighbor search around the prototype's representation.

We observe that our models learns to detect different semantic parts. Part-0 in Fig. 3 localizes the bird's breast, Part-1 the wing/body and Part-2 locates the head. We also note here that examples within a prototype are visually similar while across prototypes they are quite distinct.

5.2   Crowd-Sourced Experiments

To further evaluate whether humans can "interpret" the learned prototypes and encodings, we curate crowd sourced results via Amazon Mechanical Turk (MTurk). We designed three questions to measure different aspects of the interpretability for our model: 1) *Discriminability of parts*: Are the parts discriminative enough for humans to recognize the class? 2) *Prototype recognition*: Can humans recognize the prototypes for parts of a certain image? 3) *Part-type probability prediction*: Do humans agree with the part-type probability scores output by the model?

For the purpose of this section, we select a subset containing 10 classes of the CUB dataset. The classes are listed in Table 4. Each class has around 60 images. To simulate the FSL and ZSL scenarios where the novel classes have no samples during training, we held out two as unseen classes, and train our model on the remaining 8. The model has 3 parts and the number of prototypes in each part is set to 5. After the model is trained, the 3 parts located by our model are cropped from the original images for all classes. In each part, we select 5 examples to represent each prototype through nearest neighbor search in the seen classes.

We use these prototypes and examples to create the assignments in MTurk. Each assignment is answered by 5 different turkers. The questions and results are detailed below:

Discriminability of Parts. This question provides turkers with a collection of 3 parts identified by our model and asks them to select the class which those parts belong to. An exemplar question is shown in Fig. 4. The turker can choose one class out of four options or "None of the above". The intent of this question is to ascertain whether humans find the parts discriminative enough to distinguish between different categories. For this question we used 502 examples in total from all the 10 classes. We use the majority response of the 5 workers as the final answer for each image and consider the image to be "correct" if the final answer

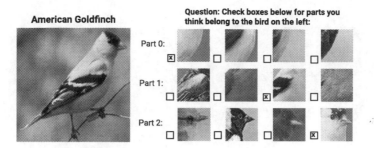

Fig. 5. Exemplar question for Prototype recognition. Turkers are asked to pick the prototypes they think belong to the given image on the left. The ground truth is marked with an 'x' in its box (best viewed in color). (Color figure online)

is the same as the ground truth class. The accuracy we obtained for all examples is 94.2%, which indicates a high probability that humans can distinguish the bird using only the parts discovered by our model. Note that our model was only trained on the 8 seen classes, but it still produced discriminative parts for the novel classes, demonstrating that the parts learned are generalizable.

Prototype Recognition. This question provides workers with an image from one of the seen classes and a set of prototypical examples for the each part. The workers are asked to choose the prototype in each part that they think belongs to the bird in the given image, as shown in Fig. 5. The question is intended to determine if humans can learn to recognize images using the prototypes learned by our model. Good accuracy would demonstrate that the prototypes are diverse and representative of different classes. We used 406 examples from seen classes for this question and in each part we also use the majority vote of the 5 answers for computing accuracy. In the experiment, the provided prototypical examples are selected based on their class instead of just the prototype since prototypes are shared between different classes and a single example may not represent the prototype. The answer is considered correct if it belongs to the same prototype as the ground truth. The accuracy for the three parts are 92.96%, 95.73%, and 96.98%, respectively, validating that humans can learn to recognize images as a collection of prototypes learned by our model.

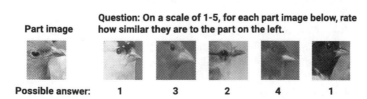

Fig. 6. Exemplar question for part-type probability prediction. Turkers are asked to choose a score for the similarity between the given part and the prototype. 1 means least and 5 means most similar (best viewed in color). (Color figure online)

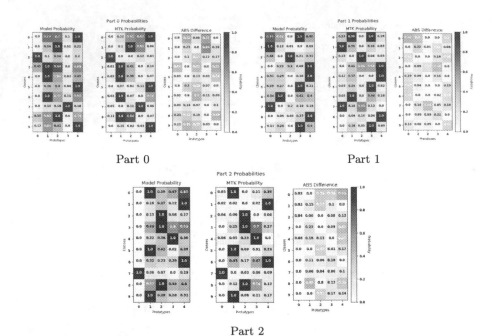

Part 0   Part 1

Part 2

Fig. 7. The class probability scores from our model (left) and the Mturk workers (middle), and their absolute difference (right).

Part-Type Probability Prediction. In this question, turkers are provided with a part example and a list of all prototypes for the same part. Turkers are asked to rate the probability on a scale of 1 to 5, 1 being least possible, that the given example belongs to a particular prototype, as shown in Fig. 6. We used 502 images from all classes per part for this experiment. For each of the 3 parts, in order to obtain the class probability score, we average the scores provided by turkers over all images belonging to a certain category. As a comparison, we also average the LDVA encoding from our model for each category. The class probability scores of the workers, our model, and their absolute differences, are visualized in Fig. 7a, b and c for the three parts, respectively. For better visualization, the probability scores are linearly scaled to lie in the range $[0, 1]$. The results confirm that human annotators largely agree with the probability that our model assigns for a part in an image belonging to a given part-type represented by prototypes. This holds true for scores from classes 0 and 3 as well, which are not seen during training. Thus the model's perception of visual similarity agrees with those of humans and this perception generalized to unseen images.

6 Conclusion

We presented an interpretable image encoding method: low dimensional visual attributes, which learns images as a group of salient parts, and represents those parts as a mixture of learned part-prototypes. This image representation is amenable to label-limited image recognition tasks like few-shot learning, zero-shot learning and domain adaptation and we found our simple unified model compares favorably to state of the art methods in these tasks. Finally, via extensive crowd sourced results, we also demonstrated that the proposed encoding is naturally interpretable by humans.

References

1. Akata, Z., Perronnin, F., Harchaoui, Z., Schmid, C.: Label-embedding for attribute-based classification. In: Proceedings of the IEEE Conference on Computer Vision and Pattern Recognition, pp. 819–826 (2013)
2. Annadani, Y., Biswas, S.: Preserving semantic relations for zero-shot learning. In: The IEEE Conference on Computer Vision and Pattern Recognition (CVPR), June 2018
3. Chen, C., Li, O., Tao, D., Barnett, A., Rudin, C., Su, J.K.: This looks like that: deep learning for interpretable image recognition. In: Advances in Neural Information Processing Systems, pp. 8930–8941 (2019)
4. Chen, L., Zhang, H., Xiao, J., Liu, W., Chang, S.F.: Zero-shot visual recognition using semantics-preserving adversarial embedding network. In: Proceedings of the IEEE Conference on Computer Vision and Pattern Recognition, vol. 2 (2018)
5. Dong, H., Fu, Y., Sigal, L., Hwang, S.J., Jiang, Y.G., Xue, X.: Learning to separate domains in generalized zero-shot and open set learning: a probabilistic perspective. arXiv preprint arXiv:1810.07368 (2018)
6. Erhan, D., Bengio, Y., Courville, A., Vincent, P.: Visualizing higher-layer features of a deep network. University of Montreal 1341, no. 3, p. 1 (2009)
7. Farhadi, A., Endres, I., Hoiem, D., Forsyth, D.: Describing objects by their attributes. In: IEEE Conference on Computer Vision and Pattern Recognition, CVPR 2009, pp. 1778–1785. IEEE (2009)
8. Finn, C., Abbeel, P., Levine, S.: Model-agnostic meta-learning for fast adaptation of deep networks. arXiv preprint arXiv:1703.03400 (2017)
9. French, G., Mackiewicz, M., Fisher, M.: Self-ensembling for visual domain adaptation. arXiv preprint arXiv:1706.05208 (2017)
10. Frome, A., Corrado, G.S., Shlens, J., Bengio, S., Dean, J., Mikolov, T., et al.: DeViSE: a deep visual-semantic embedding model. In: Advances in Neural Information Processing Systems, pp. 2121–2129 (2013)
11. Han, Z., Fu, Z., Yang, J.: Learning the redundancy-free features for generalized zero-shot object recognition. In: IEEE/CVF Conference on Computer Vision and Pattern Recognition (CVPR), June 2020
12. Hoffman, J., et al.: CyCADA: cycle-consistent adversarial domain adaptation. arXiv preprint arXiv:1711.03213 (2017)
13. Hou, R., Chang, H., Bingpeng, M., Shan, S., Chen, X.: Cross attention network for few-shot classification. In: Advances in Neural Information Processing Systems, pp. 4003–4014 (2019)

14. Huang, H., Wang, C., Yu, P.S., Wang, C.D.: Generative dual adversarial network for generalized zero-shot learning. In: Proceedings of the IEEE Conference on Computer Vision and Pattern Recognition, pp. 801–810 (2019)
15. Hull, J.J.: A database for handwritten text recognition research. IEEE Trans. Pattern Anal. Mach. Intell. **16**(5), 550–554 (1994)
16. Huynh, D., Elhamifar, E.: Fine-grained generalized zero-shot learning via dense attribute-based attention. In: Proceedings of the IEEE/CVF Conference on Computer Vision and Pattern Recognition, pp. 4483–4493 (2020)
17. Krizhevsky, A., Sutskever, I., Hinton, G.E.: ImageNet classification with deep convolutional neural networks. In: Advances in Neural Information Processing Systems, pp. 1097–1105 (2012)
18. Kumar Verma, V., Arora, G., Mishra, A., Rai, P.: Generalized zero-shot learning via synthesized examples. In: Proceedings of the IEEE Conference on Computer Vision and Pattern Recognition, pp. 4281–4289 (2018)
19. Kumar Verma, V., Arora, G., Mishra, A., Rai, P.: Generalized zero-shot learning via synthesized examples. In: The IEEE Conference on Computer Vision and Pattern Recognition (CVPR), June 2018
20. Lake, B.M., Salakhutdinov, R., Tenenbaum, J.B.: Human-level concept learning through probabilistic program induction. Science **350**(6266), 1332–1338 (2015)
21. LeCun, Y., Bottou, L., Bengio, Y., Haffner, P.: Gradient-based learning applied to document recognition. Proc. IEEE **86**(11), 2278–2324 (1998)
22. Li, D., Yang, Y., Song, Y.Z., Hospedales, T.M.: Learning to generalize: meta-learning for domain generalization. In: Thirty-Second AAAI Conference on Artificial Intelligence (2018)
23. Li, K., Zhang, Y., Li, K., Fu, Y.: Adversarial feature hallucination networks for few-shot learning. In: IEEE/CVF Conference on Computer Vision and Pattern Recognition (CVPR), June 2020
24. Li, M., Zhai, Y.M., Luo, Y.W., Ge, P.F., Ren, C.X.: Enhanced transport distance for unsupervised domain adaptation. In: IEEE/CVF Conference on Computer Vision and Pattern Recognition (CVPR), June 2020
25. Li, W., Xu, J., Huo, J., Wang, L., Gao, Y., Luo, J.: Distribution consistency based covariance metric networks for few-shot learning. In: Proceedings of the AAAI Conference on Artificial Intelligence, vol. 33, pp. 8642–8649 (2019)
26. Liu, B., Kang, H., Li, H., Hua, G., Vasconcelos, N.: Few-shot open-set recognition using meta-learning. In: IEEE/CVF Conference on Computer Vision and Pattern Recognition (CVPR), June 2020
27. Liu, M.Y., Breuel, T., Kautz, J.: Unsupervised image-to-image translation networks. In: Advances in Neural Information Processing Systems, pp. 700–708 (2017)
28. Liu, M.Y., Tuzel, O.: Coupled generative adversarial networks. In: Advances in Neural Information Processing Systems, pp. 469–477 (2016)
29. Liu, S., Chen, J., Pan, L., Ngo, C.W., Chua, T.S., Jiang, Y.G.: Hyperbolic visual embedding learning for zero-shot recognition. In: IEEE/CVF Conference on Computer Vision and Pattern Recognition (CVPR), June 2020
30. Misra, I., Gupta, A., Hebert, M.: From red wine to red tomato: composition with context. In: Proceedings of the IEEE Conference on Computer Vision and Pattern Recognition, pp. 1792–1801 (2017)
31. Munkhdalai, T., Yu, H.: Meta networks. arXiv preprint arXiv:1703.00837 (2017)
32. Netzer, Y., Wang, T., Coates, A., Bissacco, A., Wu, B., Ng, A.Y.: Reading digits in natural images with unsupervised feature learning. In: NIPS Workshop on Deep Learning and Unsupervised Feature Learning, vol. 2011, p. 5 (2011)

33. Oreshkin, B., López, P.R., Lacoste, A.: TADAM: task dependent adaptive metric for improved few-shot learning. In: Advances in Neural Information Processing Systems, pp. 721–731 (2018)
34. Purushwalkam, S., Nickel, M., Gupta, A., Ranzato, M.: Task-driven modular networks for zero-shot compositional learning. In: Proceedings of the IEEE International Conference on Computer Vision, pp. 3593–3602 (2019)
35. Russakovsky, O., et al.: ImageNet large scale visual recognition challenge (2014)
36. Rusu, A.A., et al.: Meta-learning with latent embedding optimization. arXiv preprint arXiv:1807.05960 (2018)
37. Schonfeld, E., Ebrahimi, S., Sinha, S., Darrell, T., Akata, Z.: Generalized zero-and few-shot learning via aligned variational autoencoders. In: Proceedings of the IEEE Conference on Computer Vision and Pattern Recognition, pp. 8247–8255 (2019)
38. Selvaraju, R.R., Cogswell, M., Das, A., Vedantam, R., Parikh, D., Batra, D.: Grad-CAM: visual explanations from deep networks via gradient-based localization. In: Proceedings of the IEEE International Conference on Computer Vision, pp. 618–626 (2017)
39. Simonyan, K., Vedaldi, A., Zisserman, A.: Deep inside convolutional networks: visualising image classification models and saliency maps. arXiv preprint arXiv:1312.6034 (2013)
40. Snell, J., Swersky, K., Zemel, R.: Prototypical networks for few-shot learning. In: Advances in Neural Information Processing Systems, pp. 4077–4087 (2017)
41. Sundararajan, M., Taly, A., Yan, Q.: Axiomatic attribution for deep networks. arXiv preprint arXiv:1703.01365 (2017)
42. Sung, F., Yang, Y., Zhang, L., Xiang, T., Torr, P.H., Hospedales, T.M.: Learning to compare: relation network for few-shot learning. In: Proceedings of the IEEE Conference on Computer Vision and Pattern Recognition, pp. 1199–1208 (2018)
43. Sylvain, T., Petrini, L., Hjelm, D.: Locality and compositionality in zero-shot learning. arXiv preprint arXiv:1912.12179 (2019)
44. Taigman, Y., Polyak, A., Wolf, L.: Unsupervised cross-domain image generation. arXiv preprint arXiv:1611.02200 (2016)
45. Tang, L., Wertheimer, D., Hariharan, B.: Revisiting pose-normalization for fine-grained few-shot recognition. In: Proceedings of the IEEE/CVF Conference on Computer Vision and Pattern Recognition, pp. 14352–14361 (2020)
46. Tzeng, E., Hoffman, J., Saenko, K., Darrell, T.: Adversarial discriminative domain adaptation. In: Computer Vision and Pattern Recognition (CVPR), vol. 1, p. 4 (2017)
47. Vinyals, O., Blundell, C., Lillicrap, T., Wierstra, D., et al.: Matching networks for one shot learning. In: Advances in Neural Information Processing Systems, pp. 3630–3638 (2016)
48. Wah, C., Branson, S., Welinder, P., Perona, P., Belongie, S.: The Caltech-UCSD birds-200-2011 dataset. Technical report (2011)
49. Wang, M., Deng, W.: Deep visual domain adaptation: a survey. Neurocomputing **312**, 135–153 (2018)
50. Wang, S., Chen, X., Wang, Y., Long, M., Wang, J.: Progressive adversarial networks for fine-grained domain adaptation. In: IEEE/CVF Conference on Computer Vision and Pattern Recognition (CVPR), June 2020
51. Wang, X., Yu, F., Wang, R., Darrell, T., Gonzalez, J.E.: TAFE-Net: task-aware feature embeddings for low shot learning. In: Proceedings of the IEEE Conference on Computer Vision and Pattern Recognition, pp. 1831–1840 (2019)

52. Wang, Y.-X., Hebert, M.: Learning to learn: model regression networks for easy small sample learning. In: Leibe, B., Matas, J., Sebe, N., Welling, M. (eds.) ECCV 2016. LNCS, vol. 9910, pp. 616–634. Springer, Cham (2016). https://doi.org/10.1007/978-3-319-46466-4_37

53. Chen, L., Zhang, H., Xiao, J., Liu, W., Chang, S.F.: Zero-shot visual recognition using semantics-preserving adversarial embedding network. In: Proceedings of the IEEE Conference on Computer Vision and Pattern Recognition, vol. 2 (2018)

54. Xie, S., Zheng, Z., Chen, L., Chen, C.: Learning semantic representations for unsupervised domain adaptation. In: International Conference on Machine Learning, pp. 5419–5428 (2018)

55. Xu, R., Liu, P., Wang, L., Chen, C., Wang, J.: Reliable weighted optimal transport for unsupervised domain adaptation. In: IEEE/CVF Conference on Computer Vision and Pattern Recognition (CVPR), June 2020

56. Ye, H.J., Hu, H., Zhan, D.C., Sha, F.: Learning embedding adaptation for few-shot learning. arXiv preprint arXiv:1812.03664 (2018)

57. Yu, Y., Ji, Z., Han, J., Zhang, Z.: Episode-based prototype generating network for zero-shot learning. In: IEEE/CVF Conference on Computer Vision and Pattern Recognition (CVPR), June 2020

58. Zheng, H., Fu, J., Mei, T., Luo, J.: Learning multi-attention convolutional neural network for fine-grained image recognition. In: International Conference on Computer Vision, vol. 6 (2017)

59. Zhu, P., Wang, H., Saligrama, V.: Generalized zero-shot recognition based on visually semantic embedding. In: Proceedings of the IEEE Conference on Computer Vision and Pattern Recognition, pp. 2995–3003 (2019)

60. Zhu, P., Wang, H., Saligrama, V.: Learning classifiers for target domain with limited or no labels. In: International Conference on Machine Learning, pp. 7643–7653 (2019)

61. Zhu, Y., Xie, J., Tang, Z., Peng, X., Elgammal, A.: Semantic-guided multi-attention localization for zero-shot learning. In: Advances in Neural Information Processing Systems, pp. 14943–14953 (2019)

Explainable 3D-CNN for Multiple Sclerosis Patients Stratification

Federica Cruciani[1]([envelope]) [iD], Lorenza Brusini[1] [iD], Mauro Zucchelli[2] [iD],
Gustavo Retuci Pinheiro[3] [iD], Francesco Setti[1] [iD], Ilaria Boscolo Galazzo[1] [iD],
Rachid Deriche[2] [iD], Leticia Rittner[3] [iD], Massimiliano Calabrese[4] [iD],
and Gloria Menegaz[1] [iD]

[1] Department of Computer Science, University of Verona, Verona, Italy
{federica.cruciani,lorenza.brusini,francesco.setti,
ilaria.boscologalazzo,gloria.menegaz}@univr.it
[2] Athena Project-Team, Inria Sophia Antipolis-Méditerranée,
Université Côte d'Azur, Nice, France
{mauro.zucchelli,rachid.deriche}@inria.fr
[3] MICLab, School of Electrical and Computer Engineering (FEEC), UNICAMP,
Campinas, Brazil
{gustavorp,lrittner}@dca.fee.unicamp.br
[4] Department of Neurosciences, Biomedicine and Movement, University of Verona,
Verona, Italy
massimiliano.calabreseg@univr.it

Abstract. The growing availability of novel interpretation techniques opened the way to the application of deep learning models in the clinical field, including neuroimaging, where their use is still largely underexploited. In this framework, we focus the stratification of Multiple Sclerosis (MS) patients in the Primary Progressive versus the Relapsing-Remitting state of the disease using a 3D Convolutional Neural Network trained on structural MRI data. Within this task, the application of Layer-wise Relevance Propagation visualization allowed detecting the voxels of the input data mostly involved in the classification decision, potentially bringing to light brain regions which might reveal disease state.

Keywords: 3D-CNN · LRP · MS stratification

1 Introduction

Convolutional Neural Networks (CNNs) recently gained popularity thanks to their ability in solving complex classification tasks. Especially in the last few years, they are starting to be employed to address clinical questions related to Multiple Sclerosis (MS) patients stratification based on Magnetic Resonance Imaging (MRI) data. Besides the availability of big data, one of the main bottlenecks for the use of these techniques for medical purposes is that they are notoriously hard to interpret in retrospect. This is a bottleneck that cannot be

© Springer Nature Switzerland AG 2021
A. Del Bimbo et al. (Eds.): ICPR 2020 Workshops, LNCS 12663, pp. 103–114, 2021.
https://doi.org/10.1007/978-3-030-68796-0_8

overlooked in diagnostics and treatment monitoring. In this respect, deep learning methods, including CNNs, are often criticised for being non-transparent and are still considered as "black boxes". Therefore, the availability of a means for interpreting the network decisions becomes the key element for their exploitability.

Many recent studies aimed at overcoming this limitation proposing visualization strategies. In particular, these techniques enhance the method explanaibility by highlighting, through feature visualization, characteristics of the input that strongly influence the output of the CNN. Among the available ones, the most common are briefly summarized hereafter. Backpropagation methods highlight relevant pixels by propagating the network output back to the input image space [3, 30, 36, 37] while Perturbation-based methods visualize feature relevance by comparing the CNN output with respect to an input and a modified copy of the input [42, 43]. An extensive review of the state of the art of visualization methods can be found in [41].

Among the backpropagation methods, we consider the Layerwise Relevance Propagation (LRP) as the most promising for MRI-based classification tasks. It was originally presented in [3] and then applied to visualize the most relevant features influencing CNNs decisions in [5, 11] in MRI based classification problems. There are two main reasons behind our preference. First, LRP provides a heatmap for each subject indicating the relevance of each voxel for the final classification decision, which is fundamental in the framework of precision medicine where personalized treatment is pursued. Second, LRP heatmaps have proven to be more eloquent than those returned by other backpropagation methods [5]. For example, the maps derived from guided backpropagation [39] reflect the areas of the input that are more susceptible to changes, but these might not overlap with the areas on which the CNN based the decision. Conversely, LRP returns the image-specific relevance overcoming such a limitation.

In this context, MS patients stratification would highly benefit from the employment of such a technique since the mechanisms driving the pathology are still largely unknown. The MS disease affects brain and the spinal cord and can appear with physical and cognitive disability [9, 33]. Among the identified MS phenotypes, Relapsing-Remitting (RRMS) and Progressive Multiple Sclerosis (PPMS) are the most known forms [19, 24]. The sooner the clinician can distinguish between them the sooner the patient's specific treatment can be devised [24, 27]. Demyelination and atrophy could be found in either forms but structure and patterns vary quantitatively and qualitatively [17]. This suggests that the differentiation is driven by different mechanisms [25, 33], and it has been hypothesized that the distinction may be related to the appearance of lesions in the Grey Matter (GM) since its impairment has been found associated with the early onset of the pathology [6, 8].

Some studies aimed at MS stages stratification grounding on classical statistics and white matter derived features [10, 29], while several MRI studies confirmed the GM involvement hypothesis detecting both demyelination and atrophy in cortical and deep GM structures [6, 7, 23, 31]. We could find only another work on the stratification of MS patients [28] grounding on CNNs. In particular, Marzullo *et al.* [28] combined CNN and graph metrics derived from diffusion MRI data acquisitions.

To the best of our knowledge, no attempts have still been made for exploiting 3D-CNNs and LRP visualization in the PPMS versus RRMS patients stratification task using only GM features derived from MRI. LRP maps can potentially provide hints for the interpretation of the mechanisms at the basis of the MS disease course, besides the primary classification task, opening new perspectives for diagnosis, prognosis and treatment. To achieve this aim, we propose a 3D-CNN model trained using T1-weighted (T1-w) images, with LRP heatmaps generated for every subject.

2 Materials and Methods

2.1 Population, Data Acquisition and Image Processing

The population consisted of 91 subjects, including 46 RRMS (35 females, 52.5 $\pm$ 10.4 years old) and 45 PPMS (25 females, 47.2 $\pm$ 9.5 years old) patients. Expanded Disability Status Scale (EDSS) score was 2.8 $\pm$ 1.4 and 4.8 $\pm$ 1.3 for the two groups, respectively. Group differences in age and EDSS score were tested through t-test, while differences in gender numerosity were evaluated through χ^2 test.

MRI acquisitions were performed on a 3T Philips Achieva scanner (Philips Medical Systems, the Netherlands) equipped with an 8-channel head coil. The following sequences were used for all patients: 1) 3D T1-w Fast Field Echo (TR/TE = 8.1/3 ms, FA = 8°, FOV = 240 $\times$ 240 mm^2, 1 mm isotropic resolution, 180 slices); 2) 3D Fluid-Attenuated Inversion Recovery (FLAIR) image (TR/TE = 8000/290 ms, TI = 2356 ms, flip angle = 90°, FOV = 256 $\times$ 256 mm^2, 0.9 $\times$ 0.9 $\times$ 0.5 mm^3 resolution, 180 slices). All patients were recruited in our centre according to their diagnosis based on the McDonald 2010 diagnostic criteria. The study was approved by the local ethics committee, and informed consent was obtained from all patients. All procedures were performed in accordance with the Declaration of Helsinki (2008).

For each subject, the FLAIR was linearly registered to the T1-w (FSL flirt tool) and the Lesion Prediction Algorithm [35] was used to automatically segment and fill the WM lesions in the native T1-w image. Each filled T1-w image was then imported in the FreeSurfer software [13] to perform a complete brain parcellation with 112 anatomical ROIs. The binary mask representing the GM tissue probability thresholded at 95% was derived for each subject (FSL fast tool) and applied to all the filled T1-w.

2.2 Network Architecture

The architecture chosen for our 3D-CNN was a VGG net [38]. This model has been used in combination with MRI data in few recent studies [5,22,34], and

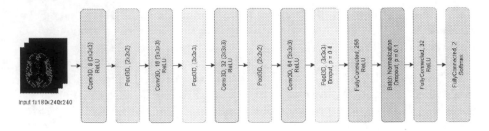

Fig. 1. 3D CNN architecture with single channel T1-w input.

it has been demonstrated to achieve comparable accuracy with respect to a ResNet model [16] in distinguishing AD patients from healthy controls [22]. The advantage of the VGG model is to easily allow the application of visualization methods such as LRP.

The structure implemented in this work consists of four volumetric convolutional blocks for feature extraction, two deconvolutional layers with batch normalization, and one output layer with *softmax* nonlinearity. More in detail, each convolutional block consists of a convolutional layer followed by *ReLU*, batch normalization and 3D pooling. A graphical representation of the 3D-CNN structure highlighting the main parameters for each layer is provided in Fig. 1.

2.3   Training, Validation and Testing

Data augmentation was performed during the training/validation phase in order to improve the generalization capabilities of our models. In detail, the data augmentation consisted of: addition of random Gaussian noise ($\mu = 0$, $\sigma = 0.1$); random affine transformation from -5 to $+5°$ in the Z axis, and from -3 to $+3°$ in the X axis; random volume translation from -3 to $+3$ voxels along each of the three axis; flipping across the X axis. In addition, clipping of the values to the 99th percentile was performed.

The CNN was trained using a 5-fold cross validation (5-fold CV) strategy over a training/validation set of 71 subjects. On each fold, the 71 subjects were randomly split in five groups, each of 14 subjects (except one of 15 subjects). The experiment was repeated five times and, for each repetition, four groups were considered as training and the remaining one was kept unseen for validation. The cross-entropy loss was optimized by means of the Adam optimizer [21] during the training phase. Twenty subjects were kept unseen and considered as testing set. In detail, the five models derived from fold of the 5-fold CV, were used to perform the prediction over the test set, and the performance metrics where computed for each of them. The test subjects did not undergo the data augmentation transformations.

In this work, true positives (TPs) and true negatives (TNs) represent the number of correctly classified PPMS and RRMS subjects, respectively. The CNN performance was reported, averaged over the five models, in terms of accuracy, sensitivity and specificity, while precision for each class was defined

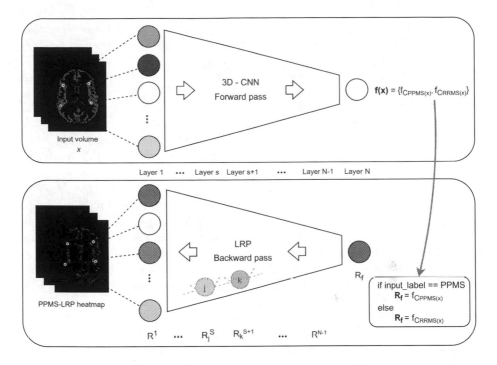

Fig. 2. Overview of LRP visualization procedure.

as precision$_{PPMS}$ = TP/(TP + FP) and precision$_{RRMS}$ = TN/(TN + FN). The whole deep learning analysis was carried out using Pytorch [32]. The computation was performed on a laptop (Ubuntu 18.6, Nvidia Geforce GTX 1050, Intel Core i7, 16 GB RAM). Torchsample wrapper was used as high-level interface.

2.4   CNN Visualization

LRP visualization was employed to identify which voxels in the input volume contributed most to the classification output. This technique is based on a backward procedure which is a conservative relevance redistribution of the output prediction probability through the CNN layers till the input volume.

The core rule of the LRP backward procedure is the relevance conservation per layer as illustrated in Fig. 2. Let s and $s + 1$ be two successive layers of the network and j and k two "neurons" of those layers, respectively. The relevance of the neuron k for the prediction $f(x)$, where x is the input, can be written as R_k^{s+1}. This relevance is redistributed to the connected "neurons" in layer s trough the following equation:

$$\sum_j R_{j \leftarrow k}^s = R_k^{s+1} \tag{1}$$

The iteration of Eq. 1 through all the CNN layers allows the decomposition of the relevance of prediction function $f(x)$, R_f, in terms of the input in the first layer.

Multiple rules can be applied for the distribution of the relevance [30]. In this work we used the β-rule [3,4], setting $\beta = 0$, hence allowing only positive contribution to the relevance score, following [5] where they demonstrated the LRP robustness relatively to the β-value. Higher β-values decompose the relevance in positive and negative contribution, the latter usually considered when dealing with patients controls classification task, not object of this study. In this work, the classification aim of differentiating two groups of patients led to the computation not only of the TPs (PPMS) related LRPs, but also the TNs (RRMS) related ones by computing the so called *winning class LRP*. In fact, to obtain LRP maps, a target class has to be defined and the resulting maps are strongly related to such class. In this work, since the two classes share the same importance, the backward procedure starts, for each subject, from the highest relative prediction probability present in the prediction function $f(x)$ (hence, there is not a fixed target class). In this way, widening the definition of LRPs given in [5] for AD, the resulting winning class LRPs will answer to two questions: (i) '*What speaks for PPMS in this subject?*', for the subjects predicted as PPMS, (ii) '*What speaks for RRMS in this subject?*' for the subjects predicted as RRMS. To compute LRP maps the iNNvestigate library [2] was used.

2.5 LRP Heatmaps Analysis

The LRP heatmaps were generated for each subject of the test set, based on the best model (in terms of accuracy) among the five derived from the 5-fold CV. After, they were registered to the standard MNI space (voxel size = 1 mm) and averaged over the two groups of patients, for visualization purposes.

Fifteen brain Regions of Interest (ROIs) were selected based on MS literature [7,12,15,18]: thalamus (Thal), caudate (Cau), putamen (Put), hippocampus (Hipp), insular cortex (Ins), temporal gyrus (TpG), superior frontal gyrus (SFG), cingulate gyrus (CnG), lateral occipital cortex (LOC), pericalcarine (PCN), lingual gyrus (LgG), cerebellum (Cer), temporal pole (TP), pallidum (Pall) and parahippocampal gyrus (PHG). The reference atlas was the Desikan-Killany available in FreeSurfer tool.

The average of the LRP derived relevance values for the 15 ROIs was computed across the correctly classified subjects of the test set.

Finally, as explorative analysis, we investigated the LRP neurological plausibility, following [11] and [5]. The Spearman correlation between the average LRP relevance for each ROI and the EDSS score was calculated together with the corresponding p-value.

3   Results

A preliminary analysis revealed that the EDSS score and the age were significantly different between RRMS and PPMS subjects ($p < 0.05$). The same held with gender numerosity ($p < 0.05$), this last observation reflecting the epidemiology of the disease.

The proposed T1-CNN achieved an average accuracy equals to 0.84 ± 0.10 over the five models derived from the 5-fold CV, one for each fold. The sensitivity and specificity were 0.74 ± 0.24 and 0.94 ± 0.08, showing that the CNN minimized the FPs, that are the wrongly classified RRMS subjects. The trend was confirmed by the precision$_{RRMS}$ which was 0.82 ± 0.14 while the precision$_{PPMS}$ was 0.94 ± 0.14.

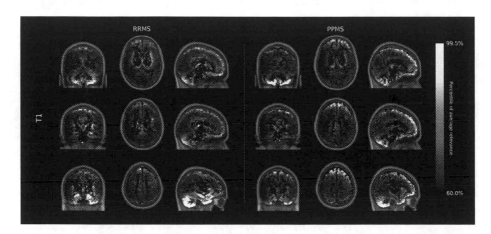

Fig. 3. LRP heatmaps obtained from the T1-CNN model. The heatmaps are shown for both RRMS and PPMS patients, and are overlaid to the MNI152 template in coronal, sagittal and axial views (columns). Each LRP map is averaged across the correctly classified RRMS and correctly classified PPMS subjects of the test set, respectively. The reported values are clipped to the range 60th–99.5^{th} percentile, calculated over the RRMS and the PPMS class group mean heatmaps.

Figure 3 shows the group LRP heatmaps, averaged over the correctly classified subjects of the test set for each class. For ease of visualization, the maps are clipped between the 60th and the 99.5^{th} percentile calculated over the respective LRP target group heatmap. As expected, considering how winning class LRP maps were calculated, high relevance was found in both PPMS and RRMS classes. Even if a widespread relevance values were present in both classes, the pattern was slightly different. In fact, the RRMS derived LRP map showed high activation in the temporal cortex and cerebellum, particularly evident in the coronal and sagittal views, respectively. On the contrary, the PPMS derived LRP map showed low relevance in the temporal lobe, while high relevance was assigned to the frontal lobe as can be observed in the sagittal view.

ROI-based analysis was performed to quantitatively assess the relevant areas for the classification task, as a first step towards the clinical validation of the outcomes. Figure 4 illustrates the size-normalized importance metrics for the correctly classified patients of the test set, separately for the two classes.

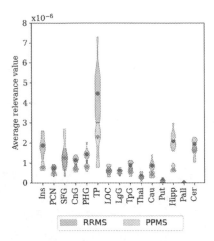

Fig. 4. Size-normalized importance metric extracted from the LRP maps. The mean relevance value for each ROI is reported for all the correctly classified PPMS and RRMS subjects in the test set. The median relevance for PPMS (orange circle) and RRMS (blue circle) groups are also shown. (Color figure online)

As previously stated for the qualitative analysis of the LRP maps, the temporal pole showed the highest relevance for both classes, as well as the highest distance between the medians, followed by the hippocampus, which moreover presents the highest gap between the two distributions. Other relevant ROIs were the insula and the cerebellum, the former showing higher distance between the medians of the distributions. The other considered ROIs showed lower relevance values and overlapped distributions, particularly evident for the superior frontal gyrus.

Finally the results of the Spearman correlation analysis between the ROIs mean relevance values and the EDSS scores are reported in Table 1. Significant negative correlations were detected for the parahippocampal gyrus, the temporal gyrus, and the hippocampus (p-value < 0.05), showing a ρ value of -0.59, -0.52, and -0.50, respectively. On the contrary, a slightly positive correlation with $\rho = 0.47$ could be found for the superior frontal gyrus.

4   Discussion

In this work we addressed the stratification problem between RRMS and PPMS subjects based on T1-w data. A 3D-CNN was proposed to this aim, and the LRP visualization technique was applied in order to highlight which are the key brain regions for correctly classifying the two patient populations. Finally, the outcomes were strengthen through a Spearman correlation between the mean relevance for each ROI and the individual EDSS scores. Distinguishing PPMS from RRMS based on GM features is one of the current challenges in MS research [26], and the identification of a biomarker allowing to capture the differences between PPMS and RRMS patients is hence one of the major challenges of personalized medicine [20].

Table 1. Spearman correlation results between the mean relevance for each ROI and the EDSS score.

	Ins	PCN	SFG	CnG	PHG
ρ	−0.42	0.16	**0.47**	−0.16	**−0.59**
p-value	0.08	0.51	**0.05**	0.53	**0.01**
	TP	LOC	LgG	TpG	Thal
ρ	−0.44	0.42	−0.40	**−0.52**	0.08
p-value	0.07	0.08	0.10	**0.03**	0.74
	Cau	Put	Hipp	Pall	Cer
ρ	−0.25	−0.43	**−0.50**	−0.13	−0.22
p-value	0.38	0.08	**0.03**	0.61	0.38

The ρ score and relative p-values (rows) are reported for each ROI (columns). The significant correlations (p-value < 0.05) are highlighted in bold.

The obtained accuracy of 0.84 ± 0.10 suggests that the combination of T1-w and CNNs can help in the classification task between MS subtypes. Performance is comparable with that presented in [28] (average precision of 0.84 and an average recall of 0.8 on a dataset of 604 acquisitions) although achieved with different methods and data acquisitions. The other classification metrics, as formalized in this work, can be strictly related to the ease of classification of each class of patients. In our results, the precision$_{PPMS}$ and the specificity were respectively close to the precision$_{RRMS}$ and the sensitivity, indicating that the CNN better minimized the FPs (the wrongly classified RRMS subjects). This highlighted a probable better characterization of RRMS subjects with respect to PPMS.

The differentiation between healthy and pathological subjects is much more common in literature. In this respect, a 3D CNN based approach was proposed by [11], showing an accuracy of 87.04% on a set of 147 fully volumetric structural MRI acquisitions. Moreover, to better interpret the CNN performance, Eitel and colleagues adopted LRP visualization. The substantial difference in the research question make these works not directly comparable to our.

Through LRP visualization it was possible to identify the regions based on which the CNN model performed the classification between the two MS subtypes. The ROIs deemed as more relevant, which were also significantly correlated with the EDSS score, are generally involved in MS pathology. The parahippocampal gyrus and the hippocampus have been shown to have high probability of focal GM demyelination in MS pathology [14,40], and the temporal gyrus has been demonstrated to be correlated with cognitive performances in MS [1], while the superior frontal gyrus has been shown to be associated with fatigue, particularly in RRMS [8]. Interestingly, the superior frontal gyrus resulted significantly correlated with EDSS despite it showed overlapping relevance between the two classes. This reasonably calls for clinical validation of the outcomes. In fact, the relevance values allowed to understand how the voxels of certain ROIs contributed to the classification, but still did not allow to identify the underlying reasons (e.g. lesion load, atrophy, etc.) [5].

Despite the promising results obtained in this study, we acknowledge that our study can be improved especially for what concerns the robustness of the outcomes, that depends on the numerosity of the sample. This limitation also affected the hyperparameters optimization, which was performed on separate sets. A comparison with different classification techniques will be object of future works.

Nevertheless, we consider these outcomes as a valuable first evidence of the potential of the proposed method in splitting apart the two MR phenotypes and providing hints on the possible subserving mechanisms of disease progression, and we leave the open issues mentioned above for future investigation.

5   Conclusions

This work corroborated the capability of T1-w combined with a 3D CNN classifier of distinguishing the different typologies of MS disease. In addition we could highlight, through the application of LRP visualization, that the CNN classification was based on clinically relevant ROIs that significantly correlated with EDSS score. From a clinical perspective, our results strengthen the hypothesis of the suitability of GM features as biomarkers for MS pathological brain tissues. Moreover, this work has the potential to address clinically important problems in MS, like the early identification of the clinical course for diagnosis, personalized treatment and treatment decision.

Acknowledgements. This work has received funding from the European Research Council (ERC) under the European Union's Horizon 2020 research and innovation program (ERC Advanced Grant agreement no. 694665: CoBCoM - Computational Brain Connectivity Mapping) and from the French government, through the 3IA Côte d'Azur Investments in the Future project managed by the National Research Agency (ANR) with the reference number ANR-10-P3IA-0002.

References

1. Achiron, A., Chapman, J., Tal, S., Bercovich, E., Gil, H., Achiron, A.: Superior temporal gyrus thickness correlates with cognitive performance in multiple sclerosis. Brain Struct. Funct. **218**(4), 943–950 (2013)
2. Alber, M., et al.: Innvestigate neural networks!. J. Mach. Learn. Res. **20**(93), 1–8 (2019)
3. Bach, S., Binder, A., Montavon, G., Klauschen, F., Müller, K.R., Samek, W.: On pixel-wise explanations for non-linear classifier decisions by layer-wise relevance propagation. PloS One **10**(7), e0130140 (2015)
4. Binder, A., Montavon, G., Lapuschkin, S., Müller, K.-R., Samek, W.: Layer-wise relevance propagation for neural networks with local renormalization layers. In: Villa, A.E.P., Masulli, P., Pons Rivero, A.J. (eds.) ICANN 2016, Part II. LNCS, vol. 9887, pp. 63–71. Springer, Cham (2016). https://doi.org/10.1007/978-3-319-44781-0_8

5. Böhle, M., Eitel, F., Weygandt, M., Ritter, K.: Layer-wise relevance propagation for explaining deep neural network decisions in MRI-based Alzheimer's disease classification. Front. Aging Neurosci. **11**, 194 (2019). https://doi.org/10.3389/fnagi.2019.00194
6. Calabrese, M., Castellaro, M.: Cortical gray matter MR imaging in multiple sclerosis. Neuroimaging Clin. **27**(2), 301–312 (2017)
7. Calabrese, M., et al.: Regional distribution and evolution of gray matter damage in different populations of multiple sclerosis patients. PloS One **10**(8), e0135428 (2015)
8. Calabrese, M., et al.: Basal ganglia and frontal/parietal cortical atrophy is associated with fatigue in relapsing-remitting multiple sclerosis. Mult. Scler. J. **16**(10), 1220–1228 (2010). https://doi.org/10.1177/1352458510376405. pMID: 20670981
9. Compston, A., Coles, A.: Multiple sclerosis. The Lancet **372**(9648), 1502–1517 (2008). https://doi.org/10.1016/S0140-6736(08)61620-7
10. De Santis, S., et al.: Characterizing microstructural tissue properties in multiple sclerosis with diffusion MRI at 7 t and 3 t: the impact of the experimental design. Neuroscience **403**, 17–26 (2019)
11. Eitel, F., et al.: Uncovering convolutional neural network decisions for diagnosing multiple sclerosis on conventional MRI using layer-wise relevance propagation. arXiv preprint arXiv:1904.08771 (2019)
12. Eshaghi, A., et al.: Progression of regional grey matter atrophy in multiple sclerosis. Brain **141**(6), 1665–1677 (2018)
13. Fischl, B.: FreeSurfer. Neuroimage **62**(2), 774–781 (2012)
14. Geurts, J.J., Barkhof, F.: Grey matter pathology in multiple sclerosis. The Lancet Neurol. **7**(9), 841–851 (2008)
15. Geurts, J.J., Calabrese, M., Fisher, E., Rudick, R.A.: Measurement and clinical effect of grey matter pathology in multiple sclerosis. The Lancet Neurol. **11**(12), 1082–1092 (2012)
16. He, K., Zhang, X., Ren, S., Sun, J.: Deep residual learning for image recognition. In: The IEEE Conference on Computer Vision and Pattern Recognition (CVPR), pp. 770–778 (June 2016)
17. Huang, W.J., Chen, W.W., Zhang, X.: Multiple sclerosis: pathology, diagnosis and treatments. Exp. Ther. Med. **13**(6), 3163–3166 (2017)
18. Hulst, H.E., Geurts, J.J.: Gray matter imaging in multiple sclerosis: what have we learned? BMC Neurol. **11**(1), 153 (2011)
19. Hurwitz, B.J.: The diagnosis of multiple sclerosis and the clinical subtypes. Ann. Indian Acad. Neurol. **12**(4), 226 (2009)
20. Inojosa, H., Proschmann, U., Akgün, K., Ziemssen, T.: A focus on secondary progressive multiple sclerosis (SPMS): challenges in diagnosis and definition. J. Neurol. 1–12 (2019). https://doi.org/10.1007/s00415-019-09489-5
21. Kingma, D.P., Ba, J.: Adam: A method for stochastic optimization. arXiv preprint arXiv:1412.6980 (2014)
22. Korolev, S., Safiullin, A., Belyaev, M., Dodonova, Y.: Residual and plain convolutional neural networks for 3D brain MRI classification. In: 2017 IEEE 14th International Symposium on Biomedical Imaging (ISBI 2017), pp. 835–838. IEEE (2017)
23. Lassmann, H.: Multiple sclerosis pathology. Cold Spring Harb. Perspect. Med. **8**(3), a028936 (2018)
24. Lublin, F.D., et al.: Defining the clinical course of multiple sclerosis: the 2013 revisions. Neurology **83**(3), 278–286 (2014)

25. Lucchinetti, C., Brück, W., Parisi, J., Scheithauer, B., Rodriguez, M., Lassmann, H.: Heterogeneity of multiple sclerosis lesions: implications for the pathogenesis of demyelination. Ann. Neurol. Off. J. Am. Neurol. Assoc. Child Neurol. Soc. **47**(6), 707–717 (2000)
26. Magliozzi, R., et al.: Inflammatory intrathecal profiles and cortical damage in multiple sclerosis. Ann. Neurol. **83**(4), 739–755 (2018). https://doi.org/10.1002/ana.25197
27. Manca, R., Sharrack, B., Paling, D., Wilkinson, I.D., Venneri, A.: Brain connectivity and cognitive processing speed in multiple sclerosis: a systematic review. J. Neurol. Sci. **388**, 115–127 (2018)
28. Marzullo, A., et al.: Classification of multiple sclerosis clinical profiles via graph convolutional neural networks. Front. Neurosci. **13**, 594 (2019)
29. Miller, D., Thompson, A., Filippi, M.: Magnetic resonance studies of abnormalities in the normal appearing white matter and grey matter in multiple sclerosis. J. Neurol. **250**(12), 1407–1419 (2003)
30. Montavon, G., Samek, W., Müller, K.R.: Methods for interpreting and understanding deep neural networks. Digit. Signal Process. **73**, 1–15 (2018)
31. Nourbakhsh, B., Mowry, E.M.: Multiple sclerosis risk factors and pathogenesis. CONTINUUM: Lifelong Learn. Neurol. **25**(3), 596–610 (2019)
32. Paszke, A., et al.: Automatic differentiation in PyTorch. In: Conference on Neural Information Processing Systems (NIPS) (2017)
33. Popescu, V., et al.: Brain atrophy and lesion load predict long term disability in multiple sclerosis. J. Neurol. Neurosurg. Psychiatry **84**(10), 1082–1091 (2013). https://doi.org/10.1136/jnnp-2012-304094
34. Rieke, J., Eitel, F., Weygandt, M., Haynes, J.-D., Ritter, K.: Visualizing convolutional networks for MRI-based diagnosis of Alzheimer's disease. In: Stoyanov, D., et al. (eds.) MLCN/DLF/IMIMIC -2018. LNCS, vol. 11038, pp. 24–31. Springer, Cham (2018). https://doi.org/10.1007/978-3-030-02628-8_3
35. Schmidt, P., et al.: An automated tool for detection of flair-hyperintense white-matter lesions in multiple sclerosis. Neuroimage **59**(4), 3774–3783 (2012)
36. Shrikumar, A., Greenside, P., Kundaje, A.: Learning important features through propagating activation differences. arXiv preprint arXiv:1704.02685 (2017)
37. Simonyan, K., Vedaldi, A., Zisserman, A.: Deep inside convolutional networks: Visualising image classification models and saliency maps. arXiv preprint arXiv:1312.6034 (2013)
38. Simonyan, K., Zisserman, A.: Very deep convolutional networks for large-scale image recognition. arXiv preprint arXiv:1409.1556 (2014)
39. Springenberg, J.T., Dosovitskiy, A., Brox, T., Riedmiller, M.: Striving for simplicity: The all convolutional net. arXiv preprint arXiv:1412.6806 (2014)
40. Vercellino, M., et al.: Demyelination, inflammation, and neurodegeneration in multiple sclerosis deep gray matter. J. Neuropathol. Exp. Neurol. **68**(5), 489–502 (2009)
41. Xie, N., Ras, G., van Gerven, M., Doran, D.: Explainable deep learning: A field guide for the uninitiated. arXiv preprint arXiv:2004.14545 (2020)
42. Zeiler, M.D., Fergus, R.: Visualizing and understanding convolutional networks. In: Fleet, D., Pajdla, T., Schiele, B., Tuytelaars, T. (eds.) ECCV 2014, Part I. LNCS, vol. 8689, pp. 818–833. Springer, Cham (2014). https://doi.org/10.1007/978-3-319-10590-1_53
43. Zintgraf, L.M., Cohen, T.S., Adel, T., Welling, M.: Visualizing deep neural network decisions: Prediction difference analysis. arXiv preprint arXiv:1702.04595 (2017)

Visualizing the Effect of Semantic Classes in the Attribution of Scene Recognition Models

Alejandro López-Cifuentes[✉][iD], Marcos Escudero-Viñolo[iD], Andrija Gajić[iD], and Jesús Bescós[iD]

Video Processing and Understanding Lab, Universidad Autónoma de Madrid, 28049 Madrid, Spain
{alejandro.lopezc,marcos.escudero,j.bescos}@uam.es, andrija.gajic@estudiante.uam.es

Abstract. The performance of Convolutional Neural Networks for image classification has vastly and steadily increased during the last years. This success goes hand in hand with the need to explain and understand their decisions: opening the black box. The problem of attribution specifically deals with the characterization of the response of Convolutional Neural Networks by identifying the input features responsible for the model's decision. Among all attribution methods, perturbation-based methods are an important family based on measuring the effect of perturbations applied to the input image in the model's output. In this paper, we discuss the limitations of existing approaches and propose a novel perturbation-based attribution method guided by semantic segmentation. Our method inhibits specific image areas according to their assigned semantic label. Hereby, perturbations are link up with a semantic meaning and a complete attribution map is obtained for all image pixels. In addition, we propose a particularization of the proposed method to the scene recognition task which, differently than image classification, requires multi-focus attribution models. The proposed semantic-guided attribution method enables us to delve deeper into scene recognition interpretability by obtaining for each scene class the sets of relevant, irrelevant and distracting semantic labels. Experimental results suggest that the method can boost research by increasing the understanding of Convolutional Neural Networks while uncovering datasets biases which may have been inadvertently included during the harvest and annotation processes. All the code, data and supplementary results are available at http://www-vpu.eps.uam.es/publications/SemanticEffectSceneRecognition/

Keywords: Convolutional Neural Networks · Attribution · Interpretability · Scene recognition · Semantic segmentation

1 Introduction

Convolutional Neural Networks (CNNs) have spread rapidly during the last years. On top of their discriminative and generative power, strategies such as

A. Del Bimbo et al. (Eds.): ICPR 2020 Workshops, LNCS 12663, pp. 115–129, 2021.
https://doi.org/10.1007/978-3-030-68796-0_9

transfer learning allow to adapt heavily and richly trained CNNs to specific tasks, partially inheriting the power of the source network but also its biases. In order to detect model biases, to help the foretelling of their behaviour in real-world applications, and to design training mechanisms in accordance with their learning processes, the success of CNNs comes together with the need to explain their decisions. In that vein, a hot research topic is the definition of methodologies for the visualization of CNNs focused on aiding human interpretation of their operation.

This paper deals with the problem of attribution, i.e. the characterization of the response of CNNs by identifying the input features responsible for model decision [11]. Most of the attribution methods can be broadly organized into four categories: Methods based on back propagation [10,11], perturbation-based methods [8,14], approximation-based methods [9] and visualizations of intermediate activations [7,12].

In this paper we focus on perturbation-based attribution methods. These methods propose to measure attribution by modifying the input RGB image and collecting and observing the effect of that perturbation in the model's output. Among others, Zeiler et al. [14] proposed to analyze the effect of systematically covering up different portions of an image with a gray square. Fong et al. [3], following the same idea, proposed to use meaningful perturbations blurring specific areas of an image with a learnable mask and extended this idea [2] by regularising the set of representative perturbations. They introduced the concept of extremal perturbations, i.e. the activation of a certain neuron in a neural network to create relevant image areas for classification. Kapishnikov et al. proposed XRAI [6]: a superpixel-based attribution method that builds upon integrated gradients to obtain perturbed versions of images. With this method the most important regions for classifying an image as an instance of a specific scene class are revealed.

Analyzed methods are limited to image classification tasks like the ImageNet Challenge [1], where there are mainly one or two objects that define the image class. Differently, for the scene recognition task, the image class is defined by several related objects and by their arrangement. Furthermore, the sets of objects that define two different scene classes generally overlap significantly; hence, measuring attribution for multiple regions is preferable. Besides, these methods are limited to a per-image analysis revealing relevant image areas (maximal activation regions), and their results are rarely studied on larger scopes than the image—e.g.. on a per-scene-class basis. Finally, there is not, to the best of our knowledge, any reported method studying the nature of the attribution regions and relating it with the model output in a fully automatic way.

To overcome these limitations we propose a perturbation-based attribution method guided by semantic segmentation. The proposed method perturbs RGB images by inhibiting specific areas according to their assigned semantic labels. By this process, the perturbation is no longer random [14] or selected by super-pixels [6]: it has a semantic meaning. Thereby, we obtain complete attribution maps, i.e. attribution scores for all pixels, not just for the relevant ones. Moreover, the particularization of the method for the scene recognition task enables us to delve deeper into scene recognition interpretability, obtaining relevant, irrelevant, and distracting semantic labels on a per-scene basis. Figure 1 graphically depicts the proposed method.

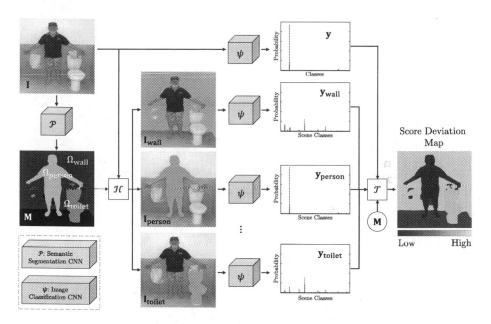

Fig. 1. Diagram of the proposed method. A given image **I** is forwarded to a trained image classification CNN Ψ obtaining prediction **y**. In parallel, **I** is mapped into regions using a semantic segmentation network $\mathcal{P}$ obtaining **M**. This segmentation is used to modify areas of **I** creating inhibited images. Each inhibited image $\mathbf{I}_l$, being l the class of the inhibited object, is forwarded to Ψ to obtain the correspondent probability distribution $\mathbf{y}_l$. Using the semantic segmentation **M**, the original prediction **y** and the set of modified $\mathbf{y}_l$, the proposed Score Deviation Map is obtained. Better viewed in color. (Color figure online)

2   Method

2.1   Preliminaries

Let **I** be a color image, and let $\Psi : \mathbb{R}^{W \times H \times 3} \to \mathbb{R}^K$ be a classification CNN model that maps **I** to a vector of non-normalized predictions $\mathbf{f} = \Psi(\mathbf{I})$, one for each of the K learned scene classes. The inference of class posterior probabilities $\mathbf{y} = [y_1, ..., y_k, ...y_K] \in \mathbb{R}^K$ is obtained from **f** by using a logarithmic normalized exponential (*logarithmic softmax*) function $\gamma(\mathbf{f}) : \mathbb{R}^K \to \mathbb{R}^K$, e.g.:

$$y_k = \gamma(\mathbf{f}) = \log\left(\frac{\exp(f_k)}{\sum_i^K \exp(f_i)}\right), \tag{1}$$

for the posterior probability of class k. Generally, $\mathbf{I}$ is classified as an instance of class k^* if $k^* = argmax_k(\mathbf{y})$.

Let Ω be the spatial support of $\mathbf{I}$, and let $\mathcal{P} : \mathbb{R}^{W \times H \times 3} \rightarrow \mathbb{N}^{W \times H}$ be a semantic segmentation model that maps $\mathbf{I}$ to $\mathbf{M}$, a region partition of $\mathbf{I}$:

$$\mathbf{M} = \mathcal{P}(\mathbf{I}) = \left\{ \Omega_1, ..., \Omega_n : \Omega = \bigcup_{j=1}^{n} \Omega_j \quad \text{s.t.} \quad (\Omega_{j_1} \cap \Omega_{j_2} = \emptyset, \forall j_1 \neq j_2) \right\}, \quad (2)$$

where each region is assigned a semantic class $\ell(\Omega_j) = l, \{l \in \mathbb{N} : 1 \leq l \leq L\}$, being L the number of semantic classes learned by model $\mathcal{P}$.

2.2   Score Deviation

To estimate the effect of each semantic class in the prediction $\Psi(\mathbf{I})$, we propose to inhibit in $\mathbf{I}$ the texture of each semantic class, leveraging on recent studies confirming the significant texture-bias in the prediction of CNN models [4].

To this aim, we define an operator $\mathcal{H}$ that, given an image, its partition, and a categorical semantic label, returns a new image $\mathbf{I}_l$ which is $\mathbf{I}$ modified by setting to a reference color value $\boldsymbol{\mu}$ the set of pixels $\mathbf{p}$ belonging to regions tagged in $\mathbf{M}$ with semantic class l:

$$\mathcal{H}(\mathbf{I}, \mathbf{M}, l) = \mathbf{I}_l, \quad \mathbf{I}_l(\mathbf{p}) = \begin{cases} \boldsymbol{\mu}, & \forall \mathbf{p} \in \{\Omega_j \quad \text{s.t.} \quad \ell(\Omega_j) = l\} \\ \mathbf{I}(\mathbf{p}), & \text{elsewhere} \end{cases} \quad (3)$$

We evaluate the effect in the prediction of the semantic class l by measuring the score deviation $s(\mathbf{I}, l)$. This score is obtained by subtracting, for the originally predicted class k^*, the inferred probability obtained for the modified image from that obtained for the original image:

$$s(\mathbf{I}, l) = y_{k^*} - y_{k^*}(l), \quad \text{where} \quad \mathbf{y}_l = \{y_1(l), ..., y_k(l), ..., y_K(l)\} = \gamma(\Psi(\mathbf{I}_l)) \quad (4)$$

As y_{k^*} and $y_{k^*}(l)$ are probabilities, $s(\mathbf{I}, l)$ is theoretically bounded in $[-1, 1] \in \mathbb{R}$. In practice, as we are evaluating $\mathbf{y}$ and $\mathbf{y}_l$ only for the class of maximum probability, obtaining large negative values is rare. Negative values of $s(\mathbf{I}, l)$ indicate prediction gains, i.e. the score of the predicted class increases after the inhibition of the areas tagged as l; hence, negative values are not indicative of the impact of these areas, but of potential hindering areas for the prediction. More relevant for measuring the impact are larger values of $s(\mathbf{I}, l)$: the larger the value, the more impactful are the regions tagged as l for the prediction, as their inhibitions harms the prediction. On the other hand, close to zero values indicate low impact, as the prediction score remains nearly unchanged.

By repeating this process for the L semantic class, we yield a vector of score deviations $\mathbf{s}(\mathbf{I}) = \{s(\mathbf{I}, l), l \in \mathbb{N} : 1 \leq l \leq L\}$.

2.3 Score Deviation Map

To visualize the attribution of each region in the input image, we propose to create a Score Deviation Map **SDM** through an operator $\mathcal{T}$ that assigns to the spatial support of each region Ω_j of the semantic segmentation **M**, the score deviation obtained after modifying the input image by inhibiting the regions tagged as $\ell(\Omega_j)$:

$$\mathcal{T}(\mathbf{M}, \mathbf{s}, l) = \mathbf{SDM}, \quad \mathbf{SDM}(\mathbf{p}) = s(\mathbf{I}, l), \forall \mathbf{p} \in \{\Omega_j \quad \text{s.t.} \quad \ell(\Omega_j) = l\} \quad (5)$$

2.4 Class-Wise Statistics

Differently than previous methods for measuring image attribution, the proposed set of scores for each image is parametrized by the semantic classes. This parametrization eases the creation of a complete non-binary attribution measure: the Score Deviation Map, where every pixel, not just the relevant ones, has an attribution score. Furthermore, it also enables the automatic extraction of class-wise relationships between scene and semantic classes.

In this paper we study three types of class-wise statistics: relevant semantic classes for the prediction, irrelevant semantic classes for the prediction, and distracting semantic classes.

Relevant Semantic Classes. Let $\mathbf{I}_k$ be the set of images predicted as instances of the scene class k, and let $\mathbf{S}_l = \{s(\mathbf{I}, l) \quad \forall \mathbf{I} \in \mathbf{I}_k\}$ be the score-set obtained by following the scoring procedure defined in Eqs. 3 and 4 for images in $\mathbf{I}_k$ and semantic class l. This process is repeated in the $\mathbf{I}_k$ set for every semantic class, yielding a set of score-sets $\mathbf{S} = \{\mathbf{S}_l, l \in \mathbb{N} : 1 \leq l \leq L\}$.

We propose to study the expectation, $\mathbb{E}(\mathbf{S}_l)$, median and standard deviation of each score-set $\mathbf{S}_l$ as class-wise statistics of the impact of semantic class l in the prediction of class k for a classification model and a dataset. Leveraging on these statistics, we define the relevant set, $\mathbf{S}^R$, as the ranked set of semantic classes obtained by arranging the score-sets according to their average score:

$$\mathbf{S}^R = \{\mathbf{S}_{(1)}, ..., \mathbf{S}_{(l)}, ..., \mathbf{S}_{(L)}\} \rightarrow \mathbb{E}(\mathbf{S}_{(1)}) \geq ... \geq \mathbb{E}(\mathbf{S}_{(l)}) \geq ... \geq \mathbb{E}(\mathbf{S}_{(L)}) \quad (6)$$

This relevance set can be shortened by using a significance score value α and removing all the score-sets which average is smaller than α. We refer to this relevant truncated set as $\mathbf{S}^R(\alpha)$.

Irrelevant Semantic Classes. For a given significance level α, we define the set of irrelevant semantic classes, $\mathbf{S}^I(\alpha)$, as the relative complement of $\mathbf{S}^R(\alpha)$ with respect to $\mathbf{S}^R$: $\mathbf{S}^I(\alpha) = \mathbf{S}^R \setminus \mathbf{S}^R(\alpha)$.

This irrelevant set can be shortened by removing all the score-sets associated to semantic classes that are low represented in the set of images $\mathbf{I}_k$. To this aim, we extract the density of semantic class l in $\mathbf{I}_k$ by dividing the number of pixels tagged as l in the partitions of the whole set $\{\mathcal{P}(\mathbf{I}), \forall \mathbf{I} \in \mathbf{I}_k\}$ by the total number of pixels in $\mathbf{I}_k$. Then, using a significance density value β, we remove all the score-sets in the irrelevant set which density is smaller than or equal to β. We refer to this irrelevant truncated set as $\mathbf{S}^I(\alpha, \beta)$.

Distracting Semantic Classes. The previous sets measure the impact of semantic classes in the prediction of a scene class, this does not require knowledge of the scene ground-truth. To extract the set of distracting semantic classes, we do require the ground-truth class, k_{GT}, for each image $\mathbf{I}$.

We define the set of distracting semantic classes $\mathbf{D}(\mathbf{I}_k)$ for the set of images $\mathbf{I}_k$ as the set of semantic classes which inhibition changes the prediction from a wrong class (i.e. a false positive) to the ground-truth one.

$$\mathbf{D}(\mathbf{I}_k) = \{l \quad \text{s.t.} \quad argmax_k(\mathbf{y}) \neq k_{GT} \wedge argmax_k(\mathbf{y}_l) = k_{GT}\} \tag{7}$$

2.5   Particularization to Scene Recognition

The described method can be used on the output activation or class prediction scores of any classification model. It can also be easily adjusted to operate on their intermediate layers. We hereinafter validate this method for a scene recognition model. Differently than image classification, scene recognition necessitates multi-focus models as it results from the coexistence of several objects and their context. Therefore, we consider it a representative model to illustrate the potential benefits of our method

3   Experimental Results

Along this section we present a series of results that arise from the proposed method. First, to ease the reproducibility of the method and results, Sect. 3.1 presents the implementation details and the adopted dataset. Then, attribution results are presented, covering results at image (Sect. 3.2) and scene class (Sect. 3.3) levels.

3.1   Implementation Details

The aim of the proposed method is to aid interpretability and understanding for any classification model and, by extension, for any scene recognition model. This means that the visual analysis is suitable for any state-of-the-art scene recognition method disregarding its architecture. The selected semantic segmentation model is also replaceable by any other approach in the literature.

To verify the capability of the method, ResNet-18 [5] trained over the training set of the Places365 dataset [15] is used as the scene recognition model, whereas for the semantic segmentation model, we rely on the UPerNet-50 network [13] trained on the ADE20K dataset [16], which encompasses samples from $L = 150$ semantic classes, including objects and stuff.

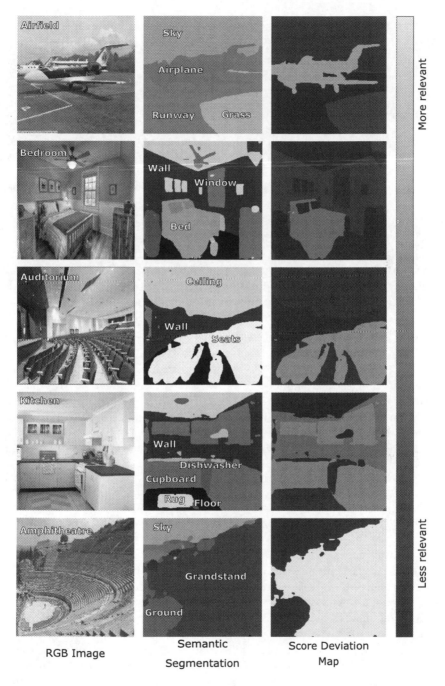

RGB Image   Semantic   Score Deviation
                    Segmentation   Map

Fig. 2. Several examples of the proposed method for a given image. Left column represents the analyzed RGB image with the predicted scene class superimposed. Middle column depicts the correspondent semantic segmentation. Right column represents the obtained Score Deviation Map. Yellowish colors in the map, i.e. $s(\mathbf{I}, l) \to 1$, represent objects/areas with higher relevance in the prediction. On the other hand, blueish colors, i.e. $s(\mathbf{I}, l) \to -1$, represent areas with lower relevance in the prediction. Better viewed in color. (Color figure online)

For all the experiments along this section the Places365 validation set [15] has been used. It includes 36000 validation images from $K = 365$ scene classes.

Finally, for the set of experiments, the mean value of ImageNet's RGB color space is used as the reference color: $\boldsymbol{\mu} = [0.485, 0.456, 0.406]$.

3.2   Score Deviation Maps

Figure 2 represents several examples of the obtained **SDM** for a given image. Yellowish colors in the **SDM** represent objects/areas whose inhibition decreases the probability—more relevant for scene prediction. On the other hand, blueish colors represent areas that do not modify the probability; hence, irrelevant for scene prediction. For the first example depicted in the top row image, the obtained **SDM** suggests that the airplane, grass and sky are the most relevant areas for predicting the image as one of the *airfield* class, whereas the runaway is irrelevant. Similar results arise for the rest of examples, where it can be observed that the bed for the *bedroom*, the seats for the *auditorium*, the cupboard and walls for *kitchen* and the grandstand for the *amphitheatre* are semantic classes that play a relevant role in the prediction of the scene classes.

3.3   Relevant, Irrelevant and Distracting Semantic Classes

As stated in Sect. 3.2, through **SDM** one can visually interpret how different areas of an image directly affect a scene prediction, similar to the maximal activation regions of previous approaches. However, in this Section we study attribution not on individual images but on the complete set of samples of a specific scene class. Through this evaluation, not only a per-image visual analysis is obtained, but also a qualitative study on which semantic classes are relevant, irrelevant, or distracting, for a specific scene class.

Relevant Semantic Classes for Scene Prediction. Figure 3 depicts an example of the relevant semantic classes for *Bedroom* and *Hotel Room* scene classes. In the top row, different RGB samples for both scenes are represented. In the bottom row, the ranked set of relevant semantics (Eq. 6) for each scene is presented using two representations: first, a word count represents the full set of relevant semantic labels $\mathbf{S}^R(\alpha = 0.00)$ using a font size relative to each $\mathbf{S}_l$ value. Second, a box-plot represents a qualitative analysis of the set; but, to ease visualization, just the most relevant semantic classes are presented, i.e. a larger α is used: $\mathbf{S}^R(\alpha = 0.01)$; see the project website for non-truncated representations.

Results from Fig. 3 lead to a two-fold analysis. First, one can obtain a reliable representation, albeit constrained by the L learnt semantic classes, of how semantic classes affect the prediction of a given scene. In this line, results for *Bedroom* suggest that the set of relevant objects learnt by the CNNs as representative of *Bedroom(s)* is primarily composed by Beds, Walls, Windows, Painting, Cushion, Person, Sofa and Dresser (sorted from a higher to a lower score). Otherwise, for the *Hotel Room* class, results suggest that Walls, Floors, Beds, Windows,

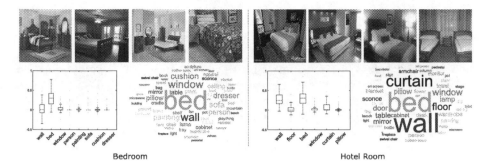

Fig. 3. Relevant Semantic Classes for *Bedroom* and *Hotel Room* scene classes. Top row represents different samples from Places365 validation set for both labels. Bottom row depicts a box-plot and a word count representation showing which objects and stuff are relevant for both classes. Better viewed in color. (Color figure online)

Curtains and Pillows are relevant. The fact that Floors are relevant might seem incoherent given that most scene classes do include floors. However, as there is no differentiation between different types of floor in the L learnt semantic labels, the relevance of this label might come from its distinctive texture features, i.e. floors in samples tagged as *Hotel Room* tend to be covered with carpets whereas *Bedrooms* samples tend to present different types of floors (e.g. wooden or parquet floors) (see Fig. 3 top row examples).

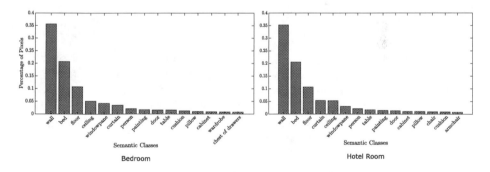

Fig. 4. Semantic classes histogram for *Bedroom* and *Hotel Room* Places365 training set. Better viewed in color. (Color figure online)

Second, as stated before, one of the main challenges in Scene Recognition is the high overlap between similar scenes. In these examples, images from *Bedroom* and *Hotel Room* have a low inter-class variability, leading to similarly composed color images. The proposed visualization allows to understand what the CNN is learning for both scenes and what is differential between them. Results for *Hotel Room* in Fig. 3 suggest that the set of relevant objects learnt by the CNNs as representative of *Hotel Room(s)* is primarily composed by Beds, Walls, Curtains,

Floors, Windows and Pillows. This relevant set and the one obtained for *Bedroom* overlap in several semantic classes (e.g. Beds and Walls). However, some semantic classes are exclusive from *Bedroom* class (e.g. Cushions) and others exclusive for the *Hotel Room* class (e.g. Curtains, Pillows and Floors). This suggests that the CNN, in order to learn different representations for both scene classes, attends to different image areas which are related to different semantic segmentation classes. The set of most populated semantic classes for these two scene classes included in Fig. 4 supports this: among the 15 top populated semantic classes in the training sets of these two classes, Curtain is the forth top populated semantic class for the *Hotel Room* scene class while it is the sixth one for the *Bedroom* class.

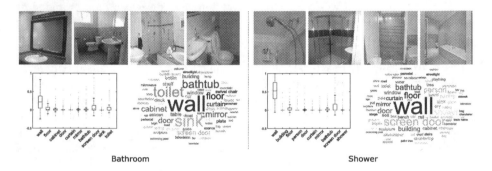

Bathroom   Shower

Fig. 5. Relevant Semantic Classes for *Bathroom* and *Shower* scene classes. Better viewed in color. (Color figure online

It is important to highlight that this analysis is constrained by the examples provided in the training dataset, as real-world representations of *Bedroom(s)* and *Hotel Room(s)* may have pillows, curtains and moquettes. However, the presented analysis can boost research on the Scene Recognition task by increasing the understanding of how the CNNs are producing their scene recognition decisions, which may be of great interest for profiling failure cases. Moreover, this analysis may be useful for uncovering dataset biases easily. These biases may have been inadvertently included during the harvest and annotation process, hindering the proper training and evaluation of scene recognition methods, as identifying them usually requires exhaustive human inspection.

Figures 5 and 6 extend this analysis to two other classes. From Fig. 5 it can be observed that set of relevant objects for *Bathroom* and *Shower* scene classes mainly differs in larger scores for Toilet and Sink for *Bathroom* and for Screen Door for *Shower*. However, the high number of shared semantic classes reveals a low inter-class variation which leads to a blurred separation between both scene classes (the model predicts 16% of *Bathroom* samples as *Shower* and 20% of *Shower* samples as *Bathroom*). As in the example in Fig. 3, the presence of Wall as the most relevant semantic class might be unexpected but bathrooms' and showers' walls might have specific cues, i.e. color, texture or materials, that make them scene discriminant.

Figure 6 shows differences for an indoor-outdoor pair of scene classes. The prediction of *Parking Garage Indoor* is mainly focused on Floors, Cars and Ceiling, whereas top relevant semantics for the *Parking Garage Outdoor* are Buildings, Roads and Sky. More examples for scene pair labels are gathered up at Link.

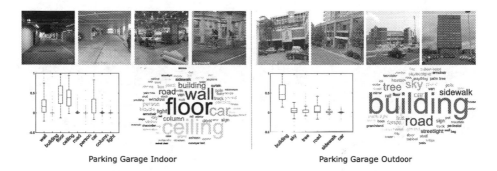

Fig. 6. Relevant Semantic Classes for *Parking Garage Indoor* and *Parking Garage Outdoor* scene classes. Better viewed in color. (Color figure online)

Irrelevant Semantic Classes for Scene Prediction. Figure 7 depicts *Bedroom, Hotel Room, Bathroom, Shower, Parking Garage Indoor* and *Parking Garage Outdoor*, irrelevant semantic classes by the use of word counts representing the irrelevant truncated sets $\mathbf{S}^I (\alpha = 0.01, \beta = 0.00)$.

Figure 7 results complement those presented in Figures 3, 5 and 6. It can be observed how relevant semantic classes for the *Hotel Room* (e.g. Floor and Curtains) are, in turn, irrelevant for the *Bedroom* scene class. For the analyzed model, it seems that the presence of these semantic classes is precisely what defines a *Hotel Room*, and so they become irrelevant for the prediction of *Bedroom*. The other word counts examples reveal how several semantic classes do not influence the scene prediction results. An interesting result, that can be just partially appreciated in the included graphs, is that Ceilings are irrelevant for all indoor scenes except for the *Parking Garage Indoor* that has an outdoor counterpart class; in this case, as depicted before in Fig. 6, the Ceiling class is relevant to disambiguate between *Parking Garage Indoor* and *Parking Garage Outdoor*. The analysis brought forth by this representation could additionally be helpful to outline, with human inspection, if irrelevant objects might be useful although the used CNN is not considering them.

Distracting Semantic Classes for Scene Prediction. Figure 8 depicts some examples of the set $\mathbf{D}$ (Eq. 7) of distracting semantic classes for miss-classified samples from the *Airplane Cabin, Aqueduct, Bedroom* and *Baseball Field* scene

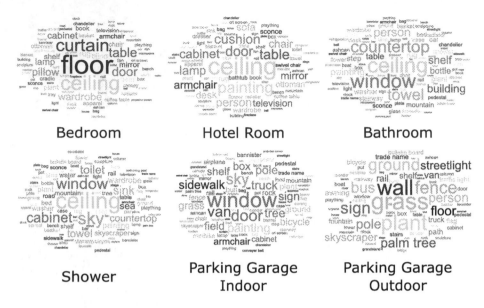

Fig. 7. Irrelevant semantic classes for *Bedroom, Hotel Room, Bathroom, Shower, Parking Garage Indoor* and *Parking Garage Outdoor* scene classes. Better viewed in color. (Color figure online)

classes. Scene classes are represented as graph nodes while semantic classes are represented as graph edges. The center node of the graph (bold font) represents the ground-truth (GT) scene class. The exterior nodes represent the CNN wrong scene predictions for the considered ground-truth class. The edge joining an exterior node with the center node represents the semantic class whose inhibition shifts the prediction to the ground-truth. The size of the edge is proportional to the times this shift happens.

Usually, profiling of miss-classified samples for a scene is carried out by analyzing which is the scene that agglutinates most of the wrong predictions (analysis of nodes from Fig. 8). This information is useful to detect problematic sets of similar scene classes, e.g. *Train Interior-Airplane Cabin, Aqueduct-Arch* or *Hotel Room-Bedroom*. However, such analysis does not provide evidences on the reasons behind the confusion. The proposed visualization strategy of distracting semantic classes might aid for the identification of problematic semantic classes, which then may lead to the definition of new tailored training schemes.

Results from Fig. 8 suggest that, for the presented scene classes, Wall is usually a distracting semantic class, suggesting a two-fold analysis. First, walls are a distracting semantic class due to their discriminative appearance. In the case of the pair *Train Interior-Airplane Cabin* scene classes, both scenes layouts might be similar, i.e. both may encompass semantic classes as persons, seats and windows. However, the color and texture cues representing a *Train Interior* wall might be, indeed, helpful to differentiate it from an *Airplane Cabin*. Second, walls are categorized as a distracting semantic class, not only for its discriminative

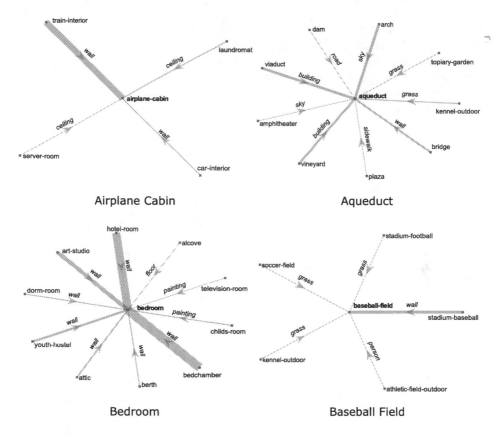

Fig. 8. Distractor semantic classes for *Airplane Cabin, Aqueduct, Bedroom* and *Baseball Field*. Scene classes are represented as graph nodes whereas semantic classes are represented as graph edges. The center node of the graph (bold node) is the ground-truth scene class. The exterior nodes represent predictions for miss-classified samples of the ground-truth class. The edge joining an exterior node with the center node represents the semantic class whose inhibition shifts the prediction to the ground-truth one. The width of the edge is proportional to the number of samples in which this change takes place. Better viewed in color. (Color figure online)

cues, but for its larger covering area with respect to other semantic classes. Inhibiting larger areas of an image might lead to a reduced set of potentially useful and discriminative features. If the model can not attend to wall areas to infer a prediction, other image locations will be taken into account producing a more discriminated prediction. The set of *art-studio-hotel-room-bedroom* and *stadium-baseball-baseball-field* scenes classes are examples of this behaviour.

4   Conclusions

This paper describes a simple yet effective approach for the problem of attribution in the image classification task, i.e. the characterization of the response of the CNNs by identifying the input features responsible for model decision. The proposed method perturbs RGB images levering on specific areas according to an assigned semantic segmentation label. Complete attribution maps are obtained for images and, moreover, when applied to the scene recognition task, a per-scene basis analysis is obtained delving a deep interpretability of relevant, irrelevant and distracting semantic labels for scenes. This analysis enables researchers to deeply profile the used CNNs and the used datasets to boost future performances.

The presented results and analysis are only the tip of the iceberg of what the proposed attribution effort might offer and we invite other researchers to explore the supplementary material that did not fit in the article. In addition, future work will continue exploring this line of research extending the number of analyzed CNNs and expanding the results to other computer vision tasks.

Acknowledgments. This study has been partially supported by the Spanish Government through its TEC2017-88169-R MobiNetVideo project.

References

1. Deng, J., Dong, W., Socher, R., Li, L.J., Li, K., Fei-Fei, L.: Imagenet: a large-scale hierarchical image database. In: Proceedings of the IEEE Conference on Computer Vision and Pattern Recognition (CVPR), pp. 248–255. IEEE (2009)
2. Fong, R., Patrick, M., Vedaldi, A.: Understanding deep networks via extremal perturbations and smooth masks. In: Proceedings of the IEEE International Conference on Computer Vision (ICCV), pp. 2950–2958 (2019)
3. Fong, R.C., Vedaldi, A.: Interpretable explanations of black boxes by meaningful perturbation. In: Proceedings of the IEEE International Conference on Computer Vision (ICCV), pp. 3429–3437 (2017)
4. Geirhos, R., Rubisch, P., Michaelis, C., Bethge, M., Wichmann, F.A., Brendel, W.: Imagenet-trained CNNs are biased towards texture; increasing shape bias improves accuracy and robustness. In: Proceedings of the International Conference on Learning Representations (ICLR) (2019)
5. He, K., Zhang, X., Ren, S., Sun, J.: Deep residual learning for image recognition. In: Proceedings of the IEEE Conference on Computer Vision and Pattern Recognition (CVPR), pp. 770–778 (2016)
6. Kapishnikov, A., Bolukbasi, T., Viégas, F., Terry, M.: Xrai: better attributions through regions. In: Proceedings of the IEEE International Conference on Computer Vision (ICCV), pp. 4948–4957 (2019)
7. Olah, C., Mordvintsev, A., Schubert, L.: Feature visualization. Distill **2**(11), e7 (2017)
8. Petsiuk, V., Das, A., Saenko, K.: Rise: randomized input sampling for explanation of black-box models. In: Proceedings of the British Machine Vision Conference (BMVC) (2018)
9. Ribeiro, M.T., Singh, S., Guestrin, C.: "Why should i trust you?" explaining the predictions of any classifier. In: Proceedings of the International Conference on Knowledge Discovery and Data Mining (SIGKDD), pp. 1135–1144 (2016)

10. Selvaraju, R., Cogswell, M., Das, A., Vedantam, R., Parikh, D., Batra, D., et al.: Visual explanations from deep networks via gradient-based localization. In: Proceedings of the IEEE Conference on Computer Vision and Pattern Recognition (CVPR), pp. 618–626 (2019)
11. Simonyan, K., Vedaldi, A., Zisserman, A.: Deep inside convolutional networks: Visualising image classification models and saliency maps. In: Proceedings of the Workshop at International Conference on Learning Representations (ICLR) (2014)
12. Ulyanov, D., Vedaldi, A., Lempitsky, V.: Deep image prior. In: Proceedings of the IEEE Conference on Computer Vision and Pattern Recognition (CVPR), pp. 9446–9454 (2018)
13. Xiao, T., Liu, Y., Zhou, B., Jiang, Y., Sun, J.: Unified perceptual parsing for scene understanding. In: Ferrari, V., Hebert, M., Sminchisescu, C., Weiss, Y. (eds.) ECCV 2018. LNCS, vol. 11209, pp. 432–448. Springer, Cham (2018). https://doi.org/10.1007/978-3-030-01228-1_26
14. Zeiler, M.D., Fergus, R.: Visualizing and understanding convolutional networks. In: Fleet, D., Pajdla, T., Schiele, B., Tuytelaars, T. (eds.) ECCV 2014. LNCS, vol. 8689, pp. 818–833. Springer, Cham (2014). https://doi.org/10.1007/978-3-319-10590-1_53
15. Zhou, B., Lapedriza, A., Khosla, A., Oliva, A., Torralba, A.: Places: A 10 million image database for scene recognition. Proc. IEEE Trans. Pattern Anal. Mach. Intell. **40**(6), 1452–1464 (2017)
16. Zhou, B., Zhao, H., Puig, X., Fidler, S., Barriuso, A., Torralba, A.: Scene parsing through ade20k dataset. In: Proceedings of the IEEE Conference on Computer Vision and Pattern Recognition (CVPR), pp. 633–641 (2017)

The Impact of Activation Sparsity on Overfitting in Convolutional Neural Networks

Karim Huesmann, Luis Garcia Rodriguez, Lars Linsen, and Benjamin Risse[✉]

Faculty of Mathematics and Computer Science,
University of Muenster, Münster, Germany
{karim.huesmann,luis.garcia,linsen,b.risse}@uni-muenster.de
https://cvmls.uni-muenster.de

Abstract. Overfitting is one of the fundamental challenges when training convolutional neural networks and is usually identified by a diverging
training and test loss. The underlying dynamics of how the flow of activations induce overfitting is however poorly understood. In this study
we introduce a perplexity-based sparsity definition to derive and visualise layer-wise activation measures. These novel explainable AI strategies reveal a surprising relationship between activation sparsity and overfitting, namely an increase in sparsity in the feature extraction layers
shortly before the test loss starts rising. This tendency is preserved across
network architectures and reguralisation strategies so that our measures
can be used as a reliable indicator for overfitting while decoupling the
network's generalisation capabilities from its loss-based definition. Moreover, our differentiable sparsity formulation can be used to explicitly
penalise the emergence of sparsity during training so that the impact of
reduced sparsity on overfitting can be studied in real-time. Applying this
penalty and analysing activation sparsity for well known regularisers and
in common network architectures supports the hypothesis that reduced
activation sparsity can effectively improve the generalisation and classification performance. In line with other recent work on this topic, our
methods reveal novel insights into the contradicting concepts of activation sparsity and network capacity by demonstrating that dense activations can enable discriminative feature learning while efficiently exploiting the capacity of deep models without suffering from overfitting, even
when trained excessively.

Keywords: Explainable AI · Sparstiy · Overfitting · Visualisation
technique · CNNs

1 Introduction

In recent years deep convolutional neural networks (CNNs) achieved state-of-
the-art performances in most computer vision applications [20,35]. The ultimate

© Springer Nature Switzerland AG 2021
A. Del Bimbo et al. (Eds.): ICPR 2020 Workshops, LNCS 12663, pp. 130–145, 2021.
https://doi.org/10.1007/978-3-030-68796-0_10

goal of training neural networks networks is to achieve high performance measures while avoiding the generalisation error, which is defined by the difference between the training and test set loss [40]. This error estimate requires that the trained model is independent of the test set (independence hypothesis) [37]. If the independence hypothesis holds [37] and generalisation error is high, then the model is suspected to have an inappropriately high variance and is therefore overfitted to the training data [41]. In fact, overfitting appears to be one of the fundamental challenges in training deep CNNs since models often tend to learn too specific features of the training set [2,13].

1.1 Related Work

In the past, a variety of strategies have been proposed to prevent overfitting, which can be roughly categorised into: (i) increasing the amount of training data; (ii) reducing the models' capacity; (iii) regularising the model parameters; and (iv) early stopping procedures. Increasing the training set can either be done by collecting additional data or by augmenting the existing set [10,16]. The reduction of the capacity is usually done by explicitly pruning learnable parameters [15,21,23,27]. In a similar fashion, regularisation can also be used to decrease the capacity of the model [19,28]. For example [28] and [4] both aim to extenuate the model complexity by using weight decay and it has also been shown that classical L1 regularisation tends to less complex models over time [25,38]. In contrast, decorrelation-based regularisers aim to employ the given capacity by reducing redundancies based on hidden features [3,6] or activations [5,9], whereas entropy-based regularisation uses the output distribution of the network to reduce overfitting [26,29]. Alternative regularisation strategies incorporate additional layers. The two most common examples are dropout [34] and batch normalisation [19]. Finally, early stopping has been studied for more than a decade to end the training before the generalisation error gets too high [30] and has recently been studied in the presence of label noise [22].

An important concept often related to overfitting is neural network sparsity, which is interpreted as an indicator of success in learning discriminative features [1] while filtering out irrelevant information, in analogy to sparsity observed in the neocortex [36]. Consequently, many of the previously mentioned pruning and regularisation techniques assume that sparse models suffer less from generalisation error [4,15,21,23,25,27,28,38]. In addition, several empirical investigations have been done to demonstrate beneficial effects of sparsity on the performance of deep neural networks [7,11,12]. However, recent experiments suggest that our comprehension of sparsity is insufficient to fully understand its underlying relationship to generalisation errors [24,42]. Interestingly, even though sparsity inevitably induces an underutilisation of the network's capacity [3] it has never been considered to be used to explain overfitting.

1.2   Contribution

Usually sparsity is referred to the property of zero-valued weights [12] and is distinguished from *activation sparsity* which counts the number of zeros after applying a non-linearity (in general ReLU) [31,39]. Most existing work on (activation) sparsity focuses on its beneficiary effects such as improved inference performances or the robustness to adversarial attacks and noise [1,11,17]. Here we propose a novel activation sparsity definition which reveals a surprising relationship between sparsity and overfitting. Our analysis suggests that high activation sparsity is a reliable indicator for an underutilisation of the potential network capacity and therefore limits the generalisation capabilities of the model which induces overfitting. To study this hypothesis we propose:

1. a perplexity-based activation sparsity definition which uses network features across neural receptive fields, yielding a novel layer-wise (i.e. targeted) sparsity measures, called *neural activation sparsity* (NAS);
2. targeted explainable AI (XAI) visualisation strategies to identify neural activation sparsity in both, convolutional and fully connected layers in real-time;
3. a regularisation strategy derived from our neural activation sparsity definition which can be used to penalise or reward neural activation sparsity in a targeted manner.

Using these techniques, we demonstrate that an increase in neural activation sparsity in all layers except the prediction layer indeed coincides with test loss-based overfitting measures. Therefore, our XAI measures can be used as an indicator for overfitting, which is independent of loss values, thus enables the detection of generalisation errors even if the independence hypothesis of the training and test data is violated. To further demonstrate this relationship, we counteract neural activation sparsity in a layer-specific fashion using a novel regularisation strategy: by penalising neural activation sparsity in the feature extraction layers we can prevent the network from overfitting while increasing the overall accuracy. We elaborate our findings by performing several experiments including common network architectures (including VGG16, ResNet50 and Xception) and regularisation strategies (L1, L2, dropout and batch normalisation). Interestingly, targeted neural activation sparsity regularisation prevents overfitting even in low training data/high model size scenarios and outperforms conventional regularisation techniques. In line with other recent work on activation sparsity [24,42] we demonstrate that neural network sparsity must not be a desirable property by definition. Instead salient and discriminative feature learning while exploiting the full capacity of the model appears to be another important dimension to effectively train deep convolutional neural networks.

2   Methods

2.1   Activation Sparsity Definition

Neural network sparsity is usually defined by the amount of weights which are exactly or close to zero [12]. Even though this quantification is inspired by observations made in real brains [36], neuroscientific sparsity definitions are based on

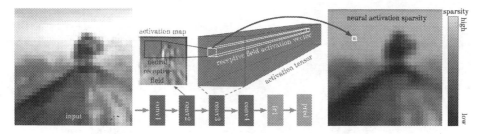

Fig. 1. NAS and NAS heatmap generation. Left: sample input image. Middle: schematic network architecture and sketch of an exemplary proximate receptive field from the conv2 layer and the corresponding receptive field activation vector in conv3 layer. Right: NAS Heatmap extracted by calculating the activation sparsity on the depicted receptive field activation vector.

neuronal activation patterns [32]. In a similar fashion sparse information propagation in the forward path of artificial neural networks can be the result of zero-valued weights or zero-valued input coefficients. Motivated by this observation we introduce a novel sparsity indicator that is purely based on the feature map activations which we refer to as *neural activation sparsity* (NAS). We note that our sparsity definition differs from existing activation sparsity definitions in two ways. Firstly, conventional activation sparsity measures count the number of zeros after the use of the non-linearity [31,39], whereas our metric is calculated before the nonlinearity is applied. As a consequence NAS is independent of the activation function (i.e. less biased) and captures both, weight- and data-induced sparsifications (i.e. more sensitive). Secondly, we measure relative neural activity values in comparison to all other feature map activations at a given neural receptive field. The neural receptive field is defined as the region of a layer's direct input that a filter is being affected by (see Fig. 1).

More formally, a layer with D filters creates a $D \times M \times N$ shaped feature tensor. Thus, the input of this layer consists of $M \cdot N = R$ receptive fields. Let $x_{d',i,j,m,n}$ be a pixel at position (i,j) and channel d' of receptive field $r_{m,n}$. The corresponding weight of filter f_d which affects this pixel is given as $w_{d',i,j,d}$. The number of pixels in $r_{m,n}$ is equal to the number of weights in f_d. Hence, the linear activation $a_{m,n,d}$ created by f_d when applied to $r_{m,n}$ is defined as

$$a_{m,n,d} = \sum_{d',i,j} w_{d',i,j,d} \cdot x_{d',i,j,m,n}. \tag{1}$$

To improve readability, we denote the results of this linear filtering as receptive field activation vectors $\mathbf{a}_k \in \mathbb{R}^D, k \in [0, R-1]$, where k is a linear index over all receptive fields computed by $k = m \cdot N + n$.

In order to define activation sparsity based on $\mathbf{a}_k$ we first transform its components into a probability-like distribution by using the Softmax function:

$$p_l(\mathbf{a}_k) = \frac{e^{a_k^l}}{\sum_m e^{a_k^m}}, \; l \in [1, ..., D] \tag{2}$$

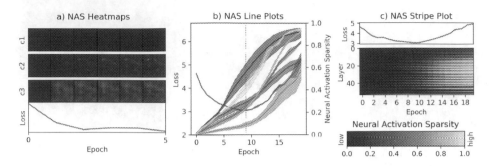

Fig. 2. Visualisations of layer NAS over time at three levels of aggregation with corresponding test loss (red): (a) *NAS Heatmaps* showing spatial sparsity distributions for 3 layers. (b) *NAS Line Plot* showing blue lines (and bands) of layer NAS values. (c) *NAS Stripe Plot* for 50 layers encoding layer NAS in 1D colour coded stripes. (Color figure online)

where a_k^l is the l-th component of $\mathbf{a}_k$. Subsequently, we calculate the perplexity for each normalised neural receptive field by

$$\rho_k = e^{H_k} \tag{3}$$

with

$$H_k = H(\mathbf{a}_k) = -\sum_{l=1}^{D} p_l(\mathbf{a}_k) \, ln(p_l(\mathbf{a}_k)). \tag{4}$$

By definition, perplexity results in values in a range between $[1, D]$. Next, we define a perplexity score τ by rescaling ρ into values ≤ 1:

$$\tau_k = \frac{\rho(\mathbf{p})_k}{D}, \tag{5}$$

where $\tau_k \in [\frac{1}{D}, 1]$. Based on this definition, the smaller/larger τ_k is, the less/more filters are activated at the neural receptive field k. Finally, we can define the neural activation sparsity by

$$s_k = 1 - \tau_k. \tag{6}$$

This activation sparsity measure reaches its maximum value $s_k = 1 - \frac{1}{D}$, if only one of the given D feature maps returns an activation a_l, $a_l \in \mathbf{a}_k$, $p_l(\mathbf{a}_k) \neq 0$, indicating lowest possible activation density for a given neural receptive field. The minimum value $s_k = 0$ can be reached, if all D feature maps return the same activation $a_l = a_m, l \neq m$, which is equivalent to the highest possible activation density and thus minimum activation sparsity.

2.2 Activation Sparsity Visualisation

In order to enable a temporal visualisation of layer NAS for a variety of CNN architectures we propose three different approaches that visually represent the time series at different levels of aggregation using geometric (lines) and colour (heatmap) encodings. These strategies are a trade-off between the level of visualised details and the underlying network depth.

The most detailed visualisation can be achieved by spatially localised colour-encodings of each NAS value for all layers. By applying the newly defined activation sparsity, we can calculate s_k for each position k in all layers, indicating how many of the layer's filters produce a comparatively high activation for the given filter input. Encoding and re-ordering all s_k into a 2D heatmap we can visualise the activation sparsity in a very detailed manner for a given input as illustrated in Fig. 2(a): High sparsity measures are given in yellow indicating that only a few filters produced high activations at the location of the respective neural receptive field. Likewise, the dark pixels indicate many highly activated filters (i.e. low NAS measures) which naturally occurs at contrast-rich locations such as edges and textured regions. Note that the same visualisation strategy can be used for fully connected layers, with the only difference that the resulting heatmap consists of a single value.

Even though NAS heatmaps enable spatial reasoning within the activation maps, this visualisation can become overloaded given many layers or training epochs. In order to provide a more concise overview of NAS values for all layers we therefore introduce the NAS Line Plot which visualise the median NAS values over all neural receptive fields for a given layer into the same illustration as shown in Fig. 2(b). Each line therefore represents the change in activation sparsity (y-axis) of an individual layer over time (x-axis), where brightness of the colour encodes the depth of the layers (early layers in dark blue and deep layers in bright blue). Furthermore, we are able to visualise uncertainties between multiple trainings by including a band, which in fact makes the plot a functional box plot over time (minimum, median, maximum). NAS Line Plots allow for effectively reading off the NAS values for each layer at each time step including their uncertainty, but they are limited to a certain amount of layers since very deep networks will lead to occluded curves.

Therefore we also provide a visualisation technique which further abstracts from the measured NAS values by means of a colour-coded 1D NAS heatmap over time (x-axis), which we refer to as NAS Stripe Plot. The NAS Stripe Plots are sorted by increasing layer depth (y-axis). As can be seen in Fig. 2(c) this visualisation encodes the least details but can be used to illustrate NAS dynamics over dozens of layers.

In Fig. 2 all NAS visualisations are superimposed with the respective test loss over time (red line) to demonstrate the impact of activation sparsity on overfitting. For NAS Heatmaps and Stripe Plots, we always applied the same colour map as shown in Fig. 2, encoding NAS values from low (dark blue, $s_k = 0$) to high (yellow, $s_k \approx 1$). Moreover these visualisations can be calculated dynamically during training so that these XAI strategies can offer deep insights into activation sparsity of a given network in real-time.

2.3 Activation Sparsity Regularisation

To test our hypothesis, that NAS is related to overfitting, we introduce a penalty term that prevents the network layers from producing sparse activations. This term is directly derived from our aforementioned activation sparsity definition and utilises the fact that perplexity is differentiable in our given ranges so that it can be used as an activity regulariser. More formally, our regularisation penalty term $\mathcal{L}_s$ is defined by

$$\mathcal{L}_s = -\sum_i \lambda_i \sum_{k=0}^{r_i} \rho_k^i, \tag{7}$$

where i loops through all layers of the network, r_i is the number of receptive fields in the respective layer and ρ_k^i refers to ρ_k as defined in Eq. 3. In the following, this regularisation is referred to as *NASReg*.

As perplexity reaches its maximum when all filters are activated in the same way, this regulariser can have the tendency to produce highly correlated filters. The trivial solution for $\mathcal{L}_s$ to be minimised is therefore to generate identical filter responses. As identical filters reduce the predictive power of neural networks, this effect has to be counterbalanced by preventing high filter correlations. Therefore we have to set $\lambda_i \geq 0$ in a way, that the perplexity is not reaching it's theoretical maximum.

2.4 Experimental Design

In our first set of experiments we used an intentionally simple base line architecture called *VanillaNet*. This basic network comprises two conv-conv-pool blocks followed by two fully connected layers and the layer sizes of conv1, conv2, conv3, conv4, and fc1 are 256, 256, 512, 512, 1024 respectively. ReLU is used as activation function across all layers except the last fully connected layer.

Next, we analysed our XAI strategies in the context of different regularisation techniques. In particular, we extended the VanillaNet by including L1, L2, dropout and batch normalisation (called *L1Net*, *L2Net*, *DropNet* and *NormNet* respectively) since these techniques are known to have an impact on sparsity. For DropNet we set the dropout rate to 0.3 for layers conv1 to fc1 and 0.5 between fc1 and prediction layer.

To study the generalisability of our metrics and visualisation strategies for state-of-the-art architectures we evaluated three very deep CNNs, namely VGG16 [33], ResNet50 [18] and Xception [8]. Moreover, the behaviour of ResNet with and without batch normalisation is analysed to further evaluate the impact of regularisation on activation sparsity of deep nets.

For a better interpretability and to reduce side effects of the experiments we have chosen a non-adaptive optimiser. Accordingly, we used vanilla Stochastic Gradient Decent without momentum and a fixed learning rate of 0.01 without learning rate scheduling. This allows us to carry out a uniform training over the entire course of the experiments. For the classification we are optimising the categorical cross-entropy loss. The experiments are trained up to 300 epochs with a batch size of 32.

During the training, we calculate NAS for each convolution and fully connected layer individually. For most of our experiments we chose the cifar-100 dataset (50,000 train and 10,000 test images), because it is very susceptible to overfitting. For one particular experiment we intentionally violated the independence hypothesis of our test dataset by creating a new testing set consisting of 5,000 train and 5,000 test images, which we mixed to generate a distorted test loss. We conducted a hyperparameter search to find appropriate values for λ_i which resulted in a strong correlation between λ_i and the size of the layers. Therefore we reduced the mean NAS via $\lambda_i = \frac{1}{r_i}$ for each layer i in all experiments. In order to add uncertainty to the results, we repeat each training 3 times.

3   Results

3.1   Relationship Between Overfitting and Activation Sparsity

To test if classical test loss based generalisation errors coincide with our NAS definition, we analysed the NAS Line Plots for multiple experiments. In Fig. 3(a) the resultant NAS Line Plots of VanillaNet on cifar-100 can be seen, which are not affected by any regularisation, thus allowing a straight-forward interpretation. Since cifar-100 is prone to overfitting if no augmentation or advanced training protocol is used, it can be seen that the test loss starts to rise quickly after epoch 4. As it is apparent in the plots, NAS also increases almost simultaneously with the test loss: Whilst the NAS in conv1 rises relatively slowly, a rapid jump can already be observed in conv2. The jump in NAS is even recognisable shortly before the test loss diverges. The observation that conv1 NAS is usually low and that higher NAS can be observed in deeper layers is in line with other work on activation sparsity (i.e. based on counting zeros after ReLU activation) [31].

Since our NAS overfitting estimation is only based on activation patterns, it does not depend on the satisfaction of the independence hypothesis [37]. To illustrate this we created a test loss which violates the independence hypothesis by including 50% dependent images to this set (Fig. 3(a); orange line). As can be clearly seen, this perturbed test loss does not allow generalisation error estimations, whereas our NAS indicators still diverge accordingly.

To further investigate our observation that NAS coincides with overfitting, we used dropout since this technique is known to reduce generalisation errors. As shown in Fig. 3(b) dropout indeed delays the divergence of the test loss and also reduces its slope. However, overfitting cannot be avoided which is also reflected in the median NAS measures throughout the layers. Moreover, all but the conv1 NAS measures saturate close to $s_k = 1$ after epoch 18 indicating a drastically reduced number of highly activated features propagating through the network. This observation, combined with the constantly increasing test loss value suggests, that the remaining features are over-adapted to the training data.

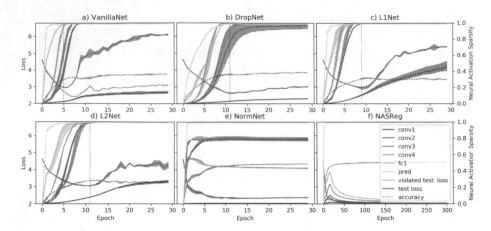

Fig. 3. NAS Line Plots for Test loss (left axis) and median NAS (right axis) over time. The dashed red lines indicate the moment of overfitting derived from the test loss. All trainings are carried out on cifar-100 dataset. (a)–(e) networks are trained for 30 epochs whereas the NASReg network in (f) is trained for 300 epochs. (Color figure online)

As theory suggests, applying L1 regularisation encourages sparse weight tensors and should therefore affect our NAS measures. As shown in Fig. 3(c), we can see a relatively steep increase of NAS in all layers compared to all other experiments. Furthermore, all layers (even conv1) quickly converge towards NAS values close to 1. Again, the moment of diverging loss and increasing NAS coincide. A similar observation can be made for L2 regularised networks (Fig. 3(d)). Even though L2 regularisation is able to shift the moment of overfitting to a later epoch, the corresponding NAS values start to rise slowly before strong generalisation errors are observable in the test loss estimates.

Adding batch normalisation layers to a given network architecture is a widely used approach to prevent overfitting [19]. In line with other work on this regularisation technique the loss does not show a noticeable divergence throughout our training as can be seen in Fig. 3(e). Similarly our NAS estimates also tend towards constant values < 1 which indicates that batch normalisation has an attenuating effect on activation sparsity over time. Note that the first layer (conv1) has no tendency towards sparsified activations throughout the entire training. We conclude that despite the different effect of batch normalisation on overfitting, the overall tendency of coinciding NAS propagation can also be observed for almost all layers.

3.2   Spatial Analysis of Activation Sparstiy

Figure 4(a) illustrates the NAS Heatmaps generated for the individual VanillaNet layers over 30 epochs of training in comparison to the corresponding test loss. Similar to the observations made in the previous section the test loss

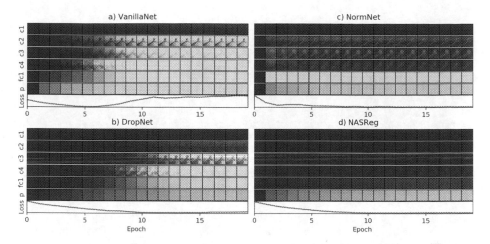

Fig. 4. NAS Heatmaps and corresponding test loss values for (a) VanillaNet, (b) Drop-Net, (c) NormNet and (d) NASReg trainings. The respective heatmaps were created after each corresponding epoch. The original input image can be seen in Fig. 1 (colour map corresponds to Fig. 2).

indicates overfitting after epoch 4 and the conv1 layer is not very susceptible to changes in NAS, whereas the other layers show increased sparsity proportional to their depth. The same phenomenon can be seen in Fig. 4(b) in which we used dropout to delay overfitting. In analogy to the previous results, the NAS measures shift accordingly to later epochs but the overall tendency of coinciding generalisation error and increasing NAS is preserved. Moreover, spatial NAS representations further reveal the location of sparsified features and therefore less activated filters.

In order to further investigate our spatial NAS visualisation strategy, we visualised these dynamics for a batch normalisation regularised network (Fig. 4(c)). Batch normalisation can effectively counteract overfitting as can be seen in both, the loss plot and the corresponding NAS heatmaps. The heatmaps reveal that the overall NAS is low and does not show a significant change over time. However, subtle features of the original input appear relatively early in deeper conv layers highlighting the strengths of this more detailed visualisation technique.

In summary, these observations suggest that a progressive escalation of NAS tends to coincide with overfitting. To further investigate both, this hypothesis and the validity of our sparsity definition, we are penalising high NAS values in a layer-wise fashion in the next experiment.

3.3   Activation Sparsity Regularisation Results

To study the impact of activation sparsity on overfitting in more detail, we applied NASReg to enforce low NAS values in individual layers except the prediction layer. Figure 3(f) shows the course of a NAS regularised training. Note that

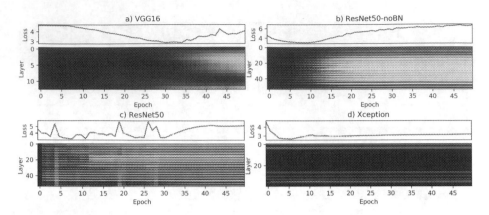

Fig. 5. NAS Stripe Plots and corresponding test loss (a) VGG16, (b) ResNet50-noBN, (c) ResNet50 and (d) Xception. Colour map equivalent to Fig. 2.

in comparison to Fig. 3(a)–(e) we substantially extended training to 300 epochs to show potential long-term effects. Since the regularisation adds a penalty term to the loss, the resultant cross-entropy loss is shown here. Juxtaposing NASReg with the other trainings, one can clearly see the effect of the regularisation on the recorded training history. VanillaNet, DropNet, L1Net and L2Net clearly start overfitting before the 20th epoch. In comparison, the NASReg test loss measures does not indicate any generalisation errors even when trained for several hundreds of epochs. Moreover this training reaches a significantly lower loss value compared to the other trainings. One can observe that the NAS regularised layers reveal a different behaviour in comparison to the other trainings: Despite the initial increase in NAS estimates the regulariser pushes all NAS measurements towards values close to zero shortly before epoch 15.

The differences between NASReg and the other trainings is also shown in Fig. 4(d). Here one can see a strong similarity to the NormNet training, which also does not suffer from overfitting in the given epochs. Since we explicitly encourage low NAS values using NASReg the heatmaps given in Fig. 4(d) comprise even lower activation sparsity values than NormNet. Moreover, we regularise fc1 so that only the final prediction layer learns to produce sparse activations, as desired for conventional classification tasks. Even though we used intentionally straight forward models the positive influence of regularised NAS can also be observed in the test accuracy: As can be seen in Fig. 3 the peak accuracy of NASReg (0.5119) outperforms VanillaNet (0.3851), DropNet (0.4034), L1Net (0.3267) and L2Net (0.2866). The smaller accuracy difference to Norm-Net (0.4947) follows the intuition that a certain degree of activation sparsity is acceptable in deeper layers.

3.4   Activation Sparsity in Common Deep Architectures

After having examined the VanillaNet baseline architecture and its regularised variations, we next investigate further NAS measurements in common deep architectures, namely VGG16, ResNet50 and Xception. The training was performed on cifar-100 using the same conditions as described in Sect. 2.4.

The VGG16 network mainly differs from VanillaNet by having a higher number of convolutional layers and a more advanced pooling strategy. In line with our hypothesis we can observe the same NAS behaviour when the network starts overfitting (Fig. 5(a)). Here, overfitting takes place at around epoch 30 and we can observe increased NAS measures especially in the middle layers shortly before epoch 30.

The ResNet architecture is another common deep CNN, consisting of multiple layers with several shortcut connections. Since batch normalisation has a strong influence on activation sparsity (see Sect. 3.1) we investigated the original regularised ResNet50 and an unregularised version (ResNet50-noBN). The main difference between ResNet50-noBN and VGG16 is the higher number of layers and the presence of shortcuts. Again, as soon as the training drifts into overfitting, the NAS starts rising significantly in most layers (see Fig. 5(b)).

When applying batch normalisation to ResNet50, we observe an impact on both the NAS and the overfitting measures (see Fig. 5(c)). Similar to the results presented for the VanillaNet (cf. Fig. 3), continuous test loss increases can be delayed while achieving better overall loss values when compared to the non-regularised version. Moreover, batch norm again stabilises many layers to constant NAS values throughout the training (cf. Sect. 3.1). However, the loss rises sharply at epoch 5, 19 and 26, which is also reflected by a sudden NAS increase for most layers. Overall a more chaotic NAS and test loss behaviour can be observed until the network starts to overfit in epoch 30.

The overall relationship between overfitting and NAS can also be confirmed in the Xception architecture (see Fig. 5(d)): When compared to VGG16 and ResNet50 the Xception network achieves best overall generalisation performance, which is also reflected in the low activation sparsity measures. Since these networks also utilise batch normalisation in most layers we can also observe stabilised NAS values over time. Interestingly, even in this complex architecture subtle overfitting tendency starting at about epoch 5 can be observed in a deeper layer as slight increases in the NAS estimates are visible at the moment of overfitting which again demonstrates the sensitivity of our XAI measures.

4   Conclusion

In this paper we introduced a more sensitive and less biased neural activation sparsity (NAS) definition which we used to derive reliable quantitative measures and layer-wise visualisation techniques to study the dynamics in CNNs during training. Interestingly, the analysis of NAS for various network types and regularisation strategies revealed a correlation between activation sparsity and overfitting. Throughout our experiments we observed a decreasing amount of discriminative features in almost all layers over time so that the influence of most neurons for the overall classification task became negligible. This observation is in line with work on the beneficiary effects of network pruning [14,24]. Potential generalisation error tendencies of heavily sparsified models were however not taken into consideration previously. Our results suggest that high activation sparsity indeed coincides with overfitting which we were able to detect on a per-layer basis. Moreover, the rise in NAS values even occurs shortly before the test loss based overfitting measures and our generalisation error estimates do not require the independence between training and test data.

Using our visualisation strategy we were able to show the network performance with respect to the utilised capacity during training. These visual investigation gave additional evidence that low NAS can be a desirable characteristic for the feature extraction layers. In contrast, the final classification layer benefits from high activation sparsity to ensure distinct classification decisions. Applying the NAS measures as a penalty term during training we derived a novel regulariser which prevents CNNs from overfitting over the entire course of training. In fact, our NAS-based regularisation technique not just supports hypothetical relationship between overfitting and activation sparsity, but also outperforms dropout and batch normalisation in our experiments.

We studied the effects of NAS in a variety of different well-known architectures and regularisation strategies and demonstrated that comparable effects can be observed across all experiments. These experiments gave additional evidence for the relation between sparsity and overfitting and revealed interesting sparsity-related activation dynamics of batch normalisation. In the future we will investigate these dynamics in more detail, experiment with more complex network architectures, analyse NAS values for adaptive optimisers such as ADAM and study the potential of our novel regulariser for overall performance improvements.

Acknowledgements. BR would like to thank the *Ministeriums für Kultur und Wissenschaft des Landes Nordrhein-Westfalen* for the AI Starter support (ID 005-2010-005). Moreover, the authors would like to sincerely thank Sören Klemm for his valuable ideas and input throughout this project and the *WWU IT* for the usage of the *PALMA2* supercomputer. This work was partially supported by the *Deutsche Forschungsgemeinschaft* (DFG) under contract LI 1530/21-2.

References

1. Ahmad, S., Scheinkman, L.: How can we be so dense? The benefits of using highly sparse representations. arXiv preprint arXiv:1903.11257 (2019)
2. Ayinde, B.O., Inanc, T., Zurada, J.M.: On correlation of features extracted by deep neural networks. In: International Joint Conference on Neural Networks (IJCNN), Proceedings, pp. 1–8 (2019)
3. Ayinde, B.O., Inanc, T., Zurada, J.M.: Regularizing deep neural networks by enhancing diversity in feature extraction. IEEE Trans. Neural Netw. Learn. Syst. **30**, 2650–2661 (2019)

4. Ayinde, B.O., Zurada, J.M.: Deep learning of constrained autoencoders for enhanced understanding of data. IEEE Trans. Neural Netw. Learn. Syst. **29**(9), 3969–3979 (2017)

5. Bao, Y., Jiang, H., Dai, L., Liu, C.: Incoherent training of deep neural networks to de-correlate bottleneck features for speech recognition. In: 2013 IEEE International Conference on Acoustics, Speech and Signal Processing, pp. 6980–6984. IEEE (2013)

6. Bengio, Y., Bergstra, J.S.: Slow, decorrelated features for pretraining complex cell-like networks. In: Advances in Neural Information Processing Systems, pp. 99–107 (2009)

7. Changpinyo, S., Sandler, M., Zhmoginov, A.: The power of sparsity in convolutional neural networks. arXiv preprint arXiv:1702.06257 (2017)

8. Chollet, F.: Xception: deep learning with depthwise separable convolutions. In: Proceedings of the IEEE Conference on Computer Vision and Pattern Recognition, pp. 1251–1258 (2017)

9. Cogswell, M., Ahmed, F., Girshick, R., Zitnick, L., Batra, D.: Reducing overfitting in deep networks by decorrelating representations. arXiv preprint arXiv:1511.06068 (2015)

10. Cubuk, E.D., Zoph, B., Mane, D., Vasudevan, V., Le, Q.V.: AutoAugment: learning augmentation strategies from data. In: IEEE Conference on Computer Vision and Pattern Recognition (CVPR), Proceedings, pp. 113–123 (2019)

11. Frankle, J., Carbin, M.: The lottery ticket hypothesis: finding sparse, trainable neural networks. In: International Conference on Learning Representations (2018)

12. Gale, T., Elsen, E., Hooker, S.: The state of sparsity in deep neural networks. arXiv preprint arXiv:1902.09574 (2019)

13. Gavrilov, A.D., Jordache, A., Vasdani, M., Deng, J.: Preventing model overfitting and underfitting in convolutional neural networks. Int. J. Softw. Sci. Comput. Intell. (IJSSCI) **10**(4), 19–28 (2018)

14. Gomez, A.N., et al.: Learning sparse networks using targeted dropout. arXiv (2019)

15. Goodfellow, I.J., Bengio, Y., Courville, A.C.: Deep Learning. Adaptive Computation and Machine Learning. MIT Press, Cambridge (2016)

16. Guo, H., Mao, Y., Zhang, R.: Mixup as locally linear out-of-manifold regularization. In: AAAI Conference on Artificial Intelligence (AAAI), Proceedings, pp. 3714–3722 (2019)

17. Guo, Y., Zhang, C., Zhang, C., Chen, Y.: Sparse DNNs with improved adversarial robustness. In: Advances in Neural Information Processing Systems, pp. 242–251 (2018)

18. He, K., Zhang, X., Ren, S., Sun, J.: Deep residual learning for image recognition. In: Proceedings of the IEEE Conference on Computer Vision and Pattern Recognition, pp. 770–778 (2016)

19. Ioffe, S., Szegedy, C.: Batch normalization: accelerating deep network training by reducing internal covariate shift. In: International Conference on Machine Learning (ICML), Proceedings, pp. 448–456 (2015)

20. Khan, A., Sohail, A., Zahoora, U., Qureshi, A.S.: A survey of the recent architectures of deep convolutional neural networks. Artif. Intell. Rev. **53**(8), 5455–5516 (2020). https://doi.org/10.1007/s10462-020-09825-6

21. Klemm, S., Ortkemper, R.D., Jiang, X.: Deploying deep learning into practice: a case study on fundus segmentation. In: Zheng, Y., Williams, B.M., Chen, K. (eds.) MIUA 2019. CCIS, vol. 1065, pp. 411–422. Springer, Cham (2020). https://doi.org/10.1007/978-3-030-39343-4_35

22. Li, M., Soltanolkotabi, M., Oymak, S.: Gradient descent with early stopping is provably robust to label noise for overparameterized neural networks. In: International Conference on Artificial Intelligence and Statistics, pp. 4313–4324. PMLR (2020)
23. Liu, Z., Li, J., Shen, Z., Huang, G., Yan, S., Zhang, C.: Learning efficient convolutional networks through network slimming. In: Proceedings of the IEEE International Conference on Computer Vision, pp. 2736–2744 (2017)
24. Liu, Z., Sun, M., Zhou, T., Huang, G., Darrell, T.: Rethinking the value of network pruning. In: International Conference on Learning Representations (2018)
25. Mehta, D., Kim, K.I., Theobalt, C.: On implicit filter level sparsity in convolutional neural networks. In: Proceedings of the IEEE Conference on Computer Vision and Pattern Recognition, pp. 520–528 (2019)
26. Miller, D.J., Rao, A.V., Rose, K., Gersho, A.: A global optimization technique for statistical classifier design. IEEE Trans. Signal Process. **44**(12), 3108–3122 (1996)
27. Molchanov, P., Tyree, S., Karras, T., Aila, T., Kautz, J.: Pruning convolutional neural networks for resource efficient inference. In: 5th International Conference on Learning Representations, ICLR 2017-Conference Track Proceedings (2019)
28. Nowlan, S.J., Hinton, G.E.: Simplifying neural networks by soft weight-sharing. Neural Comput. **4**(4), 473–493 (1992)
29. Pereyra, G., Tucker, G., Chorowski, J., Kaiser, L., Hinton, G.E.: Regularizing neural networks by penalizing confident output distributions. In: International Conference on Learning Representations (ICLR), Proceedings (2017)
30. Prechelt, L.: Early stopping - but when? In: Orr, G.B., Müller, K.-R. (eds.) Neural Networks: Tricks of the Trade. LNCS, vol. 1524, pp. 55–69. Springer, Heidelberg (1998). https://doi.org/10.1007/3-540-49430-8_3
31. Rhu, M., O'Connor, M., Chatterjee, N., Pool, J., Kwon, Y., Keckler, S.W.: Compressing DMA engine: leveraging activation sparsity for training deep neural networks. In: 2018 IEEE International Symposium on High Performance Computer Architecture (HPCA), pp. 78–91 (2018)
32. Seelig, J.D., et al.: Two-photon calcium imaging from head-fixed drosophila during optomotor walking behavior. Nat. Methods **7**(7), 535 (2010)
33. Simonyan, K., Zisserman, A.: Very deep convolutional networks for large-scale image recognition. Computational and Biological Learning Society (2015)
34. Srivastava, N., Hinton, G.E., Krizhevsky, A., Sutskever, I., Salakhutdinov, R.: Dropout: a simple way to prevent neural networks from overfitting. J. Mach. Learn. Res. (JMLR) **15**(1), 1929–1958 (2014)
35. Tu, Z., et al.: A survey of variational and CNN-based optical flow techniques. Sig. Process. Image Commun. **72**, 9–24 (2019)
36. Vinje, W.E., Gallant, J.L.: Sparse coding and decorrelation in primary visual cortex during natural vision. Science **287**(5456), 1273–1276 (2000)
37. Werpachowski, R., György, A., Szepesvári, C.: Detecting overfitting via adversarial examples. In: Advances in Neural Information Processing Systems, pp. 7856–7866 (2019)
38. Yaguchi, A., Suzuki, T., Asano, W., Nitta, S., Sakata, Y., Tanizawa, A.: Adam induces implicit weight sparsity in rectifier neural networks. In: IEEE International Conference on Machine Learning and Applications (ICMLA), Proceedings, pp. 318–325 (2018)
39. Yang, Q., Mao, J., Wang, Z., Li, H.: DASNet: dynamic activation sparsity for neural network efficiency improvement. In: 2019 IEEE 31st International Conference on Tools with Artificial Intelligence (ICTAI), pp. 1401–1405. IEEE (2019)

40. Zhang, C., Bengio, S., Hardt, M., Recht, B., Vinyals, O.: Understanding deep learning requires rethinking generalization. In: International Conference on Learning Representations (ICLR), Proceedings (2017)
41. Zhang, C., Vinyals, O., Munos, R., Bengio, S.: A study on overfitting in deep reinforcement learning. arXiv preprint arXiv:1804.06893 (2018)
42. Zhou, H., Lan, J., Liu, R., Yosinski, J.: Deconstructing lottery tickets: zeros, signs, and the supermask. In: Advances in Neural Information Processing Systems, pp. 3592–3602 (2019)

Remove to Improve?

Kamila Abdiyeva[1,2(✉)], Martin Lukac[2], and Narendra Ahuja[3]

[1] Nanyang Technological University, Singapore, Singapore
kabdiyeva@nu.edu.kz
[2] Nazarbayev University, Nur-Sultan, Kazakhstan
martin.lukac@nu.edu.kz
[3] University of Illinois at Urbana-Champaign, Champaign, USA
n-ahuja@illinois.edu

Abstract. The workhorses of CNNs are its filters, located at different layers and tuned to different features. Their responses are combined using weights obtained via network training. Training is aimed at optimal results for the entire training data, e.g., highest average classification accuracy. In this paper, we are interested in extending the current understanding of the roles played by the filters, their mutual interactions, and their relationship to classification accuracy. This is motivated by observations that the classification accuracy for some classes increases, instead of decreasing when some filters are pruned from a CNN. We are interested in experimentally addressing the following question: Under what conditions does filter pruning increase classification accuracy? We show that improvement of classification accuracy occurs for certain classes. These classes are placed during learning into a space (spanned by filter usage) populated with semantically related neighbors. The neighborhood structure of such classes is however sparse enough so that during pruning, the resulting compression bringing all classes together brings sample data closer together and thus increases the accuracy of classification.

1 Introduction

Convolutional Neural Networks (CNN) provide solutions to a range of problems, from computer vision [3], raw audio generation [15], to general data analytics [13], to name some. Each network consists of a set of layers interconnected mostly sequentially and hierarchically, in a tree-like architecture. For the case of image classification, which is of interest in this paper, the first layer receives a multi-channel image as input. Each higher layer then receives as input the multi-channel output of the previous layer. Each layer transform its input using a fixed, layer specific set of filters, and produces a multi-channel output. The outputs of the filters are combined, both linearly and non-linearly, in ways that are architecture specific, to ultimately obtain the results at the highest, output level, e.g., likelihoods that an input image belongs to a given set of classes. The core of the network is the set of filters, located in different layers and tuned to different features. Each filter offers a different degree and type of evidence for each class

A. Del Bimbo et al. (Eds.): ICPR 2020 Workshops, LNCS 12663, pp. 146–161, 2021.
https://doi.org/10.1007/978-3-030-68796-0_11

indicated by their associated weights. The weights are obtained by the network training process in order to balance the needs of different classes and provide the best average results over the entire training data, e.g., the highest average accuracy of classification of given samples from all classes. While the network thus trained is optimal for the given task, in this paper we are interested in extending the current understanding of the relationship between a filter set and the associated classification accuracy. This interest is motivated by observations we made when working on compression of CNNs: when some filters, making weak contributions to the evidence (activations) for a class, are pruned from a CNN, the classification accuracy for a substantial subset of classes increases, as against the expectation of a decrease. We wish to extend the current understanding of the roles played by the filters and their mutual interactions. In particular, we experimentally determine criteria for classification accuracy increase for certain classes as a result of pruning.

In the next section, Sect. 2, we first review related previous work. Section 3 provides an overview of the pruning algorithm which is the main technique we use to study filters and classification accuracy. Section 4 presents some definitions and measures used in the experiments. Section 5 presents the motivation and objectives of the experiments performed, their details, and their findings, vs. the questions raised in the introduction section. Section 6 presents concluding remarks.

2   Previous Work

Neural Network Visualization and Understanding. A number of attempts have been made to interpret the operation of CNNs [5,12,14,20,21]. Many of these [14,20,21] focused on explaining the functions of individual neurons. They search for the inputs/objects that maximize the response of a specific neuron, which is then seen as a 'single-cell object identifier'. Since neurons work as a network, single-neuron feature visualization provides limited insight into the understanding of neural network decision making. However, it is also challenging to analyze decisions made by groups of neurons, due to the combinatorial complexity created by the large number of network parameters. Visualization of groups of neurons was studied through visualization of activations in 2D space using PCA or t-SNE [10] compression. Lastly, in [2], in addition to single neuron visualization, authors approximate how variation in neuron value changes the logits of each class.

Pruning. Currently, available pruning methods [1,7,9,12,16,22] can be split mainly into three groups, based on weights, activations and accuracy/loss based optimizations. The simplest line of work is based on removing filters with smallest values [4]. Pruning based on activations is the closest to our approach, as it focuses on removing the least active neurons. One of such works is [8]. However, this method is not applicable in our case as the authors remove those filters that do not change the activation map, thus not providing sufficient information about the filters' contributions to a specific class. Accuracy/loss based optimization [11,18] methods try to estimate the contribution of a filter to the overall loss function or model accuracy, and usually involve a training component. Comparatively, for instance, Taylor pruning of [11] is much more efficient, but it is optimized towards the final loss function with additional retraining. Both of these criteria are not suitable for our work, as we want to investigate the original filter contribution to classification of individual classes. Besides, we do not want to affect the model accuracy by applying retraining. Hence, we use the simplest pruning method, namely, prune neurons directly related to a particular object class, as opposed to pruning based on overall data statistics.

3   Background and Definitions

In order to study the roles and relationships among filters in a convolutional network, we propose to use a simple activation-based pruning method, referred to as *Response Based Pruning (RBP)*. Below we first briefly present the main aspects and definitions related to RBP.

Let $\mathbb{F} = \{\mathbf{F}_1 ..., \mathbf{F}_k\}$ be the set of all filters in a convolutional neural network and $\mathbf{F}_i \in \mathbb{R}^{M \times M \times d}$ be a filter. Let, a subset of filters be a layer $\mathbb{L} \subset \mathbb{F}$ of a convolutional network. Let $\mathbf{B} \in \mathbb{R}^{X \times Y \times d}$ be an input tensor to $\mathbb{L}$ (X and Y are spatial dimensions). To calculate the output tensor $\mathbf{B}'$ of $\mathbb{L}$, the input tensor $\mathbf{B}$ is convolved with the set of filters $\mathbb{L} = \{\mathbf{F}_1 ..., \mathbf{F}_d\}$ (as illustrated in Fig. 1a). The output of the convolution between input tensor $\mathbf{B}$ and a single filter $\mathbf{F}_i$ is $\mathbf{R}_i \in \mathbb{R}^{X' \times Y'}$ given by Eq. 1.

$$\mathbf{R}_i = \mathbf{F}_i \odot \mathbf{B}, \text{ and } \quad \mathbf{B}'_{(:,:,i)} = \mathbf{R}_i \tag{1}$$

Definition 1 (Pruning, $\wp(\cdot)$). *As stated earlier, pruning is our main tool in this paper to study filter roles and interactions. Specifically, pruning $\mathbb{L}$ is the process of removing one or more $\mathbf{F}_i$ from $\mathbb{L}$ using some predefined criteria, resulting in a new set of filters $\wp(\mathbb{L}) = \hat{\mathbb{L}} = \{\mathbf{F}_1, \ldots, \mathbf{F}_{\hat{d}}\}$. Hence, a new output is $\hat{\mathbf{B}}' = \hat{\mathbb{L}} \odot \mathbf{B}$ with $\hat{\mathbf{B}}' \in \mathbb{R}^{X' \times Y' \times \hat{d}'}$ such that $\hat{d}' \leq d'$.*

As a pruning criteria - conditions to determine which filters to remove from the network - we propose to threshold filters' **accumulated response** values. The first step for computing the accumulated response of a filter is to compute accumulative representation of $\mathbf{R}_i$, later referred to as activation magnitude $\bar{r}_i$ (Fig. 1b) and computed for each $\mathbf{F}_i$ as follows:

$$\bar{r}_i = \sum_{x=1}^{X'} \sum_{y=1}^{Y'} \mathbf{R}_{x,y,i} \tag{2}$$

where $\bar{r} \in \mathbb{R}^{1 \times 1 \times d'}$. The schema for calculating $\bar{r}$ is shown in Fig. 1b.

Next, to perform pruning for each class separately, we split the dataset into subsets of images belonging to the same class. Let $\mathbb{D} = \{I_1, \ldots, I_n\}$ be the dataset containing the n data samples. Let $\mathbb{C} = \{c_1, \ldots, c_m\}$ be the set of all

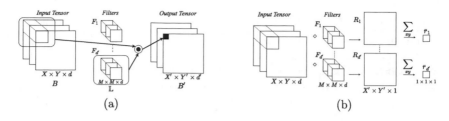

Fig. 1. (a) Convolutional layer operation and (b) computation of the activation magnitude $\bar{r}$.

object classes in the dataset. Then, $\mathbb{D}_c \subset \mathbb{D}$ be a subset of $\mathbb{D}$ containing all data samples with class label $c \in \mathbb{C}$. The number of samples in $\mathbb{D}_c$ is denoted as n', such that $n' \leq n$. Then the activation magnitude for filter $\mathbf{F}_i$ and input sample $I_j \in \mathbb{D}_c$ be $\bar{r}_i(I_j)$.

Accumulated response ($\bar{r}_i{}^c$) for class c and filter $\mathbf{F}_i$ is defined as sum of the activation magnitudes of filter $\mathbf{F}_i$ for all samples in $\mathbb{D}_c$ and computed by eq. 3

$$\bar{r}_i^c = \sum_{k=1}^{n'} \bar{r}_i(I_k) \tag{3}$$

Definition 2 (Response Based Pruning (RBP)). *Let $\bar{r}^c = \{\bar{r}_1^c, \ldots, \bar{r}_t^c\}$ be the vector of accumulated responses of all t filters in the network for class c. Also let $\bar{o}_c$ be the partially ordered set of elements $\bar{r}_l^c \in \bar{r}^c$ such that for $\bar{o}_i^c, \bar{o}_j^c \in \bar{o}_c$ we have $\bar{o}_i^c \leq \bar{o}_j^c$ if $i \leq j$. Finally let $|\bar{o}_c|$ be the cardinality of $\bar{o}_c$. Then, for any pruning ratio $\theta \in [0,1]$, RBP means removing all filters $\mathbf{F}_i$ for which $i \leq |\bar{o}_c| \cdot \theta$.*

For instance, for $\theta = 0.1$, the 10% of filters with lowest accumulated response will be removed.

4 Methodology

The experiments will throughout involve a number of measures which we list below.

Accuracy ($\mathcal{A}_c$) is the performance of a model on a class c (viewed as a binary classification problem) is computed using 4.

$$\mathcal{A}_c = \frac{tp + tn}{tp + fp + fn + tn}, \tag{4}$$

where tp stands for correctly classified samples (belonging to class c), tn stands for correctly classified samples (not belonging to class c), fn stands for misclassified samples (not belonging to class c), and fp stands for misclassified samples (belonging to class c).

Let $\bar{\mathbb{F}} = \{\mathbf{F}_i, \ldots, \mathbf{F}_n\}$ be the set of filters pruned at some θ. The set of classes with $\bar{\mathbb{F}}$ pruned be denoted as $\mathbb{C}_{\bar{\mathbb{F}}}$ and the set of filters pruned for class c be denoted as $\bar{\mathbb{F}}_c$.

Filter Similarity $(\mathcal{P})$. Two sets of filters $\mathbb{F}_{c_1}$ and $\mathbb{F}_{c_2}$ for two classes (c_1, c_2) we calculate the similarity using filter set intersection 5.

$$\mathcal{P} = \mathbb{F}_{c_1} \cap \mathbb{F}_{c_2}, \tag{5}$$

We will refer by $\bar{\mathcal{P}}$ and by $\hat{\mathcal{P}}$ to the similarity of pruned and unpruned filters respectively. If filter similarity between two classes $\mathcal{P}(c_1, c_2) \geq \sigma$, where σ similarity threshold, then classes c_1 and c_2 are referred to as highly overlapping classes.

Set of highly overlapping classes will be referred to as **Group of Classes** $\mathbb{G}$. The size of $\mathbb{G}$ and number of such sets is denoted as s and as N respectively.

Two groups $\mathbb{G}_1$ and $\mathbb{G}_2$ are said to overlap, if there is at least one class c_i such that $c_i \in \mathbb{G}_1$ and $c_i \in \mathbb{G}_2$. To measure the similarity $\mathcal{G}$ between 2 groups of classes $\mathbb{G}_1$ and $\mathbb{G}_2$ we use intersection over union metrics

$$\mathcal{G} = \frac{\mathbb{G}_1 \cap \mathbb{G}_2}{\mathbb{G}_1 \cup \mathbb{G}_2}, \tag{6}$$

Semantic Similarity $(\mathcal{S})$. We measure semantic similarity between classes using the corresponding metrics used in WordNet, e.g., in terms of distances defined with respect to the graph structure. We use Wu-Palmer [19] similarity as it provides a normalized, bounded value for the similarity, $\mathcal{S} \in (0, 1]$. To make hard decisions about similarity, we assume that if semantic similarity between two classes $\mathcal{S}(c_1, c_2) \geq \sigma$, where σ similarity threshold, then classes c_1 and c_2 are semantically related, and will be referred to as Semantically Related Neighbors (SRN). If $\mathcal{S}(c_1, c_2) < \sigma$ then classes c_1 and c_2 will be referred to as Semantically Unrelated Neighbors (SUN).

Feature Similarity $(\mathcal{F})$. In order to estimate similarity between accumulated responses of two classes ($\bar{r}^{c_1}$ and $\bar{r}^{c_2}$), we use the Euclidean distance on the PCA or t-SNE [10] projections (f) of $\bar{r}^{c_1}$ and $\bar{r}^{c_2}$ to 2D space.

$$\mathcal{F} = ||(f(\bar{r}_{c_1}) - f(\bar{r}_{c_2})|| \tag{7}$$

5   Experiments

The first set of experiments was conducted in order to observe the changes in classification accuracy at different pruning ratios θ (Sect. 5.1). We noticed that for certain values of θ there is a set of classes $\mathcal{I}$ for which classification accuracy improves (Sect. 5.1). To determine the conditions under which accuracy improves we experimentally investigated the usage and contribution of individual filters for the classification of classes in $\mathcal{I}$ (Sect. 5.2). As a result we extracted groups of most active filters specific for each class. A natural next step was to determine a) the possible overlaps of used filters between classes in $\mathcal{I}$ (Sect. 5.3) and b) the possible semantic relation between classes in $\mathcal{I}$. (Section 5.3)

We observed a) the existence of groups of classes $\mathbb{G}_{\mathbb{F}}$ for which the classification accuracy improves by pruning similar sub-set of filters (Sect. 5.4) and, b) that semantically related classes tend to prune similar sub-sets of filters (Sect. 5.4). Additionally experiments in Sect. 5.4 showed that most of the improvements is observed within small sized groups, therefore, in the following experiment we study the structure of $\mathbb{G}_{\mathbb{F}}$ in more details by looking at semantic relation with closest neighbouring classes (Sect. 5.5) and how the filter overlap with these classes changes at different θ (Sect. 5.6). The result of this experiment allowed us to determine that a) classes for which the classification accuracy is improved by pruning have in average a higher number of semantically related neighbors, and b) improved classes have on average higher increase in correlation with semantically related classes. In addition, this experiment showed that there is a clear interference between filters learned for different classes. As classification accuracy were improved by reducing filter overlap with classes which initially has high filter overlap.

For all experiments, we use AlexNet [6] trained on the ImageNet [17] dataset. The ImageNet data set contains 1000 object classes. For evaluation we used ImageNet validation set, consisting of 50000 images, and AlexNet consists of five convolutional and three fully connected layers. RBP prunes only the convolutional layers, also referred to as the feature extractor. θ is set to 0 and increased by 0.05 until reaching $\theta = 0.5$ (representing 50% pruning ratio). No retraining is performed after pruning.

5.1   Class-Wise Accuracy Changes

We applied RBP to all classes $c \in \mathbb{C}$ in the ImageNet dataset and recorded their classification accuracies $\mathcal{A}_c^\theta$ for various $\theta \geq 0$. As expected, the average accuracy $\mathcal{A}^\theta = \dfrac{\sum\limits_{c=1}^{q} \mathcal{A}_c^\theta}{q}$, where q is the total number of classes, monotonically decreases with increasing θ (Fig. 2a, green line). However, there are a significant number of classes c in the network for which $\mathcal{A}_c^\theta - \mathcal{A}_c^{\theta=0} > 0$, for some values of θ, and where $\mathcal{A}_c^{\theta=0}$ is original accuracy for the class c before pruning. Fig. 2b shows the magnitude of change (increase or decrease) in accuracy for all classes at different pruning ratios (x-axis is θ, y-axis is class, and color denotes the magnitude of change). A positive value (lighter color) represents an increase and a negative value (darker color) represents a decrease in classification accuracy. The RBP results show that in total the accuracy increases for 435 out of 1000 classes, with the average increase of 3.33%, a maximum of 17%, and a minimum of 1%. Fig. 2c reflects the number of improved classes per θ and Figure 2d shows average improvements in accuracy for each pruning threshold θ. Observe, that the highest number of improvements (Fig. 2c) is achieved at smaller $\theta = [0.05, 0.1]$, 272 and 208 respectively, while the highest average improvement (Figure 2d) in accuracy 5% is observed at large $\theta = [0.45]$. The possible reason for this phenomena is that classes which got improved at higher values of θ had strong interference from filters which were pruned only at later thresholds, and hence got bigger accuracy improvements. To investigate this phenomena in more details we need to study the contribution of each individual filter to class recognition, and what filters are getting removed by pruning.

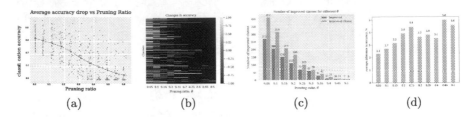

Fig. 2. (a) Average classification accuracy $\mathcal{A}$ vs pruning ratio dependency, (b) Direction of changes in accuracy for each class for different pruning ratios (light spots represent increase in accuracy), (c) Number of improved classes per threshold (relative to the original accuracy) (d) Average accuracy improvements per threshold (only improved classes considered) (Color figure online)

5.2 Identification of Filters for Each Class

The next step was to investigate the accumulated response value of each filter toward each class, and identify what groups of filters strongly contributed to each class recognition. Figure 3a shows accumulated response $\bar{r}_i^c$ of each filter $\mathbf{F}_i$ for each class c, x-axis represents $\mathbf{F}_i$, while y-xis represent classes in $\mathbb{C}$. For better visualization values of $\bar{r}_i^{\mathbb{C}}$ below -10 were set to -10. Figure 3b illustrates how many classes pruned a particular filter at threshold θ, x-axis represents $\mathbf{F}_i$ and y-xis is θ. On one hand, as can be seen from Fig. 3a, the first layer filters (0–63) contributes almost equally to the recognition of all classes and were barely pruned at any thresholds (Fig. 3b). On another hand, intermediate (64–639) and last layer (640–1152) filters are more class specific. One can also observe that at small $\theta = [0.05 - 0.15]$, only filters from intermediate layers were pruned. Only when we reach bigger $\theta \geq 0.2$ we start to prune from later layers (640–1152). One can also observe from Fig. 3a that classes 0–400 (y-axis) has high overlap in middle and later layers filters. Similar behaviours is observed for classes 414–966. Trends in Fig. 3a and Fig. 3b suggests that there are groups of classes $\mathbb{G}$ which share and prune similar sub-sets of filters. Next set of experiments will therefore provide a more precise quantitative evaluation of groups formed and intra-group filter similarity ($\mathcal{P}$).

5.3 Class-Wise Filter Overlap and Semantic Similarity

Figure 3c shows results of pruned filter similarity $\bar{\mathcal{P}}$ between all classes in $\mathbb{C}$ for $\theta = 0.2$. Initially we pruned each class independently for $\theta = 0.2$ to get $\bar{\mathbb{F}}_c$ for $\forall c \in \mathbb{C}$. Then, to generate Fig. 3c we computed pruned filter similarity $\bar{\mathcal{P}}$ between all $\bar{\mathbb{F}}_c$ of all $c \in \mathbb{C}$. Both axes in Fig. 3c represents the classes and

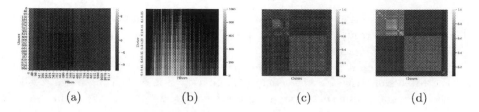

(a)   (b)   (c)   (d)

Fig. 3. (a) Accumulated Response $\bar{r}_i^c$ of each filter for each class c. (black means that the value were below -10), (b) How many classes pruned each filter $\mathbf{F}_i$ at different θ (lighter color represents higher number of classes) (c) Pruned Filter Similarity $\bar{\mathcal{P}}$ for $\theta = 0.2$, the intensity of a pixel is proportional to the number of filters that overlap for the corresponding classes (d) Semantic Similarity $\mathcal{S}$

intensity of each pixel is proportional to the number of filters that overlap for the classes corresponding to the row and column heads. Figure 3c shows that indeed there are easily identifiable groups of classes that share large numbers of filters, which support the observation made in Fig. 3a - on existence of $\mathbb{G}$. Since the filter similarity (Fig. 3c) resulted in such clear overlap pattern we pursue the study by analyzing semantic relations between classes in the dataset. Since ImageNet classes follow the WordNet class hierarchy, we measure semantic similarity using corresponding metrics used in WordNet, e.g., in terms of distances along the graph structure. We use the Wu-Palmer [19] similarity between WordNet nodes corresponding to the ImageNet class names. Figure 3d shows the magnitude of Wu-Palmer semantic similarity between all classes in $\mathbb{C}$. The high similarity in Fig. 3d and Fig. 3c hypothesizes that semantically similar classes use similar filters, and hence, prune similar filters as well.

5.4   Analysis of Groups

Non-overlapping Groups. To provide a more precise quantitative evaluation of filter overlap and grouping, we perform clustering on the classes based on pruned filter similarity $\bar{\mathcal{P}}$ (Table 1).

For each considered value of θ we calculated how many groups exists. A group of classes is formed by calculating pairwise $\bar{\mathcal{P}}(c_1, c_2)$ between all classes and then group classes for which $\bar{\mathcal{P}}(c_1, c_2) > 0.5$. As one class can belong to multiple clusters at the same time, we decided to look at two separate cases: grouping without overlap and with overlap. To form groups without overlap, for classes which belonged to multiple clusters, we assigned label based on most recent cluster.

The column entitled "Average $\bar{\mathcal{P}}$" in Table 1, shows the minimal, maximal, median and average(mean) intra-group filter overlap similarity $\bar{\mathcal{P}}$. As can be seen, the number of groups of classes sharing similar pruned filters, is decreasing with increasing θ: more pruning is done, more classes are encoded on similar groups of filters. The pruning ratio $\theta = 0.4$ resulted in a single group of classes: all learned classes were pruning similar filters and therefore the experiment stopped. Also note that the convergence of *min, max and mean* to a common value represents the filter overlap that is obtained when the network is pruned in a general and non-class specific manner. The column named "Average S" in Table 1 shows the results of computing semantic similarity S of groups of classes obtained on pruned filter similarity $\bar{P}$. The semantic similarity S is decreasing linearly with increasing θ confirming that larger groups are formed as a result of pruning: large groups of classes increasingly include classes that are less and less semantically related. Observe that in average the pruned filter similarity is growing inversely to the semantic similarity. This means that initially the average pruned filter similarity is divided among larger number of groups of classes while later larger groups have in general lower semantic similarity between classes within each group.

Table 1. Grouping based on $\bar{P} > 0.5$, * groups which had only a single class as a member were removed from the statistics

θ	Number of groups (N)*	Average $\bar{P}$				Average S			
		(min)	(max)	(median)	(mean)	(min)	(max)	(median)	(mean)
0.05	70	0.468	0.750	0.552	0.559	0.325	0.933	0.586	0.592
0.10	21	0.485	0.694	0.565	0.591	0.346	0.765	0.552	0.539
0.15	11	0.553	0.705	0.648	0.642	0.400	0.668	0.541	0.531
0.20	8	0.639	0.711	0.681	0.675	0.454	0.648	0.534	0.548
0.35	2	0.692	0.729	0.711	0.711	0.472	0.497	0.484	0.484
0.40	1	0.710	0.710	0.710	0.710	0.445	0.445	0.445	0.445

An even more detailed look in each group of classes is shown in Table 2: it shows the amount of improved classes per θ.

For every θ we split the space defined by the smallest and largest group size to four evenly sized intervals. Each row shows for every interval (from top to bottom) how many classes improved their classification accuracy (NIC), groups' sizes range (s) and how many groups are inside this interval (N). Note, that because for each θ the largest and smallest group sizes are different, the intervals are different for each θ. As can be seen from Table 2 most of the classes with improved classification accuracy for small θ are in smaller groups (containing from 1 to 19 classes per group). Total number of groups (N) at $\theta = 0.05$ and $\theta = 0.1$ in Table 1 and Table 2 is different by 26 and 2 respectively, as Table 1 excludes groups, which have only a single class inside (singleton-groups). Singleton groups were removed from Table 1 to provide a better trend statistics. Despite the fact that, according to Table 2 most of the improvements occurs for small group size, only 6 classes improved with pruning from singleton-groups. This observation can be interpreted as an indication that smaller groups offer more inter-group space that can be used for class movement during the pruning process.

Overlapping Groups. During formation of groups in the previous section, we used non-overlapping group assignment. In other words each sample belonged

Table 2. Number of improved classes (NIC) per interval. The size of group $\mathbb{G}$ is denoted as s and the total number of groups is denoted as N.

θ	N	Measure	Number of improved classes (NIC) per interval			
0.05	96	NIC	127.0	71.0	44.0	30.0
		s	[1.0, 18.5)	[18.5, 36.0)	[36.0, 53.5)	[53.5, 71.0)
		N	80	9	5	2
0.1	23	NIC	103.0	54.0	0.0	51.0
		s	[1.0, 90.5)	[90.5, 180.0)	[180.0, 269.5)	[269.5, 359.0)
		N	20	2	0	1
0.15	11	NIC	86.0	0.0	0.0	68.0
		s	[6.0, 120.8)	[120.8, 235.5)	[235.5, 350.2)	[350.2, 465.0)
		N	10	0	0	1
0.2	8	NIC	0.0	53.0	19.0	41.0
		s	[7.0, 81.2)	[81.2, 155.5)	[155.5, 229.8)	[229.8, 304.0)
		N	2	4	1	1

to a single group only. For the next set of experiments we decided to study similarity $\mathcal{G}$ between groups of classes if we assign same class to multiple groups based on pruned filter similarity $\bar{\mathcal{P}}$. To illustrate the concept lets look at the Fig. 4a. Allocating classes to all groups, which satisfied the condition $\mathcal{P}(c_i, c_j) > 0.5$ we formed $\mathbb{G}_1$, $\mathbb{G}_2$, $\mathbb{G}_3$ and $\mathbb{G}_4$. As can be seen from the Fig. 4a $\mathbb{G}_4$ has 1 and 3 classes shared with $\mathbb{G}_1$ and $\mathbb{G}_2$ respectively. In order to quantify such overlaps between groups of classes and compute $\mathcal{G}$ we used intersection over union metrics as in Eq. 6.

To accurately estimate the neighborhood of each individual class c, we created a group $\mathbb{G}_c$ for each class $c \in \mathbb{C}$ by allocating all classes with $\bar{\mathcal{P}}(c, c_i) > \sigma$. Next for $\forall \mathbb{G}_c$ we compute group-wise similarity between all formed groups and only maximum similarity with another group were recorded $\mathcal{G}_c^{max} = max_i(\mathcal{G}(\mathbb{G}_c, \mathbb{G}_{c_i}))$. Main reason for keeping only the maximum similarity with another class was to identify the existence of isolated groups, which don't have overlap with other groups of classes. However, only few groups satisfied these condition. Then we study if there is a clear distinction between groups overlap formed for improved and reduced classes. To provide separate statistics on improved/reduced classes we selected subset of improved/reduced classes and computed average similarity $\mathcal{G}'$ over corresponding to these classes $\mathcal{G}^{max}$. The procedure was repeated for $\sigma = [0.4, 0.5, 0.6]$ and resultant values are shown in Fig. 4b. One can observe from Fig. 4b that for all σ average similarity between groups for improved classes (dashed lines) is lower then for reduced accuracy classes (solid lines). In addition, one can observe that for higher σ the gap between two trends is increasing. This observation implies that for groups formed at higher similarity σ classes inside the improved groups were in a sparser space. Thus, class movement as a result of pruning has a higher chance in resulting in class-wise accuracy improvement.

Classes that have their classification accuracy reduced by pruning are thus in a denser space increasing the possibility of classification mismatch.

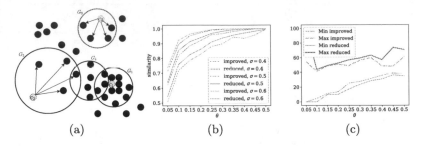

Fig. 4. (a) Schematic representation of groups of classes and their intersection (b) Average similarity ($\mathcal{G}'$) between groups of classes for $\sigma = 0.4, 0.5, 0.6$, (c) Min/Max inside group t-SNE distance for improved/reduced classes

Mapping to Lower Dimensional Space: In all the previous experiments, we considered only presence or absence of filters and their overlap for different classes. We now take into account the values of the responses (accumulated response $\bar{r}^c$). We construct a feature space from the accumulated response magnitudes $\gamma^c = \{\gamma_1^c, \cdots, \gamma_t^c\}$ for all filters in AlexNet and map them to 2D space through t-SNE [10]. We measured the average distances $\bar{\mathcal{F}}'$ between a pruned class c and all neighbors in the group. For example, lets look at Fig. 4a. Lets look closely to the group $\mathbb{G}_2$, which was formed from classes with $\mathcal{P}(c_2, c_i) > 0.5$ to c_2. As a result class c_2 got 4 neighbours. Hence, average distances $\bar{\mathcal{F}}'_{c_2}$ is computed as $\bar{\mathcal{F}}'_{c_2} = \dfrac{\sum\limits_{i=1}^{4} \bar{\mathcal{F}}(c_2, c_i)}{4}$.

Once $\bar{\mathcal{F}}'$ for all $c \in \mathbb{C}$ were computed, similarly to the previous section experiments we splitted $\mathbb{C}$ into two subsets of classes: improved (I) and reduced (R) accuracy classes. Next for each subset of classes we computed the minimum and maximum values of $\bar{\mathcal{F}}'$. Figure 4c shows the resultant values. One can observe that the minimum $\bar{\mathcal{F}}'$ for improved classes is higher then the minimum feature distance $\bar{\mathcal{F}}'$ for reduced classes. This means that classes which has neighbours too close, had smaller chances of getting improved. On the other side, maximum $\bar{\mathcal{F}}'$ for reduced classes is always higher than $\bar{\mathcal{F}}'$ for improved classes for all θ. This implies that classes which were located far away from its neighbours has small confusion with other classes, however during pruning moved closer to other classes, thus increasing confusion with other classes.

5.5   Nearest Neighbours

In order to quantify the filter and semantic overlap between classes within individual groups, we take its top-5 neighboring classes with highest filter similarity

$\bar{\mathcal{P}}$ for each class c, and calculate how many of them are semantically related. In addition, we also look at how this number is changing with increasing pruning ratio.

We count the average number of Semantically Related Neighbors (SRN: $\mathcal{S}(c_1, c_2) > 0.5$) and Semantically Unrelated Neighbors (SUN). We selected $\sigma = 0.5$ for identifying SRN and SUN, as a) identifies that c_1 and c_2 has more than half common nodes in Word-Net tree b) this value is bigger than median value in the dataset $\sigma_{median} = 0.4$.

To identify top-5 neighboring classes, the pruned filter overlap $\bar{\mathcal{P}}$ at different θ (as in Sect. 5.3) for all classes $c, c' \in \mathbb{C}$ was computed. For each class $c \in \mathbb{C}$ we take the top five classes with highest $\bar{\mathcal{P}}$. Finally for each c and its five highest closest classes we compute the semantic similarity $\mathcal{S}$. Table 3 shows the results of this experiment. The column AV shows how many neighbors are SRN and SUN in average over the whole set of classes $\mathbb{C}$. The column entitled I shows how many SRN and SUN classes are in average among the top five closes neighbors in classes that improve after pruning at θ ($\mathcal{A}_c^\theta - \mathcal{A}_c^0 > 0$). The column entitled R shows again the average number of SRN and SUN for classes for which the classification accuracy is reduced for pruning at θ ($\mathcal{A}_c^\theta - \mathcal{A}_c^0 < 0$). Finally, the column entitled Z shows the average number of SRN and SUN for classes for which the classification accuracy didn't change with pruning at θ ($\mathcal{A}_c^\theta - \mathcal{A}_c^0 = 0$).

Table 3. Average number of Semantically Related (SRN) and Unrelated (SUN) Neighbors. (I) and (R) represent average numbers for improved and reduced accuracy classes. (Z) represent average numbers for classes that didn't change classification accuracy. AV is the average number of SRN and SUN for all classes, (I), (R) and (Z) classes combined.

Pruning ratio	AV		I		R		Z	
	(SRN)	(SUN)	(SRN)	(SUN)	(SRN)	(SUN)	(SRN)	(SUN)
$\theta = 0.05$	0.786	0.214	0.807	0.193	0.787	0.213	0.744	0.256
$\theta = 0.10$	0.806	0.194	0.838	0.162	0.799	0.201	0.789	0.211
$\theta = 0.15$	0.810	0.190	0.784	0.216	0.815	0.185	0.807	0.193
$\theta = 0.20$	0.816	0.184	0.798	0.202	0.823	0.177	0.742	0.258
$\theta = 0.25$	0.822	0.178	0.795	0.205	0.825	0.175	0.807	0.193
$\theta = 0.30$	0.825	0.175	0.784	0.216	0.827	0.173	0.867	0.133
$\theta = 0.35$	0.828	0.172	0.755	0.245	0.832	0.168	0.673	0.327

On one hand, the number of semantic neighbors SRN grows with increasing θ for the AV and R cases (columns 2 and 6). We interpret this result as the fact that pruning generalizes the network decision making so that with decreased number of filters all learned classes are closer together. On the other hand, the number of semantic neighbors SRN fluctuates with increasing θ for the cases I and Z but with a general trend of increasing the number of SRN. The number of semantic neighbors SUN is complementary to SRN for each case. The changes in the number of closest semantic neighbors SRN for column I (for each θ) indicates that either a) the average number of semantic neighbors SRN is changing for every threshold or that b) the number of classes with increased classification accuracy changes. The number of SRN neighbors in R linearly increases with θ, indicating that with increasing θ new classes that previously were in I or Z move to R, as the network generalizes its knowledge to a single group (according to Table 1). In the case of the set I, the peaks of SRN indicate that classes achieved their maximum improvement by pruning: after a class gets too close to its neighbors, the classification accuracy will be reduced. This is because the classifier will misclassify it as its closest semantic neighbor. Therefore for next value of θ the average number of SRN neighbors will be decreased.

While a steady increase in number of semantic neighbours supports the hypothesis that semantic similarity and pruning filter similarity are highly related, this experiments illustrates the fact that too many SRN are actually harmful to classification. In addition, for the first two pruning ratios $\theta = 0.05$ and $\theta = 0.10$ where majority of all improved classes is observed (according to Fig. 2b), improved classes had more semantically related neighbours than the reduced accuracy classes. However when compared to other peaks of SRN neigbhors in I, the later one can be higher however the number of candidates classes c that are improved is much smaller.

One of the possible conclusion from Table 3 is that for classes for which the classification accuracy $\mathcal{A}_c$ improves, the pruning tends to group SRN together. Hence, next set of experiments targets to investigate how pruned filter similarity is changing by pruning.

5.6   Class-Wise Correlation Between Pruned Filters

Let $\bar{\mathcal{P}}(c_1, c_2)$ denote pruned filter similarity between classes c_1 and c_2 in $\mathbb{C}$. Higher is the value of $\bar{\mathcal{P}}$ higher the intersection between filters pruned for classification of c_1 and c_2.

In order to observe the similarities of filters between pruned classes in details, we look at five closest neighbors by the amount of filter overlap $\bar{\mathcal{P}}$.

Let $\bar{\mathbf{p}}^\theta = \{\bar{\mathcal{P}}_1, \ldots, \bar{\mathcal{P}}_k\}$ be a vector containing the similarity of pruned vectors between a class c and its k-closest neighbors at θ. For instance $\bar{\mathcal{P}}_1 = \bar{\mathcal{P}}(c, c_1)$.

We calculate the difference between the amplitude of $\bar{\mathbf{p}}^{\theta_\tau}$ and $\bar{\mathbf{p}}^{\theta_{\tau-1}}$ using Eq. 8, where m - number of SRN/SUN out of k neighbours. Table 4 shows the results of calculating the average changes (using Eq. 8) for $\theta = 0.05, 0.1, 0.15$ and $k = 5$.

$$DA(\bar{\mathbf{p}}^{\theta_\tau}, \bar{\mathbf{p}}^{\theta_{\tau-1}}) = \frac{1}{m}\sum_{i=1}^{m} sign(\bar{\mathcal{P}}_i^{\theta_\tau} - \bar{\mathcal{P}}_i^{\theta_{\tau-1}})_+ \text{ , where } \quad sign(x) := \begin{cases} -1, \text{if } x < 0 \\ 0, \text{if } x = 0 \\ 1, \text{if } x > 0 \end{cases}$$

$$(8)$$

Table 4. Average trends in pruned filter similarity for Semantically Related (SRN) and Unrelated (SUN) neighbors. Higher the value in the Table, higher the number of neighboring classes with which the pruned filter similarity increases. (I) and (R) represent average change in pruned filter similarity for improved and reduced classes.

Pruning ratio	AV		I		R	
	(SRN)	(SUN)	(SRN)	(SUN)	(SRN)	(SUN)
$\theta = 0.05$	0.948	0.918	0.969	0.905	0.942	0.920
$\theta = 0.10$	0.647	0.672	0.688	0.659	0.639	0.675
$\theta = 0.15$	0.572	0.590	0.654	0.642	0.562	0.583

First, observe that for $\theta = 0.05$, that $DA(\bar{\mathbf{p}}^{\theta_\tau}, \bar{\mathbf{p}}^{\theta_{\tau-1}})$ is much higher than for any next θ. This is due to the fact that for $\theta_\tau = 0.05$ the $\theta_{\tau-1} = 0.02$ and thus the interval was much smaller. This implies that for pruning at $\theta = 0.05$ most of the classes were surrounded by classes with similar pruned filters. Also note that $DA(\bar{\mathbf{p}}^{\theta_\tau}, \bar{\mathbf{p}}^{\theta_{\tau-1}})$ for (SRN) in column I is highest. As a consequence of the observation that at $\theta = 0.05$ the highest number of classes has improved classification accuracy, the results would indicate that most of improvements is coming from the distinction between SRN neighbors. In addition, note that for improved classes (I) at $\theta = 0.1$ and $\theta = 0.15$, the increase in pruned filter similarity with semantically related (SRN) neighbours is higher compared to SUN. At the same time, for the reduced (R) classes there were more increase in $\bar{\mathcal{P}}$ with semantically unrelated neighbours (SUN).

Experiments conducted in this section showed a correlation between changes in pruned filter similarity $\bar{\mathcal{P}}$ and improvement in accuracy for low values of θ. In particular, improved classes have higher increase in $\bar{\mathcal{P}}$ with semantically related neighbours, while reduced accuracy classes have higher increase in $\bar{\mathcal{P}}$ with semantically unrelated classes. The fact that we have an increase in both pruned filter similarity and accuracy indicates that the discriminative power of upruned filters improved as a result of removing similar filters between neighbouring classes. This implies that the closest neighbors are increasing their mutual filter similarity up to $\theta \leq \Theta$ so they can be distinguished by the filter response. It also can imply that by increasing $\bar{\mathcal{P}}$ with SRN, classes removing inferring filters, which is leading to accuracy improvements.

6   Discussion and Conclusions

The results presented in this work elicit several general trends. First, as shown in Experiments 5.4 the improvement in the accuracy of a set of classes due to RBP is directly related to the initial distance among the classes. Second, classes whose closest neighbors are semantically related have higher probability of being improved by RBP (Experiments 5.5). Third, as a result of RBP in Experiment 5.6 classes whose accuracy improved have more increase in pruned filter similarity with semantically related neighbours than with semantically unrelated. These observations imply that if a class is surrounded by mostly semantically related neighbors, then if the neighbors are not too close the pruning can be beneficial to the classification accuracy. This is because the compression resulting from the pruning, brings all classes closer, but also bring data samples closer together. If there is enough space between classes, the samples will be compressed enough for higher accuracy before classes will interfere with each other.

Our results could be used to design filter selection masks to increase the classification accuracy of a group of classes. Such masked networks then could be combined into ensembles for decision making. Based on our experiments, we can conclude that whether the classification accuracy for a given set of classes can be potentially improved by pruning can be determined by checking if the: classes are located sparsely, a large fraction of neighbors are semantically related, and there is an initial increase in pruned filter similarity with semantically related neighbours.

Acknowledgement. This work was funded by the FCDRGP research grant from Nazarbayev University with reference number 240919FD3936.

References

1. Anwar, S., Hwang, K., Sung, W.: Structured pruning of deep convolutional neural networks. CoRR abs/1512.08571 (2015), http://arxiv.org/abs/1512.08571
2. Carter, S., Armstrong, Z., Schubert, L., Johnson, I., Olah, C.: Activation atlas. Distill (2019)
3. Girshick, R., Donahue, J., Darrell, T., Malik, J.: Rich feature hierarchies for accurate object detection and semantic segmentation. In: Proceedings of the IEEE CVPR, pp. 580–587 (2014). https://doi.org/10.1109/CVPR.2014.81
4. Iandola, F.N., Han, S., Moskewicz, M.W., Ashraf, K., Dally, W.J., Keutzer, K.: Squeezenet: Alexnet-level accuracy with 50x fewer parameters and <0.5 mb model size. arXiv preprint arXiv:1602.07360 (2016)
5. Kindermans, P.J., et al.: Learning how to explain neural networks. ArXiv e-prints (2017)
6. Krizhevsky, A., Sutskever, I., Hinton, G.: ImageNet classification with deep convolutional neural networks. In: NIPS (2012)
7. Li, H., Kadav, A., Durdanovic, I., Samet, H., Graf, H.P.: Pruning filters for efficient convnets. CoRR abs/1608.08710 (2016). http://arxiv.org/abs/1608.08710
8. Luo, J.H., Wu, J., Lin, W.: ThiNet: a filter level pruning method for deep neural network compression. In: ICCV, pp. 5058–5066 (2017)
9. Ma, X., Yuan, G., Lin, S., Li, Z., Sun, H., Wang, Y.: ResNet Can Be Pruned 60x: Introducing Network Purification and Unused Path Removal (P-RM) after Weight Pruning, April 2019
10. van der Maaten, L., Hinton, G.: Visualizing data using t-SNE. J. Mach. Learn. Res. **9**, 2579–2605 (2008)
11. Molchanov, P., Tyree, S., Karras, T., Aila, T., Kautz, J.: Pruning convolutional neural networks for resource efficient transfer learning (2016)
12. Morcos, A.S., Barrett, D.G.T., Rabinowitz, N.C., Botvinick, M.: On the importance of single directions for generalization arXiv:1803.06959, March 2018

13. Najafabadi, M.M., Villanustre, F., Khoshgoftaar, T.M., Seliya, N., Wald, R., Muharemagic, E.: Deep learning applications and challenges in big data analytics. J. Big Data **2**(1), 1–21 (2015). https://doi.org/10.1186/s40537-014-0007-7
14. Olah, C., et al.: The building blocks of interpretability. Distill (2018)
15. van den Oord, A., et al.: WaveNet: a generative model for raw audio. In: Arxiv (2016). https://arxiv.org/abs/1609.03499
16. Raghu, M., Gilmer, J., Yosinski, J., Sohl-Dickstein, J.: SVCCA: Singular Vector Canonical Correlation Analysis for Deep Learning Dynamics and Interpretability (2017)
17. Russakovsky, O., et al.: ImageNet large scale visual recognition challenge. Int. J. Comput. Vis. **115**(3), 211–252 (2015). https://doi.org/10.1007/s11263-015-0816-y
18. Suzuki, T., et al.: Spectral-pruning: compressing deep neural network via spectral analysis (2018)
19. Wu, Z., Palmer, M.: Verbs semantics and lexical selection, pp. 133–138, January 1994
20. Yosinski, J., Clune, J., Nguyen, A.M., Fuchs, T.J., Lipson, H.: Understanding neural networks through deep visualization (2015)
21. Zhou, B., Bau, D., Oliva, A., Torralba, A.: Interpreting deep visual representations via network dissection. TPAMI **41**(9), 2131–2145 (2019)
22. Zhu, M., Gupta, S.: To prune, or not to prune: exploring the efficacy of pruning for model compression (2017). https://arxiv.org/abs/1710.01878

Explaining How Deep Neural Networks Forget by Deep Visualization

Giang Nguyen[1][✉], Shuan Chen[2], Tae Joon Jun[3], and Daeyoung Kim[1]

[1] School of Computing, KAIST, Daejeon, South Korea
{dexter.nguyen7,kimd}@kaist.ac.kr
[2] Department of Chemical and Biomolecular Engineering, KAIST, Daejeon, South Korea
shuankaist@kaist.ac.kr
[3] Ansan Institute for Life Sciences, Ansan Medical Center, Ansan, South Korea
saigram89@gmail.com

Abstract. Explaining the behaviors of deep neural networks, usually considered as black boxes, is critical especially when they are now being adopted over diverse aspects of human life. Taking the advantages of interpretable machine learning (interpretable ML), this paper proposes a novel tool called Catastrophic Forgetting Dissector (or CFD) to explain catastrophic forgetting in continual learning settings. We also introduce a new method called Critical Freezing based on the observations of our tool. Experiments on ResNet-50 articulate how catastrophic forgetting happens, particularly showing which components of this famous network are forgetting. Our new continual learning algorithm defeats various recent techniques by a significant margin, proving the capability of the investigation. Critical freezing not only attacks catastrophic forgetting but also exposes explainability.

Keywords: Explainable AI · Explainable deep learning · Catastrophic Forgetting · Continual learning

1 Introduction

Regarding human evolution, life-long learning has been considered as one of the most crucial abilities, helping us develop more complicated skills throughout the lifetime. The idea of this learning strategy is hence deployed extensively by the deep learning community. Life-long learning (or continual learning) enables machine learning models to perceive new knowledge while simultaneously exposing backward-forward transfer, non-forgetting, or few-show learning [9]. While the aforementioned properties are the ultimate goals for life-long learning systems, catastrophic forgetting or semantic drift naturally occurs in deep neural networks in life-long learning settings because they are vastly optimized upon gradient descent algorithm [3].

Catastrophic forgetting is defined as when we use a trained model on a given domain to address a new task, due to adapting to the new data samples, the

A. Del Bimbo et al. (Eds.): ICPR 2020 Workshops, LNCS 12663, pp. 162–173, 2021.
https://doi.org/10.1007/978-3-030-68796-0_12

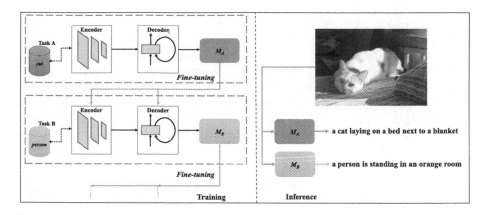

Fig. 1. Catastrophic forgetting in continual learning settings.

model forgets what it learned before on the old domain. As shown in Fig. 1, if we use fine-tuning for continual learning, the knowledge acquired from the previous task will be eradicated and the inference becomes irrelevant. In fact, the description of the cat photo is shifted from "*a cat laying on a bed next to a blanket*" to "*a person is standing in an orange room*".

Although catastrophic forgetting is tough and undesirable, research to understand this problem is rare amongst the deep learning community. The interest in understanding or measuring catastrophic forgetting does not commensurate with the number of research to deal with this problem. Kemker *et al.* [5] develop new metrics to help compare continual learning techniques fairly and directly. Nguyen *et al.* [11] study which properties cause the hardness for the learning process. By modeling the chosen properties using task space, they can estimate how much a model forgets in a sequential learning scenario, shedding light on factors affecting the error rate on a task sequence. However, these research cannot show us what is being forgotten or which components are forgetting inside the model, but revealing what properties of tasks trigger catastrophic forgetting. By comparison, our work focuses on understanding which components of a network are volatile corresponding to a given sequence of tasks to articulate catastrophic forgetting.

More specifically, this research introduces a novel approach to elaborate catastrophic forgetting by visualizing hidden layers in class-incremental learning (considered as the hardest scenario in continual learning). In this learning paradigm, the use of previous data is prohibited and instances of the incoming tasks are unseen. We develop a tool named Catastrophic Forgetting Dissector (or CFD) which automates the dissection of catastrophic forgetting, exactly pointing out which components, in a model, are causing the forgetting. We formally adopt Intersection over Union (IoU), a popular evaluation metric in detection and segmentation tasks which essentially computes the overlapping ratio between two frames, to measure the forgetting degree of deep neural networks in this paper.

The degree of forgetting is objectively measured after each class is added, thus giving us an intuition of how forgetting happens on a given part of the network.

A work from Kemker *et al.* [5] conducts experiments on state-of-the-art continual learning techniques that address catastrophic forgetting. It is demonstrated that the algorithms work, but only on weak constrains and unfair baselines, thus the forgetting problem is not fully solved and witnessed yet. They insist on the infeasibility of using toy datasets, such as MNIST [6] or CIFAR [18] in continual learning experiments. As a result, this work motivates us to choose Split MS-COCO [12] to comprehensively measure the forgetting on deep neural networks. From the results of the dissection, we try to infer the plastic components in the network to preserve the accumulated knowledge. Critical freezing protects these components by simply keeping weights unchanged while training the new network.

There are three main contributions in this work: 1) We propose a novel and pioneering method to analyze catastrophic forgetting in continual learning. 2) We introduce a new approach to mitigate catastrophic forgetting based on the findings. 3) Our extensive experiments demonstrate the efficacy of critical freezing and suggest recondite understanding about catastrophic forgetting.

2 Related Work

Feature Visualization. Contemporary interpretability methods bring us advantages to understand the decision-making process of deep neural networks, ranging from visualizing saliency maps [2,14] to transforming models into human-friendly structures [1]. In [17], deconvnets allow us to recognize which features are expected by a specific part of a network or what properties of image excite a chosen neuron the most. In stark contrast to feeding an input image to diagnose, Yosinski *et al.* [16] attempt to generate an image which maximizes the activation of a given neuron by gradient descent algorithm. Visualizing the activation of a neuron or a layer in networks helps us categorize the specific role of each block, layer, or even a node. It has been proved that the earlier layers extract local features, such as edges or colors; while deeper layers are responsible for detecting globally distinctive characteristics. Prediction Difference Analysis (PDA) [20], even more specifically, highlights pixels that support or counteract a certain class, indicating which features are positive or negative to a prediction. However, these tools only provide the computer vision, leaving the conclusion for users. This manual process cannot ensure the quality of the observation when we may have hundreds or even thousands of attribution maps. CFD automatically detects the forgetting components in a network, entirely leveraging the generated activation difference maps from PDA [20].

Catastrophic Forgetting. Many works have managed to address the forgetting problem in generative models [19], object detection [13], semantic segmentation [15], or captioning [12]. Besides, fine-tuning is considered as a baseline in [10,12,13,15] to consider the superiority of the proposed techniques. Freezing either a few specific layers or a major part of a network is proposed in [12][10], which reveals that just simply keeping some parameters unchanged can greatly help networks become robust against catastrophic forgetting. Learning without Forgetting (LwF) [7] utilizes old models to generate pseudo data, which helps the new model reach a shared low-error region of problems. Also leveraging the old networks, knowledge distillation approaches [4, 10] are formally recognized to facilitate better generalization in life-long learning via a teacher-student learning strategy. Nevertheless, algorithms are inclined to rely on external factors (e.g., input or rehearsal data, objective functions [7, 10]) while ignoring the question of why catastrophic forgetting internally happens. In this research, our algorithm is derived from catastrophic forgetting exploration.

3   Approach

Although research from [11] shows an interest in understanding catastrophic forgetting, they focus on how task properties influence the hardness of sequential learning. Hence, they are explaining based on the input data. CFD approaches the problem from an alternative perspective, trying to explain how forgetting happens over time based on the computer vision of models. In comparison, the ultimate goal of this tool is to figure out the most plastic conv layers or blocks in a network. Plasticity means a low degree of stiffness or being easy to change. Although a variety of continual learning techniques have been proposed to alleviate catastrophic forgetting, none of them takes advantage of the findings from Interpretable ML. Critical freezing is built on the top of CFD's investigation to provide an interpretable and effective approach to deal with catastrophic forgetting. In the learning process, the optimal state of the old model is employed to initialize the new network. This way mimics the working mechanism of the human brain.

3.1   Catastrophic Forgetting Dissector - CFD

To dissect the model, we visualize the activation difference maps of hidden layers with respect to a specific unit (likely in the last layer) to understand the forgetting effect. We initially hypothesized that different features of the objects could be captured and visualized by particular feature maps in different layers. By looking into each response map in one conv block, we realize diverse features, such as eyes, face shape, car wheels, or background are isolatedly recognized by different channels, which avers our hypothesis. Unfortunately, considering each feature map manually by human eyes to study the forgetting is inefficient. To solve this issue, we compare the activation difference maps of feature maps with the ground truth segmentation to choose just one representative map in each conv block when the model has been trained on the first task. When new tasks arrive, the compare activation difference maps of two old and new models, in the same conv block, to measure the forgetting degree. In general, we do not seek for the answer that what features are being forgotten, but which conv blocks are forgetting.

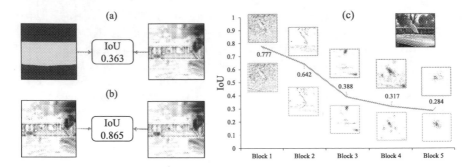

Fig. 2. (a) IoU value between the segmentation of a train and the positive features. (b) The IoU on the positive features of two representative maps. Red is evidence (or activate a unit) and blue is against (or decrease activation). (c) IoU graph and computer vision of a bird image. Yellow-bounding and blue-bounding boxes are from the old and new model respectively. (Color figure online)

The visualizations of the tool and the ground truth segmentation are simultaneously employed to infer the forgetting blocks. We assume that the semantic segmentation label of MS-COCO dataset [8] is what human eyes perceive. Next, we compare this segmentation with the computer vision of the model, particularly concentrating on positive evidence for a prediction to see how supportive features are disregarded.

The IoU value between the segmentation and evidence is calculated as shown in Fig. 2(a). On the right side of Fig. 2(a), we have an input image of a train, red dots advocate the fact that the output should be *"train"* while blue ones contradict this prediction.

Having the *m-th* activation difference map (FM) in the *l-th* block of a model M and the ground truth segmentation GT, the IoU is computed as:

$$IoU_{M,GT}(l, m) = \frac{FM(l, m) \cap GT}{FM(l, m) \cup GT} \tag{1}$$

To select the activation difference map having the largest overlap with the ground truth in *l-th* conv block, the representative map (RM) with the best IoU is $RM_{M,GT}$:

$$RM_{M,GT}(l) = argmax_m(IoU_{M,GT}(l, m)) \tag{2}$$

To understand how the computer vision changes over the training process, we compare the RMs in the new model with the RMs of the old model shown in Fig. 2(b). We compute $IoU_{M_O,GT}$ by (1) then achieve $RM_{M_O,GT}$ from (2) ($RM_{M_O,GT}$ is the representative map of the old model). The forgetting effect of each trained model is measured by the IoUs between $RM_{M_O,GT}$ and activation difference maps of M_N (M_N is the new model):

$$IoU_{M_N,M_O}(l, m) = \frac{FM(m) \cap RM_{M_O,GT}}{FM(m) \cup RM_{M_O,GT}} \tag{3}$$

Algorithm 1. CFD

1: **Input:** Sample set S, segmentation ground truth GT, old model M_O, new model M_N, number of blocks K
2: **Output:** Forgetting conv block $\mathbb{F}$
3: $i = 0$
4: $\mathrm{L} = \emptyset$
5: **repeat**
6:     $I = S[i]$
7:     $IoUs = \emptyset$
8:     $FM = PDA(I)$
9:     **for** $j = 1$ **to** K **do**
10:         $RM_{M_O,GT} \leftarrow FM$ with highest $IoU_{M_O,GT}$
11:         $RM_{M_N,M_O} \leftarrow FM$ with highest IoU_{M_N,M_O}
12:         **Append**($IoUs, max(IoU_{M_N,M_O})$)
13:     **end for**
14:     $b \leftarrow$ blocks with the highest drop in IoUs
15:     **Append**(L, b)
16:     $i = i + 1$
17: **until** $i = $ **size**(S)
18: $\mathbb{F} \leftarrow$ Most frequent block in L

Similar to the method of finding out the best map fitting with ground truth, the map representing the best memory of the original activation difference map is denoted as RM_{M_N,M_O} in (4). RM_{M_N,M_O} is determined as:

$$RM_{M_N,M_O}(l) = argmax_m(IoU_{M_N,M_O}(l,m)) \tag{4}$$

In the same block of both the old and new model, the role of a filter can be adjusted. For instance, the 50th filter in the 2nd block of the old model detects the eyes, but the same filter in the same block of the new model may consider the face. Hence, we should not make a comparison based on the index of a filter.

The workflow of CFD is given by Algorithm 1. The sample set S is particularized in Sect. 4, GT is the segmentation ground-truth from MS-COCO dataset, M_O and M_N are the old and new model for comparison respectively, and K is the number of the conv blocks in the network ($K = 5$ with ResNets). L is a list containing the most forgetting conv block with respect to all the images in S. By inputting an image I from S, we get the visualization of maps (FM) over M_O and M_N by PDA. However, we need to pick the representative activation difference map (RM) amongst thousands of maps in a conv block.

To choose the representative map RM of the jth conv block in a model, we define representative map RM to be the map having the largest overlap with the RM of the previous model (RM_{prev} in short) for the same j^{th} block. Particularly, the RM_{prev} of M_O is the ground truth because M_O is the starting model, and $RM_{M_O,GT}$ is the map at j^{th} block of M_O. Likewise, RM_{prev} of M_N at j^{th} block is $RM_{M_O,GT}$, and we obtain RM_{M_N,M_O} by comparing maps of M_N and $RM_{M_O,GT}$. The IoU values between $RM_{M_O,GT}$ and RM_{M_N,M_O} are calculated at each conv block and appended to a list $IoUs$. After calculating IoU drops through the ResNet blocks and denote the block giving the highest drop as b, we can put b as the block where the most substantial forgetting happens into a list L, tested on the input image I. Finally, we generalize on all images of S to return the most forgetting component $\mathbb{F}$.

In the juxtaposition of the old and new model, the IoUs are visually drawn to provide a bird-eye view of the forgetting trend shown in Fig. 2(c). We may argue that the conv block having the lowest IoU (block 5) is the victim of catastrophic forgetting. However, this assumption is not asserted because of the error accumulation in deep neural networks. The computer vision of deeper blocks is directly attributed to earlier conv blocks. Once forgetting occurs in the first conv block, it will be propagated throughout the entire network.

We propose to leverage IoU slopes to find the weakest block b. At a point, if the IoU drops significantly compared to the previous value, it should be the sign of catastrophic forgetting. In Fig. 2(c), a plummet of the IoU value is seen between block 2 and block 3 (0.642 to 0.388). The first thought appearing in our mind was that the 3rd is forgetting most catastrophically. It is true but we need to regard the fact that the worst map in block 3 is a result of block 2 and block 1. This finding is the foundation for our technique to prevent catastrophic forgetting.

3.2   Critical Freezing

Algorithm 2. Critical Freezing

1: **Input:** Sample set S, segmentation ground truth GT, old model M_O, new model M_N, number of blocks K
2: **Output:** optimal state θ^*
3: $M_N \leftarrow M_O$ // initialize new model by old parameters
4: $F \leftarrow$ CFD(S, GT, M_O, M_N, K)
5: **for** $i = 1$ to $F - 1$ **do**
6:     **grad**($M_N[i]$, $False$) // freeze the block i^{th}
7: **end for**
8: $\theta^* \leftarrow \underset{\hat{\theta}}{argmin}(-\sum_{i=1}^{V} Y_k^i \log \hat{Y}_k^i)$

Fine-tuning techniques play a pivotal role in training deep networks if data distribution evolves. Regarding a pre-trained model, the feature extractor which captures global information is carefully protected in adaptation. The output layer may be superseded, or the learning rate should be tweaked to a tiny number. Another dominant approach is to freeze the weights of the early layers. They are all effective yet ambiguous because we cannot ensure freezing which layers will give the best result. Using the investigation from CFD, we freeze the precursors of the most plastic conv block in a deep neural network. If a network has K conv blocks, and we find the Fth convolutional block broken, then we try to freeze earlier blocks than the Fth block. If updating the fragile components are necessary, a learning rate on those blocks should be thoroughly calibrated. The procedure of critical freezing is shown in Algorithm 2. The objective function is the standard cross-entropy loss for image captioning, $\mathbb{V}$ is the size of the vocabulary, Y_k^i is the ground truth, and $\hat{Y}_k^i$ is the prediction.

4   Experiments

We use a dataset called Split MS-COCO from [12] to reproduce catastrophic forgetting in image captioning task with incremental learning schemes. The dataset contains over 47k images for training and over 23k images for validation and testing. Regarding the incremental learning setup, a new class is introduced at each time step. Initially, we train with 19 classes to acquire the base model, followed by adding 5 classes sequentially. The captioning model is divided into an encoder and a decoder, in which the encoder is the ResNet-50, and the decoder includes an embedding layer, a single-layer LSTM, and a fully-connected layer producing a word at a time step. As CFD works on a single image, running multiple times on different and diverse input images is needed, helping us to generalize the observation of forgetting.

We choose a sample set S (*bicycle, car, motorcycle, airplane, bus, train, bird, cat, dog, horse, sheep, and cow*) from 19 trained classes. The results of CFD reinforce the fact that the 3rd conv block of ResNet is the most plastic component of this famous conv net given the learning sequence. To evaluate critical freezing, we perform fine-tuning and various schemes of freezing. In fine-tuning, the old model initializes the new model, and training is done by minimizing the loss on the new task. As the network contains two parts, encoder and decoder, we freeze them separately to specify the best freezing strategy. In addition, we choose various combinations of blocks to be frozen besides a famous baseline in continual learning experiments called LwF [7]. Two knowledge distillation techniques from [10] are also taken into comparison. The traditional scores for image captioning are considered in evaluating the superiority of critical freezing over the baselines. $BLEU4$ and $ROUGE_L$ are essentially word-overlap based metrics, while CIDEr and SPICE are more trustworthy because they give more weights on significant terms, such as verbs or nouns. Therefore, we will give discussion only on CIDEr score for conciseness.

After adding a new class, we obtain M_{20}, and M_n is the model when a total number of n classes are witnessed. In Fig. 3, the visualized results show that the first and second blocks of ResNet-50 can overall capture the outline of objects. Computer vision turns to represent more detailed features from the objects and other background features to determine the class of the input image in the deeper blocks. Also, the IoUs of different blocks in models, comparing with ground truth, are calculated by (1) and (2). The results reveal that although different models show the performance of the classification inconsistently, the $IoU_{M_n,GT}$ ($n > 19$) values are roughly similar at all the blocks, which implies that no matter the how good the performance is, the level of matching between maps of each model and the human vision is preserved (Fig. 4(a)).

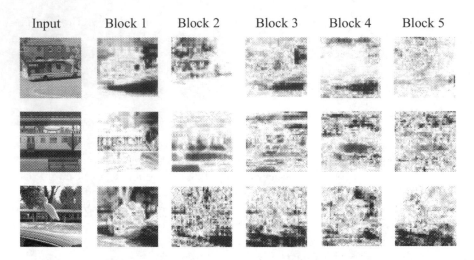

Fig. 3. Activation difference maps from convolutional blocks of ResNet-50.

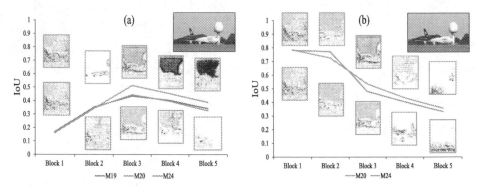

Fig. 4. (a) $IoU_{M,GT}$ of M_{19}, M_{20} and M_{24} comparing with GT. (b) $IoU_{MT,MO}$ of model M_{20} and M_{24} comparing with M_{19}.

To measure how much the forgetting occurs in the ResNet, we compute IoUs by (3) and (4). It is clearly shown in Fig. 4(b) that the IoUs between M_{20} and M_{19} are roughly equal to the corresponding figure for M_{24} and M_{19} in every block. For M_{20}, the $IoU_{M_{20},M_{19}}$ is always around 0.8 at the first block, showing that a marginal forgetting happens here. The $IoU_{M_{20},M_{19}}$ starts to drop along the blocks because the later maps are constructed by the previous maps. The forgetting effect persists and does not show which block is forgetting the most.

For M_{24}, the first block of the model still gets a high IoU comparing with M_{19} and the values decrease from the second block. Unlike the constantly decreasing trend seen in M_{20}, the decreasing rate of $IoU_{M_{24},M_{19}}$ fluctuates through the blocks and a severe drop at block 3 is observed in every testing input, suggesting that the forgetting effect might happen the most in this block. Iterating this procedure on all images of the set S reinforces that the worst forgetting happens at block 3.

Table 1. Performance when 5 classes arrive sequentially on past tasks and newly added tasks.

	Past − task				New − task			
	BLEU4	ROUGE_L	CIDEr	SPICE	BLEU4	ROUGE_L	CIDEr	SPICE
Fine-tuning	4.2	32.3	4.9	1.9	10.1	39.6	17.9	5.9
Encoder-freezing	3.8	31.5	5.2	2.0	8.8	38.4	15.1	5.1
Decoder-freezing	5.2	33.3	6.8	2.2	10.6	39.8	18.5	5.5
L1-freezing	5.2	33.5	7.9	2.4	12.0	41.1	23.4	6.4
L2-freezing	5.8	**33.6**	7.4	2.1	12.0	**41.2**	24.0	6.5
L3-freezing	4.5	32.2	6.8	2.1	10.4	39.6	20.7	6.0
L4-freezing	5.0	32.6	7.6	2.2	11.4	40.0	23.3	6.2
L5-freezing	5.4	33.0	7.4	2.3	12.1	40.4	23.3	6.2
LwF [7]	**6.4**	33.2	**9.7**	2.6	10.6	38.9	16.1	5.3
KD1 [10]	4.7	33.3	6.7	2.1	11.4	40.4	20.8	6.2
KD2 [10]	3.9	32.4	5.6	2.0	10.6	39.8	18.6	5.9
Critical freezing	5.6	33.2	9.5	**2.8**	**12.2**	40.7	**26.1**	**6.9**

While two naive approaches of freezing in [12] are also implemented, we devise critical freezing based on findings, which only freezes critical conv blocks. As shown in Table 1, precisely freezing helps to learn on both the new and old tasks much more effectively. Our freezing scheme outperforms the other approaches on new tasks by a large margin (26.1 CIDEr) while achieving comparable performance with LwF [7] on past tasks (9.5 CIDEr) although LwF [7] is far more complicated. Knowledge distillation on intermediate feature space (KD1) and output layer (KD2) [10] claims 20.8 and 18.6 CIDEr respectively. We argue that the frozen blocks contain global information derived from past tasks, which is valuable and should be accumulated during lifetime rather than changing. Fine-tuning optimizes the loss on the new task without any guidance; as a result, the model may not fall into the low-error regions of tasks. We try to freeze each conv block of the ResNet to fortify the hypothesis that properly freezing is really better than ambiguous freezing in fine-tuning schemes. Hence, critical freezing exerts a promising influence on fine-tuning techniques in deep learning.

5   Conclusion and Future Work

As the presence of catastrophic forgetting hinders the life-long learning, understanding how this phenomenon happens in computer vision is imperative. We introduce CFD to grasp catastrophic forgetting. The investigation of our tool unearths the mystical question about catastrophic forgetting.

From knowing where the forgetting issue is coming from, a new technique has been proposed focusing on plastic components of a model to moderate the information loss. The experiments illustrate the superiority of critical freezing over various freezing schemes and existing techniques. To the best of our knowledge, no work has been done for mitigating catastrophic forgetting under the supervision of Interpretable ML. By knowing which regions are needed to be kept intact, not only could the performance on the old task be largely improved, but the new task is also more conquerable. Ultimately, critical freezing could benefit a variety of fine-tuning schemes and continual learning approaches.

There are future works following our paper. Scaling this work for other tasks and deep networks can better validate the proposed continual learning algorithm's feasibility. We believe that our work results are just a starting point for a new direction to address catastrophic forgetting by interpretable methods completely. The experiments on conv blocks are coarse, which could be further refined by using conv layers, which will likely give much better results. We are choosing PDA [20] because the maps are clear; however, we can also adopt other advanced methods, such as using attribution or saliency to analyze the forgetting problem better.

Acknowledgment. This work was supported by Korea-EU Joint Research Support Project through the Ministry of Science and ICT (MSIT) and National Research Foundation of Korea (NRF-2016K1A3A7A0395205414), and the Technology Innovation Program (or Industrial Strategic Technology development Program, 2000682, Development of Automated Driving Systems and Evaluation) funded by the Ministry of Trade, Industry and Energy (MOTIE, Korea).

References

1. Che, Z., Purushotham, S., Khemani, R., Liu, Y.: Interpretable deep models for ICU outcome prediction. In: AMIA Annual Symposium Proceedings, vol. 2016, p. 371. American Medical Informatics Association (2016)
2. Dabkowski, P., Gal, Y.: Real time image saliency for black box classifiers. In: Advances in Neural Information Processing Systems, pp. 6967–6976 (2017)
3. Goodfellow, I.J., Mirza, M., Xiao, D., Courville, A., Bengio, Y.: An empirical investigation of catastrophic forgetting in gradient-based neural networks. arXiv preprint arXiv:1312.6211 (2013)
4. Hou, S., Pan, X., Change Loy, C., Wang, Z., Lin, D.: Lifelong learning via progressive distillation and retrospection. In: Proceedings of the European Conference on Computer Vision (ECCV), pp. 437–452 (2018)
5. Kemker, R., McClure, M., Abitino, A., Hayes, T.L., Kanan, C.: Measuring catastrophic forgetting in neural networks. In: Thirty-Second AAAI Conference on Artificial Intelligence (2018)
6. Kirkpatrick, J., et al.: Overcoming catastrophic forgetting in neural networks. Proc. Nat. Acad. Sci. **114**(13), 3521–3526 (2017)
7. Li, Z., Hoiem, D.: Learning without forgetting. IEEE Trans. Pattern Anal. Mach. Intell. **40**(12), 2935–2947 (2017)
8. Lin, T.-Y., et al.: Microsoft COCO: common objects in context. In: Fleet, D., Pajdla, T., Schiele, B., Tuytelaars, T. (eds.) ECCV 2014. LNCS, vol. 8693, pp. 740–755. Springer, Cham (2014). https://doi.org/10.1007/978-3-319-10602-1_48

9. Ling, C.X., Bohn, T.: A unified framework for lifelong learning in deep neural networks. arXiv preprint arXiv:1911.09704 (2019)
10. Michieli, U., Zanuttigh, P.: Incremental learning techniques for semantic segmentation. In: Proceedings of the IEEE International Conference on Computer Vision Workshops, pp. 0–0 (2019)
11. Nguyen, C.V., Achille, A., Lam, M., Hassner, T., Mahadevan, V., Soatto, S.: Toward understanding catastrophic forgetting in continual learning. arXiv preprint arXiv:1908.01091 (2019)
12. Nguyen, G., Jun, T.J., Tran, T., Kim, D.: ContCap: a comprehensive framework for continual image captioning. arXiv preprint arXiv:1909.08745 (2019)
13. Shmelkov, K., Schmid, C., Alahari, K.: Incremental learning of object detectors without catastrophic forgetting. In: Proceedings of the IEEE International Conference on Computer Vision, pp. 3400–3409 (2017)
14. Simonyan, K., Vedaldi, A., Zisserman, A.: Deep inside convolutional networks: visualising image classification models and saliency maps. arXiv preprint arXiv:1312.6034 (2013)
15. Tasar, O., Tarabalka, Y., Alliez, P.: Incremental learning for semantic segmentation of large-scale remote sensing data. IEEE J. Sel. Top. Appl. Earth Obs. Remote Sens. 12(9), 3524–3537 (2019)
16. Yosinski, J., Clune, J., Nguyen, A., Fuchs, T., Lipson, H.: Understanding neural networks through deep visualization. arXiv preprint arXiv:1506.06579 (2015)
17. Zeiler, M.D., Fergus, R.: Visualizing and understanding convolutional networks. In: Fleet, D., Pajdla, T., Schiele, B., Tuytelaars, T. (eds.) ECCV 2014. LNCS, vol. 8689, pp. 818–833. Springer, Cham (2014). https://doi.org/10.1007/978-3-319-10590-1_53
18. Zenke, F., Poole, B., Ganguli, S.: Continual learning through synaptic intelligence. In: Proceedings of the 34th International Conference on Machine Learning, vol. 70, pp. 3987–3995 (2017). JMLR.org
19. Zhai, M., Chen, L., Tung, F., He, J., Nawhal, M., Mori, G.: Lifelong GAN: continual learning for conditional image generation. In: Proceedings of the IEEE International Conference on Computer Vision, pp. 2759–2768 (2019)
20. Zintgraf, L.M., Cohen, T.S., Adel, T., Welling, M.: Visualizing deep neural network decisions: prediction difference analysis. arXiv preprint arXiv:1702.04595 (2017)

Deep Learning for Astrophysics, Understanding the Impact of Attention on Variability Induced by Parameter Initialization

Mikaël Jacquemont[1,2]([✉])[iD], Thomas Vuillaume[1][iD], Alexandre Benoit[2][iD], Gilles Maurin[1][iD], and Patrick Lambert[2][iD]

[1] CNRS, LAPP, Univ. Grenoble Alpes, Université Savoie Mont Blanc, Annecy, France
{jacquemont,vuillaume,maurin}@lapp.in2p3.fr
[2] LISTIC, Univ. Savoie Mont Blanc, Annecy, France
{alexandre.benoit,patrick.lambert}@univ-smb.fr

Abstract. In the astrophysics domain, the detection and description of gamma rays is a research direction for our understanding of the universe. Gamma-ray reconstruction from Cherenkov telescope data is multi-task by nature. The image recorded in the Cherenkov camera pixels relates to the type, energy, incoming direction and distance of a particle from a telescope observation. We propose γ-PhysNet, a physically inspired multi-task deep neural network for gamma/proton particle classification, and gamma energy and direction reconstruction. As ground truth does not exist for real data, γ-PhysNet is trained and evaluated on large-scale Monte Carlo simulations. Robustness is then crucial for the transfer of the performance to real data. Relying on a visual explanation method, we evaluate the influence of attention on the variability due to weight initialization, and how it helps improve the robustness of the model. All the experiments are conducted in the context of single telescope analysis for the Cherenkov Telescope Array simulated data analysis.

Keywords: Multitasking · Artificial neural networks · Gamma rays · Attention · Visual explanation

We gratefully acknowledge financial support from the agencies and organizations listed here: www.cta-observatory.org/consortium_acknowledgment. This project has received funding from the *European Union's Horizon 2020 research and innovation programme* under grant agreement No 653477, and from the Fondation Université Savoie Mont Blanc. This work has been done thanks to the facilities offered by the Univ. Savoie Mont Blanc - CNRS/IN2P3 MUST computing center and HPC resources from GENCI-IDRIS (Grant 2020-AD011011577) and computing and data processing ressources from the CNRS/IN2P3 Computing Center (Lyon - France). We gratefully acknowledge the support of the NVIDIA Corporation with the donation of one NVIDIA P6000 GPU for this research.

A. Del Bimbo et al. (Eds.): ICPR 2020 Workshops, LNCS 12663, pp. 174–188, 2021.
https://doi.org/10.1007/978-3-030-68796-0_13

1   Introduction

Gamma-ray astronomy aims to study astronomical phenomena (supernova remnants, dark matter annihilation...) based on the gamma radiation generated by these phenomena. The analysis of this radiation is performed through the observation of telescope images of the particle shower resulting from the penetration of high-energy particles in the atmosphere (Cherenkov effect [9], see Fig. 1).
The purpose of the image analysis is twofold:

1. identifying the gamma rays in the cosmic ray background mainly composed of protons (with a signal-to-noise ratio typically lower than 1/1000), which is a classification problem,
2. estimating the energy and direction of the identified gamma rays, which is a regression problem.

The Cherenkov Telescope Array (CTA)[1] is the next generation of Imaging Atmospheric Cherenkov Telescopes (IACTs). Composed of ∼100 telescopes of different sizes, it will improve sensitivity and accuracy in gamma-ray analysis. However, the huge amount of data (210 PB of raw data per year when in full operation) requires a shift towards new methods of analysis, in particular deep neural network approaches. The work presented in this paper is carried out on the large-scale simulation data shared within the CTA international collaboration. As ground truth is not available in the field of astrophysics, the analysis toolchains are prepared with very high-quality simulation relying on a well-known physical model of the phenomenon and on the detector simulation [2]. Besides, the first real data are just available.

In this paper, we first propose a new deep multi-task architecture, named γ-PhysNet, taking into account physics considerations and designed for single telescope gamma event analysis. We evaluate this model on the simulation data of the Large Size Telescopes 1 (LST1 [1]), the first prototype installed at the Northern CTA site in La Palma. In a second step, with the help of a visual explanation method for neural networks, we analyze the impact of attention (mechanism that reinforces relevant features) on the variability introduced by model weights initialization, and show that augmenting the network with attention improves the robustness of the model.

The rest of the paper is organized as follows. In Sect. 2, we give a short state of the art related to this work. Section 3 is a presentation of γ-PhysNet. Understanding the impact of attention mechanism and weight initialization are discussed in Sect. 4. Finally, Sect. 5 gives conclusions and some perspectives for future works.

---

[1] https://www.cta-observatory.org/.

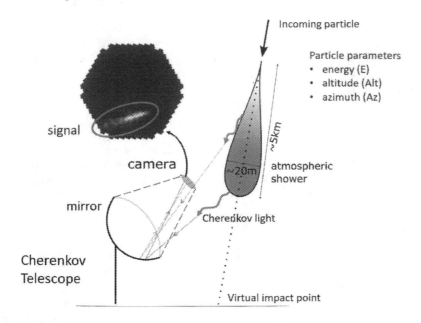

Fig. 1. Imaging Atmospheric Cherenkov Telescope. When a gamma particle enters the atmosphere, it generates an electromagnetic shower of secondary particles emitting Cherenkov light. This blue light is captured by the telescope on the ground and recorded as the signal by the camera. The event reconstruction consists in analyzing this signal to retrieve the physical parameters (type, energy, altitude, azimuth) of the primary particle. (Color figure online)

2   Related Work

Over the past decade, deep learning has emerged as the leading approach in many computer vision tasks. IACT data has not escaped this trend [16,18,20,25]. These papers present promising results, especially for gamma/proton classification. However, they have handled the different reconstruction problems as single tasks, without considering their strong interdependence. Further, multiple single task models can increase the computational cost, thus making their use complicated in our massive data context.

Multi-task Models. When dealing with a multi-task problem, it has been shown [29] that transferring knowledge across related tasks improves the generalization of the deep models with fewer data. Thus, in Multi-Task Learning (MTL), the different tasks to address are trained simultaneously, using a partially shared modeling. In hard parameter sharing architectures, the most frequently used, a whole part of the network (generally the encoder or its first layers) is shared between all tasks [22]. In soft parameter sharing architectures [4], each task is learned with its own network. Some additional layers are shared and constrained in order to encourage their weights to be similar. In MTL, balancing the tasks is the critical point. For most of the MTL related papers [15,21], this is done manually, requiring an extensive optimization process. However, adaptive methods have been proposed, with different balancing strategies such as modeling homoscedastic uncertainty for each task [12], using the task loss gradients [5], using learning progress signals as key performance indicators [6] or regarding the problem as a multi-objective optimization [24].

Complementary to MTL, the development of deep learning models integrates attention mechanisms.

Attention Mechanisms. Attention is a mechanism that helps deep learning model focus on relevant features based on a defined context through trainable weights. A distinction can be made between restricted self-attention, focusing on local spatial neighborhoods and global self-attention as a non-local operation [31]. Local and global self-attention can be considered as spatial attention mechanisms, as they capture short- and long-range dependencies in data, by weighting each pixel. On the contrary, Hu *et al.* [10] introduce a lightweight channelwise attention denoted Squeeze-and-Excitation. The squeeze operation produces descriptors for each input channel, and is followed by an adaptive recalibration, the excitation, and a scale operation that weights the input channels. Dual Attention [28] has been proposed to improve model interpretability and robustness of U-Net models for a semantic segmentation task. It combines Squeeze-and-Excitation and a simple spatial attention path. The latter first compresses the number of input channels to one, and then applies a sigmoid function to the resulting pixel values, and adds one to them to produce an attention map. This way, the spatial attention map can only increase pixel values. This map is then used to rescale the output of the Squeeze-and-Excitation. Such attention strategy then allows for the weighting of both spatial and channel-wise information in a low-cost operator.

Model Explanation. While traditional expert systems are highly interpretable and explainable, deep neural networks are often perceived as *black boxes*. Recently, the deep learning community has put an increasing effort on opening the black box. Some methods explore the role of individual neurons or linear combination of units through ablation [17,32] or optimization [19]. Others estimate the importance of input features for a particular output activation. They produce saliency maps [3,26,27] also called heatmaps in [23] for network visualization. In the rest of this paper we rely on Grad-CAM [23], a highly class-discriminative localization method that produces a heatmap of the region that is the most relevant for the model's decision. It is applicable to any network structure. The heatmaps are computed based on the last convolutional layer. In the context of multi-task learning, Grad-CAM is then especially adapted to hard parameter sharing networks that share a convolutional encoder between all tasks. In addition, when available, attention maps, produced by attention mechanisms (see previous section), can provide insights on the model regions of interest that can explain the predictions.

3   Proposed Architecture and Performance

To achieve full event reconstruction from IACT data, we propose a MTL architecture, denoted γ-PhysNet. We then compare the vanilla model to a version augmented with attention modules. Our aim is to understand model robustness against weight initialization, and the regularization effect provided by attention mechanisms. Model performances are assessed relying on different random seeds.

In this paper we restrict our analysis to a specific model with optional attention modules. This model is a performing baseline that originates from preliminary extensive comparative studies, and the scope of the paper is to study its robustness towards weight initialization variability.

3.1 γ-PhysNet Architecture

As illustrated in Fig. 2, γ-PhysNet is a hard parameter sharing architecture composed of a backbone encoder and a multi-task block inspired by the physics of the reconstruction. The network is fed with two-channel IACT data discussed in Sect. 3.2. It performs gamma rays from background noise separation, and primary particle energy and arrival direction regression as the altitude and azimuth. The regression of the virtual impact point on the ground of the particle is an auxiliary task (see Fig. 1 for the meaning of these characteristics). Even though it is not required for higher-level analysis, physics shows that this parameter provides meaningful information to solve the other tasks. The baseline backbone of γ-PhysNet is the convolutional part of a ResNet-56 [7,8], CIFAR-10 version, with full pre-activation implemented with IndexedConv [11]. The latter allows the direct processing of the hexagonal pixel images of the LST1 data used in this paper without transforming them to square pixel ones. We also propose a refined version of the model, named γ-PhysNet DA (DA for Dual Attention), that makes use of attention. Dual Attention modules are inserted into the backbone after every stage, i.e., processing scale, to benefit from attention at each feature scale. As mentioned in Sect. 2, Dual Attention is composed of a spatial attention path and a channel-wise attention path. The latter consists of a Squeeze-and-Excitation module that has a ratio parameter to control its bottleneck. An extensive study of this hyperparameter has shown that, in the context of the experiments carried out for this paper, the default ratio of 16 allows obtaining the best results. The physically inspired multi-task block finalizes the model. It is composed of a global feature network and a local feature one, both based on fully connected layers. The global feature part, dedicated to energy regression, starts with a global average pooling. This strategy follows the physics of the phenomenon, as for a given arrival direction and impact point, the amplitude of the image is roughly proportional to the primary gamma ray energy [30]. The local feature part is devoted to gamma/proton classification, and regression of the arrival direction and impact point. It is fed with the flattened feature maps produced by the backbone. The aim is to exploit local (the shape of the signal in the image) and spatial (the position and orientation of the signal) information

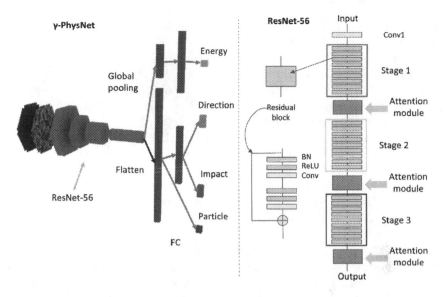

Fig. 2. γ-PhysNet. *Left:* the model architecture composed of a convolutional backbone (ResNet-56) and a physically inspired Multi-task head block based on fully connected layers (FC). The latter is divided into two paths: a global path for the energy regression and a local path for the particle type classification, the direction and the virtual impact point regression. *Right:* refined model backbone with Dual Attention modules inserted after each stage.

that is more deeply related to the particle type, its arrival direction and virtual impact point.

3.2 Experiments

Dataset. As ground truth is impossible to obtain from real data, γ-PhysNet and γ-PhysNet DA are evaluated on the *LST4 mono-trigger production* (from 2019/04/15), the reference large-scale Monte Carlo production generated by the LST international consortium for the LST1 commissioning. This dataset has been calibrated and integrated with DL1DataHandler [13]. Each sample corresponds to a single event (particle) and is composed of two-channel images: one with pixel intensities in number of photoelectrons and the other one containing per-pixel temporal information in nanoseconds. Data amplitude is not normalized since it is related to the energy of the detected particles. A data selection step is applied, following the standards in the domain and the project collaboration. It consists of a series of relatively loose selection cuts on image amplitude, shower size and truncated showers applied to the data in order to discard bad quality events that would not be reconstructed by standard methods either. The training set is finally composed of $874k$ gamma events and $506k$ proton events, the validating set $201k$ and $136k$, and the test set $209k$ and $38k$.

Training. In order to analyze the robustness of both models to parameter initialization, we repeat the experiments with six different random seeds. We define the following optimization criteria: cross-entropy loss for the classification task and the $L1$ loss for each regression task. Models are trained for 25 epochs with Adam [14] as the optimizer, and a weight decay of 10^{-4} for regularization purpose. The learning rate is set to 10^{-3}, decayed by a factor of 10 every 10 epochs. The different tasks are balanced with the uncertainty estimation method presented in [12]. In this setup, both models reach their best performance plateau on the validation set. In gamma-ray astronomy, proton events are considered as background noise. To prevent them from penalizing the learning of energy and direction regression for gamma events, we rely on a masked loss method, setting to zero the loss of the regression parameters (energy, arrival direction and impact point) when particles are protons.

Evaluation Metrics. The performance on energy and direction reconstruction tasks is measured through resolution curves. The angular resolution is defined as the 68% containment radius of the point-spread (distribution) function and the energy resolution as the 68% containment radius of the relative absolute deviation. Lower resolutions are better.

Weight initialization plays an important role in neural network performance. We then repeat the experiment six times for both models, and we illustrate the variability of these different runs by drawing the average resolution curve per energy bin, the surfaces representing the standard deviation. The latter, referred to as dispersion in this paper, serves as measure of the robustness of the models.

For the gamma/proton classification task, the overall performance of the network is given by the area under the ROC curve (AUC), the precision and the recall.

Results. As shown in Table 1, both models with and without attention have comparable results on the classification task, within the standard deviation range. However, for the energy and direction regression, as illustrated in Fig. 3, the model with Dual Attention (γ-PhysNet DA) obtains slightly better average results above 100 GeV. Furthermore, we observe that the network with attention has significantly less spread results. In particular, γ-PhysNet DA has a constantly lower dispersion on the direction reconstruction task. On the energy reconstruction one, at energies above 200 GeV, the model without attention has dispersion up to three times higher. This lower dispersion of the results of γ-PhysNet DA denotes a better robustness to parameter initialization. This will lead to a more reliable estimation of the particle parameters when we analyze real data.

Table 1. Classification performance of both models with and without attention. The AUC represents the overall performance, while the precision shows the ability of the model to discard protons (the background noise), and the recall highlights the ability of the model to retrieve gammas.

Model	AUC	Precision	Recall
γ-PhysNet	0.882 ± 0.001	0.929 ± 0.001	0.935 ± 0.007
γ-PhysNet DA	0.882 ± 0.001	0.929 ± 0.001	0.935 ± 0.005

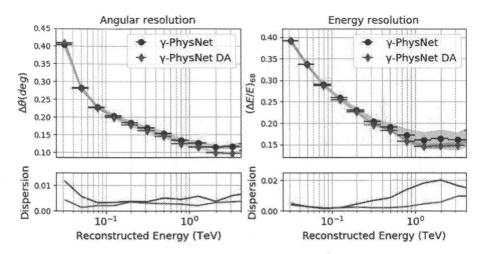

Fig. 3. Angular (*left*) and energy (*right*) resolution as a function of the energy in the LST1 energy range (lower is better). Both resolution curves represent the error of the model for the regression of respectively the direction and the energy of the detected gamma particle. The dispersion, representing the variability induced by weight initialization, is a measure of the robustness of the models.

4 Understanding the Impact of Dual Attention

As we have seen in Sect. 3.2, the addition of Dual Attention modules to γ-PhysNet improves the robustness of the model, especially for the energy and arrival direction reconstruction tasks, by reducing the dispersion due to parameter initialization during the training step. However, it has no clear impact on the classification task. To understand how and why attention acts on the model predictions, we carefully observe the Grad-CAM heatmaps produced by γ-PhysNet and γ-PhysNet DA for 25 well and badly reconstructed events of the test set. We also observe the spatial attention maps of the three Dual Attention modules. Additionally, for each input data and model seed, we combine these three spatial attention maps with the Hadamard product to obtain a global representation of the spatial attention in the model. Finally, to highlight the variability brought by the different initialization seeds for a particular event, we compute the mean and standard deviation of Grad-CAM heatmaps and spatial attention maps at the pixel level (to lighten the paper, only these means and standard deviations will be presented in the following figures).

Observation of the Grad-CAM Heatmaps and the Spatial Attention Maps. For all the 25 events analyzed, we observe a common trend in the averaged heatmaps produced by the Grad-CAM. Figure 4, Fig. 5 and Fig. 6 illustrate 3 typical examples respectively, a well-reconstructed but partially truncated gamma shower, a well-reconstructed and centered gamma shower and a badly reconstructed one. It is worth noticing that the different maps are represented using different color scales. For the classification task (denoted "class" in the figures), with or without attention, the most relevant pixels highlighted by Grad-CAM are located in the signal area. On another hand, for the regression tasks (denoted "Energy", "Altitude" and "Azimuth" in the figures) we observe different behaviors. Without attention, the most relevant ones are situated on the border of the camera, while the signal pixels are of less importance. In our understanding, this phenomenon serves as an evaluation of the signal outside of the camera, and thus not acquired, that is important for regression tasks. With attention, all the relevant pixels are located in the shower area, thus better taking into account the signal pixels and relevant information. Besides, for all tasks, the model with attention focuses on a larger part of the image. It is worth noticing that, in addition to the signal pixels themselves, pixels situated in the signal neighborhood contain useful information about the shower shape. Then, the deviation measures (denoted "std" in the figures) of Grad-CAM heatmaps highlight the same general trend related to the robustness against the initialization. Although the variability of pixel relevance is quite important in both cases, for γ-PhysNet with attention the relevant pixels fluctuate in the signal area, while without attention they vary on a larger extent between the shower area and the image boundaries.

Then, the observation of the spatial attention maps of γ-PhysNet DA shows that the action of Dual Attention is different depending on the feature scale. The output of stage 1 has the same resolution as the input data. At this scale, the attention module mainly focuses on the shower pixels, and strongly rescales their value. The value of the signal pixels is multiplied by up to 1.8 in average, while, by construction, the rescaling factor computed by the spatial attention path of Dual Attention modules ranges in [1, 2], as explained in Sect. 2. However, the attention maps are quite noisy at this scale, as also highlighted by the deviation measures. After stage 2, the attention modules also strongly favor the pixels in the signal area, and the attention maps are less noisy. Then, the last attention modules, after stage 3, have a lighter impact on the feature maps values. Finally, the observation of the combined spatial attention maps highlights that attention strongly helps the model focus on the signal pixels, which is consistent with the observation of the Grad-CAM heatmaps.

Impact of the Attention on the Classification Task. Table 1 shows no significant effect of the attention of the classification task. This can be explained by the attention and Grad-Cam heatmaps that always focus on the event shower area. More into the details, attention allows for a larger extent of the heatmaps around

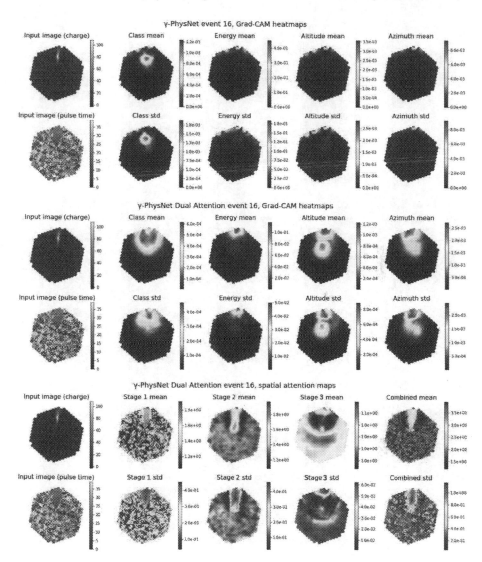

Fig. 4. Well-reconstructed gamma, event 16. The two upper rows represent the Grad-CAM heatmaps (mean and standard deviation) obtained for the vanilla γ-PhysNet, the next two rows correspond to the Grad-CAM heatmaps of γ-PhysNet DA (with attention), and the last two rows show the corresponding spatial attention maps.

the shower and also avoids interest on the noisy boundaries of the images. However since both models report similar predictions performances, one can expect that they rely on the same most contributing, shower centered, features.

Impact on the Regression Tasks. For the energy and direction reconstruction tasks, Dual Attention forces the model to focus on the shower area instead of the

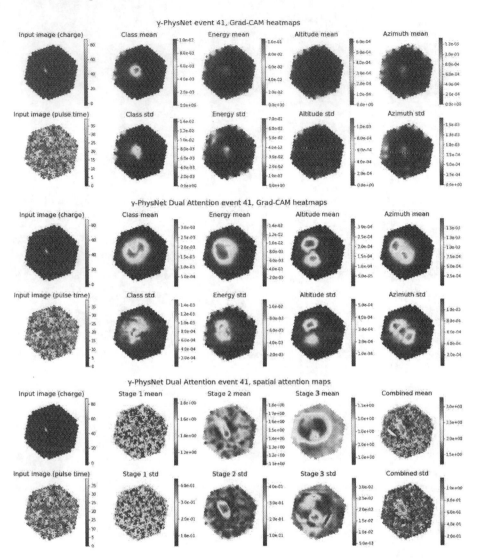

Fig. 5. Well-reconstructed gamma, event 41. The two upper rows represent the Grad-CAM heatmaps (mean and standard deviation) obtained for the vanilla γ-PhysNet, the next two rows correspond to the Grad-CAM heatmaps of γ-PhysNet DA (with attention), and the last two rows show the corresponding spatial attention maps.

image border, by strongly rescaling the signal pixels and their close neighbors. This is significant enough to improve the results of both tasks presented in Sect. 3.2, and to reduce the dispersion introduced by the parameter initialization.

Besides, it is worth noticing that for the event 16 represented in Fig. 4, the most important pixels are still on the border of the image. Indeed, the signal is truncated, and the network has learned that it is an important information to

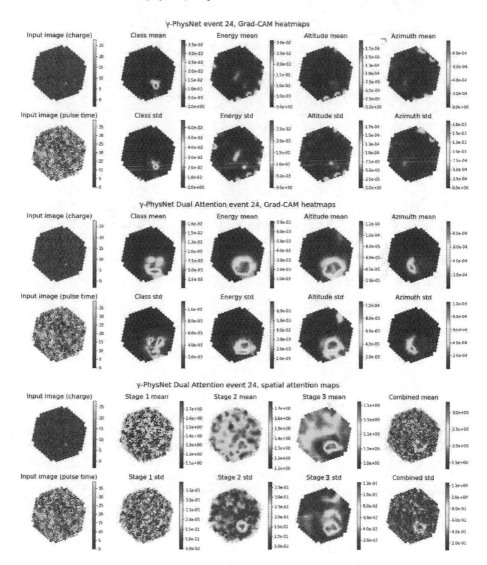

Fig. 6. Badly reconstructed gamma, event 24. The two upper rows represent the Grad-CAM heatmaps (mean and standard deviation) obtained for the vanilla γ-PhysNet, the next two rows correspond to the Grad-CAM heatmaps of γ-PhysNet DA (with attention), and the last two rows show the corresponding spatial attention maps.

take into account for the estimation of the energy and the direction of the gamma ray. However, focusing on the signal part of the image does not automatically imply a good reconstruction, as exemplified by the badly reconstructed event 24 shown in Fig. 6.

5   Conclusion

In this paper we have presented γ-PhysNet, a deep multi-task architecture for gamma-ray full-event reconstruction for IACT single telescope images. We have shown that augmenting the model with attention allows for a reduction of the performance variability induced by parameter initialization. Relying on a visual explanation method, we have then realized the first steps to understand how attention modifies the behavior of the model. In a future work, in order to deepen this analysis, we will define statistical criteria to quantify this effect. Correlating the pixels highlighted by Grad-CAM and the true signal over the whole test set is an option. We also consider analyzing statistically the distance of the relevant pixels to the shower centroid. Finally, it would also be interesting to study if the robustness brought by attention mechanisms also holds with slightly different datasets (different levels of noise, altered images, etc.).

References

1. Ambrosi, G., Awane, Y., Baba, H., et al.: For the CTA Consortium: the Cherenkov telescope array large size telescope. In: Proceedings of the 33rd International Cosmic Ray Conference, pp. 8–11 (2013). https://doi.org/10.1117/12.2054605
2. Bernlöhr, K., et al.: Monte Carlo design studies for the Cherenkov telescope array. Astropart. Phys. **43**, 171–188 (2013)
3. Cao, C., Liu, X., Yang, Y., et al.: Look and think twice: capturing top-down visual attention with feedback convolutional neural networks. In: Proceedings of the IEEE International Conference on Computer Vision, pp. 2956–2964 (2015)
4. Cao, J., Li, Y., Zhang, Z.: Partially shared multi-task convolutional neural network with local constraint for face attribute learning. In: Proceedings of the IEEE Conference on Computer Vision and Pattern Recognition, pp. 4290–4299 (2018)
5. Chen, Z., Badrinarayanan, V., Lee, C.Y., Rabinovich, A.: GradNorm: gradient normalization for adaptive loss balancing in deep multitask networks. In: Dy, J., Krause, A. (eds.) Proceedings of the 35th International Conference on Machine Learning. Proceedings of Machine Learning Research, vol. 80, pp. 794–803. PMLR (2018)
6. Guo, M., Haque, A., Huang, D.A., Yeung, S., Fei-Fei, L.: Dynamic task prioritization for multitask learning. In: Proceedings of the European Conference on Computer Vision (ECCV), pp. 270–287 (2018)
7. He, K., Zhang, X., Ren, S., Sun, J.: Identity mappings in deep residual networks. In: Leibe, B., Matas, J., Sebe, N., Welling, M. (eds.) ECCV 2016. LNCS, vol. 9908, pp. 630–645. Springer, Cham (2016). https://doi.org/10.1007/978-3-319-46493-0_38
8. He, K., Zhang, X., Ren, S., Sun, J.: Deep residual learning for image recognition. In: Proceedings of the IEEE Conference on Computer Vision and Pattern Recognition, pp. 770–778 (2016)
9. Hillas, A.: Cerenkov light images of EAS produced by primary gamma. In: International Cosmic Ray Conference, vol. 3 (1985)
10. Hu, J., Shen, L., Sun, G.: Squeeze-and-excitation networks. In: Proceedings of the IEEE Conference on Computer Vision and Pattern Recognition, pp. 7132–7141 (2018)

11. Jacquemont, M., et al.: Indexed operations for non-rectangular lattices applied to convolutional neural networks. In: Proceedings of the 14th International Joint Conference on Computer Vision, Imaging and Computer Graphics Theory and Applications, vol. 5, no. VISAPP, pp. 362–371. INSTICC, SciTePress (2019). https://doi.org/10.5220/0007364303620371

12. Kendall, A., Gal, Y., Cipolla, R.: Multi-task learning using uncertainty to weigh losses for scene geometry and semantics. In: Proceedings of the IEEE Conference on Computer Vision and Pattern Recognition, pp. 7482–7491 (2018)

13. Kim, B., Brill, A., Miener, T., Nieto, D., Feng, Q.: DL1-Data-Handler: DL1 HDF5 writer, reader, and processor for IACT data, v0.8.1-legacy (2019). https://doi.org/10.5281/zenodo.3336561

14. Kingma, D.P., Ba, J.: Adam: a method for stochastic optimization. In: Bengio, Y., LeCun, Y. (eds.) 3rd International Conference on Learning Representations, ICLR 2015, San Diego, CA, USA, 7–9 May 2015, Conference Track Proceedings (2015)

15. Luvizon, D.C., Picard, D., Tabia, H.: 2D/3D pose estimation and action recognition using multitask deep learning. In: Proceedings of the IEEE Conference on Computer Vision and Pattern Recognition (2018)

16. Mangano, S., Delgado, C., Bernardos, M.I., Lallena, M., Rodríguez Vázquez, J.J.: Extracting gamma-ray information from images with convolutional neural network methods on simulated Cherenkov telescope array data. In: Pancioni, L., Schwenker, F., Trentin, E. (eds.) ANNPR 2018. LNCS (LNAI), vol. 11081, pp. 243–254. Springer, Cham (2018). https://doi.org/10.1007/978-3-319-99978-4_19

17. Morcos, A.S., Barrett, D.G.T., Rabinowitz, N.C., Botvinick, M.: On the importance of single directions for generalization. In: 6th International Conference on Learning Representations, ICLR 2018, Vancouver, BC, Canada, 30 April–3 May 2018, Conference Track Proceedings. OpenReview.net (2018)

18. Nieto Castaño, D., Brill, A., Kim, B., Humensky, T.B., Consortium, C.: Exploring deep learning as an event classification method for the Cherenkov Telescope Array. In: 35th International Cosmic Ray Conference. ICRC, vol. 301, p. 809 (2017)

19. Olah, C., Mordvintsev, A., Schubert, L.: Feature visualization. Distill **2**(11), e7 (2017)

20. Parsons, R.D., Ohm, S.: Background rejection in atmospheric Cherenkov telescopes using recurrent convolutional neural networks. Eur. Phys. J. C **80**(5), 1–11 (2020). https://doi.org/10.1140/epjc/s10052-020-7953-3

21. Ren, Z., Jae Lee, Y.: Cross-domain self-supervised multi-task feature learning using synthetic imagery. In: Proceedings of the IEEE Conference on Computer Vision and Pattern Recognition, pp. 762–771 (2018)

22. Ruder, S.: An overview of multi-task learning in deep neural networks. arXiv preprint arXiv:1706.05098 (2017)

23. Selvaraju, R.R., Cogswell, M., Das, A., Vedantam, R., Parikh, D., Batra, D.: Gradcam: visual explanations from deep networks via gradient-based localization. In: Proceedings of the IEEE International Conference on Computer Vision, pp. 618–626 (2017)

24. Sener, O., Koltun, V.: Multi-task learning as multi-objective optimization. In: Advances in Neural Information Processing Systems (2018)

25. Shilon, I., et al.: Application of deep learning methods to analysis of imaging atmospheric Cherenkov telescopes data. Astropart. Phys. **105**, 44–53 (2019)

26. Springenberg, J.T., Dosovitskiy, A., Brox, T., Riedmiller, M.A.: Striving for simplicity: the all convolutional net. In: Bengio, Y., LeCun, Y. (eds.) 3rd International Conference on Learning Representations, ICLR 2015, San Diego, CA, USA, 7–9 May 2015, Workshop Track Proceedings (2015)

27. Srinivas, S., Fleuret, F.: Full-gradient representation for neural network visualization. In: Advances in Neural Information Processing Systems, pp. 4126–4135 (2019)
28. Sun, J., Darbeha, F., Zaidi, M., Wang, B.: Saunet: Shape attentive u-net for interpretable medical image segmentation. arXiv preprint arXiv:2001.07645 (2020)
29. Thrun, S.: Is learning the n-th thing any easier than learning the first? In: Advances in Neural Information Processing Systems, pp. 640–646 (1996)
30. Völk, H.J., Bernlöhr, K.: Imaging very high energy gamma-ray telescopes. Exp. Astron. **25**(13), 173–191 (2009)
31. Wang, X., Girshick, R., Gupta, A., He, K.: Non-local neural networks. In: Proceedings of the IEEE Conference on Computer Vision and Pattern Recognition, pp. 7794–7803 (2018)
32. Zhou, B., Sun, Y., Bau, D., Torralba, A.: Revisiting the importance of individual units in cnns via ablation. arXiv preprint arXiv:1806.02891 (2018)

A General Approach to Compute the Relevance of Middle-Level Input Features

Andrea Apicella$^{(\boxtimes)}$, Salvatore Giugliano, Francesco Isgrò, and Roberto Prevete

Dipartimento di Ingegneria Elettrica e delle Teconologie dell'Informazione,
Università degli Studi di Napoli Federico II, Naples, Italy
`and.api.univ@gmail.com`

Abstract. This work proposes a novel general framework, in the context of eXplainable Artificial Intelligence (XAI), to construct explanations for the behaviour of Machine Learning (ML) models in terms of middle-level features which represent perceptually salient input parts. One can isolate two different ways to provide explanations in the context of XAI: low and middle-level explanations. Middle-level explanations have been introduced for alleviating some deficiencies of low-level explanations such as, in the context of image classification, the fact that human users are left with a significant interpretive burden: starting from low-level explanations, one has to identify properties of the overall input that are perceptually salient for the human visual system. However, a general approach to correctly evaluate the elements of middle-level explanations with respect ML model responses has never been proposed in the literature.

We experimentally evaluate the proposed approach to explain the decisions made by an Imagenet pre-trained VGG16 model on STL-10 images and by a customised model trained on the JAFFE dataset, using two different computational definitions of middle-level features and compare it with two different XAI middle-level methods. The results show that our approach can be used successfully in different computational definitions of middle-level explanations.

Keywords: XAI · Machine Learning · Middle-level features

1 Introduction

In the last years, Machine Learning (ML) approaches have been widely used to address several challenges in Artificial Intelligence (AI), such as image [31] and text classification [11] problems, multi-target regression [25] and robot navigation [28]. However, a large part of these approaches suffers from a pervasive lack of transparency also connected to the problem of explaining their behaviour in terms that are easy to understand for human beings [18]. Indeed, it seems that the better ML systems become in terms of their performance, the harder it is to understand the underlying mechanisms and explain their behaviours [1]. For this reason, ML systems are often considered as black-box systems [1] insofar as

© Springer Nature Switzerland AG 2021
A. Del Bimbo et al. (Eds.): ICPR 2020 Workshops, LNCS 12663, pp. 189–203, 2021.
https://doi.org/10.1007/978-3-030-68796-0_14

their decisions are hard to interpret in terms of meaningful input features. Thus, generating explanations for ML system behaviours that are *understandable to human beings* is a central scientific and technological issue addressed by the rapidly growing AI research area of eXplainable Artificial Intelligence (XAI).

The literature counts various strategies to make ML systems - especially those endowed with Deep Neural Network (DNN) architectures [21] - interpretable and explainable [12,22]. XAI approaches to the explanation problem can be classified in several ways according to which properties are taken into account [1,15,23,34]. A key distinction is between *low-level* and *middle-level* input feature approaches. Low-level feature approaches to XAI attempt to explain the output of an ML system in terms of low-level features of the input such as pixels in case of image classification problems. One of the most successful methods for this type of approaches is the Layer-wise Relevance Propagation (LRP) [6], which associates a relevance value to each input element (to each pixel in the case of images) as an explanation of the ML model response. Thus, human users are left with a significant interpretive burden: starting from the relevance values of each input element (pixel), one has to identify properties of the overall input that are perceptually salient for the human visual system. A method which attempt to alleviate this drawback of low-level approaches to explanation have been proposed in [3,4], where explanations are provided in terms of middle-level properties (*atoms*) of the input which represent perceptually salient input parts [7].

A popular method which is also based on middle-level properties of the input is LIME [26], which returns a set of image parts (*superpixels*), that could have driven the ML model to the given answer. This set of superpixels can be then considered as an explanation to the ML model response. To the best of our knowledge, these types of approaches can be classified as *model-agnostic*.

Model-agnostic approaches correspond to XAI methods which are independent of the ML model to be explained [1], i.e., model-agnostic solutions are built relying only the relation between ML model inputs and outputs, without any consideration about the ML model internal state. Although this property ensures the applicability of these approaches to any ML model, on the other hand, how we will discuss more in details in Sect. 3, the explanations of the model-agnostic methods could not be fully related to the actual causal relationships between model's inputs and outputs which have contributed to the given model response. For instance, LIME returns an explanation inspecting the behaviour of the model in the neighbourhood of the input, but nothing ensures that, for that particular input instance, the answer of the classifier has a totally different explanation (for example, a particular on the background of the specific input image which the model has already seen during the training stage, making the model biased).

In this paper, we propose a new method, that we called Middle-Level Feature Relevance (MLFR), based on a variation of LRP that, instead of returning a relevance value for each input pixel, returns relevance values for a given set of middle-level features. This method can be applied whenever a) the input of a ML system can be encoded and decoded on the basis of middle-level features, and b) LRP can be applied on both the ML model and the decoder (see Sect. 3 for further details). In this sense we consider MLFR as a *a general framework* insofar as it can be applied on several different computational definitions of middle-level features as we will discuss in Sect. 3. Notice that MLFR is not a model-agnostic approach, however it can be applied to a large class of ML models as well as LRP [6], for example feedforward neural networks architectures such as shallow network and deep networks.

This paper is structured as follows. Section 2 briefly reviews the related literature; Section 3 describes the proposed architecture; experiments and results are discussed in Sect. 4; the concluding Sect. 5 summarises the main results of the proposed explanation framework and outlines some future developments.

2   Related Works

Many XAI methods have been proposed since explainability is now a sought for requirement for AI solution. The literature proposes several reviews trying to categorise/distinguish the existing methods [1,15,21,34] looking at different properties of the XAI methods. According to these categorisations, our method can be classified as a *white-box* and *local* XAI approach. White-box approaches require access to the internal structure of the ML model [1]. By contrast, black-box, or *model-agnostic*, approaches provide explanation methods which are independent of the ML model [1], i.e., they need access only to the input-output relations of the ML model. Local approaches provide explanations for each given input, while the goal of global approaches is to produce an explanation for the whole behaviour of the ML system [21].

Many model-agnostic approaches are based on *proxy-models* [8,10,24] or some type of maximisation of the ML model response with respect to the input, such as the Activation-Maximisation (AM) method [12]. Proxy models are models behaving similarly to the original model, but in a way that it is easier to explain [13]. Approaches based on AM method enables one to determine the input that makes the output of the ML model as close as possible to the model's initial response, for example, in case of classification problems, given C_k as the response of the ML model, one maximises the $P(C_k|\mathbf{x})$ with respect to $\mathbf{x}$ satisfying some constraints on $\mathbf{x}$. Notice that the explanations of the model-agnostic methods suffer from the lack of information about the actual input-output causal relationships which have contributed to the given ML model answers; thus these explanations may not be related to the specific ML model response to be explained [19].

Another critical distinction is based on the granularity level of the explanations. In fact, several XAI solutions provide explanations in terms of low-level input features. For instance, in image classification problems the output of an ML system is explained considering low-level features of the input image in terms of salience maps where to each pixel is associated a relevance value which quantifies the degree of importance of that pixel to cause the ML model response.

Among the approaches of this type, Layer-wise Relevance Propagation (LRP) [6], is the most popular in the literature. LRP is a white-box approach, although it applies to many ML models such as deep networks. Notice that it is a general framework rather than a specific method insofar as it is defined as a set of constraints that an XAI algorithm should satisfy. Thus, different XAI algorithms with different explanations may be appropriate under these constraints [6]. For example, Deep-Taylor Decomposition [21] can be interpreted as a way of obtaining LRP.

In this type of approaches, human users are left with a significant interpretive burden: starting from the relevance values of each input element (pixel), one has to identify properties of the overall input that are perceptually salient for the human visual system. Thus, to alleviate this cognitive burden, an alternative model-agnostic method, called Explanation-Maximization (EM), was proposed in [2–4]. EM, which also applies in different areas, was instantiated in the context of image classification systems. EM obtains sets of perceptually salient middle-level properties of input images by applying sparse dictionary learning techniques and a variant of AM. These middle-level properties are used as building blocks for explanations of image classifications. However, this approach suffers from the typical shortcomings of the model-agnostic ones as regards the reliability of the explanations given, as previously discussed. Among other methods using middle-level input features to build explanations about ML model responses, LIME [26] can be considered the most popular in the literature. It is model-agnostic and based on a proxy-model: it explains the output of an ML system by observing its behaviour on perturbations of its input. The input is partitioned in a collection of *components* (super-pixel in the case of images); perturbed inputs are composed of specific superpositions of these components. Perturbed inputs and outputs are used to construct a local linear model which is used as a simplified proxy for the original ML system in the neighbourhood of the input. Thus, from the proxy, it is possible to infer an explanation of the original ML model response. However, the faithfulness of the proxy with respect to the original model remains an open issue [19]. Other methods, based on LIME, as in Ribeiro et al. [27] and Guidotti et al. [14], return explanations in terms of decision rules that are used as local conditions for decisions.

The method we propose in this paper differs from the works mentioned above in the following aspects, as it can be seen as a general framework to obtain middle-level explanations analysing the actual input-output relationship defined by the ML model. Thus, different definitions of middle-level input features with different resulting solutions may be possible under this general framework. The only constraints are that the input can be encoded and decoded based on the defined middle-level input features and that LRP can be applied on both the ML model to be explained and the input decoder.

3   Middle-Level Relevance

Given an ML model M which receives an input $\mathbf{x} \in R^d$ and outputs $\mathbf{y} \in R^c$, let us suppose that $\mathbf{x}$ can be decomposed in a set of m middle-level features

$\mathbf{v}^i$ each one encoded by a value u_i. More formally, we suppose that a decoder $D : (\mathbf{V}, \mathbf{u}) \rightarrow \mathbf{x} \in R^d$ exists. Where $\mathbf{V} = \{\mathbf{v}^i\}_{i=1}^m$ is the set of $\mathbf{v}$'s middle-level features and $\mathbf{u} \in R^m$ encodes $\mathbf{x}$ in terms of the middle-level features. For example, in an image classification problem, a possible set of middle-level features can be the result of a segmentation algorithm on the input image $\mathbf{x}$ which produces a partition of $\mathbf{x}$ in m regions or partitions $\{P_i\}_{i=1}^m$. Each image's partition P_i can be represented by a vector $\mathbf{v}^i \in R^d$ such that their summation is equal to $\mathbf{x}$, in this case the decoder is a linear combination of the $\mathbf{v}^i$ with all the coefficients equal to 1, which represent the encoding of the image $\mathbf{x}$ on the basis of the m partitions (see Sect. 3.1).

Then, if we can use LRP on both M and D, we can apply it on the model M and use the obtained relevance values to apply LRP on D thus getting a relevance value for each middle-level feature. In other words, we can stack D on the top of M, thus obtaining a new model DM which receives as input $\mathbf{u}$ and outputs $\mathbf{y}$, and uses LRP propagation on DM from $\mathbf{y}$ to $\mathbf{u}$. Let us take as an example of M a neural network composed of L layers. The LRP procedure computes a set of relevance values for any given layer l composed of k_l neurons as the combination of the scores assigned to each neuron of l, representing the importance of each node for the network's output. The scores are computed by propagating the relevance values from the output layer to the input layer in a back-propagation fashion. Similarly, let us consider a shallow neural network composed of m input values u_i, d output neurons with biases equal to 0, the identity as activation functions, and one hidden layer of weights $W = V$. This network can be seen as a decoder D where the weights associated with the connections going from each input value u_i to all output neurons represent the middle-level feature vector $\mathbf{v}^i$. If we stack the shallow network/decoder D on the top of the L-layer model M, we obtain a new neural network model DM composed of $L + 1$ layers. Then, we can apply the LRP procedure on the whole DM model and obtain relevance values which designate what input's middle-level features have most contributed on the outcome y_i (see Fig. 1). In other words, we search for a relevance vector $\mathbf{r} \in \mathbb{R}^m$ which helps the user to know each middle-level feature of $\mathbf{x}$ how much has contributed to the ML model answer y_i. Note that, this approach can be generalised to any decoder to which LRP applies. For instance, we can consider any dictionary learning approach, as for example [16,17,32] (see Sect. 3.2 for more details), where each input $\mathbf{x}$ can be decomposed as $\mathbf{x} = \mathbf{V}\mathbf{u} + \epsilon$, V is a dictionary of middle-level features and ϵ is the reconstruction error vector. Also, in this case, we can notice that the decoder can be represented as a shallow neural network having the dictionary elements as weights and the biases in terms of the reconstruction error vector (see Sect. 3.2).

In the remainder of this section, we will describe two alternative ways (segmentation and dictionary learning) to obtain a decoder LRP method can be applied to, in more details. We experimentally tested our framework using both methods.

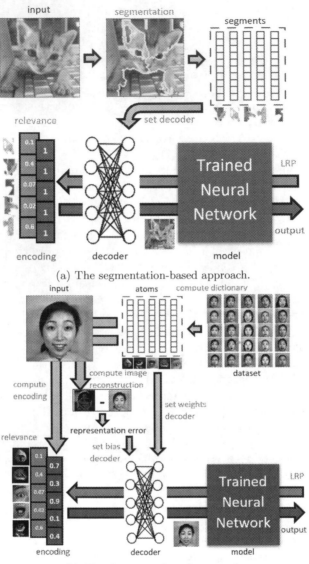

(a) The segmentation-based approach.

(b) The dictionary-based approach.

Fig. 1. A description of the proposed method (MLFR) using two different types of middle-level features. (a) After segmenting the input, the segments are used as weights for the decoder, so feeding the decoder with the 1s is equivalent to give the input image to the trained neural network. After, the LRP algorithm is used to obtain the segment relevances (see Sect. 3.1 for further details). (b) Having a dictionary, and an input encoding which best approximates the input image, we can use the dictionary and the representation error respectively as weights and bias of the decoder. So, feeding the decoder with the input encoding is equivalent to give the network the input image. After, the LRP algorithm is used to obtain the atom relevances (see Sect. 3.2 for further details).

3.1   Decoder by Super-Pixel Segmentation

Given an image $\mathbf{x} \in R^d$, we can obtain a partition of $\mathbf{x}$ composed of m elements P_h through any segmentation algorithm. We can associate to each element P_h a vector $\mathbf{pv}^h \in R^d$ such that $pv_i^h = 1$ if $x_i \in P_h$, otherwise $pv_i^h = 0$. Thus, each element P_h can be represented by the element-wise product between $\mathbf{x}$ and $\mathbf{pv}^h$, i.e., $\mathbf{v}^h = \mathbf{pv}^h \odot \mathbf{x}$, since this operation products selects all the pixels belonging to the element P_h.

Consequently, we can decompose $\mathbf{x}$ as $\mathbf{x} = \sum_{h=1}^{m} u_h \mathbf{v}^h$, with $u_h = 1$. Then, the decoder D is a linear combination of the $\mathbf{v}^h$ with all the coefficients equal to 1, which represent the encoding of the image $\mathbf{x}$ on the basis of the m partition's elements.

Following [26], in this paper we use the Quickshift segmentation algorithm [33] where the elements of the partition are called super-pixels.

We assume that a possible explanation to the output of a given classifier can be obtained in terms of relevant super-pixels, where the relevance can be computed using an LRP-based procedure.

3.2   Decoder by Sparse Dictionary Learning Methods

A sparse dictionary learning problem (see, for example, [32]) is a minimisation problem that one can formally describe as follows.

$$\arg \min_{U,V} ||X - VU||_F^2 + \gamma_1 \sum_{i=1}^{k} \Omega_V(\mathbf{v}_i) \tag{1}$$

$$\text{s.t. } \forall i, \Omega_U(\mathbf{u}_i) < \gamma_2$$

where $X \in R^{d \times n}$ is composed of n experimental observations which are expressed as column vector $\mathbf{x}^i \in R^d$, V is the dictionary, and the k columns $\mathbf{v}^i$ of V are the dictionary elements or atoms, subject to some sparsity constraint possibly. Each column of X is approximated by a linear combination of the k columns of V, subjects to some sparsity constraint potentially. Thus, $U \in R^{k \times n}$ is the matrix of the linear combination coefficients, i.e., the i-th column of U, $\mathbf{u}^i$, corresponds to the k coefficients of the linear combination of the k columns of V to approximate $\mathbf{x}^i$, the i-th column of X. Ω_V and Ω_U are some norms or quasi-norms that constrain or regularise the solutions of the minimisation problem, and $\gamma_1 \geq 0$ and $\gamma_2 \geq 0$ are parameters that control to what extent the dictionary and the coefficients are regularised.

Elements of a dictionary can be used to compute explanations of a ML model response in terms of middle-level input features [2–5].

For the experiments presented in this paper, we obtain the dictionaries from a specific sparse dictionary learning method based on SSPCA [16]. However, any dictionary learning/sparse coding method able to produce dictionaries that can be considered human-understandable can be used [2].

Given a dictionary V and an experimental observation $\mathbf{x}$ one can solve the minimisation problem as expressed in Eq. 1 with respect to the coefficients only, finding a single column vector $\mathbf{u}$. Consequently, $\tilde{\mathbf{x}} = V\mathbf{u}$ is an approximation of $\mathbf{x}$ with an error for each component equal to $\epsilon_h = x_h - \tilde{x}_h$. Then, the decoder D can be represented as a shallow neural network composed of just one weight layer W, k input values and d output neurons. Each output neuron j has the identity as activation function and the bias equal to ϵ_j. The weights associated to the connection going from the j-th input value to all the output neurons correspond to j-th V's column. Consequently, given the decomposition of $\mathbf{x}$ as $V\mathbf{u}$ the decoder D receives $\mathbf{u}$ as input and outputs $\mathbf{x}$.

4   Experimental Assessment

In this section, we describe the experiments performed and show the results obtained. We show a set of explanations produced by our approach using two different experimental setups.

The former uses as middle-level features the super-pixel segmentation schema described in Sect. 3.1; the latter adopts the sparse dictionary approach described in Sect. 3.2. For the segmentation-based experiments, we used as classifier a VGG-16 [30] neural network trained on Imagenet, and as input images a subset of the STL-10 dataset [9]. For the dictionary-based experiments, we use the JAFFE dataset [20] and a custom neural network trained from scratch with a final accuracy of the 94% on a test set. We chose to use a custom model because, to the best of our knowledge, there are no reference models for this particular dataset in the current literature. Notice that for this type of middle-level features we used a more simple dataset since dictionary learning methods on large datasets can be very expensive in terms of computational costs.

We compare the results obtained by the proposed method (MLFR) with two related methods proposed in the literature, LIME [26] and EM [2,4], and with a standard low-level feature method as LRP [6]. Notice that as we discussed in Sect. 2 the explanations returned by LIME and EM are based on features which can be considered of middle-level, but, differently from the MLFR approach, they are built in a black-box approach relying on a proxy model instead of the actual model in case of LIME, and in terms of dictionary elements by a variant of the activation-maximisation method, in case of EM. For the segmentation-based approach, we compared MLFR with LIME and LRP. For the dictionary-based approach, we compared our results with the ones produced by EM and LRP. The segments and the dictionaries are obtained respectively using Quickshift [33] (that is the same algorithm used by LIME to make the superpixel segmentation) and SSPCA [16].

A visual comparison is not enough, and to give a quantitative evaluation of our results, we use the same strategy introduced in [29] and described in Sect. 4.2.

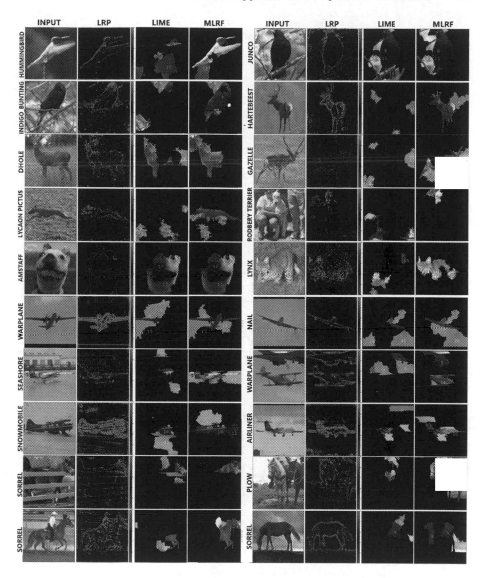

Fig. 2. Results obtained from MLFR using image segmentation (Sect. 3.1) on the STL10 dataset. For each input (1st and 5th column), we present the explanations produced by LRP method (2nd, 6th column) in terms of heatmaps (blue pixels indicate negative relevance, while red pixels indicate positive ones), LIME method (3th and 7th column) and MLFR (4rd and 8th column) as superimposition of the three superpixels with the highest relevance scores. The class returned by the classifier is reported for each input. (Color figure online)

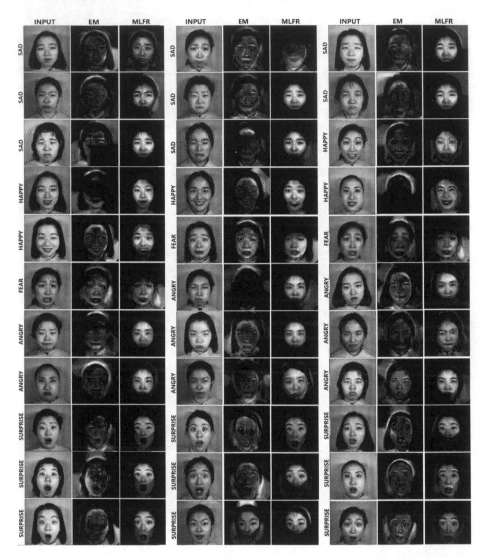

Fig. 3. Results obtained from MLFR with sparse dictionaries (Sect. 3.2) on the JAFFE dataset. For each input (1st, 4th and 7th column), we present the explanations obtained by EM method (2nd, 5th and 8th column) and MLFR (3rd, 6th and 9th column) as superimposition of the three atoms with the highest relevance scores. On the left of each input, we report the class returned by the classifier.

4.1 Qualitative Results

Some results of the two proposed strategies are shown in Fig. 2 for the superpixels-based approach and in Fig. 3 for the dictionary-based approach. To make a comparison, we also report the explanations given by LIME and LRP methods for the superpixels-based approach and EM for the dictionary-based approach. For each input, we show the superposition of the three most relevant segments/atoms for LIME, EM and MLFR, and the heatmap produced by LRP.

With respect to LIME and EM, we can show that in several cases, the explanations produced by MLFR can be considered closer to what a human being expects from a classification system. For example, we expect that the output "hummingbird" and "indigo bunting" (Fig. 2, first and second row, first column) is due mainly by the presence of the main components of a bird in the image, neglecting non-relevant part as background sprigs. Similar considerations can be done for the "hartebeest" and the "gazelle" (Fig. 2, second and third row, fifth column) and several other inputs shown in the figure. In particular, the "Bedlington Terrier" input (Fig. 2, fourth row, fifth column) provides an interesting case due to the presence of several hypothetical relevant candidates (the several human being parts) which can lead the classifier toward different classification. The proposed method, in agreement with LRP, highlights that the dog face is one of the main discriminative parts behind the classifier's choice. The different results returned by LIME can be due to several factors, such as a sub-optimal training procedure of the proxy model or the inadequacy of the proxy model in representing the real one.

Similar consideration can be done for the results shown in Fig. 3 inherent the dictionary-based approach. We show inputs for several classes of the Jaffe dataset (SAD, SURPRISE, HAPPY, FEAR, ANGRY) and the results obtained respectively by the EM method and the proposed MLFR. It is possible to see how the proposed method highlights atoms which better characterise the faces, as we would expect by an emotion classifier. MLFR highlights details concerning facial expressions as the open mouth and the eyes for the inputs classified as "SURPRISE" or the smiling expression for the input classified for "HAPPY" (for example, on the Fig. 3 see the results of the inputs on the first, fourth and seventh columns of the 5th and 8th row). The results produced by EM method, instead, seems more confused and less clear and intuitive. As far as the EM method is not based on proxy models, it is again a black-box approach based only on the input/output relations of the classifier, so without any knowledge to the real inner state of the model. Furthermore, EM needs several hyperparameters to be set, which can affect the reliability of the results produced.

Notice that for reasons of space we do not report the results obtained by LRP, since the qualitive comparison is similar to the one for the STL10 dataset.

4.2   Quantitative Evaluation

In the previous section, we show the explanations obtained in terms of the most relevant middle-level features selected by MLFR compared against the ones selected by some related works proposed in the literature. However, all the consideration we made are based only on subjective evaluations, and an objective and quantitative evaluation of the explanation methods is still an open research problem.

A possible quantitative evaluation framework was proposed in [29] with *region flipping*, a generalisation of the *pixel-flipping* measure proposed in [6]. In a nutshell, given an image classification to explain, regions of a given size are

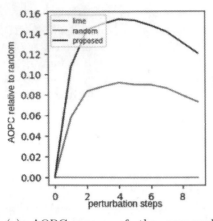

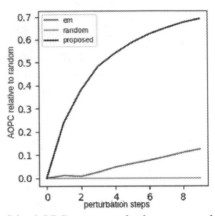

(a) AOPC curve of the proposed method (segmentation-based, section 3.1) compared with the LIME method.

(b) AOPC curve of the proposed method (DL-based, section 3.2) compared with the EM method.

Fig. 4. Comparison of the AOPC curves of the methods used in the experiments. As made in [29], all the curves have been plotted relatively to a random AOPC curve, which was obtained following a random order instead of a relevance order during the image perturbation steps.

substituted iteratively, following the descending relevance order assigned to the central pixel (MoRF, Most Relevant First) by the explanation method. At each step, the difference between the original class score returned by the model and the score returned on the perturbed input is computed, generating a curve (MoRF curve). We expect that the better the explanation method is, the stronger the difference between the scores is. Repeating this process for several images and averaging between them, it is possible to obtain the *Area Over the MoRF Perturbation Curve* (AOPC):

$$AOPC = \frac{1}{L+1} < \sum_{k=0}^{L} f(x^{(0)}) - f(x^{(k)}) >_{p(x)}$$

where $< \cdot >_{p(x)}$ is the average over the dataset images, L is the number of regions and $x^{(k)}$ is the input at k−th perturbation step. If the regions are well-ranked (so, relevant regions have a higher relevance), we expect that the resulting AOPC values are large, so we can infer that the largest the AOPC value is, the better the explanation method is. The original region-flipping method was originally defined for pixel-based heatmaps using regions of fixed size (9×9 in [29]). However, it is easily adapted to our proposed method and LIME, considering that each middle-level feature is a single region. As a perturbation scheme, we adopt the same used in [29], changing each pixel in the region with a value sampled from the Uniform distribution. In Fig. 4a we plot the AOPC curve for LIME and our proposed method on the VGG16 model, showing that MLFR outperforms LIME in terms of AOPC curve, suggesting that the former, on average, gives a more reliably relevance score respect to the latter. We hypothesise that LIME, exploiting a proxy classifier which *emulates* the real one, may not capture the real "reasons" behind the choices made by a classifier, so assigning scores to the features in a manner which not reflect the real inner state of the classifier. Similar results are shown in Fig. 4b, where the results of the proposed approach are compared with the EM method. Again, in this case, the proposed method shows better results in terms of AOPC values, giving better reliability to the explanations produced.

5   Conclusions

In this work, we propose MLFR, a novel XAI method based on middle-level features. The proposed method generalises the well-known LRP method, initially proposed for low-level features (such as pixels for image domain), to middle-level features, returning data representations which can be interpreted by a human. We describe how the proposed method can be easily adapted to several classes of middle-level features. For instance, we show how two different middle-level input representations can be suitable for the proposed method, the former based on image segments directly obtained from the input to explain, the latter on a more general set of elements which can be constructed through some dictionary learning approach. However, nothing prevents to use other representations.

To evaluate the proposed method, we adapt the quantitative measure described in [29], proposed initially for pixelwise-based methods, to middle-level feature methods, and we make a comparison with others middle-level features approaches present in literature. The results of the experiments that we carried out are encouraging, both under the qualitative point of view, giving explanations that can be easily interpretable by the human being, and the quantitative point of view, giving performances in terms of AOPC curve which are comparable to other methods present in the current literature.

Acknowledgments. The research presented in this paper was partially supported by the national project Perception, Performativity and Cognitive Sciences (PRIN Bando 2015, cod. 2015TM24JS 009).

References

1. Adadi, A., Berrada, M.: Peeking inside the black-box: a survey on explainable artificial intelligence (XAI). IEEE Access **6**, 52138–52160 (2018)
2. Apicella, A., Isgro, F., Prevete, R., Sorrentino, A., Tamburrini, G.: Explaining classification systems using sparse dictionaries. In: Proceedings of the ESANN, Special Session on Societal Issues in Machine Learning: When Learning from Data is Not Enough. Bruges, Belgium (2019)
3. Apicella, A., Isgrò, F., Prevete, R., Tamburrini, G.: Contrastive explanations to classification systems using sparse dictionaries. In: Ricci, E., Rota Bulò, S., Snoek, C., Lanz, O., Messelodi, S., Sebe, N. (eds.) ICIAP 2019, Part I. LNCS, vol. 11751, pp. 207–218. Springer, Cham (2019). https://doi.org/10.1007/978-3-030-30642-7_19

4. Apicella, A., Isgrò, F., Prevete, R., Tamburrini, G.: Middle-level features for the explanation of classification systems by sparse dictionary methods. Int. J. Neural Syst. **30**(08), 2050040 (2020)

5. Apicella, A., Isgro, F., Prevete, R., Tamburrini, G., Vietri, A.: Sparse dictionaries for the explanation of classification systems. In: PIE, p. 009. Rome, Italy (2019)

6. Bach, S., Binder, A., Montavon, G., Klauschen, F., Müller, K.R., Samek, W.: On pixel-wise explanations for non-linear classifier decisions by layer-wise relevance propagation. PloS One **10**(7), e0130140 (2015)

7. Barghout, L.: Spatial-taxon information granules as used in iterative fuzzy-decision-making for image segmentation. In: Pedrycz, W., Chen, S.-M. (eds.) Granular Computing and Decision-Making. SBD, vol. 10, pp. 285–318. Springer, Cham (2015). https://doi.org/10.1007/978-3-319-16829-6_12

8. Caccavale, R., Finzi, A.: Learning attentional regulations for structured tasks execution in robotic cognitive control. Auton. Robot. **43**(8), 2229–2243 (2019). https://doi.org/10.1007/s10514-019-09876-x

9. Coates, A., Ng, A., Lee, H.: An analysis of single-layer networks in unsupervised feature learning. In: Proceedings of the Fourteenth International Conference on Artificial Intelligence and Statistics, pp. 215–223 (2011)

10. Craven, M., Shavlik, J.W.: Extracting tree-structured representations of trained networks. In: Advances in Neural Information Processing Systems, pp. 24–30. Denver, CO, USA (1996)

11. Devlin, J., Chang, M.W., Lee, K., Toutanova, K.: BERT: Pre-training of deep bidirectional transformers for language understanding (2018)

12. Erhan, D., Bengio, Y., Courville, A., Vincent, P.: Visualizing higher-layer features of a deep network. Univ. Montreal **1341**(3), 1 (2009)

13. Gilpin, L.H., Bau, D., Yuan, B.Z., Bajwa, A., Specter, M., Kagal, L.: Explaining explanations: an overview of interpretability of machine learning. In: 2018 IEEE 5th International Conference on Data Science and Advanced Analytics (DSAA), pp. 80–89. IEEE, Turin, Italy (2018)

14. Guidotti, R., Monreale, A., Ruggieri, S., Pedreschi, D., Turini, F., Giannotti, F.: Local rule-based explanations of black box decision systems. CoRR abs/1805.10820 (2018)

15. Guidotti, R., Monreale, A., Ruggieri, S., Turini, F., Giannotti, F., Pedreschi, D.: A survey of methods for explaining black box models. ACM Comput. Surv. (CSUR) **51**(5), 93 (2018)

16. Jenatton, R., Obozinski, G., Bach, F.: Structured sparse principal component analysis. In: Proceedings of the Thirteenth International Conference on Artificial Intelligence and Statistics, pp. 366–373 (2010)

17. Lee, D.D., Seung, H.S.: Algorithms for non-negative matrix factorization. In: Advances in Neural Information Processing Systems, pp. 556–562 (2001)

18. Letham, B., Rudin, C., McCormick, T.H., Madigan, D., et al.: Interpretable classifiers using rules and Bayesian analysis: building a better stroke prediction model. Ann. Appl. Stat. **9**(3), 1350–1371 (2015)

19. Li, X.H., et al.: A survey of data-driven and knowledge-aware explainable AI. IEEE Trans. Knowl. Data Eng. (2020). https://doi.org/10.1109/TKDE.2020.2983930

20. Lyons, M., Akamatsu, S., Kamachi, M., Gyoba, J.: Coding facial expressions with Gabor wavelets. In: Proceedings, Third IEEE International Conference on Automatic Face and Gesture Recognition, pp. 200–205. IEEE Computer Society (1998)

21. Montavon, G., Samek, W., Müller, K.: Methods for interpreting and understanding deep neural networks. Digit. Signal Process. **73**, 1–15 (2018)

22. Nguyen, A., Dosovitskiy, A., Yosinski, J., Brox, T., Clune, J.: Synthesizing the preferred inputs for neurons in neural networks via deep generator networks. In: Lee, D.D., Sugiyama, M., Luxburg, U.V., Guyon, I., Garnett, R. (eds.) Advances in Neural Information Processing Systems 29, pp. 3387–3395. Curran Associates, Inc. (2016)
23. Nguyen, A., Yosinski, J., Clune, J.: Understanding neural networks via feature visualization: a survey. In: Samek, W., Montavon, G., Vedaldi, A., Hansen, L.K., Müller, K.-R. (eds.) Explainable AI: Interpreting, Explaining and Visualizing Deep Learning. LNCS (LNAI), vol. 11700, pp. 55–76. Springer, Cham (2019). https:// doi.org/10.1007/978-3-030-28954-6_4
24. Oh, S.J., Schiele, B., Fritz, M.: Towards reverse-engineering black-box neural networks. In: Samek, W., Montavon, G., Vedaldi, A., Hansen, L.K., Müller, K.-R. (eds.) Explainable AI: Interpreting, Explaining and Visualizing Deep Learning. LNCS (LNAI), vol. 11700, pp. 121–144. Springer, Cham (2019). https://doi.org/ 10.1007/978-3-030-28954-6_7
25. Reyes, O., Ventura, S.: Performing multi-target regression via a parameter sharing-based deep network. Int. J. Neural Syst. **29**, 1950014 (2019)
26. Ribeiro, M.T., Singh, S., Guestrin, C.: "Why should i trust you?": Explaining the predictions of any classifier. In: Proceedings of the 22nd ACM SIGKDD International Conference on Knowledge Discovery and Data Mining, pp. 1135–1144. KDD '16, ACM (2016)
27. Ribeiro, M.T., Singh, S., Guestrin, C.: Anchors: High-precision model-agnostic explanations. In: Thirty-Second AAAI Conference on Artificial Intelligence. New Orleans, Louisiana, USA (2018)
28. Richter, C., Vega-Brown, W., Roy, N.: Bayesian learning for safe high-speed navigation in unknown environments. In: Bicchi, A., Burgard, W. (eds.) Robotics Research. SPAR, vol. 3, pp. 325–341. Springer, Cham (2018). https://doi.org/10. 1007/978-3-319-60916-4_19
29. Samek, W., Binder, A., Montavon, G., Lapuschkin, S., Müller, K.R.: Evaluating the visualization of what a deep neural network has learned. IEEE Trans. Neural Netw. Learn. Syst. **28**(11), 2660–2673 (2016)
30. Simonyan, K., Zisserman, A.: Very deep convolutional networks for large-scale image recognition. In: International Conference on Learning Representations (2015)
31. Springenberg, J., Dosovitskiy, A., Brox, T., Riedmiller, M.: Striving for simplicity: the all convolutional net. In: Proceedings of the International Conference on Learning Representation (Workshop Track). San Diego, CA (2015)
32. Tessitore, G., Prevete, R.: Designing structured sparse dictionaries for sparse representation modeling. In: Burduk, R., Kurzynski, M., Wozniak, M., Zolnierek, A. (eds.) Computer Recognition Systems 4. Advances in Intelligent and Soft Computing, vol. 95, pp. 157–166. Springer, Heidelberg (2011). https://doi.org/10.1007/ 978-3-642-20320-6_17
33. Vedaldi, A., Soatto, S.: Quick shift and kernel methods for mode seeking. In: Forsyth, D., Torr, P., Zisserman, A. (eds.) ECCV 2008, Part IV. LNCS, vol. 5305, pp. 705–718. Springer, Heidelberg (2008). https://doi.org/10.1007/978-3-540-88693-8_52
34. Zhang, Q., Zhu, S.: Visual interpretability for deep learning: a survey. Front. Inf. Technol. Electron. Eng. **19**(1), 27–39 (2018). https://doi.org/10.1631/FITEE. 1700808

Evaluation of Interpretable Association Rule Mining Methods on Time-Series in the Maritime Domain

Manjunatha Veerappa[1,2（✉）], Mathias Anneken[1,2], and Nadia Burkart[1,2]

[1] Fraunhofer IOSB, Fraunhofer Str. 1, 76131 Karlsruhe, Germany
{manjunatha.veerappa,mathias.anneken,nadia.burkart}@iosb.fraunhofer.de
[2] Fraunhofer Center for Machine Learning, Karlsruhe, Germany

Abstract. In decision critical domains, the results generated by black box models such as state of the art deep learning based classifiers raise questions regarding their explainability. In order to ensure the trust of operators in these systems, an explanation of the reasons behind the predictions is crucial. As rule-based approaches rely on simple if-then statements which can easily be understood by a human operator they are considered as an interpretable prediction model. Therefore, association rule mining methods are applied for explaining time-series classifier in the maritime domain. Three rule mining algorithms are evaluated on the classification of vessel types trained on a real world dataset. Each one is a surrogate model which mimics the behavior of the underlying neural network. In the experiments the *GiniReg* method performs the best, resulting in a less complex model which is easier to interpret. The *SBRL* method works well in terms of classification performance but due to an increase in complexity, it is more challenging to explain. Furthermore, during the evaluation the impact of hyper-parameters on the performance of the model along with the execution time of all three approaches is analyzed.

Keywords: Association rule mining · Interpretability · Explainable artificial intelligence · Time series classification · Maritime domain

1 Introduction

For human operators in surveillance tasks, like coastguards, decision support in critical situations is crucial. While the available amount of data is steadily increasing due to e.g. the availability of inexpensive sensors, an operator can easily be overwhelmed by it. Therefore, automatic systems for supporting the decision making are increasingly used. Depending on the underlying technology, one major drawback for the acceptance of such systems is the in-explainable nature of black box models. In order to make the results of such models more interpretable, different rule mining methods are evaluated in this work.

As a large share of the world's trade is conducted by sea, a smooth and efficient voyage of all participants in sea traffic is crucial. Here, a *multilayer*

© Springer Nature Switzerland AG 2021
A. Del Bimbo et al. (Eds.): ICPR 2020 Workshops, LNCS 12663, pp. 204–218, 2021.
https://doi.org/10.1007/978-3-030-68796-0_15

perceptron (MLP) is used as classifier for the vessel types: By analysing the movement patterns of vessels, the trained model is able to distinguish common vessel types. This can be seen as a building block for more advanced decision support systems.

The structure of this paper is as follows: In Sect. 2, a brief state of the art regarding explainable artificial intelligence (XAI) methods is given. Section 3 explains the foundation towards classification, data preprocessing along with the AIS dataset, and association rule mining (ARM). Section 4 provides an insight into the three evaluated rule mining methods. A list of quality measures, that are used for comparison of the implemented methods, is stated in Sect. 5. Afterwards, in Sect. 6 the results of the experiments are illustrated. The paper finishes in Sect. 7 with a conclusion and a short outlook for future work.

2   Related Work

For decision support to be accepted in sensitive domains, trust in machine learning systems is an important factor. Therefore, it is crucial to understand why certain predictions are made by a model. For this purpose, Ribeiro et al. proposed an explanation technique called LIME (Local Interpretable Model-Agnostic Explanation) [16], that provides inside into the prediction of a single instance and is therefore suitable for a local explanation. This method tests what happens to the prediction by varying the data around the instance and trains a local interpretable model on this varied dataset. This allows us to create a picture that the model focuses on and uses to make its predictions.

Another approach for estimating the feature importance was introduced to correct Random Forest based importance measures [4] and is called "Permutation importance" [2]. In this method, feature importance is calculated by measuring how a score (i.e. accuracy, F1, etc.) decreases when a particular feature is permuted. But this method fails when correlated features are present in the dataset. To cope with this problem SHAP (Shapley Additive Explanations) [13] was introduced, which explains the output of any machine learning model. It is based on concepts borrowed from cooperative game theory.

Most of the XAI methods such as LIME, SHAP, and so on are typically highly focused on image data, text data, and tabular data. Unfortunately, the consideration of time-series is only limited for these methods. In comparison a XAI method evaluated on time-series is presented in [17]. This methods produces explanations in the form of heatmaps. The authors state, that this reliance on visual saliency masks can be quite challenging for the users to interpret.

Another work on time-series [11], where the attention mechanism concept is used to propose a deep-learning framework for interpretability. It identifies critical segments that are necessary for the classification performance. In other words, it highlights the important areas of the original data accountable for its corresponding prediction.

In healthcare, a prototype based time-series classification is proposed for interpretability [9], where prototypes are learned during the training of the classification model. These prototypes are then used to explain which features in the training data are responsible for the time-series classification.

"ShiftTree" is introduced in [10] as an interpretable model-based classification method for time-series. This method is an extension of decision tree methods, which labels different time-series by learning from the dataset. While labeling, instead of splitting the dataset using only a certain attribute, an EyeShifter operator and ConditionBuilder operator are used to move along the time axis of the time-series and compute the attributes dynamically which gives an interpretable description of the time-series.

3   Foundations

In this section, firstly, classification problems in general and the evaluated MLP model in particular are introduced. Next, information on the data acquisitions and the necessary preprocessing are given. Lastly, Association Rule Mining (ARM) is explained in brief along with its parameters.

3.1   Classification

Classification is a process of mapping the input data to discrete categories, whereas categories are often referred to as targets, labels, or classes. It can either be a binary classification or a multi-class classification problem. In this study, we are addressing a multi-class classification of maritime vessel types, i.e., to classify a vessel/ship-type based on its trajectories over time.

Given $\mathcal{X}$ as all possible inputs and $\mathcal{Y}$ as all possible outputs, multi-class classification can be defined as the mapping C_{multi} of an input $x \in \mathcal{X}$ to a single class $\hat{y} \in \mathcal{Y}$ and is given by

$$C_{\text{multi}} \colon x \mapsto \hat{y} \,. \tag{1}$$

In this study, a neural network architecture based on an MLP [14] is used as classifier. An MLP is a feed-forward neural network. It consists of one input layer, at least one hidden layer, and one output layer. The layers are connected from the input to the output layer in one direction. The input will be directly forwarded to the next layer. For each neuron in the following layer, the inputs are weighted and together with a bias are summed up. This weighted sum is used in the activation function of each neuron. The result will be fed to the next layer. At the output layer, either a decision will be made in case of testing or calculations will be further used for the back-propagation algorithm [18] in case of training.

3.2   Data Preprocessing

The dataset was recorded using the Automatic Identification System (AIS). AIS is an automated tracking system designed for the exchange of information between ships, as well as on and off-shore facilities. It was introduced as a means to prevent collisions of vessels by providing the position and other useful information to vessels in the vicinity. There are requirements for vessels to carry and use AIS, e.g. due to their capacity. Vessels with onboard transceivers will continuously broadcast information regarding the vessel together with identifiers like the Maritime Mobile Service Identity (MMSI) [15].

AIS information transmitted by a ship can be divided into three types: static information, dynamic information, and voyage information. Dynamic information consists of position, speed over ground, course over ground, heading, etc. which are sent (depending on the navigation status) at intervals of two to ten seconds While underway and three minutes otherwise, whereas static and voyage information such as ship type, vessel dimensions, draught as well as destination and ETA are sent every six minutes [15].

The vessels are divided into a set of ship-types, since most of them are relatively rare, for the evaluation only the most frequent ones (with cargo and tanker due to their similar moving patterns being fused to a single type) are used: *Cargo-Tanker, Fishing, Passenger, Pleasure-Craft,* and *Tug.*

Before the data is usable for training the classifier, preprocessing is necessary. This includes the same steps as described in [3,7]: First, the data is grouped by the attached MMSI. For each MMSI a segmentation step is performed which will result in trajectories. In this work, a trajectory T is defined as a sequence of n tuples, each containing the position P_i of an object at time t_i:

$$T = \{(t_1, P_1), (t_2, P_2), \ldots, (t_n, P_n)\}, \tag{2}$$

where the points $P_1, P_2, \ldots P_n$ are the real positions on the surface of the earth as provided by the AIS. Afterwards, the trajectories are filtered and features directly derived from the stored data and additional geographic features are calculated. As a last step normalization is performed on the resulted sequences.

The raw data for every vessel is segmented using three methods: First, if two successive samples have a time difference greater than $2\,\text{h}$, second if two successive samples have a greater spatial distance than 10^{-4} calculated in degrees, and third if the length of a trajectory exceeds the desired length. After that, if a sequence is shorter than 80 % of the sequence length, it is discarded, otherwise it is padded with zeros. As next step, all trajectories, which are stationary and which are traveling on rivers, are removed.

Nine features are extracted for each sample: Firstly, the speed over ground, the course over ground, the position in longitude and latitude (in a global and local manner) as well as the time difference between two samples can directly be used. Based on the positional feature additional features are derived: The distance to the coastline, and the distance to the closest harbour. The global position is a position normalization over the whole dataset, while the local position is a normalization over the trajectory itself. Before these steps are made, the trajectory will be moved to start in the origin in order to achieve translational invariance.

3.3 Association Rule Mining—ARM

ARM is one of the six tasks in data mining [8], which uncovers interesting relations between variables from a large dataset. A rule is basically an if-then condition/statement which has 2 items, an antecedent p and a consequent q, and takes the form $p \rightarrow q$. It can be seen as a tuple $(A, \hat{y})$, where A is a list of k predicates, the antecedents of the rule, and a prediction $\hat{y}$ as its consequent. Typically, the rules can be expressed in the form of

$$\text{IF feature}_n = \alpha \text{ AND feature}_m < \beta \text{ AND} \cdots$$
$$\text{THEN class } \hat{y}. \tag{3}$$

These rules are generated by looking for frequent patterns in data. Well known measures that are used to generate each rule are support and confidence. In general, the aim is to create association rules for which the support and confidence is greater than the user-defined thresholds.

The association rules are derived from itemsets, which consist of two or more items. Let $I = \{i_1, i_2, ..., i_m\}$ be a set of all items and $T = \{t_1, t_2, ..., t_n\}$ be a set of all transactions. The *support* S can be defined as an indication of how frequently the itemset appears in all the transactions. It is the ratio of the number of transactions that contains p and q to the total number of transactions:

$$S(p \rightarrow q) = \frac{\text{Transactions containing both } p \text{ and } q}{\text{Total number of transactions}} = \frac{frq(p, q)}{|T|} \tag{4}$$

The *confidence* C is defined as an indication of how often the generated association rule has been found to be true. It is defined as the ratio of the number of transactions that contain p and q to the number of transactions that contain p:

$$C(p \rightarrow q) = \frac{S(p \rightarrow q)}{S(p)} = \frac{frq(p, q)}{frq(p)} \tag{5}$$

Association rules are generated by using these two criteria. As for large datasets, the mining of all datasets is not necessarily feasible. Therefore, frequent pattern mining algorithms [1] are introduced to speed up the computation.

A pattern is said to be frequent if feature values are co-occurring in many transactions. A pattern can be a single feature or combination of features. In the dataset the frequency of a pattern is determined by its support [6]:

$$S(\mathcal{P}) = \{(x, \cdot) \in \mathcal{D} \mid \forall p \in \mathcal{P} \colon p(x) = \text{True}\}, \tag{6}$$

where $\mathcal{P}$ is a set of antecedents p. Algorithms for determining these patterns are called *Frequent Pattern Mining* [12]. In this study, the *Equivalence Class Transformation (ECLAT)* algorithm [21] is used to find frequent itemsets.

4 Methods

In this section, for each of the three evaluated ARM methods, a brief description is given. For the purpose of clarity, the notation found in [5] is adopted for all three methods.

4.1 Scalable Bayesian Rule Lists—SBRL

The first method is known as the *Scalable Bayesian Rule Lists (SBRL)*, which explains a model's prediction using a decision list generated by the Bayesian rule lists algorithm [20]. A decision list is a set of rules with simple if-then statements consisting of an antecedent and a consequent. Here, the antecedents are conditions on the input features and the consequent is the predicted outcome of interest.

The scheme of this method is as shown in Fig. 1a. The typical objective of a model is to find a function $f \colon \mathcal{X} \to \mathcal{Y}$, given $\mathcal{X}$ as the space of all possible inputs and $\mathcal{Y}$ as the set of all possible outputs. The dataset $\mathcal{D}$ of size N, described by

$$\mathcal{D} = \{(x_i, y_i) \mid x_i \in \mathcal{X},\, y_i \in \mathcal{Y}\}_{i=1}^{N} \tag{7}$$

consisting of the feature vectors $x_i \in X$ and the target classes $y_i \in Y$, is passed onto the data preprocessing section before training a model. The preprocessing steps include transformation, segmentation, filtering and normalization as described in Scct. 3.2. The output of the preprocessing step is continuous numeric data which is then used to train the main model. Here, the main model is a *Neural Network (NN)*, denoted by M_θ, given by its parameters $\theta \in \Theta$. The aim of the main model is to minimize the loss function $L(\theta, \mathcal{D})$, which optimizes the algorithm by estimating the classification performance:

$$\theta^* = \operatorname*{arg\,min}_{\theta \in \Theta} L(\theta, \mathcal{D}) . \tag{8}$$

Since the surrogate model in our case is an *SBRL* algorithm, which expects categorical features as an input, the output of the preprocessing data (numeric) must be converted to categorical data. To achieve this, numerical features are binned, i. e., the range of numerical values is divided into discrete intervals. For the experiment, the number of bins is varied between five and 30 bins. Now, each categorical feature shows which interval contains the original numeric value. So we obtain a new dataset $\mathcal{D}'$ of size N:

$$\mathcal{D}' = \{(x_i', M_\theta(x_i)) \mid x_i' \in X'\}_{i=1}^{N} . \tag{9}$$

The preprocessed input data x_i' along with $M_\theta(x_i)$ is then fed to the surrogate model, denoted by N_ρ, ρ being the surrogate rule list containing rules in the form of $(A, \hat{y})$. The surrogate model first mines the rules by extracting frequently occurring feature values/patterns from the dataset $\mathcal{D}'$ by using the *ECLAT* algorithm [21]. Next, the surrogate model learns a decision list from the pre-mined rules and generates high confidence rules from each frequent itemset by ensuring high posterior probability. In general, we could say that the surrogate model aims to optimize the posterior probability

$$P(d \mid x, y, \mathcal{A}, \alpha, \lambda, \eta) \propto \underbrace{P(y \mid x, d, \alpha)}_{\text{likelihood}} \underbrace{P(d \mid \mathcal{A}, \lambda, \eta)}_{\text{prior}} \tag{10}$$

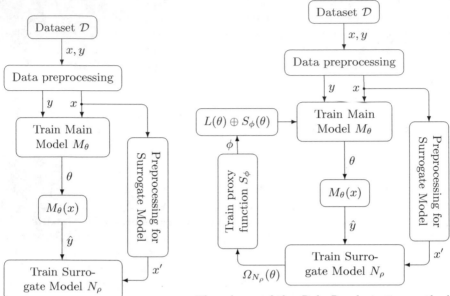

The scheme of the *SBRL* method.

The scheme of the *Rule Regularization* method [5].

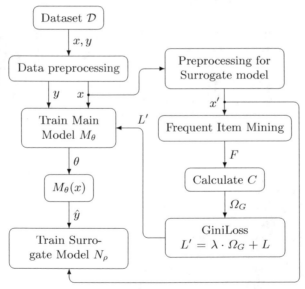

The scheme of the *Gini Regularization* method.

Fig. 1. The scheme of all three rule mining methods.

to obtain the best rule lists, where d denotes the rules in the list, λ is the desired size of the rule list, $\mathcal{A}$ is the set of pre-mined rules, η is the desired number of terms in each rule and the preference over labels α, usually set to 1 to avoid preference over target labels. Finally, with the help of a decision list, the surrogate model N_ρ that mimics the output of the main model M_θ, will be able to explain a model's prediction.

4.2   Rule-Based Regularization Method

Unlike the first method, which is an unregularized method, *Rule-based Regularization (RuleReg)* [5] is a technique where a metric for complexity that acts as a degree of explainability is obtained from the surrogate model and fed back to the training of the main model as a regularization term. This method, similar to the *SBRL*, explains a model's prediction using a decision list consisting of a set of antecedents and consequent.

The scheme of the *RuleReg* technique is shown in Fig. 1b. In contrast to the *SBRL* method, both the main model and the surrogate model are trained simultaneously. Thus, the dataset $\mathcal{D} = \{(x_i, y_i)\}_{i=1}^N$, is passed through the preprocessing steps to the main model M_θ. As usual, the main model aims at optimizing the objective function such as the loss function L. Since it is a regularization technique, the regularization term Ω is added to the actual loss L resulting in the new loss function

$$L'(\theta, \mathcal{D}) = \lambda \cdot \Omega(\theta) + L(\theta, \mathcal{D}) \,, \tag{11}$$

where λ is the regularization strength. Please note that the term Ω is derived from the surrogate model to add a penalty to the cost function.

During the training of the main model, *RuleReg* often builds a new surrogate model for every training batch and the metric Ω_{N_ρ} is calculated using the function

$$\Omega_{N_\rho}(\theta) = 1 + \sum_{(A,\hat{y}) \in \rho} |A| \,, \tag{12}$$

which sums up the number of antecedents for all rule lists. And this metric cannot be used directly in the Eq. (11) as it is not differentiable. In order to overcome the problem of the regularization term not being differentiable, a proxy function S_ϕ—here an MLP—as introduced by [19] is used to approximate Ω. Now, the actual loss function is

$$L''(\theta, \mathcal{D}) = \lambda \cdot S_\phi(\theta) + L(\theta, \mathcal{D}). \tag{13}$$

The inputs to fit the proxy function are the vectors of the main model parameters collected during the training of the main model and its corresponding complexity obtained from the surrogate model N_ρ.

And certainly, the surrogate model is fitted with the dataset $\mathcal{D}'$ of size N, $\{(x_i', M_\theta(x_i))\}_{i=1}^N$, where the numerical features are converted to categorical because of the requirement of the rule-mining algorithm such as *SBRL*.

Once both the main model and the surrogate model have been trained successfully, a surrogate rule list is generated by the surrogate model which is human-
simulatable. This is then used to explain a model's prediction.

4.3   Gini Regularization Method

Similar to the *RuleReg* method, *Gini Regularization* [6] is a regularization technique which fits a global surrogate model to a deep NN for interpretability. But
instead of repeatedly building a new surrogate model for every training batch as
in *RuleReg*, this method focuses on training only one surrogate model. In addition, a differentiable regularization term Ω allowing gradient-based optimization
is used to penalize the inhomogeneous predictions.

The scheme of this method is as shown in Fig. 1c. The dataset $\mathcal{D} =
\{(x_i, y_i)\}_{i=1}^N$ with N being the size, is fed into the preprocessing section and
then to train the main model (NN), denoted by M_θ. Before training a main
model, frequent item mining is performed on an input data x' (categorical data)
to obtain a set of frequent items F. For this purpose, the *ECLAT* algorithm [21]
is used. Once the frequent itemsets are mined, a binary matrix called *Caught-
Matrix* C is calculated using

$$C_{i,j} = \begin{cases} 1, & x_i \in F_j \\ 0, & \text{otherwise} \end{cases} , \tag{14}$$

indicating whether a datapoint is a member of the set F, i.e., if a datapoint x_i
is in frequent itemset F_j, then the *Caught-Matrix* C at i, j is 1 or 0 otherwise.
Now, a differentiable loss function L' is constructed using *Caught-Matrix* and a
classification loss function:

$$L'(\theta, D) = \lambda \cdot \Omega(\theta) + L(\theta, D), \tag{15}$$

where Ω is the regularization term obtained despite constructing a rule-based
model and λ is the regularization strength.

The main model is then trained on a dataset $\mathcal{D}$ with regard to L'. To mimic
the output of the main model, the surrogate model N_ρ is trained on a dataset
$\mathcal{D}' = \{(x_i', M_\theta(x_i))\}_{i=1}^N$ where $x' \in X'$ is the preprocessed input data. This means
the numerical features are binned in order to convert them into a categorical
data. To put in short, the surrogate model such as the SBRL algorithm then
mines the rules and generates a decision list containing set of rules, which is used
to explain a model's prediction.

5   Evaluation Metrics

Evaluating any machine learning or deep learning algorithms is an essential part
of the task. In this section, the list of quality measures that are used to compare
the performance of the three methods are listed.

F_1-*score of the main model* ($F_{1,main}$) is the harmonic mean between precision and recall of the main model M_θ, which seeks a balance between precision and recall. It is defined as

$$F_1 = 2 \cdot \frac{precision \cdot recall}{precision + recall}. \qquad (16)$$

Typically the F_1-*score* is more useful than accuracy, particularly if the class distribution is uneven. Here, the prediction function is an MLP algorithm.

F_1-*score of the surrogate model* ($F_{1,surr}$) is the harmonic mean between precision and recall of the surrogate model N_ρ and defined as shown in Eq. (16). Here, the prediction function is an SBRL algorithm, which is used to mimic the behavior of the main model M_θ.

Fidelity is an accuracy score, which measures the predictions of the surrogate model to the predictions of the main model. This metric matters the most, as the surrogate model tries to mimic the behavior of the main model.

Average Number of Rules (ANR) is the number of rules which a decision list uses to classify a single sample. It should be noted that the notion of Average Path Length (APL) is not explicitly transferable to rule lists, but for comparison purposes, APL has been replaced with ANR.

6   Experimental Results

In this section, the derived datasets and the experimental setup used for training both the main model and the surrogate model for all three methods are explained. In addition, all three methods are evaluated. Each method is evaluated on every dataset. Finally, the results are compared with the other methods and are discussed.

6.1   Datasets

The experiments are carried out on four datasets. Each dataset has been extracted from the raw AIS data as described in Sect. 3.2. All datasets use the same spatial and temporal thresholds. The only difference between the datasets is the sample count per sequence. The chosen lengths are 15, 30, 45 and 60 corresponding to 15 min, 30 min, 45 min and 60 min of data respectively, with a sampling time of 1 min. In general, each dataset has 10000 sequences with the sequence length varying depending on the chosen timespan, and each sample in turn has nine features as specified in Sect. 3.2. The target is to classify a vessel/ship-type: *Cargo-Tanker, Fishing, Passenger, Pleasure-Craft,* and *Tug*.

6.2   Experimental Setup

Through all our experiments the main model was a standard MLP. We used the same main model structure with two hidden layers for all datasets. The number of neurons present in the input layer depends on the number of features present in a dataset, as noted in Table 1, resulting in (number of samples·number of features) neurons. A *sparse categorical cross-entropy* is used as a classification loss function, *ReLU* as an activation function in all hidden layers and *softmax* for the output. The main model uses the Adam optimization algorithm with a learning-rate of 0.001. The sequences of the form (number of samples, number of features) are collapsed into a single dimension (number of samples · number of features) to fit as input for the MLP. Numerical features were binned in order to train the surrogate model. The surrogate model is trained with default hyper-parameters of *SBRL* (as pysbrl on pip), except a *support* parameter which is varied and evaluated the models performance. The *max_rule_len* parameter is chosen as 2, keeping in mind the processor and the RAM available to carry out our experiments.

6.3   Results

This study aims at evaluating the results of each method that are accurate and interpretable. Therefore, each method is implemented on every dataset and its corresponding results are shown in Table 1. It can be seen that the *SBRL* method outperforms the other two methods in terms of metrics such as $F_{1,main}$, $F_{1,surr}$, fidelity. However, the length (number of rules) of the surrogate list is relatively high, making the model more complex to interpret. *GiniReg* on the other hand, though the F_1-score of both the main model and the surrogate model is a bit less compared to *SBRL*, relatively higher fidelity is achieved and the length of the resulting surrogate list is reduced, making the behavior of the model less complex to interpret. One such example of a surrogate model on 60 min dataset is shown in Fig. 2. *RuleReg* performs the least since it generates or trains several surrogate models during the training of the main model as compared to the other two methods which train only one surrogate model on the whole. In case of *RuleReg*, It should be noted that training the models with less batch size decreases the performance of the surrogate model and with more batch size decreases the performance of the main model. Hence, choosing the correct batch size plays a major role.

We trained all three methods with variation in the *support* parameter of a surrogate model as shown in Fig. 3. We can see that for increasing *support* value the performance of the surrogate model is going down. This means the surrogate model is highly unlikely to capture the pattern of the ship trajectories with an increase in *support* value. Hence, all the models are further trained with a *support* value of 0.01.

Since we bin the numerical features before training a surrogate model, we were curious how this would impact the overall model's performance. Therefore, we trained the models with different bins (no. of discrete intervals) as shown in Fig. 4. It can be observed that the performance of all three models increases to some extent and starts decreasing gradually with an increase in the number of bins. This means the models are able to learn better if the features are categorized

Table 1. Performance of all three methods.

Method	Duration	Layers	$F_{1,main}$	$F_{1,surr}$	Fidelity	No. of rules	APL/ANR	λ
SBRL	15 min	[128,128]	**0.80**	**0.84**	0.84	52	26.50	0.0
RuleReg			0.66	0.67	0.82	46	22.71	1
GiniReg			0.74	0.76	**0.86**	**41**	**22.11**	0.05
SBRL	30 min	[256, 256]	**0.82**	**0.84**	0.85	58	25.20	0.0
RuleReg			0.70	0.71	0.81	47	23.19	10
GiniReg			0.80	0.82	**0.85**	**42**	**22.01**	0.01
SBRL	45 min	[256, 256]	**0.83**	**0.85**	0.85	59	29.50	0.0
RuleReg			0.71	0.74	0.85	42	21.52	1
GiniReg			0.80	0.81	**0.85**	**37**	**19.99**	0.01
SBRL	60 min	[512, 512]	**0.84**	**0.85**	0.85	57	29.50	0.0
RuleReg			0.69	0.70	0.81	45	22.70	1
GiniReg			0.80	0.82	**0.86**	**40**	**22.53**	0.1

IF Course_161 in (0.123, 0.164] **AND** Course_503 in (-0.00102, 0.0409]
    THEN Shiptype = Cargo-Tanker (0.95)[†]
ELSE IF (DisToharbor_186 in (0.959, 0.999]) **AND** (DisToCoast_221 in (0.369, 0.406])
    THEN Shiptype = Passenger (0.83)[†]
ELSE IF (DisToCoast_392 in (0.963, 1.0]) **AND** (Local_Y_39 in (0.04, 0.08])
    THEN Shiptype = Cargo-Tanker (0.88)[†]
ELSE IF (Speed_403 in (0.96, 1.0]) **AND** (DisToharbor_429 in (0.599, 0.639])
    THEN Shiptype = Passenger (0.94)[†]
ELSE IF (DisToharbor_276 in (0.16, 0.2]) **AND** (Global_X_288 in (0.495, 0.516])
    THEN Shiptype = Pleasure-Craft (0.65)[†]
ELSE IF (Global_Y_181 in (0.421, 0.436]) **AND** (DisToCoast_194 in (0.232, 0.27])
    THEN Shiptype = Fishing (0.40)[†]
ELSE IF (Course_17 in (0.0818, 0.123]) **AND** (Course_296 in (0.0818, 0.123])
    THEN Shiptype = Cargo-Tanker (0.91)[†]
ELSE IF (DisToCoast_374 in (0.961, 1.0]) **AND** (DisToharbor_465 in (0.919, 0.959])
    THEN Shiptype = Tug (0.79)[†]
ELSE IF (DisToCoast_32 in (0.282, 0.32]) **AND** (Course_521 in (-0.00102, 0.0409])
    THEN Shiptype = Pleasure-Craft (0.41)[†]
    ⋮

ELSE Shiptype = Cargo-Tanker (0.82)[†]

[†] predicted class with prediction probability in brackets

Fig. 2. Example Surrogate Model for 60 min AIS dataset.

into more number of discrete intervals. But it should be noted that large discrete intervals make the model fail to learn the patterns in the trajectories of the ships.

The *GiniReg* and *RuleReg* methods are regularization-based techniques and hence we trained several models with different regularization strength, λ. We can see that the number of rules in the resulting surrogate model and APL/ANR is

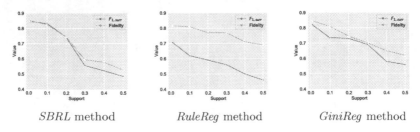

SBRL method   RuleReg method   GiniReg method

Fig. 3. The performance of the surrogate model (F_1, Fidelity) against different support parameter of the SBRL on 30 min AIS dataset.

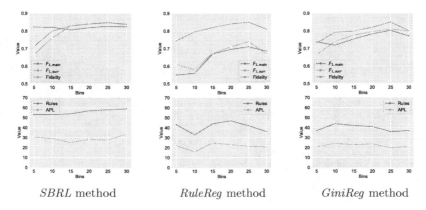

SBRL method   RuleReg method   GiniReg method

Fig. 4. The performance of both the main model and the surrogate model against different bins in the preprocessing for surrogate model on 45 min AIS dataset.

going down with an increase in λ. This indicates both these techniques make a model less complex to interpret. In case of *RuleReg*, if the strength is significantly increased to a higher value, the model would collapse into a single target output with just one default rule. However, this would not be the case in *GiniReg* technique.

In addition, we examined the runtime of all three methods on every dataset, which includes training of both the main model and the surrogate model. Table 2 represents the result in *secs* obtained in the experiments. In all the cases, *SBRL* method is faster and *RuleReg* is slower. As mentioned before, *RuleReg* generates several surrogate models compared to the other two methods which makes them relatively slow. We used an Intel(R) Core(TM) i7-5960X processor with 64 GB RAM to conduct our experiments. An increase in memory should improve the runtime of all the methods.

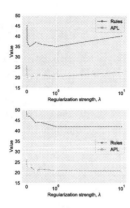

Fig. 5. Length of surrogate list and APL for increasing λ on 45 min dataset. Top: *GiniReg*, bottom: *RuleReg*.

Table 2. Runtime of all the methods

Method	Dataset	Runtime in s
SBRL	15 min	429
RuleReg		3455
Ginireg		466
SBRL	30 min	1106
RuleReg		11533
Ginireg		1537
SBRL	45 min	2142
RuleReg		20500
Ginireg		3119
SBRL	60 min	3578
RuleReg		31631
Ginireg		4316

7   Conclusion and Future Work

During this study, three ARM techniques are evaluated on time-series data in order to make the results interpretable. In our experiments, we find that the *GiniReg* technique works best on every dataset having high fidelity to the main model and a lower number of rules, making a model less complex to interpret. However, *SBRL* works better in classifying a vessel but with more number of rules in the surrogate list. *RuleReg* on the other hand achieves higher fidelity but with low performance of the main model and the surrogate model. This paper also demonstrates the impact of *support*, *bins*, *regularization* parameters on the performance of the model. In addition, the runtime of all the methods was examined, where *SBRL* was faster and *RuleReg* was a lot slower (Table 2).

Explainability or interpretability remains a very active area of research in deep learning. The major rule mining methods surveyed in this study each represent a step towards more fully understanding a deep learning model like MLP. Further work on applying these techniques to other architectures like CNN's or GRU's would be interesting.

Acknowledgment. Underlying projects to this article are funded by the WTD 81 of the German Federal Ministry of Defense. The authors are responsible for the content of this article. This work was developed in the Fraunhofer Cluster of Excellence "Cognitive Internet Technologies".

References

1. Aggarwal, C.C., Bhuiyan, M.A., Hasan, M.A.: Frequent pattern mining algorithms: a survey. In: Aggarwal, C.C., Han, J. (eds.) Frequent Pattern Mining, pp. 19–64. Springer, Cham (2014). https://doi.org/10.1007/978-3-319-07821-2_2

2. Altmann, A., Tolosi, L., Sander, O., Lengauer, T.: Permutation importance: a corrected feature importance measure. Bioinformatics **26**, 1340–1347 (2010). https://doi.org/10.1093/bioinformatics/btq134
3. Anneken, M., Strenger, M., Robert, S., Beyerer, J.: Classification of Maritime Vessels using Convolutional Neural Networks. UR-AI 2020 (2020). accepted for publication
4. Breiman, L.: Random forests. Mach. Learn. **45**(1), 5–32 (2001)
5. Burkart, N., Huber, M., Faller, P.: Forcing interpretability for deep neural networks through rule-based regularization. In: 2019 18th IEEE International Conference On Machine Learning And Applications (ICMLA), pp. 700–705 (2019)
6. Burkart, N., Huber, M., Faller, P.: Batch-wise regularization of deep neural networks for interpretability. In: 2020 IEEE International Conference on Multisensor Fusion and Integration for Intelligent Systems (MFI) (2020). accepted for publication
7. Burkart, N., Huber, M.F., Anneken, M.: Supported decision-making by explainable predictions of ship trajectories. In: Herrero, Á., Cambra, C., Urda, D., Sedano, J., Quintián, H., Corchado, E. (eds.) SOCO 2020. AISC, vol. 1268, pp. 44–54. Springer, Cham (2021). https://doi.org/10.1007/978-3-030-57802-2_5
8. Fayyad, U., Piatetsky-Shapiro, G., Smyth, P.: From data mining to knowledge discovery in databases. AI Mag. **17**(3), 37–37 (1996)
9. Gee, A., Garcia-Olano, D., Ghosh, J., Paydarfar, D.: Explaining deep classification of time-series data with learned prototypes. arXiv preprint arXiv:1904.08935 (2019)
10. Hidasi, B., Gáspár-Papanek, C.: ShiftTree: an interpretable model-based approach for time series classification. In: Gunopulos, D., Hofmann, T., Malerba, D., Vazirgiannis, M. (eds.) ECML PKDD 2011. LNCS (LNAI), vol. 6912, pp. 48–64. Springer, Heidelberg (2011). https://doi.org/10.1007/978-3-642-23783-6_4
11. Hsu, E.Y., Liu, C.L., Tseng, V.: Multivariate time series early classification with interpretability using deep learning and attention mechanism. In: Pacific-Asia Conference on Knowledge Discovery and Data Mining, pp. 541–553 (2019). https://doi.org/10.1007/978-3-030-16142-2-42
12. Letham, B., Rudin, C., McCormick, T.H., Madigan, D.: Interpretable classifiers using rules and Bayesian analysis: building a better stroke prediction model. Ann. Appl. Stat. **9**(3), 1350–1371 (2015). https://doi.org/10.1214/15-aoas848
13. Lundberg, S., Lee, S.I.: A unified approach to interpreting model predictions (2017)
14. Popescu, M.C., Balas, V.E., Perescu-Popescu, L., Mastorakis, N.: Multilayer perceptron and neural networks. WSEAS Trans. Circ. Syst. **8**(7), 579–588 (2009)
15. Raymond, E.S.: AIVDM/AIVDO protocol decoding (2019). https://gpsd.gitlab.io/gpsd/AIVDM.html. Accessed 28 Sep 2020
16. Ribeiro, M.T., Singh, S., Guestrin, C.: Why should I trust you?: Explaining the predictions of any classifier (2016)
17. Schlegel, U., Arnout, H., El-Assady, M., Oelke, D., Keim, D.: Towards a rigorous evaluation of XAI methods on time series. In: 2019 IEEE/CVF International Conference on Computer Vision Workshop (ICCVW) (2019)
18. Skorpil, V., Stastny, J.: Neural networks and back propagation algorithm. Electron Bulg Sozopol 2006 Conference Proceedings, pp. 173–177 (2006)
19. Wu, M., Hughes, M.C., Parbhoo, S., Zazzi, M., Roth, V., Doshi-Velez, F.: Beyond sparsity: Tree regularization of deep models for interpretability (2017)
20. Yang, H., Rudin, C., Seltzer, M.: Scalable Bayesian rule lists. In: International Conference on Machine Learning. PMLR, pp. 3921–3930 (2017)
21. Zaki, M.J.: Scalable algorithms for association mining. IEEE Trans. Knowl. Data Eng. **12**(3), 372–390 (2000)

Anchors vs Attention: Comparing XAI on a Real-Life Use Case

Gaëlle Jouis[1,2]([✉]), Harold Mouchère[1], Fabien Picarougne[1], and Alexandre Hardouin[2]

[1] LS2N, Université de Nantes, CNRS, 44000 Nantes, France
[2] Pôle Emploi, Direction des Systèmes d'Information, Nantes, France
gaelle.jouis@pole-emploi.fr

Abstract. Recent advances in eXplainable Artificial Intelligence (XAI) led to many different methods in order to improve explainability of deep learning algorithms. With many options at hand, and maybe the need to adapt existing ones to new problems, one may find in a struggle to choose the right method to generate explanations. This paper presents an objective approach to compare two different existing XAI methods. These methods are applied to a use case from literature and to a real use case of a French administration.

Keywords: Machine learning · Deep learning · Explainability · Attention networks

1 Introduction

Artificial Intelligence, and specifically Machine Learning, has been thriving for the past few years. Deep Learning has proven its ability to perform in many tasks, such as image processing, object recognition, and natural language processing [14]. Unlike other approaches such as linear models, deep learning models are considered as *black boxes*, because their processing is quite opaque. Hence, explaining the result of a deep learning algorithm is a difficult task.

This paper focuses on a specific real-life use case of text classification for a French Institution, *Pôle Emploi*. The classification consists in the detection of uncompliant job offers with the use of machine learning, and will later be called "LEGO". The institution has a legal duty of transparency about its algorithms and seeks to provide explanations alongside the tool's results. The "Why" and the "How" of eXplainable Artificial Intelligence (XAI) are now being tackled by the scientific community. To the best of our knowledge, proposed solutions are not systematically evaluated. Thus, choosing which method would best suit a particular AI project is not a straightforward task.

This contribution compares two different explanation methods when applied to a use case. Methods are the Anchors, a black box method, and an Attention-based white box method, both being popular and based on distinct mechanisms. The specific LEGO use case and a second use case from literature are used in this qualification process, suggesting best practices for XAI method comparison.

A. Del Bimbo et al. (Eds.): ICPR 2020 Workshops, LNCS 12663, pp. 219–227, 2021.
https://doi.org/10.1007/978-3-030-68796-0_16

2   Related Works

2.1   EXplainable Artificial Intelligence

One can regroup the numerous existing XAI approaches according to the global logic of survey papers [4,5]. Hence are defined three categories:

1. Explain a *black box* model based on its inputs and outputs.
2. Observe internal mechanisms of a system (*grey box*) after it was trained.
3. Design a transparent solution (*white box*) explaining itself.

Explaining black box models induces the use of a proxy model. One well-known method is LIME [10] and its improvement: Anchors [11]. *LIME* (Local Interpretable Model-agnostic Explanations) is an approximation of a black box model with a linear regression. The regression weights the inputs by importance. Similarly, Anchor explanation explains a result with a rule. The rule presents a set of words leading to the decision of the model. These methods are designed to explain one instance at a time and are only accurate for close examples.

Convolutional Neural Networks (CNN) internal processing has been analyzed in [13]. The authors used a neural network they named *Deconvolutional Network* to visualize patterns that activate neurons layer-wise. Also based on CNN, authors of [12] combine their works to those of [13], to detect regions and patterns of an image helping on class detection. Similar work has been done on semantic analysis with LSTM (Long Short-Term Memory) networks [7].

On the other hand, transparent solutions are inherent to the developed model. In [8], the authors create an attention-based word embedding called *Structured self-attentive embedding*. Words associated with high Attention weights are used by the model to classify the text. Another attention-based visualization is shown in [9]. Compared to black box strategies, which are approximating the trained model, Attention is a core component of this model. After training, there is no need for more computing as inference will generate Attention weights used for meaningful visualizations.

2.2   Evaluate Explanations

Evaluating explanations can be done with two main approaches: 1) Criteria and metrics, 2) User evaluation.

Criteria and Metrics. Explanations or models generating them are often evaluated with criteria and metrics in the literature. To evaluate proxy models, one mostly used criteria is fidelity to the black box model, measured with accuracy, or f1 score [5,11]. Interpretability is also measured, often as a size of the proxy model, such as number of weights [5]. The coverage can be measured as the number of instances that are in agreement with an explanation [11]. Metrics can also evaluate the explanation itself. In the case of natural language explanations, it is possible to use readability score such as the *Flesch-Reading-Ease* score, used in [3]. When required explanations are available, expected and obtained explanations can be compared as sets of features. Computing the Intersection over Union (IoU) gives a score from 0 to 1. An IoU of 1 means explanations are identical. This metric is used in [1] to evaluate interpretability in image based problems. If only a few explanations are possible, the case can be considered as a classification problem, and usual accuracy metrics can be used [2].

Evaluation based on metrics allows to work on huge test datasets. Without the need of finding users, it is also faster and cheaper to develop quantitative evaluations on any XAI method. However, explanations are designed to be an interface between algorithms and humans, hence they need to be evaluated by or with humans.

User Evaluation. When conducting a user study on model explanations, evaluation can be objective or subjective. Subjective evaluation can be a poll asking users if they are satisfied with a given explanation, or which explanation do they prefer among a couple ones [11]. They might also be asked to choose between two classifiers, one being significantly better than the other, given only their explanations [10]. These evaluations are appropriate when the purpose is improving acceptance of a model. One the other hand, objective metrics can be extracted from user studies. In [6], users are given an explanation and must predict the next output of the system. Considering user's answers as results of binary classifiers, the authors compute a Roc Curve and its Area Under Curve to measure the success of their explanations. When the user must predict the output of the model, the response time of the user can be used as a measure of the user's confidence [11].

3   Experiments

We want here to compare two explanation methods: generation of Anchors upon any model from [11] and the use of attention with a transparent model from [8]. For each following use case, a transparent attention-based model will be trained, and Anchors will be generated on the predictions of this same model. Quoting [11] for the example, lets take the sentence "This movie is not bad", which is classified "positive" by an attention-based model. The Anchor explanation would be $A = \{not, bad\} \rightarrow Positive$. Every word in the sentence would have an attention weight, and "not" and "bad" would have the highest weights.

The generation of Anchors is made with the python library developed by the authors of [11]. Following the research of [8], a neural network with a bi-LSTM and the same Attention mechanism was trained. The architecture is described in the table below (cf. Table 1). Adapting the network for each use-case resulted in some differences of dimensions, which are detailed in the 3rd and 4th columns of Table 1. The Attention mechanism results in an Attention matrix A, which is the output of the layer 5 (cf. Table 1). Words of interest are filtered using a threshold t on attention values. For the LEGO use case, when the model predicts no reject, the explanation is forced to be empty.

Table 1. Network architecture specifications of YELP and LEGO classifiers.

ID	Layer type	YELP	LEGO	Comment
1	Input Layer	300	80	Size is the number of words in texts
2	Embedding	100	300	Embedding, respectively word2vec and glove
3	BLSTM	$u - 150$	$u = 50$	Output is Hidden states H
4	Dense 0	$d_a = 350$	$d_a = 300$	*tanh* activation
5	Dense 1	$r = 1$	$r = 1$	Output is attention matrix A
6	Attention and average pooling	out: $[2u, r]$	out: $[2u, r]$	Combines attention and hidden states, $M = A^T * H$
7	Dense 2	1000		*ReLu* activation, only for YELP
8	Dense 3	5	28	Output layer

3.1 LEGO

Pôle Emploi is the french job center. One of its tools aims to automatically reject uncompliant job offers. Indeed, *Pôle Emploi* is legally bound to reject offers not complying with the Labor Code or being discriminative. Training dataset contains 480000 sentences extracted from real offers. Retrieving the reason for rejection is a multiclass classification task, with 28 topics being targeted in this study. Offers used for the training of the classifier are already labeled in *Pôle Emploi*'s database, with labels predicted by the existing rule-based system.

The classifier for this use case is similar to the one for the YELP dataset. The embedding matrix used is a 300-dimensional GloVe embedding.[1] The optimizer is Adam, with a learning rate of 0.0005. This network achieves an accuracy of 83.67% on its test set.

The existing system produces some errors. Thus, to accurately analyze explanations, a corrected test set was necessary. As the correction of labels is time-consuming, a subset of 208 sentences has been manually labeled and attributed the desired explanation. This explanation consists of highlighting keywords that led to rejection. As explanations are meaningful for uncompliant offers only, explanations for compliant offers are considered to be empty. The real world's class distribution has not been respected, and compliant explanations are underrepresented in this test set. Hence, the model's accuracy for this test set is lower and irrelevant (70.67%).

3.2 YELP

The YELP dataset contains user reviews about restaurants, associated with 1 to 5 star-ratings. The training set contains 453 600 reviews. As shown in Table 1,

---

[1] https://dl.fbaipublicfiles.com/fasttext/vectors-crawl/cc.fr.300.vec.gz.

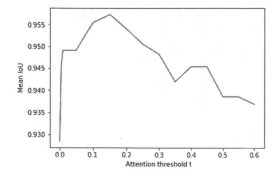

Fig. 1. Mean IoU between Attention and ground truth explanations in test set, for varying Attention threshold t. Words with Attention greater or equal to t are kept as explanation. First point is at 10^{-4}.

the embedding is a 100-dimensional English-based word2vec.[2] The optimizer is Adam, with a learning rate of 0.0005. This network achieves an accuracy of 74.63% on its test set. In comparison, authors of [8] present in their paper an accuracy of 64.21% on their own test set. As anchors explanation on large texts often leads to memory issues, anchors have been applied to a subset of 1060 reviews over the 2653 reviews of the full test set.

4   Evaluating Explanations

4.1   Quantitative Analysis

In the context of the LEGO dataset, each method is compared with ground truth. To get fair measures, stop words are not taken into account. As the evaluation of the model is not the point in this experimentation, the test set is a subset of 147 sentences over 208, that have been correctly predicted. A threshold t is used in order to filter words. t is determined by optimizing IoU on the test set, as shown in the graph in Fig. 1. The graph indicates that words with attention greater or equal to 0.15 are a good explanation in the LEGO use case.

As used in [1], IoU will allow comparing ground truth, to generated explanation, with Anchors or with Attention. Accuracy and F1-score are also displayed in Table 2, plus recall and precision used in the F1-score. Recall is an interesting metric as it is not impacted by true negatives. Anchors and Attention are also compared to one another, assuring they give similar results. With no ground truth, metrics such as accuracy and f1-score are irrelevant, as noted in Table 2. High IoU between anchors and attention explanations indicates that explanations are similar with both methods. Overall, when comparing to ground truth, Attention explanations are slightly better than Anchors, cf. Table 2.

---

[2] https://wikipedia2vec.github.io/wikipedia2vec/pretrained/.

Table 2. Evaluation of Anchors and Attention with ground truth, LEGO for correct prediction only, best result in bold.

Metric	Anchors	Attention	Anchors vs Attention
IoU	0.9377	**0.9573**	0.9471
Acc	0.9803	**0.9871**	*irrelevant*
Recall	**0.9696**	0.9641	*irrelevant*
Precision	0.9614	**0.9932**	*irrelevant*
F1	0.9540	**0.9688**	*irrelevant*

For the YELP use case, there is no expected explanation. Comparison is only possible between Anchors and Attention explanations. IoU indicates whether the given explanations are similar. Mean IoU on the successful test set is 0.2292, which shows strong differences between the two explanation methods. This can be explained by long texts and vast expected vocabulary in explanations. Hence, to assess evaluation methods in YELP use case, qualitative analysis is needed.

4.2   Qualitative Analysis

As high IoU shows similarity between two explanations, qualitative analysis can be more efficient with filtering texts with low IoU in the test set. Doing so will point out if one explanation method is more accurate when being different. Hence this filtering will be used in the following qualitative analysis for both use cases.

For the LEGO use case, Anchors explanations are shorter than Attention-based explanations. Mean lengths are respectively 0.15 and 0.33 words in the test set. The mean value is low due to empty explanations. The following table (cf. Table 3) gives a few examples where IoU is lesser than 0.5. This qualitative analysis is in agreement with the quantitative analysis, and point out Attention weights as a better explanation method for this use case. On the YELP dataset, there is no possibility to compare explanations with any wished one. Still, it is interesting to have a look at explanations for extreme reviews (1 and 5 stars, well recognized) when IoU is 0, meaning explanations are very different.

Mean explanation lengths are similar, 2.34 and 2.13 words for Anchors and Attention respectively. The first two lines of Table 4 indicates a lack of meaningful words in Anchors, hence Attention-based explanations are the best choice. The last line of Table 4 show explanations based on different but meaningful words. As average lengths are similar and Attention seems more accurate when explanations are very different, this qualitative analysis indicates that Attention-based explanations are a safer choice in this particular use case.

Table 3. LEGO texts with different explanations. Text is above other information.

Reject	Ground truth	Anchor	Attention
"Contrat a duree indeterminee - Dfd Notre agence de Saint-Medard-en-Jalles recherche une Assistante Administrative pour completer son equipe"			
Gender	['assistante administrative']	['recherche', 'Assistante', 'Jalles']	['assistante', 'administrative']
"Nous recherchons actuellement un Teleconseiller FRANCAIS / NEERLANDAIS (H/F) pour le compte de notre client, a Marcq-en-Baroeul."			
Nationality	['francais/neerlandais']	['un', 'neerlandais', 'recherchons', 'francais']	['neerlandais']

Table 4. YELP texts with different explanations. Text is above other information.

Stars	Anchor	Attention
Wow! Superb Maids did an amazing job cleaning my house. They stayed as long as it took to make sure everything was immaculate. I will be using them on a regular basis		
5	[]	['superb', 'amazing', 'everything']
For the record, this place is not gay friendly. Very homophobic and sad for 2019. Avoid at all costs		
1	['not']	['record', 'not', 'homophobic', 'sad', 'avoid']
Had the best experience buying my dress at brilliant bridal in jan 2018. Can't wait to wear my beautiful gown in oct 2018		
5	['brilliant']	['best', 'buying', 'can']

Table 5. Mentions of ratings in explanations.

Text	Stars	Prediction	Anchor	Attention
[...] An this is the reason I gave them a mere 2 stars [...]	3	2	['2', 'stars']	['2']
3 Stars is about right. [...]	3	3	['3']	['3', 'decent']
[...] Perfect amount of sweet. 5/5 bobas	5	5	['5/5', 'sweet', 'Perfect', 'great', 'all']	['5']

One interesting point is that both explanations are pointing out the same parts when reviewers mention their own rating, as shown in Table 5. For the first example, this even leads to a wrong prediction.

5   Conclusion

The upcoming multiplicity of XAI methods leads to the necessity of choosing one method that suits each specific use case. In this paper, two use cases have been developed. One is available for sharing with the community, and the second one is extracted from a real need in the french job center. The use of metrics as a way to evaluate explanations has proven to be quite useful when explanations test set is available. However, creating this data set can be expensive and needs the contribution of human experts. In this case, and if examined methods are not too many, user studies can be more relevant but are quite expensive themselves.

Another criterion that was not identified at first sight is the computing cost and time of explanations. As generating Anchors explanations was so costly, it led for one use-case to the filtering of the test set. As XAI often meets ethics, responsible AI, and even green IT, one can wonder if explanation methods such as attention mechanism can be preferred based upon efficiency criteria.

Finally, comparing various explanation methods and observing when explanations are similar or in disagreement can help to learn more about an AI model. This process might be used to evaluate the model itself.

References

1. Bau, D., Zhou, B., Khosla, A., Oliva, A., Torralba, A.: Network dissection: Quantifying interpretability of deep visual representations. In: Proceedings of the IEEE Conference on Computer Vision and Pattern Recognition, pp. 6541–6549 (2017)
2. Codella, N.C., et al.: TED: Teaching AI to explain its decisions. In: Proceedings of the 2019 AAAI/ACM Conference on AI, Ethics, and Society (2019)
3. Costa, F., Ouyang, S., Dolog, P., Lawlor, A.: Automatic generation of natural language explanations. In: Proceedings of the 23rd International Conference on Intelligent User Interfaces Companion, pp. 1–2 (2018)
4. Gilpin, L.H., Bau, D., Yuan, B.Z., Bajwa, A., Specter, M., Kagal, L.: Explaining explanations: an overview of interpretability of machine learning. In: 2018 IEEE 5th International Conference on Data Science and Advanced Analytics (DSAA), pp. 80–89 (2018)
5. Guidotti, R., Monreale, A., Ruggieri, S., Turini, F., Giannotti, F., Pedreschi, D.: A survey of methods for explaining black box models. ACM Comput. Surv. (CSUR) 51(5), 1–42 (2018)
6. Iyer, R., Li, Y., Li, H., Lewis, M., Sundar, R., Sycara, K.: Transparency and explanation in deep reinforcement learning neural networks. In: Proceedings of the 2018 AAAI/ACM Conference on AI, Ethics, and Society (2018)
7. Karpathy, A., Johnson, J., Li, F.: Visualizing and understanding recurrent networks. CoRR abs/1506.02078 (2015)
8. Lin, Z., et al.: A structured self-attentive sentence embedding. In: 5th International Conference on Learning Representations, ICLR 2017, 24–26 April 2017, Toulon, France, Conference Track Proceedings (2017)
9. Olah, C., Carter, S.: Attention and augmented recurrent neural networks. Distill (2016). https://doi.org/10.23915/distill.00001

10. Ribeiro, M.T., Singh, S., Guestrin, C.: Why should I trust you?: Explaining the predictions of any classifier. In: Proceedings of the 22nd ACM International Conference on Knowledge Discovery and Data Mining, pp. 1135–1144 (2016)
11. Ribeiro, M.T., Singh, S., Guestrin, C.: Anchors: High-precision model-agnostic explanations. In: Proceedings of the Thirty-Second AAAI Conference on Artificial Intelligence, (AAAI 2018), pp. 1527–1535 (2018)
12. Selvaraju, R.R., Cogswell, M., Das, A., Vedantam, R., Parikh, D., Batra, D.: Grad-CAM: Visual explanations from deep networks via gradient-based localization. In: The IEEE International Conference on Computer Vision (2017)
13. Zeiler, M.D., Fergus, R.: Visualizing and understanding convolutional networks. In: European Conference on Computer Vision, pp. 818–833 (2014)
14. Zou, Z., Shi, Z., Guo, Y., Ye, J.: Object detection in 20 years: a survey. arXiv preprint arXiv:1905.05055 (2019)

Explanation-Driven Characterization
of Android Ransomware

Michele Scalas[1]([⊠])[iD], Konrad Rieck[2], and Giorgio Giacinto[1][iD]

[1] University of Cagliari, Cagliari, Italy
{michele.scalas,giacinto}@unica.it
[2] Technische Universität Braunschweig, Braunschweig, Germany
k.rieck@tu-bs.de

Abstract. Machine learning is currently successfully used for addressing several cybersecurity detection and classification tasks. Typically, such detectors are modeled through complex learning algorithms employing a wide variety of features. Although these settings allow achieving considerable performances, gaining insights on the learned knowledge turns out to be a hard task. To address this issue, research efforts on the interpretability of machine learning approaches to cybersecurity tasks is currently rising. In particular, relying on explanations could improve prevention and detection capabilities since they could help human experts to find out the distinctive features that truly characterize malware attacks. In this perspective, Android ransomware represents a serious threat. Leveraging state-of-the-art explanation techniques, we present a first approach that enables the identification of the most influential discriminative features for ransomware characterization. We propose strategies to adopt explanation techniques appropriately and describe ransomware families and their evolution over time. Reported results suggest that our proposal can help cyber threat intelligence teams in the early detection of new ransomware families, and could be applicable to other malware detection systems through the identification of their distinctive features.

Keywords: Android · Ransomware · Malware detection · Interpretability · Machine learning

1 Introduction

Malware detection is one of the areas where machine learning is successfully employed due to its high discriminating power and the capability of identifying novel variants of malware samples. Typically, the problem formulation is strictly correlated to the use of a wide variety of features covering different characteristics of the entities to classify. This practice often provides considerable detection performance but hardly permits to gain insights on the knowledge extracted by the learning algorithm, and might cause detectors to learn spurious patterns, with the additional flaw of being particularly vulnerable to adversarial attacks [7,9]. This issue can be exceptionally relevant depending on the domain, such as the

© Springer Nature Switzerland AG 2021
A. Del Bimbo et al. (Eds.): ICPR 2020 Workshops, LNCS 12663, pp. 228–242, 2021.
https://doi.org/10.1007/978-3-030-68796-0_17

safety-critical cases of autonomous driving or medical diagnoses. In this sense, having the possibility to rely on explanations could improve the design process of such detectors, since they could reveal characterizing patterns, thus guiding the human expert towards the understanding of the most relevant features. Moreover, recent legislation, such as the European GDPR, enshrines the *right to explanation* for machine-made decisions. For all these reasons, research on the *interpretability* of machine learning is currently rising. This is a developing field with several contrasting concepts and methods since *explanations* can be provided for various goals and stakeholders [6,12,16].

The detection of Android ransomware represents a challenging yet illustrative domain for assessing the impact of interpretability. Ransomware represents a serious threat that acts by locking the compromised device or encrypting its data, then forcing the device owner to pay a ransom in order to restore the device functionality. The attackers typically develop such dangerous apps so that normally-legitimate components and functionalities (e.g., encryption) perform malicious behavior; thus, making them harder to be distinguished from genuine applications. Given this context, and according to our experience [13,17] and previous work, we aim to investigate if and to what extent state-of-the-art explainability techniques help to identify the features that characterize ransomware samples, i.e., the properties that are required to be present in order to combat ransomware offensives effectively. In this regard, our contribution is twofold: *i)* we present a first approach that enables a designer to select the explainability technique that is most suitable to the goal mentioned above and model agnostic as well, and *ii)* we propose practical strategies for identifying the features that characterize generic ransomware samples, specific families, and the evolution of such attacks over time. In this way, we believe that our proposal can help cyber threat intelligence teams in the early detection of new ransomware families, and could be applicable to other malware detection systems through the identification of their distinctive features. After introducing background notions about Android and ransomware attacks (Sect. 2), we provide an overview of explanation techniques, with a focus on *gradient-based* ones (Sect. 3). Our approach is then presented (Sect. 4), starting from the strategy to perform ransomware detection and followed by the rationale behind the usage of explanation techniques for identifying relevant features. Notably, tailoring such techniques to our domain and goal requires attentive checks. Therefore, in our experimental analysis (Sect. 5) we first verify their suitability, and we eventually analyze their output to extract information. Lastly, we discuss the limitations of our approach, together with the future research paths (Sect. 6).

2   Background on Android

Android applications are zipped `apk` archives composed by the following elements: *i)* the `AndroidManifest.xml` and other `xml` files that specify the application layout, *ii)* one or more `classes.dex` files, and *iii)* various resources, such as images, generic files (`assets`), and native libraries.

In this work, we analyze the `AndroidManifest.xml` and the `classes.dex` files. The former lists the app's *components*, i.e., the elements that define its structure and functionalities. For example, the screens visualized by the user are built upon an `activity`, and background tasks are executed through `services`. One of the most important sections of the Manifest comes from the list of the *permissions* requested by the application (`uses-permission` tag). In fact, the app developer has to ask the user the right to use certain functionalities. These can be related to the device (e.g., `ACCESS_NETWORK_STATE`) or functionalities (e.g., `SEND_SMS`). As regards the `classes.dex` file, it embeds the compiled source code of the applications, including all the user-implemented methods and classes.

2.1   Android Ransomware

Ransomware threats are referred to as attacks that compromise a device and make it unusable so that the attacker can extort the victim by asking a ransom to restore it. The majority of ransomware attacks for Android are based on the goal of *locking* the device screen. In this case, attackers typically take the following strategy: they create an `activity`, upon which a non-dismissable window is shown. This `activity` is forced to stay always in the foreground, and it can be restarted when killed or the device get rebooted. Moreover, they disable the navigation buttons (e.g., the *back* functionality). Newer versions of Android, primarily since API level 28 (Android Pie), have implemented countermeasures in response to this strategy, such as the *Safe Mode*, where the system blocks third-party apps from running, or the visualization of a notification in the status bar that allows disabling overlay windows. However, such recent Android versions do not reach the totality of the devices: according to the Android platform documentation, as of September 2020, 39.5% of them run Android Pie or higher. Thus, locking behavior remains a relevant threat.

Locking is generally preferred to the data encryption strategy because it does not require to operate on high-privileged data. There are, however, *crypto-ransomware* apps that perform data encryption. In this case, the attacker shows a window that could not necessarily be constantly displayed, because his main focus is to perform encryption of the user data (e.g., photos, videos, documents).

In both the cases, the created window includes a threatening message that instructs the user to pay the ransom, which will theoretically permit to *i)* suppress the permanent screen (locking case) or *ii)* decipher the data (crypto case).

3   Explanation Methods

Several studies in the past few years have proposed effective ways of explaining machine learning-based systems. Typically, their taxonomy can be made according to the following criteria [1]: *i) intrinsically-explainable* vs. *post-hoc* approaches, where machine-learning models are inherently interpretable due to their structure (e.g., decision trees) or specific methods are developed, respectively, *ii) local* vs. *global* explanations, where the former ones refer to a single prediction, while global explanations facilitate the comprehension of the whole logic of the model, and *iii) model-specific* vs. *model-agnostic* techniques, where the former ones allow interpreting only the algorithm for which they have been devised, whereas the last ones potentially apply to any model.

Since different models (e.g., SVMs, neural networks) are used for ransomware detection problems, in this work, we consider three popular *gradient-based* techniques that are all post-hoc, local, and model-agnostic. Therefore, they can be applied to any classifier, with the only requirement of having a differentiable decision function. These methods are also referred to as *attribution* techniques. As illustrated by Ancona *et al.* [5], this term means that an explanation of a sample consists of a vector, where each component is a real value—an *attribution*, or *relevance*, or *contribution*—associated with each feature. This value can be positive or negative. Therefore, in the case of a two-class setting, the sign indicates the class where the feature *moves* to.

More in detail, the three gradient-based techniques considered in this paper are: *Gradient, Gradient * Input*, and *Integrated Gradients*. The first one, also called *saliency*, consists of calculating the partial derivative of the prediction function with respect to each feature of the input sample vector. Gradient * Input has been proposed by Shrikumar *et al.* [19], which have addressed the problem of identifying the *most influential* (i.e., that has an impact on classification) features of a classifier in the case of sparse data. In fact, its computation includes the feature-wise multiplication of the gradient (the same as Gradient) to the input. In this way, features whose corresponding components are not present in the input sample exhibit a zero relevance. Lastly, Integrated Gradients, advanced by Sundararajan *et al.* [20], proposes to deal with non-linear classifiers, where the previously-described methods are not able to satisfy specific properties. Integrated Gradients also includes in its computation a *baseline*, i.e., a reference vector that models a neutral input (e.g., a black image for object recognition networks). Notably, when a zero-vector is used as the baseline and the classifier is linear, Integrated Gradients is equivalent to Gradient * Input.

4   Ransomware Detection and Explanations

In this Section, we present our method. More specifically, we illustrate the rationale behind the usual design process of Android ransomware detectors and the resulting features (Sect. 4.1); then, we describe our proposal for leveraging gradient-based techniques in the design phase (Sect. 4.2).

4.1   Detector Design

Android ransomware detection through machine learning has been studied in the literature. For example, in a previous work of us, we have shown that static analysis with a small set of System API calls alone suffices to discriminate Android ransomware samples with high accuracy [13,17]. In this paper, we aim at understanding if the features identified in such previous work turn out to be characteristic of the ransomware behavior, besides being effective for detection. We present a first proposal to point this out through explainability techniques. Therefore, within a static analysis setting, we choose to start exploring our proposed approach with a basic set up where we make use of two types of features: *i)* the occurrence of System API package calls and *ii)* the request of permissions. Before illustrating how we employ explanations for such a goal, we briefly describe the main characteristics of the chosen features in the following. First, the choice of system API calls originates from the fact that locking and encryption actions require core functionalities of the system, e.g., keeping windows constantly displayed or executing encryption routines. Building new libraries to perform these kinds of actions would be extremely inefficient. Therefore, attackers tend to rely on functions already included in the Android API system. For example, we expect the usage of APIs such as the `android.app.admin` package, which allows locking the screen or resetting the lock-screen password. For crypto-ransomware, it is likely to make use of functionalities for managing files or performing file encryption (e.g., `java.io`, `javax.crypto`). As introduced in Sect. 2, the Android operating system requires the app developer to request permission to use a particular functionality expressly. Depending on its dangerousness, that permission can be granted automatically or after explicit user agreement. This distinction is also explicitly stated in the Android platform documentation as *protection level*; therefore, it is straightforward to consider permissions as useful features.

4.2   Explaining Android Ransomware

In the following, we illustrate our proposal on how to take advantage of gradient-based explanations, aiming to identify a unique, reliable, and coherent set of relevant features that is independent of the specific *i)* model, *ii)* explanation method, and *iii)* dataset. Accordingly, we first describe the potential influence of these three elements and how we propose to address it. Then we illustrate our information extraction process.

Influencing Factors. A first concern arises around the choice of the classifiers. Since several types of them can be used with success for this detection problem, there could be as many different explanations as to the number of classifiers. For this reason, it is necessary to verify if the specific learning algorithm affects the output of the attributions. Therefore, a reasonable check to perform is to compare the explanation vectors within a set of plausible classifiers, one explanation technique at a time. Complementary to this aspect, we should get insights about which of the three explanation techniques is the most *accurate*, or to what extent they are equivalent. In this way, if all the explanations are mostly similar, it is possible only to consider one of them. Therefore, for each model, we compare its attributions across the different attribution techniques, similar to the procedure performed by Warnecke *et al.* [21]. It is worth noting that this approach gives rise to the following tricky issue: *how can we guarantee that similar attributions* *imply faithful explanations?* In this regard, in our setting, all the techniques are gradient-based, which are known to be reasonably effective; thus, we make the assumption that all of them are suitable despite their peculiarities.

The third concern comes from the influence of the data on the explanations; specifically, the possibility that the attributions are not associated with the data labeling, and, consequently, to what the model learns. For example, if attributions do not change after random ransomware samples are assigned to the trusted class, then the model would be bounded by the samples themselves, rather than by what it learned through the training phase. This aspect can be of particular interest for Gradient * Input and Integrated Gradients, where the input is part of their computation. In this case, we follow the method proposed by Adebayo *et al.* [2], where the ordinary attributions of each classifier are compared to the ones of a correspondent classifier trained with randomized labels.

Knowledge Extraction. The above concerns and our proposed answers for them allow us to approach the problem with more awareness about the caveats that these explainability techniques pose. Yet, there are a few other aspects that are worth focusing on. As the first remark, both the types of features of our setting (API calls and permission requests) are examples of *sparse* features. More specifically, each application uses only a small amount of APIs and permissions; consequently, each sample exhibits a few non-zero (used) features. Therefore, when using explanations to characterize the Android ransomware samples under test, we expect the attributions to be sparse as well. Moreover, as investigated by Lage *et al.* [11], sparsity is one of the factors that make explanations more *comprehensible* for the human expert. All other aspects being equal, we will then favor the techniques that satisfy this requirement the most.

Once a specific set of reliable attributions is established, we should find a strategy to analyze them and extract information concretely. In particular, looking at the predictions' relevance values, we aim to catch the *average* role of the features onto the samples' characterization. Since the attribution methods we have chosen provide us with a unique explanation for each prediction, it is necessary to define the concept of average in practice. Figure 1 shows an example of the distribution of the attributions obtainable with our setting, which we will describe in Sect. 5. In this Figure, two features representing two permissions are shown; they are calculated with Integrated Gradients against trusted samples for an MLP classifier. The significant aspect to observe is that, in our setting, the relevance distribution is typically bimodal. The attribution values could be zero for some samples and be condensed around a certain value level (positive if the feature converges towards the ransomware class; negative otherwise) for some others. Therefore, we could choose a synthetic metric that expresses the central tendency of this kind of distribution. In our work, *we consider the median value.* In this way, we highlight a feature as relevant when, for most of the samples, it does not exhibit a zero value. Although using a unique, synthetic measure could seem too limiting, we claim that useful information can actually be gathered by analyzing appropriate sets of samples, as we describe in Sect. 5.3.

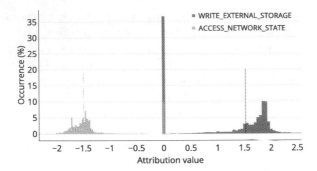

Fig. 1. Attribution distribution of two features, calculated for an MLP classifier through Integrated Gradients. Positive values associate the feature to the ransomware class, negative values to the trusted one. The dotted lines represent the median value

5   Experimental Analysis

In this Section, after illustrating the experiments' setting (Sect. 5.1), we perform preparatory tests (Sect. 5.2), which enable us to eventually analyze the generated explanations through different criteria (Sect. 5.3).

5.1   Setting

We operate in a two-class setting, where the learning algorithms are trained to classify the positive class of *ransomware* samples against the negative one of *trusted* samples. In the following, we briefly summarize the parameters and the implementation used for the experiments.

Dataset, Features, and Classifiers. We use the same dataset as [17], with 18295 trusted and 1945 ransomware samples, which span from 2011 to 2018 according to their `dex` last modification date. As explained in Sect. 2, recent Android versions limit the impact of older ransomware samples; however, these attacks are still relevant and suitable to assess the validity of our approach. The feature vector consists of 731 features. Among them, 196 represent the occurrence of the API *package* calls. We cumulate all the Android platform APIs until level 26 (Android Oreo). The remaining amount of features consists of checking the request of permissions, extracted from the `AndroidManifest.xml`: when one permission is used, we assign to the correspondent feature a 1; 0 otherwise. In this case, we cumulate the list of permissions until level 29 (Android 10). We indicate the permissions' names in capital letters. Since we want our approach to be model-agnostic, we consider three different classifiers: a linear support-vector machine (SVM) and a support-vector machine with RBF kernel (SVM-RBF), both implemented with `secml` [14]. The third classifier is a multi-layer perceptron (MLP), implemented with `Keras`. Each classifier has been trained and optimized in its parameters with a 2×5-fold cross-validation, using 50% of the dataset as the test set. Notably, we attain a 0.982 (std: 0.003) F1-macro score, which does not reach the state-of-the-art performance of a Random Forest classifier. However, the latter presents a non-differentiable decision function, thus making gradient-based techniques not usable.

Attribution Computation. The attributions are calculated on the best classifier of the first iteration from the cross-validation. To produce the explanations for SVM and SVM-RBF we use `secml`; for MLP, we use `DeepExplain` [4]. Since its implementation of Gradient does not return a signed attribution, we switch to `iNNvestigate` [3] in that case. We compute the attributions with respect to the ransomware class. Consequently, *a positive attribution value always identifies a feature that the classifier associates to ransomware.* As regards Integrated Gradients, since its computation includes an integral, this is approximated through a sum of n parts. We use $n = 130$. As a baseline, a zero-vector is used.

Correlation and Similarity Metrics. The experiments of Sect. 5.2 make use of three correlation metrics: *Pearson, cosine similarity, intersection size.* Given two attribution vectors, we consider the median value of each component over a certain set of samples, obtaining two vectors x and y that represent the input to such correlation methods. As per the first two ones, the output value lies in the range $[-1, 1]$. Intersection size follows the formulation used by Warnecke *et al.* [21]—i.e., $\mathrm{IS}(x, y) := \frac{|T_x \cap T_y|}{k}$—where T_x and T_y represent the sets of k features with the highest relevance from the attribution vectors x and y, respectively. The intersection size lies in the $[0, 1]$ range, where $\mathrm{IS} = 0$ indicates no overlap and $\mathrm{IS} = 1$ same top-k features. In our case, we choose $k = 15$. This number derives from our manual examination of the attributions since we have observed it represents the typical number of relevant features (i.e., whose values are not zero or close to) for a sample in our setting. Differently from the other two metrics, this one does not consider the sign of the attributions. Therefore, it is useful to catch the importance of a feature regardless of the assignment to a specific class.

5.2   Preliminary Evaluation

We start our investigation through a set of tests where we compare and correlate median explanation vectors according to different criteria. To make the explanation vectors under test comparable, we scale the attribution values in the range $[-1, 1]$.

Model Influence. In this first test, we correlate the attributions of the classifiers with each other, given a fixed explanation method. The results are shown in Fig. 2. It is possible to notice how the Integrated Gradients case shows particularly-high correlation values, which indicates that its explanations are quite similar to each other across the three considered classifiers. Conversely,

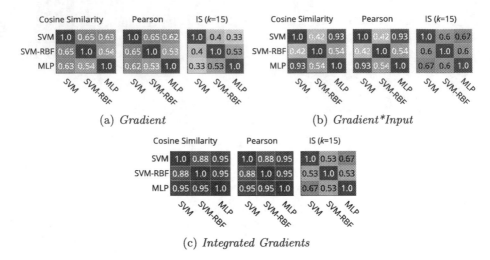

(a) *Gradient*   (b) *Gradient*Input*

(c) *Integrated Gradients*

Fig. 2. Model influence: correlation between attributions of each classifier

this is much less valid for Gradient, where each classifier provides a more dissimilar distribution of the attributions. This first result suggests that, in our setting, the impact of the specific learning algorithm to the explanations is quite modest, especially for the case of Integrated Gradients. In other words, each of the three considered classifiers could be *interchangeably* selected as the reference model for the analysis of the explanations.

Explanation Method Influence. Complementary to the previous experiment, we inspect to what extent the three explanation methods considered are similar. Therefore, for every classifier, we correlate the median attribution vectors of each technique. The results are shown in Fig. 3. This test highlights the fact that Gradient * Input and Integrated Gradients are very similar—and also equivalent for linear classifiers. On the contrary, as the previous tests have suggested as well, Gradient produces quite dissimilar explanations.

Data Influence. Finally, we evaluate the possible impact of the data on the explanations. To do so, we consider randomized labels for the samples of the training set, and we train new classifiers with these labels, forcing a 50% accuracy on the test set. Then we correlate the attribution vectors of these classifiers with those of the original ones. The results, grouped by explainability technique, are visible in Table 1. In this case, all the methods present similar results. Notably, only Gradient has nearly-to-zero correlation values, but the Pearson metric exhibits high *p-value*, making the results less reliable. Therefore, we can affirm that all the techniques, included Gradient * Input and Integrated Gradients, reflect what the model learns, without particularly being bounded by the samples.

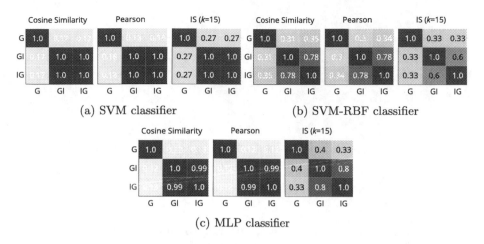

(a) SVM classifier   (b) SVM-RBF classifier

(c) MLP classifier

Fig. 3. Explanation method influence: correlation between attributions of each technique. G = Gradient, GI = Gradient * Input, IG = Integrated Gradients

Table 1. Data influence. The Pearson column also includes the p-value in brackets. CS = Cosine Similarity

Classifier	Gradient			Gradient * Input			Integrated Gradients		
	CS	Pearson	IS ($k = 15$)	CS	Pearson	IS ($k = 15$)	CS	Pearson	IS ($k = 15$)
SVM	0.01	0.02 (0.66)	0.00	0.29	0.29 (0.00)	0.27	0.29	0.29 (0.00)	0.27
SVM-RBF	0.00	−0.01 (0.81)	0.20	0.05	0.04 (0.22)	0.27	−0.22	−0.23 (0.00)	0.07
MLP	0.08	0.06 (0.09)	0.13	0.11	0.10 (0.00)	0.40	0.09	0.09 (0.01)	0.40

Overall, although all the techniques appear to be not that diverse, we have also observed by manual inspection that Gradient tends to produce less *sparse* explanations; i.e., a larger amount of features presents non-null relevance values. Ultimately, we claim the most suitable technique is, for our problem, one between Gradient * Input and Integrated Gradients.

5.3 Explanation Analysis

In this Section, we report the analysis of the explanations. Given the results from the previous Section, we examine the explanations provided by one single technique and classifier, assuming that the selected combination is representative for the detection of Android ransomware. Ultimately, *we choose the Integrated Gradients technique and the MLP classifier as such a reference.*

At this point, we aim at understanding how—on average—the features can make a distinction between the trusted and the ransomware class. Moreover, we specifically characterize the behavior of the ransomware samples and their families by associating the most relevant features to the corresponding action in the app. To do so, we group the samples according to different criteria. Differently from Sect. 5.2, the attributions are not normalized; consequently, there is no lower or upper bound to consider as reference for the magnitude of each attribution. If not stated differently, we consider the attributions calculated on all the dataset samples.

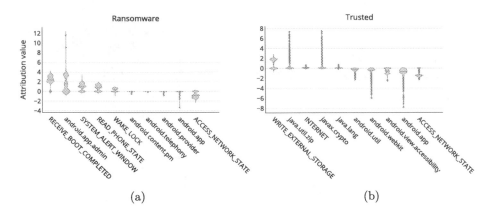

Fig. 4. Top-5 positive and top-5 negative feature attribution distribution for the ransomware (4a) and trusted (4b) samples of the dataset

Evaluation by Class. We consider the average explanations separately for the trusted and ransomware class. Figure 4 shows the distribution of the attribution values for the top-10 relevant features of the ransomware (Fig. 4a) and trusted (Fig. 4b) classes, grouped in the following manner: we sort the attribution values of each group according to the median value of each feature, and we show the top-5 features with positive values and the top-5 ones with negative values. In this way, we can inspect how the features gravitate towards one of the two classes. As a first observation, we can notice that the highest median values are associated with the features that go into the direction of the ransomware class, while trusted samples' attributions exhibit lower sparsity and much higher variance. This fact suggests that trusted samples need a higher number of features to have them described, being the set of apps much broader and diversified. Going into more detail, let us consider Fig. 4a. The top-5 positive features can be reasonably associated with the behavior of a generic malware. For example, `RECEIVE_BOOT_COMPLETED` enables an app to start after a device reboot, while `WAKE_LOCK` avoids it to be killed by the operating system. Moreover, we can see the presence of a *ransomware-specific* feature—`SYSTEM_ALERT_WINDOW`—that is a permission that allows the attacker to display an overlay window (see Sect. 2.1), and that is often tied with `android.app.admin`. The top-5 negative features, such as `ACCESS_NETWORK_STATE`, should be interpreted as typical of *non-ransomware* apps. Concerning the trusted samples, Fig. 4b shows as the most prominent feature `WRITE_EXTERNAL_STORAGE`, a permission that can be intuitively associated with crypto-ransomware apps. Other positive values (*non-trusted* features) that emerge are `javax.crypto` and `java.security`, which are characteristic of crypto-ransomware apps as well. Among the *trusted-specific* features, an illustrative example comes from `android.view.animation`, which definitely provides a set of functionalities that a ransomware developer is not interested in.

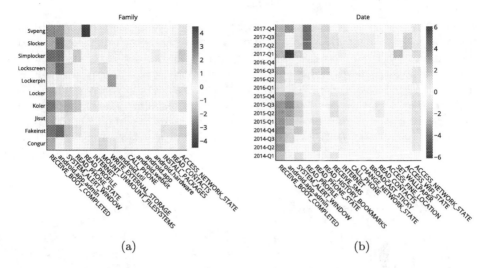

Fig. 5. Top positive (first 8 columns) and negative (last 8 columns) attributions' median values for two grouping criteria: family (a) and date (b)

Evaluation by Ransomware Family. Focusing on ransomware applications, we now inspect to what degree their different families exhibit shared and peculiar traits. `AVClass` [18] is used to extract the plausible families from the `VirusTotal` reports of each sample. Figure 5a shows the median values for the attributions of the main ransomware families of the dataset. We limit the analysis to the families with at least 30 samples, obtaining ten of them. As can be noticed by looking along the vertical axis of this plot, some features exhibit a stable relevance level across most of the families. In other words, features like `SYSTEM_ALERT_WINDOW` can be considered to be a common characteristic of all the ransomware apps. Looking at the properties of each family (rows of the plot), possible peculiarities can be noticed, such as for `Svpeng`. In this case, this family presents a strongly positive relevance of `READ_PROFILE`. To investigate the reason for that, we find a representative sample by picking the one that is closest to the median attributions, using the `cosine similarity` function. We obtain one locker ransomware[1] that, after hiding as a porn app, pretends to be the FBI enforcement and shows the victims messages that include the threat to send a supposed criminal record to their contacts, which are explicitly shown in the message. These contacts are gathered through the `READ_PROFILE` permission, which explains its relevance.

Evaluation by Ransomware Date. The analysis of the evolution of malware attacks is particularly relevant for machine learning-based detection systems, which should be carefully evaluated over time to avoid experimental bias [15]. Therefore, it could be useful to understand what features do and do not possess

---

[1] MD5: `8a7fea6a5279e8f64a56aa192d2e7cf0`.

a certain level of relevance, regardless of the ransomware evolution. To do so, we extract the last modification date from the `dex` file of each `apk`. We discard the samples with non-plausible dates (e.g., the ones with a *Unix epoch* date), and we group the remaining ones in windows of three months. The result is shown in Fig. 5b. As can be noticed, some features maintain pretty much the same relevance values over time, which makes them *resilient* to new ransomware variants. In other words, some features describe essential components for ransomware samples. Figure 5b also shows that the relevance of other features could depend on the spread of a particular family. For example, `READ_PROFILE` starts being relevant in 2017, when the previously-described `Svpeng` appeared.

6   Contributions, Limitations, and Future Work

In this work, we presented an initial proposal for a method that eases designers in finding the features that mostly characterize Android ransomware. First, we developed a set of empirical tests that allows selecting, among several combinations of explanation methods and classifiers, a unique setting that best represents the domain under analysis. Second, by looking at the *average* importance of the features within domain-specific sets of samples, we showed the Android ransomware's main traits that effectively distinguish malicious samples from legitimate ones, and the ransomware's evolution over time in terms of application components. Our work has corroborated previous evidence that API calls effectively catch the peculiar actions operated by ransomware apps. Moreover, permissions turned out to be quite impactful as well.

Concerning the limitations of our work, we claim that the two-class system we considered, where ransomware apps are evaluated against legitimate ones, does not fully capture the behavior shared with generic malware. Another limitation is related to the usage of attribution techniques, i.e., the fact that it is not possible to understand how the features interact with each other. This is one of the open issues in the field of interpretability [8,10], and we think discovering high-level *concepts* might greatly improve the understanding of the applications under analysis. As future work, we plan to refine our approach by making it more systematic and, above all, further inspecting the practical difference between each gradient-based technique. In this way, it could be possible to *combine* the complementary peculiarities of each one, instead of selecting a single technique. Lastly, being Android ransomware a case study, we aim to generalize our method to other malware detection problems.

References

1. Adadi, A., Berrada, M.: Peeking inside the black-box: a survey on explainable artificial intelligence (XAI). IEEE Access **6**, 52138–52160 (2018). https://doi.org/10.1109/ACCESS.2018.2870052
2. Adebayo, J., Gilmer, J., Muelly, M., Goodfellow, I., Hardt, M., Kim, B.: Sanity checks for saliency maps. In: Advances in Neural Information Processing Systems 31, pp. 9505–9515. Curran Associates, Inc., October 2018

3. Alber, M., et al.: iNNvestigate neural networks! August 2018. http://arxiv.org/abs/1808.04260
4. Ancona, M.: DeepExplain. https://github.com/marcoancona/DeepExplain
5. Ancona, M., Ceolini, E., Öztireli, C., Gross, M.: Gradient-based attribution methods. In: Samek, W., Montavon, G., Vedaldi, A., Hansen, L.K., Müller, K.-R. (eds.) Explainable AI: Interpreting, Explaining and Visualizing Deep Learning. LNCS (LNAI), vol. 11700, pp. 169–191. Springer, Cham (2019). https://doi.org/10.1007/978-3-030-28954-6_9
6. Barredo Arrieta, A., et al.: Explainable Artificial Intelligence (XAI): concepts, taxonomies, opportunities and challenges toward responsible AI. Inf. Fusion **58**(2019), 82–115 (2020). https://doi.org/10.1016/j.inffus.2019.12.012
7. Demetrio, L., Biggio, B., Lagorio, G., Roli, F., Armando, A.: Explaining vulnerabilities of deep learning to adversarial malware binaries. In: Proceedings of the Third Italian Conference on Cyber Security 2019. CEUR-WS.org, Pisa, February 2019
8. Ghorbani, A., Wexler, J., Zou, J., Kim, B.: Towards automatic concept-based explanations. In: Advances in Neural Information Processing Systems. pp. 9273–9282. Curran Associates Inc., Vancouver, February 2019
9. Ilyas, A., Santurkar, S., Tsipras, D., Engstrom, L., Tran, B., Madry, A.: Adversarial examples are not bugs, they are features. In: Advances in Neural Information Processing Systems 32 (NIPS 2019), pp. 125–136. Curran Associates Inc., Vancouver (2019)
10. Kim, B., et al.: Interpretability beyond feature attribution: quantitative testing with concept activation vectors (TCAV). In: 35th International Conference on Machine Learning (ICML 2018), vol. 80, pp. 2668–2677. Stockholm, July 2018
11. Lage, I., et al.: An evaluation of the human-interpretability of explanation. In: Proceedings of the AAAI Conference on Human Computation and Crowdsourcing, vol. 7, pp. 59–67. AAAI Press, Honolulu, January 2019
12. Lipton, Z.C.: The mythos of model interpretability. Queue **16**(3), 31–57 (2018). https://doi.org/10.1145/3236386.3241340
13. Maiorca, D., Mercaldo, F., Giacinto, G., Visaggio, C.A., Martinelli, F.: R-PackDroid: API package-based characterization and detection of mobile ransomware. In: Proceedings of the Symposium on Applied Computing - SAC '17, pp. 1718–1723. ACM Press, New York (2017). https://doi.org/10.1145/3019612.3019793, http://dl.acm.org/citation.cfm?doid=3019612.3019793
14. Melis, M., Demontis, A., Pintor, M., Sotgiu, A., Biggio, B.: secml: a python library for secure and explainable machine learning. arXiv preprint arXiv:1912.10013 (12 2019). http://arxiv.org/abs/1912.10013
15. Pendlebury, F., Pierazzi, F., Jordaney, R., Kinder, J., Cavallaro, L.: TESSERACT: eliminating experimental bias in malware classification across space and time. In: 28th USENIX Security Symposium (USENIX Security 19), pp. 729–746. USENIX Association, Santa Clara, August 2019
16. Preece, A., Harborne, D., Braines, D., Tomsett, R., Chakraborty, S.: Stakeholders in explainable AI. In: AAAI Fall Symposium on Artificial Intelligence in Government and Public Sector. Arlington, Virginia, USA (2018)
17. Scalas, M., Maiorca, D., Mercaldo, F., Visaggio, C.A., Martinelli, F., Giacinto, G.: On the effectiveness of system API-related information for Android ransomware detection. Comput. Secur. **86**, 168–182 (2019). https://doi.org/10.1016/j.cose.2019.06.004, https://linkinghub.elsevier.com/retrieve/pii/S0167404819301178

18. Sebastián, M., Rivera, R., Kotzias, P., Caballero, J.: AVCLASS: a tool for massive malware labeling. In: Monrose, F., Dacier, M., Blanc, G., Garcia-Alfaro, J. (eds.) RAID 2016. LNCS, vol. 9854, pp. 230–253. Springer, Cham (2016). https://doi.org/10.1007/978-3-319-45719-2_11

19. Shrikumar, A., Greenside, P., Shcherbina, A., Kundaje, A., Shcherbina, A., Kundaje, A.: Not just a black box: learning important features through propagating activation differences. In: 34th International Conference on Machine Learning, ICML 2017, vol. 7, pp. 4844–4866. JMLR.org, Sydney, NSW, Australia, May 2016. https://doi.org/10.5555/3305890.3306006

20. Sundararajan, M., Taly, A., Yan, Q.: Axiomatic attribution for deep networks. In: Proceedings of the 34th International Conference on Machine Learning, pp. 3319–3328. JMLR.org, Sidney, March 2017. http://arxiv.org/abs/1703.01365

21. Warnecke, A., Arp, D., Wressnegger, C., Rieck, K.: Evaluating explanation methods for deep learning in security. In: 5th IEEE European Symposium on Security and Privacy (Euro S&P 2020), Genova, September 2020

Reliability of eXplainable Artificial Intelligence in Adversarial Perturbation Scenarios

Antonio Galli(iD), Stefano Marrone(✉)(iD), Vincenzo Moscato(iD),
and Carlo Sansone(iD)

University of Naples Federico II, Via Claudio 21, 80125 Napoli, Italy
{antonio.galli,stefano.marrone,vincenzo.moscato,carlo.sansone}@unina.it

Abstract. Nowadays, Deep Neural Networks (DNNs) are widely adopted in several fields, including critical systems, medicine, self-guided vehicles etc. Among the reasons sustaining this spread there are the higher generalisation ability and performance levels that DNNs usually obtain when compared to classical machine learning models. Nonetheless, their black-box nature raises ethical and judicial concerns that lead to a lack of confidence in their use in sensitive applications. For this reason, recently there has been a growing interest in eXplainable Artificial Intelligence (XAI), a field providing tools, techniques and algorithms designed to generate interpretable explanations, comprehensible to humans, for the decisions made by a machine learning model. However, it has been demonstrated that DNNs are susceptible to Adversarial Perturbations (APs), namely procedures intended to mislead a target model by means of an almost imperceptible noise. The relation existing between XAI and AP is extremely of interest since it can help improve trustworthiness in AI-based systems. To this aim, it is important to increase awareness of the risks associated with the use of XAI in critical contexts, in a world where APs are present and easy to perform. On this line, we quantitatively analyse the impact that APs have on XAI in terms of differences in the explainability maps. Since this work wants to be just an intuitive proof-of-concept, the aforementioned experiments are run in a fashion easy to understand and to quantify, by using publicly available dataset and algorithms. Results show that AP can strongly affect the XAI outcomes, even in the case of a failed attack, highlighting the need for further research in this field.

1 Introduction

In recent years, Artificial Intelligence (AI) has reached a significant advance providing solutions in many application areas. In particular, there has been a massive increase in the use of Machine Learning (ML) algorithms to solve tasks

Electronic supplementary material The online version of this chapter (https://doi.org/10.1007/978-3-030-68796-0_18) contains supplementary material, which is available to authorized users.

A. Del Bimbo et al. (Eds.): ICPR 2020 Workshops, LNCS 12663, pp. 243–256, 2021.
https://doi.org/10.1007/978-3-030-68796-0_18

in different fields of science, business and social workflow. This spread is related in part to the intensification of research in Deep Learning (DL), a set of artificial neural networks characterised, among other things, by a high number of layers.

This causes deep neural networks to have a larger number of parameters, making them complex to understand and more difficult to interpret, further pushing toward the idea of considering them as obscure black-box models. Since these black-box learning models are increasingly used to make important predictions in critical contexts [5,13], the demand for transparency is growing. Indeed, the risk is to create and use decisions that are not justifiable, legitimate or simply do not allow detailed explanations of their behaviour [10].

Thus, explanations supporting the output of a model are crucial in many areas such as precision medicine, autonomous vehicles, security and finance. For the above mentioned reasons, the number of research and use of eXplainable Artificial Intelligence (XAI) is rapidly growing. The interest for XAI has also been manifested by governments, with the European Regulation on General Data Protection (GDPR) showing the important realisation of ethics [2], trust [31], prejudice [3] of IA, as well as the impact of adversarial perturbation [18] in deceiving classification decisions, especially in the case of Convolutional Neural Networks (CNNs).

The term Adversarial Perturbation (AP) refers to the whole of techniques that inject an image with a suitable, hardly perceptible, perturbation (noise) to mislead a target machine learning model. Since their introduction [9], AP algorithms have been used against a wide variety of models in several application domains [1]. Considering APs evolution and the spread of XAI in critical contexts, it was just a matter of time before researchers started working on the use of APs against XAI algorithms. On this line, a very recent work [17] proposes a black-box attack against XAI in security-critical contexts, intending to raise the attention on the problem.

This work aims to increase awareness of the risks associated with the use of XAI in critical contexts. On this line, we quantitatively analyse the impact that APs have on XAI in terms of differences in the explainability maps. Since this work wants to be just an intuitive proof-of-concept, the aforementioned experiments are run in a fashion easy to understand and to quantify, by using publicly available dataset and algorithms.

The rest of the paper is organised as follows: Sect. 2 reports the related works, analysing pros and cons of the analysis performed so far; Sect. 3 describes the considered experimental setup; Sect. 4 reports the obtained results; finally, Sect. 5 draws some conclusions.

2   Related Works

With the spread of Convolutional Neural Networks (CNNs) it was only a matter of time before researchers started analysing aspects associated with their decision making process and weakness. The former is what laid the foundation for eXplainable Artificial Intelligence (XAI) [10], a set of methods and algorithms intended to shed lights on the motivations that made an AI model to take a given decision. Similarly, Adversarial Perturbations (APs) [1] are a good example for the latter, with their ability to mislead a target CNN.

Nowadays, many researchers are introducing XAI methods as part of the development loop of machine learning models, in applications ranging from biomedical to security. For example, in [25] the authors used Grad-CAM and Guided BackPropagation (GBP) [28] to analyse the clinical coherence of the features learned by a CNN for automated grading of brain tumours in MRI. More recently, Chen et al. [4] used Gradient Class Activation Mapping (Grad-CAM) [27] to generate the explainability map of a model, showing that it focused its attention in high-dimensional bands excited by structure resonance.

Focusing on adversarial perturbations, the vast majority of the works target the development of new perturbation strategies or the design of attacks against some critical applications. Nonetheless, in some previous works, we showed that APs can also be leveraged to increase fairness and security with AI. In particular, in [20] we showed how to design an adversarial patch able to prevent ethnicity recognition in automatic face analysis, while in [21] we attacked a fingerprint authentication system to shed lights on light-heartedly use of CNN in security-critical applications.

As illustrated by the aforementioned example, XAI and APs have the potential to help the improvement of both accountability and reliability of CNNs. Some authors tried to make a step further by "contaminating XAI" with APs and vice-versa. In [16] the authors exploit XAI to make OnePixel [29] (a famous AP algorithm) more robust. On the other hand, in [8] the authors proposed a way to detect APs by means of XAI, by using the latter as a way to extract a "fingerprint" of the image.

Besides these experiments, the relation existing between XAI and APs is extremely of interest, since it can help increase AI reliability and trustworthiness of AI-based systems. On this line, in [32] the authors analysed the propagation of adversarial noise through CNNs layers, by measuring the similarity between the feature map of clean and of adversarially perturbed images. Similarly, in [6] the authors analyse how the "strength" of the noise affects the prediction accuracy. Finally, in [12] the authors demonstrated how XAI and APs are connected by a generalised form of hitting set duality, also proposing an algorithm to move from one to the other.

The latter three examples are the closest to this paper. However, each of them lacks some aspects, such as a "human interpretable" outcome [32], a quantitative analysis of the results [6] or experiments and proofs made on more realistic datasets [12].

3   Methods

To quantify the effects of APs on XAI algorithms, we defined a set of experiments intended to measure the obtained impact while producing outcomes easy to understand. To help to match the latter point, we focused on the image classification task for its intuitive interpretation. Nonetheless, to make the reported analysis rigorous, we:

- perform the experiments on Dog vs Cat [7] and UIUC Sports Event Dataset (Event8) [19], two datasets chosen for their characteristics. More in details, the first dataset represents a very human interpretable problem, consisting in the binary classification of dogs and cats images. The second dataset describes a more complex scenario, still easily interpretable by a human observer, involving the classification of images in eight different sport events categories (e.g. rowing, sailing, etc.);
- used four different CNNs, pre-trained on ImageNet and fine-tuned on the considered datasets. Among all the available networks we selected those that, for structure and characteristics, allow us to cover a wide part of the current literature in image classification. In particular, we used AlexNet [15], ResNet18 [11], ResNet34 [11] and EfficientNet-B0 [30]. Table 1 reports a brief recap of their characteristics and performance on the ImageNet dataset;
- we analysed the effects of two different adversarial perturbation algorithms, chosen for their intuitiveness (the first) and diffusion (the second). The first algorithm used is the iterative Fast Gradient Sign Method (iFGSM) [18], leveraging the sign of the prediction gradient (with respect to the input's class) to craft an additive perturbation. The second is DeepFool [22], an efficient iterative method exploiting a locally linearized version of the loss to generate a series of additive perturbations;
- considered two different versions of a XAI method, Layered Grad-CAM and Guided Grad-CAM [27]. Layered Grad-CAM calculates the target output gradients with respect to the selected layer, multiplying the average gradient for each channel by the level activations. Finally, the results are summed over all channels. On the other hand, Guided Grad-CAM is an extension of Grad-CAM which calculates the element produced by guided backpropagation with upsampled Grad-CAM attributes. In particular, the Grad-CAM attributes are calculated with respect to the layer provided in input, and the attributes are upsampled in order to match the size of the input.

Table 1. List of selected CNNs, evaluated on the ImageNet classification challenge [26]. For each network, the top-1 and top-5 error, together with the number of parameters and layers (depth) are shown. Reported numbers refer to the corresponding PyTorch [24] implementation (excluding EfficientNet, for which we refer to [30]).

Model	Top-1 error	Top-5 error	Parameters	Depth
AlexNet [15]	43.45	20.91	60,965,224	8
Resnet18 [11]	30.24	10.92	11,177,538	18
Resnet34 [11]	26.70	8.58	21,285,698	34
EfficientNet-B0 [30]	22.90	6.70	5,330,571	18

The choice of publicly available datasets and of famous and diffused architectures is intended to make the reported examples as reproducible as possible. With the same aim, we used some open-source toolboxes for both XAI and AP algorithms. In particular, the interpretation of trained models and related outputs is based on Captum [14], a library of interpretability models for PyTorch offering a series of attribution algorithms that allow understanding the importance of input characteristics, hidden neurons and layers. Similarly, for the adversarial perturbations, we used the Adversarial Robustness Toolbox (ART) [23], a Python library designed to assess machine learning security against several adversarial threats.

4   Results

Within the experimental setup described in the previous section, we run the adversarial perturbation algorithms against all the considered CNNs, trained on both datasets, evaluating the output of the XAI methods before and after the adversarial attacks (Fig. 1). To this aim, defined X_c and X_p as the explainability maps obtained on the clean and perturbed images respectively, we measure the Correlation Coefficient (CC) and the Dice Similarity Coefficient (DSC) as

$$CC = \frac{\sum \left(X_c - \overline{X_c}\right)\left(X_p - \overline{X_p}\right)}{\sqrt{\left(\sum \left(X_c - \overline{X_c}\right)^2\right)\left(\sum \left(X_p - \overline{X_p}\right)^2\right)}} \tag{1}$$

$$DSC = 2 * \frac{n(X_c \cap X_p)}{n(X_c) + n(C_p)} \tag{2}$$

where $n(\cdot)$ is the number elements in each XAI map. It is worth noting that in Eq. 1 the sum is over map elements, while in Eq. 2 X_c and X_p are binary maps obtained by thresholding (using 0.9 as threshold) the corresponding probability maps.

Since we want to measure the impact of APs on XAI in a realistic scenario, we set realistic parameters for the AP algorithms. In particular, for iFGSM method we set $\epsilon = 0.1$, while for DeepFool method we set the maximum number of iterations $i_{max} = 100$ and $\epsilon = 10^{-06}$. As a result, the adversarial attacks may not be successful for all the considered images. Therefore, the results are reported by dividing the cases in which the adversarial perturbation was successful and the cases in which it failed.

We start by reporting the boxplots for the CC and for the DSC evaluated on the explainability maps (before and after the perturbation) for all the considered CNNs, by varying the dataset, the XAI and the AP algorithms. All the plots have been drawn in couples, with green bar referring to positive XAI maps

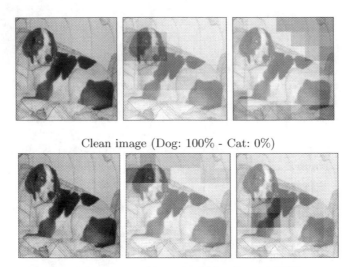

Clean image (Dog: 100% - Cat: 0%)

Perturbed image (Dog: 23.41% - Cat: 76.59%)

Fig. 1. Example of explanation maps for a clean (top row) and for a successfully perturbed (bottom row) image of a dog. In green, the explanation map for the portions of the image that have contributed to the selected output (dog in the case of the clean image, cat in the case of the perturbed image). In red, the explanation map for the portions of the image that have contributed to the non-selected output (cat in the case of the clean image, dog in the case of the perturbed image). It is worth noting that the portion of the image contributing to the predicted class is in both cases close to the dog's face. (Color figure online)

(i.e. the portion of the image that contributed to the predicted output) and red bar referring to negative XAI maps (i.e. the portion of the image that contributed to the non-predicted output).

Figures 2 and 3 report the results obtained on the Dogs vs Cats dataset, under the DeepFool attack, using the Layered Grad-CAM algorithm for successfully perturbed images (the former) and failed-attacks ones (the latter). Similarly, Figs. 4 and 5 reports the DSC measured under the same experimental settings. Results show that, in all the cases and for all the CNNs, the XAI masks strongly vary after the perturbation, for both the positive and negative masks, as well as for successful and failed attacks. Interestingly, from a visual perception perspective (Figs. 6 and 7), the portion of the image contributing to the predicted class is in both cases over the subject face (thus even when the network wrongly classifies the images into the opposite class).

Figures 8 and 9 report the same set of results, obtained for the same dataset and with the same AP algorithm, but by using Guided Grad-CAM (GGC) as XAI procedure. At a first sight, the plots seem to suggest that the perturbation

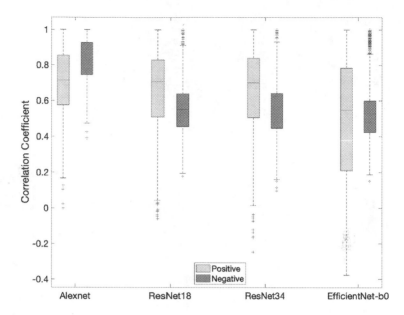

Fig. 2. Correlation Coefficient (CC) between the Layered Grad-CAM outputs before and after the execution of DeepFool, for all the images in the Dogs vs Cats dataset for which the attack succeeded.

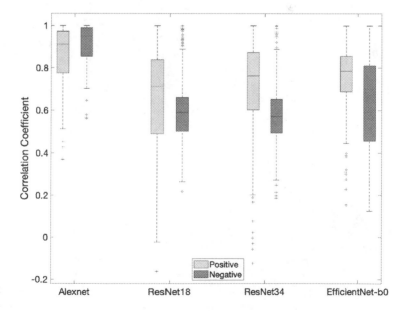

Fig. 3. Correlation Coefficient (CC) between the Layered Grad-CAM outputs before and after the execution of DeepFool, for all the images in the Dogs vs Cats dataset for which the attack failed.

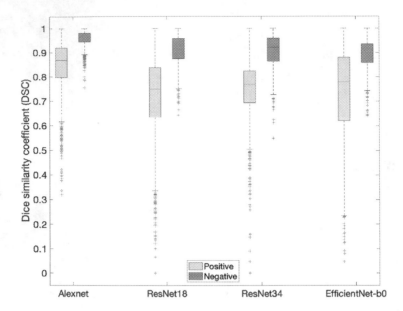

Fig. 4. Dice Similarity Coefficient (DSC) between the Layered Grad-CAM outputs before and after the execution of DeepFool, for all the images in the Dogs vs Cats dataset for which the attack succeeded.

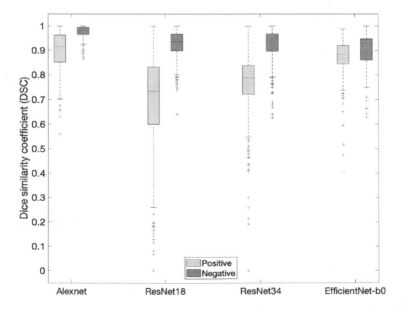

Fig. 5. Dice Similarity Coefficient (DSC) between the Layered Grad-CAM outputs before and after the execution of DeepFool, for all the images in the Dogs vs Cats dataset for which the attack failed.

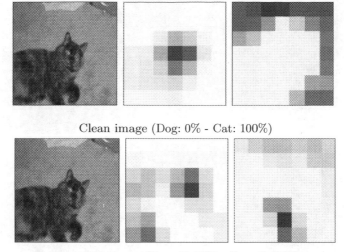

Clean image (Dog: 0% - Cat: 100%)

Perturbed image (Dog: 51.93% - Cat: 48.07%)

Fig. 6. Example of explanation maps for a clean (top row) and for a successfully perturbed (bottom row) image of a cat. In green, the explanation map for the portions of the image that have contributed to the selected output (cat in the case of the clean image, dog in the case of the perturbed image). In red, the explanation map for the portions of the image that have contributed to the non-selected output (dog in the case of the clean image, cat in the case of the perturbed image). It is worth noting that the portion of the image contributing to the predicted class is in both cases over the cat's face. (Color figure online)

did not affect this scenario. However, as clearly shown in Figs. 10 and 11, those results are because of the huge number of pixels that remained unchanged after the perturbation (as GGC works as pixel level). Indeed, if we measure the CC only over the portions of the explanation maps that actually changed, the values drop (on average) of ~0.4.

Similar results have been obtained for the FGSM perturbation algorithms and for the Event8 dataset (reported only in the supplementary material document due to paper length limits), suggesting that the number of classes and the perturbation algorithms do not change the effects that adversarial perturbations have on explainability maps.

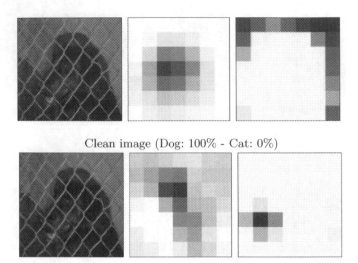

Clean image (Dog: 100% - Cat: 0%)

Perturbed image (Dog: 56.09% - Cat: 43.91%)

Fig. 7. Example of explanation maps for a clean (top row) and for an un-successfully perturbed (bottom row) image of a dog. In green, the explanation map for the portions of the image that have contributed to the selected output (dog in both cases). In red, the explanation map for the portions of the image that have contributed to the non-selected output (cat in both cases). It is worth noting that the portion of the image contributing to the predicted class is in both cases over the dog's face. (Color figure online)

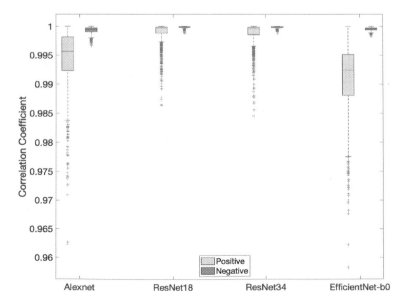

Fig. 8. Correlation Coefficient (CC) between the Guided Grad-CAM outputs before and after the execution of DeepFool, for all the images in the Dogs vs Cats dataset for which the attack succeeded.

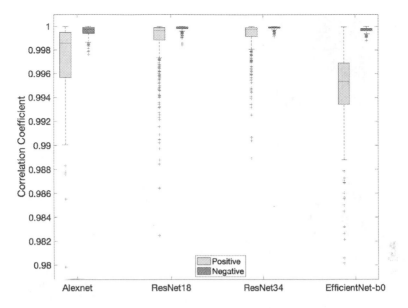

Fig. 9. Correlation Coefficient (CC) between the Guided Grad-CAM outputs before and after the execution of DeepFool, for all the images in the Dogs vs Cats dataset for which the attack failed.

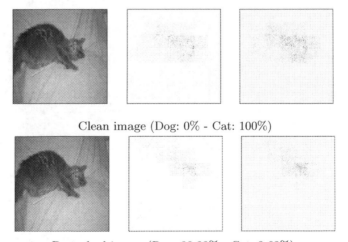

Fig. 10. Example of explanation maps for a clean (top row) and for a successfully perturbed (bottom row) image of a cat. In green, the explanation map for the portions of the image that have contributed to the selected output (cat in the case of the clean image, dog in the case of the perturbed image). In red, the explanation map for the portions of the image that have contributed to the non-selected output (dog in the case of the clean image, cat in the case of the perturbed image). It is worth noting that the portion of the image contributing to the predicted class is in both cases close to the cat's face. (Color figure online)

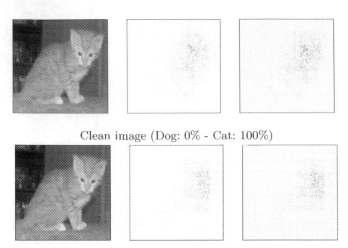

Clean image (Dog: 0% - Cat: 100%)

Perturbed image (Dog: 49.90% - Cat: 50.10%)

Fig. 11. Example of explanation maps for a clean (top row) and for an un-successfully perturbed (bottom row) image of a cat. In green, the explanation map for the portions of the image that have contributed to the selected output (cat in both cases). In red, the explanation map for the portions of the image that have contributed to the non-selected output (dog in both cases). It is worth noting that the portion of the image contributing to the predicted class is in both cases close to the cat's face. (Color figure online)

5   Conclusions

The raise of Adversarial Perturbations (APs) and the spread of eXplainable Artificial Intelligence (XAI) in critical contexts are pushing researchers in analysing the risks that the former can have on the latter. If, on one hand, some works are analysing this problematic relation [6,12,32], on the other some authors are already designing attacks in critical scenarios [17].

The aim of this paper was to increase awareness on the risks associated with the use of XAI in critical contexts by providing a quantitative analysis of the impact that adversarial perturbations have on XAI methods in terms of differences in the explainability maps. To this aim, we defined a set of experiments intended to measure the obtained impact while producing outcomes easy to understand. To help to match the latter point, we focused on the image classification task for its intuitive interpretation. Nonetheless, to make the reported analysis rigorous, we considered four different Convolutional Neural Networks (CNNs), two AP algorithms, two XAI methods and two public datasets.

Reported results show that APs can strongly affect the XAI outcomes, even in the case of a failed attack. In particular, the Correlation Coefficient (CC) and Dice Similarity Coefficient (DSC) distributions suggest not only that the injected perturbations are able to mislead the target CNN, but also that the effects on the XAI maps are not deterministic. Indeed, while the maps themselves are different before and after the perturbation, this difference is not easily perceptible by a human operator unaware of the attack, since the portion of the images that support the decision taken by the networks are almost the same. Interestingly, this happens for all the considered networks and for all the considered XAI and AP algorithms. Even the number of classes in the used dataset does not seem to affect the reported behaviour. Future works will further analyse the reported aspects, also by considering the effects on bigger datasets (with hundred of classes) and by taking into account black-box AP algorithms.

References

1. Akhtar, N., Mian, A.: Threat of adversarial attacks on deep learning in computer vision: a survey. IEEE Access **6**, 14410–14430 (2018)
2. Cath, C., Wachter, S., Mittelstadt, B., Taddeo, M., Floridi, L.: Artificial intelligence and the 'good society': the US, EU, and UK approach. Sci. Eng. Ethics **24**(2), 505–528 (2018)
3. Challen, R., Denny, J., Pitt, M., Gompels, L., Edwards, T., Tsaneva-Atanasova, K.: Artificial intelligence, bias and clinical safety. BMJ Qual. Saf. **28**(3), 231–237 (2019)
4. Chen, H.Y., Lee, C.H.: Vibration signals analysis by explainable artificial intelligence (XAI) approach: application on bearing faults diagnosis. IEEE Access **8**, 134246–134256 (2020)
5. Chugh, T., Cao, K., Jain, A.K.: Fingerprint spoof buster: use of minutiae-centered patches. IEEE Trans. Inf. Forensics Secur. **13**(9), 2190–2202 (2018)
6. Das, A., Rad, P.: Opportunities and challenges in explainable artificial intelligence (XAI): a survey. arXiv preprint arXiv:2006.11371 (2020)
7. Elson, J., Douceur, J.R., Howell, J., Saul, J.: Asirra: a captcha that exploits interest-aligned manual image categorization. In: ACM Conference on Computer and Communications Security, vol. 7, pp. 366–374 (2007)
8. Fidel, G., Bitton, R., Shabtai, A.: When explainability meets adversarial learning: Detecting adversarial examples using shap signatures. In: 2020 International Joint Conference on Neural Networks (IJCNN), pp. 1–8. IEEE (2020)
9. Goodfellow, I.J., Shlens, J., Szegedy, C.: Explaining and harnessing adversarial examples. arXiv preprint arXiv:1412.6572 (2014)
10. Gunning, D.: Explainable artificial intelligence (XAI). Defense Advanced Research Projects Agency (DARPA), nd Web, vol. 2(2) (2017)
11. He, K., Zhang, X., Ren, S., Sun, J.: Deep residual learning for image recognition. In: Proceedings of the IEEE Conference on Computer Vision and Pattern Recognition, pp. 770–778 (2016)
12. Ignatiev, A., Narodytska, N., Marques-Silva, J.: On relating explanations and adversarial examples. In: Advances in Neural Information Processing Systems, pp. 15883–15893 (2019)
13. Kelly, L., Sachan, S., Ni, L., Almaghrabi, F., Allmendinger, R., Chen, Y.W.: Explainable artificial intelligence for digital forensics: Opportunities, challenges and a drug testing case study. In: Digital Forensic Science. IntechOpen (2020)
14. Kokhlikyan, N., et al.: Captum: a unified and generic model interpretability library for pytorch. arXiv preprint arXiv:2009.07896 (2020)
15. Krizhevsky, A., Sutskever, I., Hinton, G.E.: Imagenet classification with deep convolutional neural networks. In: Advances in Neural Information Processing Systems, pp. 1097–1105 (2012)

16. Kumarl Ibrahim Ben Daya, D., Vats, K., Feng, J., Taylor, G., Wong, A.: Beyond explainability: leveraging interpretability for improved adversarial learning. In: Proceedings of the IEEE Conference on Computer Vision and Pattern Recognition Workshops, pp. 16–19 (2019)

17. Kuppa, A., Le-Khac, N.A.: Black box attacks on explainable artificial intelligence (XAI) methods in cyber security. In: 2020 International Joint Conference on Neural Networks (IJCNN), pp. 1–8. IEEE (2020)

18. Kurakin, A., Goodfellow, I., Bengio, S.: Adversarial examples in the physical world. arXiv preprint arXiv:1607.02533 (2016)

19. Li, L.J., Fei-Fei, L.: What, where and who? classifying events by scene and object recognition. In: 2007 IEEE 11th International Conference on Computer Vision, pp. 1–8. IEEE (2007)

20. Marrone, S., Sansone, C.: An adversarial perturbation approach against CNN-based soft biometrics detection. In: 2019 International Joint Conference on Neural Networks (IJCNN), pp. 1–8. IEEE (2019)

21. Marrone, S., Sansone, C.: Adversarial perturbations against fingerprint based authentication systems. In: 2019 International Conference on Biometrics (ICB), pp. 1–6. IEEE (2019)

22. Moosavi-Dezfooli, S.M., Fawzi, A., Frossard, P.: Deepfool: a simple and accurate method to fool deep neural networks. In: Proceedings of the IEEE Conference on Computer Vision and Pattern Recognition, pp. 2574–2582 (2016)

23. Nicolae, M.I., et al.: Adversarial robustness toolbox v1. 0.0. arXiv preprint arXiv:1807.01069 (2018)

24. Paszke, A., et al.: Pytorch: an imperative style, high-performance deep learning library. In: Advances in Neural Information Processing Systems, pp. 8026–8037 (2019)

25. Pereira, S., Meier, R., Alves, V., Reyes, M., Silva, C.A.: Automatic brain tumor grading from MRI data using convolutional neural networks and quality assessment. In: Stoyanov, D., et al. (eds.) MLCN/DLF/IMIMIC -2018. LNCS, vol. 11038, pp. 106–114. Springer, Cham (2018). https://doi.org/10.1007/978-3-030-02628-8_12

26. Russakovsky, O., et al.: Imagenet large scale visual recognition challenge. Int. J. Comput. Vision **115**(3), 211–252 (2015)

27. Selvaraju, R.R., Cogswell, M., Das, A., Vedantam, R., Parikh, D., Batra, D.: Grad-cam: visual explanations from deep networks via gradient-based localization. In: Proceedings of the IEEE International Conference on Computer Vision, pp. 618–626 (2017)

28. Springenberg, J.T., Dosovitskiy, A., Brox, T., Riedmiller, M.: Striving for simplicity: The all convolutional net. arXiv preprint arXiv:1412.6806 (2014)

29. Su, J., Vargas, D.V., Sakurai, K.: One pixel attack for fooling deep neural networks. IEEE Trans. Evol. Comput. **23**(5), 828–841 (2019)

30. Tan, M., Le, Q.V.: Efficientnet: rethinking model scaling for convolutional neural networks. arXiv preprint arXiv:1905.11946 (2019)

31. Weld, D.S., Bansal, G.: The challenge of crafting intelligible intelligence. Commun. ACM **62**(6), 70–79 (2019)

32. Yoon, J., Kim, K., Jang, J.: Propagated perturbation of adversarial attack for well-known CNNs: empirical study and its explanation. In: 2019 IEEE/CVF International Conference on Computer Vision Workshop (ICCVW), pp. 4226–4234. IEEE (2019)

AI Explainability. A Bridge Between Machine Vision and Natural Language Processing

Mourad Oussalah[✉]

Faculty of Information Technology, University of Oulu, CMVS, 90014 Oulu, Finland
Mourad.Oussalah@oulu.fi

Abstract. This paper attempts to present an appraisal review of explainable Artificial Intelligence research, with a focus on building a bridge between image processing community and natural language processing (NLP) community. The paper highlights the implicit link between the two disciplines as exemplified from the emergence of automatic image annotation systems, visual question-answer systems. Text-To-Image generation and multimedia analytics. Next, the paper identified a set of natural language processing fields where the visual-based explainability can boost the local NLP task. This includes, sentiment analysis, automatic text summarization, system argumentation, topical analysis, among others, which are highly expected to fuel prominent future research in the field.

Keywords: Explainable AI · Machine vision · Natural language processing

1 Introduction

Aided by the advances in computer system computational performances and learning system theory, the success of machine learning methods in the last decade has been phenomenal in various fields, especially, computer vision and natural language processing, which enhanced the prediction and automated decision-making capabilities. This has taken machine intelligence and artificial intelligence (AI) to a new frontier that witnessed the emergence of new industry standard (e.g., industry 4.0) and human-computer interaction modes where a machine guides medical diagnosis systems, creates recommender systems, makes investment decisions and instructs driverless vehicles. On the other hand, the state-of-the-art systems in many AI applications use ensembles of deep neural networks that are even more difficult to interpret, even for skilled programmer users. This negatively impacts trust. For instance, during the PwC's 2017 Global CEO Survey [1], although it is acknowledged the substantial increase of AI market to more than $15 trillion, 67% of the business leaders believe that this will impact negatively stakeholder trust levels in their industry in the next five years. This fosters the emergence of explainable AI research that seeks to ensure transparency and interpretability of machine learning and AI based algorithms. Indeed, many applications have seen a huge increase in demand for transparency from the various stakeholders involved at various levels of product pipeline. For instance, in precision-medicine, explanation is required to support system diagnosis outcome and clinical investigation; in finance and

© Springer Nature Switzerland AG 2021
A. Del Bimbo et al. (Eds.): ICPR 2020 Workshops, LNCS 12663, pp. 257–273, 2021.
https://doi.org/10.1007/978-3-030-68796-0_19

management, explanation is needed to evaluate various investment scenarios with qualitative/quantitative risk evaluations; in autonomous systems, explanation enhances fault inspection and recovery based strategies. In general stakeholders are reticent to adopt techniques that are not directly trustworthy, tractable and interpretable [2], especially given the increasing scope of ethical AI [3].

Beyond academia, since 2017, the European Union's General Data Protection Regulation (GDPR) introduced the "right to explanation" which states that a user can ask for an explanation of an algorithmic decision that was made about them [4].

Strictly speaking, the need for AI explainability was recognized well earlier, and was an inherent component of many of the first AI diagnostic systems where "IF-Then" rules and inference engine were widely employed to explain the actions of the underlined expert system for instance. This was implemented in early MYCIN systems [81] that formed the basis of many subsequent medical systems; although the exact scope and nature of these rules can be debatable. In the literature, the concept of explainability is related to transparency, interpretability, trust, fairness and accountability, among others [5]. Interpretability, often used as a synonym of explainability as well, is defined by Doshi and Kim [6] as "the ability to explain or to present in understandable terms to a human".

According to Samek et al. [7], the need of explainable systems is rooted in four points: (a) Verification of the system: Understand the rules governing the decision process in order to detect possible biases; (b) Improvement of the system: Understand the model and the dataset to compare different models and to avoid failures; (c) Learning from the system: "Extract the distilled knowledge from the AI system"; (d) Compliance with legislation (particularly with the "right to explanation" set by European Union): To find answers to legal questions and to inform people affected by AI decisions.

Lewis [8] states that "to explain an event is to provide some information about its causal history. In an act of explaining, someone who is in possession of some information about the causal history of some event – explanatory information – tries to convey it to someone else". Halpern and Pearl [9] define a good explanation as a response to a Why question, that "(a) provides information that goes beyond the knowledge of the individual asking the question and (b) be such that the individual can see that it would, if true, be (or be very likely to be) a cause of".

Miller [10] extracts four characteristics of explanations: "explanations are contrastive" (why this and not that), "explanations are selected in a biased manner (not everything shall be explained)", "probabilities don't matter" and finally "explanations are social".

Traditionally, transparency has always been at odds with performance where an increase in transparency is often translated into a decrease in system performance because of large number of parameters that require tuning [11], see Fig. 1 for exemplification. Therefore, a trade-off between the level of transparency and performance required.

Encompassing the broad scope of the explainability and its multi-disciplinary nature, this paper attempts to reconcile explainable AI research on two complementary fields: Machine Vision System (MVS) and Natural Language Processing (NLP), trying to survey the explainable AI in each field and seek complementary aspects in a way to boost fruitful XAI research in the two fields.

2   Background

We will adopt in this paper Gunning definition of Explainable Artificial Intelligence (XAI) [12]: "XAI will create a suite of machine learning techniques that enables human users to understand, appropriately trust, and effectively manage the emerging generation of artificially intelligent partners", see Fig. 1.

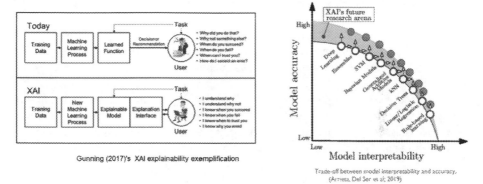

Gunning (2017)'s XAI explainability exemplification

Model interpretability

Trade-off between model interpretability and accuracy.
(Arrieta, Del Ser et al, 2019)

Fig. 1. XAI concept as described in Gunning's [12] and Performance-interpretability trade-off

This definition brings together two concepts; namely, understanding and trust that need to be addressed. Such concepts are ultimately linked to several other aspects that overlap with cognitive operations of understanding or comprehension tasks. This includes for instance causality, transferability, informativeness, fairness and confidence [13].

Regardless of the type of applications involved or the system inputs, the explanation differs according to the underlying chosen criterion. Especially, explanation methods and techniques for ML interpretability can be classified according to different criteria.

- *Pre-Model vs. In-Model vs. Post-Model*

Interpretability methods can be classified depending whether this is applied before (pre-model), during (in-model) or after (post-model) the machine-learning model [14].

Pre-model interpretability techniques tackle the data itself regardless of the employed ML model, focusing on the structure of the inputs and associated features with their visualization. Intuitive features and sparsity are some properties that help to achieve data interpretability. This includes techniques related to descriptive statistics to data visualization methods including Principal Component Analysis (PCA) [15], t-SNE (t-Distributed Stochastic Neighbor Embedding) [16], and clustering methods, such as MMD-critic [17] (Maximum Mean Discrepancy) and k-means [18]. Hence, data visualization is critical for pre-model interpretability.

In-model interpretability concerns ML models that have inherent interpretability in it, either with or without constraints, being intrinsically interpretable. Post-model interpretability refers to improving interpretability after building a model or model training (post hoc). This answers the question: what else can the model tell us?

- Model-Specific vs. Model-Agnostic

Model-specific interpretation restricts the analysis to specific model classes. For example, the interpretation of weights in a linear model is a model-specific interpretation [19]. In contrast, model-agnostic methods apply to any ML model after training phase (post-hoc), so without having access to model inner workings (i.e., weighting). By default, all post-hoc methods are model-agnostic since they were applied after the training.

In essence, two approaches can be distinguished to explain ML model prediction through either a global method that treats the group of predictions of interest as if it was the whole dataset or by applying local methods on each individual prediction followed by aggregating and joining these individual explanations afterwards [13, 20].

- *Local versus global explanation*

According to the scoop of interpretability, one distinguishes global interpretability, which concerns comprehending the entire model behavior and local interpretability, which rather focuses on a single prediction, or a single feature behavior. For instance, Yang et al's. [21] GIRP (global mode interpretation via recursive partitioning) builds a global interpretation tree. Nguyen et al. [22] advocate an activation-maximization based approach for global explanation. One of the most popular local interpretability model is LIME model [23], which enables approximating ML model in the neighborhood of any prediction of interest.

Other techniques for local explainaibility models include decomposition models (omitting some features of the original dataset and attempt to combine the effects of various features), Shapely explanations [24], sensitivity maps, saliency maps [26].

- *Type of explanation*

This includes Feature summary (either through visualization or textual input), Model internals (model specific), Data point (output data points that make the model interpretable), Surrogate intrinsically interpretable model—through approximation of ML model either locally or globally with an intrinsically interpretable model.

- *Simulatability*

This refers to comprehending how the model makes decisions, grounded on a holistic view of the data features and individual components (e.g., weights, parameters) in order to simulate the overall system.

- *Visualization and interaction*
- Popular visualization techniques applied in ML interpretability include partial-dependence plot [27], surrogate models [28, 29], individual conditional expectation [30]. Depending on the stage where the visualization techniques is conducted, one can also distinguish pre-model, in-model or post-hoc based visualization. Similarly, visualization can be performed for local or global like interpretability purpose (Table 1).

• *Approximation versus sensitivity*

Using the universal approximator property of neural network system, several interpretable approximation models have been proposed to gain insights into the functioning of the black-box of the ML model. For instance, rule-based approximation [31] approximates the decision-making process in ML model by utilizing the input and the output of the ML only. Decompositional approaches look at extracting rules at the level of individual units within ML model [32]. This includes Orthogonal search-based rule extraction proposed in [33] for medicine application. Another approximation method cited in the literature is model distillation [34], which acts as a model compression algorithm from deep network to shallow networks. DarkSight [35] combines ideas from distillation model and visualization to explain the black-box functioning.

On the other hand, sensitivity analysis [36] focuses on how black box model is influenced by its input weight perturbations. Feature importance as in Fisher et al. [37]'s Model Class Reliance or SFIMP [38] for permutation based shapely feature importance are other sensitivity like analysis for explanation tackling.

3 Link Between Image and Text in Explainability

Intuitively, the link between image and text is either explicit or implicit from several standpoints:

Purpose and Outcome Expectation
Both image processing and NLP based XAI system do share the same purpose of using ML model for classification purpose, and therefore, seeking an explanation of the ML outcome using the XAI model. They may seek a global / local, model-specific or agnostic, pre-training, in-training or post-training explanation. Although, the classification task might be different for NLP and image processing cases.

Universality of Many XAI Tools
Tools like LIME framework that enables observing the explainer function on the correctly predicted instance can be applied regardless the context of application domain (e.g., image or text based exploration). Similar reasoning applies to many visualization toolkits, e.g., heat-map that visualizes the extent to which each element contributes to the prediction result, saliency map, feature importance map, among others, that are independent of the application context.

Structure of Multimedia and Social Media Posts
With the advances in Web 2.0 technology that enabled the users to post various types of files (text, images, multimedia) and the memory efficiency for handling large scale multimedia files, the need for building a capacity to handle equally image and textual inputs

Table 1. Review of main XAI techniques

Techniques	Global (G)/Local (L)	Model Specific (Sp)/model Agnostic (A)	Pre-model, In-mode, Post-model (Po)	Approximation (Ap)/Sensitivity (S)	Visualization/Interaction	Simulatability	References
Decision trees	G	Sp	All	x			[39, 40]
LIME	L	A	Po	x	Yes	Yes	[23, 41]
Shapely explanations	L	A	Po	x	Yes	Yes	[24]
Rule extraction	G/L	A	Po	x	Yes	Yes	[43, 44]
Decomposition	L	A	Po	Ap	Yes	Yes	[32]
Activation-maximization	G/L	A	Po	x	x	x	[22]
Surrogate models	G/L	A	Po	S	Yes	x	[28, 29]
Individual conditional expectation	L	A	Po	x	Yes	x	[30]
Model distillation	G	A	Po	x	Yes	Yes	[34]
Feature importance	G/L	A	Po	Ap / S	Yes	x	[45]
Saliency map	L	A	Po	S	Yes	x	[26]
Sensitivity analysis	G/L	A	Po	S	Yes	x	[36]
Counterfactuals explanations	L	A	Po	x	Yes	x	[38]
Tree View	G/L	A	Po	x	Yes	x	[47]
Rule set	G	Sp	Po	x	Yes	x	[48]

(continued)

Table 1. (*continued*)

Techniques	Global (G)/Local (L)	Model Specific (Sp)/model Agnostic (A)	Pre-model, In-mode, Post-model (Po)	Approximation (Ap)/Sensitivity (S)	Visualization/Interaction	Simulatability	References
DecText	G/L	A	Po	x	x	x	[49]
DeepLift	G	A	Po	x	Yes	x	[50]
Layer-wise relevance propagation	G/L	A	Po	Ap	x	x	[46]
Fuzzy inference system	G	A	Po	Ap	Yes	Yes	[51]

on the same setting is growing. This motivates the development of unified frameworks in XAI to handle both types of inputs as well.

Development of Automatic Annotation Services

Automatic image annotation is the process of automatically creating textual based description for the different regions of the image highlighting the content of the images. This is especially important to identify sensitive content on online media platforms. With the advances in deep learning technology and large-scale image database, several tools were made available to scientific community for this task. This includes Google Cloud Vision [52], GoogLeNet [53], a deep learning model trained on the ILSVRC dataset.

Development of Visual Question Answering Services

Visual Question Answering (VQA) is the task of addressing open-ended questions about images; namely, given an image and a natural language question about that image, the task is to provide an accurate natural language answer, see Fig. 2 for an example. Typically, VQA requires visual and linguistic comprehension, language grounding capabilities as well as a common-sense knowledge. A variety of methods have been developed [54, 55]. In the latter, the vision component of a typical VQA system extracts visual features using a deep convolutional neural network (CNN), then linguistic components encode the question into a semantic vector using a recurrent neural network (RNN). An answer is then generated conditioned on the visual features and the question vector.

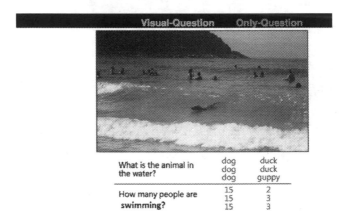

Fig. 2. Example of Visual-Question answer systems

Development of Text to Image Generation

Similarly to the previous visual question answering, the problem of explaining textual content through visual representation is also important for education and learning purposes. This has also been investigated by many computer vision scientists. Indeed, deep generative models [22] have been proposed to address the task of generating appropriate images from natural description by inferring a semantic layout, which is then converted into image using image generator. Methods based on conditional Generative Adversarial Network (GAN) have been employed in several text-to-image synthesis tasks and competitions [56, 57] and tested on large scale dataset such as birds [58], flowers [59], MS-COCO [60]. In this regard, the task of image generation is viewed as a problem of translating semantic labels into pixels. Nevertheless, the complexity of the reasoning cannot be ignored. Especially, learning a direct mapping from text to image is not straightforward and layout generator requires several constraints to enhance its practicality due to the vast amount of possibilities of potential image candidates that fit a given textual utterance, see, for instance, the example in Figs. 3, 4.

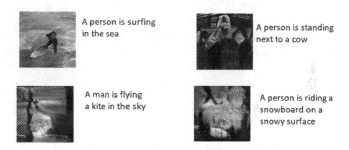

Fig. 3. Example of Text-to-Image based explanation

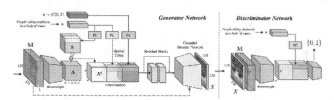

Fig. 4. Architecture for image generator conditioned on the text description and semantic layout generator in [78].

4   Potential Benefits to NLP Community

4.1   Word-Sense Disambiguation

Word-sense disambiguation aims to assign an appropriate sense to the occurrence of a word in a given context. For instance, the meaning of word "chair" in the sentence "I have been awarded a chair in Computer Science" is different from that in the sentence "I bought a chair in the city market today", where the sense of the target word "chair" is chosen among the set of senses listed in a given dictionary. Typically, standard Lesk's algorithm [61] looks into the number of overlapping words of each sense of the target word with the underlined context (sentence), so that the sense that yields the highest number of overlap is used to disambiguate the target word. Other variants of Lesk's algorithm as well as supervised and/or semi-supervised algorithms have been proposed for word-sense disambiguation tasks [62, 63, 79].

Making use of visual description raised, for instance, by text-to-image mapping can provide insights into word-sense disambiguation task. This assumes that an overall visual representation is generated for the whole sentence for each sense of the target word, and appropriate metrics are constructed to quantify the relevance and commonsense of each global visual representation.

Visualization techniques issues from XAI can also be accommodated for the word-sense disambiguation feature. For instance, various senses of target words can play the role of features and utilize LIME-like-approach to visualize the contributions of the various senses, and thereby, disambiguate accordingly. Similarly, the emergence of graph based approaches for word sense disambiguation where, in the same spirit as Navigli and Lapata [63], the senses are mapped to a graph representation where the graph is built using various connectivity algorithms such as PageRank, hyperlink induced topic search, key player problem, various senses can be ranked accordingly, and, thereby, handle disambiguation task.

4.2 Text Argumentation Theory

With the emergence of Dung's Argumentation Framework [64], a central approach for performing reasoning within argumentation in artificial intelligence and natural language processing become tenable. This opens up opportunities for legal text analysis, medical science and opinion mining. In this course, arguments are viewed as abstract entities, so that the use of argumentation semantics, i.e., criteria for finding acceptable sets of arguments, suffices to reason in an argumentative way for a variety of application scenarios. Arguments are supposed to support, contradict, and explain statements, and they are used to support decision-making. What may constitute an argument is very much context dependent. In natural language processing, this can be short utterance that fits a given ontology or might be extracted using text summarization like technique from a large or a multi-document source file. The possibility to represent both positive and negative views using the employed argumentation framework provides opportunity to sustain debate and boost interactions. Recently, abstract argumentation has been suggested to explain predictions of neural network system and diaelectrically explainable prediction [65]. This ultimately builds bridge with XAI and offers nice opportunities to use the abstract argumentation framework as a means to derive explanation and interpretability.

4.3 Sentiment Analysis

Sentiment analysis refers to the use of NLP, text analysis and computational linguistics techniques to systematically identify, extract and quantify affective states and subjective information, classifying the polarity of a given text at sentence, document or multi-document level in order to find out whether the expressed opinion is positive, negative or neutral. This has been extensively employed in a range of applications ranging from marketing to customer services to clinical medicine. Key approaches to sentiment analysis include knowledge-based techniques, which classify text based on affect categories according to presence of affect words such as happy, sad using affective lexical database of lexicon dictionary. Furthermore, supervised and machine-learning like techniques have also been populated for the same purpose [66]. Several open sources are made available for the purpose of sentiment analysis. This includes, Python NLTK, TextBlob, Pattern.en, RapidMiner, Stanford's CoreNLP, SentiStrength, among others.

Through explainability-based reasoning, sentiment analysis can be boosted a step-further to provide the reason for the sentiment score. For instance, in [67], the authors proposed layer-wise relevance propagation model for explaining recurrent network architecture for sentimentzanalysis.

Zhang et al. [68] proposed an Explicit Factor Model (EFM) based on phrase-level sentiment analysis to generate explainable recommendations.

Interestingly, the presence of contrastive statements from opinionated documents in sentiment analysis context opens up the door wide to application of more advanced argumentation system, reinforcement learning or Markov-Chain based reasoning in the same spirit as [69] inherited from question-answer system analysis. Similarly, the emergence of multimedia documents in social media platforms provides opportunities to mix-up image-analysis & text-analysis based reasoning. For instance, face-emotion recognition in videos can provide useful insights into sentiment polarity of the underlined textual input.

4.4 Topical Modelling

Since the emergence of Latent Dirichlet Allocation (LDA) [70], the task of automatic discovery of topics in a textual document has seen a new landmark. In essence, LDA introduces sparse Dirichlet prior distributions over document-topic and topic-word distributions, encoding the intuition that documents cover a small number of topics and that topics often use a small number of words. Topic models are a form of unsupervised machine learning, in that the topics and mixture parameters are unknown and inferred solely from the data where each topic is represented by its N most probable words. Humans can judge whether words of a given topic (cluster) form interpretable concept (s). Therefore, it is important to seek automatic alternative to measure the interpretability of the outputted set of words of each topic. A commonly employed approach is based on the co-occurrence analysis, stipulating that words that have high frequency of co-occurrence (either within the document under investigation or in a more wider corpus) would indicate high coherence and relatedness, as for words caught and fever for instance [71]. The development of word embedding promoted by Google researchers has also promoted the so called embedded topic model [72] where each word is modelled as a categorical distribution whose natural parameter is the inner product between a word embedding and an embedding of its assigned topic. This has shown to discover interpretable topics even with large vocabulary. On the other hand, the development of interactive topic modelling [73], where more interaction modes with system output are enabled, offers a nice setting to apply a range of visualization tools developed in the context of explainable AI for this purpose.

4.5 Automatic Textual Summarization

Automatic text summarization has been a hot topic in NLP focusing on how to summarize the main content of the document while preserving the semantic meaning and key messages conveyed by the original document in a way to reduce redundancy and maximize the diversity. Typically, two streams have been identified in the literature [74]. Extractive summarization where the summary is constituted of a selected sentences from original document through some scoring analysis mechanism that takes into account sentence similarity, location, presence of selected keywords, among others, and abstractive summarization where the summary sentences may be different from that of original documents. Extractive summarization is by far the most investigated research stream in automatic summarization. Various graph-based approaches have been put forward for extracting relevant sentences. Examples include TextRank [75] where the nodes are sentences and the edges the relations (which is context dependent, e.g., semantic similarity beyond certain threshold) between the sentence, and the importance of a given sentence is quantified using PageRank like algorithm. Similarly, latent semantic analysis [76, 77], which provides a lower dimensional representation of words, has also been applied to summarization purpose [80].

Strictly speaking, explainable research benefits summarization from both directions. First, summarization can be used as a tool to construct and identify arguments that can be used to guide the explanation process. Second, the interactive tools, LIME like approach can also be adapted to boost the sentence weighting scheme, which, in turn impact the outcome of the summarization task.

5 Conclusion

Explanation methods are a promising approach to leverage hidden knowledge about the workings of neural networks and black-box systems, promoting transparency and interpretability of the results in the light of the new data protection EU directive on the "right of explanation". This papers attempted to review the state of art of explainability methods focusing on intertwine between image processing and natural language processing fields in a way to promote fruitful development of new explanation framework. Especially, the paper highlights the implicit link between the two research fields through, e.g., automatic image annotation, visual question-answer systems, Text-To-Image generation, multimedia analytics in addition to the overall input-output like system analysis. On the other hand, this review has also identified several NLP research fields that would benefit from visual explainability based approach. This includes, wordsense disambiguation, sentiment analysis, argumentation theory, automatic text summarization and topical modelling.

There are several interesting future research directions to explore further. An interesting direction is semi-supervised learning of the model using a large set of partially annotated data. For instance, we can exploit a small number of fully annotated images and a large number of partially annotated images (*e.g.* images with only text descriptions), which allows the developed model to exploit large-scale datasets, such as the Google Conceptual Caption dataset. The paper also opens up new research directions in multimedia analytics, text summarization and abstract argumentation logic.

Acknowledgment. This work is partly supported by the H2020 YoungRes (# 823701) project, which is gratefully acknowledged.

References

1. Oxborough, C., Cameron, E.: Explainable AI, PWC report (2020). https://www.pwc.co.uk/services/risk-assurance/insights/explainable-ai.html Accessed July 2020
2. Grice, H.P.: Logic and Conversation. In: Syntax and Semantics 3: Speech arts, pp. 41–58 (1975)
3. Conati, C., Porayska-Pomsta, K., Mavrikis, M.: AI in education needs interpretable machine learning: lessons from open learner modelling. arXiv preprint arXiv:1807.00154 (2018)
4. Goodman, B., Flaxman, S.: European union regulations on algorithmic decision making and a "right to explanation." AI Mag. **38**(3), 50 (2017)
5. Abdul, A., Vermeulen, J., Wang, D., Lim, B.Y., Kankanhalli, M.: Trends and trajectories for explainable, accountable and intelligible systems: an HCI research agenda. In Proceedings of the 2018 CHI. Association for Computing Machinery, Montreal, Canada (2018). https://doi.org/10.1145/3173574.3174156
6. Doshi-velez, F., Kim, B.: A Roadmap for a Rigorous Science of Interpretability. CoRR, abs/1702.08608 (2017). https://arxiv.org/abs/1702.08608
7. Samek, W., Wiegand, T., Müller, K.R.: Explainable artificial intelligence: understanding, visualizing and interpreting deep learning models. ITU J. ICT Discoveries Spec. (1), 39–48 (2017)
8. Lewis, D.: Causal Explanation. In: Philosophical Papers. Vol II. Oxford University Press, New York, Chapter Twenty two, pp. 214–240 (1986)
9. Halpern, J.Y., Pearl, J.: Causes and explanations : a structural-model approach. Part II : Explanations. **56**(4), 889–911 (2005). https://doi.org/10.1093/bjps/axi148
10. Miller, T.: Explanation in artificial intelligence: Insights from the social sciences. Artif. Intell. **267**, 1–38 (2019). https://doi.org/10.1016/j.artint.2018.07.007
11. Arrieta, Del Ser et al. Explainable artificial intelligence (XAI): concepts, taxonomies, opportunities and challenges toward responsible AI. Inf. Fusion **58**, 82–115 (2019)
12. Gunning, D.: Explainable artificial intelligence (XAI). Technical report, pp. 1–18 (2017)
13. Lipton, Z.C.: The mythos of model interpretability. Queue **16**(3), 30:31–30:57 (2018)
14. Kim, B., Doshi-Velez, F.: Introduction to interpretable machine learning. In Proceedings of the CVPR 2018 Tutorial on Interpretable Machine Learning for Computer Vision, Salt Lake City, UT, USA (2018)
15. Jolliffe, I.: Principal component analysis. In International Encyclopedia of Statistical Science, pp. 1094–1096. Springer, Berlin (2011). https://doi.org/10.1007/978-3-642-04898-2_455
16. Maaten, L.Y.D., Hinton, G.: Visualizing data using t-SNE. J. Mach. Learn. Res. **9**, 2579–2605 (2008)
17. Kim, B., Khanna, R., Koyejo, O.O.: Examples are not enough, learn to criticize! Criticism for interpretability. In: Advances in Neural Information Processing Systems. MIT Press: Cambridge, pp. 2280–2288 (2016)
18. Hartigan, J.A., Wong, M.A.: A k-means clustering algorithm. J. R. Stat. Soc. Ser. C (Appl. Stat.) **28**, 100–108 (1979)
19. Adadi, A., Berrada, M.: Peeking inside the black-box: a survey on explainable artificial intelligence (XAI). IEEE Access **6**, 52138–52160 (2018)
20. Molnar, C.: Interpretable machine learning (2019). https://christophm.github.io/interpretable-ml-book/. Accessed July 2020

21. Yang, C., Rangarajan, A., Ranka, S.: Global model interpretation via recursive partitioning (2018). arXiv:1802.04253
22. Nguyen, A., Dosovitskiy, A., Yosinski, J., Brox, T., Clune, J.: Synthesizing the preferred inputs for neurons in neural networks via deep generator networks. Proc. Adv. Neural Inf. Process. Syst. (NIPS), 3387–3395 (2016)
23. Ribeiro, M.T., Singh, S., Guestrin, C.: Why should I trust you?: Explaining the predictions of any classifier, In: Proceedings of 22nd ACM SIGKDD International Conference on Knowledge Discovery Data Mining (2016)
24. Lundberg, S.M., Lee, S.L.: A unified approach to interpreting model predictions. Proc. Adv. Neural Inf. Process. Syst. 4768–4777 (2017)
25. Cortez, P., Embrechts, M.J.: Opening black box data mining models using sensitivity analysis. In: Proceedings of IEEE Symposium on Computational Intelligence Data Mining (CIDM), pp. 341–348 (2011)
26. Smilkov, D., Thorat, N., Kim, B., ViØgas F., Wattenberg, M.: SmoothGrad: removing noise by adding noise (2017). https://arxiv.org/abs/1706.03825
27. Green D.P., Kern, H.L.: Modeling heterogeneous treatment effects in large-scale experiments using Bayesian additive regression trees. In: Proceedings of Annual Summer Meeting Society for Political Methodology, pp. 1–40 (2010)
28. Bastani, O., Kim, C., Bastani, H.: Interpretability via model extraction (2017). https://arxiv.org/abs/1706.09773
29. Thiagarajan, J.J., Kailkhura, B., Sattigeri,P., Ramamurthy, K.N.: TreeView: peeking into deep neural networks via feature-space partitioning. (2016) https://arxiv.org/abs/1611.07429
30. Goldstein, A., Kapelner, A., Bleich, J., Pitkin, E.: Peeking inside the black box: visualizing statistical learning with plots of individual conditional expectation, J. Comput. Graph. Statist. **24**(1), 44–65 (2015)
31. Frank, E., Witten, I.H.: Generating accurate rule sets without global optimization. In: ICML 1998, pp. 144–151 (1998)
32. Robnik-Šikonja, M., Kononenko, L.: Explaining classifications for individual instances. IEEE Trans. Knowl. Data Eng. **20**(5), 589–600 (2008)
33. Etchells, T.A., Lisboa, P.J.G.: Orthogonal search-based rule extraction (OSRE) for trained neural networks: a practical and efficient approach. IEEE Trans. Neural Netw. **17**(2), 374–384 (2006)
34. Tan, S., Caruana, R., Hooker, G., Lou, Y.: Detecting bias in black-box models using transparent model distillation. https://arxiv.org/abs/1710.06169 (2018)
35. Xu, K., Park, D.H., Yi, D.H., Sutton, C.: Interpreting deep classifier by visual distillation of dark knowledge (2018). https://arxiv.org/abs/1803.04042
36. Cortez, P., Embrechts, M.J.: Using sensitivity analysis and visualization techniques to open black box data mining models. Inf. Sci. **225**, 1–7 (2013)
37. Fisher, A., Rudin, C., Dominici, F.: Model class reliance: variable importance measures for any machine learning model class, from the 'Rashomon' perspective (2018). https://arxiv.org/abs/1801.01489
38. Casalicchio, G., Molnar, C., Bischl, B.: Visualizing the feature importance for black box models (2018). https://arxiv.org/abs/1804.06620
39. Schetinin, V., et al.: Confident interpretation of Bayesian decision tree ensembles for clinical applications. IEEE Trans. Inf. Technol. Biomed. **11**(3), 312 (2007)
40. Hara, S., Hayashi, K.: Making tree ensembles interpretable (2016). https://arxiv.org/abs/1606.05390
41. Ribeiro, M.T., Singh, S., Guestrin, C.: Anchors: high-precision model-agnostic explanations. In: Proceedings of AAAI Conference on Artificial Intelligence, pp. 1–9 (2018)

42. García, S., Fernández, A., Herrera, F.: Enhancing the effectiveness and interpretability of decision tree and rule induction classifiers with evolutionary training set selection over imbalanced problems. Appl. Soft Comput. **9**(4), 1304–1314 (2009)
43. Wang, F., Rudin, C.: Falling rule lists. In: Proceedings of 18th International Confrence on Artificial Intelligence on Statistics (AISTATS), San Diego, CA, USA: JMLR W&CP, pp. 1013–1022 (2015)
44. Ras, G., Van Gerven, M., Haselager, P.: Explanation methods in deep learning: Users, values, concerns and challenges (2018). https://arxiv.org/abs/1803.07517
45. Johansson, U., König, R., Niklasson, I.: The truth is in there—rule extraction from opaque models using genetic programming. In: Proceedings of FLAIRS Conference, pp. 658–663 (2004)
46. Wachter, S., Mittelstadt, B., Russell, C.: Counterfactual explanations without opening the black box: automated decisions and the GDPR (2017). https://arxiv.org/abs/1711.00399
47. Bach, S., Binder, A., Montavon, G., Klauschen, F., Müller, K.R., Samek, W.: On pixel-wise explanations for non-linear classifier decisions by layer-wise relevance propagation. PLoS ONE **10**(7), e0130140 (2015)
48. Thiagarajan, J.J., Kailkhura, B., Sattigeri,P., Ramamurthy, K.N.: TreeView: peeking into deep neural networks via feature-space partitioning (2016). arXiv preprint arXiv:1611.07429
49. Wang, T., Rudin,C., Velez-Doshi, F., Liu, Y., Klamp, E., MacNeille, P.: Bayesian rule sets for interpretable classification. In: IEEE 16th International Conference on Data Mining (ICDM), pp. 1269–1274 (2016)
50. Boz, O.: Extracting decision trees from trained neural networks. In: Proceedings of the Eighth ACM SIGKDD International Conference on Knowledge Discovery and Data Mining, pp. 456–461. ACM (2002)
51. Shrikumar, A., Greenside, P., Shcherbina, A., Kundaje, A.: Not just a black box: learning important features through propagating activation differences (2016). arXiv:1605.01713
52. Zhou, A.M., Gan, J.Q.: Low-level interpretability and high-level interpretability: a unified view of data-driven interpretable fuzzy system modelling. Fuzzy Sets Syst. **159**(23), 3091–3131 (2008)
53. https://cloud.google.com/vision
54. Szegedy, C., et al.: Going deeper with convolutions. In: CPRV'15 (2004). arXiv preprint arxiv:1409.4842
55. Xu, H., Saenko, K.: Ask, attend and answer: exploring question-guided spatial attention for visual question answering. In: Leibe, B., Matas, J., Sebe, N., Welling, M. (eds.) ECCV 2016. LNCS, vol. 9911, pp. 451–466. Springer, Cham (2016). https://doi.org/10.1007/978-3-319-46478-7_28
56. Lu, J., Yang, J., Batra, D.: Parikh. Hierarchical question image co-attention for visual question answering. In: Advances in Neural Information Processing Systems (NIPS2016), pp 289–297 (2016)
57. Reed S. et al.: Generative adversarial text to image synthesis. In: ICML 2016, pp. 1060–1069 (2016)
58. Reed, S.E., Akata, Z., Mohan, S., Tenka, S., Schiele, B., Lee, H.: Learning what and where to draw. In: NIPS, pp. 217–225 (2016)
59. Welinder, P., et al.: Caltech-UCSD Birds 200. Technical report. CNS-TR-2010- 001, California Institute of Technology (2010)
60. Nilsback, M.E., Zisserman, A.: Automated flower classification over a large number of classes. In: Proceedings of the Indian Conference on Computer Vision, Graphics and Image Processing, pp. 722–729 (2008)

61. Lin, T.-Y., Maire, M., Belongie, S., Hays, J., Perona, P., Ramanan, D., Dollár, P., Zitnick, C.L.: Microsoft COCO: common objects in context. In: Fleet, D., Pajdla, T., Schiele, B., Tuytelaars, T. (eds.) ECCV 2014. LNCS, vol. 8693, pp. 740–755. Springer, Cham (2014). https://doi.org/10.1007/978-3-319-10602-1_48

62. Lesk, M.: Automatic sense disambiguation using machine readable dictionaries: how to tell a pine cone from an ice cream cone. In: Proceedings of SIGDOC, pp. 24–26 (1986)

63. Mihalcea, R.: Knowledge-based methods for WSD. In: Word Sense Disambiguation: Algorithms and Applications, Text, Speech and Language Technology, pp. 107–132. Springer, Dordrecht (2006). https://doi.org/10.1007/978-1-4020-4809-8_5

64. Navigli, R., Lapata, M.: Graph connectivity measures for unsupervised word sense disambiguation. In: IJCAI International Joint Conference on Artificial Intelligence, Hyderabad, India, pp. 1683–1688 (2007)

65. Dung, P.M.: On the acceptability of arguments and its fundamental role in nonmonotonic reasoning, logic programming and n-person games. Artif. Intell. **77**(2), 321–357 (1995)

66. Cocarascu, O., Stylianou, A., Cyras K., Toni, F.: Data-empowered argumentation for dialectically explainable predictions. In: 24th European Conference on Artificial Intelligence – ECAI (2020)

67. Tsytsarau, M., Palpanas, T.: Survey on mining subjective data on the web. Data Min. Knowl. Discov. **24**, 478–514 (2012)

68. Arras, L., Horn, F., Montavon, G., Muller, K.R., Samek W.: Explaining predictions of nonlinear classifiers in NLP. arXiv preprint arXiv:1606.07298 (2016)

69. Zhang Y., Lai, G., Zhang, M., Zhang, Y., Liu, Y., Ma, S.: Explicit factor models for explainable recommendation based on phrase-level sentiment analysis. In: Proceedings of the 37th ACM SIGIR, pp. 83–92 (2014)

70. Sherstov, A.A., Stone, P.: Improving action selection in MDP's via knowledge transfer. AAAI **5**, 1024–1029 (2005)

71. Blei, D.M., Lafferty, J.D.: TopicMmodels. Chapman & Hall/CRC (2009)

72. Lau, H.J., Newman, D., Baldwin, T.: Machine reading tea leaves: automatically evaluating topic coherence and topic model quality. In: EAC (2014)

73. Dieng, A.B., Ruiz, F.R., Blei, D.M.: Topic Modelling in Embedding Spaces (2019). arXiv: 1907.04907v1 cs.IR

74. Hu, Y., Boyd-Graber, J., Satinoff, B., Smith, A.: Interactive topic modeling. Mach. Learn. **95**, 423–469 (2013)

75. Nenkova A., McKeown K.: A survey of text summarization techniques. In: Aggarwal, C., Zhai, C. (eds.) Mining Text Data. Springer, Boston, MA (2012). https://doi.org/10.1007/978-1-4614-3223-4_3

76. Mihalcea, R., Tarau, P.: Textrank: bringing order into text. In: Proceedings of the conference on empirical methods in natural language processing (2004)

77. Gong, Y., Liu, X.: Generic text summarization using relevance measure and latent semantic analysis. In: Proceedings of the 24th ACM SIGIR, pp. 19– 25 (2001)

78. Steinberger, J., Jezek, K.: Using latent semantic analysis in text summarization and summary evaluation. Proc. ISIM **4**, 93–100 (2004)

79. Hong, S., Yang, D., Choi, J., Lee, H.: Interpretable text-to-image synthesis with hierarchical semantic layout generation. In: Samek, et al. (eds.): Explainable AI: Interpreting, Explaining and Visualizing Deep Learning. Springer, Germany (2019). https://doi.org/10.1007/978-3-030-28954-6

80. Mohamed, M., Oussalah, M.: A hybrid approach for paraphrase identification based on knowledge-enriched semantic heuristics. Lang. Resour. Eval. **54**(2), 457–485 (2019). https://doi.org/10.1007/s10579-019-09466-4

81. Mohamed, M., Oussalah, M.: SRL-ESA-TextSum: a text summarization approach based on semantic role labeling and explicit semantic analysis. Inf. Process. Manage. (2020). https://doi.org/10.1016/j.ipm.2019.04.003
82. Buchanan, B.G., Shortliffe, E.H.: Rule Based Expert Systems: The MYCIN Experiment of the Stanford Heuristic Programming Project. Addison-Wesley, Reading, MA (1984)

Recursive Division of Image for Explanation of Shallow CNN Models

Oleksii Gorokhovatskyi[✉] and Olena Peredrii

Simon Kuznets Kharkiv National University of Economics,
9-A Nauky Ave., Kharkiv 61166, Ukraine
oleksii.gorokhovatskyi@gmail.com, elena_peredriy@ukr.net

Abstract. In this paper, we propose the research of the recursive division approach to get an explanation for a particular decision of the shallow black box model. The core of the proposed method is the division of the image being classified into separate rectangular parts, followed by the analysis of their influence on the classification result. Such divisions are repeated recursively until the explanation of the classification result is found, or the size of parts is too small. As a result, the pair of images with complement hidden parts is discovered, the first one of which preserves both the most valuable parts and the classification result of the initial image. The second image represents the result of hiding the most valuable parts of an initial image that leads to the different classification for the binary classification problem. Experimental research (applied for Food-5K and concrete crack images datasets) proved that the quality of the proposed method might be close to LIME or even better, while the performance of recursive division is better.

Keywords: Classification explanation · Interpretation · Classification result · Shallow black box model · Recursive division · Convolutional neural network · Perturbation · Binary classification · Complement images

1 Introduction

Artificial neural networks (ANN) and, especially, convolutional neural networks (CNN) are used to solve a lot of artificial intelligence (AI) problems in computer vision, pattern recognition, and image processing domains. The black box nature of this concept is one of the most valuable drawbacks. ANN can help to deal with a huge variety of different problems effectively, but they are almost non-explainable in terms of human language [1, 2]. From the other side, there are other better explainable methods (random forest, statistical models, Bayesian nets, Markov models, etc.), but their efficiency is not so good.

Interpretation is the property of the algorithm/model to explain its decision in a human-friendly form. It forms the basis of the explainable (transparent) artificial intelligence (XAI) idea [1, 2]. Interpretations are local if they search for an explanation about a single particular input decision, and global interpretation means the availability of information about how classification decision for any arbitrary input case [3].

© Springer Nature Switzerland AG 2021
A. Del Bimbo et al. (Eds.): ICPR 2020 Workshops, LNCS 12663, pp. 274–286, 2021.
https://doi.org/10.1007/978-3-030-68796-0_20

The lack of interpretability of AI implementations generates trust problem, which is about whether a responsible person could trust automatic processing results. This problem becomes more acute in case we are talking about sensitive environments like the identification of a person, medical diagnostic and health care, safety, and security, etc.

Interpretability of the model may help to control fairness of its usage, e.g., whether this model takes into account only those features it should but not some accidental ones.

2 Shallow vs Deep Architectures

There are two main issues you need to overcome nowadays to get a successful ANN model. The first relates to the selection of network architecture and the tuning of a lot of hyperparameters. Another one is about the resources, hardware, and time required to train deep models. Interesting thoughts about the influence of deep learning models training on carbon emissions and energy consumption are provided in [4].

Here and below we refer to "shallow" architectures of ANN/CNN, if it contains up to just ten layers, including dropout ones. For sure, this term relates to the size of input images, e.g., shallow net, provided in [5] may be considered as deep enough for input size of 16×16 pixels.

Research of shallow ANN architecture usage in solving different tasks [6–12] and other methods of ANN optimization, like pruning [13, 14] shows that the accuracy of smaller nets may be close enough to deeper and state-of-the-art ANNs. Additionally, it is more convenient and effective to use tiny architectures to build cascades and ensembles of neural networks to make a cooperative decision.

3 Explanation Methods

There are different classes of methods [15] to search for an explanation. Backpropagation ones are based on measuring the influence of each pixel on the common result exploring the backpropagation of a signal. Perturbation methods (e.g., discussed in one of our previous works [16]) create some modification of initial signal (typically, in some neighborhood around it) and measure how classification result changes.

LIME (Local Interpretable Model-Agnostic Explanations) [17, 18] and SHAP (SHapley Additive exPlanations) [3, 19, 20] are amongst the most famous methods, used to search for interpretations. LIME uses the construction of a separate explainable model that uses points in a local neighborhood of the input features vector as a training set. The issues of this approach relate to the need to select some limited quantity of initial features and the overall instability [3].

Superpixel analysis was applied in LIME [17, 18] to search for explanations about the influence of separate parts of an image on the classification result. However, the effective selection of separate superpixels and combinations of them are unclear, except the brute force method. Papers [21–23] refer to iterative replacing of some image fragments preserving their mean color, but this method is computationally expensive.

"What-If" tool [24], presented by Google, demonstrates the search for the coun-terfactuals approach. One of its functions is the search of the closest vector from the existing dataset that requires minimal changes and represents other class.

The contribution of the paper is the recursive division method that explains the particular black box model decision. It doesn't require content analysis before the division of an image. This method might be used for any production-ready convolutional network model without its modification, retraining, or pruning. The result of the explanation is a pair of complement images that confirm the importance of particular image parts for making the classification decision. The investigation of the accuracy and the performance of this method shows that it is effective for shallow (tiny) architectures and may reduce computational expenses.

4 Recursive Division

Let's investigate the way to find the most important parts of images that affect a certain classification decision without analyzing of image context.

We denote by $O = B(I)$ the output vector that includes K elements (quantity of classes). This vector is the result of the classification of input image I by black box model B. We refer to C as the decision class for image I.

We split initial image I into $w \times h$ non-intersecting parts, where w is the quantity of horizontal parts, h is the quantity of vertical ones. Replacing each part with black color in turn we obtain set of images $\{I^{i,j}\}$, $i = \overline{1, w}, j = \overline{1, h}$. Worth noting, that selection of color to hide part with should not affect classification results itself.

After that we classify each of these images and retrieve output vectors $\{o^{i,j}\}$ and classification results $\{c^{i,j}\}$. We compare each result $c^{i,j}$ with the initial one C, looking for mismatches. Example of this process is illustrated in Fig. 1.

If mismatches are found, the corresponding complement $I - I^{i,j}$ images are formed and verified. We refer to the pair of images as complement if some regions of the first image are covered with distortions (e.g., filled with black color) and in the second image these distortions appear in other regions expect those in the first image.

First two perturbation images in Fig. 1 were classified as "non-food", so we build corresponding complementary images and verify them. As one can see, both are classified as "food", which corresponds to the classification result of the initial image. This means that the explanation in a form of complement images is found.

If there are few such results we leave only the most reliable one. For example that is provided in Fig. 1, first pair of perturbation and complement images has bigger absolute difference between decision values.

At the end of the stage two complementary images as well and their classification results are shown.

If all classification results $c^{i,j}$ are the same as initial C, we reassign initial image as:

$$I^* = I^{i^* j^*}, \; i^*, j^* = \underset{i,j}{argmax}(d(o^{i,j}, O)),$$

where d is the distance between vectors (e.g., Euclidean), and divide image again into w^* horizontal parts and h^* vertical ones. This case is illustrated in Fig. 2.

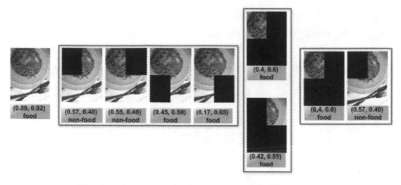

Fig. 1. Single successful stage of recursive division

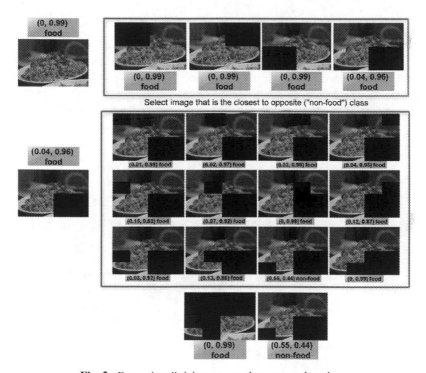

Fig. 2. Recursive division approach to get explanations

There is no sense to process very small parts of images, so searching for explanations is stopped if either width or height of part is lower than 32 pixels.

The quality of explanations found may vary on initial w and h as well as on w^* and h^* used on deeper division levels.

Manual verification of explanation result (presented in Fig. 2) is shown in Fig. 3. As one can see, left image is classified confidently. Image in the middle differs from previous one only with one black dot and result changes. Finally, the addition of the other dot changes classification result dramatically for right image.

Fig. 3. Manual verification that verifies the explanation

We perform the generation of all image combinations at the first processing step, the second step includes the building of complementary images and its verification. This may lead to cases when a successful combination of an image with hidden parts and the complementary one is absent (both classification results are of the same classes, not opposite ones). This example is shown in Fig. 4. We give one more chance in such cases with the division of the most suitable (the farthest from initial classification result) part of the image again to find more explanations. This allowed to increase the quantity of successful explanations up to 20%.

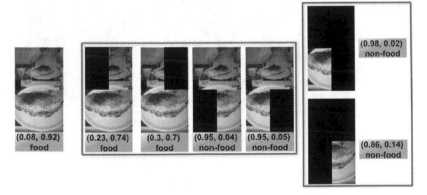

Fig. 4. Partial images and complementary ones are of the same class

5   Experimental Modelling

We created a shallow network, the architecture of it is shown in Fig. 5. It contains two convolutional layers, two maxpooling and dropout ones, one hidden dense layer with 512 neurons and the last output layer with 2 neurons for two corresponding food/non-food classes. The initial image was rescaled down to 64×64 pixels, Adam optimizer

Fig. 5. Shallow CNN used for food/non-food classification

was used, batch size during training was set up to 128 images. Keras [25] software was used for training.

We used Food-5K dataset [26] (that contains 2500 food and 2500 non-food images) for training. 3000 images were used as training ones, testing and validation sets contain 1000 of images each. According to [27], using of fine-tuned GoogLeNet (22 layered CNN) allows to achieve 99.2% accuracy.

Learning of the network (Fig. 5) has been stopped after 30 epochs, achieving accuracy 99.6% on the test set. In order to understand the dependency of explanation quality on different conditions, we performed LIME [28] explanation with 3, 5 and 10 features (1000 number of samples for the building of model have been left by default) and varied w, h, w^*, h^* values for recursive division (RD).

We confirm that the explanation by both methods is successful (as described above) only in case if hiding of meaningful parts (superpixels for LIME) of the image leads to the change of classification results and, at the same time, the classification of only these parts (hiding all another) preserves initial classification result.

5.1 UEC FOOD 100

UEC FOOD 100 dataset [29, 30] contains 14361 images and bounding box ground truth information about food location. Some images contain multiple foods or repeat in different folders, so we removed them from analysis to preserve correct comparison. 10067 images from this dataset were used. Classification accuracy for UEC FOOD 100 dataset is 81.6% (11720 images were classified as food).

LIME produced 7455 explanations, 7502 images were explained successfully by RD. 6480 images were explained by both methods at the same time. We compared average pixelwise intersection over union (IOU) value between ground truth bounding boxes and explanation results. LIME was better with $IOU_{LIME} = 0.1935$, corresponding value for RD is $IOU_{RD} = 0.1882$ (#1 in Table 1). 52% of explanations have bigger IOU value for RD. Recursive division outperforms LIME in cases when $w = h = 3$ (experiments #2 and #4 in Table 1) when 60% of explanations were better using RD.

We compared the explanation quality for LIME based on 3 and 10 features also, these results are shown in Table 2 and Table 3 correspondingly. As one can see, the results are pretty similar to previous ones. It looks like that the increasing of the number of features for LIME decreases its average IOU values.

Examples of different explanation cases are shown in Fig. 6 and Fig. 7. First column contains the initial image, second one contains its ground-truth labeling. The result of LIME explanation (built on 5 features and 1000 samples) is shown in the third column, last column contains the result of RD ($w = h = w^* = h^* = 2$). Cases, when LIME interpreter shows better (in scope of IOU) results, are shown if Fig. 6, the ones, when RD is better, are shown in Fig. 7.

Table 1. Quality Comparison of Explanations for LIME (5 features) vs RD on UEC FOOD 100 Dataset

#	Method	Average IOU	Images compared
1	LIME	**0,1935**	6480
	RD ($w = h = w^* = h^* = 2$)	0,1882	
2	LIME	0,1950	4539
	RD ($w = h = 3, w^* = h^* = 2$)	**0,2174**	
3	LIME	0,1970	5537
	RD ($w = h = 2, w^* = h^* = 3$)	**0,1976**	
4	LIME	0,2035	3836
	RD ($w = h = 3, w^* = h^* = 3$)	**0,2244**	

Table 2. Quality Comparison of Explanations for LIME (3 features) vs RD on UEC FOOD 100 Dataset

#	Method	Average IOU	Images compared
1	LIME	**0,2129**	6774
	RD ($w = h = w^* = h^* = 2$)	0,1867	
2	LIME	0,2118	4687
	RD ($w = h = 3, w^* = h^* = 2$)	**0,2161**	
3	LIME	**0,2156**	6302
	RD ($w = h = 2, w^* = h^* = 3$)	0,1963	
4	LIME	0,2196	3973
	RD ($w = h = 3, w^* = h^* = 3$)	**0,2237**	

5.2 UEC FOOD 256

We compared also LIME with RD on UEC FOOD 256 dataset [31, 32], which contains 31395 food images (27043 unique ones). The classification accuracy of the model was 87.57% (27495 "food" results).

The configuration with 5 features and 1000 samples was used to build LIME model. RD parameters were set up to $w = h = w^* = h^* = 2$. 21159 images were successfully explained by LIME, 21973 by RD, 15299 images were explained by both methods at the same time. LIME had 0.17 IOU value compared to ground-truth images, while RD had 0.1686. 6722 images were explained better by LIME, than by RD, and 8066 images vice versa, explanation for other ones were the same by both methods. When we set RD options to $w = h = 3, w^* = h^* = 2$ we received $IOU_{LIME} = 0.1688$ and $IOU_{RD} = 0.1863$ (12829 images were compared).

Table 3. Quality Comparison of Explanations for LIME (10 features) vs RD on UEC FOOD 100 Dataset

#	Method	Average IOU	Images compared
1	LIME	**0,1923**	6439
	RD ($w = h = w^* = h^* = 2$)	0,1878	
2	LIME	0,1938	4516
	RD ($w = h = 3, w^* = h^* = 2$)	**0,2167**	
3	LIME	0,1959	6302
	RD ($w = h = 2, w^* = h^* = 3$)	**0,1971**	
4	LIME	0,2027	3825
	RD ($w = h = 3, w^* = h^* = 3$)	**0,2238**	

Fig. 6. Examples of explanation results for LIME and RD for UEC FOOD 100 dataset (LIME is better)

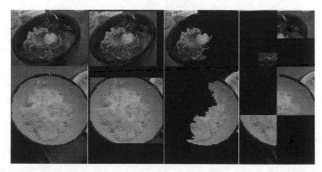

Fig. 7. Examples of explanation results for LIME and RD for UEC FOOD 100 dataset (RD is better)

5.3 Crack Dataset

We performed a comparison of both approaches for crack images presented in [33–35]. This dataset contains 20000 images without cracks and 20000 images with cracks. We split initial images into three parts: 14000 are used for training, and 3000 for validation and testing each. The same shallow net, shown in Fig. 5, has been trained, achieving accuracy 98.1% on the test set.

Crack images dataset doesn't contain ground truth labels, so we generated them for the "positive" part of the dataset. We used Otsu thresholding followed by inverting, the examples of initial images and such labels are shown in Fig. 8.

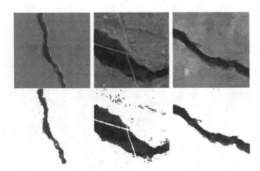

Fig. 8. Examples of initial images and generated ground truth labels for crack dataset

Superpixel-based explanation approaches are not applicable when parts of image are hidden with black color. Hiding superpixels with black immediately leads to the classification of such image as "crack". So, in this case, we hide parts of images in RD with white color.

The average IOU values for LIME and recursive division are shown in Table 4. As one can see, RD outperforms LIME in all cases.

Table 4. Quality Comparison of Explanations for LIME vs RD on Crack Dataset

#	Method	Average IOU	Images compared
1	LIME (3 features)	0,3022	806
	RD ($w = h = w^* = h^* = 2$)	**0,6534**	
2	LIME (5 features)	0,3058	755
	RD ($w = h = w^* = h^* = 2$)	**0,6559**	
3	LIME (10 features)	0,2998	777
	RD ($w = h = w^* = h^* = 2$)	**0,6544**	

Figure 9 represents examples of different explanations for the crack dataset. The following columns are shown from left to the right: initial image, generated ground-truth labeling, the result of LIME explanation (built on 5 features and 100 samples), explanation by of RD ($w = h = w^* = h^* = 2$). The first three rows represent the cases when LIME interpreter shows better results, the last three ones when RD is better.

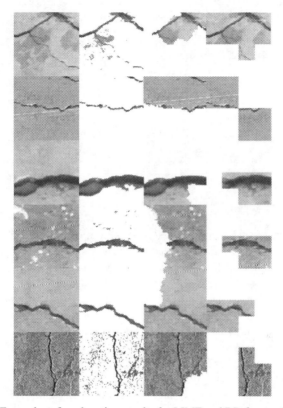

Fig. 9. Examples of explanation results for LIME and RD for crack dataset

5.4 Performance

We measured the time, required to process all images for all used datasets with LIME and RD (for the cases with the best average IOU), all results are shown in Table 5. As one can see, RD approach is 2–3 times faster than LIME.

Table 5. The performance of RD and LIME on different datasets

Dataset	Method	Time (sec.)
UEC FOOD 100	LIME (5 features, 1000 samples)	35000
	RD ($w = h = w^* = h^* = 3$)	11900
UEC FOOD 256	LIME (5 features, 1000 samples)	69700
	RD ($w = h = 3, w^* = h^* = 2$)	32000
Crack	LIME (3 features, 100 samples)	14000
	LIME (5 features, 100 samples)	13000
	LIME (10 features, 100 samples)	15000
	RD ($w = h = w^* = h^* = 2$)	4100

6 Conclusions

The building of interpretable models is a promising approach, which might make the embedding of artificial intelligence tools into sensitive data processing fields much easier.

The proposed recursive division method allows to search for an explanation of a particular black box model classification result. It builds perturbation images for input one, recursively replacing some parts of it with the specific color (in this paper we tested replacing with black and white). The choice of this color should be done properly, taking into account possible conflicts with valuable colors in the context of an image.

The division of an image without analysis of context may be useful in cases, when this analysis is slow or makes no sense (e.g., during the processing of regular images like human faces).

We apply this approach to explain the shallow convolutional neural network classification results.

The result of the recursive division approach is the pair of complement images with hidden parts, first one of which preserves both the most valuable parts and the classification result of the initial image. The second image represents the result of hiding the most valuable parts that leads to a different classification result.

We performed a comparison of this approach to the most popular LIME method based on superpixels. One of the benefits of recursive division is its performance while preserving the explanation quality at a level close to attainable by LIME.

The bottlenecks of the proposed approach relate to the necessity of w, h, w^*, h^* parameters selection. Our experiments showed that increasing the quantity of parts to split image on at first stage from 2×2 to 3×3 ($w = h = 3$) may improve explanation quality. Additionally, RD is stable and reproducible. Also, the visual representation of explanations is not so aesthetic compared to LIME.

Future research of this approach may be related to an application for multiclass shallow networks and more effective masking algorithm.

References

1. Explainable Artificial Intelligence (XAI). https://www.cc.gatech.edu/~alanwags/DLAI2016/ (Gunning)%20IJCAI-16%20DLAI%20WS.pdf. Accessed 15 March 2020
2. Explainable Artificial Intelligence (XAI). https://www.darpa.mil/attachments/XAIProgramUpdate.pdf. Accessed 15 March 2020
3. Interpretable Machine Learning. A Guide for Making Black Box Models Explainable. https://christophm.github.io/interpretable-ml-book. Accessed 15 March 2020
4. Strubell, E., Ganesh, A., McCallum, A.: Energy and policy considerations for deep learning in NLP. In: 57th Annual Meeting of the Association for Computational Linguistics, pp. 3645–3650. Florence, Italy (2018). doi: https://doi.org/10.18653/v1/P19-1355
5. Islam, R., Massicotte, D., Nougarou, F., et al.: S-ConvNet: a shallow convolutional neural network architecture for neuromuscular activity recognition using instantaneous high-density surface EMG images. In: 42nd Annual International Conference of the IEEE Engineering in Medicine & Biology Society (EMBC), pp. 744–749. Montreal, Canada (2020)
6. Gorokhovatskyi, O.: Shallow convolutional neural networks for pattern recognition problems. In: Proceedings of the Second IEEE International Conference on Data Stream Mining & Processing, pp. 459–463. Lviv, Ukraine (2018). doi: https://doi.org/10.1109/dsmp.2018.8478540
7. McDonnell, M.D., Vladusich, T.: Enhanced image classification with a fast-learning shallow convolutional neural network. In: International Joint Conference on Neural Networks (IJCNN), pp. 1–7. Killarney, Ireland (2015). doi: https://doi.org/10.1109/ijcnn.2015.7280796
8. Pan, J., McGuinness, K., Sayrol, E., et al.: Shallow and deep convolutional networks for saliency prediction. In: Proceedings of the IEEE International Conference on Computer Vision and Pattern recognition (CVPR), pp. 598–606. Las Vegas, NV, USA (2016). doi: https://doi.org/10.1109/CVPR.2016.71
9. Ba, J., Caruana, R.: Do deep nets really need to be deep? In: Advances in Neural Information Processing Systems (NIPS), pp. 2654–2662 (2014)
10. Yu, S., Wu, S., Wang, L., et al.: A shallow convolutional neural network for blind image sharpness assessment. PLoS ONE 12(5), e0176632 (2017). doi: https://doi.org/10.1371/journal.pone.0176632
11. Le, H., Cerisara, C., Denis, A.: Do convolutional networks need to be deep for text classification? In: The Workshops of The Thirty-Second AAAI Conference on Artificial Intelligence, pp. 29–36. AAAI Press, New Orleans, Louisiana, USA (2018)
12. Szegedy, C., Liu, W., Jia, Y., et al.: Going deeper with convolutions. In: Proceedings of the IEEE Conference on Computer Vision and Pattern Recognition (CVPR), pp. 1–9. Boston, MA, USA (2015). doi: https://doi.org/10.1109/cvpr.2015.7298594
13. Frankle, J., Dziugaite, G.K., Roy, D., et al.: Linear mode connectivity and the lottery ticket hypothesis. In: Proceedings of the International Conference on Machine Learning (ICML), pp. 10029–10039. Vienna, Austria (2020)
14. Frankle, J., Carbin, M.: The lottery ticket hypothesis: finding sparse, trainable neural networks. In: Seventh International Conference on Learning Representations (ICLR) (2019)
15. Wagner, J., Köhler, J.M., Gindele, T., et al.: Interpretable and fine-grained visual explanations for convolutional neural networks. In: Proceedings of 2019 IEEE/CVF Conference on Computer Vision and Pattern Recognition (CVPR), pp. 9089–9100. Long Beach, USA (2019). doi: https://doi.org/10.1109/CVPR.2019.00931
16. Gorokhovatskyi, O., Peredrii, O., Zatkhei, V., Teslenko, O.: Investigation of random neighborhood features for interpretation of MLP classification results. In: Lytvynenko, V., Babichev, S., Wójcik, W., Vynokurova, O., Vyshemyrskaya, S., Radetskaya, S. (eds.) ISDMCI 2019. AISC, vol. 1020, pp. 581–596. Springer, Cham (2020). https://doi.org/10.1007/978-3-030-26474-1_40

17. Ribeiro, M.T., Singh, S., Guestrin, C.: Why should i trust you? explaining the predictions of any classifier. In: Proceedings of the 22nd ACM SIGKDD International Conference on Knowledge Discovery and Data Mining, pp. 1135–1144. Association for Computing Machinery, New York, NY, USA (2016). doi: https://doi.org/10.1145/2939672.2939778
18. LIME - Local Interpretable Model-Agnostic Explanations. https://homes.cs.washington.edu/~marcotcr/blog/lime/. Accessed 28 September 2019
19. SHAP. https://github.com/slundberg/shap. Accessed 15 March 2020
20. Lundberg, S.M., Lee, S.: A unified approach to interpreting model predictions. In: Guyon, I., Luxburg, U.V., Bengio, S., Wallach, H., Fergus, R., Vishwanathan, S., Garnett, R. (eds.) Advances in Neural Information Processing Systems, pp. 4765 4774 (2017)
21. Zhou, B., Khosla, A., Lapedriza, A., et al.: Object detectors emerge in deep scene CNNs. In: International Conference on Learning Representations (ICLR) (2015)
22. Dabkowski, P., Gal, Y.: Real time image saliency for black box classifiers. In: Proceedings of the 31st International Conference on Neural Information Processing Systems (NIPS), pp. 6970–6979. Curran Associates Inc., New York, NY, USA (2017)
23. Seo, D., Oh, K., Oh, I.: Regional multi-scale approach for visually pleasing explanations of deep neural networks. IEEE Access **8**, 8572–8582 (2020). https://doi.org/10.1109/ACCESS.2019.2963055
24. The What-If Tool: Code-Free Probing of Machine Learning Models. https://ai.googleblog.com/2018/09/the-what-if-tool-code-free-probing-of.html. Accessed 28 Sep 2019
25. Keras. https://github.com/fchollet/keras. Accessed 30 July 2017
26. Food Image Dataset. https://mmspg.epfl.ch/downloads/food-image-datasets. Accessed 15 March 2020
27. Singla, A., Yuan, L., Ebrahimi, T.: Food/Non-food image classification and food categorization using pre-trained GoogLeNet model. In: Proceedings of the 2nd International Workshop on Multimedia Assisted Dietary Management, pp. 3–11. Association for Computing Machinery, USA (2016)
28. Lime. https://github.com/marcotcr/lime/tree/master/lime. Accessed 15 March 2020
29. UECFOOD-100 Dataset Ver.1.0. https://foodcam.mobi/dataset100.html. Accessed 15 March 2020
30. Matsuda, Y., Hoashi, H., Yanai, K.: Recognition of multiple-food images by detecting candidate regions. In: Proceedings of the IEEE International Conference on Multimedia and Expo (ICME), pp. 25–30. Melbourne, Australia (2012). doi: https://doi.org/10.1109/ICME.2012.157
31. UECFOOD-256 Dataset Ver.1.0. https://foodcam.mobi/dataset256.html. Accessed 15 March 2020
32. Kawano, Y., Yanai, K.: Automatic expansion of a food image dataset leveraging existing categories with domain adaptation. In: Agapito, L., Bronstein, M.M., Rother, C. (eds.) ECCV 2014. LNCS, vol. 8927, pp. 3–17. Springer, Cham (2015). https://doi.org/10.1007/978-3-319-16199-0_1
33. Özgenel, Ç.F., Gönenç Sorguç, A.: Performance comparison of pretrained convolutional neural networks on crack detection in buildings. In: Proceedings of the International Association for Automation and Robotics in Construction (ISARC), pp. 693–700. Berlin, Germany (2018). doi: https://doi.org/10.22260/ISARC2018/0094
34. Zhang, L., Yang, F., Zhang, Y.D., et al.: Road crack detection using deep convolutional neural network. In: Proceedings of the IEEE International Conference on Image Processing (ICIP), pp. 3708–3712. Phoenix, AZ, USA (2016). doi: https://doi.org/10.1109/ICIP.2016.7533052
35. Concrete Crack Images for Classification. https://data.mendeley.com/datasets/5y9wdsg2zt/2. Accessed 20 Oct 2019

EgoApp 2020 - 2nd Workshop on Applications of Egocentric Vision 2020

The Second Workshop on Applications of Egocentric Vision (EgoApp)

Workshop Description

Egocentric vision offers the unique manner to record actions as they are performed by the user. In this way, these recordings contain important visual data about the life of the user and bystanders. Nonetheless, egocentric vision, as compared to the conventional (3rd person) vision introduces novel computational challenges. Usual free motion of the camera causes abrupt changes in the field of view and illumination conditions. Additionally, in-the-wild nature of egocentric vision leads to frequent occlusions and objects intensive appearance variations. In this scenario, building efficient tools, enabling to look at this visual data and answering how the user manipulates certain objects, with whom interacts, how many calories consumed in a day, and for how long each of these activities lasted; are just a few examples of usability and importance of egocentric vision. In this way, related technologies act as assistive technologies not only for patients in need, but also for healthy people who seek an additional support in their daily living, i.e. by a humanoid robot. in this regard, within EgoApp besides covering the conventional topics around applications of egocentric vision, we intended to deal with visual perception of robot environment with special emphasis on methodologies and approaches for analysis of images and videos acquired from the point of view of a robot. Typically, images from robots are much lower resolution and may be affected by motion blur. Objects seen by a robot may undergo important transformations (i.e. scale and point of view), and may be partially occluded by the hands of the robot during manipulation. Overall, this pose important challenges for learning and recognition.

In recent years, the egocentric vision community made a steady progress in the scientific and technological areas. Introduction of Hololens 2.0 by Microsoft in February 2019 can be presumed as the most recent outcome of this type that introduces Mixed Reality by combining Virtual Reality, egocentric perception through vision, and inward vision for eye behaviour understanding. The second workshop on Applications of Egocentric Vision (EgoApp) aimed at contributing to this progress with bringing together diverse communities related to egocentric vision, such as computer science, robotics, and social science to discuss the current and next generation of related technologies. Both research and industry communities were invited to submit their recent outcomes in the format of a research or a position paper.

EgoApp received 6 papers long papers in total. Each paper was peer reviewed in single-blind format by two members of program committee, among which 5 papers were selected for publication and presentation at the workshop by the meta-reviewers.

November 2018

Organization

Organizing Committee

Maya Aghaei   NHL Stenden University of Applied Sciences,
                           The Netherlands
Cigdem Beyan   Istituto Italiano di Tecnologia, Italy
Fernando De la Torre   Facebook Research, USA
Vittorio Murino   Huawei Technologies, Ireland
Lorenzo Natale   Istituto Italiano di Tecnologia, Italy
Alessio Del Bue   Istituto Italiano di Tecnologia, Italy

Program Committee

Antonino Furnari   University of Catania, Italy
Beatriz Romeseiro   University of Oviedo, Spain
Dima Damen   University of Bristol, UK
Erickson R. Nascimento   Federal University of Minas Gerais, Brasil
Ronald Poppe   Utrecht University, The Netherlands
Giulia Pasquale   Istituto Italiano di Tecnologia, Italy
Alessia Vignolo   Istituto Italiano di Tecnologia, Italy

Camera Ego-Positioning Using Sensor Fusion and Complementary Method

Peng-Yuan Kao[1]([✉]), Kuan-Wei Tseng[1], Tian-Yi Shen[1], Yan-Bin Song[1], Kuan-Wen Chen[2], Shih-Wei Hu[1], Sheng-Wen Shih[3], and Yi-Ping Hung[1]

[1] National Taiwan University, Taipei, Taiwan
zbabqr@gmail.com
[2] National Chiao Tung University, Hsinchu, Taiwan
[3] National ChiNan University, Nantou, Taiwan

Abstract. Visual simultaneous localization and mapping (SLAM) is a common solution for camera ego-positioning. However, SLAM sometimes loses tracking, for instance due to fast camera motion or featureless or repetitive environments. To account for the limitations of visual SLAM, we use sensor fusion method to fuse the visual positioning results with inertial measurement unit (IMU) data based on filter-based, loosely-coupled sensor fusion methods, and further combines feature-based SLAM with direct SLAM via proposed complementary fusion to retain the advantages of both methods; i.e., we not only keep the accurate positioning of feature-based SLAM but also account for its difficulty with featureless scenes by direct SLAM. Experimental results show that the proposed complementary method improves the positioning accuracy of conventional vision-only SLAM and leads to more robust positioning results.

Keywords: Camera ego-positioning · Sensor fusion

1 Introduction

Ego-positioning is indispensable in many applications to enable the drone to navigate autonomously in unseen or indoor environments. With the advance of computer vision technology, visual ego-positioning is now one of the most appropriate solutions for drone navigation. This topic has been thoroughly studied and a variety of solutions are now available: two well-known visual ego-positioning categories are visual simultaneous localization and mapping (SLAM) and visual odometry (VO).

In visual SLAM and visual odometry, methods which use monocular cameras are called monocular visual SLAM and monocular visual odometry respectively. Researchers have proposed a variety methods for monocular visual SLAM and VO [1–3,5,6,10,15,16,18]. These can be further classified into feature-based methods and direct methods. The fundamental principle of feature-based methods is detecting feature points for each frame and matching them between consecutive frames. Direct methods in turn use the entire image information, and find a suitable camera pose by minimizing the photometric error.

© Springer Nature Switzerland AG 2021
A. Del Bimbo et al. (Eds.): ICPR 2020 Workshops, LNCS 12663, pp. 291–304, 2021.
https://doi.org/10.1007/978-3-030-68796-0_21

However, visual SLAM and VO both have drawbacks. First, when the camera moves fast, these methods can lose tracking easily due to motion blur or excessive parallax between consecutive frames. Second, for monocular methods, their map scale differs from that in the real world. Considering these drawbacks, a well-known solution is to fuse the visual ego-positioning result from the camera with inertial data from the inertial measurement unit (IMU) via sensor fusion methods [12,14,17,20,22]. In this paper, we fuse visual ego-positioning results from the camera with inertial data from the IMU via a filter-based, loosely-coupled sensor fusion method [22].

Furthermore, feature-based methods and direct methods of visual SLAM and VO have complementary advantages and disadvantages. The positioning accuracy of feature-based methods is higher than that of direct methods, but they perform poorly in featureless scenarios, usually losing tracking in this case. In contrast, although the positioning accuracy of direct methods is lower than that of feature-based methods, they still work in such featureless scenarios. Therefore, in this paper, we propose a complementary method to combine the ego-positioning results of feature-based methods and direct methods to handle featureless scenarios. Experimental results show that the proposed complementary method improves the positioning accuracy of conventional vision-only SLAM and also leads to more robust positioning results.

The rest of this paper is organized as follows. We review related work in Sect. 2 and present the sensor fusion method in Sect. 3. We present the proposed complementary ego-positioning method in Sect. 4, and in Section 5 we evaluate the sensor fusion method as well as the proposed complementary ego-positioning method. We conclude in Sect. 6.

2   Related Work

2.1   Visual Ego-Positioning

Visual ego-positioning has being well studied, two of mostly known categories of visual ego-positioning methods are visual simultaneous localization and mapping (SLAM), and visual odometry (VO). Researchers have proposed a variety methods of visual SLAM and VO these years [1–3,5,6,10,15,16,18]. ORB-SLAM [15] is a representative and classic feature-based method which provides positioning results in real time. ORB-SLAM uses ORB features, which can be computed and matched extremely quickly; the method is also invariant to scale, rotation, and limited affine changes. Furthermore, ORB-SLAM has a good loop-closing algorithm with which it optimizes the global map when closed loops are detected, which can effectively reduce the cumulative error. Using the loop-closing algorithm, ORB-SLAM is also able to quickly relocalize when it loses tracking. LSD-SLAM [2] is a classic direct SLAM method which directly operates on image intensities for both tracking and mapping, instead of using feature points to find correspondences. Semi-Direct Visual Odometry (SVO) [5] is a sparse-direct method, which detects features on the consecutive frames and uses the neighbor pixels of the detected feature to do patch matching for estimating the camera pose. Direct Sparse Odometry (DSO) [1] is also a sparse-direct method. It combines a fully direct probabilistic model (minimizing a photometric error) with consistent, joint optimization of all model parameters, including geometry represented as inverse depth in a reference frame and camera motion.

2.2   Sensor Fusion of Camera and IMU

Visual SLAM and VO have two drawbacks. First, when the camera moves rapidly, the methods lose tracking easily due to motion blur or large parallax between consecutive frames. Second, for monocular methods, the map scale is different from that in the real world. Given these drawbacks, some researchers have proposed sensor fusion methods, which estimate ego-position by fusing visual sensors and inertial sensors. In general, these methods are forms of visual-inertial odometry (VIO). VIO approaches can be divided into two categories: filter-based VIO and optimization-based VIO.

Filter-based VIO [14, 22] uses a filter to fuse visual and inertial measurements. Depending on the filter state vector, filter-based methods can be classified into tightly-coupled methods and loosely-coupled methods. Tightly-coupled methods directly consider the camera pose or information on the image as part of the filter state vector input, leading to high precision but with added computational cost [14]. Mourikis et al. [14] propose extended Kalman filter (EKF)-based real-time fusion using monocular vision and IMU; this is termed multi-state constraint Kalman filter (MSCKF). Unlike conventional EKF-based methods which put features on the image frames into the state vector, MSCKF puts camera poses into the state vector to avoid the curse of dimensionality. Experimental results show that MSCKF achieves high-precision pose estimation in real time. Loosely-coupled methods, in contrast, process the visual and inertial measurements separately to reduce computational cost. Because of this feature, loosely coupled methods are typically suited for systems with very limited resources, such as drones. Weiss et al. [22] propose a framework to enable autonomous flights of micro aerial vehicles by treating visual ego-positioning as a black box. This method is suitable for implementation on drones as it is computationally efficient and can be easily used with different visual ego-positioning algorithms.

Optimization-based VIO [12, 17, 20], in turn, estimates camera pose using an objective function to minimize the reprojection residuals and IMU residuals. Leutenegger et al. [12] propose an optimization-based VIO framework called open keyframe-based visual-inertial SLAM (OKVIS). This work applies the keyframe concept to nonlinear optimization by marginalization. Qin et al. [20] propose a nonlinear optimization-based state estimator with a loop-closing algorithm, which reduces the cumulative error and thus increases positioning accuracy. Nisar et al. [19] proposed a method called visual inertial model-based odometry (VIMO), which extends VINS-Mono by adding thrust measurements and dynamic residuals to the cost function to perform force estimation. They apply the concept of motion constraint which combines quadrotors dynamics and external forces. Their experiments on simulation shows 29% improvement on accuracy without increasing the computational time. Furthermore, in optimization-based

VIO, pre-integration [4] is a significant method, especially for drones, which is applied to process IMU data and can reduce computational costs.

Because filter-based, loosely-coupled sensor fusion methods are computationally efficient and can be easily used with different visual ego-positioning algorithms, in this paper, we use filter-based, loosely-coupled methods as our sensor fusion methods.

2.3   Complementary Ego-Positioning

Another way to overcome the drawbacks of visual SLAM and VO is to use complementary methods, i.e., combine feature-based and direct methods. Feature-based methods and direct methods each have their pros and cons. Feature-based methods enable fast tracking but do poorly in featureless scenarios. Direct methods estimate robust pose over time but come with heavy CPU demands. Complementary methods take advantage of both methods continually for robust results. Krombach et al. [11] propose a complementary ego-positioning method called the hybrid approach. Their approach uses direct method LSD-SLAM as a keyframe register for better depth estimation values. Moreover, LIBVISO2 [9], a feature-based method, keeps tracking pose due to its fast-tracking capabilities. Their experimental results show that the approach accumulates less drift than the direct method or the feature-based method.

3   Sensor Fusion of Camera and IMU

For fast computation and easily adoption of different visual ego-positioning algorithms, which is described in Sect. 2.2, we use the filtered-based, loosely-coupled VIO method. Since it requires visual measurements and IMU measurements to be processed separately, we divide the sensor fusion framework into a visual positioning module and a sensor fusion module. First, the visual positioning module estimates the initial camera pose, after which the sensor fusion module fuses the initial camera pose and IMU measurements to yield a refined camera pose and the scale of the real world. Figure 1 shows the sensor fusion framework used in this work.

3.1   Method

We use the filtered-based, loosely-coupled VIO method proposed by Weiss et al. [22], which uses an EKF framework, and estimates not only the camera pose and velocity but also the scale of the real world. The filter consists of a prediction and an update step. Below we describe in greater detail the structure of the EKF framework.

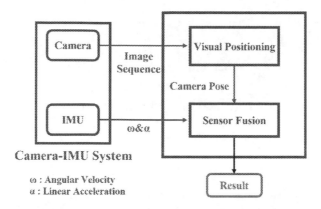

Fig. 1. Loosely-coupled sensor fusion framework

State Vector. The state vector $\mathcal{X}$ of method in [22] contains eight components. The first to the third components are the IMU position $\mathbf{p}_w^i$, the velocity $\mathbf{v}_w^i$, and the rotation $\mathbf{q}_w^i$ from the inertial world coordinate system to the IMU coordinate system. The IMU rotation is expressed in quaternion form. The fourth to the sixth components are the gyroscope bias b_ω, the accelerometer bias b_α, and a measurement scale factor λ. The seventh and the eighth components are the calibration components, which are the distance $\mathbf{p}_i^c$ between IMU and camera and the rotation $\mathbf{q}_i^c$ from the IMU coordinate system to the camera coordinate system:

$$\mathcal{X} = \left[\mathbf{p}_w^i,\ \mathbf{v}_w^i,\ \mathbf{q}_w^i,\ \mathbf{b}_\omega,\ \mathbf{b}_\alpha,\ \lambda,\ \mathbf{p}_i^c,\ \mathbf{q}_i^c\right]. \tag{1}$$

Note that this method assumes the scale factor λ and the calibration components $\mathbf{p}_i^c$ and $\mathbf{q}_i^c$ remain constant over time, that is,

$$\dot{\lambda} = 0, \quad \dot{\mathbf{p}}_i^c = 0, \quad \dot{\mathbf{q}}_i^c = 0. \tag{2}$$

Prediction Step. The IMU data is used in the prediction step for state propagation as the motion model in a basic Kalman filter. The measured angular velocity $\widehat{\boldsymbol{\omega}}$ and acceleration $\widehat{\mathbf{a}}$ data from the IMU are used to predict the system state by integration and double integration. The following differential equations govern the state:

$$\dot{\mathbf{p}}_w^i = \mathbf{v}_w^i, \tag{3}$$

$$\dot{\mathbf{v}}_w^i = \mathbf{R}_i^w\left(\widehat{\mathbf{a}} - \mathbf{b}_\alpha - \mathbf{n}_\alpha\right) - \mathbf{g}, \tag{4}$$

$$\dot{\mathbf{q}}_w^i = \frac{1}{2}\Omega\left(\widehat{\boldsymbol{\omega}} - \mathbf{b}_\omega - \mathbf{n}_\omega\right)\mathbf{q}_w^i, \tag{5}$$

where $\mathbf{b}_\alpha$ and $\mathbf{b}_\omega$ are the sensor bias of the accelerometer and gyroscope respectively; $\mathbf{n}_\alpha$ and $\mathbf{n}_\omega$ are the sensor noise of accelerometer and gyroscope respectively, which are modeled as white noise; $\mathbf{g}$ is the gravity vector in the world coordinate system; $\Omega()$ is the quaternion multiplication matrix of angular velocity; and $\mathbf{R}_i^w$ is the rotation matrix from the IMU coordinate system to the world coordinate system. Note that this method models bias as a random walk, whose derivative is white noise:

$$\dot{\mathbf{b}}_\alpha = \mathbf{n}_{\mathbf{b}\alpha}, \quad \dot{\mathbf{b}}_\omega = \mathbf{n}_{\mathbf{b}\omega}. \tag{6}$$

Update Step. The visual positioning result is used in the update step as the measurement in a basic Kalman Filter. For the position measurement $\mathbf{p}_w^c$ obtained from the visual positioning algorithm, we have the following measurement model:

$$\mathbf{p}_w^c = \lambda(\mathbf{R}_i^w \mathbf{p}_i^c + \mathbf{p}_w^i) + \mathbf{n}_p, \tag{7}$$

where $\mathbf{n}_p$ is the measurement noise modeled as white noise. The rotation measurement $\mathbf{q}_w^c$ obtained from the visual positioning algorithm is modeled as

$$\mathbf{q}_w^c = \mathbf{q}_i^c \otimes \mathbf{q}_w^i, \tag{8}$$

where $\otimes$ is the quaternion multiplication operator. Given the measurement model, the state estimation can be updated according to the Kalman filter procedure.

3.2   Camera-IMU System Calibration

The camera-IMU sensor fusion requires accurate calibration parameters of the camera-IMU system to maintain high performance. These parameters can be divided into camera-intrinsic parameters, camera-IMU-extrinsic parameters, and IMU noise parameters. Camera-intrinsic parameters are critical for the visual positioning module to achieve highly accurate camera-pose estimation. In this work, we use a well-known camera calibration method from Zhang [24]. Camera-IMU-extrinsic parameters are used to update the sensor fusion input state vector. To estimate these, we use the Kalibr toolbox [7,8,13], which is a widely used camera-IMU calibration toolbox that provides highly accurate calibration. IMU noise parameters can inform the sensor fusion system about the uncertainty of the IMU, and are important when the sensor fusion system is updating. Allan standard deviation [21] is a common method to estimate the noise parameters of the sensor.

4   Complementary Ego-Positioning

The framework of our complementary ego-positioning system is shown in Fig. 2. The framework has four main modules: a feature-based visual positioning module, a direct visual positioning module, a sensor fusion module, and a complementary fusion module. Because the feature-based method is faster and more accurate than the direct method, we use the feature-based visual positioning module as the main module and direct visual positioning module as the complementary module. First, the image sequence is fed into the main module and the complementary module to yield the camera pose. The results from the main

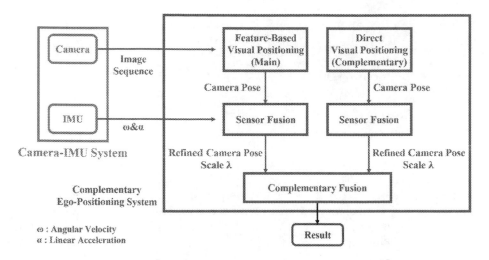

Fig. 2. Framework of proposed complementary ego-positioning system

module and complementary module are then fed into the sensor fusion module respectively, and the sensor fusion module fuses the results from these two modules with the IMU measurements to yield the main VIO result and complementary VIO result respectively. The method used in the sensor fusion module is described in detail in Sect. 3. Finally, as the feature-based method usually performs poorly or loses tracking in featureless scenarios, the complementary fusion module fuses the main and complementary VIO results to handle featureless scenarios, yielding a robust result as the final output.

4.1   3D Point Registration

To fuse the main and the complementary VIO results, they must be aligned. Although the estimated camera poses from the main module and the complementary module are unscaled, the scale can be acquired from the sensor fusion module because it can fuse the estimated camera poses from the main module and the complementary module with the IMU measurements to get the refined camera poses and the scale of the real world. Because the scale is estimated by the sensor fusion module, we can align the main and complementary VIO results as following. We have $\mathbf{p}_m$, which is one of the points in the main-VIO-result point set, $\mathbf{P}_m$, and $\mathbf{p}_c$, which is one of the points in the complementary-VIO-result point set, $\mathbf{P}_c$. Both $\mathbf{P}_m$ and $\mathbf{P}_c$ are finite-size point sets in a three-dimensional real vector space. The transformation from $\mathbf{p}_c$ to $\mathbf{p}_m$ can be formulated as

$$\mathbf{p}_m = \mathbf{R}\mathbf{p}_c + \mathbf{t}, \tag{9}$$

where $\mathbf{R}$ is a 3×3 rotation matrix and $\mathbf{t}$ is a 3×1 translation vector. We can solve the $\mathbf{R}$ and $\mathbf{t}$ by minimizing the error of the objective function:

$$\underset{\mathbf{R},\,\mathbf{t}}{\operatorname{argmin}} \sum \|\mathbf{p}_m - \mathbf{R}\mathbf{p}_c - \mathbf{t}\|^2. \tag{10}$$

After the transformation parameters $\mathbf{R}$ and $\mathbf{t}$ are estimated, we align the complementary VIO result to the main VIO result.

4.2   Complementary Fusion

In our framework, the main VIO and the complementary VIO execute in parallel. They continually output the scaled and the refined camera poses. At the same time, the complementary fusion module uses the underperformance detection algorithm to detect when the main module is underperforming (drift or lose tracking) and then fuses the main VIO result and the complementary VIO result. When the main module is working as expected, the complementary fusion module uses the main VIO result. When it underperforms, the complementary fusion module replaces the main VIO result with the complementary VIO result after aligning the complementary VIO result to the main VIO result. The alignment algorithm is presented in Sect. 4.1.

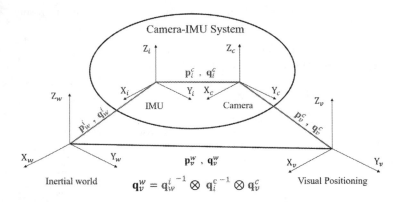

Fig. 3. Transformation relationships of coordinate systems used in sensor fusion. The red part represents the transformation relationship of the visual positioning coordinate system and camera coordinate system. The purple part represents the transformation relationship of the camera coordinate system and IMU coordinate system. The green part represents the transformation relationship of the IMU coordinate system and inertial world coordinate system. (Color figure online)

The underperformance detection algorithm previously mentioned is from [23]. It detects behavior such as pose estimation drift or tracking loss, which often result in strange camera rotation estimations. In our framework, the camera rotation is estimated by two different modules: the visual positioning module and the sensor fusion module. Figure 3 shows the transformation relationships of the coordinate systems used in the sensor fusion. Based on the relationships shown in Fig. 3, we estimate the rotation from the visual positioning coordinate system to the inertial world coordinate system, $\mathbf{q}_v^w$, for each EKF update step k by the following equation:

$$\mathbf{q}_v^w(k) = \widehat{\mathbf{q}}_w^{i^{-1}}(k) \otimes \widehat{\mathbf{q}}_i^{c^{-1}}(k) \otimes \widehat{\mathbf{q}}_v^c(k), \tag{11}$$

where $\widehat{\mathbf{q}}_v^c(k)$ is the rotation from the visual positioning coordinate system to the camera coordinate system, $\widehat{\mathbf{q}}_i^c(k)$ is the rotation from the IMU coordinate system to the camera coordinate system, and $\widehat{\mathbf{q}}_w^i(k)$ is the the rotation from the inertial world coordinate system to the IMU coordinate system.

Ideally, the camera rotation estimated by the visual positioning, $\widehat{\mathbf{q}}_v^c(k)$, and the sensor fusion, $\widehat{\mathbf{q}}_w^i(k)$, is equal. However, if the visual positioning method underperforms, there is a considerable difference between $\widehat{\mathbf{q}}_v^c(k)$ and $\widehat{\mathbf{q}}_w^i(k)$, causing the variation of $\mathbf{q}_v^w(k)$ to be high because $\widehat{\mathbf{q}}_i^c(k)$ is from the calibration and is constant in the sensor fusion framework. As the variation of $\mathbf{q}_v^w$ is slow compared to the EKF update frequency, underperformance in the main module can be detected when there is an abrupt jump in the smooth $\mathbf{q}_v^w$ estimation, $\widehat{\mathbf{q}}_v^w$:

$$\widehat{\mathbf{q}}_v^w(k) = \text{Median}\left[\mathbf{q}_v^w(i)\right], \; i = k - N \rightarrow k, \tag{12}$$

where Median[] is the median filter and N is the window size. When the EKF update step comes to $k+1$, we compare the $\mathbf{q}_v^w(k+1)$ with the past M estimates $\widehat{\mathbf{q}}_v^w$. If $\mathbf{q}_v^w(k+1)$ lies outside the 3σ error bounds of the $\widehat{\mathbf{q}}_v^w$, underperformance has occurred.

5   Experiments

In this section, we evaluate the proposed complementary ego-positioning system in two scenarios: a normal scenario and a featureless scenario. The feature-based visual positioning method we used is ORB-SLAM [15], and the direct visual positioning method we used is LSD-SLAM [2]. Both methods are the classic and representative visual SLAM methods. The experimental setup is shown in Fig. 4. We built a camera-IMU system to record data for the experiment consisting of an NGIMU and a GoPro Hero4 camera, which are mounted on a box. The camera-IMU system is shown in Fig. 4(a). The sampling rate of the NGIMU 100 Hz, and the camera was run at 30 fps. The ground truth trajectory of the camera-IMU system was taken by Vicon.

Normal Scenario. In the normal scenario, we recorded data in a regular scene full of features, as shown in Fig. 4(b). The results of this scenario on the X-Y trajectory is shown in Fig. 5. The statistics of the positioning errors and scale errors are shown in Table 1. Note that all of the trajectories are aligned to the ground truth trajectories. The alignment includes scaling, rotation, and translation. The mean and standard deviation of the positioning errors in Table 1 are estimated on the aligned trajectories. The scale errors in Table 1 are the scale ratio of the positioning algorithm trajectory by the ground truth trajectory. The results show that both ORB-SLAM and LSD-SLAM have good positioning accuracy. The positioning errors of ORB-SLAM and LSD-SLAM can be reduced by fusing with the IMU. Sensor fusion also recovers the scale of the real world. After fusing with IMU, the trajectories of ORB-SLAM and LSD SLAM become smooth and close to the ground truth trajectory. The positioning accuracy of

ORB-SLAM and ORB-SLAM + IMU is higher than the positioning accuracy of
LSD-SLAM and LSD-SLAM + IMU. With the complementary fusion method
of the proposed complementary ego-positioning system, because the main VIO
does not underperform, the final result is equal to the main VIO (ORB-SLAM
+ IMU) result.

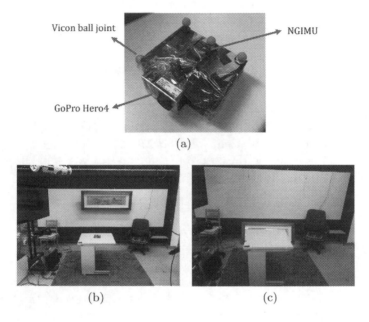

(a)

(b)   (c)

Fig. 4. Experimental setup: (a) Camera-IMU system, (b) normal scenario, and (c)
featureless scenario.

Table 1. Positioning errors and scale errors in normal scenario

	Error mean (mm)	Error stdev. (mm)	Scale error
ORB-SLAM	53.5	19.2	3.13
ORB-SLAM + IMU	49.9	17.4	0.95
LSD-SLAM	58.9	30.9	2.21
LSD-SLAM + IMU	50.9	35.3	0.95
Complementary method	49.9	17.4	0.95

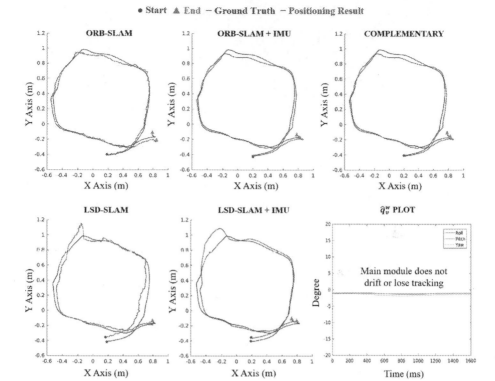

Fig. 5. X-Y trajectories of different positioning methods and plot of $\mathbf{q}_v^w$ in normal scenario

Featureless Scenario. In the featureless scenario, shown in Fig. 4(c), we removed the painting in the experiment scene of the normal scenario to simulate a featureless environment with a pure white wall. The results of this scenario on the X-Y trajectory are shown in Fig. 6. ORB-SLAM loses tracking when it comes to the white wall. With the help of fusing with IMU, ORB-SLAM does not lose tracking when it comes to the white wall. However, the trajectory of the white wall part is far from the ground truth trajectory. In contrast, LSD-SLAM and LSD + IMU is robust in the whole trajectory even though their trajectories are not very close to the ground truth trajectory. The proposed complementary ego-positioning system detects the tracking loss when it comes to the white wall and uses the complementary VIO (LSD + IMU) result to replace the main VIO (ORB-SLAM + IMU) result. The statistics of positioning errors and scale errors are shown in Table 2, according to which the positioning error of the proposed complementary ego-positioning system is the lowest.

Table 2. Positioning errors and scale errors in featureless scenario

	Error mean (mm)	Error stdev. (mm)	Scale error
ORB-SLAM	N/A	N/A	N/A
ORB-SLAM + IMU	344.4	478.7	1.01
LSD-SLAM	131.9	57.2	2.37
LSD-SLAM + IMU	125.0	52.8	1.02
Complementary method	103.0	51.3	0.95

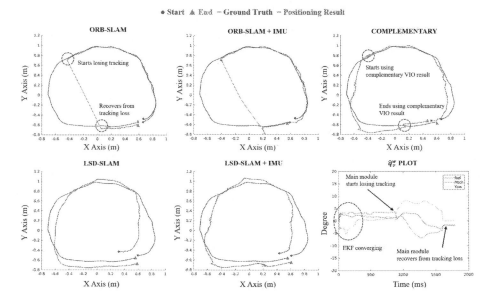

Fig. 6. X-Y trajectories of different positioning methods and plot of $\mathbf{q}_v^w$ in featureless scenario

6   Conclusion

In this paper, we propose a novel camera localization method by using sensor fusion and complementary ego-positioning. First, we use the filter-based, loosely-coupled sensor fusion to fuse the visual-positioning result with IMU measurements to yield a refined pose as well as the scale of the real world. Furthermore, we combine the ego-positioning results of feature-based SLAM and direct SLAM. Two classic and representative visual SLAM methods—ORB-SLAM and LSD-SLAM—are used in this work. ORB-SLAM is a feature-based method which is robust and accurate in normal scenes with a sufficient number of features but does poorly in featureless scenarios. LSD-SLAM is a direct method, which is less sensitive to featureless scenarios, but is less accurate than ORB-SLAM. As the two methods are complementary, the combination of ORB-SLAM and LSD-SLAM produces more robust and accurate results. The experimental results show that in normal scenarios, sensor fusion improves the visual positioning result and estimates the scale of the real world precisely. In featureless scenarios, the direct method takes over and maintains a robust result.

Acknowledgments. This work was partially supported by MediaTek and the Ministry of Science and Technology, Taiwan.

References

1. Engel, J., Koltun, V., Cremers, D.: Direct sparse odometry. IEEE Trans. Pattern Anal. Mach. Intell. **40**(3), 611–625 (2017)
2. Engel, J., Schöps, T., Cremers, D.: LSD-SLAM: large-scale direct monocular SLAM. In: Fleet, D., Pajdla, T., Schiele, B., Tuytelaars, T. (eds.) ECCV 2014. LNCS, vol. 8690, pp. 834–849. Springer, Cham (2014). https://doi.org/10.1007/978-3-319-10605-2_54
3. Engel, J., Stückler, J., Cremers, D.: Large-scale direct slam with stereo cameras. In: 2015 IEEE/RSJ International Conference on Intelligent Robots and Systems (IROS), pp. 1935–1942. IEEE (2015)
4. Forster, C., Carlone, L., Dellaert, F., Scaramuzza, D.: On-manifold preintegration for real-time visual-inertial odometry. IEEE Trans. Rob. **33**(1), 1–21 (2016)
5. Forster, C., Pizzoli, M., Scaramuzza, D.: SVO: fast semi-direct monocular visual odometry. In: 2014 IEEE International Conference on Robotics and Automation (ICRA), pp. 15–22. IEEE (2014)
6. Forster, C., Zhang, Z., Gassner, M., Werlberger, M., Scaramuzza, D.: SVO: semidirect visual odometry for monocular and multicamera systems. IEEE Trans. Rob. **33**(2), 249–265 (2016)
7. Furgale, P., Barfoot, T.D., Sibley, G.: Continuous-time batch estimation using temporal basis functions. In: 2012 IEEE International Conference on Robotics and Automation, pp. 2088–2095. IEEE (2012)
8. Furgale, P., Rehder, J., Siegwart, R.: Unified temporal and spatial calibration for multi-sensor systems. In: 2013 IEEE/RSJ International Conference on Intelligent Robots and Systems, pp. 1280–1286. IEEE (2013)
9. Geiger, A., Ziegler, J., Stiller, C.: StereoScan: dense 3D reconstruction in real-time. In: Intelligent Vehicles Symposium (IV) (2011)
10. Klein, G., Murray, D.: Parallel tracking and mapping for small AR workspaces. In: 2007 6th IEEE and ACM International Symposium on Mixed and Augmented Reality, pp. 225–234. IEEE (2007)
11. Krombach, N., Droeschel, D., Behnke, S.: Combining feature-based and direct methods for semi-dense real-time stereo visual odometry. In: Chen, W., Hosoda, K., Menegatti, E., Shimizu, M., Wang, H. (eds.) IAS 2016. AISC, vol. 531, pp. 855–868. Springer, Cham (2017). https://doi.org/10.1007/978-3-319-48036-7_62
12. Leutenegger, S., Lynen, S., Bosse, M., Siegwart, R., Furgale, P.: Keyframe-based visual-inertial odometry using nonlinear optimization. Int. J. Robot. Res. **34**(3), 314–334 (2015)
13. Maye, J., Furgale, P., Siegwart, R.: Self-supervised calibration for robotic systems. In: 2013 IEEE Intelligent Vehicles Symposium (IV), pp. 473–480. IEEE (2013)
14. Mourikis, A.I., Roumeliotis, S.I.: A multi-state constraint Kalman filter for vision-aided inertial navigation. In: 2007 IEEE International Conference on Robotics and Automation, pp. 3565–3572. IEEE (2007)

15. Mur-Artal, R., Montiel, J.M.M., Tardos, J.D.: ORB-SLAM: a versatile and accurate monocular SLAM system. IEEE Trans. Rob. **31**(5), 1147–1163 (2015)
16. Mur-Artal, R., Tardós, J.D.: ORB-SLAM2: an open-source SLAM system for monocular, stereo, and RGB-D cameras. IEEE Trans. Rob. **33**(5), 1255–1262 (2017)
17. Mur-Artal, R., Tardós, J.D.: Visual-inertial monocular SLAM with map reuse. IEEE Robot. Autom. Lett. **2**(2), 796–803 (2017)
18. Newcombe, R.A., Lovegrove, S.J., Davison, A.J.: DTAM: dense tracking and mapping in real-time. In: 2011 International Conference on Computer Vision, pp. 2320–2327, November 2011. https://doi.org/10.1109/ICCV.2011.6126513
19. Nisar, B., Foehn, P., Falanga, D., Scaramuzza, D.: VIMO: simultaneous visual inertial model-based odometry and force estimation. IEEE Robot. Autom. Lett. **4**(3), 2785–2792 (2019)
20. Qin, T., Li, P., Shen, S.: VINS-Mono: a robust and versatile monocular visual-inertial state estimator. IEEE Trans. Rob. **34**(4), 1004–1020 (2018)
21. Vukmirica, V., Trajkovski, I., Asanovic, N.: Two methods for the determination of inertial sensor parameters. Methods **3**(1) (2018)
22. Weiss, S., Achtelik, M.W., Chli, M., Siegwart, R.: Versatile distributed pose estimation and sensor self-calibration for an autonomous MAV. In: 2012 IEEE International Conference on Robotics and Automation, pp. 31–38. IEEE (2012)
23. Weiss, S., Siegwart, R.: Real-time metric state estimation for modular vision-inertial systems. In: 2011 IEEE International Conference on Robotics and Automation, pp. 4531–4537. IEEE (2011)
24. Zhang, Z.: A flexible new technique for camera calibration. IEEE Trans. Pattern Anal. Mach. Intell. **22**(11), 1330–1334 (2000)

ATSal: An Attention Based Architecture for Saliency Prediction in 360° Videos

Yasser Dahou[1(✉)], Marouane Tliba[2], Kevin McGuinness[1], and Noel O'Connor[1]

[1] Insight Centre for Data Analytics, Dublin City University, Dublin 9, Ireland
yasser.dahoudjilali2@mail.dcu.ie
[2] Institut National des Télécommunications et des TIC, Oran, Algeria

Abstract. The spherical domain representation of 360° video/image presents many challenges related to the storage, processing, transmission and rendering of omnidirectional videos (ODV). Models of human visual attention can be used so that only a single viewport is rendered at a time, which is important when developing systems that allow users to explore ODV with head mounted displays (HMD). Accordingly, researchers have proposed various saliency models for 360° video/images. This paper proposes ATSal, a novel attention based (head-eye) saliency model for 360° videos. The attention mechanism explicitly encodes global static visual attention allowing expert models to focus on learning the saliency on local patches throughout consecutive frames. We compare the proposed approach to other state-of-the-art saliency models on two datasets: Salient360! and VR-EyeTracking. Experimental results on over 80 ODV videos (75K+ frames) show that the proposed method outperforms the existing state-of-the-art.

Keywords: Omnidirectional video (ODV) · Head and eye saliency prediction · Deep learning

1 Introduction

360° video, referred to as panoramic, spherical or omnidirectional video, is a recently introduced type of multimedia that provides the user with an immersive experience. The content of ODV is rendered to cover the entire 360×180 viewing space. Humans, however, naturally focus on the most attractive and interesting field-of-views (FoV) while ignoring others in their visual field, using a set of visual operations know as visual attention. Such selective mechanisms allow humans to interpret and analyze complex scenes in real time and devote their limited perceptual and cognitive resources to the most pertinent subsets of sensory data. Inspired by this visual perception phenomenon, saliency prediction or modeling is the process that aims to model the gaze fixation distribution patterns of humans on static and dynamic scenes. Modeling visual attention in omnidirectional video is an important component of being able to deliver optimal immersive experiences. The main objective is to predict the most probable

© Springer Nature Switzerland AG 2021
A. Del Bimbo et al. (Eds.): ICPR 2020 Workshops, LNCS 12663, pp. 305–320, 2021.
https://doi.org/10.1007/978-3-030-68796-0_22

viewports in a frame reflecting the average person's head movements (HM) and eye movements (EM) reflecting the region-of-interest (RoI) inside the predicted viewport. Thus, when predicting the most salient pixels, it is necessary to predict both HM and EM for 360° video/image visual attention modeling.

Despite the remarkable advances in the field of visual attention modeling on a fixed viewport (see [3–5] for a comprehensive review), saliency prediction studies on 360° video/image are still limited. This is in part due to the comparatively small amount of research that has investigated the visual attention features that affect human perception in panoramic scenes. This is further compounded by the lack of commonly used large-scale head and eye-gaze datasets for 360° content as well as the associated difficulties of using this data compared with publicly available 2D stimuli datasets.

A recent survey conducted by Xu et al. [1] reviewed many works for predicting the HM/EM saliency maps of 360° images and video that model the probability distribution of viewports/RoIs of multiple subjects. Rai et al. [17] derived the volcano-like distribution of EM with the viewport. Results show that eye-gaze fixations are quasi-isotropically distributed in orientation, typically far away from the center of the viewport. Furthermore, ODV presents some statistical biases, as investigated in [18]. Human attention on 360° video is biased toward the equator and the front region, known as the equator bias, which could be leveraged as priors in modelling. Along with the statistical bias, a subject's attention is driven by the most salient objects in the scene. It has been shown that a smaller number of closer objects capture more human attention [19].

Motivated by this, our novel approach combines global visual features over the entire view with features derived from local patches in consecutive frames. A good set of features are those that share the minimal information necessary to perform well at the saliency task. The goal of our representation is to capture as much information as possible about the stimulus. This technique results in state-of-the-art accuracy on standard benchmarks.

The contributions of this paper are as follows:

- We demonstrate the importance of global visual attention features in achieving better saliency performance.
- A new approach, ATSal, is presented that combines an attention mechanism with expert instances for each patch location to learn effective features for saliency modelling.
- We pre-process the VR-EyeTracking [6] dataset by extracting the well annotated fixation/saliency maps from the provided raw data and make this available to others to use at this link.
- We compare our approach against a representative selection of state-of-the-art 360° approaches on both the VR-EyeTracking and Salient360! datasets.

The rest of the paper is organized as follows: Section 2 provides an overview of related 360° video saliency works. Section 3 gives a detailed description of the proposed framework. Section 4 compares the experimental results to state-of-the-art methods. Finally, we conclude this work in Sect. 5. The results can be reproduced with the source code and trained models available on GitHub: link.

2   Related Work

In this section, we present the important works related to attention modelling for 2D dynamic stimuli and 360° video/image. They mainly refer to predicting the HM/EM saliency maps of 360° video/images and can be further grouped into heuristic approaches and data-driven approaches.

2.1   2D Dynamic Saliency Models

Video saliency prediction has advanced significantly since the advent of deep learning. Recently, many works have investigated deep neural networks (DNNs) for video saliency prediction (e.g. [7–13]). SalEMA [10] added a conceptually simple exponential moving average of an internal convolutional state to the SalGAN network [14]. 3DSAL [11] performs 3D convolutions on the generated VGG-16 features, while using a weighting cuboid function to smooth the spatial features; the novel contribution is learning saliency by fusing spatio-temporal features. Unisal [7] proposed four novel domain adaptation techniques to enable strong shared features: domain-adaptive priors, domain-adaptive fusion, domain-adaptive smoothing, and Bypass-RNN. Unisal achieved the state-of-the-art results on the DHF1K benchmark [12] (e.g. AUC-J: 0.901, NSS: 2.776).

2.2   360° Heuristic Approaches

The heuristic approaches encode saliency on the 360° sphere using handcrafted features. The pioneer works by Iva et al. [15,16] generate the spherical static saliency map by combining together chromatic, intensity, and three cue conspicuity maps after normalization, through multiscale analysis on the sphere. They build the motion pyramid on the sphere by applying block matching and varying the block size. Finally, the two maps are fused to produce the dynamic saliency map on the sphere. Unfortunately, no quantitative results were provided in [15,16] since the HMD was not yet available at the time. RM3 [25] for 360° images, combines low-level features hue, saturation and GBVS features, with the high-level features present in each viewport. Unlike [15,16,25], Fang et al. [26] proposed the extraction of low-level features of color, texture luminance, and boundary connectivity from the super-pixels at multiple levels segmented from the input equirectangular projection (ERP) image.

Other works have adapted existing 2D saliency models into 360° video/ images. This approach, however, suffers from geometric distortion and border artifacts. Abreu et al. [2] introduced a fused saliency map (FSM) approach to HM saliency prediction on 360° images; they adapted SALICON [20] (a 2D image saliency prediction model) to 360° images using ERP. Lebreton et al. [21] extended the 2D Boolean Map Saliency (BMS [22]) and Graph-Based Visual Saliency (GBVS [23]) models to integrate the properties for equirectangular images, naming their approaches BMS360 and GBVS360 respectively. Maugey et al. [24] applied a 2D saliency model on each face generated under the cubemap projection (CMP). Recently, it has become easier to collect HM and EM data and thus there have emerged many end-to-end saliency prediction approaches for 360° video/images.

2.3   360° Data-Driven Approaches

Trained on recently published datasets [6,18,27,28], a number of deep neural netrowk (DNN) saliency prediction approaches for 360° video have been proposed [18,28–34]. Nguyen et al. [32] fine-tuned the PanoSalNet 2D static model on 360° video datasets to predict HM saliency map of each frame without considering the temporal dimension. The predicted saliency is enhanced by a prior filter based on an a-priori statistical bias. Cheng et al. [29] proposed a DNN-based spatial-temporal network, consisting of a static model and a ConvLSTM module to adjust the outputs of the static model based on temporal features. They also aggregated a "Cube Padding" technique in the convolution, pooling, and convolutional LSTM layers to keep connectivity between the cube faces by propagating the shared information across the views. Lebreton et al. [31] extended BMS360 [21] to V-BMS360 by adding a temporal bias and optical flow-based motion features. Hu et al. [34] proposed a deep learning-based agent for automatic piloting through 360° sports videos. At each frame, the agent observes a panoramic image and has the knowledge of previously selected viewing angles. The developed online policy allows shifting the current viewing angle to the next preferred one through a recurrent neural network. Fang et al. [35] fine tuned SalGAN [4] on the Salient360! image dataset with a new loss function combining three saliency metrics. Qiao et al. [36] proposed a Multi-Task Deep Neural Network (MT-DNN) model for head movement prediction; the center of each viewport is spatio-temporally aligned with 8 shared convolution layers to predict saliency features.

Unlike all previous approaches, Zhang et al. [28] proposed a spherical convolutional neural network, spherical U-NET, trained following the teacher forcing technique, for applying a planar saliency CNN to a 3D geometry space, where the kernel is defined on a spherical crown, and the convolution involves the rotation of the kernel along the sphere. The model input includes one frame and the predicted saliency maps of several previous frames to allow for improved modelling of dynamic saliency. The authors also defined a spherical MSE (S-MSE) loss function for training the spherical U-Net to reduce the non-uniform sampling of the ERP. Furthermore, instead of using supervised learning to learn saliency from data, Mai et al. [18] applied deep reinforcement learning (DRL) to predict HM positions by maximizing the reward of imitating human HM scanpaths through the agent's actions. The reward, which measures the similarity between the predicted and ground-truth HM scanpaths, is estimated to evaluate the action made by the DRL model. The reward is then used to make a decision on the action through the DRL model: i.e., the HM scanpath in the current frame.

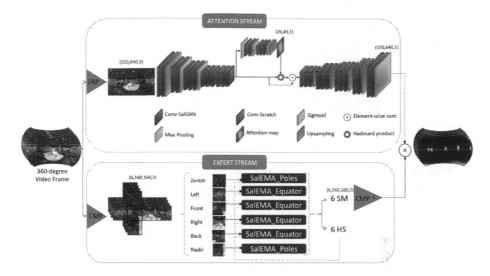

Fig. 1. Network Architecture of ATSal. The attention stream is for extracting global saliency. The experts model operates on local patches. The final saliency is obtained by pixel-wise multiplication between the two maps generated by each stream.

It is clear from the above review that the number of models targeting HM and EM 360° video visual attention modeling is still considerably limited compared with 2D video saliency prediction. There is still much work to be done to meet the specific requirements of ODV. The contributions of this paper as outlined above attempt to address this.

3 Proposed Model

This section describes our framework (see Fig. 1). The design consists of an attention model, expert models, and the fusion method.

Our approach operates in two parallel streams. One stream is dedicated to extracting global attention statistics via the attention mechanism applied on the ERP frame. This explicitly captures static saliency information allowing the second steam to learn more effective temporal features. Moreover, the expert models embed two instances of SalEMA on the cube faces, **SalEMA_Poles** for the Zenith and Nadir and **SalEMA_Equator** specialized for the equator viewports. This is motivated by findings that investigated the properties of panoramic scenes that argued that the fixations distribution is highly correlated with the locations of the viewports [36]. Thus, we adapted SalEMA weights to meet these requirements.

3.1 Attention Mechanism

Despite the strong research interest and investigations of saliency prediction over 360° stimuli, to the best of our knowledge, no previous work has exploited the global attention effect related to omnidirectional scenes in general and for head and eye saliency prediction in particular. We address this by implementing an attention mechanism in a parallel stream which is able to encode the global statistics of the 360° video/image. A dense mask is learned at the middle of the bottleneck with an enlarged receptive field, and this attention mask is combined by performing pixel-wise multiplication with the feature map followed by pixel-wise summation among the channels to obtain the final optimal latent variable representation, thereby embedding as much information as possible about the input frame.

Why an attention mechanism? Recent studies [37–40] have shown the effectiveness of attention mechanisms for several computer vision downstream tasks. In such approaches, attention is learned in an adaptive, joint, and task-oriented manner, allowing the network to focus on the most relevant parts of the input space. Similar to [12], our latent attention module extracts strong spatial saliency information and was trained on both Salient360! [41] and Sitzman [42] 360 image saliency datasets in a supervised fashion. Such a design leads to generalization of the prediction performance across different 360 saliency datasets. As shown in Fig. 2, the input is an ERP image $X \in \mathbb{R}^{640 \times 320 \times 3}$. This shape implies the preservation of the initial spherical characteristics of the data distribution, which is of ratio 2:1. However, a larger receptive field is needed to propagate each pixel-wise response to a field of 640×320 which is the sufficient condition of having the global attention. The approach is motivated by the following considerations:

Table 1. Attention model results on Salient360! validation images.

	Salient360!				
	AUC-J ↑	NSS ↑	CC ↑	SIM ↑	KLD ↓
Attention model	0.837	1.680	0.631	0.629	0.801

- As investigated in [43], human attention is driven by complementary pathways, which compete on global versus local features. Global features such as: semantics, pose, and spatial configuration, called scene layout or "gist", guides the early visual processing. In a panoramic scenario, the CMP prediction forces the model to lose the global contextual information while considering each face separately. Through the attention mechanism, the auto-encoder is forced to learn a more explicit global static representation. The global and local features are disentangled for robust predictions.
- The receptive field of the encoder needs to cover the entire input. To this end, we modified the VGG-16 encoder, by deleting the last two max pooling layers to better preserve spatial frequencies, and set the max poling layer-3 stride factor and kernel size from $(2 \rightarrow 4)$. This replaces the initial VGG-16 receptive field (212×212) with an enlarged one of (244×244) but this is

still not sufficient to cover the whole input $X \in \mathbb{R}^{640 \times 320 \times 3}$. To tackle this issue, we extended the $conv5$ layer with an attention mechanism containing several convolution layers interspersed with pooling and up-sampling operations. Given the latent variable:

$$z_1 = f_\theta(X) \in \mathbb{R}^{20 \times 40 \times 512}, \tag{1}$$

where f_θ is the encoder, the attention mechanism yields a dense attention map $M \in [0, 1]^{20 \times 40}$ with an enlarged receptive field of 676×676.

The attention module is activated with a sigmoid function, which relaxes the sum to one constraint often used in softmax based neural attention. The feature map z_1 is further enhanced by:

$$z^c = (1 + M) \circ z_1^c, \tag{2}$$

where $c \in \{1, ..., 512\}$ is the channel index and M operates as a feature wise selector on z_1, with the residual connection to keep all the useful information [44]. The optimal latent variable $z \in \mathbb{R}^{20 \times 40 \times 512}$ is fed to the decoder to learn the predicted saliency map $Y_1 \in \mathbb{R}^{640 \times 320}$. Table 2 summarizes the architecture of the attention mechanism.

Table 2. Architecture of the attention mechanism

Layer (type)	Output shape	# Parameters
MaxPool2D_1	$1 \times 512 \times 10 \times 20$	0
Conv2D_1	$1 \times 64 \times 10 \times 20$	294,976
ReLU	$1 \times 64 \times 10 \times 20$	0
Conv2D_2	$1 \times 128 \times 10 \times 20$	73,856
ReLU	$1 \times 128 \times 10 \times 20$	0
MaxPool2D_2	$1 \times 128 \times 5 \times 10$	0
Conv2D_3	$1 \times 64 \times 5 \times 10$	73,792
ReLU	$1 \times 64 \times 5 \times 10$	0
Conv2D_4	$1 \times 128 \times 5 \times 10$	73,856
ReLU	$1 \times 128 \times 5 \times 10$	0
Conv2D_5	$1 \times 1 \times 5 \times 10$	129
Upsample	$1 \times 1 \times 20 \times 40$	0
Sigmoid	$1 \times 1 \times 20 \times 40$	0

Total parameters: 516,609

3.2 Expert Models

All previous works learn the same network parameters for the six faces of the cube. However, the saliency density is mostly represented in the equator, forcing the network to over estimate fixations in the poles, which is one of the main reasons the prediction performance drops. In short, the expert stream of our framework instantiates two expert versions from SalEMA [10] and combines their results through the inverse projection to predict the final saliency. The main point of the expert stream is to predict 360° dynamic saliency viewports based on both spatiotemporal content and viewport location. Accordingly, each viewport is predicted independently with shared weights. The input frame in ERP format X is first projected to the CMP format resulting in $x_i, i \in \{1, ..6\}$. Where $x_{0,1,2,3}$ represents the front, left, right and back views, and $x_{4,5}$ are the Zenith and Nadir views. The original SalEMA was trained on DHF1K dataset using the binary cross entropy (BCE) loss and a SalGAN encoder-decoder with an added exponential moving average (EMA) recurrence. The exponential weighted average takes the state S_t output by a convolutional layer at time t. The output E_t is then propagated the next layers using a convex combination of the state S_t and previous states:

$$E_t = \alpha S_t + (1 - \alpha)E_{t-1}. \tag{3}$$

with initial $\alpha = 0.1$. We further changed the training protocol of SalEMA, by adjusting each corresponding cube face into a batch of 80 for the poles, but we kept the initial 10 for the equators; also, we kept BCE as the objective function for fine-tuning SalEMA. This is motivated by the low motion present in each viewport (see [45]). **SalEMA_Poles** was fine-tuned on batches of the faces $x_{4,5}$ to capture the underlying features on these viewports, while **SalEMA_Poles** was adapted to faces $x_{0,1,2,3}$. The generated local saliency per cube face is then inversely projected into the ERP format using CMP^{-1}; we denote $Y_2 \in \mathbb{R}^{640 \times 320}$ the generated saliency map after the inverse projection. The final saliency map Y_t is obtained after pixel wise multiplication between Y_1 and Y_2:

$$Y = Y_1 \circ Y_2 \in [0, 1]^{640 \times 320} \tag{4}$$

3.3 Loss Function for the Attention Stream

According to [46], the saliency metrics cover different aspects of the saliency map. Thus, we define the loss function as a combination between the Kullback-Leibler Divergence (KL) and the Normalized Scanpath Saliency (NSS). We denote the predicted saliency $Y_1 \in [0, 1]^{640 \times 320}$, the fixation map as $F \in \{0, 1\}^{640 \times 320}$, the dense mask at the middle of the bottleneck $M \in [0, 1]^{20 \times 40}$, and the continuous saliency map obtained after blurring F with a Gaussian filter ($\sigma = 9.35°$) as $Q_1 \in [0, 1]^{640 \times 320}$. $Q_2 \in [0, 1]^{40 \times 20}$ is the down-sampled version. The attention stream loss function is defined as follows:

$$\begin{aligned} \mathcal{L}_{\mathcal{T}}(Y_1, M, F, Q_1, Q_2) &= \alpha_1 \mathcal{L}_{\text{KL}}(Y_1, Q_1) \\ &+ \alpha_2 \mathcal{L}_{\text{NSS}}(Y_1, F) + \beta \mathcal{L}_{\text{KL}}(M, Q_2) \end{aligned} \tag{5}$$

where $\alpha_2 = \beta = 0.2$, and $\alpha_2 = 0.8$. $\mathcal{L}_{KL}$ is chosen as the primary loss:

$$\mathcal{L}_{\text{KL}}(Y_1, Q_1) = \sum_i Q_{1i} \log \left(\epsilon + \frac{Q_{1i}}{\epsilon + Y_{1i}} \right). \tag{6}$$

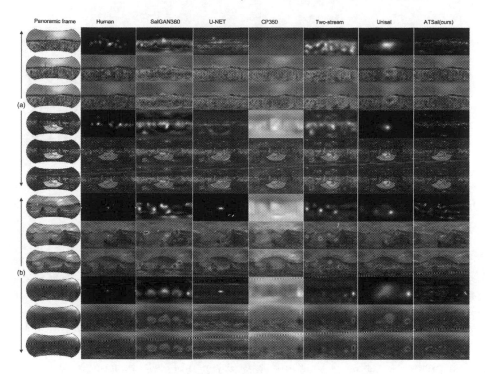

Fig. 2. Qualitative results of our ATSal model and five other competitors on sample frames from VR-EyeTracking and Salient360! datasets. It can be observed that the proposed ATSal is able to handle various challenging scenes well and produces consistent omnidirectional video saliency results.

$\mathcal{L}_{\mathrm{NSS}}$ is derived from the NSS metric, which is a similarity metric. We therefore optimize its negative:

$$\mathcal{L}_{NSS}(Y_1, F) = -\frac{1}{N} \sum_i \bar{Y}_{1i} \times F_i, \tag{7}$$

where $N = \sum F_i$ and $\bar{Y}_{1i} = (Y_{1i} - \mu(Y_{1i}))/\sigma(Y_{1i})$.

4   Experiments

4.1   Experimental Setup

Training. The attention model was trained in two stages. First, to encode static saliency, we trained the attention model on 360° images from the Salient360! and Sitzman datasets. Due to the small amount of labelled static data (103 omnidirectional images), we applied some common data augmentation techniques: mirroring, rotations, and horizontal flipping. The resulting dataset contains 2,368 360° images. Results on the images Salient360! validation set are shown in Table 1.

Fig. 3. Overlaid saliency of the attention model, experts model, and the final ATSal. It can be seen that the attention model captures more global saliency, while the experts focus on local patches. ATSal gathers both features for the final prediction.

For dynamic stimuli, we consider 2 settings: training both streams on: (i) Video-Salient360!, (ii) VR-EyeTracking. For Salient360!, we used 15 ODV for training and 04 for validation. For VR-EyeTracking, the training and testing sets include 140 and 75 videos respectively. We evaluate our model on the the test set of VR-EyeTracking and the validation sets (images and videos) of Salient360! (due to the unavailability of the reserved set after we contacted the authors), in total 79 ODVs with over 75,000 frames.

Competitors. ATSal is compared with seven models corresponding to three state-of-the-art 2D video saliency models: Unisal [7], 3DSAL [11], SalEMA [10], and four 360° specialized models: U-NET [28], CP360 [29], SalGAN360 [35], and Two-Stream [33]. This choice is motivated by the publicly available code. However, U-NET inference protocol was not discussed in the paper since the authors use the teacher forcing technique to train the model, so we feed the predicted saliency maps at time $t - 1$ into the model at time t. All models were evaluated according to five different saliency metrics: Normalized Scanpath Saliency (NSS), Kullback-Leibler Divergence(KLD), Similarity (SIM), Linear Correlation Coefficient (CC), and AUC-Judd (AUC-J). Please refer to [46] for an extensive review of these metrics.

Technical Details. The attention model is implemented in Pytorch. The Adam optimizer was used for the training with a learning rate of 10^{-5}. The attention model was trained end-to-end using a NVIDIA GTX 1080 and a 3.90 GHz I7 7820 HK Intel processor. SalEMA experts were fine-tuned with a modified input size of 160×160.

Dataset Processing. The VR-EyeTracking dataset recorded by [46], consists of 208 diverse content 4k ODVs, where the head/eye saccades were obtained from 45 participants. However, neither fixation nor saliency maps were published publicly. We processed the gaze recording to obtain the 2048×1024 fixation maps. Saliency maps were generated by convolving each fixation point (for all observers of one video) with a Gaussian filter, with $\sigma = 9.35°$ for head and eye data. The processed dataset is now available at this link.

Table 3. Comparative performance study on: Salient360! [27], VR-EyeTracking [6] datasets.

	Models	Dataset									
		Salient360!					VR-EyeTracking				
		AUC-J ↑	NSS ↑	CC ↑	SIM ↑	KLD ↓	AUC-J ↑	NSS ↑	CC ↑	SIM ↑	KLD ↓
2D models	Unisal [7]	0.746	1.258	0.206	0.190	8.524	0.764	1.798	0.314	0.281	6.767
	SalEMA [10]	–	–	–	–	–	0.772	1.790	0.320	0.284	6.532
	3DSal [11]	0.656	0.898	0.192	0.139	10.129	0.679	1.229	0.228	0.232	8.317
360° models	U-NET [28]	0.725	0.864	0.129	0.122	9.810	0.818	1.430	0331	0.247	7.070
	Cheng et al. [29]	0.819	1.094	0.175	0.213	9.313	0.735	0.914	0.171	0.179	8.879
	Salgan360 [35]	–	–	–	–	–	0.704	1.267	0.236	0.238	7.625
	Two-Stream [33]	0.787	1.608	0.265	0.179	8.252	0.827	1.906	0.346	0.254	7.127
Training setting (i)	Attention	0.827	1.397	0.222	0.168	8.225	0.795	1.338	0.255	0.229	7.405
	Experts	0.870	2.438	0.366	0.227	6.990	0.754	1.292	0.221	0.224	7.840
	Ours	**0.881**	**2.580**	**0.363**	**0.252**	**6.327**	0.801	1.590	0.265	0.255	6.571
Training setting (ii)	Attention	0.796	1.299	0.201	0.168	7.973	0.836	1.791	0.342	0.302	5.664
	Experts	0.807	1.564	0.242	0.223	7.679	0.778	1.388	0.259	0.211	7.407
	Ours	0.837	1.764	0.285	0.255	7.382	**0.862**	**2.185**	**0.363**	**0.312**	**5.561**

4.2   Results

Table 3 shows the comparative study with the aforementioned models according to the different saliency metrics on Salient360! and VR-EyeTracking datasets (4/75) test ODVs. Our model is very competitive in the two datasets: ATSal exhibits the best score for all metrics. Surprisingly, 2D approaches achieve mostly the same results as 360° specialized models; this points to the potential to consider the direct transfer of the well verified visual attention features from 2D to 360°, but also perhaps reflects the lack of large scale well-annotated 360° datasets. We invite the reader to watch the qualitative results of the proposed method in the form of a video available here.

4.3   Performance Study

VR-EyeTracking. The 75 diverse test ODVs of this dataset makes the prediction task very challenging. ATSal outperforms all competitors according to all five metrics due to the combination of global features with the attention stream, but also due to the local patches encoding the temporal domain predicted by the experts model.

Salient360!. On both distributions of the Salient360! dataset (images and videos), the proposed model gains a substantial quantitative advantage in accuracy compared with other models. This demonstrates the capacity of our model to handle a larger set of scenarios.

Encouraged by the positive results of the attention model trained on static images, and later fine-tuned for the Salient360! and VR-EyeTracking ODVs. We evaluated the model components separately on both datasets. Table 3 indicates the competitiveness of the attention model with respect to other competitors, even without the integration of the expert model. A possible explanation could relate to smaller motion effects in ODVs compared to 2D videos, where viewport locations are the most prominent features.

Figure 2 illustrates the prediction task on a sample of 360° frames from the two datasets: Salient360! and VR-EyeTracking. It can be seen that the generated saliency maps with ATSal are more comprehensive and look remarkably similar to the Ground truth maps in terms of saliency distribution. Other competitors shown in the same figure overestimate saliency in general, or overlay bias the equator/center. Furthermore, the effectiveness of ATSal in capturing the main objects in the scene is clear.

For more qualitative results, Fig. 3 shows the overlaid saliency maps on sample frames from Salient360! for the attention model, expert models, and ATSal. Two key points can be seen from these figures:

- Figure 2: ATSal predicts consistent saliency at the very beginning of each video due to the attention mechanism modeling the spatial features, while other competitors center the saliency around the equator. As the scene progresses, ATSal ignores some static regions and only focuses on other moving viewports. In video (b), all models only detect faces near the equator, while ATSal also attends to other parts of the scene.
- Figure 3: The generated saliency maps using only the attention model are sparse and cover all the possible outcomes in the scene. This is due to the enlarged receptive field of the latent space: the model tends to give a high probability to a given pixel, which makes it salient. The expert models act as a saliency selector through the pixel wise multiplication. This approach encourages not overestimating saliency, but also forces the model to generate more focused and consistent saliency regions.

Table 4. GPU inference time comparison of video saliency prediction methods (NVIDIA GTX 1080). All methods are reported based on the VR-EyeTracking benchmark [6]. Best computational performance among dedicated 360° models is shown in bold.

Model	Runtime (s)
SalGAN360 [35]	17.330
Two-stream [33]	2.061
U-Net [28]	1.802
(*) 3DSAL [11]	0.100
(*) SalEMA [10]	0.020
(*) Unisal [7]	0.010
Attention (ours)	0.050
Experts (ours)	0.170
ATSal (ours)	**0.230**

(*) 2D models.

Computational Load. Model efficiency is a key factor for real-time 360° videos application like streaming. Table 4 shows a GPU runtime comparison (processing time per 360° frame) of the different competitors on the 4K VR-EyeTracking ODVs. Compared with other 360° specialized models, ATSal is over 9× faster than Two-stream, which is the current state-of-the-art model according to the Salient360! leaderboard.

5 Conclusion

We proposed a novel deep learning based 360° video saliency model that embeds two parallel streams encoding both the global and local features. The attention model explicitly captures the global visual static saliency information through an attention mechanism at the middle of the bottleneck with an enlarged receptive field propagating the contextual pixel-wise information to the whole frame space. This design allows the expert models to learn more effective local region based saliency. The temporal domain is augmented using the simple exponential moving average (EMA).

We performed extensive evaluations on the Salient360! and VR-EyeTracking datasets, and compared the results of our model with the previous 2D and 360° static and dynamic models. The qualitative and quantitative results have shown that the proposed method is consistent, efficient, and outperforms other state-of-the-art.

Acknowledgement. This publication has emanated from research supported by Science Foundation Ireland (SFI) under Grant Number SFI/12/RC/2289_P2, co-funded by the European Regional Development Fund, through the SFI Centre for Research Training in Machine Learning (18/CRT/6183).

References

1. Xu, M., Li, C., Zhang, S., Le Callet, P.: State-of-the-art in 360 video/image processing: perception, assessment and compression. IEEE J. Sel. Top. Signal Process. **14**(1), 5–26 (2020)
2. De Abreu, A., Ozcinar, C., Smolic, A.: Look around you: saliency maps for omnidirectional images in VR applications. In: 2017 Ninth International Conference on Quality of Multimedia Experience (QoMEX), pp. 1–6. IEEE, May 2017
3. Itti, L., Koch, C.: A saliency-based search mechanism for overt and covert shifts of visual attention. Vision Res. **40**(10–12), 1489–1506 (2000)
4. Pan, J., ET AL.: SalGAN: visual saliency prediction with generative adversarial networks. arXiv preprint arXiv:1701.01081 (2017)
5. Borji, A.: Saliency prediction in the deep learning era: an empirical investigation. arXiv preprint arXiv:1810.03716. 10 (2018)
6. Xu, Y., et al.: Gaze prediction in dynamic 360 immersive videos. In: proceedings of the IEEE Conference on Computer Vision and Pattern Recognition, pp. 5333–5342 (2018)
7. Droste, R., Jiao, J., Noble, J.A.: Unified image and video saliency modeling. arXiv preprint arXiv:2003.05477 (2020)

8. Min, K., Corso, J.J.: TASED-net: temporally-aggregating spatial encoder-decoder network for video saliency detection. In Proceedings of the IEEE International Conference on Computer Vision, pp. 2394–2403. ISO 690 (2019)

9. Lai, Q., Wang, W., Sun, H., Shen, J.: Video saliency prediction using spatiotemporal residual attentive networks. IEEE Trans. Image Process. **29**, 1113–1126 (2019)

10. Linardos, P., Mohedano, E., Nieto, J.J., O'Connor, N.E., Giro-i-Nieto, X., McGuinness, K.: Simple vs complex temporal recurrences for video saliency prediction. In: British Machine Vision Conference (BMVC) (2019)

11. Djilali, Y.A.D., Sayah, M., McGuinness, K., O'Connor, N.E.: 3DSAL: an efficient 3D-CNN architecture for video saliency prediction (2020)

12. Wang, W., Shen, J., Guo, F., Cheng, M.M., Borji, A.: Revisiting video saliency: A large-scale benchmark and a new model. In: Proceedings of the IEEE Conference on Computer Vision and Pattern Recognition, pp. 4894–4903 (2018)

13. Bak, C., Kocak, A., Erdem, E., Erdem, A.: Spatio-temporal saliency networks for dynamic saliency prediction. IEEE Trans. Multimedia **20**(7), 1688–1698 (2017)

14. Pan, J., et al.: SalGAN: visual saliency prediction with adversarial networks. In: CVPR Scene Understanding Workshop (SUNw), July 2017

15. Bogdanova, I., Bur, A., Hügli, H., Farine, P.A.: Dynamic visual attention on the sphere. Comput. Vis. Image Underst. **114**(1), 100–110 (2010)

16. Bogdanova, I., Bur, A., Hugli, H.: Visual attention on the sphere. IEEE Trans. Image Process. **17**(11), 2000–2014 (2008)

17. Rai, Y., Le Callet, P., Guillotel, P.: Which saliency weighting for omni directional image quality assessment?. In: 2017 Ninth International Conference on Quality of Multimedia Experience (QoMEX), pp. 1–6. IEEE, May 2017

18. Xu, M., Song, Y., Wang, J., Qiao, M., Huo, L., Wang, Z.: Predicting head movement in panoramic video: a deep reinforcement learning approach. IEEE Trans. Pattern Anal. Mach. Intell. **41**(11), 2693–2708 (2018)

19. Sitzmann, V., et al.: Saliency in VR: how do people explore virtual environments? IEEE Trans. Visual Comput. Graphics **24**(4), 1633–1642 (2018)

20. Huang, X., Shen, C., Boix, X., Zhao, Q.: SALICON: reducing the semantic gap in saliency prediction by adapting deep neural networks. In: Proceedings of the IEEE International Conference on Computer Vision, pp. 262–270 (2015)

21. Lebreton, P., Raake, A.: GBVS360, BMS360, ProSal: extending existing saliency prediction models from 2D to omnidirectional images. Signal Process. Image Commun. **69**, 69–78 (2018)

22. Zhang, J., Sclaroff, S.: Saliency detection: a Boolean map approach. In: Proceedings of the IEEE International Conference on Computer Vision, pp. 153–160 (2013)

23. Harel, J., Koch, C., Perona, P.: Graph-based visual saliency. In: Advances In Neural Information Processing Systems, pp. 545–552 (2007)

24. Maugey, T., Le Meur, O., Liu, Z.: Saliency-based navigation in omnidirectional image. In: IEEE 19th International Workshop on Multimedia Signal Processing (MMSP). Luton 2017, pp. 1–6 (2017)

25. Battisti, F., Baldoni, S., Brizzi, M., Carli, M.: A feature-based approach for saliency estimation of omni-directional images. Signal Process. Image Commun. **69**, 53–59 (2018)

26. Fang, Y., Zhang, X., Imamoglu, N.: A novel superpixel-based saliency detection model for 360-degree images. Signal Process. Image Commun. **69**, 1–7 (2018)

27. David, EJ., Gutiérrez, J., Coutrot, A., Da Silva, M. P., Callet, P.L.: A dataset of head and eye movements for 360 videos. In: Proceedings of the 9th ACM Multimedia Systems Conference, pp. 432–437. ISO 690, June 2018

28. Zhang, Z., Xu, Y., Yu, J., Gao, S.: Saliency detection in 360 videos. In: Proceedings of the European Conference on Computer Vision (ECCV), pp. 488–503 (2018)
29. Cheng, H.T., Chao, C.H., Dong, J.D., Wen, H.K., Liu, T.L., Sun, M.: Cube padding for weakly-supervised saliency prediction in 360 videos. In: Proceedings of the IEEE Conference on Computer Vision and Pattern Recognition, pp. 1420–1429 (2018)
30. Suzuki, T., Yamanaka, T.: Saliency map estimation for omni-directional image considering prior distributions. In: 2018 IEEE International Conference on Systems, Man, and Cybernetics (SMC), pp. 2079–2084. IEEE, October 2018
31. Lebreton, P., Fremerey, S., Raake, A.: V-BMS360: a video extention to the BMS360 image saliency model. In: 2018 IEEE International Conference on Multimedia & Expo Workshops (ICMEW), pp. 1–4. IEEE, July 2018
32. Nguyen, A., Yan, Z., Nahrstedt, K.: Your attention is unique: detecting 360-degree video saliency in head-mounted display for head movement prediction. In: Proceedings of the 26th ACM International Conference on Multimedia, pp. 1190–1198, October 2018
33. Zhang, K., Chen, Z.: Video saliency prediction based on spatial-temporal two-stream network. IEEE Trans. Circuits Syst. Video Technol. **29**(12), 3544–3557 (2018)
34. Hu, H.N., Lin, Y.C., Liu, M.Y., Cheng, H.T., Chang, Y.J., Sun, M.: Deep 360 pilot: learning a deep agent for piloting through 360 sports videos. In: 2017 IEEE Conference on Computer Vision and Pattern Recognition (CVPR), pp. 1396–1405. IEEE, July 2017
35. Chao, F.Y., Zhang, L., Hamidouche, W., Deforges, O.: SalGAN360: visual saliency prediction on 360 degree images with generative adversarial networks. In: 2018 IEEE International Conference on Multimedia & Expo Workshops (ICMEW), pp. 01–04. IEEE, July 2018
36. Qiao, M., Xu, M., Wang, Z., Borji, A.: Viewport-dependent saliency prediction in 360° video. IEEE Trans. Multimed. (2020)
37. Wang, F., et al.: Residual attention network for image classification. In: Proceedings of the IEEE Conference on Computer Vision and Pattern Recognition, pp. 3156–3164 (2017)
38. Yang, Z., He, X., Gao, J., Deng, L., Smola, A.: Stacked attention networks for image question answering. In: Proceedings of the IEEE Conference on Computer Vision and Pattern Recognition, pp. 21–29 (2016)
39. Tao, A., Sapra, K., Catanzaro, B.: Hierarchical multi-scale attention for semantic segmentation. arXiv preprint arXiv:2005.10821 (2020)
40. Chen, L.C., Yang, Y., Wang, J., Xu, W., Yuille, A.L.: Attention to scale: Scale-aware semantic image segmentation. In: Proceedings of the IEEE Conference on Computer Vision and Pattern Recognition, pp. 3640–3649 (2016)
41. Rai, Y., Gutiérrez, J., Le Callet, P.: A dataset of head and eye movements for 360 degree images. In: Proceedings of the 8th ACM on Multimedia Systems Conference, pp. 205–210, June 2017
42. Sitzmann, V., et al.: How do people explore virtual environments?. arXiv preprint arXiv:1612.04335 (2016)
43. Oliva, A., Torralba, A.: The role of context in object recognition. Trends Cogn. Sci. **11**(12), 520–527 (2007)
44. He, K., Zhang, X., Ren, S., Sun, J.: Deep residual learning for image recognition. In: Proceedings of the IEEE Conference on Computer Vision and Pattern Recognition, pp. 770–778 (2016)

45. Bao, Y., Zhang, T., Pande, A., Wu, H., Liu, X.: Motion-prediction-based multicast for 360-degree video transmissions. In: 2017 14th Annual IEEE International Conference on Sensing, Communication, and Networking (SECON), pp. 1–9. IEEE, June 2017

46. Bylinskii, Z., Judd, T., Oliva, A., Torralba, A., Durand, F.: What do different evaluation metrics tell us about saliency models? IEEE Trans. Pattern Anal. Mach. Intell. **41**(3), 740–757 (2018)

Rescue Dog Action Recognition by Integrating Ego-Centric Video, Sound and Sensor Information

Yuta Ide[1], Tsuyohito Araki[1], Ryunosuke Hamada[2], Kazunori Ohno[2], and Keiji Yanai[1(✉)]

[1] Department of Informatics, The University of Electro-Communications, Tokyo, Japan
{ide-y,araki-t,yanai}@mm.inf.uec.ac.jp
[2] NICHe, Tohoku University, Sendai, Japan

Abstract. A dog which assists rescue activity in the scene of disasters such as earthquakes and landslides is called a "disaster rescue dog" or just a "rescue dog". In Japan where earthquakes happen frequently, a research project on "Cyber-Rescue" is being organized for more efficient rescue activities. In the project, to analyze the activities of rescue dogs in the scene of disasters, "Cyber Dog Suits" equipped with sensors, a camera and a GPS were developed. In this work, we recognize dog activities in the ego-centric dog videos taken by the camera mounted on the cyber-dog suits. To do that, we propose an image/sound/sensor-based four-stream CNN for dog activity recognition which integrates sound and sensor signals as well as motion and appearance. We conducted some experiments for multi-class activity categorization using the proposed method. As a result, the proposed method which integrates appearance, motion, sound and sensor information achieved the highest accuracy, 48.05%. This result is relatively high as a recognition result of ego-centric videos.

1 Introduction

A dog which assists rescue activity in the scene of disasters such as earthquakes and landslides is called a "disaster rescue dog" or just a "rescue-dog". In rescue activities in the disaster areas, trained rescue-dogs may conduct exploration as human assistants. A rescue-dog makes a pair with a human and investigates disaster areas by making use of special characteristics as a dog. Rescue-dogs can investigate even in the environments where it is difficult for a person to traverse on such as narrow spaces, crevices, and collapsed buildings. In addition, the rescue operation that relies on the dogs' developed sense of smell is possible. However, they have no language to communicate with humans. A person who pairs up with a rescue dog and gives instructions at a disaster site are called "a handler", and a handler must understand the information the rescue-dog gathered from its behavior.

At the present, a handler who directs a rescue-dog manually marks the action of the rescue-dog and orally transmits information to a commander of a rescue

A. Del Bimbo et al. (Eds.): ICPR 2020 Workshops, LNCS 12663, pp. 321–333, 2021.
https://doi.org/10.1007/978-3-030-68796-0_23

Fig. 1. A rescue dog wearing a "cyber-rescue suit" [10].

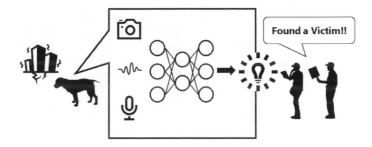

Fig. 2. During the rescue activity of a rescue dog in the disaster site, first-person (dog-centric) video, sound and sensor information are recorded by a camera, microphone and various sensors (such as inertial sensor, accelerometer and pose sensor) mounted on a cyber-dog-suit, and the proposed system recognizes the current dog's behavior from the recorded video, sound and sensor information.

team. The big problem on a joint rescue activity by a handler and a rescue-dog is lack of information on the surrounding environment and victims for triage[1]. The records by the handler are subjective, and they tend to lack objectivity. The verbal transmission also makes them less accurate.

For this situation, in Japan where earthquakes happen frequently, a research project on "Cyber-Rescue" is being organized for more efficient rescue activities. In the project, to analyze the activities of rescue dogs in the scene of a disaster, "Cyber-Dog Suits" equipped with sensors, a camera and a GPS were developed [10] (Fig. 1).

In this study, we aim to estimate the behavior of rescue-dogs using sensor data obtained from the cyber-dog suits. We analyze ego-centric videos taken by the camera mounted on the cyber-dog suits, and recognize dog activities by using not only videos but also sounds and sensor data (Fig. 2). This is expected

---

[1] "Triage" means the process of deciding who receives medical treatment first, according to how seriously the person is injured.

to make it possible to estimate what the rescue-dog is doing now automatically. The information necessary for triage is organized, and disaster rescue activities will be more efficient by the rescue-dog activity analysis.

To analyze ego-centric videos with audio and sensor data, we propose a image/sound/sensor-based four-stream CNN for dog activity recognition which integrates sound and sensor information as well as motion and appearance. We conducted some experiments for multi-class activity categorization using the proposed method. As a result, the proposed method which integrates appearance, motion sound and sensor information achieved the highest accuracy, 48.05%. This result is a relative high as a recognition result of ego-centric videos.

2   Related Work

2.1   Third-Person Activity Recognition

Two-stream CNN is a method for video classification [13]. It classifies video categories by integrating motion information represented as optical flows and appearance information. There are many kinds of researches on derived networks based on the Two-stream CNN. Convolutional Two-Stream Network Fusion [6] is one of the variant methods. The study achieved the state of the art on the standard benchmark dataset for video classification called UCF-101 by combining the output of the convolution layer of each stream and adding FC layers. In our work, we follow Two-Stream Network Fusion as the way to integrate the stream outputs, and add the two streams for audio and sensor information.

2.2   First-Person Activity Recognition

First person vision has been actively studied so far. There are so many researches such as [7,11]. Minghuang *et al.* [11] proposed a twin stream network that integrates hand segmentation, target object localization and motion. The twin stream network estimates the arm area and object locations with CNN, and integrates them with the CNN output result of the optical flow image via CNN. It is a kind of first person version of the two stream network.

Recently the large-scale egocentric video dataset, EPIC-KITCHEN [2], was released, which had been promoting the researches on ego-centric video analysis greatly [5].

2.3   Dog-Centric Activity Modeling

There are a few studies on first person video analysis from dog's view. Ehsan *et al.* [4] estimated dog activity from dog-centric video. They modeled dog activity and estimate how dogs will move. However, these studies just model dog behavior and do not estimate interaction between dogs and surroundings. They created DECADE, a dataset of ego-centric dog video and joint movements. The dataset includes 380 video clips from a camera mounted on the dog's head.

It also includes corresponding information about body position and movement. Movement were measured by inertial measurement units (IMUs), and sound was also recorded. The dataset is similar to our dataset of cyber-rescue dogs. However, they used only a video in the experiments, and did not use multi-modal information such as sound and IMU data.

Iwashita *et al.* [9] also published a Dog-Centric Activity Dataset (DCAD). This dataset is used for dog behavior classification from dog-centric movies. DCAD does not support rescue-dog specific classes, contains no audio data and assumes a single-class classification.

In our work, we extend Convolutional Two-Stream Network Fusion [6] by adding a sensor stream. In the experiments, we confirm the effectiveness of introducing sensor data for dog activity recognition.

3   Dataset

In this study, we perform multi-class activity estimation of rescue-dogs. The rescue-dog training dataset consists of a group of data collected by sensors embedded in the cyber-rescue suits that rescue-dogs wear. The dataset is still growing, and we are collecting data at the time of rescue training of rescue-dogs in the simulated disaster sites. Due to privacy and ethical issue, it does not contain the data recorded in the actual disaster sites.

It consists of about 2 min to 20 min of six movies with audio and sensor data. The dataset includes first-person videos of a handler's view and third-person videos showing a handler and a rescue dog in addition to egocentric dog videos. Since handler view videos and third-person videos do not always show the rescue dog, the dog sometimes goes into the area where it is invisible from a handler and a person recording third-person videos. Therefore, in this work, we use only dog-centric videos with audio and sensor data. As a sensor unit, Xsens Mti-300 was built in the cyber dog suits, which can record angular velocity, acceleration, geomagnetic flux, pose, pressure and temperature every 0.005 s. Among these information, we use angular velocity, acceleration and pose as sensor information.

The total time is 47 min and 5 s, the number of frames per second is 29.97fps, and the total number of frames is 84,665. Note that only two videos have sensor data the total time of which is about 20 min. We call the dataset containing only two videos with sensor data as "Sensor dataset", while we call the full dataset as "Full dataset". The videos are annotated by specifying a time range for each of 11 activity classes as shown in Table 1. Multiple classes are sometimes overlapped with each other at the same time. Therefore, we treat this task as a multi-label classification task. For example, for the scene of "rescue-dog is barking while finding a victim", two labels, *"see victim"* and *"bark"* are annotated.

Table 1. The frequencies of the 11 dog activity classes in the rescue-dog dataset.

	Bark	Cling	Command	Eat-drink	Handler	Run	See-victim	Shake	Sniff	Stop	Walk
Full	9299	3631	8035	876	7066	414	7601	1349	16573	31533	45915
Sensor	2281	1936	4903	145	3718	0	1894	405	8208	13194	14154

3.1   11 Dog Activity Classes

We explain each of the 11 classes of rescue dog activities. Their frequencies in the dataset are not uniform as shown in Table 1.

1. **bark** : The situation in which the dog is barking. Typically a rescue dog barks when finding out victims. There exists easy-to-understand phonetic features, and unique shakes in the videos occur.
2. **cling** : The situation in which a doc is sniffing with the nose close to the smell. It is more detailed than *"sniff,"* and this is labeled it always overlaps with *"sniff."*
3. **command** : The situation in which the dog is being instructed by the handler. There are various situations such as verbal instructions such as "Wait" and "Go", praises and pointing instructions.
4. **eat-drink** : The situation in which the dog is eating or drinking something. In addition to feeding success rewards for finding victims under rescue training, there are various situations such as eating grass and drinking water on the ground or a river.
5. **look at handler** : The situation in which the dog is looking at the handler. Hereinafter, this action is called just *"handler"*.
6. **run** : The situation in which the dog is running. There is a feeling of floating on the screen compared to the *walk-trot* class, and it is intense that shaking and sounds.
7. **see victim** : The situation in which the victim is appearing in the camera. Hereinafter, called *"victim"*.
8. **shake** : The situation in which the dog is vigorously waving. During this activity, sound clatters on the camera on the dog's back.
9. **sniff** : The situation in which the dog sniff surroundings. This can be the indicator that measures the dog's motivation for exploration. This action happens not only when the nose is brought close to the ground, but also when the dog smells the floating odor.
10. **stop** : The situation in which the dog is not stepping and stays in the same spot, which includes stepping on the same spot. There is little motion observed in the videos.
11. **walk-trot** : Walking, not running. The order of footing is different from *"run"* class. The dog goes forward while jumping with the front and back legs in the action of *"run,"*. During this action, the dog steps forward with the right and left legs alternately. Hereinafter, called *"walk."*

As examples, the scenes of *"see victim"* and *"stop"* are shown in Fig. 3.

Fig. 3. Examples of the ego-centric rescue-dog video dataset, which shows "*see victim*" class (upper) and "*stop*" class (lower). From the left, RGB images, optical flow images, and the sound images visualized by the MFCC spectrogram.

4   Method

In this study, we perform multi-label classification of rescue-dog activities from ego-centric dog videos, audio and sensor data. Figure 4 shows a conceptual diagram of our proposed method, which consists of four streams, a sound stream, an appearance stream, a motion stream and a sensor stream. The three streams consist of convolutional layers, the other stream consists of LSTM, and they are integrated by fully-connected (FC) layers in the same as Convolutional Two-Stream Network Fusion [6].

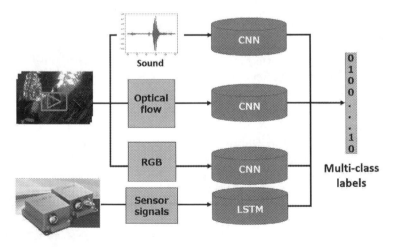

Fig. 4. Outline of the proposed method. We extract multiple information from the input video, and provide them to four different streams. The final output is multi-class labels.

The proposed network which takes two images (appearance RGB images and optical flow images), sounds and sensor data as inputs is called the image/sound/sensor-based four-stream network. The detail is shown in Fig. 5. In this study, this network is used for multi-class action estimation instead of general single-class classification.

First, we take the frame (F_t) of the RGB images out from the input video, and generate an optical flow image (O_t) between the frame, F_t, and the following frame, F_{t+1}. Next, we provide RGB images and optical flow images to the corresponding streams. Regarding sound and sensor data, we set time windows as 1.6 s the center of which corresponds to the frame provided to the RGB stream. We obtain log spectrogram with short-time Fourier transform (STFT) (S_t) from the corresponding audio part of the videos (A_t), and we provide it to the sound stream. Regarding sensor data, we used Bidirectional LSTM as the sensor stream. Finally, combine the outputs of these four streams with FC layers, and perform multi-class estimation in the last layer of the network. Action classification is performed for each frame.

In general, SoftMax CrossEntropyLoss is used as the loss function for single-class classification. Since the task of this work is multi-class estimation, Soft-MarginLoss is used. Assuming x as an output of the network, y as a target, and C as the numer of the classes, the loss function MultiLabel SoftMarginLoss for multi-class estimation is defined by the following equation:

$$loss(x, y) = -\frac{1}{C} * \Sigma_i(\{y_i\} * log((1 + exp(-x_i))^{-1})$$
$$+ (1 - y_i) * log(\frac{exp(-x_i)}{1 + exp(-x_i)})) \tag{1}$$

It is designed that the first term in Σ is used if the inferred class is correct, and the second term is used for calculation if it is incorrect. The function changes depending on the inferred label. In this study, there are 11 classes, and the output y is an 11-dimensional binary. The threshold is set to 0.5, and the class above the threshold is set as the estimated class.

4.1 The Detail of the Image/Sound/Sensor-Based Four-Stream CNN

Both input images on RGB and optical flow are (224, 224, 3) dimensions. The window size which is the unit size for activity classification is 49 frames, and a RGB image of the center frame and the corresponding optical flow image immediately after a RGB image are taken out. We fine-tune the ImageNet [3] pretrained VGG16 [12] model for both the RGB and optical flow streams. Note that we used the values of L2-norm of optical flow vectors as the third channel inputs of the optical flow stream to make the input of the optical flow stream three channels.

Regarding audio information, we extract short-term Fourier transform (SFFT) spectrogram from the 49 frames which corresponds to 0.8 s before and

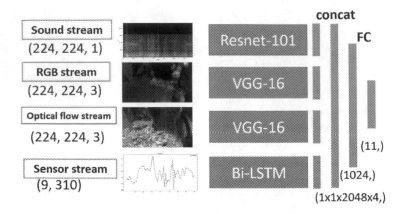

Fig. 5. Proposed method architecture of image/sound/sensor-based four-stream CNN. We provide (224,224,3) dimension images (224, 224, 1) dimension sound data, and (9, 310) dimension sensor data to each of the four stream, respectively, and get a 11-dimension output as an estimation result.

after the center frames of the window, and provide it to the sound stream. The sound stream consists of pre-trained ResNet-101 with the additional first layer which converts 1-channel to 3-channels, since spectrograms can be regarded as images. We generate a (256, 350, 1) spectrogram image using short-term Fourier transform (SFFT) from the sound data of 49 frames, resize it into (224, 224, 1) with bilinear down-sampling, and provide it into the ResNet-based sound stream. We use short-term Fourier transform (SFFT) by following Arash *et al.* [5] as sound feature representation.

As sensor data, we use acceleration, angular velocity and pose data each of which are 3 dimension with value range normalization ([-1,1]). Since the sensor recording 200 Hz, we obtain 320 points within 1.6 s window. To reduce noises, we average them for consecutive 11 frames and finally we obtain a (9, 310) sensor feature. We provide it to Bi-directional LSTM (Bi-LSTM) for feature encoding which is inspired by [8]. In contrast to a standard LSTM which only learns the forward input and makes time series predictions, with a Bi-LSTM, we learn not only in the forward direction but also in the reverse direction to make time series predictions. As a result, the Bi-LSTM can make time series predictions with higher accuracy than the normal LSTM.

The four outputs (each of them is 2048 dimension) obtained from each stream are simply concatenated in the direction of channel, and it is provided to three FC layers. The dimension of the final output of the network is 11-dimensions which is the same as the number of the activity classes annotated to the rescue-dog dataset.

5   Experiments

This section describes the experiment results with the proposed methods and discussions. We made the experiments for seeking for the best feature extraction method of sound and sensor information, and subsequently, we made experiments on the different window sizes with audio and sensor signals. Then, we compared the results of the integration with the optimal networks of sound and sensor information. Note that we used "Sensor data" for all the experiments except for the last experiments.

In all the tables showing experimental results, the accuracy for each class and the total accuracy are represented by Jaccard coefficient. Note that the Jaccard coefficient is represented by

$$\frac{TP}{FP+FN+TP}$$

and a more rigorous value can be obtained compared to the F scale. We used this coefficient to emphasize both Precision and Recall in the rescue-dog's activity estimation. Therefore in this experiments, a model with a larger Jaccard coefficient is expressed as having better accuracy. Note that "-" is displayed because Precision can not be calculated for a class that has never been estimated.

5.1   Selection of Sound Stream Network

In this subsection, we compare VGG16, ResNet-50 and ResNet-101 for the base networks of SFFT spectrogram.

Table 2 shows the results. As results, ResNet-101 with SFFT spectrogram achieved the best result. Therefore, we adopt ResNet-101 with SFFT spectrogram in this work. Sound features were relatively effective for 'bark' and 'stop', since 'bark' is directly related to sound and 'stop' is related to 'no sound' or 'less sound'

Table 2. The results with the different sound networks. (%)

Methods	Bark	Cling	Command	Eat-drink	Handler	Run	See-victim	Shake	Sniff	Stop	Walk	ALL
VGG16	64.29	0.00	**3.58**	0.00	6.51	–	**15.25**	15.25	17.02	**60.63**	70.48	39.44
ResNet-50	62.79	2.17	3.55	0.00	10.77	–	12.28	35.20	18.78	58.61	68.90	40.99
ResNet-101	66.31	**4.80**	1.76	0.00	**11.06**	–	13.49	**50.54**	**19.35**	58.66	**71.90**	**42.43**

5.2   Selection of Sound Window Size

In this study, we compare the performance with various lengths of audio windows. We compare the window size with 1.0, 1.2, 1.4, 1.6, and 2.0 s.

Table 3 shows the results, which indicates that 1.6 s is the best window size for this rescue-dog dataset.

Table 3. The results with the different time window sizes for sound features. (%)

	Bark	Cling	Command	Eat-drink	Handler	Run	See-victim	Shake	Sniff	Stop	Walk	**ALL**
1.0 s	66.31	4.80	1.76	0.00	11.06	-	13.49	50.54	19.35	58.66	71.90	42.43
1.2 s	65.24	0.00	2.89	0.00	6.48	-	7.845	55.62	14.74	59.91	66.63	38.97
1.4 s	79.02	**5.24**	0.25	0.00	12.24	-	**15.43**	21.35	17.44	59.63	67.92	40.57
1.6 s	70.51	3.44	**4.19**	0.00	6.37	-	14.96	**82.94**	**21.26**	**63.83**	73.83	**43.74**
2.0 s	**77.50**	0.00	0.11	0.00	**12.87**	-	14.14	76.84	11.48	59.73	**74.64**	42.58

5.3 Selection of Sensor Data Network

In the same way as sound networks, we made comparative experiments on different sensor network architectures for encoding sensor data.

Since the sensor data is obtained every 0.005 s (200Hz) and three kinds of three dimension sensor signals, we obtain a 200×9 feature in one second. In addition to Bidirectional LSTM (Bi-LSTM) [8], we applied a 1D convolutional network to this feature and a 2D convolutional network to a $200 \times 9 \times 1$ by adding a channel direction. We also compare the Bi-LSTM with the standard single directional LSTM.

Table 4 shows the results. Although 2D conv and LSTM achieved almost the same accuracy, the Bi-LSTM achieved the best performance. Therefore, we adopt a Bi-LSTM as an encoder of sensor data in this work. It turned out that sensor information was much less effective than sound on average, although sensor information outperformed sound for 'command', 'handler' and 'see-victim'.

Table 4. The results with the different sensor networks. (%)

	Bark	Cling	Command	Eat-drink	Handler	Run	See-victim	Shake	Sniff	Stop	Walk	**ALL**
1D CNN	0.00	0.00	3.18	0.00	0.00	-	0.00	0.00	5.949	22.95	50.18	24.57
2D CNN	0.00	0.00	**9.28**	0.00	16.21	-	8.84	0.00	16.16	26.85	47.88	25.26
LSTM	0.00	**2.01**	8.25	0.00	13.06	-	**15.97**	9.63	16.41	28.12	48.01	25.84
Bi-LSTM	0.00	1.43	8.88	0.00	**13.18**	-	15.63	**10.93**	**18.29**	**28.03**	**51.46**	**27.31**

5.4 Selection of Sensor Window Size

In the same way as the experiments on the sound window size, we compare the window size with 1.0, 1.2, 1.4, 1.6, and 2.0 s using Bi-LSTM. Table 5 shows the results, which indicate that 1.6 s achieved the best results as the time window size on the sensor data. Since the best sensor window size is the same window size as the best sound window size, we adopt 1.6 s as the time window size for both sound and sensor data.

Table 5. The results with different time window size of sensor features. (%)

	Bark	Cling	Command	Eat-drink	Handler	Run	See-victim	Shake	Sniff	Stop	Walk	**ALL**
1.0 s	0.00	1.43	8.88	0.00	13.18	-	15.63	10.93	18.29	28.03	51.46	27.31
1.2 s	0.00	4.06	8.91	0.00	13.14	-	15.84	11.89	16.70	27.00	**51.98**	27.17
1.4 s	0.00	2.48	10.22	0.00	13.89	-	17.39	11.17	17.86	29.52	49.36	27.14
1.6 s	0.00	2.47	10.71	0.00	13.94	-	16.45	10.16	16.05	**34.28**	51.12	**28.21**
1.8 s	0.00	3.78	**11.25**	0.00	11.79	-	17.30	**13.99**	**17.02**	33.76	48.62	27.60
2.0 s	0.00	**6.61**	9.37	0.00	**14.78**	-	**19.93**	2.67	14.76	34.09	47.21	26.82

5.5 Experiments by Integration of All Modalities

In this section, we made experiments by mixing of all streams including RGB, optical flow, sound and sensor data. Note that we used "Sensor data", since our proposed methods require sensor data.

In addition to our full 4-stream model, we prepare the full model using Bidirectional Gated Recurrent Unit (Bi-GRU) [1] instead of Bi-LSTM, since the training cost of GRU is smaller than that of Bi-LSTM. As a baseline, we use the model which used no sensor data. For fair comparison, we prepare our 3-stream model from which the sensor stream is excluded.

Table 6 shows the results with the four models. The proposed model with Bi-LSTM achieved the best accuracy, while the Bi-GRU model achieved the second best with the 0.54 points difference to the best one. From the table, we can see that sensor information was effective for 'sniff' and 'stop' with 8.03 points and 6.80 points improvement between our 3-stream and 4-stream models. From these results, integration of different sensor information is very important to obtain better performance. Although sensor features themselves achieved low performance, by integrating it with video and sound features, it was able to boost overall performance.

Table 6. Comparison with the baseline, ablation model and variant model. (%)

	Bark	Cling	Command	Eat-drink	Handler	Run	See-victim	Shake	Sniff	Stop	Walk	**ALL**
2-stream (RGB+opt)	16.60	0.26	**9.07**	0.00	14.30	-	36.68	39.32	14.53	45.29	72.04	41.32
3-stream (no sensor)	62.64	1.17	5.08	0.00	15.74	-	**47.99**	55.68	12.33	57.90	73.42	46.01
4-stream (Bi-LSTM)	73.86	**7.99**	3.29	0.00	14.40	-	41.03	**80.06**	20.36	**64.70**	72.55	**48.05**
4-stream (Bi-GRU)	**78.68**	1.16	3.71	0.00	18.38	-	44.77	48.86	**21.49**	59.08	**73.61**	47.51

In addition, we compare our model and the baseline with "Full dataset" which contains no sensor data. Table 7 shows that our modification on sound features improved the result by 10.92 points, which showed the effectiveness of integration of sound and video features. Especially, some actions related to sound, such as 'bark' and 'shake', are improved by 53.52 points and 51.67 points, respectively.

Table 7. Comparison using "Full dataset (no sensor data)". (%)

	Bark	Cling	Command	Eat-drink	Handler	Run	See-victim	Shake	Sniff	Stop	Walk	ALL
2-stream (RGB+opt)	11.05	1.82	4.31	0.0	**15.50**	0.0	25.91	0.0	**42.62**	70.53	66.80	43.50
3-stream (no sensor)	**64.57**	**6.25**	4.58	0.00	14.45	0.00	**45.96**	**51.67**	12.59	**74.18**	**71.48**	**54.42**

6   Conclusions

We proposed an image/sound/sensor-based four-stream CNN, and estimated the rescue-dog's behavior using the proposed network. From the experimental results, integrating sound and sensor information with ego-centric video was effective for action recognition of rescue dogs. In addition, we examined appropriate window size for sound and sensor data. As results, we found 1.6 s were the best window size for the rescue-dog dataset.

There still exists much room to improve feature extraction from dog ego-centric videos. We should consider how to extract more meaningful features. It is possible to add processing specific to dog ego-centric videos like extraction hand features from human ego-centric videos [11]. The dog region segmentation network like the hand segmentation network is applicable to dog activity estimation and expected to contribute to dog activity estimation. However, to do that, we need to create a pixel-level annotated dog ego-centric video dataset.

Increasing the amount of training data is also one of the most important issues. Training data of some actions such as 'run' and 'eat-drink' are much less than the other actions. In addition, the video data annotated with sensor data is also limited. Gathering more data is really needed to enable the proposed method work in the real rescue situation. Furthermore, although out of scope in this time, it is also required for real-time estimation for practical use.

Acknowledgement. This work was supported by JSPS KAKENHI Grant Number 17H06100 and 19H04929.

References

1. Chung, J., Gulcehre, C., Cho, K., Bengio, Y.: Empirical evaluation of gated recurrent neural networks on sequence modeling. In: Adavances in Neural Infomatoin Processing Systems Workshop on Deep Learning (2014)
2. Damen, D., et al.: Scaling egocentric vision: The EPIC-KITCHENS dataset. In: Proceedings of European Conference on Computer Vision (2018)
3. Deng, J., Dong, W., Socher, R., Li, L.J., Li, K., Fei-Fei, L.: ImageNet: a large-scale hierarchical image database. In: Proceedings of IEEE Computer Vision and Pattern Recognition (2009)
4. Ehsani, K., Bagherinezhad, H., Redmon, J., Mottaghi, R., Farhadi, A.: Who let the dogs out? modeling dog behavior from visual data. In: Proceedings of IEEE Computer Vision and Pattern Recognition (2018)
5. Evangelos, K., Arsha, N., Andrew, Z., Dima, D.: Epic-Fusion: audio-visual temporal binding for egocentric action recognition. In: Proceedings of IEEE Computer Vision and Pattern Recognition (2019)

6. Feichtenhofer, C., Pinz, A., Zisserman, A.: Convolutional two-stream network fusion for video action recognition. In: Proceedings of IEEE Computer Vision and Pattern Recognition (2016). http://arxiv.org/abs/1604.06573
7. Gedas, B., Stella, X.Y., Hyun, S.P., Jianbo, S.: Am I a baller? basketball skill assessment using first-person cameras. In: Proceedings of IEEE International Conference on Computer Vision (2016). http://arxiv.org/abs/1611.05365
8. Graves, A., Mohamed, A., Hinton, G.: Speech recognition with deep recurrent neural networks. In: Proceedings of IEEE International Conference on Acoustics, Speech and Signal Processing, pp. 6645–6649 (2013)
9. Iwashita, Y., Takamine, A., Kurazume, R., Ryoo, M.S.: First-person animal activity recognition from egocentric videos. In: Proceedings of International Conference on Pattern Recognition (ICPR) (2014)
10. Komori, Y., Fujieda, T., Ohno, K., Suzuki, T., Tadokoro, S.: Detection of continuous barking actions from search and rescue dogs' activities data. In: Proceedings of IEEE/RSJ International Conference on Intelligent Robots and Systems (IROS), pp. 630–635 (2015)
11. Minghuang, M., Haoqi, F., Kris, M.K.: Going deeper into first-person activity recognition. In: Proceedings of IEEE Computer Vision and Pattern Recognition (2016). http://www.cs.cmu.edu/~kkitani/pdf/MFK-CVPR2016.pdf
12. Simonyan, K., Vedaldi, A., Zisserman, A.: Very deep convolutional networks for large-scale image recognition. In: Proceedings of International Conference on Learning Representations (2015)
13. Simonyan, K., Zisserman, A.: Two-stream convolutional networks for action recognition in videos. In: Advances in Neural Information Processing Systems, pp. 568–576 (2014)

Understanding Event Boundaries for Egocentric Activity Recognition from Photo-Streams

Alejandro Cartas[1]([⊠])[iD], Estefania Talavera[2][iD], Petia Radeva[1][iD], and Mariella Dimiccoli[3][iD]

[1] Faculty of Mathematics and Computer Science, University of Barcelona, Gran Via de les Corts Catalanes, 585, 08007 Barcelona, Spain
{alejandro.cartas,petia.ivanova}@ub.es
[2] Bernoulli Institute, University of Groningen, Nijenborgh 9, 9747 AG Groningen, The Netherlands
[3] Institut de Robòtica i Informàtica Industrial (CSIC- UPC), C/ Llorens i Artigas 4-6, 08028 Barcelona, Spain

Abstract. The recognition of human activities captured by a wearable photo-camera is especially suited for understanding the behavior of a person. However, it has received comparatively little attention with respect to activity recognition from fixed cameras. In this work, we propose to use segmented events from photo-streams as temporal boundaries to improve the performance of activity recognition. Furthermore, we robustly measure its effectiveness when images of the evaluated person have been seen during training, and when the person is completely unknown during testing. Experimental results show that leveraging temporal boundary information on pictures of seen people improves all classification metrics, particularly it improves the classification accuracy up to 85.73%.

Keywords: Egocentric action recognition · Egocentric vision · Lifelogging

1 Introduction

Behavior understanding plays a crucial role in improving the habits of people. The activities that people perform in their daily living help in describing their lifestyle. Therefore, automatically discovering their activities is an important step towards understanding their behavior. Several approaches have addressed this problem in the literature [1–3]. However, their performance is not close to being precise and automatic.

More recently, the recognition of activities from wearable photo-cameras has gained increasing attention. These devices autonomously capture images at regular intervals of 30 s from the first-person perspective, also known as egocentric photo-streams. Since this kind of camera can be worn everywhere and are able to collect sequences over long periods of time such as days, they are well-suited not

© Springer Nature Switzerland AG 2021
A. Del Bimbo et al. (Eds.): ICPR 2020 Workshops, LNCS 12663, pp. 334–347, 2021.
https://doi.org/10.1007/978-3-030-68796-0_24

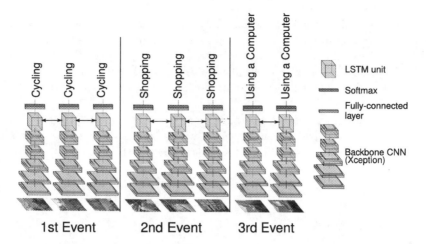

Fig. 1. Event-based activity recognition. We first extract event boundaries from a photo-stream sequence that clusters images with similar contextual and semantic features. These boundaries determine the starting and ending frames of a CNN+BLSTM architecture.

only for activity recognition but also for understanding different socio-behavioral aspects of a person [4,5].

In this work, we take a step forward in this direction by investigating the questions: *How important are event boundaries for activity recognition from egocentric photo-streams?*, and *Does the temporal coherence of segmented events from egocentric photo-streams improves the activity recognition performance at the frame-level?*. In [6], it was demonstrated that the training strategy directly affects the performance of the activity classifier. The core contribution of this work is to evaluate a training strategy for activity recognition based on temporal boundaries that define events. We believe this is a relevant problem to address in the field of egocentric vision, more specifically when analyzing egocentric photo-streams. Our work presents a rich ablation study that defines the basis for future works in the field. Our proposed model (see Fig. 1) allows evaluating our hypothesis which states that we can obtain a more robust classification of the activity occurring in the scene by the inclusion of temporal borders estimated automatically during the training process.

Since egocentric photo-streams describe what the users see throughout their daily routine, they tend to present visual patterns when performing their activities in consecutive days. This is the reason why the same location, people, and objects might appear in several photo-streams when captured by the same person. However, the images that describe such visual settings are not exactly the same, as they are not collected from the exact viewpoint and not only people but objects change over time. *Personalized* learning over the egocentric photo-streams consists of training a model using single frames or full-sequences from a set of users and later on evaluate them on the same set of users. This kind of approach has achieved high classification performance on previous works [7–9]. However, *generic* approaches are desired in order to avoid the need for the training phase. We consider the generalization capacity of the algorithm that is when the model is trained with data from a collection of users and is applicable to different ones. In this paper, we evaluate both approaches for the task of activity classification.

The remainder of the paper is organized as follows. In Sect. 2 we describe the relevant works in the field. Then, in Sect. 3 we present our event-based approach for daily activity recognition from egocentric photo-streams. Later, in Sects. 4 and 5 we describe the experimental setup and results, respectively. Finally, in Sect. 6 we outline our conclusions and possible future work.

2   Related Work

Egocentric vision has shown to be a rich source of information for the understanding of the behavior of the camera wearer. It has allowed the description of social behavior [10,11], food-related scenes [12], and routine [13], among others.

The detection of event boundaries in egocentric videos has been an object of investigation in recent years [14,15]. *Events* are generally understood as a group of sequential images that are homogeneous with respect to a given criterion. What does the criterion specify typically depends on the application at hand. Events were considered as temporal segments characterized by the same global motion and partitioned egocentric videos based on motion-features in [14]. In [15] events are intended as groups of images highlighting the presence of personal locations of interest specified by the end-user. In the domain of egocentric photo-streams events are defined as temporal semantic segments sharing semantic and contextual information [16,17].

The classification of activities has been studied through the analysis of *egocentric videos* [18–20]. In these works, the authors addressed the classification of *atomic* actions that describe a more detailed activity. For example the activity *preparing a sandwich* is composed of actions such as *get bread*, *put ham*, and *put mayonnaise*. However, the approaches addressing this problem typically rely on information such as motion and attention patterns that cannot be reliably estimated in photo-streams due to the very low frame rate (1–2 fpm).

The classification of activities from *egocentric photo-streams* has been previously addressed in multiple occasions [7–9]. In [7,9], the authors addressed the classification based on information from a single frame, by leveraging semantic and contextual features estimated via a convolutional neural network (CNN). The availability of sequences of images captured at regular intervals was later explored by integrating the temporal information in the classification by using a long short-term memory (LSTM) on the top of a CNN. In [8,21], a learning strategy based on sliding windows over the image sequence improved the testing performance of the classification model.

There have been several multi-modal approaches in the field. For instance, in [1,22,23], the authors proposed the classification of the performed activities by analyzing data collected by different sensors or audio-visual data by using different fusion strategies. The work in [24] presented a multi-modal dataset from sensor data and proposed two methods, one using crafted features and the other using deep learning.

3   Activity Recognition from Event Boundaries

In this paper, we aim to analyze and introduce a simple, but robust activity recognition pipeline for the analysis of given collections of photo-streams.

Fig. 2. One hour photo-stream sequence clustered into four consecutive event segments. Each row shows the first 15 frames of each segment.

3.1   Boundaries Detection

Events in egocentric photo-streams correspond to temporally adjacent images that share contextual and semantic features, as defined in [16]. This method relates sequential images represented as a combination of semantic and visual features extracted with a CNN. Temporal boundaries are detected when combining the grouping results obtained by under- and over-segmentation clustering methods, which are combined with graph cuts for energy optimization. We relied on such an approach to extract event boundaries from the daily visual lifelogs or photo-streams in our dataset [8], as shown in Fig. 2. As it can be observed, these events constitute a good basis for activity recognition, since typically, when the user is engaged in an activity, such as *cooking* contextual and semantic features have little variation.

3.2   Event-Based Activity Recognition

In order to exploit the temporal boundaries determined by the event segmentation, we proposed to use a recurrent neural network variant as a temporal learning mechanism. We combined the encoding produced by a CNN with a bidirectional LSTM (BLSTM) [25]. This recursive neural network evaluates a sequence in forward and backward order and merges the result. Thus, it captures patterns that might have been missed by the unidirectional version and it obtains potentially more robust representations [26]. The pipeline of our approach is shown in Fig. 1.

4   Experimental Setup

We train our models in a single training split and evaluate them in two test settings, namely *Generic* and *Personalized*. With *Generic*, we test the generalization capability of our model in images from *unseen* users during training. We want to highlight the difficulty of this task since what we consider the same class environment can be represented by completely different objects and descriptors. In contrast, in the *Personalized* setting the model is tested using images from *seen* users during training, but from different collected days.

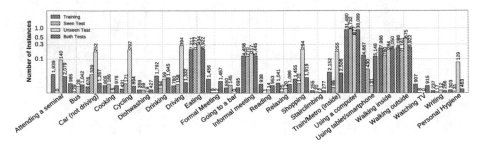

Fig. 3. Number of training/testing instances in the data splits. Note that the histograms are normalized and the vertical axis has a logarithm scale, but their corresponding value appears at top of each column.

4.1   Dataset

We carried out our experiments on the ADLEgoDataset [6], a visual lifelogging dataset collected using the Narrative Camera. This dataset consists of 125 egocentric photo-streams with 35 activity categories recorded by 15 students on their daily routine. In this dataset, most of the sequences were labeled by the camera wearer himself and the annotation process showed them consecutive frames instead of single frames to be labeled.

In order to test generalization capabilities, we divided the data into training and the two testing split sets, i.e. Generic and Personalized. These testing splits contain full-day sequences not present in the training split, and their data percentage for the unseen and seen users was around 5% and 10%, respectively. In contrast to [6], we discarded the categories that were only performed by one participant, as the model would probably overfit that category. Moreover, we also removed the categories that had less than 200 instances, since we considered that they had a few instances for training a convolutional model. This resulted in a total number of 24 categories. The number of training, seen and unseen test sequences are 91, 15, and 19, respectively. The resulting histogram of the number of photos per category and split is shown in Fig. 3.

4.2   Implementation

In order to measure the performance of our proposed pipeline for the definition of a robust activity classification model, we perform an ablation study. To this end, we trained the models CNN+RF+LSTM [21] and CNN+LSTM [27], and their bidirectional versions using daily sequences of egocentric images. For comparative purposes, we used as a baseline to train all temporal models the Xception network [28], and left its convolutional layers frozen.

Static-Image Level. The following two models were trained for static-image level classifiers training:

Table 1. Classification performance of the proposed model and the defined baseline models. We present results when the users in the test sets have been seen during training (personalized), when were hidden (generic), and their overall results. The best result is shown in bold, and the best result other than the groundtruth boundaries is highlighted in blue.

| | STILL-IMAGE LEVEL | | IMAGE-SEQUENCE LEVEL | | | | | | | | | | | | | | | |
| | CNN Xception | CNN+RF Avg. pool+pred. | CNN+RF+LSTM | | | | CNN+RF+BLSTM | | | | CNN+LSTM | | | | CNN+BLSTM | | | |
Measure			No segmentation	CES [32] segmentation	Our segmentation	GT Boundaries	No segmentation	CES [32] segmentation	Our segmentation	GT Boundaries	No segmentation	CES [32] segmentation	Our segmentation	GT Boundaries	No segmentation	CES [32] segmentation	Our segmentation	GT Boundaries
Personalized Accuracy	79.27	82.09	82.54	81.62	81.93	82.64	80.63	80.72	80.89	81.30	83.71	85.73	83.01	**86.32**	84.27	83.63	84.26	83.74
mAP	58.08	60.22	53.41	45.93	46.64	51.63	48.91	49.09	48.89	53.93	67.33	67.55	65.39	**70.11**	67.72	67.48	67.83	64.50
Macro precision	54.74	**64.67**	58.36	47.19	47.31	56.67	52.29	48.79	48.90	53.74	59.33	64.12	59.13	61.95	60.78	62.62	62.73	59.55
Macro recall	51.23	45.87	46.07	44.20	42.50	48.88	37.13	36.81	37.16	41.95	62.44	**66.81**	62.84	61.52	63.72	62.48	64.52	62.10
Generic Accuracy	72.56	74.76	73.79	71.91	72.59	75.16	65.22	66.64	66.40	70.62	82.21	81.92	80.07	**83.07**	79.21	78.31	78.49	77.92
mAP	47.80	55.59	47.07	41.74	46.76	53.97	40.92	40.51	42.92	43.59	61.77	57.78	62.58	**67.25**	59.97	61.75	60.87	56.19
Macro precision	44.10	52.21	48.40	36.10	38.69	44.41	31.87	31.91	31.87	47.01	59.69	51.15	55.55	**63.77**	57.60	57.16	53.01	53.36
Macro recall	43.61	41.62	40.10	35.67	36.58	54.85	32.32	32.41	33.11	38.40	55.22	53.11	52.45	**60.57**	54.53	52.86	50.62	52.50
Both Accuracy	77.43	80.08	80.14	78.95	79.37	80.58	76.40	76.86	76.91	78.37	83.30	84.69	82.20	**85.43**	82.88	82.17	82.68	82.14
mAP	51.39	55.96	48.33	42.12	44.18	48.67	43.95	43.84	43.98	47.24	64.17	61.65	63.61	**66.77**	63.02	62.97	63.21	59.52
Macro precision	54.63	63.98	59.77	43.60	47.31	51.98	48.49	45.33	45.27	55.22	66.64	62.16	63.01	**68.44**	63.45	65.06	63.99	60.96
Macro recall	48.00	41.71	41.70	39.78	40.19	49.75	33.20	32.98	33.22	38.01	61.00	59.68	59.29	**61.39**	56.40	55.25	56.98	56.39

CNN. We used Xception [28] as backbone CNN and we replaced the top layer with a fully-connected layer of 24 outputs. The fine-tuning procedure used Stochastic Gradient Descent (SGD) and a class-weighting scheme based on [29] to handle class imbalance. The CNN initially used the weights of a pre-trained network on ImageNet [30] that was fine-tuned. During the first 2 epochs, only the fully connected layers were optimized using a learning rate $\alpha = 1 \times 10^{-1}$, a momentum $\mu = 0.9$, and a weight decay equal to $\alpha = 5 \times 10^{-6}$. For the last epoch, the last 2 separable convolutional layers from the exit flow were also fine-tuned and the learning rate changed to $\alpha = 1 \times 10^{-3}$. In addition, the data augmentation consisted of randomly applying horizontal flips, translation and rotation shifts, and zoom operations at the frame level.

CNN+RF. One random forest (RF) having a different number of trees (100, 200, ..., 500) was trained using output layers from Xception network. Specifically, the RF was trained using as input the features extracted from the average pooling (avg. pooling) and fully-connected (FC) layers. The random forest used the Gini impurity criterion [31]. The best configuration resulted in using a number of trees equal to 200.

Image-Sequence Level. The image-sequence level models took into account temporal information and used as a backbone the previously trained models. Our event boundaries were segmented using the SR-Clustering [16]. In order to measure the importance of the temporal information in the models, we used boundaries from three other settings. As a lower bound, the first setting considered the full-day sequence (no segmentation). The second setting used event boundaries segmented using the contextual event segmentation (CES) algorithm [32] trained over the R3 dataset. As an upper bound, the last setting used the groundtruth activity boundaries.

Table 2. Mean average precision as the overlap of different IoU thresholds θ. We present results when the users in the test sets have been seen during training (personalized), when were hidden (generic), and their overall results. The best result is shown in bold, and the best result other than the groundtruth boundaries is highlighted in blue.

| | STILL-IMAGE LEVEL | | IMAGE-SEQUENCE LEVEL | | | | | | | | | | | | | | | |
| | CNN | CNN +RF | CNN+RF+LSTM | | | | CNN+RF+BLSTM | | | | CNN+LSTM | | | | CNN+BLSTM | | | |
θ	Xception	Avg. pool+pred.	No segmentation	CES [32] segmentation	Our segmentation	GT Boundaries	No segmentation	CES [32] segmentation	Our segmentation	GT Boundaries	No segmentation	CES [32] segmentation	Our segmentation	GT Boundaries	No segmentation	CES [32] segmentation	Our segmentation	GT Boundaries
Personalized																		
0.5	07.49	08.37	10.20	09.23	08.66	21.11	07.61	08.55	07.71	09.40	13.28	12.36	11.70	**24.14**	17.21	14.99	15.55	14.11
0.4	08.49	09.90	11.99	11.77	10.35	22.26	10.33	10.71	10.78	11.13	14.62	14.35	12.70	**24.80**	18.03	17.10	16.47	15.63
0.3	09.53	11.10	13.98	12.39	12.26	22.83	11.12	11.79	11.86	13.28	16.01	16.71	14.02	**25.83**	19.51	18.59	18.40	16.63
0.2	11.60	12.69	15.13	14.35	14.27	23.04	12.68	13.54	12.67	14.31	18.36	18.96	15.34	**27.68**	21.11	20.45	20.13	17.69
0.1	12.04	13.71	17.68	16.47	16.93	23.17	14.80	14.67	14.63	15.58	21.31	21.41	18.42	**28.15**	21.96	21.39	20.87	19.07
Generic																		
0.5	04.52	05.88	12.30	08.72	11.98	**32.73**	06.73	06.34	06.49	05.65	15.21	15.74	15.05	27.34	12.66	12.93	18.27	14.80
0.4	06.01	07.55	13.26	12.20	13.08	**34.25**	07.57	07.03	07.27	07.11	19.71	18.02	18.39	30.34	18.36	18.61	19.72	16.89
0.3	07.85	08.49	16.76	13.63	14.62	**34.41**	08.07	07.73	07.99	08.28	24.77	21.95	21.76	33.28	23.42	22.69	24.30	19.56
0.2	08.71	09.06	17.85	16.56	17.96	**35.02**	09.10	09.01	09.31	08.77	27.78	25.40	23.84	33.74	26.30	24.40	25.41	21.12
0.1	09.78	10.65	18.49	18.22	18.97	35.02	11.19	09.76	09.87	12.15	33.85	26.15	25.68	**35.16**	26.87	26.06	27.37	22.47
Both																		
0.5	04.50	05.83	10.25	08.21	08.14	21.23	06.35	07.03	06.24	06.67	12.51	13.61	10.84	**22.81**	13.62	12.75	14.99	12.94
0.4	05.86	07.33	11.62	10.72	09.23	22.40	07.72	08.01	07.79	08.26	14.46	15.44	12.76	**23.95**	15.89	15.45	15.93	14.32
0.3	07.12	08.63	14.28	11.77	11.29	22.86	08.55	09.08	08.98	10.42	16.99	18.66	15.20	**26.20**	18.93	18.30	18.89	15.97
0.2	08.26	09.53	15.38	13.77	13.30	23.13	09.45	10.05	09.85	11.10	19.64	21.09	16.88	**27.24**	20.66	19.77	20.30	17.16
0.1	08.97	10.81	17.24	15.47	15.55	23.24	11.46	11.24	11.00	12.90	26.23	22.60	19.95	**27.89**	21.67	21.30	21.55	18.57

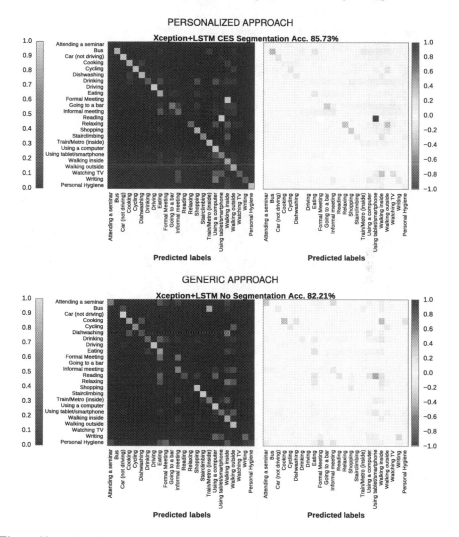

Fig. 4. Normalized confusion matrices of the best models for the seen and unseen test sets and their difference with respect to the CNN model. The increase and decrease of confidence is represented by the intensity of red and blue colors. (Color figure online)

With the purpose of making a fair comparison, the weights and outputs of the backbone models were frozen during training. All the day and event photo-stream sequences were considered as full sequences during training. All the models were trained using the SGD optimization algorithm using different learning rates, but the same momentum $\mu = 0.9$, weight decay equal to $\alpha = 5 \times 10^{-6}$, batch size of 1, and a timestep of 5.

CNN+LSTM and CNN+BLSTM. Both models removed the top layer of the Xception network and respectively added an LSTM and BLSTM layer having

256 units, followed by a fully-connected layer of 24 outputs. For both models, the learning rates were $\alpha = 1 \times 10^{-2}$ and $\alpha = 1 \times 10^{-3}$, respectively.

CNN+RF+LSTM and CNN+RF+BLSTM. These models were trained using as input the prediction of the *CNN+RF* model. Both models added an LSTM and BLSTM layer having 30 units, followed by a fully-connected layer of 24 outputs. The learning rate for both models was $\alpha = 1 \times 10^{-3}$.

4.3 Evaluation Metrics

We considered that the sequential classification of frames from a photo-stream can be seen as an action recognition and detection tasks. Therefore, we used a specific set of metrics for each task. In the case of action recognition, we considered that using only the accuracy for measuring the model performance would be misleading as the testing splits are highly imbalanced. Therefore, we also used mean average precision (mAP) and other macro metrics for precision and recall as in [6]. In the case of action detection, we measured the mAP as the overlap of intersection over the union (IoU) with different thresholds as defined in [33].

Since the event segmentation clusters contextual consecutive images and not activity boundaries, we measured their homogeneity and completeness and summarized them using the V-measure. We also used the adjusted Rand index (ARI) to measure how close to the real activity segments are.

5   Results

In Tables 1 and 2, we present the classification performance and mAP overlap of IoU for all the static and temporal models, respectively. The next subsections discuss the results in detail.

5.1   Generic Vs Personalized Learning

Since the test categories have different proportions in the personalized and generic users splits, a straight performance comparison per category between them cannot be made. Nevertheless, the temporal models can be compared with respect to their static models, as illustrated in Fig. 4. It shows the confusion matrices for the best temporal models of each test split and their difference with respect to the CNN model. It can be observed a low performance for the categories *Formal Meeting, Cooking,* and *Relaxing.* They might be due to the large intra-class variability of the category (*Relaxing*), the social context ambiguity (*Formal* and *Informal meeting*), and to the fact that same activities occur on very similar places (*Cooking* and *Dishwashing*). Additionally, the performance of these classes does not increase even using temporal methods. A comparison of all the models over the test set is presented in Table 1. It shows that the best recall scores are obtained using fully deep temporal models (CNN+LSTM and CNN+BLSTM).

5.2 Random Forest Based Models Vs. Deep Models

The results show that the deep models have a better and more robust performance than the RF based models. Although the CNN+RF improved the overall accuracy and precision of the Xception network, it decreased the rest of the evaluated macro metrics. Particularly, the recall decreased in both test splits, thus it missed a large number of test images. Furthermore, its temporal models CNN+RF+LSTM and CNN+RF+BLSTM performed consistently worse in both splits. This contrasts the results previously obtained in [21] using another dataset and it is likely due to the fact that here we are using unseen users in our test set.

5.3 LSTM Vs. BLSTM Temporal Models

The RF based and fully deep temporal models have contrasting results, as seen in Table 1. In the case of the RF based models, the bidirectional models performed worse than the unidirectional counterparts and even than its baseline model CNN+RF, thus indicating that the RF output did not provide enough information for generalization. In the case of the fully deep temporal models

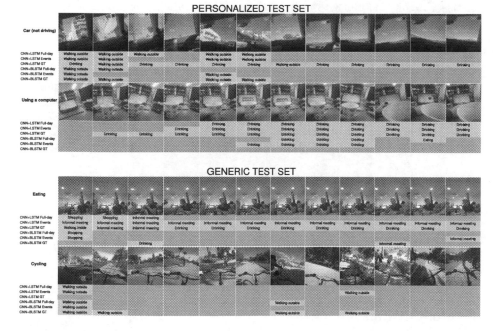

Fig. 5. Example of qualitative results obtained from personalize and generic test sets. Each row shows the first 12 frames of segmented events having only one activity. Full-day and Events refers to no-segmentation and SR-Clustering from photo-streams, correspondingly. False and true activity labels are marked in red and green, respectively. (Color figure online)

(CNN+LSTM and CNN+BLSTM), they showed improvement in all metrics and were the best in general terms. The unidirectional models achieved the highest classification accuracy in both test splits and the rest of the metrics showed a more solid classification, specifically achieving an accuracy of 85.73% and 82.21% for the Personalized and Generic test sets, correspondingly.

5.4   Event Clustering Vs. No Segmentation

We present the results of event segmentation with respect to the groundtruth activity boundaries in Table 3. They show that the event segments obtained with the CES algorithm have slightly less mixed categories with a V-measure equal to 0.936. Additionally, it shows that its clusters are closer to actual activity boundaries by having an ARI of 0.679. Their similarity of clustering performance also was reflected in achieving similar classification scores. Nevertheless, the CES algorithm obtained better performance than our segmentation algorithm for the best model CNN+LSTM (84.69% accuracy for both test splits).

The overall performance shows that the most robust performance is achieved using the CNN+LSTM with no segmentation, as shown in Table 1. Nonetheless, the results indicate that the events segmentation helps the classification when the users have been previously seen during training, and especially when they are used in conjunction with unidirectional LSTMs (achieving 85.73% accuracy as seen in Table 1). Moreover, their effect over the CNN+LSTM consistently has a better performance for higher IoU thresholds ($\theta \in \{0.2 - 0.5\}$) in both test splits, as seen in Table 2. The results show that bidirectional models are not benefited from activity boundaries provided by the groundtruth, as seen from the results presented in Table 2. Specifically, having no segmentation at all for the CNN+BLSTM model is better than the groundtruth. This might be explained as the BLSTM having a smoothing effect over mixed input categories. As a classification example over sequences, Fig. 5 shows some qualitative results.

Table 3. Activity events clustering performance. The best result is shown in bold.

Method	Homogeneity	Completeness	V-measure	Adjusted Rand index
SR clustering [16]	0.897	0.953	0.924	0.620
CES [32]	**0.905**	**0.969**	**0.936**	**0.679**

6   Conclusions

This paper addresses the effect of event boundaries for activity recognition in egocentric photo-streams, a poorly investigated topic. By using a recently published egocentric dataset acquired from 15 users, our contributions are the following. First, we propose an event-based architecture for a robust activity recognition in photo-streams. This architecture automatically segments egocentric photo-streams into subsequences with similar contextual and semantic features. These segments define the training and testing event boundaries for a CNN+BLSTM model. Second, in order to determine the effect of event boundaries, we provide a rich ablation study of different state-of-the-art methods comparing them with groundtruth boundaries and their lack of. Additionally, these tests thoroughly evaluate the generalization capabilities of these methods on a *generic* and a *personalized* training. Our results show that event boundaries benefit activity recognition performance of the CNN+LSTM when tested on users previously seen during training, thus achieving a classification accuracy of 85.73%. Moreover, our tests show that actual activity segments in the photo-stream are better classified using event boundaries for higher IoU thresholds ($\theta \in \{0.2-0.5\}$) using this architecture. The results also point that event boundaries make more robust the activity classification and detection performance of the CNN+BLSTM than not using them, but their improvement is not as good as its unidirectional counterpart. Finally, the results also indicate that event boundaries improved the detection of activity segments for temporal RF based architectures but failed to improve their classification baseline. Since activity recognition from egocentric photo-streams could be posed as a multi-classification problem, future research lines should consider the context ambiguity. For example, a person might be *eating* something while *reading* a book inside a *train*.

Acknowledgment. This work was partially funded by projects RTI2018-095232-B-C2, SGR 1742, CERCA, Nestore Horizon2020 SC1-PM-15-2017 (n 769643), Validithi EIT Health Program, and the Spanish Ministry of Economy and Competitiveness and the European Regional Development Fund (MINECO/ERDF, EU) through the program Ramon y Cajal, the national Spanish project PID2019-110977GA-I00 and the Spanish national network RED2018-102511-T. A. Cartas supported by a doctoral fellowship from the Mexican Council of Science and Technology (CONACYT) (grant-no. 366596). The authors acknowledge the support of NVIDIA Corporation for hardware donation.

References

1. Cartas, A., Luque, J., Radeva, P., Segura, C., Dimiccoli, M.: Seeing and hearing egocentric actions: How much can we learn? In: Proceedings of the IEEE International Conference on Computer Vision Workshops (2019)
2. Chen, L., Nugent, C.D.: Human Activity Recognition and Behaviour Analysis. Springer, Cham (2019). https://doi.org/10.1007/978-3-030-19408-6
3. de Jong, R.: Multimodal deep learning for the classification of human activity: radar and video data fusion for the classification of human activity (2019)
4. Bolaños, M., Dimiccoli, M., Radeva, P.: Toward storytelling from visual lifelogging: an overview. IEEE Trans. Hum.-Mach. Syst. **47**(1), 77–90 (2017)
5. Aghaei, M., Dimiccoli, M., Radeva, P.: All the people around me: face discovery in egocentric photo-streams. In: 2017 IEEE International Conference on Image Processing (ICIP), pp. 1342–1346. IEEE (2017)

6. Cartas, A., Radeva, P., Dimiccoli, M.: Activities of daily living monitoring via a wearable camera: toward real-world applications. IEEE Access **8**, 77344–77363 (2020)
7. Castro, D., et al.: Predicting daily activities from egocentric images using deep learning, pp. 75–82 (2015)
8. Cartas, A., Dimiccoli, M., Radeva, P.: Batch-based activity recognition from egocentric photo-streams. In: Proceedings of the IEEE International Conference on Computer Vision Workshops, pp. 2347–2354 (2017)
9. Cartas, A., Marín, J., Radeva, P., Dimiccoli, M.: Recognizing activities of daily living from egocentric images. In: Alexandre, L.A., Salvador Sánchez, J., Rodrigues, J.M.F. (eds.) IbPRIA 2017. LNCS, vol. 10255, pp. 87–95. Springer, Cham (2017). https://doi.org/10.1007/978-3-319-58838-4_10
10. Aghaei, M., Dimiccoli, M., Ferrer, C.C., Radeva, P.: Towards social pattern characterization in egocentric photo-streams. Comput. Vision Image Unders. **171**, 104–117 (2018)
11. Aimar, E.S., Radeva, P., Dimiccoli, M.: Social relation recognition in egocentric photostreams. In: 2019 IEEE International Conference on Image Processing (ICIP), pp. 3227–3231. IEEE (2019)
12. Talavera, E., Leyva-Vallina, M., Sarker, M.K., Puig, D., Petkov, N., Radeva, P.: Hierarchical approach to classify food scenes in egocentric photo-streams. IEEE J. Biomed. Health Inf. **24**, 866–877 (2019)
13. Talavera, E., Wuerich, C., Petkov, N., Radeva, P.: Topic modelling for routine discovery from egocentric photo-streams. Pattern Recogn **104**, 107330 (2020)
14. Poleg, Y., Arora, C., Peleg, S.: Temporal segmentation of egocentric videos. In: Proceedings of the IEEE Conference on Computer Vision and Pattern Recognition, pp. 2537–2544 (2014)
15. Furnari, A., Farinella, G.M., Battiato, S.: Temporal segmentation of egocentric videos to highlight personal locations of interest. In: Hua, G., Jégou, H. (eds.) ECCV 2016. LNCS, vol. 9913, pp. 474–489. Springer, Cham (2016). https://doi.org/10.1007/978-3-319-46604-0_34
16. Dimiccoli, M., Bolaños, M., Talavera, E., Aghaei, M., Nikolov, S.G., Radeva, P.: Sr-clustering: semantic regularized clustering for egocentric photo streams segmentation. Comput. Vision Image Underst. **155**, 55–69 (2017)
17. Dias, C., Dimiccoli, M.: Learning event representations by encoding the temporal context. In: Proceedings of the European Conference on Computer Vision (ECCV) (2018)
18. Pirsiavash, H., Ramanan, D.: Detecting activities of daily living in first-person camera views. In: Proceedings of the IEEE Computer Vision and Pattern Recognition (CVPR), pp. 2847–2854. IEEE (2012)
19. Sudhakaran, S., Lanz, O.: Attention is all we need: Nailing down object-centric attention for egocentric activity recognition. In: Proceedings of the British Machine Vision Conference (BMVC) (2018)
20. García Hernando, G., Yuan, S., Baek, S., Kim, T.-K.: First-person hand action benchmark with rgb-d videos and 3D hand pose annotations. In: The IEEE Conference on Computer Vision and Pattern Recognition (CVPR) (2018)
21. Cartas, A., Marín, J., Radeva, P., Dimiccoli, M.: Batch-based activity recognition from egocentric photo-streams revisited. Pattern Anal. Appl. (2018). https://doi.org/10.1007/s10044-018-0708-1
22. Yu, H., et al.: A multisource fusion framework driven by user-defined knowledge for egocentric activity recognition. EURASIP J. Adv. Signal Process. 2019(1), 14 (2019). https://doi.org/10.1186/s13634-019-0612-x

23. Yu, H., et al.: A hierarchical deep fusion framework for egocentric activity recognition using a wearable hybrid sensor system. Sensors **19**(3) (2019). https://www.mdpi.com/1424-8220/19/3/546
24. Song, S., et al.: Multimodal multi-stream deep learning for egocentric activity recognition. In: Proceedings of the IEEE Conference on Computer Vision and Pattern Recognition Workshops, pp. 24–31 (2016)
25. Graves, A., Schmidhuber, J.: Framewise phoneme classification with bidirectional LSTM and other neural network architectures. Neural Netw. **18**(5), 602–610 (2005). http://www.sciencedirect.com/science/article/pii/S0893608005001206
26. Chollet, F.: Deep Learning with Python, 1st edn., pp. 219–221. Manning Publications Co, Greenwich (2017)
27. Ng, J.Y.-H., Hausknecht, M., Vijayanarasimhan, S., Vinyals, O., Monga, R., Toderici, G.: Beyond short snippets: deep networks for video classification. In: Computer Vision and Pattern Recognition (2015)
28. Chollet, F.: Xception: deep learning with depthwise separable convolutions, pp. 1800–1807 (2017)
29. King, G., Zeng, L.: Logistic regression in rare events data. Polit. Anal. **9**(2), 137–163 (2001)
30. Deng, J., Dong, W., Socher, R., Li, L.-J., Li, K., Fei-Fei, L.: ImageNet: a large-scale hierarchical image database. In: CVPR09 (2009)
31. Breiman, L., Friedman, J., Stone, C.J., Olshen, R.A.: Classification and Regression Trees. CRC Press, Boca Raton (1984)
32. Garcia del Molino, A., Lim, J.-H., Tan, A.-H.: Predicting visual context for unsupervised event segmentation in continuous photo-streams. In: 2018 ACM Multimedia Conference on Multimedia Conference, pp. 10–17. ACM (2018)
33. Jiang, Y.-G.. et al.: THUMOS challenge: action recognition with a large number of classes (2014). http://crcv.ucf.edu/THUMOS14/

Egomap: Hierarchical First-Person Semantic Mapping

Tamas Suveges(iD) and Stephen McKenna(✉)(iD)

CVIP, School of Science and Engineering, University of Dundee,
Dundee DD1 4HN, UK
{t.suveges,s.j.z.mckenna}@dundee.ac.uk

Abstract. We consider unsupervised learning of semantic, user-specific maps from first-person video. The task we address can be thought of as a semantic, non-geometric form of simultaneous localisation and mapping, differing in significant ways from formulations typical in robotics. Locations, termed *stations*, typically correspond to rooms or areas in which a user spends time, places to which they might refer in spoken conversation. Our maps are modeled as a hierarchy of probabilistic station graphs and view graphs. View graphs capture an aspect of user behaviour within stations. Visits are temporally segmented based on qualitative visual motion and used to update the map, either by updating an existing map station or adding a new map station. We contribute a labelled dataset suitable for evaluation of this novel SLAM task. Experiments compare mapping performance with and without the use of view graphs and demonstrate better online mapping than when using offline clustering.

1 Introduction

First-person (egocentric) video, acquired using wearable cameras, provides data streams that lend themselves to inference and learning about everyday activities from a human-centred perspective. They have been used to analyse social interaction, focus of attention, and lifestyle behaviour, and find applications in assistive technology, health, and human-robot interaction, for example. This paper explores the use of first-person video to automatically construct a representation of a user's everyday environment in terms of locations that they frequent and their patterns of transition between, and their behaviours within, those locations. The locations in our model are conceived of as places where the

This research received funding from the UK Engineering and Physical Sciences Research Council (EPSRC grant EP/N014278/1). Maxwell J. Wilson assisted with video data acquisition. We are grateful to members of the CVIP cluster and the ACE-LP project for helpful discussions and feedback.

Electronic supplementary material The online version of this chapter (https://doi.org/10.1007/978-3-030-68796-0_25) contains supplementary material, which is available to authorized users.

A. Del Bimbo et al. (Eds.): ICPR 2020 Workshops, LNCS 12663, pp. 348–363, 2021.
https://doi.org/10.1007/978-3-030-68796-0_25

user stays for some time, often to perform a specific activity or task. They tend to correspond to places to which people might refer in narrative, e.g., my desk, the kitchen, the meeting room. We will call these locations *stations*. The aim is to dynamically learn a semantic map in terms of stations that can be used to localise the user and provide contextual information from previous visits to those stations.

As a motivating example application, consider voice output communication aids for non-speaking users. Their users often average 8–12 spoken words per minute; typical adult speech rates are 150–190 words per minute. One approach to offering a user better predictive text, and thus improved communication speed, is to leverage information about the context [1]. A user-specific map would enable that user's communication to be contextualised in terms of the stations they repeatedly visit. Other applications could include aids to compensate for memory loss and automatic visual personal history generation, potentially combined with activity recognition [2–4].

The task that we address can be thought of as a semantic, non-geometric, human-centred form of simultaneous localisation and mapping (SLAM). This is done without recourse to metric map building which is not necessary to address this task. We propose a hierarchical probabilistic model, incorporating station graphs and view graphs, and hypothesise that it can be used to perform the unsupervised mapping and localisation that we require. Each view graph captures aspects of the user's head movements while at a station. A characteristic of our map representation is that two stations can be adjacent in the station graph even if one is physically only indirectly reachable from the other; map adjacency does not imply spatial adjacency of stations. This is because the user can transition through intervening space without stopping. We identify transitions between stations based on qualitative visual motion analysis. Maps are dynamically updated, and new stations are added as they are visited for the first time.

In common with many SLAM systems, we adopt a visual bag of words feature representation with traditional features. Deep convolutional neural network representations have been used in SLAM but can perform poorly if not configured carefully for the task [5]. We leave the exploration of the use of different view representations within our framework, including the use of deep features, to future work.

The main contributions are as follows.

1. We formulate a novel first-person mapping and localisation task which requires unsupervised, sequential learning of a user-centred map in terms of semantic stations.
2. We propose a method to perform this task based on a hierarchical, probabilistic model and we report results comparing learned maps with ground-truth maps, including on a new egocentric dataset which we make available.

2   Relationship with Previous Work

In this paper, we rely solely on egocentric video sensing from a single head-mounted camera, and we focus on semantic (non-geometric) visual mapping and localisation.

2.1   Related Approaches

Appearance-based SLAM methods use visual data to construct topological maps, often employing omnidirectional cameras to ease the problem of dealing with different views of the same place [6–8]. For example, a modified incremental spectral clustering method was proposed to cluster visually similar places based on SIFT features [6]. The performance of different image descriptors has been assessed in such a setting using manually taken omnidirectional images [7]. In contrast, first-person video is usually acquired using a monocular camera with a relatively limited field of view.

Three-dimensional reconstruction is another approach to detect global loop closures, borrowed from robotics and often requiring expensive computation. Ego-Slam [9] highlights the importance of local loop closures in an egocentric video to handle significant rotation, e.g., head movements. Detected local loop closures are used to improve the accuracy of estimated camera poses, resulting in more accurate 3D reconstruction. In contrast, we use such information to build a graph representation of a station in which edges and nodes store information on head movement and visual appearance, respectively.

Furnari et al. [10,11] and Ortis et al. [12] formulate a supervised classification task rather than unsupervied SLAM. In common with [13], these are off-line solutions; we address the more challenging problem of developing an unsupervised method that can operate online.

SeqSLAM compares sequences of observations to detect loop closures [14]. First-person videos are, by their nature, generally long, so storing them and performing SeqSLAM on them in their entirety is impractical, especially as computation time exponentially increases with the length of visits.

FabMap implements a probabilistic framework for SLAM using Bayesian filtering [15]. When a loop closure is detected, FabMap updates the appearance model of a given place. This method can work well when the environment is captured at low frame-rate from a moving robot such that consecutive images are visually dissimilar enough (Consecutive images in the dataset used in [15] were acquired at positions separated by 1.5 m). Otherwise, the visual smoothness of the environment over time can cause FabMap to update a single appearance model continuously, necessitating the use of keyframe extraction in practice. Furthermore, FabMap, similarly to many other SLAM approaches, does not represent the hierarchical structure of the environment, instead defining a location as a single image.

EgoMap, the probabilistic framework we propose, uses Bayesian filtering for map inference and learning similarly to FabMap [15] but offers a more informative, hierarchical representation of the environment. We conceptualise a station as a place where the user spends time. Each station is then described as a graph of interconnected views between which the edge weights represent the probability of transition from one view to another. Hence, EgoMap differs from existing SLAM techniques by conceptualising stations, resulting in a human-centric representation. Furthermore, EgoMap offers a hierarchical representation of the user's world that allows the framework to detect loop closures at a higher, hence more general, level. Most SLAM techniques only allow image-level loop closure detection, which is useful in robotics but misses the semantic interpretation in terms of places.

2.2 Datasets

We address a novel SLAM challenge and its empirical evaluation accordingly requires an appropriate first-person video dataset. This dataset should capture the repetitive and somewhat habitual nature of everyday behaviour in which visits are made repeatedly to certain stations, often to perform specific actions. Visits to specific stations have associated user-specific visual behaviours depending on the purpose of the visit.

SLAM datasets such as KITTI 06, City Center and KAIST [16] are recorded from road vehicles often moving at relatively constant speeds. These datasets were created for a different purpose and fail to capture repetitive human behaviour in a personal environment. Similarly, those captured by robots, such as NewCollege and Robot@Home [17], focus on capturing the environment uniformly while continuously moving through it, and they fail to record everyday activity in which a person transitions between locations in a somewhat habitual manner. SLAM datasets do not capture such behaviour so are unsuitable for our purposes [18–21]. An absence of loop-closures is also common with SLAM datasets given that the environment is only captured once. Visit level loop-closures are essential to evaluate unsupervised semantic mapping. Furthermore, datasets like [19–21] have short video segments omitting the transitional sections between stations.

Many egocentric datasets focus on activity recognition [22–26]. Datasets tailored for such a task often include short video segments capturing multiple activity sequences each recorded at different stations. This setup leads to problems such as missing transitional sections and lack of loop-closures similarly to those in SLAM. Lifelogging is another intense area in ubiquitous computing [2–4], however, datasets are typically low framerate [2,4,27–29]. Those captured at high frame rate commonly document the user's life for a short period of time resulting in only a few or no loop-closures [30,31]. There are several other impressive egocentric datasets, but the number of loop closures is limited to one per station which is insufficient for our purposes [10–12]. EGO-CH [32] is an extensive egocentric video dataset for cultural heritage visitor behavioural understanding recorded by 70 different people exploring museums. This dataset is not a good match for our purposes as locations are both visually and semantically very similar. We aim to map the user in their everyday environment where stations differ in their utilization. A more relevant dataset records the everyday life of

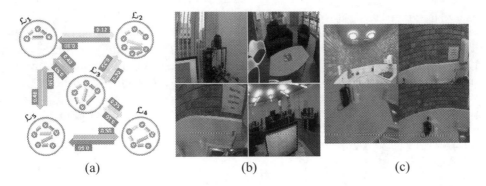

(a)   (b)   (c)

Fig. 1. (a) An illustrative map with five station nodes. Edge weights are transition probabilities. (b) Example images from four different stations in our dataset; from top left to bottom right: 3D-lab, Coffee-area, Kitchen 1, and Lab. (c) Views learned for Kitchen 1

20 subjects in their own environment using a chest-mounted camera [2] . However, due to a bias towards activity recognition, many of the users switch off the camera between activities, leading to missing transitions. Furthermore, the number of stations is often rather small (3–4). Nonetheless, we report additional, preliminary results on two of the videos from that dataset.

We contribute a dataset more suited to the challenge addressed in this paper. It includes transition segments between stations, multiple visits by a user to multiple distinct stations, and unique labels for *all* visited stations.

3   Model

3.1   Hierarchical Map

We introduce a hierarchical map structure in which stations in a map are represented in terms of view graphs. Our map can be written as a weighted directed graph $\mathcal{M} = (\{\mathcal{L}_1, ..., \mathcal{L}_M\}, \mathbf{E})$ where M is the number of stations in the map and $\mathbf{E}$ is an $M \times M$ stochastic transition matrix with $\mathbf{E}_{i,j} = P(l_{t+1} = j, | l_t = i)$ denoting the probability of transitioning from station i at time t to station j at time $t + 1$. Each station is in turn represented as a directed graph $\mathcal{L}_m = (\{\mathcal{V}_1, ..., \mathcal{V}_{N(m)}\}, \mathbf{P})$ where $N(m)$ is the number of views at that station and $\mathbf{P}$ is an $N(m) \times N(m)$ stochastic transition matrix with $\mathbf{P}_{i,j} = P(v_{t+1} = j | v_t = i)$ denoting the probability of transitioning from the jth view to the ith view at that station. Transition matrix $\mathbf{E}$ encapsulates information about the user's movement around the map whereas each $\mathbf{P}$ matrix captures information about user behaviour at a map station. This structure, illustrated in Fig. 1a, allows us to build a personalied ego-centric map for a specific user where behavioral information can be used to aid localization. Figure 1b shows examples images from four stations, and Fig. 1c shows four example view images from one of those stations.

3.2   View Representation

Each view has an associated appearance model. In our experiments we use a bag-of-words representation [33]. Each view is represented by a vector in which each element indicates the presence or absence of a 'word' in a vocabulary of size D. Let $\mathbf{z}_t = [z_1, ..., z_D]^T$ denote an observation at time t where each z_d is a binary variable. We used quantized SURF descriptors to generate binary features. Rather than model a view directly in terms of which features are likely to be observed, we introduce hidden variables similarly to [15]. A detector model relates feature existence e_d to feature detection z_d. The detector is specified by

$$
\begin{cases}
P(z_d = 1|e_d = 0), \text{false positive probability.} \\
P(z_d = 0|e_d = 1), \text{false negative probability.}
\end{cases}
\tag{1}
$$

Variable e_d can be thought of as encoding whether or not an object that generates observations of type z_d exists. We model the dth view as a D-vector, $\mathbf{v}$, the dth element of which records $P(e_d = 1)$ for that view. Each of the feature generating objects, e_d, is generated independently by the view.

4   Motion Analysis for Transition Detection

We aim to represent the user's world as a set of interconnected stations. Each station is a place in the world that the user spends time visiting. Such visits are interspersed with periods of transition characterised by, for example, sustained walking. We propose to detect when such periods of transition between visits are occurring based on qualitative visual motion analysis.

We compute frame-to-frame displacement vectors using a Lucas-Kanade feature tracker [34] on a 10×5 grid similarly to [31]. Transitions in egocentric video tend to be dominated by forward motion [9]. We assume that translation along the camera axis can be estimated by a simple zoom [35]. Equations (2) and (3) estimate the new coordinates of a point on the image plane given zoom parameter β and focal length f.

$$
X' = f[tan^{-1}\frac{X}{f}](1 + \frac{X^2}{f^2})\beta
\tag{2}
$$

$$
Y' = f[tan^{-1}\frac{Y}{f}](1 + \frac{Y^2}{f^2})\beta
\tag{3}
$$

We substantiate the coordinates of the grid cell centres and find the zoom parameter value, β^*, that gives the best fit to the estimated optical flow. Equations (2) and (3) do not decompose the motion field with respect all camera motion parameters, instead focusing on the zoom parameter. Once estimated, β^* is temporally smoothed to give $\hat{\beta}_t = s\hat{\beta}_{t-1} + (1-s)\beta_t^*$. This smoothed value is then thresholded to segment the video, detecting transition when $\hat{\beta} > T_{transition}$. We set $s = 0.99$ in all our experiments.

5   Inference

5.1   View Inference via Recursive Bayes

At time t, given an observation sequence $\mathbf{z}_{\tau:t}$ for the current visit to the mth map station, we can recursively infer the discrete random variable v_t over the $N(m)$ views,

$$P(v_t|\mathbf{z}_{\tau:t}) = \frac{P(\mathbf{z}_t|v_t)\sum_{v_{t-1}}P(v_t|v_{t-1})P(v_{t-1}|\mathbf{z}_{\tau:t-1})}{P(\mathbf{z}_t|\mathbf{z}_{\tau:t-1})}, \tag{4}$$

where the visit started at time $\tau < t$, $P(\mathbf{z}_t|v_t)$ is the current view likelihood, $P(v_t|v_{t-1})$ is the transition probability from matrix $\mathbf{P}$, and $P(\mathbf{z}_t|\mathbf{z}_{\tau:t-1})$ is the normalizing term. At the start of a visit, at time τ, a prior distribution is required over the views at a station. It would be possible to obtain this prior using weighted connections between views from different stations. However, for simplicity, we assume independence between views from different stations and use a flat prior that assigns equal probability to each view in a station at the start of a visit:

$$P(v_\tau = j|l = m) = \frac{1}{N(m)} \tag{5}$$

The view likelihood cannot be evaluated directly because of the intractability of learning the high-order conditional dependencies between appearance words. The simplest approximation is naive Bayes,

$$P(\mathbf{z}|v_t) \approx P(z_D|v_t)\dots P(z_2|v_t)P(z_1|v_t), \tag{6}$$

where,

$$P(z_d|v_t) = \sum_{s\in\{0,1\}} P(z_d|e_d = s)P(e_d = s|v_t) \tag{7}$$

5.2   Station Inference

During a visit, we can localise the user by estimating a probability distribution over map stations. At time t, given a map $\mathcal{M}$, an observation sequence $\mathbf{z}_{\tau:t}$ for the current visit, and the observation sequences, $\mathbf{Z}$, from all preceding visits, we can infer a discrete random variable, l_t, over stations,

$$P(l_t|\mathbf{z}_{\tau:t}, \mathbf{Z}) = \frac{P(\mathbf{z}_{\tau:t}|l_t)\sum_{l_{t-1}}P(l_t|l_{t-1})P(l_{t-1}|\mathbf{Z})}{P(\mathbf{z}_{\tau:t-1}|\mathbf{Z})} \tag{8}$$

where $P(\mathbf{z}_{\tau:t}|l_t)$ is the station likelihood and $P(l_t|l_{t-1})$ is the transition proba-
bility from matrix $\mathbf{E}$. Notice that the summation is constant during a visit so need only be computed once per visit. During the first visit in a video we use a flat prior over map stations:

$$P(l = m|\mathcal{M}) = \frac{1}{M} \tag{9}$$

The likelihood of a station, $P(\mathbf{z}_{\tau:t}|l_t = m)$, can be computed using the forward algorithm. Let us define a forward variable α initialized as $\alpha_\tau(v_\tau) = P(\mathbf{z}_\tau|v_\tau)P(v_\tau)$. Similarly to Eq. (4) we get the induction step:

$$\alpha_{t+1}(v_t) = P(\mathbf{z}_t|v_t) \sum_{v_{t-1}} P(v_t|v_{t-1})\alpha_t(v_{t-1}) \tag{10}$$

The likelihood at any time t' during a visit is given by the termination step:

$$P(\mathbf{z}_{\tau:t'}|l = m) = \sum_{v_{t'}} \alpha_{t'}(v_{t'}) \tag{11}$$

6   Learning

6.1   View Update

At each time step t, an association decision is made based on Eq. (4) as to which view's appearance model, $\mathbf{v}$, to update. A view model is the mean of all observations associated with it up until the current time, t. The model is sequentially updated as a moving average using Eq. (12) where γ is inversely proportional to number of updates already performed on the view. When a new view is created, its appearance model is initialized so that all words exist with marginal probability $P(e_d = 1)$ derived from the training data.

$$\mathbf{v}[d] := \gamma P(e_d = 1|\mathbf{z_t}) + (1 - \gamma)\mathbf{v}[d] \tag{12}$$

6.2   View Creation

In Sect. 5.1, we described how to compute a probability distribution over views (Eq. (4)). However, we wish to dynamically add new views to the model as appropriate. Therefore, we adjust the denominator in Eq. (4) so that the probabilities of the known views sum to less than one, leaving some probability mass assigned elsewhere. Conceptually, we would like to add a sum over all the yet to be modelled views, $\overline{v}_t$, at the station:

$$P(\mathbf{z}_t|\mathbf{z}_{\tau:t-1}) = \sum_{v_t} P(\mathbf{z}_t|v_t) \sum_{v_{t-1}} P(v_t|v_{t-1})P(v_{t-1}|\mathbf{z}_{\tau:t-1})$$
$$+ \sum_{\overline{v}_t} P(\mathbf{z}_t|\overline{v}_t) \sum_{v_{t-1}} P(\overline{v}_t|v_{t-1})P(v_{t-1}|\mathbf{z}_{\tau:t-1}) \tag{13}$$

The second summation cannot be evaluated so we adopt a mean field approximation, similarly to [15]:

$$P(\mathbf{z}_t|\mathbf{z}_{\tau:t-1}) = \sum_{v_t} P(\mathbf{z}_t|v_t) \sum_{v_{t-1}} P(v_t|v_{t-1})P(v_{t-1}|\mathbf{z}_{\tau:t-1})$$
$$+ P(\mathbf{z}_t|v_t') \sum_{v_{t-1}} P(v_t'|v_{t-1})P(v_{t-1}|\mathbf{z}_{\tau:t-1}) \tag{14}$$

Here v_t' is the average view. We adopt a uniform prior in the second term, with $P(v_t'|v_{t-1})$ the same for all views.

6.3   Station Update

To update a station, we first make a decision about the station of the user on the map, $\mathcal{M}$. To do so we calculate a MAP estimate, l_t^*:

$$l_t^* = \arg\max_m P(l = m | \mathbf{z}_{\tau:t}, \mathbf{Z}, \mathcal{M}) \tag{15}$$

After localization, we update the station's mean field $\mathbf{v}'$ as:

$$\mathbf{v}'[d] := \gamma \frac{1}{(t - \tau) + 1} \sum_{t'=\tau}^{t} P(e_d = 1 | \mathbf{z}_{t'}) + (1 - \gamma)\mathbf{v}'[d] \tag{16}$$

where $\mathbf{v}'$ is the view model of the new mean-field estimate, and γ is the weighting term inversely proportional to the number of examples already used to estimate the mean-field. Once the new mean-field is computed, we use $\mathbf{z}_{\tau:t}$ to iteratively update the station. At each timestep t', we infer $P(v_t | \mathbf{z}_{\tau:t'})$ and make a decision on the user's view in the station using Eq. (4) after which we update the station in accordance with Sects. 6.2 and 6.3.

6.4   Station Creation

Similarly to the mechanism for handling new views, we would ideally adjust the denominator of Eq. (8) to be

$$\begin{aligned} P(\mathbf{z}_{\tau:t} | \mathbf{Z}) &= \sum_{l_t} P(\mathbf{z}_{\tau:t} | l_t) \sum_{l_{t-1}} P(l_t | l_{t-1}) P(l_{t-1} | \mathbf{Z}) \\ &+ \sum_{\bar{l}_t} P(\mathbf{z}_{\tau:t} | \bar{l}_t) \sum_{l_{t-1}} P(\bar{l}_t | l_{t-1}) P(l_{t-1} | \mathbf{Z}), \end{aligned} \tag{17}$$

where $\bar{l}_t$ indexes over the yet to be modelled stations. Although, a mean-field estimation is possible it is not straightforward to estimate it. We instead use a likelihood threshold, $T_{new\ station}$, to decide when to create a new map station.

$$T_{new\ station} = \left[\sum_{\bar{l}_t} P(\mathbf{z}_{\tau:t} | \bar{l}_t) \right]^{\frac{1}{(t-\tau)+1}} \tag{18}$$

$P(\mathbf{z}_{\tau:t} | l_t)$ is computed using a recursive forward algorithm; its value is exponentially dependent on the number of observations. $T_{new\ station}$ can be interpreted as the average observation likelihood yielded by all the unknown stations for a single observation $\mathbf{z}_t$.

6.5   Transition Matrix Updates

Transition matrices $\mathbf{E}$ and $\mathbf{P}$ are updated using MAP estimation with a uniform prior over transitions. This avoids transition probabilities of zero. We implement this by initialising all transitions with a count of 5 in our experiments. Each time a transition is observed its count is incremented. Matrices $\mathbf{E}$ and $\mathbf{P}$ are obtained from these count matrices by normalisation. The effect of the prior diminishes over time.

7   Experiments and Metrics

7.1   Dataset

We recorded four hours of video, over five mornings, of a user's activity on the university campus. This activity was loosely scripted in order to ensure multiple visits were made to a range of stations. Scripts consisted of lists of stations along with suggestions for activities during station visits, e.g., make a drink, read something, collect an item from the printer. A ground-truth temporal segmentation of each video into visit and transition segments was manually annotated with reference to the scripts. The annotator was instructed to mark the start of a transition as the frame when the user appears to intentionally start moving away from the current station, and the start of a visit as the frame at which such transitional movement ends. All five videos were recorded using a head-mounted GoPro Hero 4 at 1080p resolution and 25 fps. The head mount gave us the ability to capture the approximate viewpoint of the user.

7.2   Dictionary Learning and Parameter Tuning

We used the first $10,000$ place images from the Places dataset to train our dictionary [36]. We extracted 128-dimensional SURF descriptors from each image and trained k-means on the extracted features ($k = 10,000$ as in [15]). To describe an image, we first extract SURF features, quantise using the k clusters, and construct a histogram. The final descriptor is then a binary quantized version of the obtained histogram where each bin implies presence or absence of a feature-generating object (see Sect. 3.2). We used the first video in our dataset (video 1) to tune the threshold parameter for the transitional motion detector which was then fixed ($T_{transition} = 1.008$).

7.3   Map Evaluation

To evaluate mapping performance, we aim to measure how well the predicted map approximates the ground truth map. First, predicted visit segments are matched with all ground-truth segments with which they overlap (in time). A matrix is then constructed by recording the co-occurrence frequencies between the set of ground-truth visit labels and the set of learned visit labels. Once normalised this can be considered as a joint probability distribution $P(G, L)$ where G and L are random variables over the ground-truth and the learned stations, respectively.

A measure of map quality can be obtained by computing the uncertainty a one-to-one matching process between the possible values in G and L would involve. In a perfect system, nodes co-occur exclusively, and the matching process involves no uncertainty. In other words, knowledge of one random variable provides maximum information on the other. Drifting away from the ideal case, the exclusivity disappears, and the matching process becomes difficult. To evaluate performance, we measure the mutual information (MI) as in Eq. (19) where

H is the entropy. Mutual information can be interpreted as a measure of how well a one-to-one mapping could be established between values in G and L.

$$MI(L, G) = H(L) - H(L|G) \tag{19}$$

However, MI tends to be higher when the node count is higher. This is undesirable since it prevents comparing graphs with different numbers of nodes. Therefore, we use an adjusted version of MI, AMI [37], that has been used to compare clusterings with varying numbers of clusters:

$$AMI(L, G) = \frac{MI(L, G) - E[MI(L, G)]}{\max(H(L), H(G)) - E[MI(L, G)]} \tag{20}$$

Here, E denotes the expected value. AMI takes the value of 1 when one-to-one correspondence can be established between the predicted map and the ground-truth map with certainty. On the other hand, the value is zero when the number of nodes in the predicted map is either one or equal to the number of visits.

7.4   Baseline and Ablation

We obtain baseline results by running k-means on our dataset. During clustering, we represent each visit using its mean feature vector. Notice that by doing so, we introduce the same time constraint used during inference in our system, i.e., we enforce the must-link constraint on frames from the same visit. We wish to emphasise that the offline nature of our baseline algorithm means it can access all features during clustering, greatly easing the complexity of the task. However, we believe that such a general and well-used approach provides a good baseline for comparison.

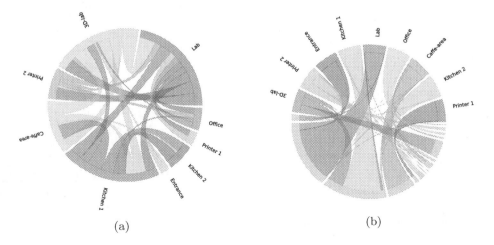

(a)   (b)

Fig. 2. Visualisations of (a) a ground-truth map, (b) visit matching between learned and ground-truth locations

Additionally, we perform an ablation experiment in which we remove the view-graph to evaluate its effect. We introduce a prohibition such that the system is only allowed to create one view per station. Such a system strongly resembles FabMap [15] with the added time-constraint.

8   Results

8.1   Visualisation

Figure 2 presents one way to visualise an example map and its correspondence with ground-truth. The ground-truth map is shown in Fig. 2a. Its nine stations are represented around the perimeter; the internal connections represent transitions that occur between those stations. Figure 2b shows a learned map and the ground-truth map together. Stations in the learned map appear around the bottom half of the circle. Connections represent the matching of visits to stations on the learned map with ground-truth stations. The size of the representation of each station in the learned map correlates with the number of visits to the station. In this example, some ground-truth stations connect with multiple nodes in the learned map. For example, *3D-lab* is matched with three nodes. This suggests that the threshold $T_{new\ station}$ was too high, causing the model to generate too many stations. On the other hand, one learned node is well-connected with both *Lab* and *3D-lab*. From Fig. 1b, we can see that these two stations have strong visual aliasing due to a computer monitor.

8.2   Quantitative Evaluation

$T_{new\ station}$ is an important free parameter in our system which indirectly controls the final station count. We report performance for different values allowing us to compare predicted maps with varying numbers of stations. In the case of k-means, the number of clusters is directly controllable hence we obtain high-resolution baseline results. We report AMI scores of three methods on our dataset in Fig. 3(a). Our partial system (without view graphs) has similar performance to the baseline k-means. However, it is important to highlight that while k-means operates in an offline manner, our partial system is still online. Furthermore, we conclude that the view graphs do have a positive effect on performance. Interestingly, we see that the best performing maps are over-segmented. One could argue that over-segmentation helps overall because ambiguous visits are not mistakenly forced into one of the known stations which would impact the system negatively in the long run given its online nature.

We also report preliminary, partial experiments in Fig. 4 on the ADL dataset published in [2]. Results were acquired by running our algorithm on the 7th and 13th video which have 6 and 3 stations, respectively. These results suggest that the hierarchical representation of the environment tends to help. However, given the low visit counts (6 and 14) and low station counts, those results are noisy.

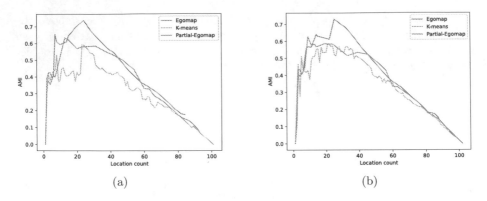

Fig. 3. AMI using (a) automatic and (b) manual segmentation

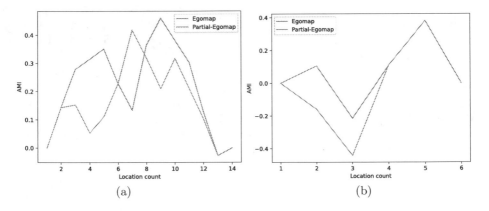

Fig. 4. Preliminary ADL results: (a) video 7 (b) video 13

To ascertain whether the qualitative motion analysis was adversely affecting results, we re-ran the experiment of Fig. 3(a) using manually segmented visits. Figure 3(b) shows the result. There is little noticeable difference from Fig. 3(a), suggesting that the motion analysis used to detect transitions between visits performs sufficiently well to support map building and semantic localisation.

9   Conclusions

We formulated a new person-centric SLAM task and described a modular, hierarchical, probabilistic framework to tackle it. Unsupervised, sequential learning of semantic, user-specific maps from first-person video enabled us to build a user-specific representation. These maps represent a network of visited stations (locations) and model each station as a network of views. We contributed a dataset and evaluated performance in terms of map correctness.

Transitions between station visits were detected using a qualitative motion analysis method and mapping performance suggested that this worked sufficiently well. Nevertheless, there is room for improvement in other modules in future work. In the view representation and likelihood function we used a quantized binary bag-of-visual-words descriptor. Although such descriptors enjoy success in various SLAM systems, they have limitations. Due to the high dimensionality of the binary feature vector, we find that matching likelihoods for two similar and two dissimilar images are too far apart in the log space often resulting in saturated probabilities. Future work could focus on finding representations where the computed likelihoods result in 'softer' probabilities. Furthermore, we note that the use of mean-field approximation for views can result in view representations at different stations that are inconsistent at a semantic level. Future work could further explore dynamic creation and merging of view nodes, and of station nodes.

References

1. Kristensson, P.-O., Lilley, J., Black, R., Waller, A.: A design engineering approach for quantitatively exploring context-aware sentence retrieval for nonspeaking individuals with motor disabilities. In: Proceedings of CHI Conference on Human Factors in Computing Systems (2020)
2. Pirsiavash, H., Ramanan, D.: Detecting activities of daily living in first-person camera views. In: IEEE Conference on Computer Vision and Pattern Recognition 2012, pp. 2847–2854 (2012)
3. Gemmell, J., Bell, C., Lueder, R.: MyLifeBits: a personal database for everything. Commun. ACM **49**, 89–95 (2006)
4. Hodges, S., et al.: SenseCam: a retrospective memory aid. In: Dourish, P., Friday, A. (eds.) UbiComp 2006. LNCS, vol. 4206, pp. 177–193. Springer, Heidelberg (2006). https://doi.org/10.1007/11853565_11
5. Hou, Y., Zhang, H., Zhou, S.: Convolutional neural network-based image representation for visual loop closure detection. In: IEEE International Conference on Information and Automation, pp. 2238–2245 (2015)
6. Valgren, C., Duckett, T., Lilienthal, A.: Incremental spectral clustering and its application to topological mapping. In: Proceedings of IEEE International Conference on Robotics and Automation, pp. 4283–4288, April 2007
7. Payá, L., Mayol, W., Cebollada, S., Reinoso, O.: Compression of topological models and localization using the global appearance of visual information. In: IEEE International Conference on Robotics and Automation (ICRA) (2017)
8. Garcia-Fidalgo, E., Ortiz, A.: Hierarchical place recognition for topological mapping. IEEE Trans. Robot. **33**(5), 1061–1074 (2017)
9. Patra, S., Gupta, K., Ahmad, F., Arora, C., Banerjee, S.: EGO-SLAM: a robust monocular SLAM for egocentric videos. In: IEEE Winter Conference on Applications of Computer Vision (WACV), pp. 31–40 (2019)
10. Furnari, A., Farinella, G.M., Battiato, S.: Recognizing personal locations from egocentric videos. IEEE Trans. Hum.-Mach. Syst. **47**(1), 6–18 (2017)
11. Furnari, A., Farinella, G.M., Battiato, S.: Temporal segmentation of egocentric videos to highlight personal locations of interest. In: Hua, G., Jégou, H. (eds.) Computer Vision: ECCV Workshops (2016)
12. Ortis, A., Farinella, G.M., D'Amico, V., Addesso, L., Torrisi, G., Battiato, S.: Organizing egocentric videos of daily living activities. Pattern Recogn. **72**, 207–218 (2017)

13. Zivkovic, Z., Booij, O., Kröse, B.: From images to rooms. Robot. Auton. Syst. **55**(5), 411–418 (2007)
14. Milford, M.J., Wyeth, G.F.: SeqSLAM: visual route-based navigation for sunny summer days and stormy winter nights. In: IEEE International Conference on Robotics and Automation (2012)
15. Cummins, M., Newman, P.: FAB-MAP: probabilistic localization and mapping in the space of appearance. Int. J. Robot. Res. **27**(6), 647–665 (2008)
16. Jeong, J., Cho, Y., Shin, Y.-S., Roh, H., Kim, A.: Complex urban dataset with multi-level sensors from highly diverse urban environments. Int. J. Robot. Res. **38**(6), 642–657 (2019)
17. Ruiz-Sarmiento, J.R., Galindo, C., González-Jiménez, J.: Robot@home, a robotic dataset for semantic mapping of home environments. Int. J. Robot. Res. **36**(2), 131–141 (2017)
18. Schubert, D., Goll, T., Demmel, N., Usenko, V., Stuckler, J., Cremers, D.: The TUM VI benchmark for evaluating visual-inertial odometry. In: International Conference on Intelligent Robots and Systems (IROS), October 2018
19. Shotton, J., Glocker, B., Zach, C., Izadi, S., Criminisi, A., Fitzgibbon, A.: Scene coordinate regression forests for camera relocalization in RGB-D images. In: Proceedings of Computer Vision and Pattern Recognition (CVPR) (2013)
20. Li, W., Saeedi, S., McCormac, J., Clark, R., Tzoumanikas, D., Ye, Q., Huang, Y., Tang, R., Leutenegger, S.: InteriorNet: mega-scale multi-sensor photo-realistic indoor scenes dataset. In: British Machine Vision Conference (BMVC) (2018)
21. Caruso, D., Engel, J., Cremers, D.: Large-scale direct SLAM for omnidirectional cameras. In: International Conference on Intelligent Robots and Systems (IROS)
22. Spera, E., Furnari, A., Battiato, S., Farinella, G.M.: EgoCart: a benchmark dataset for large-scale indoor image-based localization in retail stores. IEEE Trans. Circuits Syst. Video Technol. (2019)
23. Ragusa, F., Furnari, A., Battiato, S., Signorello, G., Farinella, G.M.: Egocentric visitors localization in cultural sites. J. Comput. Cult. Heritage (JOCCH) **12**(2), 1–19 (2019)
24. Ragusa, F., Furnari, A., Battiato, S., Signorello, G., Farinella, G.M.: Egocentric point of interest recognition in cultural sites. In: VISIGRAPP (VISAPP) (2019)
25. Bambach, S., Lee, S., Crandall, D.J., Yu, C.: Lending a hand: detecting hands and recognizing activities in complex egocentric interactions. In: International Conference on Computer Vision (ICCV), December 2015
26. Damen, D., et al.: Rescaling egocentric vision. CoRR, vol. abs/2006.13256 (2020)
27. Aghaei, M., Dimiccoli, M., Ferrer, C.C., Radeva, P.: Towards social pattern characterization in egocentric photo-streams. Comput. Vis. Image Underst. **171**, 104–117 (2018)
28. Talavera, E., Wuerich, C., Petkov, N., Radeva, P.: Topic modelling for routine discovery from egocentric photo-streams. Pattern Recogn. **104**, 107330 (2020)
29. Bolaños, M., Peris, Á., Casacuberta, F., Soler, S., Radeva, P.: Egocentric video description based on temporally-linked sequences. J. Vis. Commun. Image Represent. **50**, 205–216 (2018)
30. Lu, Z., Grauman, K.: Story-driven summarization for egocentric video. In: Proceedings of IEEE Conference on Computer Vision and Pattern Recognition, pp. 2714–2721 (2013)
31. Poleg, Y., Arora, C., Peleg, S.: Temporal segmentation of egocentric videos. In: IEEE Conference on Computer Vision and Pattern Recognition, pp. 2537–2544, June 2014

32. Ragusa, F., Furnari, A., Battiato, S., Signorello, G., Farinella, G.M.: EGO-CH: dataset and fundamental tasks for visitors behavioral understanding using egocentric vision. Pattern Recogn. Lett. **131**, 150–157 (2020)
33. Sivic, J., Zisserman, A.: Video google: a text retrieval approach to object matching in videos. In: International Conference on Computer Vision, pp. 1470–1477. IEEE (2003)
34. Lucas, B.D., Kanade, T.: An iterative image registration technique with an application to stereo vision. In: IJCAI, pp. 674–679 (1981)
35. Srinivasan, M.V., Venkatesh, S., Hosie, R.: Qualitative estimation of camera motion parameters from video sequences. Pattern Recogn. **30**(4), 593–606 (1997)
36. Zhou, B., Lapedriza, A., Khosla, A., Oliva, A., Torralba, A.: Places: a 10 million image database for scene recognition. IEEE Trans. Pattern Anal. Mach. Intell. **40**(6), 1452–1464 (2018)
37. Vinh, N., Epps, J., Bailey, J.: Information theoretic measures for clusterings comparison: is a correction for chance necessary? In: International Conference on Machine Learning (ICML) (2009)

ETTAC 2020 - Workshop on Eye Tracking Techniques, Applications and Challenges

Preface

The *1st Workshop on Eye Tracking Techniques, Applications and Challenges – ETTAC 2020 –* was held in conjunction with ICPR 2020, the 25th International Conference on Pattern Recognition, Milan, Italy, January 10–15, 2021.

Eye tracking technology is becoming more and more widespread nowadays, also thanks to the recent availability of cheap commercial devices. At the same time, novel techniques are constantly pursued to improve the precision of gaze detection, and new ways to fully exploit the potential of eye data are continuously explored. Whatever the considered use context, be it Human-Computer Interaction, user behavior understanding, biometrics, or others, pattern recognition often plays a relevant role. The purpose of the ETTAC 2020 workshop was to present recent eye tracking research that directly or indirectly exploits any form of pattern recognition.

The format of the workshop included a keynote speech followed by technical presentations. We received 14 submissions by authors from 12 countries. Through an accurate and detailed peer-review process, we selected 9 papers for presentation at the workshop (64% acceptance rate). The review process considered the quality of the articles and their scientific originality.

The accepted works covered a mix of very interesting topics: the visualization of eye tracking data through web-based tools; the influence of peripheral vibration stimuli on viewing and response tasks; the use of ultrasounds as a gaze detection technique; a comparison of eye movement patterns while looking at faces with subtle teeth imperfections; an evaluation of the stability of patients' gaze direction during Ocular Proton Therapy; synthetic gaze data augmentation to improve user calibration estimation processes; the use of temporal convolutional networks for automated eye movement classification; a study on the function of different global eye movement measures and their contribution to reading speed; and an assessment of the capability of eye tracking to classify dyslexic and non-dyslexic young adults.

The workshop program was completed by the invited talk "Eye-movement patterns and viewing biases during visual scene processing", given by Olivier Le Meur, from the Université de Rennes CNRS IRISA, Ecole Supérieure d'Ingénieurs de Rennes. Olivier Le Meur is the leader of the PERCEPT (Computational Visual Perception and Applications) team, which aims to understand and express algorithmically complex phenomena taking place in our visual system.

We would like to greatly thank the ETTAC 2020 Program Committee, whose members made the workshop possible and provided meticulous and timely reviews. We would also like to thank ICPR 2020 for hosting the workshop, and particularly the ICPR 2020 workshop chairs for their help and support.

November 2020

Organization

General Chairs

Marco Porta	University of Pavia, Italy
Pawel Kasprowski	Silesian University of Technology, Poland
Luca Lombardi	University of Pavia, Italy
Piercarlo Dondi	University of Pavia, Italy

Program Committee

Michael Burch	Eindhoven University of Technology, The Netherlands
Lucia Cascone	University of Salerno, Italy
Katarzyna Harezlak	Silesian University of Technology, Poland
Giancarlo Iannizzotto	University of Messina, Italy
Chandan Kumar	Universität Koblenz-Landau, Germany
Olivier Le Meur	University of Rennes, France
Päivi Majaranta	Tampere University, Finland
Diako Mardanbegi	AdHawk Microsystems, Canada
Carlos Morimoto	University of Sao Paulo, Brazil
Minoru Nakayama	Tokyo Institute of Technology, Japan
Michele Nappi	University of Salerno, Italy
Thies Pfeiffer	Bielefeld University, Germany
Ken Pfeuffer	Bundeswehr University Munich, Germany
Thiago Santini	University of Tübingen, Germany
Bonita Sharif	University of Nebraska, USA
Mikhail Startsev	Technical University of Munich, Germany

Additional Reviewers

Flavio Coutinho
Carlos Elmadjian
Ramin Hedeshy
Raphael Menges

Ultrasound for Gaze Estimation

Andre Golard and Sachin S. Talathi[(✉)]

Facebook Reality Labs, Redmond, WA 98052, USA
{agolard,stalathi}@fb.com

Abstract. Most eye tracking methods are light-based. As such they can suffer from ambient light changes when used outdoors. It has been suggested that ultrasound could provide a low power, fast, light-insensitive alternative to camera based sensors for eye tracking. We designed a bench top experimental setup to investigate the utility of ultrasound for eye tracking, and collected time of flight and amplitude data for a range of gaze angles of a model eye. We used this data as input for a machine learning model and demonstrate that we can effectively estimate gaze (gaze RMSE error of $1.021 \pm 0.189°$ with an adjusted R^2 score of 89.92 ± 4.9).

Keywords: Ultrasound · Eye tracking · Machine learning · CMUT

1 Introduction

Most current eye tracking methodologies use video to capture the position of the iris and/or reflected lights sources – glints [6]. As such these methods can be affected by ambient light, which will be the case with for eye tracking applications in wearables such as augmented-reality (AR). Other light-based methods such as scanning lasers, dual Purkinje and directional light sensors can likewise be affected. Speed can also be limited to 100 Hz, especially in wearables, where operating a camera at high speed would imply high power consumption. At these speeds the camera-based sensors can capture fixations but not other eye motions such as saccades, which have been implicated as markers of neurological disorders [11]. Current devices capable of measuring saccades are designed for laboratory use, and tend to lack portability. The possibility of using ultrasound for eye tracking has been raised [9]. However there was no modeling and no experimentation.

A recent paper explored the possibility of using non-contact ultrasound sensors to track fast eye movements in the field [5]. The work focused on the development of finite element simulation model to investigate the use for ultrasound time of flight data to track fast eye motions. The simulation model is based on a setup made of four transducers positioned perpendicular to the cornea. Distances are measured with each transducer receiving the reflection of its own signal. For this to be possible the device needs to be precisely positioned relative

© Springer Nature Switzerland AG 2021
A. Del Bimbo et al. (Eds.): ICPR 2020 Workshops, LNCS 12663, pp. 369–376, 2021.
https://doi.org/10.1007/978-3-030-68796-0_26

to the eye. We are interested in applications for eye tracking in AR and virtual reality (VR), where user-specific placement of the sensors is not possible. It is also to be noted that the modeling in [5] was done in the absence of occlusions. Occlusions are known to be problematic for eye tracking systems in general [3]. Furthermore, the authors [5] chose to model standard 40 kHz transducers. While these would be advantageous in terms of minimizing attenuation in air, such a system may be subject to interference from range-finding applications (typically in the 40–100 kHz range). Common range finding systems lack the resolution and short distance sensing capabilities required for eye tracking.

Another concern for our application of interest is size. Capacitative Micromachined Ultrasonic Transducers (CMUTs) operating at 500 kHz–2 MHz [7] provide a range, resolution and size that is suitable for use in VR and AR devices. This type of transducer has found numerous medical applications in both imaging and therapy. These applications are for contact ultrasound. Here, we use the devices as airborne transmitters and receivers. In this mode, the difference in impedance between air and tissue means over 99% of the ultrasound signal will be reflected by the eye surface.

While the size of transducers was a primary concern for our choice of CMUTs for the proposed study, related concerns (test bench size, power consumption) did not drive our experimental design prototype. We built a series of table top test benches to verify our ability to accurately measure distances in the appropriate range, characterize the transducers, and generate data to be used in a machine learning model to estimate gaze. As such we focus on empirically testing the hypothesis that ultrasound sensors can be used for gaze estimation in the presence of occlusions. We note that in the context of our experiments, gaze is defined by the static orientation of model eye on the goniometer. We demonstrate that ultrasound time of flight and amplitude signals can be leveraged to train a machine learning model to track gaze in such conditions. Results show that the trained model produces a regression R^2 score of 89.92% and a gaze RMSE error of $1.021 \pm 0.189°$.

We note that while there exists a vast literature on eye tracking and ultrasound [10], none has focused on using ultrasound for eye tracking. To the best of our knowledge, this paper presents the first experimental study to empirically demonstrate the feasibility for gaze estimation using ultrasound sensors.

2   Materials and Methods

In this section, we describe the bench top experimental setup for data collection, the signal processing steps to extract the ultrasound time of flight and amplitude, and the machine learning framework adopted to train a gaze estimation model.

2.1   Bench-Top Setup

We designed a series of three test benches to evaluate distance measurements, signal attenuation, transducer directionality, and our ability to estimate gaze.

In terms of electronics and data acquisition, all test benches are based on a CMUT evaluation kit from Fraunhofer IPMS (Dresden, Germany). This test kit is comprised of CMUT transducers (1.74 MHz), an amplifier, bias-tee, and associated software. These transducers fit our size and power requirements.

We first verified our ability to measure distances, as well as the signal decay due to attenuation in air given that ultrasound signal attenuation is significant at MHz frequencies [1]. We used a setup consisting of a pair of transducers aimed at a flat target attached to a linear translation stage (Test bench 1, Fig. 1A).

Next we tested the emission properties of the transducers. Our CMUTs are comprised of an array of cells connected to a single electrode and a single counter electrode. As such they act as a fixed phased array, which is expected to exhibit directionality. We tested this using a fixed transducer and one on a rotating stage (Test bench 2, Fig. 1B). The Tx transducer was rotated in 1° increments and the amplitude of the Rx signal was recorded.

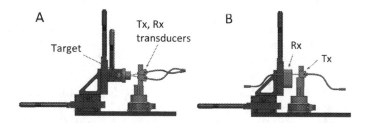

Fig. 1. CAD schema for attenuation and directionality test benches. Tx refers to transducer in transmit mode, Rx receive mode.

Our third test bench is designed for gaze estimations (Fig. 2A). As noted earlier, we define gaze in terms of the static orientation of model eye on the goniometer. The transducer side is on the right. We used a pair of transducers (one in transmit mode and one receiver) mounted on rotating stages to allow us to mimic multiple locations around a ring (or glasses frame). We acquired data for all transmit and receive locations covering 360° in 10° increments (Fig. 3C).

On the target side (left part of Fig. 2A), a standard sphere on sphere model eye (cornea radius 7.8 mm, sclera radius 11.925 mm, offset 5.6 mm) was mounted on a goniometer (Thor Labs). Gaze angles were set in one degree increments between ±5° in both up/down (ϕ) and left/right (θ) directions.

Occlusions (known to affect eye trackers) were added for realism. They consisted of a partial scanned face printed in flexible material (A40 durometer Polyjet) with a cavity to accommodate the model eye (Fig. 2B). This was mounted in front of and against the model eye and allowed the eye to move freely.

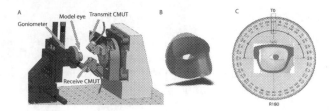

Fig. 2. A: CAD schema for the experimental bench-top setup and B: occlusions C. Transducer rotation. The receiver is fixed and the transmitter rotates around an arc. 30° steps are shown.

Our test signal consisted of a train of seven oscillations at 1.74 MHz, repeated at 2 kHz. The transmitter was moved to positions around a 180° arc opposite the receiver $(-90, -80, \ldots, 80, 90)$, Fig. 2C. Fifty runs were recorded for each transducer position. The series was repeated for all goniometer positions. The received signal was digitized at 80 MHz.

2.2   Data Analysis

Feature Engineering. In Fig. 3a, we show one raw trace, $x_i^r(t, \theta, \phi)$ $(i \in [0, 49]$ and $r \in [-90, -80, \cdots 80, 90])$, for the Ultrasound signal captured at the receiver, in response to a single test signal emitted by the transmit CMUT transducer. Figure 3b, shows the average of ten traces, defined as $\bar{x}_k^r(t, \theta, \phi) = 0.1 \sum_j^{j+10} x_j(t, \theta, \phi)$ $(k \in [0, 4])$. The ultrasound time of flight, $\tau_k^r(\theta, \phi)$, and amplitude, $a_k^r(\theta, \phi)$, signal is estimated for each $\bar{x}_k^r(t, \theta, \phi)$ as follows: the signal, $\bar{x}_k^r(t, \theta, \phi)$ is band-pass filtered in the frequency range, [1.6 MHz, 1.9 MHz] using a Butterworth filter of order 4 to generate the filtered version, $f(\bar{x}_k^r)(t, \theta, \phi)$. In Fig. 3c, we show the trace for $f^2(\bar{x}_k^r)(t, \theta, \phi)$. The ultrasound time to peak $\tau_k^r(\theta, \phi)$ and the amplitude, $a_k^r(\theta, \phi)$ is obtained by considering a time window of 45 μs around the time instance of peak value for $f^2(\bar{x}_k^r(t, \theta, \phi))$ and finding the first instance of the peak value for $\bar{x}_k^r(t, \theta, \phi)$ within the considered time window. The detected peak value represents the amplitude signal $a_k^r(\theta, \phi)$ and the time to peak recorded as the ultrasound time of flight signal, $\tau_k^r(\theta, \phi)$. In summary, for each position $\mathbf{Y} = (\theta, \phi)$ of the model eye on the goniometer, we obtain a set $k = 5$ feature vectors $\mathbf{X} \in \mathbb{R}^{36} = \{a^r, \tau^r\}_{r=[-90, -80 \cdots 80, 90]}$. Our goal for ultrasound based eye tracking is to learn a regression model, $H : \mathbf{X} \to \mathbf{Y}$; that is, given the ultrasound sensor time of flight and amplitude data, estimate two-dimensional eye gaze coordinates.

Gradient Boosted Regression Trees. From a machine learning perspective, the task of learning a gaze estimation model H is categorized as a supervised regression problem. Gradient Boosting Regression Trees (GBRT) are a powerful class of boosting algorithms for classification and regression tasks, which combine output from several weak learners into a powerful estimator. Specifically, GBRT

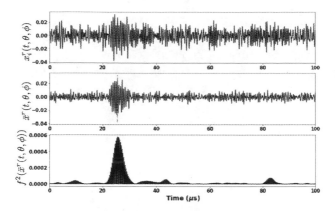

Fig. 3. Example of recorded raw time trace of ultrasound sensor signal. The top row shows an example of time trace recorded at the receive Ultrasound CMUT sensor in response to a single burst of test signal. The middle row shows averaged signal computed from the response to a set of 10 bursts of test signal. Finally the last row shows the squared filtered response signal out of a Butterworth filter. The red line indicates the time period of time-to-peak signal detection. (Color figure online)

considers additive models of the form: $F_m(x) = F_{m-1}(x) + h_m(x)$, where h_m are the basis functions modeled as small regression trees of fixed size. For each boosting iteration, a new boosting tree is added to the GBRT model, F. For our problem, we train two separate GBRT models to independently estimate the response: $\mathbf{Y} = (\theta, \phi)$ as function of the input features, $\mathbf{X} = (\tau^r, a^r)$. Assuming the GBRT model is comprised of M regression trees with T_m leaf nodes per regression tree, the GBRT model for each of the gaze regressor is given as: $F^y(X, w^y) = w_0^y + \sum_{m=1}^{M} \sum_{j=1}^{T_m} w_{jm}^y I(X \in R_{jm}^y)$, where $y = \{\theta, \phi\}$ and R_{jm}^y represents the jth disjoint partitioning of the input space for the mth regression tree for the regressor variable, y. The GBRT model weights are estimated from data as follows: $w^* = \arg \min_w \frac{1}{N} \sum_i^N L(y_i, F(\mathbf{X}_i, w))$ where, L is the squared error loss function. For an exhaustive description of GBRT, see [4,8].

3   Results

In this section we present findings from our experiments conducted using the three bench-top setups described in Sect. 2.1.

We begin by presenting our findings on the CMUT sensor characterization. Data collected using test bench setup 1, allowed us to investigate the decay characteristics of the ultrasound signal in air, see Fig. 4A. As expected, the ultrasound signal decays exponentially as a function of distance. An extrapolated fit shows it decays to zero. The distance axis shows the distance between the pair of transducers and the target (Fig. 1A). Actual travel distance is twice this measurement. The range is similar to the distances for transducers mounted on eye glasses frames, our use case scenario.

Data collected using test bench 2 (Fig. 1B) allowed us investigate whether the CMUT transducers exhibit directionality. Our findings are reported in Fig. 4B. The CMUT transducers indeed exhibit directionality with an emission cone of 10°. This applies to the transducers in both transmit and receive mode. Based

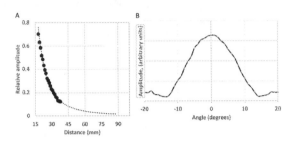

Fig. 4. CMUT sensor characterization

on the above findings we conclude that the strength of ultrasound signal at the receiver CMUT transducer will depend on two factors: distance and incident angle. As such we believe that the amplitude of the ultrasound signal at the receiver contains relevant information to contribute to our ability to estimate gaze and as shown below, our findings indeed support this claim.

We next report findings from training a GBRT model on data collected using the third test bench setup (see Fig. 2). For each model eye position on the goniometer, θ, ϕ, for a fixed receiver transducer position (180°) and for a set of 19 transmit transducer positions, we fire the ultrasound test signal 50 times, at 2 kHz and record the raw receiver signal (see Fig. 3 top row). In order to increase the strength of ultrasound response at the receiver we average 10 traces of the raw response signals at a time, to effectively generate 5 averaged ultrasound response signals, in effect acquiring data at 200 Hz. The averaged response signal is passed through a Butterworth bandpass filter and we extract two ultrasound signal features: time of flight (τ) and the amplitude at peak (a), as explained in Sect. 2.2. In total for each model eye position, we generate a total of 45 samples for each model eye position on the goniometer over the duration of the study. For the set of 36 model eye positions, we produce a total of 1620 data samples.

We train a GBRT model on these data samples, performing a 5-fold cross-validation study. The model performance is reported using an adjusted R^2 score [2] and the gaze RMSE error in degrees. Hyper-parameter search on the GBRT model parameters that produced the best adjusted R^2 score for 5-fold CV are as follows: (a) Number of regression trees: 750 (b) Tree depth: 5 and (c) Learning rate: 0.085. We obtain gaze RMSE error of 1.021 ± 0.189 and mean adjusted R^2 score of 89.922% with a standard deviation of 4.9965, suggesting that almost 90% of the data fit the regression model. Residuals analysis confirmed that the estimates obtained using the GBRT model are un-biased (data not shown). This analysis offers an empirical evidence for our claim that ultrasound sensors can be used for gaze estimation in the presence of occlusions.

In Fig. 5A and 5B, we show feature importance for the GBRT tree models trained to estimate the model eye gaze coordinates, θ (horizontal gaze) and ϕ (vertical gaze). We can see that the top two features for both horizontal and vertical gaze GBRT model are time of flight ultrasound signal followed by an amplitude feature. It has been our observation that while the time of flight component of ultrasound signal contains dominant information signal to estimate gaze (95% contribution to the regression score), the amplitude signal is also an important contributor for GBRT model to produce an adjusted-R^2 score close to 90%. In order to test this observation, we trained GBRT model using just the ultrasound time-of-flight feature and another GBRT model using just the ultrasound amplitude feature. The findings are: GBRT model trained using time-of-flight features, produces an adjusted R^2 score of 85.38 ± 5.177, where as the GBRT model trained using only the amplitude feature produces an adjusted R^2 score of 78.64 ± 8.177. In Fig. 5C, we show the mean-RMSE error (across all CV-folds) for the GBRT model. The error is biased towards the lower half of vertical gaze, primarily resulting from occlusions.

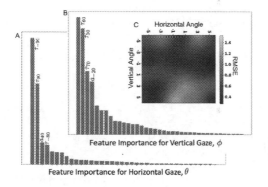

Fig. 5. Feature importance and mean-accuracy of GBRT models to estimate gaze

4   Discussion

This study is the first experimental demonstration of use for ultrasound sensors in gaze estimation. We show that ultrasonic transducers can effectively produce signals useful to resolve eye gaze, as defined by the static orientation of model eye on a goniometer, within the range tested, ±5° in both up/down (θ) and left/right (ϕ) directions. This range reflects the full deflection of our goniometer. We plan on expanding the range in future studies.

Our GBRTs show that both amplitude and time of flight contribute to our ability to estimate gaze. This is a new finding as previous modeling work dealt with time of flight alone. Two factors contribute to amplitude: attenuation and the incident angle of the incoming sound. One way to compensate for attenuation is to use the time-gain correction built in our amplifier, increasing gain over time to compensate for the signal attenuation with longer distances. When we did this (data not shown) our model performed slightly worse. This indicates that attenuation plays a role in our ability to estimate gaze, and would favor the use of high frequency transducers.

For this proof of concept we chose to average ten individual tests prior to filtering the signal and extracting peak and amplitude. This reduces the eye tracking acquisition speed from a maximum of 2 kHz to 200 Hz, which may not be sufficient to track saccadic eye motion. While this study focused on primarily testing the hypothesis that ultrasound signals can be leveraged to estimate gaze, in future works we will explore avenues to investigate the use for ultrasound in tracking fast eye motion. Specifically, we plan on using a fast-moving model eye coupled with multiple receivers operating at 2 kHz. The GBRT models will be adapted so we can test the potential of ultrasound for fast eye tracking to resolve saccades.

We are interested in investigating the feasibility for using ultrasound sensors for eye tracking in virtual and augmented reality devices. In addition to sampling speed, power consumption is an important factor to consider. The transducers are very low power, in the milliwatt range. Our current system utilizes a high speed A/D converter. This can be replaced with a low power peak detection circuit. On the compute side, GBRTs are considered low compute. In summary, this study presents data driven proof-of-principle findings to support the claim that ultrasound sensors can be used for gaze estimation.

References

1. Blackstock, D.T.: Fundamentals of Physical Acoustics. Wiley, New York (2000)
2. Dodge, Y.: The Concise Encyclopedia of Statistics. Springer, Heidelberg (2010). https://doi.org/10.1007/978-0-387-32833-1
3. Hansen, D.W., Ji, Q.: In the eye of the beholder: a survey of models for eyes and gaze. IEEE Trans. Pattern Anal. Mach. Intell. **32**(3), 478–500 (2010)
4. Hastie, T., Tibshirani, R., Friedman, J.: The Elements of Statistical Learning. Springer, Heidelberg (2011). https://doi.org/10.1007/978-0-387-84858-7
5. Kaputa, D., Enderle, J.: An ultrasound based eye tracking system. J. Biomed. Eng. Med. Devices **1**(1), 1–4 (2016)
6. Kar, A., Corcoran, P.: A review and analysis of eye-gaze estimation systems, algorithms and performance evaluation methods in consumer platforms. IEEE Access **5**, 16495–16519 (2017)
7. Khury-Yacub, B., Oralkan, O.: Capacitive micromachined ultrasonic transducers for medical imaging and therapy. J. Micromech. Microeng. **21**(5), 054004–054014 (2011)
8. Ridgeway, G.: Generalized boosted models: a guide to GBM package (2007). http://cran.r-project.org/web/packages/gbm
9. Scally, B.M., Perek, D.R.: Ultrasound/radar for eye tracking (May 2017)
10. Sánchez-Ferrer, M.L., Grima-Murcia, M.D., Sánchez-Ferrer, F., Hernández-Peñalver, A.I., Fernández-Jover, E., del Campo, F.S.: Use of eye tracking as an innovative instructional method in surgical human anatomy. J. Surg. Educ. **74**(4), 668–673 (2017)
11. Termsarasab, P., Thammongkolchai, T., Rucker, J.C., Frucht, S.J.: The diagnostic value of saccades in movement disorder patients: a practical guide and review. J. Clin. Mov. Disord. **2**(14), 1–10 (2015)

Synthetic Gaze Data Augmentation for Improved User Calibration

Gonzalo Garde[(✉)][iD], Andoni Larumbe-Bergera[(✉)][iD], Sonia Porta[(✉)][iD],
Rafael Cabeza[(✉)][iD], and Arantxa Villanueva[(✉)][iD]

Public University of Navarra (UPNA), Calle Arrosadía, 31006 Pamplona, Spain
{gonzalo.garde,andoni.larumbe,sporta,rcabeza,avilla}@unavarra.es
http://www.unavarra.es/gi4e

Abstract. In this paper, we focus on the calibration possibilitiesó of a deep learning based gaze estimation process applying transfer learning, comparing its performance when using a general dataset versus when using a gaze specific dataset in the pretrained model. Subject calibration has demonstrated to improve gaze accuracy in high performance eye trackers. Hence, we wonder about the potential of a deep learning gaze estimation model for subject calibration employing fine-tuning procedures. A pretrained Resnet-18 network, which has great performance in many computer vision tasks, is fine-tuned using user's specific data in a few shot adaptive gaze estimation approach. We study the impact of pretraining a model with a synthetic dataset, U2Eyes, before addressing the gaze estimation calibration in a real dataset, I2Head. The results of the work show that the success of the individual calibration largely depends on the balance between fine-tuning and the standard supervised learning procedures and that using a gaze specific dataset to pretrain the model improves the accuracy when few images are available for calibration. This paper shows that calibration is feasible in low resolution scenarios providing outstanding accuracies below 1.5° of error.

Keywords: Gaze estimation · Calibration · Transfer learning

1 Introduction

In the 70's one of the seminal papers about eye tracking was published [15]. This paper described a system based on the well-known pupil center-corneal reflection vector (PR-CR) and assumed a highly focused image of the eye area, i.e. a high resolution image of the eye region as is shown in Fig. 1 (left). Since then, outstanding works have been published in the field most of them persisting first, in the use of PC-CR technique and its variations and second, employing high resolution eye area images [10,16,18]. As a result of these researches, commercial solutions were developed.

As far as it is known, all of them require a subject calibration procedure consisting in asking the subject to gaze specific points in the screen. During the

© Springer Nature Switzerland AG 2021
A. Del Bimbo et al. (Eds.): ICPR 2020 Workshops, LNCS 12663, pp. 377–389, 2021.
https://doi.org/10.1007/978-3-030-68796-0_27

calibration, the system is adapted to the subject position and eye physiology. Depending of the type of system this *adaptation* process can be more or less explicitly carried out. On the one hand, the calibration of system geometry-based gaze estimation trackers permits to infer the value of different variables related to the user such as the corneal radius among other subject specific characteristics [6, 10]. On the other hand, the calibration of polynomial-based gaze estimation trackers is used in order to estimate the unknown coefficients of a polynomial, normally a second degree polynomial [2]. Regardless of the type of system, there is an agreement about the fact that a calibrated system provides better subject accuracies than the ones obtained by an average model. Outstanding accuracies below 0.5° can be found in the literature and provided by systems manufacturers.

The hardware of those systems presents some requirements. First, the use of an infrared light which provides better image quality and is responsible for the corneal glint which is key for an accurate gaze estimation. Second, in order to get a highly focused eye image, long focal lengths have to be used ~35 mm. The necessity of this special optics, infrared lighting and filters are some of the reasons that prevent high performance eye tracking from being a plug-and-play technology.

In the last decade, a sustained effort has been made by the community in order to provide a more versatile eye tracking technology that can be implemented using webcams or the mobile phone cameras. The removal of the infrared light sources and the lower focal lengths produces a drastically different subject's images as system input (see Fig. 1, right). The techniques employed for high resolution images are not longer valid in the new scenario. Thus, a new exploration field is opened for deep learning in the gaze estimation field tackled as a computer vision problem. To train a model from scratch using deep learning approach, it is necessary to employ large datasets. Sadly, to create a high quality dataset with enough number of images it's a costly process. In order to address this limitation, it is common to use a model pretrained over a large database as an initial point, which improves training time and results. Int the case of gaze estimation, works can be found in the literature showing the potential of deep learning techniques [7,8,12]. Unfortunately, the reported accuracies are far from being comparable to the ones obtained by high resolution systems, e.g. 3° to 5° [3,4]. One of the potentials assumed for deep learning it its generalization ability, that can be defined as the possibility of gaining knowledge from training data in a learning process and apply the gained knowledge on new data. It is agreed that model's generalization capability is a pursued property of the network also for gaze estimation. However, from the experience obtained for high resolution systems it is a known fact that the adaptation of the system to the specific user, i.e. calibration, results in better accuracies, which could enable the use of gaze estimation for other applications were accuracy would be critical. Hence, it is a relevant open issue how to introduce the calibration in the field of deep learning gaze estimation. The few examples found in the literature approach the problem from a fine-tuning perspective employing a few-shot training of an existing model [13,20].

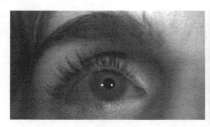

Fig. 1. Image obtained by a high resolution eye tracker using two corneal glints (left). Image obtained by a standard webcam (right) [14].

In this paper, we carry out a thorough study about user calibration for deep learning gaze estimation raised as a question between the balance required among generalization and personalization abilities of the models. This balance is measured according to its impact in the accuracy obtained for the gaze estimation system. We will study the impact of transfer learning over a model pretrained with a computer vision general database, Imagenet [5], versus the results obtained while pretraining over a gaze specialized synthetic database, U2Eyes [17], analyzing the results over a real gaze database, I2Head [14].

This paper is organized as follows, in the next section a summary of related works is performed. In Sect. 3, the working framework is presented, i.e. datasets and the main methodological specifications are provided. Then, subject calibration details are introduced in Sect. 4. The experiments configuration is explained in Sect. 5. In Sect. 6 the accuracies obtained by the different experiments are shown. Finally, the conclusions of our work are addressed.

2 Related Works

Calibration is a well-known procedure in high resolution systems. During the calibration process, the subject is asked to gaze specific points in the screen. The images acquired during calibration are automatically labelled with gazed point information and this permits to fit the gaze estimation function to the subject playing with the eye tracking system. Deep learning gaze estimation is a relatively new topic and the accuracies obtained are not comparable with the ones achieved by high resolution system. Most of the works found are related to compare the architectures to be used, labelled datasets to be used or the evaluation of the alternative training strategies of the models and less attention has been paid to personalization strategies for eye tracking systems. To follow selected relevant works addressing gaze models personalization are presented.

In one of the first relevant works, Krafka *et al.* [11] point out the relevance of using subject images during network training in order to improve the gaze estimation accuracy and its variation according to the calibration points used achieving accuracy values about 1.34 cm. In the work [20], Yu *et al.* try to construct the person-specific gaze estimation models by using few calibration points (few-shot approach). They use a VGG16 achitecture trained with ColumbiaGaze and MPIIGaze datasets. They use a more complex model using synthetic images for gaze prediction consistency. They perform the person adaptation using a few-shot scheme in which 1-5-9 samples are employed to personalize a previously pretrained model. They also confirm that the accuracy improves as the number of calibration images are increased achieving accuracies in the range [2.68°, 5°]. In this work they point out one of the main facts of deep learning gaze estimation which is the lack of labelled binocular data compared to other computer vision problems in which wide datasets area available.

An interesting approach is also described by Linden *et al.* [13]. In this work a complex model consisting in three ResNet-18 are used for three input images (both eyes and face). The network outputs for each eye are concatenated with "calibration parameters" as inputs to a fully connected module. The calibration parameters are the ones to be adjusted during the calibration procedure. Again, the improvement according to calibration points is achieved showing values about 2.76°.

As shown in this summary more attention is paid to the number of points required for calibration than to the specific computer vision domain. If calibration is required, the number of calibration points, although methodologically important, does not involve practical problems for most of the applications since high number of points can be acquired, e.g. by asking the subject to track a point in the screen.

3   Working Framework

3.1   Image Databases

The proposed synthetic framework is based on U2Eyes dataset [17]. The choice of a synthetic dataset to the detriment of a dataset with real images is motivated by the ability of synthetic datasets to provide with a large amount of images while assuring that, in all cases, the labeling is consistent and correct. As we are looking for high accuracies, we believe that this certainty is important. However, one of the main drawbacks of synthetic dataset is that, by their own nature, they have a more limited variability than the one that can be found in real datasets. Twenty different simulated subjects are provided in the public version of the dataset. The images have a resolution of 3840×2160 pixels (4K) and were created using Unity. The provided images represent the eyes area of a subject gazing at different points on a screen simulating a standard remote eye tracking session. The images are annotated with head pose and observed points information. Additionally, 2D and 3D landmarks information of both eyes is provided. For each subject 125 head positions are simulated from which two gazing grids containing 15 and 32 points are observed. Consequently, 5,875 images per user are provided resulting in a total of 120 K images. U2Eyes represents a rich appearance variation environment. The authors claim that essential eyeball physiology elements and binocular vision dynamics have been modelled. In Fig. 2 samples of the dataset are shown.

Fig. 2. Samples extracted from U2Eyes dataset.

The 3D eye model employed to generate eye images resembles the simplified eye model for gaze estimation in the literature [1]. The Line of Sight (LoS) is approximated by the visual axis that presents an angular offset, κ, with respect to the optical axis, i.e. eyeball symmetry axis of the eye (see Fig. 3). The eyeball presents individual's specific characteristics, some of them such as the angle κ cannot be inferred from the image and need to be calibrated.

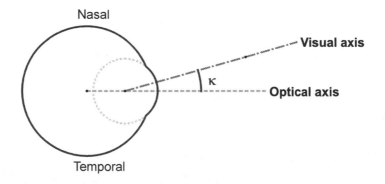

Fig. 3. Simplified model of the eye.

I2Head dataset is employed as a real benchmark in order to validate the proposed framework. I2Head is a public dataset providing images annotated with gaze and head pose data. This dataset was constructed using a magnetic sensor for pose detection and a careful setup calibration procedure. More details about the design of this dataset can be found in [14]. The dataset contains information about twelve individuals gazing two grids containing 17 and 65 points from eight different head positions, in constrained and free head movement scenarios. For each user, information about 232 ($65 \times 2 + 17 \times 6$) gazing points is provided representing a total of 2,784 points data. The range of gaze angles is approximately $20°$.

I2Head does not provides landmark information. Hence, a manual labelling of the eye region bounding box has been performed for a reduced set of images

Fig. 4. Samples extracted from I2Head dataset.

of the dataset. More specifically, the four central sessions have been selected for each user containing 164 gazing points per user. In order to perform a realistic comparison between the datasets, eye area is extracted from I2Head images. In Fig. 4 samples of the dataset are shown.

U2Eyes resembles to a large extent I2Head dataset. This is a desired quality as the importance of pretraining in a close domain for gaze estimation is studied. However, although both databases represent standard eye tracking sessions in a remote setup, some differences are found. While the camera is positioned on the top of the screen in I2Head dataset a centered position with respect to the gazing grid is selected in U2Eyes. Consequently, in U2Eyes subjects gaze points above and below the camera while all the points are placed below the camera in the I2Head dataset. In the same manner, the range of head poses is different in both datasets when referring to vertical positions. All these aspects should be taken into account when the alternative training strategies are proposed.

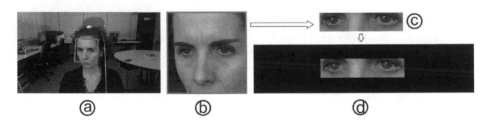

Fig. 5. Image preprocessing. The images (a) are rotated (b) so eyes are in the same line, which makes the bounding box (c) contains as meaningful information as possible. Then, a padding process (d) assures that all images have the same size before feeding them to the network.

3.2   Image Conditioning

The preprocessing applied to U2Eyes and I2Head data is described: both synthetical and real image preprocessing is equivalent, and it is shown in Fig. 5. First, the original image, (a), is rotated (b) in order to normalize the roll component. The rotation is done using the angle between the horizontal and the straight line defined by the two outer eye corners. Then, a bounding box is created using the distance between the two outer eye corners and the image is cropped (c). The rotation before cropping is necessary to prevent the gray pixels that would be present in the U2Eyes images if we would just obtain the bounding box from the original source. Finally, a black edge is added until the image size is 390 × 85 pixels (d). As the images from both datasets cover a range of well-known distances, the black edge was added to make all images the same size. Thus, the farther to the camera, the bigger the black edge, providing additional depth information to the network.

Table 1. Configurations of the different experiments according to the training mode, *U2Eyes* or *ImageNet*, and the number of users and images in the training and testing phase. The K parameter varies from 0 to 11, i.e. 0 indicates that none of the subjects of I2Head dataset has been included to train the model, except for the subject to be calibrated, and 11 indicates that all the additional subjects are present in the training phase.

Model	Train # Users/Images	Calibration # Users/Images	Total Train # Images	Test # Users/Images
ImageNet	K/K*130	1/34	K*130+34	1/130
U2Eyes	K/K*130	1/34	K*130+34	1/130

3.3   Network Architecture

The architecture of our network consists on the Resnet-18 [9] as backbone, followed by a Global Average Pooling layer and three Fully Connected Layers. As the focus of this paper is not to provide a novel architecture but to study the calibration and transfer learning process for gaze estimation, the Resnet-18 was chosen because of its performance over Imagenet [5] classification task while being simple enough to make retraining steps feasible in both, time and hardware requirements. The results obtained over Imagenet ensure that the network is able to extract meaningful features from images. The three fully connected layers at the top of the network make use of these features to compute the x and y coordinates of the look-at-points.

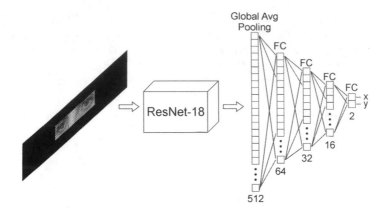

Fig. 6. Architecture proposed. The backbone consist on a Resnet-18 to extract meaningful characteristics from the image. Then, these characteristics are fed into fully connected regressor network to obtain the final gaze components.

3.4   Implementation Details

In this section, technical details for the sake of reproducibility are described. The experiment is divided into two different phases:

- A first one where a model with the same architecture as the one shown in Sect. 3.3 is trained over the synthetic dataset U2Eyes, saving the trained model, hereafter *U2Eyes-model*, to be used as the initial base for future steps. The goal with this step is to bring closer the domain in which the model is trained to the final environment.
- A second phase where the model is trained over real images obtained from the I2Head dataset in a subject calibration fashion. In this phase, we distinguish among two different situations: using the *U2Eyes-model* as initial point and starting from the Imagenet [5] weights for the Resnet-18 backbone (see Sect. 3.3).

Independently of the training phase, the steps followed to train the model and the training parameters were kept the same for all cases. The models are trained over 240 epochs, using a batch size of 128 images. The loss function employed is the euclidean distance between the estimated look-at-point and the real look-at-point, represented by the following equation:

$$Loss := \frac{1}{N} \sum_{i=1}^{N} \|p - \hat{p}\|_2, \tag{1}$$

where p is the real look-at-point, $\hat{p}$ is the estimated look-at-point, and N is the number of images per batch. Adam optimizer is used to optimize the loss function. The learning rate schedule followed is based on the Cyclic learning rate schedule [19] in a triangular manner for the first 200 epochs, fluctuating among a maximum learning rate value of 0.002 and a minimum learning rate of 0.0002, and then a linear decrease for the remaining 40 epochs where the learning rate goes from 0.0002 to 0.00002. The main specifications of the computer where the experiments were run are: CPU: Intel(R) Xeon(R) CPU E5-1650 v4 @3.60 GHz, 128 GB of RAM and a Nvidia Titan X (Pascal) GPU.

For the sake of reproducibility, the weights of the pretrained model over *U2Eyes* and a function for the model that is trained directly over the *ImageNet* weights will be available at Github[1]. It is important to remark that we are not training over U2Eyes neither over Imagenet images in this paper, we are using pretrained models over these datasets and then retraining these models over I2Head images.

4   Subject Calibration

The concept of calibration in gaze estimation refers to the process whereby a model is tuned over a given number of images from an individual to adapt to the specific parameters of that individual. This is especially crucial as there are characteristics that cannot be learned in any other way at the moment and that have a significant impact on the outcome of the regression model. Ideally, when calibrating a system for a user, the fewer images that are necessary for calibration the better, as a large number of images implicates longer calibration times and a more complicated user-machine interaction. On the other side, the improvement obtained is generally directly proportional to the number of images. As a result, a trade-off exists among the number of images, the calibration time and the final accuracy. In any case, the calibration processes work with few images if it is compared with any other approach where deep learning is used. A common strategy these days is to use few-shot training to adapt the parameters of the networks. In this paper, we focus on the advantages of pretraining in a synthetic environment where we are not limited by the number of images or the reliability of the data.

5   Experiments

The final goal of the experiment is to observe the impact of pretraining over a dataset whose domain is closer for gaze estimation before facing a real dataset and the importance of the number of images while calibrating models for gaze estimation. An approximation of the Leave-One-Out strategy is followed in order to study subject calibration. 34 images of the user to be calibrated are included in the training set together with a varying number of additional subjects extracted from I2Head dataset ranging from 0 to 11 users. For each one of these subjects in the training, 130 additional images are used. The condition of no-user-calibration is not contemplated, as the user data is always used while training. A resume of the experiments configuration is shown in Table 1.

---

[1] https://github.com/GonzaloGardeL/Synthetic-gaze-data-augmentation-for-improved-user-calibration.

6   Results

The outputs from the experiments were arranged together based on the training user configuration, and the figures and tables that are shown in this section are an average from the experiments of all users. The angular offset (in degrees) between the estimated gaze direction and subject's visual axis is used as comparison metric. This angular offset is calculated by computing the distance between the estimated point and the real point in the grid and the known distance between the real point and the user. For the sake of readability, the results from the experiments have been plotted in two different figures, Fig. 7 and Fig. 8, using both figures the results from training with 4 users as common anchor point. We highlight two cases of interest:

– Correlation between the number of training images and regressor estimation.
– Comparison of *U2Eyes* and *ImageNet* Methods.

6.1   Number of Training Images and Regressor Estimation

The regressor estimations are worse as the number of training images decreased. This is the expected behavior for this problem as by reducing the number of available images for training, it is more difficult for the network to learn the optimal parameters for the problem. In Table 2, the mean and median for each case are shown. The results are consistent for both *U2Eyes* and *ImageNet* training modes. When the number of training images is maximum (12 users in training, the calibration user + 11 additional users), outstanding results with degrees of error lower than 1.5° are obtained for the median.

6.2   *U2Eyes* and *ImageNet* Methods

At Fig. 8, we observe that the results obtained from *U2Eyes* and *ImageNet* are similar but slightly better for *ImageNet* method when the number of additional users goes from 4 to 11. One possible explanation for this behaviour could be that, if enough images are used to train the ImageNet model over the specific user, the model benefits from the more variability presented in real images rather than the more limited variability of synthetic ones. Attending to table II, the biggest difference in mean is under 0.17°. As we increase the number of training users, the obtained results from both models are better. However, when adding 3 or fewer additional users to the training, we observe in Fig. 7 that the behavior is different. The *U2Eyes* models are more robust to the lack of training images than the *ImageNet* models. The hypothesis is that, when the number of training images is low enough, the models that were pretrained in a similar domain (synthetic dataset U2Eyes in this case) are more capable to continue learning than the ones trained in a more general domain. If we compare the results in Table 2, we can observe that this difference is up to 10.16° for the median value in the case of training using only the calibration user.

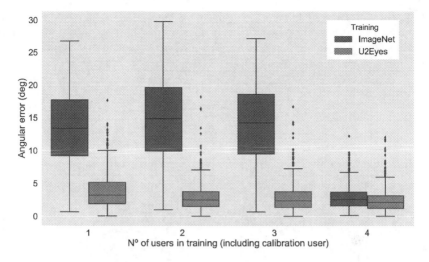

Fig. 7. Experiments when training from 1 user to 4 users. In this figure we observe that the performance of the *ImageNet* models change drastically when the number of users included in the training dataset gets reduced from a specific number. The models trained over the *U2Eyes* strategy are more robust when working with a reduced dataset.

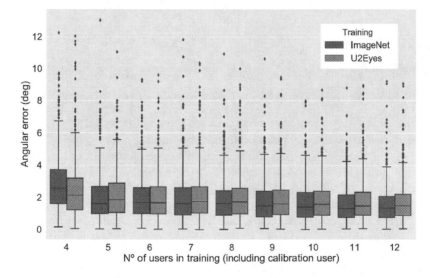

Fig. 8. Experiments when training from 4 users to 12 users. The performance of the models tends to improve as the number of training images increases. Both *ImageNet* and *U2Eyes* models have a similar behavior for each one of the cases.

Table 2. Results from the different experiments configurations. The mean and median angular errors in degrees are shown for each. The number of users in training includes the user for which the system has been calibrated. The maximum and minimum values for each one of the columns are emphasized.

Users in training	Mean (°)		Median (°)	
	Imagenet	U2Eyes	Imagenet	U2Eyes
1	13.615	**3.891**	13.401	**3.243**
2	**14.812**	2.967	**14.880**	2.522
3	14.069	2.861	14.255	2.404
4	2.867	2.488	2.567	2.149
5	2.004	2.149	1.631	1.867
6	2.028	1.965	1.675	1.667
7	1.987	2.039	1.617	1.746
8	1.877	1.968	1.639	1.724
9	1.758	1.860	1.471	1.611
10	1.681	1.818	1.412	1.588
11	1.615	1.777	**1.334**	**1.485**
12	**1.559**	**1.714**	1.344	1.486

7   Conclusions

In this paper, subject calibration based in transfer learning for low resolution systems is studied. To this end, a deep learning model and two gaze data datasets, i.e. I2Head and U2Eyes, are used containing real and synthetic images. Two experimental setups have been employed in order to validate our hypothesis. The first setup uses Imagenet as start-point while a dataset containing eye synthetic images is employed in the second one. The results presented in this paper show that a calibration strategy is possible for low resolution, achieving first-class performance when adapting a gaze estimation regressor for an specific user, yielding results close to the ones achieved in high resolution, i.e. ~1.5° which is one of the main contributions of our work. Furthermore, the importance of providing domain images during the training process has been confirmed and also the benefits of pretraining the regressor in a closer domain instead of in a more general dataset to compensate the lack of useful gaze data images, due to the difficulties in both acquiring and labeling them, that characterize gaze estimation problem.

References

1. Abass, A., et al.: Positions of ocular geometrical and visual axes in Brazilian, Chinese and Italian populations. Curr. Eye Res. **43**(11), 1404–1414 (2018). https://doi.org/10.1080/02713683.2018.1500609, pMID: 30009634

2. Cerrolaza, J.J., Villanueva, A., Cabeza, R.: Study of polynomial mapping functions in video-oculography eye trackers. ACM Trans. Comput.-Hum. Interact. **19**(2), 10:1–10:25 (2012). https://doi.org/10.1145/2240156.2240158
3. Chen, Z., Shi, B.E.: Geddnet: a network for gaze estimation with dilation and decomposition (2020). https://arxiv.org/abs/2001.09284
4. Cheng, Y., Huang, S., Wang, F., Qian, C., Lu, F.: A coarse-to-fine adaptive network for appearance-based gaze estimation (2020). https://arxiv.org/abs/2001.00187
5. Deng, J., Dong, W., Socher, R., Li, L.J., Li, K., Fei-Fei, L.: ImageNet: a large-scale hierarchical image database. In: CVPR09 (2009)
6. Guestrin, E., Eizenman, M.: General theory of remote gaze estimation using pupil center and corneal reflections. IEEE Trans. Biomed. Eng. **53**(6), 1124–1133 (2006)
7. Guo, T., et al.: A generalized and robust method towards practical gaze estimation on smart phone. In: 2019 International Conference on Computer Vision (ICCV) Workshops ICCV 2019, October 2019
8. He, J., et al.: On-device few-shot personalization for real-time gaze estimation. In: 2019 IEEE International Conference on Computer Vision (ICCV) Workshops ICCV 2019, October 2019
9. He, K., Zhang, X., Ren, S., Sun, J.: Deep residual learning for image recognition. In: 2016 IEEE Conference on Computer Vision and Pattern Recognition (CVPR) (2015)
10. Hennessey, C., Noureddin, B., Lawrence, P.: A single camera eye-gaze tracking system with free head motion. In: Proceedings of the 2006 Symposium on Eye Tracking Research & Applications, ETRA 2006, pp. 87–94. Association for Computing Machinery, New York (2006). https://doi.org/10.1145/1117309.1117349
11. Krafka, K., et al.: Eye tracking for everyone. In: Proceedings of the IEEE Conference on Computer Vision and Pattern Recognition, pp. 2176–2184 (2016)
12. Linden, E., Sjostrand, J., Proutiere, A.: Learning to personalize in appearance-based gaze tracking. In: 2019 IEEE International Conference on Computer Vision (ICCV) Workshops, ICCV 2019, October 2019
13. Linden, E., Sjostrand, J., Proutiere, A.: Learning to personalize in appearance-based gaze tracking. In: The IEEE International Conference on Computer Vision (ICCV) Workshops, October 2019
14. Martinikorena, I., Cabeza, R., Villanueva, A., Porta, S.: Introducing I2Head database. In: 7th International Workshop on Pervasive Eye Tracking and Mobile Eye based Interaction PETMEI 2007 (2018)
15. Merchant, J., Morrissette, R., Porterfield, J.: Remote measurement of eye direction allowing subject motion over one cubic foot of space. IEEE Trans. Biomed. Eng. **21**(4), 309–317 (1974)
16. Morimoto, C.H., Amir, A., Flickner, M.: Detecting eye position and gaze from a single camera and 2 light sources. In: Proceedings International Conference on Pattern Recognition, pp. 314–317 (2002)
17. Porta, S., Bossavit, B., Cabeza, R., Larumbe-Bergera, A., Garde, G., Villanueva, A.: U2eyes: a binocular dataset for eye tracking and gaze estimation. In: 2019 IEEE International Conference on Computer Vision (ICCV) ICCV 2019, October 2019
18. Shih, S.W., Liu, J.: A novel approach to 3-D gaze tracking using stereo cameras. IEEE Trans. Syst. Man Cybern. Part-B **34**(1), 234–245 (2004)
19. Smith, L.N.: Cyclical learning rates for training neural networks. In: 2017 IEEE Winter Conference on Applications of Computer Vision (WACV) (2017)
20. Yu, Y., Liu, G., Odobez, J.M.: Improving few-shot user-specific gaze adaptation via gaze redirection synthesis. In: 2019 IEEE/CVF Conference on Computer Vision and Pattern Recognition (CVPR) (2019)

Eye Movement Classification with Temporal Convolutional Networks

Carlos Elmadjian$^{(\boxtimes)}$, Candy Gonzales, and Carlos H. Morimoto

University of São Paulo, São Paulo, Brazil
{elmad,candytg,hitoshi}@ime.usp.br

Abstract. Recently, deep learning approaches have been proposed to detect eye movements such as fixations, saccades, and smooth pursuits from eye tracking data. These are *end-to-end* methods that have shown to surpass traditional ones, requiring no *ad hoc* parameters. In this work we propose the use of temporal convolutional networks (TCNs) for automated eye movement classification and investigate the influence of feature space, scale, and context window sizes on the classification results. We evaluated the performance of TCNs against a state-of-the-art 1D-CNN-BLSTM model using GazeCom, a public available dataset. Our results show that TCNs can outperform the 1D-CNN-BLSTM, achieving an F-score of 94.2% for fixations, 89.9% for saccades, and 73.7% for smooth pursuits on sample level, and 89.6%, 94.3%, and 60.2% on event level. We also state the advantages of TCNs over sequential networks for this problem, and how these scores can be further improved by feature space extension.

Keywords: Eye movement classification · Temporal convolutional networks · Feature selection

1 Introduction

Eye movement classification is a fundamental task in many areas of research, including Psychology and Human-Computer Interaction. Many social, behavioral, and user experience studies depend on the correct identification of certain eye movement events [8]. Moreover, these raw events often make up more complex activity patterns (i.e., reading [5]), and thus are an elementary step in order to understand intricate cognitive states [21,25].

Although we perform several different types of movements with our eyes [19], fixations, saccades, and smooth pursuits are the most common used for classification purposes [16]. While fixations come down as the act of staring at something, saccades and smooth pursuits are considered gaze shifts. Typically, saccades are very fast and have a short duration, while pursuits are slower and usually only triggered when following a moving target in the visual field [6] (see Fig. 1).

Supported by the São Paulo Research Foundation, grant 2015/26802-1.

A. Del Bimbo et al. (Eds.): ICPR 2020 Workshops, LNCS 12663, pp. 390–404, 2021.
https://doi.org/10.1007/978-3-030-68796-0_28

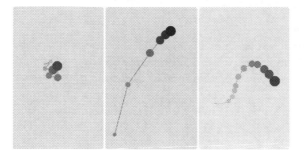

Fig. 1. Graphical representation of gaze scanpaths of fixations (left), saccades (middle), and smooth pursuit events (right). Fixations are markedly stationary, saccades present large ballistic gaze shifts, while pursuits show minor displacements, typically shaped by following a moving target.

The task of simultaneously classifying these three kinds of movements has been coined the "tertiary eye movement classification problem" (3EMCP), and it is still considered a challenging one [4]. Early solutions to this problem often relied on threshold levels for pattern segmentation [22], being later replaced by probabilistic-based models, which are considerably more robust to noise [17,23]. Only recently data-driven approaches have been employed more extensively [12, 26], becoming the current state-of-the-art.

In the realm of deep neural networks, the 3EMCP can be considered a typical sequence-to-sequence (seq2seq) problem [28], in which we want a label for each individual sample that goes into the model. Although recurrent architectures such as LSTMs and GRUs have dominated the field of seq2seq problems in the last decade, recently it has been shown that Temporal Convolutional Networks (TCNs) can outperform these recurrent models in many applications [2].

Therefore, in this work we propose a TCN model for the tertiary eye movement classification problem, and we investigate its performance, architectural advantages, and shortcomings in comparison to the 1D-CNN-BLSTM model proposed by Startsev et al. [26], which is currently the best performing model in the GazeCom dataset [7]. Additionally, we investigate the role of different features, feature scale size, and temporal windows on general model performance, and we show how deep architectures in general can benefit from these findings in the domain of eye movement classification.

2   Related Work

Although not all related algorithms and models have focused specifically on the tertiary eye movement classification problem, they all fall into one of the following categories: threshold-based methods, probabilistic methods, or data-driven models, such as deep learning approaches.

2.1   Threshold-Based Methods

Threshold-based methods are the ones that make use of threshold levels to discriminate different classes of eye movements. They are often marked by their simplicity and low computational requirements, making them suitable for real-time applications.

Velocity threshold is a widely use criterion to cut apart saccades from other eye movements, as saccades are commonly characterized by their fast displacements. Salvucci and Goldberg [22] showed that it is possible to use a simple threshold to discriminate saccades from fixations by computing the point-to-point velocity in eye data stream.

However, because a static threshold can be severely affected by noise, equipment, or user attributes, Nyström and Holmqvist [20] proposed an adaptive velocity threshold to classify fixations, saccades, and post-saccadic oscillations (PSOs), a method that is particularly less sensitive to noise level fluctuations. Since their work focused on saccade and PSO detection, fixations were treated as a negative class.

Dispersion threshold is another form of criterion found in the literature. It provides a more robust approach to detect fixations compared to the velocity threshold [22]. The idea is that we can treat fixations as consecutive samples within maximum spatial separation under a minimum duration threshold.

Berg et al. [3] demonstrated that it is also possible to use Principal Component Analysis (PCA) to establish more generic dispersion thresholds that are able to discriminate fixations, saccades, and smooth pursuits. This approach, however, is very parameter-sensitive, which makes it not so adaptive.

2.2   Probabilistic Methods

In the pursuit of methods that are less sensitive to noise and are also parameter-free, several authors proposed what we call *probabilistic* approaches.

Komogortsev and Khan [17] designed the Attention Focus Kalman Filter (AFKF) framework, which aimed to solve the 3EMCP in real-time. The AFKF framework was in fact an extension of a previous method [24], in which a Kalman filter with a χ^2-test is used to detect saccades. In this updated version, Komogortsev and Khan proposed that smooth pursuits could be treated as a negative event (i.e., neither saccades or fixations), provided they did not surpass the velocity of 140 deg/s.

A more reliable 3EMCP solution was presented by Santini et al. [23] through what they called Bayesian Decision Theory Identification (I-BDT) algorithm. The method consisted on defining priors and likelihoods for all events, and then calculating the posterior for each event, given eye velocity and movement ratio over windows according to the Bayes' rules.

2.3 Data-Driven Methods

Data-driven methods emerged with the increasing success and growth of machine learning techniques. Because models in this class are typically implicit, they tend to be more adaptive and robust than previous algorithms, often displaying a large capacity (i.e., the ability to fit a wide variety of functions).

Some of these methods resort to classical machine learning techniques, such as the one proposed by Vidal et al. [29]. They considered a set of shape features that characterize smooth pursuits as a statistical phenomenon, training a k-nearest neighbor classifier with them. Another example is the work of Zemblys et al. [31], in which they introduced a random forests-based model to detect fixations, saccades and PSOs.

With the prominence of deep learning, some authors introduced artificial neural models for this problem as well. Hoppe and Bulling [12] proposed a CNN-based end-to-end architecture to classify fixations, saccades, and smooth pursuits in a continuous gaze stream, from which frequency features are extracted to train their model. Later, Starsev et al. [26] introduced a 1D-CNN-BLSTM *seq2seq* network that also addresses the 3EMCP. Besides the three eye movement classes, they also added a "noise" class, so that the model was not forced to choose between one of the three. They showed that their 1D-CNN-BLSTM classifier outperforms 12 previous baseline models in the GazeCom dataset [1, 3, 7, 14, 15, 18], effectively becoming the current state-of-the-art.

It is also worth noting that since performance of neural networks is highly impacted by the amount of data available and its variability on training [10], some authors suggested gaze data augmentation techniques for this problem. Zemblys et al. [30] proposed gazeNet, a generative network that can create different kinds of eye movement events. More recently, Fuhl [9] introduced CNNs for raw eye tracking data segmentation, generation, and reconstruction.

Our TCN model is also part of this class. Although—to the best of our knowledge—there are no previous studies of TCNs on eye movement classification, this kind of network has already demonstrated that it can outperform recurrent architectures in a varied set of sequence modeling tasks [2]. We describe our architecture and its features in the following section.

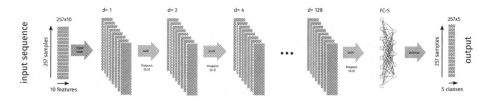

Fig. 2. Architecture of our TCN network. At each hidden state we increase dilations by a factor of 2. FC-5 represents a time-distributed fully-connected layer with 5 outputs.

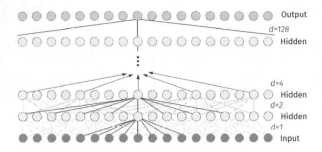

Fig. 3. Non-causal dilated convolutions using size 8 kernels, providing a large receptive field and the ability to look into the "future".

3   Model Architecture

Compared to LSTMs or GRUs, TCNs present some important advantages. TCNs are known to have longer memory than recurrent nets with the same capacity since they do not have gating mechanisms. They also have a flexible receptive field size, lower memory requirements for training, and can be trained with variable input length. Also, because TCNs have a convolutional structure, it can be more easily parallelized, meaning less training time than recurrent nets, that present a more sequential pipeline structure [2].

In broader terms, TCNs can be understood as 1D fully-convolutional networks with causal convolutions. This means that given a time instant t in a time series and a constraint y_t, then y_t can only be satisfied by $x_0, ..., x_t$, and not by $x_{t+1}, ..., x_T$ [2]. This makes them suitable for real-time applications, but also puts them in a disadvantageous position against bidirectional recurrent architectures, as they can process features in two directions.

To make up for this, we use non-causal TCNs instead, which gives our architecture the ability to look into the future at the expense of being offline. We also make use of several dilated convolutions $(1, 2, 4, 8, 16, 32, 64, 128)$, and a relatively sizeable kernel $(k = 8)$, which effectively provides us with a large receptive field (see Fig. 3). This convenience does have a cost though, as our network may require almost 2 million parameters to train. However, despite the amount of parameters required, training is comparatively fast due to its parallelized structure, roughly taking half of the time required to train the 1D-CNN-BLSTM on the same machine to reach an empirical optimum validation loss in the GazeCom dataset [7].

The schematic description of our architecture is depicted in Fig. 2. All hyperparameters were defined according to a reduced grid search with a subset of the GazeCom dataset. The TCN has a total of 128 filters, an internal dropout rate of 0.3, and uses the hyperbolic tangent activation function $(tanh)$ instead of the more commonly seen rectified linear units $(ReLU)$. Weights are initialized following a random uniform distribution, and we do not employ batch normalization between layers.

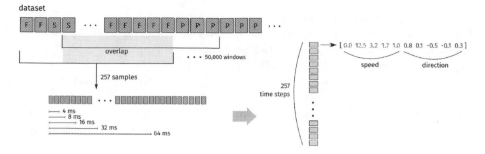

Fig. 4. Feature extraction procedure from the GazeCom dataset, according to Startsev et al. [26]. For each 257-sample window we extract speed and direction features related to each step of the sequence, using different scale sizes.

At the end of the convolutional chain, we add a fully connected layer with a softmax activation function wrapped by a timed-distributed layer, so that we can have a certain probability distribution for each eye movement pattern at all time steps. Because of our one-hot encoded targets, we use a categorical cross-entropy loss function. We also opted for the Adam optimizer [13] with a initial learning rate of 0.0001, as this configuration demonstrated a faster convergence in our grid search.

4   Evaluation

4.1   Materials

Our network implementation was based on the publicly available code base from Startsev et al. [26], but we ported all their original training and evaluation routines to Python 3. We also created a customized Python 3 version of their feature extraction tool, which was originally written in MATLAB. The architecture itself was implemented and trained using the functional API from Keras (2.3.1), which is a built-in high-level API for Tensorflow (2.0.2).

For the TCN, in particular, we used the keras-tcn package (3.1.1), available at the Python Package Index (PyPI). All the training was done distributedly on two machines with an Intel Core i7-7700 CPU with 16 GB RAM, both of them with a NVidia GeForce GTX 1070 GPU (8 GB VRAM), running on the Ubuntu 18.04 operating system.

All our code base, data, and models trained for this work are publicly available at https://github.com/elmadjian/3EMCP-with-TCNs.

4.2   Dataset

The dataset employed in this study is the GazeCom dataset [7], the same one that was used by the 1D-CNN-BLSTM model proposed by Startsev et al. It contains 18 clips from roughly 47 viewers (the number slightly varies according to the video), with labels for fixations, saccades, smooth pursuits, and noise. The labels are given based on the judgment and agreement of two experts, after observing the patterns that each user performed when watching short videos. Clips are limited to a duration of 21 s for training.

The GazeCom data was collected using 250 Hz remote eye tracker, and is constituted by 4.3 million samples, being 72.5% fixations, 10.5% saccades, 11% smooth pursuits, and 5.9% noise or blinks. The average confidence level given by the eye tracker is 99.4%. The average duration of each pattern is shown in Table 1.

Table 1. Average event duration in GazeCom dataset

	Duration (ms)	Deviation (ms)
Fixations	324.37	306.07
Saccades	46.38	22.17
Smooth pursuits	410.98	323.42
Noise	291.91	294.34

4.3   Feature Extraction

The temporal sequences that are fed to the model are formed by pre-computed multi-scale features extracted from the x and y gaze coordinates. In their original implementation, Startsev et al. considered five different temporal scales: 4, 8, 16, 32, and 64 ms. In ours, we included support to a larger set of scales (128, 256, and 512 ms) in order to investigate their role in model classification performance.

The feature extraction process is depicted in Fig. 4. All these features are created by pre-processing the entire set of raw gaze coordinates before training. Each sample consists of a fixed-size context window of roughly 1 s (257 steps), and each timestep of this window presentes the associated multi-scale set of features, which could be either acceleration, speed, or direction, or a combination of them.

Statsev et al. have also demonstrated that classification improves when features such as speed and direction are combined in training, while acceleration deteriorates performance. Thus, we use this composite of speed and direction as our baseline, but we also investigated the addition of other two common features in the time series domain: standard deviation and displacement (not to be confused with distance).

4.4   Metrics

Because the GazeCom dataset has an unbalanced distribution of classes, general accuracy measurements might lead to biased interpretations of actual model performance. That is why we evaluate our model using the F-score and intersection over union (IoU) as our two primary metrics, since they can give more weight to misclassified samples and can be more informative in terms of event correlation.

Although other useful metrics could be applied as well, for comparison fairness we have limited our evaluation scope to the same metrics used by Startsev et al. [27].

4.5 Training and Evaluation

In this work, we evaluate the general performance of our model in comparison with a state-of-the-art baseline using the same configuration and metrics; we investigate the role of increasing feature space and scale on model performance; and we take advantage of TCNs' lower memory requirements to examine model classification behavior of smooth pursuits when exposed to larger context windows of sequences.

To compare our model with the baseline, we use the same Leave-One-Video-Out (LOVO) cross-validation procedure reported by Startsev et al., in which each step of training is done with 17 clips and the model is evaluated on the remaining one. We also employ the same input setup, with a context window of 257 samples ($\sim$1 s), an overlap of 192 samples, with speed and direction features combined, and limiting the number of training sequences to 50,000, using a random permutation of sequences with the same seed. To get more stable and reproducible results, we also fix the random seed generators of the NumPy library and TensorFlow to 0.

While the baseline model was reportedly trained with a batch size of 5000 for 1000 epochs, the TCN model is trained with a batch size of 128 samples for 20 epochs. Another important difference is that our model uses the Adam optimizer, and not RMSprop. Although we did not re-train the baseline model, we ran the evaluation routines for its two trained versions available in a public repository from the authors and obtained the same reported results.

Assuming the standard feature space (SF) as the combination of speed and direction, we evaluated the TCN model performance in this aspect according to the following configurations: SF + standard deviation; SF + displacement; and SF + standard deviation + displacement. Regarding the feature scale size investigation, we evaluated the model with additional scales of 128, 256, and 512 ms. We used the same LOVO procedure while training using the same context window size, training sequences, batch size, and epochs, as reported before.

Since smooth pursuits have a typically longer duration than fixations and saccades, it has been hypothesized that larger context windows can benefit *seq2seq* models to improve its detection. To demonstrate this, we trained our model using two additional windows of 1.5 s and 2 s, using the same LOVO training procedure, but with the overlap having to be adjusted to keep the 50,000 sequences fixed. In other words, we used 385 samples with an overlap of 312 for the 1.5 s window, and 514 samples with an overlap of 470 for the 2 s window.

It is worth mentioning that larger contexts can be prohibitive for recurrent networks in terms of memory usage and computational complexity, but there were no such issues training with the TCN model. Based on these findings, we

Table 2. TCN model evaluation

Model	Fixation				Saccade				Smooth pursuit			
	F1	Prec.	Recall	EF1	F1	Prec.	Recall	EF1	F1	Prec.	Recall	EF1
TCN Model+	**0.945**	**0.929**	0.961	0.735	0.894	0.899	**0.889**	0.888	0.762	0.787	**0.739**	0.253
TCN Model+*	**0.945**	0.928	0.962	**0.900**	0.892	0.897	0.887	0.941	**0.764**	**0.791**	**0.739**	**0.608**
TCN Model	0.942	0.925	0.959	0.717	**0.899**	**0.903**	0.894	0.885	0.737	0.765	0.711	0.234
TCN Model*	0.942	0.924	0.960	0.896	0.896	0.901	0.890	**0.943**	0.739	0.769	0.711	0.602
Startsev et al. [26]	0.939	0.914	**0.967**	0.868	0.893	0.897	**0.889**	0.924	0.703	0.788	0.634	0.484
Startsev et al.*	0.939	0.914	**0.967**	0.883	0.893	0.897	**0.889**	0.935	0.703	0.789	0.634	0.537
Startsev et al. [27]	0.937	0.921	0.954	0.882	0.896	0.899	0.893	0.929	0.707	0.724	0.691	0.544
Startsev et al.*	0.937	0.921	0.954	0.892	0.896	0.899	0.892	0.939	0.708	0.725	0.692	0.576

Results for sample-level detection, except column **EF1** = Event F1 (IoU >= 0.5). Rows marked with * represent filtered output. **Prec.** = Precision. + = Our best model.

ran a final LOVO evaluation combining the best configurations provided by the study on feature space, feature scale size, and temporal window width.

Finally, we also evaluated all models with and without a domain-based knowledge filtering procedure applied to the outputs. This heuristic assumes that any event that is shorter than 12 ms is a spurious output. The filter then replaces the class of the samples belonging to this event by the the next non-spurious neighbor.

5   Results

Compared to the reported results of the 1D-CNN-BLSTM model, and using the same input constraints and training regimen, our model achieved an improved performance in all three major patterns, with an F-score of 94.2% for fixations, 89.9% for saccades, and 73.4% for smooth pursuits. This represents a gain over the best published result in the GazeCom dataset of 0.3%, 0.3%, and 3%, respectively. If considered the models further improved by window width, feature space, and feature scale size, the highest gains were of 0.6%, 0.3%, and 5.7%, respectively. A complete assessment compiling the reported results in terms of sample F1 and event detection (episode F1 with IoU > 0.5) is shown in Table 2. The TCN model marked by a + sign is the one trained with the best features, while the ones marked with a * had their output filtered.

The use of a domain-based knowledge filtering for the outputs also increased event detection scores according to the metrics proposed by Hooge et al. [11]. With smooth pursuits, in particular, the TCN models roughly tripled their event F-scores, while the models from Startsev et al. had only modest improvements. Besides, the filter effect over general sample-level scores were barely noticeable.

The evaluation on feature space and feature scale size have shown mixed results. It is clear that increasing the scale size led to an overall marginal improvement on classification performance when compared to the default 5-scale features input. However these gains did not occur consistently across scale sizes, and smooth pursuits showed the largest fluctuations. Figure 5 exhibits how the F1 and IoU values for smooth pursuits oscillated with respect to the scale size.

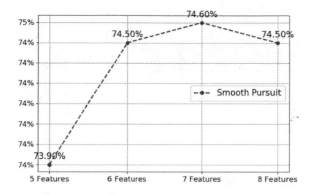

Fig. 5. Smooth pursuit F-score variation across different scale sizes.

Table 3. Feature space study

	Fixation		Saccade		SP	
	F1	EF1	F1	EF1	F1	EF1
Win 257	0.942	0.717	0.899	0.885	0.737	0.234
Win 257*	0.942	**0.896**	0.896	0.943	0.739	**0.602**
Win 257+std	0.942	0.721	**0.898**	0.890	0.738	0.239
Win 257+std*	0.942	**0.896**	0.895	**0.945**	0.739	0.601
Win 257+disp	0.942	0.728	0.896	0.880	0.738	0.252
Win 257+disp*	0.942	0.895	0.893	0.943	0.740	0.596
Win 257+std+disp	0.942	0.730	0.896	0.883	0.740	0.253
Win 257+std+disp*	0.942	**0.896**	0.894	0.944	**0.741**	0.600

EF1 = Event F1 (IoU >= 0.5), * = Filtered

Tables 3 and 4 show the results related to the feature space study and feature scale size, respectively.

The investigation on the size of temporal window partially confirmed the hypothesis that smooth pursuits detection can benefit from larger contexts. With a window size of 1.5 s (385 samples), there was an improvement of 1.3% over the 1 s window (257 samples), but with a context of 2 s (514 samples), the gain dropped to 0.7%. These results can be seen in Table 5.

A final evaluation with the best configuration in terms of features and context windows gave us the highest F1 scores achieved for smooth pursuits in the GazeCom dataset. The results were 94.5% for fixations, 89.2% for saccades, and 76.4% for smooth pursuits.

Table 4. Feature scale study

	Fixation		Saccade		SP	
	F1	EF1	F1	EF1	F1	EF1
5 Features	0.942	0.717	**0.899**	0.885	0.737	0.234
5 Features	0.942	0.896	0.896	**0.943**	0.739	0.602
6 Features	**0.943**	0.723	**0.899**	0.887	0.743	0.240
6 Features*	**0.943**	**0.897**	0.896	**0.943**	0.745	**0.613**
7 Features	0.942	0.725	0.898	0.884	0.745	0.244
7 Features*	0.942	0.896	0.895	**0.943**	**0.746**	0.597
8 Features	0.942	0.715	0.897	0.885	0.742	0.235
8 Features*	0.942	0.894	0.894	0.941	0.745	0.599

EF1 = Event F1 (IoU >= 0.5), * = Filtered

Table 5. Temporal window width

	Fixation		Saccade		SP	
	F1	EF1	F1	EF1	F1	EF1
Win 257	0.942	0.717	0.899	0.885	0.737	0.234
Win 257*	0.942	0.896	0.896	**0.943**	0.739	0.602
Win 385	**0.943**	0.708	0.899	0.884	0.749	0.227
Win 385*	**0.943**	0.898	0.897	**0.943**	**0.751**	0.602
Win 514	0.941	0.694	**0.900**	0.886	0.744	0.213
Win 514*	0.942	**0.898**	0.897	**0.943**	0.747	**0.604**

Results for varying temporal window sizes (257, 358, and 514 samples) of the TCN model. Results marked by * indicate an identical trained model with filtered output.

6   Discussion

Our results show that the TCN architecture outperforms the state-of-the-art model with the GazeCom dataset. The most significant improvement was in the classification of smooth pursuits, with a 3% performance increase, or 5.7% increase over previous published results when considering the increments on context window width, feature space, and scale size (see Fig. 6).

The investigation on feature space and scale size revealed that increasing both dimensions were somewhat beneficial to the TCN classification performance. The impact of adding novel features, although favorable, was comparatively less significant than the increase of feature scale size, as the latter provided comparatively higher scores on the GazeCom dataset, particularly with respect to smooth pursuits.

The improvement, though, was not consistent with size increments. It could be argued that saccade detection had no improvement at all, while smooth pursuits had the highest scores with a 7-scale size instead of the largest 8-scale one.

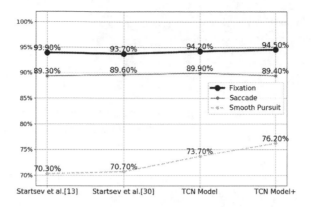

Fig. 6. Results of our TCN model for fixations, saccades, and smooth pursuits (SP), along with the reported results from the 1D-CNN-BLSTM model.

Based on our experiments, it is still not clear whether the network capacity was not appropriate for a larger set of input scales using the same hyperparameters, or whether these inputs naturally have a detrimental effect on training when reaching a certain length.

A similar phenomenon was observed when examining the effect of larger context windows. Although training with both 1.5-s and 2-s temporal windows resulted in improved classification performance, the evaluation on the 1.5-s context presented the general highest scores. It is clear that smooth pursuits had an increased detection rate with larger contexts, but these results do not support the hypothesis that smooth pursuit classification scores increase proportionally with window size.

The filter heuristics also demonstrated to be fundamental when it comes to event detection with TCNs. This improvement could be explained by the fact that convolutional architectures are not favored by the sequential learning constraints of recurrent nets, thus often tainting an event block with one or other wrong predictions. This, of course, can be harmful depending on the metric chosen for event assessment, but it barely affects sample-level classification accuracy.

Compared to other architectures, the TCN is also clearly advantageous in terms of memory usage and training time, since TCNs do not make use of cell gates and have a convenient structure for parallel processing on GPUs. Contrary to LSTMs or GRUs, it could also learn from an arbitrary input length, but our current findings do not suggest that this would not necessarily result in a superior classification performance.

Another consideration is that our TCN model was not designed for online classification, but this would be possible by simply reverting the current configuration to *causal* convolutions. This would obviously result in more modest scores, since the network effectively ceases to be bidirectional. However, because evaluation on TCNs is potentially faster than on recurrent models with the similar memory requirements, TCNs could be a more appropriate choice for real-time applications with high frame rates.

7   Conclusion

In this work we designed a temporal convolutional network for the problem of automated eye movement classification. We demonstrated that our model was capable of surpassing the previous state-of-the-art architectures on the same dataset using the same metrics. Moreover, we highlighted several additional advantages of TCNs over preceding recurrent models, such as lower memory footprint, faster training, and the ability of learning sequences of arbitrary length.

Additionally, the research on feature space, feature scale size, and context window width revealed that such extrinsic factors can also play an important role on model performance, marginally improving predictions in all classes, though these improvements were not consistent with factor size increments. Overall, we witnessed the highest classification gain with smooth pursuits, which are the most underrepresented class in the GazeCom dataset.

References

1. Agtzidis, I., Startsev, M., Dorr, M.: In the pursuit of (ground) truth: a hand-labelling tool for eye movements recorded during dynamic scene viewing. In: 2016 IEEE Second Workshop on Eye Tracking and Visualization (ETVIS), pp. 65–68 (2016)
2. Bai, S., Kolter, J.Z., Koltun, V.: An empirical evaluation of generic convolutional and recurrent networks for sequence modeling. CoRR abs/1803.01271 (2018). http://arxiv.org/abs/1803.01271
3. Berg, D.J., Boehnke, S.E., Marino, R.A., Munoz, D.P., Itti, L.: Free viewing of dynamic stimuli by humans and monkeys. J. Vis. **9**(5), 19 (2009). https://doi.org/10.1167/9.5.19
4. Berndt, S., Kirkpatrick, D., Taviano, T., Komogortsev, O.: Tertiary eye movement classification by a hybrid algorithm. CoRR abs/1904.10085 (2019). http://arxiv.org/abs/1904.10085
5. Campbell, C.S., Maglio, P.P.: A robust algorithm for reading detection. In: Proceedings of the 2001 workshop on Perceptive User Interfaces, pp. 1–7 (2001)
6. Cassin, B., Rubin, M.L., Solomon, S.: Dictionary of Eye Terminology, vol. 10. Triad Publishing Company, Gainsville (1984)
7. Dorr, M., Martinetz, T., Gegenfurtner, K.R., Barth, E.: Variability of eye movements when viewing dynamic natural scenes. J. Vision **10**(10), 28 (2010). https://doi.org/10.1167/10.10.28
8. Duchowski, A.T.: Gaze-based interaction: a 30 year retrospective. Comput. Graph. **73**, 59–69 (2018). https://doi.org/10.1016/j.cag.2018.04.002
9. Fuhl, W.: Fully convolutional neural networks for raw eye tracking data segmentation, generation, and reconstruction (2020)
10. Goodfellow, I.J., Bengio, Y., Courville, A.C.: Deep Learning: Adaptive computation and Machine Learning. MIT Press, Cambridge (2016). http://www.deeplearningbook.org/

11. Hooge, I., Niehorster, D., Nyström, M., Andersson, R., Hessels, R.: Is human classification by experienced untrained observers a gold standard in fixation detection? Behav. Res. Methods **50**(5), 1864–1881 (2018). https://doi.org/10.3758/s13428-017-0955-x
12. Hoppe, S., Bulling, A.: End-to-end eye movement detection using convolutional neural networks. CoRR abs/1609.02452 (2016). http://arxiv.org/abs/1609.02452
13. Kingma, D.P., Ba, J.: Adam: a method for stochastic optimization. In: Bengio, Y., LeCun, Y. (eds.) 3rd International Conference on Learning Representations, ICLR 2015, San Diego, CA, USA, 7–9 May 2015, Conference Track Proceedings (2015). http://arxiv.org/abs/1412.6980
14. Komogortsev, O., Gobert, D., Jayarathna, S., Koh, D., Gowda, S.: Standardization of automated analyses of oculomotor fixation and saccadic behaviors. IEEE Trans. Biomed. Eng. **57**, 2635–2645 (2010). https://doi.org/10.1109/TBME.2010.2057429
15. Komogortsev, O., Karpov, A.: Automated classification and scoring of smooth pursuit eye movements in the presence of fixations and saccades. Behav. Res. Methods **45** (2012). https://doi.org/10.3758/s13428-012-0234-9
16. Komogortsev, O.V., Karpov, A.: Automated classification and scoring of smooth pursuit eye movements in the presence of fixations and saccades. Behav. Res. Methods **45**(1), 203–215 (2013). https://doi.org/10.3758/s13428-012-0234-9
17. Komogortsev, O.V., Khan, J.I.: Kalman filtering in the design of eye-gaze-guided computer interfaces. In: Jacko, J.A. (ed.) HCI 2007. LNCS, vol. 4552, pp. 679–689. Springer, Heidelberg (2007). https://doi.org/10.1007/978-3-540-73110-8_74. http://dl.acm.org/citation.cfm?id=1769590.1769667
18. Larsson, L., Nyström, M., Andersson, R., Stridh, M.: Detection of fixations and smooth pursuit movements in high-speed eye-tracking data. Biomed. Signal Process. Control **18**, 145–152 (2015). https://doi.org/10.1016/j.bspc.2014.12.008, http://www.sciencedirect.com/science/article/pii/S1746809414002031
19. Leigh, R.J., Zee, D.S.: The neurology of eye movements. OUP USA (2015)
20. Nyström, M., Holmqvist, K.: An adaptive algorithm for fixation, saccade, and glissade detection in eyetracking data. Behav. Res. Methods **42**(1), 188–204 (2010). https://doi.org/10.3758/BRM.42.1.188
21. Peters, C., Pelachaud, C., Bevacqua, E., Mancini, M., Poggi, I.: A model of attention and interest using gaze behavior. In: Panayiotopoulos, T., Gratch, J., Aylett, R., Ballin, D., Olivier, P., Rist, T. (eds.) IVA 2005. LNCS (LNAI), vol. 3661, pp. 229–240. Springer, Heidelberg (2005). https://doi.org/10.1007/11550617_20
22. Salvucci, D.D., Goldberg, J.H.: Identifying fixations and saccades in eye-tracking protocols. In: Proceedings of the 2000 Symposium on Eye Tracking Research & Applications, ETRA 2000, pp. 71–78. ACM, New York (2000). https://doi.org/10.1145/355017.355028, http://doi.acm.org/10.1145/355017.355028
23. Santini, T., Fuhl, W., Kübler, T., Kasneci, E.: Bayesian identification of fixations, saccades, and smooth pursuits. In: Proceedings of the Ninth Biennial ACM Symposium on Eye Tracking Research & Applications, ETRA 2016, pp. 163–170. ACM, New York (2016). https://doi.org/10.1145/2857491.2857512, http://doi.acm.org/10.1145/2857491.2857512
24. Sauter, D., Martin, B.J., Di Renzo, N., Vomscheid, C.: Analysis of eye tracking movements using innovations generated by a kalman filter. Med. Biol. Eng. Comput. **29**(1), 63–69 (1991). https://doi.org/10.1007/BF02446297
25. Shepherd, S.: Following gaze: Gaze-following behavior as a window into social cognition. Front. Integr. Neurosci. **4**, 5 (2010). https://doi.org/10.3389/fnint.2010.00005, https://www.frontiersin.org/articles/10.3389/fnint.2010.00005

26. Startsev, M., Agtzidis, I., Dorr, M.: 1D CNN with BLSTM for automated classi-fication of fixations, saccades, and smooth pursuits. Behav. Res. Methods **51**(2), 556–572 (2019). https://doi.org/10.3758/s13428-018-1144-2

27. Startsev, M., Agtzidis, I., Dorr, M.: Sequence-to-sequence deep learning for eye movement classification. In: Perception, vol. 48, pp. 200–200. Sage Publications LTD., London (2019)

28. Sutskever, I., Vinyals, O., Le, Q.V.: Sequence to sequence learning with neural networks. In: Ghahramani, Z., Welling, M., Cortes, C., Lawrence, N.D., Wein-berger, K.Q. (eds.) Advances in Neural Information Processing Systems 27: Annual Conference on Neural Information Processing Systems 2014, Montreal, Quebec, Canada, 8–13 December 2014, pp. 3104–3112 (2014). http://papers.nips.cc/paper/5346-sequence-to-sequence-learning-with-neural-networks

29. Vidal, M., Bulling, A., Gellersen, H.: Detection of smooth pursuits using eye move-ment shape features. In: Proceedings of the Symposium on Eye Tracking Research and Applications, ETRA 2012, pp. 177–180. ACM, New York (2012). https://doi.org/10.1145/2168556.2168586, http://doi.acm.org/10.1145/2168556.2168586

30. Zemblys, R., Niehorster, D.C., Holmqvist, K.: gazenet: End-to-end eye-movement event detection with deep neural networks. Behav. Res. Methods **51**, 840–864 (2018)

31. Zemblys, R., Niehorster, D.C., Komogortsev, O., Holmqvist, K.: Using machine learning to detect events in eye-tracking data. Behav. Res. Methods **50**(1), 160–181 (2018)

A Web-Based Eye Tracking Data Visualization Tool

Hristo Bakardzhiev, Marloes van der Burgt, Eduardo Martins,
Bart van den Dool, Chyara Jansen, David van Scheppingen, Günter Wallner,
and Michael Burch$^{(\boxtimes)}$

Eindhoven University of Technology, Eindhoven, The Netherlands
{h.bakardzhiev,m.p.a.v.d.burgt,e.j.costa.martins,b.c.v.d.dool,
c.w.p.jansen}@student.tue.nl
{g.wallner,m.burch}@tue.nl

Abstract. Visualizing eye tracking data can provide insights in many research fields. However, visualizing such data efficiently and cost-effectively is challenging without well-designed tools. Easily accessible web-based approaches equipped with intuitive and interactive visualizations offer to be a promising solution. Many of such tools already exist, however, they mostly use one specific visualization technique. In this paper, we describe a web application which uses a combination of different visualization methods for eye tracking data. The visualization techniques are interactively linked to provide several perspectives on the eye tracking data. We conclude the paper by discussing challenges, limitations, and future work.

Keywords: Eye tracking · Information visualization · Multiple linked views

1 Introduction

Eye tracking data appears in a variety of fields such as psychology [19,24], marketing [17], or computer science [1]. It can give insights in the fixation points, their duration and sequential order, and more. Based on this information, a better understanding of certain processes can be achieved, such as how people read a sentence [20], how advertisements can be made more effective [21], or how to improve a metro map [9].

While recording the data is rather simple with today's technology, visualization poses challenges due to the complexity of the data. It needs to be processed in order to be readable and understandable by a human. Quantitative examination of the data can be valuable to process these amounts of data but usually requires certain knowledge of the data beforehand. If the analysis is more exploratory in nature, however, interactive visualizations have proven to be a suitable means to support interpretations of patterns in the data over space, time, people, and stimuli. While many visualization techniques are available they are typically provided separately and may not be straightforward to use.

© Springer Nature Switzerland AG 2021
A. Del Bimbo et al. (Eds.): ICPR 2020 Workshops, LNCS 12663, pp. 405–419, 2021.
https://doi.org/10.1007/978-3-030-68796-0_29

The main goal of this research is to create a web-based tool that is freely accessible, simple to use, and thus enables both experts and non-experts to visualize eye tracking data in multiple linked ways [8,11]. It is intended for static stimuli displayed on screens. Hence, video stimuli or data recorded by mobile eye-tracking devices are not taken into account. The current version of the tool includes four different views, namely an areas-of-interest (AOI) timeline, a gaze plot, a heatmap, and a scarf plot.

The remainder of this paper is structured as follows. After briefly discussing already existing research, the data handling will be described and each of the four views will be illustrated and explained. This is followed by a short explanation of the web application itself. Next to that, the workflow and a use case are described. Finally, we discuss the approach and its current limitations, then we conclude with possible future work.

2   Related Work

The visualization of eye tracking data has been in focus of research for quite some time (see [2]). In this paper, we propose a web-based tool to increase accessibility to otherwise often difficult to obtain tools. Several web-based tools for eye tracking data already exist [8,11]. These tools make use of different specific views, for instance, a hierarchical flow visualization [7], a Sankey diagram [10], heatmaps [4,25] or a combination of heatmaps, gaze stripes, and attention clouds [11]. In contrast, we propose a modular tool, currently featuring four different visualizations but which can be extended with other visualizations in the future.

A crucial aspect of eye tracking data are fixation points, i.e. the moments of visual intake [22]. However, saccades, i.e. rapid eye movements, are equally important [13]. As such, we focus on a combination of point-based and AOI-based visualization techniques [2]. Point-based techniques use spatial and temporal information of the recorded data whereas AOI-based visualization techniques focus on objects or regions of interest [2]. AOI-based techniques can give a quick, clear overview but the choices made during the definition of AOIs influence the outcome [15]. Therefore, combining both point-based as well as AOI-based visualization techniques is expected to allow the user to retrieve valuable insights by being able to view the data from both perspectives.

As visualization, interaction with eye tracking data can be challenging due to its complexity. For this reason we follow the interaction principles for information visualization [26] which can be categorized as select, explore, reconfigure, encode, abstract/elaborate, filter, and connect.

3   Data Handling

In this section we describe aspects of data preparation and processing.

3.1   Data Validation

The tool allows users to upload eye tracking data via `zip` files, that include the eye tracking data in form of `csv` files as well as images of the stimuli on which the eye tracking data is based. This data is verified first to ensure that the uploaded dataset is in the correct format and complete, i.e. all required columns are present in the `csv` file and that the data in those columns is of the correct type. Finally, the dataset is checked for internal consistency.

3.2   Clustering

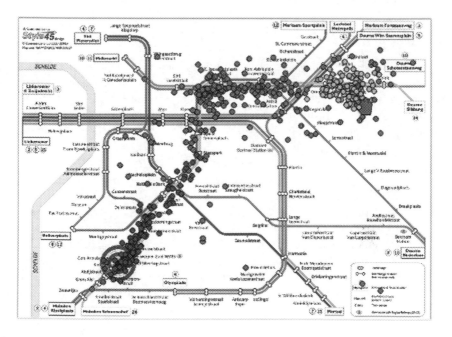

Fig. 1. Overview of the partitioning of the areas of interest. Each cluster is represented by a unique color. Three clusters are visible (points not belonging to any cluster are grayed out). (Color figure online)

Areas of interest (AOIs) are often used in eye tracking data visualizations. There are at least two ways of acquiring them: either by clustering or by letting users manually select AOIs and mapping points to them. By default, our tool uses the *meanshift* [14] algorithm for clustering as no user input is required. Two additional algorithms are also offered, namely *k-means* and *HDBSCAN* [18], both of which require some user input, namely the number of clusters k or the minimum amount of points in a cluster in case of HDBSCAN. Whatever clustering result is generated automatically, the user can modify it and interactively deselect points from a cluster or remap points to other clusters as well. This puts the user in-the-loop to take advantage of both automatic processing and the user's practical experience.

Where *meanshift* automatically partitions all data points into clusters, *k*-means does so for a fixed amount of clusters while in case of *HDBSCAN* points may not belong to any cluster. Lastly, the user is able to manually select AOIs and use those in other visualizations. Offering different options allows the user to more freely explore different settings for AOI creation. The tool provides an overview of the clustered data points superimposed over the stimulus (as can be seen in Fig. 1 and Fig. 2 ❶). The color of a data point indicates the AOI (cluster) it belongs to. This color is used consistently across all visualizations (e.g., also in the AOI timeline and the scarf plot).

3.3   Heatmap Data

The heatmap is based on the fixation points. For that purpose, a grid (whose grid size is user-definable) with the intensity values for the heatmap is created by iterating over each cell of the grid and checking whether any fixation points are within a cell, determining the intensity value over the whole grid. Such intensity values build a scalar field that can further be smoothed by applying a reconstruction filter [5].

3.4   Caching

To save processing time and offer a smooth user experience all the data process-ing and clustering of it are cached whenever possible. A lot of data processing has to be done to get it prepared for the interactive visualizations. Calculat-ing this data costs valuable processing time, and repeating it every time a user requests that data can impact user experience, in particular for user interactions. Therefore, most of the data processing and clustering are cached and saved to mitigate delays.

4   Visualization Techniques

The tool offers four visualizations that provide information complementary to each other and reveal different aspects of the data (see Fig. 2). In the following, each visualization will be described along with the interactions it offers. Lastly, we describe the general interaction possibilities implemented in all four views.

4.1   AOI Timeline

The AOI timeline is a visualization that combines multiple factors into one explanatory graph. The implementation of the current AOI timeline can be seen in Fig. 3 and Fig. 2 ❷. Vertically, all selected or computed AOIs are located in the same order as they were given (just by given IDs, no special order precomputed).

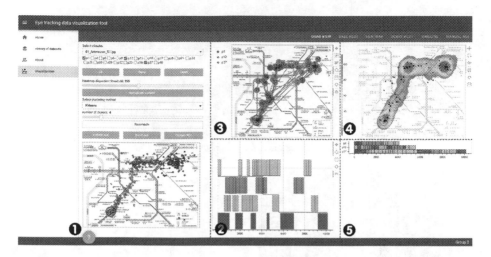

Fig. 2. All visualizations can be shown next to each other as multiple coordinated views. Interacting with one view automatically highlights the elements under investigation in all of the other views (in case the user wishes to see that). The views can be moved around and arranged by the users based on their demands.

The user can also place a screenshot for each AOI to better set it in context to the shown stimulus in the eye tracking study. Consequently, each AOI has a representative horizontal line for the progress over time. In the AOI timeline we use the same color coding as for the AOI definitions in the corresponding stimulus. The time axis is running from left to right (older time points to the left, newer ones to the right).

If one or more participants looked into one of the defined AOIs, a color-coded rectangle is shown with the horizontal extent of the time it is fixated by one or more participants. This visualization gives an overview about all AOIs and when they have been attended to visually and for how long. To see who looked at an AOI, user interaction is required, for example, by hovering over an AOI rectangle. Since each AOI cluster is shown in a separate row we can easily compare the visual attention strategies and identify in which order AOIs have been investigated over time.

The color coding is configurable by the user. Selecting an AOI sequence over time indicates the participants involved in that sequence (black line in Fig. 3). As a drawback we identify the fact that the total number of participants paying visual attention to a specific AOI is not visible in the diagram.

A user can also select an AOI to mark all participants who gazed at it for the selected time. Participants can also be added and removed to focus on different subsets of the eye movement data or make comparisons.

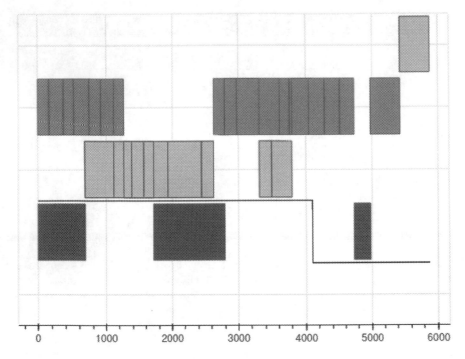

Fig. 3. An AOI timeline showing four AOIs under investigation. The AOI in the top row is only visually attended towards the end, maybe it is related to a solution of a given task in the eye tracking experiment. A black line can be added interactively to explore the participants and fixation durations over time in a certain AOI sequence. (Color figure online)

4.2   Gaze Plot

Gaze plots (cf. Fig. 2 ❸) are visualizations that show the order in which participants looked at which point of the stimuli. Furthermore, by varying the size of the circles, the fixation time can also be represented. However, if too many fixation points need to be shown, clutter and overplotting can occur [2].

Multiple solutions to overplotting in gaze plots have been proposed such as bundling the scan paths [23] when there are many data points with high similarity or reducing the number of objects being rendered on the screen by either limiting the amount of data that is visualized or by removing the circles in the visualization and using other methods to determine the order of the scan path. In our case, the user is able to select which participants' data is being shown to allow the user to handle potential clutter in case of large amounts of data. For example, Fig. 4 shows a gaze plot with the fixation order of one participant. If the scanpath gets longer or if the visual attention behaviors of many participants are inspected at the same time we typically get visual clutter effects, hence a combination with another visualization is required.

In terms of interactions, it is possible to select a node, which highlights the point and all corresponding points in the other plots. By selecting a node, detailed information will be shown such as which participant fixated there, how long the participant looked at this location, and the coordinates of this point relative to the stimulus. It is also possible to filter the participants who have viewed this stimulus. This allows for reduced clutter when the data from a large number of participants is rendered at once.

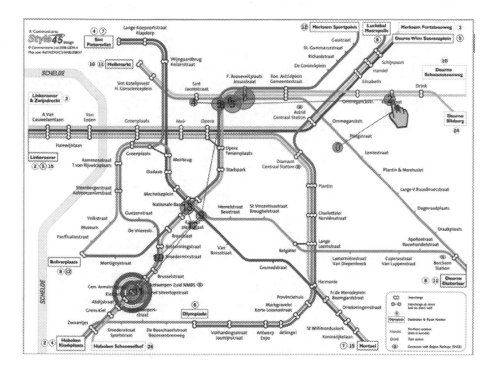

Fig. 4. A gaze plot showing the fixation order of one participant.

4.3 Heatmap

Heatmaps, sometimes also called visual attention maps in the context of eye tracking, give a visual overview of all fixations in order to support the investigation of which areas attracted more or less attention. Visual attention maps are powerful for visualizing large amounts of data at once while being easy to read. However, without real experience in eye tracking, users often misinterpret what is being shown or draw invalid conclusions [4,16] due to the fact that the temporal information is not displayed. Another issue with heatmaps is the difficulty of visual interpretation due to being overlaid on the stimulus, i.e. important context information might get lost, hence a combination with another visualization is beneficial.

There are numerous ways to create heatmaps, all with different intended purposes [3,12,25]. Figure 5 (and Fig. 2 ❹, respectively) shows an absolute fixation count heatmap. It counts the number of fixations in a certain radius and maps the counted number to a color.

A fixation or a group of fixations can be selected and highlighted to keep track of the fixation when switching between plots or zooming in or out. With a dispersion threshold slider the user can vary the radius used to calculate the heatmap. A smaller threshold will result in smaller hotspot areas, i.e. the spatial extent of the visually attended areas, whereas a larger threshold has the opposite effect. It is possible to move the plot in all directions to have different parts visible. When the mouse hovers over a point, information will be shown such as the x- and y-coordinates of the fixation and its duration. It is also possible to zoom in or out to see more or less detail. Users can also be selected to show only their specific fixations on the heatmap.

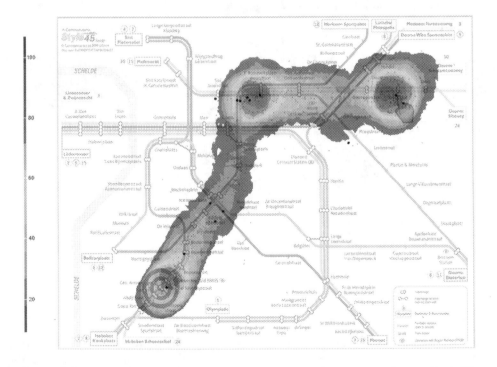

Fig. 5. A heatmap showing the computed scalar values by using a color gradient. The red spots have a large scalar value, i.e. many fixation points are located there. On the left, a color bar is included to show how many fixations must be present within the chosen radius to show a certain color. (Color figure online)

4.4   Scarf Plot

Scarf plots (see Fig. 6 and Fig. 2 ❺) are visualizations that show the AOIs being gazed at over time. An AOI-based approach offers a simplification of the data. Thus while being less detailed it gives an easier overview of the data. Furthermore, by showing multiple participants at once, trends can be spotted that occur between multiple participants. However, scarf plots are limited in the amount of AOIs that they can display, as with an increasing number of AOIs differentiation between the colored bars becomes more difficult.

In the design of the visualization we took several considerations into account. First, the different AOIs should be clearly distinguishable to allow for easy comparison between different participants and to be able to see trends. Lastly, the AOIs should be clearly denoted and linked to the scarf plot.

Important aspects to be considered for this visualization are the clear distinction between different AOIs and allowing for easy comparison between different participants to see trends and countertrends. Another design consideration is the difference between total time for different participants and the appropriate scaling necessary that allows for correct comparison.

By selecting an AOI the times when it was gazed at by participants will be highlighted as well as the location of it. By being able to manually change the AOIs, overriding the clustering, the user has fine-grained control of what is actually considered to be an AOI in a specific situation. By hovering over a bar segment, information will be given about the AOI it represents, the duration, start and stop times, and the exact location of the data point. When selecting a bar segment, the exact point that represents this bar segment will be shown on the stimulus in any of the linked visualizations in which the stimulus is represented.

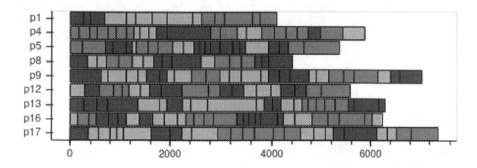

Fig. 6. A scarf plot showing which fixation belongs to which cluster.

4.5   General Interactions

The following general interactions are also available within the tool:

- Tapping or mouse clicking functionality is implemented which enables users to select certain rectangular segments of interest. This will render all other points in gray to highlight the selection.
  All views are linked and marking a selection in one view does it in the others as well.
- Each view can be saved as image with a legend embedded.
- Users can zoom in and out on each view to get more or less details.
- Hovering to reveal additional information is supported in each plot as a details-on-demand feature.
- Participants can be added and removed dynamically while the diagrams get updated.
- The clustering method can be selected as either *Meanshift*, *k-means*, or *HDB-SCAN*. The number of clusters can manually be changed and clusters can be defined by selecting points and assigning them to a certain cluster.

5   Web Application Architecture

For the front-end of the web application, *Vue.js* is being used (*Vue.js* uses a combination of *HTML*, *CSS*, and *JavaScript*), together with several modules such as *Vuetify*. The front-end communicates with the *Flask* back-end (*Flask* uses *Python*) through *Axios* requests and URL parameters. *Flask* itself runs a *Bokeh* server used to render the interactive visualizations in the web browser. The content is rendered on the server-side and then sent directly to the client of the user, thus little computation is done on the user's device.

Data processing is done on demand when possible. This way users only have to wait for the data processing that is necessary for them. It is cached whenever possible to reduce loading times for data that has already been used before. The caching includes the data frame and the computations needed for the graphs.

Briefly, when the website is visited a *Vue* front-end is rendered. When a `zip` file is uploaded then a check is performed to verify whether the file is not corrupt and has the necessary structure. If successful, the caching starts and its results are saved on the server. Afterwards, once the computations are complete, the rendered content is forwarded to the user's client. Once the file is uploaded the user is automatically redirected from the home page of the tool to the page with the visualizations. At this page, users have different options to interact with the visualizations (cf. Sect. 4). Furthermore, the front-end includes fail-safes such as rerouting the users if they try to visit pages that have been disabled.

6   Use Case: Metro Map of Antwerp

In this section we give some examples of the usage of the different types of visualizations and why combining those four is beneficial. For that purpose we use the metro maps eye tracking dataset generated by Burch et al. [9]. The dataset contains various colored and gray-scale metro maps from different cities, of which we here focus on the colored and gray-scale map of Antwerp.

To get an initial overview of the data, we start with observing the heatmap of the colored version of the metro map (see Fig. 5) as it gives a clear and useful overview, even when the dataset becomes larger. We can observe three main spots, corresponding to the start location (bottom left), the destination (top right), and an intermediate station. The end-point is watched relatively more in the colored version compared to the black-white version of the same route (not shown). Also it can be seen that there are only a few fixation points not within close proximity of the route.

Next, to focus on the differences between specific participants and between the different types of the map we take a look at the gaze plot. For example, from the gaze plot of $P1$ (cf. Fig. 4) we can see that the fixations of $P1$ begin around the starting point (bottom left), then lead to the center where a transfer could be needed. Towards the end of the saccade the user fixates the end point, but after visiting the end point, the final fixations focus on the part between the middle and the end point.

From the scarf plot of $P1$ (see Fig. 6, top bar), it seems as if she/he first focused on the start point (dark blue cluster, see also Fig. 1), then the center point (orange cluster), and then the end point (light blue cluster) as those are the spots of the areas of interest. While less specific as the gaze plot, this gives an overall idea of the focus points of the participant. Also, most other participants (cf. Fig. 6) show much more changing of fixations between the areas of interest. These participants are most likely to check where they need to go and then look back to see what possible routes they can take. The sequence of the areas of interest is different for every participant. Most go back two or three times to see if the metro lines are connected or to check if their task solution was correct. The duration of the gaze patterns of all participants is at least 4 s. With the normalized scarf plot (not shown) it can be seen that near the end of the gaze pattern more participants focus on the end point of the route. Interesting to note is that this pattern is not visible at all in the black-white version of the same stimulus. The time spent finding a route is longer and the time spent at the starting point is also longer on average.

The AOI timeline (not depicted) can be used to show the combination of a selected number of participants. This makes it easier to observe general trends. The heatmap and gaze plot show this already for the locations of the fixation points but the timeline shows the switching between areas of interest over time for all the selected participants. Also it can be observed which part of the selected users is still watching the stimulus after a certain period of time. In the colored version all the participants are finished after ten seconds, while in the black-white version a part of the group is finished after thirteen seconds and a few are even not finished after more than sixteen seconds. Also, the areas of interest at one-third and two-thirds of the route are visited many times, but always only briefly. The beginning, end, and center points are visited for much longer periods of time but not as often as the one-third point of the route.

7   Discussion and Limitations

In the following we discuss different aspects of the tool and reflect on current limitations.

7.1   Front-End and Back-End Decisions

The choice for both *Vuetify* and *Bokeh* seemed as a good option but during building the tool it was found that the library which could be used to connect the two easily was not available anymore. Therefore, the implementation of *Bokeh* in *Vuetify* did not go as smoothly as planned. A framework had to be built around *Bokeh* to get it to work nicely, which was very time-consuming. For future iterations we thus intent to use a different combination of front-end and back-end.

7.2   Performance

The *Flask* back-end of the visualization tool mostly uses *Python* to create the visualizations and to process the data. The data processing together with the calculation of data needed for the visualization takes a few seconds to complete. Switching between stimuli takes a couple of seconds while uploading a file can take 10 s and longer, depending on the size of the file. Although we have made improvements regarding the performance – for example, by implementing caching – the loading times can still be too slow. This problem could be fixed by switching to a faster back-end. This would, however, complicate making the visualizations with *Bokeh*, as the libraries are for a large part not compatible. After discussing performance issues we decided it would be best to try and improve our existing back-end instead of switching to faster options. This does mean the visualizations have a delayed response to the changing of settings, such as switching stimuli.

7.3   Uploading

As noted earlier, there are certain requirements for the `zip` file that can be uploaded. This `zip` file must contain a csv file with the collected data and a separate folder with images. Moreover, the column names and types of data in these columns need to match with specific requirements. This currently decreases the accessibility of the tool as users will have to convert their data in order to use it. Supporting more file types or providing a file format converter in the future will make the tool more accessible and user-friendly.

7.4   Interactions

As previously described there are multiple interactions implemented in the tool. Some of these interactions could be improved and some useful interactions are not yet supported in the tool. For example, saving the plot will download a `png` image of the plot in its current state but it does currently not show the parameter settings to recreate the picture. It is also not possible to save a picture of multiple plots in one view. *Bokeh* also has some limitations when it comes to implementing interactions. Similar to the saving aspect, there are other interactions that we believe could be improved upon or be added to the visualizations.

Also, only one image stimulus can be shown at the same time. This makes it more difficult for the user to compare two different stimuli. This can be a desired feature by the user if a dataset contains multiple slightly different stimuli such as in the use case earlier. Currently the user has to save the images and then can compare the two stimuli manually. Giving the user the option to show two stimuli at the same time below or next to each other would allow to draw more conclusions directly within the tool.

7.5   Interface

Some pages were re-designed a couple of times to improve their appearance. However, the page showing the visualizations still offers room for improvement. Especially, the scroll bar which is needed to see all the possible interaction methods is not ideal. Using more columns or resizing the views differently could be a solution for this. The part where the visualizations are shown could be smaller to give the interaction methods more space.

The less optimal look of the visualization page may decrease the user experience. Also, some parts of the visualization page may not be entirely straightforward. These aspects will need to be assessed in a user study to ensure that the usability and user experience matches the needs of the intended target audience.

7.6   Views

Four different views with the possibility to focus on different aspects of the data were implemented. Short explanations about the views are provided as well as information about how to interact with the views. Adding more views in a well-arranged format can make the web page more useful. By adding extra views, the user has more possibilities and can choose which views to use. Extra views can give the user more insight but may also cause confusion. Therefore, a good distinction between the views and a clear explanation of them is needed.

While the AOI timeline is useful for multiple participants at the same time it is not for selecting all participants at the same time. The difference between the scarf plot and the AOI timeline is therefore a bit smaller than previously expected. The scarf plot is useful for specific participants or a small group of participants while the AOI timeline is useful for a combination of a small group of participants.

8   Conclusion and Future Work

In this paper we proposed on online tool to assist with the analysis of eye tracking data. It includes different types of interactive visualizations. Customization options, such as being able to choose the clustering method, allow the users to analyze their data in different ways. The front-end design utilizes the same style and widgets as many popular websites and thus should be intuitive to navigate. Having said that, a user study still needs to be performed to assess the simplicity, usability, and practicality of the tool. Apart from this, future work will need to focus on performance to support a more responsive design and to reduce loading times. Four visualizations were included based on literature and our aim to offer different perspectives onto the data. However, future iterations could include more visualizations such as transition graphs (cf. [6]). Future work could also focus on including more interactions, such as hovering over a point to show relevant information for this point in all views, instead of just information in a single view. Similarly, simultaneously zooming could prove useful.

References

1. Bailly-Salins, I., Luga, H.: Artistic 3D object creation using artificial life paradigms. In: Butz, A., Fisher, B., Krüger, A., Olivier, P., Owada, S. (eds.) SG 2007. LNCS, vol. 4569, pp. 135–145. Springer, Heidelberg (2007). https://doi.org/10.1007/978-3-540-73214-3_12
2. Blascheck, T., Kurzhals, K., Raschke, M., Burch, M., Weiskopf, D., Ertl, T.: Visualization of eye tracking data: a taxonomy and survey: visualization of eye tracking data. Comput. Graph. Forum (2017). https://doi.org/10.1111/cgf.13079
3. Blignaut, P.J.: Visual span and other parameters for the generation of heatmaps. In: Morimoto, C.H., Istance, H.O., Hyrskykari, A., Ji, Q. (eds.) Proceedings of the 2010 Symposium on Eye-Tracking Research & Applications, ETRA 2010, Austin, Texas, USA, 22-24 March 2010, pp. 125–128. ACM (2010). https://doi.org/10.1145/1743666.1743697
4. Bojko, A.A.: Informative or misleading? Heatmaps deconstructed. In: Jacko, J.A. (ed.) HCI 2009. LNCS, vol. 5610, pp. 30–39. Springer, Heidelberg (2009). https://doi.org/10.1007/978-3-642-02574-7_4
5. Burch, M.: Time-preserving visual attention maps. In: Proceedings of Intelligent Decision Technologies, pp. 273–283 (2016)
6. Burch, M.: Interaction graphs: visual analysis of eye movement data from interactive stimuli. In: Krejtz, K., Sharif, B. (eds.) Proceedings of the 11th ACM Symposium on Eye Tracking Research & Applications, ETRA 2019, pp. 89:1–89:5. ACM (2019). https://doi.org/10.1145/3317960.3321617
7. Burch, M., Kumar, A., Mueller, K.: The hierarchical flow of eye movements. In: Proceedings of the 3rd Workshop on Eye Tracking and Visualization, ETVIS, pp. 3:1–3:5. ACM (2018)
8. Burch, M., Kumar, A., Timmermans, N.: An interactive web-based visual analytics tool for detecting strategic eye movement patterns. In: Proceedings of the 11th ACM Symposium on Eye Tracking Research & Applications (2019)

9. Burch, M., Netzel, R., Ohlhausen, B., Woods, R., Weiskopf, D.: User performance and reading strategies for metro maps: an eye tracking study. Spl Issue Eye Track. Spat. Res. Spat. Cogn. Comput. Interdisc. J. **17** (2016). https://doi.org/10.1080/13875868.2016.1226839

10. Burch, M., Timmermans, N.: Sankeye: a visualization technique for AOI transitions. In: Proceedings of the Symposium on Eye Tracking Research and Applications, ETRA, pp. 48:1–48:5. ACM (2020)

11. Burch, M., Veneri, A., Sun, B.: Eyeclouds: a visualization and analysis tool for exploring eye movement data. In: Proceedings of the 12th International Symposium on Visual Information Communication and Interaction. Association for Computing Machinery, New York (2019)

12. Duchowski, A.T., Price, M.M., Meyer, M.D., Orero, P.: Aggregate gaze visualization with real-time heatmaps. In: Morimoto, C.H., Istance, H.O., Spencer, S.N., Mulligan, J.B., Qvarfordt, P. (eds.) Proceedings of the 2012 Symposium on Eye-Tracking Research and Applications, ETRA 2012, Santa Barbara, CA, USA, 28–30 March 2012, pp. 13–20. ACM (2012)

13. Fuchs, A., Kaneko, C., Scudder, C.: Brainstem control of saccadic eye movements. Ann. Rev. Neurosci. **8**, 307–337 (1985). https://doi.org/10.1146/annurev.ne.08.030185.001515

14. Fukunaga, K., Hostetler, L.: The estimation of the gradient of a density function, with applications in pattern recognition. IEEE Trans. Inf. Theory **21**(1), 32–40 (1975)

15. Hessels, R.S., Kemner, C., van den Boomen, C., Hooge, I.T.C.: The area-of-interest problem in eyetracking research: a noise-robust solution for face and sparse stimuli. Behav. Res. Methods **48**(4), 1694–1712 (2015). https://doi.org/10.3758/s13428-015-0676-y

16. Holmqvist, K.: Eye Tracking: A Comprehensive Guide to Methods and Measures. Oxford University Press, Oxford (2011)

17. Lohse, G.L.: Consumer eye movement patterns on yellow pages advertising. J. Advertising **26**(1), 61–73 (1997)

18. Malzer, C., Baum, M.: A hybrid approach to hierarchical density-based cluster selection (2019)

19. Mather, G.: Foundations of Sensation and Perception. Psychology Press, London (2009)

20. Matlin, M., Farmer, T.: Cognition. Wiley, New York (2017)

21. Muñoz-Leiva, F., Hernández-Méndez, J., Gómez-Carmona, D.: Measuring advertising effectiveness in travel 2.0 websites through eye-tracking technology. Physiol. Behav. **200**, 83–95 (2019)

22. Nyström, M., Holmqvist, K.: An adaptive algorithm for fixation, saccade, and glissade detection in eyetracking data. Behav. Res. Methods **42**, 188–204 (2010)

23. Peysakhovich, V., Hurter, C., Telea, A.: Attribute-driven edge bundling for general graphs with applications in trail analysis. In: Liu, S., Scheuermann, G., Takahashi, S. (eds.) Proceedings of IEEE Pacific Visualization Symposium, PacificVis, pp. 39–46. IEEE Computer Society (2015)

24. Rosenbaum, D.: Human Motor Control. Elsevier Science, New York (2009)

25. Spakov, O., Miniotas, D.: Visualization of eye gaze data using heat maps. In: Electronics and Electrical Engineering 2, vol. 74, pp. 55–58 (2007)

26. Yi, J.S., Kang, Y., Stasko, J., Jacko, J.A.: Toward a deeper understanding of the role of interaction in information visualization. IEEE Trans. Visual. Comput. Graph. **13**(6), 1224–1231 (2007)

Influence of Peripheral Vibration Stimulus on Viewing and Response Actions

Takahiro Ueno and Minoru Nakayama$^{(\boxtimes)}$ (iD)

Tokyo Institute of Technology, Meguro, Tokyo 152-8552, Japan
nakayama@ict.e.titech.ac.jp

Abstract. Changes in perceptional performance and attention levels in response to vibration motion stimulus in the peripheral field of vision were observed experimentally. Viewers were asked to respond to the dual tasks of detecting a single peripheral vibration while viewing a consequence task in the central field of vision. A hierarchical Bayesian model was employed to extract the features of viewing behaviour from observed response data. The estimated parameters showed the correct answer rate tendency, vibration frequency dependence, and time series for covert attention. Also, the estimated frequency of microsaccades was an indicator of the temporal change in latent attention and the suppression of eye movement.

Keywords: Peripheral vision field · Visual attention · Eye movement · Bayesian model

1 Introduction

The human field of vision is classified into central and peripheral fields of vision using the distribution of retinal ganglion cells [1]. The properties of peripheral vision are quick response to motion, though other properties such as resolution, and object and colour recognition are inferior to the central field of vision [2]. These characteristics have been taken into account during the design of information displays which use peripheral vision perceptual ability to enhance viewing functions. Recently, this information has been used in the design of head mounted displays (HMD) [3–5].

Visual perception ability in the peripheral field of vision while viewing objects in the central field of vision is sometimes measured using responses to peripheral vibration stimuli. One study employed a set of peripheral vibration stimuli in 12 directional areas, and response ability was measured by the percentage of correct detection of stimuli [6]. The results suggested a difference in perception ability exists between the upper and lower fields of vision. If the difference in visual processing of area of vision or direction of vibration can be confirmed, the activity of the MT (middle temporal) field of the brain may be different, and

© Springer Nature Switzerland AG 2021
A. Del Bimbo et al. (Eds.): ICPR 2020 Workshops, LNCS 12663, pp. 420–428, 2021.
https://doi.org/10.1007/978-3-030-68796-0_30

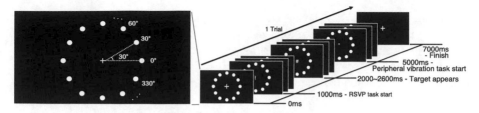

Fig. 1. Stimuli Presentation procedure

the difference may influence motion perception and eye movement because they are driven by MT activation [1].

Also, the level of visual attention and areas toward which attention is paid affect microsaccades, which appear during eye movement fixation, so that the latent visual attention may stimulate eye movement [7,8]. Therefore, the properties of eye movement may reflect the viewer's attention behaviour, including visual perception of stimuli in the peripheral field of vision.

This paper will address the relationship between peripheral vibration perception performance and eye movement behaviour during viewing, in order to examine the ability to respond to a task while paying attention to the peripheral field of vision. In this analysis, changes of microsaccade frequency are evaluated as a response to the level of visual attention.

2   Experiment

The experimental design was based on a previous study [6]. The experimental task consists of a dual task, namely the detection of an object using peripheral vibration while searching for numerical characters in the central field of vision, and a presentation diagram is shown in Fig. 1.

2.1   Visual Stimuli

The experiment's two tasks are defined as the central vision task and the peripheral vision task. The details are as follows.

- Task during central area of vision viewing: The central field of vision viewing task is based on a RSVP (Rapid Serial Visual Presentation) task where the object is to find single numerical characters from among randomised sequences of letters of the alphabet shown between 1000 and 7000 ms. The visual angles of a letter is 2.5° The target numerical characters appear 2 or 3 times between 2000 and 2600 ms.
- Peripheral field of vision viewing task: Twelve small dots (size: 2°) are placed on a circle (radius: 25° angle of vision) every 30°, and one of the dots is vibrated within a radius of 1px (0.054°) at 5 frequency levels (5, 10, 15, 20 and 25 Hz). The colour of the dots is white and background is black. All of

the dots are displayed during each trial, and the vibration appears between 5000 and 7000 ms. Subjects were asked to report the direction of vibration of the dot in relation to the centre orally.

Table 1. Percentage correct for peripheral task (%)

Angles	Frequency				
	5Hz	10Hz	15Hz	20Hz	25Hz
0°	100.0	100.0	100.0	94.1	68.4
30°	100.0	100.0	100.0	70.6	68.4
60°	100.0	100.0	88.9	70.0	15.8
90°	100.0	94.4	90.0	57.9	35.0
120°	100.0	100.0	90.0	83.3	70.0
150°	100.0	100.0	100.0	78.9	78.9
180°	100.0	100.0	100.0	100.0	84.2
210°	100.0	95.0	94.7	100.0	47.4
240°	100.0	100.0	100.0	61.1	66.7
270°	100.0	100.0	100.0	70.0	55.0
300°	95.0	100.0	94.7	85.0	75.0
330°	100.0	95.0	100.0	89.5	50.0
Means	99.6	98.7	96.5	80.0	59.6

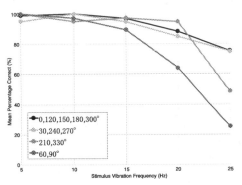

Fig. 2. Mean percentage correct by vibration frequency

2.2   Experimental Procedure

The experimental tasks were explained to all subjects, with the focus on the central field of vision task of viewing displays of characters in four trial exercises. The number of trials was 120 (12 directions × 5 levels × 2 trials), and these were divided into three sets with 5 min breaks between each set.

The stimulus was displayed on a 27 in. LCD monitor (EIZO:EV2736W-Z), with subjects 330 mm away from the monitor, and seated using a chin rest. Eye movements are measured 400 Hz using an eye tracker (Arrington:BCU400) in order to observe which regions are viewed by subjects, and to track microsaccades. The visual angles of the display were 84° × 54°

2.3   Subjects

Ten paid participants, who were aged between 21 and 22 (M = 9, F = 1) and possessed sufficient visual acuity and colour perception, took part in this experiment. All subjects participated in an instruction session before the experiment and provided their written consent in order to participate.

3   Results

In the results, 1200 trials were recorded, but 41 of these were omitted because the eye movement responses were outside the range of measurement of the experiment.

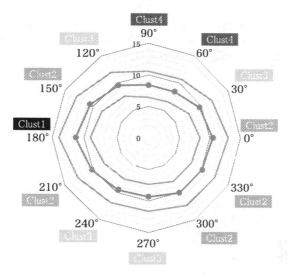

Fig. 3. Posterior distribution of parameters for directional angle PO

3.1 Percentage Correct of the Task of Peripheral Field of Vision Viewing

The ability to view objects in the peripheral field of vision is evaluated using the percentage of correct responses to the peripheral task. The results are summarised in Table 1. The table shows a tendency for the rate of correct responses to decrease as the frequency of vibration in all directions increases. In order to reduce the dimension of direction, a cluster analysis was applied to the percentage of correct responses using a k-means method. Four clusters were extracted with colour labels, as shown in Fig. 2. The mean percentages for the four clusters are summarised in Fig. 2. The relationship between the clusters is still unclear

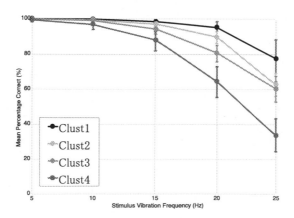

Fig. 4. Frequency dependence of each cluster

because the order of the correct response rates is not simple. As some experimental factors may interact with each other, a statistical modelling technique is introduced to diminish the influence of these factors [10]. Details of the modelling procedure, which uses a hierarchical Bayesian model, are explained in the following section.

3.2 Hierarchical Bayesian Modelling

The mean percentage of correct responses (θ) is hypothesised as binary data Y using a Bernoulli distribution, as shown in the following Eq., (1).

$$Y \sim Bernoulli\,(\theta) \tag{1}$$

The independent variables for the percentage correct (θ) are also hypothesised as follows: the fixed effect of vibration frequency F, the variable effect of the factor of direction PO, the individual factor rID, and the order effect rTR. Logit function is introduced as a link function, as shown in the Eq., (2). Here, β_1 is a coefficient for F.

$$logit\,(\theta) = \beta_1 \times F + PO + rID + rTR \tag{2}$$

Distributions of these variables are given as normal distributions, and both the similarity between neighbours and the differential relationship are considered to be the factor of direction and the order effect in the experiment. The factor of direction is defined as $i = 0, \ldots, 12$. Also, the individual factor has a common deviation and the overall mean is set to 0. The variables can be noted as follows:

$$PO_i \sim Normal\,(PO_{i-1}, sPO)\,(i = 1, 2, \ldots, 12)$$
$$rID_j \sim Normal\,(0, sID)\,(j = 1, 2, \ldots, 10)$$
$$rTR_k \sim Normal\,(rTR_{k-1}, sTr)\,(k = 1, 2, \ldots, 120) \tag{3}$$

Model parameters were estimated using the Markov Chain Monte Carlo technique, and EAP (estimated as a posterior) estimation was used to calculate the mean of the parameter samples obtained from between 500 and 4000 periods in each of the four independent MCMC chains. The convergence of the calculation was evaluated using the index ($\widehat{R} \leq 1.1$).

The estimated parameters for the distribution of posterior probability for the factor of direction PO are summarised in Fig. 3. The magnitude of the parameters indicates the contribution of the effect. The factors for direction are classified into four groups ("Clust1"–"Clust4") using cluster analysis based on the k-means method. These groups are indicated in Fig. 3. Mean percentage correct, which is based on the estimated parameters, is summarised in Fig. 4. The plots indicate the median of each distribution and the error bars indicate the confidence interval of 95%. The overall tendencies for the rate of percentage correct to be the highest for vibration in a leftward horizontal direction, and for the rates for both the upper and lower fields of vision to be the lowest is confirmed. These results clearly emphasise this tendency when compared to the results in Fig. 2.

3.3   Analysis of Microsaccades

Attention levels during viewing behaviour were estimated using the frequency of microsaccades. The experimental frequencies were extracted from eye movement observations using Microsaccade toolbox [9]. The observed frequency Y_t is calculated each 100 ms, and the temporal changes are summarised in Fig. 5.

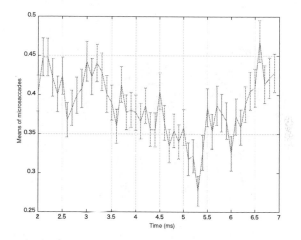

Fig. 5. Temporal change of appearance of microsaccades

The observed temporal microsaccade frequency is defined using a state space model. A parameter μ is defined as a state variable with white noise which is defined as the normal distribution $N(0, \sigma_\eta^2)$. The frequency of observation y_t consists of the state μ and the measurement error ε_t is defined as another normal distribution $N(0, \sigma_\varepsilon^2)$. Using these definitions, the microsaccade frequency Y_t at time t is estimated using a Poisson distribution. The formulae can be noted as follows:

$$\mu_{t+1} = \mu_t + \eta_t, \quad \eta_t \sim Normal\left(0, \sigma_\eta^2\right)$$
$$log(y_t) = \mu_t + \varepsilon_t, \quad \varepsilon_t \sim Normal\left(0, \sigma_\varepsilon^2\right)$$
$$Y_t \sim Poisson\left(y_t\right) \tag{4}$$

All parameters were also estimated using the previous procedure for estimating the parameters. The estimated microsaccade frequencies for the levels of attention during the experimental task and during viewing were extracted. The temporal change is summarised in Fig. 6. The vertical axis indicates the EAP values corresponding to the frequency of microsaccades noted as $\exp(EAP)$. The bold line indicates the median of the distribution and the grey zone indicates where the confidence interval is 95%. The initial period, which is illustrated in blue, indicates the first task in the central field of vision between 2000 and 2600 ms. The red area indicates the start of the peripheral viewing task around

5000 ms. The frequency of microsaccades drops off after the two task events, which suggests that level of attention paid to the tasks suppresses the frequency of microsaccades. In regards to the above results, the estimated frequency of microsaccades may reflect the level of attention during viewing both the central and peripheral fields of vision.

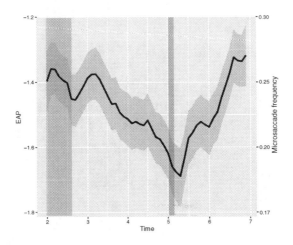

Fig. 6. Temporal change of estimated MS frequency

4   Discussion

In the results of the experiment, the percentage of correct detection of the peripheral vibration direction of origin decreases with the frequency of the vibration. The same tendency is shown in the results of statistical estimation, and the influence of both the upper and lower fields of vision is clearly emphasised using the estimated parameters for the factor of direction. The spatial distribution of parameters of the factor of direction seems to be a flat ellipse, and it shifts to the left of centre. This bias may appear in response to the neuron activity in the MT area of the brain, which exerts dominance for motion in specific directions [1]. However, the mechanism of the bias and its influence should be examined carefully in a further experiment. Since the subjects react to a peripheral stimulus vibrating in a radial direction, the vibration may be perceived as directional motion.

Additionally, the frequency suppression of microsaccades can be an index of the level of attention for visual stimuli. This occurs between 2000 and 2600 ms after the appearance of the stimuli in the central field of vision begins, and just after the peripheral vibration begins at 5000 ms. Also, the frequency decreases between 3000 and 5000 ms, after the appearance of the previous suppression. As the microsaccade frequency may reflect latent levels of attention, such as mental workload or expectation, the estimated information shows the situation change of the viewer's mental processing.

5   Conclusion

In this study, eye movement and microsaccades were analysed in order to evaluate perceptional response and attention behaviour during the appearance of peripheral vibration stimulus. The following points were examined:

1. In order to evaluate perceptional performance during peripheral vibration, correct responses were extracted as factor contributions using a hierarchical Bayesian model with fixed and variable effects. Also, the peripheral regions were classified into four fields of vision using cluster analysis. The results suggest that both the upper and lower fields of vision have relatively lower rates of correct response depending on the frequency of the vibration.
2. The frequency of temporal microsaccades during the experiment progress was estimated as the level of attention of the viewer using a state space model. The estimated frequency shows the temporal change in latent attention and the suppression of eye movement. In particular, the effect was significant after the appearance of the stimuli.

Various stimuli presented in the peripheral field of vision may affect both attention levels and eye movement behaviour during the viewing of specific information. A detailed analysis of this will be the subject of our further study.

Acknowledgement. This research was partially supported by the Japan Society for the Promotion of Science (JSPS), Grant-in-Aid for Scientific Research (KAKEN, 20H01718: 2020–2022).

References

1. Vision Society of Japan (ed.): Sikaku Jyouhou Syori Handbook. Asakura Shoten, Tokyo, Japan (2000)
2. Fukuda, T.: The functional difference between central vision and peripheral vision in motion perception. J. ITE-J **33**(6), 479–484 (1979)
3. Kishishita, N., Orlosky, J., Kiyokawa, K., Mashita, T., Takemura, H.: Investigation on the peripheral visual field for information display with wide-view see-through HMDs. Trans. VRSJ. **19**(2), 121–130 (2014)
4. Ishiguro, Y., Rekimoto, J.: Peripheral vision annotation: noninterference information presentation method by using gaze information. J. IPSJ **53**(4), 1328–1337 (2012)
5. Matsui, K., Nakamura, S.: Influence on time evaluation by presenting visual stimulus in peripheral vision. J. IPSJ **59**(3), 970–978 (2018)
6. Shimura, M., Suzuki, H., Shimomura, Y., Katuura, T.: Perception of visual motions stimulation in peripheral vision during eye fixation. Jpn. J. Physiol. Anthropol. **20**(2), 95–102 (2015)
7. Endo, S., Kohama, T., Noguchi, D.: Continuous inhibition of microsaccades in attentional concentration. ITE Tech. Report **37**(12), 51–54 (2013)
8. Engbert, R., Kliegl, R.: Microsaccades uncover the orientation of covert attention. Vision Res. **43**(9), 1035–1045 (2003)

9. Engbert, R., Sinn, P., Mergenthaler, K., Trukenbrod, H.: Microsaccade toolbox 0.9. (2015). http://read.psych.uni-potsdam.de
10. Kubo, T.: Introduction to Statistical Modelling for Data Analysis. Iwanami Shoten, Tokyo, Japan (2012)

Judging Qualification, Gender, and Age of the Observer Based on Gaze Patterns When Looking at Faces

Pawel Kasprowski[1]([envelope]) [iD], Katarzyna Harezlak[1] [iD], Piotr Fudalej[2] [iD],
and Pawel Fudalej[3]

[1] Silesian University of Technology, Akademicka 16, Gliwice, Poland
pawel.kasprowski@polsl.pl
[2] Department of Orthodontics and Dentofacial Orthopedics, School of Dental
Medicine, University of Bern, Bern, Switzerland
[3] Private Practice, Warsaw, Poland

Abstract. The research aimed to compare eye movement patterns of people looking at faces with different but subtle teeth imperfections. Both non-specialists and dental experts took part in the experiment. The research outcome includes the analysis of eye movement patterns depending on the specialization, gender, age, face gender, and level of teeth deformation. The study was performed using a novel, not widely explored features of eye movements, derived from recurrence plots and Gaze Self Similarity Plots. It occurred that most features are significantly different for laypeople and specialists. Significant differences were also found for gender and age among the observers. There were no differences found when comparing the gender of the face being observed and levels of imperfection. Interestingly, it was possible to define which features are sensitive to gender and which to qualification.

Keywords: Eye tracking · Gaze patterns · Faces observation · Age estimation

1 Introduction

By registering eye movements of people observing images, it is possible to obtain much interesting information. On the one hand, it is possible to learn something about the observers - their knowledge, intentions, anxiety, etc. On the other side, by registering eye movements of several observers looking at the same image, it is also possible to learn something about the picture - if the content is interesting, shocking, which parts of the image are the most interesting, etc.

This work was supported by Silesian University of Technology, Rector's Pro-Quality Grant Number: 02/100/RGJ20/0002 and Statutory Research funds of Department of Applied Informatics, Silesian University of Technology, Gliwice, Poland (02/100/BK_20/0003).

A. Del Bimbo et al. (Eds.): ICPR 2020 Workshops, LNCS 12663, pp. 429–439, 2021.
https://doi.org/10.1007/978-3-030-68796-0_31

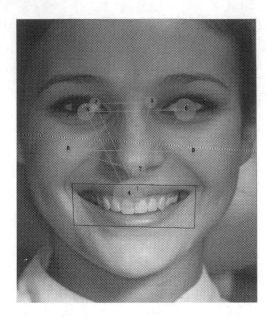

Fig. 1. A scan-path of a typical face observation

Registering eye movements while observing other people's faces is one of the most popular experiments because face observing patterns are very specific for humans. The ability to follow and analyze somebody's face is one of the first skills achieved by a newborn baby. During our whole life, we train observation of faces to recognize people's intentions, moods, etc. Lack of this ability may be considered a severe disadvantage. The analysis of eye movement patterns during face observation has been used to diagnose autism [4] or Alzheimer's disease [12]. The pattern is also supposed to be idiosyncratic [3,8], different for races [2] and age [11], and changes if the observer knows the face being observed [7].

It is well known that people typically start by looking at the other people's eyes and then look at the mouth and nose area. It is called a 'face triangle'. However, subtle differences in this pattern may reveal information about the observer and the face being observed. It is the central assumption of the research described in this paper. We presented faces of people with and without various teeth imperfections to two groups of participants: dentists and non-specialists without any connection with dentistry. Contrary to the previous research that showed that people tend to look longer at teeth when imperfections are visible [9], this time, the differences were subtle and barely distinguishable even for specialists.

Our first assumption was that eye movement patterns of dentists and laypeople will be distinguishable. We also expected that eye movement patterns would depend on the level of teeth imperfections - especially for the dentists' group. At the same time, we wanted to explore if the eye movement patterns depend on the gender and age of both people being observed and observers.

Many papers show differences in eye movement patterns between novices and specialists, e.g., radiographers [10], or chess experts [13]. Some works were also devoted to the dentists' gaze patterns - e.g., when they looked at CT images [14]. However, to the best of our knowledge, there was no published research concerning differences between non-specialists and dentists while looking at face images. In the case of gender, some evidence of different women's and men's gaze patterns has been shown in [5] - which revealed that women are better at recognizing familiar faces.

However, most papers cited above compared gaze patterns using only traditional criteria such as the number and duration of fixations and area of interest (AOI) analysis. Our paper analyses also additional, relatively new, and unexplored measures based on recurrence plots [1] and Gaze Self-Similarity Plots [6]. Therefore, this paper's contribution is two-fold: (1) it explores the previously unchecked problem of comparing dentists with laypeople when looking at faces, and (2) it introduces novel and yet unexplored techniques to perform this comparison.

2   Methods and Material

The experimental design consisted of a presentation of 48 human faces with three levels of dental imperfections (16 faces for each level). Every face was presented for 6 s. The participants' task was to just freely observe the pictures and try to judge the attractiveness of the person being observed.

The same presentation was shown to 53 participants, including 25 non-specialists and 28 dental specialists. Participants' eye movements were recorded during each trial utilizing The Eye Tribe eye tracker with 60 Hz sampling rate. It gave about 360 subsequent gaze points for each 6-s recording - called an *observation* in the subsequent text.

The data registered during the experiment were analyzed to remove observations with improper gaze points (e.g., when a person closed eyes for some time or turned away her eyes). Observations for which there were less than 250 gaze points were removed from the dataset. Finally, 1883 observations were available for further analyses, including 929 observations of specialists and 954 observations of non-specialists. The dataset consisted of 654 observations from women and 1229 from males, and 1188 observations of female faces and 695 observations of male faces.

Every image of the face used during the experiment was processed to define two areas of interest (AOI): mouth and incisor teeth. The time to gaze at these AOIs and the overall time of staring at them were calculated for each observation. Additionally, typical eye movement signal properties such as fixation number and average fixation duration were measured.

The next step was the calculation of four measures used to quantify eye movement recordings based on the recurrence plot defined in [1]. Given a sequence of N fixations:

- **Recurrence** represents the percentage of recurrent fixations (i.e., how often the observer refixates previously fixated image positions).
- **Determinism** represents repeating fixation patterns.
- **Laminarity** measures how often the same areas of a scene are repeatedly fixated.
- **Center of recurrence mass** (CORM) measures how close the recurrent fixations points are situated.

Due to space limits, we do not present details about the way these four measures are calculated, which may be found in [1].

The next group of measures included the features derived from Gaze Self Similarity Plots (GSSP) [6]. At first, the co-occurrence matrix was calculated for every GSSP, and then the contrast, homogeneity, and uniformity were calculated.

- **Homogeneity** gives information to what extend nearby gazes are placed in similar locations.
- **Contrast** reveals long jumps (saccades) from one gaze point to another.
- **Uniformity** measures gaze pairs repetitions. It is high when the GSSP contains similar areas, which means that the same paired values with the same arrangement repeatedly appear in the image.

All three features were calculated for $[1, 1]$ offset. Please refer to [6] for calculation details.

The last group of features included the coverage - the whole image was divided into $N \times N$ areas and the **coverageN** was calculated using the Eq. 1.

$$COV_N = \frac{\sum_i^N \sum_j^N \left(\exists Fix \in area(i,j)\right)?1:0}{N \times N} \tag{1}$$

All examined features are summarized in Table 1.

3   Results

The research aimed to check if some particular observer's features influence the way the image is being observed. The second aim was to check if the content of the image influences gaze patterns. Therefore, we defined three independent features describing the observer: qualification, gender, and age and two independent features describing the image: the level of imperfection and *imgGender* - gender of a person on the image (see Table 1). It was first checked if there are statistically significant differences in these groups for dependent variables (all gaze-related features). According to the Kolmogorov-Smirnov test, all variables were normally distributed. Therefore, for variables with only two possible values (*qualification, gender* and *imgGender*) the t-Student test was used, and for variables with more than two possible values (age and level) the ANOVA test was used with Bonferroni correction. For the sake of readability, values of the homogeneity and uniformity were multiplied by $10e3$ and $10e5$, respectively.

Table 1. The features taken into account.

Feature	Description
	Independent features
gender	Gender of the observer
age	Age of the observer
qual	Qualification of the observer (layman, specialist)
level	Level of imperfection (1–3)
imgGender	Gender of a person on the image
	Gaze related features
fixNum	Number of fixations
fixAvgDur	Average fixation duration
sacAvgLen	Average saccade length
sacLen	Summary of saccades length
mouthTimeto	Time before focusing the mouth AOI
mouthTime	The overall time of gazing at mouth AOI
incisTimeTo	Time before focusing the incisors AOI
incisTime	The overall time of gazing at incisors AOI
rec	Reccurence
det	Determination
lam	Laminarity
corm	Center of recurrence mass
coverage5	Coverage of the image in 5×5 grid
coverage7	Coverage of the image in 7×7 grid
coverage10	Coverage of the image in 10×10 grid
contrast	GSSP contrast
homog	GSSP homogeneity
uniformity	GSSP uniformity

3.1 Observer Related Variables

The results analysis starts with discussing features related to the observer, namely: qualification, gender, and age.

Qualification. We verified the hypothesis that eye movement patterns are different for specialists and laypeople. Average values of features and standard deviations were calculated, and then the t-Student test was used to decide if the differences are significant. As it is visible in Table 2, this hypothesis has been confirmed as nearly all analyzed features (apart from *fixAvgDur*) occurred to be significantly different between groups.

Table 2. Features values - differences for laypeople and specialists.

Feature	Laymen	Specialists	t(1883)	p-value	
fixNum	14,6	15,4	−3,289	0,001	**
fixAvgDur	345,9	359,4	−0,704	0,482	
sacAvgLen	6,9	4,7	20,024	0	***
sacLen	100,2	70,6	14,976	0	***
mouthTimeto	2253,2	1054	14,12	0	***
mouthTime	986	1977,4	−14,818	0	***
incisTimeto	3991,3	2574,8	13,573	0	***
incistime	428,5	962,7	−10,353	0	***
rec	13,1	21,3	−12,178	0	***
det	30,8	46,1	−9,167	0	***
lam	51,6	80,4	−14,702	0	***
corm	4,8	8,1	−8,822	0	***
coverage5	0,21	0,17	13,204	0	***
coverage7	0,14	0,11	11,043	0	***
coverage10	0,08	0,07	10,17	0	***
contrast	102,4	186,6	7,23	0	***
homog	332,3	290,6	13,25	0	***
uniformity	202,4	220,3	−2,18	0,03	*

It is not surprising that for the chosen AOIs (mouth and teeth), the observation is longer, and *timeto* values are shorter for specialists. However, it is interesting to notice that other features exhibit significant differences as well. The only exception is *uniformity*, which is similar for both groups.

Gender. The next research question was if the eye movement patterns depend on the gender of the observer. As was already stated in the Introduction, it has been confirmed previously for other datasets. As there were significant differences between specialists and laypeople, we decided to perform the t-Student test independently for both groups. The results are presented in Table 3 and Table 4. There are significant differences in most features depend on the observer's gender in both groups.

Interestingly this time, contrary to the previous case, the values of *recurrence* and *contrast* are not significantly different, while the *uniformity* may be considered as a feature that can reliably distinguish both genders.

Age of the Observer. Observers were divided into four groups differing with age: (20–30, 30–40, 40–50, 50+). It occurred that for most features the result of

Table 3. Gender differences for non-specialists.

Feature	Female	Male	t(954)	p-value	
fixNum	12,9	15,6	−10,36	0	***
fixAvgLen	422,7	297,5	9,85	0	***
sacAvgLen	7,4	6,6	4,32	0	***
sacLen	95,5	103,2	−2,62	0,01	**
mouthTimeTo	2051,8	2380,2	−2,35	0,02	*
mouthTime	1409,1	719,2	8,31	0	***
incisTimeTo	4076	3937,9	0,93	0,35	
incisTime	587,1	328,4	4,35	0	***
rec	13,4	13	0,57	0,57	
det	27,9	32,7	−2,17	0,03	*
lam	39	59,5	−7,73	0	***
corm	5,3	4,5	2,73	0,01	**
coverage5	0,2	0,22	−4,02	0	***
coverage7	0,13	0,14	−4,52	0	***
coverage10	0,08	0,08	−4,1	0	***
contrast	90,1	110,2	−1,76	0,08	
homog	372,6	306,8	19,62	0	***
uniformity	236,12	181,1	5,89	0	***

ANOVA test revealed significant differences: $F(3, 1883) > 4.8, p < 0.01$. Only for *corm* feature the effect was less significant with $F(3, 1883) = 3.268, p = 0.021$.

3.2 Image Properties

The second group of properties included properties related to the observed image - the different level of imperfection (*level*) and the gender of a person on the image (*imgGender*). However, this time neither the ANOVA test conducted for *level* nor t-Student test performed for *imgGender* showed significant differences in the results (Table 5).

3.3 Classification

Disclosing the importance of differences in eye movement features for specialists and non-specialists, males and females, and the observer's age was the motivation factor to verify the possibility of identifying the observer's qualifications based on his/her visual pattern during a single observation of a face.

For this purpose, we applied a simple k-nearest neighbor algorithm with $k = 7$. The algorithm predicts the given observation's class based on the classification of k nearest training observations. The model was tested using classic

Table 4. Gender differences for specialists.

Feature	Female	Male	t(954)	p-value	
fixNum	13	16,4	−7,69	0	***
fixavgDur	662,8	225,1	8,67	0	***
sacAvgLen	5,2	4,5	4,39	0	***
sacLen	72,1	70	0,65	0,52	
mouthTimeTo	893,3	1125,2	−2,1	0,04	*
mouthTime	2997	1526,1	11,58	0	***
incisTimeTo	2359,8	2669,9	−1,87	0,06	
incisTime	1452,6	745,8	6,56	0	***
rec	21,9	20,9	0,76	0,45	
det	34,7	51,1	−6,47	0	***
lam	66,6	86,5	−6,66	0	***
corm	10,3	7,2	3,27	0	**
coverage5	0,16	0,17	−1,77	0,08	
coverage7	0,11	0,11	−2,49	0,01	*
coverage10	0,06	0,07	−3,45	0	***
contrast	167,6	194,9	−1,25	0,21	
homog	334,2	271,3	13,36	0	***
uniformity	295,8	186,8	7,07	0	***

10-fold cross-validation repeated ten times. The results presented in Table 6 confirm the previous findings that the observer's qualification and gender may be estimated using the features defined in Table 1.

The last test was an attempt to predict the observer's age. The task was more difficult than the previous ones because it was 1 out of 4 classification. The confusion matrix for the dataset is presented in Table 7. It may be noticed that the best results were obtained for the participants belonging to the group 40–50. However, the overall accuracy was about 58%.

4   Summary

The research presented in this paper aimed to analyze if and how eye movement features depend on the properties of a person being examined and the properties of the image being observed. The detailed analysis confirmed that significant differences in eye movement patterns might be found for qualification and gender. Probably the most interesting finding was that *contrast* and *homogeneity* proved to be useful in differentiating the level of expertise, while *uniformity* depended on the gender of a person.

Table 5. Features values for images containing women and men (*imgGender*) - the results for specialists.

Feature	Female	Male	t(929)	p-value	
fixNum	15,4	15,3	0,39	0,7	
fixavgDur	357,9	361,9	−0,11	0,91	
sacAvgLen	4,8	4,5	1,87	0,06	
sacLen	72,8	66,8	2,21	0,03	*
mouthTimeTo	1098,3	977,4	1,14	0,26	
mounthTme	1910,2	2093,8	−1,58	0,11	
incisTimeTo	2655,8	2434,4	1,41	0,16	
incisTime	918,6	1039	−1,28	0,2	
rec	20,9	21,8	−0,74	0,46	
det	46,3	45,8	0,18	0,86	
lam	81,4	78,8	0,86	0,39	
corm	8	8,4	−0,63	0,53	
coverage5	0,17	0,16	1,81	0,07	
coverage7	0,11	0,11	−0,19	0,85	
coverage10	0,07	0,07	0,84	0,4	
contrast	177,8	201,8	−1,08	0,28	
homog	289,1	293,2	−0,84	0,4	
uniformity	219,2	221,4	−0,17	0,86	

Table 6. Results of classification for all two-class features.

Feature	Accuracy	Precision	Recall	F1-score
qual	79,4%	80,8%	78,1%	79,4%
qual/fem	86,4%	85,9%	83,4%	84,7%
qual/male	78,3%	79,8%	78,9%	79,4%
gender	77,6%	86,8%	80,4%	83,5%
gender/lay	80,6%	84,6%	83,9%	84,2%
gender/spec	78,4%	90,6%	80,7%	85,4%
imGen	57,0%	21,2%	35,9%	26,7%
imGen/spec	59,2%	27,1%	41,2%	32,7%
imGen/lay	57,5%	22,2%	37,9%	28,0%

It was impossible to find any significant dependencies regarding the type of an image - probably because the images represented the same kind of stimulus (face) and were characterized by similar features.

Table 7. Confusion matrix for age classification for non-specialists.

	20–30	30–40	40–50	50+
20–30	108	50	21	9
30–40	88	211	34	27
40–50	19	18	220	4
50+	2	8	2	35

The main limitation of the presented results is the vague meaning of the novel features being analyzed. The semantics of the presented REC and GSSP features is for now not clear. More studies of these features are necessary to define what they represent precisely. The research presented in this paper shows the meaningfulness of these features; however, their values are still not as easy to interpret as average fixation duration or AOI gazing time.

Future work will include tests using other datasets and more in-depth analysis of the novel features. It is planned to check if these features could be used to distinguish a type of observed images or to identify people.

Acknowledgement. This work was supported by Silesian University of Technology, Rector's Pro-Quality Grant No: 02/100/RGJ20/0002 and Statutory Research funds of Department of Applied Informatics, Grant No: 02/100/BK_20/0003.

References

1. Anderson, N.C., Bischof, W.F., Laidlaw, K.E., Risko, E.F., Kingstone, A.: Recurrence quantification analysis of eye movements. Behav. Res. Methods **45**(3), 842–856 (2013)
2. Blais, C., Jack, R.E., Scheepers, C., Fiset, D., Caldara, R.: Culture shapes how we look at faces. PloS One **3**(8), e3022 (2008)
3. Cantoni, V., Galdi, C., Nappi, M., Porta, M., Riccio, D.: GANT: gaze analysis technique for human identification. Pattern Recogn. **48**(4), 1027–1038 (2015)
4. Dalton, K.M., et al.: Gaze fixation and the neural circuitry of face processing in autism. Nature Neurosci. **8**(4), 519–526 (2005)
5. Hall, J.K., Hutton, S.B., Morgan, M.J.: Sex differences in scanning faces: Does attention to the eyes explain female superiority in facial expression recognition? Cognit. Emotion **24**(4), 629–637 (2010)
6. Kasprowski, P., Harezlak, K.: Gaze self-similarity plot-a new. J. Eye Mov. Res. **10**(3), 1–14 (2017)
7. Kasprowski, P.: Mining of eye movement data to discover people intentions. In: Kozielski, S., Mrozek, D., Kasprowski, P., Małysiak-Mrozek, B., Kostrzewa, D. (eds.) BDAS 2014. CCIS, vol. 424, pp. 355–363. Springer, Cham (2014). https://doi.org/10.1007/978-3-319-06932-6_34
8. Kasprowski, P., Harezlak, K.: The second eye movements verification and identification competition. In: IEEE International Joint Conference on Biometrics (IJCB), pp. 1–6. IEEE (2014)

9. Kasprowski, P., Harezlak, K., Fudalej, P., Fudalej, P.: Examining the impact of dental imperfections on scan-path patterns. In: Czarnowski, I., Howlett, R.J., Jain, L.C. (eds.) IDT 2017. SIST, vol. 73, pp. 278–286. Springer, Cham (2018). https://doi.org/10.1007/978-3-319-59424-8_26
10. Kasprowski, P., Harezlak, K., Kasprowska, S.: Development of diagnostic performance & visual processing in different types of radiological expertise. In: Proceedings of the 2018 ACM Symposium on Eye Tracking Research & Applications, p. 40. ACM (2018)
11. Liu, S., Quinn, P.C., Wheeler, A., Xiao, N., Ge, L., Lee, K.: Similarity and difference in the processing of same-and other-race faces as revealed by eye tracking in 4-to 9-month-olds. J. Exp. Child Psychol. **108**(1), 180–189 (2011)
12. Mendez, M.F., Mendez, M., Martin, R., Smyth, K.A., Whitehouse, P.J.: Complex visual disturbances in Alzheimer's disease. Neurology **40**(3 Part 1), 439–439 (1990)
13. Reingold, E.M., Charness, N., Pomplun, M., Stampe, D.M.: Visual span in expert chess players: evidence from eye movements. Psychol. Sci. **12**(1), 48–55 (2001)
14. Suwa, K., Furukawa, A., Matsumoto, T., Yosue, T.: Analyzing the eye movement of dentists during their reading of CT images. Odontology **89**(1), 0054–0061 (2001)

Gaze Stability During Ocular Proton Therapy: Quantitative Evaluation Based on Eye Surface Surveillance Videos

Rosalinda Ricotti[1]([✉]) [iD], Andrea Pella[1], Giovanni Elisei[1], Barbara Tagaste[1],
Federico Bello[1], Giulia Fontana[1], Maria Rosaria Fiore[2], Mario Ciocca[3],
Edoardo Mastella[3], Ester Orlandi[2], and Guido Baroni[1,4]

[1] Bioengineering Unit, Clinical Department, National Center for Oncological Hadrontherapy
(CNAO), Strada Campeggi, 53, 27100 Pavia, Italy
{rosalinda.ricotti,andrea.pella,giovanni.elisei,barbara.tagaste,
federico.bello,giulia.fontana,guido.baroni}@cnao.it,
rosalinda.ricotti@gmail.com

[2] Radiation Oncology, Clinical Department, National Center for Oncological Hadrontherapy
(CNAO), Pavia, Italy
{mariarosaria.fiore,ester.orlandi}@cnao.it

[3] Medical Physics Unit, Clinical Department, National Center for Oncological Hadrontherapy
(CNAO), Pavia, Italy
{mario.ciocca,edoardo.mastella}@cnao.it

[4] Department of Electronics, Information and Bioengineering, Politecnico di Milano University,
Milan, Italy

Abstract. Ocular proton therapy (OPT) is acknowledged as a therapeutic option
for the treatment of ocular melanomas. OPT clinical workflow is deeply based on
x-ray image guidance procedures, both for treatment planning and patient setup
verification purposes. An optimized eye orientation relative to the proton beam
axis is determined during treatment planning and it is reproduced during treatment by focusing the patient gaze on a fixation light conveniently positioned in
space. Treatment geometry verification is routinely performed through stereoscopic radiographic images while real time patient gaze reproducibility is qualitatively monitored by visual control of eye surface images acquired by dedicated
optical cameras. We described an approach to quantitatively evaluate the stability
of patients' gaze direction over an OPT treatment course at the National Centre of Oncological Hadrontherapy (Centro Nazionale di Adroterapia Oncologica,
CNAO, Pavia, Italy).

Pupil automatic segmentation procedure was implemented on eye surveillance
videos of five patients recorded during OPT. Automatic pupil detection performance was benchmarked against manual pupil contours of four different clinical
operators. Stability of patients' gaze direction was quantified. 2D distances were
expressed as percentage of the reference pupil radius.

R. Ricotti and A. Pella—Contributed equally to this study and should be con-sidered as co-first
authors.

A. Del Bimbo et al. (Eds.): ICPR 2020 Workshops, LNCS 12663, pp. 440–452, 2021.
https://doi.org/10.1007/978-3-030-68796-0_32

Valuable approximation between circular fitting and manual contours was observed. Inter-operator manual contours 2D distances were in median (interquartile range) 3.3% (3.6%) of the of the reference pupil radius. The median (interquartile range) of 2D distances between the automatic segmentations and the manual contours was 5.0% (5.3) of the of the reference pupil radius. Stability of gaze direction varied across patients with median values ranging between 6.6% and 16.5% of reference pupil radius.

The measured pupil displacement on the camera field of view were clinically acceptable. Further developments are necessary to reach a real-time clip-less quantification of eye during OPT.

Keywords: Ocular proton therapy · Gaze detection · Eye tracking

1 Introduction

Ocular proton therapy (OPT) is acknowledged as a favorable therapeutic option for the treatment of ocular melanomas, especially for lesions located close to organs at risk such as macula and optic disk [1–4].

OPT clinical workflow makes extensive use of image guidance procedures, regardless the different technological methodologies adopted for delivering OPT [5]. The localization of the target volume during treatment planning and dose delivery is indirectly addressed by the surgical implantation of radiopaque tantalum clips on the eye globe surface prior to the irradiation [6]. As reported in a recent publication [5], reference clips are usually sutured in close proximity of the tumor site. Anatomical measurements of the diseased eye and the location of the implanted clips are processed by a dedicated treatment planning system (TPS), that computes the optimal gaze direction (expressed in polar/azimuth angles), in order to maximize the dose distribution inside the target volume, while sparing as much as possible the surrounding organs at risk [7]. The patient actively participates during set-up and irradiation by looking at a fixation light, conveniently positioned in space in order to reproduce the planned gaze alignment. At the time of treatment, proper alignment of the eye is verified and iteratively corrected using repeated radiographic imaging of the tantalum clips current configuration. In parallel, gaze reproducibility is qualitatively monitored by visual control of eye surface images acquired by dedicated optical cameras. Clinical operators outline convenient ocular features on a reference eye image to detect eventual eye misalignments or shifts during irradiation. In case of eye misalignment during treatment, beam delivery is manually gated off [5].

Alongside the described common clinical practice, systems and procedures for non-invasive and quantitative monitoring of eye motion during OPT have been investigated. These strategies mainly implement the feature extraction technique to localize in space and/or to quantitatively monitor the stability of the gaze during OPT treatments [8–11]. In addition, more sophisticated approaches provide the tridimensional position and orientation of the monitored eye through the analysis of specific ocular features extracted from the video images captured by two optical cameras (in particular pupil center and cornea center of curvature). These parameters may be used to arrange a coordinate frame rigidly attached to the eyeball, thus providing absolute eye localization for treatment geometry verification [12–17].

The National Centre of Oncological Hadrontherapy (Centro Nazionale di Adroterapia Oncologica, CNAO, Pavia, Italy) has introduced an OPT treatment protocol for intraocular lesions since August 2016, adapting a general-purpose horizontal proton beamline to treat also ocular diseases [18] and developing a dedicated platform for patient positioning and motion monitoring [19]. A complete description of hardware and software systems installed at CNAO and their integration in the clinical workflow was presented by our group in [19]. In particular, [19] described an eye tracking device (ETS) which had a dual purpose: first, to provide an aid for the patient to maintain a stable gaze along the planned direction with a light emitting diode visible through a reflecting mirror placed in front of the patient's eye; second, to monitor involuntary eye motion by means of a stereo-camera system embedded in the same device, providing real-time optical imaging of the eye surface. The integration of the fixation light and the monitoring optical camera in a single device represents a novel solution and grants optimal visibility of the ocular surface as the video cameras were placed in axis with the fixation diode. ETS capabilities were not fully exploited in clinical routine, since the videos recorded by the device are currently used for surveillance purposes, only. In this study we present a method designed to quantitatively evaluate the stability of gaze direction during OPT at CNAO, based on a fully automatic segmentation procedure of the pupil on the eye surface images recorded by one stereo-camera embedded in the ETS.

2   Material and Methods

2.1   Patient Data

Clinical protocol for ocular melanoma at the National Centre for Oncological Hadrontherapy (CNAO, Pavia, Italy) prescribes a total dose of 60Gy equally divided in 4 consecutive daily fractions. We retrospectively collected clinical data and surveillance videos recorded by the ETS during the setup procedures and treatment delivery of five patients (P1–P5, see Table 1), who were diagnosed with choroidal melanoma and underwent OPT in our facility between January and July 2020. Inclusion criteria for this preliminary study foreseen the visibility of the entire pupil in the video, thus excluding from this analysis particular cases in which the eye bulb resulted partially occluded due to the prescribed gaze direction and ETS position in space.

2.2   Automatic Pupil Detection Algorithm

As previously mentioned, the stream of eye images acquired by the ETS along the course of treatment was collected and processed, in order to quantitatively estimate the patient's capacity to maintain the nominal gaze angle. Infrared videos were recorded in RGB24 AVI format, with a resolution of 640×512 pixels and a frame rate of 12 Hz. Images were stored in real time in a dedicated workstation at the time of treatment and made available for off-line analysis.

Table 1. Patient data. Clinical details of patients' cohort. Daily delivery time indicates the average duration of the videos analyzed over the four treatment fractions.

	Diseased eye	Prescribed gaze direction (Polar/azimuthal angles) [°]	Daily mean (std) delivery time[s]
P1	Right	28/0	193.8 (8.9)
P2	Left	28/110	163.8 (18.9)
P3	Left	28/0	184.6 (41.8)
P4	Left	30/90	226.7 (40.9)
P5	Left	29/0	123.1 (10.9)

A custom routine for video analysis was developed in MATLAB (MatWorks, Natick, MA, USA - Image Processing Toolbox: Version 9.5) and operated in two subsequent steps: 1) processing the images to highlight the borders of desired features; 2) apply the Hough Transformation in a framework of pre-defined geometrical constraints (Fig. 1). The desired outcome was a unique circular profile fitting the pupil edges.

The image contrast of each video frame was firstly enhanced by histogram optimization, rescaling the original grayscale interval of 25–50 to 0–250 (pixels with intensity values out of threshold range were consequently saturated). The threshold value to minimize the intraclass variance of black and white pixels was selected according to Otsu's method and images were binarized [20]. A morphological filter (closing) with a circular 8-connected structuring elements was chosen to reduce white noise. Residual pupil reflections were removed by a flood-fill operation. A Circular Hough Transform (CHT) was then applied. We choose the MATLAB built-in implementation of CHT because of its robustness in the presence of noise, occlusion and varying illumination.

We iteratively applied the CHT method to detect a plausible pupil structure in each video frame. We fixed the function sensitivity at 0.98 in order to introduce an adequate grade of flexibility in the searching routine. The main variable of the iterative process was the magnitude of circles radii to be detected. It was set to range in intervals from a minimum value of 40 pixels to a fixed value of 75 pixels, with increasing steps of 5 pixels. During each iteration, a rank of the relative circle strengths was stored, as the center of the estimated circumferences.

The stopping condition was reached when a twofold circumstance was satisfied: a proper performance in metric at the biggest value of radii. Since the pre-processing of frames produced high-contrasted images, the center of the pupil was supposed to be roughly estimated in the majority of the iterations, while changing the magnitude interval of searched radii. The collection of the closest circles was set as reference and in between this group the one with the biggest radii was considered as a candidate to surrogate the pupil (Fig. 1).

2.3 Validation

In clinical routine, prior to the treatment delivery, patients are asked to look at the fixation light. Pausing the video stream of ETS on a single frame, operators are facilitated to draw

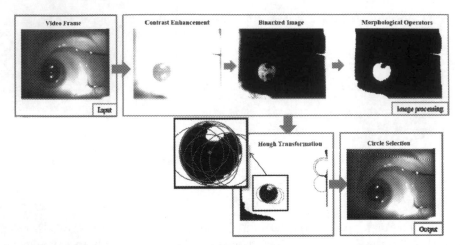

Fig. 1. Block diagram of the proposed algorithm. In the Circular Hough Transformation block, the green circles have the highest magnitudes of the accumulator array peaks (metric) in correspondence of three different explored radius ranges, while blue circles indicate all the circles detected by the Circular Hough Transformation. In the Circle Selection block the circle with the highest relative strength in correspondence of the biggest radii range was considered as a candidate to surrogate the pupil. (Color figure online)

the external contour of the pupil. This manual contour is used both as a reference to refine the setup and its visualization is maintained during the treatment delivery.

In order to validate our method in a clinical like scenario, we selected a single frame extracted from the setup video recorded for P1 to P5. To highlight any potential difference in inter-operator contouring variability, we asked 4 different operators to trace the pupil at the best of their capabilities. A total of 80 manual contours (mC: manual contours) referring to 5 patients, 4 setup frames and 4 different operators were tested.

Each manual contour was fitted by a circular regression (mCF: manual circle fitting) and the corresponding coefficient of determination (R-squared) was calculated. We quantified the goodness-of-fit of manual pupil contours to a circle as an indicator of the applicability of the proposed method since it is based on circular features detection. The 2D distances between the centers of each mCF were calculated to assess the inter-observer variability.

In addition, in order to evaluate the performance of the proposed method, the 2D distance between the center of each mCF and the center of the circle automatically detected by the described algorithm (aCD: automatic circle detection) was calculated.

To guarantee comparability of data, results are presented as percentage of the radius of the circle automatically detected by the proposed algorithm.

In Fig. 2 the testing dataset is presented. Graphical representation of manual contours (mC), circle fitting manual contours (mCF) and circle automatically detected by the described algorithm (aCD) is presented.

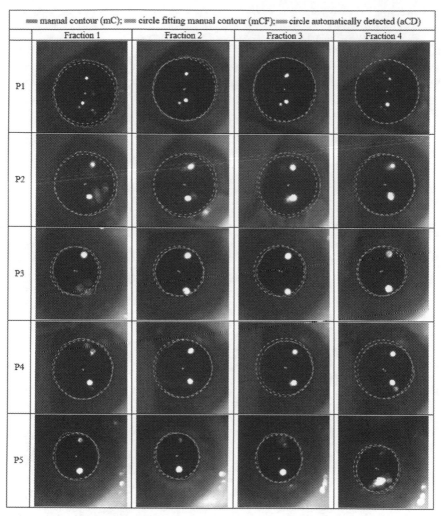

Fig. 2. Validation Testing Dataset: 20 video frames extracted from the setup video recorded for P1–P5 in the 4 treatment fractions with superimposed the manual contours (mC) traced by one representative operator (yellow). The circles fitting manual contours (mCF) are show in blue. The circles automatically detected by the described algorithm (aCD) are shown in red. (Color figure online)

2.4   Evaluation of Pupil Position Stability

Videos recorded during beam delivery in each of the 4 treatment fractions of P1–P5 were collected and retrospectively analyzed. To mimic the manual contouring in the evaluation of our approach we had to define a frame of reference. The first available frame after the start of irradiation was selected to automatically define the reference position of the pupil, as described in the previous paragraph.

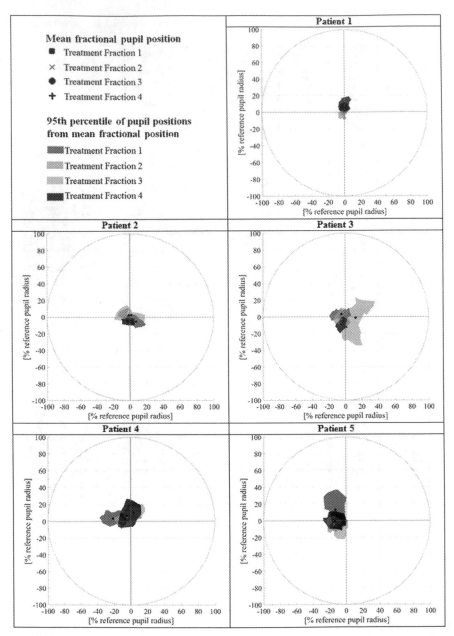

Fig. 3. Schematic representation of pupil motion throughout treatment fractions for each patient in the camera field of view. Graphical markers indicate the mean pupil position over a specific treatment fraction. Colored areas enclose the 95th percentile of pupil position from the mean fractional position. (Color figure online)

Throughout the treatment fraction, the center of the circle fitting the pupil was automatically extracted every 10 frames corresponding to approximately 0.8 s. We arbitrary opted for this time span to better highlight eventual gaze deviations and to optimize computational workload.

Stability of gaze direction was measured and it is presented in next paragraphs as the 2D distance between the center of the circle at reference position and the center of the circles automatically detected in the remaining frames. 2D distances were expressed as the percentage of the radius of the reference setup pupil. A statistical analysis based on Kruskal-Wallis test was performed to investigate the 2D pupil motion across patients.

3 Results

3.1 Validation

The median R-squared indicator of all circles fitting manual pupil contours (mCF) was 0.97 and ranged between 0.62 and 1.00, thus confirming a valuable approximation between circular fitting and manual contours.

The median 2D distances between the centers of each corresponding mCFs traced by different operators was 3.3% with an interquartile range of 3.6% and ranged between 0.4%–10.7% of the automatically detected circle radius.

The distribution of 2D distances between the centers of the circle automatically detected (aCD) and the centers of each corresponding mCFs had median equal to 5% and an interquartile range of 5.3% ranging between 0.3 and 13.3% of the automatically detected circle radius.

Results of validation testing are shown separately for each patient in Table 2 along with the patient-specific reference pupil radii expressed in pixels.

3.2 Evaluation of Pupil Position Stability

2D distances between the centers of the circle at reference position and the centers of the circles automatically detected along the corresponding video frames are summarized in Fig. 3. The red crossed circle represents the reference setup pupil as identified at the beginning of each treatment fraction in the camera field of view; graphical markers indicate the mean pupil position over a specific treatment fraction while the colored areas enclose the 95th percentile of pupil position from the mean fractional position.

In Fig. 4 the distributions of the 2D distances between the centers of the circle at reference setup position and the centers of the circles automatically detected during treatment fraction is showed.

Stability of gaze direction varies across patients with median values ranging between 6.6% (P1) and 16.5%(P5) of reference pupil radius. Similarly, the interquartile ranges of the 2D distances varies between 5.5% (P1) and 10.0% (P5).

The Kruskal-Wallis test rejected the hypothesis of equal median values for the 2D pupil motion in the 5 considered patients ($P < < 0.001$). In particular, on post-hoc analysis, P3, P4, P5 individually had mean ranks significantly different from all patients, while P1 and P2 did not have mean ranks significantly different from each other.

Table 2. Results of method validation expressed separately for each patient (P1–5). Validation was arranged in the evaluation of (**1**) method applicability according to the R-squared indicator of all circles fitting manual pupil contours (mCF) (**2**) inter-operator contour variability according to the distances between the centers of each corresponding mCFs (**3**) automatic method performance according to 2D distances between centers of the circle automatically detected (aCD) and the centers of each corresponding mCFs. Patient-specific reference pupil radii expressed in pixels are reported.

	Method applicability	Inter-operator variability	Method performance	Reference pupil radius
	mCF R-squared median(min-max)	mCF centers distances Median (iqr) [min-max] [%radius]	mCF-aCD centers distances Median (iqr) [min-max] [%radius]	Median [min-max][pixel]
P1	0.98 (0.70 – 1.00)	1.4 (1.3) [0.4 – 6.0]	2.4 (2.3) [0.3 – 4.7]	71.9 [70.0 – 73.1]
P2	0.99 (0.62 – 1.00)	3.8 (3.0) [0.9 – 9.2]	4.7 (3.0) [1.1 – 8.6]	68.4 [67.2 – 68.5]
P3	0.98 (0.77 – 1.00)	3.7 (3.0) [0.6 – 7.0]	8.2 (3.3) [3.5 – 10.7]	56.8 [55.2 – 58.3]
P4	0.95 (0.74 – 1.00)	4.3 (4.0) [1.9 – 9.4]	9.6 (6.5) [1.8 – 13.3]	67.1 [66.4 – 67.3]
P5	0.95 (0.65 – 1.00)	3.5 (3.9) [0.5 – 10.7]	6.4 (3.3) [1.5 – 10.4]	52.8 [51.9 – 54.1]

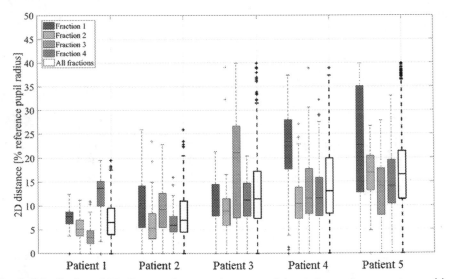

Fig. 4. Distribution of 2D distances between the center of the circle at reference setup position and the center of the circles automatically detected during treatment fractions.

4 Discussion

A relevant parameter of an OPT treatment plan consists of the optimal gaze direction (polar and azimuth angles) to minimize the dose to critical structures and thus to achieve the desired target coverage. As a result, the patient actively participates in all the clinical procedures by looking at a fixation light aiming at reproducing the optimal planned gaze direction during set-up and irradiation phases. Patient position is verified and iteratively corrected using radiographic images of tantalum clips, and real time monitored by visual control of the eye bulb acquired by dedicated cameras [19]. To guarantee the reproducibility of the gaze direction during treatment, operators are required to outline convenient ocular features on the eye images to detect misalignments or shifts that may occur during irradiation.

The presented study proposed a preliminary approach to quantitatively evaluate the stability of gaze direction over an OPT treatment course at CNAO of five patients, relying on an automatic segmentation procedure of the pupil. The bi-dimensional eye localization has been intended as an indirect measure of the 3D eye motion.

A limitation of this study is represented by the selection of patient cohort, whose prescribed gaze direction reproduced by the ETS guaranteed the visibility of the entire pupil in all the video frames under consideration. Since our method aimed at detecting a unique circular feature fitting the pupil edge, the absence of visual occlusions represented a strong favorable condition. Nevertheless, this preliminary evaluation allowed us to underline reliable results concerning gaze stability. The presented method was based on a well-established approach for pupil segmentation through Circular Hough Transform widely investigated in the eye tracking research area [21, 22]. Towards a fully automatic procedure, pre-processing of images as extracted by the video recorded during OPT was necessary as a first step. Image contrast enhancement was refined according to the analyzed video lighting condition and the range of radii for the circular objects was defined according to plausible pupil dimensions. Since image contrast enhancement was based on histogram mapping of a fixed range of gray intensity values, further algorithm improvements envisage the use of automatically adaptive parameters in accordance to the characteristics of the environment (different light conditions, shadows and reflections, for example). Others and more comprehensive and accurate approaches as large scale optimization or Deep Learning techniques are recently been investigated to face these issues [23–25]. Actually, as reported by [24], the state-of art of eye detection techniques can be classified as shape-based, feature-beased, appearance-based and hybrid methods. In addition to such conventional methods, existing works also utilize the deep learning approaches for the pupil detection while using hierarchical image patterns to enhance and eliminate artefacts with Convolutional Neural Networks (CNNs).

In our opinion, a relevant step towards the definition of a reliable automatic segmentation technique was the inter-operator analysis. Different clinical operators verified the proposed algorithm for pupil detection, benchmarking its performance against the manual pupil contours traced on setup video frames. No significant differences were noticed, while an inter-observer variability was observed to be patient dependent (Kruskal-Wallis: p-value $= 0.0001$), privileging the best visibility of the eye bulb on screen. Manual contours traced by operators on the pupil of P1 were significantly more similar to each other than the manual contours traced on the pupils of the other patients (median of mCF centers distances for P1 $= 1.4\%$ Table2). Furthermore, the inter-operator variability of the manual contours traced on the pupils of other patients were higher and comparable (median of mCF centers distances $> 3.5\%$ Table2). This could be a consequence of the increased pupil sharpness of P1 in the analysed video frames. Not surprisingly, the more the video images were blurred, the more the inter-operator variability increased, suggesting the potential impact of a robust automatic procedure in the clinical scenario.

The goodness-of-fit of manual pupil contours to a circle as an indicator of the proposed method applicability was a second aspect. Even if results were satisfying, broadening the dataset evaluation might require stepping towards higher grade of polynomial in shape estimation and fitting [12, 14].

The evaluation of gaze stability over treatment fractions did not show significant time-trend. Since fatigue and relaxation of the eye muscles is common in OPT, these results were quite unexpected. The absence of progressive misalignments in the position of the pupil is probably due to the clinical procedures implemented during beam delivery: the patient is asked to look steady towards the fixation light at intervals that rarely overcome 30 s circa. In between different sessions, the patient is able to rest, thus mitigating fatigue effects.

At this time, a noteworthy limitation of this study is the lack of geometrical calibration of the ETS cameras. Pupil displacement throughout the analyzed video frames could be expressed in terms of percentage of the reference pupil radius as automatically detected by the algorithm. Patient-specific reference pupil radii are expressed in pixels in Table 2. However, the reported results can be interpreted according to offline pixel-spacing measurements performed on a checkbox phantom composed of squares of 10 mm width. ETS cameras have a fixed optics and their use is foreseen in a well-defined depth in space: the eye bulb must be distant from the ETS case from a minimum of 40 to a maximum of 100 mm circa. Out of these boundaries, the quality of images rapidly degrades. We built a basic test fixing the ETS and moving the checkboard along its normal axis, stopping and acquiring images at different distances (40, 75 and 100 mm from the ETS mirror). Results reported a correspondence of 0.06 ± 0.01 mm/pixel. It might be assumed that the measured pupil displacement on the camera field of views are within the clinical CTV margin expansion of 2.5 mm imposed systematically by the treating planning system.

Further developments are necessary to reach a real-time clip-less quantification of eye position and orientation for treatment geometry verification and motion monitoring during OPT. Optimization of eye setup with respect to the cameras embedded in the ETS will allow the processing of images with patient pupil in focus, resulting in a more accurate pupil detection both manual and automatic.

The main advantage of the work is the possibility of using the simple method presented for ensuring the reproducibility of gaze direction during treatment. The real time estimation of a figure of merit describing eye stability during treatment could be used to guide a computer-controlled eye movement gated treatment or to implement automatic beam stopping procedures in case eye motion overcoming a clinical pre-defined threshold are detected.

References

1. Olsen, D.R., Bruland, O.S., Frykholm, G., Norderhaug, I.N.: Proton therapy – a systematic review of clinical effectiveness. Radiother Oncol. **83**, 123–132 (2007)
2. Wang, Z., et al.: Charged particle radiation therapy for uveal melanoma: a systematic review and meta-analysis. Int. J. Radiat. Oncol. Biol. Phys. **86**(1), 18–26 (2013)

3. Maschi, C., Thariat, J., Herault, J., Caujolle, J.: Tumor response in uveal melanomas treated with proton beam therapy. Clin. Oncol. **28**, 198–203 (2015)
4. Sikuade, M.J., et al.: Outcomes of treatment with stereotactic radiosurgery or proton beam therapy for choroidal melanoma. Eye **29**(9), 1194–1198 (2015)
5. Hrbacek, J., et al.: Practice patterns analysis of ocular proton therapy centers: the international OPTIC survey. Int. J. Radiat. Oncol. Biol. Phys. **95**(1), 336–343 (2016). https://doi.org/10.1016/j.ijrobp.2016.01.040. Epub 2016 Jan 28. PMID: 27084651.
6. Carnicer, A., Angellier, G., Thariat, J., Sauerwein, W., Caujolle, J.P., Herault, J.: Quantification of dose perturbations induced by external and internal accessories in ocular proton therapy and evaluation of their dosimetric impact. Med. Phys. **40**(6), 061708 (2013). https://doi.org/10.1118/1.4807090. PMID: 23718587
7. Goitein, M., Miller, T.: Planning proton therapy of the eye. Med. Phys. **10**(3), 275–283 (1983). https://doi.org/10.1118/1.595258. PMID: 6308407.
8. Jaywant, S.M., Osei, E.K., Ladak, S.: Stereotactic radiotherapy in the treatment ofocular melanoma: a noninvasive eye fixation aid and tracking system. J. Appl. Clin. Med. Phys. **4**(2), 156–161 (2003). https://doi.org/10.1120/jacmp.v4i2.2531. PMID: 12777151; PMCID: PMC5724480.
9. Shin, D., Yoo, S.H., Moon, S.H., Yoon, M., Lee, S.B., Park, S.Y.: Eye tracking and gating system for proton therapy of orbital tumors. Med. Phys. **39**(7), 4265–4273 (2012). https://doi.org/10.1118/1.4729708. PMID: 22830760
10. Petersch, B., Bogner, J., Dieckmann, K., Potter, R., Georg, D.: Automatic real-time surveillance of eye position and gating for stereotactic radiotherapy of uveal melanoma. Med. Phys. **31**(12), 3521–3527 (2004). https://doi.org/10.1118/1.1824195. PMID: 15651635
11. Gong, C., et al.: Precise delineation and tumor localization based on novel image registration strategy between optical coherence tomography and computed tomography in the radiotherapy of intraocular cancer. Phys. Med. Biol. **64**(12), 125009 (2019). https://doi.org/10.1088/1361-6560/ab0ddf. PMID: 30844768
12. Guestrin, E.D., Eizenman, M.: General theory of remote gaze estimation using the pupil center and corneal reflections. IEEE Trans. Biomed. Eng. **53**(6), 1124–1133 (2006 Jun). https://doi.org/10.1109/TBME.2005.863952.Erratum.In:IEEETransBiomedEng. 2006Aug;53(8):1728. PMID: 16761839
13. Fassi, A., Riboldi, M., Forlani, C.F., Baroni, G.: Optical eye tracking system for noninvasive and automatic monitoring of eye position and movements in radiotherapy treatments of ocular tumors. Appl. Opt. **51**(13), 2441–2450 (2012). https://doi.org/10.1364/AO.51.002441. PMID: 22614424
14. Via, R., et al.: Optical eye tracking system for real-time noninvasive tumor localization in external beam radiotherapy. Med. Phys. **42**(5), 2194–2202 (2015). https://doi.org/10.1118/1.4915921. PMID: 25979013
15. Wyder, S., Hennings, F., Pezold, S., Hrbacek, J., Cattin, P.C.: With gaze tracking toward non-invasive eye cancer treatment. IEEE Trans. Biomed. Eng. **63**(9), 1914–1924 (2016). https://doi.org/10.1109/TBME.2015.2505740. Epub 2015 Dec 4 PMID: 26660515
16. Via, R., et al.: Noninvasive eye localization in ocular proton therapy through optical eye tracking: a proof of concept. Med Phys. **45**(5), 2186–2194 (2018). https://doi.org/10.1002/mp.12841. Epub 2018 Mar 23 PMID: 29493800
17. Wyder, S., Cattin, P.C.: Eye tracker accuracy: quantitative evaluation of the invisible eye center location. Int. J. Comput. Assist. Radiol. Surg. **13**(10), 1651–1660 (2018). https://doi.org/10.1007/s11548-018-1808-5
18. Ciocca, M., et al.: Design and commissioning of the non-dedicated scanning proton beamline for ocular treatment at the synchrotron-based CNAO facility. Med. Phys. **46**(4), 1852–1862 (2019). https://doi.org/10.1002/mp.13389. Epub 2019 Feb 14 PMID: 30659616

19. Via, R., et al.: A platform for patient positioning and motion monitoring in ocular proton therapy with a non-dedicated beamline. Phys. Med. **59**, 55–63 (2019). https://doi.org/10.1016/j.ejmp.2019.02.020. Epub 2019 Mar 2 PMID: 30928066

20. Otsu, N.: A threshold selection method from gray-level histograms. IEEE Trans. Syst. . Man Cybern. **9**(1), 62–66 (Jan. 1979). https://doi.org/10.1109/TSMC.1979.4310076

21. Bozomitu, R.G., Păsărică, A., Cehan, V., Lupu, R.G., Rotariu, C.: Coca, Implementation of eye-tracking system based on circular Hough transform algorithm. In: 2015 E-Health and Bioengineering Conference (EHB), Iasi, 2015, pp. 1–4 (2015). https://doi.org/10.1109/EHB.2015.7391384

22. Setiawan, M.T., Wibirama, S., Setiawan, N.A.: Robust pupil localization algorithm based on circular hough transform for extreme pupil occlusion. In: 2018 4th International Conference on Science and Technology (ICST), Yogyakarta, 2018, pp. 1–5 (2018). https://doi.org/10.1109/ICSTC.2018.8528286.

23. Yiu, Y.H., et al.: DeepVOG: open-source pupil segmentation and gaze estimation in neuroscienceusing deep learning. J. Neurosci. Methods **324**, 108307 (2019). https://doi.org/10.1016/j.jneumeth.2019.05.016. Epub 2019 Jun 6. PMID: 31176683.

24. Khan, W., Hussain, A., Kuru, K., Al-Askar, H.: Pupil localisation and eye centre estimation using machine learning and computer vision. Sensors (Basel). **20**(13), 3785 (2020). https://doi.org/10.3390/s20133785

25. Harezlak, K., Kasprowski, P.: Application of eye tracking in medicine: a survey, research issues and challenges. Comput Med Imaging Graph. **65**, 176–190 (2018). https://doi.org/10.1016/j.compmedimag.2017.04.006. Epub 2017 May 30 PMID: 28606763

Predicting Reading Speed from Eye-Movement Measures

Ádám Nárai[1], Kathleen Kay Amora[1,2], Zoltán Vidnyánszky[1], and Béla Weiss[1(✉)]

[1] Brain Imaging Centre, Research Centre for Natural Sciences, Budapest, Hungary
weiss.bela@ttk.hu
[2] Multilingualism Doctoral School, University of Pannonia, Veszprém, Hungary

Abstract. Examining eye-movement measures makes understanding the intricacies of reading processes possible. Previous studies have identified some eye-movement measures such as fixation time, number of progressive and regressive saccades as possible major indices for measuring silent reading speed, however, not quite intensively and systematically investigated. The purpose of this study was to exhaustively reveal the functions of different global eye-movement measures and their contribution to reading speed using linear regression analysis. Twenty-four young adults underwent an eye-tracking experiment while reading text paragraphs. Reading speed and a set of twenty-three eye-movement measures including properties of saccades, glissades and fixations were estimated. Correlation analysis indicated multicollinearity between several eye-movement measures, and accordingly, linear regression with elastic net regularization was used to model reading speed with eye-movement explanatory variables. Regression analyses revealed the capability of progressive saccade frequency and the number of progressive saccades normalized by the number of words in predicting reading speed. Furthermore, the results supported claims in the existing literature that reading speed depends on fixation duration, as well as the amplitude, number and percentage of progressive saccades, and also indicated the potential importance of glissade measures in deeper understanding of reading processes. Our findings indicate the possibility of the applied linear regression modeling approach to eventually identify important eye-movement measures related to different reading performance metrics, which could potentially improve the assessment of reading abilities.

Keywords: Reading speed · Silent reading · Eye tracking · Eye movements · Saccades · Fixations · Glissades · Linear regression · Elastic net regularization · Modeling

1 Introduction

Reading, which is shaped through years of exposure to text and formal teaching, is an essential marker of literacy and has a pivotal role in our today's society [1]. Most learn how to read naturally with explicit instruction although around 5–10% of the population experience reading difficulties due to developmental dyslexia, a learning disability characterized by problems in word recognition accuracy and fluency as well as decoding

© Springer Nature Switzerland AG 2021
A. Del Bimbo et al. (Eds.): ICPR 2020 Workshops, LNCS 12663, pp. 453–466, 2021.
https://doi.org/10.1007/978-3-030-68796-0_33

and spelling skills [2]. Reading processes can be sensitive to low-level visual features (e.g. configural text properties, letter-spacing, font characteristics), linguistic characteristics (e.g. word frequency and length) and high-level cognitive processes (e.g. attention) [3–5]. However, reading is not restricted to the involvement of these domains, but it is rather characterized by interplay of these factors with a series of active oculomotor processes employing eye movements such as saccades, glissades and fixations that subserve successful reading mechanisms [6]. Reading competence improves developmentally and can be measured by many factors, one of these is through assessing reading speed. Reading speed is a compound measure of reading expertise, and the rate at which individuals read can largely affect their capacity to process written information.

Most screening tools used to evaluate reading performance and to categorize good from poor readers rely on these cognitive, linguistic and motor (e.g. written and oral) processes that subserve reading through pen-and-paper tests. However, more work is still needed to develop methods that assess the potential of natural reading for improving the screening methods [7, 8]. Few studies have attempted to address this issue by investigating the capability of eye-movement features in detecting poor readers using a machine learning approach based on eye-tracking data recorded during reading text with default [7, 8] and modulated inter-letter spacing [9]. Despite the limited studies that investigated behavioral reading measures and eye movements in different populations and conditions, to the best of our knowledge, no study attempted to investigate the relationship of reading speed and eye movements systematically and exhaustively. Thus, in this study, we assessed how different global eye-movement measures influence reading speed in natural paragraph reading. Our study explores a broad spectrum of eye-movement measures including properties of fixations, saccades and corrective eye movements called glissades using linear modeling with different explanatory variable sets obtained for young adults. By doing this, we aim to contribute to deeper understating of oculomotor underpinning of reading and to creating an advanced modeling framework which can eventually improve the assessment and screening of people with reading difficulties.

1.1 Eye Movements and Reading Speed

Several models were developed for eye-movement prediction [10, 11], however, these mainly focused on saccade programming, in essence answering the questions of where and when to move the eyes during reading. These models can provide predictions for saccade timing based on the words' length, frequency and predictability in a given context, however, they are not suitable for direct investigation of the relationship between eye-movement measures and reading speed in general. Namely, testing the effects of reading mode (oral or silent) or configural text properties on eye-movement characteristics and reading performance is not implemented in these approaches. Accordingly, these models are not suitable for investigation of the effects of e.g. reading mode or letter-spacing modulation.

Nevertheless, a few studies investigated the relationship of reading speed and eye movements in adolescents [12], typically-developing 12 year-old children [3], and typical and poor adult readers [4] in either or both silent and oral reading of connected texts. Krieber and colleagues found in their study on adolescents that eye-movement measures during reading also depend on the reading mode [12]. Beginning readers learn how to read orally first then eventually progressing to, preferring, and becoming faster in silent reading as they become more skilled [12, 13]. Silent reading showed shorter fixation times by approximately 50 ms (225 ms vs 275 ms), longer average saccadic amplitudes (7–9 letters vs 6–7 letters) and less progressive saccades and regressions than oral reading [6, 12–14], thus affecting reading speed. Some studies also suggest that silent reading could be less demanding than oral reading probably due to additional costs brought by oculomotor movements syncing with articulatory processes in the case of oral reading [12, 14]. Additionally, Søvik and colleagues found significant intercorrelations between silent reading speed and eye-movement measures such as recognition span (average number of words in a fixation), average fixation time and number of progressive and regressive saccades in children, with the latter three measures exhibiting negative intercorrelations with reading speed, which means that shorter fixation times and less progressive and regressive saccades characterize fast readers compared to slow readers [3]. However, in multiple regression analyses for both silent and oral reading speeds, Søvik and colleagues found significant differences among the same eye-movement measures apart from number of progressive saccades. Rayner and colleagues only investigated silent reading speed in fast and slow readers among university students and showed similar results. They measured four eye-movement parameters that affect reading speed during silent reading, wherein fast adult readers also exhibited shorter fixation times, less number of forward and backward fixations, and longer saccade length than slow readers [4].

Dyslexic readers showed compromised reading speed and accuracy during word reading [15] and silent sentence reading tasks [16]. These dyslexic readers showed similar eye-movement parameters as slow readers with longer and more fixations and shorter saccades than typical peers [17]. However, differences in eye-movement patterns during reading in dyslexics are mostly not caused by oculomotor dysfunctions but are probably more related to visual processes affected by specific text characteristics and manifested through the behavior of eye-movement measures [18, 19]. These variations could result from varying linguistic (e.g. effect of word frequency, word length [20], syllabic complexity [16], etc.) and orthographic properties of text in different languages. Hutzler and Wimmer showed that languages with more regularities (e.g. German) exhibited fewer regressions than a more opaque orthography (e.g. English), but have longer fixations than other languages despite similar orthography (e.g. Italian) due to increased syllabic complexity in German [16].

1.2 Effects of Inter-letter Spacing Modulation on Reading

Spacing manipulations can also affect reading speed. To date, results have been mixed regarding this topic, wherein reduced intra-word/inter-letter spacing could either facilitate or hinder reading. Rayner and colleagues found that reduced intra-word spacing resulted in faster reading times, exhibiting shorter and fewer fixations, longer saccades and less regressive fixations than normal intra-word spacing in a sentence reading study in typical and poor adult readers [4]. However, in their paradigm, they combined the reduced intra-word spacing ($\times 0.9$ times the normal spacing) with increased inter-word spacing, which could aid facilitation of reading.

Contradictory to their result, the authors also explained that decreasing the intra-word/inter-letter spacing in a text can potentially deter efficient identification [4]. This kind of manipulation may increase visual processing demands by increasing the amount of information in a single fixation, hence recruiting more neural resources for proper execution that is reflected in longer fixation durations and smaller saccades compared to the default inter-letter spacing condition [5]. This situation holds true in a study on older adults reading condensed text ($\times 0.8$–0.9 times the normal spacing), resulting in longer reading times characterized by increased number of normal fixations and lengthened average fixation durations. The authors attributed this difficulty to crowding as older adults are more sensitive to it [21]. On the other hand, doubling the inter-letter spacing seems to decrease the duration of fixations and increase the amplitude of saccades. However, this modulation of eye-movement measures is accompanied with the reduction of reading speed compared to the normal spacing condition during silent paragraph reading in young adults without reading difficulties [5]. Contrary to this finding, extra-large letter spacing improves oral text reading speed and accuracy of dyslexic children most probably due to their sensitivity to crowding [22]. Nevertheless, the oculomotor underpinning of these positive effects on behavioral measures remained unclear.

2   Methods

2.1   Participants

This study was conducted on 24 young adults (11 female). The participants were 20–26 years old with 22.33 years average and 1.78 years standard deviation. All participants were native speakers of Hungarian, reported having typical reading skills and had normal or corrected-to-normal vision.

2.2   Apparatus

Eye-tracking (ET) data was recorded from the left eye using an iView X™ Hi-Speed 1250 system (SensoMotoric Instruments GmbH, Teltow, Germany) with 1250 Hz sampling rate. EEG data were acquired using a BrainAmp Standard amplifier with a 64-channel actiCAP active electrode system and the BrainVision Recorder 1.2 software (Brain Products GmbH, Munich, Germany), with 500 Hz sampling rate. See ref. [5] for further information about the experimental setup.

2.3   Stimuli and Experimental Procedure

Participants were instructed to read 32 Hungarian text paragraphs silently at their own pace. The paragraphs were presented line-by-line either with normal inter-letter spacing (NS; ~$0.31°$ spacing size), minimal spacing (MS; 0.707 times the NS spacing) or double spacing (DS; 2 times the NS spacing). To assure that participants read the texts carefully and to assess their reading comprehension, a single sentence test statement was presented after each paragraph, and participants had to report with a mouse button press whether the test sentence was true (left button) or false (right button). See ref. [5] for further information about the presented stimuli and the experimental paradigm. Here, the relationship between the reading speed and eye-movement measures was assessed for the default inter-letter spacing size (NS), results for the altered spacing conditions (MS and DS) are to be provided elsewhere.

2.4 Data Analysis

Eye-movement measures such as properties of fixations, saccades and glissades were extracted on a text line basis using a velocity-based adaptive algorithm [23] with default settings and 50 °/sec initial peak velocity detection threshold. Using text properties, raw ET data and the output of the adaptive algorithm, reading speed and a set of 23 global eye-movement measures (see Table 1) were estimated at subject level by pooling the data across the text lines presented with normal spacing. ET data processing was performed in MATLAB R2016b (The MathWorks Inc., Natick, MA, USA) with custom scripts based on the toolbox provided by dr. Marcus Nyström.

Before modeling the reading speed with eye-movement measures, reading comprehension of participants and correlations between the investigated variables were evaluated. Reading speed may depend on the level of comprehension. Namely, participants who pay less attention to the reading task may achieve higher reading speed at the cost of lower comprehension performance. The potential confounding effect of text comprehension on reading speed was investigated by correlating the two measures, and neither the Pearson ($r_P = -0.12$, $p = 0.57$) nor the Spearman correlation coefficient ($r_S = -0.15$, $p = 0.47$) was found to be significant. Furthermore, to select an appropriate approach for modeling of reading speed with eye-movement measures, the correlation between dependent and independent variables as well as the multicollinearity between the explanatory variables were tested. Besides the Pearson correlation coefficients (r_P), Spearman's rank correlation coefficients (r_S) were also considered to investigate the presence of nonlinear relationships and the potential side-effects of bivariate outliers on the estimation of correlation coefficients. The obtained results indicated a weak nonlinear relationship for two eye-movement measures and strong multicollinearity between several independent variables (see Sect. 3.1 for details). Accordingly, linear regression with elastic net regularization [24] (ENET) was selected as a modeling approach. This model applies a linear combination of the L1 and L2 penalties to aid model interpretation by selection of variables and to control the multicollinearity between the variables.

Reading speed (Med_rspeed) was modeled with four different sets of eye-movement measures (see Set 1–4 columns in Table 1). Set 1 contained all the 23 eye-movement measures, while the frequency (Freq_fsacc, Freq_bsacc) and the word-normalized number of saccades (Med_fsnum_wnum, Med_bsnum_wnum) were excluded from Set 2 and Set 3, respectively, since these measures may closely resemble reading speed and may mask the effect of other eye-movement measures. Finally, in Set 4, we excluded both the frequency and word-number measures of saccades. For the ENET model, we used the ElasticNetCV class implemented in the scikit-learn package (version 0.23.2) with 10-fold cross-validation, 20 l1_ratio values from 0.1 to 1 equally spaced on a logarithmic scale and 20 alpha values set automatically. Predictor variables and reading speed were z-scored before modeling. Model performance was evaluated by taking the median of the R^2 (coefficient of determination) scores derived from 10-fold cross-validation, referred

Table 1. List of dependent (DV) and independent variables used for modeling of reading speed with eye-movement measures. Inclusion of independent variables in different sets of explanatory variables (Sets 1–4) is marked by X.

Abbreviation	Set 1	Set 2	Set 3	Set 4	Definition
Med_rspeed	DV	DV	DV	DV	Median of word number divided by the reading time
Med_fixdur	X	X	X	X	Median of fixation durations
Perc_fsacc	X	X	X	X	Percentage of progressive (forward) saccades
Perc_fsacc_gliss/Perc_bsacc_gliss	X	X	X	X	Percentage of progressive (forward)/regressive (backward) saccades followed by a glissade (among progressive/regressive saccades)
Perc_fsacc_fgliss/Perc_bsacc_fgliss	X	X	X	X	Percentage of progressive (forward)/regressive (backward) saccades followed by a progressive glissade (among progressive/regressive saccades followed by a glissade)
Med_fsaccamp/Med_bsaccamp	X	X	X	X	Median amplitude of progressive (forward)/regressive (backward) saccades
Freq_fsacc/Freq_bsacc	X		X		Number of progressive (forward)/regressive (backward) saccades divided by reading time
Med_saccpdetth	X	X	X	X	Median of saccade peak detection thresholds

(continued)

Table 1. (*continued*)

Abbreviation	Set 1	Set 2	Set 3	Set 4	Definition
Med_fsaccdur/Med_bsaccdur	X	X	X	X	Median duration of progressive (forward)/regressive (backward) saccades
Med_fglissdur/Med_bglissdur	X	X	X	X	Median duration of progressive (forward)/regressive (backward) glissades
Med_fglissamp/Med_bglissamp	X	X	X	X	Median amplitude of progressive (forward)/regressive (backward) glissades
Med_fsnum_wnum/Med_bsnum_wnum	X	X			Median number of progressive (forward)/regressive (backward) saccades per word
Med_saccpvel	X	X	X	X	Median number of saccade peak velocity
Perc_lvel_gliss	X	X	X	X	Percentage of low-velocity glissades
Med_lvglisspvel/Med_hvglisspvel	X	X	X	X	Median peak velocity of low/high-velocity glissades

to as cross-validated R^2 (R^2_{CV}) from now on. Significance testing of ENET regression weights was performed by generating a null distribution of regression weights, retraining the same model (including hyperparameter selection with cross-validation) on 1000 random permutations of the dependent variable. P values were defined as the fraction of permuted results (maximized in 1) that were more extreme than or equal to the true coefficient.

3 Results

3.1 Correlation Analyses

Several eye-movement measures significantly correlated with reading speed both with Pearson (Fig. 1, first row) and Spearman correlation analysis (Fig. 1, first column), indicating linear correlations fairly robust against bivariate outliers (also supported by the inspection of z-scored distributions of reading speed and eye-movement measures in Fig. 2 (a)). The three eye-movement measures having the strongest correlations with reading speed, namely word-normalized number of progressive saccades

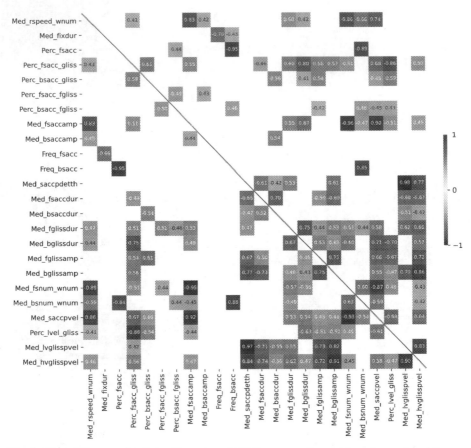

Fig. 1. Correlation matrix of significant (p < 0.05) Spearman (lower triangular part) and Pearson (upper triangular part) correlation coefficients obtained for reading speed (first column and first row) and the investigated eye-movement variables. For the definition of eye-movement measures see Table 1.

(Med_fsnum_wnum: $r_P/r_S = -0.86/-0.89$, p < 0.00001), amplitude of progressive saccades (Med_fsaccamp: $r_P/r_S = 0.83/0.83$, p < 0.00001) and peak velocity of saccades (Med_saccpvel: $r_P/r_S = 0.74/0.86$, p ≤ 0.000035) also showed strong intercorrelation with each other (see Fig. 1), indicating a high degree of multicollinearity between these variables. Furthermore, word-normalized number of regressive saccades (Med_bsnum_wnum: $r_P/r_S = -0.66/-0.59$, p ≤ 0.0023), duration of progressive glissades (Med_fglissdur: $r_P/r_S = 0.50/0.47$, p ≤ 0.021), duration of regressive glissades (Med_bglissdur: $r_P/r_S = 0.43/0.44$, p ≤ 0.035), amplitude of regressive saccades (Med_bsaccamp: $r_P/r_S = 0.42/0.45$, p ≤ 0.040) and percentage of regressive saccades followed by a glissade (Perc_fsacc_gliss: $r_P/r_S = 0.41/0.43$, p ≤ 0.047) also significantly correlated with reading speed. Two eye-movement measures, percentage of low-velocity glissades (Perc_lvel_gliss: $r_S = -0.41$, p = 0.048) and peak velocity of high-velocity

glissades (Med_hvglisspvel: $r_S = 0.46$, $p = 0.024$) exhibited moderate, but still significant correlation with reading speed only in the case of Spearman's rank correlation coefficient, suggesting nonlinear relationships for these glissade-related variables. Significant
correlations between the eye-movement measures exhibited a very similar pattern for
Pearson and Spearman correlation coefficients (Fig. 1, upper and lower triangles of the
correlation matrix, excluding the first row and the first column) implying a potentially
high degree of multicollinearity in our data, thus the application of the ENET model
with L2 norm for controlling multicollinearity and an L1 norm to aid interpretation is
well founded.

3.2   Regression Using All Eye-Movement Measures (Set 1)

First, we trained an ENET model using hyperparameter selection with cross-validation (α
$= 0.0101$, ll_ratio $= 0.53$) on all eye-movement measures as predictors (Set 1) explaining
nearly 90% of the variation in reading speed ($R^2_{CV} = 0.8787$). Our model predicted a
significant increase in reading speed with increasing amplitude (Mcd_fsaccamp: $\beta =$
$+0.53$, $p = 0.013$) and frequency (Freq_fsacc: $\beta = +0.43$, $p = 0.011$) of progressive
saccades, as shown in Fig. 2 (b), Set 1 column. In contrast to these measures, word-
normalized number of progressive saccades had a significant negative regression weight
(Med_fsnum_wnum: $\beta = -0.40$, $p = 0.021$) indicating that participants with lower
word-normalized number of progressive saccades were expected to read faster. Finally,
an increase in the percentage of progressive saccades (Perc_fsacc) predicted a marginally
significant increase of reading speed ($\beta = +0.14$, $p = 0.053$).

3.3   Regression Using Different Subsets of Eye-Movement Measures (Set 2–4)

Since the frequency of saccades (Freq_fsacc and Freq_bsacc) may closely resemble
reading speed and may mask the effect of other eye-movement measures, we excluded
them in Set 2. The retrained model ($\alpha = 0.0142$, ll_ratio $= 0.78$) explained about 51%
of the variation in reading speed ($R^2_{CV} = 0.5059$). Compared to the results obtained
for Set 1, using the Set 2 collection of eye-movement measures the regression weight of
progressive saccade amplitude (Med_fsaccamp) became somewhat weaker ($\beta = +0.35$,
$p = 0.023$), while the weight of the word-normalized number of progressive saccades
(Med_fsnum_wnum) remained similar ($\beta = -0.47$, $p = 0.021$). Contrary to Set 1, the
percentage of progressive saccades (Perc_fsacc) reached the level of significance ($\beta =$
$+0.32$, $p = 0.031$) and fixation duration (Med_fixdur) also had a significant effect on
reading speed ($\beta = -0.40$, $p = 0.015$), suggesting that participants with shorter fixations
read faster. Finally, the duration of regressive glissades (Med_bglissdur) had a marginally
significant negative effect on reading speed ($\beta = -0.18$, $p = 0.051$).

Omitting the normalized saccade number measures (Med_fsnum_wnum and
Med_bsnum_wnum) instead of saccade frequency measures (Set 3), the retrained model
($\alpha = 0.0105$, ll_ratio $= 1.00$) was able to explain nearly 80% of the variance in reading
speed ($R^2_{CV} = 0.7872$). Compared to Set 1, the weight of progressive saccade frequency
(Freq_fsacc) was similar in Set 3 ($\beta = +0.47$, $p = 0.007$), the percentage of progressive
saccades (Perc_fsacc) became significant ($\beta = +0.18$, $p = 0.043$) and the weight of
the progressive saccades amplitude measure (Med_fsaccamp) became higher ($\beta = +$

0.96, p = 0.003). The model trained with the omission of both saccade frequency and normalized saccade number measures (Set 4, α = 0.0345, l1_ratio = 0.63) explained only 44% of the variance in reading speed (R^2_{CV} = 0.4398). Set 4 resulted in similar significant regression weights (Med_fixdur: β = −0.37, p = 0.017; Perc_fsacc: β = + 0.38, p = 0.023) as Set 2, with the exception of progressive saccade amplitude, that exhibited a higher regression weight for Set 4 (Med_fsaccamp: β = +0.76, p = 0.003).

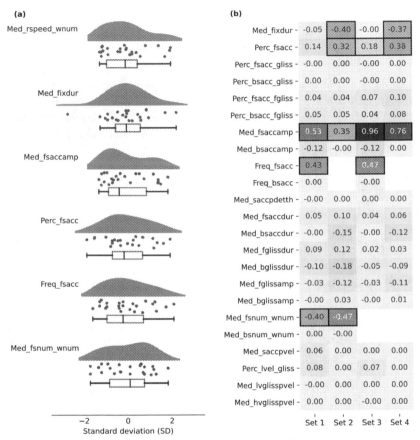

Fig. 2. Panel (a) shows raincloud plots depicting z-scored median reading speed (Med_rspeed_wnum), median fixation duration (Med_fixdur), median amplitude of progressive saccades (Med_fsaccamp), percentage of progressive saccades (Perc_fsacc), frequency of progressive saccades (Freq_fsacc) and number of progressive saccades normalized by the number of words (Med_fsnum_wnum). Whiskers on boxplots depict 1.5 times the interquartile range. Panel (b) presents the regression weights obtained for different eye-movement measure sets. Black rectangles mark significant regression weights. For the definition of eye-movement measures and different sets (Set 1, Set 2, Set 3 and Set 4) of explanatory variables see Table 1.

4 Discussion

The phenomena behind reading, from identifying visual features to higher-level cognitive processes, can be explained and evaluated through studying eye-movement measures. One of the many reading measures that reflect reading performance is reading speed. A handful of studies [3, 4, 14] characterize fixation time, saccade length, number of progressive and regressive saccades as possible indices for silent reading speed during sentence reading tasks, but to date, only few studies explored various reading measures in a more in-depth manner [7, 8]. Thus, the objective of this study was to investigate a wide spectrum of eye-movement measures including several properties of fixations, saccades and glissades and their relationship with reading speed using linear regression analysis.

Our correlation analyses suggested a high degree of collinearity between eye-movement measures which we were able to remedy by using a linear modeling approach with elastic net regularization and by testing different sets of explanatory variables. We trained different linear regression models to examine the relationship between reading speed and four subsets of our eye-movement measures to reveal which eye-movement measures and to what extent these contribute to reading speed. Our results reveal that primarily three features of progressive saccades (amplitude, frequency, and number per word) drive reading speed, with an additional smaller effect of progressive saccade percentage (see Set 1 results). As participants make larger and more frequent progressive saccades, their reading speed increases, whereas more progressive saccades per word makes their reading slower. This result is partially in line with the study of Søvik and colleagues in which they found a negative correlation between silent reading speed and number of progressive saccades in children [3].

The increase of fixation duration also negatively impacts reading speed [3, 4, 12–14], however, frequency measures of saccades can easily mask this effect due to their strong dependence on fixation duration. As expected, our results based on explanatory variable sets without saccade frequency measures (Set 2 and Set 4) supported several studies in different populations which also found the negative effect of longer fixation duration on reading speed [3, 4, 12–14]. With the omission of saccade frequency measures (Set 2), fixation duration and the percentage of progressive saccades become the two defining eye-movement explanatory variables of reading speed besides the consistent contribution of progressive saccade amplitude. The significant contribution of fixation duration to the explanation of reading speed variance after the exclusion of the progressive saccade frequency measure can be explained by the significant negative correlation between these two explanatory variables. However, the increase of regression weight observed for the percentage of progressive saccades is more likely the result of the strong negative correlation between regressive saccade frequency and the percentage of progressive saccades. On the other hand, with the omission of normalized saccade number measures (Set 3), the contribution of progressive saccade amplitude becomes more prevalent while the effect of the other measures stays essentially the same, which is most probably the result of the strong negative correlation present between the amplitude and the normalized number of progressive saccades. Excluding both saccade frequency and normalized saccade number measures from independent variables (Set 4), a model resembling the results obtained by Set 2 and Set 3 explanatory variables emerged.

Considering the coefficient of determination measure obtained for the model with Set 1 explanatory variables ($R^2_{CV} = 0.8787$), we found that global eye-movement measures investigated in this study may explain even up to ~ 90% of variance in reading speed. Moreover, the R^2_{CV} coefficients of linear regression models based on Set 2 ($R^2_{CV} = 0.5059$), Set 3 ($R^2_{CV} = 0.7872$) and Set 4 ($R^2_{CV} = 0.4398$) eye-movement measures suggest a contribution of about ~ 40% and ~ 10% of the total variance in reading speed for saccade frequency and normalized saccade number measures, respectively.

Interestingly, with the omission of saccade frequency (but not word-normalized saccade number) measures (Set 2), we found a moderate negative contribution of regressive glissade duration to reading speed reflecting lower reading speed for participants with longer regressive glissades. The potential importance of glissades in reading is also indicated by our recent finding according to which the dispersion of forward glissade duration might contribute to the detection of dyslexia using a machine learning framework based on eye-movement correlates of text paragraph reading [8, 9]. However, further investigations are needed to reveal the role of glissades in oculomotor processes subserving reading.

The finding that dispersion and not the central tendency of forward glissade duration contributes to data-driven classification of dyslexic and control readers [8, 9] suggests that besides the central tendency measures, dispersion-like eye-movement measures might also play a part in predicting reading performance metrics such as reading speed.

Generally, our results obtained by training linear models with regularization replicated the findings of previous studies that investigated the relationship between specific eye-movement measures and reading speed. Furthermore, we revealed additional eye-movement measures contributing to reading speed, which can allow better characterization of oculomotor processes underpinning reading. We conclude that reading speed mainly depends on the frequency, amplitude, normalized number and percentage of progressive saccades, as well as on fixation duration.

Even though we investigated the relationship between reading speed and eye-movement correlates in paragraph reading with normal inter-letter spacing only, the same modeling approach could be applied to assess how modulation of letter spacing can affect this relationship in typical and poor readers (e.g. persons with dyslexia). To address this question, eye-tracking data corresponding to reading of text with reduced and increased inter-letter spacing [5, 8, 9] could be used. Moreover, this analysis framework could also be expanded to identify the relationship between eye-movement measures and different reading performance metrics (reading accuracy, reading fluency) aside from reading speed. This expansion could lead to a more natural way of assessing reading performance. Furthermore, this knowledge could also contribute to the development of advanced training approaches aimed at improving the reading abilities of poor readers.

Acknowledgments. This research was supported by the Hungarian Scientific Research Fund (grant number: K112093), the Hungarian Brain Research Program 2.0 (grant number: NAP 2.0 4001-17919), by the KEP-5/2019 grant and the Neo-PRISM-C project funded by the European Union Horizon 2020 Program (H2020-MSCA-ITN-2018) under the Marie Skłodowska-Curie Innovative Training Network (Grant Agreement No. 813546).

References

1. Conklin, K., Pellicer-Sánchez, A., Carrol, G.: Eye-tracking: A Guide for Applied Linguistics Research. Cambridge University Press, Cambridge (2018)
2. Lyon, G.R., Shaywitz, S.E., Shaywitz, B.A.: A definition of dyslexia. Ann. Dyslexia **53**, 1–4 (2003). https://doi.org/10.1007/s11881-003-0001-9
3. Søvik, N., Arntzen, O., Samuelstuen, M.: Eye-movement parameters and reading speed. Read. Writ. **13**, 237–255 (2000). https://doi.org/10.1023/A:1026495716953
4. Rayner, K., Slattery, T.J., Bélanger, N.N.: Eye movements, the perceptual span, and reading speed. Psychon. Bull. Rev. **17**, 834–839 (2010). https://doi.org/10.3758/PBR.17.6.834
5. Weiss, B., Knakker, B., Vidnyánszky, Z.: Visual processing during natural reading. Sci. Rep. **6**, 26902 (2016). https://doi.org/10.1038/srep26902
6. Schotter, E.R., Rayner, K.: The work of the eyes during reading. In: The Oxford Handbook of Reading, pp. 44–59. Oxford University Press, New York (2015)
7. Benfatto, M.N., Seimyr, G.Ö., Ygge, J., Pansell, T., Rydberg, A., Jacobson, C.: Screening for dyslexia using eye tracking during reading. PLoS One **11**, e0165508 (2016). https://doi.org/10.1371/journal.pone.0165508
8. Szalma, J., Weiss, B.: Data-driven classification of dyslexia using eye-movement correlates of natural reading. In: ACM Symposium on Eye Tracking Research and Applications, pp. 1–4. ACM, Stuttgart (2020). https://doi.org/10.1145/3379156.3391379
9. Szalma, J., Amora, K.K., Vidnyánszky, Z., Weiss, B.: Investigating the effect of inter-letter spacing modulation on data-driven detection of developmental dyslexia based on eye-movement correlates of reading: a machine learning approach. In: Del Bimbo, A., et al. (eds.) ICPR 2021 Workshops. LNCS, vol. 12663, pp. xx–yy. Springer, Cham (2021). https://doi.org/10.1007/978-3-030-68796-0_34
10. Reichle, E.D., Rayner, K., Pollatsek, A.: The E-Z Reader model of eye-movement control in reading: comparisons to other models. Behav. Brain Sci. **26**, 445–476 (2003). https://doi.org/10.1017/S0140525X03000104
11. Engbert, R., Nuthmann, A., Richter, E.M., Kliegl, R.: SWIFT: a dynamical model of saccade generation during reading. Psychol. Rev. **112**, 777–813 (2005). https://doi.org/10.1037/0033-295X.112.4.777
12. Krieber, M., et al.: Eye movements during silent and oral reading in a regular orthography: basic characteristics and correlations with childhood cognitive abilities and adolescent reading skills. PLoS One **12**, e0170986 (2017). https://doi.org/10.1371/journal.pone.0170986
13. Rayner, K.: Eye movements in reading and information processing: 20 years of research. Psychol. Bull. **124**, 372–422 (1998). https://doi.org/10.1037/0033-2909.124.3.372
14. Rayner, K.: The 35th Sir Frederick Bartlett Lecture: eye movements and attention in reading, scene perception, and visual search. Q. J. Exp. Psychol. **62**, 1457–1506 (2009). https://doi.org/10.1080/17470210902816461
15. De Luca, M., Borrelli, M., Judica, A., Spinelli, D., Zoccolotti, P.: Reading words and pseudowords: an eye movement study of developmental dyslexia. Brain Lang. **80**, 617–626 (2002). https://doi.org/10.1006/brln.2001.2637
16. Hutzler, F., Wimmer, H.: Eye movements of dyslexic children when reading in a regular orthography. Brain Lang. **89**, 235–242 (2004). https://doi.org/10.1016/S0093-934X(03)00401-2
17. Prado, C., Dubois, M., Valdois, S.: The eye movements of dyslexic children during reading and visual search: impact of the visual attention span. Vis. Res. **47**, 2521–2530 (2007). https://doi.org/10.1016/j.visres.2007.06.001
18. Rayner, K.: Do faulty eye movements cause dyslexia? Dev. Neuropsychol. **1**, 3–15 (1985). https://doi.org/10.1080/87565648509540294

19. De Luca, M., Di Pace, E., Judica, A., Spinelli, D., Zoccolotti, P.: Eye movement patterns in linguistic and non-linguistic tasks in developmental surface dyslexia. Neuropsychologia **37**, 1407–1420 (1999). https://doi.org/10.1016/S0028-3932(99)00038-X

20. Loberg, O., Hautala, J., Hämäläinen, J.A., Leppänen, P.H.T.: Influence of reading skill and word length on fixation-related brain activity in school-aged children during natural reading. Vis. Res. **165**, 109–122 (2019). https://doi.org/10.1016/j.visres.2019.07.008

21. Li, S., et al.: Adult age differences in effects of text spacing on eye movements during reading. Front. Psychol. **9** (2019). https://doi.org/10.3389/fpsyg.2018.02700

22. Zorzi, M., et al.: Extra-large letter spacing improves reading in dyslexia. Proc. Natl. Acad. Sci. **109**, 11455–11459 (2012). https://doi.org/10.1073/pnas.1205566109

23. Nyström, M., Holmqvist, K.: An adaptive algorithm for fixation, saccade, and glissade detection in eyetracking data. Behav. Res. Methods **42**, 188–204 (2010). https://doi.org/10.3758/BRM.42.1.188

24. Zou, H., Hastie, T.: Regularization and variable selection via the elastic net. J. R. Stat. Soc. Ser. B Stat. Methodol. **67**, 301–320 (2005). https://doi.org/10.1111/j.1467-9868.2005.00503.x

Investigating the Effect of Inter-letter Spacing Modulation on Data-Driven Detection of Developmental Dyslexia Based on Eye-Movement Correlates of Reading: A Machine Learning Approach

János Szalma[1], Kathleen Kay Amora[1,2], Zoltán Vidnyánszky[1], and Béla Weiss[1(✉)]

[1] Brain Imaging Centre, Research Centre for Natural Sciences, Budapest, Hungary
weiss.bela@ttk.hu
[2] Multilingualism Doctoral School, University of Pannonia, Veszprém, Hungary

Abstract. Developmental dyslexia is a reading disability estimated to affect between 5 to 10% of the population. However, current screening methods are limited as they tell very little about the oculomotor processes underlying natural reading. Accordingly, investigating the eye-movement correlates of reading in a machine learning framework could potentially enhance the detection of poor readers. Here, the capability of eye-movement measures in classifying dyslexic and control young adults (24 dyslexic, 24 control) was assessed on eye-tracking data acquired during reading of isolated sentences presented at five inter-letter spacing levels. The set of 65 eye-movement features included properties of fixations, saccades and glissades. Classification accuracy and importance of features were assessed for all spacing levels by aggregating the results of five feature selection methods. Highest classification accuracy (73.25%) was achieved for an increased spacing level, while the worst classification performance (63%) was obtained for the minimal spacing condition. However, the classification performance did not differ significantly between these two spacing levels (p = 0.28). The most important features contributing to the best classification performance across the spacing levels were as follows: median of progressive and all saccade amplitudes, median of fixation duration and interquartile range of forward glissade duration. Selection frequency was even for the median of fixation duration, while the median amplitude of all and forward saccades measures exhibited complementary distributions across the spacing levels. The results suggest that although the importance of features may vary with the size of inter-letter spacing, the classification performance remains invariant.

Keywords: Developmental dyslexia · Reading · Inter-letter spacing · Machine learning · Support vector machine · Eye-movement features · Feature selection

1 Introduction

Developmental dyslexia is a reading disability characterized by decreased word recognition speed and accuracy, impaired fluency in reading and decoding [1]. Between 5

© Springer Nature Switzerland AG 2021
A. Del Bimbo et al. (Eds.): ICPR 2020 Workshops, LNCS 12663, pp. 467–481, 2021.
https://doi.org/10.1007/978-3-030-68796-0_34

and 10% of the population is often estimated to be affected [2]. The early detection of dyslexia is important as some of the adverse effects can be mitigated [3] enabling training programs to enhance phonological skills and letter knowledge that can have long-lasting benefits.

However, common behavioral tests used for screening of dyslexia say very little about the oculomotor processes that underlie natural reading. Dyslexic readers have been shown to make longer and more fixations, more saccades, particularly more regressive saccades, and their mean saccade amplitude is shorter (for a comprehensive review, see [4]). Accordingly, research into eye-movement correlates of natural reading could contribute to a deeper understanding of reading difficulties and could also improve early detection of developmental dyslexia.

Dyslexics are sensitive to crowding, a perceptual phenomenon where the surrounding letters of the text negatively influence the perception of the central target [5–7]. To remediate reading difficulties due to crowding, the effects of inter-letter spacing modulation were investigated. However, results have been mixed regarding the relationship of eye-movement measures in response to different inter-letter spacing modulations. In silent sentence reading tasks, reduced inter-letter spacing ($\times 0.9$ the normal spacing) has been found to facilitate faster reading with shorter fixation times, lower number of fixations, longer saccades and lower number of regressive fixations than normal spacing in typical young adults [8]. However, this kind of manipulation may also increase visual load in older adults by compressing more information into a single fixation leading to crowding issues, which may lead to longer fixation times, smaller saccades and more fixations, that can hamper reading speed [9]. Moreover, young adults in paragraph reading tasks showed increased fixations, smaller saccades yet faster reading [10]. On the other hand, increased inter-letter spacing also generated different results. Skilled readers could benefit from increased inter-letter spacing unless the increase is more than the critical letter spacing, which could lead to a slower reading speed [5, 11]. Moreover, in silent sentence reading tasks, young adults read faster in increased inter-letter spacing (below critical letter spacing) than the normal spacing condition with shorter average fixation durations for progressive and regressive saccades [11]. However, contrary to this result, going beyond the critical letter spacing showed interesting effects. Double inter-letter spacing led to increased reading times characterized by reduced fixation duration and increased saccadic amplitudes [10]. Extra-large letter spacing has also been found to improve reading accuracy and speed on dyslexic children in a behavioral task as it addresses crowding issues [7, 12]. Therefore, this topic about the effect of inter-letter spacing modulations on eye-movement measures remained widely debated as results may vary depending on population, tasks, stimuli and text manipulations. Although there are studies exploring inter-letter spacing modulations and eye-movement measures in skilled readers like those cited above; to the best of our knowledge, none has been done yet on dyslexics in a natural reading context.

Recently, several research groups attempted to develop data-driven frameworks for the detection of dyslexia based on eye-movement characteristics and machine learning. On a sample of 193 (103 dyslexics, selected as the bottom 5% of a larger sample; 90 controls matched on gender, class, language and non-verbal skills, and exhibiting average or better reading performance) 9–10 year-old children, Benfatto and colleagues

[13] achieved 95.4% classification accuracy using a linear Support Vector Machine (SVM) classifier [14] and Recursive Feature Elimination (RFE) feature selection [15]. They found the following features as the most significant: mean duration of progressive and regressive fixations, standard deviation of regressive fixation durations, central tendency and dispersion measures of regressive and progressive saccade properties. Asvestopoulou and colleagues conducted their experiments on 69 participants (32 dyslexic, 37 control) between 8.5 and 12.5 years [16]. Using the Least Absolute Shrinkage and Selection Operator (LASSO) [17] feature selection, the most important measures were: mean and median saccade amplitude, number of short forward (progressive) saccades (less than 100 pixels, about 5 letters) and the number of refixated words. They achieved 97.1% classification accuracy using a linear SVM classifier. Rello and Ballesteros selected 97 subjects (48 dyslexic, 49 control) aged 10 to 50 years [18]. Using a linear SVM classifier, they achieved a classification performance of 80.4% accuracy, but they did not perform any data-driven feature importance estimation. The features they found to be important were: reading time, mean of fixation duration, and age. We have previously shown [19] that dyslexic and control young adults can also be classified with a 75.75% classification accuracy based on eye-movement measures obtained for silent reading of isolated sentences. We used RFE as a feature selection technique to rank the features based on their importance to the detection of dyslexic subjects. The features with most contributions were: interquartile range (IQR) of the number of fixations, number of progressive saccades and number of all saccades normalized by the number of words, IQR of progressive glissade (corrective eye movements that occur after saccades) duration, median of progressive, regressive and all saccade amplitudes, IQR of regressive glissade amplitude, median of regressive saccade peak velocity, IQR of reading speed and frequency of regressive saccades. To our knowledge, this is the only study that investigated the capability of eye-movement measures in data-driven detection of developmental dyslexia on a pure adult sample.

Literature on data-driven classification of dyslexic and control subjects suggests that eye-movement measures shown to be significantly affected by inter-letter spacing modulation also play a pivotal role in achieving best classification accuracies. However, classification results of the aforementioned studies were based on eye-tracking (ET) data recorded during reading text with default spacing. Accordingly, it remains unclear whether the modulation of eye-movement measures with decrease and/or increase of inter-letter spacing could contribute to improvement in detecting poor readers. To address this shortcoming, in this study, we tested the capability of eye-movement measures in detecting dyslexic young adults based on their eye-tracking data acquired during reading of isolated sentences presented at five different letter spacing levels. Besides evaluating the classification performance, we also assessed the importance of eye-movement measures in achieving best classification accuracies across the spacing levels. To avoid the potential bias of a particular feature selection method, we determined the importance of features by aggregating the results of five feature selection methods.

2 Materials and Methods

2.1 Materials

This study is based on the eye-tracking data of 24 dyslexic (mean and standard deviation age: 24.79 ± 3.47 years; 12 female) and 24 control (age: 23.04 ± 2.52 years; 12 female) young adults. All participants were native speakers of Hungarian and had normal or corrected-to-normal vision. None of the participants had any history of neurological or psychiatric diseases. Dyslexic participants were recruited based on their official diagnosis of developmental dyslexia, and control subjects were selected in a way to match the dyslexics at group level considering age, gender, and level of education. The study was approved by the Committee of Science and Research Ethics of the Medical Research Council and the ethical approval was issued by the Health Registration and Training Center (092,026/2016/OTIG). All methods were carried out in accordance with the approved guidelines and subjects gave written informed consent before starting the experiment.

Participants read isolated Hungarian sentences while their eye movements were recorded. The sentences were selected from the Hungarian Electronic Library (https://mek.oszk.hu). Each sentence was 140–145 characters long, started with a capital letter, contained only words with lemma and word frequencies greater than 0.01 per million, and had neither numerical characters nor special characters other than commas. Text was presented on a 23.5″ liquid crystal display (LG Electronics Inc. 24M47VQ-P) with a resolution of 1920 × 1080 pixels and a refresh rate of 60 Hz using 13 pt Courier New font. The viewing distance was 56 cm. Black text was presented on a 53.3°× 30° (degrees of visual angle) white background. Depending on the level of inter-letter spacing, sentences consisted of one or two text lines that were presented line-by-line. The inter-letter spacing was modulated from 0.7 to 1.9 times (5 levels: Sp1 (×0.7), Sp2 (×1), Sp3 (×1.3), Sp4 (×1.6), Sp5 (×1.9); 50 sentences/spacing level) the normal spacing. In the normal spacing condition, the average character width was ~ 0.23° and the spacing size was ~0.26°. After 25% of sentences, a test statement about the last read sentence was randomly shown, and participants had to report if the statement was true or false by pressing the J or F keyboard buttons, respectively. Eye-tracking data was recorded from the left eye using an iView XTM Hi-Speed 1250 system (SensoMotoric Instruments GmbH, Teltow, Germany) at 1250 Hz sampling rate. Calibration was performed using the built-in randomized 13-point routine with a vertically squeezed calibration area to move the fixation points closer to the horizontal midline where text lines were presented during this experiment. Prior to presentation and after reading of text lines, ET precision and accuracy was validated.

2.2 Methods

Feature Extraction. An adaptive algorithm [20] with default parameter values was used to extract eye-movement characteristics. This approach was partly chosen because of its ability to detect glissades and because, by taking into account the local noise level, it relies on adaptive estimation of threshold values. A collection of 65 features (see the Supplementary Material available at [21]) was defined for all the five spacing levels based on eye-tracking data, the output of the adaptive algorithm and the presented stimuli. The set of features included central tendency (median) and dispersion (IQR) statistics of saccade, glissade and fixation measures obtained after pooling of measures across text lines presented with the same spacing size: duration of saccades, glissades and fixations; amplitude, maximum velocity and acceleration of saccades and glissades; number of saccades and fixations normalized by the number of words. The median frequency of saccades and glissades was also estimated. Progressive (left-to-right or forward) and regressive (right-to-left or backward) eye movements were considered together and separately and the median of their proportion was also calculated. The median and IQR of the mean signal noise, standard deviation of the signal noise and the saccade peak detection threshold as well as the percentage of saccades followed by glissades were also assessed. The set of features was almost identical to the one we used in our previous study [19]. For the main analysis, only two measures were excluded related to reading speed since recent studies indicated that around 90% [22] or even more [23] of variation in reading speed could be explained by different properties of eye movements subserving reading. For the extraction of features, MATLAB R2016b (The MathWorks Inc., Natick, MA, USA) was used with customized scripts based on the toolbox provided by dr. Marcus Nyström.

As a final preprocessing step all features were normalized between 0 and 1 after pooling the measures of the two groups, and a linear SVM classifier [14] was used for the classification of dyslexic and control subjects based on the normalized features.

Feature Selection. Classification performance can be improved by selecting and combining the features. Here, ranking of features and best feature subsets were obtained using different classification performance metrics and five feature selection techniques: forward and backward sequential feature selection (FSFS, BSFS), SVM-based recursive feature elimination (RFE) [15], LASSO [17] and elastic net [24] (ENet). SFS methods are wrapper techniques using a linear SVM classifier with the C hyperparameter set to 1 to evaluate the feature combinations based on classification accuracy. Evaluation of SFS methods was carried out with 10-fold cross-validation that was repeated 10 times. RFE utilizes the internal weights of the SVM to remove the feature with the lowest weight at every iteration, while LASSO and ENet are linear regression-based regularization methods. RFE, LASSO and ENet best feature subsets were obtained applying a 10-fold cross-validation.

Using the feature selection techniques as feature ranking methods, the accuracy of classification can also be considered as a function of the number of features. Although LASSO and ENet provide only the best feature subsets by default, it is also possible to rank the features based on the corresponding coefficient values. Note that a zero coefficient is assigned to features not included in the best subset, which means that a ranking cannot be established for all features.

For default and optimized C values, the performance of the feature combinations selected by the feature selection methods was estimated using a 10-fold cross-validation repeated 10 times.

Hyperparameter Optimization. Optimization of the C hyperparameter was carried out using a greedy search algorithm in the 10^{-3} to 10^3 range. Every candidate C value was evaluated using a 10-fold cross-validation repeated 10 times. For further details, see the Supplementary Material [21].

Cross-validation. Overfitting may occur for small sample sizes when standard k-fold cross-validation is used for model parameter optimization [25]. To address this issue, the whole analysis pipeline including hyperparameter optimization and feature selection was implemented using nested tenfold stratified cross-validation repeated 10 times [26]. The randomization of cross-validation was seeded to make the results reproducible and comparable between the spacing conditions and selection methods.

To evaluate the magnitude of overfitting that could occur as a result of hyperparameter optimization and feature selection, a standard (non-nested) stratified 10 times repeated 10-fold cross-validation was also considered. In this case, the optimization of the C hyperparameter and the selection of features were performed using the entire dataset without separating test sets. The validation of the classifiers with the selected hyperparameter values and feature sets was performed on the same validation datasets with 10 times repeated 10-fold cross-validation.

Classification, feature selection and C parameter optimization were performed using custom Python scripts based on scikit-learn [27] and mlxtend libraries [28].

Performance Metrics of Classification. The nested cross-validation scheme requires a different training set for every iteration, which means that feature selection methods can select different features across the iterations. To determine best feature subsets and ranking of features, different performance metrics were used to aggregate the results over the cross-validation iterations.

Best subset accuracy (BSA) only considers the feature combinations that were found to be the best by a given feature selection method for each iteration. The cross-validated classification performance is estimated by taking the mean and standard deviation of these classification accuracy scores across the iterations.

Ranked max accuracy (RMA) assesses the rankings of features generated by the feature selection techniques. The rankings of features are generated for each iteration by first considering the features with the highest ranking score and then adding the remaining features one-by-one in a rank-wise decreasing fashion. RMA measures are calculated by averaging the classification accuracy across the iterations and taking the maximum of these mean accuracies across the combinations of features with different numbers of features. Even though this metric may be somewhat positively biased, it allows analysis of classification accuracy as a function of the number of features. Note that this average over the cross-validation iterations is often not possible for LASSO and ENet, as these methods do not provide a full ranking of features.

Per iteration max accuracy (PIMA) also assesses the ranked feature combinations as the RMA. However, it takes the maxima across feature combinations with different feature numbers for all iterations, and the cross-validated model performance is given by taking the mean and standard deviation of these maxima over the iterations.

To assess whether the classification capability of two classifiers differs significantly, Kappa analysis [29] was applied. Confusion matrices were generated by adding up the confusion matrices of cross-validation folds and averaging these matrices across the cross-validation repetitions.

Feature Importance Metrics. To assess the importance of features, four feature performance metrics were used.

Individual classification accuracy (IA) is estimated for all features separately by training SVM classifiers on single features using a tenfold stratified cross-validation repeated 10 times.

Selection frequency describes how often a feature chosen by a specific selection method has been selected over the cross-validation iterations.

The added classification accuracy (AA) shows the average change in classification accuracy obtained by adding a given feature to the combination of features. Order of feature addition was based on feature rankings. Note that feature ranking corresponds to feature removals in the case of the feature elimination techniques (RFE and BSFS), but we still regard it as a consecutive feature addition to calculate added classification accuracy. The baseline for features that were added first was chance classification (50%). The estimation of AA is in practice never applicable for all features in every iteration in the case of LASSO and ENet selections, since these feature selection methods assign a zero coefficient for every feature not included in their regression models. Added accuracies were averaged over cross-validation iterations.

The fourth feature importance metric, the leave-out accuracy decrease (LOAD) describes the average accuracy change when a given feature is excluded from a feature set. It is negated so that a positive tendency would indicate that excluding the feature is detrimental. Compared to added classification accuracy, this metric does not utilize the feature ranking but for a given feature combination excludes every feature one-by-one to calculate the leave-out accuracy change. Leave-out accuracies were averaged over all cross-validation iterations.

3 Results

The different cross-validation and accuracy aggregation metrics applied in this study provide thorough information about the models' classification capabilities across different letter spacing levels. The disparity between the standard and nested cross-validations sheds some light on the extent of the dataset overfitting.

SVM using standard cross-validation achieved a higher classification accuracy compared to the nested cross-validation for every feature number (see Fig. 1) and with respect to each accuracy metric (see Fig. 2). The numerical maximum was estimated by the per iteration max accuracy (PIMA) that was always the highest out of the three considered performance metrics, but it does not represent the generalization capability of the models. Best subset accuracy (BSA) reflects the ability of the feature selection methods to select the best feature combinations based on the validation sets at each iteration, while ranked maximum accuracy (RMA) uses the feature rankings generated by the selection methods. This data surplus resulted in higher RMA compared to the best subset metric in the case of RFE, LASSO and ENet (Fig. 2).

With standard cross-validation, results averaged across the letter spacing levels, all feature selection methods first showed increasing tendencies, then reached max ranked accuracy with less than 20 features (83.67% with 5 features for FSFS, 84.24% with 8 features for BSFS, 82.21% with 15 features for RFE) and finally decreased.

With nested cross-validation, the classification accuracy of RFE and FSFS reached their maxima (69.78% and 69.3%, respectively) with only a few features (1 and 6, respectively) and then decreased. BSFS showed increasing tendencies throughout reaching a maximum of 66.63%.

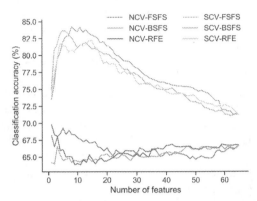

Fig. 1. Standard (SV) and nested (NCV) cross-validation classification accuracy of FSFS, BSFS and RFE feature selection methods averaged across the letter spacing levels as a function of the number of features. LASSO and ENet are excluded as they do not provide valid rankings for all 65 features.

We also evaluated which feature selection methods achieved the best classification accuracy across the letter spacing levels (Fig. 2). With standard cross-validation, BSFS achieved the highest classification accuracy for all performance metrics, closely followed by FSFS then by RFE, ENet and LASSO. In the case of nested-cross validation, the disparity between the feature selection methods was much lower. The FSFS method achieved the highest classification accuracy considering all performance metrics (68.11%, 72.2% and 82.38% for best subset, ranked max and per iteration max, respectively), however, the difference between the FSFS and the worst feature selection method was only ~3.5% for BSA and ~4% for RMA.

The effects of hyperparameter optimization were clearly beneficial in the case of standard cross-validation. Regarding feature selection methods, the highest improvement was achieved by RFE, LASSO and ENet feature selection methods (Fig. 3 left). Considering the optimization effects averaged across the feature selection methods, the highest improvement could be seen for the Sp2 condition followed by Sp1 (Fig. 3 right). In the case of the nested-cross validation, the results are mixed. Nested hyperparameter optimization always improved PIMA, whereas letter spacing and the feature selection method influenced the changes in RMA and BSA measures. In spacing conditions Sp1 and Sp3, both RMA and BSA decreased after hyperparameter optimization. In Sp2 condition, BSA decreased but RMA increased. Lastly, in Sp4 and Sp5 conditions, both metrics increased. Regarding feature selection methods, after hyperparameter optimization, both BSA and RMA were higher using BSFS and lower using FSFS. For RFE and LASSO, BSA decreased while RMA increased after hyperparameter optimization. However, for ENet, the results showed the opposite tendency.

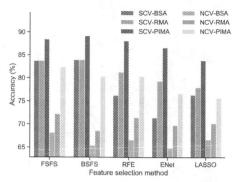

Fig. 2. Best subset (BSA), ranked max (RMA) and per iteration max accuracy (PIMA) metrics averaged across the letter spacing conditions for all feature selection methods (FSFS, BSFS, RFE, ENet and LASSO), using standard (SCV) and nested (NCV) cross-validation without C optimization.

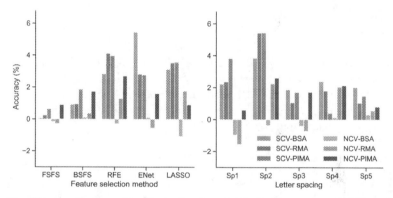

Fig. 3. The difference between C optimized and non-optimized best subset (BSA), ranked max (RMA) and per iteration max (PIMA) accuracies averaged across letter spacing levels (left) and feature selection methods (right), using standard (SCV) and nested (NCV) cross-validation.

For further analysis, we only considered the BSA performance metric as it is the most accurate estimation of the classifiers' generalization capability. Figure 4 shows that both with nested and standard cross-validations, classification accuracy maxima for conditions Sp2, Sp3 and Sp4 are achieved by FSFS. For nested cross-validation, FSFS reaches the maximum accuracy in condition Sp5 as well. The highest classification accuracy obtained for condition Sp4 (73.25%) did not differ significantly from the classification accuracy achieved by the default spacing condition (Sp2, 70.16%, p = 0.71) and the lowest performance found for the minimal spacing size (Sp1, 63.08%, p = 0.28).

To check which features are the most essential for the detection of poor readers, we looked at features that were selected the most often across the feature selection methods and letter spacing conditions both with standard and nested cross-validation (Fig. 5). Out of the first 11 features, 9 were the same in both cross-validation schemes. The

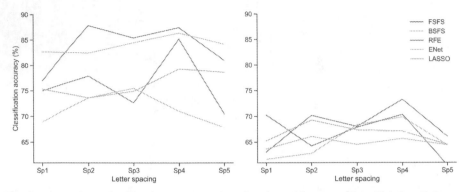

Fig. 4. Best subset classification accuracy as a function of letter spacing (Sp) for all feature selection methods (FSFS, BSFS, RFE, ENet and LASSO) with standard (left) and nested (right) cross-validation without C optimization.

most frequently selected features with nested cross-validation were: median of saccade amplitude (frequency: 59.96%, IA: 71.78%, AA: 8%, LOAD: 2.7%), median of forward saccade amplitude (frequency: 59.32%, IA: 72.2%, AA: 12.5%, LOAD: 2.9%), median of fixation duration (frequency: 37.44%, IA: 63%, AA: 0.3%, LOAD: 0%) and IQR of forward glissade amplitude (frequency: 37.42%, IA: 47.63%, AA: 2.5%, LOAD: 2.3%). Note that while the IQR of forward glissade amplitude had a chance level classification accuracy individually, combining it with other measures had a beneficial effect, while all other measures had a high IA.

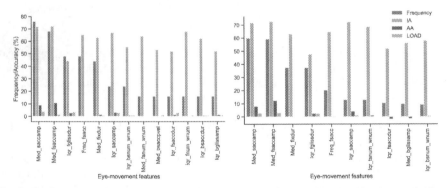

Fig. 5. Performance of eye-movement features aggregated across feature selection methods and letter spacing levels for standard (left) and nested (right) cross-validation. Selection frequency and individual accuracy (IA) of features with a frequency of 40 at least (chosen by 2 feature selections) were first averaged over the feature selection methods and then across letter spacing levels. Aggregated added accuracy (AA) and leave-out accuracy decrease (LOAD) metrics were calculated by taking the average of AA and LOAD values over the feature selection methods weighted by the selection frequency and then averaging across letter spacing levels again weighted by the selection frequency of corresponding features. Features are ordered by their selection frequency. For the definition of features see the Supplementary Material [21].

It is also important to assess how the most frequently selected features were distributed across letter spacing levels (Fig. 6). One can observe that the median of saccade amplitude shows a decreasing tendency over spacing levels Sp1 and Sp3 and stagnates after that, while the median of progressive saccade amplitude increases over Sp1 and Sp3 and then stagnates. The median of fixation duration was selected roughly the same number of times (between 35 and 50) for all spacing levels. In the case of the IQR of progressive glissade duration, no clear tendencies could be observed. Note that out of these four features, three were the same (median of fixation duration was replaced by median of forward saccade number normalized by the number of words) when results of the best feature selection method (FSFS) were considered separately (see [21], Supplementary Fig. 1).

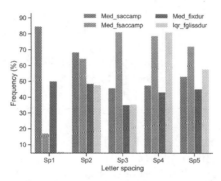

Fig. 6. Selection frequency of the four most frequently selected features as a function of letter spacing (Sp). Features were chosen based on nested cross-validation results averaged across feature selection methods and letter spacing levels. For the definition of features see the Supplementary Material [21].

Besides the features that are relevant across all letter spacing levels, we also analyzed measures that were selected only in particular spacing conditions with at least a frequency of 40% (chosen by 2 feature selection methods) using nested cross-validation. These features were: median backward glissade amplitude in Sp1 (frequency: 49.6%, IA: 56.25%, AA: −2.8%, LOAD: 0.5%), IQR of the total saccade number normalized by the number of words in Sp2 (frequency: 64.8%, IA: 68.6%, AA: 1.5%, LOAD: − 0.5%), and IQR of progressive saccade duration (frequency: 52.8%, IA: 52%, AA: − 3.4%, LOAD: 0.7%) with the IQR of the number of regressive saccades normalized by the number of words (frequency: 46.6%, IA: 56.9%, AA: 1.25%, LOAD: 0.05%), in condition Sp5. No such features were found for spacing levels Sp3 and Sp4.

4   Discussion

In this study, we have tested eye-movement correlates of natural reading for detection of developmental dyslexia in young adults using a data-driven approach and eye-tracking data acquired during reading of isolated sentences that were presented with five letter spacing levels. Applying five different feature selection methods, we have shown that combination of eye-movement features improves classification accuracy and selection of features can reduce the complexity of classification models, making the models more interpretable. By using standard and nested cross-validation, we have shown that overfitting is present in all letter spacing conditions and feature selection methods. As standard cross-validation represents a positively biased estimate of classification accuracy, we intend to discuss only nested cross-validation results in detail. Hyperparameter optimization increased classification accuracy of standard cross-validation considering all performance metrics, and especially for LASSO, ENet and RFE feature selection methods. In the case of nested cross-validation, results varied with letter spacing and feature selection technique, but in general, hyperparameter optimization did not improve the classification performance. Out of the five feature selection methods utilized, FSFS tended to achieve the highest classification accuracy. However, using nested cross-validation without C optimization, the average performance of FSFS across the letter spacing levels was only 3.5% and 4% better than the worst method considering best subset and ranked max metrics, respectively.

We have shown that even though maximum nested BSA of 73.25% could be reached in spacing Sp4, this performance is not significantly better compared to normal spacing (Sp2, 70.16%, p = 0.72) and the worst performing minimal spacing condition (Sp1, 63.08%, p = 0.28). The difference of classification performance between the letter spacing levels was even lower in the case of RMA and PIMA. Despite the insignificance, we could discuss the tendencies shown by the FSFS method in comparing different spacing conditions. According to the results, Sp1 is the worst performing spacing with 63.08% BSA. Sp1 has a reduced spacing ($\times 0.7$ times the normal spacing) which increases crowding of letters. Dyslexics have long been reported to be sensitive to crowding [6, 7], hence the expectation for the group to perform poorly in this kind of spacing. However, this relatively lower classification accuracy of Sp1 compared to other spacing modulations could be due to controls having more difficulties than expected. Thus, the differences between the two groups diminished and were not fully demarcated by the model. This setup could also add more visual load to both groups by increasing the amount of information in a single fixation, thus recruiting more resources for proper execution [10], making it harder, despite a modest 63.08% accuracy, for the model to delineate between typical and poor readers compared to other spacing. However, spacing 4 ($\times 1.6$ times the normal spacing) showed the best accuracy (73.25%). Even though increase in inter-letter spacing seemed to be beneficial for both dyslexic and typical readers, going beyond a critical letter spacing point may be detrimental to reading [5, 10, 11] for both groups but could be more disadvantageous for dyslexics as they are hypothesized to have a shorter perceptual span than experienced readers [4]. Similar to minimal spacing Sp1, typical readers would also have difficulties in reading the text with extra-large spacing Sp5 as longer words may be outside their visual/perceptual span [5] and go beyond and goes beyond the critical point for spacing. This condition might have required both groups to exhibit similar eye-movement behaviors such as short fixations due to lower crowding but exhibited multiple fixations for longer words. This behavior could have led to the difficulties of the model to completely distinguish the two groups apart. This assumption could explain the model's drop in accuracy for this spacing.

We also found that the most prominent features were similar across all letter spacing conditions. Median of forward and all saccade amplitudes, median of fixation duration and IQR of forward glissade duration were the most frequently selected considering all feature selection methods and letter spacings. Taking only the best feature selection method (FSFS) into consideration, three out of these four measures were still the most frequently selected ones, with median of forward saccade number per word number replacing median of the fixation duration. Central tendency of saccade amplitude (both forward and all saccades) and fixation duration were already shown to differ significantly for dyslexic readers [4] who tend to make shorter saccades and longer fixations. The presence of the IQR of forward glissade duration and forward saccade number divided by word number might reflect a difference between the two groups in adapting the reading processes from one sentence to another, with dyslexic readers having lower IQR values. The significance of the glissade-related measure in combination with other features also might reflect that the reading pattern differences of control and dyslexic participants can manifest at the level of fine oculomotor processes. Features that were often selected for one spacing condition only, did not have both a positive AA and LOAD, showing that these features were not always clearly beneficial for that spacing. By including reading speed and performance measures, three out of four most frequently selected features remained the same with the median of the reading speed replacing the median of fixation duration (for details see [21], Supplementary Figs. 2, 3, 4). However, no significant increase in classification accuracy could be achieved after inclusion of basic behavioral measures (see Fig. 4 and Supplementary Figs. 3, 4) indicating no additional orthogonal information in these features. This result is in agreement with the finding that suggests high predictability of reading speed based on eye-movement measures [22, 23].

Despite the promising classification results achieved in this study, the linear SVM classifier might perform poorly in exploiting nonlinearities that could be potentially present in the data. Accordingly, classification paradigms with shallow nonlinearity could enhance the detection of reading difficulties based on eye-movement measures. However, to test this assumption, a larger sample with participants suffering from different subtypes of developmental dyslexia would have to be collected. Carrying out training and optimization procedures on a larger sample could also reduce overfitting and improve the generalizability of the classification frameworks. Moreover, a large sample with random sampling would also allow for the estimation of regression models. Instead of providing binary information only, regression models could predict the level of reading difficulties from behavioral and eye-movement measures. Data-driven reduction of feature dimensionality could also mitigate overfitting and pooling the best performing features from different spacing levels could result in a better performing classifier compared to any given spacing condition. Finally, for early detection of developmental dyslexia, the translational capability of the classification framework developed here for adults would have to be investigated on children.

Acknowledgements. The authors thank Dávid Farkas and dr. Dénes Tóth for their assistance in preparation of text stimuli and data collection. This research was supported by the Hungarian Scientific Research Fund (grant number: K112093), the Hungarian Brain Research Program 2.0 (grant number: NAP 2.0 4001-17919), by the KEP-5/2019 grant and the Neo-PRISM-C project funded by the European Union Horizon 2020 Program (H2020-MSCA-ITN-2018) under the Marie Skłodowska-Curie Innovative Training Network (Grant Agreement No. 813546).

References

1. Shaywitz, S.E., Shaywitz, B.A.: Dyslexia (specific reading disability). Biol. Psychiatry **57**(11) (2005). https://doi.org/10.1016/j.biopsych.2005.01.043
2. Habib, M.: The neurological basis of developmental dyslexia: an overview and working hypothesis. Brain **123**(12) (2000). https://doi.org/10.1093/brain/123.12.2373
3. Snowling, M.J., Hulme, C.: Interventions for children's language and literacy difficulties. Int. J. Lang. Commun. Disord. **47**(1) (2012). https://doi.org/10.1111/j.1460-6984.2011.00081.x
4. Rayner, K.: Eye movements in reading and information processing: 20 years of research. Psychol. Bull. **124**(3) (1998). https://doi.org/10.1037/0033-2909.124.3.372
5. Chung, S.T.L.: The effect of letter spacing on reading speed in central and peripheral vision. Vis. Psychophys. Physiol. Opt. **43**(4), 1270–1276 (2002). https://doi.org/10.1097/00006324-200012001-00034
6. Spinelli, D., De Luca, M., Judica, A., Zoccolotti, P.: Crowding effects on word identification in developmental dyslexia. Cortex **38**(2), 179–200 (2002). https://doi.org/10.1016/S0010-9452(08)70649-X
7. Zorzi, M., et al.: Extra-large letter spacing improves reading in dyslexia. Proc. Natl. Acad. Sci. U.S.A. **109**(28), 11455–11459 (2012). https://doi.org/10.1073/pnas.1205566109
8. Rayner, K., Slattery, T.J., Bélanger, N.N.: Eye movements, the perceptual span, and reading speed. Psychon. Bull. Rev. **17**, 834–839 (2010). https://doi.org/10.3758/PBR.17.6.834
9. Li, S., et al.: Adult age differences in effects of text spacing on eye movements during reading. Front. Psychol. **9** (2019). https://doi.org/10.3389/fpsyg.2018.02700
10. Weiss, B., Knakker, B., Vidnyánszky, Z.: Visual processing during natural reading. Sci. Rep. **6**, 26902 (2016). https://doi.org/10.1038/srep26902
11. Perea, M., Gomez, P.: Subtle increases in interletter spacing facilitate the encoding of words during normal reading. PLoS One **7**(10), 1–7 (2012). https://doi.org/10.1371/journal.pone.0047568
12. McCandliss, B.D.: Helping dyslexic children attend to letters within visual word forms. Proc. Natl. Acad. Sci. **109**(28), 11064–11065 (2012)
13. Nilsson Benfatto, M., Öqvist Seimyr, G., Ygge, J., Pansell, T., Rydberg, A., Jacobson, C.: Screening for dyslexia using eye tracking during reading. PLoS One **11**(12), e0165508 (2016)
14. Cortes, C., Vapnik, V.: Support-vector networks. Mach. Learn. **20**(3) (1995). https://doi.org/10.1023/A:1022627411411
15. Guyon, I., Weston, J., Barnhill, S., Vapnik, V.: Gene selection for cancer classification using support vector machines. Mach. Learn. **46**(1–3) (2002). https://doi.org/10.1023/A:1012487302797
16. Asvestopoulou, T., et al.: DysLexML: screening tool for dyslexia using machine learning (2019). https://arxiv.org/abs/1903.06274
17. Tibshirani, R.: Regression shrinkage and selection via the LASSO. J. Roy. Stat. Soc. Ser. B (Methodol.) **58**(1) (1996). https://doi.org/10.1111/j.2517-6161.1996.tb02080.x
18. Rello, L., Ballesteros, M.: Detecting readers with dyslexia using machine learning with eye tracking measures. In: W4A 2015 - 12th Web for All Conference (2015). https://doi.org/10.1145/2745555.2746644
19. Szalma, J., Weiss, B.: Data-driven classification of dyslexia using eye-movement correlates of natural reading. In: ACM Symposium on Eye Tracking Research and Applications, pp. 1–4. ACM, Stuttgart (2020). https://doi.org/10.1145/3379156.3391379

20. Nyström, M., Holmqvist, K.: An adaptive algorithm for fixation, saccade, and glissade detection in eyetracking data. Behav. Res. Methods **42**(1) (2010). https://doi.org/10.3758/BRM. 42.1.188
21. Szalma, J., Amora, K.K., Vidnyánszky Z., Weiss, B.: Supplementary Material. https://gitlab. com/wb-papers/ettac2020
22. Nárai, Á., Amora, K.K., Vidnyánszky Z., Weiss, B.: Predicting reading speed from eye-movement measures. In: Del Bimbo, A., et al. (eds.) ICPR 2021 Workshops. LNCS, vol. 12663, pp. 453–466 (2021). https://doi.org/10.1007/978-3-030-68796-0_33
23. Krieber, M., et al.: Eye movements during silent and oral reading in a regular orthography: basic characteristics and correlations with childhood cognitive abilities and adolescent reading skills. PLoS One **12**, e0170986 (2017). https://doi.org/10.1371/journal.pone.0170986
24. Zou, H., Hastie, T.: Regularization and variable selection via the elastic net. J. Roy. Stat. Soc. Ser. B Stat. Methodol. **67**(2) (2005). https://doi.org/10.1111/j.1467-9868.2005.00503.x
25. Hastie, T., Tibshirani, R., Friedman, J.: The Elements of Statistical Learning, 2nd edn., Springer, New York (2009). https://doi.org/10.1007/978-0-387-84858-7
26. Vabalas, A., Gowen, E., Poliakoff, E., Casson, A.J.: Machine learning algorithm validation with a limited sample size. PLoS One **14**(11) (2019). https://doi.org/10.1371/journal.pone. 0224365
27. Pedregosa, F., et al.: Scikit-learn: machine learning in Python. J. Mach. Learn. Res. **12**, 2825–2830 (2011)
28. Raschka, S.: MLxtend: providing machine learning and data science utilities and extensions to Python's scientific computing stack. J. Open Source Softw. **3**(24) (2018). https://doi.org/ 10.21105/joss.00638
29. Congalton, R.G., Green, K.: Assessing the Accuracy of Remotely Sensed Data: Principles and Practices. CRC Press, Boca Raton (2019)

FAPER - International Workshop on Fine Art Pattern Extraction and Recognition

Preface

The International Workshop on Fine Art Pattern Extraction and Recognition (FAPER) was intended to provide an international forum for those wishing to present advancements in the state of the art, innovative research, ongoing projects, and academic and industrial reports on the application of visual pattern extraction and recognition for better understanding and fruition of fine arts. Cultural heritage, and in particular fine art, is of inestimable importance for the cultural, historical, and economic growth of our societies. Fine art is developed primarily for aesthetic purposes and is mainly concerned with paintings, sculptures and architecture. In recent years, due to technological improvements and drastic decreases in costs, a large-scale digitization effort has been made, leading to a growing availability of large digitized fine art collections. This availability, coupled with recent advances in pattern recognition and computer vision, has opened new opportunities for computer science researchers to assist the art community with automatic tools to analyse and further understand fine arts, as well as to support the restoration and preservation process of artworks. Among other benefits, a deeper understanding of fine arts has the potential to make them more accessible to a wider population, both in terms of fruition and creation, thus supporting the spread of culture.

The workshop solicited contributions from diverse areas such as pattern recognition, computer vision, artificial intelligence and image processing. The workshop was organized in conjunction with the 25th International Conference on Pattern Recognition (ICPR 2020). Due to the COVID-19 pandemic, the main conference and all associated workshops were fully virtual.

We received 15 submissions for reviews, from authors belonging to 7 distinct countries. After a thorough review process, 14 papers were selected for presentation at the workshop. Each paper received 3 reviews and the review process focused on the quality of the papers, their scientific novelty, the significance of their content and their applicability to the cultural heritage field. The acceptance of the papers was the result of the discussion and agreement of the reviewers.

The accepted papers offer various contributions focusing on different fine arts including painting, sculpture, architecture, photography and historical documents. On the one hand, some contributions address and review the problem of the high-level semantic analysis and interpretation of the artwork. This is faced in terms of the representation of the content of the bare scene, but also in terms of the colors and focal points chosen by the artist, as well as the emotions that arouse to the sight. On the other hand, further contributions focus on solutions for the preservation and restoration of fine arts. Novel methods for archiving, reconstructing, restoring and virtually navigating into different types of artworks are proposed, as well as for analyzing the status and type of materials used. On many occasions, the contributions describe specific relevant case studies, underlining the uniqueness of each individual artist and artwork.

The workshop program was completed by an invited talk on machine and deep learning methods for the semantic segmentation of heritage 3D data. The talk was given by Fabio Remondino from the FBK - Bruno Kessler Foundation, a public research center located in Trento, Italy. In addition to reviewing and comparing various methods, along with a recent benchmark, the talk presented a multi-level multi-resolution approach and reported some generalization results.

Last but not least, we would like to thank the Program Committee, whose members made the workshop possible with their rigorous and timely review process. Moreover, we would like to thank the IAPR Technical Committee 19 - Computer Vision for Cultural Heritage Applications and Journal of Imaging - MDPI for sponsoring and promoting the event.

January 2021

Gennaro Vessio
Giovanna Castellano
Fabio Bellavia

Organization

Chairs

Gennaro Vessio	University of Bari, Italy
Giovanna Castellano	University of Bari, Italy
Fabio Bellavia	University of Palermo, Italy

Program Committee

Gabriella Casalino	University of Bari, Italy
Moises Diaz	Universidad del Atlántico Medio, Spain
Eufemia Lella	Exprivia S.p.A.
Fabrizio Balducci	University of Bari, Italy
Nicole Dalia Cilia	University of Cassino and Southern Lazio, Italy
Andrea Pazienza	Exprivia S.p.A.
Eleonora Bernasconi	Sapienza University of Rome, Italy
Matteo Stefanini	University of Modena and Reggio Emilia, Italy
Petia Radeva	Universitat de Barcelona, Spain
Matteo Tomei	University of Modena and Reggio Emilia, Italy
Eva Cetinic	Rudjer Boskovic Institute, Croatia
Miguel Ceriani	University of Bari, Italy
Xi Shen	ParisTech, France
Giosuè Lo Bosco	University of Palermo, Italy
Lorenzo Seidenari	University of Florence, Italy
Marco Fanfani	University of Florence, Italy
Fabio Remondino	FBK, Italy
Eleonora Grilli	FBK, Italy

A Brief Overview of Deep Learning Approaches to Pattern Extraction and Recognition in Paintings and Drawings

Giovanna Castellano⊕ and Gennaro Vessio(✉)⊕

Department of Computer Science, University of Bari "Aldo Moro", Bari, Italy
{giovanna.castellano,gennaro.vessio}@uniba.it

Abstract. This paper provides a brief overview of some of the most relevant deep learning approaches to visual art pattern extraction and recognition, particularly painting and drawing. Indeed, recent advances in deep learning and computer vision, coupled with the growing availability of large digitized visual art collections, have opened new opportunities for computer science researchers to assist the art community with automatic tools to analyze and further understand visual arts. Among other benefits, a deeper understanding of visual arts has the potential to make them more accessible to a wider population, both in terms of fruition and creation, thus supporting the spread of culture.

Keywords: Cultural heritage · Visual arts · Deep learning · Computer vision · Literary review

1 Introduction

Visual arts play a strategic role for the cultural, historic and economic growth of our societies [25]. They stimulate interest and can change the way we look at the world around us. They tell stories that words cannot capture. Visual arts are also vital for children's learning, as they can help students form their creativity while developing their personality [21].

In the last few years, due to technology improvements and drastically declining costs, a large-scale digitization effort has been made, leading to a growing availability of large digitized visual art collections. This availability, coupled with the recent advances in deep learning and computer vision, has opened new opportunities for computer science researchers to assist the art community with automatic tools to analyze and further understand visual arts. Among other benefits, a deeper understanding of visual arts has the potential to make them more accessible to a wider population, both in terms of fruition and creation, thus supporting the spread of culture.

The ability to recognize meaningful patterns in visual artworks inherently falls within the domain of human perception. Recognizing stylistic and semantic attributes of an artwork, in fact, originates from the composition of the colour,

A. Del Bimbo et al. (Eds.): ICPR 2020 Workshops, LNCS 12663, pp. 487–501, 2021.
https://doi.org/10.1007/978-3-030-68796-0_35

texture and shape features visually perceived by the human eye. In the past years, this task has been computationally tackled by using hand-crafted features (e.g., [7,23,34]). However, despite the promising results of feature engineering techniques, early attempts were affected by the difficulty of capturing explicit knowledge about the attributes to be associated with a particular artist or artwork. Such a difficulty arises because this knowledge is typically associated with implicit and subjective expertise human observers may find hard to verbalize and conceptualize.

Conversely, representation learning approaches, such as those on which deep learning models typically rely, can be the key to tackling the problem of extracting useful representations from low-level colour and texture features. These representations can assist in various art-related tasks, ranging from object detection in paintings to artistic style categorization, useful for examples in museum and art gallery websites.

This paper aims at providing a brief overview of some of the most relevant works investigating the application of deep learning-based approaches to visual art pattern extraction and recognition. Visual arts are developed primarily for aesthetic purposes, and are mainly concerned with painting, drawing, photography and architecture. In this paper, we restrict our focus only to painting and drawing, as two of the most studied visual arts.

This literary review is intended to provide the reader not only with a state-of-the-art and future perspective on the topic, but also with some guidelines that the reader may find useful for entering this line of research. For this reason, the paper is divided into two main parts. The first part, which is reported in Sect. 2, describes some available datasets and the deep learning methods typically used. The second part, which is reported in Sect. 3, discusses the main research trends. It is worth remarking that some of the concepts discussed in Sect. 2 are redundant with the content of Sect. 3; nevertheless, we believe this organization contributes to improving readability. Finally, Sect. 4 concludes the paper and outlines directions for further research on the topic.

2   Main Datasets and Deep Learning Approaches

This Section briefly reviews some of the most relevant datasets, as well as the basic principles of the main deep learning methods adopted in this context.

2.1   Datasets

A schematic description of some of the most commonly used and relevant datasets is provided in Table 1.

WikiArt[1] (formerly known as WikiPaintings) is currently one of the largest online collections of digitized paintings available. It integrates a broad set of metadata including style, period and series. The artworks it includes span a wide

---

[1] https://www.wikiart.org.

Table 1. Schematic overview of some of the most frequently used and relevant datasets.

Dataset	# artworks	Main task
WikiArt	~170,000	Classification and retrieval
Art500k	~550,000	Classification and retrieval
Rijksmuseum	~650,000	Classification and retrieval
The MET	~400,000	Classification and retrieval
People-Art	~4,500	Object recognition and detection
BAM!	~65,000,000	Object recognition and detection
SemArt	~20,000	Multi-modal retrieval
Artpedia	~3,000	Multi-modal retrieval

range of periods, with a particular focus on the modern and contemporary art. WikiArt has been a frequent choice for creating datasets in many of the recent studies and has contributed to several art-related research projects. The dataset is continuously growing and includes not only paintings but also sculptures, sketches, posters, etc. At the time of writing, the WikiArt dataset comprises around 170,000 artworks attributed to 171 art movements (some samples are shown in Fig. 1). Analogously, Art500k [28] is a large-scale visual art dataset with over than 550,000 digital artworks with rich annotations. It provides, in fact, detailed labels not only related to artist and genre but also to event, place and historical figure. All images were mainly scraped from a few websites, including WikiArt itself, and are low resolution copies of the original artworks.

In addition to these projects, some museums begun to make available to developers, researchers and enthusiasts their artwork collections. For example, the Rijksmuseum of Amsterdam made available (the first API for data collection was launched in 2013) extensive descriptions of more than a half a million art historical objects, hundreds of thousands of object photographs and the complete library catalogue. The dataset was introduced as part of a challenge and consisted of around 100,000 photographic reproductions of the artworks exhibited in the museum. Since then, the digitally available content has been updated. The Rijksmuseum uses controlled vocabularies to unambiguously describe its collection and bibliographic datasets. These thesauri contain information about, for example, people, locations, events and concepts. Currently, the museum is developing technologies to allow users to make optimal use of Linked Open Data. Similarly, on February 2017, the Metropolitan Museum of Art of New York City, colloquially "The MET", made all the images of public-domain works in its collection available under Creative Commons open access license.[2] In particular, the museum made available for download more than 406,000 images of artworks representing more than 5,000 years of art from all over the world, from the classic age to contemporary works.

---

[2] https://www.metmuseum.org.

Fig. 1. Sample digital artworks from WikiArt.

All the datasets mentioned above are mainly designed to perform classification and retrieval tasks. A few datasets, instead, have been enriched with precise information on objects, for object recognition and detection purposes. This is the case, for example, of the People-Art dataset, which provides bounding boxes for the single "person" category [42]. The authors claim that the reason for only labeling people is that they occur more frequently than any other object class. A similar purpose is pursued by the Behance-Artistic-Media (BAM!) dataset [43], built from Behance, that is a portfolio website for contemporary commercial and professional artists, containing over ten million projects and 65 million images. Artworks on Behance span many fields, such as sculpture, painting, photography, graphic design, graffiti, illustration, and advertising. Unlike other datasets, BAM! collects a rich vocabulary of emotion, media, and content attributes; in particular, six content attributes are considered, corresponding to popular PASCAL VOC categories: bicycle, bird, car, cat, dog, people.

Finally, to accommodate a multi-modal retrieval task where paintings are retrieved in accordance with an artistic text, and vice versa, a few datasets provide not only metadata attributes but also artistic comments or descriptions, such as those that commonly appear in catalogues or museum collections. This is the case of SemArt [16] and Artpedia [36]. The main difference between them is that Artpedia distinguishes *visual* sentences, describing the visual content of the work, from *contextual* sentences, describing the historical context of the work.

2.2 Deep Learning Approaches

Deep learning refers to a class of machine learning techniques that exploits hierarchical architectures of information processing layers for feature learning and pattern recognition [26]. The main advantage over classic machine learning algorithms is the ability of deep learning models to learn features that can be relevant for the task at hand directly from data. This is desirable especially in *perceptual* problems, such as aesthetic perception, as mimicking skills that humans feel natural and intuitive has been elusive for machines for a long time.

Indeed, deep learning has a fairly long history, the basic concept of which originates from artificial neural network research. The neural network paradigm was popularized in the 1980s thanks to the introduction of the well-known back-propagation algorithm, which allows a network to update its parameters in an effective way. However, due to the lack of large-scale training data and limited computation power, neural networks went out of fashion in the early 2000s. In the last years, the availability of large annotated datasets, such as ImageNet, and the development of high performance parallel computing systems, such as GPUs, have boosted a revival of deep learning with breakthroughs in historically difficult tasks, notably image classification and natural language processing.

A rich family of deep learning techniques has been proposed [27]: among these, the most commonly used in the art domain are discussed below.

Convolutional Neural Networks. Since their appearance, Convolutional Neural Networks (CNNs) have revolutionized image processing and are now almost universally used in computer vision applications [24]. They are much better suited for image data than traditional multi-layer perceptrons, thanks to their ability to retain the spatial input information as it propagates forward. The two main building blocks of CNNs, in fact, which are convolutional layers and pooling layers, are respectively able to detect the presence of features throughout an image and guarantee, to some extent, a translation invariance property. When used in the painting domain, a CNN can learn to recognize an artist's visually distinctive features by adapting its filters to respond to the presence of these features in a digital painting. The fully-connected layers typically stacked on top of the convolutional/pooling layers can then be used to translate the presence and intensity of the filter responses into a single confidence score for an artist. In this way, a high confidence score is indicative of the presence of a strong response, while a low score indicates that responses are weak or non-existent. A classic example is PigeoNET, a CNN conceived for an artist attribution task based on digital artwork training data [41]. When enriched with a feature visualization technique, such a network can show the regions of the input image that contributed most to the correct artist attribution, especially in case of multiple authorship. More recently, multi-task models have begun to gain popularity, which provide an effective method to solve separate tasks (artist attribution, period estimation, etc.), tackling them simultaneously. Sharing data representation among tasks, in fact, allows the model to exploit the "semantic entanglement" among them to achieve better accuracy [37].

Object Detectors. Object detection systems involve not only recognizing and classifying an object in an image, but also localizing where the object is by drawing a rectangular bounding box around it. This clearly makes object detection more difficult than traditional image classification. Generic object detection frameworks can be mainly categorized into two classes. The first one includes models that generate region proposals at first and then classify each proposal into different categories. This two-step process was pioneered by the well-known R-CNN model [18]. The second class concerns those models that regard object detection as a regression or classification problem, adopting a unified process to achieve categories and locations directly in one step. One of the most popular frameworks that falls in this class is the YOLO object detection family [30]. A trade-off should be considered between the two classes, as region proposal based methods usually perform better, while regression based methods are faster at the expense of decreased accuracy. The main problem encountered when using object detectors on artistic images is the so-called *cross-depiction* problem, that is the problem of detecting objects regardless of how they are depicted (photographed, painted, drawn, etc.). Most methods tacitly assume a photographic input, both at training and test time; however, any solution that does not generalize well regardless of its input depiction is of limited applicability.

Generative Adversarial Networks. Generative Adversarial Networks (GANs), firstly proposed by Goodfellow et al. in [20], represent an emerging paradigm for unsupervised deep learning. They are characterized by a pair of networks, typically consisting of convolutional and/or fully-connected layers, which are in competition against each other. The first network, generally referred to as the *generator*, creates fake images, with the aim of making them as realistic as possible. The second network, called the *discriminator*, receives both real and fake images, with the aim to tell them apart. The two networks are trained simultaneously: when the generator is able to perfectly match the real data distribution, then the discriminator is maximally fooled, predicting 0.5 for all input images. As generative models learn to capture the statistical distribution of data, this allows for the synthesis of samples from the learned distribution. In the specific context of computational creativity, GANs allow practitioners to automatically create a form of art [14].

3   Main Research Trends

The studies involving deep learning approaches for pattern extraction and recognition in paintings and drawings can be broadly classified in accordance with the task being solved. These tasks outlined some main research trends and directions: they are discussed in the following subsections.

3.1   Artwork Attribute Prediction

One of the tasks most frequently faced by researchers in the visual art domain is learning to recognize some artwork attributes (artist, genre, period, etc.) from their *visual style*. Automatic attribute prediction can support art experts in their work on painting analysis and in organizing large collections of paintings. In addition, the widespread diffusion of the mobile technology encouraged the tourism industry in developing applications that are able to automatically recognize art-work attributes in order to provide visitors with relevant information. Although the concept of visual style is rather difficult to define rigorously, distinct styles are recognizable to human observers and are often evident in different painting schools. Artistic visual styles, such as Impressionism, Romanticism, etc., indeed, are characterized by distinctive features which allow artworks to be grouped into related art movements. In other words, every artwork has a visual style "idiosyncratic signature" [3] which relates it to other similar works.

The papers investigating this topic can be further categorized depending on the use of either one single model for each individual attribute prediction or a multi-task model aimed at predicting different attributes simultaneously.

Single-Task Methods. Thanks to their ability to capture not only color distribution, but also higher level features related to object categories, features automatically extracted by a CNN can easily surpass traditional hand-crafted features when tackling an artwork attribute prediction task. One of the first works on this topic, namely the research presented by Karayev et al. in [22], in fact, showed how a CNN pre-trained on PASCAL VOC, i.e. an object recognition and detection dataset, is quite effective in attributing the correct painting school to an artwork. The authors explain this behaviour observing that object recognition depends on object appearance, thus the model learns to re-use these features for image style. In other words, they suggest style is highly content-dependent.

As mentioned above, another seminal work in this context is the research presented in [41], in which van Noord et al. proposed PigeoNET: a CNN trained on a large collection of paintings to perform the task of automatic artist association based on visual characteristics. These characteristics can also be used to reveal the artist of a precise area of an artwork, in the case of multiple authorship of a same work. We observe that the classification of an artist's unique characteristics is a complex task, even for an expert. This can be explained considering that there can be low inter-variability among different artists and high intra-variability in the style of the same artist.

In [32], Saleh and Elgammal developed a model that is capable of predicting not only style, but also genre and artist, based on a metric learning approach. The goal is to learn similarity measures optimized on the historical knowledge available on the specific domain. After learning the metric, the raw visual features are projected into a new optimized feature space on which standard classifiers are trained to solve the corresponding prediction task. In addition to classic visual descriptors, the authors also made use of features automatically learned by a CNN. Also in [38], Tan et al. focused on the three tasks of style, genre and artist classification, and conducted training on each task individually. Interestingly, they also visualized the neurons' responses in the genre classification task, highlighting how neurons in the first layer learn to recognize simple features, while, as layers go deeper, neurons learn to recognize more complex patterns, such as faces in portraits (Fig. 2(a)).

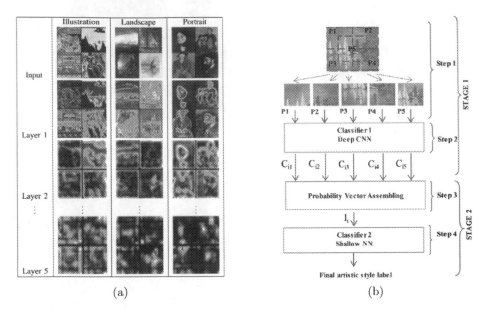

Fig. 2. (a) Visualization of the neurons' response in a genre classification task [38]. (b) Two-stage style classification model proposed in [33].

Cetinic et al. [10] conducted an extensive experimentation to investigate the effective transferability of deep representations across different domains. Interestingly, one of their main findings is that fine-tuning networks pre-trained for scene recognition and sentiment prediction yields better performance in style classification than fine-tuning networks pre-trained for object recognition (typically ImageNet).

In [11], Chen et al. further advances the research on the use of CNNs for style classification, moving from the observation that different layers in existing deep learning models have different feature responses for the same input image. To take full advantage of information from different layers, the authors propose an adaptive cross-layer model that combines responses from both lower and higher layers to capture style. Finally, another contribution was made by Sandoval et al. [33], who proposed a two-stage image classification approach to improve style classification. In the first stage, the method splits the input image into patches and uses a CNN model to classify the artistic style for each patch. Then, the probability scores given by the CNN are incorporated into a single feature vector which is fed as an individual input to a shallow neural network model that provides the final classification (see Fig. 2(b)). The main intuition of the proposed method is that the single patches work as independent evaluators of different portions of the same image; the final model ensembles those evaluations to make the final decision. As is usually the case in this research, confusion was found between historically similar styles.

Multi-Task Methods. The methods described above address each prediction task individually. Tackling multiple tasks with a single end-to-end trainable model can aid in training efficiency and improve classification performance if there is a correlation between different representations of the same input for different tasks. A popular multi-task method in this domain is OmniArt [37]: it basically consists of a multi-output CNN model in which there is a shared convolutional base for feature extraction and separate output layers, one for each task. The overall training is carried out by minimizing an aggregated loss obtained as a weighted combination of the separate losses.

A different approach was adopted in [4] by Belhi et al. who present a multimodal architecture that simultaneously takes both the digital image and textual metadata as inputs. The three-channel image goes through the convolutional base of a standard ResNet; some metadata, particularly information on genre, medium and style, are one-hot-encoded and given as an input to a shallow feed-forward network. Higher level visual and textual features are concatenated and used to feed the final classification layer. Experimental results indicate that the multi-modal classification system outperforms the individual classification in most cases.

Garcia et al. [15] move a step further by combining a multi-output model trained to solve attribute prediction tasks based on visual features and a second model based on non-visual information extracted from artistic metadata encoded by using a knowledge graph (see Fig. 3). In short, a knowledge graph is a complex graph that is capable of capturing unstructured relationships between the data represented in the graph. The second model based on the constructed graph is therefore intended to inject "context" information to improve the performance of the first model. Indeed, at test time, the context embeddings obtained by computing the knowledge graph cannot be obtained from samples that were not included as nodes, thus the modules that process this information are thrown away. However, the assumption is that the main classification model has been forced to learn how to incorporate some contextual information during training. It is worth noting that the proposed method is successfully used by the authors to perform both painting classification and retrieval.

3.2   Object Recognition and Detection

Another task frequently addressed by the research community working in this field is finding objects in artworks. Object recognition and detection in artworks can help solve large-scale retrieval tasks as well as support the analyses made by historians. Art historians, in fact, are often interested in finding out when a specific object first appeared in a painting or how the portrayal of an object evolved during time. A pioneering work in this context has been the research reported in [12] by Crowley and Zisserman. They proposed a system that, given an input query, retrieves positive training samples by crawling Google Images on-the-fly. These are then processed by a pre-trained CNN and used in conjunction with a pre-computed pool of negative features to learn a real-time classifier. The classifier finally returns a ranked list of paintings containing the queried object.

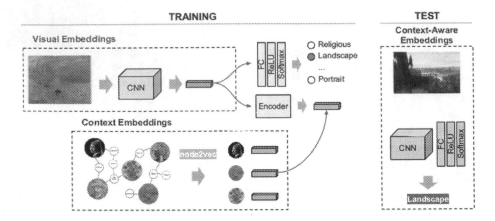

Fig. 3. The method proposed in [15] combining both visual and context embeddings.

In this context, Cai et al. [5,6] were among the firsts to emphasize the importance of tackling the *cross-depiction* problem in computer vision, i.e. recognizing and detecting objects regardless of whether they are photographed, painted, drawn, and so on. The variance across photos and artworks is greater than either domains when considered alone, thus classifiers usually trained on natural images may find difficulties when dealing with painting images, due to the domain shift. Given the unlimited range of potential depictions of a same object, the authors recognize that learning the specificity of each depiction is not a candidate solution, but learning the abstraction different depictions have in common so that they can be recognized independently of their depiction.

Crowley and Zisserman [13] improved on their previous work by shifting from image-level classifiers, i.e. those that take the overall image as an input, to object detection systems, which are assumed to improve the detection of small objects that are particularly prevalent in paintings. The findings of their experimental study provided evidence that detectors can find many objects in paintings that were likely to be overlooked. Westlake et al. [42] improved upon this line of research by showing how a CNN only trained on photos can lead to overfitting; conversely, fine-tuning on artworks allows the model to better generalize to other artwork styles. To evaluate their proposal, the authors used the People-Art dataset, purposely realized for the task of people detection. To push forward research in this direction, Wilber et al. [43] does not restrict their focus only on people, but propose to use the previously mentioned BAM! dataset, which is designed to provide researchers with a large benchmark dataset to expand the current state-of-the-art of computer vision to the visual art domain.

More recently, Gonthier et al. [19] focused on more specific objects or visual attributes that may be useful to art historians, such as ruins or nudity, and iconographic characters, such as the Virgin, Jesus, etc. These categories are unlikely to be inherited directly from photographic databases. To overcome this problem, the authors propose a "weakly supervised" approach that can learn to detect objects by only relying on image-level annotations. The goal is to detect new, unseen objects with minimal supervision.

As can be realistically supposed, the approaches discussed are more successful with artworks that are "photo-realistic" by nature, but can fail or show degraded performance when used on more abstract styles such as Cubism [17].

3.3 Content Generation

The last task we explore in this overview is the generation of art by machines. This is a central problem in the Artificial Intelligence community, as making a machine capable of displaying creativity on a human level (not only in painting, but also in poetry, music, and so on) is widely recognized as an expression of intelligence. Traditional literature on computational creativity developed systems for art generation based on the involvement of human artists in the generation process. More recently, the advent of the Generative Adversarial Network paradigm has allowed researchers to develop systems that do not put humans in the loop but make use of prior human products in the learning process. This is consistent with the assumption that even human experts utilize prior experience and their knowledge of past art to develop their own creativity.

In [14], Elgammal et al. proposed CAN (Creative Adversarial Network): a variant of a classic GAN architecture which aims to create art by maximizing the deviation from established styles and minimizing the deviation from art distribution. In other words, the model "tries to generate art that is novel, but not too novel". Deviating from established styles is important, as a classic GAN would "emulate" the prior data distribution showing limited creativity. The effectiveness of CAN was assessed by involving the judgment of human evaluators, who regularly confused the generated art with human art. Examples of images generated by CAN are shown in Fig. 4. Of course, the machine has no semantic understanding of the subject matter, since its learning is based only on exposure to prior art.

Similarly, Tan et al. [39] proposed ArtGan: a GAN variant in which the gradient information with respect to the label is propagated from the discriminator back to the generator for better learning representation and image quality. Additional architectural novelties are introduced in the model generation. Qualitative results show that ArtGan is capable of generating plausible-looking artworks based on style, artist and genre.

Fig. 4. Examples of images generated by CAN, ranked as highly plausible by human experts [14].

4   Concluding Remarks and Future Directions

The growing availability of large digitized artwork collections has given rise to a new, intriguing research area where computer vision and visual arts meet. The new research area is framed as a sub-field of the constantly growing *digital humanities*, which aims to bring together digital technologies and humanities. Applications are countless and range from information retrieval in digital databases to the design of novel human-computer interaction paradigms.

It is worth remarking that there are at least two (implicit) assumptions made by researchers in this field. First, the input to deep learning models are assumed to be faithful photographic reproductions of actual paintings. While this can be generally considered true, it is worth mentioning that reproduction is highly dependent on the quality of illumination, the relative distance from the artwork when the photo is taken, etc., which may hamper the following feature extraction process if standard criteria are not followed during digitization. Therefore, caution should be used when using digitized images, especially considering that the problems mentioned above can be exacerbated by the reduction in size and normalization process images usually undergo before being fed to CNN models. The second assumption is that digital artworks will be treated in the same way as traditional digital images when provided as an input to CNNs when used as feature extractors. Even this assumption can be trusted, especially if CNN models are asked to find both low-level and high-level visual features to perform tasks as diverse as style, genre, and artist recognition. However, when these models are asked to recognize or even detect objects regardless of how they are depicted, performance drops dramatically.

As is usually the case in deep learning applications, the real success of these models is that they automatically project raw pixel values into meaningful embeddings where patterns of interest begin to emerge. However, although this representation capability can be enhanced with visualization techniques, such as attention and saliency maps, which provide a means to highlight the neurons' response to some input features, explaining the rationale behind what the algorithm discovers is still very difficult. Very recent works are investigating *neuro-symbolic* approaches, in which knowledge bases are used to guide the learning process of deep neural networks [1,2]. This hybrid approach has the potential to bridge the gap between visual perception and reasoning, and may play a role in enabling a machine to mimic the complex human aesthetic perception, the underlying processes of which are still largely unknown. Filling this gap can foster the dialogue between computer vision enthusiasts and humanists that currently seems to lack [29].

We warn the reader that this overview does not purport to be comprehensive but, for space reasons, deliberately ignored some other research topics falling under this umbrella, such as artistic influence discovery (e.g., [8,9,31]), near-duplicate detection (e.g., [35]) and image-to-image translation (e.g., [40]). A future extension could provide the reader with a more exhaustive literary review.

Acknowledgement. Gennaro Vessio acknowledges funding support from the Italian Ministry of Education, University and Research through the PON AIM 1852414 project.

References

1. Aggarwal, G., Parikh, D.: Neuro-symbolic generative art: a preliminary study. arXiv preprint arXiv:2007.02171 (2020)
2. Amizadeh, S., Palangi, H., Polozov, O., Huang, Y., Koishida, K.: Neuro-symbolic visual reasoning: Disentangling "visual" from "reasoning". arXiv preprint arXiv:2006.11524 (2020)
3. Bar, Y., Levy, N., Wolf, L.: Classification of artistic styles using binarized features derived from a deep neural network. In: Agapito, L., Bronstein, M.M., Rother, C. (eds.) ECCV 2014. LNCS, vol. 8925, pp. 71–84. Springer, Cham (2015). https://doi.org/10.1007/978-3-319-16178-5_5
4. Belhi, A., Bouras, A., Foufou, S.: Leveraging known data for missing label prediction in cultural heritage context. Appl. Sci. **8**(10), 1768 (2018)
5. Cai, H., Wu, Q., Corradi, T., Hall, P.: The cross-depiction problem: computer vision algorithms for recognising objects in artwork and in photographs. arXiv preprint arXiv:1505.00110 (2015)
6. Cai, H., Wu, Q., Hall, P.: Beyond photo-domain object recognition: Benchmarks for the cross-depiction problem. In: Proceedings of the IEEE International Conference on Computer Vision Workshops, pp. 1–6 (2015)
7. Carneiro, G., da Silva, N.P., Del Bue, A., Costeira, J.P.: Artistic image classification: an analysis on the PRINTART database. In: Fitzgibbon, A., Lazebnik, S., Perona, P., Sato, Y., Schmid, C. (eds.) ECCV 2012. LNCS, vol. 7575, pp. 143–157. Springer, Heidelberg (2012). https://doi.org/10.1007/978-3-642-33765-9_11
8. Castellano, G., Lella, E., Vessio, G.: Visual link retrieval and knowledge discovery in painting datasets. Multimedia Tools Appl. (2020, in press)
9. Castellano, G., Vessio, G.: Towards a tool for visual link retrieval and knowledge discovery in painting datasets. In: Ceci, M., Ferilli, S., Poggi, A. (eds.) IRCDL 2020. CCIS, vol. 1177, pp. 105–110. Springer, Cham (2020). https://doi.org/10.1007/978-3-030-39905-4_11

10. Cetinic, E., Lipic, T., Grgic, S.: Fine-tuning convolutional neural networks for fine art classification. Expert Syst. Appl. **114**, 107–118 (2018)
11. Chen, L., Yang, J.: Recognizing the style of visual arts via adaptive cross-layer correlation. In: Proceedings of the 27th ACM International Conference on Multimedia, pp. 2459–2467 (2019)
12. Crowley, E.J., Zisserman, A.: In search of art. In: Agapito, L., Bronstein, M.M., Rother, C. (eds.) ECCV 2014. LNCS, vol. 8925, pp. 54–70. Springer, Cham (2015). https://doi.org/10.1007/978-3-319-16178-5_4
13. Crowley, E.J., Zisserman, A.: The art of detection. In: Hua, G., Jégou, H. (eds.) ECCV 2016. LNCS, vol. 9913, pp. 721–737. Springer, Cham (2016). https://doi.org/10.1007/978-3-319-46604-0_50
14. Elgammal, A., Liu, B., Elhoseiny, M., Mazzone, M.: CAN: creative adversarial networks, generating "art" by learning about styles and deviating from style norms. arXiv preprint arXiv:1706.07068 (2017)
15. Garcia, N., Renoust, B., Nakashima, Y.: ContextNet: representation and exploration for painting classification and retrieval in context. Int. J. Multimedia Inf. Retr. **9**(1), 17–30 (2020). https://doi.org/10.1007/s13735-019-00189-4
16. Garcia, N., Vogiatzis, G.: How to read paintings: semantic art understanding with multi-modal retrieval. In: Leal-Taixé, L., Roth, S. (eds.) ECCV 2018. LNCS, vol. 11130, pp. 676–691. Springer, Cham (2019). https://doi.org/10.1007/978-3-030-11012-3_52
17. Ginosar, S., Haas, D., Brown, T., Malik, J.: Detecting people in cubist art. In: Agapito, L., Bronstein, M.M., Rother, C. (eds.) ECCV 2014. LNCS, vol. 8925, pp. 101–116. Springer, Cham (2015). https://doi.org/10.1007/978-3-319-16178-5_7
18. Girshick, R., Donahue, J., Darrell, T., Malik, J.: Rich feature hierarchies for accurate object detection and semantic segmentation. In: Proceedings of the IEEE Conference on Computer Vision and Pattern Recognition, pp. 580–587 (2014)
19. Gonthier, N., Gousseau, Y., Ladjal, S., Bonfait, O.: Weakly supervised object detection in artworks. In: Leal-Taixé, L., Roth, S. (eds.) ECCV 2018. LNCS, vol. 11130, pp. 692–709. Springer, Cham (2019). https://doi.org/10.1007/978-3-030-11012-3_53
20. Goodfellow, I., Pouget-Abadie, J., Mirza, M., Xu, B., Warde-Farley, D., Ozair, S., Courville, A., Bengio, Y.: Generative adversarial nets. In: Advances in Neural Information Processing Systems, pp. 2672–2680 (2014)
21. van de Kamp, M.T., Admiraal, W., van Drie, J., Rijlaarsdam, G.: Enhancing divergent thinking in visual arts education: effects of explicit instruction of metacognition. Br. J. Educ. Psychol. **85**(1), 47–58 (2015)
22. Karayev, S., et al.: Recognizing image style. arXiv preprint arXiv:1311.3715 (2013)
23. Khan, F.S., Beigpour, S., Van de Weijer, J., Felsberg, M.: Painting-91: a large scale database for computational painting categorization. Mach. Vis. Appl. **25**(6), 1385–1397 (2014)
24. Krizhevsky, A., Sutskever, I., Hinton, G.E.: Imagenet classification with deep convolutional neural networks. In: Advances in Neural Information Processing Systems, pp. 1097–1105 (2012)
25. Leavy, P.: Handbook of Arts-Based Research. Guilford Publications, New York (2017)
26. LeCun, Y., Bengio, Y., Hinton, G.: Deep learning. Nature **521**(7553), 436–444 (2015)
27. Liu, W., Wang, Z., Liu, X., Zeng, N., Liu, Y., Alsaadi, F.E.: A survey of deep neural network architectures and their applications. Neurocomputing **234**, 11–26 (2017)

28. Mao, H., Cheung, M., She, J.: DeepArt: learning joint representations of visual arts. In: Proceedings of the 25th ACM International Conference on Multimedia, pp. 1183–1191. ACM (2017)
29. Mercuriali, G.: Digital art history and the computational imagination. Int. J. Digit. Art Hist. Issue 3 2018: Digit. Space Architect. **3**, 141 (2019)
30. Redmon, J., Farhadi, A.: YOLOv3: an incremental improvement. arXiv preprint arXiv:1804.02767 (2018)
31. Saleh, B., Abe, K., Arora, R.S., Elgammal, A.: Toward automated discovery of artistic influence. Multimedia Tools Appl. **75**(7), 3565–3591 (2014). https://doi. org/10.1007/s11042-014-2193-x
32. Saleh, B., Elgammal, A.: Large-scale classification of fine-art paintings: learning the right metric on the right feature. arXiv preprint arXiv:1505.00855 (2015)
33. Sandoval, C., Pirogova, E., Lech, M.: Two-stage deep learning approach to the classification of fine-art paintings. IEEE Access **7**, 41770–41781 (2019)
34. Shamir, L., Macura, T., Orlov, N., Eckley, D.M., Goldberg, I.G.: Impressionism, expressionism, surrealism: automated recognition of painters and schools of art. ACM Trans. Appl. Percept. (TAP) **7**(2), 8 (2010)
35. Shen, X., Efros, A.A., Aubry, M.: Discovering visual patterns in art collections with spatially-consistent feature learning. In: Proceedings of the IEEE Conference on Computer Vision and Pattern Recognition, pp. 9278–9287 (2019)
36. Stefanini, M., Cornia, M., Baraldi, L., Corsini, M., Cucchiara, R.: Artpedia: a new visual-semantic dataset with visual and contextual sentences in the artistic domain. In: Ricci, E., Rota Bulò, S., Snoek, C., Lanz, O., Messelodi, S., Sebe, N. (eds.) ICIAP 2019. LNCS, vol. 11752, pp. 729–740. Springer, Cham (2019). https://doi.org/10.1007/978-3-030-30645-8_66
37. Strezoski, G., Worring, M.: OmniArt: multi-task deep learning for artistic data analysis. arXiv preprint arXiv:1708.00684 (2017)
38. Tan, W.R., Chan, C.S., Aguirre, H.E., Tanaka, K.: Ceci n'est pas une pipe: a deep convolutional network for fine-art paintings classification. In: 2016 IEEE International Conference on Image Processing (ICIP), pp. 3703–3707. IEEE (2016)
39. Tan, W.R., Chan, C.S., Aguirre, H.E., Tanaka, K.: Improved ArtGan for conditional synthesis of natural image and artwork. IEEE Trans. Image Process. **28**(1), 394–409 (2018)
40. Tomei, M., Cornia, M., Baraldi, L., Cucchiara, R.: Art2Real: unfolding the reality of artworks via semantically-aware image-to-image translation. In: Proceedings of the IEEE Conference on Computer Vision and Pattern Recognition, pp. 5849–5859 (2019)
41. Van Noord, N., Hendriks, E., Postma, E.: Toward discovery of the artist's style: learning to recognize artists by their artworks. IEEE Signal Process. Mag. **32**(4), 46–54 (2015)
42. Westlake, N., Cai, H., Hall, P.: Detecting people in artwork with CNNs. In: Hua, G., Jégou, H. (eds.) ECCV 2016. LNCS, vol. 9913, pp. 825–841. Springer, Cham (2016). https://doi.org/10.1007/978-3-319-46604-0_57
43. Wilber, M.J., Fang, C., Jin, H., Hertzmann, A., Collomosse, J., Belongie, S.: BAM! The behance artistic media dataset for recognition beyond photography. In: Proceedings of the IEEE International Conference on Computer Vision, pp. 1202–1211 (2017)

Iconographic Image Captioning for Artworks

Eva Cetinic[(✉)] [iD]

Rudjer Boskovic Institute, Bijenicka cesta 54, 10000 Zagreb, Croatia
ecetinic@irb.hr

Abstract. Image captioning implies automatically generating textual descriptions of images based only on the visual input. Although this has been an extensively addressed research topic in recent years, not many contributions have been made in the domain of art historical data. In this particular context, the task of image captioning is confronted with various challenges such as the lack of large-scale datasets of image-text pairs, the complexity of meaning associated with describing artworks and the need for expert-level annotations. This work aims to address some of those challenges by utilizing a novel large-scale dataset of artwork images annotated with concepts from the Iconclass classification system designed for art and iconography. The annotations are processed into clean textual description to create a dataset suitable for training a deep neural network model on the image captioning task. Motivated by the state-of-the-art results achieved in generating captions for natural images, a transformer-based vision-language pre-trained model is fine-tuned using the artwork image dataset. Quantitative evaluation of the results is performed using standard image captioning metrics. The quality of the generated captions and the model's capacity to generalize to new data is explored by employing the model on a new collection of paintings and performing an analysis of the relation between commonly generated captions and the artistic genre. The overall results suggest that the model can generate meaningful captions that exhibit a stronger relevance to the art historical context, particularly in comparison to captions obtained from models trained only on natural image datasets.

Keywords: Image captioning · Vision-language models · Fine-tuning · Visual art

1 Introduction

Automatically generating meaningful and accurate image descriptions is a challenging task that has been extensively addressed in the recent years. This task implies recognizing objects and their relationship in an image and generating syntactically and semantically correct textual descriptions. In resolving this task, significant progress has been made using deep learning based - techniques. A prerequisite for this kind of approach are large datasets of semantically related image

© Springer Nature Switzerland AG 2021
A. Del Bimbo et al. (Eds.): ICPR 2020 Workshops, LNCS 12663, pp. 502–516, 2021.
https://doi.org/10.1007/978-3-030-68796-0_36

and sentence pairs. In the domain of natural images, several well-known large-scale datasets are commonly used for caption generation, such as the MS COCO [22], Flickr30 [41] and Visual Genome [20] dataset. Although the availability of such datasets enabled remarkable results in generating high quality captions for photographs of various objects and scenes, the task of generating image captions still remains difficult for domain-specific image collections. In particular, in the context of the cultural heritage domain, generating image captions is an open problem with various challenges. One of the major obstacles is the lack of a truly large-scale dataset of artwork images paired with adequate descriptions. It is also relevant to address what kind of description would be regarded as "adequate" for a particular purpose. Considering for instance Erwin Panofsky's three levels of analysis [25], we can distinguish the "pre-iconographic" description, "iconographic" description and the "iconologic" interpretation as possibilities of aligning semantically meaningful, yet very different textual descriptions with the same image. While captions of natural images usually function on the level of "pre-iconographic" descriptions, which implies simply listing the elements that are depicted in an image, for artwork images this type of description represent only the most basic level of visual understanding and is often not considered to be of great interest.

In the context of artwork images, it would be more interesting to generate "iconographic" captions that capture the subject and symbolic relations between objects. Creating a dataset for such a complex task requires expert knowledge in the process of collecting sentence-based descriptions of images. There have been some attempts to create such datasets, but those existing datasets consist only of a few thousand images and are therefore not suitable to train deep neural models in the current state-of-the-art setting for image captioning. However, there are several existing large-scale artwork collections that associate images with keywords and specific concepts. The idea of this work is to use a concatenation of concept descriptions associated with an image as textual inputs for training an image captioning model. Recently an interesting large-scale artwork dataset has been published under the name "Iconclass AI Test Set" [27]. This dataset represents a collection of various artwork images assigned with alphanumeric classification codes that correspond to notations from the Iconclass system [9]. Iconclass is a classification system designed for art and iconography and is widely accepted by museums and art institutions as a tool for the description and retrieval of subjects represented in images. Although the "Iconclass AI Test Set" is not structured primarily as an image captioning dataset, each code is paired with its "textual correlate" - a description of the iconographic subject of the particular Iconclass notation. Therefore the main intention of this work is to extract and preprocess the given annotations into clean textual description and create the "Iconclass Caption" dataset. This dataset is then used to fine-tune a pre-trained unified vision-language model on the down-stream task of image captioning [42]. Transformer-based vision-language pre-trained models currently represent the leading approach in solving a variety of tasks in the intersection of computer vision and natural language processing. This paper represents a first attempt to employ the aforementioned approach on a collection of artwork images with the goal to generate image captions relevant in the context of art history.

2   Related Work

The availability of large collections of digitized artwork images led to an increase of interest in the employment of deep learning-based techniques for a variety of different tasks. Research in this area most commonly focuses on addressing problems related to computer vision in the context of art historical data, such as image classification [4,29], visual link retrieval [3,31], analysis of visual patterns and conceptual features [6,11,14,33], object and face detection [10,36], pose and character matching [19,24] and computational aesthetics [5,18,30].

Recently however there has been a surge of interest in topics that deal with not only visual, but both visual and textual modalities of artwork collections. The pioneering works in this research area mostly addressed the task of multi-modal retrieval. In particular, [15] introduced the SemArt dataset, a collection of fine-art images associated with textual comments, with the aim to map the images and their descriptions in a joint semantic space. They compare different combinations of visual and textual encodings, as well as different methods of multi-modal transformation. In projecting the visual and textual encodings in a common multimodal space, they achieve the best results by applying a neural network trained with cosine margin loss on ResNet50 features as visual encodings and bag-of-word as textual encodings. The task of creating a shared embedding space was also addressed in [1] where the authors introduce a new visual semantic dataset named BibleVSA, a collection of miniature illustrations and commentary text pairs, and explore supervised and semi-supervised approaches to learning cross-references between textual and visual information in documents. In [35] the authors present the Artpedia dataset consisting of 2930 images annotated with visual and contextual sentences. They introduce a cross-modal retrieval model that projects images and sentences in a common embedding space and discriminates between contextual and visual sentences of the same image. A similar extension of this approach to other artistic datasets was presented in [8].

Besides multi-modal retrieval, another emerging topic of interest is visual question answering (VAQ). In [2] the authors annotated a subset of the ArtPedia dataset with visual and contextual question-answer pairs and introduced a question classifier that discriminates between visual and contextual questions and a model that is able to answer both types of questions. In [16] the authors introduce a novel dataset AQUA, which consists of automatically generated visual and knowledge-based QA pairs, and also present a two-branch model where the visual and knowledge questions are handled independently.

A limited number of studies contributed to the task of generating descriptions of artwork images using deep neural networks and all of them rely on employing the encoder-decoder architecture-based image captioning approach. For example, [34] proposes an encoder-decoder framework for generating captions of artwork images where the encoder (ResNet18 model) extracts the input image feature representation and the artwork type representation, while the decoder is a long short-term memory (LSTM) network. They introduce two image captioning datasets referring to ancient Egyptian art and ancient Chinese art, which contain 17,940 and 7,607 images respectively. Another very recent work [17] presented a novel captioning dataset for art historical images consisting of 4000 images across 9 iconographies, along with a description for each image consisting of one or more paragraphs. They used this dataset to fine-tune different variations of image captioning models based on the well known encoder decoder approach introduced in [39].

Influenced by the success of utilizing large scale pre-trained language models like BERT [13] for different tasks related to natural language processing, there has recently been a surge of interest in developing Transformer-based vision-language pre-trained models. Vision-language models are designed to learn joint representations that combine information of both modalities and the alignments across those modalities. It has been shown that models pre-trained on intermediate tasks with unsupervised learning objectives using large datasets of image-text pairs, achieve remarkable results when adapted to different down-stream tasks such as image captioning, cross-modal retrieval or visual question answering [7,23,37,42]. However, to the best of our knowledge, this approach has until now not been explored for tasks in the domain of art historical data.

3   Experimental Setup

3.1   Iconclass Caption Dataset

In our experiment we use a subset of 86 530 valid images from the "Iconclass AI Test Set" [27].This is a very diverse collection of images sampled from the Arkyves database[1]. It includes images of various types of artworks such as paintings, posters, drawings, prints, manuscripts pages, etc. Each image is associated with one or more codes linked to labels from the Iconclass classification system. The authors of the "Iconclass AI Test Set" provide a json file with the list of images and corresponding codes, as well as an Iconclass Python package to perform analysis and extract information from the assigned classification codes. To extract textual descriptions of images for the purpose of this work, the English textual descriptions of each code associated with an image are concatenated. Further preprocessing of the descriptions includes removing text in brackets and some recurrent uppercased dataset-specific codes. In this dataset, the text in brackets most commonly includes very specific named entities, which are considered a noisy input in the image captioning task. Therefore, when preprocessing the textual items, all the text in brackets is removed, even at the cost of sometimes removing useful information. Figure 1 shows several example images from the Iconclass dataset and their corresponding descriptions before and after preprocessing. Depending on the number of codes associated with each image, the

---

[1] www.arkyves.org.

final textual descriptions can significantly vary in length. Also, because of the specific properties of this dataset, the image descriptions are not structured as sentences but as a list of comma-separated words and phrases.

Original description: Madonna: i.c. Mary with the Christ child, flowers: rose, historical persons (portraits and scenes from the life) (+ half-length portrait)
Clean description: Madonna: i.e. Mary with the Christ-child, flowers: rose, historical persons .

Original description: adult woman, manuscript of musical score, writer, poet, author (+ portrait, self-portrait of artist), pen, ink-well, paper (writing material), codex, inscription, historical events and situations (1567), historical person (MONTENAY, Georgette de) - BB - woman - historical person (MONTENAY, Georgette de) portrayed alone, proverbs, sayings, etc. (O PLUME EN LA MAIN NON VAINE)
Clean description: adult woman, manuscript of musical score, writer, poet, author , pen, ink-well, paper , codex, inscription, historical events and situations , historical person, woman - historical person portrayed alone, proverbs, sayings.

Original description: plants and herbs (HELLEBORINE), plants and herbs (LUPINE),
Clean description: plants and herbs .

Fig. 1. Example images from the Iconclass dataset and their corresponding descriptions before and after preprocessing.

Because of this type of structure, and because of having only one reference caption for each image, the Iconclass Caption dataset is not a standard image captioning dataset. However, having in mind the difficulties of obtaining adequate textual descriptions for images of artworks, this dataset can be considered a valuable source of image-text pairs in the current context. Particularly because of the large number of annotated images that enables training deep neural models. In the experimental setting, a subset of 76k items is used for training the model, 5k for validation and 5k for testing.

3.2   Vision-Language Model

In this work the unified vision-language pre-training model (VLP) introduced in
[42] is employed. This model is denoted as "unified" because the same pre-trained
model can be fine-tuned for different types of tasks. Those task include both
vision-language generation (e.g. image captioning) and vision-language understanding (e.g. visual question answering). The model is based on an encoder-
decoder architecture comprised of 12 Transformer blocks. The model input consist of the image embedding, text embedding and three special tokens that indicate the start of the image input, the boundary between visual and textual
input and the end of the textual input. The image input consist of 100 object
classification aware region features extracted using the Faster RCNN model [28]
pre-trained on the Visual Genome dataset [20]. For a more detailed description
of the overall VLP framework and pre-training objectives, the reader is refered to
[42]. The experiments introduced in this work employ as the base model the VLP
model pre-trained on the Conceptual Captions dataset [32] using the sequence-
to-sequence objective. This base model is fine-tuned on the Iconclass Caption
Dataset using recommended fine-tuning configurations, namely training with a
constant learning rate of 3e−5 for 30 epochs. Because the descriptions in the
Iconclass Caption Dataset are on average longer than captions in other caption
datasets, when fine-tuning the VLP model, the maximum number of tokens in
the input and target sequence is modified from the default value (20) to a new
higher value (100).

4   Results

4.1   Quantitative Results

To quantitatively evaluate the generated captions, standard language evaluation
metrics for image captioning on the Iconclass Caption test set are used. Those
include the standard 4 BLEU metrics [26], METEOR [12] ROUGE [21] and
CIDEr [38]. The BLUE, ROUGE and METEOR are metrics that originate from
machine translation tasks, while CIDEr was specifically developed for image caption evaluation. The BLUE metrics represent n-gram precision scores multiplied
by a brevity penalty factor to assess the length correspondence of candidate and
reference sentences. ROUGE is a metric that measures the recall of n-grams and
therefore rewards long sentences. Specifically ROUGE-L measures the longest
matching sequence of words between a pair of sentences. METEOR represents
the harmonic mean of precision and recall of unigram matches between sentences
and additionally includes synonyms and paraphrase matching. CIDEr measures
the cosine similarity between TF-IDF weighted n-grams of the candidate and
the reference sentences. The TF-IDF weighting of n-grams reduces the score of
frequent n-grams and appoints higher scores to distinctive words. The results
obtained using those metrics are presented in Table 1.

Although the current results cannot be compared with any other work
because the experiments are performed on a new and syntactically and semantically different dataset, the quantitative evaluation results ar included to serve as

Table 1. Table captions should be placed above the tables.

Evaluation metric	Iconclass Caption test set
BLEU 1	14.8
BLEU 2	12.8
BLEU 3	11.3
BLEU 4	10.0
METEOR	11.7
ROUGE-L	31.9
CIDEr	172.1

a benchmark for future work. In comparison with current state-of-the-art caption evaluation results on natural image datasets (e.g. BLEU4 $\approx$ 37 for COCO and $\approx$30 for Flickr30 datasets) [40, 42], the BLUE scores are lower for the Iconclass dataset. A similar behaviour is also reported in another study addressing iconographic image captioning [17]. On the other hand, the CIDEr score is quite high in comparison to the one reported for natural image datasets (e.g. CIDEr $\approx$116 for COCO and $\approx$68 for Flickr30 dataset) [40, 42].

However, it remains questionable how adequate these metrics are in assessing the overall quality of the captions in this particular context. All of the reported metrics mostly measure the word overlap between generated and reference captions. They are not designed to capture the semantic meaning of a sentence and therefore often lead to poor correlation with human judgement. Also, they are not appropriate for measuring very short descriptions which are quite common in the IconClass Caption dataset. Moreover, they do not address the relation between the generated caption and the image content, but express only the similarity between the original and generated textual descriptions. The generated caption could be semantically aligned with the image content but represent a different version of the original caption and therefore have very low metric scores. In Fig. 2, several such examples from the Iconclass Caption test set are presented.

Those examples indicate that the existing evaluation metrics are not very suitable in assessing the relevance of generated captions for this particular dataset. Therefore a qualitative analysis of the results is also required in order to better understand potential contributions and drawbacks of the proposed approach.

4.2 Qualitative Analysis

For the purpose of qualitative analysis, examples of images and generated captions on two datasets are analyzed. One is the test set of the Iconclass Caption dataset that serves for direct comparison between the generated captions and ground-truth descriptions. The other dataset is a subset of the WikiArt painting collection, which does not include textual descriptions of images but has a broad set of labels associated with each image. This enables the study of the

Ground-truth: sea.
Caption: sailing - ship, sailing - boat.

BLEU 1: 2.49e-16
BLEU 2: 2.88e-16
BLEU 3: 3.46e-16
BLEU 4: 4.51e-16
METEOR: 0.16
ROUGE: 0.0
CIDEr: 0.0

Ground-truth: apostle, unspecified, key.
Caption: head turned to the right, historical persons.

BLEU 1: 1.43e-16
BLEU 2: 1.54e-16
BLEU 3: 1.68e-16
BLEU 4: 1.85e-16
METEOR: 0.0
ROUGE: 0.0
CIDEr: 0.0

Ground-truth: arms, fingers.
Caption: hand.

BLEU 1: 3.67e-16
BLEU 2: 1.16e-11
BLEU 3: 3.67e-10
BLEU 4: 2.06e-09
METEOR: 0.0
ROUGE: 0.0
CIDEr: 0.0

Ground-truth: palace, king, New Testament, adoration of the kings: the Wise Men present their gifts to the Christ-child.
Caption: New Testament.

BLEU 1: 0.00055
BLEU 2: 0.00055
BLEU 3: 5.53e-16
BLEU 4: 5.53e-07
METEOR: 0.0552
ROUGE: 0.184
CIDEr: 0.051

Fig. 2. Examples of images from the Iconclass Caption test set, their corresponding ground-truth and generated captions and the values of evaluation metrics for those examples.

relation between generated captions and other concepts, e.g. genre categorization of paintings, as well as gives an insight into how well the model generalizes to a different artwork dataset.

Iconclass Caption Test Set. To gain a better insight into the generated image captions, in Fig. 3 several examples are shown. The presented image-text pairs are chosen to demonstrate both successful examples (the left column) and failed examples (the right column) of generated captions.

Analysis of the failed examples indicates an existing "logic" in those erroneous captions, as well as demonstrates underlying biases within the dataset. For instance, in the Iconclass Caption training test there are more than thousand examples that include the phrase "New Testament" in the description. There-

Ground-truth: historiated initial , printed historiated initial , printed matter , Roman script ; scripts based on the Roman alphabet
Caption: historiated initial , printed historiated initial , printed matter , Roman script ; scripts based on the Roman alphabet

Ground-truth: device , printed matter.
Caption: historiated initial , printed historiated initial , printed matter , Roman script ; scripts based on the Roman alphabet.

Ground-truth: 'New Testament, Christ in the house of Martha and Mary , Martha complains to Christ about Mary.
Caption: New Testament.

Ground-truth: hoofed animals: deer, Classical Mythology and Ancient History, the sacrifice of Iphigenia.
Caption: New Testament , the assumption of Mary : she is borne into heaven by angels.

Ground-truth: 'crustaceans: lobster, molluscs: oyster, glass, rummer, table-cloth.
Caption: crustaceans : lobster , molluscs : oyster , fruits : lemon , fruits : orange , fruits : peach , fruits : walnut , table - cloth , fruit , fruit , grape .

Ground-truth: glass, rummer, meat; still life of meat, tools, aids, implements crafts and industries: knife.
Caption: crustaceans : lobster , molluscs : oyster , fish ; still life of fishes.

Ground-truth: 'founder of the Order of Friars Minor , Francisof Assisi; possible attributes: book, crucifix, lily, skull, stigmata.
Caption: male saints.

Ground-truth: saints, St. Jerome as Doctor of the Latin Church in his study with book, pen and ink; lion and cardinal's hat beside him, study; 'studiolo'; library.
Caption: saints , the penitent harlot Mary Magdalene ; possible attributes : book , crown , crown of thorns , crucifix , jar of ointment , mirror , musical instrument , palm - branch , rosary , scourge , book.

Fig. 3. Examples of images from the Iconclass Caption test set, their corresponding ground-truth and generated captions. Examples shown in the left column represent successfully generated captions, while examples shown in the right column demonstrate wrongly generated captions.

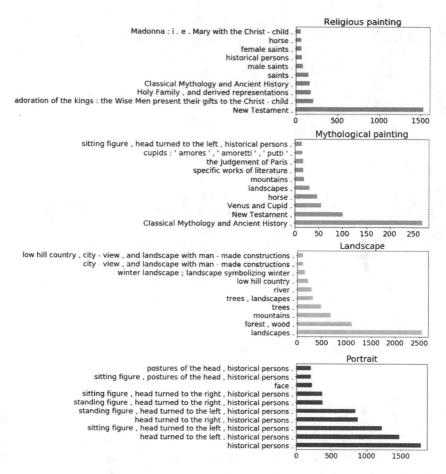

Fig. 4. Distribution of most commonly generated descriptions in relation to four different genres in the WikiArt dataset.

fore images that include structurally similar scenes, particularly from classical history and mythology, are sometimes wrongly attributed as depicting a scene from the New Testament. This signifies the importance of balanced examples in the training dataset and indicates directions for possible future improvements. The Iconclass dataset is a collection of very diverse images and apart from the Iconclass classification codes, there are currently no other metadata available for the images. Therefore it is difficult to perform an in-depth exploratory analysis of the dataset and the generated results in regard to attributes relevant in the context of art history such as the date of creation, style, genre, etc. For this reason, the fine-tuned image captioning model is employed on a novel artwork dataset - a subset of the WikiArt collection of paintings.

Jan van Hemessen, Christ Driving Merchants from the Temple, 1556
Iconclass caption: New Testament .
Flickr caption: A painting of a group of people .
Coco caption: A painting of a group of people dancing .

Giovanni Bellini, Madonna Enthroned Cherishing the Sleeping Child, 1475
Iconclass caption: Madonna : i . e . Mary with the Christ - child , sitting figure , historical persons .
Flickr caption: A woman holding a baby .
Coco caption: A painting of a woman holding a child .

Jan Gossaert, Adam and Eve in Paradise, 1527
Iconclass caption: Adam and Eve holding the fruit .
Flickr caption: Four naked men are standing in the mud .
Coco caption: A couple of men standing next to each other .

Fig. 5. Examples from the WikiArt dataset with captions generated by models fine-tuned on the Iconclass, Flickr and COCO datasets.

WikiArt Dataset. In order to explore how the model generalizes to a new artwork dataset, a subset of 52562 images of paintings from the WikiArt[2] collection is used. Because images in the WikiArt dataset are annotated with a broad set of labels (e.g. style, genre, artist, technique, date of creation, etc.), the study of the relation between the generated captions on those labels is performed as one method of qualitative assessment. Figure 4 shows the distribution of most commonly generated descriptions in relation to four different genres. From this basic analysis it is obvious that the generated captions are meaningful in relation to the content and the genre classification of images.

To understand the contribution of the proposed model in the context of iconographic image captioning, it is interesting to compare the Iconclass captions with captions obtained from models trained on natural images. For this purpose, two models of the same architecture but fine-tuned on the Flickr 30 i MS COCO datasets are used. Figure 5 shows several examples from the WikiArt dataset with corresponding Iconclass, Flickr and COCO captions. It is evident that the other two models generate results that are meaningful in relation to the image content but do not necessarily contribute to producing more fine-grained and context-aware descriptions.

---

[2] www.wikiart.org.

5   Conclusion

This paper introduces a novel model for generating iconographic image captions. This is done by utilizing a large-scale dataset of artwork images annotated with concepts from the Iconclass classification system designed for art and iconography. To the best of our knowledge, this dataset has not yet been widely used in the computer vision community. Within the scope of this work, the available annotations are processed into clean textual descriptions and the existing dataset is transformed into a collection of suitable image-text pairs. The dataset is used to fine-tune a transformer-based visual-language model. For this purpose, object classification aware region features are extracted from the images using the Faster RCNN model. The base model in our fine-tuning experiment is an existing model, called the VLP model, that is pre-trained on a natural image dataset on an intermediate tasks with unsupervised learning objectives. Fine-tuning pre-trained vision-language models represents the current state-of-the-art approach for many different multimodal tasks.

The captions generated by the fine-tuned models are evaluated using standard image captioning metrics. Unlike in other image captioning datasets which usually contain several short sentences, the ground-truth descriptions of the Iconclass dataset significantly vary in length. Because of the specific properties of the Iconclass dataset, standard image captioning evaluation metrics are not very informative regarding the relevance and appropriateness of the generated captions in relation to the image content. Therefore, the quality of the generated captions and the model's capacity to generalize to new data are further explored by employing the model on another artwork dataset. The overall quantitative and qualitative evaluation of the results suggests that the model can generate meaningful captions that capture not only the depicted objects but also the art historical context and relation between subjects. However, there is still room for significant improvement. In particular, the unbalanced distribution of themes and topics within the training set result in often wrongly identified subjects in the generated image descriptions. Furthermore, the generated textual descriptions are often very short and could serve more as labels rather than captions. Nevertheless, the current results show significant improvement in comparison to captions generated from artwork images using models trained on natural image caption datasets. Further improvement can potentially be achieved with fine-tuning the current model on a smaller dataset with more elaborate ground-truth iconographic captions.

References

1. Baraldi, L., Cornia, M., Grana, C., Cucchiara, R.: Aligning text and document illustrations: towards visually explainable digital humanities. In: 2018 24th International Conference on Pattern Recognition (ICPR), pp. 1097–1102. IEEE (2018)
2. Bongini, P., Becattini, F., Bagdanov, A.D., Del Bimbo, A.: Visual question answering for cultural heritage. arXiv preprint arXiv:2003.09853 (2020)

3. Castellano, G., Vessio, G.: Towards a tool for visual link retrieval and knowledge discovery in painting datasets. In: Ceci, M., Ferilli, S., Poggi, A. (eds.) IRCDL 2020. CCIS, vol. 1177, pp. 105–110. Springer, Cham (2020). https://doi.org/10.1007/978-3-030-39905-4_11

4. Cetinic, E., Lipic, T., Grgic, S.: Fine-tuning convolutional neural networks for fine art classification. Expert Syst. Appl. **114**, 107–118 (2018)

5. Cetinic, E., Lipic, T., Grgic, S.: A deep learning perspective on beauty, sentiment, and remembrance of art. IEEE Access **7**, 73694–73710 (2019)

6. Cetinic, E., Lipic, T., Grgic, S.: Learning the principles of art history with convolutional neural networks. Pattern Recogn. Lett. **129**, 56–62 (2020)

7. Chen, Y.C., et al.: UNITER: learning universal image-text representations. arXiv preprint arXiv:1909.11740 (2019)

8. Cornia, M., Stefanini, M., Baraldi, L., Corsini, M., Cucchiara, R.: Explaining digital humanities by aligning images and textual descriptions. Pattern Recogn. Lett. **129**, 166–172 (2020)

9. Couprie, L.D.: Iconclass: an iconographic classification system. Art Libr. J. **8**(2), 32–49 (1983)

10. Crowley, E.J., Zisserman, A.: In search of art. In: Agapito, L., Bronstein, M.M., Rother, C. (eds.) ECCV 2014. LNCS, vol. 8925, pp. 54–70. Springer, Cham (2015). https://doi.org/10.1007/978-3-319-16178-5_4

11. Deng, Y., Tang, F., Dong, W., Ma, C., Huang, F., Deussen, O., Xu, C.: Exploring the representativity of art paintings. IEEE Trans. Multimed. (2020)

12. Denkowski, M., Lavie, A.: Meteor Universal: language specific translation evaluation for any target language. In: Proceedings of the Ninth Workshop on Statistical Machine Translation, pp. 376–380 (2014)

13. Devlin, J., Chang, M.W., Lee, K., Toutanova, K.: BERT: pre-training of deep bidirectional transformers for language understanding. arXiv preprint arXiv:1810.04805 (2018)

14. Elgammal, A., Liu, B., Kim, D., Elhoseiny, M., Mazzone, M.: The shape of art history in the eyes of the machine. In: 32nd AAAI Conference on Artificial Intelligence, AAAI 2018, pp. 2183–2191. AAAI press (2018)

15. Garcia, N., Vogiatzis, G.: How to read paintings: semantic art understanding with multi-modal retrieval. In: Proceedings of the European Conference on Computer Vision (ECCV) (2018)

16. Garcia, N., et al.: A dataset and baselines for visual question answering on art. arXiv preprint arXiv:2008.12520 (2020)

17. Gupta, J., Madhu, P., Kosti, R., Bell, P., Maier, A., Christlein, V.: Towards image caption generation for art historical data. In: AI Methods for Digital Heritage, Workshop at KI2020 43rd German Conference on Artificial Intelligence (2020)

18. Hayn-Leichsenring, G.U., Lehmann, T., Redies, C.: Subjective ratings of beauty and aesthetics: correlations with statistical image properties in western oil paintings. i-Perception **8**(3), 2041669517715474 (2017)

19. Jenicek, T., Chum, O.: Linking art through human poses. In: 2019 International Conference on Document Analysis and Recognition (ICDAR), pp. 1338–1345. IEEE (2019)

20. Krishna, R., et al.: Visual genome: connecting language and vision using crowd-sourced dense image annotations. Int. J. Comput. Vision **123**(1), 32–73 (2017)

21. Lin, C.Y.: ROUGE: a package for automatic evaluation of summaries. In: Text Summarization Branches Out, pp. 74–81 (2004)

22. Lin, T.-Y., et al.: Microsoft COCO: common objects in context. In: Fleet, D., Pajdla, T., Schiele, B., Tuytelaars, T. (eds.) ECCV 2014. LNCS, vol. 8693, pp. 740–755. Springer, Cham (2014). https://doi.org/10.1007/978-3-319-10602-1_48

23. Lu, J., Batra, D., Parikh, D., Lee, S.: ViLBERT: pretraining task-agnostic visiolinguistic representations for vision-and-language tasks. In: Advances in Neural Information Processing Systems, pp. 13–23 (2019)

24. Madhu, P., Kosti, R., Mührenberg, L., Bell, P., Maier, A., Christlein, V.: Recognizing characters in art history using deep learning. In: Proceedings of the 1st Workshop on Structuring and Understanding of Multimedia heritAge Contents, pp. 15–22 (2019)

25. Panofsky, E.: Studies in Iconology. Humanistic Themes in the Art of the Renaissance. Harper and Row, New York (1972)

26. Papineni, K., Roukos, S., Ward, T., Zhu, W.J.: BLEU: a method for automatic evaluation of machine translation. In: Proceedings of the 40th annual meeting of the Association for Computational Linguistics, pp. 311–318 (2002)

27. Posthumus, E.: Brill Iconclass AI test set (2020)

28. Ren, S., He, K., Girshick, R., Sun, J.: Faster R-CNN: towards real-time object detection with region proposal networks. In: Advances in Neural Information Processing Systems, pp. 91–99 (2015)

29. Sandoval, C., Pirogova, E., Lech, M.: Two-stage deep learning approach to the classification of fine-art paintings. IEEE Access **7**, 41770–41781 (2019)

30. Sargentis, G., Dimitriadis, P., Koutsoyiannis, D., et al.: Aesthetical issues of leonardo da vinci's and pablo picasso's paintings with stochastic evaluation. Heritage **3**(2), 283–305 (2020)

31. Seguin, B., Striolo, C., diLenardo, I., Kaplan, F.: Visual link retrieval in a database of paintings. In: Hua, G., Jégou, H. (eds.) ECCV 2016. LNCS, vol. 9913, pp. 753–767. Springer, Cham (2016). https://doi.org/10.1007/978-3-319-46604-0_52

32. Sharma, P., Ding, N., Goodman, S., Soricut, R.: Conceptual captions: a cleaned, hypernymed, image alt-text dataset for automatic image captioning. In: Proceedings of the 56th Annual Meeting of the Association for Computational Linguistics (Volume 1: Long Papers), pp. 2556–2565 (2018)

33. Shen, X., Efros, A.A., Aubry, M.: Discovering visual patterns in art collections with spatially-consistent feature learning. In: Proceedings of the IEEE Conference on Computer Vision and Pattern Recognition, pp. 9278–9287 (2019)

34. Sheng, S., Moens, M.F.: Generating captions for images of ancient artworks. In: Proceedings of the 27th ACM International Conference on Multimedia, pp. 2478–2486 (2019)

35. Stefanini, M., Cornia, M., Baraldi, L., Corsini, M., Cucchiara, R.: Artpedia: a new visual-semantic dataset with visual and contextual sentences in the artistic domain. In: Ricci, E., Rota Bulò, S., Snoek, C., Lanz, O., Messelodi, S., Sebe, N. (eds.) ICIAP 2019. LNCS, vol. 11752, pp. 729–740. Springer, Cham (2019). https://doi.org/10.1007/978-3-030-30645-8_66

36. Strezoski, G., Worring, M.: OmniArt: a large-scale artistic benchmark. ACM Trans. Multimed. Comput. Commun. Appl. (TOMM) **14**(4), 1–21 (2018)

37. Tan, H., Bansal, M.: LXMERT: learning cross-modality encoder representations from transformers. arXiv preprint arXiv:1908.07490 (2019)

38. Vedantam, R., Lawrence Zitnick, C., Parikh, D.: CIDEr: consensus-based image description evaluation. In: Proceedings of the IEEE Conference on Computer Vision and Pattern Recognition, pp. 4566–4575 (2015)

39. Vinyals, O., Toshev, A., Bengio, S., Erhan, D.: Show and tell: A neural image caption generator. In: Proceedings of the IEEE Conference on Computer Vision and Pattern Recognition, pp. 3156–3164 (2015)
40. Xia, Q., et al.: XGPT: cross-modal generative pre-training for image captioning. arXiv preprint arXiv:2003.01473 (2020)
41. Young, P., Lai, A., Hodosh, M., Hockenmaier, J.: From image descriptions to visual denotations: new similarity metrics for semantic inference over event descriptions. Trans. Assoc. Comput. Linguist. **2**, 67–78 (2014)
42. Zhou, L., Palangi, H., Zhang, L., Hu, H., Corso, J.J., Gao, J.: Unified vision-language pre-training for image captioning and VQA. In: AAAI, pp. 13041–13049 (2020)

Semantic Analysis of Cultural Heritage Data: Aligning Paintings and Descriptions in Art-Historic Collections

Nitisha Jain, Christian Bartz(✉), Tobias Bredow, Emanuel Metzenthin, Jona Otholt, and Ralf Krestel

Hasso Plattner Institute, University of Potsdam, 14482 Potsdam, Germany
{nitisha.jain,christian.bartz,tobias.bredow,emanuel.metzenthin,
jona.otholt,ralf.krestel}@hpi.de

Abstract. Art-historic documents often contain multimodal data in terms of images of artworks and metadata, descriptions, or interpretations thereof. Most research efforts have focused either on image analysis or text analysis independently since the associations between the two modes are usually lost during digitization. In this work, we focus on the task of alignment of images and textual descriptions in art-historic digital collections. To this end, we reproduce an existing approach that learns alignments in a semi-supervised fashion. We identify several challenges while automatically aligning images and texts, specifically for the cultural heritage domain, which limit the scalability of previous works. To improve the performance of alignment, we introduce various enhancements to extend the existing approach that show promising results.

Keywords: Cultural heritage · Natural language processing · Computer vision

1 Introduction

Digitized collections of cultural artifacts provide an interesting opportunity for deeper analysis and understanding of our heritage and culture. Several cultural institutions around the world have made continued efforts to digitize their cultural resources and make them widely available for access and analysis by scholars, as well as interested audiences. Massive volumes of art-historic archives have been scanned and digitized by museums and galleries as part of the OpenGlam[1] initiative. These digital collections comprise art catalogues, magazines and art books that contain multimodal data, namely texts and images. For instance, images of paintings are often accompanied by their titles and textual descriptions in these materials.

N. Jain and C. Bartz—Both authors contributed equally.

[1] openglam.org.

© Springer Nature Switzerland AG 2021
A. Del Bimbo et al. (Eds.): ICPR 2020 Workshops, LNCS 12663, pp. 517–530, 2021.
https://doi.org/10.1007/978-3-030-68796-0_37

In order to derive useful insights from these resources, many attempts are being made to leverage machine learning techniques. Several works have focused on deriving useful information and systematic representations from text alone [6,8,17,22,32,36]. On the other hand, previous work has paid attention to image analysis techniques for the depicted artworks [9,20,35,37]. However, both research directions typically overlook the rich information embedded in joint analysis of multiple modalities. An important example is the structure and associations of the paintings with their descriptions, that are present in the original resources but usually lost during the digitization process. In this work, we bring attention to the task of aligning the images with their corresponding texts in the context of digitized art collections. As detailed previously [1], one of the most important benefits of image and text alignment is to facilitate multimodal search and retrieval of artworks from online digital archives, by leveraging the textual, as well as image features in conjunction. Additionally, enriching the digital resources with multimodal meta-data can improve results for individual text analysis and image analysis tasks. For example, image classification is difficult for paintings, especially those depicting portraits, and classification models can greatly benefit from textual cues for such cases.

The alignment of images and texts in digitized collections is a non-trivial task due to various challenges that are unique to the cultural heritage domain, including diverse formats, lack of training data, etc. Moreover, different datasets require customizations to the alignment techniques. For instance, varying ratios and types of images and texts are found in different art-historic datasets. On the one hand, art books have longer texts in the context of a few paintings or art styles, artists and so on. On the other hand, auction or exhibition catalogues contain mostly images of paintings or artifacts and shorter texts, mainly title, artist, date, *etc.* Due to this variability, scaling of any existing technique across different datasets becomes difficult.

Within the scope of an ongoing project on multimodal analysis of cultural heritage datasets, we collaborate with the Wildenstein Plattner Institute (WPI)[2] that was founded to promote scholarly research on cultural heritage collections. We have been provided access to a large digitized collection compiled and maintained by WPI. This collection consists of scanned pages of art-historic documents ranging from sales catalogues to art magazines from the 19th century up to today. We refer to our dataset as WPI-Art in the rest of the paper.

Although there are a few existing approaches on image and text alignment (see related work, Sect. 2), we found that none of the current techniques performed well on the WPI-Art dataset due to several novel challenges (see Sect. 3). Therefore, we explored several enhancements over existing approaches for overcoming these challenges in the context of the WPI-Art dataset. More specifically, due to the lack of annotated training datasets we follow an approach, introduced by Cornia *et al.* [5], for identifying the correct alignment. We first extract text and image content from the digitized dataset and derive semantic features from both separately, and then perform semantic alignment to match the

---

[2] https://wpi.art/.

artwork images with their correct texts. Building on the work of Cornia *et al.* , we improve the results with several new additions for semantic analysis such as augmenting texts with thesauri tokens, using bag-of-words (BoW) and N-grams representations for text, as well as using the technique of neural style transfer for the images (Sect. 4). In our experimental results (see Sect. 5), we show that our proposed enhancements do not only improve results on the WPI-Art dataset, but also on the commonly used SemArt dataset [14].

The specific contributions of this work are as follows: (1) Define distinct challenges for the task of aligning artwork images with their text descriptions in art-historic collections. (2) Reproduce and evaluate an existing semi-supervised approach for image and text alignment on our WPI-Art dataset. (3) Enhance the approach with several customizations for text analysis and image analysis techniques, improving the performance on the WPI-Art and SemArt datasets.

2   Related Work

The multimodal nature of the problem domain we are dealing with is rooted in two modalities. On the one hand, computer vision methods are used for image analysis. On the other hand, methods from the field of natural language processing are leveraged for attaining semantic understanding of the texts. In this section we present related work in the field of image and text alignment.

The overall task of aligning images and texts in a multimodal retrieval setting has been under active research in the past few years [5,11,12,14,21,26]. All of the proposed methods attempt to seek a function that embeds the features of images and texts in a common semantic space [26]. Thereafter, retrieval algorithms search for images and texts that are close to each other in this embedding space. While several methods were introduced to perform alignment of photos and their corresponding texts [21,26,29], quite a number of methods have been introduced to achieve the same for images of artworks and their corresponding descriptions [5,11–14].

Many of these proposed methods only work with supervised learning techniques that require full annotation of a large training dataset [11,12,14,26]. Garcia *et al.* [14] introduced such a supervised retrieval model. They compare multiple methods for embedding images and texts into a common semantic subspace together with different techniques of matching the embedded features of images and texts in the same space. The authors further enhance their proposed model with contextual features, such as the category of depicted scene, the artist's name, or the timeframe of the painting [12,13]. Furthermore, they propose to use knowledge graphs to enrich the embeddings of their input images.

To train supervised models for the retrieval of artworks and their corresponding descriptions, Garcia *et al.* [14] introduce the SemArt dataset consisting of 21 384 paintings paired with textual descriptions. Furthermore, Stefanini *et al.* [34] introduced the Artpedia dataset that consists of approximately 3000 images of paintings paired with textual descriptions. Although the Artpedia dataset is smaller than the SemArt dataset, it contains much more interesting content.

Each sentence that is paired with an image is further classified as a sentence that describes the visual content of the image, or a sentence that provides art-historical information about the image. The SemArt dataset lacks such a categorization which makes it difficult to apply this dataset for multimodal retrieval, since several images only contain texts without any description of the visual content. Although the Artpedia dataset seems to be the natural choice for the development of a system, its small size kept us from using it in our experiments.

Apart from fully supervised models, Cornia *et al.* [5] proposed an unsupervised approach for aligning paintings and their corresponding descriptions. They first train an image to text matching model on the standard COCO [28] image captioning dataset in a fully supervised setting. Thereafter, they use the Maximum Mean Discrepancy (MMD), as well as images and texts from the SemArt dataset (without any annotations) to adapt the supervised model in a manner that the embeddings of paintings and texts match, although the model has only been trained on the COCO dataset.

The approach presented in this paper is based on the work of Cornia *et al.* Owing to the lack of availability of large annotated training data, their approach fits quite well for our use case. We also include the SemArt dataset in our evaluations to enable fair comparison of our reproduction of their model, as well as to demonstrate the improvements from our proposed enhancements, as discussed in Sect. 4.

3   Challenges for Image and Text Alignment in the Cultural Heritage Domain

Due to the variety and diversity of the available art-historic material, restoring lost associations between artwork images and texts is a non-trivial task. In this section we discuss and illustrate the most prominent challenges that we encountered while working with the WPI-Art dataset.

Loss of Formatting. Due to a variety of formats within our digital collections, we found several examples where there is no one-to-one mapping between the images and texts. Figure 1 shows a common scenario where there are several different text segments, but only one of them is aligned to the image. In this case, it is important to correctly identify which text is associated with the image and take the information about missing associations into account while learning the alignment. To further compound the problem, the irregular text spacing in such old documents makes it difficult to clearly separate the different texts after extraction through OCR via text segmentation techniques. The identification of correct and relevant text segments is also important for art books having longer discussions not only about the artworks, but also about the artists, art styles, *etc.* Moreover, useful formatting cues such as the numbers matching the images with the text segments, are also lost after text extraction from page scans. Without such cues, in many cases it is challenging to perform the alignment, even for human annotators.

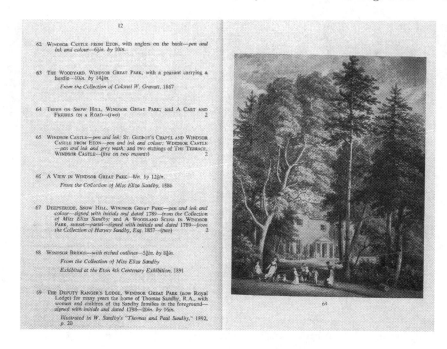

12

62 WINDSOR CASTLE FROM ETON, with anglers on the bank—*pen and ink and colour*—6½*in. by* 10*in.*

63 THE WOODYARD, WINDSOR GREAT PARK, with a peasant carrying a bundle—10*in. by* 14½*in.*
    From the Collection of Colonel W. Gravatt, 1867

64 TREES ON SNOW HILL, WINDSOR GREAT PARK; and A CART AND FIGURES ON A ROAD—(*two*)   2

65 WINDSOR CASTLE—*pen and ink;* ST. GEORGE'S CHAPEL AND WINDSOR CASTLE FROM ETON—*pen and ink and colour;* WINDSOR CASTLE —*pen and ink and grey wash,* and *two etchings of* THE TERRACE, WINDSOR CASTLE—(*five on two mounts*)   2

66 A VIEW IN WINDSOR GREAT PARK—8*in. by* 12½*in.*
    From the Collection of Miss Eliza Sandby, 1886

67 DEEPSTRODE, SNOW HILL, WINDSOR GREAT PARK—*pen and ink and colour—signed with initials and dated* 1789—*from the Collection of Miss Eliza Sandby;* and A WOODLAND SCENE IN WINDSOR PARK, *sunset—pastel—signed with initials and dated* 1789—*from the Collection of Harvey Sandby, Esq.* 1857—(*two*)   2

68 WINDSOR BRIDGE—*with etched outlines*—5¾*in. by* 8⅜*in.*
    From the Collection of Miss Eliza Sandby
    Exhibited at the Eton 4th Centenary Exhibition, 1891

69 THE DEPUTY RANGER'S LODGE, WINDSOR GREAT PARK (now Royal Lodge) for many years the home of Thomas Sandby, R.A., with women and children of the Sandby families in the foreground— *signed with initials and dated* 1798—20*in. by* 16*in.*
    Illustrated in W. Sandby's "Thomas and Paul Sandby," 1892, *p.* 20

69

Fig. 1. Mapping difficulties

A calm with a yacht at anchor in the centre with numerous figures firing a salute a row boat with fifteen figures on the right in front and numerous small craft and boats beyond ...

A sloop with numerous figures in the centre lowering sail in collision with another vessel ; a barque beyond on the right ; a man-of-war shortening sail in a gale on the left.

Fig. 2. Similar depictions in images

Granularity. The complexity of the task also varies depending on the level of granularity - whether the alignment is being performed for a single page of the resource, the whole catalogue/book, or for the whole collection. Different levels face different types of challenges. For instance, a single page of an art catalogue can contain multiple images depicting the same scenery. Generally, in a catalogue, images of paintings showing similar depictions are grouped together. Post-digitization, it becomes difficult to identify the correct associations since the features obtained from image analysis and text analysis are quite similar for such cases. Minute differences in depictions, colors, tones, and style need to be recognized for distinguishing the different mappings and therefore the feature extraction needs to be quite elaborate in such a scenario. On the other hand, when performing alignment for images and texts from an entire catalogue or collection, all artworks are placed together in a single corpus. This may bring

Fig. 3. Semantic ambiguity in Images

together artwork images from different pages with very similar depictions and descriptions as shown in Fig. 2, making the task of alignment equally challenging.

Lack of Semantic Pointers. For the WPI-Art dataset, we encountered several cases where the textual descriptions, including the painting titles, fail to contain useful information to enable the alignment with the correct images. As discussed in [23], the identification of titles of artworks in textual descriptions is a non-trivial task itself for which existing Named Entity Recognition (NER) tools show sub-optimal performance. Even if these titles can be identified, there are several instances where the titles and even the description text for an artwork do not sufficiently describe the depictions of the painting, as would be identified by an image captioning model. One prominent example is that of portrait paintings where the texts usually elaborate on the person being portrayed, rather than describe the artwork depiction itself. Figure 3 illustrates a few portraits of different women in similar white attire. Even when some indicative features are present, it is challenging to perform alignment due to the overlapping features in the images. In the absence of fine-grained semantic features for guidance, the task of identifying the correct alignment becomes several magnitudes harder.

Training Data Unavailability. Machine learning algorithms require sizeable training data to learn models for performing specific tasks. There are several annotated datasets for the task of aligning image datasets comprising of photographs with texts [28]. However, the same is not true for our use case where the matching has to be performed for images of artworks and paintings. Although we leverage the few available datasets in this work [14], the existing models and techniques do not scale well to our dataset due to differences in image features, length of text descriptions, as well as formatting styles. Image analysis is harder for artworks due to the ambiguity of depiction and interpretation for several artworks, especially in the modern art genre. Due to this ambiguity, annotations need to be more precise as well as larger in size for the effective training of machine learning models. The unavailability of such annotated training datasets prevents the applicability of existing techniques for art-historic datasets and necessitates the need for further efforts in this direction.

4   Alignment Approach

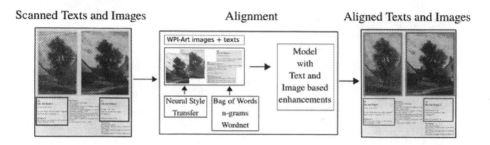

Fig. 4. Overview of our approach

In this section, we discuss our approach for the alignment of artwork images to associated texts and describe the different enhancement techniques in detail. In our previous work [1] we envisioned a framework for aligning images and texts. The overall framework, including the enhancements made in this work is shown in Fig. 4.

To apply any existing approaches on the WPI-Art dataset which consists of scanned catalogue pages, as a first step, we perform the automatic extraction of images and texts. Image extraction is performed by using the image localization algorithm from the OpenCV library [3]. We employ the Tesseract OCR engine [33] for the extraction of textual content from the scans and store it as plain text files.

Due to the lack of large annotated datasets in the art domain, we adopted the approach of Cornia *et al.*, which leverages the knowledge from the supervised training of an image-text alignment model trained on non-art documents. After training the supervised alignment model, an unsupervised method based on Maximum Mean Discrepancy is used to align the feature distributions of the unsupervised dataset with the feature distribution of the supervised training set. In this case, the COCO dataset, which consists of photos of common objects, was used as the supervised training dataset and the SemArt dataset was considered as the unsupervised training dataset. In the approach presented by Cornia *et al.* two types of neural networks are used to encode the data. Images are encoded using a pretrained ResNet-152 [18] architecture, while texts are encoded using a Gated Recurrent Unit (GRU) [4]. Furthermore, words are embedded using pre-trained word embeddings (either Glove [31] or FastText [2]). The output of the encoders is passed through one linear layer each, resulting in an embedding vector for each text description or image respectively. The embedding layers need to be trained such that the vectors of a matching text-image pair end up close in the semantic space whilst embeddings of other negative pairs are separated apart. In order to achieve this, two batches of training samples are fed through the networks at each step: a supervised batch (from the COCO dataset) and an unsupervised batch (from SemArt). A triplet hinge loss is used as the loss function. The loss gets reduced over the batch samples either by using a mean or sum operation. The unsupervised batch is used to guide the resulting embeddings towards the target domain of artworks. For this, the Maximum Mean Discrepancy (MMD) loss is used for aligning the distributions of the unsupervised text and image samples embedded with the current state of the model.

In the rest of the section, we discuss the techniques that we have explored for improving the performance of the model by Cornia *et al.*, specifically on the WPI-Art dataset.

4.1   Word Encodings

Since the textual descriptions in our dataset are often composed of short sentences (this is especially true for painting titles), a complex word representation model based on word sequences is not a good way to encode the text. Previous work has also shown that a simple BoW encoding for texts outperformed more complex methods [14]. Therefore, we implemented the BoW encoding for the texts, replacing the GRU encoding in Cornia *et al.* We further extended this technique and used bigrams encoding for the texts, so as to capture the semantics at phrase level as well.

4.2   Vocabulary Augmentation

In order to maximize the information from the textual excerpts and thus increase the chance of aligning the correct images, we enhanced the textual data using a thesaurus. We use WordNet [30] to generate synonyms from the terms in the text descriptions and added these to the training data. The primary motivation for this technique being, two semantically similar terms, that are not trivially matched by the model could be anchored around a shared synonym and hence nudge the model towards matching this pair better.

4.3   Neural Style Transfer

Paintings and photographs follow very different distributions in semantic space [5]. Due to this, conventional deep learning models that are trained on photographic datasets do not work well on art-related images. Convolutional neural networks (CNNs) for image recognition are typically biased towards texture in their input data [16]. Artworks, however, include varying types of brush strokes that may have no relation to the actual objects depicted in the image.

In the absence of large annotated datasets, we leverage the technique of Neural Style Transfer (NST) to bridge the gap between the datasets of photographs and paintings.

First introduced by Gatys et al. [15], neural style transfer describes the task of rendering a given input image (content image) in the "style" of another input image (style image), while retaining the content of the content image and applying the style of the style image. In the past years, several other neural style transfer mechanisms have been proposed [24] and successfully applied. In our work, we explored using the same technique as Geirhos et al. for image classification, using a stylized version of the ImageNet dataset [7], for improving the retrieval results on the WPI-Art dataset.

5   Results and Discussion

In this paper, our focus is on the application of multimodal retrieval for evaluating the alignment of images and texts extracted from art-historic datasets. We evaluate the approach introduced by Cornia et al. [5] and show how our proposed enhancements can help to boost the performance of the baseline approach. In this section, we first introduce our experimental setup. Subsequently, we describe the datasets that we use for training and evaluation. Lastly, we show the results of our experiments on the SemArt dataset and WPI-Art dataset.

5.1   Experimental Setup

In our experiments, we followed the network design introduced by Cornia et al. [5]. For the extraction of image features we used a ResNet-152 [18] model pre-trained on the ImageNet dataset [7]. For the encoding of text, we used a GRU [4], while we generated embeddings of our vocabulary using pre-trained word vectors. As long as not stated otherwise, we trained our models for 30 epochs, used the Adam optimizer [25] with a learning rate of $2 \cdot 10^{-4}$, and a batch size of 128. For evaluation, we calculate and report Recall@5 at the sample size 100, of the respective test datasets. We release our code and models for further experimentation[3].

5.2   Datasets

We used different datasets for training and evaluation of our models. For the training of the supervised part of our model, we followed Cornia et al. and used the Microsoft COCO [28] dataset, totalling 83 000 samples for training. For training the unsupervised part of the model, we used the train split of the SemArt dataset [14], which accounts for 19 244 samples for training. For evaluation, we used the validation split of the SemArt dataset and a subset of

---

[3] https://github.com/HPI-DeepLearning/semantic_analysis_of_cultural_heritage _data.

the WPI-Art dataset. Thw WPI-Art dataset consists of 93 images of paintings and their corresponding descriptions that we extracted from scans of auction catalogues provided by the Wildenstein Plattner Institute.

5.3 Results

We performed a range of different experiments. First, we attempted to reproduce the results of Cornia *et al.* and created a baseline that was used to illustrate the effect of our enhancements (see row 1 in Table 1 for our baseline results). Subsequently, we performed experiments using our proposed enhancements introduced in Sect. 4.

Table 1. Results of our experiments on the SemArt and WPI-Art evaluation datasets with a sample size of 100 or 93, respectively and a batch size of 32 for the BoW bigrams approach. We report Recall@5 as our evaluation metric. **Bold font** indicates the overall best result.

Method	Text retrieval		Image retrieval	
	SemArt	WPI-Art	SemArt	WPI-Art
Baseline	0.08	0.20	0.11	0.20
unigram BoW	0.21	0.25	0.26	0.29
unigram BoW + Style Transfer	0.20	0.17	0.27	0.23
unigram BoW + WordNet	0.24	0.20	0.28	0.27
bigram BoW	**0.30**	**0.34**	**0.34**	**0.34**

Enhancing the Text Encoding. Our first enhancement to the baseline model was to replace the GRU text encoder with a simpler BoW encoding, as used in [14]. Using this simple approach of text encoding we were able to improve the performance of our model by a large margin. We further adjusted the text encoding with bag-of-words to consider bigrams instead of single words, which lead to improvements in the results, as can be seen in rows 2 and 5 of Table 1. The results show that a simple text pre-processing technique is better suited for the alignment task since the bag-of-words approach can skip learning the word sequences in the descriptions.

An additional technique that we applied on the text encoding part, was to enrich the text data with a thesaurus. As already described in Sect. 4.2, we enriched our vocabulary using synonyms extracted from the WordNet [10] hierarchy. Table 1 (see row 4) shows that enriching the vocabulary with Word-Net helped to improve our results on the SemArt dataset although not on the WPI-Art dataset. We conclude that enriching descriptions with synonyms is a promising technique for enabling the alignment of images to texts. Using vocabulary enrichment increases the probability for the text embedding model to find concepts that can be embedded close to the concepts obtained by the image feature extractor.

Enhancing the Image Encoding. Besides improving the text analysis, we also introduced improvements on the image encoding side. Here, we used neural style transfer for the creation of a stylized version of ImageNet, as described in Sect. 4.3. Unfortunately, using a pre-trained image encoder on stylized images did not improve results, as can be observed in Table 1 (see row 2). One reason for this could be the stylization of only the training data for the feature extractor. The stylization of the images used for training the supervised part of the alignment model could likely improve results, however this is open for future work.

Table 2. Recall@5 on the SemArt (different sample sizes) and WPI-Art evaluation datasets for bigrams BoW approaches using different batch sizes (in parenthenses).

Method	Text retrieval					Image retrieval				
	100	300	500	1000	WPI-Art	100	300	500	1000	WPI-Art
bigrams BoW (128)	0.27	0.14	0.10	0.05	0.32	0.28	0.14	0.09	0.05	0.34
bigrams BoW (64)	0.27	**0.19**	**0.15**	**0.10**	**0.34**	0.33	0.19	**0.16**	0.11	**0.40**
bigrams BoW (32)	**0.30**	**0.19**	**0.15**	0.09	**0.34**	**0.34**	**0.24**	0.12	**0.12**	0.34

Batch Size Experiments. Until this point, our improvements already showed substantial improvements over the baseline. Next, we experimented with different batch sizes. Previous work has shown that large batch sizes can harm generalization [19]. A batch size of 128 being quite large, we performed additional experiments with lower batch sizes than 128. From the results in Table 2, it can be seen that decreasing the batch size indeed helped the model to generalize and provided us with our best results on the SemArt and WPI-Art datasets.

Reproducing the Existing Approach. Since the code or models from Cornia et al. [5] was unavailable, we attempted to reproduce their results for this work. Table 3 shows our replication results (denoted as "baseline"), the results reported by Cornia et al. as well as the results of our best performing model. Despite following the design of their system, as outlined in Sect. 5.1, as closely as possible, our replication of their setup did not show the same results, with our baseline having a considerably lower Recall@5. The reason for this is not clear,

Table 3. Recall@5 on the SemArt evaluation datasets for Cornia et al., our re-implementation as baseline, and our best approach. We evaluate on different sample sizes (100, 300, 500, 1000) for retrieval.

Method	Text Retrieval				Image Retrieval			
	100	300	500	1000	100	300	500	1000
Cornia et al. [5]	**0.34**	**0.19**	0.12	**0.09**	0.32	0.17	**0.12**	0.07
Baseline	0.08	0.04	0.03	0.02	0.11	0.06	0.04	0.02
bigrams BoW	0.30	**0.19**	**0.15**	**0.09**	**0.34**	**0.24**	**0.12**	**0.12**

it is highly probable that small technical nuances that could not be directly inferred from the paper were missing in our setup. However, with the help of our enhancement techniques, we were able to improve the results to be on par with the results reported by Cornia *et al.* This shows that our proposed enhancements can prove valuable in improving the performance of existing approaches substantially.

6   Conclusion

In this paper, we presented our approach on aligning artwork images to their corresponding descriptions in the digitized art-historic corpus of the Wildenstein Plattner Institute. We showed that analyzing digitized art-historic corpora poses many challenges. One of the greatest challenges is the availability of annotated training data for the training of deep models for multimodal retrieval. To this end, we proposed to leverage a previously introduced, semi-supervised approach that we further extended with various enhancements. The results of our experiments show that though the results of the previous approach could not be fully reproduced, our chosen approach and enhancements are viable and promising on the dataset under consideration.

Future Work. There is ample scope for several improvements based on this work that can lead to performance gains. In this work, we have evaluated the gains of our enhancements individually, in future work we want to further investigate combinations of our proposed enhancements. We also think that further experiments with neural style transfer could prove helpful. In this paper, we have considered stylizing the training data for the feature extractor but have not stylized the COCO dataset that was used as supervised training set, this could lead to potential problems in the distribution alignment phase and could be explored further. On the text analysis side, a possible improvement would be to additionally incorporate a dataset that contains less contextual information, but more descriptions of artworks, such as the Artpedia dataset [34]. Furthermore, a larger dataset extracted from the corpus of the WPI could be of help, since the training dataset does not have to contain matched pairs of artworks and descriptions. Finally, it might be possible to improve our experimental results by following a different unsupervised domain adaptation approach, as used by Lee *et al.* [27].

Acknowledgement. We thank the Wildenstein Plattner Institute for providing access to their art-historic archives.

References

1. Bartz, C., Jain, N., Krestel, R.: Automatic matching of paintings and descriptions in art-historic archives using multimodal analysis. In: Proceedings of the International Workshop on Artificial Intelligence for Historical Image Enrichment and Access (AI4HI), pp. 23–28 (2020)

2. Bojanowski, P., Grave, E., Joulin, A., Mikolov, T.: Enriching word vectors with subword information. Trans. Assoc. Comput. Linguist. **5**, 135–146 (2017)
3. Bradski, G., Kaehler, A.D., Opencv, D.: Dobb's journal of software tools. OpenCV Libr **25**, 120 (2000)
4. Cho, K., et al.: Learning phrase representations using RNN encoder-decoder for statistical machine translation. In: Proceedings of the Conference on Empirical Methods in Natural Language Processing, (EMNLP), pp. 1724–1734 (2014)
5. Cornia, M., Stefanini, M., Baraldi, L., Corsini, M., Cucchiara, R.: Explaining digital humanities by aligning images and textual descriptions. Pattern Recogn. Lett. **129**, 166–172 (2020)
6. de Boer, V., Wielemaker, J., van Gent, J., Hildebrand, M., Isaac, A., van Ossenbruggen, J., Schreiber, G.: Supporting linked data production for cultural heritage institutes: the Amsterdam museum case study. In: Simperl, E., Cimiano, P., Polleres, A., Corcho, O., Presutti, V. (eds.) ESWC 2012. LNCS, vol. 7295, pp. 733–747. Springer, Heidelberg (2012). https://doi.org/10.1007/978-3-642-30284-8_56
7. Deng, J., Dong, W., Socher, R., Li, L., Li, K., Fei-Fei, L.: ImageNet: a large-scale hierarchical image database. In: Proceedings of the Conference on Computer Vision and Pattern Recognition (CVPR), pp. 248–255 (2009)
8. Dijkshoorn, C., Jongma, L., Aroyo, L., Van Ossenbruggen, J., Schreiber, G., ter Weele, W., Wielemaker, J.: The rijksmuseum collection as linked data. Semantic Web **9**(2), 221–230 (2018)
9. Elgammal, A., Liu, B., Kim, D., Elhoseiny, M., Mazzone, M.: The shape of art history in the eyes of the machine. In: Proceedings of the Conference on Artificial Intelligence (AAAI) (2018)
10. Fellbaum, C.: WordNet: An Electronic Lexical Database. MIT Press, Cambridge (1998)
11. Garcia, N., Renoust, B., Nakashima, Y.: Context-aware embeddings for automatic art analysis. In: Proceedings of the International Conference on Multimedia Retrieval (ICMR), pp. 25–33. ICMR '19, Ottawa ON, Canada, June 2019
12. Garcia, N., Renoust, B., Nakashima, Y.: Understanding art through multi-modal retrieval in paintings. arXiv:1904.10615 [cs], April 2019
13. Garcia, N., Renoust, B., Nakashima, Y.: ContextNet: representation and exploration for painting classification and retrieval in context. Int. J. Multimed. Inf. Retrieval **9**(1), 17–30 (2019). https://doi.org/10.1007/s13735-019-00189-4
14. Garcia, N., Vogiatzis, G.: How to read paintings: semantic art understanding with multi-modal retrieval. In: Proceedings of the ECCV Workshops (Workshop on Computer Vision for Art Analysis), pp. 676–691 (2018)
15. Gatys, L.A., Ecker, A.S., Bethge, M.: A Neural Algorithm of Artistic Style. arXiv:1508.06576 [cs, q-bio] (2015)
16. Geirhos, R., Rubisch, P., Michaelis, C., Bethge, M., Wichmann, F.A., Brendel, W.: ImageNet-trained CNNs are biased towards texture; increasing shape bias improves accuracy and robustness. In: Proceedings of the International Conference on Learning Representations, September 2018
17. Harris, M., Levene, M., Zhang, D., Levene, D.: Finding parallel passages in cultural heritage archives. J. Comput. Cultural Heritage **11**(3), 1–24 (2018)
18. He, K., Zhang, X., Ren, S., Sun, J.: Deep residual learning for image recognition. In: Proceedings of the Conference on Computer Vision and Pattern Recognition (CVPR), pp. 770–778 (2016)

19. Hoffer, E., Hubara, I., Soudry, D.: Train longer, generalize better: closing the generalization gap in large batch training of neural networks. In: Advances in Neural Information Processing Systems (NIPS), pp. 1731–1741 (2017)

20. Huang, X., Zhong, S.h., Xiao, Z.: Fine-art painting classification via two-channel deep residual network. In: Advances in Multimedia Information Processing (PCM), pp. 79–88 (2018)

21. Huang, Y., Wang, L.: ACMM: Aligned cross-modal memory for few-shot image and sentence matching. In: Proceedings of the International Conference on Computer Vision (ICCV), pp. 5774–5783 (2019)

22. Hyvönen, E., Rantala, H.: Knowledge-based relation discovery in cultural heritage knowledge graphs. In: Proceedings of the Digital Humanities in the Nordic Countries Conference (DHN), pp. 230–239 (2019)

23. Jain, N., Krestel, R.: Who is Mona L.? identifying mentions of artworks in historical archives. In: Doucet, A., Isaac, A., Golub, K., Aalberg, T., Jatowt, A. (eds.) TPDL 2019. LNCS, vol. 11799, pp. 115–122. Springer, Cham (2019). https://doi.org/10.1007/978-3-030-30760-8_10

24. Jing, Y., Yang, Y., Feng, Z., Ye, J., Yu, Y., Song, M.: Neural style transfer: a review. Trans. Vis. Comput. Graph. **26**(11), 3365–3385 (2019)

25. Kingma, D.P., Ba, J.: Adam: a method for stochastic optimization. In: Proceedings of the International Conference on Learning Represenations (ICLR), San Diego (2015)

26. Kiros, R., Salakhutdinov, R., Zemel, R.S.: Unifying Visual-Semantic Embeddings with Multimodal Neural Language Models. arXiv:1411.2539 [cs] (2014)

27. Lee, C.Y., Batra, T., Baig, M.H., Ulbricht, D.: Sliced Wasserstein discrepancy for unsupervised domain adaptation. In: Proceedings of the Conference on Computer Vision and Pattern Recognition (CVPR), pp. 10285–10295 (2019)

28. Lin, T.-Y., et al.: Microsoft COCO: common objects in context. In: Fleet, D., Pajdla, T., Schiele, B., Tuytelaars, T. (eds.) ECCV 2014. LNCS, vol. 8693, pp. 740–755. Springer, Cham (2014). https://doi.org/10.1007/978-3-319-10602-1_48

29. Liu, Y., Guo, Y., Liu, L., Bakker, E.M., Lew, M.S.: CycleMatch: a cycle-consistent embedding network for image-text matching. Pattern Recogn. **93**, 365–379 (2019)

30. Miller, G.A.: WordNet: An electronic lexical database. MIT press (1998)

31. Pennington, J., Socher, R., Manning, C.D.: Glove: global vectors for word representation. In: Proceedings of the 2014 Conference on Empirical Methods in Natural Language Processing (EMNLP), pp. 1532–1543 (2014)

32. Segers, R., et al.: Hacking History via Event Extraction. In: Proceedings of the International Conference on Knowledge Capture (K-CAP), pp. 161–162 (2011)

33. Smith, R.: An overview of the Tesseract OCR engine. In: Proceedings of the International Conference on Document Analysis and Recognition (ICDAR), pp. 629–633 (2007)

34. Stefanini, M., Cornia, M., Baraldi, L., Corsini, M., Cucchiara, R.: Artpedia: a new visual-semantic dataset with visual and contextual sentences in the artistic domain. In: Image Analysis and Processing (ICIAP), pp. 729–740 (2019)

35. Thomas, C., Kovashka, A.: Artistic object recognition by unsupervised style adaptation. In: Proceedings of the Asian Conference on Computer Vision (ACCV), pp. 460–476 (2019)

36. Van Hooland, S., Verborgh, R.: Linked Data for Libraries, Archives and Museums: How to Clean. Link and Publish your Metadata, Facet Publishing (2014)

37. Yang, S., Oh, B.M., Merchant, D., Howe, B., West, J.: Classifying digitized art type and time period. In: Proceedings of the Workshop on Data Science for Digital Art History (DSDAH) (2018)

Insights from a Large-Scale Database of Material Depictions in Paintings

Hubert Lin[1]($\boxtimes$), Mitchell Van Zuijlen[2], Maarten W. A. Wijntjes[2], Sylvia C. Pont[2], and Kavita Bala[1]

[1] Computer Science Department, Cornell University, Ithaca, USA
hubert@cs.cornell.edu
[2] Perceptual Intelligence Lab, Delft University of Technology, Delft, The Netherlands

Abstract. Deep learning has paved the way for strong recognition systems which are often both trained on and applied to natural images. In this paper, we examine the give-and-take relationship between such visual recognition systems and the rich information available in the fine arts. First, we find that visual recognition systems designed for natural images can work surprisingly well on paintings. In particular, we find that interactive segmentation tools can be used to cleanly annotate polygonal segments within paintings, a task which is time consuming to undertake by hand. We also find that FasterRCNN, a model which has been designed for object recognition in natural scenes, can be quickly repurposed for detection of materials in paintings. Second, we show that learning from paintings can be beneficial for neural networks that are intended to be used on natural images. We find that training on paintings instead of natural images can improve the quality of learned features and we further find that a large number of paintings can be a valuable source of test data for evaluating domain adaptation algorithms. Our experiments are based on a novel large-scale annotated database of material depictions in paintings which we detail in a separate manuscript.

Keywords: Artistic material depictions · Large-scale data · Segmentation · Classification · Interpretability · Domain adaptation

1 Introduction

Deep learning has enabled the development of high performing recognition systems across a variety of image-based tasks [15,17,50]. These systems are often trained on natural photographs with applications in real world recognition like self-driving. Furthermore, applying recognition systems to large collections of images can also reveal cultural trends or give us insight into the visual patterns in the world (e.g. [26,29,32]). Human-created images, such as paintings, are particularly interesting to analyze from this perspective. Artistic depictions can reveal insights into culturally relevant ideas throughout time, as well as insights into human visual perception through the realism depicted by skilled artists.

© Springer Nature Switzerland AG 2021
A. Del Bimbo et al. (Eds.): ICPR 2020 Workshops, LNCS 12663, pp. 531–545, 2021.
https://doi.org/10.1007/978-3-030-68796-0_38

Whereas most computer vision systems focusing on digital art history is concerned with *object* recognition (e.g., [11]), it is the depiction of *space* and *materials* that visually characterize the course of art history. The depiction of space has had considerable attention in scientific literature [20,34,37,46] while recently the depiction of materials has gained scientific interest [5,38,47,48]. Therefore, it is interesting to investigate the interplay between deep learning systems designed for natural image analysis and the rich visual information found in paintings, especially with respect to artistic depictions of materials.

This remainder of this paper is organized into three parts. In Sect. 2, we briefly describe the dataset that subsequent experiments are based on. In Sect. 3, we explore how deep learning systems that have been primarily developed for use on natural photographs can be used to analyze paintings. Specifically, we explore (a) segmentation and (b) detection of materials in paintings. Recognition of materials in paintings can be useful for digital art history as well as general public interest. In Sect. 4, we explore how paintings can be a useful source of data from which better recognition systems can be built. Specifically, we investigate (c) the generalizability and interpretability of classifiers trained on paintings, and we investigate (d) the role that a large-scale painting dataset can play in evaluating visual recognition models.

2   Dataset

All experiments in this paper utilize data from a large-scale annotated database of material depictions in paintings. Extensive details and analysis of this database will be available in a separate manuscript. For context and completeness, we summarize a few relevant details here. The dataset consists of 19K high resolution paintings downloaded from the online collections of international art galleries, which span over 500 years of art history. The galleries with corresponding number of paintings are: The Rijksmuseum (4,672), The Metropolitan Museum of Art (3,222), Nationalmuseum (3,077), Cleveland Museum of Art (2,217), National Gallery of Art (2,132), Museo Nacional del Prado (2,032), The Art Institute of Chicago (936), Mauritshuis (638), and J. Paul Getty Museum (399). The distribution of paintings by year is shown in Fig. 1. The dataset includes crowd-sourced extreme click [35] bounding box annotations over 15 material categories, which are further delineated into 50 finegrained categories. Figure 2 shows a few examples of the annotated bounding boxes available in the dataset.

3   Using Computer Vision to Analyze Paintings

Research in computer recognition systems have focused primarily on natural images. For example, semantic segmentation benchmarks (of objects, 'stuff', or materials) [2,3,7,14,21,25] emphasize parsing in-the-wild photos, with applications in robotics, self-driving, and so forth. However, the analyses of paintings can also benefit from the use of visual recognition systems. Paintings can encode both cultural and perceptual biases, and being able to analyze paintings at scale

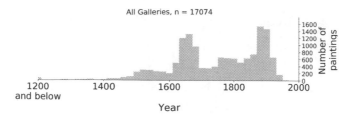

All Galleries, n = 17074

Fig. 1. Year Distribution of Paintings in Dataset. Each bin equals 20 years. There are peaks in the paintings in the1700s and 1900s. The former corresponds to the European golden ages; it is less clear what explains the latter peak.

Fig. 2. Examples of annotated bounding boxes. Left to Right: Liquid, Fabric, Ceramic, Metal, and Food.

can be useful for a variety of scientific disciplines including digital art history and human visual perception.

In this section, we explore the effectiveness of interactive segmentation methods (which can be used to select regions of interest in photographs for the purpose of image editing or data annotation) when applied to paintings. We also explore how well an *object* bounding box detector can be finetuned to detect *materials* depicted in unlabelled paintings, which could be used for content-based retrieval.

3.1   Extracting Polygon Segments with Interactive Segmentation

Polygon segmentation masks are useful for reasoning about boundary relationships between different semantic regions of an image, as well as the shape of the regions themselves. However, annotating segmentations is expensive and many modern datasets rely on expensive manual annotation methods [2,7,10,25,51]. Recent work has focused on more cost effective annotation methods (e.g. [4,24,27,31]). The use of interactive segmentation methods that transform sparse user inputs into polygon masks can ease annotation difficulty. For paintings, it is unclear whether these methods (especially deep learning methods trained on natural images) would perform well. Semantic boundaries in paintings likely have a different, and more varying structure than in photos. Paintings can have ambiguous or fuzzy boundaries between objects or materials [33] which can potentially be problematic for color-based methods. This can be due to variations in artistic style which can emphasize different aspects of depictions – for example, Van Gogh uses lines and edges to create texture, but such edges could potentially appear as boundaries to a segmentation model. In this experiment, we study the difficulty of segmenting paintings and whether innovations are necessary for existing methods to perform well.

Experimental Setup. We experiment with GrabCut [40] (an image-based approach) and DEXTR [31] (a modern deep learning approach). We evaluated the performance of these methods against 4.5k high-quality human annotated segmentations from [52]. The inputs to these methods are generated from the extreme points of the regions we are interested in. We use a variant of the GrabCut initialization proposed in [35], as well as a rectangular initialization for reference. For DEXTR, we consider models pretrained on popular object datasets [14, 25] as a starting point.

Results. We found that both GrabCut and DEXTR perform quite well on paintings. Surprisingly, DEXTR transfers quite well to materials in paintings despite being trained only with natural photographs of objects. The performance of DEXTR can be further improved by finetuning on COCO with a smaller learning rate (10% of original learning rate for 1 epoch). Finetuning DEXTR on Grabcut segments or iteratively finetuning with output of DEXTR does not seem to yield further improvements. The performance is summarized in Table 1, and samples are visualized in Fig. 3.

Table 1. Segmentation Performance. Grabcut Extr is based on [35] with small modifications: (a) minimum cost boundary is computed with the negative log probability of a pixel belonging to an edge; (b) in addition to clamping the morphological skeleton, the extreme points centroid and extreme points are clamped; (c) GC is computed directly on the RGB image. DEXTR [31] is pretrained on Pascal-SBD and COCO. Note that Pascal-SBD and COCO are natural image datasets of objects, but DEXTR transfers surprisingly well across both visual domain (paintings vs. photos) and annotation categories (materials vs. objects).

Segmentation mean IOU (%)

Grabcut Rectangle	Grabcut Extr	DEXTR Pascal-SBD	DEXTR COCO	DEXTR Finetuned
44.1	72.4	74.3	76.4	78.4

DEXTR Finetuned IOU By Class (%)

Animal	Ceramic	Fabric	Flora	Food
76.9	86.8	79.1	77.0	87.5

Gem	Glass	Ground	Liquid	Metal
74.4	83.2	69.6	73.0	75.5

Paper	Skin	Sky	Stone	Wood
86.1	78.9	78.5	81.7	67.4

Fig. 3. Extreme Click Segmentations. Left to right: Original Image, Ground Truth Segment, Grabcut Extr Segment, DEXTR COCO Segment. Both Grabcut and DEXTR use extreme points as input. For evaluation, the extreme points are generated synthetically from the ground truth segments. In practice, extreme clicks can be crowdsourced. Bottom-right corner shows the IOU for each segmentation.

3.2   Detecting Materials in Unlabeled Paintings

To allow the public to view and interact with art collections, museums and galleries provide extensive online functionality to search and navigate through the collections. Currently, to our knowledge, no online collections allows online visitors to query the collection for depicted *materials* within painting, which can be of interest to the public. Furthermore, depiction of materials plays a crucial role in characterizing art history. Detecting materials within novel paintings will be particularly beneficial to digital art historians who study materials such as stone [1,13] or skin [6,22]. Having access to specific materials can also digital art historians to compare these depictions directly with respect to painting style or technique. We experiment with automatic bounding box detection to ease access to material depictions in unlabelled collections.

Experimental Setup. We train a FasterRCNN [39] bounding box detector to localize and label material boxes with on 90% of annotated paintings in the dataset, and evaluate on the remaining 10%. Default COCO hyperparameters from [49] are used. Given the non-spatially-exhaustive nature of the annotations, many detected bounding boxes will not be matched against labelled ground truth boxes. However, the dataset is exhaustively annotated at an image level, and therefore, we report image-level accuracies. This can be interpreted as the accuracy of the model in tagging each image with the types of materials present. The validity of each localized box can be further quantified through a user study, but we did not perform this study at this time.

Results. Table 2 shows the performance. We found that the FasterRCNN model is able to accurately detect materials in paintings by finetuning on the annotated bounding boxes directly without any changes to the network architecture or training hyperparameters. It is certainly promising to see that an algorithm designed for object localization in natural images can be readily applied to material localization in paintings. A qualitative sample of detected bounding boxes is given in Fig. 4. To improve the spatial-specificity of the detected materials, it can be interesting to train an instance detector like MaskRCNN on segments extracted using methods discussed in the previous section. It would also be useful to combine material recognition with conventional object-based detection to extract complementary forms of information that improve the ability for users to filter data by their specific needs.

Table 2. Image-level Detection Accuracy. Bounding boxes are detected with FasterRCNN trained on paintings. Because the dataset is not exhaustively annotated spatially, image-level accuracy is reported instead of box precision and recall. Overall, images are tagged with the correct materials with high accuracy.

Animal	Ceramic	Fabric	Flora	Food
85.6	92.7	66.0	85.0	94.9
Gem	Glass	Ground	Liquid	Metal
88.4	91.3	86.5	86.4	70.7
Paper	Skin	Sky	Stone	Wood
92.4	70.2	89.4	74.8	74.9

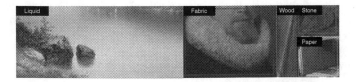

Fig. 4. Detected materials in Unlabeled Paintings. Automatically detecting materials can be useful for content retrieval and for filtering online galleries by viewer interests.

4   Using Paintings to Build Better Recognition Systems

In recent work for machine perception systems, art has been used in various ways. Models that learn to convert photographs into painting-like or sketch-like images have been studied extensively for their application as a tool for digital artists [18]. Recent work has shown that such neural style transfer algorithms can also produce images that are useful for training robust neural networks [16]. Artworks have also been used directly to evaluate the robustness of neural networks under "domain shifts" in which a model trained to recognize objects from photographs are shown artistic depictions of such objects instead [23,36].

We use the dataset of material depictions in paintings to explore two directions. First, we hypothesize that the perceptually focused depictions of artists can allow neural networks to learn better cues for classification. We find that learning from paintings can improve the interpretability of the cues it uses for its predictions. In a second experiment, we investigate the utility of a large-scale painting dataset as a benchmark for computer vision models under domain shifts when more data is available than is typical in existing domain adaptation benchmark datasets. We find that existing domain adaptation algorithms can fail to behave as expected in this setting.

4.1   Learning Robust Cues for Finegrained Fabric Classification

The task of distinguishing between images of different semantic content is a standard recognition task for computer vision systems. Increasing attention is being given to "fine-grained" classification where a model is tasked with distinguishing images of the same broad category (e.g. distinguishing different species of birds or different types of flora [43–45]). Fine-grained classification is particularly challenging for deep learning systems. Such a task depends on recognizing specific attributes for each finegrained class; in comparison, classifiers can perform well on coarse-grained classification by relying on context alone. We hypothesize that the painted depictions of materials can be beneficial for this task. Since some artistic depictions focus on salient cues for perception through perceptual shortcuts [8,12,30], it is possible that a network trained on such artwork is able to learn a more robust feature representation by focusing on these cues.

Experimental Setup. We experiment with the task classifying cotton/wool versus silk/satin. The latter can be recognized through local cues such as highlights on the cloth; such cues are carefully placed by artists in paintings. To understand whether artistic depictions of fabric allow a neural network to learn better features for classification, we train a model with either photographs or paintings. High resolution photographs of cotton/wool and silk/satin fabric and clothing (dresses, shirts) are downloaded and manually filtered from publicly available photos licensed under the Creative Commons from Flickr. In total, we downloaded roughly 1K photos. We sample cotton/wool and silk/satin samples from our dataset to form a corresponding dataset of 1K paintings.

Generalizability of Classifiers. Does training with paintings improve the generalizability of classifiers? To test cross-domain generalization, we test the classifier on types of images that it has not seen before. A classifier that has learned more robust features will perform better on this task than one that has learned to classify images based on more spurious correlations. We test the trained classifiers on both photographs and paintings.

Interpretability of Classifier Cues. Are the cues used by each classifier interpretable to humans? We produce evidence heatmaps with GradCAM [41] from the feature maps in the network before the fully connected classification layer. We extract high resolution feature maps from images of size 1024 × 1024 (for a feature map of size 32 × 32. The heatmaps produced by GradCAM show which regions of an image the classifier uses as evidence for a specific class. If a classifier has learned a good representation, the evidence that it uses should be more interpretable for humans. For both models, we compute heatmaps for test images corresponding to their ground truth label. We conduct a user study on Amazon Mechanical Turk to find which heatmaps are preferred by humans. Users are shown images with regions corresponding to heatmap values that are above 1.5 standard deviations above the mean. Figure 5 illustrates an example. Our user study resulted in responses from 85 participants, 57 of which were analyzed after quality control. For quality control, we only kept results from participants who spent over 1 s on average per task item.

Fig. 5. Classifier Cues. Left to Right: Original Image, Masked Image (Painting Classifier), and Masked Image (Photo Classifier). The unmasked regions represent evidence used by the classifiers for predicting "silk/satin" in this particular image.

Results. We find that the classifier trained with paintings exhibits better cross-domain generalization, and uses cues that humans prefer over the photo classifier. This suggests that paintings can improve the robustness of classifiers for this task of fabric classification.

Generalizability of Classifiers. In Table 3, the performance of the two classifiers are summarized. We find that both classifiers perform similarly well on the domain they are trained on. However, when the classifiers are cross-domain data, we find that the painting-trained classifier performs better than the photo-trained classifier. This suggests that the classifier trained on paintings has learned a more generalizable feature representation for this task.

Interpretability of Classifier Cues. Overall, we find that the classifier trained on paintings uses evidence that is better aligned with evidence preferred by humans (Table 4 and Fig. 6). Due to domain shifts when applying classifiers to out-of-domain images, we would expect the cues selected by the painting classifier to be preferable on paintings, and the cues selected by the photo classifier to be preferable on photos. Interestingly, this does not hold for photos of satin/silk (column 2 of Table 4) – we find that users equally prefer the evidence selected by the painting classifier to the evidence selected by the photo classifier. This suggests that either (a) the painting classifier has learned the "correct" human-interpretable cues for recognizing satin/silk, or (b) that the photo classifier has learned to classify satin/silk based on some spurious contextual signals. We asked users to elucidate their reasoning when choosing which set of cues they preferred. In general, users noted that they preferred the network which picks out regions containing the target class. Therefore, it seems that the network trained on paintings has learned better to distinguish fabric through the actual presence of such fabrics in the image over other contextual signals.

Taken together, our results provide evidence that a classifier trained on paintings can be more robust than a classifier trained on photographs. It would be interesting to explore this further. A limitation of this study is the relatively small number of data samples, and very limited number of material types (two: cotton/wool and silk/satin) that we explored. Are there other materials or objects which deep neural networks can learn to recognize better from paintings than photographs?

Table 3. Classifier Generalization. Classifiers are trained to distinguish cotton/wool from silk/satin. One classifier is trained on photographs and another classifier is trained on paintings. Both classifiers perform similarly well on images of the same type they were trained on, but the classifier trained on paintings performs better on photographs than vice versa. This suggests that the features learned from paintings are more generalizable for this task on this set of data.

	Photo → Photo	Painting→ Painting
MEAN F1 Score	79.6%	80.5%
	Photo → Painting	Painting→ Photo
MEAN F1 Score	49.5%	57.8%

4.2   Benchmarking Unsupervised Domain Adaptation

In unsupervised domain adaptation (UDA), models are trained on a 'source' dataset with annotated labels as well as an unlabeled 'target' dataset. The goal is to train a model which performs well on unseen target dataset samples. Existing domain adaptation benchmark datasets for classification focus primarily on object recognition and tend to be limited in number of data samples, with most class categories containing on the order of 1000 samples or fewer (for example, refer to Table 1 of [36]). In contrast, the dataset we use here has the unique properties of (a) focusing primarily on material classification and (b) containing on the order of 10–30K for 9 of the 15 annotated classes (e.g. fabric, wood), with the remainder in the range of 2K–5K (e.g. ground). This positions this data as a valuable addition for benchmarking for UDA algorithms.

Table 4. Human Agreement with Classifier Cues. On average, humans prefer the cues used by the painting-trained classifier to make its predictions over the cues used by the photo-trained classifier. Interestingly, the human judgements also indicate that the painting-trained classifier uses cues that are just as good to the cues used by the photo-trained classifier for silk/satin photos despite never seeing a silk/satin photo during training. A pictorial representation of the results is given in Fig. 6.

	Cotton/Wool Photos	Silk/Satin Photos	Cotton/Wool Paintings	Silk/Satin Paintings	MEAN
Photo Classif. Preferred	64.7 ± 3.5%	48.9 ± 3.1%	26.8 ± 2.5%	39.1 ± 2.1%	44.9 ± 1.9%
Painting Classif. Preferred	35.3 ± 3.5%	51.1 ± 3.1%	73.2 ± 2.5%	60.9 ± 2.1%	55.1 ± 1.9%

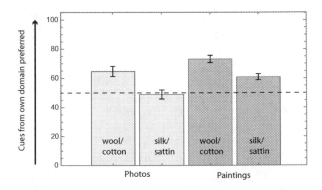

Fig. 6. Human Agreement with Classifier Cues. Pictorial representation of user study results from Table 4. The y-axis represents how often humans prefer the cues from a classifier trained on the same domain as the test images. It is clear that humans prefer the painting classifier for paintings more than they prefer the photo classifier for photos. Furthermore, the painting and photo classifiers are equally preferred for silk/satin photos despite the painting classifier never seeing a photo during training.

Experimental Setup. For this study, we focus on a family of domain adaptation algorithms which aim to explicitly minimize feature discrepancy across the source and target domains. Existing work has shown that class-conditional UDA in which labels are estimated for target domain samples during training can be better than class-agnostic UDA where adaptation is performed without using any estimated label information at all. We choose CDD [19] and MMD [28, 42] as representative methods for class-conditional and class-agnostic discrepancy minimization. All methods are trained with default settings from publicly available source code for CDD, which includes the use of domain batch normalization [9]. We selected 10 material categories: ceramic, fabric, foliage, glass, liquid, metal, paper, skin, stone, and wood. For our painting dataset, we sampled as-class-balanced-as-possible from these classes to form a dataset with 10K samples and a dataset with 60K samples. A corresponding photograph dataset is constructed from Opensurfaces/MINC/COCO with 10K and 60K samples as well.

Results. We find that the studied domain adaptation algorithms can indeed behave differently than would be expected from results on existing benchmark datasets. This is could due to more data being available or a more difficult domain shift than conventional adaptation benchmark datasets.

Effect of Dataset Size. Results are summarized in Table 5. With the conventional 1K samples per class, we confirm domain adaptation yields gains over source-only as found on existing benchmark datasets. In contrast to results on existing benchmarks however, we find that class-conditional adaptation does not necessarily outperform class-agnostic adaptation. We hypothesize this occurs due to failures in target label estimation for the class-conditional case – we discuss this further below. Next, with 6K samples per class (which is 6× more data samples per class than conventional UDA benchmarks), we find that source-only (i.e., no adaptation) performs very competitively. In fact, source-only strictly outperforms adaptation for Painting to Photo transfer in this data regime! This result suggests that domain adaptation is useful in lower data regimes, but source-only is a competitive alternative when more data is available. We leave a deeper exploration of this phenomenon to future work.

Effect of Class Label Estimation. As found above, class-conditional adaptation can underperform class-agnostic adaptation despite utilizing more information. As class-conditional adaptation depends on estimated target labels, large domain shifts that hamper label estimation can harm adaptation. To confirm this, we consider two experiments: CDD with intraclass discrepancy minimization only (instead of both intraclass minimization and interclass maximization), and CDD with ground truth labels (i.e., perfect label estimation). Results are in Table 6. In both cases, we see performance improves. In the case where perfect label estimation is assumed, then CDD does outperform intraCDD and MMD as found on existing datasets. Therefore, estimating class labels for domain adaptation is useful in practice, but only if the labels are estimated sufficiently well.

Table 5. Effect of Dataset Size. UDA from photo (source) to painting (target) and painting (source) to photo (target). Source-only refers to a reference baseline where no adaptation is used. The gap between source-only and UDA decreases as data samples increases from 1K images per class to 6K images per class. Furthermore, in contrast to behavior found on existing benchmark datasets, the class-conditional method of CDD does not necessarily outperform the class-agnostic counterpart MMD.

ResNet18 1K imgs/class per domain	Photo → Painting	Painting → Photo
Source-Only	35.2	46.9
MMD	46.1 (+10.9)	56.4 (+9.5)
CDD	40.5 (+5.3)	57.4 (+10.5)
ResNet18 6K imgs/class per domain	Photo → Painting	Painting → Photo
Source-Only	38.7	53.6
MMD	43.5 (+4.8)	51.5 (-2.1)
CDD	35.6 (-3.1)	49.4 (-4.2)

Table 6. Effect of Class Label Estimation. Reducing the reliance class label estimation improves class-conditional UDA when label estimation for target data is poor. We find that IntraCDD (which considers only intraclass discrepancy) outperforms CDD (which considers both intraclass and interclass discrepancy). Using ground truth (GT) labels with CDD (i.e., assuming perfect class label estimation) recovers performance gains over intraCDD and MMD. MMD does not require class label estimation, and so its performance not suffer in the case of poor label estimation.

ResNet18 1K imgs/class per domain	Photo → Painting	Painting → Photo
MMD	46.1 (+10.9)	56.4 (+9.5)
IntraCDD	44.4 (+9.2)	58.5 (+11.6)
CDD	40.5 (+5.3)	57.4 (+10.5)
IntraCDD w/ GT labels	57.6 (+22.4)	64.4 (+17.5)
CDD w/ GT labels	61.6 (+26.4)	72.5 (+25.6)

5   Conclusion

In this paper, we explored how modern deep learning tools developed for natural images can be used to analyze paintings, and in turn, how paintings can be used to improve deep learning systems in a series of experiments. Our findings suggest that progress in visual perception for natural images can benefit systems used for fine art analysis, and having access to the visual information encoded in paintings can be fruitful for building more generalizable perception systems.

Acknowledgements. This work was funded in part by Google, NSF (CHS-1617861 and CHS-1513967), NSERC (PGS-D 516803 2018), and the Netherlands Organization for Scientific Research (NWO) project 276-54-001.

References

1. Augart, I., Saß, M., Wenderholm, I.: Steinformen. De Gruyter, Berlin, Boston (2018). https://doi.org/10.1515/9783110583618. https://www.degruyter.com/view/title/535173
2. Bell, S., Upchurch, P., Snavely, N., Bala, K.: OpenSurfaces: a richly annotated catalog of surface appearance. ACM Trans. Graph. **32**(4), 1 (2013). https://doi.org/10.1145/2461912.2462002. http://dl.acm.org/citation.cfm?doid=2461912.2462002
3. Bell, S., Upchurch, P., Snavely, N., Bala, K.: Material recognition in the wild with the materials in context database. In: Computer Vision and Pattern Recognition (CVPR) (2015)
4. Benenson, R., Popov, S., Ferrari, V.: Large-scale interactive object segmentation with human annotators. In: Proceedings of the IEEE Conference on Computer Vision and Pattern Recognition, pp. 11700–11709 (2019)
5. Beurs, W.: "De groote waereld in't kleen geschildert, of Schilderagtig tafereel van's weerelds schilderyen. Kortelijk vervat in ses boeken: Verklarende de hooftverwen, haare verscheide mengelinge in oly, en der zelver gebruik...". By Johannes en Gillis Janssonius van Waesberge (1692)
6. Bol, M., Lehmann, A.S.: Painting skin and water: towards a material iconography of translucent motifs in early Netherlandish painting. In: Rogier van der Weyden in context: papers presented at the Seventeenth Symposium for the Study of Underdrawing and Technology in Painting held in Leuven, 22–24 October, pp. 215–228. Peeters (2012)
7. Caesar, H., Uijlings, J., Ferrari, V.: Coco-stuff: Thing and stuff classes in context. In: Proceedings of the IEEE Conference on Computer Vision and Pattern Recognition, pp. 1209–1218 (2018)
8. Cavanagh, P.: The artist as neuroscientist. Nature **434**(7031), 301–307 (2005). https://doi.org/10.1038/434301a
9. Chang, W.G., You, T., Seo, S., Kwak, S., Han, B.: Domain-specific batch normalization for unsupervised domain adaptation. In: Proceedings of the IEEE Conference on Computer Vision and Pattern Recognition, pp. 7354–7362 (2019)
10. Cordts, M., et al.: The cityscapes dataset for semantic urban scene understanding. In: Proceedings of the IEEE Conference on Computer Vision and Pattern Recognition, pp. 3213–3223 (2016)
11. Crowley, E.J., Zisserman, A.: The state of the art: object retrieval in paintings using discriminative regions. In: British Machine Vision Conference (2014)
12. Di Cicco, F., Wijntjes, M.W., Pont, S.C.: Understanding gloss perception through the lens of art: combining perception, image analysis, and painting recipes of 17th century painted grapes. J. Vis. **19**(3), 1–15 (2019). https://doi.org/10.1167/19.3.7
13. Dietrich, R.: Rocks depicted in painting & sculpture. Rocks Miner. **65**(3), 224–236 (1990)
14. Everingham, M., Van Gool, L., Williams, C.K., Winn, J., Zisserman, A.: The pascal visual object classes (VOC) challenge. Int. J. Comput. Vision **88**(2), 303–338 (2010)
15. Garcia-Garcia, A., Orts-Escolano, S., Oprea, S., Villena-Martinez, V., Martinez-Gonzalez, P., Garcia-Rodriguez, J.: A survey on deep learning techniques for image and video semantic segmentation. Appl. Soft. Comput. **70**, 41–65 (2018)
16. Geirhos, R., Rubisch, P., Michaelis, C., Bethge, M., Wichmann, F.A., Brendel, W.: Imagenet-trained CNNs are biased towards texture; increasing shape bias improves accuracy and robustness. arXiv preprint arXiv:1811.12231 (2018)

17. Hafiz, A.M., Bhat, G.M.: A survey on instance segmentation: state of the art. International Journal of Multimedia Information Retrieval pp. 1–19 (2020)
18. Jing, Y., Yang, Y., Feng, Z., Ye, J., Yu, Y., Song, M.: Neural style transfer: a review. IEEE Trans. Vis. Comput. Graph. **26**, 3365–3385 (2019)
19. Kang, G., Jiang, L., Yang, Y., Hauptmann, A.G.: Contrastive adaptation network for unsupervised domain adaptation. In: Proceedings of the IEEE Conference on Computer Vision and Pattern Recognition, pp. 4893–4902 (2019)
20. Kemp, M., et al.: The science of art: optical themes in western art from brunelleschi to seurat (1990)
21. Kuznetsova, A., et al.: The open images dataset v4: Unified image classification, object detection, and visual relationship detection at scale. arXiv preprint arXiv:1811.00982 (2018)
22. Lehmann, A.S.: Fleshing out the body: The'colours of the naked'in workshop practice and art theory, 1400–1600. Nederlands Kunsthistorisch Jaarboek **59**, 86 (2008)
23. Li, D., Yang, Y., Song, Y.Z., Hospedales, T.M.: Deeper, broader and artier domain generalization. In: Proceedings of the IEEE International Conference on Computer Vision, pp. 5542–5550 (2017)
24. Lin, H., Upchurch, P., Bala, K.: Block annotation: Better image annotation with sub-image decomposition. In: Proceedings of the IEEE International Conference on Computer Vision. pp. 5290–5300 (2019)
25. Lin, T.-Y., Maire, M., Belongie, S., Hays, J., Perona, P., Ramanan, D., Dollár, P., Zitnick, C.L.: Microsoft COCO: common objects in context. In: Fleet, D., Pajdla, T., Schiele, B., Tuytelaars, T. (eds.) ECCV 2014. LNCS, vol. 8693, pp. 740–755. Springer, Cham (2014). https://doi.org/10.1007/978-3-319-10602-1_48
26. Lin, Z., Sun, J., Davis, A., Snavely, N.: Visual chirality. In: Proceedings of the IEEE/CVF Conference on Computer Vision and Pattern Recognition, pp. 12295–12303 (2020)
27. Ling, H., Gao, J., Kar, A., Chen, W., Fidler, S.: Fast interactive object annotation with curve-gcn. In: Proceedings of the IEEE Conference on Computer Vision and Pattern Recognition, pp. 5257–5266 (2019)
28. Long, M., Cao, Y., Wang, J., Jordan, M.: Learning transferable features with deep adaptation networks. In: International Conference on Machine Learning, pp. 97–105. PMLR (2015)
29. Mall, U., Matzen, K., Hariharan, B., Snavely, N., Bala, K.: Geostyle: discovering fashion trends and events. In: Proceedings of the IEEE International Conference on Computer Vision, pp. 411–420 (2019)
30. Mamassian, P.: Ambiguities and conventions in the perception of visual art. Vision. Res. **48**(20), 2143–2153 (2008). https://doi.org/10.1016/j.visres.2008.06.010
31. Maninis, K.K., Caelles, S., Pont-Tuset, J., Van Gool, L.: Deep extreme cut: from extreme points to object segmentation (2017). http://arxiv.org/abs/1711.09081
32. Matzen, K., Bala, K., Snavely, N.: Streetstyle: exploring world-wide clothing styles from millions of photos. arXiv preprint arXiv:1706.01869 (2017)
33. van Eikema, M.H.: Hommes: The contours in the paintings of the oranjezaal, huis ten bosch' (2005)
34. Panofsky, E.: Perspective as Symbolic Form. Princeton University Press, Princeton (1927/2020)
35. Papadopoulos, D.P., Uijlings, J.R.R., Keller, F., Ferrari, V.: Extreme clicking for efficient object annotation. Int. J. Comput. Vis. (2017). https://doi.org/10.1109/ICCV.2017.528. http://arxiv.org/abs/1708.02750

36. Peng, X., Bai, Q., Xia, X., Huang, Z., Saenko, K., Wang, B.: Moment matching for multi-source domain adaptation. In: Proceedings of the IEEE International Conference on Computer Vision, pp. 1406–1415 (2019)
37. Pirenne, M.H.: Optics, painting & photography. Cambridge University Press
38. Pottasch, C.: Frans van mieris's painting technique as one of the possible sources for willem beurs's treatise on painting. Art & Perception, pp. 1–17, 13 June 2020. https://doi.org/10.1163/22134913-bja10013.   https://brill.com/view/journals/artp/aop/article-10.1163-22134913-bja10013/article-10.1163-22134913-bja10013.xml
39. Ren, S., He, K., Girshick, R., Sun, J.: Faster R-CNN: towards real-time object detection with region proposal networks. In: Advances in Neural Information Processing Systems, pp. 91–99 (2015)
40. Rother, C., Kolmogorov, V., Blake, A.: "grabcut" interactive foreground extraction using iterated graph cuts. ACM Trans. Graph. (TOG) 23(3), 309–314 (2004)
41. Selvaraju, R.R., Cogswell, M., Das, A., Vedantam, R., Parikh, D., Batra, D.: Grad-cam: visual explanations from deep networks via gradient-based localization. In: Proceedings of the IEEE International Conference on Computer Vision, pp. 618–626 (2017)
42. Tzeng, E., Hoffman, J., Zhang, N., Saenko, K., Darrell, T.: Deep domain confusion: Maximizing for domain invariance. arXiv preprint arXiv:1412.3474 (2014)
43. Van Horn, G., Mac Aodha, O., Song, Y., Cui, Y., Sun, C., Shepard, A., Adam, H., Perona, P., Belongie, S.: The inaturalist species classification and detection dataset. In: Proceedings of the IEEE Conference on Computer Vision and Pattern Recognition, pp. 8769–8778 (2018)
44. Wah, C., Branson, S., Welinder, P., Perona, P., Belongie, S.: The caltech-ucsd birds-200-2011 dataset (2011)
45. Wei, X.S., Wu, J., Cui, Q.: Deep learning for fine-grained image analysis: a survey. arXiv preprint arXiv:1907.03069 (2019)
46. White, J.: The birth and rebirth of pictorial space, Cambridge MA (1957)
47. Wiersma, L.: Colouring – material depiction in flemish and dutch baroque art theory. Art & Perception, pp. 1–23, 22 April 2020. https://doi.org/10.1163/22134913-bja10005. https://brill.com/view/journals/artp/aop/article-10.1163-22134913-bja10005/article-10.1163-22134913-bja10005.xml
48. Wijntjes, M.W.A., Spoiala, C., de Ridder, H.: Thurstonian scaling and the perception of painterly translucency. Art Perception, 1–24, 04 Sep 2020. https://doi.org/10.1163/22134913-bja10021. https://brill.com/view/journals/artp/aop/article-10.1163-22134913-bja10021/article-10.1163-22134913-bja10021.xml
49. Wu, Y., Kirillov, A., Massa, F., Lo, W.Y., Girshick, R.: Detectron2 (2019)
50. Ye, M., Shen, J., Lin, G., Xiang, T., Shao, L., Hoi, S.C.: Deep learning for person re-identification: a survey and outlook. arXiv preprint arXiv:2001.04193 (2020)
51. Zhou, B., Zhao, H., Puig, X., Fidler, S., Barriuso, A., Torralba, A.: Scene parsing through ade20k dataset. In: Proceedings of the IEEE conference on Computer Vision and Pattern Recognition, pp. 633–641 (2017)
52. van Zuijlen, M.J., Pont, S.C., Wijntjes, M.W.: Painterly depiction of material properties. J. Vision 20(7), 7–7 (2020)

An Analysis of the Transfer Learning
of Convolutional Neural Networks
for Artistic Images

Nicolas Gonthier[1,2（✉）] [iD], Yann Gousseau[1], and Saïd Ladjal[1]

[1] LTCI - Télécom Paris - Institut Polytechnique de Paris, 91120 Palaiseau, France
{nicolas.gonthier,yann.gousseau,said.ladjal}@telecom-paris.fr
[2] Université Paris Saclay, 91190 Saint-Aubin, France

Abstract. Transfer learning from huge natural image datasets, fine-tuning of deep neural networks and the use of the corresponding pre-trained networks have become de facto the core of art analysis applications. Nevertheless, the effects of transfer learning are still poorly understood. In this paper, we first use techniques for visualizing the network internal representations in order to provide clues to the understanding of what the network has learned on artistic images. Then, we provide a quantitative analysis of the changes introduced by the learning process thanks to metrics in both the feature and parameter spaces, as well as metrics computed on the set of maximal activation images. These analyses are performed on several variations of the transfer learning procedure. In particular, we observed that the network could specialize some pre-trained filters to the new image modality and also that higher layers tend to concentrate classes. Finally, we have shown that a double fine-tuning involving a medium-size artistic dataset can improve the classification on smaller datasets, even when the task changes.

Keywords: Transfer learning · Convolutional neural network · Art analysis · Feature visualization

1 Introduction

Over the last decade, numerous efforts have been invested in the digitization of fine art, yielding digital collections allowing the preservation and remote access to cultural heritage. Such collections, even when available online, can only be fruitfully browsed through the metadata associated with images. In recent years, several research teams have developed search engines dedicated to fine arts for different recognition tasks: Replica [21] for visual similarity search or the Oxford Painting Search [5] for semantics recognition of arbitrary objects. Often, those search engines are based on convolutional neural networks (CNN). Transfer learning from large-scale natural image datasets such as ImageNet, mostly by

---

Supported by the "IDI 2017" project funded by the IDEX Paris-Saclay, ANR-11-IDEX-0003-02 and Télécom Paris.

A. Del Bimbo et al. (Eds.): ICPR 2020 Workshops, LNCS 12663, pp. 546–561, 2021.
https://doi.org/10.1007/978-3-030-68796-0_39

fine-tuning large pre-trained networks, has become a de facto standard for art analysis applications. Nevertheless, there are large differences in dataset sizes, image style and task specifications between natural images and the target artistic images, and there is little understanding of the effects of transfer learning in this context. In this work, we explore some properties of transfer learning for artistic images, by using both visualization techniques and quantitative studies. Visualization techniques permit to understand what the networks have learned on specific artistic datasets, by showing some of their internal representations or giving hints at what aspects of artistic images are important for their understanding. In particular, we will see that the networks can specify some pre-trained filters in order to adapt them to the new modality of images and also that the network can learn new, highly structured filters specific to artistic images from scratch. We also look at the set of the maximal activation images for a given channel to complete our observation.

Quantitative results can confirm some intuitive facts about the way networks are modified during fine-tuning. To quantify the amount of change experienced by networks in different fine-tuning modality, we rely on feature similarity and the ℓ_2 distance between models. We also compute metrics (overlapping ratio and entropy) on the maximal activation images set to this end. Moreover we experimentally show that fine-tuning first a pretrained ImageNet model on an intermediate artistic dataset may lead to better performance than a direct fine tuning on the target small artistic dataset (for a different tasks). Let us emphasize that the goal of this work is not to provide state-of-the-art classification performances, but rather to investigate the way CNNs are modified by classical fine-tuning operations in the specific case of artwork images.

2 Related Work

Our analysis of the adaptation of a deep network to artistic databases uses already well-established tools and methods. In the following we describe these methods and list the relevant related works.

2.1 Deep Transfer Learning for Art Classification Problems

Transfer learning consists in adapting a model trained on a large image database (such as ImageNet [19]) for a new task. This method is the de facto standard when faced with relatively small datasets and has proven its relevance in many works. Two main modalities are possible for transfer learning. The first consists in taking the penultimate output of the pre-trained network to make it the input of a simple classifier [6]. In the following, we refer to this approach as the *off-the-shelf* method. The second option consists in *fine-tuning* (FT) the pre-trained network for the new task [9]. One can also argue that the bare architecture of a successful network is in itself a form of transfer learning, as this architecture has proven its relevance to the task of image classification.

On bigger datasets, one can fine-tune the weights to adapt the network to a new task. This approach is by far the most used one. For the domain of artistic images, it has been used for style classification [2,12,27], object recognition in drawings [30] or iconographic characters [13], people detection across a variety of artworks [28], visual link retrieval [21], author classification [15,20] or several of those tasks at the same time [1].

More precisely, [27] show that fine-tuning a CNN pretrained on ImageNet outperforms off-the-shelf and training from scratch strategies for style, genre or artist classification. In [2], the authors evaluated the impact of domain-specific weight initialization and the kind of fine-tuning used (number of frozen layers for instance) for different art classification tasks. They compared different pre-training with different natural images datasets. They have shown that the bigger (in terms of training images and number of labels), the better will be the results.

A midway strategy between directly fine-tuning a pre-trained network and the mere use of the final network features, when the dataset is small, is to have a two phase fine-tuning, the first one with a relatively large dataset of artworks and the second on the target dataset. This strategy was shown to be helpful in [20], using the Rijksmuseum dataset for the first fine-tuning. Their findings suggest that the double fine-tuned model focuses more on fine details to perform artist attribution.

In this work, we will look at the two ways of fine-tuning and the various effects they have on what the network learns to adapt itself to artworks. When using a double fine-tuning, the middle dataset will always be the RASTA dataset (described below). We will also look at the transfer of the bare architecture, which means initializing the weights to random values. Intermediate strategies such as partial freezing of the network will also be studied.

2.2   Deep Convolutional Neural Network Understanding

The deep learning community has provided several tools for trying to better understand deep CNNs: feature visualization [7,17] and attribution [22]. Feature visualization answers questions about what a deep network is responding to in a dataset by generating examples that yield maximum activation. Nevertheless, to achieve visually good results and output results that are understandable by humans, it is a necessity to add some constraints [17] to the optimization, thus avoiding getting adversarial structured noise. Based on those works, several papers have proposed methodology to determine the way the different features contribute to a classification [18] by mixing it with attribution methods. Visualization of the optimized images also permits regrouping the filters of the first layers of an InceptionV1 model in some comprehensible groups [16]. Such works [7,16,17] tend to show that a CNN learns meaningful features (for instance eye detector or dog head detector) whereas others show that those networks are primarily detecting textures [8]. By looking at the channel responses, the authors of [27] concluded that lower layers learn simple patterns and higher ones, complex object parts such as portrait shape. In [24], the authors look at the feature visualizations and attributions of a small convolutional network trained on an artistic dataset. Some of the characteristic patterns of the classes (as the circle shape for portrait class) can be found in the visualizations. In [25], the authors visualize the impact of the fine-tuning of a network on fine-grained datasets. They demonstrate various properties of the transfer learning process such as the speed and characteristics of adaptation, neuron reuse and spatial scale of the represented image features on natural images datasets. Another way to understand the inner structure of networks is to compute feature similarity between different layers or different models. The recent work [11] proposes to do this through Centred Kernel Alignement (CKA), a measure that we will use later in this work.

2.3 Datasets

Most artistic datasets only contain style or author metadata [12,27] instead of depicted objects or iconographic elements. Some datasets are specific to a given class of objects such as person in paintings [28] or to concepts that are specific to art history [3]. In [29], an annotated database of 2.2M contemporary artworks from Behance (website of portfolios from professional artists) is introduced, on which it is shown that fine-tuning improves recognition performances. The OmniArt dataset introduced in [23] contains 1M historical artworks of 4 different types (from craft to paintings). Those two large-scale datasets are not openly accessible yet and no models pretrained on them has been shared to the community. For our experiments we use three datasets which come from different research works. The first one contains the largest number of samples and comes from the WikiArt website. It contains 80,000 images tagged with one among 25 artistic styles [12] and is named *RASTA*. Many other works referred to this dataset as the "WikiArt paintings" [27] but this variant contains only 25 classes instead of 27. Due to its size and large diversity, we will mainly use this dataset in the experimental section. The second one is the *Paintings* Dataset introduced in [4], made of 8629 British painting images with 10 different labels corresponding to common objects.The last dataset is the *IconArt* dataset from [10] composed of 5955 painting images from Wikicommons with 7 iconographic labels, for instance angel or the crucifixion of Jesus. These two datasets are designed for object classification, similarly to ImageNet.

3 Analyzing CNNs Trained for Art Classification Tasks

In this work, we investigate the effect of fine-tuning in the case of artistic images. In order to do so, we rely both on visualization techniques and quantification of the change the network undergoes. Our experimental results are organized in five sections. First, we consider an Inception V1 network [26] pre-trained on ImageNet and fine-tuned on RASTA for artistic style classification (Sect. 3.1). Then we consider the same architecture with a random initialization (from scratch) trained on RASTA (Sect. 3.2). The Sects. 3.3 and 3.4 are dedicated to the classification performance and the evaluation of the changes implied by the training on RASTA. Finally, we studied the same architecture pre-trained on ImageNet and then fine-tuned first on RASTA and then on a smaller art dataset for object classification (Sect. 3.5) to see how using an intermediate art dataset can help.

Feature Visualization. The first visualization technique we use consists in generating *optimized images*, as introduced in [17]. These images are obtained by maximizing the response to a given channel. The entire feature map at a given layer can be decomposed in two spatial dimensions and one dimension depending on the convolutional kernels. A *channel* denotes one element according to this last dimension. We use the Lucid framework for visualizing convolutional channels via activation maximization. We use Lucid's 2D FFT image representation with decorrelation and 2048 iterations of the gradient ascent.

Maximal Activation Images. We devise another indicator that might be useful for the analysis of the transformation that a network undergoes during its transfer to a different domain. This indicator is the evolution of the *maximal activation images*. For a given channel, we compute the *top 100* images in the target dataset that trigger it the most. We also compute the information *entropy* over classes for each top 100 images, in order to evaluate the clustering power of the corresponding channel. The entropy is defined as $\frac{1}{maxE} \sum_{classes} -p_c log_2(p_c)$ with p_c the fraction of images in the top 100 belonging to the class c and $maxE$ the maximal entropy with this number of classes. Moreover, the top 100 can be computed twice, once at the beginning and once at the end of the fine-tuning. The percentage of the images that lie in both sets is an indicator of how much the channel has drifted during its adaptation. These percentages are named *overlapping ratio* in the following. They are, in many cases, much higher than what we would expect from a random reshuffling of the dataset. Besides, the combination of this indicator with the visualization technique from [17] leads to several findings that we will present thereafter.

Experimental Setup. All our visualization experiments use the InceptionV1 [26] CNN (also called GoogLeNet). It is a 22 layers with only 7M parameters thanks to the introduction of Inception modules. The last layer of the network is replaced by a fully connected layer with the number of outputs corresponding to the dataset at hand and where activation function is a softmax for RASTA or a sigmoid for Paintings and IconArt datasets. The loss function is the usual cross-entropy in the first case, and the sum over the classes of binary cross-entropy in the two others. The InceptionV1 network is the classical and efficient choice for feature visualization by optimization [17] although it no longer produces the best classification performances. We ran experiments with a various number of hyperparameters such as the learning rate for the last layer (classification layer), the learning rate for the transferred layers, the use of a deep supervision, the maximum number of epochs or the possible use of random crops within the input image. The input size of the network is 224×224. For all experiments, we selected the model with the best loss value on the corresponding validation set.

In the following sections, we analyze how the networks have been modified by fine-tuning processes. We present qualitative observations using optimized images and the maximal activation images, as well as quantitative evaluations relying on the ℓ_2 norm of the difference between convolution kernels and the linear CKA measure [11].

3.1   From Natural to Art Images

The first feature visualizations we report have been obtained by fine-tuning on the RASTA classification dataset an InceptionV1 architecture protrained on ImageNet with different sets of hyperparameters.

Low-Level Layers are Only Slightly Modified by the Fine-Tuning. The first observation is that low-level layers from the original network trained on ImageNet are hardly modified by the new training on RASTA. This fact will be confirmed by the CKA measure (see Fig. 5) and the overlapping ratio of the top 100 maximal activation images (see Fig. 6a) in Sect. 3.4.

Mid-Level Layers Adapt to the New Dataset. Some of the filters have been modified to the specificity of the new dataset by the fine-tuning process, as illustrated in Figs. 1i to 1k. In these figures are displayed for some channels, the optimized images defined in the second paragraph of Sect. 3. The model learned a red and blue drapery detector, a blue mountain one and a house pediment one. It is worth mentioning that other channels are hardly modified by the fine-tuning process. First, among the 70k training samples, some maximal activation images are present in the top 100 both before and after fine-tuning Those images are surrounded by a green line in the last row of Fig. 1. Second, in those maximal activation images, we can recognize the pattern that emerged in the optimized image (when we compare the third and last rows). For instance, in the third column of Fig. 1, a flower-like structure is transformed into a house pediment one. Finally, we observe that the detector fine-tuned on RASTA concentrates images with this specific pattern (last row of Fig. 1). The first group of images of the last row contains characters with a blue dress (as the Mary character), the second one blue mountains and the last one buildings depicted with some perspective. On the other hand, for other channels, the pattern is already present in the optimized image and the detector is slightly adapted to the new dataset. This appears in the form of a minor modification of the optimized image. An arch detector within the pretrained ImageNet model has been modified to detect bigger arches as it can be seen in Fig. 1l. The maximal activation images before the fine-tuning already was composed of many buildings images. In this case, the overlapping ratio between the two sets of maximal activation images is equal to 46%. Nevertheless, we highlight those visualizations but the reader must keep in mind that some channels are not modified by the fine-tuning or are not interpretable at all[1].

---

[1] The reader can find more feature visualizations at https://artfinetune.telecom-paris. fr/data/.

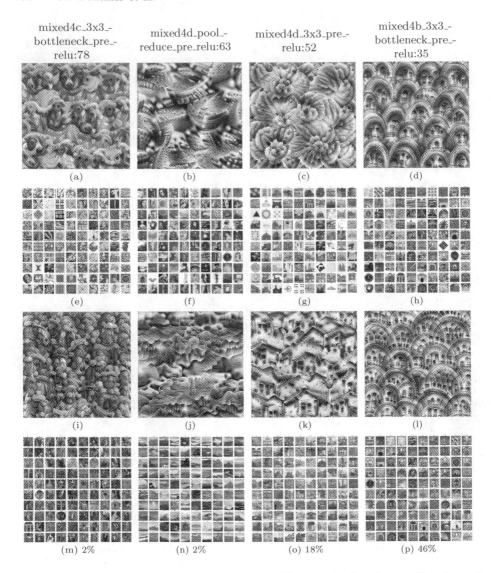

Fig. 1. First row: optimized images for InceptionV1 pretrained on ImagneNet. Second row: top 100 maximal activation examples for the same model. Third and fourth rows: optimized images and maximal activation examples for the same channel of the model fine-tuned on RASTA. The images surrounded by a green line are already present in the top 100 of the pretrained model. The overlapping ratio between the two sets of maximal activation images is displayed at the bottom of each column. (Color figure online)

Learned Filters Have a High Variability. We ran 2 distinct fine-tunings for each of the 5 considered optimization schemes named Mode A to E[2]. The initial last layer is different as well as the order of the images in the mini-batches during the training process. From a same starting point (the ImageNet weights) but for different hyper-parameters, the training process may sometimes converge to similar optimized images. On the contrary, two optimizations with the same hyper-parameters (same mode) may lead to very different detectors. Those phenomena are illustrated in Fig. 2. For this given channel, according to the mode and occurrence of the fine-tuning, one can recognize houses (Fig. 2a), flowers (Fig. 2e), a mix of houses or more abstract patterns (Fig. 2i). ImageNet pre-trained filters seem to be a good initialization for learning useful new filters adapted to the artistic style classification and they also permit to learn a variety of new filters. The percentage of overlap between the set of maximal activation images before and after fine-tuning seems to be correlated to the amount of visual change.

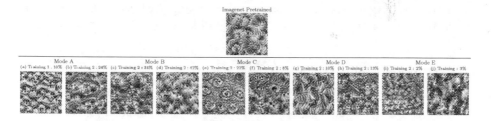

Fig. 2. Optimized Image for a given channel (mixed4d "_3x3 "_pre "_relu:52) with different trainings. The overlapping ratio between the two sets of maximal activation images is displayed on top of the images.

High-Level Filters Concentrate Images From the Same Classes. The visualizations of high-level layers (near the classification output) are more difficult to interpret, as illustrated in Fig. 3. The network seems to mix different visual information from the previous layers. Nevertheless, the group of images with maximal activation for those 2 given channels gather images from the same artistic style after fine-tuning. The first channel is mostly fired by Ukiyo-e images (Fig. 3b), the second one gathers western renaissance artworks (Fig. 3d). There is no visual clue to such clustering in the optimized images. In the last image, one may see some green tree in front of a blue sky and some drapery. The fact that Early_Renaissance, High_Renaissance and Mannerism_(Late_Renaissance) classes are clustered together maybe due to their strong visual similarity. Deep model commonly mislabels one of these as another, as mentioned in [12].

---

[2] A slight extension of this work is available at https://arxiv.org/abs/2011.02727 with the differences between the optimization schemes and more visualization experiments.

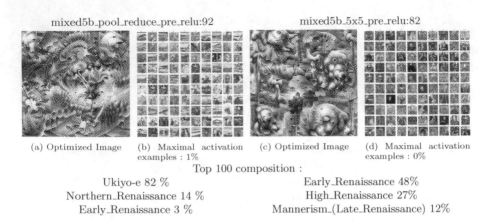

mixed5b_pool_reduce_pre_relu:92   mixed5b_5x5_pre_relu:82

(a) Optimized Image   (b) Maximal activation   (c) Optimized Image   (d) Maximal activation
                        examples : 1%   examples : 0%

Top 100 composition :

Ukiyo-e 82 %   Early_Renaissance 48%
Northern_Renaissance 14 %   High_Renaissance 27%
Early_Renaissance 3 %   Mannerism_(Late_Renaissance) 12%

Fig. 3. Optimized Images and Maximal Activation Examples for two high level layers for the model fine-tuned on RASTA. The overlapping ratio between the set of maximal activation images before and after fine-tuning is displayed under the images. The percentage of the 3 most common class is displayed below. (Color figure online)

3.2   Training from Scratch

Mid-Level Detectors can be Learned from Scratch When Low-Level Layers are Transferred from ImageNet. The next experiment consists in fine-tuning a network whose low-level layers are initialized using the training on ImageNet and frozen whereas the mid and high-level layers are initialized randomly. In this case, the network is able to learn useful and comprehensible mid-level detectors such as drapery or checkerboard as illustrated in Figs. 4a and 4b. This phenomenon is most likely triggered by the low-level layers inherited from the ImagNet training, but the emergence of such structured detectors with a relatively small-sized dataset is relatively surprising.

The Optimized Images are More Difficult to Interpret with a Full Training from Scratch. A network trained fully from scratch seems yields the same kind of low-level filters that the ones pretrained on ImageNet whereas the mid and high-level layers provide optimized images that are much more difficult to interpret, see Figs. 4c and 4d. A possible explanation is that the network may not need to learn very specific filters given its high capacity. The training of the network provides filters that are able to fire for a given class such as Ukiyo-e (Fig. 4g) or Magic_Realism (Fig. 4h) without being interpretable for humans.

3.3   Classification Performance

Even though the goal of this work is not to reach the best possible classification performance, we display the corresponding results in Table 1 to further characterize the considered fine-tuning. From this table, one sees that a simple and short fine-tuning of a pre-trained model yields to a better performance than the

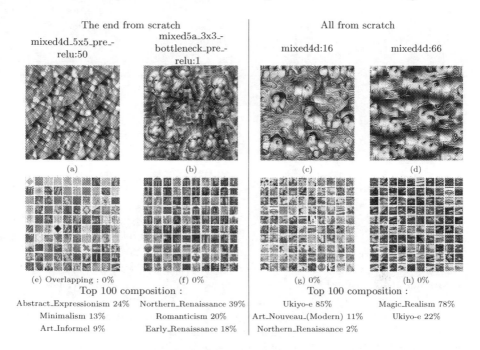

The end from scratch

All from scratch

mixed4d_5x5_pre_-
relu:50

mixed5a_3x3_-
bottleneck_pre_-
relu:1

mixed4d:16

mixed4d:66

(a)   (b)   (c)   (d)

(e) Overlapping : 0%   (f) 0%   (g) 0%   (h) 0%

Top 100 composition :   Top 100 composition :

Abstract_Expressionism 24%	Northern_Renaissance 39%	Ukiyo-e 85%	Magic_Realism 78%
Minimalism 13%	Romanticism 20%	Art_Nouveau_(Modern) 11%	Ukiyo-e 22%
Art_Informel 9%	Early_Renaissance 18%	Northern_Renaissance 2%	

Fig. 4. Optimized Image and Maximal activation examples from different mid-level layers. On the left: fine-tuning is performed starting from low-level layers initialized from ImagNet and upper layers initialized at random. On the right, the fine-tuning is fully performed from scratch (randomly initialized layers). The overlapping ratio between the set of maximal activation images before and after fine-tuning is displayed under the images. The percentage of the 3 most common class is displayed below.

off-the-shelf strategy. The former method is based on extracting features from the ImageNet pretrained model and training the last layer. The features extracted may be too specific to the ImageNet classification task and the classification head too small. With training from scratch, we failed to obtain a model as good as the ImageNet pretraining. This can be due to the relatively small size of the RASTA dataset. Some data augmentation and a longer training was required to reach 45.29% Top1 accuracy. This experiment confirms Lecoutre et al. [12] conclusions for another deep architecture. We conclude this section by observing that a simple way to improve results is to simply average the prediction of three models trained with different strategies (see last row of Table 1).

3.4 Quantitative Evaluation of the CNNs Modification

In order to quantify some of the previous observations, we make use of the linear CKA [11] as a measure of similarity between two output features at a given layer, for two instances of a network. For computational reason, we used the global spatial average of each channel. The results are shown in Fig. 5. We can observe a decreasing of the CKA when the depth of the layers increases, when

Table 1. Top-k accuracies (%) on RASTA dataset [12] for different methods. The hyperparameters are different between the methods.

Method	Top-1	Top-3	Top-5
Off-the-shelf InceptionV1 pretrained on ImageNet	30.95	58.71	74.10
FT of InceptionV1 pretrained on ImageNet (Mode A training 1)	**55.18**	**82.25**	**91.06**
Training from scratch the end of the model with pretrained frozen low-level layers	50.35	78.04	88.42
InceptionV1 trained from scratch	45.29	73.44	84.67
Ensemble of the 3 previous models	*58.76*	*83.99*	*92.23*

we compare the pretrained model with its fine-tuned version (dark blue line). This is a confirmation of what we observed previously with the optimized images (Sect. 3.1). The fine-tuned models are the closest ones according to the green and light blue lines. The high level layers of those models are closed because those models have been trained on the same dataset from the same initialization point. The CKA also decreases with layers when we compare one model from scratch to its random initialization (purple and orange curves). The values of CKA present here are higher than the ones obtained in [14] for X-ray images. In the case of the model trained from scratch, we even observe several orders of magnitude of difference. This confirms and quantifies the fact that the structure of artistic images is closer to the one of natural images when compared to X-ray images.

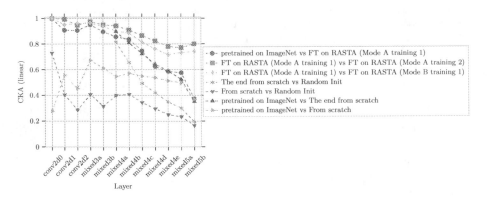

Fig. 5. CKA computed on RASTA test set for different models trained or fine-tuned on RASTA train set. (Color figure online)

In addition to feature similarity, we also look at the distance between two models in the parameter space in Table 2 (as in the recent work [14]). We can see that the fine-tuned models are still close one to another and also close to the ImageNet pretrained initialization. In contrast, the models trained from scratch are much farther away from their initialization.

We also observe the evolution of the overlapping ratio between the ImageNet pretrained model and the fine-tuned one for the top 100 maximal activation images in Fig. 6a. We can see a monotonic decrease of this ratio with the depth

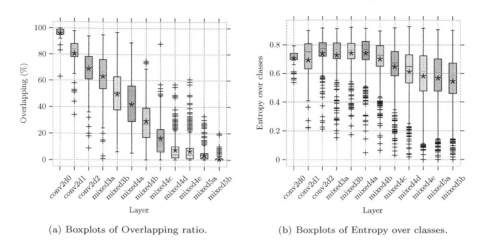

(a) Boxplots of Overlapping ratio.   (b) Boxplots of Entropy over classes.

Fig. 6. Boxplots of some metrics on the top 100 maximal activation images for the model fine-tuned on RASTA (Mode A1). For each box, the horizontal orange line corresponds to the average result and the star to the median.

Table 2. Mean over all layers of the ℓ_2 norm of the difference between convolutional kernels between two models

NetA	NetB	mean ℓ_2 norm
Pretrained on ImageNet	FT on RASTA (Mode A training 1)	1.26
FT on RASTA (Mode A training 1)	FT on RASTA (Mode B training 1)	1.24
FT on RASTA (Mode A training 1)	FT on RASTA (Mode A training 2)	1.23
The end from scratch	Its Random initialization	6.52
From scratch	Its Random initialization	8.13

of the layer. This is another illustration of the fact that the high level layers are more modified by the fine-tuning. The behavior is the same if we consider the top 1000 maximal activation images. One also observes that channels with low overlapping ratio seem to correspond to optimized images that are more modified by the fine-tuning. This fact should be investigated further and could yield a simple way to browse through optimized images. Finally, and in order to quantify the class concentration described in Sect. 3.1, we display the entropy over classes, (Fig. 6b), showing a decreasing of the average entropy with the layer depth, starting roughly in the middle of the network architecture.

3.5 From One Art Dataset to Another

Table 3 compares the classification results obtained for the object classification task on the Paintings dataset [4] and on the IconArt dataset [10] when using a model pretrained on ImageNet or fine-tuned on RASTA dataset (from an ImageNet initialization or from scratch). On the contrary to [20] where they compared the pretraining on the Rijkmuseum dataset and ImageNet for the Antwerp dataset, the task is not the same between the two artistic datasets:

classification of the artistic style versus object classification. Once again the fine-tuning strategy is better than the off-the-shelf one. The most important observation is that the double fine-tuning (first using RASTA, then using the considered dataset) outperforms the direct fine-tuning using only the dataset at hand. The filters learned on RASTA seem to be more adapted to other artistic datasets and ease the transfer in these two cases (IconArt and Paintings) where the datasets are relatively small. Finally, a model only trained on RASTA (last row of the two tables) will not provide a good initialization point for fine-tuning, neither for IconArt, nor for Paintings. This is most probably due to the size of the RASTA dataset.

Table 3. Mean Average Precision (%) on Paintings [4] and IconArt test sets [10].

Method	Paintings	IconArt
Off-the-shelf InceptionV1 pretrained on ImageNet	56.0	53.2
Off-the-shelf InceptionV1 pretrained on ImageNet and RASTA	52.4	54.4
FT of InceptionV1 pretrained on ImageNet (Mode A training 1)	64.8	59.2
FT of InceptionV1 pretrained on ImageNet and RASTA	**65.6**	**67.4**
FT of InceptionV1 trained from scratch on RASTA the end of the model with pretrained frozen low-level	59.6	59.4
FT of InceptionV1 trained from scratch on RASTA	49.1	50.1

In Table 4, we use the two previously mentioned metrics to compare the different models fine-tuned on the IconArt and Paintings datasets. The model fine-tuned on a small art dataset will stay similar to its ImageNet pretrained initialization (with a CKA of 0.89 or 0.91 for the IconArt and Paintings datasets). A fine-tuning on the large RASTA dataset changes more the network ($CKA = 0.77$ and ℓ_2 norm $= 1.26$). A double fine-tuning permits to go even further from the original pretrained weights ($CKA = 0.73$ and 0.76). As already mentioned, this method provides the best classification performance.

Table 4. Mean linear CKA (on IconArt or Paintings test set) and mean ℓ_2 norm between models.

Nets/Small art dataset used:		IconArt		Paintings	
NetA	NetB	Mean CKA	Mean ℓ_2 norm	Mean CKA	Mean ℓ_2 norm
Pretrained on ImageNet	FT on small art dataset	0.90	0.14	0.91	0.15
Pretrained on ImageNet	FT on RASTA + FT on small dataset	0.73	1.61	0.76	1.67
FT on RASTA (Mode A)	FT on RASTA + FT on small dataset	0.79	0.78	0.77	0.86
The end from scratch on RASTA	The end from scratch on RASTA + FT on small dataset	0.70	0.91	0.72	1.01
From scratch on RASTA	From scratch on RASTA + FT on small dataset	0.83	0.27	0.79	0.52

In the case of the model trained from scratch (two last lines of Table 4), the change between initialization and optimal model is also large due to the randomness of the initialization but those models are worst in terms of classification.

4   Conclusion

In this work, we have investigated the effect of fine-tuning a network pre-trained on ImageNet using artistic datasets. We made use of visualization techniques and quantitative assessments of the changes of the networks. Among other things, we have shown that some of the intermediate layers of the networks exhibit easily recognizable patterns that appear to be more related to art images than the patterns learned on natural images, while lower layers of the network are hardly changed. We have also shown that higher layers tend to concentrate classes after fine-tuning. Eventually, we have also shown that a double fine-tuning involving a medium size artistic dataset can help the classification of small-sized artistic datasets in accordance with visual patterns more related to the domain. The classification tasks between the two artistic datasets do not need to be identical. In our case, the intermediate task is style classification whereas the final one is object classification. This study provides some insights on the way networks are modified by fine-tuning in the case of artistic databases. Several of the findings in this work necessitate further confirmation, possible on larger databases [23,29]. Another perspective would be to go further in the use of feature visualization, as it is done in [16,18]. For instance, it could be more informative to look at the patches that fire a given channel rather than the whole input image as in [18]. In [16], the authors claim for universality in different deep convolutional architectures and it is of interest to check if the same is true for artistic datasets.

References

1. Bianco, S., Mazzini, D., Napoletano, P., Schettini, R.: Multitask painting categorization by deep multibranch neural network. Exp. Syst. Appl. **135**, 90–101 (2019)
2. Cetinic, E., Lipic, T., Grgic, S.: Fine-tuning convolutional neural networks for fine art classification. Exp. Syst. Appl. **114**, 107–118 (2018)
3. Cetinic, E., Lipic, T., Grgic, S.: Learning the principles of art history with convolutional neural networks. Pattern Recogn. Lett. **129**, 56–62 (2019)
4. Crowley, E.J., Zisserman, A.: In search of art. In: Agapito, L., Bronstein, M.M., Rother, C. (eds.) ECCV 2014. LNCS, vol. 8925, pp. 54–70. Springer, Cham (2015). https://doi.org/10.1007/978-3-319-16178-5_4
5. Crowley, E.J., Zisserman, A.: The art of detection. In: Hua, G., Jégou, H. (eds.) ECCV 2016. LNCS, vol. 9913, pp. 721–737. Springer, Cham (2016). https://doi.org/10.1007/978-3-319-46604-0_50
6. Donahue, J., et al.: DeCAF: a deep convolutional activation feature for generic visual recognition. In: International Conference on Machine Learning (2014)
7. Erhan, D., Bengio, Y., Courville, A., Vincent, P.: Visualizing higher-layer features of a deep network. Univ. Montreal **1341**(3), 1 (2009)

8. Geirhos, R., Rubisch, P., Michaelis, C., Bethge, M., Wichmann, F.A., Brendel, W.: ImageNet-trained CNNs are biased towards texture; increasing shape bias improves accuracy and robustness. In: ICLR (2019)

9. Girshick, R., Donahue, J., Darrell, T., Malik, J.: Rich feature hierarchies for accurate object detection and semantic segmentation. In: IEEE Conference on Computer Vision and Pattern Recognition (2014)

10. Gonthier, N., Gousseau, Y., Ladjal, S., Bonfait, O.: Weakly supervised object detection in artworks. In: Leal-Taixé, L., Roth, S. (eds.) ECCV 2018. LNCS, vol. 11130, pp. 692–709. Springer, Cham (2019). https://doi.org/10.1007/978-3-030-11012-3_53

11. Kornblith, S., Norouzi, M., Lee, H., Hinton, G.: Similarity of neural network representations revisited. In: ICML (2019)

12. Lecoutre, A., Negrevergne, B., Yger, F.: Recognizing art style automatically in painting with deep learning. In: Asian Conference on Machine Learning. JMLR: Workshop and Conference Proceedings (2017)

13. Madhu, P., Kosti, R., Mührenberg, L., Bell, P., Maier, A., Christlein, V.: Recognizing characters in art history using deep learning. In: Proceedings of the 1st Workshop on Structuring and Understanding of Multimedia heritAge Contents, SUMAC 2019, pp. 15–22.ACM (2019)

14. Neyshabur, B., Sedghi, H., Zhang, C.: What is being transferred in transfer learning? In: Advances in Neural Information Processing Systems, vol. 33 (2020)

15. van Noord, N., Postma, E.: Learning scale-variant and scale-invariant features for deep image classification. Pattern Recogn. **61**, 583–592 (2017)

16. Olah, C., Cammarata, N., Schubert, L., Goh, G., Petrov, M., Carter, S.: An overview of early vision in InceptionV1. Distill **5**(4) (2020)

17. Olah, C., Mordvintsev, A., Schubert, L.: Feature visualization. Distill **2**(11), e7 (2017)

18. Olah, C., et al.: The building blocks of interpretability. Distill **3**(3), e10 (2018)

19. Russakovsky, O., et al.: ImageNet large scale visual recognition challenge. Int. J. Comput. Vis. **115**(3), 211–252 (2015)

20. Sabatelli, M., Kestemont, M., Daelemans, W., Geurts, P.: Deep transfer learning for art classification problems. In: Workshop on Computer Vision for Art Analysis ECCV, Munich, pp. 1–17 (2018)

21. Seguin, B., Striolo, C., diLenardo, I., Kaplan, F.: Visual link retrieval in a database of paintings. In: Hua, G., Jégou, H. (eds.) ECCV 2016. LNCS, vol. 9913, pp. 753–767. Springer, Cham (2016). https://doi.org/10.1007/978-3-319-46604-0_52

22. Simonyan, K., Vedaldi, A., Zisserman, A.: Deep inside convolutional networks: visualising image classification models and saliency maps. In: ICLR, pp. 1–8 (2014)

23. Strezoski, G., Worning, M.: OmniArt: a large-scale artistic benchmark. ACM Trans. Multimedia Comput. Commun. Appl. (TOMM) - Spec. Sect. Deep Learn. Intell. Multimedia Anal. **14**(4), 1–21 (2018)

24. Strezoski, G., Worring, M.: Plug-and-Play Interactive Deep Network Visualization. Visual Analytics for Deep Learning, VADL (2017)

25. Szabó, R., Katona, D., Csillag, M., Csiszárik, A., Varga, D.: Visualizing transfer learning. In: ICML Workshop on Human Interpretability in Machine Learning (2020)

26. Szegedy, C., et al.: Going deeper with convolutions. In: Proceedings of the IEEE Conference on Computer Vision and Pattern Recognition (CVPR) (2015)

27. Tan, W.R., Chan, C.S., Aguirre, H.E., Tanaka, K.: Ceci n'est pas une pipe: a deep convolutional network for fine-art paintings classification. In: 2016 IEEE International Conference on Image Processing (ICIP), pp. 3703–3707 (2016)

28. Westlake, N., Cai, H., Hall, P.: Detecting people in artwork with CNNs. In: Hua, G., Jégou, H. (eds.) ECCV 2016. LNCS, vol. 9913, pp. 825–841. Springer, Cham (2016). https://doi.org/10.1007/978-3-319-46604-0_57
29. Wilber, M.J., Fang, C., Jin, H., Hertzmann, A., Collomosse, J., Belongie, S.: BAM! The behance artistic media dataset for recognition beyond photography. In: IEEE International Conference on Computer Vision (ICCV), pp. 1211–1220 (2017)
30. Yin, R., Monson, E., Honig, E., Daubechies, I., Maggioni, M.: Object recognition in art drawings: transfer of a neural network. In: 2016 IEEE International Conference on Acoustics, Speech and Signal Processing (ICASSP), pp. 2299–2303 (2016)

Handwriting Classification for the Analysis of Art-Historical Documents

Christian Bartz(✉) , Hendrik Rätz , and Christoph Meinel

Hasso Plattner Institute, University of Potsdam, 14482 Potsdam, Germany
{christian.bartz,christoph.meinel}@hpi.de,
hendrik.raetz@student.hpi.de

Abstract. Digitized archives contain and preserve the knowledge of generations of scholars in millions of documents. The size of these archives calls for automatic analysis since a manual analysis by specialists is often too expensive. In this paper, we focus on the analysis of handwriting in scanned documents from the art-historic archive of the Wildenstein Plattner Institute. Since the archive consists of documents written in several languages and lacks annotated training data for the creation of recognition models, we propose the task of handwriting classification as a new step for a handwriting OCR pipeline. We propose a handwriting classification model that labels extracted text fragments, *e.g.*, numbers, dates, or words, based on their visual structure. Such a classification supports historians by highlighting documents that contain a specific class of text without the need to read the entire content. To this end, we develop and compare several deep learning-based models for text classification. In extensive experiments, we show the advantages and disadvantages of our proposed approach and discuss possible usage scenarios on a real-world dataset.

Keywords: Computer vision · Deep learning · Cultural heritage · Art history · Archive analysis

1 Introduction

Archives contain a wealth of documents that are highly valuable for historical research since they have been gathered over a long period of time (typically several centuries or decades). Digitization helps to preserve documents, which only exist on paper, by converting the documents into a format that can be copied and distributed without quality loss. However, simply digitizing documents does not provide additional value for research. The digitized documents are only available in the form of digital images, thus preventing a direct search of their content. Data that is of interest includes, but is not limited to, the content of printed texts, handwritten texts, and depicted objects in images. The extraction of such

C. Bartz and H. Rätz—Equal contribution.

metadata is a time and labor-intensive task, which can be done by humans, but becomes infeasible very quickly once an archive contains millions of documents.

Thanks to recent advances in machine learning and computer vision [9, 16, 28], it is possible to automate the task of analyzing digitized data of an archive. In our work, we focus on the analysis of handwriting because it may contain thoughts or the contents of personal communication. Additionally, it might provide extra information that cannot be found elsewhere, such as prices of artworks at an auction. In our work, we analyze the digitized data of the art-historical archive of the Wildenstein Plattner Institute (WPI)[1], whose archive contains information that is, *e.g.*, of interest when researching the provenance of works of art. Optical Character Recognition (OCR) is the tool of choice to recognize handwritten text contained in the digitized documents. In a typical setting, an OCR system first locates all regions that contain printed or handwritten text and then it recognizes the content of words, groups of words, or entire lines of text.

Modern approaches for OCR make use of deep learning methods for successful recognition of text [26, 28] (more on related work can be found in Sect. 2). However, methods based on deep learning require a large amount of annotated training data for the language the model is to be applied to. The availability of such data is crucial for the creation of modern deep-learning-based handwriting recognition models. Therefore, it is not directly possible to apply research results for handwriting recognition [13, 28] on the archive of the WPI because no annotated data is available. To extract information without fully recognizing the textual content of a given text snippet, we propose to classify images of text based on their visual structure. Such a classification provides researchers with information about the type of text in their documents, *e.g.*, a page does not only contain words but also dates or other identifiers. This helps them to identify and filter documents and pages quickly by specifying the type of information they are looking for.

In this paper, we introduce and evaluate several approaches for text classification. On the one hand, we propose to train a softmax classifier with a fixed number of classes. On the other hand, we propose to learn a model that uses metric learning to embed images of handwriting. This model arranges the images in a way that those with similar structure are located close to each other, while positioning structurally different images far from each other (more on our models can be found in Sect. 3). In our experiments (see Sect. 4), we show that our models perform well on different datasets. The softmax classifier outperforms the metric learning approach, but the metric learning approach is by far more flexible and can be used in a more general setting. The contributions made in this paper can be summarized as follows: 1) An in-depth analysis of handwriting classification for the analysis of archival data. 2) Introduction of methods for successfully synthesizing training data, such as numbers or dates, which are not or rarely contained in existing datasets for handwriting recognition. 3) We

---

[1] https://wpi.art.

provide our trained models and our code to the research community for further experimentation[2].

2   Related Work

Handwriting recognition is a field of OCR that has actively been researched over the past decades [2,5,22,24,27,28]. In this section, we will introduce work from the area of handwriting recognition and also existing work in the area of handwriting classification.

Handwriting Recognition. Online handwriting recognition describes the task of recognizing handwritten characters based on the recorded movement information of a person writing characters. The field of online handwriting recognition has been researched very actively in the past and is still of interest to the community [5,22,24]. However, in the area of archival analysis, we do not have access to online writing data because the handwriting data is only available in image form.

Offline handwriting recognition revolves around the task of recognizing handwriting in images of text. Over time, approaches shifted from using Hidden Markov Models [3,8] to the usage of deep neural networks in conjunction with recurrent neural networks [2,13,27,28]. The proposed models reach state-of-the-art results with character errors rates as low as 8% [2] on the IAMDB dataset [20]. However, these results can only be achieved for handwriting of a specific language (English in the case of the IAM dataset) while using a large amount of data for the training of the recognition model. When trying to use a system on another language, such as French or Italian, an entirely new model, which requires a large amount of annotated training data, needs to be created. This problem gets even more severe when dealing with documents containing older scripts or words that are not used anymore.

Handwriting Classification. To alleviate the problem of missing training data and to allow at least some insight into the data, classifying text snippets based on their visual structure could be a viable alternative. To the best of our knowledge, not much research has been done in that direction. Mandal *et al.* [19] propose a method that takes text snippets as input and locates dates within documents. In their paper, they try to find month words, such as "Jan" or "October", using handcrafted features. Additionally, they identify digits using gradient-based features in conjunction with a Support Vector Machine.

3   Method

The task of handwriting classification enables us to analyze handwriting without the need to directly recognize textual content. This enables analysis of

---

[2] https://github.com/hendraet/handwriting-classification.

handwritten documents from different languages by looking at the structure of the depicted handwriting. With our models, we try to discern handwritten words from numbers, dates, and also alphanumeric strings. Existing handwriting databases (*e.g.*, the IAM Handwriting Database (IAMDB) [20]) contain a large amount of handwritten text but hardly any numbers, dates, or alphanumeric strings. In this section, we first introduce a strategy to synthesize enough data for the training of our models. Then, we introduce our first model, which is a simple softmax classifier. Additionally, we train an embedding model based on metric learning since we hypothesize that such a model is more flexible than a softmax classifier with a fixed number of classes.

3.1 Handwriting Synthesis

Existing datasets, such as the well-known IAM datasets (IAMDB [20], IAM Historical Handwriting Database (IAM-HistDB) [6,7]), rarely contain numbers, dates, or alphanumeric strings. The largest of the IAM datasets, the IAMDB dataset, contains 115320 images of words but only 454 images where numbers are displayed. The unavailability of numbers, dates, and alphanumeric strings poses a problem for our approach. A solution to this problem is the usage of synthetic but realistically looking handwriting. Approaches for the generation of synthetic handwriting exist, but synthetic datasets, such as the IIIT-HWS [15] dataset, also only contain a small amount of samples that are not words.

To overcome the problem of missing handwritten numbers and dates, we adapt the *GANwriting* model proposed by Kang *et al.* [12]. The GANwriting model is based on a conditional Generative Adversarial Network (cGAN) that produces realistic looking handwriting conditioned on input styles. Furthermore, the model is able to synthesize words or character combinations that have not been part of the train set. A structural overview of the model can be seen in Fig. 1. In the following, we describe the most important parts of the model and our changes to it.

Generator. The generator of the GANwriting model takes two inputs. The first set of inputs are multiple images depicting handwritten words of one author. These inputs are passed to the style encoder, which extracts the stylistic features of the handwriting.

The second input is a vector with a one-hot-encoded representation of the input characters. This input is passed through the content encoder, generating two outputs. The first output is a character-wise encoding that is concatenated with the extracted stylistic features, which are subsequently used to steer the generation of the characters in the resulting image. Here, we adapted the model and increased the maximum allowable word length from **seven** characters to a maximum of **twenty five** characters, by introducing a novel padding strategy. In a second step, the content encoder generates parameters that are used by the decoder to perform Adaptive Instance Normalization (AdaIN) [11].

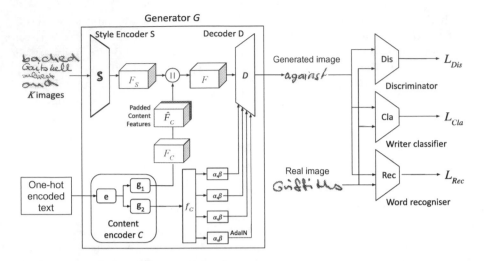

Fig. 1. Structural overview of the GANwriting generator model. The model consists of a generator that receives the text to be generated and a set of K images that define the desired style. The generated images are assessed by three models: a discriminator, a writer classifier, and a word recognizer.

Style and content features are used to guide the decoder model in the generation of handwriting, which is rendered in the style of the input images while containing all required characters.

Discriminator. In the GANwriting model, not one but three models are used for assessing the quality of the generated image. The first model is a discriminator that tries to determine whether a given input image is fake or real. The second model is a writer classifier, whose task is to determine the author of a given handwriting sample. Thus, it forces the generator to make use of the stylistic information passed to the style encoder and asserts that synthesized images use the provided style. The third model is a text recognition model, which is used to force the generator to create handwriting that is readable while containing the expected content. For further information about the three models used to assess the quality of the generator, please refer to the GANwriting paper [12].

Data Generation with the GANwriting Model. The described model can be used to generate new handwriting images, to generate handwritten numbers, and dates, we still need some examples of these types of data. Since the available datasets do not contain enough of these samples, we used another mechanism to synthesize simple numbers and dates that we use for the training of our adapted GANwriting model. To produce these samples, we make use of online handwriting data from the IAM On-line Handwriting Database (IAMONDB) [17]. Here, we extract the strokes of individual digits, as well as the strokes for dots and dashes. We then generate numbers and dates by concatenating the gathered strokes and rendering them on a white canvas, thus transforming the online to offline data. It is important to note that we can not combine the strokes of different authors because the GANwriting model learns to mimic the style of one author per generated sample. Using synthesized data with strokes from different authors would, therefore, lead to unsatisfactory results. The strokes that are used during synthesis do not contain any information about stroke thickness or color of the stroke because online data only contains information about movements while writing. Thus, this information is artificially generated and added before the rendering process to simulate a broader variety of writing styles. We then use the newly generated dates and numbers together with the already existing word images from the IAMDB dataset for the training of the GANwriting model.

3.2   Handwriting Classification Networks

Besides data, we need classification approaches for categorizing given handwritten texts. In the following, we introduce two different architectures for the classification of handwriting. On the one hand, we propose the usage of a softmax-based classifier. On the other hand, we propose to use a distance-based model that can be used to embed images in a way that the Euclidean distance can be used as a similarity measure. Using such an embedding model, we can determine clusters and classify new samples based on their location in these clusters.

Softmax Classifier. Our first model is a ResNet-18 [10] based network with a softmax classifier, which can discern the classes present in our experiments (see Sect. 4). We train the model using softmax cross entropy as loss function. Classifiers trained with softmax cross entropy are very strong multi-class classification models, but they are quite inflexible. For instance, it is not possible to simply add a new class to the classifier without retraining the whole network. To mitigate this issue, we propose another approach for text classification.

Distance-Based Model. In our distance-based model we also make use of a ResNet-18 feature extractor. However, we increase the number of the neurons of the final linear classification layer and omit the softmax activation. Therefore, the model transforms an input image into an embedding, which is a vector with 512 dimensions. We train our model to produce embeddings that are similar to each other if the input images depict the same type of content (*e.g.*, words, dates, numbers, ...). To learn the parameters of the model we make use of the triplet loss function [23]. When training a model with triplet loss, the model takes a triplet of samples as input. The three samples are called *anchor*, *positive*, and *negative*, where anchor and positive belong to the same class and negative represents a different class. The objective of a model trained using triplet loss is to minimize the Euclidean distance between the anchor and positive sample, while maximizing the Euclidean distance between the anchor and the negative sample. Effectively, the model groups samples of the same class, while it positions those of different classes far from each other.

Based on a properly trained triplet loss model, it is possible to group embeddings of samples in clusters based on their class. A sample can now be classified using multiple strategies. The first strategy (we refer to this as the *naive* approach) is to use two widely used algorithms: k-means [18] for clustering and kNN [1] for classification. We first cluster the embeddings of unseen samples and determine the centroids of the found clusters. To fit the kNN model, we then use a set of support embeddings, *i.e.*, embeddings where the class is known, and determine the class of the clusters based on the embedded support samples.

Another possible approach for classification is to use distance-based thresholding [23]. In distance-based thresholding the distances of the embeddings of a questioned sample and a support sample are compared. If the distance of the questioned sample to the support sample is greater than a predefined threshold, the sample is classified as not belonging to the support sample's class. However, if the distance is lower than the predefined threshold, the sample is classified as belonging to the class of the support sample. Using such a *hard decision* threshold is impractical, because the threshold needs to be calculated for each model and each class individually, rendering the proposed distance-based model inflexible when handling new and unseen data.

A better approach is to produce *soft decisions* based on Log-Likelihood Ratios (llrs) [4]. Opposed to the hard decision based on a threshold, llrs provide a relative score reflecting a confidence. The idea is that the llr determines how likely it is that a calculated distance d is observed for a sample of class A (target trial) or class B (non-target trial). To determine the likelihood, it is necessary to compute the distance distributions for the two classes beforehand by using a validation/support set. The logarithm of the ratio of those likelihoods then forms the llr. The llr was designed with the application of two-class classification in mind. However, they can also be used in a multi-class setting, where the llr is calculated in a one-vs-all approach for all classes.

The distance-based approach is very flexible. If the embedding network learns to extract meaningful features that describe the structure of the underlying text, it is theoretically possible to classify samples of classes unseen during training Such a behavior is not possible when using a softmax-based classifier, since the classifier would need to be retrained for each new class, which means that enough training data needs to be gathered.

4   Results and Discussion

In this section, we present the results of our experiments on multiple datasets. We show that our proposed models are feasible for usage on synthetic and real data. Furthermore, we discuss the advantages of our proposed models, especially their generalization capabilities and their ability to handle classes that have not been seen during training. First, we introduce the datasets we used for our experiments. Subsequently, we provide some information about our experimental setup. Last, we present the results of our experiments in addition to the insights we draw from them.

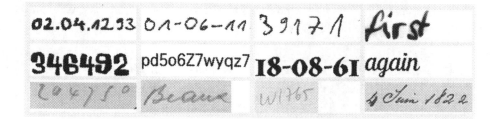

Fig. 2. Visualization of samples from all datasets used in this work. In the first row, we show samples from the GANwriting dataset, which were synthesised using the GAN-writing model. The second row depicts (printed) samples, which, together with samples from the GANwriting dataset, form the 5CHPT dataset. The last row shows samples from the WPI dataset, which solely consists of real images from archival documents and is used for evaluation only.

4.1 Datasets

In our experiments, we use multiple datasets for the evaluation of our proposed models. These datasets contain different kinds of samples distributed over various classes. On the one hand, we use two different synthetic datasets for training and preliminary evaluation. On the other hand, we employ a dataset consisting of real samples from the archive of the Wildenstein Plattner Institute for evaluation purposes only. We show some samples from each dataset in Fig. 2.

Synthetic Datasets. As already mentioned in Sect. 3.1, getting access to a large amount of labeled training data is very difficult, if not impossible. Hence, we devise methods to synthesize data that we can use for the training of our proposed models. Here, we create two different datasets. The first dataset consists of samples synthesized by our adaption of the GANwriting model (see Sect. 3.1). This dataset consists of synthetic handwriting samples from three classes (words, numbers and dates), totaling in 7920 samples that are equally distributed over the classes. The second dataset adds two more classes: alphanumeric strings and five-digit numbers that resemble zip codes. In addition to synthetic handwritten text, this dataset includes samples of synthetic printed text. We decided to also add printed text, as the model should be trained for classifying images of text, based on the visual structure of the contained texts. We argue that adding printed text leads to extra variety in our samples, which helps our model to generalize better because the structure of handwritten text and printed text for, *e.g.*, dates, is similar. Since the dataset consists of 5 classes and contains handwritten, as well as printed text, we refer to it as Five Classes Handwritten and Printed Text (5CHPT) dataset. In total, the dataset consists of 26400 samples, equally distributed over the five classes.

WPI Dataset. Besides the synthetic datasets that we use for training and validation of our models, we also gathered a dataset from the archive of the WPI. This dataset consists of 272 images of handwritten text, showing numbers (112

Table 1. Evaluation results for our proposed models on all of our datasets. We report accuracy, precision, recall, and F1 score. **Bold font** indicates the best result on the corresponding dataset.

Dataset	Model	Accuracy (%)	Precision (%)	Recall (%)	F1 Score
GANwriting	Naive	**99.62**	**99.62**	**99.62**	**0.9962**
	LLR	99.24	99.25	99.24	0.9924
	Softmax	**99.62**	**99.62**	**99.62**	**0.9962**
5CHPT	Naive	74.32	73.31	74.32	0.7456
	LLR	79.89	99.25	99.24	0.7999
	Softmax	**90.00**	**90.62**	**90.00**	**0.9004**
WPI	Naive	**58.33**	49.82	**58.33**	**0.5263**
	LLR	25.76	32.96	25.76	0.2771
	Softmax	37.50	**60.61**	37.50	0.4086

samples), words (108 samples), alphanumeric strings (31 samples), and dates (21 samples). We depict some of the samples in the last row of Fig. 2. Please note, we first binarize images from this dataset before feeding them to our models.

4.2   Experimental Setup

The model we use to synthesize handwriting samples is based on Lei Kang's Pytorch implementation[3] of the GANwriting paper [12]. Our adapted version that additionally can handle date generation is also freely available on GitHub[4]. We train our GANwriting model in two rounds for 3000 and 6000 epochs, respectively, using a batch size of 16 and a GPU with a total of 12 GB of RAM. We use Adam [14], as our optimizer, with a learning rate of 10^{-4} for discriminator and generator and 10^{-5} for writer classifier and content recognizer. We implement the classification models using the deep learning framework Chainer [25] and provide our code on GitHub[5]. Here, we also use a GPU with a total of 12 GB of RAM, Adam with a learning rate of 10^{-4}, and a batch size of 128. We train these models for 20 epochs.

4.3   Results on the GANwriting Dataset

In our first experiments, we assess whether our overall approach of classifying handwriting is feasible and test it on our GANwriting dataset, which consists of images from three different classes. The results (see the first rows of Table 1) show that all of our three approaches can correctly classify samples from the GANwriting dataset. When looking at a visualization of the predicted clusters

---

[3] https://github.com/omni-us/research-GANwriting.
[4] https://github.com/hendraet/research-GANwriting/tree/support-date-generation.
[5] https://github.com/hendraet/handwriting-classification.

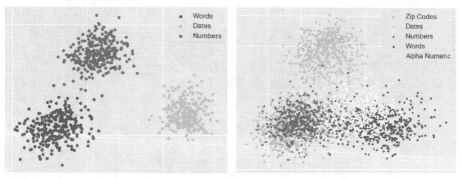

(a) PCA of samples in GANwriting dataset   (b) PCA of samples in 5CHPT dataset

Fig. 3. Comparison of embeddings on our synthetic training datasets. Embeddings produced by the model trained on the GANwriting dataset are shown in a, whereas embeddings of the model trained on the 5CHPT dataset are shown in b. The visualizations are obtained by performing a PCA [21].

(see Fig. 3a), we can see that the model is able to cluster the input samples into three distinct clusters. Hence, the naive method relying on k-Means and kNN, as well as the llr method perform very well. We can also observe that the visual structure of dates differs significantly from the structure of numbers and words because the cluster of dates is positioned far away from the other clusters.

4.4   Results on the 5CHPT Dataset

In our next series of experiments, we trained our models on the 5CHPT dataset. We examine whether our models can handle a wider variety of classes that are more similar to each other than the classes in the last experiment. We present the results of these experiments in the second row of Table 1. The results show that the model using a softmax classifier outperforms the embedding models by a large margin.

Consulting the visualization of the predicted clusters in Fig. 3b, we can identify the reason for the comparatively poor performance of the embedding-based models. Although individual clusters are visible, the clusters for zip codes, numbers, alphanumerics and words can not be distinguished clearly. This is not unexpected considering the nature of the underlying classes. Zip codes are a sub-class of numbers and alphanumerics are a superclass of words and numbers. This complicates the clustering process for our embedding models, whereas the softmax model can rely on different features and push the samples into more distinct categories. However, the embeddings of our date images form their own distinct cluster, showing that our embedding models indeed learn to cluster based on the structure of the given text sample.

The results on this dataset show the limitations of our classification approach. Classification only makes sense for distinguishing visually dissimilar classes from

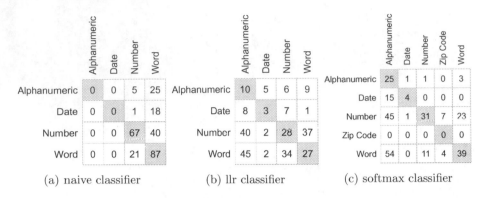

Fig. 4. Confusion matrices for our different classifiers on the WPI dataset. Rows refer to the actual class, whereas columns refer to the predicted class. The confusion matrix of the softmax model also includes the zip code class because it was trained on the 5CHPT dataset and is therefore restricted to classifying exactly five classes.

each other in a coarse way. A fine-grained classification is only possible with a full recognition pipeline with additional analysis steps, such as named entity recognition.

4.5   Results on the WPI Dataset

Following our experiments on the 5CHPT dataset, we evaluate the models trained on the 5CHPT dataset on the dataset that contains real images from the art-historical archive of the WPI. The results (see third row of Table 1) show that applying our trained models to the WPI dataset leads to severe performance degradations. Here, our naive model seems to perform best, which is an interesting result.

On closer examination, the reasons for the seemingly better performance of the naive model become apparent. Looking at the confusion matrix of the naive approach (see Fig. 4a), we can observe that the naive model is not able to identify alphanumerics and dates at all (F1 score of 0 for both classes). The confusion matrix clearly shows that the naive classifier can only identify two classes. We conclude that the model is not able to embed the samples of the WPI dataset so that they form distinct clusters. Hence, the k-Means algorithm is only able to find two clusters: one for words and one for numbers. This leads to a superior accuracy because the dataset is imbalanced and those two classes contain a majority of the samples. Therefore, the negative impact of misclassifying dates or alphanumeric strings is comparatively small. The llr classifier, on the other hand, is able to find at least some instances of each class. It also shows the most balanced misclassifications, which is mainly due to a poor clustering performance of the underlying embedding model. Finally, the softmax classifier incorrectly identifies many samples as alphanumeric strings, which is technically correct because these are a superclass of words, numbers, and dates. This mis-

Table 2. Evaluation results for our proposed models when adding a new and unseen class to the classification task. The first row shows the results of our models on the training set with only two classes, while the second row shows the classification result of our models when adding a third, unseen class to the classification task.

Experiment	Model	Accuracy (%)	Precision (%)	Recall (%)	F1 Score
Two classes	Naive	**98.48**	**98.49**	**98.48**	**0.9848**
	LLR	93.75	94.32	93.75	0.9373
Three classes	Naive	65.66	49.33	65.66	0.5472
	LLR	**79.63**	**76.37**	**75.63**	**0.7520**

classification is severe and could be avoided by using training data that is more similar to the data encountered in the real archive.

All in all, the results show that the softmax model can generalize best on unseen data, although it does not reach the best results in our evaluation. The naive and llr approach fail in this scenario because the embedding model is not able to embed images of similar structure close to each other. Although the llr classifier shows even worse results than the softmax classifier, it is still a better choice than the naive approach because it is able to categorize samples into each available class.

However, it should be mentioned that the llr approach and naive approach might perform better under different circumstances. For finding the clusters, both approaches need a set of support samples whose class is known. For the experiments on the WPI dataset, we use samples from the 5CHPT dataset as support. These samples are quite different to the samples of the WPI dataset, as can be seen in Fig. 2. We argue that our results could be improved if we had access to more labeled data that we can use for fine-tuning the embedding models. We leave this open for future work.

4.6 Classification of an Additional Unseen Class

In Sect. 3.2, we argued that our embedding models are a good solution if we want to classify samples as classes that we did not use during training. Naturally, a softmax-based classifier cannot do so without retraining. However, a model based on embeddings can be used for such a task because only a small labeled support set has to be available for finding clusters of the newly added class. The results of this additional experiment (see Table 2) show that our embedding approaches are indeed able to handle new and unseen classes. Although the classification accuracy decreases, the model based on Log-Likelihood Ratios is able to successfully distinguish between the three classes despite only encountering two classes during training. This result indicates that our proposed embedding models are more flexible than our softmax-based approach.

In the end, it will depend on the specific use-case, which of our proposed models should be employed. If training data is available and the number of classes can be determined beforehand, it is better to use the softmax approach. In case there is no training data for a specific class or the number of classes can not be defined in advance, it makes more sense to use the more flexible llr approach, although it might not be as accurate as the softmax model.

5   Conclusion

In this paper, we presented a novel approach for automatic classification of handwritten text. The task of handwriting classification itself deals with categorizing a given image of handwritten text into classes such as dates, numbers, or words without explicitly recognizing the content of the text. Therefore, it is easier to gather and reuse existing training data for different languages because the classification is based on the visual structure of the text and not the exact content. It also allows us to process scans of documents in multi-lingual archives that use the same alphabet (*i.e.* Latin).

To alleviate the problem of missing training data, we propose to use methods for the synthesis of such data. We propose three different approaches for handwriting classification and train them on our synthesized training data. On the one hand, we propose to use a model based on a softmax classifier. This model performs best in our experiments and should be used if enough training data is available and the number of classes is known in advance. On the other hand, we introduce two approaches based on an embedding model trained with triplet loss. In general, these models perform worse than the softmax model. However, the results show that they offer more flexibility because they can be applied in situations, where only a few training samples are available and the number of classes is not known in advance.

In the future, we want to further investigate the behavior of our embedding models if more support samples for unseen data are available. Further, we want to investigate how we can improve the generation and classification of clusters so that we can close the gap to the softmax model and use all advantages of our embedding models.

Acknowledgments. We thank the Wildenstein Plattner Institute for providing us with access to their art-historical archive and their expertise.

References

1. Altman, N.S.: An introduction to kernel and nearest-neighbor nonparametric regression. Am. Stat. **46**(3), 175–185 (1992). https://doi.org/10.1080/00031305.1992.10475879
2. Bhunia, A.K., Das, A., Bhunia, A.K., Kishore, P.S.R., Roy, P.P.: Handwriting recognition in low-resource scripts using adversarial learning. In: 2019 IEEE/CVF Conference on Computer Vision and Pattern Recognition (CVPR), pp. 4767–4776 (2019)

3. Bluche, T., Ney, H., Kermorvant, C.: Tandem HMM with convolutional neural network for handwritten word recognition. In: 2013 IEEE International Conference on Acoustics, Speech and Signal Processing, pp. 2390–2394, May 2013. https:// doi.org/10.1109/ICASSP.2013.6638083, iSSN: 2379-190X

4. Brümmer, N., du Preez, J.: Application-independent evaluation of speaker detection. Comput. Speech Lang. **20**(2), 230–275 (2006). https://doi.org/10.1016/j.csl. 2005.08.001

5. Carbune, V., et al.: Fast multi-language LSTM-based online handwriting recognition. Int. J. Doc. Anal. Recogn. (IJDAR) **23**, 89–102 (2020)

6. Fischer, A., Frinken, V., Fornés, A., Bunke, H.: Transcription alignment of Latin manuscripts using hidden Markov models. In: Proceedings of the 2011 Workshop on Historical Document Imaging and Processing, HIP 2011, pp. 29–36. Association for Computing Machinery, New York, September 2011. https://doi.org/10.1145/ 2037342.2037348

7. Fischer, A., Keller, A., Frinken, V., Bunke, H.: Lexicon-free handwritten word spotting using character HMMs. Pattern Recogn. Lett. **33**(7), 934–942 (2012). https://doi.org/10.1016/j.patrec.2011.09.009

8. Giménez, A., Khoury, I., Andrés-Ferrer, J., Juan, A.: Handwriting word recognition using windowed Bernoulli HMMs. Pattern Recogn. Lett. **35**, 149–156 (2014). https://doi.org/10.1016/j.patrec.2012.09.002

9. He, K., Gkioxari, G., Dollar, P., Girshick, R.: Mask R-CNN. In: 2017 IEEE International Conference on Computer Vision (ICCV), pp. 2961–2969 (2017)

10. He, K., Zhang, X., Ren, S., Sun, J.: Deep residual learning for image recognition. In: Proceedings of the IEEE Conference on Computer Vision and Pattern Recognition, pp. 770–778 (2016)

11. Huang, X., Belongie, S.: Arbitrary style transfer in real-time with adaptive instance normalization. In: 2017 IEEE International Conference on Computer Vision (ICCV), pp. 1501–1510 (2017)

12. Kang, L., Riba, P., Wang, Y., Rusiñol, M., Fornés, A., Villegas, M.: GANwriting: Content-Conditioned Generation of Styled Handwritten Word Images. arXiv:2003.02567 [cs], March 2020, arXiv: 2003.02567

13. Kang, L., Toledo, J.I., Riba, P., Villegas, M., Fornés, A., Rusiñol, M.: Convolve, attend and spell: an attention-based sequence-to-sequence model for handwritten word recognition. In: Brox, T., Bruhn, A., Fritz, M. (eds.) GCPR 2018. LNCS, vol. 11269, pp. 459–472. Springer, Cham (2019). https://doi.org/10.1007/978-3-030-12939-2_32

14. Kingma, D.P., Ba, J.: Adam: a method for stochastic optimization. In: Bengio, Y., LeCun, Y. (eds.) 3rd International Conference on Learning Representations, ICLR 2015, San Diego, CA, USA, 7–9 May, 2015, Conference Track Proceedings (2015)

15. Krishnan, P., Jawahar, C.V.: Generating Synthetic Data for Text Recognition. arXiv:1608.04224 [cs], August 2016, arXiv: 1608.04224

16. Krizhevsky, A., Sutskever, I., Hinton, G.E.: ImageNet classification with deep convolutional neural networks. In: Pereira, F., Burges, C.J.C., Bottou, L., Weinberger, K.Q. (eds.) Advances in Neural Information Processing Systems 25, pp. 1097–1105. Curran Associates, Inc. (2012)

17. Liwicki, M., Bunke, H.: IAM-OnDB - an on-line English sentence database acquired from handwritten text on a whiteboard. In: Eighth International Conference on Document Analysis and Recognition (ICDAR 2005), vol. 2, pp. 956–961, August 2005. https://doi.org/10.1109/ICDAR.2005.132, iSSN: 2379-2140

18. Lloyd, S.: Least squares quantization in PCM. IEEE Trans. Inf. Theory **28**(2), 129–137 (1982). https://doi.org/10.1109/TIT.1982.1056489

19. Mandal, R., Roy, P.P., Pal, U., Blumenstein, M.: Multi-lingual date field extraction for automatic document retrieval by machine. Inf. Sci. **314**, 277–292 (2015). https://doi.org/10.1016/j.ins.2014.08.037

20. Marti, U.V., Bunke, H.: The IAM-database: an English sentence database for offline handwriting recognition. Int. J. Doc. Anal. Recogn. **5**(1), 39–46 (2002). https://doi.org/10.1007/s100320200071

21. Pearson, K.: LIII. On lines and planes of closest fit to systems of points in space. The London, Edinburgh, and Dublin Philosophical Magazine and Journal of Science **2**(11), 559–572 (1901), publisher: Taylor & Francis

22. Plamondon, R., Srihari, S.: Online and off-line handwriting recognition: a comprehensive survey. IEEE Trans. Pattern Anal. Mach. Intell. **22**(1), 63–84 (2000). https://doi.org/10.1109/34.824821

23. Schroff, F., Kalenichenko, D., Philbin, J.: FaceNet: a unified embedding for face recognition and clustering. In: 2015 IEEE Conference on Computer Vision and Pattern Recognition (CVPR), pp. 815–823 (2015)

24. Tappert, C., Suen, C., Wakahara, T.: The state of the art in online handwriting recognition. IEEE Trans. Pattern Anal. Mach. Intell. **12**(8), 787–808 (1990). https://doi.org/10.1109/34.57669

25. Tokui, S., Oono, K., Hido, S., Clayton, J.: Chainer: a next-generation open source framework for deep learning. In: Proceedings of Workshop on Machine Learning Systems (LearningSys) in The Twenty-ninth Annual Conference on Neural Information Processing Systems (NIPS) (2015)

26. Ul-Hasan, A., Shafait, F., Breuel, T.: High-Performance OCR for Printed English and Fraktur using LSTM. Networks (2013). https://doi.org/10.1109/ICDAR.2013.140

27. Wigington, C., Stewart, S., Davis, B., Barrett, B., Price, B., Cohen, S.: Data augmentation for recognition of handwritten words and lines using a CNN-LSTM network. In: 2017 14th IAPR International Conference on Document Analysis and Recognition (ICDAR), vol. 01, pp. 639–645, November 2017. https://doi.org/10.1109/ICDAR.2017.110, iSSN: 2379-2140

28. Wigington, C., Tensmeyer, C., Davis, B., Barrett, W., Price, B., Cohen, S.: Start, follow, read: end-to-end full-page handwriting recognition. In: Ferrari, V., Hebert, M., Sminchisescu, C., Weiss, Y. (eds.) ECCV 2018. LNCS, vol. 11210, pp. 372–388. Springer, Cham (2018). https://doi.org/10.1007/978-3-030-01231-1_23

Color Space Exploration of Paintings Using a Novel Probabilistic Divergence

Shounak Roychowdhury[✉]

Department of Computer Science, Texas State University, San Marcos, TX, USA
s_r546@txstate.edu

Abstract. It is strange to think of a world without color. Color adds profound richness and spectacular variety to the phenomenon of visual experience. This paper explores the latent color space used by artists through various well-known paintings. We compare the paintings' color spaces by introducing a novel probabilistic divergence to evaluate the separation (divergences) between two paintings in their color spaces. Our results show that there is a significant divergence in color spaces of the works created at different periods of history.

Keywords: Paintings · Color space · Probabilistic divergences

1 Introduction

Since antiquity, artists have relied on natural colors as colors add richness and vibrancy to their artworks. It is evident from the prehistoric paintings of hand-prints of bison and horses found in Spanish and French caves [1,2]. Designs and pictures imprinted on Greek pottery, especially on the vases and amphoras, show how the ancient Greeks painters effectively used red and black pigments to colorize them. They adorned these pictures to tell stories of their gods and heroes [3,4]. Art history shows that even before the Renaissance, the artists were using colors derived from minerals and semi-precious stones, such as lapis lazuli, azurite, orpiment, cinnabar, and other organic compounds. Evidence is found in Giotto's frescos in the Scrovegni Chapel in Padua, Italy [5]. Painters of Renaissance and post-Renaissance, leading to the Baroque period, continued to use naturally occurring chemicals. With the industrial revolution came the explosion of various tints and shades of various colors from synthetic pigments and dyes. The availability of a new gamut of colors also led artists to explore new ways of playing with light and shade by the end of the 19th century. These days, it is easy to generate more than a million colors spread throughout the spectrum of light in the computational world. Thus, we have moved from a limited artist palette of yesteryears to a nearly infinite palette of the modern digital reality.

The research question inquired in this paper is how to compare paintings from their color palette perspective. Our approach is to find a distance measure in the color spaces of the two paintings. We can use the digital palette to compare the palettes of paintings of different eras.

A. Del Bimbo et al. (Eds.): ICPR 2020 Workshops, LNCS 12663, pp. 577–588, 2021.
https://doi.org/10.1007/978-3-030-68796-0_41

The second section reviews the color theory. The third section examines the color space as a probabilistic model. The fourth section proposes a new probabilistic distance model that is symmetric, unlike some of the well-known probabilistic divergences. The fifth section discusses the experimental results – of a few natural colors and a select group of paintings by various artists spanning the last two millennia. We select these pictures purely from the color space point of view.

2   The Color Theory

This section briefly reviews the central aspect of the color theory. A recent paper on complementary colors by Pridmore touches on the historical background [8]. Albers [6] describes the relativity of colors, how colors influence each other. In [7] O'Conner discusses the harmonies of color. Wyszecki and Stiles analyze the properties of color starting from it light sources, to visual measurement of color, and color scales and more [12]. Palmer presents the computational description of color perception, where he discusses different theories of color vision such as trichromatic theory, dual process theory, and opponent process theory [11].

In 1666 Newton showed a concrete physical description of light. Using a triangular prism, he showed that the white light is composed of several components of light and each of these lights had specific colors, ranging from red to violet [13]. He also found that it is possible to recreate the white light by combining red, green, and blue color components by using multiple prisms. Thereby, he termed red, green, and blue as called primary colors. Other colors, such as yellow, orange, indigo, and violet, are observed as physical phenomena.

However, in 1810 Goethe proposed his theory of colors from the perspective of color perception and color experience defined by human cognition and traits [14]. His work had influenced painters like Turner [16] and Kandinsky [15]. At the same time, many of his contemporaries disavowed his color theory as a valued theory. Despite this, it is interesting to note that he was the first person to propose the color magenta, also known as purple, as a cognitive phenomenon because magenta is not a real color as it does not exist in the light spectrum. The color wheel that we know has magenta as a complementary color to green. Young showed that purple is an equal mixture of red and blue whereas violet is a mixture of two parts blue and three parts red [17].

In 1839, Chevreul, a French industrial chemist, identified the simultaneous contrast sensation: how two different color objects can affect each other [18]. For example, Fig. 1a shows that the same gray value looks lighter in the blue background than the one in the yellow background. This theory positively influenced Impressionist and post Impressionist painters who wanted to bring out contrasting features using complementary colors. Later in the twentieth century, following Young's [17] ideas on photoreceptors, it became clear how the eye perceives colors through rods and cones in the retina.

From a more practical point of view, the color theory provides a set of guidelines for an artist to generate a spectrum of colors based on three different

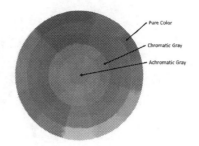

Simultaneous contrast of the same gray value in context of complementary colors.

Color wheel with chromatic grays and achromatic gray.

Fig. 1. Simultaneous contrast and color wheel. (Color figure online)

parameters: value, hue, and chroma. The value deals with lightness or darkness of a color. The hue is pure color. The chroma represents the saturation of the color. For example, the hue of color red has a dominating wavelength of approximately 625–740 nm. When a pinch of white (tint) or black (shade) to the red color, red color shifts towards light-red or dark-red. Note that white and black colors are not true colors. They represent lightness and darkness values. A mixture of white and black produces gray, which is called tone. Furthermore, the addition of gray (tone) color to any pure color reduces pure color saturation. Figure 1b shows the color wheel. Colors projected at the perimeter of the color wheel are pure saturated colors. Moving toward the center of the wheel the color changes from chromatic grays to achromatic gray. Figure 1b shows the approximate range of chromatic gray. The chromatic gray is formed by adding complementary colors, and that shade of gray is affected by the tinge of one of the dominant colors among the complementary colors. In the centermost area of the wheel, the complementary colors create a zone of achromatic gray. The gray level value determines the lightness and the darkness of colors.

3   RGB Color Space

A color image has three channels for each of the three color components Red, Green, and Blue. Thus, we can create a three-dimensional volume (color cube) to describe the component values as Cartesian coordinates in a Euclidean space. In a standard RGB cube, the range of each component is between 0 and 1. Each component has a value between 0 to 255 instead of 0 and 1 to avoid floating-point errors in our model. There are $16,777,216 = 256^3$ tuples in the cube. Each tuple represents a specific and unique color. Therefore, the color cube is a repository of all possible colors.

Figure 2 shows RGB color cube. Let the point A in this cube is a tuple whose value is (0,0,0), and it is pure black. Similarly, the diagonal point G is a tuple whose value is (255,255,255), and it is pure white. All the points along the

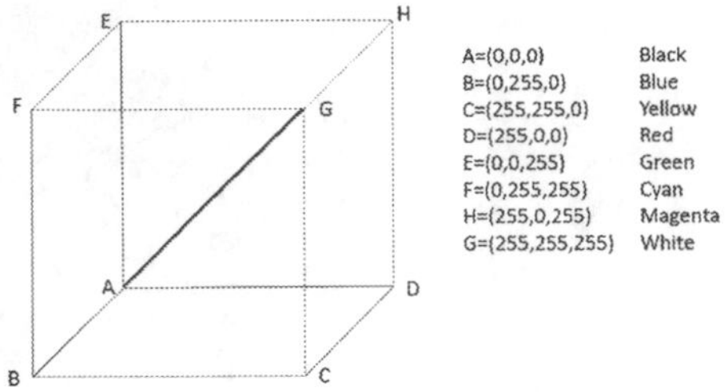

A=(0,0,0)   Black
B=(0,255,0)   Blue
C=(255,255,0)   Yellow
D=(255,0,0)   Red
E=(0,0,255)   Green
F=(0,255,255)   Cyan
H=(255,0,255)   Magenta
G=(255,255,255) White

Fig. 2. RGB color cube. The diagonal AG represents the values of achromatic grayscale. A is pure black (0,0,0) and G is pure white (255,255,255). The middle of the cube is achromatic gray value of (127,127,127).

diagonal are the grayscale values. The tuple at the center of the cube is gray and has a value of (127,127,127). The corner points B, D, and E are primary colors: red, green, and blue. The remaining corner points F, C, and H are secondary colors: cyan, yellow, and magenta.

Painting is an image of 3 color channels (RGB), with M rows and N columns. We convert the three-dimensional image into a vector. Extract the red component of an image by accessing $r = image[i, j, 0]$. Similarly, extract the green and the blue components of an image by accessing $g = image[i, j, 1]$ and $b = image[i, j, 2]$ respectively. Use the r, g, and b to construct a vector V whose index i is,

$$i = r + 256 * g + 256 * 256 * b. \tag{1}$$

Suppose, α_i be number of times the ith color appears in image, store it in $V[i]$, such that

$$V[i] = \alpha_i, \tag{2}$$

for all values of M and N. Thus, this colossal vector V represents the color content of the image. In order words, each painting has its color spectrum. Normalize V to V'.

$$V'[i] = \frac{\alpha_i}{\sum_{i=1}^{256^3} \alpha_i}, \tag{3}$$

The normalization leads us to treat an image as a probability density function in the color space, which further implies that each image has a unique probability density function in terms of colors used therein. We use these probability density functions in probabilistic divergences to measure the distance between different paintings' probability density functions.

In the next section, we briefly review well-known probabilistic divergences that are often used in information theory [9].

4   Probabilistic Divergence Measure

Probabilistic Divergence Measure are computed between two probability distribution functions, such that $p(x_i) = P(X = i)$ and $q(x_i) = P(X' = i)$, where X and X' are two random variables.

The Kulback-Liebler divergence is also popularly known as KL-divergence is mostly used in information theory and its applications such communications [9], machine learning [10] etc. The KL-divergence is defined as followed:

$$D_{KL}(p||q) = \sum_{i=1}^{N} p(x_i) log\left(\frac{p(x_i)}{q(x_i)}\right) \tag{4}$$

It is clear that $D_{KL}(p||q)$ is not symmetric, i.e., $D_{KL}(p||q) \neq D_{KL}(q||p)$. The Jensen-Shannon divergence a symmetrized and smoothed version of $D_{KL}(p||q)$, and

$$D_{JSD}(p||q) = \frac{1}{2}D(p||m) + \frac{1}{2}D(q||m), \tag{5}$$

where $m(x_i) = \frac{p(x_i)+q(x_i)}{2}$. The Hellinger distance [19] is given by:

$$D_H(p||q) = \frac{1}{\sqrt{2}}\sqrt{\sum_{i=1}^{N} \sqrt{p(x_i)} - \sqrt{q(x_i)}}. \tag{6}$$

The Bhattacharya distance [20] is given by:

$$D_{Bhatt}(p||q) = \sqrt{\sum_{i=1}^{N} \sqrt{p(x_i)}\sqrt{q(x_i)}}. \tag{7}$$

5   A Novel Probabilistic Divergence Measure

In this section we propose a novel parameterized probabilistic divergence measure that we use in finding the distance between two paintings.

The proposed parameterized probabilistic divergence measure is given by:

$$D^*(p||q:m) = -log\left(\frac{\sum_{i=1}^{N} p^m(x)q(x) + p(x)q^m(x)}{\sum_{i=1}^{N}(p^{m+1}(x) + q^{m+1}(x))}\right), \tag{8}$$

for $m \in \{1, ..., \infty\}$.

When $m = 1$ then (8) is reduced to simple equation that is given below:

$$D^*(p||q:1) = -log\left(\frac{\sum_{i=1}^{N} 2p(x)q(x)}{\sum_{i=1}^{N}(p^2(x) + q^2(x))}\right). \tag{9}$$

When $m = 2$ then (8) is reduced to simple equation that is given below:

$$D^*(p||q:2) = -log\left(\frac{\sum_{i=1}^{N} p^2(x)q(x) + q^2(x)p(x)}{\sum_{i=1}^{N}(p^3(x) + q^3(x))}\right). \tag{10}$$

Unlike $D_{KL}(p||q)$, $D^*(p||q,m)$ is symmetric, which is obvious by interchanging p and q. Also, it may be noted that the triangle inequality does not hold. In other words, $D(p||r) \geq D(p||q) + D(q||r)$, which implies that this divergence is not a metric.

In the next section, we will use this novel divergence and compare results for various paintings.

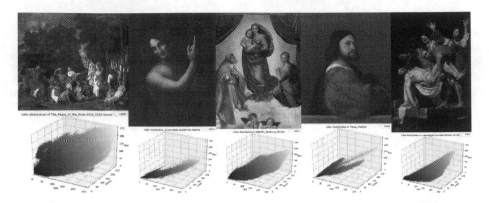

Fig. 3. A selection of classical paintings (left to right): 1) "The Feast of the Gods" by Bellini, 2) "St. John the Baptist" by Leonardo Da Vinci, 3) "Sistine Madona" by Raphael, 4) "A Man with a Quilted Sleeve" by Titian, 5) "The Entombment of Christ" by Caravaggio. (Color figure online)

6   Experiments and Results

Here we compare the color spaces of some selected paintings.

6.1   Classic Masters

Figure 3 shows five paintings by classic masters. From left to right, we see the following paintings in the following order. Bellini's *The Feast of the Gods* is a study in blues and reds [21]. Leonardo Da Vinci's *St. John the Baptist* [23] shows the controlled power of using two colors. We see the effective use of Malachite in *Sistine Madona* by Raphael [22]. Titian's portrait of *A Man with a Quilted Sleeve* is a study in the bluish-gray color theme [24]. Similarly, Caravaggio's *The entombment of christ* shows the power of a limited palette, of white and the earth tones.

Table 1 shows the divergences computed for different paintings. The $D_1^* = 5.744$ and $D_2^* = 7.331$ between Bellini's and daVinci's paintings. The color spaces of these two paintings clearly show that daVinci's paintings forms a subset of Bellini's painting in the color space. Similarly comparing Raphael's and Titian's paintings shades of bluish grays are more common than shades of yellow ochre, and has $D_1^* = 4.101$ and $D_2^* = 6.250$ compared to KL-divergence is 5.346. Again, JS-Div, Hellinger, and Bhattacharya divergences have low variances.

6.2   Modern Masters

This subsection explores the divergences of five modern masters' color spaces, focusing on a period of fifty years from 1860 to 1910. See Fig. 4.

The first painting is a still life by Cezzane that shows a table, napkins, and a basket of fruits painted sometime between 1895–1900 [26]. There is hardly any pure blue color, but the use of chromatic bluish-grey is evident. Red and yellow

Table 1. This table shows the distance computed for different classical painting with limited palette.

	KL-Div	JS-Div	Hellinger	Bhatt	D_1^*	D_2^*
Titian-Portrait & Caravaggio	10.384	0.625	1.229	0.131	5.575	8.670
Titian-Portrait & Bellini	3.694	0.547	1.024	0.276	3.670	5.570
Titian-Portrait & daVinci	8.862	0.621	1.205	0.148	4.843	6.626
Titian-Portrait & Raphael	5.346	0.581	1.111	0.214	4.101	6.250
Caravaggio & Bellini	5.590	0.575	1.107	0.217	6.031	7.992
Caravaggio & daVinci	13.045	0.637	1.252	0.114	6.914	9.593
Caravaggio & Raphael	3.897	0.491	0.915	0.353	4.405	6.049
Bellini & daVinci	10.266	0.641	1.249	0.117	5.744	7.331
Bellini & Raphael	6.198	0.475	0.911	0.356	1.598	2.605
daVinci & Raphael	8.589	0.621	1.223	0.135	6.565	8.468

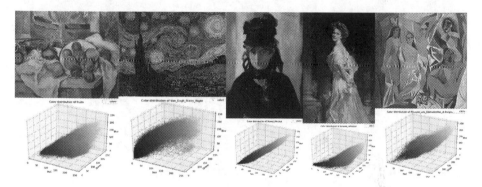

Fig. 4. This figure shows five paintings by five modern masters (left to right). 1) "Still life" by Cezzane, 2) "The starry night" by Van Gogh, 3) "portrait for Bertha Morisot" by Manet, 4) "Lady Nancy Astor" by Sargent, 5) "Les Demoiselles d'Avignon" by Picasso. (Color figure online)

colors and relative shades dominate the painting. The second painting is *The starry night* by Van Gogh. The painting's color space clearly shows the range of color ranging from deep blue to light blue shades. There are, in fact, two clusters: 1) with blue and black colors and 2) with mid-tones of yellow. The third picture is by Manet. In 1872, Manet painted a portrait for Bertha Morisot while she was mourning the death of her father. It is work that has gray dominance and colors cluster around the diagonal. It shows the limited palette used by Manet. The fourth painting in this list is *Lady Nancy Astor*, was a British Parliament member. Sargent painted her in 1906. The color palette is dominated by earth tones, especially around the color of burnt sienna and shades of yellows. *Les Demoiselles d'Avignon* is our last painting by Picasso in 1907 [25]. This painting does not have a traditional perspective, and distortion of perspective in this

Table 2. This table shows the distance computed for different paintings with expanded palette by modern masters.

	KL-Div	JS-Div	Hellinger	Bhatt	D_1^*	D_2^*
VanGogh & Cezzane	9.399	0.649	1.303	0.079	3.475	4.462
VanGogh & Manet	10.927	0.645	1.265	0.106	4.721	5.725
VanGogh & Sargent	11.881	0.686	1.381	0.024	6.262	7.144
VanGogh & Picasso	8.823	0.656	1.317	0.069	4.205	5.259
Cezzane & Manet	10.372	0.633	1.267	0.104	7.529	13.130
Cezzane & Sargent	9.546	0.618	1.234	0.127	4.629	8.647
Cezzane & Picasso	8.660	0.668	1.339	0.053	4.791	5.601
Manet & Sargent	15.396	0.685	1.389	0.018	9.568	13.596
Manet & Picasso	12.263	0.672	1.355	0.042	8.179	13.351
Sargent & Picasso	9.913	0.687	1.382	0.023	6.473	7.398

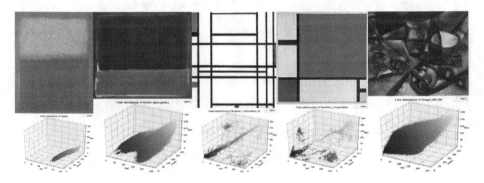

Fig. 5. This paintings by three abstract masters (left to right): 1) "untitled" by Rothko, 2) "untitled" by Rothko, 3) "B288.317" by Mondrian 4) "B219" by Mondrian, 5) "Nature morte" by Chagall .

composition makes it a seminal work to the development of cubism and later art movements. The pigments used are lead white, bone black, vermilion, cadmium yellow, cobalt blue, emerald green, and native earth pigments (such as brown ochre).

Table 2 shows divergences between the selected paintings of modern masters. When Manet's painting of Bertha Morisot is compared with Cezzane' painting of the fruits we get $D_1^* = 7.529$ and $D_2^* = 13.130$, and the KL-divergence is 10.372. Also, when Manet's painting is further compared with Sargent's and Picasso's paintings we get $D_1^* = 9.568$ and $D_2^* = 13.596$, and $D_1^* = 7.529$ and $D_2^* = 13.130$ respectively.

6.3   Abstract Masters

Among the abstract masters, we compare paintings by Rothko, Mondrian, and Chagall in Fig. 5 [27]. Because of the use of unique color palettes, we choose these images here for our study. On the surface, the observer sees a few colors in paintings by Rothko, but there are many shades underneath [28]. It is well-known that Rothko used to wash with thin layers of colors of different tonalities before settling into one final color [29]. On the other hand, Mondrian used very selected colors in his paintings and nearly used the colors in a geometric sense. Unlike Rothko and Chagall and other artists in general, he did not mix paints. Therefore, the third and fourth color cubes show distinct patches of color space, unlike any other. These two paintings are similar to the Trafalgar Square series [31]. One can see Mondrian's catalogue raisone [30] to glance through his works. Shades of deep blues, shades of red primarily dominate the last painting. Chagall painted this still-life painting titled *Nature morte* in 1912.

Table 3. This table shows the distances computed for different paintings with a limited palette by abstract masters.

	KL-Div	JS-Div	Hellinger	Bhatt	D_1^*	D_2^*
Rothko-1 & Mondrian-1	11.439	0.685	1.378	0.025	8.556	12.708
Rothko-1 & Mondrian-2	11.585	0.689	1.394	0.015	14.951	22.794
Rothko-1 & Chagall	12.404	0.641	1.284	0.092	6.946	9.529
Rothko-1 & Rothko-2	12.108	0.669	1.343	0.050	7.094	11.692
Mondrian-1 & Mondrian-2	11.316	0.641	1.264	0.106	6.220	7.065
Mondrian-1 & Chagall	13.544	0.670	1.335	0.056	7.436	11.704
Mondrian-1 & Rothko-2	12.928	0.674	1.363	0.037	8.670	13.670
Mondrian-1 & Chagall	17.227	0.678	1.358	0.040	12.926	20.905
Mondrian-1 & Rothko-2	16.002	0.679	1.373	0.029	16.836	20.086
Chagall & Rothko-2	9.747	0.689	1.389	0.018	11.215	13.435

Table 3 shows the divergences computed with the paintings of abstract masters. Compare Rothko-1 and Mondrian-1 and Rothko-1 and Mondrian-2, we find that D_1^* and D_2^* are significantly different from KL-divergence. It is interesting to note that KL-divergence is more than D_1^* and D_2^* for Mondrian-1 and Mondrian-2. When we only compare all the KL-divergences, the observed variance is 5.9092295, and in contrast, the variances of divergence measures D_1^* is 13.547674 and D_2^* is 26.83838.

7   Related Works

This brief section shows a few related works in the area of color space, color palettes, color image-segmentation, and color transformation. Vallari et al.

discuss the problem of colorimetric fidelity of digitized color slides of fine art paintings [36]. In another work [37] they experiment with 3CCD color detectors for color measurement on works of fine art without resorting to any small amount of destruction of the artwork. Gramazio et al. present an evaluation of a web-based tool, termed Colorgorical, for creating customizable color palettes for a practitioner [35]. Ma and Wang propose a color image descriptor, called color distance histogram, for color image indexing and retrieval [33]. Guo and Guo study the color image morphology technique using a vectorized ordering scheme based on distance measurements in the HSI color space, applied to edge detection [32]. Wesolkowski and Fieguth discuss a probabilistic color distance measure based on hypothesis testing to achieve shading invariance in image segmentation [34]. Sidorov studies the problem of creating a uniform of color space concerning perceptual color space using deep learning [38].

8   Conclusion

This paper contributes two things: firstly, we introduce a new parametric probabilistic divergence measure and secondly, we focus on the color space of a painting and not on the painting itself. We introduce the application of the novel probabilistic divergence to color space in order to understand the differences of palettes, which can be used as an annotated feature for the automated classification of paintings. Another interesting thing that emerges from this study is the usage of color spaces or color palettes used by painters through different times and eras.

References

1. Guthrie, R.D.: The Nature of Prehistoric Art. University of Chicago Press, Chicago (2006)
2. Curtis, G.: The Cave Painters: Probing the Mysteries of the World's First Artists. Alfred A. Knopf, New York (2006)
3. Beazley, J.D.: Attic Red-figure Vase-Painters, 2nd edn. Clarendon Press, Oxford (1963)
4. Boardman, J.: The History of Greek Vases: Potters, Painters, Pictures. Thames & Hudson, New York (2001)
5. Derbes, A., Sandona, M.: The Usurer's Heart: Giotto, Enrico Scrovegni, and the Arena Chapel in Padua. Pennsylvania State University Press, University Park (2008)
6. Albers, J.: Interaction of Color. Yale University Press, London (2006). Revised and Expanded Edition
7. O'Connor, Z.: Color harmony revisited. Color Res. Appl. **35**(4), 267–273 (2010)
8. Pridmore, R.W.: Complementary colors: a literature review. Color Res. Appl., 1–7 (2020). https://doi.org/10.1002/col.22576
9. Cover, T.M., Thomas, J.A.: Elements of Information Theory, 2nd edn. Wiley, New York (2006)
10. Bishop, C.M.: Pattern Recognition and Machine Learning. Springer, Boston (2006). https://doi.org/10.1007/978-1-4615-7566-5

11. Palmer, S.E.: Vision Science: Photons to Phenomenology. MIT Press, Cambridge (1999)
12. Wyszecki, G., Stiles, W.S.: Colour Science: Concepts and Methods, Quantitative Data and Formulae. Wiley Series in Pure and Applied Optics, 2nd edn. Wiley, NY (1982)
13. Newton, I.: Opticks: or, a treatise of the reflections, refractions, inflexions and colours of light., Printed for Sam. Smith, and Benj. Walford, London, (1704)
14. von Goethe, J.W.: Theory of Colours, trans. Charles Lock Eastlake. MIT press, Cambridge (1982)
15. Short, C.: The Art Theory of Wassily Kandinsky, 1909–1928: The Quest for Synthesis. Peter Lang, New York (2010)
16. Finley, G.E., Turner, J.M.W.: Angel in the Sun: Turner's Vision of History. McGill-Queen's University Press, Montreal (1999)
17. Young, T.: Bakerian lecture: on the theory of light and colours. Phil. Trans. R. Soc. Lond. **92**, 12–48 (1802)
18. Chevreul, M.E., Margulis, D.: On the Law of Simultaneous Contrast of Colors. MCW Publishing, Louisville (2020)
19. Pardo, L.: Statistical Inference Based on Divergence Measures. Chapman and Hall/CRC, New York (2006)
20. Bhattacharyya, A.: On a measure of divergence between two statistical populations defined by their probability distributions. Bull. Calcutta Math. Soc. **35**, 99–109 (1943)
21. Plesters, J.: The Feast of the Gods: Conservation, Examination, and Interpretation. Studies in the History of Art, vol. 40 (1990)
22. Raphael, Sistine Madonna (1518). https://colourlex.com/project/raphael-sistine-madonna/
23. Zollner, F.: Leonardo da Vinci. The Complete Paintings and Drawings, Cologne (2003)
24. Jaffé, D. (ed.): Titian. The National Gallery Company, Yale, London (2003)
25. Picasso, P.: Les Demoiselles d'Avignon: Museum of Modern Art, NY, USA. https://www.moma.org/calendar/galleries/5135
26. Cezanne, P.: Table, napkin, and fruit, The Barnes Foundation, Merion, Pennsylvania, US, (1895–1900)
27. Ross, C.: Abstract Expressionism: Creators and Critics: An Anthology. Abrams, New York (1990)
28. Cassell, J.: Rothko's Subtler Shades. USA Today, 7 May 1984
29. Sandler, I.: Mark Rothko: Paintings, 1948–1969. Pace Gallery, New York (1983)
30. Robert, P.W., Joosten, J.M.: Piet Mondrian: Catalogue Raisonne (1998). http://catalogue.pietmondrian.nl/
31. Mondrian, P.: MoMA, New York. https://www.moma.org/collection/works/79879
32. Guo, X., Guo, B.: Color image morphology based on distances in the HSI color space. In: ISECS International Colloquium on Computing, Communication, Control, and Management, Sanya, pp. 264–267 (2009)
33. Ma, K.K., Wang, J.: Color distance histogram: a novel descriptor for color image segmentation. In: 7th International Conference on Control, Automation, Robotics and Vision, ICARCV 2002, Singapore, vol. 3, pp. 1228–1232 (2002)
34. Wesolkowski, S., Fieguth, P.: A probabilistic shading invariant color distance measure. In: 15th European Signal Processing Conference, Poznan, pp. 1907–1911 (2007)

35. Gramazio, C.C., Laidlaw, D.H., Schloss, K.B.: Colorgorical: creating discriminable and preferable color palettes for information visualization. IEEE Trans. Vis. Comput. Graph. **23**(1), 521–530 (2017)
36. Vallari, M., Chryssoulakis, Y., Chassery, J.M.: A colour study approach through colour measurements on slides of art paintings. Color Res. Appl. **22**(5), 0361–2317, 326–334 (1997)
37. Vallari, M., Chryssoulakis, Y., Chassery, J. M.: In situ colour measurement on works of fine art using a non-destructive methodology. J. Soc. Dyers Colourists 113(9), 0037–9859 (1997)
38. Sidorov O.: Novel approach to uniformization of a color space via generic deep learning-based transformation. In: 2018 Colour and Visual Computing Symposium (CVCS), Gjøvik (2018)

Identifying Centres of Interest in Paintings Using Alignment and Edge Detection

Case Studies on Works by Luc Tuymans

Sinem Aslan[1]([⊠]) (iD) and Luc Steels[2] (iD)

[1] International Computer Institute, Ege University, Izmir, Turkey
siinem@gmail.com

[2] Catalan Institute for Advanced Studies (ICREA), Institute for Evolutionary Biology (UPF-CSIC), Barcelona, Spain
steels@arti.vub.ac.be
http://akademik.ube.ege.edu.tr/~aslan/,
https://www.icrea.cat/Web/ScientificStaff/Steels-Luc-539

Abstract. What is the creative process through which an artist goes from an original image to a painting? Can we examine this process using techniques from computer vision and pattern recognition? Here we set the first preliminary steps to algorithmically deconstruct some of the transformations that an artist applies to an original image in order to establish centres of interest, which are focal areas of a painting that carry meaning. We introduce a comparative methodology that first cuts out the minimal segment from the original image on which the painting is based, then aligns the painting with this source, investigates micro-differences to identify centres of interest and attempts to understand their role. In this paper we focus exclusively on micro-differences with respect to edges. We believe that research into where and how artists create centres of interest in paintings is valuable for curators, art historians, viewers, and art educators, and might even help artists to understand and refine their own artistic method.

1 Introduction

There is already a significant body of research investigating artistic paintings using techniques from pattern recognition, computer vision and AI. For example, some researchers have used deep learning to extract patterns from a series of paintings in order to obtain a statistical model of the painter's style and then

This work was made possible thanks to a 'scientist in residence of an artist studio' grant to Luc Steels and Studio Luc Tuymans. The residency was funded by the European Commission's S+T+ARTS programme, set up by DG CONNECT. It was organized by BOZAR, a Belgian art centre located in Brussels, and GLUON, a Brussels organisation facilitating art-science interactions. Additional funding for this research has come from the H2020 EU project MUHAI on Meaning and Understanding in AI.

create new images in the same style [15]. Others use neural networks for classifying paintings [3] or semantic web technology for organizing large collections based on rich ontologies so that these collections can be searched in more powerful ways [2]. In addition, many projects have been using image processing to assist in conservation work, artist identification, detection of forgery, and many other applications [4]. This paper focuses on a new, complementary aspect of art investigation, which attempts to *understand the artistic creation process through AI modeling.*

We start from the hypothesis that an artist tries to stimulate a process of narrative creation in the viewer and uses the expressive means available in the chosen medium. In the case of painting, this includes objects and figures being depicted, lines, colors, contrast, composition, blurring of background, etc. The artist is in a sense engaged in a form of cognitive engineering [5], manipulating the mental processes of viewers by shaping their sensory experiences and memory recalls. The creation of an artistic painting is therefore more than the application of a particular style to an existing image, as done in deep generative adversarial neural network experiments [15]. A style can certainly be recognized by current AI technology and even replicated, but the creation of an artwork is more than achieving formal appearances in a particular style. It is about choosing a pertinent subject, transforming images into more powerful ones, and evoking a web of meanings in the viewer.

Consequently, the interpretation of an artwork has a strong similarity with the *understanding* of a text and the creation of an artwork is similar to the *production* of a text, with the important difference that many of the meanings expressed or invoked by paintings or works in other media, like music or dance, are pre-verbal. They concern conceptualizations, emotions, moral values and perspectives that are not so easy to put into words. These meanings resonate with viewers at a subconscious level and, partly for this reason, they may evoke a stronger reaction from the viewer than obtainable from a purely rational text. Art works activate the non-rational, non-cognitive areas of the brain, such as the emotion system [11] or the social brain [21].

A work of art is complex and rich because it evokes the different levels of meaning (formal, factual, expressional, cultural, intrinsic) at the same time and the meanings at each level intimately interact with others [13]. Moreover which set of meanings resonates with one viewer is usually not the same as those resonating with another viewer or with those originally felt or intended by the artist, simply because everybody has their own episodic and semantic memory, their own prior experiences of artworks, their own social context and psychological state when viewing, experiencing and interpreting an artwork. There is therefore no objectively 'correct' set of meanings and it would be futile to develop an AI system that would extract such a set. However, this paper will try to show that we can nevertheless study *artistic methods*, i.e. the kind of transformations an artist performs on a real scene or a found image in order to induce meanings in the viewer.

An important part of the artistic painting method consists in the introduction of visual *centres of interest*, attention getters which guide meaning invocation. They are instantiated partly by what is being represented, for example, an iconic image of a well known person which is appropriated by the artist, such as the well-known image of Marilyn Monroe used by Andy Warhol. Partly there are objects or parts of objects where the human vision system naturally pays attention to, for example the eyes of a face. And in addition, artists often introduce deviations from what is expected, for example they deform the nose on a face, or they use devices such as contrast, bright colors, sharp edges, blurring of background, flattening out of 3d effect, etc.

There is often a first most salient centre of attention, called the primary focal point, which pulls the viewer into the painting. For example, in the case of Fig. 1 (left), the focal point is clearly the right eye and to a second degree the lips. The primary focal point introduces an organizing perspective from which the gaze of the viewer starts its exploration. Then there are additional focal points, as the viewer's eye gaze glances over the different parts of the painting.

In earlier work in collaboration with Björn Wahle [17], we already used various computer vision methods to investigate how saliency identifies the primary focal point. The saliency detection methods we tried on the Tuymans paintings were either low-level, in the sense that they estimate saliency based on general statististical properties of the visual image, or based on the use of supervised neural network training. The results of applying these algorithms were mixed. MSI-Net provides the most reliable first suggestions of focal points but falls short of several interest regions that viewers or painters spontaneously point to [10].

In this paper we introduce a complementary new and quite different methodology to study which areas in a painting are interest centres. The methodology is based on comparing an original source image (for example a photograph) with the painting based on it and deconstructing the interventions the painter undertook to transform one into the other. Many contemporary painters expressly use existing images from popular culture to make contact with their audience and thus comment on contemporary media culture. Our comparative methodology contains four steps:

(i) Locate the original image, either directly from the painter or searching information resources like images available on the world wide web or in image repositories using reverse image search.

(ii) Align the painting with the original image. This involves finding the minimal set of *macro-operations* performed by the artist, such as cutting, rotating, or scaling so that the contents of the painting are optimally aligned with the corresponding segment in the original image.

(iii) Zoom in on regions where there have been *micro-transformations* focusing on specific aspects of the painting, for example changes in shape, blurring, changes in illumination, edges differences, color changes, etc. The difference map between original image and painting for each of these aspects provides us with hypotheses what areas may be centres of interest and triggers inquiries in their possible meaning.

(iv) Importantly we then want to understand the meanings of these macro- and micro-transformations. This cannot be done at the moment with AI but introspection and conversations with the artist will help us to move in this direction in the future. In any case we have found that the suggestions coming out of the previous steps are very illuminating because they tell us where to look. They have certainly enriched the experience of paintings for the present authors.

2   Case Studies

The present paper reports the first results from applying our comparative methodology using paintings by the contemporary Flemish painter Luc Tuymans. Working with a living artist makes it possible to validate our hypotheses about what the centres of interest are in a particular painting and they can tell us whether AI techniques have yielded anything worthwhile, not only for viewers, curators or art historians but also for those creating artworks themselves.

Luc Tuymans is considered to be one of the most important contemporary painters at the moment [20]. He has done solo exhibitions at some of the most prestigious and influential art centres in the world such as the MOMA in New York, the Palazzo Grassi in Venice, the MCA Museum of Contemporary Art in Chicago, BOZAR in Brussels, the Städel Museum in Frankfurt, the National Art Museum of Beijing, etc. We have been fortunate because we have a direct and recurrent contact with this painter and have access to the relevant parts of his digital archives. Moreover Luc Tuymans is very articulate in describing his own artistic method as well as the methods used by other painters [19].

We have constructed a general interactive pipeline of pattern recognition, computer vision and AI algorithms to apply our methodology and processed several paintings by Luc Tuymans. Here we only focus on those parts of the pipeline that involve alignment and edge detection. The paintings we have studied in detail so far have come from the solo exhibition of Luc Tuymans at the Palazzo Grassi in Venice (2019–2020) but we have also done experiments on all the paintings Luc Tuymans documented in his Catalogue Raisoné [12]. Given space limitations, we focus in this paper mainly on one specific painting, entitled K., shown in Fig. 1 (left) where the focus on edge difference maps has been fruitful. But we also show a second example, entitled Secrets, shown in Fig. 8, where a focus on edge differences has yielded less results, mainly because the changes at the edge level are too numerous - hence we get too many possible centres of interest.

3   Step I. Finding the Original Image

Due to direct contacts with the artist, we have had access to several original sources for the Palazzo Grassi paintings, including the one for K. (see Fig. 1, right). But we also wondered whether, with the massive availability of images on the web and the sophistication of current image recognition technology, it was possible to find the original source image using *reverse image search* with the painting as a key.

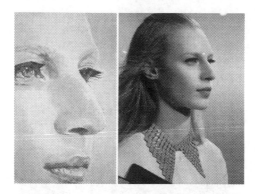

Fig. 1. Left: 'K.' by Luc Tuymans, 2017, oil on canvas. 135 × 80, 2 cm. Andrew Xue Collection, Singapore. Right: Source image as provided by the artist.

Interestingly, a reverse image web search with the painting K. did not deliver anything close to a possible source image for K., even though the source was also available on the web (see below). It appears that there are properties of artistic paintings which make the use of reverse image search algorithms difficult, whereas a human observer immediately recognizes that the painting on the left of Fig. 1 depicts the woman shown on the right. The issue of domain adaptation has become a recent hot topic in computer vision research but we have not applied these new methods yet [23].

On the other hand, once an original source image is available, reverse image search systems, like the one provided by Google or Bing, *are* able to locate this original and its variants, even if the provided original image is only a segment within a larger image or parts of the original image are not included. Thus using the original image in Fig. 1 (right), we found the actual context of the original image. It turned out to come from an advertising campaign by Dior (see Fig. 2), showing a clothing line designed by fashion designer Raf Simons and photographed by Willy Vanderperre, both alumni of the Antwerp art academy where Tuymans studied as well. The scene has been set up on the Normandy coast in France. Notice that in the advertisement, the top hair of K. is cut out which is not the case in the original image for K. provided by the painter.

Finding the original image of a painting is of interest from an art-history point of view and it provides important cues as to the factual and cultural meaning of the painting. This kind of fashion advertisement imagery - not necessarily this particular image - is familiar to everybody through magazines and posters and it reflects contemporary culture. Luc Tuymans expropriates the esthetic elements and the staging of the fashion models but at the same time removes completely the original context in order to create a timeless image.

4   Step II. Aligning the Painting and the Original

The next step in our methodology is to align the original image with the painting. This is a very non-trivial image processing problem. For this paper, we did a manual selection of a possible candidate image, cutting out a segment that left out as much as possible of the material that was not in the painting, because we found that the vision algorithms we tried do not work well when there was too much additional extra material in the source image.

Fig. 2. Image from the Dior Autumn-Winter 2015 campaign with clothes designed by Raf Simons and photography by Willy Vanderperre. The fashion model to the left, the basis of K., is Julia Nobis.

Given a good candidate, the alignment problem becomes similar to the so called *image registration task* [9] which is widely used in medical imaging, automated manufacturing, satellite navigation, and many other application fields for comparing or integrating data acquired from different sensors, at different times, or with different depth or viewpoints. Image registration algorithms fuse multimodal information or detect changes on such images. Given a set of two images, the one that will be transformed is called the *moving image*, and the one that is left unchanged, is called the *reference image*.

In the present investigation, we view the original image (the photograph) as the moving image and try to align it to the painting by progressively transforming the original image. The painting is therefore the reference image in image registration terminology. This is the perspective of the painter because the painter transforms the original image into a painting. Conversely, we can start from the painting, which now becomes the moving image, and try to align it to the original image, which now becomes the reference image, by transforming the painting to look similar to the photograph. This is in a sense the perspective from the viewer who sees the painting and then tries to align it with an image stored in his or her episodic memory. Both approaches yield interesting results, but in this paper we focus mainly on the painter's perspective only.

Image registration has been discussed intensely in the computer vision literature and many algorithms exist, primarily feature-based or intensity-based methods [9]. Feature-based methods aim to find a correspondence between image features such as interest points, lines, and contours, while intensity-based methods aim to align pixel patterns via correlation or similarity metrics. In this paper, we will rely only on the multi-modal intensity-based registration method, implemented using the Matlab Registration Estimator App with its default parameters.[1]

We also experimented with the feature-based approach trying to detect the candidate features on source and target images by various well-known algorithms, in particular, the *Maximally stable extremal region method* (MSER) [7] and the *Speeded up Robust Features Method* (SURF) [1]. However, we found that the output of the feature-based approaches performed poorly for the alignment task, possibly due to the significant gap between source and target images, as one is a photograph and the other a painting. Using features from these classical methods leads to the detection of too many low quality interest points to yield effective alignment (Fig. 3).

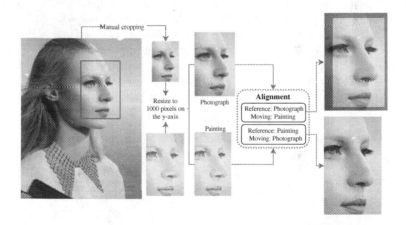

Fig. 3. Flow diagram for image alignment of K. The top show the 'viewer's perspective', using the painting as moving image and the photograph as reference image, and at the bottom, we show the 'painter's perspective' with the photography as moving image and the painting as reference image. To show the overlay, the painting is rendered using a purple color and the original photograph using green. (Color figure online)

We operationalized alignment using a best-first search algorithm, as used for example in [18]. The Mattes mutual information metric [14] is used to compute the similarity between source and target. It is shown in [14] that this metric leads to better alignment than the Mean Squares metric when the goal is to align

---

[1] https://www.mathworks.com/help/images/register-images-using-the-registration-estimator-app.html.

images from different modalities using rigid transformations, which is the case here. The algorithm searches for a set of transformation parameters that produce the best possible alignment result. Given a matrix of transformation parameters M, called the parent, a number of variations $M_1, \ldots M_n$, called the children, are generated, at first using aggressive perturbations. The perturbations include shape-preserving transformations like *rotation, translation, isotropic scaling*, and *reflection*. If a child M_i's parameters yield a better alignment, then it becomes the new parent on the next iteration. But if a parent still yields a better result, it remains as a parent and new children are computed with less aggressive changes to the parent's matrix.

5   Step III. Micro-transformations

Once we have adequately aligned the original image with the painting, it becomes possible to inquire about the micro-transformations that the painter has introduced and their function. These variations have happened for different visual aspects, e.g. color, contrast, figure orientation, contours, etc. and so we need to first isolate these aspects from the image. In the rest of this paper we only look at edges, which means that we investigate which additional edges or edge variations the painter has introduced, The flow diagram of this pipeline is illustrated in Fig. 4. We have experimented with two algorithms, a traditional edge detection method, namely the *Sobel Isotropic 3×3 gradient operator* (SOBEL), and a deep neural network known as the *Traditional Inspired Network* (TIN) recently introduced by Wibisono and Hang [22]. The SOBEL edge detection method has

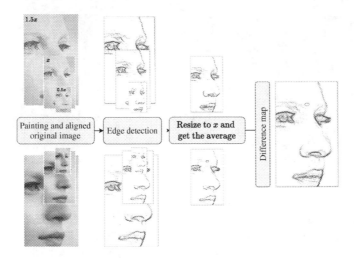

Fig. 4. Flow diagram for edge detection. It shows the edge maps for K. on top for the painting and below for the original image at different scales based on the TIN method. The difference map is shown with purple for the photograph, green for the painting and black when edges overlap. (Color figure online)

been a very popular and widely used algorithm in image processing since 1968 [16]. It is based on derivation of a simple and computationally efficient gradient operator. In order to calculate the approximations of derivatives for horizontal and vertical intensity changes, the gray-scaled input image is convolved with two 3×3 kernels as follows :

$$G_x = \begin{bmatrix} +1 & 0 & -1 \\ +2 & 0 & -2 \\ +1 & 0 & -1 \end{bmatrix} * I \quad G_y = \begin{bmatrix} +1 & +2 & +1 \\ 0 & 0 & 0 \\ -1 & -2 & -1 \end{bmatrix} * I$$

where I denotes the input image in grayscale, G_x and G_y are two images which at each point contain the vertical and horizontal derivative approximations. Then, the resulting gradient approximations are combined to have the gradient magnitude at each point in the image, using $G = \sqrt{G_x^2 + G_y^2}$. Subsequent images showing the results of the Sobel Method in this paper, display this gradient magnitude G.

Deep neural network frameworks have originally been designed for high-level computer vision tasks such as object recognition or scene understanding through semantic segmentation. Edge detection is a more local and simpler task so that a lightweight deep learning network can provide high quality edges with reduced computational complexity. This approach has been adopted by the *Traditional Method Inspired Network* (*TIN*) proposed very recently by Wibisono and Hang [22] with reported state of the art accuracy performances on the BSDS500 test set. The framework is composed of three modules, i.e., *Feature Extractor*, *Enrichment*, and *Summarizer*, which roughly correspond to gradient, low pass filter, and pixel connection in the traditional edge detection schemes. The pre-training of the TIN method was performed on three datasets of natural images BSDS500, In our experiment, we used the published code[2] by the authors and we used their pretrained model on the aforementioned datasets for the proposed architecture TIN2, since higher performances were reported by TIN2 compared to TIN1 in [22]. To make a fair comparative analysis between the SOBEL and TIN methods, we applied the same post-processing operation, namely *Non-Maximum Suppression* (NMS), to both edge-detection methods, i.e. we computed edge maps at different scales, $1.5x$, $1x$, $0.5x$, for both the origin and target, took the average of these maps, and resized the edge maps to the original image size, i.e., $x = 1000$. As mentioned in [22], this procedure provides better-located edges.

Finally, we compute the edge difference maps for further analysis. Figure 5 shows the outcome after thresholding in order to binarize the edge map so that the significant edges stand out more. Before such a thresholding operation, SOBEL had provided a more noisy edge detection map than TIN. However, after thresholding we observe that while some edges detected by TIN were preserved, some edges detected by the SOBEL method where removed. As TIN preserved better significant edges, we proceed for further analysis with the edges detected by the TIN method.

---

[2] https://github.com/jannctu/TIN.

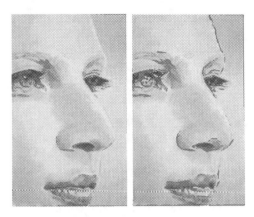

Fig. 5. Comparison of two edge detection methods, taking the painter's perspective (going from photograph to painting). The painting edges are in green and the photograph edges in purple. Left: the difference map for the SOBEL method. Right: the difference map for the TIN method. We see that the TIN method provides clearer edges showing the variations introduced by the painter in a clearer way. (Color figure online)

We now can compute centres of interest, being those areas on the painting for which there are significant differences between the two edge maps. The algorithm proceeds in three steps: [i] Compute first the bounding boxes around the thresholded edges *only* contained in the painting, so neither in the picture only nor in both. Only those edges are retained which form an area containing more than a points (pixels) with a perimeter containing more than p points. The bounding box is extended slightly (with an addition of c). [ii] Concate neighbors of bounding boxes by merging overlapping boxes from step [i] into larger boxes. [iii] Step [ii] is iterated until there are no overlapping bounding boxes. The different parameters a, p, and c allow us to tune these steps to get more or fewer centres of interest. Results are shown in Fig. 6. (i) shows the result of step [i] with $a = 100$, $p = 70$, and $c = 0.0023$. (ii) shows the result of step [i] projected on the painting. (iii) shows the result of applying step [ii] for two iterations at which point there are no more overlapping bounding boxes.

We see in Fig. 6, (iii) that the following centres are proposed: (a) the lips area at the bottom, specifically the right side of the lips ('right' from the perspective of the person being depicted), (b) the right eye and the area around it, specifically the region where the eyebrow reaches the top of the nose, the pupil and the line under the right eye, (c) the nose area with the nostril and the curve at the right wing of the nose, (d) the left eye, particularly the corner with the nose, and (e) the region above the left eye.

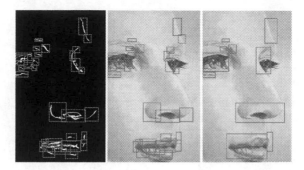

Fig. 6. Computing the centres of interest based on edge difference maps. (i) Aggregation of edge differences. (ii) Projection of aggregation on painting. (iii) Expansion of bounding boxes.

6   Step IV. Deconstructing Possible Meanings

Do these newly discovered centres of interest make any sense? A closer look at the original photograph and the painting shows that there is actually a subtle difference in facial expression between the photograph and the painting. This becomes clearer if we compare the centres of interest projected on the edge map of the painting (ii) and the photograph (iii) (see Fig. 7).

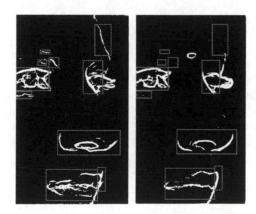

Fig. 7. Edge maps with centres of intrest (TIN method). (i) Projection on edge map of painting, (ii) Projection on edge map of original aligned photograph.

We see that on the painting, the facial expression of K. is more open and presents a weak smile, whereas on the photograph, the expression is more sturdy and closed. The more open facial expression is achieved by very subtle changes. The left corner of the lips in the painting is curled upward, the nostril more pronounced, the eye pupil bigger, the eyebrows showing a clearer V-shape, and the line under the left eye being more visible. These changes are subtle and unconscious to the viewer but they have an impact on the interpretation process, as they all point to a more open weakly smiling facial expression.

To see whether this interpretation has any validity. It is instructive to consider a 'gold standard' narrative about painting K. offered by Marc Donnadieu, chief curator of the Musée de l'Elysée in Lausanne and published in the guidebook of the La Pelle exhibition at the Palazzo Grassi in Venice: [6]

"The artist was inspired by advertising billboards he saw in Panama, which feature women's faces that have been smoothed out to the point of erasing their personality. As a filmmaker would do, he zoomed on this face so close that it is partially cut out and incomplete. By moving his 'paintbrush camera' so close he treats this female face as if it was an object, which is precisely the purpose of advertising, in particular when selling beauty products. This approach renders the face empty, almost dead, especially because it is not contextualized. But by zooming this way, the artist also highlights the gaze of this woman who has been so objectified that she doesn't even have a name, just a letter, K. And her gaze is very expressive, as if she tried to exist beyond the image and the commercial profit that is sought through her. She seems defiant, aware that she is exploited and ready to stand up as she looks far ahead, maybe towards a future where women will not be treated as objects. The treatment is smooth, flat, and the pastel colors highlight the contrast between the artificial aspect of advertising imagery and the humanity of all women. K's mouth is shut, but she smiles discreetly and her silence speaks volumes."

The painting may be inspired by billboards in Panama on beauty products, although we have seen that the direct inspiration are fashion models from an advertising campaign of Dior. Nevertheless the way women are represented is undoubtly similar. There is an *objectification* [8] of the human body, more concretely in this case of the human face. This objectification is present in the photography but even more so in the painting: The extreme focus on the face so that there is an almost complete elimination of the context, the use of pastel color, the flat treatment of the skin to smoothen out details that make natural faces alive, the choice of a letter K. for the title of the painting, instead of a real name. Marc Donnadieu mentions expressional meanings like: 'smile discreetly', 'defiant', 'expressive gaze' which confirm the subtle changes in lips, eyes, eyebrows and nose that the edge-based comparative methodology detected. This example therefore illustrates the idea that AI methods can act like a microscope that draws attention to interest regions and helps us see details that would otherwise remain unconscious.

7   A Second Case Study

We now show very briefly a second example from the 2019–2020 Palazzo Grassi solo exhibition by Luc Tuymans, a painting entitle Secrets. It depicts one of the main figures of the Nazi regime, Albert Speer, who has always denied any knowledge of the Holocaust atrocities. Figure 8 shows first the painting as well as the source image, which has been cropped from a larger image that shows Speer in full Nazi regalia. Figure 8 shows next the results of using the same alignment process as used for K., both for aligning the picture on the painting and the painting on the picture.

Fig. 8. From left to right: (i) painting, (ii) original photograph, (iii) alignment picture on painting (iv) aligning of painting on picture.

We see that the alignment algorithm works very well, even though this case is much more challenging as the face is slightly rotated, stretched along the y-axis and squeezed along the x-axis. Figure 9 shows the results of edge detection using the TIN method with the difference map projected on the photograph. Again the results are very satisfactory. Finally, Fig. 10 shows the same operations as in Fig. 6, now on the edge difference map of 'Secrets'.

Again we have to ask whether the regions identified through this process function as meaningful centres of interest. Unfortunately there are clearly too many regions to allow a meaningful analysis, mainly because there are a lot of changes that the artist has made to the original source image. As a consequence the merging of the bounding boxes results after several iterations into

Fig. 9. From left to right: (i) edges from painting, (ii) edges from aligned photograph, (iii) edge difference map painter's perspective.

Fig. 10. Computing the centres of interest based on edge difference maps. (i) Aggregation of edge differences. (ii) Projection of aggregation on painting. (iii) Expansion of bounding boxes.

one big bounding box encompassing almost the complete painting. Nevertheless the changes are all purposeful. They have to do with making the face more geometric, closed-off, inward-looking and in denial. We conjecture that other means of showing the centres of interest based on edge difference might give a more useful result and are currently researching them.

8   Conclusions

It is well known that painters never attempt to paint exactly a chosen image (or a real world scene) but transform it to achieve an artistic purpose - except in artistic movements where realism is in itself an artistic statement, like in hyper-realistic art. This paper reported on attempts to deconstruct algorithmically what transformations a contemporary painter carried out and discussed in how far paying attention to the regions identified by this process helps us in the construction of a narrative capturing the meanings invoked by a painting. AI algorithms are used here as microscopes that allow us to look in detail at transformations which are normally only experienced at a subconscious level.

This paper focused on edge differences only. In one case study (the painting entitled K.), the regions found through comparing edge differences indeed point to centres of interest that can be interpreted. In the second case study ('Secrets') alignment and edge detection worked well but useful conclusions in terms of centres of interest could not be reached. These examples show that the comparative method is only at its first beginning. There are other dimensions of transformation that must be studied in equal detail and color is the most likely candidate. More generally, a lot of hard, but certainly fascinating, work remains to see how far the type of analysis proposed here can help to recognize and label the objects in a painting, detect the general mood, the emotions being expressed by the depicted figures, and much more, all in the service of supporting narrative construction in viewers.

References

1. Bay, H., Ess, A., Tuytelaars, T., van Gool, L.: Speeded-up robust features. Comput. Vis. Image Underst. **110**, 346–359 (2008)
2. de Boer, V., et al.: Amsterdam museum linked open data. Semantic Web **4**(3), 237–243 (2013)
3. Cetinica, E., Lipica, T., Grgicb, S.: Fine-tuning convolutional neural networks for fine art classification. Expert Syst. Appl. **114**, 107–118 (2018)
4. Corenlis, B.: Image processing for art investigation. Electron. Lett. Comput. Vis. Image Anal. **14**(3), 13–15 (2015)
5. Dewey, R.: Hack the Experience. New Tools for Artists from Cognitive Science. Brainstorm Books, Punctum Books, Goleta Ca (2018)
6. Donnadieu, M.: La Pelle, exhibition guide. Palazzo Grassi, Venice (2019)
7. Donoser, M., Bishof, H.: Efficient maximally stable extremal region (MSER) tracking. In: Proceedings of the 2006 Conference on Computer Vision and Pattern recognition (CVPR). Computer Vision Foundation (2006)
8. Fredrickson, B., Roberts, T.A.: Objectification theory. Toward understanding women's lived experiences and mental health risks. Psychol. Women Q. **21**, 173–206 (1997)
9. Goshtasby, A.A.: 2-D and 3-D Image Registration: for Medical, Remote Sensing, and Industrial Applications. Wiley, New York (2005)
10. Kroner, A., Senden, M., Driessens, K., Goebel, R.: Contextual encoder-decoder network for visual saliency prediction. Neural Netw. **129**, 261–270 (2020)
11. Ledoux, J.: The Emotional Brain. Simon and Schuster, New york (1996)
12. Meyer-Hermann, E.: Catalogue Raisonné of Paintings by Luc Tuymans. David Zwirner Books, Yale University Press, New Haven (2019)
13. Panofsky, E.: Studies in Iconology. Humanistic Themes in the Art of the Renaissance, p. 1972. Oxford University Press, Oxford (1939)
14. Rahunathan, S., Stredney, D., Schmalbrock, P., Clymer, B.D.: Image registration using rigid registration and maximization of mutual information. In: 13th Annual Medicine Meets Virtual Reality (2005)
15. Semmo, A., Isenberg, T., Doellner, J.: Neural style transfer: a paradigm shift for image-based artistic rendering? In: Proceedings of the Symposium on Non-Photorealistic Animation and Rendering. ACM (2017)
16. Sobel, I., Feldman, G.: A 3×3 isotropic gradient operator for image processing. A talk at the Stanford Artificial Project, pp. 271–272 (1968)
17. Steels, L., Wahle, B.: Perceiving the focal point of a painting with AI. Case studies on works of Luc Tuymans. In: 12th International Conference on Agents and Artificial Intelligence. Scite Press, Setubal, Portugal (2020)
18. Styner, M., Brechbuhler, C., Szckely, G., Gerig, G.: Parametric estimate of intensity inhomogeneities applied to MRI. IEEE Trans. Med. Imaging **19**(3), 153–165 (2000)
19. Tuymans, L.: The Image Revisited. In Conversation with Boehm, G., Clark, T., and De Wolf, H. Ludion, Brussels (2018)
20. Loock, U., Aliaga, J.-V., Spector, N.: Luc Tuymans. Phaidon, London (1996)
21. Vilarroya, O., i Argemon, F.F. (eds): Social Brain Matters: Stances on the Neurobiology of Social Cognition. Brill, Amsterdam (2007)
22. Wibisono, K., Hang, H.M.: Traditional method inspired deep neural network for edge detection. In: IEEE International Conference on Image Processing (ICIP), pp. 678–682 (2020)
23. Wilson, G., Cook, D.J.: A survey of unsupervised deep domain adaptation. ACM Trans. Intell. Syst. Techn. (TIST) **11**(5), 1–46 (2020)

Attention-Based Multi-modal Emotion Recognition from Art

Tsegaye Misikir Tashu[1,2]($\boxtimes$) and Tomáš Horváth[1,3]

[1] Faculty of Informatics, Department of Data Science and Engineering, Telekom Innovation Laboratories, ELTE Eötvös Loránd University, Pázmány Péter sétány 1/C, Budapest 1117, Hungary
{misikir,tomas.horvath}@inf.elte.hu
[2] Kombolcha Institute of Technology College of Informatics, Wollo University, 208 Kombolcha, Ethiopia
[3] Faculty of Science Institute of Computer Science, Pavol Jozef Šafárik University in Košice, Jesenná 5, 040 01 Košice, Slovakia

Abstract. Emotions are very important in dealing with human decisions, interactions, and cognitive processes. Art is an imaginative human creation that should be appreciated, thought-provoking, and elicits an emotional response. The automatic recognition of emotions triggered by art is of considerable importance. It can be used to categorize artworks according to the emotions they evoke, recommend paintings that accentuate or balance a particular mood, and search for paintings of a particular style or genre that represent custom content in a custom state of impact. In this paper, we propose an attention-based multi-modal approach to emotion recognition that aims to use information from both the painting and title channels to achieve more accurate emotion recognition. Experimental results on the WikiArt emotion dataset showed the efficiency of the model we proposed and the usefulness of image and text modalities in emotion recognition.

Keywords: Emotion recognition · Emotion analysis · Multi-modal

1 Introduction

Art is an imaginative human creation, which should be appreciated, make people think, and evoke an emotional response [11]. Emotion is a psycho-physiological process that can be triggered by conscious and/or unconscious perception of objects and situations and is related to a variety of factors such as mood, temperament, personality, disposition, and motivation [20]. Emotions are very important in dealing with human decisions, in interaction, and in the cognitive process [18]. As technology advances and our understanding of emotions progresses, the need for automated systems for the recognition of emotions is growing [20].

Several types of research on the automatic analysis of works of art have been carried out, covering a wide range of tasks. These include the inferring of painting

© Springer Nature Switzerland AG 2021
A. Del Bimbo et al. (Eds.): ICPR 2020 Workshops, LNCS 12663, pp. 604–612, 2021.
https://doi.org/10.1007/978-3-030-68796-0_43

styles [8], the study of influences between artists and art movements [22], the distinction between authentic drawings and imitations, the automatic generation of artworks [19], and the evaluation of evoked emotions [14,26]. There have been several attempts to develop approaches to the analysis of people's emotional experience in reaction to artworks [14,26]. Most of these studies use computer vision and machine learning approaches to categorize artworks emotionally [14,26] and to identify the parts of the paintings that are responsible for evoking certain emotions [23].

Recently, the performance of automatic emotion recognition has continuously improved thanks to the advancement of computer vision processing and natural language processing methods. However, due to the abstract concept and the many ways to express emotions, automatic emotion recognition is still a difficult task. The automatic recognition of emotions caused by art is of considerable importance since it can be used to categorize art paintings according to the emotions they evoke, recommend paintings that accentuate or balance a particular mood, and search for paintings of a particular style or genre that represent custom content in a user-defined state of effect [11]. In this paper, we propose an attention-based multi-modal emotion recognition approach that aims to use information from both the painting and title channels to achieve a more robust and accurate recognition.

2   Related Work

In this section, we will give a short overview of previous works on uni-modal and multi-modal emotion recognition, as well as emotion recognition in Art Paintings.

2.1   Modalities in Emotion Recognition

The initial attempts to recognize human emotions were mostly unimodal. The most frequently studied modality was facial expressions [5], speech or voice expressions [16], body gestures [12], and physiological signals such as respiratory and cardiac signals [7]. Multi-modal emotion recognition was investigated using classifiers such as Support Vector Machines (SVM), and linear and logistic regression [2,17]. With the development of larger data sets, deep learning architectures were developed and explored [6,10,13,25].

2.2   Emotion Recognition from Art

Yanulevskaya et al. [23] proposed an approach to categorize emotions from art paintings based on the aggregation of local image statistics and SVM. Machajdik et al. [9] introduced a unified framework for classifying artworks by combining low-level visual characteristics with high-level concepts from psychology and art theory. In the paper [24], a "bag-of-visual-words" model combined with SVM was introduced also by Yanulevskaya et al. [24] to classify abstract paintings into positive or negative emotions. Sartori et al. [15] introduced a common learning framework for recognizing emotions in abstract paintings that integrates both visual and textual information.

Due to several reasons, most of the works in emotion recognition from art paintings are uni-modal. Using information from different modalities might boost model accuracy in emotion recognition. In this work, we propose an attention-based multi-modal emotion recognition approach that aims to use information from both the painting and title channels to achieve a more robust and accurate recognition.

2.3   Proposed Multi-modal Fusion Model

Here, text and image are treated as two modalities. The weighted modality fusion technique is used to make full use of the two modalities. In the following paragraph and subsections both text vectors and image vectors will be defined the weighted fusion technique briefly introduced.

For the imaging modality, the pre-trained and fine-tuned ResNet [4] model is used to obtain 14×14 regional vectors of the art image defined as the raw image vectors averaged to get the image vector. Bidirectional Gated Recurrent Unit (Bi-GRU) is utilized to obtain the text vectors. The raw text vectors are the concatenated forward and backward hidden states for each time step of the Bi-GRU, while the text feature vector is the average of the above raw vectors.

The refined vectors of two modalities are combined into one vector with a weighted average instead of simple concatenation in the process of modality fusion. Lastly, the fused vector is pumped into a two-layer fully-connected neural network to obtain a classification result. More details of our model are provided below.

2.4   Image Feature Representation

The ResNet-50 [4] model is used to obtain representations of Art images. The last fully-connected (FC) layer of the pre-trained model is chopped and replaced with a new one for the sake of model fine-tuning. Following the work of [1,21], an input image I is re-sized to 448×448 and divided into 14×14 regions. Each region $I_i (i = 1, 2, \ldots, 196)$ is then sent through the ResNet model to obtain a regional feature representation, a.k.a. a raw image vector. The final image feature vector (V) is obtained by the average of all regional image vectors.

$$V = \frac{\sum_{i=1}^{N_r} ResNet(I_i)}{N_r} \tag{1}$$

where $ResNet(I_i)$ is the row image vector extracted via ResNet, N_r (set to 196 in this work) is the number of regions as in [21]. V is the average of all regional image vectors.

2.5   Text Feature Representation

The sequence of word embeddings learned using the embedding layer is passed to a Bi-GRU network layer. The gated recurrent unit (GRU) was recently introduced as an alternative to the LSTM to make each recurrent unit to adaptively capture dependencies of different time scales [3]. Similarly to the LSTM unit, the GRU has gating units that modulate the flow of information inside the unit, however, without having a separate memory cell. The updates performed at each time step $t \in \{1, ..., T\}$ in a GRU are as follows:

$$Z_t = sigmoid(W_z X_t + U_z h_{t-1}) \tag{2}$$

$$r_t = sigmoid(W_r X_t + U_r h_{t-1}) \tag{3}$$

$$\hat{h}_t = tanh(W_h X_t + U_h(r_t \odot h_{t-1})) \tag{4}$$

$$h_t = (1 - Z_t) \odot h_{t-1} + Z_t \odot \hat{h}_t \tag{5}$$

where $W_z, W_r, W_h, U_r, U_z, U_h, U_o$ are the weight matrices, $\odot$ is an element-wise multiplication. The activation h_t at time t is a linear interpolation between the previous activation h_{t-1} and the candidate activation $\hat{h}_t$. An update gate Z_t decides how much the unit updates its activation or content. The reset gate (r_t) is used to control access to the previous state h_{t-1} and compute a proposed update $\hat{h}_t$. When off (r_t close to 0), the reset gate effectively makes the unit act as if it is reading the first symbol of an input sequence, allowing it to forget the previously computed state. The final text feature vector A is the arithmetic average of hidden states in each time step.

$$A = \frac{\sum_{i=1}^{L} h_t}{L} \tag{6}$$

2.6   Attention Layer

Similar to [1,21], the image and title are connected by calculating the similarity between image and title features at all pairs of image-locations and title-locations. Specifically, given an image feature map V and the title representation A, the affinity matrix C is calculated as

$$C = tanh(A^T W_b V) \tag{7}$$

Once the affinity matrix is computed, it can be used as a feature to learn to predict the image and title attentions as follows:

$$H^V = tanh(W_v V + (W_A A)C)$$
$$a^V = softmax(w_{hv}^T H^v) \tag{8}$$

$$H^A = tanh(W_A A + (W_v V)C)$$
$$a^A = softmax(w_{hA}^T H^A) \tag{9}$$

where W_v, W_A, w_{hv}, w_{hA} are the weight parameters. a^v and a^A are the attention probabilities of each image region v_n and word in title a_t. The affinity matrix C transforms title attention space to image attention space (vice versa for C^T). Based on the above attention weights, the image and title attention vectors are calculated as the weighted sum of the image features and title features, i.e.,

$$\hat{V} = \sum_{n=1}^{N} a_n^v V_n$$
$$\hat{A} = \sum_{n=1}^{T} a_t^A A_t \tag{10}$$

2.7   Classification Layer

A two-layer fully-connected neural network is used as the classification layer. The activation function of the hidden layer and the output layer are Relu and Softmax functions, respectively. The loss function used is the categorical cross-entropy.

3   Experiment and Results

3.1   Dataset

Mohammad and Kiritchenko [11] created the WikiArt Emotions Dataset which includes emotion annotations for more than 4000 pieces of art from four western styles (Modern Art, Post-Renaissance Art, Renaissance Art and Contemporary Art) and 22 style categories. The art is annotated via crowd-sourcing for one or more of twenty emotion categories. The final result of closely-related emotion sets were arranged in three sets, such that "positive", "negative" and "mixed or other", as shown in Table 1.

3.2   Training Details

The pre-trained ResNet model available within Keras is used for image and the Glove word embedding for text was used to extract row feature vectors. Parameters of the pre-trained ResNet model and Parameters of word embeddings are fixed during training. Adam optimizer was used to optimize the loss function. The best performing hyper-parameters are listed in Table 2. 70% of the data is used as a training set, 10% as the validation set, and 20% as the test set.

3.3   Baseline

– Bi-LSTM (Text Only): Bi-LSTM is one of the most popular methods for addressing many text classification problems. It leverages a bidirectional LSTM network for learning text representations and then uses a classification layer to make a prediction.

Table 1. Main characteristics of the dataset used in the experiment.

Polarity	Emotion category	Instances
Positive	Gratitude, happiness, humility,love, optimism, trust	2578
Negative	Anger, arrogance, disgust, fear, pessimism, regret, sadness, shame	838
Other or Mixed	Agreeableness, anticipation, disagreeableness, surprise, shyness, neutral	689

Table 2. The best performing hyper-parameters used for the neural networks determined by using grid search.

Hyper-parameters	Values
ResNet FC size	512
Batch size	32
Number of BGRU hidden units	128
Dropout rate	0.4
Number of epochs	40
Learning rate	0.001
Word embedding dimensions	50

– CNN (Image Only): CNN with six hidden layers was implemented. The first two convolutional layers contain 32 kernels of size 3 × 3 and the second two convolutional layers have 64 kernels of size 3 × 3. The second and fourth convolutional layers are interleaved with max-pooling layers of dimension 2×2 with a dropout of 0.3. Then a fully-connected layer with 256 neurons and a dropout of 0.4 is followed.

3.4   Results

The proposed method was compared with the two baseline methods based on (1) 2D-CNN network for image emotion recognition, (2) Bi-LSTM network for text emotion recognition, respectively. As shown in Table 3, the proposed method improves the baseline uni-modal methods employing a single type of features and achieves an emotion classification accuracy of 74.10% based on the WikiArt emotion dataset.

Compared with the text-based uni-modal method, the presented approach wins by 8.3% more gains and 5.8% more gains as compared to the uni-modal image-based network. The significant improvement validates the importance of extracting multi-modal information in recognizing and analyzing human emotion. For comparison on multi-modal methods, the proposed approach outperforms the direct concatenation and the so-called without concatenation approaches showing the advantage of weighted concatenation and the importance of retaining the similarity between image and text modalities. The proposed method outperforms the baseline models in terms of classification accuracy which means the use of pre-trained models with attention network is reasonable. The experimental result demonstrates the effectiveness of the proposed method in the emotion classification task.

Table 3. Performance on test set in terms of the accuracy on the three polarities.

Model	Channel	Accuracy	Loss
CNN	Image	0.683	0.663
Bi-LSTM	Title	0.658	0.810
ResNet+GRU without attention	Image, Title	0.713	0.710
ResNet+GRU with attention	Image, Title	0.741	0.130

4   Conclusion

In this paper, we propose an attention-based fusion model to fully exploit two modalities (images and text) to address the challenging multi-modal task of emotion recognition from art paintings. The Experimental results on the WikiArt dataset showed the effectiveness of the proposed model and the usefulness of the two modalities. In future work, we will include other modalities, such as image attributes in the emotion recognition task, and will also investigate other better approaches that are more robust and accurate in emotion recognition.

Acknowledgements. This research is supported by the ÚNKP-20-4 New National Excellence Program of the Ministry for Innovation and Technology from the source of the National Research, Development and Innovation Fund. Supported by Telekom Innovation Laboratories (T-Labs), the Research and Development unit of Deutsche Telekom.

References

1. Cai, Y., Cai, H., Wan, X.: Multi-modal sarcasm detection in Twitter with hierarchical fusion model. In: Association for Computational Linguistics, Florence, Italy, pp. 2506–2515, July 2019. https://doi.org/10.18653/v1/P19-1239
2. Castellano, G., Kessous, L., Caridakis, G.: Emotion recognition through multiple modalities: face, body gesture, speech. In: Peter, C., Beale, R. (eds.) Affect and Emotion in Human-Computer Interaction. LNCS, vol. 4868, pp. 92–103. Springer, Heidelberg (2008). https://doi.org/10.1007/978-3-540-85099-1_8
3. Chung, J., Gülçehre, Ç., Cho, K., Bengio, Y.: Empirical evaluation of gated recurrent neural networks on sequence modeling. CoRR abs/1412.3555 (2014)
4. He, K., Zhang, X., Ren, S., Sun, J.: Deep residual learning for image recognition. In: 2016 IEEE Conference on Computer Vision and Pattern Recognition (CVPR), pp. 770–778 (2016)

5. Khalfallah, J., Slama, J.B.H.: Facial expression recognition for intelligent tutoring systems in remote laboratories platform. Procedia Comput. Sci. **73**, 274–281 (2015). International Conference on Advanced Wireless Information and Communication Technologies (AWICT 2015)
6. Kim, Y., Lee, H., Provost, E.M.: Deep learning for robust feature generation in audiovisual emotion recognition. In: 2013 IEEE International Conference on Acoustics, Speech and Signal Processing, pp. 3687–3691 (2013)
7. Knapp, R.B., Kim, J., André, E.: Physiological signals and their use in augmenting emotion recognition for human-machine interaction. In: Cowie, R., Pelachaud, C., Petta, P. (eds.) Emotion-Oriented Systems. Cognitive Technologies, pp. 133–159. Springer, Heidelberg (2011). https://doi.org/10.1007/978-3-642-15184-2-9
8. Liu, G., et al.: Inferring Painting Style with Multi-task Dictionary Learning, pp. 2162–2168. AAAI Press (2015)
9. Machajdik, J., Hanbury, A.: Affective image classification using features inspired by psychology and art theory. In: Association for Computing Machinery, New York, NY, USA, pp 83–92 (2010). https://doi.org/10.1145/1873951.1873965
10. Majumder, N., Hazarika, D., Gelbukh, A., Cambria, E., Poria, S.: Multimodal sentiment analysis using hierarchical fusion with context modeling. Knowl.-Based Syst. **161**, 124–133 (2018)
11. Mohammad, S., Kiritchenko, S.: WikiArt emotions: an annotated dataset of emotions evoked by art. In: Proceedings of the Eleventh International Conference on Language Resources and Evaluation (LREC 2018), European Language Resources Association (ELRA), Miyazaki, Japan, May 2018
12. Navarretta, C.: Individuality in Communicative Bodily Behaviours, pp. 417–423, January 2012. https://doi.org/10.1007/978-3-642-34584-537
13. Ren, M., Nie, W., Liu, A., Su, Y.: Multi-modal correlated network for emotion recognition in speech. Vis. Inform. **3**(3), 150–155 (2019)
14. Sartori, A., Culibrk, D., Yan, Y., Sebe, N.: Who's afraid of ITTEN: using the art theory of color combination to analyze emotions in abstract paintings. In: MM 2015, Association for Computing Machinery, New York, NY, USA, pp. 311–320 (2015). https://doi.org/10.1145/2733373.2806250
15. Sartori, A., Yan, Y., Özbal, G., Salah, A.A.A., Salah, A.A., Sebe, N.: Looking at Mondrian's Victory Boogie-woogie: What Do I Feel? pp. 2503–2509. AAAI Press (2015)
16. Scherer, K., Johnstone, T., Klasmeyer, G.: Handbook of Affective Sciences - Vocal expression of emotion, pp. 433–456, January 2003
17. Sikka, K., Dykstra, K., Sathyanarayana, S., Littlewort, G., Bartlett, M.: Multiple kernel learning for emotion recognition in the wild. In: Association for Computing Machinery, New York, NY, USA, pp. 517–524 (2013). https://doi.org/10.1145/2522848.2531741
18. Sreeshakthy, M., Preethi, J.: Classification of human emotion from deap EEG signal using hybrid improved neural networks with cuckoo search. BRAIN Broad Res. Artif. Intell. Neurosci. **6**(3–4), 60–73 (2016)
19. Szegedy, C., et al.: Going deeper with convolutions. In: 2015 IEEE Conference on Computer Vision and Pattern Recognition (CVPR), pp. 1–9 (2015)
20. Tripathi, S., Beigi, H.S.M.: Multi-modal emotion recognition on IEMOCAP dataset using deep learning. CoRR abs/1804.05788 (2018)
21. Wang, P., Wu, Q., Shen, C., van den Hengel, A.: The VQA-machine: learning how to use existing vision algorithms to answer new questions. In: 2017 IEEE Conference on Computer Vision and Pattern Recognition (CVPR), pp. 3909–3918 (2017)

22. Wang, Y., Takatsuka, M.: SOM based artistic styles visualization. In: 2013 IEEE International Conference on Multimedia and Expo (ICME), pp. 1–6 (2013)
23. Yanulevskaya, V., van Gemert, J.C., Roth, K., Herbold, A.K., Sebe, N., Geusebroek, J.M.: Emotional valence categorization using holistic image features. In: 2008 15th IEEE International Conference on Image Processing, pp. 101–104 (2008)
24. Yanulevskaya, V., et al.: In the eye of the beholder: employing statistical analysis and eye tracking for analyzing abstract paintings. In: Association for Computing Machinery, New York, NY, USA, pp. 349–358 (2012). https://doi.org/10.1145/2393347.2393399
25. Yoon, S., Byun, S., Dey, S., Jung, K.: Speech emotion recognition using multi-hop attention mechanism. In: ICASSP 2019–2019 IEEE International Conference on Acoustics, Speech and Signal Processing (ICASSP), pp. 2822–2826 (2019)
26. Zhao, S., Gao, Y., Jiang, X., Yao, H., Chua, T.S., Sun, X.: Exploring principles-of-art features for image emotion recognition. In: Association for Computing Machinery, New York, NY, USA, pp. 47–56 (2014). https://doi.org/10.1145/2647868.2654930

Machines Learning for Mixed Reality
The Milan Cathedral from Survey to Holograms

Simone Teruggi$^{(\boxtimes)}$ (ID) and Francesco Fassi (ID)

3DSurveyGroup-ABCLab-Politecnico di Milano, Via Ponzio 31, 20133 Milan, Italy
{simone.teruggi,francesco.fassi}@polimi.it

Abstract. In recent years, a complete 3D mapping of the Cultural Heritage (CH) has become fundamental before every other action could follow. Different survey techniques outputs could be combined in a 3D point cloud, completely describing the geometry of even the most complex object. These data very rich in metric quality can be used to extract 2D technical elaborations and advanced 3D representations to support conservation interventions and maintenance planning.

The case of Milan Cathedral is outstanding. In the last 12 years, a multi-technique omni-comprehensive survey has been carried out to extract the technical representations that are used by the Veneranda Fabbrica (VF) del Duomo di Milano to plan its maintenance and conservation activities.

Nevertheless, point cloud data lack structured information such as semantics and hierarchy among parts, fundamentals for 3D model interaction and database (DB) retrieval. In this context, the introduction of point cloud classification methods could improve data usage, model definition and analysis.

In this paper, a Multi-level Multi-resolution (MLMR) classification approach is presented and tested on the large dataset of Milan Cathedral. The 3D point model, so structured, for the first time, is used directly in a Mixed Reality (MR) environment to develop an application that could benefit professional works, allowing to use 3D survey data on-site, supporting VF activities.

Keywords: Machine Learning · Classification · Cultural heritage · Mixed reality · HoloLens2 · Point cloud

1 Introduction

The work here presented is a further step of the research activity[1] for years conducted in collaboration with the "VF del Duomo di Milano[2]" for the digitalization of the Cathedral. This article wants to describe the latest developments of the work both concerning the survey operations that led to the acquisition of a complete and highly resolute point cloud of the entire Cathedral, and about its future and futuristic use in VR/AR/MR systems,

---

[1] Conducted by Politecnico di Milano, ABC department, Group 3Dsurvey.

[2] *"The "Veneranda Fabbrica del Duomo di Milano" is an ecclesiastical body endowed with legal personality by ancient statutory determination with the purpose of worship and religion, which excludes all profit-making activities. Its earliest regulations were issued on 16 October 1387 at the behest of Gian Galeazzo Visconti."* [1]

© Springer Nature Switzerland AG 2021
A. Del Bimbo et al. (Eds.): ICPR 2020 Workshops, LNCS 12663, pp. 613–627, 2021.
https://doi.org/10.1007/978-3-030-68796-0_44

and the process of classification of the point cloud of the Cathedral functional for this purpose.

In particular, the article aims to show how the technological advancement in the field of surveying in the last 12 years has allowed the complete digitization of a vast and complex building at very high resolution, providing millimetric detail, and how this data can be effectively used in the maintenance processes without post-elaboration but in an efficient way.

The heart of the research is addressing the issues of point cloud classification as an indispensable step to be truly functional in their use. Assigning to the point cloud models a semantic meaning allows to segment them in their distinctive elements, to be able to visualize and use them individually in different groups or sets, according to the needs, and above all, to be able to use them within MR systems as a complete and accurate 3D.

The first part of the article presents the survey operations, and the obtained point cloud briefly. The second part describes the results obtained in the classification process, and finally, in the third part, are presented the very first developments of a MR system that is being implemented ad hoc to support site activities.

2   Milan Cathedral Survey. A Brief Overview

The survey of the Milan Cathedral has now been underway for 12 years and is now almost complete. The history of the survey of the Cathedral can be considered the best example of the evolution not only of measurements techniques, from 2008 to the present day but also of the way of using the survey data in maintenance activities and of the slow and still ongoing natural transition from a two-dimensional to a purely three-dimensional way of thinking and operating in CH field.

It can be divided into two phases. The first one (2008 to 2015) is the one that allowed the survey and modelling of the Main Spire and other parts of the Cathedral following, or better anticipating, the site activities. The second phase, still being completed (2015–2020) is the survey of the entire Cathedral.

The objective of the first phase was to produce all the documents necessary to support construction site activities. By documents, we mean the classical two-dimensional representations typical of the architecture generally used for the design and the realization of the interventions. It was immediately clear from the beginning that classical survey methods, therefore, at the time, the use of total-stations for the direct measurement of the features strictly necessary to those representations, was inadequate for the VF's projects. It was impossible to identify a priori a pre-established number of section plans and their exact positions; the needs of the site imposed the exigency to have that type of metric information everywhere and immediately available at the time of need. Because of the complex, distinctive and varied characteristics of the architectures, a small number of plans or sections in a predefined theoretical position were not enough to plan the restorations works accurately. The idea was to create a three-dimensional model accurate enough to allow the manual or semi-automatic extraction of 2D views at a max scale of 1:50, thus guaranteeing centimetric detail and measurement tolerance. In this way, it was possible to extract the necessary representations in a concise space of time in functions of the daily demands of the construction site.

The survey operation was conducted mainly with digital close-range photogramme-try, firstly modelling the structure with stereo-plotting techniques and then completing the modelling phase with manual measurements, triangulation scanners and the first attempts of Structure From Motion (SFM) techniques [2].

The final product of this activity was a complete 3D NURBS model of all the central spire (and other parts of Milan Cathedral). It was divided into all the marble ashlars that make up the structures: every single ashlar is a closed three-dimensional model.

The work was structured in this way to meet the VF's needs allowing to have a graphic, metric, accurate and detailed support in every point of the structure under exam-ination. At that time, the photogrammetric elaboration techniques, the impossibility of using the laser scanner on marble, and a genuinely complex reality-based modelling pro-cess made the work a real research challenge. On the other side, the project allowed us to understand the importance of using 3D within the maintenance practices of monumental architecture. From the beginning, it was clear that 3D would not only be a technical and technological game, but it could be instrumental within the more than consolidated modus operandi of the VF. It allowed to have a scalable overview of the entire structure, to select and represent different views and objects from time to time, to calculate sur-faces and volumes of complex and massive structures speeding up metric calculations, to design scaffolding of the different spire yards.

At the end of this phase, it was clear that the significant effort to build a colossal reality-based 3D model it had to be translated in something useful not only within the technical operation but which could also be used by other operators. Restorers, historians, archivists, installers, decision-makers could benefit from a complete, detailed and even accurate representative product. The 3D model could also serve as a basis for a conditional information system that the staff of the Veneranda Fabbrica could use to catalogue, collect, store, and georeference information speeding up the communication between the operators, facilitating the maintenance of the data and their updating in real-time. These were the main objectives that led to the development of a web-based information platform, the WEBBIM3D [3]. It was created to visualize the complete 3D model or parts of it and to consult and insert information and images related to the displayed items [4]. The system could also be used on the construction site and can certainly be a prime example of a Building Information Modeling (BIM) web platform for sharing information [5].

Noble objectives, strong motivation, and a successful result, but the way to get to have such complete and accurate 3D, was long, arduous, and, in the end, uneconomical. For this reason, the second phase of the survey work on the Cathedral of Milan takes an entirely different path. The idea of modelling every part of the Cathedral prefers to be abandoned, with the idea to build a complete, resolute, and accurate 3D data point cloud model. This approach is possible by taking advantage of developments in surveying techniques, especially SFM techniques and 3D point clouds visualization. The final idea is to use surveying products directly in the VF activities without going through the modelling phase.

Pursuing this path has meant surveying the entire Cathedral in all its parts and producing a three-dimensional model in the form of a cloud of points of the entire building.

The purposes and the final usage scopes are the same that also characterized the first phase of research. So, the final point cloud should have a very high resolution to extract metric information at centimetre accuracy; it should be uniform both in terms of the type of resolution and accuracy.

The survey was conducted in circa three years using scanner techniques for the interiors and close-range photogrammetry for the exteriors. The internal scan was obtained using the C10 scanner for the noble internal areas of the Cathedral, and Leica Geosystems HDS7000 for the service spaces, internal site areas, cellars, storage, and religious service areas. The new Leica Geosystems RTC360 was also tested to scan problematic internal areas as narrow passages and staircases.

The internal main noble spaces were acquired with special care positioning the instrument both from the ground and from one or two upper levels in the function of the height of the nave, using a lifting platform. This approach was necessary to avoid shadow areas created by the gigantic capitals and to guarantee a uniform resolution of 5 mm everywhere on the high walls, pillars, and vaults [6].

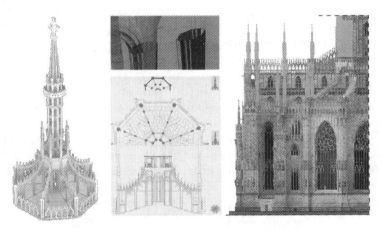

Fig. 1. Survey elaboration product, from left to right: 3D NURBS model of the Main Spire, 2D technical drawings, high-resolution orthophoto of the Apse.

Only for the noble internal spaces, 246 scans were collected for a total of 2.1 billion points. Totally 1283 scans were necessary to complete the scanner survey giving a considerable point cloud of circa 59 billion points. The external facades, roofs and spires were surveyed using close-range photogrammetry because more flexible in open spaces respect to the scanner technique allowing a multiscale acquisition at a different height from terrain level to 60 m high. The product was here a metric coloured point cloud of all the external parts of circa 1.2 billion of points and high-resolution orthoimages of the facades (Fig. 1) [7].

Some external parts that cannot be reached by the photogrammetric survey, as passages, ramps and little staircases that connected different roofs levels, were acquired using Leica RTC360 and testing different alternative techniques [8].

The final point cloud at the end is characterized by circa 60 billion points with a uniform resolution of 5mm mainly divided in 3 big separated but geofenced point clouds corresponding to the exteriors, the interiors, and the underground spaces.

Firstly, the point cloud was used to completely renovating the technical representative park of the VF producing classic plans and sections in sufficient number to have a global and complete representation of the Cathedral. The operation of extracting this vector information from the top clouds is an entirely manual process. The second step was to assign to the cloud the right to be defined as a 3D model: segmenting it in its constituent elements and assigning semantic meaning to every single point. This process has been obtained classifying the cloud of points with a method based on a Multi-layer Multi-resolution (MLMR) approach combined with a Machine Learning (ML) algorithm [9].

3 Multi-level Multi-resolution Classification

The semantic segmentation of the 3D dataset allows the direct use of the point cloud in the project decision-making process, and it is preparatory to 3D model reconstruction (Computer Aided System (CAD) or BIM) and classical 2D elaborations. Furthermore, the semantically segmented model can be used directly to build a MR application. It allows avoiding a time consuming and difficult modelling phase that brings a lowering in detail of the original survey data.

In the field of Cultural Heritage, the 3D classification of point cloud data has been experimented in different applications as support to scan-to-BIM processes [10–12], for monitoring and restoration activities [13, 14], to support maintenance intervention planning [15–17] and for damage detection [18, 19]. In most cases, it is generally presented as a manual operation of subdivision of the datasets. In case of a large dataset, it is a laborious and expensive operation, that moreover brings to a high degree of subjectivity, non-repeatability, and non-reproducibility of the process, which could be as time-consuming as the 3D modelling phase itself.

In recent years, significant progress has been made in automatic classification processes using Artificial Intelligence as ML and Deep Learning (DL) methods, which, on the contrary, are objective, replicable and repeatable.

First, the two methods are different both, in terms of the type of approach to the data, and in terms of the initial requests to be able to conduct the classification. Standard supervised ML techniques require the algorithms to take as input some manually annotated parts of the point cloud, together with the so-called "features", geometric or radiometric attributes selected by the operator to facilitate learning and the distinction of the classes sought. On the other hand, DL strategies provide for the automatic generation of features, which they learn thanks to the use of vast amounts of annotated input data not necessarily belonging to the case in question. This is precisely the critical aspect of using this method: it is not easy to have a sufficiently large amount of pre-annotated 3D point cloud data of architectural objects from the literature. This is both because the point cloud data is a relatively new type of data, not yet universally used, and because architectural objects, especially those in the CH world and especially considering their three-dimensional representation, are incredibly complex, of varied forms, and therefore not standardizable. One could assume that each element is unique.

To address the lack of architectural data useful for training algorithms, a collection (ArCH) of annotated architectural point clouds was recently released [20]. To facilitate the annotation process Murtiyoso and Grussenmeyer [21] have developed a series of mathematical functions through which it is possible to isolate some specific architectural classes within the point cloud, such as columns and beams.

In the DL area, Pierdicca et al. [22], trained a Dynamic Graph Convolutional Neural Network (DGCNN) supported by significant features (colours and normals) on the ArCH dataset. The resulting model was then tested in two different ways: on a partially tagged dataset and an unseen scene, providing promising results.

Nowadays, in the field of CH, the ML approach seems to be the winning one because the method can be scaled and parameterized on the specific case study. Grilli et al. [23] proposed a supervised ML approach that transfers classification information from 2D textures to 3D models. The same authors applied supervised training directly on the point clouds, training a Random Forest (RF) classifier with geometric features explicitly designed for architecture [24, 25].

A comparison paper on the classification of architectural point clouds using ML or DL techniques was also recently published [26]. From the article, it emerged that the results obtained with ML and DL are comparable in terms of accuracy, although the times used in the ML are still far lower than in the DL methods.

Considering the complexity and peculiarity of Milan's Cathedral dataset, it was decided to take as a starting point the ML approach proposed by Grilli and Remondino [25], as it is easily adaptable to new architectural classes during the algorithm training.

3.1 Methodology

The complexity of the Milan Cathedral forces to solve two main issues: the size of the data that makes the calculation process challenging in computational terms. A subsampling of the point cloud could help manage the high number of points but would lower the level of detail of the original dataset. A large number of semantic classes to be identified at the same time quickly leads to classification errors: some initial experiments have shown that the higher the number of classes, the lower the accuracy of the classification [9].

Considering the problems mentioned above and the necessity to produce a segmented dataset for visualization in an MR application, it was considered appropriate to implement the single-step methodology presented by Grilli et al. [25], dividing the classification process into several stages following an MLMR approach. In the proposed methods, each element can be classified in an increasingly way, based on the resolution of the point cloud used at the corresponding level, and then interpolated to a higher resolution version. The process is iterative, and the last level of classification will correspond to the full resolution point cloud. Furthermore, the sub-sampling of the point cloud will depend on both the complexity of the object to be classified and the elements to be recognized [9]. Following the logical subdivision of the Milan's Cathedral dataset on four levels [5], the macro-categories of objects (the architectural macro-elements) allow a lower resolution, while the higher resolution is used at object level for more detailed elements (Fig. 2).

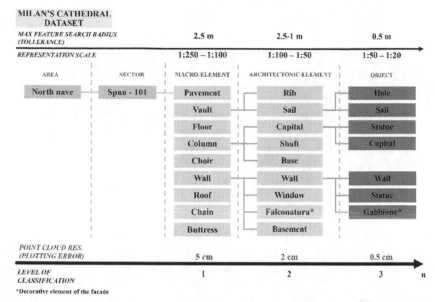

Fig. 2. Milan's Cathedral dataset subdivision with semantic classes corresponding to each classification level. The diagram has the purpose of providing indications in terms of the geometric resolution of the point cloud and geometric features used in each phase of the classification. The parameters (resolution and radii of the features) may vary case by case, depending on the characteristics and dimensions of the objects. However, it can be noted that they correspond to the smallest detail that can be represented at a given scale of representation and its metric tolerance, in a logic of representation at an increasing level of detail.

3.2 Classification

The geometric features selected to train the ML model to the automatic recognition of architectural elements are the so-called "covariance features" [27], which allow to highlight the local geometric characteristics of the 3D data. In this way, the local behaviours of the cloud are highlighted such as "linearity", "planarity" and "sphericity" or even the "surface variation" and "anisotropy". The choice of the right geometric features and the radius around the point on which to calculate them is fundamental for the purpose of identifying the architectural elements [24].

In addition to the selection of geometric features, some parts of each dataset, at each classification level, must be manually annotated to train the Random Forest algorithm [28]. Figure 3a shows the training sets used at the first classification level (resolution 5 cm) of the Milan Cathedral. The dataset is composed by 30 million points, the training sample is made up of about 2.5 million "labelled points" for the external surfaces and about 2.6 million "labelled points" for the internal spaces.

The performance of the classification has been assessed using traditional ML metrics (Precision, Recall and F1 score) [29]. These metrics are obtained from the direct comparison between automatic prediction and manual annotation of the same portion of the cloud. Correctly predicted values as well as erroneous ones, are taken into consideration.

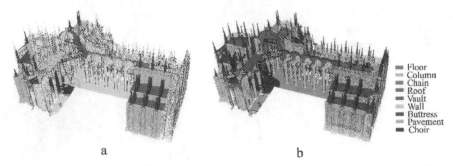

▪	Floor
▪	Column
▪	Chain
▪	Roof
▪	Vault
▪	Wall
▪	Buttress
▪	Pavement
▪	Choir

a   b

Fig. 3. Classification level 1, on the left manually annotated portion to train the RF classifier, on the right final prediction result on the whole dataset.

Applying the hierarchical approach, the Milan Cathedral point cloud has been classified on three levels. At the first level, the classification was performed on a point cloud with a resolution of 5 cm, calculating geometric features with a radius between 20 cm and 2.5 m, Fig. 3b shows the result at this first classification level of the Cathedral dataset. Macro-elements (such as column, vault, floor etc.) are well highlighted on the point cloud with satisfactory results (Precision 94.7%, Recall 95%, F1-score 93.78%).

Errors were mainly due: to occluded parts and to the choir area. Occluded parts resulted in incomplete geometries on the point clouds. When extracting geometric features those parts behaved anomaly in respect to complete similar objects.

The choir proved problematic as well because of the ethereogeneity of its parts resulting in classification noise in surrounding areas.

At the second classification level, after having transferred the classification coming from the first level to a point cloud with a resolution of 2 cm, the previously identified macro-elements have been divided into architectural elements (Precision 99%, Recall 98%, F1-score 99.3%), reducing to 10 cm and 1 m min./max search radii of geometric features.

Finally, the third level of classification aims at the subdivision of each component in its monolithic architectonic objects (such as statues, gothic decorations, etc.). In this case, therefore, the full resolution point cloud was used, searching for features with minimum and maximum radii of 0.5 and 5 cm respectively (Precision 92%, Recall 88.5%, F1-score 91.8%) (Fig. 4) [9]. The calculation time for geometric features extraction varies with the size of the point cloud, the number of features and their search radius. Regarding the first level of classification, on a workstation with an 18-core processor, the training phase for the Milan Cathedral took about 5 min (2.5 million points), while it took 43 s to classify the remaining point cloud (12 million points).

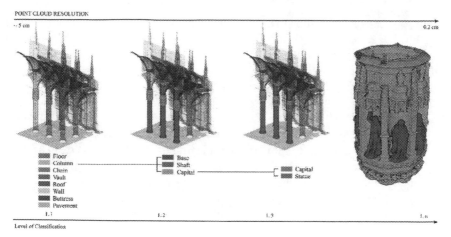

Fig. 4. MLMR classification results with corresponding semantic classes on Milan Cathedral dataset. The first level corresponds to the subdivision of the architecture in its constituent macro elements, the second level to the subdivision of architectonic elements and the third level to the subdivision in objects (e.g. statues of the gigantic capitals). Point cloud resolution at all levels has been selected considering the dimensions of elements to be classified and necessities for MR visualization.

4   Mixed Reality System[3]

4.1   MR to Support Maintenance Works in Complex Architecture

MR, as defined by Milgram et al. [30] in 1995, refers to all those applications that lay in between the real world and the virtual one. Augmented Reality and Augmented Virtuality are a subset of MR.

MR systems proved beneficial in many different fields: industry [31], navigation [32], medicine [33]. In all these fields of application, it brought a rationalization in the working process, a reduction in time and an increase in efficiency. Even in the world of CH, these systems could potentially give an enormous contribution in terms of exchange and dissemination of information among the many practitioners working on a particular case study. Nevertheless, the applications of MR are, to date, relegated to tourism and education activities [34]. These applications work on the possibility to project a 3D model on the reality adding info about history and curiosity or showing past versions and historical transformations. Up to date, there is not a real implemented application to use MR system inside maintenance operation. All cases coming from literature consists of laboratory experiments and studies of possibilities. Even systems applied and tested in real scenarios are prototypes, meaning that the research on the topics is still very active and far from conclusion.

The motivations for this delay in the use of mixed reality systems in the world of CH are mainly due to the complexity to produce these models and to the amount of data that

---

[3] https://polimi365-my.sharepoint.com/:f:/g/personal/10323083_polimi_it/EhYS8zRzYmBPi6t d4HZxJ6YB0hPp8o4wFNfb9Pbxp9HV0Q?e=VsJiIG

need to be processed, in addition to a congenital latency of the world of cultural heritage to take advantage of technological innovations. However, it is true that the modelling phase, necessary to create a reality-based 3D model, is not as easy for CH objects as for standardized industrial pieces. Modelling a so complex object usually is time-consuming and uneconomical and introduces an unsupervised degree of subjectivity and lower the initial metric content of the survey.

The presented MLMR semantic segmentation process give the possibility to rationally subdivide and structure the survey point cloud, enabling its use for interaction and DB connection and retrieval. It permits to identify and highlight the main architectural components in the point cloud, allowing to use them directly, skipping the time-consuming manual modelling phase entirely. The direct use of 3D point cloud model in an MR system makes the process of information acquisition and its final use quick and almost direct, without too many intermediate steps that make, as it is so far, all the digital process of knowledge laborious, demanding and unattractive, although desired and necessary.

In Milan Cathedral, an MR system could have a significant impact because it would provide a tool for instant access to information during routine inspection operations. The system should allow round trip access to the data allowing the consultation of georeferenced information but also the insertion of new data and update in real-time. Moreover, it would make it possible to consult geometrical data (also 2D) coming from the survey directly on-site and visualize the hidden objects and details, walls thickness, to check planarity and verticality, to count objects as statutes or marble ashlar and to inspect elements at the highest resolution directly on the scene. The possibility to share info in real-time with other operators is another essential feature of an MR system that could facilitate the exchange of information between operators.

4.2   The Developed Prototype

In line with the necessities to support maintenance work coming from the building site of Milan Cathedral, a first application prototype has been designed.

It has been developed in Unity 3D environment [35] using the MRTKv2 [36] libraries as an interface with the HoloLens 2 device from Microsoft [37]. It is a Head-Mounted Display that through a series of lenses can project 3D models on the reality allowing to interact with them as with real objects.

The presented classification process allows using the structured point cloud inside HoloLens 2 as the 3D basis for application development. The same point cloud resolutions used during the MLMR classification are here employed to ease the computational requirements necessary to render the scene on the device (Fig. 5). The display of the 3D point models, through the transparent screen of the device, works on the principle that a lower resolution point model will retain a good visualization quality if seen from the right distance. It allows using full resolution only in those situations where it is necessary to visualize elements at great detail from a close distance.

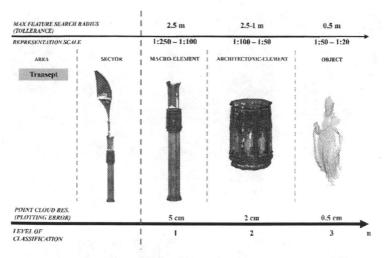

MAX FEATURE SEARCH RADIUS (TOLLERANCE)			2.5 m	2.5-1 m	0.5 m
REPRESENTATION SCALE			1:250 – 1:100	1:100 – 1:50	1:50 – 1:20
AREA		SECTOR	MACRO-ELEMENT	ARCHITECTONIC-ELEMENT	OBJECT
Transept					
POINT CLOUD RES. (PLOTTING ERROR)			5 cm	2 cm	0.5 cm
LEVEL OF CLASSIFICATION			1	2	3 n

Fig. 5. Milan Cathedral subdivision schema for MR application. It is possible to see how the point cloud produced during the classification process (right of the red line) are used at different resolution step to enable their visualization through the HoloLens2. Sectors and Areas (left of the red line) are obtained by aggregation of different macro-elements and different sectors, respectively. (Color figure online)

The device allows to interact with holograms using four main types of hand gestures: hand ray[4] or touch for far and near interaction, air tap[5] to select and air tap and hold to grab holograms. These gestures have been used ad hoc to give the user the possibility to interact with the segmented point cloud that can be navigated, moved, rotated, and scaled at will.

After starting the application, the user is presented with the point cloud of the concerned sector at low resolution (5 cm resolution), together with a small main menu. At this stage, it is possible to move, scale, and rotate the whole sector displayed or it is possible, by touching the corresponding key on the menu bar, to split the sector in its constituting macro-elements, without changing point cloud resolution. Using the hand ray gesture, these macro-elements can be singularly highlighted and touched to isolate and display the correspondent item through its higher resolution point model (2 cm resolution). This macro-element can be displayed and manipulated with its related information attached, or the user can split it in its constituting architectonic elements at the same resolution. These elements, as during the previous step, can be highlighted and touched to turn on their isolated higher resolution version (0.5 cm resolution).

The process is iterative up to the single object instance. This is displayed at full resolution (e.g. statues and ornaments) or, in those cases where it is still necessary a 3D modelling phase (e.g. marble blocks), with its 3D mesh representation (Fig. 6). It

---

[4] The HoloLens 2 device works on the possibility to track hands movements with its cameras, when it recognizes that an hand is present in the rendering area it will project a dashed line in the direction to which the hand is pointing.

[5] Air tap interaction consists in touching the index finger with the thumb of the same hand and immediately releasing them while the HoloLens 2 is tracking their position.

Fig. 6. Point cloud displayed through the HoloLens 2 on-site. From left to right: sector (5 cm resolution), macro-element highlight (5 cm resolution), macro-element (2 cm resolution), architectonic element highlight (2 cm resolution), architectonic element (0.5 cm resolution).

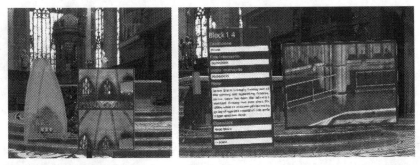

Fig. 7. The information displayed with different 3D point cloud; every level of visualization could have information attached independently from point cloud resolution, classification level, or model type.

is important to note that it is possible to attach different information to the displayed object independently from the segmentation level displayed and the type of 3D model displayed (3D point cloud or 3D mesh model) (Fig. 7). Test of 1:1 scale superimposition at on the real objects directly in the Cathedral has been already done to set up a good visualization quality and good persistence of the experience.

5   Conclusion and Future Works

The article aims to describe the most actual part of the research work carried out by 3DSurveyGroup in collaboration with the "Veneranda Fabbrica del Duomo di Milano". The work presents the final stage of the geometrical survey of the Cathedral and some concrete proposals developed at the applied research level for the effective use of these 3D data within the VF's activities. The development of ML techniques allows to classify and segment the 3D point cloud assigning name and surname to each point belonging to the different architectural element. The classification results show how classified point clouds can facilitate the understanding of complex architectural structures, becoming possible tools to support the restoration, maintenance, and management of structures on-site without the need for subsequent synthesisations, as classical 3D modelling. The process is semi-automatic, and for this reason, it is fast, objective, and repeatable; the results show that it is also reliable. We prefer to use the ML approach instead of the DL approach because we are convinced that the cognitive contribution of an expert operator is essential at the beginning of the process. Precisely, because the CH is varied, no absolute generalizations can be made, the expert operator who knows the property in question requires the effort of defining the classes and the choice of training and validation sets (annotation of the data). These steps are crucial for adapting the process to different case studies and different purposes. The classification phase can be considered an indispensable step to use the semi-raw point cloud as a real 3D model. Finally, we describe the first steps taken to use this type of data in an MR system. The development of the prototype application showed the feasibility of the presented work. On this topic, many are the future works already in the program. One of this is to develop a system able to place correctly and automatic the 1:1 3D models in the real world with the possibility to share the generated coordinate system and to allow multiuser experience.

Acknowledgement. The authors would like to thank all the colleagues who have participated in the past and are now collaborating in the Milan Cathedral project. A special thanks to Ing. Francesco Canali, yard director of "Veneranda Fabbrica del Duomo di Milano". Thanks to the colleagues of FBK of Trento 3DOM, Fabio Remondino and Eleonora Grilli with whom the research on the ML classification of the Cathedral of Milan has been carried out and more in-depth presented in [9].

References

1. Veneranda Fabbrica Homepage. https://www.duomomilano.it/en/infopage/veneranda-fabbrica-del-duomo-di-milano/68/. Accessed 21 Oct 2020
2. Fassi, F., Achille, C., Fregonese, L.: Surveying and modelling the main spire of milan cathedral using multiple data sources. Photogram. Rec. **26**, 462–487 (2011)
3. Fassi, F., Achille, C., Mandelli, A., Rechichi, F., Parri, S.: A new idea of BIM system for visualization, WEB sharing and using huge complex 3D models for facility management. In: International Archives of the Photogrammetry, Remote Sensing and Spatial Information Sciences, vol. XL-5/W4, pp. 359–366 (2015)
4. Rechichi, F., Mandelli, A., Achille, C., Fassi, F.: Sharing high-resolution modules and information on the WEB: the WEB module of BIM3DSG system. In: International Archives of the Photogrammetry, Remote Sensing and Spatial Information Sciences, vol. XLI-B5, pp. 703–710 (2016)
5. Fassi, F., Parri, S.: Complex architecture in 3D: from survey to web. Int. J. Heritage Digit. Era **1**(3), 379–398 (2012)
6. Achille, C., Fassi, F., Mandelli, A., Perfetti, L., Rechichi, F., Teruggi, S.: From a traditional to a digital site: 2008–2019. The history of Milan Cathedral surveys. In: Daniotti, B., Gianinetto, M., Della Torre, S. (eds.) Digital Transformation of the Design, Construction and Management Processes of the Built Environment. RD, pp. 331–341. Springer, Cham (2020). https://doi.org/10.1007/978-3-030-33570-0_30
7. Perfetti, L., Fassi, F., Gulsan, H.: Generation of gigapixel orthophoto for the maintenance of complex buildings. Challenges and lesson learnt. In: International Archives of the Photogrammetry, Remote Sensing and Spatial Information Sciences, vol. XLII-2/W9, pp. 605–614 (2019)

8. Mandelli, A., Fassi, F., Perfetti, L., Polari, C.: Testing different survey techniques to model architectonic narrow spaces. In: International Archives of the Photogrammetry, Remote Sensing and Spatial Information Sciences, vol. XLII-2/W5, pp. 505–511 (2017)
9. Teruggi, S., Grilli, E., Russo, M., Fassi, F., Remondino, F.: A hierarchical machine learning approach for multi-level and multi-resolution 3D point cloud classification. Remote Sens. 12(16), 2598 (2020)
10. Reboli, D., Pučko, Z., Babič, N.Č, Bizjak, M., Mongus, D.: Point cloud quality requirements for scan-vs-BIM based automated construction progress monitoring. Autom. Constr. 84, 323–334 (2017)
11. Son, H., Kim, C.: Semantic as-built 3D modelling of structural elements of buildings based in local concavity and convexity. Adv. Eng. Inform. 34, 114–124 (2017)
12. Bassier, M., Yousefzadeh, M., Vergauwen, M.: Comparison of 2D and 3D wall reconstruction algorithms from point cloud data for as-built BIM. J. Inf. Technol. Constr. (ITcon) 25(11), 173–192 (2020)
13. Apollonio, F.I., et al.: A 3D-centered information system for the documentation of a complex restoration intervention. J. Cult. Heritage 29, 89–99 (2018)
14. Croce, V., Caroti, G., De Luca, L., Piemonte, A., Véron, P.: Semantic annotation of heritage models: 2D/3D approaches and future research challenges. In: The International Archives of Photogrammetry, Remote Sensing and Spatial Information Science, vol. 43, pp. 829–836 (2020)
15. Sánchez-Aparicio, L.J., Del Pozo, S., Ramos, L.F., Arce, A., Fernandes, F.M.: Heritage site preservation with combined radiometric and geometric analysis of TLS data. Automation in Construction 85, 24–39 (2018)
16. Valero, E., Bosché, F., Forster, A.: Automatic segmentation of 3D point cloud of rubble masonry walls and its application to building surveying Repair and Maintenance. Autom.Constr. 96, 29–39 (2018)
17. Roussel, R., Bagnéris, M., De Luca, L., Bomblet, P.: A digital diagnosis for the <<Autumn>> statue (Marseille, France): photogrammetry, digital cartography and construction of a thesaurus. In: International Archives of Photogrammetry, Remote Sensing and Spatial Information Science, vol. XLII-2/W15, pp. 1039–1046 (2019)
18. Mizoguchi, T., et al.: Quantitative scaling evaluation of concrete structures based on terrestrial laser scanning. Autom. Constr. 35, 263–274 (2013)
19. Kashani, A.G., Graettinger, A.J.: Cluster-based roof covering damage detection in ground-based lidar data. Autom. Constr. 58, 19–27 (2015)
20. Matrone, F., et al.: A benchmark for large-scale heritage point cloud semantic segmentation. In: International Archives of Photogrammetry, Remote Sensing and Spatial Information Science, vol. XLIII-B2, pp. 1419–1426 (2020)
21. Murtiyoso, A., Grussenmeyer, P.: Virtual disassembling of historical edifices: experiments and assessments of an automatic approach for classifying multi-scalar point clouds into architectural elements. Sensors 20(8), 2161 (2020)
22. Pierdicca, R., et al.: Point cloud semantic segmentation using deep learning framework for cultural heritage. Remote Sens. 12(6), 1005 (2020)
23. Grilli, E., Dininno, D., Marsicano, L., Petrucci, G., Remondino, F.: Supervised segmentation of 3D cultural heritage. In 2018 3rd Digital Heritage International Congress (Digital-HERITAGE) Held Jointly with 2018 24th International Conference on Virtual Systems & Multimedia (VSMM 2018), San Francisco, CA, USA, pp. 1–8. IEEE (2018)
24. Grilli, E., M. Farella, E., Torresani, A., Remondino, F.: geometric features analysis for the classification of cultural heritage point clouds. In: International Archives of Photogrammetry, Remote Sensing and Spatial Information Science, vol. XLII-2/W15, pp. 541–548 (2019)
25. Grilli, E., Remondino, F.: Machine learning generalization across different 3D architectural heritage. ISPRS Int. J. Geo-Inf. 9(6), 379 (2020)

26. Matrone, F., Grilli, E., Martini, M., Paolanti, M., Pierdicca, R., Remondino, F.: Comparing machine and deep learning methods for large 3D heritage semantic segmentation. ISPRS Int. J. Geo-Inf. **9**(9), 535 (2020)
27. Blomley, R., Weinmann, M., Leitloff, J., Jutzi, B.: Shape distribution features for point cloud analysis – a geometric histogram approach on multiple scales. In: ISPRS Annals of Photogrammetry, Remote Sensing and Spatial Information Sciences, vol. 2, no. 3, p. 9 (2014)
28. Breimann, L.: Random forests. Mach. Learn. **45**(1), 5–32 (2001)
29. Goutte, C., Gaussier, E.: A probabilistic interpretation of precision, recall and F-score, with implication for evaluation. In: Losada, D.E., Fernández-Luna, J.M. (eds.) ECIR 2005. LNCS, vol. 3408, pp. 345–359. Springer, Heidelberg (2005). https://doi.org/10.1007/978-3-540-31865-1_25
30. Milgram, P., Takemura, H., Utsumi, A., Kishino, F.: Augmented reality: a class of displays on the reality-virtuality continuum. Telemanipulator Telepresence Technol. **2351**, 282–292 (1995)
31. De Pace, F., Manuri, F., Sanna, A.: Augmented reality in Industry 4.0. Am. J. Comput. Sci. Inf. Technol. **06**(01), 1–7 (2018)
32. Fraga-Lamas, P., Fernandez-Carames, T. M., Blanco-Nova, O., Vilar-Montesinos, M. A.: A review of industrial augmented reality systems for the Industry 4.0 Shipyard. IEEE Access **6**, 13358–13375 (2018)
33. Desselle, M.R., Brown, R.A., James, A.R., Midwinter, M.J., Powel, S.K., Woodruff, M.A.: Augmented and virtual reality in surgery. Comput. Sci. Eng. **22**(3), 18–26 (2020)
34. Blanco-Pons, S., Carrion-Ruiz, B., Duong, M., Chartrand, J., Fai, S., Luis Lerma, J.: Augmented reality markerless multi-image outdoor tracking system for the historical buildings on parliament hill. Sustainability **11**(16), 4268 (2019)
35. Unity 3D Homepage. https://unity.com/. Accessed 22 Oct 2020
36. MRTKv2 GitHub page. https://github.com/microsoft/MixedRealityToolkit-Unity. Accessed 22 Oct 2020
37. HoloLens 2 Homepage. https://www.microsoft.com/it-it/hololens/hardware. Accessed 22 Oct 2020

From Fully Supervised to Blind Digital Anastylosis on DAFNE Dataset

Paola Barra[1]([envelope]) [iD], Silvio Barra[2][iD], and Fabio Narducci[1][iD]

[1] Department of Computer Sciences, University of Salerno, Fisciano, Italy
{pbarra,fnarducci}@unisa.it
[2] Department of Electrical and Information Technology Engineering (DIETI),
University of Naples Federico II, Naples, Italy
silvio.barra@unina.it

Abstract. Anastylosis is an archaeological term consisting in a reconstruction technique whereby an artefact is restored using the original architectural elements. Experts can sometimes imply months or years to carry out this task counting on their expertise. Software procedures can represent a valid support but several challenges arise when dealing with practical scenarios. This paper starts from the achievements on DAFNE challenge, with a traditional template matching approach which won the third place at the competition, to arrive to discuss the critical issues that make the unsupervised version, the blind digital anastylosis, a hard problem to solve. A preliminary solution supported by experimental results is presented.

Keywords: Digital anastylosis · Fresco reconstruction · DAFNE dataset · Supervised and blind approach

1 Introduction

In the past history, there have been several events involving archaeological, historical and artistic sites devastated and destroyed by natural disasters (earthquakes, tsunamis and fires); the recent fire to the Notre-Dame cathedral represents a typical example of huge historical and artistic loss, which in addition has caused several structural damages to the infrastructure of the cathedral itself [23]. Given the high seismic risk of the territory, joint to the countless natural and historic sites, Italy has a sad history behind, regarding destruction of cultural attractions. One of the saddest event has been the September '97 earthquake which has destroyed the St. Francis of Assisi Cathedral, causing the devastation of many frescoes among which some from Giotto and Cimabue. The two above mentioned are significant examples of the interest that digital anastylosis had and might have as a support tool for experts during the reconstruction of archaeological findings. Several ambitious interdisciplinary projects have been undertaken to push the frontiers of research on hardware, software, and human computer interaction to develop tools that digitally support the traditional work

A. Del Bimbo et al. (Eds.): ICPR 2020 Workshops, LNCS 12663, pp. 628–642, 2021.
https://doi.org/10.1007/978-3-030-68796-0_45

of archaeologists and their co-workers in related fields [2, 22]. The professions and the skills involved in a typical excavation site are interdisciplinary, ranging from anthropologists and archaeologists to geologists and geodesists. Dealing with such a wide range of problems and heterogeneous difficulties puts the research in computer vision, especially geometry processing, in a privileged position to support the traditional work in all of the above fields. In this paper, we explore the difficulties of addressing the fresco reconstruction task in an unsupervised scenario, in which no references of the archaeological findings are available. This work is a step forward with respect to a previous work [6], in which a supervised approach to the digital reconstruction of frescoes was proposed.

The paper is organised as follows: Sect. 2 discusses similar approaches in the literature dealing with digital cultural heritage reconstruction; Sect. 3 discusses the peculiarities of DAFNE challenge; Sect. 4 introduces the difficulties of a blind approach to frescoes reconstruction from fragments while Sect. 5 discusses the experimental results obtained in both supervised and unsupervised version of the problem. Section 6 provides conclusion as well as insights and future research lines of the proposed work.

2   Related Works

One of the challenges characterising the reconstruction of the archaeological objects is working with a large number of fragments that are found in excavation sites [12], and determining the correct matches between them [11]; this problem is well referenced as anastylosis. In several conditions, the work of archaeologists is made hard because of the presence of gaps among fragments which complicates the work of matching them together [18]. Therefore, numerous studies proposed methods and techniques to achieve reliable and suitable solutions to this class of problems. The digital anastylosis can be both 2D (paintings, frescoes, ancient documents and similar) [6] and 3D (e.g., sculptures, vases and buildings) [10]. In both cases, the problem is looking for fragments that match each other and together rebuild the original look of the object. In ideal conditions, all fragments recompose the original artefact perfectly but in practical scenarios the reconstruction task is far from being such simple. Lost and damaged fragments, very small pieces (up to become dust) and the effect of time make the problem very challenging to face with. Many studies have focused on the issue of archaeology to find a solution based on two-dimensional images and three-dimensional models, whereas some of the researchers were interested in the proposed methods of classifying fragments into groups and reconstructing the archaeological objects. Most of work focused on finding pairwise matches between adjacent fragments by using surface colour [18] and texture properties, like Smith et al. [19] did to classify two-dimensional fragments. Similarly, Makridis and Daras [16] made considerations on the matching of features of the front and rear of the pottery to improve the classification accuracy based on colour information and local texture features. On the same research line, Leitao and Stolfi [13] exploited the boundary information and contours of ceramic fragments. Geometrically

unknown objects to reassemble thin artefacts via photometric properties of the
boundary contour have been considered in [9]. Colour and boundary adjacency
has been also analysed in [24] for 2D image reconstruction, while Tan et al. [21]
reconstructed the pixels surrounding the target to improve the probability of
successfully matching the fragments. Under strict assumptions, the problem of
digital image reconstruction can be considered as a clustering task, so grouping
the fragments according the structural features, as it happens in other computer
vision disciplines, like object recognition [15] and biometrics [1,5]. Yingand Gang
[14] exploited fuzzy logic on the basis of surface texture properties for clustering
ceramic fragments. However, when dealing with detailed paintings or complex
geometries, simple grouping of pieces can be very ineffective. Moreover, considering that gaps among pixels may reasonably exist and archaeological findings
could not cover the whole original artefact, the digital anastylosis becomes significantly harder to fix by automatic software solutions in practical conditions.

3   The DAFNE Challenge

DAFNE Challenge (Digital Anastylosis of Frescoes challeNgE)[1] has been
launched in 2019 by the Computer Vision and Multimedia Lab of University
of Pavia to highlight the importance of cultural heritage assets conservation,
and promoting restoration of artworks that would otherwise be lost forever, due
for example to a destructive phenomena such as earthquakes, wars or vandal-
ism acts. In particular, it focuses on reconstruction of frescoes from collection of
fragments. The goal of the challenge was developing tools enabling digital reconstruction of heavily damaged frescoes, supporting their restoration through the
solution of the *puzzles* formed by the remaining fragments, often mixed with
spurious elements.

The DAFNE dataset[2] has been specifically built for the DAFNE challenge;
it has been divided in training and testing dataset in order to meet the needs of
those who aimed at developing learning based approaches; the former contains 62
frescoes, each composed by 18 different fragments tessellations. Each tessellations
consists of a set of fragments to reassemble the original fresco (whose ground
truth image is also provided) and a file containing the ground truth location
and rotation of each fragments. Some of the tessellations may contain spurious
fragments, i.e. fragments which do not belong to the reference fresco. The testing
dataset consists of 3 frescoes[3]. Frescoes have variable dimensions, as well as the
fragments, which do not match neatly, but an erosion degree is applied, such
simulating the real scenarios in which the contours of the collapsed fragments
are often indented and some space between is present.

---

[1] https://vision.unipv.it/DAFchallenge/DAF-notice.html.
[2] Available from the link https://vision.unipv.it/DAFchallenge/DAFNE_dataset/
dataset_download.html.
[3] The solution to the testing frescoes has been released after the competition.

Fig. 1. In this picture the fresco *Camera Picta* by Mantegna from DAFNE dataset has shown. On the left, a piece of the collection belonging to the fresco and the green links with the keypoint of the original fresco.

3.1 The Supervised Approach

In [6] a supervised approach to the DAFNE challenge is proposed; it is based on three main steps:

- SIFT application: SIFT features are extracted both from the fresco and from the fragments. The former phase returns a certain number of keypoint matches, which are ordered according to a confidence metric; only the best two matches are kept, whereas the other ones are discarded. In Fig. 1 an example of SIFT matching between a single fragment and the fresco is shown;
- fragment rotation: since the fragments have a random rotation degree applied, the second step is in charge of recovering the original orientation of the fragment. This is done by computing a rotation transformation of the fragment, as shown in Fig. 2.
- once the location coordinates and rotation degrees are found, the fragment can be properly located. These steps are repeated for each fragment of a given tessellation.

The experimental results summarised at Sect. 5 shows that, even when highly supervised, the digital anastylosis is an error-prone problem. However, significantly high level of performances can be achieved. The difficulties arise when dealing with practical scenarios, where no references are available and data may be corrupted. The Sect. 4 discusses in more details and more formally the points that make the blind anastylosis a problem hard to resolve.

4   Blind Digital Anastylosis

The above described approach considers the typical situation in which we are provided with the reference image of the fresco to reconstruct. In a real scenario, this only happens when the fresco is known and well documented.

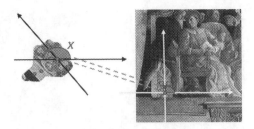

Fig. 2. How a piece is properly rotated once the matching has been found. According to the strongest and more reliable keypoints (red in figure) the transformation to overlap them on the original fresco is computed. (Color figure online)

This simplifies a lot the anastylosis, even though some difficulties still remain, like the presence of gaps between the fragments and the potential presence of plain surfaces, which are quite hard to place without any shape-driven reference. The situation becomes unfairly harder when one aims at restoring a fresco or a sculpture, in cases in which the reference image is not available. In such situations, we refer to this problems as Blind Digital Anastylosis. Besides sharing the same difficulties of the canonical digital anastylosis, many more are added; moreover, the existing ones are further tangled and made more challenging and intricate to address. Few examples in this field are discussed in [20], where a computer assisted procedure allows to match pieces of Pompeian frescoes. Similarly, the work by Andreoli [4] shows how the knowledge on Romanian frescoes pictorial style can contribute to ease the work of matching the fragments. In general, the blind digital anastylosis problem is a special case of jigsaw puzzle. Compared to a regular jigsaw puzzle, however, the challenge of reconstruction a drawing from a small number of remaining and deteriorated fragments is harder. A fully automatic solution can be considered feasible only if the collection of fragments is complete. More details on this aspect are provided in Sect. 4.1. In the following, the issues related to the blind digital anastylosis are described; in particular, three main aspects are discussed: (i) the lack of a reference image, (ii) the missing/spurious fragments and (iii) the non-neat match between fragments. Also, a potential preliminary solution is proposed and described.

4.1 Blind Digital Anastylosis Like a Hard Jigsaw Puzzle Problem

Blind digital anastylosis is highly controversial. How can faithfully reconstruct a fresco, or in general a archaeological object, if no drawings could guide the process? The colours and the texture of the fragments can sometimes provide insights on the artistic style and the epoch of the artwork. Similarly, other findings in the same archaeological site or historical region can provide a rough idea of the expected appearance. To achieve a trusty anastylosis result an accurate study of the remaining original fragments is expected. Which brings to consider the problem as a "puzzle"; hence trying to put pieces together in the correct way. In fact, the 2D anastylosis can be mainly considered as an alternative

Fig. 3. The images are extracted from the DAFNE training dataset and show three frescoes by Giotto. From left to right: *Adoration of the Magi*, *The Raising of Lazarus* and *The Entry into Jerusalem*.

view point of Jigsaw Puzzle Problem (JPP) which consists in tiling puzzle that requires the assembly of often oddly shaped interlocking and mosaiced pieces. Often JPP solvers use chromatic information as well as geometric shape [8] to find matches among pieces. In a classical interpretation of the problem, JPP solver can use linear programming and can be computed in linear time. This is true when the size of the puzzle is known *a priori* and there are no missing pieces and, more importantly, the shape of the pieces is regular among all pieces [25]. In such a case, the bottleneck is just represented by the computation of all pairwise matches which takes quadratic time ($O(n^2)$) on the number n of fragments. From simple solutions based on colour similarity up to deep neural networks approaches [17], when the problem is faced under the assumption of regular squared fragments, significantly high results have been reported in the literature. Growing in complexity, e.g., as mentioned before introducing missing pieces or randomly shaped fragments, the problem becomes a NP-complete problem since it can be demonstrated that Set Partition Problem is reducible to JPP [3]. Moreover, the random shape of the fragments introduces a higher order of uncertainty because the number of possible rotations of the pieces can be ideally infinite thus explaining the exponential trend of complexity growing of the problem. As a consequence of that, achieving an automatic solution which is both computationally sustainable and accurate becomes unfeasible. In the following sections the main points that have been considered in this study and that make the blind anastylosis an hard problem to resolve are discussed.

Lack of a Reference. The reference image provides lots of insights about the actual location of a fragment: first of all, potential ambiguity in fragments' positioning can be nimbly solved; secondly, in presence of spurious fragments, it results easy to visually state whether it belongs to a certain fresco or not. As a consequence, it becomes easier to develop a method which can rely on the presence of a ground truth image. Regarding the dataset provided for the DAFNE challenge, a further help is given from the fact that the single fragments respect the dimension of the original fresco image, therefore no scaling is needed. This eases the positioning of the fragments, since:

– the entire set of fragments of a given fragmentation set fits perfectly the dimensions of the fresco (which are known, since we are provided with the reference image).
– even if we are unsure about the rotation degrees of the fragment, we still can apply a brute force approach to find the proper one, trying to match the underlying image.

In real scenarios, unfortunately, one could not take for granted the availability of documentation supporting the reconstruction; in fact, whether in cases of very renowned frescoes, and cultural heritage in general, many documents and images are available, in many situations, only partial documentation is accessible; occasionally these can be totally missing. Now in the light of these considerations, one can imagine how hard it can be the work of archaeologists and operators, which have to face with the reconstruction of a fresco, a sculpture or a vase, which has been decomposed in several (three dimensional) fragments, some very small, and of which no reference is available. In Blind Digital Anastylosis, regarding the DAFNE dataset, the lack of a reference does not allow the use of feature extraction methods, joint with feature matching approaches. Therefore, it would not be possible to automatically approximate the location of a fragment on the reference fresco image. In addition, it is not possible at all to evaluate whether a fragment (or a group of) is properly posed (in terms of x/y positioning and rotation), since the ground truth information do not have meaning anymore; a sort of evaluation can be done only relating a fragment position with its neighbors. Unfortunately, the inaccurate positioning of a single fragment may influence the overall evaluation.

Missing and Spurious Fragments. Following a natural disaster, most of the artistic damage is caused by the rescue means, which in rush for saving potential lives, pass on the ruins, so further crashing fragments, or even making dust of them. Missing fragments are a severe problem, not only for the artistic loss, but also because they may serve as a reference for locating the position of other fragments. This hardens a lot the anastylosis, both in real and in digital working environments. Analogously, but from a different point of view, spurious fragments may create confusion during the reconstruction, especially when the fragments belong to frescoes from the same historic period or even the same artist, thus resulting similar. An example is shown in Fig. 3. The three frescoes are named, in the order, *Adoration of the Magi*, *The Raising of Lazarus* and *The Entry into Jerusalem* and are three wonderful frescoes by Giotto located in the Scrovegni Chapel, Padua (ITALY). How it is possible to see, the style of painting and the semantic structure of the fresco are basically the same, and all of the three are surrounded with a brown frame; also, the tone of the colours are quite the same. The images are taken from the DAFNE training dataset. The missing and spurious fragments' issues are further complicated when:

– the reference image or supporting documentation is missing, therefore there are no hints about the original fresco;
– the fragments come from plain sections, without features which could help to locate the proper location of the fragment.

In Fig. 4, three fragments belonging to three different frescoes are shown: in particular, the piece A, B and C belong respectively to the first, second and third fresco in Fig. 3. Even though the surrounding frame can give some indications about their location in the fresco (all of them are located on the outer border of the image), it is still complicated to precisely state the location.

Non-neat Match Between Fragments. Last issue, but not least, the collapsed fragments of frescoes present an indented contour, which is really hard to make fit one each other to perfection; in addition, often, there is no contact point between two adjacent fragments, forcing to suppose the matching according to the visual characteristic of the fragments. For these reasons, matching two fragments results really hard to accomplish. This situation is faithfully mirrored in the DAFNE dataset, since on each fragment is applied an erosion, thus avoiding the perfect match between fragments, as well as reducing the size of the fragment itself.

4.2   A Preliminary Approach

Any approach developed for a supervised condition is inherently unsuitable to be used in the blind version of the digital anastylosis problem, mainly for the issues described in the previous section. Here, a light solution based on contours features matching is proposed (Fig. 5). It is based on the assumption that gaps among fragments may exist and they do not cover the whole surface of the fresco. On the other hand, however, it supposes that the fragments provide insights that support the visual inspection of the final results and its correctness. In other words, this means that a match among pairs of pieces can be found. Given a set of irregular fragments belonging to a fresco (without scaling or rotating and without spurious), for each fragment the RGB value of the contour pixels is extracted. In Fig. 6A and 6B, the extraction of the contour of two fragments is shown. Each pair of RGB value arrays was compared for all available fragments. For each fragment, therefore, the matching percentage is extracted with the contour of all the other fragments of the fresco. Once the pair with the highest matching percentage is selected, the Euclidean distance between equal pair of pixels is calculated to determine the fitness of matches found (Fig. 6B). In Fig. 6B, let $S = \{s_1, s_2, ..., s_i, ...s_n\}$ be the set of contour pixels of the first fragment and $P = \{p_1, p_2, ..., p_j, ...p_m\}$ be the set of contour pixels of the second fragment.

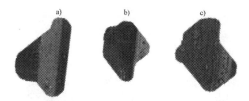

Fig. 4. Three fragments extracted from the DAFNE dataset. They all belong to Giotto frescoes, respectively to *Adoration of the Magi*, *The Raising of Lazarus* and *The Entry into Jerusalem*.

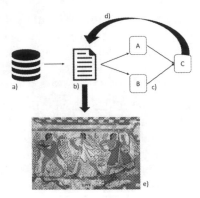

Fig. 5. a) Dataset with fragments belonging to a fresco. b) Extraction of the contour from each fragment and calculation of the matching percentage for each pair of fragments within the dataset. c) Extraction of the two fragments A and B with higher matching percentage and union in a new fragment C. d) Updating the list of percentages by adding the new fragment C and deleting the information relating to A and B. e) Repetition of the whole sequence until a single fragment, ie the reconstructed final fresco, is present in the list.

If the pixels with the same value are such that $s_i = p_i$ and $s_j = p_j = p_m$ then it must be verified that the Euclidean distance between pixels in each pair are also equal. In such a case, those pixel pairs are more likely to be part of the fit than other pairs. Let $d(s_1, s_2)$ be the Euclidean distance between two pixels $s1$ and $s2$ of the same fragment. As it can be seen in Fig. 6B, it results that the Euclidean distance $d(s_i, s_j)$ is equal to $d(p_i, p_j)$. This suggests that the pairs of pixels (s_i, p_i) and (s_j, p_j) are potentially correct matches between the two fragments. Conversely, the Euclidean distance $d(s_i, s_j)$ is not equal to $d(p_m, p_j)$ even if the features s_i and p_m match each other, taken singularly. Therefore these pairs will be discarded as potential matches. This approach inherently fixes the problem of spurious fragments in a very simplistic way. Spurious fragments do not belong to the reference fresco and therefore such an exact match is hard to be found. On the other hand, this does not guarantee that a spurious fragment is such to never show a perfect overlapping of features with original fragments or even with other spurious fragments. Our experimental results show that the proposed approach has an ability to discard spurious fragments but aimed considerations and experimental observations are necessary on this topic.

This comparison is done for each pair of pixels that verifies the conditions explained above. In presence of more than a matching two pairs of pixels per matching remain that are those with the highest Euclidean distance similarity; in our example s_i with p_i and s_j with p_j. As a result of the matching a new fragment is created (Fig. 6C), which is inserted into the original set of the fragments, and the fragments just combined are eliminated. The algorithm can start again from scratch, until convergence is reached, which means obtaining a single fragment

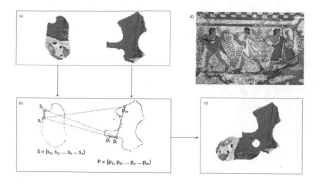

Fig. 6. a) two examples of fragments that have the highest percentage of contour matching; b) calculation of the distance between the same pixels belonging to two different fragment contours; c) union of the two fragments based on the pixels that match; D: the final fresco of the two fragments examined.

representing recomposed fresco (Fig. 6D) or a partial reconstruction when not other matches can be found.

5   Experimental Results

The results presented in this section are mainly focused on the experimentation carried out on the supervised approach, which was submitted to the DAFNE challenge and got the third place in the ranking list of the winners. As discussed in the previous sections, the DAFNE challenge is a fully supervised problem where the scenario considers that the reference picture is available. Even though this limits the challenge at a traditional template matching problem, the task is less trivial than expected. Fragments can sometimes be very small or texture-less thus resulting hard to locate and place in the correct way.

The results here presented refer to 540 tessellations: 30 different frescoes, each with 18 different fragment configurations. The strength of our method lies in always obtaining 0 spurious elements for each fresco; the proposed approach never positions a fragment on the picture if it does not belong to the fresco. On the other hand, there is a relatively low average percentage of original fragments well positioned corresponding to 26%, which are however correctly overlapped at 96% on average. Table 1 shows the results achieved on DAFNE dataset according to different conditions. The mean average results are reported in terms of percentage of fragment sets and true fragments, meaning the fragments that belong to the picture. False positive (FP) at fragment level and pixel level are reported. As said above, the constraints of the proposed approach are so strict that a fragment is posed on the fresco only when they are all satisfied. This is the reason why the false positive rate reported during the experimentation is always equal zero, which explains the robustness against spurious pieces. On the other hand, the strong selection of matching features can refuse a fragment belonging to the fresco, marking it also as a spurious.

Table 1. Results achieved on DAFNE dataset. The table summarises the average results over a total of more than 500 different tessellations of frescoes as well as collects the results achieved on specific tessellations in terms of highest and lowest parameter partitions. For each fresco, the number of fragments composing that particular tessellation and the number of fragments properly (TP) anche wrongly (FP) positioned are indicated. The false positives are expressed both in terms of fragments and in terms of pixels in the last two columns.

	Fresco	Number of fragments	TP(frags)	FP (frags)	FP (pixels)
Highest rate true frags.	Mantegna Camera picta	163	112 (68.71%)	0	2.09
Lowest rate true frags.	Giotto Massacre of the Innocents	1500	8 (0.53%)	0	2.02
Largest frag. set	Fra Angelico Cristo deriso	2103	199 (9.46%)	0	5.55
Smallest frag. set	Vasari Paul III Farnese	85	38 (44.71%)	0	2.32
Highest px error	Piero della Francesca Exaltation of the Cross	430	51 (11.86%)	0	22.45
Lowest px error	Nebbia Traslazione reliquie	556	150 (26.98%)	0	0.79
Mean	–	472.62	106.3 (26.35%)	0	4.62

The correctness of the fragments chosen and positioned onto the fresco is calculated with the Jaccard index; let A be the position of the ground truth and B the proposed position, the Jaccard index $J(A, B)$ is calculated as follows:

$$J(A, B) = \frac{|A \bigcap B|}{|A \bigcup B|} = \frac{|A \bigcap B|}{|A| + |B| - |A \bigcap B|}, 0 \leq J(A, B) \leq 1 \qquad (1)$$

Figure 7 shows examples of reconstructed frescoes; in particular, the top images are related to the fresco *Camera picta*[4] by Andrea Mantegna, which is the fresco with the highest percentage of correct fragments (68.71%). The bottom images are instead related to the reconstructed fresco *Massacre of Innocents*[5] by Giotto, which is the fresco with the lowest percentage of correct fragments (0.53%). Looking at the ground-truth, it is rather clear how significantly harder is the reconstruction for Giotto's fresco compared to Mantenga's one. The fragments of the former are so small that they have very ambiguous SIFT features as well as they appear similar in shape. This condition creates the premises for a error-prone matching which is confirmed by the low TP rate achieved.

Considering the results achieved on the supervised approach, one can reasonably expect that the unsupervised version of the problems is significantly more complex (as discussed in Sect. 4) and experimental results cannot achieve a competitive level of performance. Due to the lack of the reference image and its properties (e.g., the size of the drawing, and the absolute positioning of

---

[4] The fresco is "Mantenga - Camera picta 2019-2-20 17.27.40" in the DAFNE dataset.
[5] The fresco is "Giotto - Massacre of the Innocents 2019-2-16 16.13.48" in DAFNE dataset.

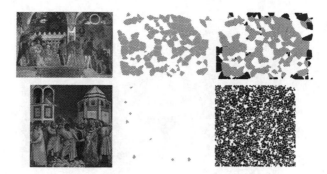

Fig. 7. Reconstruction of *Camera picta* by Mantenga and *Massacre of the Innocents* by Giotto with the comparison with the ground truth. The three images related to each fresco show respectively the final reconstruction of the fresco (on the left), the mask of the properly positioned fragments (in the middle) and the pixels of the solution that do not match the ground truth (highlighted in red in the last image).

the fragments) the unsupervised approach is characterised by a higher level of uncertainty. Moreover, in presence of gaps among pieces or missing pieces such a probability of error grows so rapidly to turn the blind anastylosis into a NP-Complete problem. The preliminary experimental results obtained on a test sample (a fresco from the Murecine excavation shown in Fig. 8), show that the proposed method is quite effective looking for pairwise matches in a collection of fragments and it progressively assembles the original fragments with the ones assembled at previous iterations. The experimentation is solely based on a visual inspection of the obtained results since the replica of DAFNE conditions makes harder a formal discussion. Further improvements of the proposed blind approach and a wider experimentation should be performed to assess the promising preliminary results achieved.

6   Conclusions

Archaeologists and experts working on original excavation findings are quite often put in front of the critical problem of matching small pieces of a painting or a sculpture to reconstruct the original appearance. Digital anastylosis undoubtedly represents a valid support to such a purpose. Even if digital anastylosis shares some issues and difficulties of puzzle solving problems, it is an authentic unsupervised task that can be very hard to resolve, up to becoming NP-complete under low assumptions. In fact, several approaches have been presented and discussed in the literature, but they are all built around hypothesis that are not compliant with real and practical scenario. One of this example is represented by the DAFNE competition, which proposed a challenge founded on the reconstruction of frescoes by providing both original and spurious fragments. It consisted in a supervised problem since the original frescoes were all given, along with the

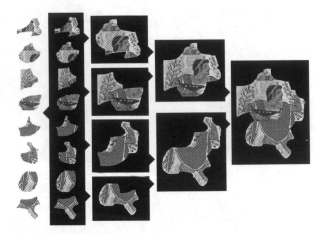

Fig. 8. Picture showing the blind reconstruction process starting from a collection of fragments (leftmost in the picture). The original fragments are expanded, meaning that the contour pixels are generated on the basis of the available pixels. From the expanded fragments, the matching process takes place.

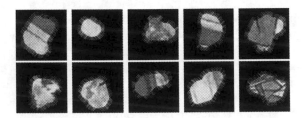

Fig. 9. The generation of missing contouring pixels based on the knowledge on visible pixels in a fragment.

ground truth information (position and rotation) of the fragments. The experimental results are achieved on a template matching proposal, based on the SIFT features extracted by the pieces. The experimentation suggests that the method is very robust, since besides positioning an acceptable percentage of fragments, it never gets wrong, by positioning a spurious element in the wrong fresco. This paper focuses the attention on the unsupervised version of the DAFNE challenge. It does not consider the presence of a reference image, along with the original position of the fragment, thus resulting an authentic unsupervised problem and closer to real conditions for experts working on excavations. The issues that arise are discussed, up to reduce to the NP-complete set of problems. However, on the basis of some assumptions (the guarantee that matching points can be found between pairs of fragments), a contour-based approach is proposed and applied to a homemade test bed which is compliant with the constraints and the hypothesis of DAFNE supervised challenge. The promising results achieved in terms of matching among pieces and the progressively reconstruction from assembled pieces opens to possible further improvement which takes into consideration the use of generative approaches, like generative adversarial networks or hidden Markov model. They can expand the contours of each fragments by predicting the visual properties of surrounding pixels so to contribute to increase the matching probability of pieces that do not match each other due to lack of information. An exemplary expansion of visible pixels to generate missing information is depicted in Figs. 8 and 9. Preliminary experimental observation carried out on this kind of approaches confirm the inherent difficult nature of blind digital anastylosis in presence of missing pixels and it deserves an aimed attention. Similarly, spurious fragments represent another critical factor for which special considerations have to be done and specific solutions designed. Generalisation is very difficult to achieve since the solutions strongly depend on the fresco and its pictorial epoch/style. Future works may imply the use of multi resolution contour definition [7], to alleviate the problematic caused by the irregular contours of the fragments.

References

1. Abate, A.F., Barra, P., Barra, S., Molinari, C., Nappi, M., Narducci, F.: Clustering facial attributes: narrowing the path from soft to hard biometrics. IEEE Access **8**, 9037–9045 (2020). https://doi.org/10.1109/ACCESS.2019.2962010
2. Abate, A.F., Barra, S., Galeotafiore, G., Díaz, C., Aura, E., Sánchez, M., Mas, X., Vendrell, E.: An augmented reality mobile app for museums: virtual restoration of a plate of glass. In: Ioannides, M., Fink, E., Brumana, R., Patias, P., Doulamis, A., Martins, J., Wallace, M. (eds.) EuroMed 2018. LNCS, vol. 11196, pp. 539–547. Springer, Cham (2018). https://doi.org/10.1007/978-3-030-01762-0_47
3. Altman, T.: Solving the jigsaw puzzle problem in linear time. Appl. Artif. Intell. Int. J. **3**(4), 453–462 (1989)
4. Andreoli, M.: Mosaics of frescoes: digital photogrammetry, raster representation, pigment analysis and metrology of a flavian wall painting on the caelian hill (rome). Cambridge Archaeol. J. **24**(2), 233–248 (2014)
5. Anzalone, L., Barra, P., Barra, S., Narducci, F., Nappi, M.: Transfer learning for facial attributes prediction and clustering. In: Wang, G., El Saddik, A., Lai, X., Martinez Perez, G., Choo, K.-K.R. (eds.) iSCI 2019. CCIS, vol. 1122, pp. 105–117. Springer, Singapore (2019). https://doi.org/10.1007/978-981-15-1301-5_9
6. Barra, P., Barra, S., Nappi, M., Narducci, F.: Saffo: a sift based approach for digital anastylosis for fresco reconstruction. Pattern Recogn. Lett. (2020). https://doi.org/10.1016/j.patrec.2020.07.008, http://www.sciencedirect.com/science/article/pii/S0167865520302543
7. Chacón, P., Wriggers, W.: Multi-resolution contour-based fitting of macromolecular structures. J. Mol. Biol. **317**(3), 375–384 (2002)
8. Chung, M.G., Fleck, M.M., Forsyth, D.A.: Jigsaw puzzle solver using shape and color. In: ICSP'98. 1998 Fourth International Conference on Signal Processing (Cat. No. 98TH8344), vol. 2, pp. 877–880. IEEE (1998)
9. Dellepiane, M., Niccolucci, F., Serna, S.P., Rushmeier, H., Van Gool, L., et al.: Reassembling thin artifacts of unknown geometry. In: Proceedings of the 12th International Conference on Virtual Reality, Archaeology and Cultural Heritage, pp. 51–61. Euro Graphics Association Aireola-Ville, Switzerland (2011)

10. Díaz-Marín, C., Vendrell-Vidal, E., Aura-Castro, E., Abate, A.F., Sánchez-Belenguer, C., Narducci, F.: Virtual reconstruction and representation of an archaeological terracotta statue. In: 2015 Digital Heritage, vol. 2, pp. 699–702. IEEE (2015)
11. Du, G., Zhou, M., Yin, C., Wu, Z., Shui, W.: Classifying fragments of terracotta warriors using template-based partial matching. Multimed. Tools Appl. 77(15), 19171–19191 (2018)
12. Du, G., Zhou, M., Yin, C., Zhang, J., Wu, Z., Shui, W.: An automatic positioning algorithm for archaeological fragments. In: Proceedings of the 15th ACM SIGGRAPH Conference on Virtual-Reality Continuum and Its Applications in Industry-Volume 1, pp. 431–439 (2016)
13. Leitao, H.C., Stolfi, J.: Measuring the information content of fracture lines. Int. J. Comput. Vision 65(3), 163–174 (2005)
14. Li-Ying, Q., Ke-Gang, W.: Kernel fuzzy clustering based classification of ancient-ceramic fragments. In: 2010 2nd IEEE International Conference on Information Management and Engineering, pp. 348–350. IEEE (2010)
15. Lowe, D.G.: Local feature view clustering for 3d object recognition. In: Proceedings of the 2001 IEEE Computer Society Conference on Computer Vision and Pattern Recognition. CVPR 2001, vol. 1, pp. I-I, December 2001. https://doi.org/10.1109/CVPR.2001.990541
16. Makridis, M., Daras, P.: Automatic classification of archaeological pottery sherds. J. Comput. Cultural Heritage (JOCCH) 5(4), 1–21 (2013)
17. Paumard, M.M., Picard, D., Tabia, H.: Jigsaw puzzle solving using local feature co-occurrences in deep neural networks. In: 2018 25th IEEE International Conference on Image Processing (ICIP), pp. 1018–1022. IEEE (2018)
18. Rasheed, N.A., Nordin, M.J.: Classification and reconstruction algorithms for the archaeological fragments. J. King Saud Univ. Comput. Inf. Sci. 26(5), 204–215 (2018)
19. Smith, P., Bespalov, D., Shokoufandeh, A., Jeppson, P.: Classification of archaeological ceramic fragments using texture and color descriptors. In: 2010 IEEE Computer Society Conference on Computer Vision and Pattern Recognition-Workshops, pp. 49–54. IEEE (2010)
20. Tammisto, A., Danielli, C., Häyhä, H.: Poster: developing the digital puzzling and reconstruction system for second style fresco fragments from the house of marcus lucretius (ix, 3, 5.24) in pompeii. In: Nuove ricerche archeologiche nell'area Vesuviana (scavi 2003–2006): Atti del Convegno Internazionale, Roma 1.-3.2. 2007, pp. 544–545 (2008)
21. Tan, T.K., Boon, C.S., Suzuki, Y.: Intra prediction by template matching. In: 2006 International Conference on Image Processing, pp. 1693–1696. IEEE (2006)
22. Thuswaldner, B., Flöry, S., Kalasek, R., Hofer, M., Huang, Q.X., Thür, H.: Digital anastylosis of the octagon in ephesos. JOCCH 2(1), 1–1 (2009)
23. Vannucci, P., Maffi-Berthier, V., Stefanou, I., Masi, F.: Structural integrity of notre dame cathedral after the fire of april 15th (2019)
24. Youguang, W., Li, X., Li, M.: Color and contour based reconstruction of fragmented image. In: 2013 8th International Conference on Computer Science & Education, pp. 999–1003. IEEE (2013)
25. Yu, R., Russell, C., Agapito, L.: Solving jigsaw puzzles with linear programming. arXiv preprint arXiv:1511.04472 (2015)

Restoration and Enhancement of Historical Stereo Photos Through Optical Flow

Marco Fanfani[1] , Carlo Colombo[1] , and Fabio Bellavia[2]([envelope])

[1] Department of Information Engineering, Università degli Studi di Firenze,
Firenze, Italy
{marco.fanfani,carlo.colombo}@unifi.it
[2] Department of Math and Computer Science, Università degli Studi di Palermo,
Palermo, Italy
fabio.bellavia@unipa.it

Abstract. Restoration of digital visual media acquired from repositories of historical photographic and cinematographic material is of key importance for the preservation, study and transmission of the legacy of past cultures to the coming generations. In this paper, a fully automatic approach to the digital restoration of historical stereo photographs is proposed. The approach exploits the content redundancy in stereo pairs for detecting and fixing scratches, dust, dirt spots and many other defects in the original images, as well as improving contrast and illumination. This is done by estimating the optical flow between the images, and using it to register one view onto the other both geometrically and photometrically. Restoration is then accomplished by data fusion according to the stacked median, followed by gradient adjustment and iterative visual consistency checking. The obtained output is fully consistent with the original content, thus improving over the methods based on image hallucination. Comparative results on three different datasets of historical stereograms show the effectiveness of the proposed approach, and its superiority over single-image denoising and super-resolution methods.

Keywords: Image denoising · Image restoration · Image enhancement · Stereo matching · Optical flow · Gradient filtering

1 Introduction

Photographic material of the XIX and XX centuries is an invaluable source of information for historians of art, architecture and sociology, as it allows them to track the changes occurred over the decades to a community and its living environment. Unfortunately, due to the effect of time and bad preservation conditions, most of the survived photographic heritage is partially damaged, and needs restoration, both at the physical (cardboard support, glass negatives, films, etc.) and digital (the image content acquired through scanners) levels. Dirt, scratches,

© Springer Nature Switzerland AG 2021
A. Del Bimbo et al. (Eds.): ICPR 2020 Workshops, LNCS 12663, pp. 643–656, 2021.
https://doi.org/10.1007/978-3-030-68796-0_46

discoloration and other signs of aging strongly reduce the visual quality of the photos [1]. A similar situation also holds for the cinematographic material [10].

Digital restoration of both still images and videos has attracted considerable interest from the research community in the early 2000s. This has led to the development of several tools that improve the visual quality. Some approaches rely on the instantiation of noise models, which can either be fixed a-priori or derived from the input images [3,16,18]. Other approaches detect damaged areas of the image and correct them according to inpainting techniques [6]. Self-correlation inside the image, or across different frames in videos, is often exploited in this context, under the assumption that zero-mean additive noise cancels out as the available number of image data samples increases [4,5,7]. A similar idea is exploited by super-resolution techniques, that enhance image quality by pixel interpolation [14,23]. In recent years, the algorithmic methods above have been sided by methods based on deep learning, that can infer the image formation model from a training set in order to inject this information into the final output—a process called image hallucination [19,21,24]. Although the final image may often alter the original image data content, and hence cannot be fully trusted (e.g., in the medical diagnosis domain), from the visual point of view the hallucination methods can give aesthetically pleasing results (see Fig. 1).

Stereoscopy has accompanied photography since its very birth in the nineteenth century, with ups and downs in popularity through time. Notwithstanding the lesser spread of stereo photography with respect to standard (monocular) photography, many digital archives with thousands of stereo images exist, some of which are freely available on the web. Stereo photos have a richer content than standard ones, as they present two different views of the same scene, thus explicitly introducing content redundancy and implicitly embedding information about scene depth. This characteristic can be exploited also in digital noise removal, enhancement and restoration, since a damaged area in one image can be reconstructed from the other image, provided that the correspondences between the two images are known. At a first glance, the above mentioned approach looks similar to that of video restoration from multiple video frames, in which the scene is acquired in subsequent time instants from slightly changed viewpoints. However, stereo images have their own peculiarities, and actually introduce in the restoration process more complications than video frames, which in movies typically exhibit an almost static and undeformed background, differently from stereo pairs. As a matter of fact, although several advances have been recently made in stereo matching and dense optical flow estimation [17], the problem is hard and far to be fully solved, especially in the case of very noisy and altered images such as those generated by early photographic stereo material. To the best of the authors' knowledge, stereo photo characteristics have been employed only for the super-resolution enhancement or deblurring of modern, clean photos [9,22,25]. On the other hand, the image analysis and computer vision approaches developed so far for historical stereo photos mainly aimed at achieving (usually in a manual way) better visualizations or 3D scene reconstructions [8,11,15], with no attempt at restoring the quality of the raw stereo pairs.

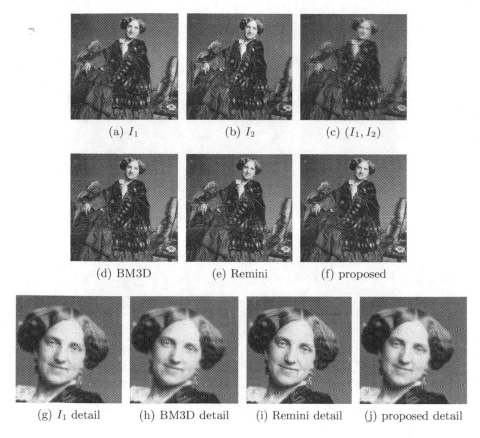

(a) I_1 (b) I_2 (c) (I_1, I_2)

(d) BM3D   (e) Remini   (f) proposed

(g) I_1 detail   (h) BM3D detail   (i) Remini detail   (j) proposed detail

Fig. 1. An example of historical stereo pair images, I_1 and I_2, also superimposed as anaglyph in (c). The enhancement of I_1 according to several methodologies is also shown. In particular, although producing visually impressive results, the deep super-resolution method Remini - Photo Enhancer (https://play.google.com/store/apps/details?id=com.bigwinepot.nwdn.international) (e) does not preserve the true input image, adding fictitious details. Indeed, a closer look at (i) reveals alterations with respect to the original face expression (g), accentuating the smile and introducing bush-like textures on the left part of the hair. Best viewed in color, the reader is invited to zoom in the electronic version of the manuscript in order to better appreciate the visual differences.

This paper proposes a new approach to clean-up and restore the true scene content in degraded historical stereo photographs, working in a fully automatic way. With respect to existent single image methods, damaged image areas with scratches or dust can be better detected and fixed, thanks to the availability of more sampled data points for denoising. In addition, the correct illumination can be restored or enhanced in a way akin to that of High Dynamic Range Imaging, where the images of the same scene taken at different exposure levels are used in order to enhance details and colors [12]. For this scope the optical flow, estimated with a recent state-of-the-art deep network [17], is used to synthesize corresponding scene viewpoints in the stereo pair, while denoising and restoration is carried out using non-deep image processing approaches. The entire process is superseded by scene content consistency validation, used to check critical stereo matching mispredictions that were previously unresolved by the network. Our approach aims to obtain an output which is fully consistent with the original scenario captured by the stereo pair, in contrast with the recent super-resolution and denoising approaches based on image hallucination.

The rest of the paper is organized as follows: Sect. 2 introduces the proposed approach. An experimental evaluation and comparison with similar approaches is reported in Sect. 3. Finally, conclusions and future work are discussed in Sect. 4.

2   Method Description

Given a pair of stereo images I_1 and I_2, the aim of the process is to output a defect-free version of one image of the pair (referred to as the reference) by exploiting the additional information coming from the other image (denoted as auxiliary). For convenience, the reference is denoted as I_1 and the auxiliary image as I_2, but their roles can be interchanged. Images are assumed to be single channel graylevel and ranging in $[0, 255]$. Code is freely available online.[1]

2.1   Auxiliary Image Point-Wise Transfer

As first step, the recent state-of-the-art Recurrent All-Pairs Field Transforms (RAFT) deep network [17] is used to compute the optical flow map pair (m_x, m_y), so that a synthesized image based on the content of I_2 and registered onto I_1 can be obtained

$$\tilde{I}_{2\to1}(x,y) = I_2(x + m_x(x,y), y + m_y(x,y)) \tag{1}$$

by transferring pixel intensity values from I_2 into the view given by I_1. Notice that in the case of perfectly rectified stereo images it holds everywhere that $m_y(x,y) = 0$. However the stereo alignment for the photos under consideration is far from perfect due to the technological limitations of the period, hence both the maps m_x and m_y are considered. RAFT optical flow estimation is not completely accurate, nor it does preserve the map inversion when exchanging the input image order. Hence, a further flow mapping pair (m'_x, m'_y) can be obtained by switching the two input images, which can be employed to synthesize a second image according to

$$\tilde{I}'_{2\to1}(x,y) = I_2(x - m'_x(x,y), y - m'_y(x,y)) \tag{2}$$

The final synthesized image $I_{2\to1}$ is then obtained by choosing the intensity value of each pixel (x,y) as the one from $\tilde{I}_{2\to1}(x,y)$ and $\tilde{I}'_{2\to1}(x,y)$ that minimizes the sum of absolute errors with respect to I_1 on a 5×5 local window centered on the pixel (compare the 2nd, 3th and 4th columns of Fig. 2).

---

[1] https://drive.google.com/drive/folders/1DRsKLrlKJs9AnCMBceDSDm9VBS ftNRi3.

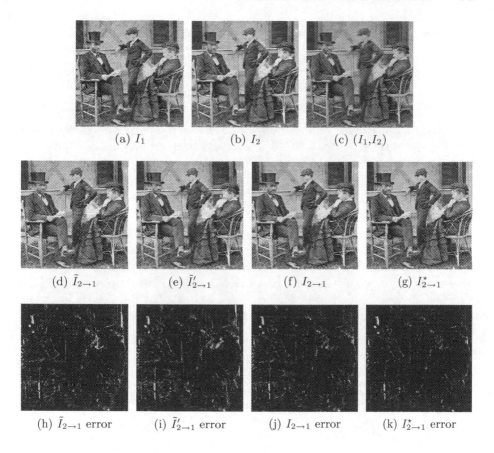

(a) I_1 (b) I_2 (c) (I_1, I_2)

(d) $\tilde{I}_{2\to1}$ (e) $\tilde{I}'_{2\to1}$ (f) $I_{2\to1}$ (g) $I^\star_{2\to1}$

(h) $\tilde{I}_{2\to1}$ error   (i) $\tilde{I}'_{2\to1}$ error   (j) $I_{2\to1}$ error   (k) $I^\star_{2\to1}$ error

Fig. 2. Auxiliary image point-wise transfer and color correction steps, errors are reported with respect to I_1 while (c) shows the input stereo pair as anaglyph. Best viewed in color, the reader is invited to zoom in the electronic version of the manuscript in order to better appreciate the visual differences.

2.2   Color Correction

Due to the technical limitations of old the photographic instrumentation, illumination conditions between the two stereo images can differ noticeably. For instance, flash lamp and, even more, flash powder did not provide each time uniform and identical illumination conditions, and it was not infrequent that a single camera was moved in two different positions in order to simulate a stereo setup instead of having two synchronized cameras [8]. Moreover, discoloration of the support due to aging can be present. In order to improve the final result, the state-of-the-art color correction method named Gradient Preserving Spline with Linear Color Propagation (GPS/LCP) presented in [2] is employed to correct the illumination of $I_{2\to1}$ according to I_1, thus obtaining the new image $I^\star_{2\to1}$ (see Fig. 2, last column). This method is able to preserve the image content and works also in the case of not perfectly aligned images. Clearly, if $I_{2\to1}$ presents better illumination conditions than I_1, it is also possible to correct I_1 according to $I_{2\to1}$.

2.3   Data Fusion

Given the reference image I_1 and the synthesized one obtained from the auxiliary view $I_{2\to1}^{\star}$ after the illumination post-processing, the two images are blended into a new image I_{12} according to the stacked median

$$I_{12} = \nabla(I_1 \cup I_{2\to1}^{\star}) \tag{3}$$

Formally, the stacked median $\nabla(\{I\})$ of a set of images $\{I\}$ is defined so that the intensity value of the resulting image located at pixel (x, y) is given by the median computed on the union of the 3×3 local windows centered at (x, y) on each image of the set. With this operator, dirt, scratches and other signs of photographic age or damages are effectively removed from I_{12}, but high frequency details can be lost in the process, due to the 3×3 filtering. These are re-introduced by considering a blended version of the gradient magnitude

$$d_{m_{12}} = \nabla(\nabla(M(I_1)) \cup \nabla(M(I_{2\to1}^{\star}))) \tag{4}$$

obtained as the two-step stacked median of eight possible gradient magnitudes, four for each of the I_1 and $I_{2\to1}^{\star}$ images. Each gradient magnitude image in the set $M(I)$ for a generic image I is computed as

$$d_m = (d_x^2 + d_y^2)^{\frac{1}{2}} \tag{5}$$

pixel-wise, where the image gradient direction pairs (d_x, d_y) are computed by the convolution of I with the following four pairs of kernel filters

$$\left\{ \left(\begin{bmatrix} 0 & 0 & 0 \\ 0 & -1 & 1 \\ 0 & 0 & 0 \end{bmatrix}, \begin{bmatrix} 0 & 1 & 0 \\ 0 & -1 & 0 \\ 0 & 0 & 0 \end{bmatrix} \right), \left(\begin{bmatrix} 0 & 0 & 1 \\ 0 & -1 & 0 \\ 0 & 0 & 0 \end{bmatrix}, \begin{bmatrix} 1 & 0 & 0 \\ 0 & -1 & 0 \\ 0 & 0 & 0 \end{bmatrix} \right), \left(\begin{bmatrix} 0 & 0 & 0 \\ 1 & -1 & 0 \\ 0 & 0 & 0 \end{bmatrix}, \begin{bmatrix} 0 & 0 & 0 \\ 0 & -1 & 0 \\ 0 & 1 & 0 \end{bmatrix} \right), \left(\begin{bmatrix} 0 & 0 & 0 \\ 0 & -1 & 0 \\ 1 & 0 & 0 \end{bmatrix}, \begin{bmatrix} 0 & 0 & 0 \\ 0 & -1 & 0 \\ 0 & 0 & 1 \end{bmatrix} \right) \right\} \tag{6}$$

Notice that $d_{m_{12}} \neq \nabla(M(I_{12}))$ in the general case. Consider for now only a single derivative pair (d_x, d_y) of I_{12}: Each pixel intensity $I_{12}(x, y)$ is incremented by a value $v(x, y)$ so that

$$(d_x + v)^2 + (d_y + v)^2 = d_{m_{12}}^{\ 2} \tag{7}$$

pixel-wise, that gives the a twofold solution

$$v^{\star} = \pm(2d_x d_y - d_{m_{12}}^{\ 2})^{\frac{1}{2}} - d_x - d_y \tag{8}$$

The final solution $v(x, y)$ is chosen as 0 in the case $v^{\star}(x, y)$ is complex or, otherwise, as the one among the two possible solutions with the minimum absolute value, in order to alter I_{12} as little as possible, thus obtaining the final image $I_{12\uparrow} = I_{12} + v$ (see Fig. 3). Actually, the average of the four allowable derivative pairs is used to get the final $v(x, y)$ values.

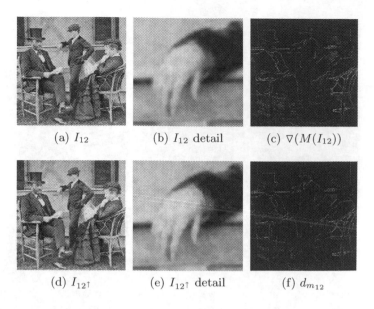

(a) I_{12} (b) I_{12} detail   (c) $\nabla(M(I_{12}))$

(d) $I_{12\uparrow}$ (e) $I_{12\uparrow}$ detail   (f) $d_{m_{12}}$

Fig. 3. Data fusion step. Best viewed in color, the reader is invited to zoom in the electronic version of the manuscript in order to better appreciate the visual differences.

2.4   Refinement

As already noted for the first step, the optical flow may be not perfect, causing the presence of wrong data in the image synthesis and hence in the data fusion process described in the previous step. To solve this issue, an error-driven image correction is introduced that consists of two sub-steps. The first one is the detection of the image region that needs to be adjusted, done by considering a 11×11 local window on $(I_1 - I_{12\uparrow})^2$ centered at (x, y). If on this window the root squared average of the values lower than the 66% percentile (i.e., the inliers) is higher than a predefined threshold $t = 16$, pixel (x, y) is selected to be corrected. Optionally, the obtained mask B can be smoothed using a Gaussian kernel followed by binarization. Selection by percentile has shown to be more robust than working on the whole window. For the second sub-step, data fusion is repeated on the masked pixels by substituting $I^{\star}_{2 \rightarrow 1}$ with $I_{12\uparrow}$ in the input. Since $I_{12\uparrow}$ is a sort of average between I_1 and $I^{\star}_{2 \rightarrow 1}$, repeating data fusion between I_1 and $I_{12\uparrow}$ on masked pixels will push these more towards I_1. If this refined image $I_{\bar{1}2\uparrow}$ still contains regions to be adjusted according to the first sub-step, the second refinement sub-step is repeated again (see Fig. 4). A maximum of four iterations are allowed, as it was verified experimentally that data fusion roughly converges to I_1 within this number of steps. Actually, the current mask is morphologically dilated by a disk with radius proportional to the number of the remaining steps for better results.

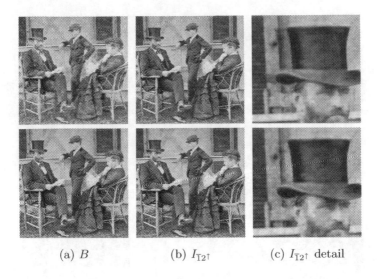

(a) B (b) $I_{\bar{1}2\uparrow}$ (c) $I_{\bar{1}2\uparrow}$ detail

Fig. 4. Refinement step. First (top row) and last (bottom row) detection and adjustment sub-steps. The red and blue masks correspond respectively to make the selection with or without the proposed outlier rejection filtering, (c) is the final denoised image. It can be shown by inspecting the detail that the ghosting effect is gradually eliminated. Best viewed in color, the reader is invited to zoom in the electronic version of the manuscript in order to better appreciate the visual differences.

3   Evaluation

3.1   Dataset

In order to evaluate the proposed approach we built a new dataset including historical stereo pairs from different sources. The left frames of the selected stereo pairs are shown as reference in Fig. 5.

A first set of seven stereo pairs belongs to the collection of stereograms by Anton Hautmann, one of the most active photographers in Florence (Italy) between 1858 and 1862, courtesy of Photothek des Kunsthistorischen Instituts in Florenz—Max-Planck-Institut. Part of Hautmann's collection is described in [8]. The seven stereo pairs used in this work depict different viewpoints of Piazza Santissima Annunziata in Florence as it was in the middle of the XIX century. Inspecting these photos (see Fig. 5, red frames), it can be noticed that the image quality is very poor: the pairs are quite noisy, have poor definition, low contrast, saturated or blurred areas and also show scratches and stains.

A second set of five images was collected from the U.S. Geological Survey (USGS) Historical Stereoscopic Photos account on Flickr[2], and includes natural landscapes (see Fig. 5, green frames), except for the last one which includes also two horsemen with their mounts. Noise affects these images as with the first set, but also strong vignetting effects are present.

---

[2] https://www.flickr.com/photos/usgeologicalsurvey/.

Fig. 5. Left frames of the noisy stereo pair datasets. Image frames for Hautmann's, USGS and Stereoscopic Photos datasets are respectively in red, green and blue. Best viewed in color and zoomed in onto the electronic version of the manuscript. (Color figure online)

A third set, including ten stereo pairs, was instead gathered from the Stereoscopic History Instagram account[3] (see Fig. 5, blue frames). The first five images are landscape pictures of urban and natural scenes, while the last five pairs are individual or group portraits. This set is the most challenging one, since strong noises affect the images, evidently corrupting the content.

3.2 Compared Methods

The proposed approach was compared against Block Matching 3D (BM3D) [7] and the Deep Image Prior (hereafter denoted DP) architecture [19], two state-of-the-art single image denoising methods. For BM3D, the legacy version was employed, since according to our preliminary experiments the new version including correlated noise suppression did not work well for our kind of images. The BM3D σ parameter, the only one present, was set to 7 and 14, that according to our experiments gave the best visual results. In particular $\sigma = 14$ seems to work better than $\sigma = 7$ in the case of higher resolution images. Besides applying the standard BM3D on the reference image, a modified version of it was deployed in order to allow BM3D to benefit from the stereo auxiliary data. Since BM3D

---

[3] https://www.instagram.com/stereoscopichistory/.

exploits image self-correlation to suppress noise, this modified BM3D generates auxiliary sub-images by siding two corresponding 96×96 patches from I_1 and $I_{2 \to 1}^{\star}$, runs BM3D on each sub-image and then reconstructs the final result collecting those blocks from each sub-image corresponding to the 32×32 central I_1 patches. No difference in the result outputs with respect to the standard BM3D were detected, which plausibly implies that corresponding patches for I_1 and $I_{2 \to 1}^{\star}$ are not judged as similar by BM3D. In the case of DP, the input can be rescaled due to network constraints, and borders were cropped: These missing parts were replaced with the original input image.

3.3   Results

Figures 6 and 7 show some results for a visual qualitative evaluation—the reader is invited to inspect the full-resolution images of the whole dataset included in the additional material (see Footnote 1). No quantitative evaluations have been reported since, lacking of ground-truth clean data, image quality measurements requiring a reference image such as the Structural Similarity Index (SSIM) [20] cannot be extracted, while non-reference quality measures such as the Blind/Referenceless Image Spatial Quality Evaluator (BRISQUE) [13] are

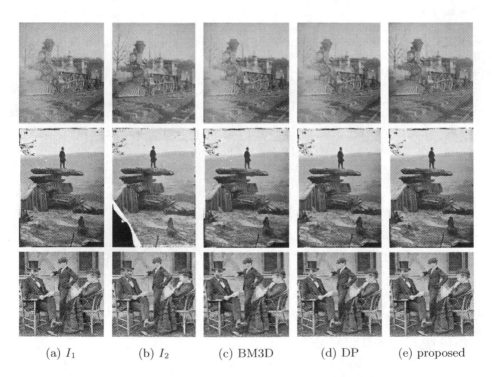

(a) I_1 (b) I_2 (c) BM3D   (d) DP   (e) proposed

Fig. 6. Visual comparison on the whole image. Best viewed in color, the reader is invited to zoom in the electronic version of the manuscript in order to better appreciate the differences.

not modeled for old camera model statistics nor are able to judge the removal and restoration of damaged image areas.

According to the results, BM3D and DP seem to often oversmooth relevant details in the image, with BM3D producing somewhat better results than DP. In any case, these methods are not able to detect and compensate for dust, scratches and other kinds of artefacts, that conversely may be enhanced in the process, as one can check by inspecting the dust spots and the sketches on the two images. This is not the case of the proposed method that, exploiting the stereo correspondences, is able to fix these issues. Our method can also enhance the image contrast, as it happens for the dark spot under the right arcade in Fig. 7, 2nd row. In more severe cases, better results can be obtained by forcing

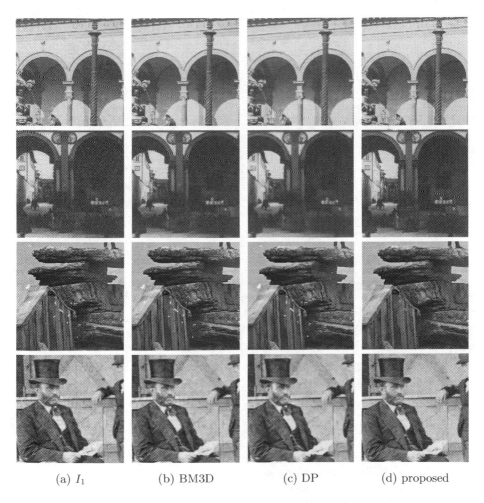

(a) I_1 (b) BM3D   (c) DP   (d) proposed

Fig. 7. Visual comparison on image details. Best viewed in color, the reader is invited to zoom in the electronic version of the manuscript in order to better appreciate the differences.

the illumination of the auxiliary image into the reference (see Sect. 2.2), as shown in Fig. 6, 1st row. Nevertheless, the proposed method also has some limitations. In particular, finer high-frequency texture details can sometimes disappear in low-resolution images, due to the use of 3×3 windows in the stacked median (see Sect. 2.3) in conjunction with an inaccurate optical flow estimation, as in Fig. 7, 3th row. Indeed, the proposed method strongly depends upon a correct identification of the optical flow, and although its wrong estimation is generally handled well (see Sect. 2.4), as for the tube hat of Fig. 7, last row, some spurious ghosting artefacts can sometimes arise, as those around the light pole in Fig. 7, 1st column.

4   Conclusion and Future Work

This paper proposed a novel method for the fully automatic restoration of historical stereo photographs. By exploiting optical flow clues, the auxiliary view of the stereo frame is geometrically and photometrically registered against the reference view. Restoration is carried out by fusing the data information available from both images according to the stacked median approach followed by gradient adjustments in order to better preserve finer details. Finally, an iterative refinement is performed in order to remove artefacts due to errors in the flow estimation guided by a visual consistency check.

Results on historical stereo pairs show the effectiveness of the proposed approach, that is able to remove most of the image defects including dust and scratches, without excessive smoothing of the image content. The proposed method works better than its single-image denoising competitors, thanks to the ability of exploiting stereo information. As a matter of fact, single-image methods have severe limitations in handling damaged areas, and usually produce more blurry results.

Future work will be addressed to investigate novel solutions to refine the optical flow in order to reduce pixel mismatch, but also to consolidate both theoretical and practical aspects of the stacked median. In particular, further and general applications will be explored, as well as new methods for improving the gradient refinement. Additionally, explicit solutions to embed other methods such as BM3D into our approach and to identify damaged image areas on a single stereo frame will be studied in order to let the system better weights the local contributions of a frame in producing the final output. Finally, the proposed method will be extended and adapted to cinematographic images and historical film restoration.

Acknowledgment. This work was supported by the Italian Ministry of University and Research (MUR) under the program PON Ricerca e Innovazione 2014–2020, cofunded by the European Social Fund (ESF), CUP B74I18000220006, id. proposta AIM 1875400, linea di attività 2, Area Cultural Heritage.

The Titan Xp used for this research was generously donated by the NVIDIA Corporation.

We would like to thank Drs. Costanza Caraffa and Ute Dercks at Photothek des Kunsthistorischen Instituts in Florenz – Max-Planck-Institut for allowing the reproduction of the photos in this paper. Hautmann's collection digital scans: ©Stefano Fancelli/KHI.

References

1. Ardizzone, E., De Polo, A., Dindo, H., Mazzola, G., Nanni, C.: A dual taxonomy for defects in digitized historical photos. In: 10th International Conference on Document Analysis and Recognition, pp. 1166–1170 (2009)
2. Bellavia, F., Colombo, C.: Dissecting and reassembling color correction algorithms for image stitching. IEEE Trans. Image Process. **27**(2), 735–748 (2018)
3. Besserer, B., Thiré, C.: Detection and tracking scheme for line scratch removal in an image sequence. In: European Conference on Computer Vision (ECCV2004), pp. 264–275 (2004)
4. Buades, A., Lisani, J., Miladinović, M.: Patch-based video denoising with optical flow estimation. IEEE Trans. Image Process. **25**(6), 2573–2586 (2016)
5. Chen, F., Zhang, L., Yu, H.: External patch prior guided internal clustering for image denoising. In: IEEE International Conference on Computer Vision (ICCV2015), pp. 603–611 (2015)
6. Criminisi, A., Perez, P., Toyama, K.: Object removal by exemplar-based inpainting. In: IEEE Conference on Computer Vision and Pattern Recognition (CVPR2003), vol. 2 (2003)
7. Dabov, K., Foi, A., Katkovnik, V., Egiazarian, K.: Image denoising by sparse 3D transform-domain collaborative filtering. IEEE Trans. Image Process. **16**(8), 2080–2095 (2007)
8. Fanfani, M., Bellavia, F., Bassetti, G., Argenti, F., Colombo, C.: 3D map computation from historical stereo photographs of Florence. In: IOP Conference Series: Materials Science and Engineering, vol. 364, p. 012044 (2018)
9. Jeon, D.S., Baek, S., Choi, I., Kim, M.H.: Enhancing the spatial resolution of stereo images using a parallax prior. In: IEEE Conference on Computer Vision and Pattern Recognition (CVPR2018), pp. 1721–1730 (2018)
10. Kokaram, A.C.: Motion Picture Restoration: Digital Algorithms for Artefact Suppression in Degraded Motion Picture Film and Video. Springer-Verlag (1998). DOIurl10.1007/978-1-4471-3485-5
11. Luo, X., Kong, Y., Lawrence, J., Martin-Brualla, R., Seitz, S.: KeystoneDepth: Visualizing history in 3D (2019)
12. McCann, J.J., Rizzi, A.: The Art and Science of HDR Imaging. Wiley, Hoboken (2011)
13. Mittal, A., Moorthy, A.K., Bovik, A.C.: No-reference image quality assessment in the spatial domain. IEEE Trans. Image Process. **21**(12), 4695–4708 (2012)
14. Nasrollahi, K., Moeslund, T.B.: Super-resolution: a comprehensive survey. Mach. Vis. Appl. **25**(6), 1423–1468 (2014)
15. Schindler, G., Dellaert, F.: 4D cities: analyzing, visualizing, and interacting with historical urban photo collections. J. Multimed. **7**(2), 124–131 (2012)
16. Stanco, F., Tenze, L., Ramponi, G.: Virtual restoration of vintage photographic prints affected by foxing and water blotches. J. Electron. Imaging **14**, 043008 (2005)
17. Teed, Z., Deng, J.: RAFT: recurrent all-pairs field transforms for optical flow. In: European Conference on Computer Vision (ECCV2020) (2020)

18. Tegolo, D., Isgrò, F.: A genetic algorithm for scratch removal in static images. In: International Conference on Image Analysis and Processing (ICIAP2001), pp. 507–511 (2001)
19. Ulyanov, D., Vedaldi, A., Lempitsky, V.: Deep image prior. In: IEEE Conference on Computer Vision and Pattern Recognition (CVPR2018) (2018)
20. Wang, Z., Bovik, A.C., Sheikh, H.R., Simoncelli, E.P.: Image quality assessment: from error visibility to structural similarity. IEEE Trans. Image Process. **13**(4), 600–612 (2004)
21. Wang, Z., Chen, J., Hoi, S.C.H.: Deep learning for image super-resolution: a survey. IEEE Trans. Patt. Anal. Mach. Intell. (2020). https://ieeexplore.ieee.org/document/9044873
22. Yan, B., Ma, C., Bare, B., Tan, W., Hoi, S.: Disparity-aware domain adaptation in stereo image restoration. In: IEEE Conference on Computer Vision and Pattern Recognition (CVPR2020), pp. 13176–13184 (2020)
23. Yang, J., Wright, J., Huang, T.S., Ma, Y.: Image super-resolution via sparse representation. IEEE Trans. Image Process. **19**(11), 2861–2873 (2010)
24. Zhang, Y., Tian, Y., Kong, Y., Zhong, B., Fu, Y.: Residual dense network for image restoration. IEEE Trans. Patt. Anal. Mach. Intell. (2020). https://ieeexplore.ieee.org/document/8964437
25. Zhou, S., Zhang, J., Zuo, W., Xie, H., Pan, J., Ren, J.S.: DAVANet: stereo deblurring with view aggregation. In: IEEE Conference on Computer Vision and Pattern Recognition (CVPR2019), pp. 10988–10997 (2019)

Automatic Chain Line Segmentation
in Historical Prints

Meike Biendl[1](✉), Aline Sindel[1,2], Thomas Klinke[3], Andreas Maier[1],
and Vincent Christlein[1]

[1] Pattern Recognition Lab, FAU Erlangen-Nürnberg, Erlangen, Germany
{meike.biendl,aline.sindel,andreas.maier,vincent.christlein}@fau.de
[2] Germanisches Nationalmuseum, Nuremberg, Germany
[3] Cologne Institute of Conservation Sciences (CICS), TH Köln, Köln, Germany
thomas.klinke@th-koeln.de

Abstract. The analysis of chain line patterns in historical prints can
provide valuable information about the origin of the paper. For this task,
we propose a method to automatically detect chain lines in transmitted
light images of prints from the 16th century. As motifs and writing on
the paper partially occlude the paper structure, we utilize a convolutional neural network in combination with further postprocessing steps
to segment and parametrize the chain lines. We compare the number of
parametrized lines, as well as the distances between them, with reference
lines and values. Our proposed method is an effective method showing
a low error of less than 1 mm in comparison to the manually measured
chain line distances.

Keywords: Line segmentation · Line detection · Chain lines ·
Historical prints · Paper structure

1 Introduction

In the 16th century, the paper that was used for printed artworks, such as wood
cuts or etchings, was scooped by hand. Apart from analyzing the motif itself,
e.g. concerning its degree of wear, also characteristics of the paper pattern can
give hints to locate the possible date of origin.

To create paper by hand, a mold with a porous screen is dipped into a vat
of pulp made of macerated rag fibers suspended in water. The screen is made of
closely spaced "laid" wires and perpendicular wider spaced "chain" wires. The
paper is formed by the remaining layer of rag fibers on the screen. On its surface
a grid pattern, imprinted from the wires, is visible [4]. In Fig. 1a an illuminated
image section of a paper with horizontal laid lines caused by the laid wires and
a vertical chain line formed by a chain wire can be seen.

M. Biendl and A. Sindel—Contributed equally to this paper.

© Springer Nature Switzerland AG 2021
A. Del Bimbo et al. (Eds.): ICPR 2020 Workshops, LNCS 12663, pp. 657–665, 2021.
https://doi.org/10.1007/978-3-030-68796-0_47

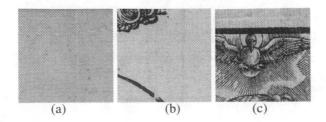

(a)   (b)   (c)

Fig. 1. Paper structure in historical prints using transmitted light photography: (a) plain paper with horizontal laid lines and a vertical chain line, chain and laid lines in (b) and (c) are partly occluded by artworks.

The distances between the parallel chain lines are approximately 25–30 mm, but vary across the screen. For every mold, the chain lines form a unique pattern. Paper created by the same mold show a similar pattern of chain lines, whereas papers from different origins have different line sequences [3]. Images formed by the same mold are called *moldmates* [4]. These moldmates can be identified by analyzing the recorded wire features and can help in dating the artworks.

The goal of this paper is to automatically detect the chain lines in transmitted light images of German prints from the 16th century as manual tracing of the lines is time consuming. The paper structure can be revealed with transmitted light, i.e. the contrast of chain lines and laid lines is enhanced. However, the motif printed with dark ink partly occludes the paper structure and the lines are not always clearly visible, see Fig. 1b,c. Therefore, we use a neural network to automatically segment the chain lines in the artworks and then locate and parameterize the lines using an agglomerative clustering and RANSAC [2] based approach in comparison to using the Hough transform.

2   Related Work

To digitalize the paper structure of historical prints, e.g. transmitted light photography, transmitted infrared photography, beta-radiography or thermography can be used. Chain lines are recognizable in the images of all these modalities. By using transmitted light photography additional image processing might be necessary due to interferences like ink that remain visible. These interferences disappear in the images using the other modalities. However, transmitted light photography is faster, cheaper and easier to handle.

There are a few approaches for automated segmentation of chain lines of paper. Van der Lubbe et al. [5] assumed straight and vertical chain lines for chain line detection in radiography. They use uniform filtering and morphological opening and closing operators as pre-processing and apply a vertical projection to detect the vertical lines as peaks of the projection. Atanasiu [1] detected the density of laid lines by using 2-D discrete fast Fourier transform. In a pre-processing step, emboss edge-enhancing high-pass filter reduces noise, but beforehand the orientation of the laid lines must be known. Van Staalduinen et al. [7] presented a method for moldmate matching based on chain and laid line detection. The chain distances are computed based on the shadow around the chain lines using a combination of discrete Fourier transform and Radon transform assuming straight and equidistant lines. Hiary et al. [3] used back-light scanning and image processing such as mathematical morphological operations to extract watermarks and automatically convert them to graphical representations. In an intermediate step they perform chain line detection using Radon transform and rotate the image to upright the chain lines. Johnson et al. [4] proposed an approach for chain line pattern matching to find moldmates among Rembrandt's prints in beta radiographs. They assume straight, but not necessarily parallel lines. The angle to rotate the chain lines to vertical is obtained by applying Radon transform. Then, the lines are detected using a vertical filter and Hough transform.

3   Method

Our proposed method for detecting chain lines in transmitted light images of prints is illustrated in Fig. 2. First, a line segmentation network is trained that predicts mask images containing the line segments. Then, some further image processing steps are applied to extract the chain lines from the line segments.

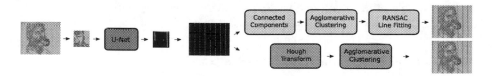

Fig. 2. Chain line segmentation pipeline: patch extraction, line segmentation network and postprocessing steps for line parametrization based on the line segment predictions. Image: *Martin Luther as Junker Jörg*, Hans Sebald Beham (attributed), Germanisches Nationalmuseum, Nuremberg, St. N. 365

3.1   Line Segmentation Network

The segmentation of the lines is performed by a neural network on patch-level. Therefore, we employ the U-net architecture which consists of a contracting path and a symmetric expansive path with convolutional and pooling layers as well as rectified linear units (ReLU). An advantage of this network is that only a few training samples are needed [6].

Our dataset contains images with chain lines distributed either horizontally or vertically at approximately the same distances. For manual annotation of the lines, we selected two points on each line for parametrization as illustrated in Fig. 3a,b. With this knowledge, corresponding mask images are created which contain only the segmented lines (Fig. 3c) and serve as labels for training and as ground truth for the final evaluation.

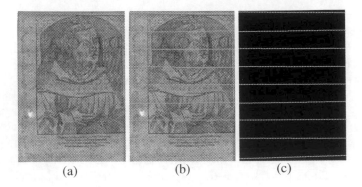

(a)   (b)   (c)

Fig. 3. (a) Transmitted light image, (b) image with segmented lines and (c) corresponding mask image. Image: *Martin Luther as Augustinian monk*, Unknown, after Lucas Cranach the Elder, Staatsbibliothek Bamberg, 22-64 B 21

The network is trained by minimizing the binary cross-entropy loss computed between the predicted mask and the labeled mask image patches.

During inference, the U-Net outputs a mask image patch for every test image patch. The whole mask image is reassembled from the predicted mask patches. Due to the occlusions by the printed motifs, the network predictions do not contain complete lines, but smaller line segments. Therefore, in additional post-processing steps the chain lines are extracted from the predicted mask images.

3.2   Line Detection and Parameterization

For the detection and parametrization of the lines from the mask images, we used two different approaches.

The first approach applies the method connected components where the pixels are grouped into connected line segments. With a Sobel filter the orientation of the lines (horizontal or vertical) is determined and line segments that have the wrong orientation or contain only a few points are discarded. Since the number of chain lines is unknown, the mean Euclidean distances between the line segments are determined. 75% of the maximum Euclidean distance between two neighbouring segments is used as a distance threshold in agglomerative clustering with Ward linkage to calculate the approximate number of lines. With this knowledge, the line segments corresponding to each line are grouped into larger point clouds. Then, the RANSAC method is used to fit a line through each point cloud. This method is used since it is very robust against outliers [2].

Secondly, we apply a voting based approach, i.e. we compute the Hough transform on the mask images. The Hough transform detects a line for large and straight line segments, which results in several predicted lines for each chain line. Then, agglomerative clustering is used in the same manner to group and merge nearby lines.

For visualization, we superimpose the predicted lines from the two approaches onto the original images. Due to the distance between the lines, their distance to the edges and their slope, the lines are categorized in probable and improbable lines, which we color differently to allow a quick evaluation.

4   Evaluation

4.1   Dataset

The dataset consists of high-resolution gray-scale transmitted light images of prints from the 16th century including portraits of Martin Luther and contemporaries collected within the research project "Critical catalogue of Luther portraits (1519-1530)" by the Germanisches Nationalmuseum Nürnberg, FAU Erlangen-Nürnberg and TH Köln. For the dataset creation, we selected 59 images in which the chain lines were recognizable by the human eye. We manually annotated the chain lines by selecting two points on each line and fitted a straight line through them to generate mask images (Fig. 3). The sharp edges of the annotated lines in the mask images are removed by applying a Gaussian filter with a standard deviation of 3. The images are divided into 47 images for the training process and 12 images for testing. Due to the high-resolution of the images, we split the images into smaller image patches of size 512×512. For training, we extract the patches by using an overlap stride of the half patch size. Patches without segmented lines are not considered for training, but data augmentation is used to obtain more samples. The total number of training patches (8550) is randomly split into a training set of 75% and a validation set of 25%. The test dataset is also divided into patches but without overlap resulting in 313 patches.

4.2   Implementation Details and Evaluation Metrics

The U-net model is trained from scratch for 30 epochs by using Adam optimizer, a learning rate of $\eta = 1 \cdot 10^{-4}$, batch size of 5 and He-initialization for the convolutional layers. We use data augmentation such as rotation by $90°$ to produce the same number of vertical and horizontal lines.

For evaluation, we compare the number of predicted lines using Precision, Recall and F_1 score, the mean pixel differences of chain line positions and the mean difference of the chain distance intervals in mm. Therefore, we convert the pixel distances in mm by scaling the images based on the manually measured width of the artwork.

4.3   Results

An example of a test image and the corresponding predicted mask is shown in Fig. 4a,b and Fig. 6a,b. It can be seen that the image contains noise and instead of continuous lines there are only line segments visible. The additional image processing steps (connected components + RANSAC or Hough transformation) transform the line segments into straight lines. The resulting images with segmented lines can be seen in Fig. 4c,d.

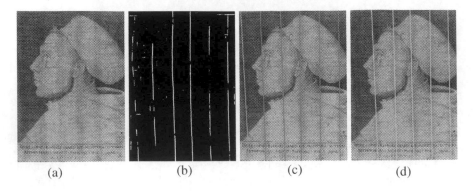

(a)   (b)   (c)   (d)

Fig. 4. (a) Transmitted light test image, (b) mask image, images with predicted lines from (c) RANSAC colored in blue (probable) and orange (improbable) and (d) Hough transformation colored in green. Image: *Martin Luther as Augustinian monk*, Lucas Cranach the Elder, Klassik Stiftung Weimar, DK 183-83

Table 1. Evaluation of precision, recall and F_1 score of chain lines.

	All	RANSAC probable	Hough	Manually measured	Ground truth
Sum of lines	92	86	84	87	89
TP	89	86	84	87	89
FN	0	3	5	2	0
FP	3	0	0	0	0
Precision	0.967	1	1	1	1
Recall	1	0.966	0.944	0.978	1
F_1 **score**	0.983	0.983	0.971	0.989	1

To measure the quality of these approaches the number of detected lines are compared in Table 1. We compare our method with line distances that were measured by hand by an art technologist, i.e. directly using the physical paper and the ground truth annotations that were manually annotated on the digital images. For our approach with connected components and RANSAC, a distinction is made between all predicted lines and the lines the algorithm declares as probable. Regarding all detected lines, our RANSAC based approach detects all 89 lines from the test dataset leading to a F_1 score of 0.983. In addition, it locates three additional lines (see column 2 in Table 1). The extra lines only appear at the border of three of the images, because the edges of the prints appear brighter in transmitted light and can be falsely recognized as lines. Regarding only the probable lines, the RANSAC based approach misses out three lines (see column 3 in Table 1), but has no false-positives resulting in the same F_1 score of 0.983. These missing lines were categorized as improbable lines, because they either have a smaller distance to the nearest line or their slope is too steep or they are not fully visible. Two examples for improbable lines marked in orange can be seen in Fig. 4c where the orange line on the left runs not as vertical as the others or in Fig. 6c where the orange line on the bottom is only partly visible. The approach using the Hough transform finds less correct lines than RANSAC in both cases (all or only probable lines). For the Hough approach, all of the predicted lines are marked as probable and the corresponding F_1 score is 0.971 which is slightly smaller than for the RANSAC based approach. The manual measurement of the lines only skips two lines that are either partly or hardly visible and achieves the best F_1 score of 0.989. Our method using RANSAC performs similar with only a slightly lower F_1 score, yet in a more efficient way due to its automatic design.

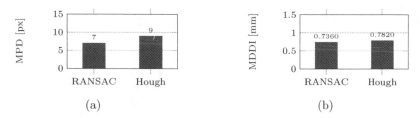

Fig. 5. Comparison of (a) the mean pixel difference (MPD) of line locations (predicted, ground truth labels) and (b) the mean difference of distance intervals (MDDI) between predicted distances and manually measured distances. (Color figure online)

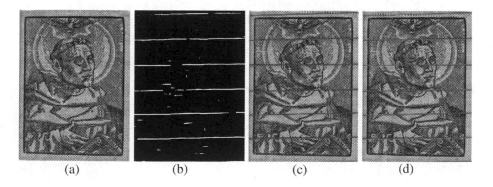

Fig. 6. (a) Transmitted light test image and (b) corresponding predicted mask, image with manually labeled lines (violet) and (c) predicted lines by RANSAC (blue, orange) and (d) lines computed by Hough transform (green). Image: *Martin Luther as Augustinian monk*, Unknown, after Hans Baldung Grien, Germanisches Nationalmuseum, Nuremberg, H 4763 (Color figure online)

Further, we compare the position of the lines by calculating the mean pixel difference between the predicted lines and corresponding ground truth lines in Fig. 5a. The mean pixel difference between the ground truth values and the images obtained by using connected components and RANSAC is 7 pixel and for the images with Hough lines the mean pixel error leads to a slightly larger value of 9 pixel. An example of an image with predicted lines by RANSAC (blue, orange) and by Hough (green) in comparison with the manually labeled image (violet) can be seen in Fig. 6.

In Fig. 5b the distance between the subsequent lines (chain intervals) are compared to the hand-measured chain distances. The mean error that is made by the algorithms between the segmented chain lines is quite small and lies at 0.736 mm for our RANSAC based approach and slightly higher at 0.782 mm for the lines detected by the Hough transformation.

Our method achieves a good performance, but there is a limitation since it can only segment straight lines. For cases, where the wire was bent which is resulting in a curved chain line, our method cannot determine an exact line but only an approximation, for instance the first line in Fig. 4c. But with our categorization into probable and improbable lines, the art technologists or historians can have a second look on the improbable lines and reject or accept them.

5   Conclusion

We presented a method for chain line segmentation in historical prints using deep learning. We trained a U-net for line segmentation and proposed some postprocessing steps to localize and parameterize the lines. We showed for our art test dataset, that our approach using U-net in combination with connected components and RANSAC performed best and was able to detect all lines, but also detected some additional ones. As the distances between those lines and the lines next to them are noticeable smaller, those additional lines were marked as improbable and can be reviewed by the art historians.

Further, comparing the chain line distance intervals from the predicted distances and the manually measured distances demonstrated a low error of less than 1 mm. The automatic chain line segmentation and distance measurement gives the opportunity to compare a larger number of historical prints and drawings by one artist or art workshop. Thus, future work could comprise analyzing the chain distance patterns and perform clustering or similarity search to identify moldmates.

References

1. Atanasiu, V.: Assessing paper origin and quality through large-scale laid lines density measurements. In: 26th Congress of the International Paper Historians Association, pp. 172–184 (2002)
2. Fischler, M.A., Bolles, R.C.: Random sample consensus: a paradigm for model fitting with applications to image analysis and automated cartography. Commun. ACM **24**, 381–395 (1981)
3. Hiary, H., Ng, K.: A system for segmenting and extracting paper-based watermark designs. Int. J. Digit. Libr. **6**(4), 351–361 (2007). https://doi.org/10.1007/s00799-007-0008-7

4. Johnson, C.R., Sethares, W.A., Ellis, M.H., Haqqi, S.: Hunting for paper moldmates among rembrandt's prints: chain-line pattern matching. IEEE Sig. Process. Mag. **32**, 28–37 (2015)
5. van der Lubbe, J., Someren, E., M., R.: Dating and authentication of rembrandt's etchings with the help of computational intelligence. In: ICHIM (2001)
6. Ronneberger, O., Fischer, P., Brox, T.: U-net: convolutional networks for biomedical image segmentation. In: Navab, N., Hornegger, J., Wells, W.M., Frangi, A.F. (eds.) MICCAI 2015, Part III. LNCS, vol. 9351, pp. 234–241. Springer, Cham (2015). https://doi.org/10.1007/978-3-319-24574-4_28
7. van Staalduinen, M., van der Lubbe, J.C.A., Backer, E., Paclík, P.: Paper retrieval based on specific paper features: chain and laid lines. In: Gunsel, B., Jain, A.K., Tekalp, A.M., Sankur, B. (eds.) MRCS 2006. LNCS, vol. 4105, pp. 346–353. Springer, Heidelberg (2006). https://doi.org/10.1007/11848035_46

Documenting the State of Preservation of Historical Stone Sculptures in Three Dimensions with Digital Tools

Efstathios Adamopoulos[1]([⊠]) [iD] and Fulvio Rinaudo[2] [iD]

[1] Department of Computer Science, University of Turin, Corso Svizzera 185, 10149 Turin, Italy
efstathios.adamopoulos@unito.it
[2] Department of Architecture and Design, Polytechnic University of Turin,
Viale Pier Andrea Mattioli 39, 10125 Turin, Italy
fulvio.rinaudo@polito.it

Abstract. Protection of stone heritage requires detailed records of the state-of-preservation to ensure accurate decision-making for conservation interventions. This short paper explores the topic of using digital tools to better visualize and map in three-dimensional (3D) representations the deterioration state of stone statues. Technical photography, geomatics techniques, and 3D visualization approaches are combined to propose reproducible and adaptable solutions that can support the investigation of historical materials' degradation. The short paper reports on the application of these multi-technique approaches regarding a bust sculpture from the *Accademia Carrara* in Bergamo (Italy).

Keywords: Spectral imaging · Structured Light Scanning · Photogrammetry · 3D visualization · Decay mapping · Stone heritage

1 Introduction

A significant part of our tangible heritage is made of stone and continually undergoes decay, which creates significant challenges for ensuring its preservation over time [1]. Stone is subjected to degradation, which can be caused by external or internal factors [2]. The exposure to external environments triggers various degradation phenomena, leading to the decay of the stone matrix, resulting in loss of the original details and colors [3]. Detailed analysis and monitoring of deterioration patterns can contribute to the knowledge of the degradation mechanisms and effectively assist the decision-making process regarding necessary conservation interventions.

Traditional approaches for evaluating and representing the preservation state for stone statues involve visual inspection and analog two-dimensional (2D) sketching of deterioration maps. Nevertheless, the stone degradation's exhaustive characterization requires time-consuming multi-technique diagnostical campaigns with spectroscopic and chemical methods, including non-invasive and invasive analyses [4, 5]. However, the heightened interest in ensuring the sustainability of stone heritage on a broad scale

© Springer Nature Switzerland AG 2021
A. Del Bimbo et al. (Eds.): ICPR 2020 Workshops, LNCS 12663, pp. 666–673, 2021.
https://doi.org/10.1007/978-3-030-68796-0_48

dictates the design and implementation of cost-effective, flexible—and relatively auto-matic—workflows for assessing and visualizing the state of conservation. Towards this direction, geomatics can provide useful solutions by offering digital tools for agile geo-metric and radiometric recording and 3D processing of the documented data that can help understand heritage objects' condition.

Recent technological advancements have enabled the acquisition of suitable and rich data for cultural heritage documentation. Photogrammetric recording approaches employing structure-from-motion (SfM) algorithms have become quite common for her-itage studies due to their capability of restituting 3D geometry from oblique imagery, estimating the camera's geometry without the need for predefined sets of control points or prior calibration, and due to the reduced needs for supervision and user-expertise [6, 7]. Semi-automated workflows combining SfM, dense multi-view reconstruction (DMVR), and 3D meshing algorithms have been frequently applied to record the condi-tion of stone sculptures and high reliefs for conservation purposes [8, 9] and to support interventions through virtual restoration and 3D printing of missing parts [10–12]. Also, Structured-Light Scanning (SLS) has significant advantages for implementing stone her-itage documentation. SLS systems are easy to use, compact, lightweight, and provide dense resolution and high accuracy results [6, 13, 14]. However, the approaches men-tioned above frequently focus only on the 3D shape of stone heritage and the volume of material loss but do not examine the deterioration patterns. To faithfully represent degraded surface microstructure, different shading and rendering techniques can be adopted for the digital models [15].

Detailed condition assessment of stone objects has often been associated with labor-intensive analog or computer-aided design (CAD)-based mapping, which requires well-trained personnel [16]. Restorers often use mapping software, which still uses 2D maps or images as a reference and is therefore useful only for relatively planar historic sur-faces, such as walls or façades. Commercial 3D mapping software does not always provide satisfactory results and is not user-friendly [17]. On the contrary, approaches centered on segmenting 3D models based on the surface [18] or reflectance [19] prop-erties present greater accuracy and represent the real situation about deterioration more closely. Detailed 3D mapping can be achieved by classifying color and spectral infor-mation, by segmenting exported orthophoto-mosaics or UV maps and projecting the classification results back onto the 3D model of an object [20]. Specifically, the use of near-infrared (NIR) intensity textures can be of great value for decay mapping [21].

2 Overview and Methods

This short article discusses applying the techniques mentioned above for 3D digitization, visualization, and mapping of the state of preservation of stone heritage, through the case study of a bust of Franz Joseph I of Austria from the *Accademia Carrara di Bergamo* (Fig. 1). The authors aim to present the progress made in the experimentation with digitization and computational methods to evaluate workflows for accurate and less labor-intensive for conservation planning.

The object's geometric recording was performed with a structured-light system and with digital photogrammetric approaches to obtain diverse data types. SLS was performed with a handheld STONEX F6-SR structured-light scanner. Imagery for SfM/DMVR approach-based reconstruction was robustly captured with a modified Canon Rebel SL1 camera, employing an 18.0 MP CMOS sensor. A UV-NIR-cut external filter was used for the color images, and a NIR-pass filter (700–1400 nm) was used to capture near-infrared reflectance images. The Mantis Vision Echo Software 1.2.0 was used for SLS, while Agisoft Metashape Professional 1.5.1 was utilized for the photogrammetric processing.

Post-processing of the scanned 3D point clouds, application of different visualization techniques, and segmentation of the 3D models based on RGB and near-infrared textures were performed in CloudCompare, as well as the metric validation of the photogrammetric results. The classification of images and models' textures was implemented in MATLAB through K-means clustering-based image segmentation, using k-means++ algorithm for cluster center initialization. The number of clusters was chosen by roughly identifying the number of present deterioration patterns, according to the 'Illustrated glossary on stone deterioration patterns' [22] and by considering that at least one cluster should correspond to the healthy materials' surface.

Fig. 1. A view of the bust of Franz Joseph I.

3   Application and Results

The scanning of the busts' complex geometry resulted in many partial 3D point clouds that had to be co-registered through an Iterative Closest Point (ICP) algorithm and merged into a single point cloud. The resulting point cloud was cleaned, denoised, and then meshed (Poisson Surface Reconstruction). Despite the incomplete digitization inside the Echo Software, the visualization of the NIR intensities recorder by the structured-light scanner could give a decent first idea of the weathering stages on the bust's surface (Fig. 2). In addition to that, the SLS-derived model contained less surface noise than the ones produced with photogrammetric procedures.

The 3D models generated with image-based approaches from RGB and NIR imagery were metrically validated by comparing them to the ground-truth model produced with SLS. In both cases, mean Hausdorff distances estimated with the appropriate measurement tool in CloudCompare ranged below 1 mm. Furthermore, the two models had between them remarkably similar density, surface characteristics, and the distances calculated between the two surfaces were, on average less than 0.5 mm.

Shading of meshes' surfaces was based on approximate normal rendering with the Eye-Dome Lighting (EDL) shader, approximate ambient occlusion rendering with the Screen space ambient occlusion (SSAO) [23] shader, and applying Sobel filtering [24] over anisotropic diffusion filtered images to obtain gradient maps of the surface. The results, shown in Fig. 3, and particularly rendering according to SSAO and gradient vectors gave more interpretable visualizations of the surface's characteristics.

Fig. 2. Partial SLS-produced model textured with the F6 SR scanner intensities.

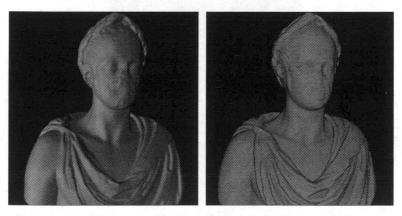

Fig. 3. Visualizations of digital model in CloudCompare with approximated normal rendering using SSAO shader (left) and Sobel filter-based solution (right).

Photogrammetrically-produced models are illustrated in Fig. 4. After transferring the NIR intensities from the texture mosaic image-file to the model's surface triangles, a direct segmentation of the weathering stages was achieved by directly segmenting in 3D according to the grayscale values. This segmentation had good correspondence with the real-life situation about degradation, as seen in Fig. 5. The segmented surfaces' area could be measured, which has significant value for the conservation interventions' efficient planning.

Fig. 4. Digital models produced with image-based techniques: untextured (left), textured (right), produced with RGB imagery (top), and with NIR imagery (bottom).

Fig. 5. Direct 3D segmentation of the model based on NIR texture to visualize stone weathering stages (darkest tone translates to a higher level of weathering).

The detailed classification of the deterioration patterns in 3D was implemented with two different techniques. The first included exporting RGB and NIR 2D ortho-mosaics of the bust's surface, blending them to create a multi-spectral pseudo-colored image, then classifying it with an unsupervised method, and finally back-projecting the 2D classification results onto the 3D object. The second technique was based on the NIR texture's direct unsupervised classification (Fig. 6). Results from the first implementation were more easily interpretable as specific segmented areas had an apparent correspondence to a particular type of deterioration. However, the projection of the classified ortho-mosaic onto the model created few gaps in the textured product due to the occlusions caused by complex geometry. Multiple partial classified ortho-mosaics on convenient planes would be needed to cover the full object and avoid the occlusions as much as possible. The second technique provided a classification covering the complete object without occlusion problems. However, in this case, results were not as easily interpretable because of errors created during the classification—due to areas that presented the same decay patterns but were unconnected on the texture image.

Fig. 6. 3D classification of deterioration using the near-infrared texture. Blue-colored areas correspond to healthier material, while green corresponds to biodeterioration and black crusts, and orange to stone patina.

4 Discussion and Conclusions

This paper presented digital approaches for visualizing the state of preservation for stone sculptures by combining contemporary image and SLS-based reconstruction approaches, rendering, and computational techniques. The different types of shaded visualization provided useful qualitative ways of interpreting the degradation of stone in 3D. However, the surface's segmentation based on thresholding of NIR intensities and 3D classification based on multi-spectral textures proved to have a significant advantage over the time-consuming analog mapping and 2D approaches which do not have metric qualities. Additionally, 3D classification approaches have the advantage that the identified deteriorated areas can be measured, providing important input for the decision-making on conservation interventions. The authors aim to explore further the methods described here by involving more intricate supervised classification techniques based on the conservators' input and machine learning algorithms. Additionally, the authors are interested in expanding the experimentation through interactive 3D visualization and by annotating information about the conservation state and historical information.

Acknowledgments. This project has received funding by the European Union's Framework Program for Research and Innovation Horizon 2020 under the H2020–Marie-Skłodowska Curie Actions–COFUND scheme (Grant Agreement 754511) and by the banking foundation *Compagnia di San Paolo*.

The authors would like to acknowledge the *Accademia Carrara di Bergamo*, and the *Fondazione Centro Conservazione e Restauro dei Beni Culturali 'La Venaria Reale'* for the generous concession of permission to publish the results about Emperor Franz Joseph I of Austria's bust.

References

1. Doehne, E.F., Price, C.A.: Stone Conservation: An Overview of Current Research. Getty Conservation Institute, Los Angeles (2010)
2. Steiger, M., Charola, A.E., Sterflinger, K.: Weathering and deterioration. In: Siegesmund, S., Snethlage, R. (eds.) Stone in Architecture, pp. 227–316. Springer, Heidelberg (2011). https://doi.org/10.1007/978-3-642-14475-2_4
3. Rosado, T., Silva, M., Galvão, A., Mirão, J., Candeias, A., Caldeira, A.T.: A first insight on the biodegradation of limestone: the case of the world heritage convent of christ. Appl. Phys. A **122**(12), 1–7 (2016). https://doi.org/10.1007/s00339-016-0525-6
4. Hatzigiannakis, et al.: Monitoring and mapping of deterioration products on cultural heritage monuments using imaging and laser spectroscopy. In: Moropoulou, A., Korres, M., Georgopoulos, A., Spyrakos, C., Mouzakis, C. (eds.) TMM_CH 2018. CCIS, vol. 962, pp. 419–429. Springer, Cham (2019). https://doi.org/10.1007/978-3-030-12960-6_29
5. Mascalchi, M., Osticioli, I., Cuzman, O.A., Mugnaini, S., Giamello, M., Siano, S.: Diagnostic campaign and innovative conservation treatments carried out on the statue "La Speranza" by Odoardo Fantacchiotti. In: Calcagnile, L., Daponte, P. (eds.) Proceedings of the 3rd TC-4 International Conference on Metrology for Archaeology and Cultural Heritage, pp. 520–524. IMEKO, Budapest (2017)
6. Georgopoulos, A., Stathopoulou, E.K.: Data acquisition for 3D geometric recording: state of the art and recent innovations. In: Vincent, M.L., López-Menchero Bendicho, V.M., Ioannides, M., Levy, T.E. (eds.) Heritage and Archaeology in the Digital Age. QMHSS, pp. 1–26. Springer, Cham (2017). https://doi.org/10.1007/978-3-319-65370-9_1
7. Aicardi, I., Chiabrando, F., Maria Lingua, A., Noardo, F.: Recent trends in cultural heritage 3D survey: the photogrammetric computer vision approach. J. Cult. Herit. **32**, 257–266 (2018). https://doi.org/10.1016/j.culher.2017.11.006
8. Pomaska, G.: Monitoring the deterioration of stone at mindener museum's lapidarium. Int. Arch. Photogramm. Remote. Sens. Spatial Inf. Sci. **XL-5/W2**, 495–500 (2013). https://doi.org/10.5194/isprsarchives-XL-5-W2-495-2013
9. Koehl, M., Fuchs, M.: 3D modelling of architectural blocks and antique sculptures for the conservation and the promotion of archaeological heritage – experiments in Alsace. Int. Arch. Photogramm. Remote Sens. Spatial Inf. Sci. **XLII-2-W15**, 625–632 (2019). https://doi.org/10.5194/isprs-archives-XLII-2-W15-625-2019
10. Apollonio, F.I., Ballabeni, M., Bertacchi, S., Fallavollita, F., Foschi, R., Gaiani, M.: From documentation images to restauration support tools: a path following the neptune fountain in bologna design process. Int. Arch. Photogramm. Remote Sens. Spatial Inf. Sci. **XLII-5/W1**, 329–336 (2017). https://doi.org/10.5194/isprs-archives-XLII-5-W1-329-2017
11. Di Paola, F., Milazzo, G., Spatafora, F.: Computer-aided restoration tools to assist the conservation of an ancient sculpture. the colossal statue of zeus enthroned. Int. Arch. Photogramm. Remote Sens. Spatial Inf. Sci. **XLII-2/W5**, 177–184 (2017). https://doi.org/10.5194/isprs-archives-XLII-2-W5-177-2017.
12. Tucci, G., Bonora, V., Conti, A., Fiorini, L.: High-quality 3D models and their use in a cultural heritage conservation project. Int. Arch. Photogramm. Remote Sens. Spatial Inf. Sci. **XLII-2/W5**, 687–693 (2017). https://doi.org/10.5194/isprs-archives-XLII-2-W5-687-2017.

13. Morena, S., Barba, S., Álvaro-Tordesillas, A.: Shining 3D einscan-pro, application and validation in the field of cultural heritage, from the chillida-leku museum to the archaeological museum of Sarno. Int. Arch. Photogramm. Remote Sens. Spatial Inf. Sci. **XLII-2/W18**, 135–142 (2019). https://doi.org/10.5194/isprs-archives-XLII-2-W18-135-2019.

14. Patrucco, G., Rinaudo, F., Spreafico, A.: A New Handheld Scanner for 3D Survey of Small Artifacts: The Stonex F6. 8 (2019)

15. Apollonio, F.I., Gaiani, M., Basilissi, W., Rivaroli, L.: Photogrammetry driven tools to support the restauration of open-air bronze surfaces of sculptures: an integrated solution starting from the experience of the neptune fountain in Bologna. Int. Arch. Photogramm. Remote Sens. Spatial Inf. Sci. **XLII-2/W3**, 47–54 (2017). https://doi.org/10.5194/isprs-archives-XLII-2-W3-47-2017.

16. Siedel, H., Siegesmund, S.: Characterization of stone deterioration on buildings. In: Siegesmund, S., Snethlage, R. (eds.) Stone in Architecture, pp. 349–414. Springer, Heidelberg (2014). https://doi.org/10.1007/978-3-642-45155-3_6

17. Ansel, J., Gerling, C., Hofmeister, S., Schick, S.: Zwei Heiligenfiguren aus der katholischen Marienkirche in Bad Mergentheim. Ein außergewöhnliches Restaurierungsprojekt und der Testlauf für eine 3-D-Dokumentation. Denkmalpflege in Baden-Württemberg– Nachrichtenblatt der Landesdenkmalpflege 45(3), 157–163 (2016).

18. Pfeuffer, C., Rahrig, M., Snethlage, R., Drewello, R.: 3D mapping as a tool for the planning of preservation measures on sculptures made of natural stone. Environ. Earth Sci. **77**(8), 1–2 (2018). https://doi.org/10.1007/s12665-018-7479-2

19. Adamopoulos, E., Rinaudo, F.: Near-infrared modeling and enhanced visualization, as a novel approach for 3D decay mapping of stone sculptures. Archaeol. Anthropol. Sci. **12**(7), 1–2 (2020). https://doi.org/10.1007/s12520-020-01110-5

20. Grilli, E., Remondino, F.: Classification of 3D digital heritage. Remote Sens. **11**, 847 (2019). https://doi.org/10.3390/rs11070847

21. Adamopoulos, E., Rinaudo, F.: enhancing image-based multiscale heritage recording with near-infrared data. IJGI **9**, 269 (2020). https://doi.org/10.3390/ijgi9040269

22. ICOMOS-ISCS. Illustrated glossary on stone deterioration patterns. Ateliers 30 Impression, Champigny-sur-Marne (2008)

23. Ritschel, T., Grosch, T., Seidel, H.-P.: Approximating dynamic global illumination in image space. In: Proceedings of the 2009 symposium on Interactive 3D graphics and games - I3D 20'09. p. 75. ACM Press, Boston (2009). https://doi.org/10.1145/1507149.1507161

24. Pratt, W.K.: Digital Image Processing. John Wiley & Sons, Inc., Hoboken (2007). https://doi.org/10.1002/0470097434

FBE2020 - Workshop on Facial and Body Expressions, micro-expressions and behavior recognition

Workshop on Facial and Body Expressions, micro-expressions and behavior recognition (FBE2020)

FBE is a venue for researchers working in the field of human behavior understanding. The workshop has a specific focus on low-level characteristics, either facial or related to the human body, aiming at understanding high level concepts, such as recognizing actions or emotions.

In general, low-level expressions and behaviors are more difficult to recognize than high-level ones, due to the fine-grained nature of the problem. It is also a fact that with the recent technological advancement, the means of data acquisition and processing have also dramatically improved, enabling new applications and analyses. To reliably understand facial micro-expressions, for example, there are both spatial and temporal issues to take into account. On the one hand it is necessary to either acquire and process high-resolution images or rely on different kinds of data such as high-quality depth maps. On the other hand, micro-expressions occur over an extremely short timespan (<500 ms) and might not even be detectable with conventional low-framerate cameras. If some years ago it was not possible to acquire these kind of data and process them, now it certainly is.

The first edition of the Workshop of Facial and Body Expressions, micro-expressions and behavior recognition (FBE2020) was scheduled to be held in Milan, Italy, in conjunction with the International Conference on Pattern Recognition (ICPR) 2020 and then moved online due to the outburst of the Covid19 pandemic. The format of the workshop included a keynote speaker followed by technical presentations.

The workshop received 11 submissions, with authors belonging to 12 different institutions worldwide. After an accurate peer-review process, 7 papers were selected for publication at the workshop. The acceptance rate was of 63%. Among the accepted papers, 5 are full length papers and 2 are short papers.

The review process focused on scientific novelty, overall quality and relevance for the topics covered by the workshop. Each paper was reviewed by at least 2 experts in the field with a single-blind reviewing policy. The accepted papers mostly focused on deep learning techniques for either facial expression recognition, micro-expression recognition or action recognition.

The workshop program was completed by an invited talk by Prof. Matti Pietikäinen from the University of Oulu, Finland.

We would like to thank the FBE2020 Program Committee, whose members made the workshop possible by ensuring timely and precise reviews.

January 2021

Organization

FBE2020 Workshop Chairs

Federico Becattini	University of Florence, Italy
Vittorio Murino	University of Verona, Italy
Federico Pernici	University of Florence, Italy
Moi Hoon Yap	Manchester Metropolitan University, UK

Website Chair

Andrea Ferracani	University of Florence, Italy

Program Committee

Nazre Batool	Scania CV AB, Sweden
Carmen Bisogni	Università degli Studi di Salerno, Italy
João Cardia	Faculdade de Tecnologia do Estado de São Paulo, Brazil
Tong Chen	Southwest University, USA
Hongying Meng	Brunel University, UK
Madhumita Takalkar	University of Technology, Australia
Tiberio Uricchio	University of Florence, Italy

Additional Reviewer

Ferrari Claudio	University of Florence, Italy

FBE 2020 Organizers

Federico Becattini
University of Florence
Viale Morgagni 65, Firenze, 50134, Firenze, Italy
E-mail: federico.becattini@unifi.it

Vittorio Murino
University of Verona
Ca' Vignal 2, Strada Le Grazie 15, 37134 Verona, Italy
E-mail: vittorio.murino@univr.it

Federico Pernici
University of Florence
Viale Morgagni 65, Firenze, 50134, Firenze, Italy
E-mail: federico.pernici@unifi.it

Moi Hoon Yap
Manchester Metropolitan University
John Dalton Building, Chester Street, Manchester, M1 5GD, UK
E-mail: M.Yap@mmu.ac.uk

Motion Attention Deep Transfer Network for Cross-database Micro-expression Recognition

Wanchuang Xia[1], Wenming Zheng[2(✉)], Yuan Zong[2], and Xingxun Jiang[2]

[1] School of Cyber Science and Engineering, Southeast University,
Nanjing 210096, China
xiawanchuag@seu.edu.cn
[2] School of Biological Science and Medical Engineering, Southeast University,
Nanjing 210096, China
{wenming_zheng,xhzongyuan,jiangxingxun}@seu.edu.cn

Abstract. Cross-database micro-expression recognition is a great challenging problem due to the short duration and low intensity of micro-expressions from different collection conditions. In this paper, we present a Motion Attention Deep Transfer Network (MADTN) that can focus on the most discriminative movement regions of the face and reduce the database bias. Specifically, we firstly combine the motion information and facial appearance information to obtain the discriminative representation by merging the optical flow fields between three key-frames (the onset frame, the middle frame, the offset frame) and the facial appearance of the middle frame. Then, the deep network architecture extracts cross-domain feature with the superiority of the maximum mean discrepancy(MMD) loss so that the source and target domains have a similar distribution. Results on benchmark cross-database micro-expression experiments demonstrate that the MADTN achieves remarkable performance in many micro-expression transfer tasks and exceed the state-of-the-art results, which show the robustness and superiority of our approach.

Keywords: Micro-expression recognition · Deep learning · Optical flow · Transfer learning

1 Introduction

Micro-expressions can reveal true information in social life, which are unconscious and spontaneous facial movements during the time a person emerge emotion but intentionally or involuntarily tries to hide genuine emotion [8]. Therefore, micro-expression recognition has great value in different fields, including lie detection [34], clinical diagnosis [35], business negotiation [36]. This has attracted increasing researchers to analyze micro-expression. Nevertheless, compared to ordinary facial expressions, the duration of a micro-expression is usually very short which is between one twenty-fifth to one half of a second [7]. Moreover, the muscle movements of micro-expressions also have locality and low intensity

A. Del Bimbo et al. (Eds.): ICPR 2020 Workshops, LNCS 12663, pp. 679–693, 2021.
https://doi.org/10.1007/978-3-030-68796-0_49

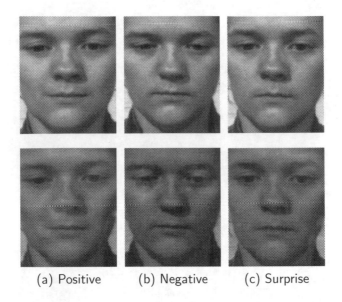

(a) Positive   (b) Negative   (c) Surprise

Fig. 1. Examples of the middle frame and the motion attention representation in the SMIC-HS database. The first row are the middle frames of a micro-expression sequence.The second row are RGB images that R channel is the optical flow fields between the onset frame and the middle frame of video clip, G channel denote gray image of the middle frame, and B channel is the optical flow fields between the middle frame and the offset frame. (Color figure online)

characteristics [34]. So micro-expressions recognition lack discriminative feature representations. The low intensity and short duration of micro-expressions make its recognition a very difficult task for people, even with professional training [11]. Thus, it is necessary to build an automatic micro-expression recognition system by using machine learning and computer vision techniques.

In recent years, many researchers have proposed a series of algorithms based on the characteristics of micro-expressions. In the work of [31], Park et al. proposed using the Eulerian Motion Magnification (EMM) [38] to exaggerate subtle change in the micro-expression video. Temporal interpolation method (TIM) [43] and Sparsity-Promoting Dynamic Mode Decomposition (DMDSP) [18] was employed to solve asymmetrical length of micro-expression video in [22–24]. Due to local binary pattern on three orthogonal planes (LBP-TOP) [42] could encode spatio-temporal variations, Pfister et al. chosen it to extract micro-expression representation [33]. Subsequently, Wang et al. [37] proposed local Binary Pattern with Six Interception Points (LBP-SIP) by reducing redundant information in LBP-TOP. Later on, lots of spatio-temporal descriptors were employed in micro-expression recognition, such as Spatio-temporal Completed Local Quantized Patterns (STCLQP) [16], Spatio-temporal LBP with Integration Projection (STLBP-IP) [15], Histogram of Oriented Gradient-TOP (HOG-TOP) [24]. Optical Flow (OF) [14] can readily portray motion information displayed in the micro-expression video. Several works were proposed based on OF, for example, Main Directional Mean Optical Flow (MDMO) [27], Facial Dynamics Map (FDM) [39], Bi-Weighted Oriented Optical Flow (Bi-WOOF) [26]. Meanwhile, with deep learning widely prevailing in the visual task, it is obstacle for micro-expressions recognition by deep learning that lack large spontaneous micro-expressions database. Current popular spontaneous micro-expressions datasets are small, such as SMIC [25], CASME II [40]. Due to characteristics of micro-expressions, it is very hard to collect many spontaneous micro-expressions sample. Some works [19,20,32] explored to utilize neural networks in micro-expression recognition task.

Nevertheless, the above work mainly assumes that training(source) set and test(target) set satisfy the same distribution. This assumption is hard to conform with practical situations because samples recorded with different equipment under diverse backgrounds, illumination, angle. Without taking this into account, model trained on the source domain may fail to generalize well to the sample in the target domain. To alleviate this problem, transfer learning leverages the source domain with label information, and transfers the knowledge of the source domain to the unlabeled target domain [6]. Therefore, Zong et al. firstly investigate cross-database micro-expression recognition in [44–46] to alleviate distribution shift across domains.

In order to construct more discriminative and robustness features, we propose Motion Attention Deep Transfer Network (MADTN) for cross-database micro-expression recognition in this paper. Intuitively, people perceive micro-expressions by observing facial muscle movements in a video instead of only an image. Inspired by the intuition, MADTN perceives facial movement and pays attention mainly to the variational facial regions. Figure 1 illustrates the synthetic image of optical flow fields and facial appearance information. Optical Flow can obviously display the variational regions of the face. As can be shown in Fig. 1(a), movements occur in the corners of the mouth and the tip of the nose. Thus MADTN is able to focus on the discriminative regions of facial image. Firstly, we estimate facial deformations between the middle frame and the onset or offset frame in a micro-expression sequence. Then, the motion information is weighted to different regions of the face by Convolution Neural Network (CNN). Finally, we are able to reduce the feature distribution gap between domains by inserting the MMD loss into CNN. In this paper, our main contributions are summarized as follows:

- We propose Motion Attention Deep Transfer Network (MADTN) to conduct cross-database micro-expression recognition. MADTN can perceive the motion regions of the face and reduce the distribution shift between source and target domain.
- Visualized results show that the optical flow algorithm is effective in depicting facial muscle movement. With the integration of optical flow fields and facial appearance information, it can generate a discriminative feature representation, see Fig. 1. We only select three frames from the video clips to cut down redundant information in sequence, and optical flow with them display

larger degrees of motion information that contribute to the representation more discriminating.

- Experiment results demonstrate the superiority and robustness of the proposed MADTN over other state-of-the-art methods on two benchmark tasks.

2   Related Work

Motion information can effectively improve the performance of micro-expression recognition. Several approaches were proposed based on Optical Flow(OF), which can readily portray motion information. MDMO [27] calculate the main direction of OF in each region of interest (ROI), including local statistics and spatial location information. FDM [39] extracts the motion information of micro-expression in a different granularity that iteratively calculates the principal OF direction of the local facial dynamic. BI-WOOF [26] was weight the Histogram of the Oriented Optical Flow (HOOF) [3] by multiplying with OF magnitude and optical strain magnitude of each ROI. These approaches utilize OF based the ROI level, thus it is important to choose appropriate ROI. However, improper ROI which include different motion direction may damage motion information that only considers the single direction of in ROI. In addition, these methods only consider motion information but neglect facial information. Combining motion information and facial information can accurately indicate the facial region where the movement occurs. In computer vision community, the attention mechanism [17] is proposed to weight different ROI and highlight the representations of task-related location. Compare with existing attention model that added attention module in the network, our approach adopts optical flow to produce the attention maps. In this paper, we weight facial information by OF information at the pixel level to generate more discriminative representation.

Deep learning has been shown to be effective in extracting features but is fairly new to this community. Because the lack of micro-expression samples limits the development of deep learning on micro-expression recognition. Kim et al. [20] attempt to utilize CNN and Long Short-Term Memory (LSTM) encoding micro-expression sequence and the network was designed relatively shallower. Peng et al. adapt micro-expression video clips and its OF information to train a 3D-CNN model that named Dual Temporal Scale Convolutional Neural Network (DTSCNN) [32] Enriched Long-term Recurrent Convolutional Network (ELRCN) [19] stack video frame, OF and optical strain with adjacent frames based channel level and feature level. Inspired from the above idea, this paper utilizes CNN to learning discriminative representation that combines facial image and OF information. A larger pixel's movement could contribute to more discriminative representation, thus we calculate OF between the onset or offset frame and the middle frame. The duration of a micro-expression video is usually very short which less than one half of a second, so the peak of micro-expression are more easily captured by high-speed cameras. On the one hand, OF in adjacent frame is too subtle to discriminative. On the other hand, it may not be robust enough to noise so that not accurately depict facial muscle movements.

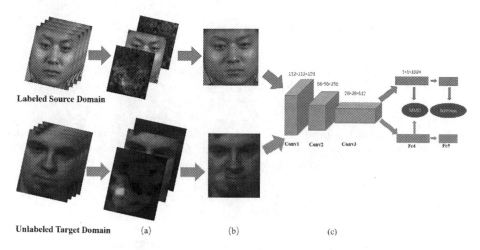

Fig. 2. Overview of the proposed Motion Attention Deep Transfer Network (MADTN) for unsupervised cross-domain micro-expression recognition. We select three frames(the onset frame, the middle frame, the offset frame) from a micro-expression sequence to produce more discriminative representation. Our method leverages the representation by backpropagating the MMD loss between features in addition to cross entropy loss. (a) two optical flow fields between the onset or offset frame and the middle frame, the gray image of the middle facial frame. (b) a synthesis RGB image consist of three gray images in (a). (c) Deep Transfer Network. The blue and orange arrows denote the source domain and target domain, respectively. (Color figure online)

To satisfy the practice application, cross-database micro-expression recognition is worthy to investigate that mitigate the domain shift between source data and target data. Zong et al. [44] proposed Target Sample Re-Generator (TSRG) to regenerate samples that have the same or similar distribution. In the work of [45], Zong et al. attempt to bridge the feature distribution shift by proposing the auxiliary set selection model (ASSM) and transductive transfer regression model (TTRM). MMD can measure the feature distribution distances, thus we utilize MMD to minimizing the distribution distance between the source domain and target domain.

3   Methodology

In this section, we introduce our proposed Motion Attention Deep Transfer Network (MADTN) for cross-database micro-expression recognition, which utilizes CNN to learn the discriminative representation that combines motion information and facial appearance information. Due to the discrepancy between databases, we embed MMD in the deep convolution network to learning domains-invariant features.

3.1   Motion Attention Representation

Optical Flow could effectively encode the spatio-temporal displacement in the micro-expression video. In this paper, we detect facial location by MTCNN [41] in the onset frame of a micro-expression video. In order to better preserve the micro-expression related information, we crop face region from the onset frame which up to the top of the forehead, down to the bottom of the chin. According to the common facial bounding box in the onset frame, we crop a facial image from other frames of the video so that not hamper the motion information. On the one hand, micro-expressions have a very short duration, which makes sure that the faces of other frames exist in the relative facial position of the onset frames. On the other hand, if every frame was detected facial location, different facial bounding box will result in face displacement. So optical flow does not represent facial muscle movement, it would have a negative effect on optical flow approximation. The optical flow estimation algorithm [9] infers the motion of an object by tracking the displacement of mass points in a sequence. Given two frames in a video clip, the corresponding points on them satisfy the following equation:

$$I(x, y, t) = I(x + \Delta x, y + \Delta y, t + \Delta t) \tag{1}$$

where $I(x, y, t)$ is intensity at pixel point (x, y) in frame at time t, after Δt time, the piont move $(\Delta x, \Delta y)$ that exist in another frame. According to Eq. (1), we could define the optical flow constraint equation:

$$I_x V_x + I_y V_y + I_t = 0 \tag{2}$$

where I_x, I_y, I_t are the partial derivatives of the intensity function. V_x and V_y are the horizontal and vertical components of the optical flow, which are defined as follow:

$$V = \left[V_x = \frac{dx}{dt}, V_y = \frac{dy}{dt} \right]^T \tag{3}$$

Due to obviously discrepancy exists between variations of the onset to the middle and the middle to the offset in a micro-expression sequence, we calculate optical flow between the onset frame and the middle frame, as well as between the middle frame and the offset frame. As can be seen in Fig. 3.(b), movement appears in the left corner of the mouth. The last row is the RGB image in Fig. 3 by concatenating the onset-middle optical flow image, the middle frame and the middle-offset optical flow image. We could observe the variations region of the face with the naked eye in the image. After such processing, we can obtain more discriminative features. As has been mentioned before, we treat a video clip as an image so that reduces redundant information in sequence.

3.2   Deep Transfer Network

Due to the powerful feature extraction capability of Convolutional Neural Network (CNN), we designed MADTN with three convolutional layers and two fully connected layers, see Fig. 2. Max pooling operation is used to reduce dimensionality after every convolutional layer. And after each layer, Leaky Rectified Linear Unit (LReLU) [29] is adopted to increase nonlinearity of model so that improve the fitting ability of the network.

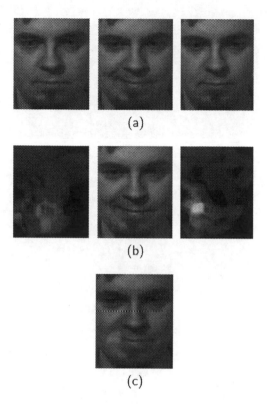

Fig. 3. Extracting motion attention representation from a video sequence sample. From left to right, (a) are the onset frame, the middle frame, the offset frame in a video sequence, respectively. (b) are the optical flow fields between the onset frame and the middle frame, the gray image of the middle image, the optical flow fields between the middle frame and the offset frame. (c) is an RGB image that synthesis from three gray images in (b). (Color figure online)

Directly utilizing this model trained on source domain to test samples in target domain usually results in poor performance because of database discrepancy. MMD [1] can measure the discrepancy between two domain by calculating the distance based on probability distributions in the reproducing kernel Hilbert space(RKHS). Therefore, we embedded MMD in the first fully connected layer of the network so as to produce domain-invariant features. The MMD can be defined as:

$$\mathrm{MMD}\left[D_s, D_t, \mathcal{F}\right] := \sup_{f \in \mathcal{F}}(\mathbf{E}_{D_s}\left[f(x^s)\right] - \mathbf{E}_{D_t}\left[f(x^t)\right]) \tag{4}$$

where $\mathbf{E}_{D_s}$ and $\mathbf{E}_{D_t}$ denote the expectations of source domain D_s and target domain D_t, respectively. If their distribution is similar, MMD $[D_s, D_t]$ would close to zero. To satisfy practice calculation, MMD also is expressed as:

$$\text{MMD}\,[D_s, D_t, \mathcal{H}] = \|\frac{1}{N_s}\sum_{i=1}^{N_s}\kappa(d_i^s) - \frac{1}{N_t}\sum_{i=1}^{N_t}\kappa(d_i^t)\|_{\mathcal{H}} \tag{5}$$

Because RKHS is often a high-dimensional or even infinite-dimensional space, the corresponding kernel chooses the Gaussian kernel,

$$\kappa(d^s, d^t) = \exp(-\frac{\|d^s - d^t\|^2}{2\delta^2}) \tag{6}$$

According to the above assumptions, the unbiased estimator of MMD^2 $[D_s, D_t, \mathcal{H}]$ was proposed:

$$\begin{aligned}\text{MMD}^2\,[D_s, D_t, \mathcal{H}] =& \frac{1}{N_s(N_s-1)}\sum_{i\neq j}^{N_s}\kappa(d_i^s, d_j^s)\\&+ \frac{1}{N_t(N_t-1)}\sum_{i\neq j}^{N_t}\kappa(d_i^t, d_j^t)\\&- \frac{2}{N_sN_t}\sum_{i,j=1}^{N_s,N_t}\kappa(d_i^s, d_j^t)\end{aligned} \tag{7}$$

By adding the MMD loss into the network, the total loss function of MADTN becomes as follows:

$$L_{\text{all}} = L_s(\Phi(x^s), y^s) + \lambda\text{MMD}^2\,[D_s, D_t, \mathcal{H}] \tag{8}$$

where $L_s(\Phi(x^s), y^s)$ denotes cross-entropy loss function of the source domain, and λ is hyper-parameter to trade off these two loss functions. Through joint

Table 1. Results(mean F1-score/accuracy) based on the TYPE-I experiments, which a series of transfer tasks between three subsets of the SMIC database. For short, H = SMIC-HS, V = SMIC-VIS, N = SMIC-NIR. The bold elements correspond to the best results

Method	$H \to V$	$V \to H$	$H \to N$	$N \to H$	$V \to N$	$N \to V$	Average
Baseline[2]	0.8002/80.28	0.5421/54.27	0.5455/53.52	0.4878/54.88	0.6186/63.38	0.6078/63.38	0.6003/61.62
IW-SVM[13]	0.8868/88.73	0.5852/58.54	0.7469/74.65	0.5427/54.27	0.6620/69.01	0.7228/73.24	0.6911/68.07
TCA[30]	0.8269/83.10	0.5477/54.88	0.5828/59.15	0.5443/57.32	0.5810/61.97	0.6598/67.61	0.6238/64.01
GFK[12]	0.8448/84.51	0.5957/59.15	0.6977/70.42	0.6197/**62.80**	0.7619/76.06	0.8142/81.69	0.7223/72.44
SA[10]	0.8037/80.28	0.5955/59.15	0.7465/74.65	0.5644/56.10	0.7004/71.83	0.7394/74.65	0.6917/69.44
STM[4,5]	0.8253/83.10	0.5059/51.22	0.6628/66.20	0.5351/56.10	0.6427/67.61	0.6922/70.42	0.6440/65.78
TKL[28]	0.7742/77.46	0.5738/57.32	0.7051/70.42	0.6116/62.60	0.7558/76.06	0.7579/76.06	0.6964/69.92
TSRG[44]	**0.8869/88.73**	0.5652/56.71	0.6484/64.79	0.5770/57.93	0.7056/70.42	0.8116/81.69	0.7128/71.23
DRFS-T[47]	0.8643/85.92	0.5767/57.32	0.7179/71.83	0.6163/61.59	0.7286/73.24	0.7732/77.46	0.7128/71.23
DRLS[47]	0.8604/85.92	0.6120/60.98	0.6599/66.20	0.5599/55.49	0.6620/69.01	0.5771/61.97	0.6552/66.60
RSTR[46]	0.8721/87.32	0.6401/64.02	0.7466/74.65	0.5765/57.32	0.7506/76.06	0.8428/84.51	0.7381/73.98
MADTN(ours)	0.8302/83.11	**0.6704/66.46**	**0.7641/77.44**	**0.6252/62.21**	**0.8435/84.52**	**0.8732/87.30**	**0.7678/76.84**

training the loss functions, it not only can learn discriminative representation about micro-expression, but also can reduce the difference between the source and the target domains. The experiment details are presented in the next section.

Table 2. Results(mean F1-score/accuracy) based on the TYPE-II experiments, which a series of transfer tasks between the CASME II database and one subsets of the SMIC(HS, VIS, NIR) database. For short, C = CASME II, H = SMIC-HS, V = SMIC-VIS, N = SMIC-NIR. The bold elements correspond to the best results

Method	$C \rightarrow H$	$H \rightarrow C$	$C \rightarrow V$	$V \rightarrow C$	$C \rightarrow N$	$N \rightarrow C$	Average
Baseline[2]	0.3697/45.12	0.3245/48.46	0.4701/50.70	0.5367/53.08	0.5295/52.11	0.2368/23.85	0.4112/45.55
IW-SVM[13]	0.3541/41.46	0.5829/62.31	0.5778/59.15	0.5537/54.62	0.5117/50.70	0.3456/36.15	0.4876/50.73
TCA[30]	0.4637/46.34	0.4870/53.08	0.6834/69.01	0.5789/59.23	0.4992/50.70	0.3937/42.31	0.5177/53.45
GFK[12]	0.4126/46.95	0.4776/50.77	0.6361/66.20	0.6056/61.50	0.5180/53.52	0.4469/46.92	0.5161/54.31
SA[10]	0.4302/47.56	0.5447/62.31	0.5939/59.15	0.5243/51.54	0.4738/47.89	0.3592/36.92	0.4877/50.90
STM[4,5]	0.3604/43.90	0.6115/63.85	0.4015/52.11	0.2715/30.00	0.3523/42.25	0.3850/41.54	0.3982/45.61
TKL[28]	0.3829/44.51	0.4661/54.62	0.6042/60.56	0.5378/53.08	0.5392/54.93	0.4248/43.85	0.4925/51.93
TSRG[44]	0.5042/51.83	0.5171/60.77	0.5935/59.15	0.6208/63.08	0.5624/56.34	0.4105/46.15	0.5348/56.22
DRFS-T[47]	0.4524/46.95	0.5460/60.00	0.6217/63.38	0.6762/68.46	0.5369/56.34	0.4653/50.77	0.5498/57.65
DRLS[47]	0.4924/53.05	0.5267/59.23	0.5757/57.75	0.5942/60.00	0.4885/49.83	0.3838/42.37	0.5102/53.71
RSTR[46]	0.5297/54.27	0.5622/60.77	0.5882/59.15	0.7021/70.77	0.5009/50.70	0.4693/50.77	0.5587/57.74
MADTN(ours)	**0.6100/62.79**	**0.7486/77.54**	**0.7056/70.41**	**0.7304/72.85**	**0.7305/73.24**	**0.7403/75.98**	**0.7109/72.14**

4 Experiments

We evaluate the proposed Motion Attention Deep Transfer Network by cross-domain micro-expression recognition tasks on SMIC [25] , CASME II [40]. And we keep the same experiment protocols with [46] to guarantee fair comparison.

4.1 Databases

SMIC [25] has three subsets SMIC-HS, SMIC-VIS and SMIC-NIR, which collected from three distinct cameras: a high-speed camera with 100 fps, a normal visual camera with 25 fps, a near-infrared camera with 25 fps, respectively. All samples were divided into three categories which are Positive, Negative and Surprise. SMIC-HS contains 164 samples from 16 subjects, while SMIC-VIS and SMIC-NIR have 71 samples belonging to the last eight subjects from all subjects.

CASME II [40] consists of 257 samples video sequences of 26 subjects belonging to seven classes: Happy, Disgust, Repression, Sad, Fear, Surprise and Others. The frame rate of all sample videos is up to 200 fps. In cross-database classification task, the different databases should have same labels. According to the definition of the label in SMIC, we relabel the samples from CASME II, Happy samples are relabeled to the Positive(32 samples), Disgust, Sad and Fear are given the Negative(73 samples), and the Surprise(25 samples) stays unchanged.

4.2   Implementation Details

To produce discriminative representations, we synthesize a RGB image by utilizing optical flow fields and appearance information. Optical flow fields have the horizontal components V_x and the vertical components V_y which expressed in the Cartesian coordinate system. Optical Flow indicates the direction and intensity of frame pixel movement, so we transform the Cartesian coordinate $V = (V_x, V_y)$ into the Polar coordinate $V = (r, \theta)$, where r and θ are the amplitude and orientation of the optical flow, respectively. In the HSV representation model, Hue H typically measured in degrees $[0°, 360°]$, as well as Saturation S and Value V measured on the range $[0, 1]$. In order to form an image, we set the value of V to 1 and assigned r, θ to S, H, respectively. Then we convert the image to a grayscale image, see Fig. 3(b).

In order to avoid overfitting problems, we select the 20% frames in the middle of a training(source) set video clip as the middle frame but the test(target) set only selected the most middle frame in a video clip. This increases the diversity of sample due to the different degrees of facial muscle movement. In addition, each sample randomly rotated between the angles $[-30°, 30°]$. And our network was designed relatively shallow. All images were resized to 112×112 pixels before inputting to the network, as well as in [46]. We optimize our model by Adam [21] solver with learning rate 2×10^{-4}. The batch size is set to 32 for each domain. We set the MMD penalty parameter λ to equal 2 in every experiment. Zong et al. [46] establish a benchmark cross-database micro-expression recognition(CDMER) experimental evaluation protocol, which contains two kinds of CDMER tasks: TYPE-I, TYPE-II. TYPE-I denote experiments between three subset of SMIC(SMIC-HS(H), SMIC-VIS(V), SMIC-NIR(N)), i.e., $H \rightarrow V$, $V \rightarrow H$, $H \rightarrow N$, $N \rightarrow H$, $V \rightarrow N$, $N \rightarrow V$. TYPE-II indicate experiments between the selected CASME II(C) and SMIC including $C \rightarrow H$, $H \rightarrow C$, $C \rightarrow V$, $V \rightarrow C$, $C \rightarrow N$, $N \rightarrow C$. Experiments are measured using mean F1-score and Accuracy. Mean F1-Score is the F1-score of each class divided by the number of classes without consideration of every class size, which provides a reasonable metric in the class imbalanced data.

4.3   Results

The results on TYPE-I, TYPE-II experiments and comparisons with other methods are reported in Table 1, Table 2. To fair comparison, the results of other methods directly reported from [46] on TYPE-I, TYPE-II. Our proposed MADTN model has state-of-the-art overall performance than all the comparison methods in average mean F1-score and average accuracy. Especially in the TYPE-II experiment, our method is superior to the highest average mean F1-score/accuracy of [46] by 0.1522/14.4%. Furthermore, MADTN substantially outperforms the comparison methods on most of the experiments, and with larger rooms of improvement. In addition, some comparison methods outperform MADTN at $H \rightarrow V$. SMIC-HS and SMIC-VIS are very similar that samples was collected from same environment, and the frame rate is the main difference between them.

Hence other methods can achieve a relatively good result at $H \rightarrow V$. While motion information in some samples of SMIC-VIS is not obvious enough, probably because of the low frame rate, see Fig. 4. It may not capture the peak and valley of micro-expression in normal-speed(24fps) camera. It make MADTN to have a relatively poor performance. Distinct motion information is very critical to train our approach for a remarkable performance.

Fig. 4. Samples in the SMIC-VIS database

It is worth noting that three subsets of SMIC are very similar in many respects, their difference is recorded by different cameras. Nevertheless, SMIC and CASME II are much more different due to collected by different researchers. Hence, the TYPE-II task is more difficult than the TYPE-I. As shown in Table 1, Table 2, It can demonstrate that the result of all methods in the TYPE-II and TYPE-III task are much lower than those in the TYPE-I task. We notice that the performance of other method drop sharply from the TYPE-I task to the TYPE-II task, while the result of MADTN has only a small drop. These results demonstrate the strong robustness of our proposed method. This could be caused by enhancing feature more discriminating and alleviating distribution discrepancy.

4.4   Ablation Analysis

To look more deeply into our model, we conduct an extensive ablation experiment to study how components of MADTN affect performance. Firstly, we evaluate these variant ingredients of Motion Attention Feature on $C \rightarrow H$, $C \rightarrow V$ experiments following the same setting. In order to keep invariable network architecture, we set it to equal zero if an ingredient has not existed. The results are shown in Table 3, that the *Face* denotes a grayscale image of the middle frame in a video clip, the *onOF* represent optical flow fields between the onset frame and the middle frame, the *offOF* signify optical flow fields between the middle frame and the offset frame. We compared *Face* and *onOF-offOF* to verify benefit of motion representation. The promotions of *onOF-offOF* suggest that facial encoded representation has fallen behind in reflecting micro-expression compared with motion representation. Comparing the *onOF-Face* and the *onOF-Face-offOF*, transformation during micro-expression vanishing may benefits the performance. It may be because larger muscle movement occurs in the last half of the video clip. With the help of facial and motion representations, the *onOF-Face-offOF* achieves the best performance than others. This is because the optical flow enables the model to attention movement-related facial regions. Facial information can help to reduce the impact of motion bias on different faces.

Table 3. Experimental result(mean F1-score/accuracy) of our method with different input features on $C \rightarrow H$, $C \rightarrow V$ and $H \rightarrow N$. The *Face* denotes facial appearance information of the middle frame, the *onOF* denotes optical flow fields between the onset frame and the middle frame, the *offOF* denotes optical flow fields between the middle frame and the offset frame

Input	$C \rightarrow H$	$C \rightarrow V$	$H \rightarrow N$
Face	0.4115/42.07	0.4715/52.10	0.4673/52.10
onOF-Face	0.5598/56.69	0.6207/61.96	0.5713/57.76
onOF-offOF	0.5858/59.13	0.6520/64.79	0.7352/73.24
onOF-Face-offOF	0.6100/62.79	0.7056/70.41	0.7641/77.44

Then, we validate the effectiveness of the MMD loss on an ablation experiment that eliminates the effect of the MMD loss. Specifically, we demonstrate particular cross-dataset results on $C \rightarrow H$ and $C \rightarrow V$ in terms of different value λ, see Fig. 5. We can observe that the accuracy reach the maximum at $\lambda = 2$ and then fall off. Figure 5 display the promoting effect of the supervision of the cross-entropy loss and the MMD loss. It demonstrates that the MMD loss can help MADTN to alleviate the distribution shift between source and target domains and to enhance performances of our method.

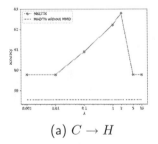   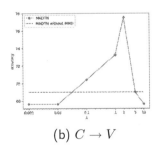

(a) $C \rightarrow H$ (b) $C \rightarrow V$

Fig. 5. Performances w.r.t λ on $C \rightarrow H$ and $C \rightarrow V$

5   Conclusion

In this paper, Motion Attention Deep Transfer Network (MADTN) has been presented to conduct unsupervised cross-database micro-expression recognition.

We select three frames into micro-expression sequences such that can reduce redundant information, then combine their motion information and facial appearance information to pay more attention to facial regions that occur muscle movement. What's more, deep transfer network has proposed to bridge the distribution discrepancy between source and target domains which increase the robustness of our method. Experiments on two benchmark tasks show that the MADTN achieves remarkable performance in many transfer tasks and outperforms all other counterparts, demonstrating the robustness and superiority of our approach.

Acknowledgements. This work was supported in part by the National Key Research and Development Program of China under Grant 2018YFB1305200, in part by the National Natural Science Foundation of China under Grant 61921004, Grant 61902064, Grant 81971282, Grant U2003207, and Grant 62076064, and in part by the Fundamental Research Funds for the Central Universities under Grant 2242018K3DN01.

References

1. Borgwardt, K.M., Gretton, A., Rasch, M.J., Kriegel, H.P., Schölkopf, B., Smola, A.J.: Integrating structured biological data by kernel maximum mean discrepancy. Bioinformatics **22**(14), e49–e57 (2006)
2. Chang, C.C., Lin, C.J.: LIBSVM: a library for support vector machines. ACM Trans. Intell. Syst. Technol. (TIST) **2**(3), 1–27 (2011)
3. Chaudhry, R., Ravichandran, A., Hager, G., Vidal, R.: Histograms of oriented optical flow and binet-cauchy kernels on nonlinear dynamical systems for the recognition of human actions. In: 2009 IEEE Conference on Computer Vision and Pattern Recognition, pp. 1932–1939. IEEE (2009)
4. Chu, W.S., De la Torre, F., Cohn, J.F.: Selective transfer machine for personalized facial action unit detection. In: Proceedings of the IEEE Conference on Computer Vision and Pattern Recognition, pp. 3515–3522 (2013)
5. Chu, W.S., De la Torre, F., Cohn, J.F.: Selective transfer machine for personalized facial expression analysis. IEEE Trans. Pattern Anal. Mach. Intell. **39**(3), 529–545 (2016)
6. Csurka, G.: Domain Adaptation in Computer Vision Applications, vol. 8. Springer, Heidelberg (2017). https://doi.org/10.1007/978-3-319-58347-1
7. Ekman, P.: Telling Lies: Clues to Deceit in the Marketplace, Politics, and Marriage, revised edn. WW Norton & Company, New York (2009)
8. Ekman, P., Friesen, W.V.: Nonverbal leakage and clues to deception. Psychiatry **32**(1), 88–106 (1969)
9. Farnebäck, G.: Two-frame motion estimation based on polynomial expansion. In: Bigun, J., Gustavsson, T. (eds.) SCIA 2003. LNCS, vol. 2749, pp. 363–370. Springer, Heidelberg (2003). https://doi.org/10.1007/3-540-45103-X_50
10. Fernando, B., Habrard, A., Sebban, M., Tuytelaars, T.: Unsupervised visual domain adaptation using subspace alignment. In: Proceedings of the IEEE International Conference on Computer Vision, pp. 2960–2967 (2013)
11. Frank, M., Herbasz, M., Sinuk, K., Keller, A., Nolan, C.: I see how you feel: training laypeople and professionals to recognize fleeting emotions. In: The Annual Meeting of the International Communication Association. Sheraton New York, New York City (2009)

12. Gong, B., Shi, Y., Sha, F., Grauman, K.: Geodesic flow kernel for unsupervised domain adaptation. In: 2012 IEEE Conference on Computer Vision and Pattern Recognition, pp. 2066–2073. IEEE (2012)
13. Hassan, A., Damper, R., Niranjan, M.: On acoustic emotion recognition: compensating for covariate shift. IEEE Trans. Audio Speech Lang. Process. **21**(7), 1458–1468 (2013)
14. Horn, B.K., Schunck, B.G.: Determining optical flow. In: Techniques and Applications of Image Understanding, vol. 281, pp. 319–331. International Society for Optics and Photonics (1981)
15. Huang, X., Wang, S.J., Zhao, G., Piteikainen, M.: Facial micro-expression recognition using spatiotemporal local binary pattern with integral projection. In: Proceedings of the IEEE International Conference on Computer Vision Workshops, pp. 1–9 (2015)
16. Huang, X., Zhao, G., Hong, X., Zheng, W., Pietikäinen, M.: Spontaneous facial micro-expression analysis using spatiotemporal completed local quantized patterns. Neurocomputing **175**, 564–578 (2016)
17. Itti, L., Koch, C.: Computational modelling of visual attention. Nat. Rev. Neurosci. **2**(3), 194–203 (2001)
18. Jovanović, M.R., Schmid, P.J., Nichols, J.W.: Sparsity-promoting dynamic mode decomposition. Phys. Fluids **26**(2), 024103 (2014)
19. Khor, H.Q., See, J., Phan, R.C.W., Lin, W.: Enriched long-term recurrent convolutional network for facial micro-expression recognition. In: 2018 13th IEEE International Conference on Automatic Face & Gesture Recognition (FG 2018), pp. 667–674. IEEE (2018)
20. Kim, D.H., Baddar, W.J., Ro, Y.M.: Micro-expression recognition with expression-state constrained spatio-temporal feature representations. In: Proceedings of the 24th ACM International Conference on Multimedia, pp. 382–386 (2016)
21. Kingma, D.P., Ba, J.: Adam: a method for stochastic optimization. arXiv preprint arXiv:1412.6980 (2014)
22. Le Ngo, A.C., Liong, S.T., See, J., Phan, R.C.W.: Are subtle expressions too sparse to recognize? In: 2015 IEEE International Conference on Digital Signal Processing (DSP), pp. 1246–1250. IEEE (2015)
23. Le Ngo, A.C., Oh, Y.H., Phan, R.C.W., See, J.: Eulerian emotion magnification for subtle expression recognition. In: 2016 IEEE International Conference on Acoustics, Speech and Signal Processing (ICASSP), pp. 1243–1247. IEEE (2016)
24. Li, X., et al.: Towards reading hidden emotions: a comparative study of spontaneous micro-expression spotting and recognition methods. IEEE Trans. Affect. Comput. **9**(4), 563–577 (2017)
25. Li, X., Pfister, T., Huang, X., Zhao, G., Pietikäinen, M.: A spontaneous micro-expression database: inducement, collection and baseline. In: 2013 10th IEEE International Conference and Workshops on Automatic Face and Gesture Recognition (FG), pp. 1–6. IEEE (2013)
26. Liong, S.T., See, J., Wong, K., Phan, R.C.W.: Less is more: micro-expression recognition from video using apex frame. Signal Process. Image Commun. **62**, 82–92 (2018)
27. Liu, Y.J., Zhang, J.K., Yan, W.J., Wang, S.J., Zhao, G., Fu, X.: A main directional mean optical flow feature for spontaneous micro-expression recognition. IEEE Trans. Affect. Comput. **7**(4), 299–310 (2015)
28. Long, M., Wang, J., Sun, J., Philip, S.Y.: Domain invariant transfer kernel learning. IEEE Trans. Knowl. Data Eng. **27**(6), 1519–1532 (2014)

29. Maas, A.L., Hannun, A.Y., Ng, A.Y.: Rectifier nonlinearities improve neural network acoustic models. In: Proceedings of ICML, vol. 30, p. 3 (2013)
30. Pan, S.J., Tsang, I.W., Kwok, J.T., Yang, Q.: Domain adaptation via transfer component analysis. IEEE Trans. Neural Netw. **22**(2), 199–210 (2010)
31. Park, S.Y., Lee, S.H., Ro, Y.M.: Subtle facial expression recognition using adaptive magnification of discriminative facial motion. In: Proceedings of the 23rd ACM International Conference on Multimedia, pp. 911–914 (2015)
32. Peng, M., Wang, C., Chen, T., Liu, G., Fu, X.: Dual temporal scale convolutional neural network for micro-expression recognition. Front. Psychol. **8**, 1745 (2017)
33. Pfister, T., Li, X., Zhao, G., Pietikäinen, M.: Recognising spontaneous facial micro-expressions. In: 2011 International Conference on Computer Vision, pp. 1449–1456. IEEE (2011)
34. Porter, S., Ten Brinke, L.: Reading between the lies: identifying concealed and falsified emotions in universal facial expressions. Psychol. Sci. **19**(5), 508–514 (2008)
35. Russell, T.A., Chu, E., Phillips, M.L.: A pilot study to investigate the effectiveness of emotion recognition remediation in schizophrenia using the micro-expression training tool. Brit. J. Clin. Psychol. **45**(4), 579–583 (2006)
36. Salter, F., Grammer, K., Rikowski, A.: Sex differences in negotiating with powerful males. Hum. Nat. **16**(3), 306–321 (2005)
37. Wang, Y., See, J., Phan, R.C.-W., Oh, Y.-H.: LBP with six intersection points: reducing redundant information in LBP-TOP for micro-expression recognition. In: Cremers, D., Reid, I., Saito, H., Yang, M.-H. (eds.) ACCV 2014. LNCS, vol. 9003, pp. 525–537. Springer, Cham (2015). https://doi.org/10.1007/978-3-319-16865-4_34
38. Wu, H.Y., Rubinstein, M., Shih, E., Guttag, J., Durand, F., Freeman, W.: Eulerian video magnification for revealing subtle changes in the world. ACM Trans. Graph. (TOG) **31**(4), 1–8 (2012)
39. Xu, F., Zhang, J., Wang, J.Z.: Microexpression identification and categorization using a facial dynamics map. IEEE Trans. Affect. Comput. **8**(2), 254–267 (2017)
40. Yan, W.J., Li, X., Wang, S.J., Zhao, G., Liu, Y.J., Chen, Y.H., Fu, X.: CASME II: an improved spontaneous micro-expression database and the baseline evaluation. PloS one **9**(1), e86041(2014)
41. Zhang, K., Zhang, Z., Li, Z., Qiao, Y.: Joint face detection and alignment using multitask cascaded convolutional networks. IEEE Signal Process. Lett. **23**(10), 1499–1503 (2016)
42. Zhao, G., Pietikainen, M.: Dynamic texture recognition using local binary patterns with an application to facial expressions. IEEE Trans. Pattern Anal. Mach. Intell. **29**(6), 915–928 (2007)
43. Zhou, Z., Zhao, G., Pietikäinen, M.: Towards a practical lipreading system. In: CVPR 2011, pp. 137–144. IEEE (2011)
44. Zong, Y., Huang, X., Zheng, W., Cui, Z., Zhao, G.: Learning a target sample regenerator for cross-database micro-expression recognition. In: Proceedings of the 25th ACM International Conference on Multimedia, pp. 872–880 (2017)
45. Zong, Y., Zheng, W., Cui, Z., Zhao, G., Hu, B.: Toward bridging microexpressions from different domains. IEEE Trans. Cybern. **50**, 5047–5060 (2019)
46. Zong, Y., Zheng, W., Hong, X., Tang, C., Cui, Z., Zhao, G.: Cross-database micro-expression recognition: a benchmark. In: Proceedings of the 2019 on International Conference on Multimedia Retrieval, pp. 354–363 (2019)
47. Zong, Y., Zheng, W., Huang, X., Shi, J., Cui, Z., Zhao, G.: Domain regeneration for cross-database micro-expression recognition. IEEE Trans. Image Process. **27**(5), 2484–2498 (2018)

Spatial Temporal Transformer Network for Skeleton-Based Action Recognition

Chiara Plizzari[✉], Marco Cannici, and Matteo Matteucci

Politecnico di Milano, Milan, Italy
chiara.plizzari@mail.polimi.it,
{marco.cannici,matteo.matteucci}@polimi.it

Abstract. Skeleton-based human action recognition has achieved a great interest in recent years, as skeleton data has been demonstrated to be robust to illumination changes, body scales, dynamic camera views, and complex background. Nevertheless, an effective encoding of the latent information underlying the 3D skeleton is still an open problem. In this work, we propose a novel Spatial-Temporal Transformer network (ST-TR) which models dependencies between joints using the Transformer *self-attention* operator. In our ST-TR model, a Spatial Self-Attention module (SSA) is used to understand intra-frame interactions between different body parts, and a Temporal Self-Attention module (TSA) to model inter-frame correlations. The two are combined in a two-stream network which outperforms state-of-the-art models using the same input data on both NTU-RGB+D 60 and NTU-RGB+D 120.

Keywords: Representation learning · Graph CNN · Self-attention · 3D skeleton · Action recognition

1 Introduction

Skeleton-based activity recognition is achieving increasing interest in recent years thanks to advances in 3D skeleton pose estimation devices, both in terms of accuracy and resolution. Algorithms and neural architectures for extracting context-aware fine-grained spatial-temporal features, capable of unlocking the true potential of skeleton based action recognition, however, are still lacking in the literature. The most widespread method to perform skeleton-based action recognition has become Spatial-Temporal Graph Convolutional Network (ST-GCN) [16], since, being an efficient representation of non-Euclidean data, it is able to effectively capture spatial (intra-frame) and temporal (inter-frame) information. However, ST-GCN models have some structural limitations, some of them already addressed in [2,10,13,14]: (i) The topology of the graph representing the human body is fixed for all layers and all the actions, preventing the extraction of rich representations. (ii) Both the spatial and temporal convolutions are implemented from a standard 2D convolution. As such, they are limited

© Springer Nature Switzerland AG 2021
A. Del Bimbo et al. (Eds.): ICPR 2020 Workshops, LNCS 12663, pp. 694–701, 2021.
https://doi.org/10.1007/978-3-030-68796-0_50

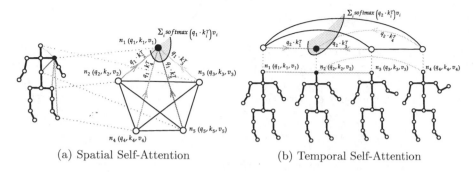

(a) Spatial Self-Attention   (b) Temporal Self-Attention

Fig. 1. Spatial Self-Attention (SSA) and Temporal Self-Attention (TSA). Self-attention operates on each pair of nodes by computing a weight for each of them representing the strength of their correlation. Those weights are used to score the contribution of each body joint n_i, proportionally to how relevant the node is w.r.t. the other ones.

to operate in a local neighborhood. (iii) As a consequence of (i) and (ii), correlations between body joints not linked in the human skeleton, e.g., the left and right hands, are underestimated even if relevant in actions such as "clapping".

In this paper, we face all these limitations by employing a modified Transformer self-attention operator. Despite being originally designed for Natural Language Processing (NLP) tasks, the flexibility of the Transformer self-attention [15] in modeling long-range dependencies, make this model a perfect solution to tackle ST-GCN weaknesses. Recently, Bello et al. in [1] employed self-attention on image pixels to overcome the locality of the convolution operator. In our work, we aim to apply the same mechanism to joints representing the human skeleton, with the goal of extracting adaptive low-level features modeling interactions in human actions both in space, through a Spatial Self-Attention module (SSA), and time, through a Temporal Self-Attention module (TSA) module. Authors of [3] also proposed a Self-Attention Network (SAN) to extract long-term semantic information; however, since they focus on temporally segmented clips, they solve the locality limitations of convolution only partially.

Contributions of this paper are summarized as follows:

- We propose a novel two-stream Transformer-based model, employing *self-attention* on both the spatial and temporal dimensions
- We design a *Spatial Self-Attention* (SSA) module to dynamically build links between skeleton joints, representing the relationships between human body parts, conditionally on the action and independently from the natural human body structure. On the temporal dimension, we introduce a *Temporal Self-Attention* (TSA) module to study the dynamics of joints along time too[1]
- Our model outperforms the ST-GCN [16] baseline, and outperforms previous state-of-the-art methods using the same input data on NTU-RGB+D [6,12].

---

[1] Code at https://github.com/Chiaraplizz/ST-TR.

2   Spatial Temporal Transformer Network

We propose *Spatial Temporal Transformer (ST-TR)*, an architecture using the Transformer self-attention mechanism to operate both on space and time. We develop two modules, *Spatial Self-Attention (SSA)* and *Temporal Self-Attention (TSA)*, each one focusing on extracting correlations in one of the two dimensions.

2.1   Spatial Self-Attention (SSA)

The SSA module applies self-attention *inside each frame* to extract low-level features embedding the relations between body parts, i.e., computing correlations between each pair of joints in every single frame independently, as depicted in Fig. 1a. Given the frame at time t, for each node i^t of the skeleton, a *query* vector $\mathbf{q}_i^t \in \mathbb{R}^{dq}$, a *key* vector $\mathbf{k}_i^t \in \mathbb{R}^{dk}$ and a *value* vector $\mathbf{v}_i^t \in \mathbb{R}^{dv}$ are first computed by applying trainable linear transformations to the node features $\mathbf{n}_i^t \in \mathbb{R}^{C_{in}}$, shared across all nodes, of parameters $\mathbf{W}_q \in \mathbb{R}^{C_{in} \times dq}$, $\mathbf{W}_k \in \mathbb{R}^{C_{in} \times dk}$, $\mathbf{W}_v \in \mathbb{R}^{C_{in} \times dv}$. Then, for each pair of body nodes (i^t, j^t), a *query-key dot product* is applied to obtain a weight $\alpha_{ij}^t \in \mathbb{R}$ representing the strength of the correlations between the two nodes. The resulting score α_{ij}^t is used to weight each joint value $\mathbf{v}_j^t$, and a weighted sum is computed to obtain a new embedding for node i^t, as in the following:

$$\alpha_{ij}^t = \mathbf{q}_i^t \cdot \mathbf{k}_j^{t\,T}, \forall t \in T, \qquad \mathbf{z}_i^t = \sum_j softmax_j \left(\frac{\alpha_{ij}^t}{\sqrt{d_{\mathrm{k}}}} \right) \mathbf{v}_j^t \qquad (1)$$

where $\mathbf{z}_i^t \in \mathbb{R}^{C_{out}}$ (with C_{out} the number of output channels) constitutes the new embedding of node i^t.

Multi-head self-attention is finally applied by repeating this embedding extraction process H times, each time with a different set of learnable parameters. The set $(\mathbf{z}_{i_1}^t, ..., \mathbf{z}_{i_H}^t)$ of node embeddings thus obtained, all referring to the same node i^t, is finally combined with a learnable transformation, i.e., $concat(\mathbf{z}_{i_1}^t, ..., \mathbf{z}_{i_H}^t) \cdot \mathbf{W}_o$, and constitutes the output features of SSA.

Thus, as shown in Fig. 1a, the relations between nodes (i.e., the α_{ij}^t scores) are dynamically *predicted* in SSA; the correlation structure is not fixed for all the actions, but it changes adaptively for each sample. SSA operates similar to a graph convolution on a fully connected graph where, however, the kernel values (i.e., the α_{ij}^t scores) are predicted dynamically based on the skeleton pose.

2.2   Temporal Self-Attention (TSA)

Along the temporal dimension, the dynamics of each joint is studied separately *along all the frames*, i.e., each single node is considered as independent and correlations between frames are computed by comparing features of the same body joint along the temporal dimension (see Fig. 1b). The formulation is symmetrical to the one reported in Eq. (1) for SSA:

$$\alpha_{ij}^v = \mathbf{q}_i^v \cdot \mathbf{k}_j^v \quad \forall v \in V, \qquad \mathbf{z}_i^v = \sum_j softmax_j \left(\frac{\alpha_{ij}^v}{\sqrt{d_k}} \right) \mathbf{v}_j^v \qquad (2)$$

where i^v, j^v indicate the same joint v in two different instants i, j, $\alpha_{ij}^v \in \mathbb{R}$, $\mathbf{q}_i^v \in \mathbb{R}^{dq}$ is the query associated to i^v, $\mathbf{k}_j^v \in \mathbb{R}^{dk}$ and $\mathbf{v}_j^v \in \mathbb{R}^{dv}$ are the key and value associated to joint j^v (all computed using trainable linear transformations as in SSA), and $\mathbf{z}_i^v \in \mathbb{R}^{C_{out}}$ is the resulting node embedding. An illustration of TSA is depicted in Fig. 1b. Multi-head attention is applied as in SSA. The network, by extracting inter-frame relations between nodes in time, can learn to correlate frames apart from each other (e.g., nodes in the first frame with those in the last one), capturing discriminant features that are not otherwise possible to capture with a standard convolution, being this limited by the kernel size.

2.3   Two-Stream Spatial Temporal Transformer Network

To combine the SSA and TSA modules, a two-stream architecture named 2s-ST-TR is used, as similarly proposed by Shi et al. in [14] and [13]. In our formulation, the two streams differentiate on the way the self-attention mechanism is applied: SSA operates on the spatial stream (named S-TR stream), while TSA on the temporal one (named T-TR stream). On both streams, simple features are first extracted through a three-layers residual network, where each layer processes the input on the spatial dimension through graph convolution (GCN), and on the temporal dimension through a standard 2D convolution (TCN), as in ST-GCN [16]. SSA and TSA are applied on the S-TR and on the T-TR stream in substitution to the GCN and TCN feature extraction modules respectively (Fig. 2). Each stream is trained using the standard cross-entropy loss, and the sub-networks outputs are eventually fused together by summing up their softmax output scores to obtain the final prediction, as in [13,14].

Spatial Transformer Stream (S-TR). In the spatial stream (Fig. 2), self-attention is applied at the skeleton level through a SSA module, which focuses on spatial relations between joints, and then its output is passed to a 2D convolutional module with kernel K_t on temporal dimension (TCN), as in [16], to extract temporally relevant features, i.e., $\mathbf{S\text{-}TR}(x) = Conv_{2D(1 \times K_t)}(\mathbf{SSA}(x))$. Following the original Transformer structure, the input is pre-normalized passing through a Batch Normalization layer [4,11], and skip connections are used, which sum the input to the output of the SSA module.

Temporal Transformer Stream (T-TR). The temporal stream, instead, focuses on discovering inter-frame temporal relations. Similarly to the S-TR stream, inside each T-TR layer, a standard graph convolution sub-module [16] is followed by the proposed Temporal Self-Attention module, i.e., $\mathbf{T\text{-}TR}(x) = \mathbf{TSA}(GCN(x))$. In this case, TSA operates on graphs linking the same joint along all the time dimension (e.g., all left feet, or all right hands).

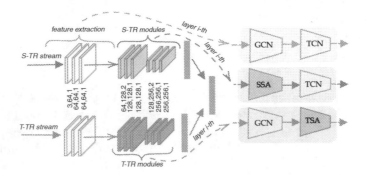

Fig. 2. The 2s-ST-TR architecture. On each stream, the first three layers extract simple features. On the S-TR stream, at each subsequent layer, SSA is used to extract spatial information, followed by a 2D convolution on time dimension (TCN). On the T-TR stream, at each subsequent layer, TSA is used to extract temporal information, while spatial features are extracted by a standard graph convolution (GCN) [16]

3   Model Evaluation

3.1   Datasets

NTU RGB+D 60 and NTU RGB+D 120. The NTU RGB+D 60 (NTU-60) dataset is a large-scale benchmark for 3D human action recognition [12]. Skeleton information consists of 3D coordinates of 25 body joints and a total of 60 different action classes. The NTU-60 dataset follows two different criteria for evaluation. In *Cross-View Evaluation* (X-View), the data is split according to the camera from which the action is taken, while in *Cross-Subject Evaluation* (X-Sub) according to the subject performing the action. NTU-RGB+D 120 [6] (NTU-120) is an extension of NTU-60, with a total of 113,945 videos and 120 classes. It follows two evaluation criteria: *Cross-Subject Evaluation (X-Sub)* is the same used in NTU-60, while in *Cross-Setup Evaluation (X-Set)* training and testing samples are split based on the parity of the camera setup IDs.

3.2   Experimental Settings

Using PyTorch framework, we trained our models for a total of 120 epochs with batch size 32 and SGD as optimizer. The learning rate is set to 0.1 at the beginning and then reduced by a factor of 10 at the epochs {60, 90}. Moreover, we preprocessed the data with the same procedure used by Shi et al. in [14] and [13]. In order to avoid overfitting, we also used *DropAttention* [17], a dropout technique introduced by Zehui et al. [17] for regularizing attention weights in Transformer. In all of these experiments, the *number of heads* for multi-head attention is set to 8, and d_q, d_k, d_v embedding dimensions to $0.25 \times C_{out}$ in each layer, as in [1]. We did not perform a grid search on these parameters.

Table 1. a) Accuracy (%) comparison of S-TR and T-TR, and their combination (ST-TR) on NTU-60, w and w/o bones. b) Parameters of SSA and TSA modules

(a)

Method	Bones	X-Sub	X-View
ST-GCN [16]		85.7	92.7
S-TR		86.4	94.0
T-TR		86.0	93.6
ST-TR		88.7	95.6
S-TR	✓	87.9	94.9
T-TR	✓	87.3	94.1
ST-TR	✓	89.9	96.1

(b)

Module	Params [$\times 10^4$]
GCN [16]	19.9
SSA	17.8
TCN [16]	59.0
TSA	17.7

3.3 Results

To verify the effectiveness of our SSA and TSA modules, we compare separately the S-TR stream and T-TR stream against the ST-GCN [16] baseline, whose results on NTU-60 [12] are reported in Table 1 using our learning rate scheduling.

As far as it concerns the SSA, S-TR outperforms the baseline by 0.7% on X-Sub, and by 1.3% on X-View, demonstrating that self-attention can be used in place of graph convolution, increasing the network performance while also decreasing the number of parameters. On NTU-60 the S-TR stream achieves slightly better performance (+0.4%) than the T-TR stream, on both X-View and X-Sub (Table 1a). This can be motivated by the fact that SSA in S-TR operates on 25 joints only, while on the temporal dimension the number of correlations is proportional to the huge number of frames. Table 1b shows the difference in terms of parameters between a single GCN (TCN) and the corresponding SSA (TSA) module, with $C_{in} = C_{out} = 256$. Especially on the temporal dimension, TSA results in a decrease in parameters, introducing 41.3×10^4 less than TCN. The combination of the two streams achieves 88.7% of accuracy on X-Sub and 95.6% of accuracy on X-View, outperforming the baseline ST-GCN by up to 3% and surpassing other two-stream architectures (Table 2). Classes that benefit the most from self-attention are "playing with phone", "typing", and "cross hands" on S-TR, and those involving long-range relations or two people, i.e., "hugging", "point finger", "pat on back", on T-TR. These require to correlate along the entire action, giving empirical insight on the advantage of the proposed method.

As adding bones information demonstrated leading to better results in previous works [13,14], we also studied the effect of our self-attention module on combined joint and bones information. For each node $\mathbf{v}_1 = (\mathbf{x}_1, \mathbf{y}_1, \mathbf{z}_1)$ and $\mathbf{v}_2 = (\mathbf{x}_2, \mathbf{y}_2, \mathbf{z}_2)$, the bone connecting the two is calculated as $\mathbf{b}_{\mathbf{v}_1, \mathbf{v}_2} = (\mathbf{x}_2 - \mathbf{x}_1, \mathbf{y}_2 - \mathbf{y}_1, \mathbf{z}_2 - \mathbf{z}_1)$. Joint and bone information are concatenated along the channel dimension and then fed to the network. At each layer, the size of the input and output channels is doubled as in [13,14]. The performance results are shown again in Table 1a; all previous configurations improve when bones are added as input. The latter fact highlights the flexibility of our method, which is capable of adapting to different input types and network configurations.

Table 2. Comparison with state-of-the-art accuracy (%) of S-TR, T-TR, and their combination (ST-TR) on NTU-60 (a) and NTU-120 (b)

(a)

NTU-60

Method	Bones	X-Sub	X-View
ST-GCN [16]		81.5	88.3
1s-AGCN [14][10]		86.0	93.7
1s Shift-GCN [2]		87.8	95.1
SAN [3]		87.2	92.7
ST-TR (Ours)		**88.7**	**95.6**
2s-AGCN [14]	✓	88.5	95.1
DGCNN [13]	✓	89.9	96.1
2s Shift-GCN [2]	✓	89.7	96.0
MS-G3D [10]	✓	**91.5**	**96.2**
ST-TR (Ours)	✓	89.9	96.1

(b)

NTU-120

Method	X-Sub	X-Set
ST-LSTM [7]	55.7	57.9
GCA-LSTM [8]	61.2	63.3
RotClips+MTCNN [5]	62.2	61.8
Pose Evol. Map [9]	64.6	66.9
1s Shift-GCN [2]	80.9	83.2
S-TR (Ours)	78.6	80.7
T-TR (Ours)	78.4	80.5
ST-TR (Ours)	**81.9**	**84.1**

4   Comparison with State-of-the-Art

We compare our methods on NTU-60 and NTU-120 w.r.t. other methods which make use of joint or joint+bones information on a one- or two-stream architecture, as we also did, for a fair comparison (Table 2). On NTU-60, ST-TR without bones outperforms all the state-of-the-art models not using bones, including 1s-AGCN and SAN [3], which uses self-attention too. Similarly, our ST-TR with bones outperforms all previous two-stream methods that use bones information as well, i.e., 2s-AGCN and 2s Shift-GCN. On NTU-120, the model based only on joint information outperforms all state-of-the-art methods making use of the same information. The competitive results validate the superiority of our method over architectures relying on convolution only.

5   Conclusions

In this paper, we propose a novel approach that introduces Transformer self-attention in skeleton activity recognition as an alternative to graph convolution. Through experiments on NTU-60 and NTU-120, we demonstrated that our Spatial Self-Attention module (SSA) can replace graph convolution, enabling more flexible and dynamic representations. Similarly, the Temporal Self-Attention module (TSA) overcomes the strict locality of standard convolution, leading to global motion pattern extraction. Moreover, our final Spatial-Temporal Transformer network (ST-TR) achieves state-of-the-art performance on NTU-RGB+D w.r.t. methods using same input information and streams setup.

References

1. Bello, I., Zoph, B., Vaswani, A., Shlens, J., Le, Q.V.: Attention augmented convolutional networks. In: Proceedings of the IEEE International Conference on Computer Vision, pp. 3286–3295 (2019)

2. Cheng, K., Zhang, Y., He, X., Chen, W., Cheng, J., Lu, H.: Skeleton-based action recognition with shift graph convolutional network. In: Proceedings of the IEEE/CVF Conference on Computer Vision and Pattern Recognition, pp. 183–192 (2020)
3. Cho, S., Maqbool, M., Liu, F., Foroosh, H.: Self-attention network for skeleton-based human action recognition. In: The IEEE Winter Conference on Applications of Computer Vision, pp. 635–644 (2020)
4. Ioffe, S., Szegedy, C.: Batch normalization: accelerating deep network training by reducing internal covariate shift. arXiv preprint arXiv:1502.03167 (2015)
5. Ke, Q., Bennamoun, M., An, S., Sohel, F., Boussaid, F.: Learning clip representations for skeleton-based 3D action recognition. IEEE Trans. Image Process. **27**(6), 2842–2855 (2018)
6. Liu, J., Shahroudy, A., Perez, M.L., Wang, G., Duan, L.Y., Chichung, A.K.: NTURGB+D 120: a large-scale benchmark for 3D human activity understanding. IEEE Trans. Pattern Anal. Mach. Intell. **42**, 2684–2701 (2019)
7. Liu, J., Shahroudy, A., Xu, D., Wang, G.: Spatio-temporal LSTM with trust gates for 3D human action recognition. In: Leibe, B., Matas, J., Sebe, N., Welling, M. (eds.) ECCV 2016. LNCS, vol. 9907, pp. 816–833. Springer, Cham (2016). https://doi.org/10.1007/978-3-319-46487-9_50
8. Liu, J., Wang, G., Duan, L.Y., Abdiyeva, K., Kot, A.C.: Skeleton-based human action recognition with global context-aware attention LSTM networks. IEEE Trans. Image Process. **27**(4), 1586–1599 (2017)
9. Liu, M., Yuan, J.: Recognizing human actions as the evolution of pose estimation maps. In: Proceedings of the IEEE Conference on Computer Vision and Pattern Recognition, pp. 1159–1168 (2018)
10. Liu, Z., Zhang, H., Chen, Z., Wang, Z., Ouyang, W.: Disentangling and unifying graph convolutions for skeleton-based action recognition. In: Proceedings of the IEEE/CVF Conference on Computer Vision and Pattern Recognition, pp. 143–152 (2020)
11. Nguyen, T.Q., Salazar, J.: Transformers without tears: improving the normalization of self-attention. arXiv preprint arXiv:1910.05895 (2019)
12. Shahroudy, A., Liu, J., Ng, T.T., Wang, G.: NTU RGB+D: a large scale dataset for 3D human activity analysis. In: Proceedings of the IEEE Conference on Computer Vision and Pattern Recognition, pp. 1010–1019 (2016)
13. Shi, L., Zhang, Y., Cheng, J., Lu, H.: Skeleton-based action recognition with directed graph neural networks. In: Proceedings of the IEEE Conference on Computer Vision and Pattern Recognition, pp. 7912–7921 (2019)
14. Shi, L., Zhang, Y., Cheng, J., Lu, H.: Two-stream adaptive graph convolutional networks for skeleton-based action recognition. In: Proceedings of the IEEE Conference on Computer Vision and Pattern Recognition, pp. 12026–12035 (2019)
15. Vaswani, A., et al.: Attention is all you need. In: Advances in Neural Information Processing Systems, pp. 5998–6008 (2017)
16. Yan, S., Xiong, Y., Lin, D.: Spatial temporal graph convolutional networks for skeleton-based action recognition. In: Thirty-Second AAAI Conference on Artificial Intelligence (2018)
17. Zehui, L., et al.: DropAttention: a regularization method for fully-connected self-attention networks. arXiv preprint arXiv:1907.11065 (2019)

Slow Feature Subspace for Action Recognition

Suzana R. A. Beleza[1]([✉]) and Kazuhiro Fukui[1,2]

[1] Graduate School of Science and Technology, University of Tsukuba,
Tsukuba, Japan
`suzana@cvlab.cs.tsukuba.ac.jp`
[2] Center for Artificial Intelligence Research (C-AIR), University of Tsukuba,
Tsukuba, Japan
`kfukui@cs.tsukuba.ac.jp`

Abstract. This paper proposes a framework for human action recognition using a combination of subspace-based methods and slow feature analysis (SFA). Subspace-based methods can compactly model the distribution of multiple images from a video by a low dimensional subspace even when few data is available. However, the temporal information of the video is lost after generating the subspace using principal component analysis (PCA). In contrast, PCA-SFA, which is a variant of SFA, can produce a valid video descriptor as a basis of a slow feature space from a given image sequence. In the proposed framework, we extract a valid video descriptor from an input video by conducting PCA-SFA, and then transform the descriptor into a subspace by using PCA. This new representation of slow feature subspace includes temporal dynamic information. Thus, we can compare two sequences and perform classification by simply calculating the similarity between their slow feature subspaces. The effectiveness of our framework is demonstrated through extensive experiments with two publicly available datasets, KTH action and the Chinese sign language dataset (isolated SLR500).

Keywords: Human action recognition · Slow feature analysis · Subspace-based methods

1 Introduction

Human action recognition has recently received renewed attention in the computer vision field due to the advent of new technologies and, consequently, new applications for surveillance, human-machine interaction, assistive technologies, and others [2, 20, 23]. The algorithms used for these applications have some challenges (e.g., over-fitting, data occlusion) which are posed due to data scarceness and the computational complexity of the problem. Recently, subspace-based approaches are being applied to minimize various challenges on action recognition.

Subspace-based methods are well known for their ability to approximate well the data distribution, in terms of the least mean square, using compact

A. Del Bimbo et al. (Eds.): ICPR 2020 Workshops, LNCS 12663, pp. 702–716, 2021.
https://doi.org/10.1007/978-3-030-68796-0_51

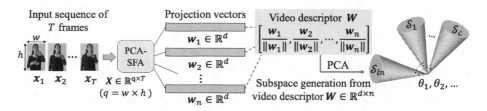

Fig. 1. Conceptual diagram of the proposed method. A video descriptor W is extracted from the T frames of a video X using PCA-SFA, by selecting the first n projection vectors w. Then, a compact slow feature subspace $\mathcal{S}_{in}$ is generated by applying PCA to the video descriptor W. After that, the similarity is calculated using the canonical angles $\{\theta\}$ between the input subspace $\mathcal{S}_{in}$ and each class subspace $\mathcal{S}_c$, where $c = \{1, .., C\}$ and C is the number of classes. Finally, $\mathcal{S}_{in}$ is assigned to the class with the highest similarity.

subspaces [4–6] even when the dataset is scarce. Besides, as they are image set classifiers, they can easily handle the frames of a video using an image set [18].

On the other hand, this image set's temporal dynamic information is lost while generating the subspace using principal component analysis (PCA). To increase the methods' success rate, it is necessary to introduce a mechanism to exploit the time dynamics of a sequence in the subspace. Therefore, we propose a framework in this paper for action recognition using a combination of subspace-based methods and slow feature analysis (SFA) [8,21].

SFA [21] is a method that finds a set of valid projection vectors (i.e., linear mapping function) that extract features that slowly change along time from a given image sequence. These slow features represent an essential temporal structure of the image sequence after removing unnecessary details. As a variant of SFA, PCA-SFA [8] gives attention to the projection vectors instead of slow feature vectors, considering that they also represent the temporal structure of the sequence without depending on the length of the video. PCA-SFA uses a set of projection vectors as an effective video descriptor for classification tasks of image sequences. Besides, PCA-SFA can address the over-fitting problem of SFA under small sample size (SSS). Motivated by the advantages above, we utilize PCA-SFA to improve the efficiency of our framework.

The conceptual diagram of the proposed method is shown in Fig. 1. A set of n projection vectors W, to which we refer as video descriptor, is extracted for each video X using PCA-SFA. In this process flow, the dimension of the projection vectors d is equal to the image dimension q, since only raw images are being used. Next, to achieve a compact subspace representation, we apply PCA without data-centering to the set of projection vectors in W, generating the slow feature subspace $\mathcal{S}_{in}$. Thus, we can precisely compare two distinct actions by calculating the similarity using the canonical angles $\{\theta\}$ between the input slow feature subspace $\mathcal{S}_{in}$ and the class slow feature subspaces $\mathcal{S}_c$. These class subspaces $\mathcal{S}_c$ are generated from a set of video descriptors $\{W_i^c\}_{i=1}^m|_{c=1}^C$, where

m is the number of videos and C is the number of classes. Finally, we perform classification by assigning the input subspace to the class with the highest similarity.

This method is expected to increase the classification accuracy of traditional subspace-based methods due to its ability to characterize the temporal dynamics of the action. Besides, our method also inherits the ability to handle data scarceness from the use of PCA-SFA.

The rest of this paper is organized as follows. In Sect. 2, we introduce the current literature on human action recognition regarding SFA and subspace-based methods. After that, we discuss our proposed approach in Sect. 3. Next, the details of the experiments and the recognition results are shown in Sect. 4. Then, we present our final considerations and future work in Sect. 5.

2   Related Work

This section will describe the SFA and subspace-based methods, which are the central techniques of the proposed method.

2.1   Slow Feature Analysis for Action Recognition

The human brain perception uses high-level abstraction to reduce unnecessary information from input signals and build a representation of the scenario with the remaining information. The slowness principle is a concept created to mimic this ability at a computational level [20].

This principle aims to extract slowly varying signals from a fast varying input signal to recover the source's essential information. For example, consider an object (source) on a table and two types of signals to represent it. The first signal varies very fast because it is being captured by a high-resolution camera (sensor), which is sensitive to the smallest changes of the object (e.g., light, rotation, translation). The second signal represents the brain perception of the video information. This signal is significantly smoother than the first one because it represents the object's essential information, which changes slowly along the time. This way, the main challenge of the slowness principle is recovering the essential information of the source independent of the sensor used to capture the source signal [3,20].

According to this principle, the SFA [21] method computes the slowest varying elements of a time series. This method has been useful for video analysis and action recognition [8,20,23]. However, it suffers from over-fitting when the number of frames of a video is smaller than their dimension. This dimension indicates the number of pixels in an image or the dimension of a feature vector extracted from a convolutional neural network (CNN). PCA-SFA [8] was recently proposed to solve this small sample size problem of SFA and was shown to be effective for action recognition.

2.2 Subspace-Based Methods for Action Recognition

Image set classification methods have recently gained special attention due to their ability to represent several types of data (e.g., videos, multi-view images) [18]. In this category, we can highlight subspace-based methods known by their robustness in representing high dimensional data using a low dimensional subspace. They can approximate the training data distribution well, in terms of the least mean square, while reducing the computational cost of the algorithm [4,5].

Several new methods based on subspaces have been developed for action recognition using videos for several applications. An approach for gait recognition was created applying CMSM and CNN features, achieving high classification accuracy [12]. However, this approach still does not implement any sequence descriptor to exploit the relationship between the video frames.

Recently, an approach was created for motion recognition using randomized time warping to represent a video sequence with subspaces and perform classification on the Grassmann manifold. This method has achieved competitive results for the datasets used [19]. Among several subspace-based methods existent, MSM, CMSM, KMSM and KCMSM are the most used ones. Following, we will briefly explain each of them.

Mutual Subspace Method

The mutual subspace method (MSM) is an image set classification method that has achieved high performance for action recognition. Figure 2 shows a conceptual diagram of MSM, which can be formally defined as follows. Given a N_1-dimensional subspace $\mathcal{S}_1$ and a N_2-dimensional subspace $\mathcal{S}_2$ in d-dimensional vector space, where $N_1 \leq N_2$, the canonical angles $\{0 \leq \theta_1, ..., \theta_{N_1} \leq \frac{\pi}{2}\}$ between the $\mathcal{S}_1$ and $\mathcal{S}_2$ are recursively defined as follows [1,7]:

$$\cos \theta_i = \max_{\mathbf{u} \in \mathcal{S}_1} \max_{\mathbf{v} \in \mathcal{S}_2} \mathbf{u}^\top \mathbf{v} = \mathbf{u}_i^\top \mathbf{v}_i,$$
$$s.t. \|\mathbf{u}_i\|_2 = \|\mathbf{v}_i\|_2 = 1, \mathbf{u}_i^\top \mathbf{u}_j = \mathbf{v}_i^\top \mathbf{v}_j = 0, i \neq j, \tag{1}$$

where $\mathbf{u}_i$ and $\mathbf{v}_i$ are the canonical vectors forming the i-th smallest canonical angle θ_i between $\mathcal{S}_1$ and $\mathcal{S}_2$. The j-th canonical angle θ_j is the smallest angle in the direction orthogonal to the canonical angles $\{\theta_k\}_{k=1}^{j-1}$.

The canonical angles can be calculated from the orthogonal projection matrices onto subspaces $\mathcal{S}_1$ and $\mathcal{S}_2$. Let $\{\mathbf{\Phi}_i\}_{i=1}^{N_1}$ be the basis vectors of $\mathcal{S}_1$ and $\{\mathbf{\Psi}_i\}_{i=1}^{N_1}$ be the basis vectors of $\mathcal{S}_2$. The projection matrices $\mathbf{P}_1$ and $\mathbf{P}_2$ are calculated as $\sum_{i=1}^{N_1} \mathbf{\Phi}_i \mathbf{\Phi}_i^\top$ and $\sum_{i=1}^{N_2} \mathbf{\Psi}_i \mathbf{\Psi}_i^\top$, respectively. $\cos^2 \theta_i$ is the i-th largest eigenvalue of $\mathbf{P}_1^\top \mathbf{P}_2$ or $\mathbf{P}_2^\top \mathbf{P}_1$. Alternatively, the canonical angles can be easily calculated by applying the singular value decomposition (SVD) to the orthonormal basis vectors of the subspaces. The geometric similarity between two subspaces $\mathcal{S}_1$ and $\mathcal{S}_2$ is defined by using the canonical angles, as in Eq. 2.

$$\text{sim}(\mathcal{S}_1, \mathcal{S}_2) = \frac{1}{N_1} \sum_{i=1}^{N_1} \cos^2 \theta_i . \tag{2}$$

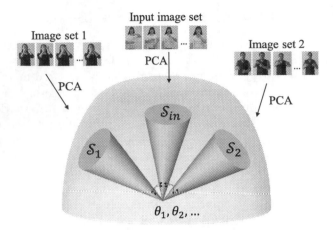

Fig. 2. Conceptual diagram of MSM. On MSM, each image set is represented as a subspace after applying PCA. The canonical angles formed between two subspaces are used to measure their similarity. The input subspace $\mathcal{S}_{in}$ is then assigned to the class with the highest similarity.

After calculating the similarities, MSM assigns an input subspace $\mathcal{S}_{in}$ to the most similar class subspace $\{\mathcal{S}_c\}_{c=1}^{C}$.

Constrained Mutual Subspace Method

The constrained mutual subspace method (CMSM) is an extension of MSM created to increase the class separability by limiting the shared information between classes. In MSM, the subspaces are created independently of each other. Although these subspaces can make a good approximation of the training data distribution, it is not possible to assume that they are optimal for classification purposes [6].

In CMSM, the components with common information between class subspaces $\{\mathcal{S}_c\}_{c=1}^{C}$ are discarded by projecting the subspaces into a generalized difference subspace (GDS) [6]. Therefore, CMSM performs classification based only on exclusive characteristics of the class, increasing the classification accuracy.

Kernel Mutual Subspace Method

The kernel mutual subspace method (KMSM) [13] performs MSM in a reproducing kernel Hilbert space to handle non-linear data distributions. In this space, the dimensions are extremely high; consequently, it is challenging to compute the projections directly. Therefore, a kernel PCA (KPCA) [14] is performed by a kernel trick. The Gaussian radial basis function is a commonly used kernel functions defined as $k(x_i, x_j)$ in Eq. 3, where x_i and x_j belong to the training input, and σ^2 is the kernel bandwidth parameter.

$$k(x_i, x_j) = \exp\left(-\frac{\|x_i - x_j\|^2}{2\sigma^2}\right). \tag{3}$$

Kernel Constrained Mutual Subspace Method

The kernel constrained mutual subspace method (KCMSM) [6] performs KMSM on the kernel GDS (KGDS). In KCMSM, the KGDS is generated from the non-linear subspaces created by KPCA. After that, the image set is projected onto the generalized difference subspace. Then, the standard PCA is applied to these projections to create new linear subspaces. In summary, the key idea of KCMSM is to generate new subspaces using KGDS to extract the difference components of the original subspaces created by KPCA. KGDS uses the same kernel trick formulated in Eq. 3.

3   Proposed Method and Framework

In this section, we introduce the proposed method and the framework used for action recognition.

3.1   Subspace Representation of Slowly Varying Components

The slow feature analysis (SFA) is an unsupervised algorithm used for representing the smoothest (i.e., slowest) varying elements of a time series and has recently become a powerful method for video analysis. Nevertheless, the original formulation of SFA suffers from the effects of the small sample size (SSS) problem.

Frequently, features of videos are extracted to facilitate the analysis and recognition of human actions. These features are extracted throughout the video sequence, which can be defined as $\boldsymbol{X} = [\boldsymbol{x}_1, \ldots, \boldsymbol{x}_T]$ of T feature vectors $\boldsymbol{x}_t \in \mathbb{R}^d$ with the time index t and dimension d. The SFA calculates the projection vector $\mathbf{w} \in \mathbb{R}^d$, which is a mapping function of the features $\boldsymbol{x}_t$, such that the output signal $y_t = \mathbf{w}^\top \boldsymbol{x}_t + b$ slowly changes through the sequence under the following constraints: zero mean $\frac{1}{T} \sum_{t=1}^T y_t = 0$, unit variance $\frac{1}{T} \sum_{t=1}^T y_t^2 = 1$ and decorrelation $\frac{1}{T} \sum_{t=1}^T y_t^{(i)} y_t^{(j)} = 0 \ \forall i < j$ where $y_t^{(i)} = \mathbf{w}_i^\top \boldsymbol{x}_t + b_i$ is the i-th output value by the i-th projection $\mathbf{w}_i$. This formulation leads to the generalized eigenvalue problem in Eq. 4;

$$\left(\sum_t \dot{\boldsymbol{x}}_t \dot{\boldsymbol{x}}_t^\top \right) \mathbf{w} = \lambda \left(\sum_t (\boldsymbol{x}_t - \boldsymbol{\mu})(\boldsymbol{x}_t - \boldsymbol{\mu})^\top \right) \mathbf{w}, \qquad (4)$$

where $\boldsymbol{\mu}$ is the mean $\boldsymbol{\mu} = \frac{1}{T} \sum_t \boldsymbol{x}_t$ and $\dot{\boldsymbol{x}}_t$ is the differential vector on t responsible for exploiting the time structure of the sample, it is practically computed as $\dot{\boldsymbol{x}}_t = \boldsymbol{x}_{t+1} - \boldsymbol{x}_t$.

For action recognition, the datasets frequently have $T < d$, which affects the SFA eigenvalue problem of Eq. 4. To deal with this SSS problem, Kobayashi [8] integrated the PCA into the SFA, creating the PCA-SFA method. This method minimizes the problem of a sample $\{\boldsymbol{x}_t\}_{t=1}^T$ of $T < d$ that can have an arbitrary form when projected due to over-fitting. The PCA-SFA regularizes the projection vector $\mathbf{w}$ to follow the PCA subspace of the frames/features sequence to extract their temporal information via SFA effectively.

Formally, the eigenvalue problems of PCA and SFA are equivalent to minimization problems that share the same denominator. Therefore, it is possible to join the two methods using the Eq. 5.

$$\min_{\mathbf{w}} \frac{\mathbf{w}^\top \left(\eta I + \sum_t \dot{\mathbf{x}}_t \dot{\mathbf{x}}_t^\top\right) \mathbf{w}}{\mathbf{w}^\top \left\{\sum_t (\mathbf{x}_t - \boldsymbol{\mu})(\mathbf{x}_t - \boldsymbol{\mu})^\top\right\} \mathbf{w}} \Leftrightarrow$$

$$\left(\eta I + \sum_t \dot{\mathbf{x}}_t \dot{\mathbf{x}}_t^\top\right) \mathbf{w} = \lambda \left(\sum_t (\mathbf{x}_t - \boldsymbol{\mu})(\mathbf{x}_t - \boldsymbol{\mu})^\top\right) \mathbf{w} , \tag{5}$$

where η is a balancing (regularization) parameter between PCA and SFA that is defined as $\eta = \frac{1}{T} \sum_t \|\dot{x}\|_2^2$. This parameter becomes higher for the smaller-sized samples and lower for the larger-sized ones. In our experiments, η was defined empirically as being twice the original value, $\eta = 2\frac{1}{T} \sum_t \|\dot{x}\|_2^2$.

The PCA-SFA [8] is efficiently computed in the case of SSS as follows. First, the features are centered by using $\mathbf{X} - \boldsymbol{\mu}\mathbf{1}^\top$, where $\mathbf{X} \in \mathbb{R}^{d \times T}$ ($T \ll d$) with the features vectors $\mathbf{x}_t$ as its columns. Second, the SVD is applied to the centered sequence $\mathbf{X} - \boldsymbol{\mu}\mathbf{1}^\top = \mathbf{U}\boldsymbol{\Sigma}\mathbf{V}^\top$ where $\mathbf{U} \in \mathbb{R}^{d \times r}$, $\boldsymbol{\Sigma} \in \mathbb{R}^{r \times r}$, $\mathbf{V} \in \mathbb{R}^{T \times r}$ and $r(< T)$ indicates the rank, usually $r = T - 1$. Then, Eq. 5 can be rewritten using Eq. 6 by reparameterizing the projection vector as $\mathbf{w} = \mathbf{U}\boldsymbol{\Sigma}^{-1}\boldsymbol{\alpha}$.

$$\boldsymbol{\Sigma}^{-1}\mathbf{U}^\top \left(\eta I + \sum_t \dot{\mathbf{x}}_t \dot{\mathbf{x}}_t^\top\right) \mathbf{U}\boldsymbol{\Sigma}^{-1}\boldsymbol{\alpha} = \lambda\boldsymbol{\alpha}, \Leftrightarrow$$

$$\left(\eta\boldsymbol{\Sigma}^{-2} + \boldsymbol{\Sigma}^{-1}\mathbf{U}^\top \sum_t \dot{\mathbf{x}}_t \dot{\mathbf{x}}_t^\top \mathbf{U}\boldsymbol{\Sigma}^{-1}\right) \boldsymbol{\alpha} = \lambda\boldsymbol{\alpha}. \tag{6}$$

By solving the eigenvalue problem above, we can find the eigenvector $\boldsymbol{\alpha}$ and calculate $\mathbf{w}$. After that, it is necessary to sort $\mathbf{w}$ in ascending order using the eigenvalues in λ. Hence, the first projection vector $\mathbf{w}_1$ will correspond to the 1st order temporal and the last one to the T-th order one.

In our proposed method, we consider several projection vectors $\mathbf{w}$ to create the video descriptor $\boldsymbol{W}$, using the equation below.

$$\boldsymbol{W} = \left[\frac{\mathbf{w}_1^\top}{\|\mathbf{w}_1\|_2} \cdots \frac{\mathbf{w}_n^\top}{\|\mathbf{w}_n\|_2}\right]^\top \in \mathbb{R}^{d \times n}, \tag{7}$$

where the number of columns $n \in \{1, \ldots, T\}$ corresponds to the number of projection vectors in $\boldsymbol{W}$. After selecting n, $\boldsymbol{W}$ is normalized so that each column has norm equals 1. Then, PCA without data-centering is applied again to the normalized $\boldsymbol{W}$ to generate a single slow feature subspace for each class or input set. Finally, the traditional subspace-based methods can be used to perform classification. Next, we explain the proposed framework that combines the slow feature subspace with the traditional subspace-based methods for action recognition.

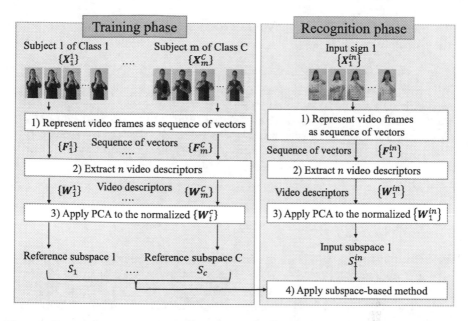

Fig. 3. The process flow of the proposed framework is divided into training and recognition. In the training phase, video descriptors are extracted by PCA-SFA. After that, subspaces are modeled to each class using the normalized video descriptors. In the recognition phase, a subspace is modeled from the input video descriptors and classified using a subspace-based method.

3.2   Proposed Framework for Action Recognition

In our framework, videos are defined as $\{X_i^c\}_{i=1}^m|_{c=1}^C$, where $X_i^c \in \mathbb{R}^{q \times T}$, m is the number of samples and C is the number of classes. Furthermore, the dimension of the frames is $q = h \times w$, where h is the height and w is the width of the videos. The feature vectors (e.g., raw images, CNN features) of the videos are defined as $\{F_i^c\}_{i=1}^m|_{c=1}^C$, where $F_i^c \in \mathbb{R}^{d \times T}$. In this scenario, d can be equal to q, if raw images are used, or d can be equal to CNN feature vectors' dimension, if CNN features are extracted for each frame. Finally, the video descriptors are defined as $\{W_i^c\}_{i=1}^m|_{c=1}^C$ and W_i^c is obtained in Eq. 7.

Figure 3 shows the flowchart of our framework, which is divided into training and recognition phases. In the training phase, there are three steps:

1. The videos $\{X_i^c\}$ are represented as feature vectors $\{F_i^c\}$.
2. The video descriptor $\{W_i^c\}$ is obtained by selecting the n first projection vectors extracted from the feature vectors $\{F_i^c\}$.
3. Each class subspace $\mathcal{S}_c$ is generated by applying PCA (or KPCA) to all normalized video descriptors of the corresponding class $\{W_i^c\}$.

Depending on the subspace-based method used for classification, we can also apply KPCA to build the subspaces. Next, the recognition phase is divided into:

1. The input video $\{X_1^{in}\}$ is represented as feature vectors $\{F_1^{in}\}$.
2. The video descriptor $\{W_1^{in}\}$ is obtained by selecting the n first projection vectors extracted from the feature vectors $\{F_1^{in}\}$.
3. The input subspace $\mathcal{S}_1^{in}$ is generated by applying PCA (or KPCA), without data-centering, to the normalized $\{W_1^{in}\}$.
4. One of the subspace-based methods are applied to perform further operations with the subspaces and assign the video to the class with the highest similarity.

4   Experimental Results and Discussions

This section evaluates the proposed framework with the following traditional subspace-based methods: MSM, CMSM, KMSM and KCMSM. We performed two sets of experiments. In the first set, we used the KTH action dataset [15] to evaluate the effectiveness of our framework on human action recognition using raw images. In the second set, we used the Chinese sign language dataset (isolated SLR500) [9–11,22] with VGG-19 features before and after fine-tuning to evaluate the framework's consistency with CNN features. Besides, we also compare the results of our framework with the results of the fine-tuned VGG-19 model. Moreover, we compare different approaches to model the class subspaces: using a single class subspace or multiple class subspaces to represent the training samples of a class.

4.1   Experiment with KTH Action Dataset

In this section, we present the experimental results obtained for the KTH action dataset [15]. This dataset of videos has six classes, which are exemplified in Table 1. These actions were performed by 25 individuals on different scenarios: outdoors, outdoors with zoom variation, outdoors with different clothes and indoors. The six classes and the four filming conditions have four samples each. In our experiments, we resized the images to 16×16 pixels.

We performed 10-fold cross-validation with 10 subjects for training and 15 for testing for each class. For the experiments with our method, we defined n as 5, 8 and 10. For the experiments with KTH raw, we considered only the 20 first frames of the videos.

Table 2 shows the classification accuracy for the KTH action dataset. The results show that all subspace-based methods achieve higher results with our method. In particular, KCMSM achieved the highest classification accuracy of 73.7% with 10 projection vectors, enhancing this method's result by approximately 8% compared to the results with the raw dataset. These results show that the proposed method can improve the performance of the traditional subspace-based methods even when raw images are used.

Table 1. Examples of KTH action dataset.

Class	Example	Class	Example
Boxing		Running	
Handclapping		Jogging	
Handwaving		Walking	

Table 2. Classification accuracy (%) for KTH action.

Data	MSM	CMSM	KMSM	KCMSM
KTH raw	67.3 ± 3.3	67.1 ± 3.9	67.6 ± 2.2	65.8 ± 2.1
Projection vectors (5)	67.0 ± 2.6	65.7 ± 2.1	71.4 ± 1.4	72.0 ± 1.9
Projection vectors (8)	68.8 ± 1.7	67.6 ± 2.1	72.1 ± 1.1	72.2 ± 2.0
Projection vectors (10)	$\mathbf{71.1 \pm 2.3}$	69.7 ± 2.1	$\mathbf{73.1 \pm 1.2}$	$\mathbf{73.7 \pm 2.3}$

4.2 Experiments with Isolated SLR500 Dataset

The Chinese sign language dataset (isolated SLR500) [9–11,22] consists of 500 signs, each performed by 50 subjects, resulting in 25000 videos. Each RGB video has a resolution of 1280×720 pixels and was filmed at 30 fps. The distance between the signers and the Kinect 2.0 is approximately 1.5 m. We randomly sampled 10 signs with their 50 subjects for our experiments, resulting in a subset of 500 videos. For simplicity, only the first 50 frames of each video were considered. Table 3 shows some examples of the 10 classes used in this experiment.

Feature Extraction

The features were extracted from block five of VGG-19 [16] before and after fine-tuning. To reduce the features' dimensionality, we applied global average pooling, obtaining feature vectors of 512 dimensions.

For fine-tuning, we defined the learning rate (LR) as $1e-5$ after performing a small experiment in one fold using the LR finder [17]. Furthermore, we also utilized stochastic gradient descent as an optimizer, 50 epochs and a batch size of 32. After that, we replaced the model's old fully connected (FC) layer with a new one and fine-tuned it to recognize the ten classes of our problem. Next, the CNN was retrained with the block immediately before the FC layers unfrozen.

We extracted features from 50 sequential frames of each video before and after fine-tuning the CNN. Afterward, these features were grouped following the

Table 3. Examples of Isolated SLR500 dataset.

Class	Example	Class	Example
Goal		Short	
Clue		Swell	
Public Welfare		Brother	
Development		Grandmother	
Composition		Soda	

sequence of the original video. To summarize, there are two datasets; and each has 500 samples with 50 feature vectors of 512 dimensions.

Action Recognition Using the Proposed Framework

In this experiment, we performed 10-fold cross-validation and split the set of features into training (300), validation (100) and evaluation (100). Furthermore, we varied the number n of projection vectors in 5, 8, 10, 20 and 50 to find an appropriate representation for the samples. We evaluated the performance of our method combined with four subspace-based methods: MSM, CMSM, KMSM and KCMSM with features before and after fine-tuning VGG-19.

Table 4 shows the results for features extracted before fine-tuning the CNN. By modeling the subspaces directly from the CNN features, the highest classification accuracy is from MSM with 63.9% accuracy. However, the best result was achieved by our method with KMSM (78.6%), using 5 projection vectors as a video descriptor. It shows that few projection vectors are necessary to increase the accuracy of this model in approximately 16%, compared to the results obtained with only CNN features.

Table 5 shows the results for the features extracted after fine-tuning the VGG-19 model. Using subspaces generated from only CNN features, the best classification accuracy was achieved using KMSM (67.6%). However, KMSM achieved 80.7% accuracy, using 8 projection vectors. This result also shows that few projection vectors are necessary to improve the performance of all subspace-based methods. In both experiments, KCMSM improved approximately 19% when compared to using it with the CNN features.

In addition, we also performed the classification task using the fine-tuned VGG-19, without using the subspace-based methods. In this scenario, we extracted the softmax layer's predictions for the ten classes and calculated the

Table 4. Classification accuracy (%) of subspace-based methods for pre-trained VGG-19 features.

Data	MSM	CMSM	KMSM	KCMSM
CNN features	63.9 ± 3.3	60.9 ± 3.8	62.7 ± 3.4	57.7 ± 4.0
Projection vectors (5)	69.5 ± 3.5	64.3 ± 4.3	$\mathbf{78.6 \pm 3.8}$	$\mathbf{77.3 \pm 5.5}$
Projection vectors (8)	$\mathbf{73.9 \pm 3.7}$	66.9 ± 5.6	77.2 ± 3.5	76.8 ± 4.5
Projection vectors (10)	73.0 ± 3.3	$\mathbf{71.6 \pm 6.5}$	76.9 ± 2.3	75.6 ± 4.5
Projection vectors (20)	67.8 ± 3.6	66.5 ± 5.6	69.5 ± 3.1	66.4 ± 5.6
Projection vectors (50)	51.6 ± 4.4	47.9 ± 4.8	61.2 ± 4.5	54.2 ± 3.9

Table 5. Classification accuracy (%) of subspace-based methods for fine-tuned VGG-19 features.

Data	MSM	CMSM	KMSM	KCMSM	Softmax
Raw isolate SLR500	–	–	–	–	30.7 ± 3.9
CNN features	59.8 ± 5.5	60.4 ± 4.4	67.6 ± 5.9	59.3 ± 4.0	–
Projection vectors (5)	71.4 ± 3.9	64.7 ± 7.1	79.5 ± 3.4	$\mathbf{78.6 \pm 4.0}$	–
Projection vectors (8)	70.2 ± 3.9	66.8 ± 4.5	$\mathbf{80.7 \pm 4.4}$	77.1 ± 2.2	–
Projection vectors (10)	$\mathbf{73.0 \pm 4.1}$	$\mathbf{67.5 \pm 4.2}$	80.6 ± 3.1	77.9 ± 4.0	–
Projection vectors (20)	67.9 ± 4.2	66.6 ± 5.0	72.2 ± 2.6	67.6 ± 2.6	–
Projection vectors (50)	53.9 ± 4.5	52.3 ± 6.7	68.7 ± 3.3	67.1 ± 4.2	–

vector's average value for each video. Then, we selected the class that had the largest value as the predicted label of the video, obtaining a classification accuracy of 30.7% for VGG-19.

This low result might have two main reasons. The first reason is the data scarceness, which might be affecting the generalization of the CNN. The second one is the single-frame classification, as different videos can have similar frames, it could generate misclassification. Our results suggest that our proposed method and framework have some advantages over deep learning models, such as:

1. The videos can be modeled and compared regardless of the number of frames.
2. A whole video can be represented by a subspace.
3. The order of the frames can be represented by projection vectors generated by PCA-SFA embedded in the subspace.
4. The effects of the small sample size problem can be also minimized.

Evaluation of the Class Subspaces Modeling

In step 3 of our framework, we generate a single subspace to each of the ten classes of our training set. To evaluate the most suitable data representation, we also conducted experiments using one subspace for each class sample. For example, if a class has 30 samples, we will have 30 subspaces, one for each sample. After that, we perform k-nearest neighbor (kNN) classification based on the subspaces similarity in Eq. 2 for k set as 5, 20 and 30. The rest of the framework is kept the same. Besides, we only evaluate MSM's performance in this experiment.

The experimental results can be seen in Tables 6 and 7 for features extracted before and after fine-tuning the VGG-19. We indicate results for a single subspace per class as "Our+MSM" and results for one subspace per sample as "kNN+MSM". Both tables show that our method achieved the best results independently of the number of projection vectors utilized.

Table 6. Classification accuracy (%) of kNN+MSM for pre-trained VGG-19 features.

Data	Our+MSM	kNN+MSM (k = 5)	kNN+MSM (k = 20)	kNN+MSM (k = 30)
Projection vectors (5)	**69.5 ± 3.5**	64.2 ± 3.7	69.3 ± 2.2	67.5 ± 4.0
Projection vectors (8)	**73.9 ± 3.7**	58.6 ± 3.1	68.8 ± 3.3	71.0 ± 3.6
Projection vectors (10)	**73.0 ± 3.3**	59.8 ± 3.5	64.7 ± 4.9	69.2 ± 3.0
Projection vectors (20)	**67.8 ± 3.6**	54.2 ± 6.0	59.7 ± 4.6	60.2 ± 3.7
Projection vectors (50)	**51.6 ± 4.4**	36.9 ± 3.6	45.9 ± 4.5	48.3 ± 5.3

Therefore, the proposed method (i.e., a single subspace per class) achieved the highest accuracy rates for the analyzed dataset. We hypothesize that a single subspace per class can better generalize the classes' diversity, while modeling a single subspace per sample might introduce noise by considering the sample specific information that does not characterize the whole class.

Table 7. Classification accuracy (%) of kNN+MSM for fine-tuned VGG-19 features.

Data	Our+MSM	kNN+MSM (k = 5)	kNN+MSM (k = 20)	kNN+MSM (k = 30)
Projection vectors (5)	**71.4 ± 3.9**	68.5 ± 5.6	69.2 ± 4.2	68.9 ± 4.0
Projection vectors (8)	**70.2 ± 3.9**	66.0 ± 5.6	67.8 ± 2.9	69.4 ± 3.8
Projection vectors (10)	**73.0 ± 4.1**	66.0 ± 6.1	67.8 ± 2.9	67.4 ± 4.7
Projection vectors (20)	**67.9 ± 4.2**	55.7 ± 4.7	58.5 ± 4.8	58.9 ± 4.5
Projection vectors (50)	**53.9 ± 4.5**	39.8 ± 3.4	49.4 ± 4.7	49.9 ± 4.0

5   Conclusion and Future Work

This paper proposed a framework for action recognition jointly using subspace-based methods and SFA. The experimental results showed that our framework could improve the action recognition independently of using raw images or CNN features to represent the video frames. Besides, our framework outperformed the accuracy results of the fine-tuned VGG-19 model. Furthermore, utilizing a single subspace to represent the whole class variability produces higher classification accuracy than using multiple subspaces. Our results showed that our framework achieved the highest accuracy with both datasets. For future work, it is necessary to investigate the use of a kernel function in the first steps of the video descriptor to improve the representation of the data non-linearity.

Acknowledgments. This work was supported by JSPS KAKENHI Grant Number 19H04129 and the Japanese Ministry of Education, Culture, Sports, Science, and Technology (MEXT) scholarship.

References

1. Afriat, S.N.: Orthogonal and oblique projectors and the characteristics of pairs of vector spaces. In: Mathematical Proceedings of the Cambridge Philosophical Society, vol. 53, pp. 800–816 (1957)
2. Aslan, M.F., Durdu, A., Sabanci, K.: Human action recognition with bag of visual words using different machine learning methods and hyperparameter optimization. Neural Comput. Appl. **32**(12), 8585–8597 (2020)
3. Berkes, P., Wiskott, L.: Applying slow feature analysis to image sequences yields a rich repertoire of complex cell properties. In: Dorronsoro, J.R. (ed.) ICANN 2002. LNCS, vol. 2415, pp. 81–86. Springer, Heidelberg (2002). https://doi.org/10.1007/3-540-46084-5_14
4. Cheok, M.J., Omar, Z., Jaward, M.H.: A review of hand gesture and sign language recognition techniques. Int. J. Mach. Learn. Cybern. **10**(1), 131–153 (2019)
5. Fukui, K.: Subspace methods. In: Ikeuchi, K. (ed.) Computer Vision, pp. 777–781. Springer, Boston (2014). https://doi.org/10.1007/978-0-387-31439-6_708
6. Fukui, K., Maki, A.: Difference subspace and its generalization for subspace-based methods. IEEE Trans. Pattern Anal. Mach. Intell. **37**(11), 2164–2177 (2015)
7. Hotelling, H.: Relations between two sets of variates. In: Kotz, S., Johnson, N.L. (eds.) Breakthroughs in Statistics. SSS, pp. 162–190. Springer, New York (1992). https://doi.org/10.1007/978-1-4612-4380-9_14
8. Kobayashi, T.: Feature sequence representation via slow feature analysis for action classification. In: Proceedings of the British Machine Vision Conference (BMVC), pp. 125.1–125.13 (2017)
9. Liu, T., Zhou, W., Li, H.: Sign language recognition with long short-term memory. In: 2016 IEEE International Conference on Image Processing (ICIP), pp. 2871–2875 (2016)
10. Pu, J., Zhou, W., Li, H.: Sign language recognition with multi-modal features. In: Chen, E., Gong, Y., Tie, Y. (eds.) PCM 2016. LNCS, vol. 9917, pp. 252–261. Springer, Cham (2016). https://doi.org/10.1007/978-3-319-48896-7_25
11. Pu, J., Zhou, W., Zhang, J., Li, H.: Sign language recognition based on trajectory modeling with HMMs. In: Tian, Q., Sebe, N., Qi, G.-J., Huet, B., Hong, R., Liu, X. (eds.) MMM 2016. LNCS, vol. 9516, pp. 686–697. Springer, Cham (2016). https://doi.org/10.1007/978-3-319-27671-7_58
12. Sakai, A., Sogi, N., Fukui, K.: Gait recognition based on constrained mutual subspace method with CNN features. In: 2019 16th International Conference on Machine Vision Applications (MVA), pp. 1–6 (2019)

13. Sakano, H., Mukawa, N.: Kernel mutual subspace method for robust facial image recognition. In: KES 2000, Fourth International Conference on Knowledge-Based Intelligent Engineering Systems and Allied Technologies, Proceedings (Cat. No. 00TH8516), vol. 1, pp. 245–248 (2000)
14. Schölkopf, B., Smola, A., Müller, K.R.: Nonlinear component analysis as a kernel eigenvalue problem. Neural Comput. **10**(5), 1299–1319 (1998)
15. Schuldt, C., Laptev, I., Caputo, B.: Recognizing human actions: a local SVM approach. In: Proceedings of the 17th International Conference on Pattern Recognition 2004, ICPR 2004, vol. 3, pp. 32–36 (2004)
16. Simonyan, K., Zisserman, A.: Very deep convolutional networks for large-scale image recognition. arXiv preprint arXiv:1409.1556 (2014)
17. Smith, L.N.: Cyclical learning rates for training neural networks. In: 2017 IEEE Winter Conference on Applications of Computer Vision (WACV), pp. 464–472 (2017)
18. Sogi, N., Nakayama, T., Fukui, K.: A method based on convex cone model for image-set classification with CNN features. In: 2018 International Joint Conference on Neural Networks (IJCNN), pp. 1–8 (2018)
19. Souza, L.S., Gatto, B.B., Xue, J.H., Fukui, K.: Enhanced Grassmann discriminant analysis with randomized time warping for motion recognition. Pattern Recogn. **97**, 107028 (2020)
20. Sun, L., Jia, K., Chan, T.H., Fang, Y., Wang, G., Yan, S.: DL-SFA: deeply-learned slow feature analysis for action recognition. In: Proceedings of the IEEE Conference on Computer Vision and Pattern Recognition, pp. 2625–2632 (2014)
21. Wiskott, L., Sejnowski, T.J.: Slow feature analysis: unsupervised learning of invariances. Neural Comput. **14**(4), 715–770 (2002)
22. Zhang, J., Zhou, W., Xie, C., Pu, J., Li, H.: Chinese sign language recognition with adaptive HMM. In: 2016 IEEE International Conference on Multimedia and Expo (ICME), pp. 1–6 (2016)
23. Zhang, Z., Tao, D.: Slow feature analysis for human action recognition. IEEE Trans. Pattern Anal. Mach. Intell. **34**(3), 436–450 (2012)

Classification Mechanism
of Convolutional Neural Network
for Facial Expression Recognition

Yongpei Zhu, Hongwei Fan, and Kehong Yuan[✉]

Graduate School at Shenzhen, Tsinghua University, Shenzhen 518055, China
zhuyp20@mails.tsinghua.edu.cn,yuankh@sz.tsinghua.edu.cn

Abstract. With the development of deep learning, the structures of convolutional neural networks (CNNs) are becoming more complex and the performance of expression recognition is getting better. However, the classification mechanism of CNN is still a black box. The main problem is that CNNs have a great number of parameters, which makes it difficult to analyze them clearly. In this paper, we explain the essence of deep learning from the perspective of manifold geometry. The main purpose of deep learning especially CNN is to learn the probability distributions on manifolds. And we design a neural network based on the facial expression recognition to explore the classification mechanism of CNN. By using the deconvolution visualization method, we qualitatively verify that the trained CNN forms a detector for specific facial action unit (FAU) and each neuron of CNN is a specific manifold feature extractor for facial images. Moreover, we design a distance function to measure the differences of activation value distributions on the same feature map of FAU. The greater the distance, the more sensitive the feature map is to the FAU. The results show that the mapping relationship between FAUs and feature maps of CNN is determined, the trained CNN has generated an internal detector for each FAU to extract the facial manifold feature.

Keywords: Convolution Neural Networks · Deconvolution visualization · Manifolds · Expression recognition · Facial action unit

1 Introduction

In recent years, CNNs in deep learning [1] used for feature extraction and classification have become extensive, gaining higher accuracy and stronger robustness. As more sophisticated network structures are designed, many image classification problems in computer vision have been well solved, for example, facial expression recognition problems with some open datasets have been greatly improved in the accuracy. However, in many cases CNN is used as a black box and its internal classification mechanism is not clear. Most time people try to improve the performance of the network only through their experience and constant trial, which is not conducive to the improvement of neural network.

© Springer Nature Switzerland AG 2021
A. Del Bimbo et al. (Eds.): ICPR 2020 Workshops, LNCS 12663, pp. 717–729, 2021.
https://doi.org/10.1007/978-3-030-68796-0_52

Several groups began to look into this black-box problem since a review was published by Castelvecchi in 2016 [2]. Selvaraju et al. [10] used the gradients of any target concept, flowing into the final convolutional layer to produce a coarse localization map highlighting important regions in the image for predicting the concept. Fong and Vedaldi [11] proposed a general framework for learning different kinds of explanations for any black box algorithm and specialised the framework to find the parts of an image which were the most responsible for a classifier decision. Chattopadhyay et al. [12] proposed Grad-CAM++ that could provide better visual explanations of CNN model predictions, in terms of better object localization as well as explaining occurrences of multiple object instances in a single image.

The purpose of this paper is to provide a reasonable explanation for the classification mechanism of CNNs. According to the manifold distribution theory [9], high-dimensional data is distributed near low-dimensional manifolds such as facial images with specific probability distribution, and deep learning has the strong ability to approach nonlinear mapping. Deep learning especially CNNs can extract the manifold structure from facial images and express the global prior knowledge with manifolds, specifically, encoding and decoding mapping, which are implied in the weights of the neurons in CNNs. Each neuron of CNN is a specific manifold feature extractor from the geometric view.

Therefore, the contributions of this paper are the following: First, we explained the essence of deep learning from the perspective of manifold geometry and designed a CNN model for facial expression recognition, aiming to analyze and verify the classification mechanism of CNN. By using the deconvolution visualization method, we discovered that CNN forms a detector for the specific FAU in the training stage and each neuron of CNN is a specific manifold feature extractor for facial images. Moreover, we designed a distance function to measure the differences of activation distributions on the same feature map of FAU. The greater the distance, the more sensitive the feature map is to the FAU. The mapping relationship between FAUs and feature maps is determined.

2   Manifolds in Deep Learning

2.1   Encoder and Decoder

Manifold is the most basic concept in topology and differential geometry [9], which is essentially a space composed of many Euclidean spaces. One of the main purposes of deep learning is to learn encoding and decoding mapping. Autoencoder is a very basic deep learning model for learning manifold structures. As shown in Fig. 1, the autoencoder is a feedforward network, with equal input and output dimensions, and both input and output are background spaces $\mathcal{X}$. There is a bottleneck layer in the middle, and the output space of the bottleneck layer is the feature space $\mathcal{F}$. The network is symmetric about the bottleneck layer, and the left network is used to represent the encoding mapping, denoted as $\varphi_\theta : \mathcal{X} \to \mathcal{F}$, the right network is used to represent the decoding mapping, denoted as $\psi_\theta : \mathcal{F} \to \mathcal{X}$. The loss function is equal to the norm L^2 of the input and output images. We take dense samples on manifolds, and get training sample set $X = \{x_1, x_2, x_3, \ldots, x_k\}$ to train the network. We use the reconstructed manifold $\tilde{S} := \psi_\theta \circ \varphi_\theta(S) = \psi_\theta(\varphi_\theta(S))$ ($\circ$ represents the transformation between encoding and decoding mapping) to approximate the data manifold S, namely,

$$\min_\theta \sum_{i=1}^{k} \| x_i - \psi_\theta \circ \varphi_\theta(x_i) \|^2 \tag{1}$$

The training of CNN is also regarded as the process of learning the manifold structure. CNN can extract the manifold features from facial images, specifically, encoding and decoding mapping, which are implied in the weights of neurons. The forward propagation process of CNN, such as convolution and pooling, can be regarded as the encoding mapping, while the inverse process, such as upsampling and deconvolution, can be regarded as the decoding mapping. So we explain the learning mechanism of CNN with the example of facial expression recognition via the deconvolution visualization method.

Fig. 1. Encoder and decoder.

2.2 Traditional Expression Recognition Method

One of the traditional expression recognition methods is based on Facial Action Units (FAUs) that derived from the Facial Action Coding System (FACS) [5] which is used to divide the movement regions of facial muscles. The FAUs in Table 1 are composed of recognizable facial changes caused by the simultaneous movements of several facial muscles. Almost all facial expressions can be decomposed into the combinations of different FAUs in Fig. 2. In traditional methods, it is common to design a detector for each FAU. The expressions are classified according to the detection results which are showed in Fig. 3. In practice, it is very difficult to design a detector for each FAU manually with high accuracy and efficiency. The reason why CNN can classify facial expressions exactly is that it can learn the manifold features automatically from the facial images. So, this paper proposes the following hypothesis, the trained CNN has generated the internal detector for each FAU to extract the facial manifold features.

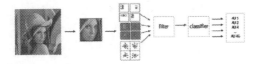

Fig. 2. Expression encoding.

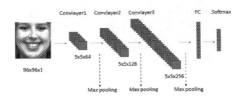

Fig. 3. Traditional method to detect the FAU.

3   Proposed Model

In order to analyze the mechanism of CNN on learning facial manifolds, one CNN model with shallow layer is designed in this section.

3.1   Model Design

The model adopts a typical feedforward neural network structure. As shown in Fig. 4, the image size of input layer is 96×96. There are three convolution layers in the network. The number of convolution kernel is 64, 128, 256 respectively. The design of gradually increasing the numbers of convolution kernels is a common method. That means the features become more abstract and the high-level features formed by the combination of low-level features will be increased as the numbers of layers increase. The size of each convolution kernel is 5×5. Each convolution layer is followed by a ReLU activation layer and a 2×2 maxpooling layer. Then the output will connect to the full connection layer with 1024 hidden neurons, and finally followed by softmax layer as the classification output.

Fig. 4. Model network structure.

4   Classification Mechanism Analysis of the Network

4.1   Deconvolution Visualization

In Sect. 3, we obtain a model for the expression classification. The classification mechanism of this model is discussed in this section. We use deconvolution visualization method [4] to map the largest activation response in the feature map of different layers to the pixel space of original image, and explore the regions which have the most important impact on the classification. As an visualization method, deconvolution visualization enables us to understand the role played by each layer and the potential problems of the model.

It is a common practice to obtain an intuitive understanding of network through visual features [6], but it is usually limited to the first layer which directly maps to the image. For the response of a neuron in a high-level feature, it needs to apply deconvolution method [7] to map back to its corresponding pixel space. For example, in order to visualize the n-layer neural activation value a, firstly it is necessary for the input image to be propagated forward through the network. Next, the n-layer neurons other than the activation value a are set to 0, then the image of the activated neurons in the original pixel space is visualized through deconvolution. Let the input image, the convolution kernel, the output be x, C and y, respectively. The convolution operation can be represented as:

$$y = Cx \tag{2}$$

In backpropagation, we can get $\frac{\partial Loss}{\partial y}$ from a deeper network.

$$\frac{\partial \text{Loss}}{\partial x_j} = \sum_i \frac{\partial \text{Loss}}{\partial y_i} \frac{\partial y_i}{\partial x_j} = \sum_i \frac{\partial \text{Loss}}{\partial y_i} C_{i,j} = C_{*,j}^T \frac{\partial \text{Loss}}{\partial y} \tag{3}$$

$$\frac{\partial \text{Loss}}{\partial x} = \begin{bmatrix} \frac{\partial \text{Loss}}{\partial x_1} \\ \frac{\partial \text{Loss}}{\partial x_2} \\ ... \\ \frac{\partial \text{Loss}}{\partial x_n} \end{bmatrix} = \begin{bmatrix} C_{*,1}^T \frac{\partial \text{Loss}}{\partial y} \\ C_{*,2}^T \frac{\partial \text{Loss}}{\partial y} \\ ... \\ C_{*,n}^T \frac{\partial \text{Loss}}{\partial y} \end{bmatrix} = \begin{bmatrix} C_{*,1}^T \\ C_{*,2}^T \\ ... \\ C_{*,2}^T \end{bmatrix} \frac{\partial \text{Loss}}{\partial y}$$

$$= C^T \frac{\partial \text{Loss}}{\partial y} \tag{4}$$

In this section, we use deconvolution visualization method to visualize the activation values on the corresponding feature map of the third convolution layer in the network. The deconvolution process of the activation value of the feature map is shown in Fig. 5. The activation value i is an activation in the feature map j generated by the third convolution layer. By deconvolution of the activation value i, the receptive field (block a) is mapped on the original map and the corresponding deconvolution response (block b) can be obtained. From above deconvolution process, we can conclude that the map represented by block b can enhance the activation value i. Therefore, it can be considered that the network structure associated with the feature map j in which the activation value i is located constitutes a detector of the map represented by block b.

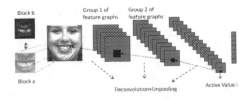

Fig. 5. Deconvolution visualization of activation values.

Table 1. Comparison of deconvolution response maps with FAU

Number of FAU	FAU image	Type	The deconvolution response with the maximum activation value in the feature map
1		Original	
		Deconvolution	
16		Original	
		Deconvolution	
6		Original	
		Deconvolution	
26		Original	
		Deconvolution	
2		Original	
		Deconvolution	
27		Original	
		Deconvolution	

4.2   Facial Action Units

The process of this experiment is as follows:

- Input all the training images into the network in turn.
- For each image, record the maximum activation value and the corresponding position of each image in 256 feature maps of the third convolution layer.
- For each feature map, take the images corresponding to the former nine maximum activation values.
- Using deconvolution method, the response of original image space corresponding to each activation value is calculated.
- At the same time, original image area corresponding to the activation value is calculated.

Finally, the receptive fields and the responses of deconvolution corresponding to the former nine maximum values of each feature map in the third convolution layer are obtained. Some deconvolution visualizations of the feature map are selected which are shown in Table 1. These are the response of original image space corresponding to the activation value of feature maps after deconvolution in the even line and the receptive field corresponding to original image in the odd line. It can be clearly seen that:

(1) The image areas corresponding to the maximum response value of a feature map are basically in the similar image type. And the activation map of original image pixel space corresponding to its deconvolution is also very similar to this image type.

(2) The image obtained by deconvolution is very similar to the FAU.

Therefore, we can draw the following preliminary conclusions, through training the network, the model gradually forms some specific detectors, which can extract the manifold features of images. Some of the detected shapes are very similar to those FAUs. The number of output feature maps from the third convolution layer is 256, which is equivalent to 256 feature detectors. The number of these feature detectors is far more than the number of FAUs, so the division of facial regions is more detailed. FAU16, FAU26 and FAU27 from Table 1 show the mouth shape selected from the deconvolution feature map and FAU. It can be seen that the trained network can detect a variety of facial mouth shapes. Compared with the three mouth shapes defined in the FAU, the convolution network can detect different types of mouth shapes. Compared with the process of designing the detector manually, deep learning method automatically completes feature extraction of data during the training stage and forms the detectors for specific image features (manifold features).

This section presents the internal mechanism of the network with deconvolution visualization. The similarity between network-formed detector and FAU is also determined. And the following section we demonstrate the relationship between the formed detectors and FAUs.

5   Experiments and Results

From the above section, we can observe that some feature maps are very similar to the FAUs. In this section, the correlation between deconvolution feature map and FAU is verified and the one-to-one correspondence between deconvolution feature map and FAU is proved. That is to say, for a certain FAU, the most closely associated feature map is obtained.

5.1   Dataset and Implementation

The dataset used in this experiment is the extended Cohn-Kanade database (CK+) [3]. The CK+ dataset contains 327 face sequences whose labels contain the following seven expressions: anger, contempt, disgust, fear, joy, sadness and surprise. The labels of each face image are composed of both the expression labels and the labels of FAUs that constitute the expressions.

The hyperparameters of the model are as follows: batchsize is set to 64, momentum is set to 0.9, weight decay parameter is 0.0001, learning rate is 0.001 and the weights of CNN are initialized by Gaussian distribution with mean value 0 and variance 1. In order to avoid overfitting, data augmentation and dropout are adopted. The full connection layer is dropout with a probability value 0.5.

To increase the reasonability of comparison, the first frame of each image sequence is treated as a neutral expression and other images are treated as the datasets. In the augmentated dataset, 200 images are selected as the testing set, the remaining images are used as the training set. The expression images here consist of the images of facial areas. According to the coordinates of feature points of each image given by the CK+ dataset, the areas surrounded by four largest feature points, namely the upper, lower, left and right, are selected as the facial images.

In this section, data preprocessing and augmentation are as follows:

- Rotate the image randomly between the angles (−15, +15).
- Flip the image at random.
- Normalize the image to the size of 99×99.
- Cut the image randomly to 96×96.
- Standardize the image, that is, subtract the average value then divide by the standard deviation from each pixel of the image.

5.2   Criteria for Distance Measurement

This section proposes the following hypothesis, for a particular feature map i in the network, the feature map i represents the detector of the FAU j. S is a collection of images containing the FAU j and S^c is a collection of images without the FAU j. $F_a(S)$ represents the response of S through the network in the feature map a and $F_a(S^c)$ represents the response of S^c through the network in the feature map a. And the distance between $F_a(S)$ and $F_a(S^c)$ is $D(F_a(S), F_a(S^c))$, namely,

$$D(F_i(S), F_i(S^c)) = \max(D(F_a(S)), F_a(S^c)) \quad a = 1, ..., 256 \tag{5}$$

That is, the maximum distance between $F_a(S)$ and $F_a(S^c)$ should be $D(F_i(S), F_i(S^c))$. This hypothesis is reasonable, because in generally for the detector i of the FAU j, if S contains an FAU j then the response $F_i(S)$ is larger, otherwise the response $F_i(S^c)$ is larger. Therefore, the distance $D(F_i(S), F_i(S^c))$ should be the maximum distance in all the feature maps for the detector i. Therefore, for a given FAU j, the feature map i that maximizes $D(F_a(S), F_a(S^c))$ is most closely associated with the FAU j. Namely, the network structure associated with the feature map i constitutes a detector for the FAU j.

In addition to provide facial expression labels, the CK+ database also provides the label for FAU image. Through the FAU label, the correlation between the spatial feature of the original image (i.e. deconvolution feature map) and the FAU can be verified. The activation value distribution of the image with FAU j is the most different from that of the image without FAU j in the feature map i. Let $F_{Li(x)}$ be the activation value of the ith feature map of image x in the L layer. Here we set the third convolution layer, namely $L = 3$. S is a collection of images containing the FAU j and S^c is a collection of images without the FAU j.

$$R_{ij}(x) = P(F_{3i}(x|S)) \qquad (6)$$

$$Q_{ij}(x) = P(F_{3i}(x|S^c)) \qquad (7)$$

$Q_{ij}(x)$ and $R_{ij}(x)$ are the probability distributions with the FAU j and without the FAU j in the feature map i respectively. The common method for measuring the distance between two distributions is to calculate the KL divergence between them.

KL Distance [8] **(Relative Entropy):** A measure of the difference between two probability distributions of the same event space. The formula is as follows:

$$D(R||Q) = \sum_{x \in X} R(x) \log(\frac{R(x)}{Q(x)}) \qquad (8)$$

When R and Q are the same distribution, the KL distance is 0. And the greater difference of R and Q distribution, the greater the KL distance. In this section, the distance between $Q_{ij}(x)$ and $R_{ij}(x)$ does not strictly conform to the definition of KL distance:

(1) The probability distributions represented by $Q_{ij}(x)$ and $R_{ij}(x)$ cannot be obtained.

(2) $Q_{ij}(x)$ and $R_{ij}(x)$ are inputs from different datasets.

To solve the above problems, the following distance function is designed in this section:

Step 1: Let the activation value of the feature map i be $R_i(x)$ and $Q_i(x^c)$, where x belongs to the former n images in which the activation value response of the image set S is greatest in the feature map i, and x^c belongs to the former n images in which the activation value response of the image set S^c is greatest in the feature map i. And we use activation values $P_i(x)$ and $Q_i(x^c)$ approximate the distributions of two datasets in response to the feature map i, namely,

$$R_i(x_1) > R_i(x_2) > ... > R_i(x_n) \qquad (9)$$

$$Q_i(x^c_1) > Q_i(x^c_2) > ... > Q_i(x^c_n) \qquad (10)$$

Step 2: These activation values $R_i(x)$ and $Q_i(x^c)$ are shown as follows:

$$D(R||Q) = \sum_{k=1}^{n} R_i(x_k) \log\left(\frac{R_i(x_k)}{Q_i(x^c_k)}\right) \qquad (11)$$

Its property is similar to that of KL distance. The closer the response of two datasets in the feature map i (i.e. $R_i(x)$ and $Q_i(x^c)$), the smaller the distance, and vice versa. Because the distance is asymmetrical, namely,

$$D(R||Q) \neq D(Q||R) \qquad (12)$$

So the final distance function is as follows:

$$D_i(R||Q) = D(R||Q) + D(Q||R) \tag{13}$$

$$D_i(R||Q) = \sum_{k=1}^{n} R_i(x_k) \log\left(\frac{R_i(x_k)}{Q_i(x^c{}_k)}\right)$$
$$+ \sum_{k=1}^{n} Q_i(x^c{}_k) \log\left(\frac{Q_i(x^c{}_k)}{R_i(x_k)}\right) \tag{14}$$

The distance of FAU j in the feature map i is $D_{ij}(Q_{ij}||R_{ij})$. In this experiment, we select $n = 9$. Namely, the former nine images with the greatest response value in the feature map i are selected for the datasets which contain the FAU j and without the FAU j respectively. And the distance is calculated as:

$$D = D_{ij}(Q_{ij}||R_{ij}) \tag{15}$$

The distance is calculated for all 256 feature maps and the corresponding feature map with the maximum distance is selected:

$$\max(D_{ij}(Q_{ij}||R_{ij})), \quad i = 1,...,256 \tag{16}$$

5.3   Results

Figure 6 shows the distances of partial FAUs on the third convolution layer. It shows that the distance of FAU1 is the largest when $i = 113$. And the deconvolution feature map with the largest distance corresponding to the FAU in Fig. 6 are shown in Table 2. Take FAU1 as an example, it is highly consistent with the deconvolution image of feature map 113. At this point, we obtain the mapping relationship between the FAU1 and feature map 113, and we conclude that the network structure associated with the feature map 113 is the detector of the FAU1. By calculating the distance D_j of activation value distribution of FAU j in different feature maps, the mapping between FAUs and feature maps is established successfully.

Therefore, the network does learn the manifold feature of images and generate the specific detector to detect the FAU. We verify that the principle of CNN is based on the combination of manifolds in expression recognition, classifying the objective by detecting the specific FAU. And this mechanism has a similar performance in other classification tasks.

In this section, by calculating the response of FAUs on different feature maps, the distance function D is designed to measure the relationship between FAUs and feature maps. The subjective results obtained in Sect. 4.1 are verified experimentally. It not only confirms that the trained network forms the detector of specific image, but also obtains the mapping relation between the detectors and the designated FAUs.

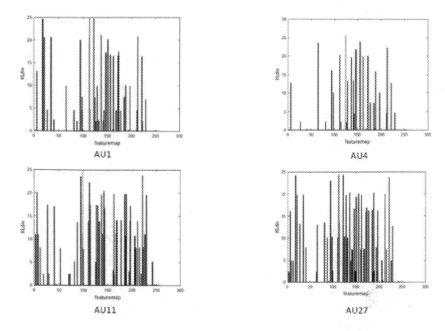

Fig. 6. The distances corresponding to FAU1, FAU4, FAU11, FAU27.

Table 2. The corresponding deconvolution feature map of FAU in Fig. 6

Number of FAU	FAU image	Type	The deconvolution response with the maximum activation value in the feature map
1		Original	
		Deconvolution	
16		Original	
		Deconvolution	
6		Original	
		Deconvolution	
26		Original	
		Deconvolution	
2		Original	
		Deconvolution	
27		Original	
		Deconvolution	

In this experiment, the result also illustrates that CNN (deep learning) can extract the manifold structure (two-dimensional facial feature map) from image data (facial expression images) and express the overall prior knowledge in the form of a manifold, specifically, the encoding (forward propagation) and decoding (deconvolution visualization) mapping, which are implied in the weights of the neurons (activation values) in CNN.

6   Conclusions

In this work, we analyze the essence of deep learning from the perspective of manifold geometry and verify the principle of expression classification based on a CNN model. The connection between CNN and traditional facial expression recognition method by constructing the detector is established. And the principle of CNN in classification is verified intuitively, the trained CNN forms the detector of specific image. By calculating the distance function of FAUs on different feature maps, we establish the corresponding relationship between the feature maps and FAUs synchronously, which further supports the proposed hypothesis on the classification principle of CNN. This conclusion has been verified in the expression classification problem, which can be inferred to be equally applicable in other issues.

References

1. LeCun, Y., Bengio, Y., Hinton, G.: Deep learning. Nature **521**(7553), 436–444 (2015)
2. Castelvecchi, D.: Can we open the black box of AI? Nat. News **538**(7623), 20–23 (2016)
3. Lucey, P., Cohn, J.F., Kanade, T., Saragih, J., Matthews, I.: The extended cohn-kanade dataset (ck+): a complete dataset for action unit and emotion-specified expression. In: Proceedings of the IEEE Conference on Computer Vision and Pattern Recognition Workshops (CVPRW), pp. 94–101(2010)
4. Zeiler, M.D., Fergus, R.: Visualizing and understanding convolutional networks. In: European Conference on Computer Vision, pp. 818–833 (2014)
5. Ekman, P., Friesen, W.V.: Facial Action Coding System (FACS): A Technique for the Measurement of Facial Movement. Consulting Psychologists Press, Berkeley (1978)
6. Donahue, J., Jia, Y., Vinyals, O., Hoffman, J.: Decaf: a deep convolutional activation feature for generic visual recognition. In: International conference on Machine Learning, pp. 647–655 (2014)
7. Erhan, D., Bengio, Y., Courville, A., Vincent, P.: Visualizing higher-layer features of a deep network. Univ. Montreal **1341**(3), 1–23 (2009)
8. Tibshirani, R., Hastie, T.: Local likelihood estimation. J. Am. Stat. Assoc. **82**(398), 559–567 (1987)

9. Lei, N., Luo, Z.X., Yau, S.T., Gu, X.F.: Geometric Understanding of Deep Learning. arXiv preprint arXiv: 1805.10451(2018)
10. Selvaraju, R.R., Cogswell, M., Das, A., Vedantam, R., Parikh, D., Batra, D.: Grad-CAM: visual explanations from deep networks via gradient-based localization. In: International Conference on Computer Vision (ICCV) (2017)
11. Fong, R.C., Vedaldi, A.: Interpretable explanation of black boxes by meaningful perturbation. In: International Conference on Computer Vision (ICCV) (2017)
12. Chattopadhyay, A., Sarkar, A., Howlader, P., Balasubramanian, V.N.: Grad-cam++: improved visual explanations for deep convolutional networks. In: IEEE Winter Conference on Applications of Computer Vision (WACV) (2018)

Applying Delaunay Triangulation Augmentation for Deep Learning Facial Expression Generation and Recognition

Hristo Valev[1,2(✉)] [ID], Alessio Gallucci[3] [ID], Tim Leufkens[1] [ID],
Joyce Westerink[1,3] [ID], and Corina Sas[2] [ID]

[1] Philips Research, High Tech Campus 34, 5656 AE Eindhoven, The Netherlands
h_valev@outlook.com
[2] Lancaster University, Bailrigg, Lancaster LA1 4YW, UK
[3] Technical University Eindhoven,
Groene Loper 3, 5612 AE Eindhoven, The Netherlands

Abstract. Generating and recognizing facial expressions has numerous applications, however, those are limited by the scarcity of datasets containing labeled nuanced expressions. In this paper, we describe the use of Delaunay triangulation combined with simple morphing techniques to blend images of faces, which allows us to create and automatically label facial expressions portraying controllable intensities of emotion. We have applied this approach on the RafD dataset consisting of 67 participants and 8 categorical emotions and evaluated the augmentation in a facial expression generation and recognition tasks using deep learning models. For the generation task, we used a deconvolution neural network which learns to encode the input images in a high-dimensional feature space and generate realistic expressions at varying intensities. The augmentation significantly improves the quality of images compared to previous comparable experiments and it allows to create images with a higher resolution. For the recognition task, we evaluated pre-trained Densenet121 and Resnet50 networks with either the original or augmented dataset. Our results indicate that the augmentation alone has a similar or better performance compared to the original. Implications of this method and its role in improving existing facial expression generation and recognition approaches are discussed.

Keywords: Facial expressions · Augmentation · Deep learning · Emotions

1 Introduction

Generating and recognizing facial expressions has numerous applications ranging from medical ones, such as inferring character [1], emotional states and intent [2],

This work has been supported by AffecTech: Personal Technologies for Affective Health, Innovative Training Network funded by the H2020 People Programme under Marie Skłodowska-Curie grant agreement No 722022.

© Springer Nature Switzerland AG 2021
A. Del Bimbo et al. (Eds.): ICPR 2020 Workshops, LNCS 12663, pp. 730–740, 2021.
https://doi.org/10.1007/978-3-030-68796-0_53

detection of diseases [3] to authentication and biometrics [4], designing affective interfaces [5–8] and virtual avatars [9,10] and computer graphics [11]. State of the art uses machine- and deep-learning methods to achieve impressive results [12,13]. However, most approaches are able to recognize or synthesize facial expressions as a categorical state with few recent works being able to also account for varying emotion intensities [14,15]. This is important as facial expressions' meaning varies at different intensities and such approaches need to be able to distinguish the intensity portrayed emotion accurately [16].

While both facial expression recognition and generation approaches have achieved impressive results in recent years, humans are still better recognizing subtle facial expressions [17]. A reason for that is the scarce number of datasets consisting of labeled nuanced expressions. In fact, correctly classifying subtle facial expressions poses a few key challenges: 1) facial expressions displaying low intensity of emotion can share certain similarities with other expressions, 2) dissimilarity in the display of emotion between different people and 3) imbalanced sample distribution for expressions and subjects [18].

In this paper, we explore an existing method for blending faces applied on a facial expression dataset and evaluate it in a generation and recognition tasks. First, we elucidate on the steps required to create an augmented dataset, then present the results from both tasks and discuss the implications of this method for improving upon both facial expression generation and recognition challenges and outline further use-cases.

2   Dataset

In order to train the models, we are using the Radboud Faces Database (RafD) [19]. The dataset consists of 8040 colored images with 681×1024 resolution including 67 persons – 57 adults and 10 children. The dataset is labeled for person's identity, gender, ethnicity, facial expression, eye gaze direction, and camera angle. For the purpose of simplifying the method and evaluation described herein, we only used images of front-facing facial expressions, omitting angles different than $90°$. Furthermore, we are also only including images of adults which results in 1336 images.

3   Augmented Dataset

In this section we outline the pre-processing steps required to create the augmented dataset. For the preprocessing steps of alignment, centering and cropping we used the python libraries dlib, imutils and OpenCV2. For computing the Delaunay triangulation and affine transform we used OpenCV2.

Fig. 1. On the left is a successful augmentation portraying happiness with 0.3 intensity. On the right is an unsuccessful augmentation.

3.1   Alignment, Centering and Cropping

In the first phase, we detect and locale 68 landmarks with dlib. The landmarks are then used to align all the images with the FaceAligner class from imutils with rigid registration. Generally, the images in the RafD dataset are well aligned, however, there is still a benefit in using the aligner as we noticed a slight tilt in some of them. This has yielded some improvements, particularly for features such as the eyes and mouth, since it ensures that those are stacked on the same spatial coordinates in every image. Finally, detected faces are cropped out of the original image with output dimensions of 550×550 pixels.

3.2   Computing Delaunay Triangulation and Transform

To generate the augmented dataset, we computed a Delaunay triangulation on the aligned and centered images by re-identifying landmark points using dlib after applying the preprocessing steps described earlier. Computing the Delaunay triangulation can be done in multiple ways [20]. We have used OpenCV's implementation for *calculateDelaunayTriangles*, *similarityTransform*, *warpAffine* and *warpTriangle* as it allows to easily reproduce the steps. The point-to-point correspondence registration is trivial, since the landmarks descriptive of facial features are an ordered set. We found the similarity transform between the two point clouds facilitating a rotation, translation and scaling for each triangle in the Delaunay triangulation. Subsequently, by computing the transformation for all triangles, the images are morphed together, where the texture blending is controlled by a factor between $[0, 1]$ weighing each image's contribution to resulting pixel values. To create the augmented dataset, we have applied this method per expression and within subjects. For each emotion, we took the neutral and a 'target' one, where as a result of the blending, for example at a factor of 0.5, the result would portray the 'target' expression at half intensity. The algorithm can also be applied to produce varying levels of intensities by adjusting the blending factor.

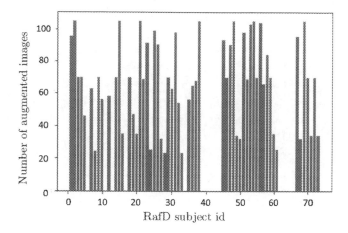

Fig. 2. Augmentations per subject (as referenced by their ids in the dataset) without artefacts. Optimally, we expect 105 images per subject for the $[0.3, 0.7]$ intensity range descriptive of 5 intensities, 7 emotions and 3 eye gaze directions.

We created expression intensities between 0.3 and 0.7 at increments of 0.1 as expressions with no (neutral expression) or maximum intensity are already contained within the original dataset. By applying this augmentation per person and then per expression, while using the neutral expression as a baseline, our approach yielded 6840 images. In some cases, mostly for the neutral expression for particular subjects, the augmentation produces visual artefacts, which makes them unsuitable for use (see Fig. 1). Figure 2 depicts the amount of augmented images created per subject. Noticeable is that there are clusters with near-similar amount of augmentations, due to the fact that the visual artefacts manifested on particular images, which rendered any blends thereof unusable. Excluding unsuccessful augmentations, the final augmented dataset consisted of 3848 images. Table 1 visualizes the distribution of created augmentations according to expression and intensity of displayed emotion. It consists of mostly evenly distributed number of augmentations for intensities. There are also less samples for sad, angry and contemptuous facial expressions in contrast to happy, disgusted, fearful and surprised ones.

3.3 Limitations

Visual artefacts expressed as solid black regions produced by the transformation were mostly localized in the area around the mouth, such that the subsequent interpolation between both sets of points fails (see Fig. 1). In our approach we are blending expressions within subjects, this was observed in nearly half of the generated augmentations. Those images need to be discarded from the final dataset as they will likely severely hamper the performance in the subsequent generation and recognition tasks. Using this approach, we are able to align facial

Table 1. Augmented images without artefacts per step

Emotion\Label	0.3	0.4	0.5	0.6	0.7
Happy	122	122	122	122	122
Sad	98	98	100	99	98
Angry	93	91	85	81	77
Contemptuous	103	102	102	98	99
Disgusted	122	122	122	122	122
Fearful	119	118	119	119	119
Surprised	122	122	122	122	122
Total	779	775	772	763	759

features together and create a blended image, however, regions, which lie outside the face contours are simply added and averaged together. Consequently, hairstyles of all blended subjects are visible in the resulting images (see Fig. 1). This effect is marginal in this case, as subjects in the RafD mostly have the same hairstyle in their depictions of different facial expressions.

4   Facial Expression Generation Task

The model we used in the generation task is a deconvolutional decoder network, previously used for morphing of objects [21]. The relative simplicity of the model allows to better control and interpret the output, in contrast to more sophisticated GANs. Training images are encoded in a high-dimensional latent space, whereby novel representations are created by varying the input parameters and iterating over it. The original model includes as an additional output a segmentation mask, which unnecessarily complicates the model and was removed. We implemented the model in tensorflow as it gives us more flexibility in fine-tuning individual layers and applying minor optimizations. For training, we used both the original RafD dataset and the augmented one. The model loss is computed based on the labels from the original dataset and the soft labels created by the augmentation. We used an early-stopping criterion, which concluded the training after 96 epochs.

Figure 3 displays the results from the generative model for the facial expressions of happiness, sadness, disgust, anger, fear, surprise and contempt each presented in successive rows. Images on the left depict expressions at their maximum intensity and each subsequent image to the right represents a decrement of 0.1 in portrayed emotion intensity towards the neutral expression.

The model was able to produce realistic-looking depictions of facial expressions for all emotion intensities with particular facial features appearing crisp and detailed. We discovered experimentally that using instance normalization produced significantly better results to batch normalization. Furthermore, uneven class distribution, as expected, plays a role when the amount of augmented

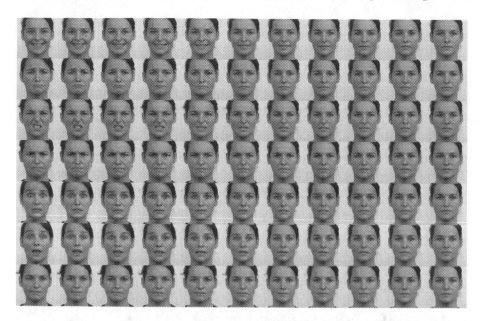

Fig. 3. Output from the generative model trained on the original and augmented datasets. Images on the right depict the neutral expression while those on the left – the facial expressions for happiness, sadness, disgust, anger, fear, surprise and contempt at maximum intensity. The intermediary images are samples in-between at increments of 0.1.

training samples outweighs the original dataset resulting in the model learning artefacts from the augmentation. The number of samples between the augmented and original datasets is at a proportion of approximately 3:1. We, therefore, balanced the training set to a uniform distribution by oversampling the originals, which mediated the best results.

In contrast, faces generated only with the original RafD dataset appear blurred and the intermediary expressions are rather ambiguous. Omitting the augmentation does not provide sufficient training data for the generative model to learn textures such as those for teeth. In this case, the model substitutes textures for teeth for those of lips or skin in intermediary expressions for emotions such as anger and happiness. This hints at the observation that the network does not learn the meaning behind facial expressions or rather the interaction between individual features, albeit it learns low-level and in subsequent layers high-level representations in order to adequately generate them. Using the augmentation alone does not create perfect synthetic facial expressions either as it is prone to artefacts itself (i.e. shadows when blending images of people with different hair styles). Using the augmentation in combination with the original dataset provides suitable synthetic images for the model to learn accurate approximations for intermediary facial expressions. This is also the case for subjects in the dataset, for which there were relatively few augmentations available as previously elaborated on why.

5   Facial Expression Recognition Task

To establish whether the augmentation can improve results for facial expression recognition classification, we designed a downstream task evaluating the quality of the augmentation. In this manner we can compare the performance efficacy of networks trained on the original dataset and the augmentation. We used the DenseNet121 [22] and ResNet50 [23] networks as they have achieved impressive results in various classification tasks. A suitable metric for evaluating generative models is the Classification Accuracy Score (CAS) [24]. Both DenseNet121 and ResNet50 have been pre-trained on ImageNet [25]. For ground truth, we used the soft labels for the facial expression intensities as generated by the augmentation. It is important to note that, while the soft labels (e.g. intensities of emotions) in the original dataset are either 1 or 0 as there are no intermediary expressions, the augmented one only consists of ones in the intensity range [0.3, 0.7] as shown (see Table 1). For training, we split both original and augmented datasets in a 90% training- and 10% test-sets stratified according to subject. For testing, since we are evaluating the augmentation as a downstream task, we are only using the test-set from the original dataset, which as mentioned above includes only binary labels. We have also adapted the classification for the DenseNet121 and ResNet50 models to predict 7 classes, representing expressions available in the dataset, in place of the default 1000 classes. For training parameters we used ADAM optimizer [26] with $\beta_1 = 0.9$, $\beta_2 = 0.99$, $\epsilon = 10^{-8}$, learning rate $\alpha = 0.001$ and no weight decay. We also evaluated an additional augmentation strategy where in A) we are not using any augmentation and in B) we are further using standard augmentations consisting of rotation (+-30), scaling with a random factor between (0.8 and, 1.2) and shear random factor (0.9 and, 1.1). The results of our experiment can be seen in Table 2.

Table 2. Facial expression recognition results from Resnet50 and Densenet121 models where Augmented and Original refer to the RafD dataset and A) is no additional augmentation and B) is applying rotation (+-30), scaling with a random factor between (0.8 and, 1.2) and shear random factor (0.9 and, 1.1).

	Densenet121		Resnet50	
	Augmented	Original	Augmented	Original
A	0.965	0.965	0.972	0.965
B	0.993	0.958	0.958	0.972

While the performance for the RafD dataset are reaching human level of performance (recognizing simple emotions in high resolution images is a relatively simple task for deep learning models), the results hold true also for the augmented data. In addition, using only the augmented images performs better, or on pair, compared to the original images in every situation except for Resnet50 B). An interesting observation is that augmented images do not include facial expressions at maximum intensity but have been evaluated on such. This implies that training on augmented images featuring medium intensities of portrayed emotions was sufficient to classify those at maximum intensity as well. In our case, cross-entropy with soft labels is not symmetric due to the fact that 1) soft-labels in the augmentation weigh towards the neutral expression and 2) the augmentation for certain expressions is more prone to artefacts (i.e. sadness and anger), which results in a unbalanced training samples between classes. Contrary to our belief, however, this did not appear to hamper the CAS scores for the model trained only on augmented images. This is a positive result, as it implies that the networks learn class distribution on- or almost on-par and in some cases even better compared to using the original dataset, which makes both datasets practically interchangeable for training.

6   Discussion

In this paper we have presented a known approach for blending images of faces and explored its use to augment existing facial expression datasets to create labeled expressions portraying varying intensities of emotion. We evaluated the augmentation in a facial expression generation and recognition tasks and our results indicate significant improvements in generating facial expressions when using the augmentation in addition to the original dataset. In a facial expression recognition task, the original and augmented datasets can be used interchangeably as both achieve near-similar levels of classification accuracy. There are benefits to using this augmentation for a wider set of tasks, in particular for networks which also aim to recognize intensities of facial expression beyond categorical classification.

Some further considerations when using this technique are that the method can also be applied in a person-agnostic manner as long as facial feature landmarks can be correctly identified. For the purposes of our evaluation, we applied the augmentation only within subjects, but this can be done for an arbitrary amount of identities. Those blended pseudo-identities would still be of sufficient quality to be reliably used. A potential benefit is that with an increase of blended identities, artefacts caused by the augmentation method are reduced, which in turn allows the generation of larger automatically labeled datasets. Recently, it has also been a topic of discussion that a lot of datasets are biased and are not representative for group diversity. This method can be particularly useful to correct for this bias by generating morphed samples for underrepresented genders and ethnicities which in turn can be helpful in producing less biased algorithms.

Holistic-based facial-expression recognition approaches can benefit from such augmentation as well. It can provide plausible samples for training, which can help discriminative models to learn more accurate decision boundaries between classes, thus reducing misclassification errors for nuanced facial expressions. Currently, more expressive features of the face are weighted such that they disproportionately influence classification. Alternatively, the presented method can be used in recognition tasks to strengthen the interdependence of formant facial features contributing to individual facial expressions.

7   Future Work

In further work, we aim to evaluate this approach on datasets, ideally containing ambiguous and nuanced expressions. We also aim to evaluate the effectiveness of this method in more challenging tasks, such as images with low-resolution, under different lighting conditions or with occlusions. In addition, we would also like to conflate both generation and recognition experiments in a downstream task, evaluating whether a combination of the generative model output trained on augmented data can further improve the augmentation quality. In turn, this can be used to also improve the performance of facial expression recognition tasks. Finally, we would also like to investigate whether training a classification model with augmented data for intermediary intensities can also improve recognition results for nuanced expressions.

8   Conclusion

We have evaluated an effective and inexpensive method to create a labeled augmented facial expression dataset with varying intensities of emotion from a categorically labeled one. We have detailed the steps required for its creation and explored potential caveats when working with the augmented data such as uneven sample distribution of labeled classes, particularly when working with soft labels. The simplicity of the method makes it easily applicable for facial expression recognition and generation tasks. The augmentation relying on a geometric transformation makes experiments using this approach easily reproducible. The application of this augmentation can address contemporary problems in deep learning algorithms related to improvements in nuanced facial expression recognition and generation, uneven sample distribution and debiasing facial expression datasets.

References

1. Cogsdill, E.J., Todorov, A.T., Spelke, E.S., Banaji, M.R.: Inferring character from faces: a developmental study. Psychol. Sci. **25**(5), 1132–1139 (2014)
2. Buck, R.: Social and emotional functions in facial expression and communication: the readout hypothesis. Biol. Psychol. **38**(2–3), 95–115 (1994)
3. Kruszka, P., et al.: 22q11. 2 deletion syndrome in diverse populations. Am. J. Med. Genet. Part A **173**(4), 879–888 (2017)
4. Chang, K.I., Bowyer, K.W., Flynn, P.J.: Multiple nose region matching for 3D face recognition under varying facial expression. IEEE Trans. Pattern Anal. Mach. Intell. **28**(10), 1695–1700 (2006)
5. Valev, H., Leufkens, T., Sas, C., Westerink, J., Dotsch, R.: Evaluation of a self-report system for assessing mood using facial expressions. In: Cipresso, P., Serino, S., Villani, D. (eds.) MindCare 2019. LNICST, vol. 288, pp. 231–241. Springer, Cham (2019). https://doi.org/10.1007/978-3-030-25872-6_19
6. Sanches, P., et al.: HCI and affective health: taking stock of a decade of studies and charting future research directions. In: Proceedings of the 2019 CHI Conference on Human Factors in Computing Systems, pp. 1–17 (2019)

7. Colombo, D., et al.: The need for change: understanding emotion regulation antecedents and consequences using ecological momentary assessment. Emotion **20**(1), 30 (2020)
8. Alfaras, M., et al.: From biodata to somadata. In: Proceedings of the 2020 CHI Conference on Human Factors in Computing Systems, pp. 1–14 (2020)
9. Hu, L., et al.: Avatar digitization from a single image for real-time rendering. ACM Trans. Graph. (ToG) **36**(6), 1–14 (2017)
10. Gallucci, A., Znamenskiy, D., Petkovic, M.: Prediction of 3D body parts from face shape and anthropometric measurements. J. Image Graph. **8**(3), 67–74 (2020)
11. Lombardi, S., Saragih, J., Simon, T., Sheikh, Y.: Deep appearance models for face rendering. ACM Trans. Graph. (TOG) **37**(4), 1–13 (2018)
12. Chu, C., Zhmoginov, A., Sandler, M.: Cyclegan, a master of steganography. arXiv preprint arXiv:1712.02950 (2017)
13. Choi, Y., Choi, M., Kim, M., Ha, J.W., Kim, S., Choo, J.: StarGAN: unified generative adversarial networks for multi-domain image-to-image translation. In: Proceedings of the IEEE Computer Society Conference on Computer Vision and Pattern Recognition, pp. 8789–8797 (2018)
14. Ding, H., Sricharan, K., Chellappa, R.: Exprgan: Facial expression editing with controllable expression intensity. arXiv preprint arXiv:1709.03842 (2017)
15. Pumarola, A., Agudo, A., Martinez, A.M., Sanfeliu, A., Moreno-Noguer, F.: Ganimation: anatomically-aware facial animation from a single image. In: Proceedings of the European Conference on Computer Vision (ECCV), pp. 818–833 (2018)
16. Rychlowska, M., Jack, R.E., Garrod, O.G., Schyns, P.G., Martin, J.D., Niedenthal, P.M.: Functional smiles: tools for love, sympathy, and war. Psychol. Sci. **28**(9), 1259–1270 (2017)
17. Yitzhak, N., et al.: Gently does it: humans outperform a software classifier in recognizing subtle, nonstereotypical facial expressions. Emotion **17**(8), 1187 (2017)
18. Le Ngo, A.C., Phan, R.C.-W., See, J.: Spontaneous subtle expression recognition: imbalanced databases and solutions. In: Cremers, D., Reid, I., Saito, H., Yang, M.-H. (eds.) ACCV 2014. LNCS, vol. 9006, pp. 33–48. Springer, Cham (2015). https://doi.org/10.1007/978-3-319-16817-3_3
19. Langner, O., Dotsch, R., Bijlstra, G., Wigboldus, D.H., Hawk, S.T., Van Knippenberg, A.: Presentation and validation of the radboud faces database. Cogn. Emotion **24**(8), 1377–1388 (2010)
20. Lee, D.-T., Schachter, B.J.: Two algorithms for constructing a delaunay triangulation. Int. J. Comput. Inf. Sci. **9**(3), 219–242 (1980)
21. Dosovitskiy, A., Springenberg, J.T., Tatarchenko, M., Brox, T.: Learning to generate chairs, tables and cars with convolutional networks. IEEE Trans. Pattern Anal. Mach. Intell. **39**(4), 692–705 (2016)
22. Huang, G., Liu, Z., Van Der Maaten, L., Weinberger, K.Q.: Densely connected convolutional networks. In: Proceedings of the IEEE Conference on Computer Vision and Pattern Recognition, pp. 4700–4708 (2017)
23. He, K., Zhang, X., Ren, S., Sun, J.: Deep residual learning for image recognition. In: Proceedings of the IEEE Conference on Computer Vision and Pattern Recognition, pp. 770–778 (2016)

24. Ravuri, S., Vinyals, O.: Classification accuracy score for conditional generative models. In: Advances in Neural Information Processing Systems, pp. 12268–12279 (2019)
25. Russakovsky, O., et al.: Imagenet large scale visual recognition challenge. Int. J. Comput. Vis. **115**(3), 211–252 (2015)
26. Kingma, D.P., Ba, J.: Adam: A method for stochastic optimization. arXiv preprint arXiv:1412.6980 (2014)

Deformable Convolutional LSTM for Human Body Emotion Recognition

Peyman Tahghighi[1(✉)], Abbas Koochari[2], and Masoume Jalali[2]

[1] School of Electrical and Computer Engineering, University of Tehran, Tehran, Iran
Peyman.Tahghighi@ut.ac.ir
[2] School of Mechanics, Electrical Power and Computer, Islamic Azad University,
Science and Research Branch, Tehran, Iran

Abstract. People represent their emotions in a myriad of ways. Among the most important ones is whole body expressions which have many applications in different fields such as human-computer interaction (HCI). One of the most important challenges in human emotion recognition is that people express the same feeling in various ways using their face and their body. Recently many methods have tried to overcome these challenges using Deep Neural Networks (DNNs). However, most of these methods were based on images or on facial expressions only and did not consider deformation that may happen in the images such as scaling and rotation which can adversely affect the recognition accuracy. In this work, motivated by recent researches on deformable convolutions, we incorporate the deformable behavior into the core of convolutional long short-term memory (ConvLSTM) to improve robustness to these deformations in the image and, consequently, improve its accuracy on the emotion recognition task from videos of arbitrary length. We did experiments on the GEMEP dataset and achieved state-of-the-art accuracy of 98.8% on the task of whole human body emotion recognition on the validation set.

Keywords: Human emotion recognition · Deformable convolutions · Convolutional long short-term memory · Recurrent Neural Networks · Long short-term memory

1 Introduction

Understanding and interpreting human emotions from videos have many different applications especially in the field of Human Computer/Robotic Interaction (HCI/HRI) [14]. Humans can represent different emotions by their behavior using verbal and non-verbal signs during a conversation. Generally, human communication can be classified as verbal and nonverbal. The verbal communication includes voice and its tune, while nonverbal includes body movement, facial expression and gestures [6,12].

So far, many researchers have tried to analyze and classify emotion from a single image or a stream of frames. For instance, Jain *et al.* [8], used images of

© Springer Nature Switzerland AG 2021
A. Del Bimbo et al. (Eds.): ICPR 2020 Workshops, LNCS 12663, pp. 741–747, 2021.
https://doi.org/10.1007/978-3-030-68796-0_54

the face and a deep convolutional neural network (CNN) based on ResNet [7] for classification of emotions based on human faces, while [10] used a similar idea to classify whole body emotion. Nevertheless, both of these methods were based on fixed images, while we are trying to classify emotion from videos. Moreover, Jeong *et al.* [9] used 3D CNNs on a stream of facial videos for classification, but their method was limited to facial videos. Considering whole human body emotion recognition, Ahmed *et al.* [1] used features extracted from human body movement to classify different emotions, while Santhoshkumar *et al.* [13] used features extracted from two consecutive frames using their difference. Some other methods relied on multi modalities such as video and audio. For instance, Chen *et al.* [3] leveraged both audio and video in a multiple feature fusion method to classify videos. However, in this paper, we try to use video frames only and the whole human body to classify emotions.

Motivated by the recent research on deformable 2D convolutions [4,17] which showed its effectiveness in classification and object recognition, in this paper, we tried to incorporate deformable convolutions into the core of ConvLSTMs [15] in order to improve its flexibility to detect and extract features from a given frame. That is to say, since the offsets in the deformable convolutional layer allow free deformation of the sampling grid (receptive field) in comparison to fix grid in regular convolution layers, they can perform better at capturing and focusing on the salient part of frames. Furthermore, we combined deformable ConvL-STMs with 3D convolutions to extract both long-term and short-term spatio-temporal features from videos. Afterward, we used a shallow 2D CNN architecture to extract features from each 2D spatio-temporal feature map individually and finally, we used feature fusion for final classification. We experimented with GEMEP [2] dataset which contains 145 videos representing 17 different emotions and achieved state-of-the-art accuracy of 98.8% on the validation set.

2   Method

2.1   Input Preprocessing

Different individuals may represent different emotions at various speeds. Hence, videos in our dataset contain an arbitrary number of frames and we had to set all videos to a fixed number of frames. One of the ways was to split each video into an array of videos with fixed frames, but one clip sometimes cannot represent the whole emotion. Consequently, we used the idea of Uniform sampling with temporal jitter [16] to fix the length of all videos to 32 frames. If the length of one video was less than 32, we repeated the last frame. Moreover, we reduced the original frame size of videos from 720×576 to 112×112 to reduce the parameter size of our network.

2.2   Network Architecture

As can be seen in Fig. 1, our network is consists of three major components which in this section we elaborate on each of them thoroughly.

3D CNN Component. Inspired by [16], since 3D convolutions can perform better at learning local and short-term spatio-temporal features, in the first layer we used a 3D CNN component. As can be seen in Fig. 2a, we only used two max pooling operations which only one of them shrinks the video length. Consequently, this component only focuses on the short-term spatio-temporal features and we leave the learning of long-term spatio-temporal features to the deformable convolutional LSTMs.

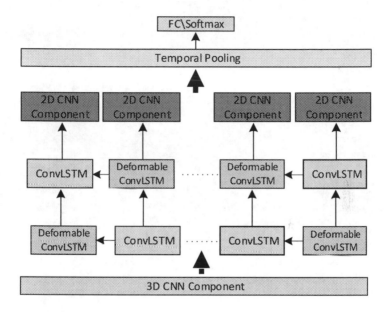

Fig. 1. Network architecture for emotion classification.

Deformable Convolutional LSTMs. Recurrent Neural Networks (RNNs) and LSTMs are more suitable for learning long-term spatio-temporal features [16]. Nevertheless, ConvLSTMs are inherently limited to model large, unknown transformations since we use regular CNNs with a fixed receptive field at the core of them. Hence, so as to improve the robustness of traditional ConvLSTMs to these transformations, we used deformable 2D convolutions in the core of ConvLSTMs. Additionally, since deformable convolutions require a large number of parameters, we could not use them instead of every normal ConvLSTM layer. Consequently, we decided to use deformable ConvLSTMs on certain frames only. Since the characters usually start to represent the emotion after some frames and salient parts for classification usually happen in the middle parts of a video, we decided to choose frames after 25% of video have passed, after half of the video has passed and after 75% of video have passed. In each of these parts, we chose three different frames. Moreover, as stated in [16], we removed the convolutional structure of all gates except for the input-to-state gate for spatio-temporal feature fusion which we used deformable 2D convolutions.

2D CNN Component. So far, we have reduced the spatial dimension of our input to 28×28, but already, we have learned short-term and long-term spatio-temporal features. Therefore, in this part, we try to learn and focus on spatial features only using a 2D CNN component. As can be seen in Fig. 2b we have chosen a shallow network with three convolutional and average pooling layers. After this stage, we did a final global average pooling for final feature fusion among all frames before using a fully connected layer for final classification.

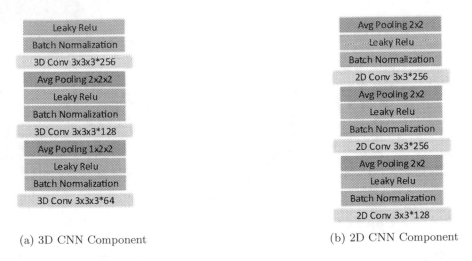

(a) 3D CNN Component　　　　　　　(b) 2D CNN Component

Fig. 2. (a) 3D CNN component that is used to extract short-term spatio-temporal features. (b) 2D CNN component which acts as the final classification layer.

3　Experiments

3.1　Dataset

For experimental studies, we used the GEMEP dataset which contains 145 videos representing 17 different emotions which are called *compound emotions* in the literature [5]. The different emotion classes are admiration, amusement, tenderness, anger, disgust, despair, pride, anxiety, interest, irritation, joy, contempt, fear, pleasure, relief, surprise and sadness. Since the number of videos for training our network was insufficient for training a deep neural network, we did data augmentation. For augmentation, we translated each frame to four different corners by 25 pixels, rotated each video between $-30°$ to $30°$, used gaussian filter with different intensities and changed the brightness. Finally, we had 9052 videos which since there were not any standard division into training and validation set for this dataset, we decided to use 80% for training and 20% for validation. Some frames of the dataset utilized in this work are depicted in Fig. 3.

Fig. 3. Some examples of the utilized GEMEP dataset in our experiments.

Table 1. Comparison between using deformable ConvLSTM and normal ConvLSTM. Note that we only applied deformable ConvLSTM to 9 different frames.

	Accuracy
Normal ConvLSTM	96.38
Deformable ConvLSTM	**98.8**

3.2   Comparison Between Deformable ConvLSTM and ConvLSTM

In this section, we compare the result of using normal ConvLSTM and deformable ConvLSTM. Since deformation may happen in any given image, it makes it difficult for a fixed size receptive field to focus on the salient parts of the image. On the other hand, deformable convolutions due to their flexible nature can easily focus on these deformed parts and extract features using their arbitrary shaped receptive field. As can be seen in Table 1, even though we used deformable ConvLSTM only on a limited number of frames (9 frames) we were able to achieve a higher classification accuracy in comparison to normal ConvLSTM which prove their effectiveness.

3.3   Comparison Between Other Methods

As can be seen in Table 2, our method based on deformable ConvLSTMs outperformed other methods in terms of accuracy. For comparison, we selected methods that used the whole human body for classification. The method in [10] used a deep architecture for classification using images extracted from videos. The superior result of our approach indicates that in some frames the emotion may become ambiguous and by using spatio-temporal features we can clarify this ambiguity and achieve higher accuracy. Additionally, both MBMIC [13] and HOG-KLT [11] used frame difference to extract temporal features. However, results show that using 3D convolutions and ConvLSTMs for learning and extracting spatio-temporal features is the superior choice.

4   Conclusion

In this paper, we proposed a method for the classification of human whole-body emotion from videos. In the first layer, we used 3D convolutions to extract

Table 2. Comparison between our proposed method and other methods on the GEMEP dataset. Note that we only chose approaches which considered whole human body and the results of our method is based on validation set.

	Accuracy
Ours	**98.8**
FDCNN (Image) [10]	95.4
MBMIC [13]	94.6
HOG-KLT [11]	95.9

short-term spatio-temporal features. Afterward, motivated by the recent success of deformable 2D convolutions we incorporated these flexible convolutions in the core of normal ConvLSTMs to form deformable ConvLSTMs. Because the receptive in these forms of convolutions are adjustable, it gives the network more freedom to extract features from different regions of a given frame. Finally, we used a shallow 2D convolutional network to further extract features from the 2D features map and used a final feature fusion. Results using GEMEP dataset show a state-of-the-art result of 98.8% accuracy on the validation set.

In future works, we will try to study the effectiveness of our deformable ConvLSTMs on other classification tasks which involve videos such as human gesture recognition or facial emotion recognition. Additionally, we will explore with different frame selection strategies for using deformable ConvLSTMs so as to find the optimal choice.

References

1. Ahmed, F., Bari, A., Gavrilova, M.: Emotion recognition from body movement. IEEE Access **8**, 11761–11781 (2019). https://doi.org/10.1109/ACCESS. 2019.2963113
2. Bänziger, T., Scherer, K.: Introducing the geneva multimodal emotion portrayal (gemep) corpus. Blueprint for Affective Computing: A Sourcebook (2010)
3. Chen, J., Chen, Z., Chi, Z., Fu, H.: Facial expression recognition in video with multiple feature fusion. IEEE Trans. Affect. Comput. **9**, 38–50 (2016). https://doi. org/10.1109/TAFFC.2016.2593719
4. Dai, J., et al.: Deformable convolutional networks (2017)
5. Du, S., Martinez, A.: Compound facial expressions of emotion: from basic research to clinical applications. Dial. Clin. Neurosci. **17**, 443–455 (2015)
6. Glowinski, D., Dael, N., Camurri, A., Volpe, G., Mortillaro, M., Scherer, K.: Toward a minimal representation of affective gestures. T. Affect. Comput. **2**, 106–118 (2011). https://doi.org/10.1109/T-AFFC.2011.7
7. He, K., Zhang, X., Ren, S., Sun, J.: Deep residual learning for image recognition (2015)
8. Jain, D., Shamsolmoali, P., Sehdev, P.: Extended deep neural network for facial emotion recognition. Pattern Recogn. Lett. **120**, 69–74 (2019). https://doi.org/10. 1016/j.patrec.2019.01.008

9. Jeong, D., Kim, B.G., Dong, S.Y.: Deep joint spatiotemporal network (djstn) for efficient facial expression recognition. Sensors **20**(7) (2020). https://doi.org/10.3390/s20071936, https://www.mdpi.com/1424-8220/20/7/1936

10. Rajaram, S., Geetha, M.: Deep learning approach for emotion recognition from human body movements with feedforward deep convolution neural networks. Procedia Comput. Sci. **152**, 158–165 (2019). https://doi.org/10.1016/j.procs.2019.05.038

11. Santhoshkumar, R., Kalaiselvi Geetha, M.: Vision-based human emotion recognition using HOG-KLT feature. In: Singh, P.K., Pawłowski, W., Tanwar, S., Kumar, N., Rodrigues, J.J.P.C., Obaidat, M.S. (eds.) Proceedings of First International Conference on Computing, Communications, and Cyber-Security (IC4S 2019). LNNS, vol. 121, pp. 261–272. Springer, Singapore (2020). https://doi.org/10.1007/978-981-15-3369-3_20

12. Rajaram, S., Geetha, M.K., Arunnehru, J.: SVM-KNN based emotion recognition of human in video using hog feature and KLT tracking algorithm. Int. J. Pure Appl. Math. **117**, 621–634 (2017)

13. Santhoshkumar, R., Geetha, M.K.: Emotion recognition on multi view static action videos using multi blocks maximum intensity code (MBMIC). In: Smys, S., Iliyasu, A.M., Bestak, R., Shi F. (eds.) New Trends in Computational Vision and Bio-inspired Computing, pp. 1143–1151. Springer, Cham (2020). https://doi.org/10.1007/978-3-030-41862-5-116

14. Sharma, G., Dhall, A.: A survey on automatic multimodal emotion recognition in the wild. In: Phillips-Wren, G., Esposito, A., Jain, L.C. (eds.) Advances in Data Science: Methodologies and Applications. Intelligent Systems Reference Library, vol. 189, pp. 35–64. Springer, Cham (2021). https://doi.org/10.1007/978-3-030-51870-7-3

15. Shi, X., Chen, Z., Wang, H., Yeung, D.Y., Wong, W.K., Woo, W.C.: Convolutional LSTM network: A machine learning approach for precipitation nowcasting (2015)

16. Zhang, L., Zhu, G., Shen, P., Song, J.: Learning spatiotemporal features using 3dcnn and convolutional LSTM for gesture recognition. In: Proceedings of the IEEE International Conference on Computer Vision Workshops, pp. 3120–3128 (2017). https://doi.org/10.1109/ICCVW.2017.369

17. Zhu, X., Hu, H., Lin, S., Dai, J.: Deformable convnets v2: More deformable, better results (2018)

Nonlinear Temporal Correlation Based Network for Action Recognition

Hongsheng Li, WeiWei Zhang, Guangming Zhu[✉], Liang Zhang, Peiyi Shen, and Juan Song

School of Computer Science and Technology, Xidian University, Xi'an, People's Republic of China
gmzhu@xidian.edu.cn

Abstract. Action recognition, a trending topic in current research, is important for human behavior analysis, virtual reality, and human computer interaction. Recently, Some of the latest works have achieved impressive results in action recognition by decomposing 3D convolutions into temporal and spatial convolutions, respsctively. Modelling the temporal features is important for action recognition. In this paper, we reconsider the decomposing of convolution operations. In the previous temporal convolution operations, the temporal features are extracted by simple linear transformation, and the temporal relations among adjacent frames are not fully considered. Therefore, we propose a novel temporal structure, namely, Nonlinear Temporal Extractors, to replace the existing 1D temporal convolutions. On the one hand, this operation can extract temporal features by considering the relation along the time dimension. On the other hand, this enhances network's representation ability by increasing the nonlinearity of the network. Finally, we perform experiments on the common action classification datasets, including UCF-101, HMDB-51, and mini-Kinetics-200. Experimental results show the effectiveness of our proposed structure.

Keywords: Human action recognition · Spatio-temporal convolution · Correlation-based method

1 Introduction

Since the introduction of the deep convolutional neural networks (CNNs), a breakthrough has been made in the field of computer vision. With effective architectures [12,13,25], CNNs have been able to reach or exceed human capabilities for visual recognition in still images. Inspired by the success of 2DCNN in image classification, some researchers have attempted to apply 2DCNN for action recognition and achieved certain results of action recognition task compared with hand-crafted methods [16,20,28].

Video signals are 3D tensors wherein spatial and temporal information get coupled. 3DCNNs, presumed to be a natural method to understand videos, have

A. Del Bimbo et al. (Eds.): ICPR 2020 Workshops, LNCS 12663, pp. 748–763, 2021.
https://doi.org/10.1007/978-3-030-68796-0_55

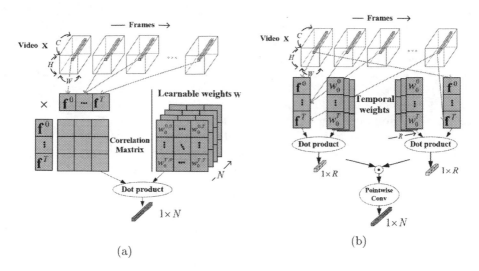

Fig. 1. Correlation based feature learning. × represents out product. The orange vectors represent a single pixel of the feature extracted from the previous convolutions or frames. Here, we ignore the spatial position and only focus on the features at different times in a certain position. The green matrix in (a) represents the correlation matrix between the vectors, and the blue matrix represents the weights of the correlation matrix, and the new features are obtained by the combination of correlations. The blue vectors in (b) represent the kernels of temporal convolutions, which will convolve on the input features. (Color figure online)

been proposed to model spatial–temporal features. Current 3DCNNs [14] for video classification, which jointly model the spatial–temporal information via 3D convolutional kernels, treat the spatial and temporal dimensions uniformly. Each layer of this structure, which has been proven to be effective, combines spatial and temporal information, thereby enabling spatial–temporal information to be fused at different levels. C3D [26] builds a shallow network by stacking 3D convolutions. In general, the more layers the network has, the better the performance it can achieve. To explore deeper 3D networks, R3D [11] borrows an architecture from the ResNet [12] and extends it from 2D to 3D ones. Similarly, I3D [2] extends 2D to 3D architecture, but uses the Inception structure [25] and utilizes a novel initialization method that bootstraps parameters from the pretrained ImageNet models. However, the immediate side effect of all 3DCNNs is the huge amount of computation and memory requirements, making it extremely difficult to train the network and achieve further optimization.

Many researchers have focused on the spatial–temporal separable network to pursue a more efficient and effective method for action recognition. The spatial–temporal separable ConvNet [19,24,27,30] is a factorization of 3D convolutional kernels and uses 2D ConvNet and 1D ConvNet to capture spatial information and temporal information, respectively. One of its advantages is that it has fewer parameters after than before decomposition. The reduction of parameters make it easier to optimize for the spatial–temporal separable network. In addition, the separation of spatial convolution and temporal convolution doubles the number of nonlinear layers, which can represent more complex features. Many effective network structures [3,32] are found in 2DCNNs, and applying such networks to 3DCNNs is also a hot topic being discussed in the literature.

By observing the spatial–temporal separable network, we find that the 1D temporal convolutions can be used to model temporal information and motion patterns. However, features from different times are processed only by first-order addition operations. We argue that although nonlinear transformation can be achieved by the continuous superposition of linear transformation and non-linear rectification, extracting a temporal feature by simple linear transformations is not effective enough. Thus, we design a slightly complex but more efficient temporal layer, namely, the Nonlinear Temporal Extractor (NTE), which attempts to introduce high-dimensional features to be a basic block. Unlike spatial–temporal separable network, we directly increase the non-linear ability of each layer of the temporal convolution. Compared with normal 1D temporal convolutions, the NTE can extract temporal feature from the correlation between adjacent frames, making it easier to achieve better for action recognition.

The primary contributions of this work can be summarized as follows. First, we propose a novel temporal block that learns temporal representation effectively and efficiently with multiplicative interaction rather than a weighted summation. Second, we comprehensively evaluate our method on large-scale datasets, such as mini-Kinetics-200 [30], UCF-101 [23], and HMDB-51 [15]. Experiments show that our architecture enhances the temporal feature learning and outperforms the conventional C3D model and its variants.

2   Related Work

In recent years, the video classification problem has gradually become the focus of machine vision research. Many studies adopted different methods to extract the key spatial temporal features. These methods are primarily divided into two categories as described below.

In order to solve the first problem mentioned above, Qiu *et al.* introduced P3D [19] with three variants of bottleneck buildings, which decomposed the standard 3D convolutional layer (with $3 \times 3 \times 3$ convolutional filters) into a combination of spatial convolutional layer (with $1 \times 3 \times 3$ convolutional filters, equal to 2DCNN block) and temporal convolutional layers (with $3 \times 1 \times 1$ convolutional filters) [19]. The three variants result from different orders of convolution: the temporal one following the spatial one, the temporal one with the spatial one in parallel, and the spatial one with the temporal in residual way. Combining these different variants, P3D achieves the best results. Similarly, Xie et al. factorized the standard 3D convolution operation into Inception 3D architecture along spatial and temporal dimensions [30]. S3D has a slightly higher accuracy and fewer parameters than I3D. Tran et al. proposed R(2+1)D, which replaces the standard 3D convolutional layer in a similar way but has the same parameters with 3DCNN [27]. Zhou *et al.* integrated the 3DCNN with 2DCNN to learn the spatial–temporal features [34]. All of the methods mentioned in this subsection can utilize the weights that are pre-trained on ImageNet to initialize the spatial part of the convolution. As a result, the training of the network becomes relatively easier.

3 Proposed Network

In this section, we first introduce the details of our proposed method. Moreover, we describe the construction of three novel temporal extractors (NTE-A, NTE-B, and NTE-C) (3.2), which use more effective feature mapping to extract temporal features compared with others. Finally, we introduce our entire network structure for action recognition.

3.1 Spatial-Temporal Separable Convolution

Spatial–temporal separable networks decompose standard 3D convolutions into spatial 2D convolutions and temporal 1D convolutions, which are used to extract spatial features and temporal features, respectively. Suppose we have the input video $\mathbf{X}$, each video is represented by a 4D tensor of size $T \times H \times W \times C$, where T and $H \times W$ are the temporal and spatial resolutions, respectively and C is the number of channels. During the spatial-temporal operations, the spatial 2D filters is firstly implemented on the videos, which can be formulated as:

$$\mathbf{F}^t(p,q) = \sum_{i,j} \mathbf{S}(i,j)\mathbf{X}^t(p+i,q+j) \tag{1}$$

where (i,j) is the spatial location, F is the obtained feature which is the same temporal size as the input, and S is the spatial kernel of size $1 \times H \times W$. In the following temporal convolutions, 1D temporal kernels conduct an inner product operation on the 2D spatial feature map along the temporal dimension. In this process, the same operation is performed for the features of different spatial positions. Thus for simplicity, we denote $\mathbf{F}$ at any position (p,q) as $\mathbf{f}$. Thus $\mathbf{f}$ become a vector of size $C \times T$. The temporal convolution is formulated as:

$$\mathbf{y}_c^t = \sum_{\tau=-\Delta_t}^{\Delta_t} \mathbf{W}_c^\tau \mathbf{f}^{t+\tau} \tag{2}$$

where $\mathbf{y}_c^t$ is the output tensor of the c-th temporal 1D filters at the t-th time step, and $\mathbf{W}_c^\tau$ and Δ_t are the weight and receptive field of temporal convolutions.

3.2 Correlation Based Feature Learning

Following Eq. (2), the temporal feature between the adjacent frames is just calculated by a linear combination of their current feature. However, the features obtained in this way have the following drawbacks: **when the value of one point is larger than that of another point, the effect of the change of the other point on the output feature is negligible.**

Principle of the Correlation Based Feature. We argue that compared to still images, videos implicitly contain a salient cue that is changes of features over time. Whether the feature signals become stronger, weaker, or unchanged, it represents a pattern of feature over time. These patterns reflect the correlation between frames. In order to represent these patterns, we designed our operators with the help of correlation. In statistics, correlation shows the strength and direction of the relationship between two random variables. As we all know, the multiplication operation of the two variables can better reflect the correlation between such variables. As shown in Fig. 1(a), we define the correlation matrix as:

$$Corr_t(\tau_1, \tau_2) = (\mathbf{f}^{t+\tau 1})^\top \mathbf{f}^{t+\tau 2} \tag{3}$$

Each point in the matrix (green matrix in Fig. 1(a)) represents the correlation feature between the two feature points, which also represents the correlation between two frames. Although we have now obtained the correlation of features at different times, not all correlations are useful for recognition tasks, and we need to selectively extract the imformation. Here we use a learnable parameter to extract a specific pattern.

$$\mathbf{y}_n^t = \sum_{\tau 1=-\Delta_t}^{\Delta_t} \sum_{\tau 2=-\Delta_t}^{\Delta_t} \mathbf{W}_n^{\tau 1, \tau 2}(Corr_t(\tau_1, \tau_2)) \tag{4}$$

where $\mathbf{y}_n^t$ is the n-th relation calculated by a specific combination of correlations between features from three frames with weight $\{\mathbf{W}_n^{\tau 1, \tau 2} : \tau 1, \tau 2 \in [-\Delta_t, \Delta_t], n \in [1, N]\}$ and we call it correlation based feature (CF).

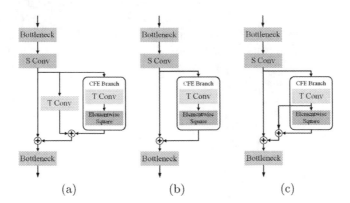

Fig. 2. Three types of NTE blocks. T Conv and S Conv represent spatial convolution and temporal convolution, respectively. CFE represents the correlation based feature extractors. Three NTE variants introduce different combinations of temporal 1D convolutions and correlation based extractors.

However, Eqs. (3) and (4) are not well implemented using current convolution operators. Therefore we perform Canonical Polyadic Decomposition [9]

(CP decomposition) for $\mathbf{W}_n^{\tau 1,\tau 2}$. CP decomposition, which is quite similar to the singular value decomposition (SVD) of matrices, approximates a tensor with a sum of a series of rank-one tensors. For example, given the third-order tensor $\mathbf{W} \in \mathbb{R}^{I,J,K}$, we can rewrite it as:

$$\mathbf{W} = \sum_{r=1}^{R} \boldsymbol{\alpha}_r \otimes \boldsymbol{\beta}_r \otimes \boldsymbol{\gamma}_r \tag{5}$$

where $\boldsymbol{\alpha}_r \in \mathbb{R}^I, \boldsymbol{\beta}_r \in \mathbb{R}^J, \boldsymbol{\gamma}_r \in \mathbb{R}^K, r \in [1,R]$ are three rank-one tensors and $\otimes$ represent the tensor product. Elementwise, the weight $\mathbf{W}_n^{\tau 1,\tau 2}$ in (4) can be rewritten as:

$$\mathbf{W}_n^{\tau 1,\tau 2} = \sum_{r=1}^{R} \alpha_r^{\tau 1} \beta_r^{\tau 2} \gamma_{n,r} \tag{6}$$

Where each element in the matrix $\mathbf{W}$ can be expressed as the sum of a series of vector element products.

Thus, Eq. (4) can be rewritten as follows:

$$
\begin{aligned}
\mathbf{y}_n &= \sum_{\tau 1=-\Delta_t}^{\Delta_t} \sum_{\tau 2=-\Delta_t}^{\Delta_t} \left(\sum_{r=1}^{R} \alpha_r^{\tau 1} \beta_r^{\tau 2} \gamma_{n,r} \right) \mathbf{f}^{t+\tau 1} \mathbf{f}^{t+\tau 2} \\
&= \sum_{r=1}^{R} \gamma_{n,r} \underbrace{\sum_{\tau 1=-\Delta_t}^{\Delta_t} (\alpha_r^{\tau 1} \mathbf{f}^{t+\tau 1})}_{Pa} \underbrace{\sum_{\tau 2=-\Delta_t}^{\Delta_t} (\beta_r^{\tau 2} \mathbf{f}^{t+\tau 2})}_{Pb}
\end{aligned}
\tag{7}
$$

where $\mathbf{y}_n$ is rewritten as a combination of multiplicative interactions between part Pa and Pb followed by a pointwise convolution. The part Pa and Pb can be easily implemented using 1D temporal convolutions. In order to simplify our calculation process and reduce parameters, we set $\alpha_r^{\tau 1} = \beta_r^{\tau 2}$. In this way, the process shown in Eq. (7) is decomposed into the following steps.

$$\mathbf{v}_r^t = \sum_{\tau=-\Delta_t}^{\Delta_t} \alpha_r^{\tau} \mathbf{f}^{t+\tau} \tag{8}$$

$$\mathbf{p}_r^t = \mathbf{v}_r^t \odot \mathbf{v}_r^t \tag{9}$$

$$\mathbf{y}_n^t = \sum_{r=1}^{R} \gamma_{n,r} \mathbf{p}_r^t \tag{10}$$

where $\odot$ is a element-wise product. The input features are first convolved by 1D temporal convolutions to obtain intermediate features $\mathbf{v}_r^t$ and then the feature makes an element-wise product of itself. Finally, a pointwise convolution is applyed to merge the feature in different channels. The entire process is the same as described in Fig. 1(b).

Backpropagation of the Correlation Based Feature Extractor. Next we introduce how to perform back propagation of our correlation based feature extractor. We use L and δ^l to denote the final loss function and error at layer l. And we use $l_\mathbf{y}$, $l_\mathbf{p}$ and $l_\mathbf{v}$ denote the layer described by the Eq. (8), (9), (10), respectively. In the process of back propagation, the error at layer $l_\mathbf{y}$ is denote as $\delta^{l_\mathbf{y}}$, and it can be formulated as :

$$\delta_n^{l_\mathbf{y}} = \frac{\partial L}{\partial \mathbf{y}_n} \tag{11}$$

With $\delta^{l_\mathbf{y}}$, we can recursively compute the error $\delta_r^{l_\mathbf{p}}$ at layer $l_\mathbf{p}$ and $\delta^{l_\mathbf{v}}$ at layer $l_\mathbf{v}$:

$$\delta_r^{l_\mathbf{p}} = \frac{\partial L}{\partial \mathbf{p}_r} = \sum_n \frac{\partial L}{\partial \mathbf{y}_n^t} \frac{\partial \mathbf{y}_n^t}{\partial \mathbf{p}_r} = \sum_n \delta_n^{l_\mathbf{y}} \frac{\partial(\gamma_{n,r} \mathbf{p}_r^t)}{\partial \mathbf{p}_r} = \sum_n \delta_n^{l_\mathbf{y}} \gamma_{n,r} \tag{12}$$

$$\delta_r^{l_\mathbf{v}} = \frac{\partial L}{\partial \mathbf{v}_r^t} = \frac{\partial L}{\partial \mathbf{p}_r} \frac{\partial \mathbf{p}_r}{\partial \mathbf{v}_r^t} = 2\delta_r^{l_\mathbf{p}} \mathbf{v}_r^t \tag{13}$$

Then, the gradients of the weights at each layers can thus be computed using the computed $\delta^{l_\mathbf{y}}$, $\delta_r^{l_\mathbf{p}}$ and $\delta_r^{l_\mathbf{v}}$:

$$\frac{\partial L}{\partial \gamma_{n,r}} = \frac{\partial L}{\partial \mathbf{y}_n^t} \frac{\partial \mathbf{y}_n^t}{\partial \gamma_{n,r}} = \delta_r^{l_\mathbf{y}} \frac{\partial(\gamma_{n,r} \mathbf{p}_r^t)}{\partial \gamma_{n,r}} = \delta_r^{l_\mathbf{y}} \mathbf{p}_r^t \tag{14}$$

$$\frac{\partial L}{\partial \alpha_r^\tau} = \frac{\partial L}{\partial \mathbf{v}_r^t} \frac{\partial \mathbf{v}_r^t}{\partial \alpha_r^\tau} = \delta_r^{l_\mathbf{v}} \frac{\partial(\alpha_r^\tau \mathbf{f}^{t+\tau})}{\partial \alpha_r^\tau} = \delta_r^{l_\mathbf{v}} \mathbf{f}^{t+\tau} \tag{15}$$

With these gradients, we can update the weights by gradient descent algorithm.

3.3   NTE Block Design

Consequently, we merge our CF extractors into traditional spatial-temporal separable networks and propose three basic temporal blocks called and create novel network structures by stacking such modules. An illustration of our new spatial–temporal blocks are shown in Fig. 2.

3.4   Nonlinear Temporal Networks

NTE-A. We added our CF extractor branch to the original spatial–temporal separable convolution structures to obtain better results. As shown in Fig. 2(a), our first block, NTE-A, consists of spatial convolutions and temporal modules. In the temporal module, two parallel branches are identified: the original temporal 1D convolution and a branching of our proposed CF extractor. In this form, we use NTE to obtain correlation based features and a standard temporal convolution to obtain first-order temporal features. However, the weight of our CF extractor and the weight of standard temporal convolution are not shared,

Table 1. Architectures of 3D ResnNet-50, P3D and our two NTE Networks.
NTE is to replace all the blocks with our NTE block, and NTE* is to replace one block in each level. The dimensions given for filters are time, height, and width, and the numbers in {} represent the number of channels in each layer of convolutions

Type	3D ResNet-50 size/stride	P3D size/stride	NTE Net size/stride	NTE* Net size/stride	Output size
3D Conv	$3 \times 7 \times 7/(1,2)$	$3 \times 7 \times 7/(1,2)$	$3 \times 7 \times 7/(1,2)$	$3 \times 7 \times 7/(1,2)$	$16 \times 112 \times 112$
	Maxpool/(1, 2)	Maxpool/(1, 2)	Maxpool/(1, 2)	Maxpool/(1, 2)	
conv-1	$\begin{bmatrix} 1 \times 1 \times 1, 64 \\ 3 \times 3 \times 3, 64 \\ 1 \times 1 \times 1, 256 \end{bmatrix} \times 3$	$\begin{bmatrix} 1 \times 1 \times 1, 64 \\ 1 \times 3 \times 3, 64 \\ 3 \times 1 \times 1, 64 \\ 1 \times 1 \times 1, 256 \end{bmatrix} \times 3$	$\begin{bmatrix} NTE - A/B/C, \\ \{64, 64, 64, 256\} \end{bmatrix} \times 3$	$\begin{bmatrix} 1 \times 1 \times 1, 64 \\ 1 \times 3 \times 3, 64 \\ 3 \times 1 \times 1, 64 \\ 1 \times 1 \times 1, 256 \end{bmatrix} \times 2$ $\begin{bmatrix} NTE - A/B/C, \\ \{64, 64, 64, 256\} \end{bmatrix} \times 1$	$16 \times 56 \times 56$
conv-1	$\begin{bmatrix} 1 \times 1 \times 1, 128 \\ 3 \times 3 \times 3, 128 \\ 1 \times 1 \times 1, 512 \end{bmatrix} \times 4$	$\begin{bmatrix} 1 \times 1 \times 1, 128 \\ 1 \times 3 \times 3, 128 \\ 3 \times 1 \times 1, 128 \\ 1 \times 1 \times 1, 512 \end{bmatrix} \times 4$	$\begin{bmatrix} NTE - A/B/C, \\ \{128, 128, 128, 512\} \end{bmatrix} \times 4$	$\begin{bmatrix} 1 \times 1 \times 1, 128 \\ 1 \times 3 \times 3, 128 \\ 3 \times 1 \times 1, 128 \\ 1 \times 1 \times 1, 512 \end{bmatrix} \times 3$ $\begin{bmatrix} NTE - A/B/C, \\ \{128, 128, 128, 512\} \end{bmatrix} \times 1$	$8 \times 28 \times 28$
conv-1	$\begin{bmatrix} 1 \times 1 \times 1, 256 \\ 3 \times 3 \times 3, 256 \\ 1 \times 1 \times 1, 1024 \end{bmatrix} \times 6$	$\begin{bmatrix} 1 \times 1 \times 1, 256 \\ 1 \times 3 \times 3, 256 \\ 3 \times 1 \times 1, 256 \\ 1 \times 1 \times 1, 1024 \end{bmatrix} \times 6$	$\begin{bmatrix} NTE - A/B/C, \\ \{256, 256, 256, 1024\} \end{bmatrix} \times 6$	$\begin{bmatrix} 1 \times 1 \times 1, 256 \\ 1 \times 3 \times 3, 256 \\ 3 \times 1 \times 1, 256 \\ 1 \times 1 \times 1, 1024 \end{bmatrix} \times 5$ $\begin{bmatrix} NTE - A/B/C, \\ \{256, 256, 256, 1024\} \end{bmatrix} \times 1$	$4 \times 14 \times 14$
conv-1	$\begin{bmatrix} 1 \times 1 \times 1, 512 \\ 3 \times 3 \times 3, 512 \\ 1 \times 1 \times 1, 2048 \end{bmatrix} \times 3$	$\begin{bmatrix} 1 \times 1 \times 1, 512 \\ 1 \times 3 \times 3, 512 \\ 3 \times 1 \times 1, 512 \\ 1 \times 1 \times 1, 2048 \end{bmatrix} \times 3$	$\begin{bmatrix} NTE - A/B/C, \\ \{512, 512, 512, 2048\} \end{bmatrix} \times 3$	$\begin{bmatrix} 1 \times 1 \times 1, 512 \\ 1 \times 3 \times 3, 512 \\ 3 \times 1 \times 1, 512 \\ 1 \times 1 \times 1, 2048 \end{bmatrix} \times 2$ $\begin{bmatrix} NTE - A/B/C, \\ \{512, 512, 512, 2048\} \end{bmatrix} \times 1$	$2 \times 7 \times 7$
pooling	spatial-temporal global average pooling				$1 \times 1 \times 1$
fc	$2048 \times num\_classes$				

thus increasing the amount of parameters. Besides, there are two pointwise convolutions with a element-wise sum in between, which seems to us that the same effect can be obtained by integrating the previous convolution into the latter. Therefore, we remove the convolution in the CF extractor branch, and the last pointwise convolution is responsible for the cross-channel information fusion and adjusting the number of channels. In the NTE-B and NTE-C module, we also used the same configuration as in NTE-A.

NTE-B. To avoid side effects and to verify the effect of our relation branch independently, we consider whether the original temporal 1D convolution branch is necessary. Thus, we design the second structure shown in Fig. 2(b). We completely replace the original temporal 1D convolutions with our CF extractor. The parameter amount of such structure is the same as that of the original spatial–temporal separable convolution structure, but the features obtained by 1D standard temporal convolution are discarded.

NTE-C. As we want to combine the advantages of both structures and avoid the defects of both structures, we thus design the third block (Fig. 2(c)) by adding the proposed CF extractor to P3D block in a residual manner. Consequently, we can either use the original 1D convolution structure or add our new temporal feature extractor by sharing parameters. Compared with the first block, this block has an extra identity mapping from the end of temporal 1D convolution.

In this paper, we choose the ResNet-50 as our default backbone because of its good performance. First, we showed the detail of ResNet-50; then, we designed two groups of networks which only differ in the number of NTE blocks (Table 1). In the NTE network, each building block has been replaced by a NTE block, whereas in the second one, we only replaced four blocks. In each group, different networks can be constructed by stacking different basic blocks (NTE-[A/B/C]).

4   Experiments

In this section, we design some experiments to validate the various methods we introduced in previous sections. We first train and validate our methods on the mini-Kinetics-200 dataset created by [30] due to limitations in computing resources. We show our result on benchmark dataset for action recognition: UCF-101 [23] and HMDB-51 [15].

4.1   Datasets

The mini-Kinetics-200 has 200 categories, each with 400 training and 25 validation examples, resulting in 80K training examples and 5K validation examples in total. This dataset is a subset of Kinetics-400 dataset and Kinetics-400 is one of the largest video datasets of human action, which has approximately $240K$ training videos and $20K$ validation videos of 400 human actions. UCF101 [23] is a large dataset for human action recognition with 101 action classes, over 13 labeled clips, and 27 h of video data. It also contains three training/test splits, each including approximately $9.5K$ training and $3.7K$ test clips. HMDB-51 [15] is collected from digitized movies and YouTube and has 51 action categories that contain approximately $7K$ manually annotated clips.

4.2   Experimental Setup

During training, we sample 32 frames with two sampling steps from a random initial temporal position in each video. Then, we resize the shorter side of each frame to 256 and crop a 224×224 region at a random location. We also randomly flip frames horizontally and normalize the R, G, B channels with a mean of $[0.485, 0.456, 0.406]$ and a variance of $[0.229, 0.224, 0.225]$. During inference, we sample 10 examples from each video with an equal temporal interval, after which we take 224×224 center crops from the resized frames. The predictions are calculated from the average scores of the 10 examples.

Table 2. Ablations study on mini-Kinetics-200 validation set.

Model	Test	Accuracy	Model size	FLOPs
3D-ResNet-50	Clip	65.09%	33.4M	54.1G
	Video	73.25%		
P3D	Clip	65.93%	28.1M	32.9G
	Video	73.36%		
NTE-A	Clip	68.27%	31.8M	37.2G
	Video	76.18%		
NTE-A*	Clip	68.63%	29.1M	34.4G
	Video	77.14%		
NTE-B*	Clip	68.17%	28.1M	33.0G
	Video	76.06%		
NTE-C*	Clip	**70.37%**	28.1M	33.0G
	Video	**78.42%**		

4.3 Ablation Study

We compare our variants with the normal spatial–temporal separable networks (P3D [19]) to validate the effectiveness of our basic block (Fig. 2). Limited by computational power, we choose to validate our method on the mini-Kinetics-200 dataset. For P3D [19] and our new architecture, we utilize the ResNet-50 as our default backbone. Table 2 shows the results achieved by our networks with different NTE blocks.

Comparisons Between Variants. Our network differs from P3D [19] networks in basic blocks. P3D [19] uses traditional spatial-temporal convolutions as the basic block, whereas our network replaces these with the blocks shown in Figs. 2(a), 2(b) and 2(c). The experimental result shows that when P3D is equipped with NTE building blocks (whether fully equipped or partially equipped), compared with P3D, the accuracy of our network has been greatly improved, thus indicating the advantage of our NTE blocks in extracting temporal features. Among the networks we designed, NTE-B* has the same amount of parameters as P3D [19]; the former considers the high-order temporal features based on correlation, and the latter is based on standard first-order temporal features. However, the high accuracy of NTE-B* validates the capacity of correlation-based temporal features. Compared with NTE-B*, NTE-A* considers both temporal features in the form of independent parameters. The good performance of NTE-A* indicates that the two corresponding temporal feature structures are effective and can complement each other. Simultaneously, we noticed that NTE-C* has the highest accuracy among the networks we introduced. The results indicate that considering both temporal features in the form of shared parameters reduces the number of parameters, thus generating better results.

4.4 Study on the Change of Accuracy

Figure 3 show the the accuracy of some categories in mini-kinetics-200. Figure 3(a) shows the five categories with the highest accuracy, Fig. 3(b) shows the five categories with the lowest accuracy, and Fig. 3(c) shows the five categories with the greatest accuracy improvement. For the categories with the highest accuracy, our NTE network can still maintain the highest accuracy, which proves that the NTE module can retain the effective features extracted in the traditional spatiotemporal convolutions. The categories with the lowest accuracy also have a significant improvement over the results of P3D and C3D, which proves that the new features we introduced are an effective supplement to the original features. In addition, among the five categories with the greatest improvement in accuracy, their common feature is that they have repeated actions over time, and there is a clear correlation between the actions before and after, and these actions are the key features of action recognition. Therefore, after introducing our NTE module, the recognition accuracy of these categories can be significantly improved.

Number of NTE Blocks. We also verified the effectiveness of different numbers of modules in terms of accuracy. As shown in Table 2, despite having more NTE layers, the video accuracy of NTE-A is 0.96% lower than that of NTE-A*. This finding indicates that high-order temporal features obtained by stacking too many NTE layers cannot be used for video classification and may even slightly affect the performance of the network. When too many NTE layers are added, the non-linear capability of the network will be excessively increased, resulting in the proportion of basic features in the features being too small, which will cause negative effects.

4.5 Comparison with State-of-art on Mini-Kinetics-200 Datasets

Table 3. Top-1 Action recognition accuracy on mini-Kinetics-200 validation set. The results of 3D ResNet' and P3D' were obtained by re-training on the mini-Kinetics-200 dataset, and the results of I3D were obtained from [30].

Model	Backbone	Accuracy
3D ResNet'	ResNet-50	73.18%
P3D'	ResNet-50	73.36%
WTBN C2D [17]	ResNet-18	69.0%
WTBN C3D [17]	ResNet-18	67.2%
Fast-S3D [30]	Inception	78.0%
S3D [30]	Inception	**78.42%**
I3D [30]	Inception	78.4%
MARS+RGB+FLOW(16 frames) [5]		73.5%
NTE-C*	ResNet-50	**78.42%**

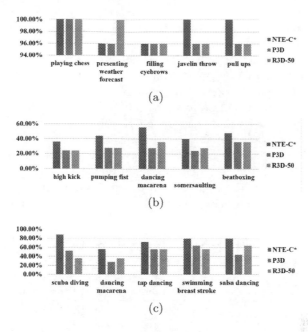

Fig. 3. Classification accuracy of different categories. (a): The five categories with the highest accuracy. (b): The five categories with the lowest accuracy. (c): The five categories with the greatest accuracy improvements.

Table 3 shows our results compared with some state-of-the-art methods. We retrain 3D Resnet and P3D [19] on mini-kinetics-200 datasets, and initialize 3D Resnet using the initialization method introduced by I3D and the spatial branch in P3D [19] with weight on ImageNet. The training process is the same as that described in Sect. 4.2. To be fair, we only take RGB images as input. Results show that our methods outperform 3D Resnet and P3D by 5.28% and 5.06%, respectively, with similar architectures. The NTE block can also bring an improvement for P3D. Our network also achieves the comparable performance of S3D and I3D with Inception architecture, but our structure is more flexible and can be applied to any other spatial–temporal separable networks. Besides, MARS are trained using 16-frame clips, and use optical flow as a second modality. From the experimental results, we still have 4.9% higher accuracy than MARS.

4.6 Comparison with State-of-art on UCF-101 and HMDB-51

We also conduct transfer learning experiments on the UCF-101 [23] and HMDB-51 [15] datasets. We use the models trained on the mini-Kinetics-200 dataset as initialization. During training, we adopted the same settings as those in the mini-Kinetics-200. The results are summarized in Table 4. For fair comparison, we consider methods that only use RGB input. Results show that our NTE network outperforms the C3D network, both on the UCF-101 dataset and the HMDB-51 dataset. Compared with the current optimal I3D network, when the two are pre-trained on the mini-kinetics-200 dataset, our NTE-C* model is 2.5% and 5.1% higher than I3D [2] on UCF-101 [23] and HMDB-51 [15], respectively, but is 1.5% and 3.7% lower than I3D when pre-trained on Full Kinetics. In the spatial–temporal separable convolutions, our network is remarkably better than P3D [19] with the same amount of parameters and obtains comparable performance with R(2+1)D, which have more parameters (33.3M) than our network (28.1M). Compared with the latest MARS [5] and EvaNet [18] methods, our accuracy is lower than their results. Because they are pretrained on full Kinetics-400 and use a large number of frames. MARS extracts temporal features by simulating optacal flow to improve the accuracy of action recognition, which we extract temporal features by introducing temporal correlation, which is more effective.

Table 4. Comparison with the state-of-the-art on UCF-101 and HMDB-51. The accuracies are averaged over three splits.

Model	Video pretrain	UCF-101	HMDB-51
TLE [8]		86.9%	63.2%
TSN [29]		85.7%	54.6%
Two-stream+LSTM [33]		88.6%	
ST-ResNet [4]		82.2%	43.4%
C3D [26]	Sports 1M	82.3%	51.6%
MiCT-RGB [34]	Sports 1M	88.9%	63.8%
C3D [26]	Kinetics	89.8%	62.1%
P3D [19]	Kinetics	88.6%	
R(2+1)D [27]	Kinetics	96.8%	74.5%
I3D-RGB [2]	Kinetics	95.6%	74.8%
MARS [5]	Kinetics	**97.4%**	79.3%
EvaNet [18]	Kinetics		**82.7%**
I3D-RGB [2]	MiniKinetics	91.8%	66.4%
NTE-C*	MiniKinetics	**94.1%**	**71.5%**

5   Conclusion

In this paper, we attempted to explore a more efficient temporal feature extractor from the correlation of features in time dimension and propose the NTE network. The results on action recognition datasets demonstrate that, by introducing the correlation of spatial features between different times, the network can extract temporal features more effectively than by directly implementing linear transformation on spatial features. In addition, our NTE building block can be flexibly combined with the current spatial temporal separable convolution to obtain better results compared with the original basis. In the future, we shall conduct the following work. First, more combinations of temporal 1D convolution shall be investigated, and our NTE block will be tested to obtain a better result. Second, we will attempt to introduce more input modalities, such as optical flow information. Third, we will investigate the extraction of keyframes from the video instead of evenly sampling from the video.

References

1. Camgoz, N.C., Hadfield, S., Koller, O., Bowden, R.: Using convolutional 3D neural networks for user-independent continuous gesture recognition. In: 2016 23rd International Conference on Pattern Recognition (ICPR), pp. 49–54. IEEE (2016)
2. Carreira, J., Zisserman, A.: Quo vadis, action recognition? A new model and the kinetics dataset. In: proceedings of the IEEE Conference on Computer Vision and Pattern Recognition, pp. 6299–6308 (2017)
3. Chollet, F.: Xception: deep learning with depthwise separable convolutions. In: Proceedings of the IEEE Conference on Computer Vision and Pattern Recognition, pp. 1251–1258 (2017)
4. Christoph, R., Pinz, F.A.: Spatiotemporal residual networks for video action recognition. Adv. Neural Inf. Process. Syst. 3468–3476 (2016)
5. Crasto, N., Weinzaepfel, P., Alahari, K., Schmid, C.: MARS: Motion-augmented RGB stream for action recognition. In: Proceedings of the IEEE Conference on Computer Vision and Pattern Recognition, pp. 7882–7891 (2019)
6. Diba, A., et al.: Temporal 3D convnets: new architecture and transfer learning for video classification. arXiv preprint arXiv:1711.08200 (2017)
7. Diba, A., Pazandeh, A.M., Van Gool, L.: Efficient two-stream motion and appearance 3D CNNs for video classification. arXiv preprint arXiv:1608.08851 (2016)
8. Diba, A., Sharma, V., Van Gool, L.: Deep temporal linear encoding networks. In: Proceedings of the IEEE Conference on Computer Vision and Pattern Recognition, pp. 2329–2338 (2017)
9. Domanov, I., Lathauwer, L.D.: Canonical polyadic decomposition of third-order tensors: reduction to generalized eigenvalue decomposition. SIAM J. Matrix Anal. Appl. **35**(2), 636–660 (2014)
10. Feichtenhofer, C., Pinz, A., Zisserman, A.: Convolutional two-stream network fusion for video action recognition. In: Proceedings of the IEEE Conference on Computer Vision and Pattern Recognition, pp. 1933–1941 (2016)
11. Hara, K., Kataoka, H., Satoh, Y.: Learning spatio-temporal features with 3D residual networks for action recognition. In: Proceedings of the IEEE International Conference on Computer Vision Workshops, pp. 3154–3160 (2017)
12. He, K., Zhang, X., Ren, S., Sun, J.: Deep residual learning for image recognition. In: Proceedings of the IEEE Conference on Computer Vision and Pattern Recognition, pp. 770–778 (2016)

13. Huang, G., Liu, Z., Van Der Maaten, L., Weinberger, K.Q.: Densely connected convolutional networks. In: Proceedings of the IEEE Conference on Computer Vision and Pattern Recognition, pp. 4700–4708 (2017)

14. Ji, S., Yang, M., Yu, K.: 3D convolutional neural networks for human action recognition. IEEE Trans. Patt. Anal. Mach. Intell. **35**(1), 221–31 (2013). https://doi.org/10.1109/TPAMI.2012.59, https://www.ncbi.nlm.nih.gov/pubmed/22392705

15. Kuehne, H., Jhuang, H., Garrote, E., Poggio, T., Serre, T.: HMDB: a large video database for human motion recognition. In: 2011 International Conference on Computer Vision, pp. 2556–2563. IEEE (2011)

16. Laptev, I., Marszalek, M., Schmid, C., Rozenfeld, B.: Learning realistic human actions from movies. In: 2008 IEEE Conference on Computer Vision and Pattern Recognition, pp. 1–8. IEEE (2008)

17. Li, Y., Song, S., Li, Y., Liu, J.: Temporal bilinear networks for video action recognition. In: Proceedings of the AAAI Conference on Artificial Intelligence, vol. 33, pp. 8674–8681 (2019). https://doi.org/10.1609/aaai.v33i01.33018674

18. Piergiovanni, A., Angelova, A., Toshev, A., Ryoo, M.S.: Evolving space-time neural architectures for videos. In: Proceedings of the IEEE International Conference on Computer Vision, pp. 1793–1802 (2019)

19. Qiu, Z., Yao, T., Mei, T.: Learning spatio-temporal representation with pseudo-3D residual networks. In: proceedings of the IEEE International Conference on Computer Vision, pp. 5533–5541 (2017)

20. Scovanner, P., Ali, S., Shah, M.: A 3-dimensional sift descriptor and its application to action recognition. In: Proceedings of the 15th ACM International Conference on Multimedia, pp. 357–360 (2007)

21. Simonyan, K., Zisserman, A.: Two-stream convolutional networks for action recognition in videos. In: Advances in Neural Information Processing Systems, pp. 568–576 (2014)

22. Simonyan, K., Zisserman, A.: Very deep convolutional networks for large-scale image recognition. arXiv preprint arXiv:1409.1556 (2014)

23. Soomro, K., Zamir, A.R., Shah, M.: Ucf101: a dataset of 101 human actions classes from videos in the wild. arXiv preprint arXiv:1212.0402 (2012)

24. Sun, L., Jia, K., Yeung, D.Y., Shi, B.E.: Human action recognition using factorized spatio-temporal convolutional networks. In: Proceedings of the IEEE International Conference on Computer Vision, pp. 4597–4605 (2015)

25. Szegedy, C., et al.: Going deeper with convolutions. In: Proceedings of the IEEE Conference on Computer Vision and Pattern Recognition, pp. 1–9 (2015)

26. Tran, D., Bourdev, L., Fergus, R., Torresani, L., Paluri, M.: Learning spatiotemporal features with 3D convolutional networks. In: Proceedings of the IEEE International Conference on Computer Vision, pp. 4489–4497 (2015)

27. Tran, D., Wang, H., Torresani, L., Ray, J., LeCun, Y., Paluri, M.: A closer look at spatiotemporal convolutions for action recognition. In: Proceedings of the IEEE conference on Computer Vision and Pattern Recognition, pp. 6450–6459 (2018)

28. Wang, H., Kläser, A., Schmid, C., Liu, C.L.: Action recognition by dense trajectories. In: CVPR 2011, pp. 3169–3176. IEEE (2011)

29. Wang, L., et al.: Temporal segment networks: towards good practices for deep action recognition. In: Leibe, Bastian, Matas, Jiri, Sebe, Nicu, Welling, Max (eds.) ECCV 2016. LNCS, vol. 9912, pp. 20–36. Springer, Cham (2016). https://doi.org/10.1007/978-3-319-46484-8_2

30. Xie, S., Sun, C., Huang, J., Tu, Z., Murphy, K.: Rethinking spatiotemporal feature learning for video understanding. arXiv preprint arXiv:1712.04851, vol. 1(2), p. 5 (2017)

31. Xingjian, S., Chen, Z., Wang, H., Yeung, D.Y., Wong, W.K., Woo, W.C.: Convolutional lSTM network: a machine learning approach for precipitation nowcasting. In: Advances in Neural Information Processing Systems, pp. 802–810 (2015)
32. Yu, F., Koltun, V.: Multi-scale context aggregation by dilated convolutions. arXiv preprint arXiv:1511.07122 (2015)
33. Yue-Hei Ng, J., Hausknecht, M., Vijayanarasimhan, S., Vinyals, O., Monga, R., Toderici, G.: Beyond short snippets: deep networks for video classification. In: Proceedings of the IEEE Conference on Computer Vision and Pattern Recognition, pp. 4694–4702 (2015)
34. Zhou, Y., Sun, X., Zha, Z.J., Zeng, W.: MiCT: Mixed 3D/2D convolutional tube for human action recognition. In: Proceedings of the IEEE Conference on Computer Vision and Pattern Recognition, pp. 449–458 (2018)

Author Index

Printed in the United States
By Bookmasters